1001 BATTLES

THAT CHANGED THE COURSE OF WORLD HISTORY

1001 BATTLES

THAT CHANGED THE COURSE OF WORLD HISTORY

GENERAL EDITOR **R. G. GRANT**

PREFACE BY **BRIGADIER GENERAL ROBERT DOUGHTY**

UNIVERSE

A Quintessence Book

First published in the United States of America in 2011 by
UNIVERSE PUBLISHING
A Division of Rizzoli International Publications, Inc.
300 Park Avenue South
New York, NY 10010
www.rizzoliusa.com

2011 2012 2013 2014 / 10 9 8 7 6 5 4 3 2 1

ISBN: 978-0-7893-2233-3

Library of Congress Control Number: 2010932889

QSS.BATT

This book was designed and produced by
Quintessence Editions Ltd.
226 City Road
London EC1V 2TT
www.1001beforeyoudie.com

Project Editor	Philip Contos
Editors	Becky Gee, Frank Ritter
Designers	Tom Howey, Rod Teasdale
Production Manager	Anna Pauletti

Editorial Director	Jane Laing
Publisher	Tristan de Lancey

Color reproduction by Chroma Graphics Pte Ltd., Singapore.
Printed in China by Toppan Leefung Printing Ltd.

CONTENTS

PREFACE
By Brigadier General Robert Doughty

More than any other human activity, battles have shaped world history. Julius Caesar's victory over the combined Gallic tribes in the Battle of Alesia in 52 BCE, for example, marked a turning point in the Gallic Wars and opened the way for Roman laws and language to spread across Europe. Similarly, Constantine I's victory near the Tiber River at the Milvian Bridge in 312 set the stage for Christianity to become the official religion of the Roman Empire. Battles have shaped the boundaries and destinies of countries all around the world. In many ways the United States was defined by battles fought at such places as Concord (1775), Trenton (1776), Saratoga (1777), and Yorktown (1781).

As *1001 Battles That Changed the Course of World History* shows, the nature and scale of battles have varied greatly over the centuries. Many were one in a series of battles or a campaign, such as the Battle of Seven Pines in the Peninsula Campaign (1862). Others were a single, climactic war-winning victory—Sadowa (Königgrätz) in 1866, for example. Some battles involved huge forces from many states (Leipzig, 1813), while others involved small forces from two opposing armies (Cowpens, 1781). Many battles were decisive victories (Fall of France, 1940), while some had a "winner" only in name (Verdun, 1916). In the eighteenth century, battles at times consisted of commanders maneuvering their troops until they had an advantage over an opponent and could force a surrender without a costly fight. Commanders such as the Duke of Marlborough at Blenheim (1704) and Frederick the Great at Leuthen (1757), however, demonstrated a willingness to fight and suffer heavy losses when necessary.

Important battles have also occurred on the sea and in the air. In the greatest naval battle since Trafalgar (1805), the Japanese destroyed almost the entire Russian fleet at the battle of Tsushima (1905). The destruction of Japanese air carriers and crews at the battle of Midway (1942) marked the turning point in the Allied offensive in the Pacific. In sharp contrast, Germany and the United States failed to achieve decisive success in the air battles, respectively, of Britain (1940) and Rolling Thunder (1965). Greater success with air power came in the initial aerial attack in Desert Storm (1991) and in the Kosovo Bombing (1999).

Differences in weapons, terrain, weather, and circumstances have made each battle unique. U.S. military leaders in the Union and Confederate forces, for example, often tried to mimic the methods of Napoleon, but new weapons and different terrain made Gettysburg (1863) very different from Austerlitz (1805). Leaders have also molded battles; Ulysses S. Grant demonstrates clearly the ability of a commander to form an army and fight a battle according to his own command style and goals.

Usually battles are a discrete event with a clear beginning and an end. And most commanders—and their political leaders—think they understand the consequences of victory or defeat. Some battles, however, have had results that were unimaginable at the time of the fighting. Had Germany, for example, won the First Battle of the Marne (1914), the history of Europe and the world could have been dramatically different.

Nonetheless, numerous similarities exist between different battles. All involve fighting. All involve heroic sacrifice, and some involve craven cowardice. And, even in the computer age, all involve uncertainty. My own experience illustrates this. In February 1969 I was an adviser to a Vietnamese armored cavalry troop that along with other Vietnamese forces (another cavalry troop, an infantry battalion, and a Ranger company) wandered into the space between elements of two North Vietnamese divisions that had infiltrated into South Vietnam. The two divisions were poised to leapfrog one over the other in an assault on the city of Quang Ngai. The North Vietnamese had not planned an operation as large as the Tet Offensive (1968) but wanted to capture the world's attention. We knew something was happening because we had found weapons caches, rice stocks, and freshly dug graves, but we did not anticipate any significant action until we unexpectedly encountered a wall of fire from a wood line shortly before our scheduled departure from the field. Over the next few days we were surrounded by the North Vietnamese, who were surprised to find a heavy combat force in their center. Although we suffered significant casualties, particularly in the infantry battalion, we completely disrupted the North Vietnamese attack and destroyed a large portion of their forces. A serendipitous move into a wood line produced a hard-fought battle that kept the enemy from seizing an important South Vietnamese city.

Like our fight near Quang Ngai and like thousands of others, battles involve uncertainty, friction, and violence. Yet, victory usually goes to the side with the best commanders, troops, weapons, and position. Battles, like life and death, are not mere games of chance.

Natchitoches, Louisiana

INTRODUCTION
By R. G. Grant, General Editor

As a callow young man, I once foolishly suggested to an American general that a long, arduous operation in which he had fought might, at times, have been "boring." With politeness and restraint that did him credit, the general replied that although many and various adjectives might be accurately applied to combat, "boring" was definitely not among them. Even people who deplore war should be prepared to acknowledge the enduring fascination of battles, whether fought with spears, bows, and swords, or with helicopter gunships and assault rifles. Nor is their appeal any mystery, for battles raise life to an unequalled dramatic pitch, whether their focus is heroism and courage, or futility and waste of life.

Battles are historically important as well as intense and exciting. Armed combat has always been available as a final arbiter in human affairs. Clashes of ideas, societies, or civilizations are not necessarily resolved by force of arms, but they can be. This fact has shaped the evolution of the human world. Societies capable of producing superior weaponry, or of mobilizing greater resources for warfare, have often survived while others—possibly superior in virtue or cultural sophistication—have perished. It is questionable whether the Spanish conquistadores who destroyed the Aztec and Inca empires of Mexico and Peru in the sixteenth century represented a superior civilization, but it is beyond doubt that they came from a superior military tradition. Sometimes in history, that is all that matters. At their most dramatic, battles have constituted massive throws of the dice, with the fate of individuals, nations, and whole civilizations gambled on an afternoon's slaughter. Historians, in general no lovers of drama, often prefer to stress the plodding long-term factors that they believe eventually decide the shape of the future. But for those people in the thick of historical events—enjoying the fruits of victory or suffering the dire consequences of defeat—there is never any doubt that the outcome of warfare matters very much indeed.

Many battles stand out as events at crossroads, where different possible futures lay open, the path taken depending upon a military outcome. A famous example is the Battle of Tours (confusingly, also known as the Battle of Poitiers) in 732 AD. In the century preceding the battle, Muslim armies had extended the realm of Islam from Arabia to northern Spain. At Tours, the Christian Franks defeated Muslim raiders, who never advanced as far north again. Eighteenth-century historian Edward Gibbon suggested that, had the battle gone the other way, "the Koran would now be taught in the schools of Oxford, and her pulpits might demonstrate to a circumcised people the sanctity and truth of the revelation of Mahomet." Many historians since have queried Gibbon's judgment, but an Islamic conquest of northern Europe was certainly not beyond the bounds of possibility.

Leaping forward to the twentieth century, the consequences of the First Battle of the Marne in 1914 were momentous. In the early weeks of what became World War I, German armies stood on the verge of victory over France and Britain. Had they triumphed at the Marne, the war might have been over by Christmas 1914, and the subsequent history of Europe would have been changed. There would have been no Russian Revolution in 1917, no Nazi government in Germany in the 1930s, no World War II. But the Marne was an Allied victory: the German armies were forced back, military stalemate ensued, and so did the actual history of the twentieth century. Another alternative time line is proposed by novelist Robert Harris in his book *Fatherland*, in which the Soviet Union's victory over Germany at the Battle of Stalingrad in 1942–43 never happens. Consequently, Hitler wins World War II and is still ruler of the German Reich and Europe in the 1960s.

A relatively small number of battles have evident epic influence on history, but the long-term consequences of less prominent clashes can be greater than is immediately obvious. The naval battles of the seventeenth century Anglo-Dutch Wars may seem trivial in their short-term results, but Britain's rise to global naval supremacy at the expense of the Dutch was immensely important to history: it led to the founding of the British Empire and, arguably, caused the Industrial Revolution to take the form it did. A great number of battles have been influential on a more local scale. They have determined the political map of the world, establishing frontiers and allowing states to found or uphold independence. The southern borders of the United States might be significantly different had Mexican armies performed better in battles fought in the 1840s. And if the Confederates had won at the Battle of Gettysburg (1863) in the American Civil War, it is not impossible that two countries would inhabit the current territory of the United States, one of them having upheld slavery at least into the twentieth century.

In selecting a list of history's most significant battles, the first question that I could not avoid was: what constitutes a battle? A satisfactory answer requires common sense rather than pedantry. In its purest sense, "battle" refers to a style of warfare that largely vanished in the course of the nineteenth century. Two armies faced each other across a chosen battlefield and fought until one side won and the other fled. The action was tightly circumscribed in time and space; usually lasting less than a day and conducted within visual range of each side's commanders. Yet even in the centuries when pitched battles were fought in this manner, prolonged sieges of walled cites and fortresses constituted an alternative form of combat; one often far more common than battles in an open field. Skirmishes and ambushes were also time-honored styles of combat, especially when the forces were unequal, making a weaker side unwilling to face its enemy in open battle. Where sieges, skirmishes, or ambushes are historically significant, there seemed no good reason to deny them the status of "battles."

In modern times, the increasing size of armies—and the ability to keep them supplied and under coordinated command—has enabled generals to conduct military operations of greater geographical extent, lasting almost continuously for months. This has led to "operation" largely replacing "battle" in formal military terminology. Again, there seemed no good reason to resist the popular use of the word "battle" for the prolonged combats at the Somme and Verdun in 1916, for example, or in Normandy in 1944. Aerial combat by its nature has a different structure from combat on land or sea, but it was not just propaganda that led the fighting over southern England in 1940 to be dubbed the "Battle of Britain": it had adequate unity of time, place, and purpose to be deemed a battle. In contrast, the so-called "Battle of the Atlantic" in World War II—the struggle to keep Allied transatlantic supply lines open against attack by submarines, aircraft, and warships—seemed to stretch the "battle" concept too far, with combat dispersed over more than five years and an entire ocean. Somewhere a line had to be drawn.

A considerable number of battles pick themselves for a list of history's most significant: they would be agreed by any informed selection committee. But many choices I have made are personal and could be controversial. Men, and sometimes women, have been fighting for thousands of years, resulting in an excess of actions from which to choose. The American Civil War alone generated 300 encounters that could be described as "battles," all of them at least of local significance and making a contribution to the outcome of the war. Inevitably, I have left out many battles that could justifiably be included. Although size is an important consideration, I have also given weight to other factors. A battle may be included as the masterpiece of a famous general, or because it was the first or most striking use of a particular tactic or technology. The World War I Battle of Flers-Courcelette in 1916 would not justify inclusion for its negligible impact on the stalemated trench warfare of the Western Front, but must be included as the first use of tanks; an innovation of great consequence indeed. Some battles are significant not singly, but as part of a sequence: the short-term result of each is purely military—such as the raising of a siege or the advance of one side at the expense of the other—but the series eventually results in victory for one side. Other battles have a prominent place in national mythology—the victories of Alexander Nevsky for Russians, the Alamo for Americans—that may exceed their objective importance, but their legendary status in itself justifies inclusion.

The aim of the entries in this book is, straightforwardly, to give a clear account of the course of each battle in its essential outline. Where battles exist in sequences—indicated by backward and forward links on the page—it would have been tedious to repeat basic background information in every entry. Reading them in sequence will show each battle in context.

An attempt has been made, where possible, to indicate the number of people engaged in a battle and the scale of losses. Such figures are an enduring problem for military historians. Until modern times, it can be assumed that all figures are estimates, sometimes no better than guesses. Historians have taken great pains to check, and where necessary correct, contemporary estimates—proving, for example, the exaggeration of medieval battle counts—but, if no one was counting at the time, accuracy is hardly possible. Even in modern times, anyone who has followed public disputes about the death toll from fighting in Iraq since 2003 will be aware of how widely estimates can vary. The reasons for this range from the pressure to produce propaganda—deliberate distortion—to the many practical problems in casualty counting. For example, does a man who dies of his battle wounds six months later count as killed or wounded in the battle? What if he dies the following day? What if, like one unfortunate American at the Battle of Manila Bay (1898), he dies of a heart attack because the excitement is too much for an already sickly organ? American deaths in that battle can be given as zero or one, depending on a decision on that point. For modern battles, fought by bureaucratic societies, you might expect exact figures to be available, yet the American death toll in the D-day landings continues to be a matter of dispute after more than forty years of historical research. This book's contributors strove to provide the most credible figures available, but readers should not be unduly surprised if they see different figures cited in other sources.

I have set out to cover the widest range of warfare, both geographically and temporally. The book is organized by date; so, followed from start to finish, it offers a panorama of the development of fighting techniques and of technological progress through history. Its geographical range means that battles from different parts of the world are often juxtaposed to interesting effect—reminding us, for example, that wars were being fought in Mexico, China, and northern Europe while Americans were focused on their Civil War. Every reader should find some unexpected material, as well as a useful ready reference to well-known battles. Many, I hope, will be inspired to find out more about the encounters listed in these pages, so that the book will serve as the starting point of an exploration, stimulating curiosity and opening new areas of interest.

Index of Battles

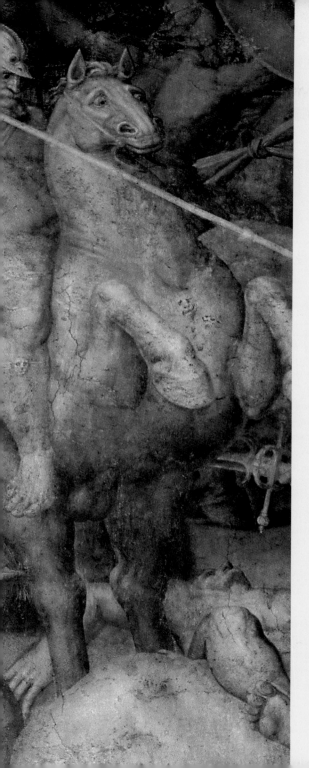

Anglo-Saxon Wars
Assyrian Wars
Babylonian Wars
Breton-Frankish War
Byzantine Iberian War
Byzantine-Bulgarian Wars
Byzantine-Gothic War
Byzantine-Sassanid Wars
Byzantine-Vandalic War
Carthage's Mercenary War
Charlemagne's Wars
China's Spring and Autumn Period War
China's Three Kingdoms Wars
China's Warring States Period
Chinese-Xiongnu War
Chu-Han War
Conquests of Alexander
Cretan War
Early Roman Wars
First Punic War
Frankish Wars
Gallic Wars
Goguryeo-Sui War
Greco-Persian Wars
Islamic Civil War
Israelite Wars
Jewish-Roman Wars
Jin Dynasty Wars
Korea's Three Kingdoms Wars
Lulin Rebellion
Macedonian Conquest of Greece
Magyar Incursions
Peloponnesian War
Rise of Islam
Roman Civil War
Roman Conquest of Britain
Roman Servile War
Roman-Alamanni Conflict
Roman-Germanic Wars
Roman-Parthian Wars
Roman-Persian Wars
Rome's Cimbrian War
Rome's Dacian Wars
Rome's War with Palmyra
Saxon Wars
Scandinavian Wars
Second Punic War
Shang-Zhou War
Sulla's Civil Wars
Sumerian City-state Wars
Syrian Wars
Theban Wars
Third Punic War
Trojan War
Vietnamese-Chinese War
Viking Raids
Wars of Alexander's Successors
Wars of Ancient Egypt
Wars of Arab Expansion
Wars of Constantine I
Wars of Mauryan India
Wars of Roman Decline
Wars of Roman Expansion
Wars of the Persian Empire

Detail from a sixteenth-century fresco by Niccolò dell'Abbate showing close combat at Pharsalus (48 BCE).

Lagash Fights Umma c. 2450 BCE

The first wars known to history took place about 4,500 years ago in Sumer, southern Mesopotamia—part of modern-day Iraq. Described in fragmentary detail on a monument—the Stele of the Vultures—the clash between the Sumerian city-states of Lagash and Umma is the earliest recorded battle.

Lagash was ruled by Eannatum, an aggressive king with imperial ambitions. Eannatum entered into dispute with neighboring Umma over ownership of irrigated land that lay between the two cities. According to the Stele of the Vultures (now in the Louvre in Paris), he consulted the protector god of Lagash, Ningirsu, who promised the king that if he went to war his enemy's corpses would be heaped to the base of heaven. Thus encouraged, Eannatum led an army against Umma.

The king rode in a primitive four-wheeled chariot pulled by asses, followed by the ranks of his helmeted foot soldiers clad in kilts and armed with spears. As the men of Umma emerged from their walled city to confront the invaders, Eannatum climbed down from his chariot to lead his soldiers into battle on foot. The Lagash army fought in a disciplined, tight formation, the infantry advancing with leveled spears over the bodies of their fallen foes. Some of the Umma soldiers must have been armed with bows because Eannatum is shown on the stele being struck by an arrow. The wound was not fatal. The Lagash army triumphed and Eannatum imposed a humiliating peace on defeated Umma, reducing the city to tributary status.

Erected to celebrate this triumph, the stele gloatingly represents vultures feasting on the bodies of the enemy dead. Later in his reign, Eannatum extended his rule over a wide area—including all of Sumer—although Lagash soon lost its regional ascendancy after his death. **RG**

Losses: Umma, probably 100 to 200 dead (most of its army); Lagash, minimal

The oldest known historiographic document—one side of this stele charts the events of the battle.

Megiddo   c. 1457 BCE

One of three famous battles fought near the town of Megiddo in modern-day Israel (see 609 BCE and 1918 CE), this was the first great victory of Egypt's all-conquering Pharaoh Tuthmosis III. A leader of military genius, Tuthmosis created an Egyptian empire of unprecedented scale.

Shortly after Tuthmosis succeeded to the throne, a coalition of Canaanite kingdoms led by the king of Kadesh challenged Egyptian dominance in Syria and Palestine. Learning that the Canaanite army had advanced to Megiddo, Tuthmosis set out from Egypt to meet the challenge. The progress of the campaign was recorded by the pharaoh's secretary and later carved on the walls of the Temple of Amun in Karnak.

The key to victory was speed of movement. Tuthmosis's army advanced 125 miles (201 km) across the desert to Gaza in ten days, before turning north into Palestine. Between the Egyptians and their enemies on the Megiddo

plain lay the rocky Mount Carmel ridge. Tuthmosis's generals argued for marching around the ridge, but the pharaoh insisted on taking the direct route over the top—via the narrow Aruna pass—and ignored the risk of being ambushed. He achieved total surprise, debouching onto the plain behind the Canaanite forces. The Egyptians drew up in full battle array, Tuthmosis an impressive figure in the center on "a chariot of electrum with all his weapons of war." The Canaanites had no stomach for a fight and soon fled. The citizens of Megiddo closed their gates, but fleeing soldiers were hauled ingloriously over the city walls to safety as Egyptian soldiers stopped to plunder abandoned baggage. This indiscipline denied Tuthmosis a total victory, and Megiddo only surrendered after a laborious seven-month siege. **RG**

Losses: Unknown; possibly 10,000 soldiers engaged on each side

Kadesh 1275 BCE >

⬆ *On the Seventh Pylon in Karnak, Egypt, Tuthmosis III is depicted smiting his prisoners.*

Kadesh 1275 BCE

In one of the world's largest chariot battles, fought beside the Orontes River, Pharaoh Rameses II sought to wrest Syria from the Hittites. There was a day of carnage as some 5,000 chariots charged into the fray, but no outright victor. The battle led to the world's first recorded peace treaty.

Resolved to pursue the expansionist policy introduced by his father, Seti I, Rameses invaded Hittite territories in Palestine and pushed on into Syria. Near the Orontes River, his soldiers captured two men who said they were deserters from the Hittite force, which now lay some way off, outside Aleppo. This was reassuring, since the impetuous pharaoh had pushed well ahead of his main army with an advance guard of 20,000 infantry and 2,000 chariots. Unfortunately, the "deserters" were loyal agents of his enemy. Led by their High Prince, Muwatalli, the Hittites were at hand—with 40,000 foot soldiers and 3,000 chariots—and swiftly attacked. Their heavy, three-horse chariots smashed into the Egyptian vanguard, scattering its lighter chariots and the ranks behind. An easy victory seemed assured, and the Hittites dropped their guard and set about plundering their fallen enemy. Calm and determined, Rameses quickly remarshalled his men and launched a counterattack.

With their shock advantage gone, the Hittite chariots seemed slow and ungainly; the lighter Egyptian vehicles outmaneuvered them with ease. Rameses, bold and decisive, managed to pluck from the jaws of defeat if not victory, then at least an honorable draw. Both sides claimed Kadesh as a triumph, and Rameses had his temples festooned with celebratory reliefs. In truth, the outcome was inconclusive. So much so that, fifteen years later, the two sides returned to Kadesh to agree to a non-aggression pact—the first known example in history. **MK**

Losses: Unknown

◁ *Megiddo c. 1457 BCE*　　　　　　*Megiddo 609 BCE* ▷

　　　An account of the battle, as recorded on papyrus by Rameses II c. 1275 BCE.

Troy 1250 BCE

No war has had a more tenacious hold over the Western imagination than that of the Siege of Troy, as related in Homer's *Iliad*. It was long assumed to be the stuff of legend, yet it has recently been suggested that it might be a part of history as well.

When Aphrodite, Greek goddess of love, promised the most beautiful woman in the world to Prince Paris of Troy, neither worried too much about the fact that she was already married. Paris set sail for Greece, abducted Helen of Sparta, and carried her home with him. He did not fear—or even consider—the consequences, which were to be grave indeed. Helen's husband, Menelaus, called together all the heroes of Greece's cities: men such as his brother Agamemnon, king of Mycenae; Achilles, all but invulnerable to wounds; and Ajax, invincible in war. Setting off across the Aegean, the Greeks laid siege to Troy. Periodically, Trojan warriors

such as Hector emerged to trade defiant speeches with the enemy and engage them in small-scale skirmishes and duels. Finally, despairing of taking the city by storm, the Greeks followed a stratagem proposed by the cunning Odysseus: pretending to withdraw and lift the siege, they left a large wooden horse, apparently as a propitiatory gift for the Trojans. After the horse had been drawn into the city, concealed warriors emerged from its hollow body at night to open the gates to the Greeks—now back in force.

In 1868, German archeologist Heinreich Schliemann claimed to have found the site of Troy on a headland between the Aegean Sea and the Dardanelles at Hisarlik, Turkey. Scholars, long skeptical, now agree that this city may well have been an outpost of the Hittite Empire, and that it could quite easily have come into conflict with the mercantile power of Mycenae. **MK**

Losses: Unknown

⬆ *The Trojan horse and Greek soldiers carved in relief on a Greek amphora from 640 BCE.*

Gilboa 1100 BCE

Muye 1046 BCE

The Battle of Gilboa, narrated in the Bible, is famous for Saul's last suicidal stand in the face of Philistine attack. Although the dramatic biblical account is perhaps not fully reliable, historians agree that a newly united kingdom of Israel fought for its survival here.

The Shang dynasty, rulers of China for half a millennium, went out with a whimper. Although certainly a historic turning point, the Battle of Muye was—in truth—a one-sided struggle. Most Shang troops refused to fight, and the few who did were overwhelmed and slaughtered.

Saul was the first ruler of the double kingdom of Israel and Judah (the former in the north, the latter in the south of the modern country). The marriage was an uneasy one, although unity was to some extent enforced by the impending presence of external enemies—most notably the Philistines. The new king led victorious campaigns against the Philistines and another tribe, the Amalekites, yet the removal of these outside threats allowed internal squabbles to resurface. The emergence of David may be seen in this light: the man who started out Saul's protégé and ended up his rival belonged to the tribe of Judah, so his political powerbase was in the south. It is unclear how far we should believe the biblical accounts of his early clash with Goliath, of Saul's growing envy, or of Crown Prince Jonathan's self-abnegating love for David. It does seem perfectly possible, however, that—in his lust for power—the young Judaean pretender made common cause with the Philistines.

Apparently emboldened, the Philistines renewed their campaign against Israel. Saul marched his men to the heights of Gilboa, a rocky ridge above the Jordan Valley. It seemed a commanding position, but the Philistines charged up the hillside and stormed the Jewish positions. Rather than be taken prisoner, Saul threw himself on his own sword and died. A triumph for the Philistines, then, but the real victor was David, who was now able to crown himself king of Israel. **MK**

The achievements of the Shang dynasty over half a millennium had been incredible: they had built a viable state and maintained an extraordinary Bronze Age culture. By the middle of the eleventh century, however, a dynasty in long-term decline was in a desperate state. Under King Wen, the Zhou were poised to supplant the Shang as China's leading power.

Di Xin, the king of the Shang, had gone so far as to imprison Wen—in the hope of canceling out the threat he posed—before releasing him in return for a ransom. He then tried to co-opt Wen's loyalty by making him his "western overlord." But Wen refused to be bought and rose in rebellion, and although he died in 1050 BCE, his son, King Wu, continued the struggle against the Shang.

The ruling dynasty's problems were now compounded by popular unrest at home, in a kingdom that was collapsing into chaos. Although in theory Di Xin commanded half a million men, the king was scarcely able to muster any sort of army to resist Wu's troops when they approached his capital, Yin, in 1046 BCE. Driven to recklessness by what seemed a hopeless plight, Di Xin issued arms to 170,000 slaves, calling on them to defend "their" kingdom—to no one's great surprise, they went straight over to the enemy. Demoralized, his regular troops deserted in droves—many defecting to the cause of the Zhou. Those who stayed true were put to the sword by Wu's advancing army. **MK**

Losses: Unknown

Losses: Shang, unknown but extremely high; Zhou, light

Lachish 701 BCE ▶

Chengpu 632 BCE ▶

Qarqar 853 BCE

In the ninth century the Assyrians, the most ruthless fighting people of ancient Mesopotamia, were expanding their empire by conquest. At Qarqar, Shalmaneser III's invading Assyrian troops were met by the allied forces of a dozen Syrian kings in possibly the largest battle the world had yet seen.

In keeping with Babylonian tradition, the campaigning season for the Assyrians began once the harvest month of *Ajarus* had concluded—in what we would think of as mid-May. At this point in 853 BCE, Shalmaneser set out from Nineveh, leading his troops westward into Syria in order to follow through on conquests he had made in previous campaigns. These included the city of Halman (Aleppo), which he now took as his base, striking out to the southwest into Hamath, in central Syria.

This time, though, his enemies were more organized. Hamath's King Irhuleni had banded together with eleven other local rulers, including Ahab of Israel, and their combined force prepared to meet the invaders on the plains beside the Orontes River. The armies were large, although the claim in Assyrian inscriptions that 100,000 Assyrians faced 70,000 Syrians is likely exaggerated. Records show that the Syrian force included chariots, horsemen, and 1,000 Arabs mounted on dromedaries— not only the first mention of camel warfare but also the earliest reference in the historical record to the existence of the Arabs as a nation. The Assyrian inscriptions proclaim the battle a glorious triumph for Shalmaneser. This cannot be quite true, because further Syrian campaigns had to be fought in the years that followed. Even so, the momentum was now clearly with the Assyrians, who soon took control of territory up to the Mediterranean coast, from southern Turkey to Gaza. **MK**

Losses: Assyrian, no reliable figures; Syrian, allegedly 14,000 casualties

Lachish 701 BCE [>]

A ninth-century BCE ornamental ivory plaque from the palace of Shalmaneser III at Nimrud, Assyria.

Lachish 701 BCE

Lachish was the second city of the kingdom of Judah. Assyrian King Sennacherib led his army into Judah in order to punish a revolt against his authority. The episode is well known because it figures both in the Bible and in an Assyrian pictorial record that shows siege engines and the use of terror against civilians.

"Their arrows are sharpened and their bows drawn … and their chariot wheels spin like a whirlwind." For the Prophet Isaiah, the Assyrians were the wrath of God. Sennacherib, however, was simply trying to teach subjects across his empire an important lesson. One such subject, Judah's King Hezekiah, had joined up with other local rulers (possibly with Egyptian support) in a concerted attempt to throw off the dominance of Assyria. This defiance could not be tolerated by Sennacherib; others would feel emboldened if it went unpunished.

The Assyrians were masters of siege warfare. Friezes from the Royal Palace at Nineveh show engineers hacking at the walls of Lachish while archers—protected by large curved shields—provide covering fire. In other scenes, an elaborately constructed siege tower is wheeled up an earth ramp to attack the walls with a battering ram, and soldiers attempt to scale the walls with ladders.

The length of the siege is unknown, but its aftermath was bloody. The Nineveh reliefs show the defeated men being tortured and executed; some impaled on stakes while others plead for their lives. The Assyrians habitually emptied captured cities of their population by massacre and mass deportation. The treatment of Lachish was designed to send a message to Hezekiah and his supporters in Jerusalem, but a subsequent Assyrian siege of the Judaean capital ended in failure. **MK**

Losses: Unknown; large numbers of civilians killed and displaced

◁ *Qarqar 853 BCE*　　　　　　　　　*Nineveh 612 BCE* ▷

Chengpu 632 BCE

Between the eighth and fifth centuries BCE, in the era known in China as the Spring and Autumn Period, powerful armies spearheaded by charioteers clashed in battles between rival Chinese kingdoms. One of the largest encounters was fought between the southern state of Chu and its northern rival Jin at Chengpu.

The Spring and Autumn Period saw China's Eastern Zhou dynasty emperors nominally holding sway, but in practice they were being pushed around by local warlords. By the seventh century BCE, effective power was becoming concentrated on the kings of Jin, in Shanxi, in the valley of the Yellow River, while the kings of Chu were coming to prominence in the Yangtze basin to the south. By 633 BCE, King Cheng of Chu felt confident enough to attack the state of Song—a key Jin ally. Duke Wen of Jin responded by invading Chu's allies Wei and Cao. Open war broke out—the Jin ruler leading a vast army boasting 700 chariots to meet the forces of Chu and its allies. The exact geographical location of Chengpu, the site where Chinese annals say the armies clashed, is not known.

According to the annals, Duke Wen believed the enemy's right wing was its weak point, so sent the chariots of his own left wing hurtling forward in a smashing charge. Their chariot horses clad in tiger skins, the charioteers scattered the Chu right wing and were able to come at the enemy center. The increasingly demoralized Chu force was now under sustained attack from two sides, which became three and finally four as the Jin right wing moved around to encircle them. Remnants of the Chu escaped through a precipitate retreat, but the defeat at Chengpu was complete enough to definitively check Chu ambitions to attain overall ascendancy in China. **MK**

Losses: Unknown

◁ *Muye 1046 BCE*　　　　　　　　　*Maling 342 BCE* ▷

◀ *An eighth-century BCE alabaster relief showing one of the defense towers in Lachish.*

Nineveh 612 BCE

Determined to end Assyrian dominance in Mesopotamia, Babylonia led an alliance in an attack against the Assyrian capital, Nineveh. The city was comprehensively sacked after a three-month siege, and Assyrian King Sinsharushkin was killed. Although his successors clung to power for a while, the days of Assyrian ascendancy were gone.

In the early centuries of the second millennium BCE, Babylon had been the dominant power in Mesopotamia and the Middle East. Since then, the city had been increasingly marginalized. Its pride remained, and it had several times attempted to rise up against Assyrian domination, but it had never been close to succeeding. In 626 BCE, however, a new king, Nabopolassar, sensed that the hold of Assyria's rulers was weakening.

It took Nabopolassar ten years to expel Assyrian forces from Babylonia itself, and in 616 BCE he led an invasion of Assyria. By then, other discontent peoples were eager to enlist in the Babylonian cause, including several from what is now Iran. Soon, Nabopolassar was heading an army that included the people of Susa—a city-state in the foothills of the Zagros mountains—and the Scythians, mounted nomads (and formidable cavalrymen) from the steppe. The Medes, a people from the plains of northwestern Iran, marched south to take the Assyrians' original home city of Assur in 614 BCE, after which they too struck an alliance with Nabopolassar.

Together, under Babylonian leadership, the allies moved against the Assyrian capital, Nineveh. Resistance was fierce, and it was three long months of fighting before it fell. The city was sacked, and Assyria's King Sinsharushkin killed. Even then, the Assyrians rallied around a new, would-be ruler, Ashuruballit, but he was finally defeated in 608 BCE. **MK**

Megiddo 609 BCE

The second major battle fought at Megiddo, in modern-day Israel, occurred when King Josiah of Judah made a bold attempt to rebuild the kingdom of Israel amid the crumbling ruins of Assyrian power. However, the Egyptian Pharaoh Necho II defeated and deposed him for his pains, and Egypt became the dominant force in Palestine.

After Solomon's death in 926 BCE, the kingdom of Israel had broken into two: Judah in the south; Samaria in the north. The dream of reuniting the realm remained, but—with Assyrian power apparently irresistible—it was one that the Jews realized would have to wait. However, after Nabopolassar's triumph at Nineveh, Judah's King Josiah saw his historic opportunity: the Assyrian Empire was progressively imploding. When Pharaoh Necho II marched his army eastward to offer his Assyrian ally assistance, Josiah resolved to prevent their getting through. He planned to intercept the Egyptian army as it crossed a narrow pass near the city of Megiddo: in those rugged uplands, the Jews should have had the advantage of surprise.

In the event, Josiah's plan worked to the extent that he was able to get his army into position, but the advancing Egyptians simply swept his force aside. If the biblical account (II Chronicles 35) is to be believed, Josiah was wounded by an archer at Megiddo and was taken to Jerusalem, where he died. Marching on to Mesopotamia, the pharaoh was defeated by Nabopolassar's Babylonians at Charchemish—the vacuum Josiah had hoped for was created, but of course he was no longer there to take advantage. His son, Jehoahaz, succeeded him, but was deposed by Necho on his homeward journey in favor of his more tractable brother, Jehoiakim. Egypt was now the real power in Palestine. **MK**

Losses: Unknown

◁ *Lachish 701 BCE*   *Megiddo 609 BCE* ▷

Losses: Unknown

◁ *Kadesh 1275 BCE*   *Fall of Jerusalem 587 BCE* ▷

 From the palace at Nineveh, a seventh-century BCE relief of Assyrian soldiers in a chariot.

Fall of Jerusalem   587 BCE

Rebelling against foreign domination, King Zedekiah of Judah defied Nebuchadnezzar II, ruler of the newly dominant regional power Babylon. The rebellion ended in even worse disaster for the Jews than their earlier revolt against the Assyrians because they were subjected to an unprecedented mass exile, known as the "Babylonian Captivity."

Jehoiakim, installed on Judah's throne by the Egyptian pharaoh Necho II after the Battle of Megiddo, had tried to stand out against the expansion of Babylonian power. In 597 BCE, accordingly, Nebuchadnezzar II of Babylon had taken Jerusalem after a short siege, and replaced Jehoiakim with a puppet of his own.

King Zedekiah, too, hankered after the authority of a real king, however, and in 587 BCE he tried to break away. Alone, his people could do nothing, but Zedekiah went behind Babylonian backs to make an alliance with Egypt's Pharaoh Apries, who agreed to assist the Jews if they rebelled. Apries was as good as his word: unfortunately, however, the army he sent into Judah was quickly and easily dispatched by Nebuchadnezzar's forces, who could now concentrate entirely on the errant kingdom of Judah and its capital. "A lion has arisen from its lair, to make your land a desert . . . and reduce your cities to ruins," lamented the prophet Jeremiah (Jeremiah 4:7).

After about eighteen months, Jerusalem's defenders were finally starved into submission. Zedekiah's two sons were captured and executed before his eyes—which were then put out. The king was led off to exile in Babylon, accompanied by up to 10,000 of his nation's aristocratic, religious, and scholarly elite: Nebuchadnezzar was determined to destroy not just the spirit but the very identity of the Jews, as well. **MK**

"Raise the signal to go to Zion! Flee for safety without delay! For I am bringing disaster from the north, even terrible destruction."

Jeremiah 4:6

⬆ *This cuneiform tablet from Babylon records Nebuchadnezzar II's capture of Jerusalem and campaign against the king of Egypt.*

Losses: Many thousands dead; 10,000 Jews deported to Babylon

◁ *Megiddo 609 BCE*   *Opis 539 BCE* ▷

Sardis 546 BCE

The defeat of King Croesus of Lydia by Persian ruler Cyrus II at Sardis was a major step forward in the rise of the Persian Empire. The victory was achieved against heavy odds through Cyrus's calm resourcefulness, the discipline of his men, and a remarkable use of camels as both a martial and an olfactory deterrent.

Cyrus II belonged to the Achaemenid dynasty, claiming descent from the mythical hero Achaemenes. As of the mid-sixth century BCE, his house no longer had the illustrious empire that its lineage warranted, but Cyrus set out to change this. In 550 BCE, the king of the Persians encouraged the neighboring Medes to rise up against Astyages, their ruler. When he then invaded their land, he was greeted as a liberator. Croesus, ruler of Lydia, in modern-day Turkey, was Astyages' brother-in-law. He marched into Media to avenge Astyages, but Cyrus's soldiers defeated him at the Battle of Pteria.

Pursuing the fleeing Lydians into the heart of their own country, the Persians found themselves outnumbered when Croesus called up all his reserves. Famous for his wealth, the Lydian ruler could marshal impressive forces, reportedly just over 100,000 to the Persians' 50,000. Cyrus formed his army into a vast defensive square, surrounded by the camels from his baggage train. The onrushing Lydian cavalry fanned out as though to enfold the square in a classic encircling movement, but soon realized that they had spread themselves too thin. Worse, their horses shied away in panic at the strange sight and smell of the Persian camels, an effect that Cyrus had noticed earlier at Pteria. Croesus's army broke and scattered; the king withdrew to his capital Sardis, but it was taken by the Persians after a two-week siege. **MK**

Losses: Unknown

Opis 539 BCE

After his emphatic victory at Sardis, Persian ruler Cyrus II continued to expand his newly founded empire. His crushing victory over the Babylonians at Opis in 539 BCE removed the last significant block to Persian power in West Asia and confirmed Cyrus as one of history's greatest empire builders.

Nabonidus became king of Babylon, the major power in Mesopotamia, in 556 BCE, and the events of his reign were carefully recorded in the *Chronicle of Nabonidus*. But, ironically, the king has endured as a peripheral player in his own history, which is read nowadays chiefly for what it tells us about the career of Cyrus. Understandably, perhaps, Nabonidus's scribes did not feel like dwelling on the events of 539 BCE—year seventeen of their master's reign. They concede that Nabonidus's army was comprehensively defeated at Opis, a city on the banks of the Tigris, north of Babylon, but give no details of the fighting. There was clearly much destruction in the wake of the battle, as the chronicle speaks of massacre and plunder after the Persian victory. The defeat of Nabonidus appears to have triggered a popular uprising against his rule. With the people up in arms and Nabonidus's soldiers deserting him in droves, the nearby city of Sippar was "taken without a blow being struck," according to the chronicle. The way then lay open to Babylon itself.

Writing at a much later date, the Greek historian Herodotus claimed that Cyrus had his men drain the moat around the capital so that they could get across and storm its walls. The contemporary chronicle, however, seems to suggest that Babylon fell without a fight. The victory left Cyrus with an empire stretching from Central Asia to the Mediterranean. **MK**

Losses: Unknown

Opis 539 BCE [>]   [<] Sardis 546 BCE   Marathon 490 BCE [>]

Rome 508 BCE

The story of their forefathers' fight against Etruscan tyrants was told by Romans over generations, but historians are divided over whether it actually took place. Yet the legend records one verifiable truth: Rome's emergence as an independent state.

The Etruscans are known as Italy's first advanced civilization, famous for their richly decorated tombs. However, the Romans did their best to bury the reputation of a line of kings who for generations had held their forefathers in subjection. Some time around 509 BCE, the citizens of the Latin city rose up and expelled the king, Lucius Tarquinius Superbus, the seventh—and, as it turned out, the last—of the Etruscan line.

When Superbus returned, it was with his kinsmen's backing. Marching south, the Etruscan army took the Romans by surprise, approaching from behind the Janiculum, a hill to the west across the Tiber. Farmers raced for the safety of the Sulpician Bridge—the only crossing point into the city—as the enemy appeared above. No resistance had been prepared, and the capture of Rome seemed a formality until Horatius Cocles came up with an impulsive plan.

Taking up positions at the far end of the bridge, he and two friends—Spurius Lartius and Titus Herminius—stood side by side. In the narrow confines of the bridge, they were able to hold the advancing Etruscans back, while their comrades worked frantically to demolish the bridge behind them. Finally the two friends were forced to retreat, but Horatius held on a few moments longer before leaping into the Tiber and swimming back to safety. **MK**

Losses: Unknown

River Allia 390 BCE ▶

This sarcophagus relief shows the Greek hoplite infantry taking the upper hand in the Battle of Marathon. ⬇

Marathon   August or September 490 BCE

At the Bay of Marathon the army of the city-state of Athens defeated an invasion of Greece by Persian King Darius. Western historians have traditionally represented Marathon as a crucial victory for European civilization over Asiatic despotism.

By 500 BCE the Persian Empire had expanded to include modern Turkey and Macedonia. Greece was ruled by various city-states, of which Athens and Sparta were dominant. In 499 BCE Athens supported a rebellion against Persian rule by a group of Greek cities in Asia Minor. Having defeated this rebellion Darius resolved to conquer Greece itself.

In late summer 490 BCE, a Persian army—supported by 600 ships—came ashore at Marathon, 25 miles (40 km) from Athens, and Athens sent its army of 10,000 men—supported by a contingent from Plataea—to confront the landing force. After a five-day standoff, the battle commenced.

Although outnumbered by the Persians, the Athenians decided to attack. The Greek forces were based around hoplite infantry: armored Athenian citizens carrying a large shield and a long stabbing spear. They charged the Persians at a run, braving a hail of arrows. According to Greek historian Herodotus, the Persians thought the Athenians were mad to attack a superior force "without support of cavalry or archers." Although initially thrown back by the Persians in the center, the Greeks soon had the better of the hand-to-hand fighting. The Persians broke and fled to their ships with the hoplites in hot pursuit. According to Greek tradition, the messenger Pheidippedes ran to Athens carrying news of the victory—the original "marathon." **DS**

Losses: Persian, 6,000 of 20,000; Greek, 200 of 10,000

◁ *Opis 539 BCE*   *Thermopylae 480 BCE* ▷

Artemisium August 480 BCE

When the Persians invaded Greece in 480 BCE, their massive land army was accompanied by an equally outsize fleet. While a Spartan-led force tried to block the Persians on land at Thermpoylae, a parallel sea battle was fought off the Greek coast at Artemisium.

The Greek city-states, led by Sparta and Athens, had equipped themselves with a substantial fleet of triremes. Each of these nimble vessels was rowed into battle by 170 oarsmen. The boats carried only a handful of soldiers, and their offensive weapon was a heavy ram protruding from the bow below the waterline. In battle, a trireme sought to outmaneuver the enemy, using skillful rowing by its oarsmen; it would then move in to crush the enemy hull by ramming it.

Led by the Spartan Eurybiades and the Athenian Themistocles, a fleet of some 300 Greek triremes—half of them Athenian—assembled to block the Straits of Artemisium between Euboea island and the Greek mainland. The Persians cleverly sought to trap the Greek fleet by sending 200 of their ships around the seaward side of Euboea. The Greeks might have been caught between this force and the main Persian fleet, but the plan went wrong when a sudden storm destroyed almost all of the 200-ship detachment. The Persians still had plenty of vessels left, and—after two days of skirmishing—sought a full-scale battle. They bore down in a huge sickle formation upon the bay where the Greek fleet was based. The Greeks rowed out to attack, hoping to smash through the Persian line. Fighting raged all day, with heavy losses on both sides. In the evening, the two fleets withdrew to repair damage and bury their dead. Afterward, the Greeks headed south to Salamis, where the decisive naval battle of the war would be fought. **RG**

Losses: Greek, 100 ships of 300; Persian, 200 ships of 900

◁ *Marathon 490 BCE*   *Salamis 480 BCE* ▷

Thermopylae August 480 BCE

Ten years after the defeat at Marathon, the Persian invasion of Greece was resumed by King Xerxes in 480 BCE. A Spartan-led Greek army tried to block the Persian advance at the pass of Thermopylae but was defeated despite brave resistance against overwhelming odds.

Persian King Xerxes led a vast army overland from the Dardanelles, accompanied by a substantial fleet moving along the coast. His forces quickly seized northern Greece. The alliance of Greek city-states, led by Athens and Sparta, then tried to halt Persian progress on land at the narrow pass of Thermopylae and at sea nearby in the straits of Artemisium.

The Greek army was led by the Spartan king, Leonidas. He had perhaps 7,000 men and faced some 70,000 enemies. The armored Greek infantry held a line only a few dozen yards long between a steep hillside and the sea. This constricted battlefield prevented the Persians bringing their superior numbers to bear. The Greeks threw back two days of fierce Persian attacks, imposing heavy casualties while suffering relatively light losses themselves. Xerxes despaired of a breakthrough until he learned of a hill path that his troops could use to outflank the enemy line. On the third day, the Persians attacked via this route, brushed aside the Greek flank guard, and annihilated the parts of the Greek army that did not withdraw in time.

Leonidas and his 300-man bodyguard are said to have refused to retreat because it was contrary to Spartan law and custom. They staged a final suicide attack in which they were wiped out. Meanwhile, the largely Athenian Greek naval force received news of the defeat at Thermopylae and withdrew from Artemisium after a drawn battle with the Persian fleet. **DS**

Losses: Greek, 3,000; Persian, up to 20,000

◁ *Marathon 490 BCE*   *Salamis 480 BCE* ▷

A fifth-century BCE marble sculpture of the Spartan king, Leonidas.

Salamis   23 September 480 BCE

After defeating the Greeks on land at Thermopylae, King Xerxes of Persia continued his invasion of Greece. Most of the Greek armies retreated into southern Greece, but their fleets assembled at Salamis, where they decisively defeated a Persian naval attack.

After Thermopylae, the Persians advanced their large army toward Athens. Greatly outnumbered, the Greek alliance withdrew its army across the narrow isthmus of Corinth into the Peloponnese and set up defenses there. The people of Athens mostly evacuated their city, which was captured and burned by the Persians, and moved to the island of Salamis in the Bay of Eleusis nearby.

Under the leadership of Themistocles, Athens had built up a substantial fleet in the years before the war began. Joined by contingents from some twenty other city-states, they had fought the drawn Battle of Artemisium against the Persian fleet at the same time as Thermopylae. The allied fleet then reassembled in the Bay of Salamis, and Themistocles persuaded the leaders of the various contingents to stay and offer battle. According to ancient sources, the "Persian" force, which included contingents from Phoenicia and Egypt—as well as King Xerxes' Greek allies—had 1,200 ships and the Greek alliance some 370, about half of them Athenian; modern assessments suggest that the true strengths were about 600 and 200, respectively.

Xerxes might have done better to have blockaded the Greeks inside the bay and used the bulk of his fleet to take his army across to the Peloponnese to outflank the Greek defenses and finish the war on land. Instead, he ordered a naval attack, and had his throne set up on a hill overlooking the bay so that he could watch the action unfold.

All the ships on both sides were powered principally by oars. Most of the crews were oarsmen but each ship also carried a smaller number of marines, able to lead boarding actions. The most important type of ship was the narrow-beamed and maneuverable trireme, powered by three banks of oars. It was fitted with a ram at the bow, which could sink an enemy ship or be used to shear off an enemy vessel's oars, leaving it helpless.

As the huge Persian force moved into the confined waters of the bay, its lines became disorganized; Themistocles may have fooled the Persians into attacking at a time when the seas were choppy seas, which would have disrupted their advance. The smaller Greek force had room to maneuver and began a series of well-coordinated ramming and boarding attacks that reduced the Persian formation to chaos and gradually picked off more and more of their ships. Fierce fighting continued throughout the day, but eventually the remainder of the Persian fleet retreated in disorder. With winter approaching and his supply lines now vulnerable to Greek attack, Xerxes decided to return home with much of his army, but he left part of it in northern Greece to continue the war the following year.

Salamis marked the turning point in Persian attempts to expand to the west, confirmed when they were defeated at Plataea in 479 BCE. Instead, for the next couple of centuries, Greece would dominate the eastern Mediterranean lands, and with this dominance would come the flowering of the Hellenic civilization from which much of modern Western culture is ultimately derived. **DS**

Losses: Greek, 40 ships; Persian, 200 ships; human casualties unknown

◁ *Thermopylae 480 BCE*   *Plataea 479 BCE* ▷

Plataea July 479 BCE

Following the Greek naval success at the Battle of Salamis in 480 BCE, Persian King Xerxes left Greece with much of his army. However, his general, Mardonius, remained in northern Greece to continue the fight. The war's deciding encounter at Plataea the next summer proved to be a crushing Greek victory.

Although Xerxes had returned to Asia and the Persian fleet had retreated to the eastern Aegean (and would be defeated there in 479 BCE), Mardonius still had a vast army, substantially larger than the Greek alliance's force. After initial maneuvers, Mardonius established a base at Plataea in the territory of Persia's ally, Thebes. The Greek army, under the Spartan Pausanius, assembled on hills near the Persian camp to confront them.

At first, neither side wanted to make a full-scale attack, but the Persian cavalry successfully raided Greek supply routes and blocked some of the springs that provided their water supply. Pausanius therefore decided on a night move to a new position. This maneuver did not go as planned, and when dawn broke the Greek force was strung out and disorganized. Mardonius saw his opportunity and attacked. This offensive gave the Greeks the chance they needed. At close quarters their well-armed hoplite infantry gradually gained the upper hand. Mardonius himself was killed in action with the Spartans, and the leaderless Persians then broke and fled. As always in an ancient battle, the casualties of a routing army were horrific. Thousands of Persians were slaughtered on the retreat or in their camp; what was left of the Persian army withdrew north into Thessaly. Fighting between Greeks and Persians continued for many years, but the Persians never invaded Greece again. **DS**

Losses: Persian, 30,000 of 100,000; Greek, 2,000 of 40,000

◁ Salamis 480 BCE

Pylos July 425 BCE

In the Peloponnesian War, Athens, Sparta, and their respective allies contested supremacy in Greece and the eastern Mediterranean. Sparta was usually stronger on land and Athens at sea. At Pylos, an Athenian naval success led to the surrender of a Spartan land force, an almost unprecedented event.

From around 460 BCE, Athens and its allies in the so-called Delian League—mainly island and coastal states around the Aegean—fought a series of wars against Sparta and its allies, based predominantly in the Peloponnese and other parts of mainland Greece. Backed by its great trading wealth, Athens was dominant at sea and the city itself was strongly fortified. Athens thus held out against repeated Spartan land invasions.

From around 426 BCE a new Athenian leader, Cleon, began a more aggressive strategy, stepping up raids on the coast of the Peloponnese. In the course of these operations, a small Athenian force set up a base in the summer of 425 BCE at Pylos, on the Bay of Navarino, on the southwest coast. Faced with this threat close to their home city, the Spartans attacked.

A three-stage battle followed. At first, superior Spartan forces attacked the Greek camp on land, but were soon beaten off. Next the main Athenian fleet arrived, defeated the Spartan fleet, and captured a number of its ships. This left a small Spartan army cut off on the island of Sphacteria in the bay. After peace negotiations failed, the Athenians attacked the island and forced the Spartans to surrender. Those surrendering included more than one hundred of Sparta's elite warrior class, an outcome that was a shocking blow to Spartan prestige and an inspiration to Athens and its allies as the war continued. **DS**

Losses: 300 Spartan and allied troops surrender; other losses unknown

Delium 424 BCE ▷

Delium   November 424 BCE

With Sparta's efforts in the Peloponnesian War limited by the defeat at Pylos the previous year, Athens continued its strategy of taking the fight to the enemy in 424 BCE with an invasion of Boeotia. The attack was heavily defeated at Delium by Boeotian forces, led by its principal city, Thebes, under the command of Pagondas.

In 424 BCE Athens planned converging attacks on Boeotia, an area immediately to the northwest of Athenian territory, but in the end only one attack was carried out in full. An Athenian fleet landed an army under Hippocrates at Delium, where the Athenians planned to set up a fortified base. Once established, the main Athenian force moved off from the base and the shadowing enemy force decided to attack, inspired by the Theban leader Pagondas.

Each side had about 7,000 hoplite heavy infantry, which had formed the backbone of all Greek armies for many years. However, by this time, Greek armies were becoming more varied in composition, and their tactics more sophisticated. Both sides had a cavalry contingent—with the 1,000 Boeotians outnumbering their enemies approximately two to one—and both had strong light infantry forces, although these seem to have played little part in the fighting.

When the battle began, Pagondas made his right wing overwhelmingly strong and it soon crushed its immediate opponents. Meanwhile, on the opposite flank, the Athenians gained an advantage—despite some of their troops mistakenly attacking each other—but were then sent into retreat by a surprise cavalry attack. In the aftermath, the Athenians abandoned the base at Delium and sailed home. The defeat at Delium was one of several setbacks for Athens that led to a peace agreement in 421 BCE. **DS**

Losses: Athenian, 1,200; Boeotia and allied, 500

◁ *Pylos* 425 BCE   *Syracuse* 413 BCE ▷

Syracuse   September 413 BCE

The peace of Nicias of 421 BCE did not end the Peloponnesian War. Within a few years, new Athenian leaders were looking for conquests among Sparta's allies on Sicily, an important source of grain supplies for the Spartan confederation. Athens sent a massive expeditionary force to attack Syracuse, but it was eventually annihilated.

Athens's Sicilian expedition set off in 415 BCE, inspired by the idea that capturing Syracuse might bring dominance over Sicily as a whole and supply the resources that Athens would need to win its long war with Sparta. Although the initial Athenian force was very strong—with 130 triremes, 5,000 hoplite infantry, and numerous supporting ships and lighter troops—it began operations with a halfhearted attack on the city. In the spring of 414 BCE, commanded by Nicias—a rather indecisive general who had opposed making the expedition in the first place—it settled down to besiege Syracuse. Sparta and its allies sent troops and a fleet to Sicily, and a series of inconclusive land and sea battles around Syracuse followed.

Athens responded with thousands of reinforcements but they too failed to break the deadlock. Yet more enemy troops arrived from the Peloponnese, and the Athenian commanders finally decided to leave—but it was too late. The Syracusans and their allies gained the upper hand in a naval engagement in the harbor and established a blockade. In a series of hard-fought naval battles in September 413 BCE, they burned or sank all the trapped Athenian ships. The Athenian army tried to escape overland, abandoning its many sick and wounded, but it was brought to battle and defeated. The survivors were captured and sold into slavery. Athens was gravely weakened yet its war with Sparta continued. **DS**

Losses: Athenian, at least 40,000 dead or captured; Sicilian and Spartan, unknown

◁ *Delium* 424 BCE   *Arginusae* 406 BCE ▷

Arginusae 406 BCE

Aegospotami 405 BCE

In the continuing Peloponnesian War, the action focused around the islands of the Aegean, where Sparta—with Persian help—was challenging Athens's previous naval dominance. Athens was struggling, but new tactics helped win an important victory at Arginusae.

Sparta's victory at Aegospotami led, within months, to the end of the Peloponnesian War. Athens's last fleet was wiped out in a surprise attack, and, shortly after, the triumphant Spartan forces surrounded Athens by land and sea, eventually starving the city into surrender.

By 406 BCE Sparta had a larger fleet in action in the Aegean than Athens. In the first phase of fighting, the undermanned main Athenian fleet was trapped in the harbor at Mytilene, on the island of Lesbos, off the coast of Asia Minor. Athens scraped together a relief force of about 150 triremes, manned in large part by freed slaves. This was sent to meet the Spartan force near the Arginusae islands, between Lesbos and the Asian mainland. The Spartans had about 120 ships in action after part of their fleet was left to hold the other Athenian force in Mytilene. In order to offset the inexperience of their crews, the Athenian commanders devised a new two-line formation to make it harder for the Spartan ships to make ramming attacks. They also managed to concentrate their superior numbers against the wings of the Spartan fleet. Spartan resistance was gradually worn down, many of their ships were sunk, and their commander, Callicratidas, was killed. The remains of the Spartan fleet fled.

Both Athens and Sparta were riven by political rivalries. In the aftermath of the battle, six of the successful Athenian commanders were executed for failing to rescue the crews of damaged ships (there was a storm). For its part, rather than restore the previously successful commander Lysander, the governing faction in Sparta offered generous peace terms, which the Athenians unwisely rejected. **DS**

Athens was heavily dependent on grain supplies from the Black Sea region and relied on its fleet to keep the sea lanes open. Following their defeat at Arginusae, the Spartans revived their Persian alliance, which helped them rebuild their fleet, and reappointed the noted admiral Lysander to command. In the early stages of the 405 BCE campaign, he slipped past the Athenian fleet in the Aegean and set up a secure and well-supplied base at a town on the south side of the Dardanelles strait, blocking the route to the Black Sea. The pursuing Athenian fleet established its base on the north side of the strait, but on an open beach without a nearby source of supplies.

Ancient writers give two different versions of the battle that followed. According to one account, Lysander caught a detachment of the Athenian fleet when it was out on a supply mission and then overwhelmed the rest of the Athenian forces. The other, more likely, account says that the Athenians had beached their ships and sent most of their crews inland to find food. Lysander took the initiative and the Spartans attacked, capturing most of the Athenian ships with little fighting.

However it happened, the result was clear. Only a handful of the Athenian ships escaped, and thousands of Athenian sailors were taken prisoner and subsequently executed. The Athenians tried to continue the war but it was a hopeless cause without grain supplies. They surrendered in March 404 BCE. **DS**

Losses: Athenian, 25 ships; Spartan, 70 ships; casualties unknown

◁ Syracuse 413 BCE   Aegospotami 405 BCE ▷

Losses: Athenian, 150 ships, 3,000 prisoners executed; Spartan, very few ships or men

◁ Arginusae 406 BCE

River Allia   390 BCE

"There was nothing to remind one of Romans either among the generals or the private soldiers. They were terrified."

Roman historian Livy, c. 27–25 BCE

⬆ *Sculpted relief of the sacred geese in flight in front of the temple of Juno Moneto, Capitoline Hill, Rome.*

The Romans' sense of their special destiny—defending civilization against savage barbarism—was reinforced by their first unfortunate encounter with the Celts, led by Brennus. After weeks of heavy losses, Rome's innermost defenses were only saved after a night attack that set Gallic raiders against a goddess and her geese.

A warrior elite of central European origin, known as the Celts or Gauls, had by the middle of the first millennium BCE expanded west into France and Spain and east into the Balkans. As Brennus, chief of the Gallic tribe the Senones, came over the Alps with an army some 20,000 strong, Rome was ill-prepared. The Romans were all too conscious of the culture clash. "You do not face a Latin or Sabine foe who, once you have beaten him, will become your ally," Consul Marcus Popilius Caenas warned his troops on the banks of the River Allia, a few miles northeast of Rome. "We have drawn our swords against wild beasts whose blood we must shed or spill our own." These words were written for him later by the Roman historian Livy, but he very likely expressed himself in much these terms.

Rome's center, strong and seasoned troops fighting in a spear-armed phalanx, held firm before a ferocious charge. But the more inexperienced soldiers on either flank broke and ran, allowing the center to be encircled and cut down. The Gauls then advanced on the city itself. Bursting their way in, they sacked and plundered for weeks on end while Rome's last defenders cowered in the Capitol. A night attack on this stronghold was reportedly thwarted when the sacred geese of Juno's temple cackled the alarm. The Gauls were finally forced to withdraw by an epidemic of the plague and negotiated an end to the siege. **MK**

Losses: Unknown

◁ *Rome 508 BCE*   *Trifanum 338 BCE* ▷

Leuctra 6 July 371 BCE

Fought in Boeotia, Greece, the Battle of Leuctra made Thebes the leading military power among the Greek city-states, ending the long dominance of Sparta. The battle also marked a revolutionary advance in battlefield tactics and demonstrated the effectiveness of homosexuality as a form of bonding for elite troops.

Thebes defied the Spartans by leading a league of Boeotian city-states that Sparta was determined to suppress. A force of Spartan and other Peloponnesian troops was thus sent to attack Thebes, which hastily prepared to defend itself with its Boeotian League allies. Although the Thebans were outnumbered and their allies were unreliable, Theban general Epaminondas persuaded his colleagues that they should give battle on the plain at Leuctra.

Thebes was strong in cavalry but its infantry phalanx looked certain to lose against the experienced Spartans. Epaminondas improvised a major departure from Greek military convention. Traditionally the armored hoplite phalanx fought in a block twelve deep, with the best troops in the place of honor on the right. But Epaminondas packed his hoplites on the left of his line in a column about fifty deep, fronted by the Theban Sacred Band, an elite body of 150 homosexual couples. The center and right of his line, weak and depleted, he held back from contact with the Spartan phalanx, screened by skirmishers and horsemen. Advancing obliquely to the attack, the Thebans delivered a crushing blow to the Spartan right, smashing it apart with heavy losses. The rest of the Peloponnesian forces, exposed to attack from the flank, put up little resistance. Sparta suffered above all a blow to its prestige, which encouraged allies and subject states to drift away from its orbit. **RG**

Losses: Theban, 300 of 8,500; Spartan,1,000 of 12,000

Mantinea 362 BCE ▶

Mantinea 4 July 362 BCE

After their triumph at Leuctra, the Thebans were opposed by an alliance of other Greek city-states, including Athens and Sparta. The showdown between Thebes and its rivals at Mantinea was the largest battle ever fought between Greek cities. It left the inspired Theban general Epaminondas dead and Greece leaderless.

In summer 362 BCE, with typical daring, Epaminondas took the offensive against the powerful anti-Theban alliance. He invaded the Peloponnese and, after a surprise attack on Sparta itself failed, moved to threaten Sparta's ally, the city of Mantinea. When the Mantineans were joined by Spartan and Athenian troops, Epaminondas decided to seek battle on a plain in front of the city.

He relied on a variant of the oblique attack that had succeeded so well at Leuctra. His cavalry on the flanks, supported by lightly equipped infantry runners dispersed among the horsemen, drove off the enemy's mounted troops. Meanwhile, the Theban hoplite infantry marched in a column across the face of the enemy infantry line, then performed a smart wheel and crashed with spear and shield into enemy right, where the Mantineans were positioned. The powerful blow was too much for the Mantinean hoplites, who fled. In the thick of the fighting, however, Epaminondas had a spear driven into his body. He died on the battlefield. His death was a crushing setback for Thebes. Instead of following up the victory by imposing their hegemony on the Greek city-states, the Thebans withdrew almost as if defeated. Without a dominant power, Greece soon proved defenseless against the aggression of Philip II of Macedon. Only twenty-seven years later, Thebes was utterly laid to waste by Philip's son, Alexander the Great. **RG**

Losses: Each side lost 1,000 of 25,000

◀ Leuctra 371 BCE

Maling 342 BCE

The Battle of Maling, in Henan Province, was fought between the armies of the warring Chinese kingdoms of Qi and Wei during the Warring States Period. It is a famous example of the tactical genius of the Qi general Sun Bin, who achieved an overwhelming victory through a subtle combination of deception and maneuver.

Sun Bin was originally a general in the service of the state of Wei. Falsely accused of treason, he was mutilated by the removal of his kneecaps. The consequent disability prevented him riding a horse but did not stop him escaping to offer his services as a military strategist to the state of Qi. Sun Bin became principal adviser to the Qi military commander Tian Ji.

In 342 BCE the Wei army, led by Sun Bin's rival Pang Juan, attacked the kingdom of Han, Qi's ally. Instead of coming to Han's assistance directly, Sun Bin recommended an attack on the Wei capital, Daliang. This forced the king of Wei to recall Pang Juan's army from Han, where it had been on the verge of victory. The Wei forces were too strong for the Qi army to confront directly, so Sun Bin devised a deception plan. As Pang Juan approached, the Qi forces withdrew from Wei, drawing Pang into pursuit.

Each time the Wei army overran the site of a camp the Qi had recently left, it found abandoned weaponry and evidence of a decreasing number of camp fires. Pang thus assumed, as Sun Bin intended, that the Qi army was shrinking through desertion. To speed up the pursuit, Pang forged ahead with his fleetest cavalry. At a narrow pass, Qi archers waited in ambush. The Wei cavalry was slaughtered by crossbow bolts, and the rest of the Wei army was put to flight. Pang Juan died, either committing suicide or killed in the battle. **RG**

Losses: No reliable figures; one source gives Wei losses at 100,000, but this is a vast exaggeration

◁ Chengpu 632 BCE Changping 260 BCE ▷

Trifanum 338 BCE

Given the historic glories to come, the early rise of the Romans now seems entirely inevitable. In reality, however, this was far from the truth. In 338 BCE, a twofold assault—at Mount Vesuvius and Trifanum—by the Campanians and the allied cities of the Latin League came very close to destroying Rome for good.

Rome had earned its ascendancy in Italy leading the resistance to the invading Gauls. Men such as Titus Manlius had performed epic deeds of strength and courage. His honorific title "Torquatus" referred to the torc or neckring he had taken from the giant Gaul he had killed in single combat. In recognition of his achievements, he had been given the office of dictator in Rome.

However, former allies felt that Rome was taking dictatorial powers itself. Originally, it had been one of several cities in the Latin League, an alliance first formed for the fight against the Etruscans in the sixth century BCE. By 339 BCE, though, Roman arrogance had alienated not only its Latin neighbors but also its sometime friends in Campania, farther to the south. The Latin cities demanded recognition of their equal status within the alliance, and when that was not forthcoming they joined the Campanians and attacked the Romans from the south.

The two sides met beneath Mount Vesuvius, where the Romans were saved from defeat by Torquatus's heroics: he mounted a horse and galloped into the enemy's midst, causing complete confusion. In 338 BCE, Torquatus took the offensive. With his army strengthened by auxiliaries sent by the Samnites—fierce tribal warriors from the Apennine mountains—he advanced to Trifanum, near Caserta in Campania. A crushing triumph in the battle that followed assured Roman dominance in central Italy. **MK**

Losses: Unknown

◁ River Allia 390 BCE Sentinum 295 BCE ▷

Chaeronea   Aug or Sept 338 BCE

This decisive encounter in Boeotia established the increasing power of Macedon as the leading state in Greece and brought to an end the independent status of the Greek city-states. The tactics used at the Battle of Chaeronea would later be perfected by the young prince Alexander, who came to be known as "the Great."

King Philip II of Macedon had been gradually increasing his control over the independent city-states of Greece. In 338 BCE he took advantage of an obscure religious dispute to declare war on Athens. Led by orator Demosthenes, Athens formed an alliance with Thebes and smaller states. Philip marched against Thebes and was met by the allied army in a valley at Chaeronea. The allies placed the elite Theban Sacred Band on their right, with the Thebans and the minor allies in the center and Athenians on the left. Philip placed his main phalanx of heavy infantry in the center. On the right wing he commanded the elite hypaspist infantry, and on the left he placed his seventeen-year-old son, Alexander, in sole command of the cavalry.

The battle opened with an advance by the Macedonian phalanx and hypaspists. The phalanx then stood firm while the hypaspists withdrew, luring the Athenians forward. The minor allies moved with the Athenians, opening up a gap between themselves and the Thebans. Alexander led his cavalry into this gap, fanning out to attack the Thebans and allies in flank and rear. Philip then halted his withdrawal and ordered a general advance against the crumbling Athenians. The isolated Sacred Band was surrounded and massacred. The victory confirmed Macedon's position as the most powerful state in Greece. **RM**

Losses: Allied, 4,000 dead and 8,000 captured of 35,000; Macedonian, unknown, minor casualties

◁ *Mantinea 362 BCE*

Granicus 334 BCE ▷

Granicus   May 334 BCE

The first victorious engagement of Alexander the Great's invasion of the Persian Empire established the Macedonians on enemy soil. It allowed Alexander to replenish his empty supply stores and encouraged some key Greek states to rebel against the Persians. However, the battle very nearly cost Alexander his life.

After succeeding his father as king of Macedon, Alexander continued the planned invasion of the Persian Empire. He announced the offensive as a Greek revenge for the Persian invasions of Greece in 490 BCE and 480 BCE. His army consisted chiefly of Macedonians, but with some allied Greeks. By crossing into Asia before the campaigning season, it caught the Persians off guard.

Alexander gambled that winning an early victory would allow him to gather supplies for his troops from conquered territory as the harvest ripened. Although advised by Greek mercenary Memnon of Rhodes to fall back and starve Alexander into retreat, the Persian commander Arsames decided to confront the invaders on the Granicus River, east of the Dardanelles. Alexander led a charge of his elite Companion cavalry across the steep-sided stream, but the Persian cavalry launched a countercharge, and Alexander was surrounded and disarmed. His companions rescued him, and the rest of the Macedonian forces succeeded in joining the fight.

After a tough struggle, Alexander's heavy cavalry broke through the Persian army, the Macedonian phalanx followed through the gap, and the Persians fled. Greek mercenaries serving in the Persian army tried to surrender, but Alexander treated them as traitors. Half died in battle; the rest were sent as chained slaves to work in Macedonian mines. **RM**

Losses: Macedonian, 400 dead and 2,000 wounded of 40,000; Persian, 5,000 dead and 2,000 captured of 50,000

◁ *Chaeronea 338 BCE*

Issus 333 BCE ▷

Issus November 333 BCE

The key victory of Alexander the Great's invasion of the Persian Empire saw the Macedonians defeat the main Persian army led by Darius III. Fighting against heavy odds—they were outnumbered four to one—Alexander's forces triumphed through superior leadership, morale, and tactics.

Having won at the Battle of Granicus, Alexander spent the following months establishing Macedonian control over the provinces of Asia Minor. He sent a strong advance guard, under the veteran Parmenio, to hold the city of Issus in northern Syria through which any army sent from Persia would need to advance.

In November 333 BCE, Alexander's scouts brought news that a vast army drawn from many provinces of the Persian Empire was advancing north through Syria. Alexander joined Parmenio and went to meet it. However, the Persian leader, Darius, had marched his army through the mountains to get behind Alexander, thus cutting his supply lines. Alexander turned back to confront the Persians and brought them to battle at the River Pinarus. He had 22,000 armored infantry equipped with long spears and trained to fight in a line sixteen men deep. The front six men held their spears forward to create an impenetrable hedge of points, while those behind added momentum and muscle power. This phalanx could either stand like a rock or advance with a steady, rhythmic march to roll over any formation in front of it, while about 13,000 lightly armed infantry guarded the phalanx flanks. The 6,000 cavalrymen were used as a battering ram to smash a gap in enemy formations and exploit weaknesses.

The Persian army was composed of 10,000 elite "Immortals" and 10,000 Greek mercenary hoplites, both heavy infantry, plus about 8,000 heavy and 10,000 light

Persian leader Darius, facing Alexander on horseback, is supported by infantry with pikes in this first-century BCE mosaic. ⬇

cavalry, and perhaps as many as 80,000 light infantry skirmishers. Darius put his cavalry on the right along the coast where the land was more suitable for horses. The center was held by the heavy infantry, of which Darius took personal command. The left wing consisted of the Persian light infantry who formed a vast mass of men extending into a range of low, broken hills. Alexander put his deputy Parmenio on the coast with half his cavalry. The center was held by the armored phalanx. Alexander himself commanded the elite Companion cavalry on the right. A force of light infantry and some cavalry was to Alexander's right to face the extreme Persian left.

The battle opened with the Persian cavalry crossing the River Pinarus and pushing back Parmenio, who withdrew in good order. Meanwhile the Macedonian phalanx had advanced, causing the Persian heavy infantry to edge back. Alexander spotted a weakness in the enemy line where the heavy infantry met the lighter left flank forces. He charged into the space with his Companion cavalry, burst through to the Persian rear, and then wheeled left to where he could see Darius and the Persian senior commanders. Lacking a reserve to hold off Alexander and his horsemen, Darius fled. Alexander let him go, instead attacking the rear of the Persian heavy infantry formations. The Persian army collapsed into confusion and then fled, suffering many casualties as they tried to escape into the hills to the north and east. Alexander captured the Persian camp, in which he found Darius's wife, mother, and daughters—whom he treated well—along with huge amounts of booty. **RM**

Losses: Macedonian, 6,000 dead and wounded of 30,000 engaged; Persian, 20,000 of 120,000 engaged

◁ *Granicus 334 BCE*　　　　　　　　*Gaugamela 331 BCE* ▷

Gaugamela (Arbela) 1 Oct 331 BCE

Alexander the Great completed his conquest of Darius III's Persian Empire with an extraordinary victory achieved against a numerically superior army on ground chosen by the Persians. As at Issus, the aggression of the Macedonian cavalry led by Alexander carried the day.

Alexander the Great spent a year after Issus securing his grip on the western provinces of the Persian Empire, while Darius raised a new army from the central core of his empire and awaited the invader in Mesopotamia. Alexander took up the challenge, embarking on the long march eastward in spring 331 BCE.

As Alexander approached, Darius drew up his army on a broad plain where his superior numbers would have maximum effect. He had the ground cleared of obstacles so that his force of 200 chariots could charge unhindered. His army also included Indian war elephants. Rejecting the option of a night attack, Alexander boldly advanced to take on the formidable Persian host in open battle.

The combat began with the Macedonian infantry phalanx advancing to face the Persian center, driving off chariot attacks. Alexander was leading the cavalry on the Macedonian right. He took his horsemen farther to the right, threatening to outflank the left of the Persian line. The Persians moved left to block the outflanking move, but this opened a gap between their left and center. Alexander sent his light infantry to hold the Persian left wing while he wheeled his cavalry about and charged into the gap. He broke through, widening the gap so that his heavy infantry could follow. Darius fled to avoid capture, and the Persian army began to collapse. Darius was later murdered by one of his satraps, and Alexander took the Persian capital Babylon. **RM**

Losses: Macedonian, 700 of 47,000; Persian, possibly 20,000 of 100,000

◁ Issus 333 BCE   Hydaspes 326 BCE ▷

Hydaspes Late spring 326 BCE

The fight on the banks of the Hydaspes River in India was the closest Alexander the Great came to defeat. His feared Companion cavalry was unable to subdue fully the courageous King Porus. Hydaspes marked the limit of Alexander's career of conquest; he died before he could launch another campaign.

After conquering the Persian Empire, Alexander decided to probe into northern India. King Porus of Paurava blocked Alexander's advance at a ford on the Hydaspes River (now the Jhelum) in the Punjab. The forces were numerically quite evenly balanced, although Alexander had more cavalry and Porus fielded 200 war elephants.

Alexander divided his army, leaving a small force with Craterus facing Porus on the ford while taking most of the army to cross a second ford 17 miles (27 km) away. When Porus learned that Alexander had advanced over the river, he marched to attack. Porus put his cavalry on the flanks and infantry in the center, with the elephants in front. Alexander posted his heavy infantry in a phalanx in the center, led the right wing cavalry himself, and sent the left wing cavalry under Coenus on a wide, outflanking ride behind a hill.

In the center, the Macedonian phalanx was almost broken by the charging elephants, but eventually drove them off, only to face the Indian infantry. Alexander attacked on the right, but failed to find a gap to exploit with his horsemen. When Coenus returned to the battlefield at the rear of the Indians, Alexander was able to defeat the Indian cavalry and encircle the infantry. Porus reformed his infantry into a defensive block and then offered to surrender if granted generous terms. Alexander agreed Porus could remain king of Paurava but imposed tribute. **RM**

Losses: Macedonian, 1,000 of 41,000; Indian, 12,000 dead and 9,000 captured of 50,000

◁ Gaugamela 331 BCE   Ipsos 301 BCE ▷

⟵ *An eighteenth-century ivory relief depicting a scene from the Battle of Gaugamela.*

Ipsos 301 BCE

Alexander the Great's sudden death in Babylon in 323 BCE left his leading generals locked in decades of squabbling over the spoils of his empire. At Ipsos, Antigonus—long in the ascendant—was finally overpowered by the combined forces of his rivals, and particularly by their strength in elephants.

With a powerbase at the heart of Alexander's empire in Asia Minor, Syria, and Palestine, Antigonus appeared to have the upper hand among the *diadochi* (successors). His son, Demetrius, had taken Athens and southern Greece, but others opposed their primacy: Lysimachus, ruler of Macedon and Thrace; Seleucus, who had established himself as king across Mesopotamia, Persia, and other eastern territories; and Cassander, whose father Antipater had taken charge of Alexander's homeland in Macedon.

The last great *diadochus*—Ptolemy, ruler of Egypt—was still struggling to rebuild his armies after Antigonus's invasion of 306 BCE. This experience convinced the successors of the need to offer concerted resistance. In 301 BCE, accordingly, Lysimachus and Cassander came together with Seleucus to do battle with Antigonus and Demetrius in open grassland near Ipsos, Phrygia, in the center of what is now Turkey.

Skirmishers engaged before the heavy infantry pushed slowly together from both sides; Demetrius drove forward, with the elite of the Antigonid cavalry, from the right flank. His attempted encirclement was thwarted when Seleucus deployed his elephants as a living wall. Antigonus's own seventy-odd elephants had given him a clear edge over rivals in earlier rounds, but Seleucus had 400 animals, and this made the difference. As the allied infantry pressed their advantage in a storm of arrows, slingshot, and other missiles, Antigonus was caught and killed by a javelin. **MK**

Losses: Unknown

[<] *Hydaspes 326 BCE*   *Raphia 217 BCE* [>]

Sentinum 295 BCE

Gallic chariots spearheaded a strong if motley coalition, united in its resolve to stop the rise of Rome. Instead, the Romans emerged as the victors in this battle and the dominant power in the Italian peninsula, demonstrating the effectiveness of their new military organization, the legion.

Although beaten in two earlier wars, the Samnite mountain warriors of the Apennines were determined to check the apparently inexorable expansion of Roman influence. In near desperation, they formed an ecumenical alliance that included not only the neighboring Umbrians and Etruscans but also Celtic tribes from the north Italian plains and Alpine foothills. They set out to meet the Romans in central Italy.

Facing an army that was almost double their own size, the Romans mounted small-scale diversionary attacks against Etruria and Umbria: these succeeded in drawing away the armies of those two peoples. This still left the legions outnumbered by about 40,000 to 50,000 men by the time battle commenced. Led on the left by Decius Mus and on the right by his friend and fellow consul Fabius Rullianus, the Roman army faced a daunting task.

A series of headlong chariot charges by the Gauls very nearly broke their resolve. On the left, however, sensing that his men's resistance was close to crumbling, Decius Mus plunged into the thick of the Celt attack. He was killed, but his heroic self-sacrifice inspired his troops into action and they finally held firm. (Legend holds that his father and son also sacrificed themselves in battle.)

On the right, meanwhile, Fabius was faring far better against the Samnites. With his infantry having softened up the enemy ranks, he was able to bring up reinforcements and, at last, deploy his powerful cavalry, who cut down the Samnites mercilessly as they fled. **MK**

Losses: Roman, 8,000; Samnites and allied, 25,000 dead

[<] *Trifanum 338 BCE*   *Asculum 279 BCE* [>]

Asculum 279 BCE

The original "Pyrrhic victory" saw the renowned Greek general, Pyrrhus of Epirus, carry all before him in a battle with the stubborn Romans—but at a cost in lives that could not be sustained. "One more such victory," Pyrrhus reportedly said, "and we are undone." The unbroken rise of Rome continued.

Pyrrhus of Epirus reigned over a rugged kingdom in northwest Greece. To the west, in southern Italy, cities founded as trading colonies by Greeks in centuries past were worried by the relentless rise of Roman power. At the invitation of one of these cities, Tarentum, Pyrrhus brought an army to Italy. As well as the Greeks, Samnites, Etruscans, and Umbrians—long-standing enemies of Rome—flocked to his standard.

Pyrrhus's army was typical of the eastern Mediterranean: armored infantry—fighting with long spears in a tight phalanx—cavalry, and war elephants. He defeated the Roman legions, who had never confronted elephants before, at Heraclea in 280 BCE. But far from giving in, the Romans assembled a fresh army and resumed the offensive the following year. They brought with them an array of ingenious spiked chariots, traps, and flares intended to stop Pyrrhus's elephants.

The armies met on wooded, hilly terrain at Asculum in Apulia. On the first day, Pyrrhus's infantry drove back the legions, but his allies proved less robust and his elephants were ineffective in woodland. On the second day, Pyrrhus succeeded in driving the Romans into the open, where the elephants' lumbering advance overcame the Roman anti-elephant devices. The legions succumbed to the combined pressure of the phalanx, and the pachyderms finally put them to flight. The victory was without long-term effect—bar the genesis of the phrase "Pyrrhic victory"—and Pyrrhus left Italy for good in 275 BCE. **MK**

> *"[This] Lernean Hydra . . . grows two heads for each one cut off."*
>
> *Pyrrhus on the Roman army*

Losses: Roman, 8,000; Epirian, 3,000, including key officers

◁ Sentinum 295 BCE   Mylae 260 BCE ▷

A Roman copy of a Greek bust of Pyrrhus, king of Epirus, found in the ancient town of Herculaneum.

Kalinga Campaign 265 BCE

The conquest of the kingdom of Kalinga by India's Mauryan Empire was bought at the expense of much bloodshed: casualties were horrific on both sides. Appalled and sickened, one of world history's great warrior kings became a convert to Buddhism and a man of peace.

The empire built by Chandragupta Maurya in the final quarter of the fourth century BCE expanded steadily under his successors. Chandragupta's grandson, Ashoka, was the greatest of these. Ashoka, who reigned from 272 BCE, held sway over most of the Indian subcontinent along with Afghanistan and Baluchistan. But he was angry that the kingdom of Kalinga, in what is now Orissa, on India's east coast, had thus far held out against Mauryan might. In addition, it had taken advantage of Ashoka's absorption in campaigns against far-southern kingdoms to make incursions into the territories of the Mauryan Empire in the east.

Ashoka attacked in 265 BCE, in overwhelming force: his army is said to have been 400,000 strong. Kalinga could muster only a fraction of that number in its defense, although some 700 elephants helped to even the balance a little, and its soldiers defended their homeland with the utmost courage.

This, however, only provoked the invaders to ever more brutal acts of savagery: many thousands of civilians are believed to have been massacred as the Mauryans sought to break the resolve of the Kalingans. The campaign culminated in a confrontation on and around the Dhauli hill on the banks of the Daya River, which is said to have run red with the blood of those slain. Ashoka was so shocked at what he had done that he became a Buddhist and forswore all future conflict. **MK**

Losses: Mauryan, 10,000; Kalingan, 150,000, including civilians

Detail from the Buddhist monument commissioned by Ashoka at the Great Stupa in Sanchi, India. ⬆

Changping 260 BCE

At Changping, the lengthy rivalry between the kingdoms of Qin and Zhao reached a bloody showdown. The battle is not only remembered as a milestone toward the unification of China under the Qin dynasty, but also as one of the greatest atrocities of all time.

The Warring States Period in Chinese history covers the time between 475 and 221 BCE: the title is as accurate as it is stark. States did, indeed, war pretty much ceaselessly, and the stronger states expanded at the expense of their weaker neighbors. During this period, military philosophy was modernizing and the old heroic ethos was being shed, along with the chariot. Technology had been transformed by the introduction of iron: sharp and durable blades could be mass produced, and vast numbers of infantrymen and trained cavalry could be armed.

By the third century BCE, the situation had shaken down, and only two major players were left in the game: the western state of Qin and Zhao, whose territories lay farther north. When Qin invaded Han in 265 BCE, its desperate rulers appealed to Zhao for help: the two powers were now on a collision course. Zhao's commander Lian Po led 500,000 troops into the disputed area. There, faced with a Qin army more than 600,000 strong, he dug in—in a series of fortified camps—awaiting reinforcements.

However, the Qin cut off their enemy, preventing any help from arriving and setting a siege that they kept up for three full years. Finally, Lian Po's men were forced to break out for a battle which—starved and weakened as they were—they were ill-equipped to fight. Not surprisingly, they soon surrendered. Not satisfied, Qin commander Bai Qi wanted the potentially powerful army removed from the strategic equation and had 400,000 prisoners executed, burying them alive. **MK**

Losses: Zhao, 450,000; Qin, 250,000

◁ Maling 342 BCE   Julu 207 BCE ▷

⬆ *Life-size terra-cotta warriors were constructed to guard the mausoleum of the first Qin emperor.*

Mylae 260 BCE

Having become increasingly dominant on the Italian mainland, Rome proceeded to challenge Carthage—a trading empire based in north Africa—for control of Sicily. At Mylae, a newly created Roman fleet used novel tactics to defeat the more experienced Carthaginian sailors.

Rome had risen to control much of Italy as a land power and began its war with Carthage with victories on land in Sicily. Maintaining these new conquests required naval power, so Rome rapidly built its first fleet of ships. Like all warships of the era, these were oar-powered. However, the Romans were aware that their sailors and oarsmen were unlikely to be skilled enough to employ ramming tactics, so they equipped their ships to bring about a boarding action where their familiar land warfare techniques could be used. They fitted their vessels with a new secret weapon: the *corvus*, in effect a combined grappling hook and gangplank, so that their marines could rush aboard and capture any Carthaginian ship that came close, a position the Carthaginians needed to adopt if they were to use their traditional ramming methods.

In 260 BCE the two fleets fought near the small island of Mylae, off northeastern Sicily. Both sides had 120 to 130 ships, but the Carthaginians attacked confidently at first, expecting their greater experience of naval warfare to prevail. Instead, the Carthaginian ships found themselves unexpectedly being grappled and boarded, whether they attacked head-on or tried to maneuver more subtly. After almost half of their ships had been captured or sunk, the Carthaginians retreated.

The consul Gaius Duilius had won Rome's first notable naval victory. His opponent, Hannibal Gisco, was recalled to Carthage and crucified for incompetence. **DS**

Losses: Carthaginian, 50 ships; Roman, unknown

◁ *Asculum* 279 BCE   *Cape Ecnomus* 256 BCE ▷

Cape Ecnomus 256 BCE

Building on its success in land battles on Sicily and in naval encounters such as Mylae, Rome decided to continue the First Punic War by invading north Africa and attacking Carthage directly. Both sides built massive fleets, which met off southern Sicily, with a significant Roman victory as the result.

The fleets that fought the Battle of Cape Ecnomus were truly huge, with both sides having up to 350 vessels carrying 150,000 crewmen and soldiers. The resulting encounter was one of the largest battles of the ancient world and one of the biggest naval combats in history.

Although Rome's navy was new, it was capable of maintaining ordered formations, and the Carthaginians had still not worked out a good counter to the Roman *corvus* and related boarding tactics. As the Romans moved west along Sicily's south coast, they adopted a wedge formation, with their joint commanders—the consuls Marcus Atilius Regulus and Lucius Manlius Volso—leading the two frontline squadrons. Behind came transport ships and a reserve force. The Carthaginians came to meet them in a single, long line abreast, intending to use an encircling maneuver by their flanking squadrons to strike into the Roman transport fleet.

The battle developed as a series of separate actions, each of them hard-fought. Using their now standard boarding methods, the two consuls' squadrons sank or captured many of their opponents from the Carthaginian center force, driving the rest into retreat. Then the whole Roman force concentrated against the other parts of the Carthaginian fleet to complete their victory. Consul Regulus subsequently led an invasion of Carthage's homeland but, after early success, he was defeated the next year and most of his army wiped out. **DS**

Losses: Carthaginian, 94 ships; Roman, 24 ships

◁ *Mylae* 260 BCE   *Drepana* 249 BCE ▷

⬅ *Detail from* Triumph of Rome Over Sicily After the Battle of Mylae *by Jacopo Ripanda, c. 1508–13.*

Drepana   249 BCE

Although it had suffered disastrous naval losses in recent storms, Rome continued its offensive strategy, with land attacks on Carthage's strongholds on Sicily. During a siege of Lilybaeum, the supporting fleets fought near Drepana; Rome was heavily defeated after ignoring ill omens.

While Roman forces were attacking Lilybaeum (modern Marsala), Carthaginian commanders at nearby Drepana (modern Trapani) were able to send supplies to the beleaguered garrison by sea. The Roman consul commanding the operation, Publius Claudius Pulcher, decided to make a surprise attack on the Carthaginian fleet while it was in harbor at Drepana. However, the night approach to the enemy harbor went badly wrong and, as day broke, the Roman fleet was strung out in a disorganized, straggling line nearby. This gave the Carthaginians the chance to move out of the harbor into the open sea, where they would have room to maneuver.

According to ancient writing, Publius Claudius consulted the omens at this point, as was customary during battle. When the sacred chickens refused to eat (which would have predicted a victory), he ordered them thrown overboard with the comment, "Well, let them drink." In the battle that followed, the better organized Carthaginian fleet picked off Claudius's scattered ships one by one. Claudius escaped, to stand trial in Rome—not for the defeat, but for his sacrilegious behavior toward chickens.

Another part of the Roman navy was wrecked in a storm the same year, bringing Rome's naval losses since 255 BCE to 600 or 700 ships and up to 200,000 men. Rome continued the fight on land on Sicily but abandoned major naval operations until around 242 BCE. **DS**

Losses: Roman, 90 ships captured or sunk, 25,000 men dead or captured; Carthaginian, unknown but very slight

◁ *Cape Ecnomus* 256 BCE   *Agates Islands* 241 BCE ▷

Agates Islands   10 March 241 BCE

Carthaginians and Romans had been fighting on Sicily since 265 BCE. With the war in its third decade, both sides' resources were depleted. Rome made a last effort and built a fleet to attack Carthage's remaining strongholds on the island. Carthage's hastily raised relief force was crushed.

After several years of inconclusive, small-scale fighting on Sicily, Roman leaders decided to make a final bid to win the war. They built a new fleet of 200 ships, financed by contributions from wealthy citizens, and in 242 BCE sent it to Sicily under the command of the consul Gaius Lutatius Catulus. With no Carthaginian fleet on hand to oppose him, Catulus began the campaign by blockading the Carthaginian strongholds of Drepana and Lilybaeum. He also made the best of his opportunity to train his sailors and marines to a high standard.

Belatedly, the Carthaginians raised a fleet of 250 warships and transports and sent it off to Sicily the next spring, carrying men and supplies for the threatened garrisons. Catulus sailed to meet them near the Agates Islands off Sicily's westernmost tip. This time the Romans had a clear qualitative advantage: the Carthaginian crews were inexperienced and their ships heavily laden, while the Romans had prepared their fleet fully for battle. Although fought in heavy weather, which had proved disastrous for Roman fleets in the recent past, the battle could have only one outcome. About half the Carthaginian ships were captured or sunk.

With its only active army now isolated on Sicily and unable to build a new fleet, Carthage gave up the struggle and made peace, but the bitter enmity between Rome and Carthage remained. **DS**

Losses: Carthaginian, 120 ships captured or sunk; Roman, 25 ships sunk

◁ *Drepana* 249 BCE   *Utica* 238 BCE ▷

Utica   238 BCE

Having lost the First Punic War against Rome, the north African city of Carthage found itself unable to pay the wages of the mercenaries whom it had hired during the conflict. The mercenaries revolted, putting Carthage in grave peril until it was saved by Hamilcar Barca.

The mercenaries were led by Spendius and Mathos, two veteran soldiers. They won the support of many Libyans, who felt oppressed by Carthaginian rule. Utica, one of the few cities that stayed loyal to Carthage, was placed under siege by the mercenaries. After a first attempt at lifting the siege ended in disaster, the Carthaginians handed the task of organizing a fresh relief force to Hamilcar Barca.

Hamilcar was advancing across the plains around the River Macaras when he was attacked by Spendius and a large part of the besieging army. The Carthaginian column was led by elephants, cavalry, and light infantry, while the heavy infantry were in the rear. Hamilcar had his elephants and cavalry hold the enemy assault while he drew up his heavy infantry, then signaled them to retreat quickly. The jubilant rebels surged forward, losing all formation as they did so. The Carthaginian heavy infantry then attacked, breaking the rebel forces. The retreating rebels were pursued ruthlessly by Hamilcar's cavalry, who overran the rebel camp and thus raised the Siege of Utica.

The war lasted another two years, but the rebels no longer had any realistic chance of success. Spendius and Mathos were crucified, and the victory over the mercenaries gave Hamilcar a dominant position in Carthage. He was able to mount an offensive in Spain, the first step of a planned revenge on Rome that was carried through by Hamilcar's son, Hannibal, in the Second Punic War. **RM**

Losses: Rebel, 6,000 dead and 2,000 captured of 25,000; Carthaginian, unknown, but minor losses of 10,000

◁ *Agates Islands 241 BCE*   *Trebbia 218 BCE* ▷

Trebbia   December 218 BCE

The slaughter at Trebbia revealed for the first time the military skills of the Carthaginian Hannibal, arguably the finest field commander of all time. Hannibal's victory brought allies to his standard and established his army on Italian soil, where it would remain for the next fifteen years.

The Second Punic War was fought between Rome and Carthage for control of the western Mediterranean. The war began in 219 BCE when Rome broke a treaty agreement. The Carthaginian commander, Hannibal Barca, decided to march his army from Spain to northern Italy, crossing the Alps to arrive there in 218 BCE with 26,000 men and a small number of elephants.

In December, a large Roman army led by Sempronius arrived, cowed the local Celts into loyalty, and marched to the attack. Sempronius forded the icy Trebbia River, then deployed his 32,000 heavy infantry in line with 6,000 light infantry skirmishing ahead and 4,000 cavalry on the flanks. Hannibal had 20,000 heavy infantry in line with 7,000 light infantry ahead and 10,000 cavalry, plus the elephants on the flanks. A further 2,000 light troops hid in a wood on the right flank. The Roman attack drove in the Carthaginian skirmishers, then fell upon the heavy infantry in the center. When the heavy infantry were engaged, Hannibal unleashed the men in hiding to attack the rear of the Roman army, while his much larger cavalry forces swept the Roman cavalry off the field and then joined the assault on the vulnerable rear. Sempronius formed his veteran legions, about 10,000 men, into a hollow square and led them to the fortified town of Piacenza, leaving the rest of his army to be butchered. Winter weather then closed in, forcing Hannibal to break off his siege of Piacenza. **RM**

Losses: Carthaginian, minor losses of 40,000 engaged; Roman, about 28,000 of 42,000 engaged

◁ *Utica 238 BCE*   *Lake Trasimene 217 BCE* ▷

Raphia 22 June 217 BCE

Ptolemy IV, ruler of Egypt, and Antiochus III, leader of the Seleucid Empire in Asia—both descendants of Alexander the Great's Macedonian generals— fought for control of Syria and Palestine. One of the largest battles in the ancient world, Raphia included a memorable clash between massed war elephants.

The Ptolemaic and Seleucid armies, totaling some 130,000 men, met in the Sinai desert south of Gaza. They drew up in traditional Macedonian formation, with dense-packed, armored infantry phalanxes in the center, flanked by lightly equipped skirmishers and cavalry. On the wings were elephants, with soldiers mounted in towers on their backs.

Antiochus had about one hundred large elephants from India, Ptolemy some seventy smaller African forest elephants. According to Roman historian Polybius, the rival beasts clashed head to head, pushing and goring one another with their tusks. The African elephants were fearful of their larger cousins, however, and soon fled to the rear, trampling on Ptolemy's soldiers in their panic. But success in the elephant contest did not bring the Seleucids victory. The battle was decided by the infantry.

While Antiochus led a successful cavalry charge on the right—the traditional place of honor for a commander— Ptolemy positioned himself in the center, inspiring his men to fight, Polybius tells us, "with alacrity and spirit." Ptolemy had strengthened his infantry by training native Egyptians to fight alongside his Macedonians. Pressing forward in compact masses with their long sarissa spears, they drove back the Seleucid phalanxes. As the Seleucid left also gave way, Antiochus had to admit defeat. The battle had no long-term consequences: by 200 BCE Antiochus had absorbed Syria and Palestine into his empire. **RG**

Losses: Unknown

◁ *Ipsos 301 BCE*   *Magnesia 190 BCE* ▷

Lake Trasimene 24 June 217 BCE

Hannibal's victory over the Roman army of Gaius Flaminius remains, in terms of numbers of men, the largest ambush in history. In the run-up to the battle, Hannibal pulled off the earliest known example of a strategic turning movement. The battle showed how an innovative use of terrain could bring victory.

After his victory at Trebbia, Hannibal—the commander of the Carthaginian invasion of Italy—persuaded the Celtic tribes of the Po Valley to rise against Rome and march south. The Romans raised a new army, under the command of Gaius Flaminius, with orders to avoid a pitched battle against Hannibal. After some weeks of skirmishing, Hannibal marched around Flaminius toward the rich lands of Apulia. Flaminius gave chase.

On the shores of Lake Trasimene, the road squeezed between the lake to the south and a crescent of wooded hills to the north. As part of his innovative strategy, Hannibal hid his men in the wooded hills then sent some horsemen miles to the east to light hundreds of campfires to make Flaminius think he was far behind the Carthaginians. Soon after dawn, Flaminius marched into the trap. As the head of the column reached the end of the crescent of hills, Hannibal sent his heavy infantry to block the road ahead, while the Celtic infantry marched down to block the road behind. The light infantry and cavalry then swept down from the hills. Only the Roman advance guard formed into battle order and managed to fight its way out over the hills to the north, but the rest were trapped. In the four hours of fighting that followed, Flaminius and most of his men were killed. Those who surrendered were sold into slavery by Hannibal to raise funds to pay his Celts. **RM**

Losses: Carthaginian, 2,500 of 50,000; Roman, 19,000 dead and 12,000 captured of 40,000

◁ *Trebbia 218 BCE*   *Cannae 216 BCE* ▷

The Battle of Lake Trasimene by Flemish artist Leonard Thiry (c. 1500–c. 1550).

Cannae   2 August 216 BCE

This was the bloodiest day in military history. More men fell at Cannae than on the first day of the Somme in 1916 or in any day's fighting on Hitler's Eastern Front. Hannibal's flawless double envelopment maneuver is still studied at military colleges, and modern commanders seek to emulate it.

In the spring of 216 BCE, the Carthaginian commander Hannibal marched south through Italy hoping to persuade the allies of Rome to abandon their allegiance. He seized the supply depot at Cannae, thus blocking the route between Rome and her allies to the southeast.

The Romans elected two new consuls—Gaius Terrentius Varro and Lucius Aemilius Paullus—to lead a combined army of 40,000 Roman legionaries, with 40,000 allied infantry and about 2,500 cavalry. The consuls agreed to hold tactical command on alternate days. Hannibal awaited them with a force of 40,000 heavy infantry, 6,000 light infantry, and 10,000 cavalry. Arriving at Cannae, the Romans built a fortified camp. Hannibal sent his cavalry to

"Of all that befell the Romans and Carthaginians … the cause was one man and one mind: Hannibal."

Polybius, The Histories

stop the Romans collecting water from the River Aufidus. On the third day, Varro had command and marched out to fight, arranging his infantry in depth hoping to use them to smash through the thinner Carthaginian line. He maneuvered his columns so that Hannibal was backed against the river, where the Carthaginians would have less room for their cavalry to operate. Varro put his few cavalry on the flanks with orders to hold off the enemy horsemen. Hannibal, meanwhile, had drawn up his forces with the Celtic and Spanish infantry holding the center.

The veteran African infantry were on either flank. On the far right and left were positioned the cavalry, which greatly outnumbered the Roman horses.

The battle began as Varro hoped. The cavalry on the flanks engaged in a desultory skirmish, while the Roman heavy infantry advanced and pushed back Hannibal's infantry. But Hannibal had guessed Varro's intentions when he saw the Roman dispositions. He had put his men with their backs to the river so that they had access to fresh water, and the hot wind would blow dust into the Roman's faces. As the Celtic and Spanish infantry fell back, the Romans advanced into a crescent-shaped bulge within which they became increasingly disordered and closely packed. On Hannibal's order, the Carthaginian cavalry attacked in earnest, driving the Roman horsemen from the field with heavy loss. At the same time, the African infantry wheeled inward and began pushing against the flanks of the Roman infantry, compressing the crowded legionary ranks even further. When the Carthaginian cavalry returned from chasing the enemy horsemen, they charged into the rear of the Roman infantry, who were now surrounded.

Thirsty, hot, dusty, and crowded together, the Romans were virtually helpless. The killing went on until darkness fell, when the survivors cut their way out of the trap and fled to the nearby fortified town of Canusium. Other Roman survivors included the fleeing cavalry, the guard left at the camp, and a few detachments absent on the day of battle. Paullus was killed, but Varro escaped. The Greek-speaking states of southern Italy and Sicily renounced their alliances with Rome, as did Macedon. However, Rome's other allies remained loyal. When Hannibal offered peace on moderate terms, the Roman senate refused. The war continued. **RM**

Losses: Carthaginian, 5,700 of 56,000 engaged; Roman, 48,200 dead and 4,500 captured of 86,000 engaged

◁ *Lake Trasimene* 217 BCE   *Syracuse* 214 BCE ▷

A fifteenth-century illuminated manuscript by Jean Fouquet depicting the Battle of Cannae. ➜

Cy commance la fame des grans : dures
batailles qui furent y moult long temps entre
les Rommains et ceulx de la noble cité de Cartage.
Sumeure adoncques ne auoit
oncques eu hayne entre ceulx
de cartage et ceulx de Romme
ne chose nulle par quoy par
quoy il peuft auoir entreulx estoyt ne ba
taille Grendroit su la premiere estincelle
alumee qui tant aut puis et enforca que
apeine se pouroit croire ceulx qui louent
et entendent Les Cartaines respondirent
aux messaiges de tarente quilz boulentiers
leur aideroient et seruoient a leur amour :
a leur concordance en toutes les manieres
quilz audeu ne valour leur pouroient Lors

furent les oste somons en cartaise et par
toute libe et passerent mer aleurs baisse
aulz Tant firent quilz bindrent ala Cite
de Tarente Ceulx de Romme enuoierent
encontre eulx sitost comme ilz le seurent
ne iry ot une longue parolles tausce e
puis que les oste sentreapprouherent ainsi
se combatirent les Rommains et les carta
remene moult autrement ensemble Mais
les cartesemens y furent desconfiz acelle
premiere foiz et sen retournerent moult
dolens et moult tristes Carilz ne cuidoie
nue deuant ceste auenture que nulle ce
tiens les peuffent surmonter ne vaincre
Mais adoncques seurent Ilz certainement
que les rommains les pouroient bien cha

Syracuse 214–212 BCE

Fought as part of the Second Punic War between Rome and Carthage, the capture of Syracuse by Rome marked the end of the independence of the Greek cities in southern Italy and Sicily. It also led to the death of the noted mathematician and inventor Archimedes, who took part in the city's defense.

In 214 BCE the pro-Roman king, Hiero II of Syracuse, died and a republic was founded. The new government rebuffed Rome, allied itself to Carthage, and declared war. A Roman army and fleet, led by Marcus Claudius Marcellus, arrived to lay siege. Syracuse was a strongly defended city with a large harbor, and Marcellus brought in ships equipped with siege towers and scaling ladders to assault the city from the port.

Inside Syracuse, Archimedes devised a number of counter measures. One was a powerful hook mounted on a rotating crane that could lift Roman ships out of the water and capsize them. He is said to have also developed a curved mirror that could focus the rays of the sun onto Roman ships and set them on fire. Soon Roman crews refused to approach the walls, and the siege settled down into a blockade. A Carthaginian army attempted to relieve Syracuse but was decimated by disease, while the Romans drove off a Carthaginian fleet.

In 212 BCE Marcellus took advantage of a festival to the goddess Artemis to send an elite squad of soldiers under cover of night to scale the walls and open the gates. In the sack that followed, a Roman soldier found Archimedes in his study working on a mathematical problem. Archimedes told the soldier to leave him alone, and was later killed. The central fortress of Syracuse held out for a few weeks, but eventually fell. **RM**

Losses: Roman, unknown; Syracusan, 5,000 (the entire garrison) plus a large proportion of the civilian population

◁ Cannae 216 BCE   Metaurus 207 BCE ▷

Metaurus 207 BCE

The defeat of the Carthaginian Hasdrubal on the banks of the Metaurus paved the way for the eventual victory of Rome in the Second Punic War. The victory was largely due to the innovative actions of the Roman officer Claudius Nero, who thus established the fortunes of his family.

By 207 BCE the campaign of the Carthaginian commander in Italy, Hannibal, was stagnating because of a lack of men, money, and siege equipment. His brother, Hasdrubal, set off from Spain with the much-needed reinforcements.

Hasdrubal had reached the River Metaurus in Italy when he met a Roman army led by Marcus Livius. Hasdrubal put his cavalry on the right next to the river and fielded the Spanish and mercenary infantry in the center. The less reliable Celtic infantry were on the left, their front protected by a deep ravine. Livius drew up his legions in line with his horsemen on the left to face the Carthaginian cavalry. His second in command, Claudius Nero, had command of the right wing. The battle began by the river as the opposing cavalry clashed, followed by the infantry in the center. The left wing of the Roman infantry was pushed back and appeared in danger of breaking. Claudius Nero left the right flank thinly protected along the ravine and marched most of his men right around the back of the Roman army, past the threatened section of line, and along the river banks to fall on the Carthaginian right flank.

The Carthaginian cavalry fled, allowing Claudius Nero to roll up the Carthaginian infantry, pinning it against the steep hills. Hasdrubal was killed—his head was cut off and taken south to be hurled into Hannibal's camp under cover of darkness. **RM**

Losses: Carthaginian, 20,000 dead and 30,000 captured of 56,000; Roman, 8,000 dead of 40,000

◁ Syracuse 214 BCE   Zama 202 BCE ▷

Julu 207 BCE

In 221 BCE, Qin Shi Huangdi unified China under his rule, thus becoming the first emperor of China. His dynasty did not, however, survive for long after his death in 210 BCE. The Battle of Julu ensured the fall of the Qin, opening the way for the subsequent rise of the Han dynasty.

The kingdoms into which China had been divided before the Qin ascendancy revolted against Qin Shi Huangdi's successors. The Qin forces were still overwhelmingly strong, but the Chu kingdom rebels discovered a general of remarkable vigor and brutality in Xiang Yu.

When a vast Qin army, under general Zhang Han, besieged the Zhao city of Julu, Xiang led a much smaller force against them. To inspire his soldiers with fighting spirit, he confronted them with a choice between victory or starvation. They were made to destroy all except three days' marching rations. If they wanted any more food or water, they would have to take it from the Qin army. The desperate soldiers duly fought like tigers. Xiang placed himself across the Qin supply lines, repeatedly defeating them as they attempted to break through. The Qin army began to crumble, while other rebel forces flocked to join Xiang. Before long, the Qin leadership fell to in-fighting. Threatened with execution for alleged treachery, Zhang Han surrendered his entire army to Xiang.

In imitation of a massacre carried out by the Qin at Changping half a century earlier, Xiang buried his mass of prisoners alive. The fear and distrust inspired by his cruelty played a large part in preventing Xiang enjoying the ultimate fruit of his victory. Instead, he was defeated eventually by the Han leader Liu Bang, who founded a new dynasty in 202 BCE. **RG**

"Mastering swordsmanship allows me to face only one opponent . . . I want to learn how to defeat 10,000."

Xiang Yu

A nineteenth-century painting of a Han dynasty general: his weapons were some of the earliest to be made from iron and steel.

Losses: No reliable figures: Chu allegedly fielded 30,000, suffering light losses; Qin allegedly had 300,000, all killed in battle or subsequent massacre

Changping 260 BCE   Mobei Campaign 119 BCE

Zama 19 October 202 BCE

The defeat of Carthaginian commander Hannibal by Roman general Scipio Africanus marked the end of Carthage as an independent power and the defeat of the last major threat to Roman hegemony in the western Mediterranean. Hannibal went on the run, and was hunted down by Rome twenty years later.

After a series of brilliant victories in Italy, Carthaginian commander Hannibal was ground down by a lack of supplies and money. In 204 BCE, a Roman army under Publius Cornelius Scipio landed in Africa and easily defeated the local Carthaginian troops. In response, the Carthaginians recalled Hannibal and raised a fresh army. The two armies met on the plains of Zama outside Carthage. Hannibal placed 30,000 poorly trained infantry in the center in two lines, with his 10,000 veterans from Italy in the rear and 6,000 experienced cavalry on the flanks, while eighty war elephants were positioned ahead of the army. Scipio arranged his Roman legions in the center, with Italian cavalry on the left and north African cavalry on the right.

The battle began with a charge of the elephants. The Roman infantry opened lanes in their ranks along which the elephants were allowed to pass to the rear, where trained elephant killers dispatched them. On the flanks, Scipio's cavalry drove the Carthaginian cavalry off the field. Hannibal's first two infantry lines attacked and inflicted heavy losses on the Roman infantry before they were driven off. He was sending forward his third line of veterans to defeat the Roman infantry when some of the Roman left wing cavalry returned, charged his rear, and so disrupted the attack that it ended in disaster for Hannibal. Scipio imposed devastating peace terms that crushed Carthage as a real power. **RM**

Losses: Carthaginian, 20,000 dead and 26,000 captured of 48,000 engaged; Roman, 6,500 of 43,000 engaged

◁ Metaurus 207 BCE

Carthage 146 BCE ▷

Chios 201 BCE

The naval defeat of Philip V of Macedon at Chios was the last large-scale naval battle between fleets sent out by independent Greek states. At the time, it was thought that it had secured independence for the smaller states, but in fact it only opened the way for Roman domination of Greece.

With Rome busy fighting Carthage, King Philip V of Macedon took the opportunity to increase his territory and power in Greece and around the Aegean. By 201 BCE only Rhodes and Pergamum remained hostile. Philip laid siege to Pergamum, but was driven off. He was retreating in his fleet toward his base on Samos when the fleets of Pergamum and Rhodes came into sight.

Philip had fifty-three cataphract ships—large oared galleys with enclosed sides—plus about 150 lembi, small galleys with open decks. King Attalus of Pergamum had about fifty medium and large oared galleys; Theophiliscus of Rhodes had about seventy. Both sides formed up in line abreast and advanced. Theophiliscus hoped to use his skilled crews to outmaneuver the larger Macedonian ships and ram them, while Philip hoped to use his lembi to hamper the enemy's movements and leave them easy prey for his large but cumbersome cataphracts.

On the allies' left wing, Attalus engaged in a melee with the Macedonian right wing, which hung in the balance until Philip brought up his reserve squadron. Attalus fled, though many of his ships remained in action. The more skilled Rhodian crews evaded the lembi and outmaneuvered the Macedonian cataphracts, ramming and sinking many of them. The death of Theophiliscus did nothing to slow the Rhodian attacks. Returning from driving off Attalus, Philip realized he faced defeat and drew his remaining ships off in good order. **RM**

Losses: Macedonian, 92 ships sunk, 7 captured of 200 engaged; Greek allied, 6 ships sunk, 2 captured of 130

Cynoscephalae 197 BCE ▷

◀ *Detail from* The Battle of Zama, *painted by Giulio Romano 1570–80.*

Cynoscephalae 197 BCE

At Cynoscephalae, the tactical system developed by Alexander the Great, which had dominated warfare in the eastern Mediterranean, came up against the Roman legions. The victory of the more flexible, sword-armed Romans heralded the end of the use of the massed infantry phalanx in ancient warfare.

Having defeated Carthage at Zama, Rome turned against Philip V of Macedon. It suited Rome to keep Greece divided into small states rather than have it united into a single powerful rival.

The Roman and allied Greek army, commanded by Titus Quinctius Flaminius, was marching toward Scotusa searching for Philip's army. A foggy dawn found the two armies on opposite sides of the Cynoscephalae hills unaware of each other's position. Both Flaminius and Philip sent scouts into the hills, where they clashed. Philip gained the high ground first, while Flaminius formed up his army on the lower southern slopes of the hills. Flaminius placed most of his Roman legions on the left; other Romans, plus the Greek allied infantry, more Greek horsemen, and war elephants were on the right. Philip sent his right wing phalanx and cavalry to attack, ordering his center and left wing to follow as soon as they could. Philip's right phalanx pushed back the Roman infantry. Meanwhile, Flaminius's right fell upon the Macedonian center and left as they were forming up.

The Macedonians fled, pursued by the Greek allies. The Romans on the right flank turned to assault Philip's right wing phalanx in the rear. Unable to face about, the Macedonians broke formation and fled. The smaller Greek states were free of Macedonian rule, although time would prove that Rome had ambitions of her own in the area. **RM**

Losses: Macedonian, 5,000 dead and 1,000 captured of 34,000; Roman, 2,000 of 26,000

◁ Chios 201 BCE   Magnesia 190 BCE ▷

Magnesia 190 BCE

With Macedon humbled, Rome posed as the champion of the small Greek states and declared war on the Seleucid Antiochus III. The peace treaty imposed by Rome after their victory at Magnesia robbed Antiochus of his western provinces and almost bankrupted his treasury.

A Roman and Greek army, led by Lucius Cornelius Scipio, invaded the Seleucid Empire and found Antiochus waiting at Magnesia in Lydia (in modern Turkey).

Scipio had 20,000 Roman heavy infantry, which he placed on his left wing. The allied Greek heavy infantry formed the right wing. Light infantry skirmished in front, while 3,000 Greek cavalry were divided equally between either flank, and sixteen war elephants were held in reserve. Antiochus placed 16,000 men, armed in Macedonian style, in a solid phalanx in the right center along with war elephants. On their flanks were heavy cavalry, flanked by light cavalry and infantry. In front of the army were placed chariots and archers mounted on camels, which opened the battle by charging.

On the right this drove off Scipio's cavalry, but on the left the attack failed. Scipio's horsemen counterattacked and drove the light infantry from the field. Antiochus sent forward his phalanx to hold the Roman heavy infantry while he led a charge of heavy cavalry to exploit the gap opened by his chariots. The Roman infantry, trained to move and operate in smaller groups, were able to form a defensive line and hold the charge. Meanwhile, Scipio's right wing cavalry came back from the pursuit and assaulted the Seleucid phalanx in the rear. The unwieldy phalanx was unable to respond effectively and, after much fighting, the Seleucid survivors surrendered. **RM**

Losses: Seleucid, 50,000 dead and captured of 70,000 engaged; Roman, 349 of 25,000 engaged; Greek allied, casualties unknown

◁ Cynoscephalae 197 BCE   Pydna 168 BCE ▷

Pydna 22 June 168 BCE

The Battle of Pydna marked the destruction of the kingdom of Macedon, once ruled by Alexander the Great, and the final defeat of the Macedonian tactical system that had once carried all before it. As a result, Rome dominated Greece and the whole eastern Mediterranean.

Rome declared war on King Perseus of Macedon in 171 BCE, fearing he aimed to oust them from control of Greece. In 168 BCE, Lucius Aemilius Paullus invaded Macedon and met Perseus at Pydna.

Paullus fell back in order to have low hills behind him. He put 15,000 heavy infantry in the center with 10,000 allied infantry on their flanks. He divided 4,000 cavalry between the flanks and put 22 war elephants on the far right wing. Perseus put his 25,000-strong Macedonian-style phalanx of tight-packed, spear-armed infantry in the center, with the elite 3,000 guard infantry on its left and light infantry to its right. On his left he put 1,000 cavalry and on the right had 4,000 horsemen under his personal command.

Perseus ordered the phalanx to attack and waited for an opportunity to use his cavalry in a battle-winning charge. The phalanx drove the Romans back, but when the phalanx reached uneven ground, the tight formation began to break up. The Roman legionaries, wielding their short swords, pushed into the gaps to defeat the Macedonians at close quarters. The Roman cavalry charged, driving off the Macedonian left, but were held on the other flank. When Perseus was wounded his cavalry fled, allowing the Roman horsemen to close in. Perseus and his family were kept prisoners in Rome until they died. Macedonia was first divided into four republics, then annexed to Rome. **RM**

Losses: Macedonian, 25,000 dead or captured of 44,000 engaged; Roman, 1,000 of 38,000 engaged

[<] *Magnesia 190 BCE*

Carthage 146 BCE

The destruction of Carthage was an act of Roman aggression prompted as much by motives of revenge for earlier wars as by greed for the rich farming lands around the city. The Carthaginian defeat was total and absolute, instilling fear and horror into Rome's enemies and allies.

Under the treaty ending the Second Punic War, signed after the Battle of Zama, Carthage had to seek Roman permission before waging war. That treaty expired in 151 BCE, so when Rome's ally Numidia annexed land from Carthage, a Carthaginian army marched to defend it. Rome declared this event to be an act of war and laid siege to Carthage.

The Roman army, led by Manius Manlius, made little impact as the Carthaginians raised an army, converted the city into an arms factory, and held out. About 140,000 of Carthage's women and children were evacuated by sea to seek refuge in friendly states. In 147 BCE, the Roman senate sent a new commander, Scipio Aemilianus, with orders to take the city by storm. He defeated the Carthaginian field army and built a mole to block the city's harbor. The end came in the spring of 146 BCE after the besiegers made a breach in the city walls. The Roman soldiers poured in, only to find that each street had been barricaded and every house fortified. The Romans had to clear the houses one by one.

By the eighth day, the last pockets of Carthaginian resistance collapsed. Last to fall was the Temple of Eshmun, where the wife of the Carthaginian commander, Hasdrubal, sacrificed her sons in front of the Romans, then killed herself. Scipio ordered the city to be burned, then demolished. **RM**

Losses: Carthaginian, 62,000 dead and 50,000 enslaved of 112,000 present in the city; Roman, 17,000 of 40,000

[<] *Zama 202 BCE*

Mobei Campaign 119 BCE

In the second century BCE, Han dynasty China was under constant threat from the Xiongnu, a confederation of fierce nomadic horsemen raiding from beyond the frontiers of the empire. In 119 BCE Chinese Emperor Wu sent a military expedition across the Gobi desert to destroy the Xiongnu.

The scale of the military effort was an astonishing demonstration of the power of Han China, even if financing the expedition meant almost ruining the population with extra taxation. Two columns of cavalry and infantry, each some 150,000 strong, were dispatched on different routes, hoping to make contact with the main Xiongnu forces under their leader Chanyu. It was the column led by General Wei Qing that, after an impressive march of some 500 miles (805 km) across inhospitable terrain, found Chanyu waiting north of the Gobi. Wei had divided his army on the march and now faced potential disaster as tens of thousands of Xiongnu horsemen attacked his exhausted, depleted army. Forming their carts into vast circles as a defensive barrier, the Chinese deployed their massed crossbowmen—drilled in rapid-fire tactics—to mow down the charging cavalry. Arrows shot from the nomads' composite bows took a toll on the defenders, but the horsemen failed to break through.

At dusk, Wei sent his own cavalry unobserved in an encircling movement around both flanks of the Xiongnu host. Outmaneuvered, Chanyu was forced to flee as his army fell into disarray. Victorious on the battlefield, Wei pressed on into the Orkhon Valley, destroying the key Xiongnu fortress of Zhao Xin. The blow to the morale and physical resources of the Xiongnu was so great that they never fully recovered as a fighting force. **RG**

"They saw five-colored banners flying from the Chanyu's fort, and several hundred men in armor."

Han Shu (History of the Han Dynasty)

⬆ *Detail from a work by Han Kan, showing a stableman tending his horse after battle.*

Losses: No reliable figures: Chinese, 20,000; Xiongnu, 90,000

◁ Julu 207 BCE   Kunyang 23 CE ▷

Aquae Sextiae 102 BCE

A Roman victory that followed a string of defeats, the Battle of Aquae Sextiae confirmed the military genius of consul Gaius Marius and reestablished Rome's military supremacy. Marius was responsible for reforms of the Roman military system that turned the legions into a permanent professional army.

From the north German coast, the Ambrones and their allies (the Cimbri and Teutones) were of mixed Celtic-Germanic origins. Wandering and pillaging across Europe, they defeated four Roman armies. Marius, who had risen from obscurity to fame through military successes, was called back from campaigning in Africa to cope with the crisis.

In 102 BCE Marius's army of 40,000 legionaries met about 140,000 Ambrones and Teutones at Aquae Sextiae (Aix-en-Provence). The battle began by chance when a Roman patrol encountered some Ambrones and was defeated. The Ambrones followed up by advancing in numbers, but they were met by a Roman relief force and defeated in their turn. Two days later, the Ambrones launched an assault on the Roman camp. Marius had posted 3,000 men in a wood some miles away, keeping his main force behind the timber stockades and earthworks of his camp. The initial onslaught of the Ambrones was halted and driven back. At this point, the 3,000 men advanced from the wood to attack the disorganized Ambrones. Marius sallied out with most of his men, trapping the Ambrones between his two forces and slaughtering them.

After a further defeat for the Cimbri at Vercellae in 101 BCE, the threat of the Celto-Germanic tribes was overcome. Marius used his power to begin reforms that favored the poorer citizens, making him an early member of the group that became known as "populares." **RM**

Losses: Roman, fewer than 1,000 of 40,000; Ambrones, 40,000 dead and 100,000 prisoners of 140,000—including women and children

Colline Gate November 82 BCE

Contemporaries thought that the great victory won by Sulla at the Colline Gate and the reforms that followed had settled the social and political disputes that threatened to tear apart the Roman Republic. In fact, they set the scene for the even greater and more wide-ranging civil wars to come.

In 83 BCE a Roman civil war broke out between the "populares," who favored reforms to benefit the poorer citizens, and the "optimates," who opposed them. Lucius Cornelius Sulla and the optimates had gained the upper hand by the autumn of 82 BCE when a large army of Samnites, a central Italian state favoring the democratic reformers, laid siege to Rome itself.

Sulla sent his cavalry on ahead to skirmish with the Samnites who were camped outside the Colline Gate, the northernmost gate in the city walls. Sulla and the infantry arrived on the morning of 1 November, having marched all night, and formed up for battle. Sulla commanded the left-wing legions, while the right wing was under the command of Marcus Licinius Crassus. The Samnites advanced under their king, Pontius Telesinus, and soon had Sulla backed up against the city walls. Crassus then detached one unit and led them around the flank of the Samnite army to attack them in the rear. This caused enough confusion to allow Sulla to push forward.

When Pontius was killed, the Samnites fled. Sulla then marched into Rome and asked the senate to appoint him dictator. As the senate debated the motion, Sulla had the Samnite prisoners murdered in an adjoining street. "It is just some malefactors suffering for their crimes," Sulla commented when the screams interrupted the debate. He won the vote and became dictator of Rome. **RM**

Losses: Unknown, but it was later said that 40,000 bodies lay buried beside the Colline Gate

Colline Gate 82 BCE ▷   ◁ Aquae Sextiae 102 BCE   Defeat of Spartacus 71 BCE ▷

Defeat of Spartacus 71 BCE

The career of the escaped Roman slave Spartacus has been used as a symbol of freedom against oppression in recent years, but at the time was seen as a slave rebellion that quickly degenerated into banditry. The final battle was a victory for training and discipline over numbers and fervor.

Spartacus led a group of fellow gladiators out of captivity in Capua in 73 BCE and into the mountains. There they were soon joined by as many as 100,000 slaves fleeing servitude across southern Italy. By late summer 71 BCE, Spartacus and his escaped slaves were camped at Rhegium. A Roman army of about 40,000 under Marcus Licinius Crassus, who had fought at the Colline Gate, blocked all routes out of the peninsula while warships patrolled the seas.

Spartacus tried to negotiate terms of surrender, but Crassus refused. Spartacus then broke through the southern end of the Roman lines and led his followers northeast. The large group of escaped slaves began to fragment as stragglers fell out and others dispersed into the hills. Crassus and his legions gave chase. They caught up with the rear of Spartacus's column near Strongoli. Isolated groups of slaves began attacking the Roman column in a series of uncoordinated rushes. Spartacus halted his march, forming his men up in a line blocking a valley. Crassus formed his legions up in three lines and attacked all along the front at the same time. The fighting lasted for some hours, ending in Roman victory. Most of the slaves were killed on the battlefield, but 6,000 prisoners were later crucified along the Appian Way between Rome and Capua. The fate of Spartacus is unknown, although he is presumed to have died with his followers. **RM**

Losses: Roman, few losses of 40,000; slave rebel, 50,000 dead or captured

◁ *Colline Gate 82 BCE*　　　　*Invasion of Britain 55 BCE* ▷

Sambre (Selle) July 57 BCE

From 59 BCE, as governor of Transalpine Gaul, Julius Caesar embarked on campaigns of conquest that extended Roman rule over the Celtic tribes of northwest Europe. His career nearly came to a swift end, however, when his legions were caught off guard by tribal warriors in what is now Belgium.

Caesar led eight legions in his campaign against the Belgic tribes, laying waste to their territory as he advanced. A number of tribes—most prominent among them the Nervii and the Atrebates—refused to be cowed and prepared an ambush by a river, traditionally identified as the Sambre but now believed to be the Selle.

Caesar arrived with six of his legions and set about making camp. Many soldiers scattered to find materials; others were engaged in constructing a ditch and rampart. A mass of Belgic warriors emerged from concealment in woods on the other side of the river, waded through the shallow water, and attacked the disorganized Romans. Showing their high level of training, the legionaries hastily formed an improvised defensive line, responding to trumpet calls and gathering to the nearest standard.

Two legions on the Roman right were especially hard-pressed. Surrounded by the Nervii, they were forced back into such a dense mass that they could hardly wield their arms. Caesar, by his own account, grabbed a shield from a legionary and strode into the front line, urging the men to spread out and inspiring them to continued resistance. Meanwhile, on the Roman left, Titus Labienus—one of Caesar's most trusted lieutenants—had routed the Belgic warriors in front of him, pursuing them across the river. He led his legionaries back to attack the Nervii from the rear. Trapped, most of the Belgic warriors were massacred. **RG**

Losses: Roman, 2,500 casualties of 30,000; Belgic, 5,000 to 50,000 casualties of 25,000–150,000

Invasion of Britain 55 BCE ▷

➐ *Detail from a copper engraving (1630) showing the Roman army overcoming Spartacus and his gladiators.*

Invasion of Britain August–September 55 BCE

The Roman invasion of Britain in 55 BCE, led by Julius Caesar, ended in a bloody stalemate. Caesar tried a second invasion the following year, but once more was forced to retreat having gained little. The Romans did not land successfully in Britain for nearly another hundred years.

During Julius Caesar's conquest of Gaul, men and supplies from Britain had been sent to aid the Gauls, and a number of fugitives had fled to Britain. Caesar decided to attack Britain in revenge.

The Roman general set sail from Boulogne on 23 August, with the seventh and tenth legions—about 10,000 men—plus some auxiliary troops. The next day he arrived off Dover, but a large British army was visible on top of the cliffs. Caesar sailed northeast to reach a wide beach at what is now Deal. The men were reluctant to land because British cavalry and chariots were on the beach. The standard bearer of the tenth legion leaped into the surf and the rest of the legion followed, rather than see their eagle lost. Caesar built a fortified camp and opened negotiations with the local Cantium tribal leaders. However, when a high tide combined with a heavy storm swamped or wrecked many of Caesar's beached ships, the Celts broke off all negotiations.

A Roman foraging party was ambushed, which encouraged the British to mount a major assault on the fort, but this was driven off with heavy loss. The local rulers then promised to hand over hostages if Caesar went back to Gaul. Caesar shipped his men back to Gaul, but only to regroup and return the following summer. This second invasion proved to be a slightly more successful campaign, but Caesar again left having exacted tribute and hostages. Britain remained free of Roman rule. **RM**

Losses: Roman, 500 of 12,000 engaged; British, 2,000 of 40,000

[<] *Sambre* 57 *BCE*　　　　　　　　　　　*Alesia* 52 *BCE* [>]

　　A fifteenth-century Flemish book illumination showing ship's carpenters building Caesar's invasion fleet.

Carrhae 53 BCE

The Parthian Arsacid dynasty created a powerful Asian empire that stretched from eastern Turkey to Iran. At the Battle of Carrhae, the Parthian mounted archers proved superior to the heavy infantry of the Roman legions. The Romans were especially disturbed by their tactic of pretended flight.

In 53 BCE, Marcus Licinius Crassus, the veteran of the Colline Gate and Spartacus campaigns, launched an unprovoked invasion of the Parthian Empire in order to boost his political career in Rome. Crassus advanced over the desert toward Mesopotamia. As he neared Carrhae, Crassus sighted a Parthian cavalry army. He formed his 35,000 heavy infantry into a large, hollow square that could not be outflanked and placed his 4,000 cavalry inside the square, while sending his 4,000 light infantry forward to skirmish.

Led by the nobleman Surena, the Parthians opened the attack with 9,000 horse archers driving the light infantry back into the square, then shooting at the heavy infantry while staying out of range of the Roman spears. Crassus sent his son, Publius, with about 1,500 cavalry to drive off the horse archers. The Parthians fell back, pretending to flee but instead luring Publius toward a force of 1,000 heavily armed cataphract cavalry (armored horsemen), who ambushed the Romans and wiped them out.

Thinking that the horse archers were gone, Crassus ordered his square to advance, only to come under a renewed attack by the horse archers. They were soon joined by the cataphracts, who mounted a series of charges that lasted until nightfall.

The next day, Surena invited Crassus to a meeting to discuss terms for a truce. Crassus was killed at the meeting, after which his army attempted to retreat back to friendly territory, although very few of them made it. **RM**

Losses: Roman, 20,000 dead and 10,000 captured of 43,000 engaged; Parthian, 1,000 of 11,000

⬆ *Detail from a book illustration highlighting the superiority of the Parthian horse archers.*

Alesia September 52 BCE

The Siege of Alesia and the battles that raged around it are often considered to be the finest military exploits in the career of Julius Caesar. His victory completed the Roman conquest of Gaul and made Caesar powerful enough to embark on the civil wars that would make him dictator of Rome.

By 52 BCE, the Roman conquest of Gaul was almost complete, accomplished by Julius Caesar. The Gallic tribes, however, were bitter and rebellious. When they found a new leader in Vercingetorix of the Averni, the tribes united in an uprising against Roman rule.

Caesar attacked Vercingetorix's capital at Gergovia, but was repulsed. After a prolonged campaign, he succeeded in forcing Vercingetorix and about 60,000 men to defend the fortified hilltop town of Alesia. Caesar decided to starve Vercingetorix into surrender, and ordered his men to construct a timber and earthen wall, 12 feet (3.6 m) high and 11 miles (18 km) long, to enclose the town: a circumvallation. The Gauls launched

> *"[Alesia] gave him an opportunity of showing greater instances of his valor and conduct than any other contest had done."* Plutarch, on Caesar

constant raids against the building works, but as the works neared completion, a strong force of cavalry burst through and rode off. Caesar guessed that the horsemen had been sent to fetch help, so he began a second rampart, this time facing outward to form a wall of contravallation. The outer wall was similar to the inner one, but longer at 14 miles (22.5 km). There was one section of this wall where a deep ravine and large boulders made it impossible to build a continuous wall. Caesar sought to hide the spot by a fold in the wall. The

Roman camps were placed between the two walls. In order to keep what food remained for his fighting men, Vercingetorix forced out of the gates all the women and children, in the expectation that they would be allowed through the Roman lines. Caesar refused to let the refugees pass, so they had no choice but to camp between the two armies, and slowly starved.

In late September, the expected relief army of Gauls arrived, commanded by Commius of the Atrebates and Vercassivellaunos of the Averni. The next day, Commius launched an attack on the wall of contravallation. Seeing the move, Vercingetorix attacked from the inside. The Romans managed to beat off the attacks, which were renewed the next night. On 2 October, Vercassivellaunos attacked the weak spot in the Roman outer wall, with Vercingetorix again assaulting the inner wall. Caesar realized the attack would be difficult to beat off and poured reinforcements into the area. He then sent infantry out of the inner wall to attack Vercingetorix, although this achieved little. The Roman lines were on the verge of breaking. Caesar led 6,000 of his cavalry out of the outer walls and rode around to attack the rear of the attacking column led by Vercassivellaunos. The Gauls broke and ran, pursued closely by the Roman cavalry who overran the Gauls' camp and drove the troops for miles, with great slaughter.

The next day, Vercingetorix opened talks with Caesar, offering to surrender if the lives of his men were spared. Caesar agreed, although Vercingetorix was sent to Rome in chains. Five years later, he formed part of Caesar's triumphal parade and was then executed by strangulation. Caesar used his fame and spoils from the wars in Gaul to aid a bid for power in Rome, in which he was supported by his loyal legionaries. **RM**

Losses: Roman, 12,800 of 60,000; Gallic, unknown number of dead and 40,000 captured of 180,000

◁ *Invasion of Britain* 55 BCE   *Dyrrachium* 48 BCE ▷

Alesia Besieged by Julius Caesar *by sixteenth-century German artist Melchior Feselen.* ➡

QVANTA STRA
GE VIRVM SVBLI
MIS ALEXIA CESSIT
CÆSAREIS AQVI
LIS. PICTA TABEL
LA NOTAT

Dyrrachium   Early July 48 BCE

In 49 BCE Julius Caesar, fresh from his conquests in Gaul, marched an army into Italy, crossing the Rubicon and capturing Rome. This triggered a civil war in which Caesar's main opponent was the general Pompey the Great. At Dyrrachium Caesar was defeated, but Pompey did not exploit his success.

Now in control of Italy, Caesar sailed his legions across the Adriatic to face an army that Pompey had formed in Greece. In order to capture supplies for his army, Caesar marched on Pompey's large depot at the port of Dyrrachium, in modern-day Albania. He was starting to build siege works when Pompey arrived with a relief force that was far larger in numbers than Caesar's army, although the troops were less experienced.

Weeks of skirmishing followed, as Caesar's engineers sought to surround Pompey's army with fortifications. Finally, Pompey assaulted Caesar's siege lines close to where they met the sea. This area, on Caesar's left, was held by the ninth legion. Pompey's infantry attacked in large numbers, driving the legion back with heavy loss. Caesar countered by sending in 4,000 reinforcements, led by Mark Antony, who charged Pompey's disordered legions and drove them back. Meanwhile, Pompey sent a large force of infantry and some 3,000 cavalry marching to outflank Caesar's right wing. Caesar at first ordered the legions on that wing to stand firm, but then—seeing for himself the danger of being outflanked—ordered a retreat that soon became a disordered rout.

Pompey did not pursue Caesar's forces as he had achieved his objectives in raising the siege and denying Caesar much-needed supplies. This was a serious error, because it allowed Caesar's veterans to fall back to regroup and so continue the campaign. **RM**

"Today the victory had been the enemy's—had there been any one among them to gain it."

Julius Caesar, 48 BCE

⬆ Caesar and Pompey, painted by Italian artist Taddeo di Bartolo.

Losses: Caesar, fewer than 1,000 of 15,000; Pompey, 2,000 of 45,000

◁ Alesia 52 BCE   Pharsalus 48 BCE ▷

Pharsalus 9 August 48 BCE

The Battle of Pharsalus was the decisive clash of the civil war fought between armies led by Julius Caesar and Pompey the Great. The battle showed the values of discipline and training in a close-quarter fight, Caesar's battle-hardened veterans winning despite being heavily outnumbered.

Having failed to capture the supply center of Dyrrachium, Caesar marched his army into Thessaly looking for food. Pompey followed, hoping to starve Caesar's veteran army rather than face it in battle. However, Pompey was ordered by his political masters to attack Caesar's much smaller army in order to finish the campaign quickly.

Pompey put his numerous but inexperienced infantry in dense formations, which he felt could be better maintained in combat. His right flank was on the River Enipeus, so he posted his cavalry on the left. He planned to engage Caesar's infantry in the center, use his 7,000 cavalry to sweep aside Caesar's few horsemen, then veer the cavalry around to attack the infantry in the rear. These plans were betrayed to Caesar. He placed his tough tenth legion on the right, the position of greatest danger, and put 5,000 light infantry under cover behind his cavalry.

The battle began with the main infantry formations clashing in the center. Pompey's cavalry attacked Caesar's horses, who fought for a while before suddenly riding off. This allowed Caesar's light infantry to deluge Pompey's cavalry with javelins and slingshot. The unexpected assault drove Pompey's horsemen back, allowing the tenth legion to get onto the left flank of Pompey's infantry. When Caesar threw in his reserves, Pompey's center collapsed and the battle was won. Pompey sought refuge in Egypt, but was murdered on the orders of Pharaoh Ptolemy XIII. **RM**

> *"This was the end of the Roman republic and the beginning of Caesar's autocracy."*
>
> Julius Caesar

Losses: Caesar, 1,200 of 28,000; Pompey, 6,000 of 45,000

 Detail from a sixteenth-century fresco by Niccolò dell'Abbate showing close combat at Pharsalus.

◁ *Dyrrachium 48 BCE*   *Thapsus 46 BCE* ▷

Thapsus 6 April 46 BCE

After his victory at Pharsalus, Julius Caesar needed to secure the wealthy provinces of north Africa. Victory at Thapsus achieved this objective and ensured Caesar would be victorious in this civil war. The battle is also notable as the last large-scale use of war elephants outside of India.

When Caesar invaded what is now Tunisia and laid siege to the city of Thapsus, Quintus Entellus Scipio marched to relieve the siege with his ally, King Juba of Numidia. Scipio placed his infantry in the center with his cavalry on the right flank. Juba put his light infantry on Scipio's left and his cavalry on their left. The elephants were placed on both the extreme left and extreme right. Caesar was outnumbered and drew up his heavy infantry in thinner ranks. He put his few cavalry on the flanks, interspersed with light infantry and archers.

The battle began with Caesar's archers dashing forward to shoot at the elephants, aiming for the eyes. On his left flank this caused the elephants to flee, disrupting Scipio's cavalry. On Caesar's right, however, the elephants charged first and inflicted casualties on the fifth legion before they were driven off. The infantry then advanced to close-quarters fighting. Juba held his cavalry back on Scipio's left, while on Scipio's right his disordered cavalry were swept away by Caesar's horsemen. When Caesar's cavalry returned to attack the rear of Scipio's infantry, Juba marched his men off the battlefield leaving his ally to his fate.

About 10,000 of Scipio's infantry fell back to their overnight camp and offered to surrender, but Caesar refused and had them killed. Although the civil war continued, Caesar's enemies no longer had any real prospect of success. **RM**

Losses: Caesar, 1,000 of 40,000; Scipio and Numidian, 30,000 dead and captured of 45,000

[<] Pharsalus 48 BCE   Philippi 42 BCE [>]

Philippi 3 and 23 October 42 BCE

The climactic battle in the war that followed the assassination of Julius Caesar in 44 BCE, Philippi saw the final destruction of those who favored the old Republican constitution of Rome. The battle was a brutal killing match with much confusion and little generalship on either side.

Caesar loyalists Mark Antony, Octavian Caesar, and Marcus Lepidus formed a triumvirate. They seized control of Rome and the empire's western provinces, then set off to defeat Caesar's killers, Marcus Brutus and Gaius Cassius, who had joined with other opponents of Caesar—the optimates—in raising the eastern provinces of the empire.

In late September, Antony and Octavian found the enemy, led by Brutus and Cassius, entrenched in the gap between an impassable marsh and unscalable cliffs near Philippi in Greece. On 3 October, Antony and Octavian launched a frontal assault. Octavian's troops were repulsed in disorder, and Brutus captured his camp. Antony broke through Cassius's defenses, but had to pull back to aid Octavian. Cassius, however, committed suicide thinking that his army had lost the battle. Brutus took over command of Cassius's forces and the fighting ended inconclusively. Antony then began building a fortified causeway across the marsh to outflank Brutus's defenses.

On 23 October, Brutus launched an assault on the causeway, which developed into a general action between the armies. The confined space between marsh and mountain did not allow the cavalry to play much role, so the infantry slogged it out at close quarters. Eventually Brutus's army broke and ran. Brutus pulled about a third of his army back in good order, but Antony's cavalry surrounded them. Brutus committed suicide, and his men surrendered. **RM**

Losses: Triumvirate, unknown of 100,000; Brutus and Cassius, unknown, although all survivors surrendered and the army of 100,000 ceased to exist

[<] Thapsus 46 BCE   Naulochus 36 BCE [>]

Naulochus   3 September 36 BCE

After Roman dictator Julius Caesar was murdered in 44 BCE, Sextus Pompeius, the son of Caesar's dead rival Pompey the Great, seized control of Sicily. The naval Battle of Naulochus ensured the defeat of Sextus and left Octavian Caesar and Mark Antony in control of the entire Roman Empire.

In 36 BCE Octavian launched an invasion of Sicily, with the support of a fleet led by Marcus Vipsanius Agrippa. Sextus knew that his only hope of defeating Octavian was to establish command of the sea. He had the advantage of veteran crews able to maneuver their galleys skillfully and ram opponents. But Agrippa had a new invention, the harpax: a grapnel shot from a catapult that hooked onto an enemy ship. This device would enable him to haul alongside Sextus's ships and board them with his superior force of soldiers.

The two fleets met off the coast of Sicily. Agrippa arranged his ships in two lines facing east. Sextus, likewise, formed in two lines. The battle began with Agrippa's right wing edging back as if trying to avoid the rams of the enemy. When Sextus's ships were sufficiently far advanced, the harpax was deployed, entangling the entire left wing of Sextus's fleet in a boarding battle they could not win. Meanwhile, Agrippa spread his formation to outflank the right wing of Sextus's fleet, driving the enemy ships back toward the already entangled galleys near the shore. The confusion in Sextus's fleet caused all formation to be lost, and Agrippa's ships closed in for the kill, hurling rocks from onboard catapults and shooting arrows down onto the decks from raised towers. Sextus escaped with seventeen ships, but was later executed after surrendering. **RM**

Losses: Sextus Pompeius, 28 ships sunk and 105 captured of 150; Marcus Agrippa, 3 ships sunk of 175

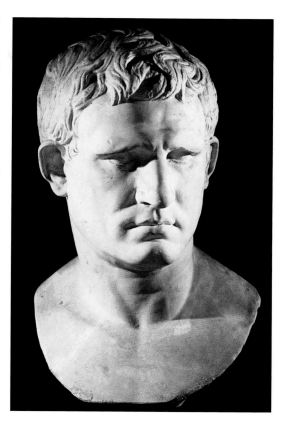

"He was a man of distinguished character, unconquerable by toil, loss of sleep, or danger."

Velleius Paterculus, on Marcus Agrippa

🔼 *A copy after a first-century-BCE marble bust of Marcus Vipsanius Agrippa.*

◀ Philippi 42 BCE   Actium 31 BCE ▶

Actium 2 September 31 BCE

The victory of Octavian Caesar at Actium made him master of the Mediterranean and the entire Roman world. He used his position to introduce reforms that destroyed the old Roman Republic and ushered in the new era of an all-powerful emperor. The battle also ended the independence of Egypt and led to the death of its famous queen, Cleopatra VII.

Soon after Naulochus, Mark Antony and Octavian Caesar fell out because both wanted to dominate the Roman Empire alone. Moreover, Mark Antony had divorced Octavian's sister to marry Queen Cleopatra VII of Egypt. By the end of 32 BCE, Antony's forces were concentrated around the Ambracian Gulf in western Greece. It seems his plan was to lure Octavian to invade Greece, then destroy his fleet in a pitched battle in order to cut the supply lines to Italy and the west. Octavian's army would then face starvation.

Antony's fleet of 500 ships was twice as large as Octavian's, and his ships were larger and heavier. In the spring, Octavian crossed to Greece with an army of perhaps 80,000 men and marched to occupy the north shore of the Gulf of Ambracia. Disaster struck Antony's forces in the form of a virulent outbreak of malaria. Most of his land army was unfit for battle, and he could crew only half his fleet. Instead of Octavian being isolated, it was Antony who was trapped by his opponent's fleet—commanded by Marcus Agrippa—and faced with starvation. Antony decided to abandon Greece. His main army was ordered to march to Macedonia, while other detachments were sent to garrison the key cities of Greece and Asia Minor. Antony then led his remaining ships out to break through the Octavian naval blockade. Antony arranged his fleet in three squadrons and took command of the northern, right flank squadron.

Cleopatra's Egyptian squadron was held back. Agrippa drew up his fleet in three squadrons, taking command of the left wing facing Antony's ships.

The battle began in the north, as Antony and Agrippa clashed ships. Shortly after midday, the afternoon breeze sprang up from the northeast. The signal for retreat was hoisted on Cleopatra's flagship, and the Egyptian squadron sailed off to the southwest. Antony's southern squadron swiftly followed, throwing their battle towers, catapults, and other heavy equipment overboard to lighten the ships and increase speed. Soon Antony's central squadron was also making sail, although Agrippa's captains had by now spotted the move and were closing in to try to stop the escape. Antony fell back to get his ships between those of Agrippa and the fleeing Egyptians. The battle continued until nightfall, when Antony left his flagship for a smaller, faster ship and hurried off to join Cleopatra.

Octavian later claimed that Cleopatra had sailed off in panic and that Antony had fled to be with his sultry lover. But it was probably a maneuver that Antony had planned in advance to get as many of his ships away as possible—and to save his main treasure, which was on Cleopatra's ships. Whatever the truth, the results were dramatic. Most of Antony's eastern allies abandoned him and made peace with Octavian. Most city garrisons chose to surrender on terms as soon as Octavian arrived at their gates. By August 30 BCE, Antony realized that he was utterly defeated and committed suicide. Cleopatra also killed herself a few days later, and Egypt was swallowed by Rome. **RM**

Losses: Octavian, unknown of 250 ships engaged; Antony, more than 100 ships sunk or captured of 250 engaged

⟨ *Naulochus 36 BCE*

M·CAELIVS
M·L·
PRIVATVS

M·CAELIVS
M·L·
THIAMINVS

M·CAELIO·T·F·LEM·BON
O·LEG·XIIX·ANN·LIII
CIDIT·BELLO·VARIANO·OSSA
NFERRE·LICEBIT·P·CAELIVS·T·F
LEM·FRATER·FECIT

Teutoburg Forest Autumn 9 CE

The massacre of three entire Roman legions, along with significant auxiliary units and cavalry, by German tribes ensured that the lands east of the Rhine were never incorporated into the Roman Empire. It was from here that the fatal barbarian invasions would come to destroy the empire almost four centuries later.

Rome had recently occupied large areas east of the Rhine. Arminius, a chief of the Cherusci tribe who had been granted Roman citizenship and fought as an auxiliary of the Roman legions, told the Roman military commander, Varus, of a minor uprising.

In fact, Arminius had formed an alliance of all major German tribes and was leading Varus into an ambush. Varus left his base, near Minden, heading northwest. As the Roman column entered the Teutoburg Forest, near Osnabruck, Arminius slipped away to join his waiting army. In the midst of the forest, the Roman column was attacked suddenly by huge numbers of Germans, catching the Romans out of battle formation. About half the Romans survived the initial ambush and next day marched south. They found their route blocked by a large earth and timber rampart lined by Germans at what is now Kalkriese. The Romans attacked, but were driven off. The Roman cavalry then fled, only to be hunted down over the days that followed.

One group of legionaries surrendered and, after a few had been sacrificed to the German gods, the rest were enslaved. Another group reached the fort at Aliso where they joined the garrison. Aliso held out under Lucius Caedicius until the onset of winter caused the Germans to go home, allowing the survivors to march back to Roman territory and bring with them news of the disaster. **RM**

Losses: Roman, about 35,000 dead or enslaved of 36,000; German, unknown, but minimal

Argentoratum 357 ▷

Kunyang July 23 CE

The Han dynasty had ruled China for some two hundred years when, in 9 CE, the usurper Wang Mang announced the foundation of the Xin dynasty. But Wang's rule soon alienated many of his subjects, and the humiliating defeat of his forces at the Battle of Kunyang ensured the rapid restoration of a Han emperor.

By 23 CE various descendants of the Han imperial family had emerged as pretenders to the Chinese throne. One of these was Liu Xiu, who led the rebel forces that captured the castle of Kunyang in Henan province. Wang Mang sent a massive Xin army to attack Kunyang, led by his generals Wang Yi and Wang Xun. Liu Xiu slipped out of the castle as the Xin army approached. While the two Wangs besieged Kunyang, he raised an army for a counterattack.

The Xin army became demoralized as the siege dragged on, and the castle's defenders maintained a stout defense. When Liu Xiu reappeared with fresh forces, his troops were still too few in number to appear to have any chance against the Xin. But the balance of morale had shifted in favor of the rebels. No doubt seeing their soldiers' uncertainty, the Wangs resolved to regain the initiative by leading in person an attack on Liu Xiu with their best 10,000 men.

It was a disastrous mistake. The Xin elite force was decimated, and Wang Xun was killed. The rest of their army made no attempt to help them and, faced with an aggressive sortie by the Kunyang garrison, threw down their arms and fled. The tide of the war had set against the Xin. Soon after, Wang Mang was killed in his imperial palace, his head kicked around like a ball by the people. In 25 CE Liu Xiu ascended the throne as Han Emperor Guangwu. **RG**

Losses: No reliable figures

◁ Mobei Campaign 119 BCE　　　　　Red Cliffs 208 ▷

← *The cenotaph of Marcus Caelius, an officer who died in the ambush at Teutoburg Forest.*

Medway 43 CE

The first major recorded battle of the Roman invasion of Britain under the orders of the emperor Claudius, the battle is thought to have been fought at a crossing of the River Medway, near the modern-day city of Rochester in Kent, England, and it raged for nearly two days.

The British force was led by two brothers: Togodumnus, king of the Catuvellauni, and Caratacus, a chieftain of the same tribe. The Roman invasion force, under the command of Aulus Plautius, consisted of four legions, a force approximately 20,000 strong. On hearing of the Roman landing at Richborough, British resistance united behind the leadership of the two brothers and, after two indecisive skirmishes in eastern Kent, the British force met the advancing Romans at the River Medway.

Cassius Dio, a Roman historian, describes how a detachment of Celtic Roman auxiliaries swam across the river and attacked the British chariot horses, surprising the Britons and causing panic. Using this initial advantage, Vespasian (a future Roman emperor) crossed the river with a large force but was unable to press home a victory. The battle continued to rage all day without any decisive result. On the second day, the Romans launched a daring attack under the command of Gnaeus Hosidius Geta, who was almost killed in the fighting that followed. However, Geta's troops rallied around their commander and the Britons were eventually overcome, with the bulk of the British force taking flight. The fact that the battle lasted for two days indicates that it must have been a significant encounter. However, the British were not yet conquered and fell back to the River Thames, where Togodumnus was defeated, dying shortly afterward. Caratacus continued resistance until beaten at Caer Caradoc in 50 CE. **TB**

Losses: No reliable figures

Watling Street 61 CE ▷

Watling Street 61 CE

In this final decisive battle of Boudica's revolt against Roman rule in Britain, a large British force was routed by the heavily outnumbered Romans, under the command of Gaius Suetonius Paulinus. The battle marked the end of resistance to Roman rule in southern Britain, which was to last until 410.

When King Prasutagus of the Iceni died, he left his lands to be divided between his daughters and the emperor, Nero. However, the Romans ignored Prasutagus's will and seized his lands, flogged his widow Boudica, and raped their daughters. While the Roman governor, Suetonius, was campaigning in Anglesey, Boudica led the Iceni in rebellion. She attacked Camulodunum (Colchester), where her troops slaughtered thousands and set fire to the temple of Claudius, killing those who sheltered inside. She then turned her attention on London, burning the city and killing anyone who could not escape. Suetonius gathered his forces, amassing around 10,000 men.

Boudica's rebel forces and Suetonius's outnumbered but well-drilled army met on the Roman road called Watling Street, near Wroxeter in Shropshire. Roman rule in Britain was in the balance, so Suetonius had to choose his battleground carefully: a narrow gorge protected his flanks and a forest protected his rear. With open plains to the front, Boudica was forced to engage the Romans in a massive frontal charge that was funneled into a tight mass and cut down by volleys of javelin. Once the Britons were in disarray, Suetonius ordered his forces forward in typical Roman wedge-shaped formation. Despite their numbers the poorly armed Britons were no match for superior Roman discipline, armor, and weaponry. As the Britons retreated, the ring of wagons belonging to their families impeded their escape and they were massacred. **TB**

Losses: According to Roman sources: British, 80,000 men, women, and children; Roman, 400

◁ *Medway 43 CE*   *Mons Graupius 84 CE* ▷

Jerusalem 70 CE

The fall of Jerusalem was a pivotal moment in the first Jewish-Roman war. It resulted in the destruction of the ancient temple of Solomon and much of the surrounding city by a fire started by the Roman army under the command of the future emperor Titus.

The Jewish-Roman war of 66 to 73 CE was the first of three rebellions by Jews against Roman rule in Judaea and is referred to as "The Great Revolt." The revolt started in 66 CE, following religious tensions between Greeks and Jews, but soon involved protests against taxation and attacks on Roman citizens. Shocked by the defeat of a legion under the command of Gallus, Emperor Nero sent military commander Vespasian, with a force of 60,000, to ensure that order was restored.

Despite victories elsewhere, Jerusalem proved difficult to take. Vespasian's son, Titus, surrounded the city with a wall and a trench, and anyone caught trying to escape was crucified. Titus then put pressure on the food and water supply by allowing pilgrims to enter the city in order to celebrate Passover but not letting them out.

After a number of failed attempts to attack the city, the Romans set about the destruction of Jerusalem's formidable defenses with a battering ram. Having breached these defenses, the Romans fought their way from street to street. Many Zealots sought sanctuary in the ancient temple of Solomon and in the fortress of Antonia. The Romans finally overwhelmed the fortress, and the ancient temple was destroyed by fire in the ensuing battle, reputedly against the wishes of Titus.

The destruction of the temple is still mourned by Jews in the annual fast of Tisha B'Av, and the fall of Jerusalem is celebrated in Rome's Arch of Titus. **TB**

Losses: According to Jewish historian Josephus, Jewish, 1.1 million dead and 97,000 enslaved; Roman, unknown

Masada 73 CE

"Children, and old men, and profane persons, and priests were all slain in the same manner."

Flavius Josephus, War of the Jews

A book illumination from the fourteenth century shows the army and citizens of Jerusalem fending off the initial Roman attack.

Masada 73 CE

After the fall of Jerusalem, Emperor Titus returned to Rome and received a triumphant welcome. At the same time, the Romans began to restore order in Judaea by putting down any final resistance and regaining control of the last few strongholds held by Zealots. The last and longest of these final encounters was the Siege of Masada.

Only a small number of Zealots escaped the massacre of men, women, and children when Jerusalem fell in 70 CE. Some of those who escaped—members of the extremist Sicarii sect—settled in the apparently impregnable mountaintop fortress of Masada.

The Romans, commanded by Lucius Silva, laid siege to Masada, building a circumvallation wall around the mountain. A blockade would have been lengthy, however, because the defenders had plentiful food and water supplies. So the Romans also set about building a massive earth ramp on the western side of the fortress. Built under constant fire from the defenders, the ramp was 1,968 feet (600 m) long and rose 200 feet (61 m) to the fortress walls. The Romans then pushed a siege tower up the ramp. Equipped with a ram, this soon battered a breach in the wall. When the Romans entered the fortress, however, they discovered that its 960 inhabitants had committed mass suicide, preferring death at their own hands to slavery or execution. Jewish historian Josephus claimed to have been given a full account of the siege by two women who survived by hiding inside a drain. The witnesses claimed that, because suicide was against Jewish belief, the Sicarii had drawn lots to kill each other, with the last man the only one to take his own life. Masada was the last act of the Jewish war. The Jews became scattered into areas around the Mediterranean with many thousands being sold into slavery. **TB**

Losses: Sicarii, 1,000; Roman, unknown

◁ *Jerusalem 70 CE*

Mons Graupius 84 CE

The Roman province of Britannia—Roman Britain— had an open frontier to the north, where people whom the Romans called "Caledonians" lived. In 84 CE Gnaeus Julius Agricola, governor of Britannia and an experienced military commander, led an army northward into what is now Scotland in order to subdue the Caledonian tribes.

There is much debate over the location of the Battle of Mons Graupius, a name given to the encounter by the historian Tacitus, who was Agricola's son-in-law. The archeology points to the most likely locations as being either Kempstone Hill or Megray Hill in Kincardineshire.

Tacitus writes that a Roman army of approximately 20,000 faced a Caledonian force of 30,000, led by a figure Tacitus refers to as Calgacus. The Caledonians held higher ground and were assembled in a horseshoe formation. Agricola kept his valuable legionaries in reserve, using auxiliaries from Batavia and Tungria to bear the brunt of the fighting. These formidable swordsmen slowly forced their way up the side of the hill. The Caledonians tried to outflank the advancing enemy but were themselves outflanked by the attacking Roman auxiliary cavalry. Approximately 10,000 Caledonians were ruthlessly slaughtered. The rest were pursued into nearby woodland where many escaped. The victory allowed the Romans to claim control of all of Britain, but northern Scotland in reality always remained outside their empire.

The battle is perhaps best known for the speech attributed to Calgacus by Tacitus, which ends: "To robbery, slaughter, plunder, they give the lying name of empire; they make a solitude and call it peace." However, it is unlikely that such a speech was made and it is more likely that Tacitus was writing a lesson for home consumption against what he saw as Roman decadence and ruthlessness. **TB**

Losses: According to Tacitus: Caledonian, 10,000; Roman, 360

◁ *Watling Street 61 CE*

Sarmizegetusa 106

The Siege of Sarmizegetusa was the final decisive encounter of the five-year war between the Roman Empire—led by the emperor, Trajan—and the kingdom of Dacia, led by King Decebalus. The siege was brought about by Decebalus's repeated attempts to break the various terms imposed by his treaties with Rome.

The Dacian Wars were key campaigns in the Roman Empire's expansion in the east of Europe. The emperor Domitian had won victories against Decebalus more than twenty years earlier, but it is the emperor Trajan who is best known for finally conquering the Dacians.

Decebalus continually flouted the terms of his treaty with Rome and war broke out in 101. Rome's victory resulted in Dacia being reduced to the status of a client kingdom, thus extending the Roman Empire north and east of the Danube River. However, Decebalus again decided to resist Roman rule, and in 105 he launched an invasion. Trajan's campaign, referred to as the Second Dacian War, is celebrated on Trajan's Column in Rome, which depicts scenes including the building of a large bridge over the Danube; the Siege of Sarmizegetusa; and the suicide of Decebalus. The column also records how the Romans bombarded the Dacian capital with siege weaponry; how a Roman assault was fought back by Dacian defenders; and how the Dacians finally surrendered after the Romans had cut off their water supply.

Decebalus escaped with many of his followers, but committed suicide rather than face capture and the humiliation of being paraded through the streets of Rome before his certain execution. The Romans leveled the Dacian capital and founded a new city approximately 25 miles (40 km) away, which survived until it was destroyed by the Goths. **TB**

"[Decebalus] was shrewd in his understanding of warfare and shrewd also in the waging of war."

Dio Cassius, Roman historian

Losses: No reliable figures

↑ These scenes from Trajan's Column depict Sarmizegetusa being set on fire (above) and the advancing Roman armies (below).

Red Cliffs 208

Han dynasty minister Cao Cao attempted to maintain the unity of the Chinese Empire by marching with a large army into the rebellious south. His defeat in a river battle, fought on the Yangtze at the Red Cliffs, initiated the period of disunity in China known as the Three Kingdoms.

The aim of Cao Cao's military expedition was to subdue the regional warlords Liu Bei and Sun Quan. The strength of Cao's army was overwhelming, but he needed to win control of the Yangtze. Neither he nor his troops had any experience of fighting on water. Advancing to the Yangtze overland, however, they captured a river fleet in port and embarked to sail downstream. Although outnumbered, Liu Bei and Sun Quan decided to stand and fight, hoping their superior experience of riverine warfare would give them the advantage.

Cao was soon in trouble. Encountering the unfamiliar disease environment of southern China, much of his army fell sick. Also, in preliminary skirmishes, his troops had difficulty fighting while standing on rocking decks. In order to create a more stable fighting platform, Cao had groups of boats lashed together. Zhou Yu, the commander of the combined forces of Liu and Sun, ordered an attack with fireships. Loaded with dry reeds, large vessels were sailed toward Cao's immobilized fleet and set ablaze by their crews, who rapidly disembarked to small boats. A large part of Cao's fleet was destroyed by fire, with heavy loss of life.

The shock of this disaster, combined with the depredations of disease, persuaded Cao to order a hasty withdrawal northward. China became divided into three kingdoms, each under the control of one of the combatants at the Red Cliffs: Cao in Wei, Liu in Shu, and Sun in Wu. **RG**

Losses: Unknown

[<] *Kunyang 23 CE*　　　　　　　*Wuzhang Plains 234* [>]

Wuzhang Plains 234

The most famous military commander of China's Three Kingdoms period (220–280) was Zhuge Liang of the kingdom of Shu. His death at the Battle of the Wuzhang Plains was a triumph for the kingdom of Wei, achieved through patient refusal to follow the dictates of the heroic warrior ethos.

From 228, Zhuge Liang embarked on a series of "Northern Expeditions," seeking to defeat Wei and create a unified Chinese Empire. These expeditions encountered major logistical difficulties, involving marches through mountain terrain and across areas where food supplies were sparse. Zhuge Liang's fifth Northern Expedition in 234 was the result of three years' preparation, but Wei commander Sima Yi had also been organizing his army, in particular improving food supplies so a large force could be sustained in the field for a long period.

As Zhuge Liang advanced northward, Sima Yi established his army in an impregnable defensive position along the line of the Wei River. The two armies settled down to a standoff through the summer months. Despite being taunted by Zhuge Liang for his cowardice, Sima Yi obeyed orders from the king of Wei to remain within his fortifications and avoid combat. The Shu forces were gradually worn down by this battle without fighting, demoralized and decimated by hardship and disease. Among the victims was Zhuge Liang himself, who died in camp. This was the final blow for the Shu army's morale. They initiated a withdrawal to carry their venerated leader's body home. Sima Yi hesitated to mount a pursuit, unsure whether Zhuge Liang was truly dead (he suspected a ploy to draw him into the open). There was in any case no need, for the Shu were thoroughly defeated and fought among themselves as they returned disconsolately through the mountain passes. **RG**

Losses: Unknown

[<] *Red Cliffs 208*　　　　　　　*Fei River 383* [>]

Edessa 260

Greece's wars with Persia have acquired all but mythic status in the Western tradition, confirming European superiority over oriental ways. Less well-reported are the triumphs of the later Sassanid Persian Empire over Rome, culminating in the crushing defeat of Emperor Valerian at Edessa.

"A great battle took place beyond Carrhae and Edessa between us and Caesar Valerian," reads the inscription carved on a rocky outcrop at Naqsh-e Rustam in Iran. "We took him prisoner with our own hands," it goes on: a flagrant boast, but well-justified.

The Sassanid emperor Shapur I had invaded Roman Mesopotamia and Syria in about 240: the Romans fought back, defeating the Persians at Resaena in 243. That the Romans now sued for peace owed more to grubby politics than military necessity: Philip the Arab, who had assassinated Gordian III and seized the imperial throne for himself, needed a chance to secure his position without outside pressure.

However, Shapur continued his depredations in the eastern parts of the Roman Empire, taking a number of territories. As emperor from 253, Valerian resolved to win these back. According to the Naqsh-e Rustam inscription, his army was 70,000 strong, and at first it seems to have made real headway. By the time the men reached Edessa (in what is now southeastern Turkey, near the Syrian border), they were beginning to flag, however. Valerian decided that his troops should hole up in the city, to which Shapur immediately laid siege. An outbreak of plague here cut a swath through what was soon a severely weakened Roman army. When Valerian led a deputation to Shapur's camp to negotiate a settlement, he was captured with his staff and taken back to Persia as a prisoner. **MK**

Losses: Roman, more than 60,000; Persian, minimal

Ctesiphon 363 >|

Immae and Emesa 272

One of the boldest rebellions against Roman domination was led by Zenobia, warrior queen of Palmyra in Syria. Her revolt was dealt a hammerblow at the Battle of Immae, where legionary discipline prevailed. The Palmyrenes' rearguard action at Emesa was a heroic but hopeless last stand.

King Odenathus of Palmyra was a contented client of the Romans. In return for his loyalty, they let him rule his Syrian desert realm. But his wife, Zenobia, was made of sterner stuff: in 267, newly widowed, she proclaimed Palmyra an independent kingdom. Beset by other difficulties—in Spain and Gaul, in Germany, the Balkans, and the Black Sea region—Rome could not stop her rapidly extending her domains, which soon stretched from Asia Minor to Egypt. By 271, however, Emperor Aurelian was reestablishing control. He wrote off Dacia, defeated the Goths, and took back the Balkans. Crossing into Asia Minor and moving on to Syria, he met the main Palmyrene force at Immae, outside Antioch.

Like other Middle Eastern peoples of the time, the Palmyrenes relied on the strength of their *clibanarii* (cataphract-style cavalry), which were heavily armored and equipped with lances. They felt confident of brushing aside Aurelian's more lightly armed horsemen and breaking his infantry. As it happened, though, the Roman cavalry ran rings around the Palmyrene heavyweights, wearing them down in the desert heat. Forced to flee, they rallied at Emesa, where it seemed things would go according to plan. The *clibanarii* defeated the Roman cavalry. Palestinian auxiliaries then galloped in, however, and soft mail armor offered no protection against the clubs they carried. The Palmyrene cataphracts fled, and the defeated Zenobia was taken to Rome and paraded in Aurelian's triumph. **MK**

Losses: Unknown

Milvian Bridge 312 >|

Milvian Bridge   28 October 312

The battle fought at Milvian Bridge outside Rome was a crucial moment in a civil war that ended with Constantine I as sole ruler of the Roman Empire and Christianity established as the empire's official religion. Constantine's conversion to the Cross may have been prompted by a dream of victory.

By the beginning of the fourth century, the Roman Empire was gradually imploding. Faction fighting and civil war had become endemic. In 306 Constantine was declared emperor at York, but Maxentius claimed the imperial title in Rome. In 312, marching on Rome, Constantine prepared to do battle with his rival's forces where they were awaiting him beside the River Tiber at the Milvian Bridge, a vital crossing point that had been partially dismantled to block the attackers.

On 27 October, the night before the battle, it is said that Constantine had a dream: he saw the sun—the object of his own worship—overlain by the figure of a cross. Beneath it was inscribed the simple message *in*

> "He saw with his own eyes in the heavens a trophy of the cross arising from the light of the sun."

Eusebius, on Constantine's vision

hoc signo vinces, which translates as "In this sign, prevail." Constantine needed no further persuasion. The next morning he ordered his men to paint crosses upon their shields. They then marched into war, accordingly, as "Christian soldiers."

Constantine's conversion, it has often been said, smacked more of superstition than religious awakening. Less often noted is the emperor's modesty. His victory owed as much to his skillful generalship as to any savior. Realizing that Maxentius had placed his troops too close

to the river, which was in their rear, he hurled his cavalry against the enemy horsemen with the utmost force. Maxentius's cavalry buckled before the impact and broke ranks. In other circumstances this would have been nothing more than a setback: here, however, with no room to remarshal their ranks, the confusion was complete. Constantine then ordered his infantry to push forward against Maxentius's infantry, who were forced to fall back and found themselves without room to maneuver.

The stone-built bridge had been reduced in width in order to keep Constantine's forces back, so Maxentius's men had crossed the Tiber via an improvised pontoon construction. This had been fine for men and horses making their way slowly and carefully in the days before the battle. As a means of escape during the stress of battle, however, it was wholly inadequate. Maxentius's decision to retreat was catastrophic. His intention was to make a strategic withdrawal, protecting the flower of his force so that he would be able to mount a successful defense of Rome from the city walls. But with only a narrow strip of stone and a rocking, heaving pathway of wood as a crossing, the retreat across the Tiber became a rout as Constantine's men surged forward from their rear. Maxentius himself appears to have been among those who drowned.

Constantine took Rome on 29 October. Some men offered sacrifices to the ancestral gods, but he remained true (at least in his fashion) to Christianity. He eventually made what had been an obscure sect the official religion of the Roman Empire. He was a less faithful friend to Rome itself, though. In relocating the imperial capital to Byzantium (which he renamed Constantinople in his own honor), he was merely bowing to the inevitable, with barbarian pressure on the western provinces increasing year by year. **MK**

Losses: Unknown

◁ *Immae and Emesa 272*　　　　　*Argentoratum 357* ▷

Pieter Lastman's painting of 1613 depicts the chaos as Maxentius and his men become trapped. ➤

Argentoratum 357

By the fourth century, the Roman legions were struggling to hold the empire's frontiers against "barbarian" invaders. As the Battle of Argentoratum showed, however, the discipline of the legion infantry was still more than a match for the free-form ferocity and individual courage of Germanic tribal warriors.

In Gaul, a major threat to the Roman Empire was posed by the Alamanni: a grouping of tribes from central Germany that had banded together under a war leader called Chnodomar. Along with similar confederations, including the Franks and the Burgundians, they had been steadily encroaching upon Gaul and, by the 350s, were streaming across the Rhine frontier more or less unhindered.

Julian, a young caesar (deputy emperor), was responsible for restoring security along the Rhine. He had inadequate numbers of troops, because the Roman legions were overstretched, but their equipment and training were far superior to the Alamanni. Julian's force of some 13,000 legionaries and auxiliaries met Chnodomar's warriors, possibly numbering 35,000, near Strasbourg. The battle started badly for the Romans. Chnodomar sent men forward on foot to creep among the Roman cavalry and stab at their horses. Disconcerted, the Roman horsemen broke and fled when the Germanic cavalry charged. But the Roman infantry held firm as the Alamanni warriors attacked ferociously. The front line of legionaries locked shields to create a continuous wall, thrusting with their spears underneath the shield wall to fend off attack. Behind them other troops kept up a rain of missiles on the Alamanni. Exhausted and suffering heavy losses, the Alamanni broke and ran. The Romans pursued them as far as the Rhine, where many drowned. Julian's victory aided his rise to become emperor three years later. **MK**

"Forward, most fortunate of all Caesars, whither your lucky star guides you; in you at last we feel that both valor and good counsel are in the field."

Roman standard bearer at Argentoratum

A fourth-century bust of Emperor Julian, now in the Louvre in Paris.

Losses: Roman, 243; Alamanni, 6,000

◀ Milvian Bridge 312

Ctesiphon 363 ▶

Ctesiphon 363

Adrianople 378

Julian, the young hero of Argentoratum, badly overplayed his hand a few years later when he tackled Shapur II's Sassanid Persian forces. The Romans won on the battlefield, but then faced a Persian scorched-earth policy. The campaign ended with the Roman army exhausted and demoralized, and Julian dead.

The emphatic defeat of Emperor Valens by the Goths at Adrianople revealed Roman vulnerability to "barbarian" attack. Fourth-century historian Ammianus Marcellinus wrote: "Never, since the Battle of Cannae, has there been such slaughter." Yet the Roman Empire in the east survived and fought back after this disaster.

Julian, now emperor, was an attractive, charismatic figure: a man who lived his life on a heroic scale, a reckless romantic in search of striking gestures and epic triumphs. How else to explain the Persian campaign of 363 when, conscious of his weakness, Shapur II had already sued for peace? And what of Julian's decision, on reaching the Persian capital Ctesiphon after sailing up the Tigris, quite literally to burn his boats?

The Persian army awaiting the Romans outside the city was an intimidating sight: long lines of cataphracts (armored cavalry), their weaponry glinting in the sun. Undaunted, though, Julian had his cavalry form a crescent, the wings enveloping the enemy. The Romans gained an unexpected victory, but Julian's siege engines had gone up in flames with his fleet. There was no way that he could hope to lay siege to Ctesiphon. Instead, he decided to strike deep into Persia, from where Shapur was advancing with another army. Harried by the Persians, who had burned all the crops, the Romans were soon hungry and morale was low. The Persians were happy to avoid a head-on clash.

Julian decided to withdraw, sweeping around northward into Anatolia, but the Persian attacks continued, and, in one of these—at Samsarra—he was mortally wounded. His army limped home, decimated by starvation, disease, and enemy attack: never had a "victorious" army returned in so forlorn a state. **MK**

Of Germanic origin, the Goths had settled territories to the north of the Black Sea. In the fourth century, they spilt westward in great numbers, dislodged by the emergence of the ferocious Huns from the Central Asian steppe. The Visigoths (Western Goths) were allowed into the Roman Empire as immigrants, to settle in frontier territories in Bulgaria and Thrace. The Ostrogoths (Eastern Goths) were denied permission to settle inside the empire, but crossed the frontier anyway. Relations with Roman officialdom soon deteriorated and the Goths rose in revolt.

Having taken control along the Danube, the Visigoths—led by Fritigern—and the Ostrogoths—commanded by Alatheus and Saphrax—headed toward Constantinople. Valens, Roman emperor in the east, led a large force out of the city to meet them. At Adrianople (now Edirne), they found Fritigern's Visigoths camped atop a hill, their wagons ringing the summit in an impromptu fortress. Complacent Roman commanders launched the assault without waiting for the order; detachments came on piecemeal and the Roman forces milled around in confusion. In this disordered state they were charged by the Ostrogoth horsemen who, according to Ammianus, "descended from the mountain like a thunderbolt." The mass of Valens's army was surrounded and slaughtered. Valens himself was among the tens of thousands killed. Yet by 382, under Valens's successor Theodosius, the Goths were driven back to Thrace and peace achieved. **MK**

Losses: Roman, 70; Persian, 2,500

[<] *Edessa 260*

Adrianople 378 [>]

Losses: Roman, 20,000; Gothic, unknown

[<] *Ctesiphon 363*

Frigidus 394 [>]

Fei River 383

Frigidus 394

In the fourth century, China was disintegrating under the effect of barbarian invasion and civil war. Self-styled "heavenly prince" Fu Jian, founder of the "Former Qin" dynasty, saw his expansionist enterprise stopped in its tracks in this epic encounter in China's Anhui province, decided by the use of psychological warfare.

At the Battle of Frigidus, the Christian emperor Theodosius may have summoned the help of a divine wind in defeating Eugenius, his pagan rival, but he showed a most ungodly cynicism in his calculations. No matter, his unexpected victory ensured that the Roman Empire would be for a time reunited under the cross of Christ.

An effective warlord, Fu Jian had gobbled up territories north of the Yangtze and then began extending his empire southward. His way was blocked by the kingdom of the Eastern Jin, led by Xiaowu. Having taken the Jin satellite states of Former Yan and Sichuan, Fu Jian advanced on the borders of Eastern Jin itself. Xiaowu could muster only 80,000 men to meet the Former Qin army, estimated in ancient sources as 900,000 strong. However, while Xiaowu's troops were a disciplined elite, Fu Jian's men were a rabble of reluctant conscripts from various conquered kingdoms.

Fu Jian formed his army up on the north bank of the Fei River; the Jin camped on the other side. The river was too deep to be crossed at this point, so the Jin generals sent a message asking the Qin to move upriver to where they could cross and engage them. The Qin commanders were doubtful—moving so huge an army would not be easy—but Fu Jian agreed, planning to destroy the Jin as they reached his side of the river.

Fu Jian's troops were unnerved by the movement they were ordered to make. The word spread in the ranks that it was a retreat. Sensing their enemy's confusion, the Jin cried out that the Qin were defeated, and in no time the rumor had become a reality. As Fu Jian's army fled in a disorganized mob, the Jin pursued, massacring their helpless foes. **MK**

Vast, unwieldy, and increasingly weak, the Roman Empire had come to be governed as two separate entities: a Western section centered on Rome, and an Eastern one ruled from Constantinople. The desire to bring the two together coincided in the closing decades of the fourth century with a final stand by the defenders of Rome's pagan traditions. When, in 392, Eugenius seized power in Rome, he set out to reinstate the reign of Jupiter across the empire as a whole. Theodosius, Valens's successor in the east, set out to stop him.

For Theodosius, as for Valens, the Visigoths represented both a vital asset and a danger. He needed their military strength but feared their power. As he marched his army out to meet Eugenius's men in a pass beside the chilly Frigidus River in the Slovenian mountains, he placed his Goths in the vanguard. All day they charged and charged again, against an enemy who remained unbudging. By nightfall, well over 3,000 had been killed. But if the power of the Visigoths had been broken, Theodosius's had hardly been advanced: Eugenius was poised for victory.

The next day, however, supposedly in response to the Christian emperor's prayers, a strong wind whipped up sand and blew it into the faces of the pagan army. So strong was the storm, it was said, that it turned their arrows in flight and sent them back upon them. Theodosius claimed a complete—and unexpected—triumph. **MK**

Losses: Former Qin, more than 150,000; Eastern Jin, unknown but minimal

Losses: Unknown

[<] Wuzhang Plains 234

Salsu River 612 [>]

[<] Adrianople 378

Sack of Rome 410 [>]

A folio from the ninth-century Canon of the Councils showing Emperor Theodosius in Constantinople. ➜

hunc sinodu̅ actu̅ e̅ constantino
poli sub theo   dosio maiore. et
paribʒ;   congregati.
                   condēnatione
                   macedonii ne
                   retic   ci et
                   qualit
                   statuer̅
                   impe
                   ra
                   tor

domnus   theodosi
ur mai   or imperat̅
        cristianissimus

Sack of Rome 24 August 410

Châlons 451

"Rome, once the capital of the world, is now the grave of the Roman people," wrote Saint Jerome of a cataclysm that no one could have predicted. After several generations of Roman superiority and arrogance, the Visigothic "barbarian" mercenaries reminded their erstwhile masters of where the real military power lay.

Emerging from the depths of Central Asia, the Huns were nomadic horsemen with a well-merited reputation for ferocity. United under the leadership of the ruthless warlord Attila, they threatened the tottering Roman Empire. But on the Catalaunian Plains of northern Gaul, the Romans showed that these savage warriors could be beaten.

Alaric, leader of the Visigoths, had been left embittered by the experience at the Battle of Frigidus. For years he waged war on the Eastern Roman Empire; yet the Western Empire feared the Visigoths' anger, too—so much so that in 402 the Romans moved their capital from Rome to the more readily defensible Ravenna, in northeastern Italy. That same year, Alaric invaded Italy, but was turned back by the great general Flavius Stilicho at Pollentia in Piedmont. Another Gothic warlord, Radagaisus, was stopped by Stilicho in 406, but the Visigoths kept coming. By 408 Alaric was back in Italy, besieging Rome.

The Huns were born to the saddle and raised to fight; they scorned the softness of the settled populations they preyed upon. For more than a century, Rome had been experiencing their indirect impact, as refugee peoples spilled westward before their advance. In the 440s, under the command of Attila, they had ravaged the Eastern Roman Empire; improbably, a family quarrel brought Attila farther west. Princess Honoria, sister of the Western emperor, Valentinian III, resented the arrangements made for her marriage and pettishly wrote to Attila for help. He took her letter as an offer of marriage—with half the Western Roman Empire by way of dowry—and headed west with a vast army to claim his prize.

Even now, the Romans hoped to bring the tenacious Visigoths back into harness as defenders of the empire. Several barbarian peoples, from Germanic warriors such as the Vandals and Sueves to Asiatic nomads such as the Alans and the Huns, had crossed the Rhine and now roamed and ransacked at will beyond the Alps. Alaric was ready to compromise with Rome: he offered to spare the city in return for the promise of an annual payment and a place in the official military hierarchy of the empire. Yet, with Rome itself at stake, Emperor Honorius haughtily refused.

The Romans by now had reached an accommodation with the Visigoths, settling them in Gaul to help assure its security. The Visigoth king, Theodoric I, and the Roman commander, Flavius Aetius, surprised the Huns as they laid siege to Aurelianum (Orléans). Withdrawing to open country, the Huns prepared to do battle, but their confidence was shaken when their priests divined a serious defeat. When battle was joined, the Huns made a rush for a ridge that ran across the plain, but the Romans and Goths were first to this high ground. Falling back in confusion, the Hunnish vanguard disrupted the advance of those behind and the initiative was lost. Attila was cornered in his camp but survived. He died two years later, and the Hun menace disappeared with him. **MK**

On the night of 24 August 410, rebel slaves, a suborned official, or some other unknown party quietly opened the gates of Rome to admit the Visigoths. They embarked on a three-day spree of plunder and destruction that left the Eternal City a smoking ruin. **MK**

Losses: Unknown

◁ *Frigidus 394*   *Châlons 451* ▷

Losses: Unknown

◁ *Sack of Rome 410*

Vouillé 507

The victory at Vouillé by Clovis, king of the Franks, established the Franks as the dominant power in what had been the Western Roman Empire. It also marked the definite rise of Catholicism as the version of Christianity preferred by the Germanic peoples, ousting the Aryanism favored by the defeated Visigoths.

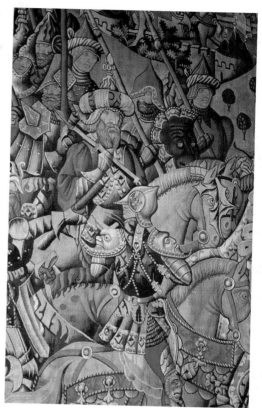

By 507 what had been the Western Roman Empire had been carved up between a number of mostly Germanic tribes and rulers. Of these, the two most powerful were the Goths who ruled Italy, Spain, and southern France and the Franks who held northern France, the Low Countries, and western Germany. Clovis united the Franks under his Merovingian dynasty in the 490s, and in 498 converted to Catholicism. Clovis and his army crossed the River Loire, probably at Tours, in late spring 507. He was met at Vouillé by Alaric II, ruler of the Visigoths.

At this battle the Franks fought exclusively on foot using the traditional Germanic combination of round shield and long spear. They were famous for their use of the "francisca," a light throwing axe with a short haft. Battles opened with a deadly shower of franciscas being hurled at the enemy. The Goths were similarly armed, but preferred a broad-bladed knife to the francisca. Very little is known specifically about the course of the battle at Vouillé, but it seems that several Gothic nobles either abandoned Alaric or switched to support Clovis. They were probably alienated by Alaric's attempts to centralize power in the royal family and take it away from the traditionally powerful nobles. Alaric was killed during the battle, allegedly by Clovis himself. The Franks captured large amounts of booty. Clovis took over all of southwestern France, with only the coastal strip around Narbonne remaining in Gothic hands. **RM**

"They clashed their shields, shouted their approval, [and] they raised Clovis up on a shield and made him their ruler."

Gregory of Tours

Losses: Unknown

Vezeronce 524 ▶

 Tapestry detail showing Clovis (center) advancing toward Vouillé—from a series at the Palais du Tau in Reims c. 1440.

Vezeronce   25 June 524

This battle marked the destruction of the Burgundians as an independent power; thereafter they would be subsumed within the growing Frankish domain. Both sides fought primarily on foot, but the Franks seem to have had a force of cavalry armed with shield and lance.

After being briefly united under Clovis I, the Franks were divided once again as each of Clovis's four sons took a share of their father's lands. In 523, the four—Theudoric, Childebert, Clothaire, and Chlodomir—joined forces to attack the Burgundians of southeastern France. Their mother, and Clovis's wife, was Clothilde, a Burgundian princess. It is likely that the brothers believed they had a claim to the Burgundian crown, but in any case probably sought revenge for the murder of their grandfather, King Chilperic II of Burgundy, at the hands of his brother Gundobad, whose son Sigismund was king of Burgundy in 524.

Sigismund and his sons were captured and taken back to Orléans by Chlodomir. The brothers were debating how best to divide their conquest when Sigismund's brother, Godomar, mustered a new Burgundian army and drove out the Franks occupying Burgundy. Chlodomir ordered the death of Sigismund and his sons before marching south alongside Theudoric. Most Franks and Burgundians fought on foot with shield, spear, and sidearm. The Franks also raised horsemen from the towns they had conquered, but whether they fought as cavalry or dismounted for battle is not clear. Details of the battle fought at what is now Vezerone-Curtin are vague. Frankish sources claim it as a victory that saw the utter defeat of the Burgundians. However, Chlodomir was killed in the fighting and Godomar remained in control of at least part of Burgundy until his death in 534. **RM**

Dara   530

Dara was a significant battle in the Iberian War fought between the Byzantine (Eastern Roman) Empire, ruled by Justinian, and the Persian Sassanid Empire. It is chiefly remembered as the first victory in the spectacular military career of the great Byzantine general, Belisarius.

Belisarius had worked his way up through the ranks of the Roman army. He served in the imperial bodyguard of Justin I and was given responsibility to expand the role of the bodyguard into a more capable fighting unit. Belisarius developed the bucellarii: a well-trained, heavy-armored cavalry force armed with broadswords.

In 527 Belisarius was trusted by the new emperor, Justinian, with the command of the Byzantine army in the east to deal with the threat posed by the expansion of the Sassanid Empire. Belisarius soon proved himself to be a talented commander, with his bucellarii forming the central core of his army. In 530 he decided to engage the larger Persian army in a major battle.

The battle at Dara lasted for two days, with the first day taken up by a series of challenges between the Byzantine and Persian champions. On the second day, the Persians took the initiative and attacked the Byzantine left flank, crossing defensive trenches, but were forced to retreat. Undeterred, they then attacked the right flank, using their elite lancers, the immortals. The Byzantines were pushed back and, fearing defeat, Belisarius ordered his bucellarii to attack. The force of the cavalry attack broke the Persian line in two and thousands were slaughtered. Sassanid expansion had been checked, although in 531 Belisarius was defeated at Callinicum and the Byzantines were forced to pay tribute to Persia in exchange for an uneasy peace. **TB**

Losses: Unknown

⟨ *Vouillé 507*   *Volturnus 554* ⟩

Losses: Byzantine, unknown; Sassanid, 10,000

Ad Decimum 533 ⟩

A Byzantine School mosaic of Emperor Justinian I and his retinue of officials, guards, and clergy.

MAXIMIANVS·

Ad Decimum 533

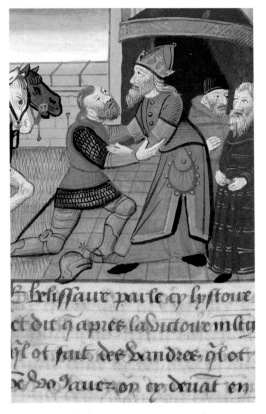

After saving the Byzantine Empire from the threat of Sassanid expansion and putting down a rebellion against Justinian in Constantinople, Belisarius took command of a huge land and sea expedition to north Africa as part of Justinian's drive to restore the Roman Empire to its former glory.

In 530 King Hilderic, ruler of the Vandal kingdom in north Africa, was overthrown by a Vandal noble, Gelimer. The Byzantine emperor Justinian had maintained friendly relations with Hilderic, who had renounced the heretical Arian Christianity embraced by most Vandals. Gelimer was an Arian, and many religious refugees soon began to arrive in Constantinople, fleeing his persecution. This was the perfect pretext for Emperor Justinian to attempt to subject north Africa, once an integral part of the Roman Empire, to his rule.

Belisarius landed his huge invasion force in modern-day Libya and proceeded to march along the coast to Carthage, which at the time was the Vandal capital. The forces of Belisarius and Gelimer clashed at the ten-mile marker from Carthage, giving rise to the name of the battle. The Romans outnumbered Gelimer's army by almost two to one, but for a time it appeared that Belisarius would be defeated. However, Gelimer failed to press home his advantage and paused in order to bury his brother's body. Belisarius regrouped his forces and counterattacked, routing the Vandals and capturing Carthage, where he was welcomed by the predominantly Roman population. Victory at Ad Decimum was followed by success at Tricamarum in December of the same year. Belisarius's victories handed Justinian control of much of north Africa and the western Mediterranean, a vital stage in the emperor's campaign to restore the Western Roman Empire. **TB**

"Piloting the great fleet / I swept the Afric coasts / And scattered the Vandal hosts / Like dust in a windy street."

Henry Wadsworth Longfellow, "Belisarius"

↑ *An illustration from a fifteenth-century French manuscript showing Justinian I receiving Belisarius.*

Losses: Unknown

◁ *Dara 530*　　　　　　　　　　　　　　　　*Rome 537* ▷

Rome 537–538

The desire of Emperor Justinian to restore the full extent of the Roman Empire led to a struggle for control of Italy between his Byzantine army, led by Belisarius, and the kingdom of the Ostrogoths. Belisarius liberated Rome from the Goths, but then had a hard fight to hold the city.

Belisarius began his campaign to reconquer Italy with victory in Sicily. He then crossed into Italy at Rhegium and lay siege to Naples. In the autumn of 537, he took Naples and marched on Rome. To the Ostrogoths, it was obvious that the populace favored Belisarius, so they left as Belisarius triumphantly entered the ancient capital.

Belisarius had a defensive ditch dug outside the walls and prepared the city for siege. The Ostrogoths built seven camps around the city and destroyed aqueducts that supplied fresh water. On the eighteenth day, they attacked with siege towers but were pushed back. Belisarius decided to dig in and sent for reinforcements, occasionally launching small sorties to wear down the morale of the Goths. Finally, after many weeks of attrition, Roman reinforcements arrived. The Ostrogoths were suffering from plague and famine as much as the Romans and sought a truce, offering parts of southern Italy in return for Rome. However, realizing that the tide was turning in his favor, Belisarius waited as the condition of the Ostrogoths deteriorated still more. In desperation, the Goths attempted to storm the city, but they were defeated.

In the meantime a Roman army under the command of John won several victories, effectively cutting the Goths off. After almost 400 days, the Goths abandoned the siege in order to defend their capital of Ravenna. As they withdrew, Belisarius pursued them and routed them at the Milvian Bridge outside Rome. **TB**

Losses: Unknown

◁ Ad Decimum 533

Taginae 552 ▷

Taginae 552

Taginae was the decisive encounter of the Gothic War. The battle was fought between the Byzantine forces of Justinian, commanded by the elderly eunuch Narses, and the Goths, under King Totila. The battle ended with a suicidal charge by the Goths into the Roman lines.

As plague swept across and weakened the Roman Empire in 542, the Goths sought to reassert their authority in Italy under King Totila. Large parts of Italy were captured by the Goths during the 540s, despite attempts by Belisarius to gain the upper hand. The last of Belisarius's campaigns, in 547, was hampered by the jealousy of Justinian, who starved the renowned general of supplies. It was an unlikely new commander, the seventy-four-year-old court eunuch Narses, who took up the fight with the Goths.

Narses landed a vast army at Salona in Greece in 551 and proceeded to march around the coast into northern Italy. He then turned inland toward Rome, encountering Totila's army at Taginae, about 30 miles (48 km) northeast of modern-day Perugia. Narses was defensive, even though he had superiority in numbers, and after a number of minor skirmishes and challenges initiated by Totila, the Gothic king decided to play for time while waiting for reinforcements. Strengthened by the arrival of fresh troops, Totila launched his reckless attack. Totila's cavalry charged headlong into the crescent-shaped ranks of the Romans, coming under massive archery fire from both sides. The Goths took disastrous casualties and, as the attack faltered, Narses ordered an advance that destroyed the Gothic army. At some point during the ensuing chaos, Totila was killed. Narses took Rome and followed up Taginae with victory at Mons Lactarius, ending Gothic rule in Italy. **TB**

Losses: Unknown

◁ Rome 537

Volturnus 554 ▷

Volturnus 554

The battle fought between the Byzantine Empire and an army of Franks, Goths, and Alemanni at the Volturnus River in southern Italy was part of the ongoing struggle by Emperor Justinian to reconquer the provinces of the Western Roman Empire. The result was a triumph for Justinian's eunuch general, Narses.

After their defeat by Narses at Tabadrginae and Mons Lactarius in 552, the Goths sought aid from the Franks in their struggle to oust the Byzantines from Italy. Led by two brothers, Leutharis and Butilinus, a force of more than 60,000 Franks and Goths invaded Italy in 553. By 554, the force had swept into central Italy, sacking towns as it went and dividing into two formidable armies. Leutharis had no desire to stay in Italy and retreated, weighed down by plunder. However, he was defeated by the Byzantine general Artabanes and later died of plague along with much of his remaining army.

Butilinus formed a strong defensive position on the banks of the Volturnus River in Campania, where he was soon confronted by Narses and a force of 20,000 Byzantines and mercenaries. Narses arranged his army in battle formation similar to that used at Taginae, with his formidable archers supporting his infantry. Butilinus attacked and penetrated the Byzantine lines, which had been weakened by the defection of mercenary troops. Fearing the worst, Narses ordered his mounted archers to attack. Charging from the wings of the crescent, they outflanked Butilinus and attacked him from behind. Completely surrounded, the Franks were cut down and almost all of their army slain, including Butilinus. The battle was a triumph for the Byzantine Empire, but it would take eight more years before Justinian could rightly claim to be the master of Italy. **TB**

Losses: Unknown

◁ *Taginae 552*

Nineveh 626 ▷

Deorham 577

In the Cotswold hills outside the city of Bath, southwest England, three kings died fighting in defense of Romano-British culture against the encroachment of Germanic Saxon invaders. The British defeat confirmed the rise of the Anglo-Saxon kingdom of Wessex as the dominant power in southern England.

The settlement of Britain by Saxon and other Germanic peoples had begun in eastern England in the first few decades after the withdrawal of Roman troops from the province in around 410. This early settlement was followed by a general resurgence of Saxon expansion into the south and west of England from the 530s, leading to the creation of the kingdom of Wessex.

The three kings who made a stand against the rising power of Wessex at the Battle of Deorham were Condidan, Commagil, and Farinmagil, representing respectively the important Romano-British towns of Cirencester, Gloucester, and Bath. The Saxons were probably led by their king, Ceawlin, whose reign is associated with military expansion at the expense of the Britons. Although there is little solid information on the battle, it is speculated that Ceawlin adopted a position on a ridge dominating the surrounding country, forcing the Britons to attack in order to dislodge him.

All three kings seem to have been killed in the battle, which was a major disaster for the Romanized Britons. Victory at Deorham meant that the Saxons now controlled territory from the Avon Valley to the Bristol Channel, which thrust a wedge between the Britons of Wales and those of Cornwall. Indeed, for some historians, the battle's key long-term significance is that it began the process in which the Britons split into two distinct linguistic groups of Welsh and Cornish. **TB**

Losses: Unknown

⊖ *A graphic depiction (1890) by Alexander Zick showing the Romans overpowering the Goths.*

Salsu River 612

Badr 624

Fought between the northern Korean kingdom of Goguryeo and Sui dynasty China, the Battle of Salsu River reputedly resulted in the deaths of almost all Chinese combatants. Even if contemporary accounts exaggerate the scale of the defeat, it was certainly a crushing blow for Chinese emperor Yangdi.

The rise of Islam against the Pagan tribes of Mecca was a vital development in military history, as well as in the history of religion and society. The Prophet Muhammad was a skilled war leader as well as the founder of a faith, and at Badr his religion was spread by the sword.

The Sui dynasty had reunified China after centuries of division, restoring its regional dominance. Goguryeo, however, refused to accept Chinese overlordship. After several previous attempts to intimidate the Koreans had failed, in 612 Emperor Yangdi mounted a military expedition of unprecedented size.

Chinese chronicles tell us that more than a million combat troops marched from Beijing, with their supply train straggling for 200 miles (322 km) along the road. Arriving in Goguryeo, this host was soon bogged down in sieges of a number of fortresses, stoutly defended on the orders of Korean commander Eulji Mundeok. Seeking to regain the strategic initiative, Yangdi ordered a third of his forces to advance on the Goguryeo capital, Pyongyang. The Chinese detachment was soon in trouble, harassed by Korean guerrillas, and their supply lines exposed to attack. At the Salsu River, Eulji Mundeok prepared a trap. He dammed the river before the Chinese arrived, lowering the water level to tempt them to ford it. When they were halfway across, he breached the dam, releasing a wall of water that swept away thousands of Chinese soldiers. The Goguryeo army then fell upon the disorganized fleeing Chinese army, allowing few to escape. Yangdi soon called off the entire expedition. His rule did not long survive this ignominious defeat, which was financially disastrous as well as militarily humiliating. The Sui dynasty was overthrown by the Tang dynasty in 618. **RG**

The Battle of Badr was a key moment in Muhammad's armed struggle against Mecca's pagan tribes. In 622 Muhammad and his followers had emigrated from Mecca to Medina. From his new base Muhammad began raiding Meccan caravan routes. This provoked the Meccan tribes into sending an army to confront Muhammad's Muslims.

Like many ancient battles, the encounter is said to have been preceded by combat between the individual champions of both sides; the Muslim champions were victorious. The battle proper started with an exchange of volleys of arrows, resulting in heavier casualties being suffered by the Meccan army. Muhammad gave the order to charge, throwing stones at his enemies in a traditional Arabic gesture. The Koran states that the Meccan lines broke under the force of Muhammad's attack and speaks of angels descending from heaven to slay the fleeing enemy. A number of important Meccan leaders were among those killed, including Muhammad's main rival, Amr ibn Hisham. The armies involved were not large: fewer than 400 Muslims and around 1,000 Meccan fighters. Yet the victory at Badr was an important milestone in the establishment of Islam. It raised Muhammad's status among the Medina tribes that supported him and convinced his followers that victory over powerful and wealthy Mecca was truly possible. The victory was not destined to be swift, but by 630 Muhammad was able to march into Mecca as a conqueror. **TB**

Losses: Chinese, allegedly 302,300 casualties of 305,000; Korean, unknown

Losses: Meccan, 100; Muslim, fewer than 20

[<] Fei River 383   Baekgang 663 [>]

Firaz 634 [>]

A sixteenth-century miniature of the Battle of Badr from Siyar-i-Nabi (Life of the Prophet).

تعالی دن سکا دسور اولدکم پیک فرشته ایله انم مسلمانلغه
یاری قلم ردی رسول حضرتنه سو ندردی کافر جری اول دم سنمغه

بشلدلرسب اول دنکم اول نکم البس قجدوغی وقت قریش کو کلنه
قورقندی اکنچی سبب اول نکم کافرلر که کله هیبت و تو ردی یه

Nineveh   12 December 626

Nineveh was a triumph for the Byzantine Empire and its ruler, Heraclius, over the Sassanid Persians. It seemed to offer the Byzantines the prospect of peace and prosperity after years of struggle to survive. Instead, Heraclius's victory unwittingly opened the way for the expansion of Islam.

The last of many Byzantine-Sassanid wars began in 603. Under the incompetent and corrupt rule of the usurper Phocas, the Byzantine Empire was at first unable to defend itself against the offensive launched by the Persian king, Khosrau II, who swiftly conquered Egypt and gained control of the Mediterranean coast of the Arabian Peninsula. Simultaneously attacked by Slavs and Avars from the north, the Byzantines seemed on the point of collapse. Then, in 610, Byzantine general Heraclius overthrew Phocas. An inspired organizer and military leader, Heraclius slowly turned the tide, and the Sassanid Empire was forced onto the defensive. In an attempt to regain the ascendancy, the Sassanids attacked Constantinople in 626. However, Heraclius won a comprehensive victory and followed this up with an invasion of the territory of the much-weakened Persia. He advanced with a force reputed to be in the region of 60,000, laying waste to the countryside as he went. By late 626, Heraclius had crossed the Zab River, in what is now Kurdish Iraq, and was threatening Khosrau's palace at Dastagird.

Heraclius positioned his army on a plain with his camp near the ruins of the ancient city of Nineveh. The Byzantines would, therefore, have the advantage of open space in which to deploy their force of heavy-armored horsemen, the cataphracts. Khosrau had entrusted the command of his force of 10,000 to his Armenian general, Rhahzadh. The battle commenced under the cover of fog.

This was a serious problem for the Sassanid army, which relied on the accurate targeting of missiles from row upon row of ballistas. The fighting continued unbroken for eleven hours. At one point, it is said, Heraclius engineered a trick in which he pretended to retreat and when the Persians gave chase turned his troops, causing chaos in the now broken Persian lines.

At the height of the battle, Rhahzadh apparently challenged Heraclius to personal combat, which ended when Heraclius struck off the Sassanid commander's head with a single blow. With Rhahzadh dead, the Sassanid army soon lost faith and fled. Heraclius's army plundered treasure as it moved farther into Persian territory unopposed. The defeated Khosrau II was overthrown and gruesomely murdered by his son Kavadh-Siroes, and a truce was agreed between the two exhausted empires. The Byzantines gained land and what they believed to be a portion of the true cross of Christ that had fallen into Sassanid hands at the Siege of Jerusalem in 614.

When Heraclius returned to Constantinople, displaying the sacred fragment of the cross and a group of captured elephants to please the crowd, it seemed as if the future of the Byzantine Empire was assured. Ironically, the eventual significance of the battle turned out to be very different from what was expected. With the resources of his own empire depleted and the Sassanid Empire crippled, Heraclius's victory created a power vacuum into which armies from Arabia, riding under the banner of Islam, were able to surge forward in the following decades. Thus Nineveh led the way to centuries of armed struggle between the Byzantium Empire and Islam. **TB**

Losses: Byzantine, unknown; Sassanid, 5,000

◁ *Volturnus 554*　　　　　　　　*Firaz 634* ▷

Firaz January 634

The Battle of Firaz was a decisive encounter in the Arab conquest of Mesopotamia. It was fought between the forces of the Muslim Arab commander Khalid ibn al-Walid and a much larger army formed from an alliance of the Byzantine Empire, the Sassanid Persian Empire, and Christian Arabs.

Khalid ibn al-Walid was a Meccan of the Quraish tribe, who had originally opposed Muhammad. After conversion to Islam, he became one of history's most successful commanders and is remembered for his numerous victories against the armies of the Byzantine Roman Empire and its allies during his conquest of Arabia, Mesopotamia, and Syria.

Firaz was a key battle in the Arab conquest of the Sassanid Persian Empire, following the death of the Prophet Muhammad. After a series of defeats had weakened the Sassanids, Khalid sought to take their capital Ctesiphon. However, he received intelligence that a huge force had combined to challenge him and that the army had gathered at the border city of Firaz. Rather than take the Persian capital directly, Khalid marched his army of around 20,000 men to Firaz and fought an army of more than 100,000 in order to destroy finally Persian and Byzantine power in Mesopotamia.

Upon arrival at Firaz, Khalid saw that the opposing army had already crossed the River Euphrates. As the two armies clashed, Khalid ordered his extreme flanks to move out and outflank the Byzantines and Persians. Khalid's army successfully managed this and, in so doing, seized control of the bridge over the river. With the Romans and Persians trapped between the river and Khalid's army, the alliance army was destroyed, and many tens of thousands were killed. Khalid had effectively completed his conquest of the Persian Empire. **TB**

Losses: Unknown

[<] *Badr 624*

Yarmuk 636 [>]

Yarmuk 20 August 636

After the devastating blow to the Sassanid Persians at Firaz, the Muslim Arab forces, under the command of Khalid ibn al-Walid, took on the army of the Christian Byzantine Empire at Yarmuk near the border of modern-day Syria and Jordan. The major battle was to continue for six days.

After the victory at Firaz, Khalid had virtually conquered Mesopotamia. Seeking to halt Muslim expansion, the Byzantines rallied all available forces. Byzantine Emperor Heraclius, the victor of Nineveh, allied himself with the Sassanids, the two empires seeking to pool their depleted resources to stop the Arab advance.

For his part, Heraclius assembled a large army of Byzantines, Slavs, Franks, and Christian Arabs and stationed them at Antioch in northern Syria. Heraclius sought to stall any battle by exploring diplomatic options while he waited for more forces to arrive from his Sassanid ally. Meanwhile, alarmed that the Byzantine-led force had assembled in Syria while Muslim forces were fragmented into at least four separate groups, Khalid called a council of war and successfully argued that the entire Arab army be united to face Heraclius.

When the two armies met, it was Heraclius's intention to exercise caution and wear the Muslims down by a series of small engagements. But the Sassanids never arrived and, after six days' attritional fighting, Khalid drew the Byzantines into a large-scale pitched battle. This ended with the Byzantines retreating in disarray, charged by the Arabs with a sand-laden wind behind them. Many of the fleeing Byzantine troops fell to their deaths over a narrow ravine. Yarmuk was Khalid's greatest victory and ended Byzantine rule in Syria. Heraclius was forced to concentrate on the defense of Anatolia and Egypt. **TB**

Losses: Byzantine allied, 40,000; Arab, 5,000

[<] *Firaz 634*

Qadissiya 637 [>]

Qadissiya   1 June 637

Three years after the Muslim Arab defeat of the Sassanid Persians at Firaz, the Arabs mounted a second invasion of Sassanid territory to quell a Persian resurgence and counteroffensive. The battle led to the lasting conquest of the Sassanid Empire by the Muslim Rashidun caliphate.

While Khalid ibn al-Walid led a united force against Heraclius and the Byzantine army at Yarmuk, the Sassanid Persians launched a counterattack against the Muslims in Persia. The Muslims responded by launching a second invasion of Mesopotamia, led by Saad ibn-Abi Waqqas, a cousin of the Prophet Muhammad. Waqqas invaded Iraq with instructions from Caliph Umar to be cautious and to use the experience of his commanders.

On entering Iraq, Waqqas camped at Qadissiya. There, he awaited orders from the caliph, who sought to bolster the invasion force by redeploying veteran troops from Libya as soon as the Byzantine threat had been suppressed. While Waqqas awaited reinforcements, the Persians confronted him and camped nearby.

For three months, the two leaders negotiated and an offer to convert to Islam was made to the Persians, who rejected it. By winter, the tension was unbearable and the two armies clashed. The first day began with a series of duels, followed by a Persian arrow volley and a mounted elephant attack that inflicted serious casualties on the Muslim lines and almost gained victory for the Persians.

On the second day, the reinforcements that Umar had promised finally arrived. The extra troops shifted the balance of the battle and, although fighting raged for three more days, the Sassanid cause was hopeless. The Sassanid dynasty was fatally weakened, and the Arabs later took the Persian capital of Ctesiphon after a two-month siege. **TB**

> "*Of great concern was Persia's inability to replenish its ranks with trained professional manpower.*"
> Kaveh Farrokh, Sassanian Elite Cavalry AD 224–642

Losses: Sassanid Persian, 35,000; Rashidun caliphate, 8,000

◁ Yarmuk 636   The Masts 655 ▷

A Bukara-style manuscript from 1600 in which a soldier is decapitated at the Battle of Qadissiya.

القرآن ثم ربعد اساطير بلاها ورخارف جلاها وقال اركبوا فيها بسم الله مجراها
ومرساها ثمة نفس نفس المغرمين او عباد الله للمكرمين وقال اما انا

The Masts 655

At the Battle of the Masts, fought in the eastern Mediterranean, the Byzantine fleet—commanded by Emperor Constans II—clashed with a Muslim Arab naval force under Abdullah bin Saad bin Abi Sarh. The victory of the Arab fleet confirmed it as a formidable new Mediterranean sea power.

Inspired by Islam, Arab armies were established as the dominant military force on land in the Middle East by the 640s, but the Byzantine Empire remained the dominant force at sea. However, recent conquests gave the Arabs control of Egypt and Syria, with ports that were major centers of shipbuilding and seafaring.

Syria's governor, future Umayyad Caliph Muawiyah, and Egypt's governor, Abdullah bin Saad, set about the construction of war galleys. The Muslims used their ships to attack and take the strategic island of Cyprus in 649.

In 655, they launched a combined land and sea attack upon Byzantine-ruled Anatolia (Turkey). While Muawiyah struck overland into Cappadocia, a fleet under Abdullah bin Saad sailed along the Anatolian coast, threatening Byzantine ports. Emperor Constans assembled a large imperial fleet, possibly numbering up to 500 vessels, and sailed from Constantinople to seek out the Arab navy.

The fleets clashed off Phoenix (modern-day Finike), southwest Anatolia. Although outnumbered, the Arabs attacked, their archers loosing volleys of arrows as they approached Byzantine galleys. The Byzantines were more skillful sailors and superior at maneuvering, but as the rival fleets locked together—creating the forest of masts that gave the battle its name—and ships were boarded, the Arabs' superiority at fighting with sword and dagger gave them the advantage. Constans escaped, but his navy was shattered. **TB**

Losses: Byzantine, 400 ships; Arab, unknown but heavy

◁ Qadissiya 637   First Arab Siege of Constantinople 674 ▷

Baekgang 27–28 August 663

Much of the history of Korea has been dictated by its location between China and Japan. The Battle of Baekgang occurred when Yamato rulers sent a fleet to counter mounting Chinese dominance in the Korean peninsula. A Japanese defeat condemned the Korean kingdom of Goguryeo to extinction.

Under the Tang dynasty, China was growing in population, prosperity, and military power, but Goguryeo had remained unsubdued by Chinese attacks from the north. The existence of two smaller Korean kingdoms, Silla and Baekje, to the south of Goguryeo offered China a potential second front. The Chinese allied with Silla and transported troops by sea to invade Goguryeo's ally, Baekje.

The Japanese imperial court felt threatened by the prospect of Chinese control of Korea. They assembled a fleet to carry 40,000 troops to aid the Baekje army. Chinese and Silla forces were besieging Churyu, the Baekje capital. The Japanese fleet sailed to the mouth of the Geum River, intending to pass up the river and land troops to relieve Churyu. But a smaller Chinese fleet blocked the river entrance. Maintaining a disciplined formation in enclosed waters, the Chinese prevented the Japanese bringing their superior numbers to bear. Twice rebuffed on consecutive days, Japan's fleet became disorganized and exhausted. The Chinese counterattacked, encircling the Japanese and setting fire to many of their ships with burning arrows. Thousands of Japanese soldiers drowned.

In the aftermath of the battle, Baekje was defeated. Trapped between its enemies to the north and south, Goguryeo was overrun as Chinese-backed Silla went on to conquer the whole of Korea. The Japanese, meanwhile, prepared elaborate coastal defenses against a Chinese seaborne onslaught that never materialized. **RG**

Losses: Japanese, 400 ships of 800, 10,000 casualties; Chinese, unknown of 170 ships engaged

◁ Salsu River 612   Kwiju 1019 ▷

The victorious Muslim Arab naval force at the Battle of the Masts.

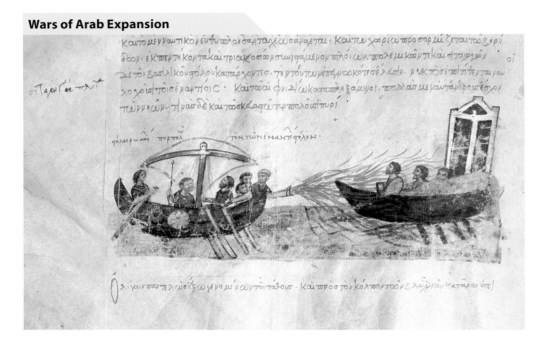

First Arab Siege of Constantinople 674–677

The defeat of the Byzantine navy by the Arabs at the Battle of the Masts left the Byzantine capital Constantinople at potential risk of attack from the sea. The four-year Arab siege that started in 674 was a naval operation and was defeated by a new naval weapon: Greek fire.

In the years after the Battle of the Masts, the Arab world was plunged into civil war, until the establishment of the Umayyad caliphate ruled by Muawiyah I. Under the Umayyads, the Arab drive to conquest was resumed.

In 674, the Arabs—established at a base on the shore of the Sea of Marmara—began to mount a series of attacks on Constantinople from the sea, using their galleys as platforms for large catapults that could hurl rocks a considerable distance toward the city's fortifications. However, the city's defense was solid and well organized by Emperor Constantine IV, and the Theodosian Walls—built under the rule of Emperor Theodosius II in the fifth century—proved impregnable. Instead the Arabs sought to starve the city by blockading major Byzantine supply routes into the Bosphorus. The Byzantine fleet was forced to sortie and engage Arab ships in an urgent attempt to break the blockade.

A new incendiary weapon was deployed for the first time: a burning liquid called "Greek fire." The invention is attributed to an architect named Kallinikos, who had come to Constantinople in the early 670s. Greek fire was deployed from the bow of Byzantine ships and forced by a siphon through a bronze tube aimed directly at the enemy. With this early form of flamethrower, the Byzantines won a crucial victory in the Sea of Marmara in 677, which broke the Arab blockade. With winter approaching, and no means of breaching the city walls, the Arabs decided to withdraw. **TB**

Losses: Unknown

◄ The Masts 655   Karbala 680 ►

Byzantine illustration showing how Greek fire was deployed against Arab ships. ⬆

Karbala   10 October 680

The Battle of Karbala was one of the most significant moments in the development of the Muslim world. Bringing about the death of Husayn ibn Ali, a grandson of the Prophet Muhammad, the battle resulted in the permanent split between the Shiite and Sunni branches of Islam.

When Yazid I succeeded his father Muawiyah I to become Umayyad caliph—the leader of the Islamic world—sections of the population that were loyal to the grandson of Muhammad rebelled in the city of Kufah, on the banks of the Euphrates River. They invited the grandson—Husayn ibn Ali—to join them, promising to proclaim him caliph in Iraq. On hearing this, Husayn set out from Mecca with most of his family, expecting to be received triumphantly by the citizens of Kufah.

In the meantime, Yazid had sent Ubayd Allah, the governor of Basra, to restore order. When Husayn reached Karbala, a small town to the west of the Euphrates, he

was confronted by a huge army. Husayn gave battle, expecting to receive aid from his supporters in Kufah. Unfortunately for Husayn, no such aid arrived and he was slain, along with many members of his family.

When news of the violent death of Muhammad's grandson reached Kufah, those who had invited him were ashamed at the part that they had played in the tragedy. As news spread quickly, Yazid and his supporters were regarded as murderers and their names have ever since been cursed by Shia Muslims. The death of Husayn is one of the most significant events in fueling the spread of Shia Islam, and its anniversary—the tenth day of the first month in the Islamic calendar—is observed as a day of public mourning. The tomb of the decapitated martyr Husayn ibn Ali, in Karbala, is to Shia Muslims one the holiest places in the world. **TB**

Losses: Unknown

⟨ *First Arab Siege of Constantinople 674*   *Guadalete 711* ⟩

⬆ *Husayn's half-brother, Abbas, is the central figure in this oil painting by Abbas Al-Musavi.*   2450 BCE–999 CE | **113**

Guadalete 711

Having conquered north Africa, the triumphant armies of Islam set their sights upon expansion into Spain. At Guadalete, an invading Arab and Berber force—led by Tariq ibn Ziyad—inflicted a crushing defeat upon the Christian Visigoths of Hispania—led by King Roderic—leaving Spain wide open to Muslim conquest.

The years from around 705 had seen an increasing number of Muslim raids on Spain from north Africa, leaving many coastal settlements in ruins. The invasion led by Tariq may have been the culmination of a series of operations across the Straits of Gibraltar.

At this time, Christian Hispania was far from united. Roderic, who was fighting a war against the Basques when news of the invasion reached him, rushed south to face the Muslim attack, gathering troops from rival clans as he went. The exact site of the battle is unknown, but it is thought to have been in the modern-day province of Cadiz, near the mouth of the Guadalete River. Tariq's army probably consisted primarily of Berber cavalry recruited in north Africa, fighting under Arab commanders. They would have adopted the hit-and-run skirmishing tactics that were common to light horsemen during this period.

No detailed description of the battle exists. Many of the sources attribute the defeat of the Visigoths to treachery among clan leaders who planned to depose Roderic. If this is the case, their treachery backfired, resulting in their own deaths as well as that of their king in the general Christian debacle. The disappearance of Roderic and most of his nobility at a stroke cleared the way for the rapid fall of the Visigothic kingdom to Muslim forces and the capture of Toledo. The Iberian peninsula would remain a primarily Muslim territory for four centuries. **TB**

Covadonga c. 720

Covadonga was a small-scale clash between Islamic Moors and a force of Christians from Asturias in northern Spain—led by their king, Don Pelayo. It guaranteed the survival of a Christian foothold in Iberia and is sometimes described as the start of the "Reconquista"—the reconquest of Spain from the Muslims.

When Don Pelayo was elected king of Asturias around 718, he drew upon the climate of ill feeling among his subjects toward the Moors and instigated a rebellion, refusing to pay tribute. Rather than a single engagement, Covadonga can be seen as the final act in a series of rebellions starting in 718 and lasting for two to three years. During this time Pelayo had successfully repulsed attempts by the Moors to reassert control in Asturias.

However, in 720, a large force was sent to Asturias to deal with the problem and, after a series of minor defeats, Pelayo was forced to retreat into the mountains. Here he formed a defensive position in a gorge flanked by steep sides. Pelayo's force was probably fewer than 500 men, but the terrain meant that a large frontal attack was impossible. On arrival, Al-Kama, the Moorish leader, sent surrender terms to Pelayo, who refused to accept them.

Al-Kama ordered his attack and sent his elite troops into the gorge. The Asturians fired arrows from both sides of the gorge inflicting terrible casualties on the Moors, who were then pushed back by a sudden counterattack led by Pelayo. As the Moors retreated, they were attacked by the Asturians, whose numbers were suddenly swelled by villagers who saw that victory might be possible.

Victory at Covadonga and the subsequent rout of the retreating Moors secured the independence of Asturias. This ensured that one small part of Iberia remained under Christian control. **TB**

Losses: Unknown

Losses: Unknown

◁ Guadalete 711

Covadonga c. 720 ▷

Tours 732 ▷

Tours (Poitiers) 732

The battle fought on ground between Tours and Poitiers in central France in 732 has often been described as one of the most crucial military encounters in world history. The victory of Frankish leader Charles Martel over the emir of Córdoba may have prevented Christian Europe succumbing to Muslim invasion.

After their conquest of the Iberian peninsula, Muslim forces pushed northward into southern Gaul. They set up a new capital at the port of Narbonne, and—despite the brief respite brought about by Odo of Aquitaine's victory at Toulouse in 721—much of Aquitaine and Bordeaux was lost to their advance.

Odo was no friend of the Franks and sought at first to secure the future of his realm by forming an alliance with the Moors. However, any hope that the alliance would ensure lasting security was dashed when a civil war in Muslim Iberia resulted in the ascendancy of Abdul al-Rahman, emir of Córdoba. The victorious emir sought

"[R]oll victorious on / Till, like the Orient, the subjected West / Should bow in reverence at Mohammed's name . . ."

Robert Southey, "Roderick"

to renew the conquest of Gaul. In desperation, Odo turned to Charles Martel, the power behind the throne in the Merovingian Frankish kingdom. Charles agreed an alliance on the condition that Odo consented to Frankish sovereignty over his kingdom. As the Muslim forces advanced northward toward the River Loire, they won a victory over Odo at the Battle of the River Garonne. When news of Odo's defeat reached Charles, he gathered his forces and resolved to meet the advancing Arabs at a location of his own choosing.

Historians have speculated that Abdul al-Rahman had become complacent after the ease of his victories in southern Gaul. To him, it appeared that much of the old territory of the Western Roman Empire lay prone at his feet. However, in Charles Martel, the Franks had a commander who was no barbarian. He had studied the tactics of Alexander the Great and the great commanders of the Roman Empire. Charles resolved to resist the invaders with a disciplined force of armored warriors who, although riding to the battlefield, would fight dismounted in a tight defensive formation.

Some 12 miles (19 km) north of Poitiers, Abdul al-Rahman's army—consisting of fast-moving horsemen —was confronted with a large force of Franks and Burgundians that had secured high ground with woodland that would hinder the Muslim cavalry. Martel's men were arranged in a large square defended on all sides with shields, swords, and spears. After several days of skirmishing, the lure of the riches of nearby Tours tempted Abdul al-Rahman to a frontal assault. This was what Charles had wanted. The Muslim horsemen, forced to charge uphill, made repeated attempts to break the Frankish lines, but each time the Franks stood firm. The battle turned when news spread that the Franks had attacked the Muslim camp and were carrying off treasure looted at Bordeaux. The Muslim cavalry broke off their latest charge and headed for camp. Chaos ensued. Abdul al-Rahman found himself surrounded by the Christian forces and was killed.

Charles Martel's victory raised him to hero status in the Christian world, but it would take many more years to force the Muslims back into Iberia. However, Gaul was preserved for Christianity, and Martel's survival laid the foundations of the Carolingian dynasty in the Frankish kingdom, with Charles's grandson, Charlemagne, anointed as emperor of the Romans in 800. **TB**

Losses: Umayyad, 10,000; Frankish, fewer than 1,000

◁ *Covadonga c. 720*   *Roncesvalles 778* ▷

Charles Martel (with ax) and Abdul al-Rahman (in white) clash in a nineteenth-century painting of Tours. ➔

Talas July 751

The battle between China and the Muslim Abbasid caliphate at the Talas River, in modern-day Khazakhstan, was arguably a turning point in world history. It may have ensured that Central Asia became part of the Islamic world and advanced the transfer of Chinese technology to the West.

Under the rule of Tang dynasty emperor Xuanzong, China was extending its zone of influence westward across Asia. A confrontation with Arab armies carrying the Islamic faith eastward was almost inevitable. When a Chinese army under a Korean-born general, Gao Xianzhi, crossed the Pamirs, local Uighur rulers asked the Arabs, already installed in Samarkand, to protect them.

Contradictory accounts exist of the battle that followed. The Arab army, led by Ziyad ibn Salih, was joined by Uighurs and Tibetans, giving it numerical superiority. Gao Xianzhi's army consisted of a small Chinese nucleus aided by numerous locally recruited auxiliaries. The confrontation lasted five days. The decisive moment came when the Chinese were attacked from the rear by a force of Turkic nomad horsemen, the Karluks. According to Chinese accounts, these Karluks were traitors who had been fighting under Gao Xianzhi but changed sides. Arab versions represent the Karluks as simply allies of the Arabs arriving late in the battle. Either way, the Chinese were put to flight, leaving behind thousands dead or taken prisoner. Tradition states that among the Chinese prisoners were two experts in papermaking who, put to work in Samarkand, introduced paper to the Islamic world, from whence it spread to Christian Europe. Shortly after the battle, Tang China was plunged into civil war and expansionist projects were abandoned. Over following centuries, the Turkic and Iranian peoples of Central Asia were Islamicized. **RG**

Losses: Chinese, unknown of 30,000 of 100,000 engaged; Arab, unknown of 100,000 to 200,000 engaged

Roncesvalles (Roncevaux) 15 Aug 778

The defeat of Roland, commander of the rearguard of Charlemagne's army, in a high mountain pass in the Pyrenees became part of legend, celebrated in the "Song of Roland," the oldest work in the canon of French literature. And his opponents were not Muslims, as the legend narrates, but Basques.

In 778 Charlemagne, king of the Franks, led an ill-fated campaign intended to extend his influence—and that of Christendom—in the Iberian peninsula, which had been under Muslim rule since 711. Charlemagne was invited into Iberia by the Muslim leaders of Barcelona, Gerona, and Zaragoza who felt threatened by the Umayyad emir of Córdoba. Charlemagne hoped to use divisions within Muslim-controlled territory to assert his authority there.

On arrival at Barcelona and Gerona, Charlemagne was welcomed, but the emir of Córdoba unseated the rebel ruler of Zaragoza, replacing him with one of his own supporters. After a brief siege of Zaragoza, Charlemagne was bought off by the new ruler and headed for home with a large amount of gold. The Basques were fierce mountain fighters trained to use guerrilla tactics in their native Pyrenees. They watched Charlemagne's army cross a mountain pass near Roncevaux, the valuable baggage at the rear of the column escorted by Roland's men. When the main body of Charlemagne's troops was sufficiently distant, the Basques engaged the rearguard. Roland's Franks were ill-adapted to fighting in mountain terrain and were almost annihilated, without Charlemagne realizing what was happening. Roland was among those killed, and the Basques captured the gold gained at Zaragoza. The defeat deterred Charlemagne from further campaigns in Iberia and ensured that the Basque region continued to be a source of trouble for the Carolingians. **TB**

Losses: Unknown

◁ Tours 732

Jengland 851 ▷

Lindisfarne 8 June 793

The Viking raid on the monastery of Lindisfarne, off the coast of Northumbria, sent shockwaves through Anglo-Saxon England. For here was a new foe that had no respect for the Christian church and was obviously heathen. Viking raids continued to terrorize England for more than 200 years.

Precisely why the Vikings erupted out of their homelands in Scandinavia at this time is still a matter of debate. A rising population, poor harvests, and improvements in shipbuilding allowing long-distance navigation are all possible causes. It is more likely, however, that once a few intrepid warriors had raided their peaceful neighbors and returned home laden with booty, others organized more frequent raids to enrich themselves.

Viking raids were simple but deadly campaigns. Navigating their fast longships across the North Sea in perhaps as little as two days, the Vikings made use of their shallow draft to sail directly onto beaches or up inland rivers. Once ashore, the warriors terrorized and pillaged the local community.

Lindisfarne was not the first Viking raid on England; they had previously raided Portland in Dorset in 789, but the monastery—a center of Christian learning in the region—was undefended and very exposed. The kingdom of Northumbria, of which it was a part, was peaceful, secure, and unprepared for the danger it now faced from the sea. Alcuin, a Northumbrian scholar serving in Charlemagne's court in Aachen, noted, "The heathens poured out the blood of saints around the altar, and trampled on the bodies of saints in the temple of God, like dung in the street." The monks were killed or taken off as slaves, while the treasures of the monastery were carried home in triumph. **SA**

Losses: Unknown

Paris 885 ▷

Pliska 26 July 811

The rising power of the Bulgars—under the formidable Khan Krum—threatened the security of the Byzantine Empire. An expedition mounted by Byzantine emperor Nicephorus I laid waste the Bulgar capital Pliska, but Krum was to wreak terrible vengeance upon Nicephorus and his army.

In May 811 Nicephorus and his son, Stauracius, led a formidable army into Bulgarian territory. Unable to resist such a powerful host in open battle, Krum tried to negotiate, but Nicephorus was bent on teaching the Bulgars a brutal lesson. His army swept aside Bulgarian resistance and easily captured Pliska.

The destruction unleashed upon the city and its surrounding countryside was brutal: men, women, and children were massacred, animals and crops destroyed. Having accomplished his mission, Nicephorus turned for home, his route taking him through the Balkan mountains. Carelessly, he entered the narrow Verbiza pass without sending out scouts to reconnoiter the surrounding heights. The Bulgars, who had shadowed every Byzantine move, sprang a trap. Working swiftly under cover of darkness, they barricaded both ends of the pass. Bulgar fighters controlled the steep sides of the rocky gorge.

On 26 July they attacked, rushing down the slopes and rolling boulders down onto their enemy. The Byzantines fled southward, many drowning as they attempted to cross a torrent, others burning to death as they fought to cross a wooden barricade that had been set ablaze. Only a handful of survivors returned to Constantinople; Nicephorus was not among them. Stauracius was carried home, paralyzed by a neck wound that killed him after six months' agony. Krum had Nicephorus's skull mounted in silver and used it as a drinking cup. **RG**

Losses: Byzantine, most dead of 60,000; Bulgar, unknown

Kleidion 1014 ▷

CUM SEDEAT CAROLVS MAGNO COR ONATVS HONORE
EST IOSIAE SIMILIS PARQUE THEODOSIO

Jengland 22 August 851

The seemingly unstoppable expansion of the Frankish domains was brought to a sudden halt by a Breton force at Jengland, where mobile cavalry proved to be superior to armored, but static, infantry. The resulting treaty was a constitutional fudge, but it defined the boundaries of Brittany down to the present day.

When Duke Nominoe of Brittany died in 851, the Frankish emperor, Charles the Bald, took the opportunity to assert imperial rule. He mustered an army of 4,000 armored Frankish infantry, plus 1,000 more lightly armed Saxon foot soldiers, and invaded Brittany. He did not take with him any of the cavalry that the Franks could raise from the richer towns within their territory.

The new duke of Brittany, Erispoe, ambushed the invaders at Jengland as they advanced up the old Roman road from Nantes. The Breton horsemen charged and threw javelins into the ranks of the Franks. They then withdrew swiftly in an attempt to entice the infantry into pursuit. Any Franks or Saxons who broke ranks were rapidly overwhelmed and cut down. The battle ended at dusk but began again soon after dawn. The second day was spent in desultory skirmishing as Frank losses mounted steadily. After dark, Charles the Bald slipped away with a small guard, leaving his army to its fate. When his absence was noticed, the Franks fled, only to be hunted down by the pursuing Breton horsemen.

At the Treaty of Angers, agreed a few weeks later, Charles the Bald recognized Erispoe to be king of Brittany with greatly expanded borders. Erispoe recognized Charles to be emperor and accepted a purely nominal overlordship. The borders of Brittany agreed at Angers have varied little over the centuries. **RM**

Losses: Frankish, 2,000 dead and wounded of 5,000; Breton, unknown but just under 1,500 engaged

◁ Roncesvalles 778

Hafrsfjord c. 872

Norwegians traditionally date the unification of their country under a single royal dynasty to the bloody victory of King Harald Fairhair at the bay of Hafrsfjord. In truth this battle was only the most dramatic event in an ongoing process that commenced in about 820 and reached completion around 1035.

For some generations, the kings of Vestfold had been uniting the states of southeastern Norway by war, marriage, and diplomacy. Other rulers of small kingdoms, earldoms, and petty states became so alarmed by the growing power of Vestfold that they united in a concerted effort to destroy its king, Harald Fairhair.

The key mover in the alliance was King Eirik of Hordaland, supported by King Sulke of Rogaland, King Kjotve the Rich of Agder, and Earl Sote. The allies formed a large fleet and sailed south to find Harald Fairhair. Harald's fleet was in Hafrsfjord, a large bay near Stavanger that had only a narrow entrance from the sea. It would seem that Harald's ships met the allies just inside the narrow entrance, dispatching them a few at a time as they entered the fjord. Eirik and Sulke were both killed, but a famous warrior named Thor Haklang managed to get his ship alongside that of Harald and led a dramatic boarding that proved to be a prolonged and bloody climax to the battle.

Thor was killed, and the allies lost heart after their heavy losses. Kjotve gathered the surviving ships and men in the shelter of a small island (possibly Kjerten) and then headed home unmolested by Harald's fleet. Harald thereafter ruled most of southern Norway and exacted tribute from much of the north, although his rule did not extend that far. **RM**

Losses: Unknown

Svolder 1000 ▷

A regal portrait of Charles the Bald on his jewel-encrusted throne holding an orb and scepter.

Edington   6–12 May 878

The arrival of a Danish "great army" in East Anglia in 865 marked the start of a new phase of Viking attacks on Britain. Previously, the Vikings had come to raid and settle around the coast; this force came to conquer. Only the victory of Alfred the Great at Edington saved Anglo-Saxon independence.

After the Anglo-Saxon kingdoms of East Anglia, Mercia, and Northumbria had been conquered by the Danish army, Wessex in southern England held out against the invaders. Alfred came to the throne after his brother, King Aethelred I, was killed fighting the Danes in 871. The new king benefited from a lull in the onslaught until 876, when Danish attacks resumed in earnest. Reinvading Wessex, they captured Wareham and, in 877, occupied Exeter. Alfred succeeded in forcing the Danes to withdraw to Mercia, but the reprieve was brief.

In January 878, under their leader Guthrum, the Danes struck back with a surprise attack against Alfred at his winter fortress at Chippenham. The king was lucky to escape, taking refuge with a handful of followers in the depths of the Somerset marshes at Athelney. There he built a fort that he used as a base for guerrilla warfare, while building up his forces. In May 878 he rode out to challenge the Danes at Edington (Ethandun) outside the now Danish-held fortress of Chippenham. Alfred's warriors, fighting on foot, confronted the Danes with a dense shield wall. The battle raged until, in the words of his biographer, Asser, Alfred "overthrew the pagans with great slaughter, and smiting the fugitives, he pursued them as far as the fortress." His victory was decisive, forcing Guthrum to withdraw from Wessex and agree to the division of England. Alfred's Wessex controlled the south and west, Viking Danelaw the north and east. **SA**

Paris   25 November 885–October 886

The year-long Viking siege of Paris, at the time the capital of the kingdom of the West Franks, was notable as the first occasion on which the Vikings dug themselves in for a long siege, rather than conduct a hit-and-run raid or fight a battle. Their failure to capture the city marked a turning point in French history.

The Vikings first rowed up the Seine to attack Paris in 845 and returned three times in the 860s. Each time they looted the city or were bought off with bribes. In 864 the Franks built bridges across the river to deter these raiding parties: two footbridges crossing the river to the city situated on the Île de la Cité.

The island city was recently fortified, but the Frankish kingdom was weak and unable to defend itself properly. Taking advantage of this weakness, the Vikings attacked Paris again with a large fleet in 885. Duke Odo of Francia, who controlled the city, prepared for the attack by erecting two towers to guard each bridge. His own force was small, probably numbering no more than 200 men. Their request for tribute refused, the Vikings besieged the city, attacking the northeast tower with catapults and other war machines. They set alight three ships to burn down the wooden bridge, weakening it enough for it to be swept away by heavy rains in February 886. The tower was eventually captured, but by then the Vikings had moved on to pillage the surrounding countryside. The Parisians took the chance to replenish their supplies and seek help from outside. During the summer, the Vikings made a final attempt to take the city, but were soon surrounded by a Frankish army led by Charles the Fat. Rather than fight, he paid the Vikings 700 pounds of silver to lift the siege and sent them off to ravage Burgundy, then in revolt against Frankish rule. **SA**

Losses: Unknown

◁ *Lindisfarne 793*   *Brunanburh c. 937* ▷

Losses: Unknown

◁ *Lindisfarne 793*   *Clontarf 1014* ▷

Brunanburh c. 937

Despite much confusion about the battle's location, and even some about its date (the year varies from 934 to as late as 939), the significance of Brunanburh is without doubt. Here the kings of Wessex confirmed their leadership of a united English kingdom and achieved dominance throughout the British Isles.

In 925 Athelstan succeeded his father Edward the Elder as king of Wessex. He completed the conquest of Danish-held northern England begun by his father and achieved the homage of both the Welsh and of Constantine II, king of Scotland. Constantine, however, chaffed against English dominance and constructed a series of alliances across the islands. He married his daughter to Olaf Guthfrithsson, the Viking king of Dublin and former king of York, and thus became allied to the Viking earls of Northumbria. Constantine was already related to Owen, king of the independent kingdom of Strathclyde in southwest Scotland. It was this coalition of Scots, Irish, and Northumbrian Danes that fought against Athelstan in 937.

The location of the battlefield of Brunanburh is still highly debatable, with possibilities suggested as far apart as southwest Scotland and southwest England. It is likely that the battle actually took place either in Northumbria or at Bromborough on the Wirral in Cheshire. The coalition erected a large wooden stockade protected by a deep trench, which was stormed by Athelstan's army. Some sources claim that the English sent out a cavalry charge, which is unlikely because their army would have been entirely infantry, so perhaps these horsemen were mercenaries from elsewhere. The battle raged all day until the English triumphed, the coalition losing five "kings" and seven Viking jarls, or chieftains. Two of Athelstan's cousins and an English bishop were also killed. **SA**

Losses: Unknown

◁ *Edington 878*

Maldon 991 ▷

Bach Dang 938

The river Battle of Bach Dang has a proud place in Vietnamese national tradition, because it confirmed the country's independence from China after more than a millennium of foreign domination. The victory of the lightly equipped Vietnamese represented a triumph of guile and skill over superior brute force.

Vietnam was first subjected to Chinese domination under the Han dynasty in 111 BCE. Interrupted by a number of revolts, Chinese domination continued until the disintegration of the Tang dynasty in the early tenth century. The area of northern Vietnam known as Giao Chi asserted its autonomy as southern China split into warring kingdoms.

In 938 Liu Yan, ruler of a kingdom he named Southern Han, decided to reassert Chinese authority over Giao Chi. He sent an army to invade Giao by sea. Led by Liu Yan's son, Liu Hongcao, the expedition planned to sail up the Bach Dang River, which would carry the troops into the heart of the Red River Delta. The Vietnamese leader Ngo Quyen anticipated this plan. He had a line of iron-tipped poles driven into the riverbed across the mouth of the river. At high tide, when the tips of the poles were hidden under water, Ngo Quyen sent small boats out toward the Chinese fleet. When the boats turned and fled into the river, the Chinese were lured into pursuit. As the tide fell, the large Chinese ships were caught on the iron spikes. Immobilized, they were attacked by swarms of Vietnamese fighters.

About half the Chinese troops are said to have been killed, many by drowning. Among the dead was Liu Hongcao. His grieving father abandoned the bid to dominate Giao. The following year Ngo Quyen was proclaimed king of Vietnam. **RG**

Losses: Chinese, possibly 100,000 dead

Chi Lang 1427 ▷

Lechfeld (Augsburg) 955

Maldon August 991

The Hungarian Magyar tribes were pagan Asian horsemen who advanced westward in the tenth century, threatening Christian Europe with invasion. At the Battle of Lechfeld the king of the Germans, Otto I, secured a decisive victory that halted Magyar expansion.

Battles are won and lost for sometimes the strangest of reasons. In the case of the Battle of Maldon, fought on the marshy coastland of Essex in eastern England, misplaced Anglo-Saxon confidence contributed to a crushing defeat at the hands of a Viking invasion force.

Up until the Battle of Lechfeld, it appeared that the kings of Germany had no answer to the continued advance of the Hungarian Magyars. In 955 Otto I barely managed to assemble a force of 10,000 to face the Magyars, who outnumbered the Germans by five to one.

Otto advanced along the River Lech toward Augsburg and maneuvered his army in order to make a Magyar retreat difficult. The Magyars attacked first, rushing across the Lech with a cavalry charge that sent Otto's troops into panic. Otto was surrounded as Magyar horsemen began to pick off his troops. Defeat looked certain but the Magyars broke off to loot German supplies. Otto counterattacked, routing those who had dismounted to take the supplies and causing the Magyar cavalry to retreat. This turnaround raised the morale of the Germans, who rallied and charged as arrows rained down. The German charge broke the Magyar lines. With the Magyar mounted archers unable to utilize their rapid attack-and-fire tactics, the battle became a desperate encounter with troops engaged in hand-to-hand combat. The deciding factor was the inability of the Magyars to fight to their strengths due to the loss of their cavalry. The Magyars were routed on the field and hunted down during their retreat.

The reputation of the Magyars as an almost invincible fighting force was broken at Lechfeld, and their raids into Western Europe ceased. Otto I came to be known as Otto the Great and was later crowned Holy Roman Emperor. The Magyars eventually converted to Christianity and founded the kingdom of Hungary. **TB**

From the 980s onward, a new wave of Danish Viking raids took place against the recently united English kingdom, ruled since 978 by Aethelred II. In the summer of 991, a Danish raiding fleet commanded by Olaf Tryggvason—the future king of Norway—sailed south along the eastern coast of Essex. The raiders made landfall on Northey Island, a low-lying island in the Blackwater estuary connected to the mainland by a tidal causeway.

The events that followed are narrated in the Anglo-Saxon poem, "The Battle of Maldon." The earl of Essex, Byrhtnoth, rode out with his thegns, or personal retainers, and the local militia to confront the invaders, taking up a strategic position at the landward end of the causeway. When the tide went out, the Danes marched along the causeway but were prevented from reaching the mainland by the English force. Battle in such restricted circumstances was impossible, so Tryggvason proposed that his raiders be allowed to march onto the mainland so that both sides could join battle. For some reason—because he thought he would win or for some idea of fair play—Byrhtnoth agreed to the request.

The battle that then took place was fierce and bloody, but ended when the earl was killed by a spear. His thegns fought on around his body until they too were killed. The Danish victory was total, and Essex was now in the hands of the Danes. Within a couple of decades, all of England was under Danish rule. **SA**

Losses: German, 2,000; Magyar, 5,000 (in German sources)

Losses: Unknown, but around 3,000 fought on each side

◁ *Brunanburh c. 937*

Ashingdon 1016 ▷

↩ *An illustration of the Battle of Lechfeld by Sigismund Meisterlin in the Augsburg Chronicle (1457).*

Albigensian Crusade
Anglo-Saxon Wars
Anglo-Scottish Wars
Aztec Wars
Bohemian-Hungarian War
Breton Succession War
Burgundian War
Byzantine-Bulgarian Wars
Byzantine-Seljuk Wars
Castilian Civil War
Fifth Crusade
First Barons' War
First Crusade
Fourth Crusade
French Invasion of Flanders
French Jacquerie
Genoese-Venetian Wars
Genpei War
Go-Daigo Rebellion
Goryeo-Khitan Wars
Guelf-Ghibelline War
Hapsburg-Bohemian War
Hundred Years' War
Hussite Wars
Imperial Wars in Italy
Italian City-state Wars
Italian Wars
Ming Rebellion
Mongol Invasions
Norman Conquests
Northern Crusades
Onin War
Ottoman Wars
Pisan-Genoese War
Portuguese Independence War
Portuguese Reconquista
Russo-Tatar Wars
Scandinavian Wars
Scottish Independence Wars
Second Barons' War
Second Crusade
Seventh Crusade
Song-Jurchen War
Spanish Reconquista
Swedish-Novgorod War
Swiss-Hapsburg Wars
Third Crusade
Timur's Wars
Vietnamese Revolt
Viking Raids
War of Bouvines
War of the Sicilian Vespers
Wars of Crusader States
Wars of Kublai Khan
Wars of Teutonic Knights
Wars of the Roses
Welsh Revolt

1000–1499

A sixteenth-century Persian illumination of the Battle of Panipat (1526).

Svolder September 1000

The death of Christian king Olaf Tryggvason at Svolder led to the division of Norway between pagan rulers who sought to halt Christianity and the unification of the country. Their efforts proved in vain—within thirty-five years Norway was a united Christian kingdom under Olaf's son, Magnus.

The growing power of a united Norway under Olaf Tryggvason alarmed King Sweyn Forkbeard of Denmark, King Olaf Eiríksson of Sweden, and Earl Eirik Hákonarson of Lade. The actual cause of war was a dispute over the dowry of Olaf Tryggvason's Danish wife, Thyri.

Olaf traveled to Wendland in the Baltic region to seek allies and was traveling home when his fleet was confronted off Svolder Island (probably modern Rugen) in early September. Olaf was abandoned by the mercenary Jomsvikings that he had hired, leaving him with only eleven ships to face the allied fleet, which numbered either 80 or 139 ships, according to different sources. Olaf lashed his ships together, placing his own ship *Long Serpent* in the center.

The battle began with an assault by the ships of Sweyn Forkbeard, which was driven off, as was an attack by Olaf Eiríksson. Earl Eirik then maneuvered his ships so that he attacked Olaf's line on the flank, thus massing his forces against a single ship. Eirik's men cleared that ship, then cut it free, and gathered round the next in line. The Swedes and Danes copied these tactics on the other flank. The Norwegians were driven back until only the *Long Serpent* remained. After bitter fighting the Danes managed to get a foothold on the ship and began fighting their way toward the stern where Olaf stood. Olaf then leaped overboard, apparently drowning, and his surviving men surrendered. **RM**

Losses: Norwegian, 800 dead or captured; Allied Danes, Swedes, and others, unknown

◁ *Hafrsfjord c.872*

Clontarf 23 April 1014

The Vikings had been a presence in Ireland since the tenth century, with Dublin as their main port. The local Gaels were too divided to drive them out. Brian Boru, Gaelic king of Munster, confronted the Dublin Vikings at Clontarf, north of Dublin, in a battle that cost him his life.

In 1002 Brian Boru claimed leadership of all the Gaels as High King of Ireland. His claim to supremacy was resisted by Máel Mórda mac Murchada, Gaelic king of Leinster, who formed an alliance with his cousin Sigtrygg Silkbeard, the leader of the Dublin Vikings. The two men were joined by Viking mercenaries from the Orkney Islands and a rebel king from the Irish province of Ulster, while Boru was assisted by around 1,000 friendly Vikings and foreign mercenaries.

In April 1014 Boru attempted to capture Dublin, but the Vikings and Leinstermen took to their ships and sailed north to Clontarf, where battle was joined. Boru himself declined to fight, as the day of the battle was Good Friday, a Christian day of fasting and prayer.

Though the Vikings on both sides were generally better armed than the Gaels, the battle eventually swung in favor of Boru's army. Unable to reach their ships on the coast or to cross the River Liffey south to the safety of Dublin, almost all Boru's Viking enemies were slaughtered. One small group, however, led by Brodir, a Manx Viking, hid in the woods near Dublin. They discovered Brian Boru praying in his tent and killed him and his retainers. Deprived of their charismatic leader, the victorious Irish Gaels were unable to unite their kingdom, while the defeated Vikings retained their hold over Dublin. Fighting between the various rival Irish kingdoms continued as before. **SA**

Losses: Vikings and Leinstermen, up to 6,000 of 7,000; Irish, 4,000 of 7,000

◁ *Paris 885*

Kleidion 29 July 1014

Byzantine emperor Basil II became known as "the Bulgar-Slayer" after his crushing defeat of the Bulgarian Empire at Kleidion in the Belasitsa mountains. His decision to blind ninety-nine out of every hundred Bulgar prisoners taken in the battle ranks as one of history's vilest war atrocities.

The Byzantines had fought the Bulgars for centuries. At the start of the eleventh century, both the Bulgarian Empire of Czar Samuel and Basil's Byzantine Empire were strong, expansionist powers. Basil had the better of fighting in the first decade of the new millennium, however, and by 1014 sensed a chance to finish the Bulgars off.

Basil led a Byzantine army from Constantinople into the mountains of southwest Bulgaria. Czar Samuel decided to block his advance at the mountain pass of Kleidion. The Bulgarians built a system of wooden palisades across the pass, behind which their army occupied an apparently impregnable position. Basil's general Nicephorus Xiphias devised a plan to outflank the Bulgarian defenses. He led a detachment unobserved across a mountain ridge and emerged behind Czar Samuel's army. As Xiphias attacked from the rear, Emperor Basil led a frontal assault on the Bulgarian palisades. In the rout that followed, some of the Bulgars managed to flee. The rest were either slaughtered or taken prisoner. The prisoners numbered somewhere between 8,000 and 15,000 men. Basil had ninety-nine out of every hundred blinded: each hundredth man was left a single eye and entrusted with leading ninety-nine blinded colleagues home. The Bulgarian emperor Samuel died later in the year, reputedly of a heart attack after witnessing the mutilation of his army. Four years later Basil completed the conquest of the Bulgars, and the Byzantine Empire once again reached as far as the Danube. **TB**

> *"By leading his men along difficult paths, [Nicephorus Xiphias] was able to encircle the enemy and 'suddenly attacked the Bulgars from the rear, yelling and making a frightening noise.'"*

Theodoros Korres, Byzantine Macedonia (324–1025)

Losses: No reliable figures

🔽 *A depiction of the Bulgarians' defeat by the Byzantines and Czar Samuel's death, from the twelfth-century Manasses Chronicle.*

◁ *Pliska 811*   *Manzikert 1071* ▷

poploꝝ mltitudine· in parte danoꝝ pugnabant·
erāt et nimiſ fīaꞇ infirmat· At tū p̄ma die belli
id e· viī· kꞇ tulij tam aſpꝝ tātꝗꝫ cruent̄ extit pre
tium· ut uſꝗꝫ excitꝰ ꝑ laſſitudine diuci pugnare
non ualeuꞇ ſole tā occidente uoluntate ſpontanea
ſe abī uicem diuiſerc· Sed die poſtea rex eadmūdꝰ
danoſ oēſ ꝑtuliſſec· ſi inq̄ dux eadria fīdei ꞃ
fuiſſeꞇ· Siquidē cum utriuſ̄ uehemenꞇ pugna
recꝰ· z angloſ ſortioꝛeſ ē͛ oſpiciē͛· q̄dam uir re
gi eadmūdo oſimillim̄ capite amputato z aꞇtu
leuauꝰ· et clamauiꞇ diceꞇ· Vos angli amiſſo capi
te ſꞃuſtꝝ pugnatis· ꝑapuel fugite· en rex eadmūdi
cap̄ hic ꜹeneo manib3· fugite fugite eſſeuoꞇ· Q̄os ang
gli audierꞇ· moſtantꝰ eꝶ ſpio exterrerūt· Illi
to eꝥ rex nuiſeꞇ ꝑpto· aiꝏ extuleꝝt angli z dano
aꝯ nuꞇ incedebant incedebant· nultos erenꝰ ꝑt̄ueruꞇ
z ſuſmiſ uiridꞝ cranieꞇ ꝗ crepuſculū uſꝗꝫ noctiꞇ acc
ter ꝑ̄iceruꞇ· Qc aduenience· digsti ſunt ut p̄re
ſpontanea uoluntace· At ū plꝯimū noctiſ ꝑceſſiꞇ
cnuto ſuoſ ſub ſilentio e caſtꝝ abire ꝯepiꞇ· z riſuꞇ
londonia iꞇ arꝛipienſ z ad naueſ ſuas uenienꞇ:iu
uentꞇ icēm londoniaꝝ obſeꞇ· Qc rex eadmūdꝰ

Mane autē ſco cum rex eadmūdꝰ cnutone̅ e͛ue
danoſ ⸫pit aufugiſſe· in weſtaꝛomam ꝛeuꞇat
maioꝛem exritum collectuꝰ· Cui ſtrenuitacem ꞇ
inquiꞇ dux eadria ꝯpientꝰ· uemꞇ ad eum frandi
lenꞇ ut eum ꝑderꞇ inſtincꞇu cnutonis· z pace icꞇ
eos ꝯfirmata regi fidelitatem ꝥ uiuiſeꞇ· Iſeaꝗ rex
eadmūdꝰ uice ꞇꞃa exciꞇ aggꝛat̄· cuiꞇ lond
nieuꝰ obſeꞇoſ libauiꞇ· danoſ ad naueſ fuganꞇ z
aꝥ bremſoꝛediam thanꝛfe ſtuun tuſleuꞇ cum dani
ꝯro plium gnꝰſſeꞇ·⸫ni turpiꞇ de campo fugauꞇ
uictoꝛiam ſibi ꞇhaſta z gladio ꝯparuꞇ z Ꞅeruꞇ belli
dꞁꝰ optimuꝰ· Cnuto ū ad naueſ fugienꞇ cauꞇa
ꝑdaturꝰ extiꞇ· bont̄ quem rex eadmūdꝰ
exritū duceꞇ iuxta otteford cum hoſtibꝫ plium
nuiſiꞇ· At illi ꝑetū eiꝰ non Ꞅerenꞇ ꞇꝺa dederūt
z ī ſeptꞁam īſulam fugam feceꝝt· ꞇunc rex eadmū
diꞇ in weſtſexam ꝑficiſcenꞇ· cnutonis ꝑgiſſimū gꝛam
ꞇ exploꝛauiꞇ· ſe cnuto ꞇuriam ꝑdaturꝰ aſcendiꞇ· exi
crtu ſuo peioꝛa poꝛibꝫ facꞇ ꝯepiꞇ· At rex eadmūdiꞇ
aꝥ eſſeldunam hoſtiꞇ audacꞇ occurrenꞇ⸫pheiꞇ in
ſiduꞁ acieꞇ ꞁuꞇꝝ· turuiaſ circuiuiꞇ· monuꞇ ut
me moꝛeſ p̄ſtine uirtutis z uictoꝛie· ſeſe reguꝶꞇ
ſuū m ab auaricia barbaroꝝ defendanꞇ· Nam cū
illiꞇ ſeie cercaꞁ affirmat iu꞉ꞇ poſſe· quoꞇ dna
ſe po uiceꞇꞇꞇ· Cu ꞃo mꞇa ſuoſ m e꞉ꞇ q̄dam pla

macie cnutonm aduolam clamoꝛem acieꝝ
extruauit hoꝛrendū· ſto ibi inꞇ parcꝯ g ſluetiꞇ
ꝗiſſimuꞇ· q̄ cū p̄diꞇoꝝ dux eadria aciec danoꝝ iū
dereꞇ idcinatꝰ· eum cuiuo cū ꝑcaꞇ ad cnuto
nem̅ fugiꞇ ut ꝑꞁ fiac Ꞅuiſoꞁ ⸫ploeiruꞇ· unde
dam foꝛnioꝛeſ effecꞇi· nimiāꞇ ex angloꞁ ſtrage
feceꝝt· Coꝛrueꝝt enim ex parte angloꝛ duceſ
nobileſ alatricuꞇ z godſmnuꞇ· uſꞇrecelloꞇ z filiuꞇ
eiꝰ echelmoldꝰ z ꝺn amiꞇ echelmuīꞇ· caduoch
quoꝗ doꝛkeceuſilienꞇ epc z abbaꞇ hſiuꞇ· cū coꝛ
fere anglie nobilitace· qui nū̄ antea ꞇimo ꝑ
lio tanꞇa cladem ab hoſtibꝫ accepeꞇ· ꞇā aute
hoc bellum iꞃeſto ſc̄i luc e euīgliſte· cnuto ꝗ
in ſua ꝑe eadem die ducum z uiroꝛ nobili
urꞇepabile ſuſtinuiꞇ decmentū· De ſeda uicꞇo

P oſt hoc· lāꞇabile plium in quo uꞇa regi ead
ꝰpter nobileſ coꝛrueruꞇ inꞇecſiꞇ paucꝯ nuidꝰ·
diebꝰ· miſericurꝰ e rex eadmūdꝰ in cnutonem ꞇ
gloſunentꝰ pumeiā iam p̄dał agmicem· Conue
nerunꞇ icaꝗꝫ ad craiꞁ in loco ꝗ dicꞇ hurſtedꞇ
dꞇ regiꞇ· ū eadmūdꝰ in occidentali parte ſaluī
ne ſluminiꞇ cum ſuiꞇ z cnuto ꞇoꝛentiali· pꞇeciꝰ
ſinꞇ oſtrūctꝰ· ſe ſe uiriliꞇ ſparaueꝛt ad pugnā·
ſe cum acieſ hinc inde diſpoſite erant ad gcur
rendū· iniꞇ dux eadricuꞇ magnatiꝫ quo
caꞇuꞇ in hanc uocem̅· prupiꞇ diceꞇ· O inſula
ti nobileſ z armiꞇ potenteꞇ· cuꝛ toꞇienſ ībel
lo moꝛi̅uꞇ ꝑ regibꝫ nꞇiꞇ· cum ipꞇi nob monenꞇbꝫ
ꞃ regnū̅ optenemꝰ· ū anari̅e ſue fine ſponꞇanꞇ·
Pugnent ꝗſolo· plꞇ꞉neꞇo ſingſarꞇ· regnare oꞇ
dunꞇ· Que e iſta regnandi libido· qc anglia uꝶ
duobꝫ ū ſufficiꞇ· ſue olim octo regibꝫ ſatiꞇ ſuiꞇ
Iſeaꝗ uꞇ ſoli oponanꞇ uꞇ ſoli꞉ ꝥ regno decernꞇ·
Placuiꞇ autē h ſu̅a oibꝫ· z ad regeſ ꝑem delatum
arbitrum ipſi oſenciendo approbabanꞇ· Eꞇ autē inſu
la ꞇ ipſiuꞇ ſluminiꞇ medioſita eiue olenueie applaꞇ
ad ꝗu regeſ ꞇuꞁuecti ſplendidiſſuniꞇ· p̄equiruꞇ ar
niꝰ· ubi꞉ꞇꝗꝫ ſpectante plꞇo· cꝛamen ineunꞇ ſingula
re· At ubi haſtarum roburꞇ tam inꞇuce i piu
gencium regiꞇ ꝗu foꝛtiſſimoꝝ· obitu clipeoꝛ dept
educꞇiꞇ eunſibꝫ ſeſe guiuꞇ· Ꞅerienꞇ· accerꝯ ac dui
gladiu ꞇem agitrel· uꞇ eadmūdiꞇ cnutonꞇ ſoꝛu̅
ꝑpec· ꜱura capita galeaca eiuel ciuiꞇeꞇ· eꝗ colliſi
one ſcintille pꝛupiruꞇ· Vbi ū illud robuſtiſſimu̅
pectuꞇ eadmundi eꝛ ipo bellandi moꞇu nā ſucceſ
diꞇ· z ſanguine ꞇealeſcente factiꞇ ꝛobuſtioꝛ· dex
ꞇram eleuaꞇ· enſem nibe· canca uehemꞇia meaꝯp

Augli   dedmund freu lac   Cnuto rege dace   Dac

Ashingdon 18 October 1016

More than two centuries after the first Viking raids against the English coast, the Danes conquered the whole of England. The decisive Battle of Ashingdon, however, while giving them victory, did not deliver them the throne. As often happens in history, an unforeseen event finally delivered the prize.

In 991 and again in 1003 Sweyn Forkbeard of Denmark invaded England, exploiting the weak rule of Aethelred II (known as "the Unready" or "Redeless," because he refused to take advice from his "rede" or council). In 1013 Sweyn managed to conquer the entire country, sending Aethelred into exile in Normandy, France.

Sweyn ruled England for only a year, dying in 1014. His son, Canute, succeeded him, but the English nobles restored Aethelred to the throne. Two years later, in 1016, Aethelred died. The English nobles then chose his son, Edmund Ironside, as his successor, while the Danes again chose Canute. War broke out between the two sides; Edmund won at Pen in Somerset and drove Canute away from besieging London, but fought an inconclusive battle at Sherston in Wiltshire. The two sides met again at Ashingdon in Essex, where the battle was evenly fought until Edmund's Mercian allies fled the field. As the English battle line broke, Canute's troops cut them down.

With the battle lost, Edmund agreed with Canute to divide England between them, Edmund ruling the south, Canute the north. Six weeks later, Edmund suddenly died. With the majority of the English nobility killed at Ashingdon, the English agreed to recognize Canute as their king. England now became part of a large Danish empire, as Canute succeeded his elder brother as King of Denmark and southern Sweden in 1019 and conquered Norway in 1028, ruling this vast empire with skill and wisdom until his death in 1035. **SA**

Kwiju 1019

The conflict between the forces of the Khitan Liao dynasty and the Korean kingdom of Goryeo at Kwiju is seen as one of the three most important battles in Korean history—the others being the battles of Salsu River and Hansando. Kwiju preserved Korean independence from a most dangerous neighbor.

During the tenth century, most of Korea was united under the kingdom of Goryeo. In the same period the Khitan, nomadic horsemen from the Mongolian steppe, won control of much of northern China, where they ruled as the Liao dynasty. From 993 the Khitan staged a number of large-scale invasions of Goryeo, failing to subdue its independence despite military successes. In winter 1018 an estimated 100,000 Liao soldiers—a mix of Khitan mounted bowmen and Chinese peasant conscripts—crossed the Yalu River. Goryeo was able to mobilize twice that number of men in its defense, but most were poorly trained militia fighting on foot with basic equipment.

Command of the Goryeo forces was assumed by Gang Gam-chan, a respected scholar and bureaucrat who had reached the age of seventy-one without acquiring any military experience. This unlikely general failed to stop the invaders advancing toward the Goryeo capital Kaesung, but succeeded in subjecting them to constant harassment as they progressed ever farther into hostile territory. The Khitan commander, Xiao Baiya, became increasingly uneasy, until his nerve broke and he turned his army for home. Waiting with his main force at the fortress of Kwiju, General Gang Gam-chan attacked the exhausted, hungry Liao troops as they withdrew.

Xiao's army evaporated; his men either killed, taken prisoner, or disappearing in pursuit of self-preservation. Gang Gam-chan was celebrated as a national hero and Goryeo's continued existence ensured. **RG**

Losses: No reliable figures

⟨ *Maldon 991*

Stamford Bridge 1066 ⟩

Losses: Goryeo, no reliable figures; Liao, 90,000

⟨ *Baekgang 663*

⟵ *An illustration from Matthew Paris's* Chronica Majora, *depicting Canute in combat with Edmund Ironside.*

Civitate   18 June 1053

The Normans' domination over southern Italy was established at the Battle of Civitate (also known as Civitella del Fotore) and in the subsequent treaties agreed by Pope Leo IX. Contemporaries believed that the fighting established the superiority of heavily armed cavalry over infantry or light cavalry on the field of battle.

Norman knights went to southern Italy as mercenaries to fight Muslim raiders in Sicily and North Africa, but they soon established themselves as landowners. In 1053 Pope Leo IX hired 700 Swabian infantry and marched south with his ally, Duke Rudolf of Gaeta, to muster anti-Norman forces and join with a Byzantine army at Apulia. Leo and Rudolf had 6,000 men when they were met by 3,000 Norman cavalry and 500 local infantry at Civitate. Rudolf put the Swabian mercenaries on a low hill with the Italian allies on

their left. The Normans formed three divisions of cavalry led by Richard of Aversa on the right, Humphrey of Hauteville in the center, and Humphrey's brother, Robert Guiscard, on the left. The local infantry raised by the Normans guarded the camp. The Normans advanced across a plain, then charged. The Italian allies fled, to be pursued by Richard's men, who pillaged the papal camp. The Swabians held Humphrey's charge, inflicting heavy losses. Robert moved to support his brother, forcing the Swabians to adopt close-order defensive formation. The return of Richard's men allowed the Normans to overwhelm the Swabians. The citizens of Civitate then handed over the pope, who agreed to a series of treaties in exchange for his freedom. **RM**

Losses: Norman, 500 of 3,000 cavalry (infantry not engaged); Papal, 1,500 of 6,000

Hastings 1066 ▶

A nineteenth-century painting captures the moment when an arrow fatally pierced the throat of King Harald Hadrada (center). ⬇

Stamford Bridge   25 September 1066

Were it not totally overshadowed by a more famous confrontation that took place at Hastings three weeks later, the Battle of Stamford Bridge between King Harold II of England and an invading Viking army led by King Harald Hadrada of Norway would be remembered as the last time the Vikings attempted to conquer England.

In January 1066 Edward the Confessor, King of England, died, having named Harold Godwinson, Earl of Wessex, as his successor. Harold had earned the undying hostility of his brother Tostig, who had been ejected, with his brother's approval, from his earldom in Northumbria the previous year. The vengeful Tostig formed an alliance with Harald Hadrada, King of Norway, promising to support Harald's attempt to conquer England in return for regaining his earldom. The two crossed the North Sea with a fleet of 300 ships and sailed up the Humber River. Once ashore, the Viking army defeated an army led by the new Earl of Northumbria in alliance with the Earl of Mercia and occupied York. King Harold of England formed an army to repel the invasion and on 16 September left London for the north, reaching Stamford Bridge, just east of York, in only nine days. The two armies drew up the next day. An English offensive was soon reversed by a Viking counteroffensive led by Harald that almost turned the battle in their favor. Harald, however, was killed by an arrow in the throat. In response, Harold offered his brother peace, but Tostig fought on, encouraged by the arrival of Viking reinforcements. But the new arrivals were exhausted and soon fell in fighting during which Tostig was killed. **SA**

Losses: Viking, 4,000 of 5,000; English, unknown

◁ *Ashingdon 1016*   *Hastings 1066* ▷

Hastings   14 October 1066

Few battles have so changed the course of a nation's history as the Battle of Hastings. The Anglo-Saxon rulers of England lost their throne and their country to Norman invaders, who transformed their new kingdom. Yet the battle was a close-run event, its outcome undecided until late in the day.

The future king of England, Edward the Confessor—so-called because of his piety—had lived for twenty-five years with his Norman mother in northern France. When he finally became king in 1042, Edward retained many Norman advisers. His marriage was childless and in 1051 he promised the throne to William, Duke of Normandy. On his deathbed in January 1066, however, Edward changed his mind and chose his brother-in-law, Harold Godwinson, Earl of Wessex, as his successor. When Harold became king, William was incensed

and prepared to invade England. Delayed during the summer by unfavorable winds, William finally set sail from Normandy on 27 September, landing at Pevensey in southern England the following day. Harold, however, was in the north of England, recovering from his victory three days before at Stamford Bridge against an invading Viking army. On hearing the news of a second invasion, he hurriedly marched south to London, covering 200 miles (322 km) in less than five days. Spending five more days in the capital to rest his exhausted troops and gather reinforcements, he then continued south, reaching Senlac Hill, some eight miles (13 km) northwest of Hastings on the south coast, on 13 October.

In the early morning of 14 October, Harold formed up his army ten to twelve deep in a defensive position along a ridge. He probably commanded around 9,000 foot soldiers and a few cavalry. The Norman army, assembled

A detail from the Bayeux Tapestry shows Harold II struck by an arrow in the eye before being killed by the sword of a mounted knight (right).

400 yards (365 m) away at the bottom of the ridge, may have numbered 15,000 men. This army was more varied in composition, with archers, a few crossbowmen—the weapon making one of its first appearances in a medieval European battle—pikemen, and mounted knights.

The battle commenced at 9:00 AM when the Normans advanced up the hill, archers and crossbowmen in the front, pikemen in the middle, and cavalry knights in the rear. The archers opened fire, but as they had to fire uphill, their arrows mostly missed their targets. The pikemen then charged but were thrown back by volleys of javelins and rocks. A cavalry charge was also thrown back, the left wing retreating in panic and pursued by English infantry. Panic began to spread in the Norman ranks, with some believing that William had been killed. Pulling off his helmet to show his face, William rallied his troops and attacked the pursuing English, soon overwhelming them.

He then led another cavalry charge against the center of the English line, but was repulsed.

With stalemate threatening, William commanded his men to pretend to retreat. Harold ordered his troops to hold their positions, but a few ran after the Normans and were cut down. The rest of the English held their lines on top of the ridge and, despite increasing tiredness, withstood repeated Norman assaults. At this point, William ordered his archers to fire high over the English lines so that their arrows and bolts would rain down on them. One arrow apparently struck Harold in the eye. The English line gave way and the Normans soon captured the ridge. The Battle of Hastings was theirs. **SA**

Losses: Norman, 2,000 of 7,000–15,000; English, 4,000 of 9,000

◁ Stamford Bridge 1066

Manzikert 26 August 1071

Toledo 1085

The defeat of Emperor Romanos IV Diogenes by the Seljuk Turks under Sultan Alp Arslan (meaning "Heroic Lion" in Turkish) at Manzikert was a mortal blow to the Byzantine Empire. Anatolia was soon lost to the Turks and Byzantine power went into slow, but terminal, decline.

The Siege of Toledo was a key moment in the struggle between the Christians and Muslims in the Iberian Peninsula. The city was the capital of the Taifa kingdom of al-Andalus and its fall to King Alfonso VI of Castile spurred the Reconquista, the Christian conquest of Muslim Spain.

In 1071 the Muslim Seljuks, who originated from central Asia, were threatening western Anatolia. Romanos IV Diogenes led an army on a long march across Anatolia to recapture the Byzantine fortress of Manzikert (now Malazgirt), which had fallen to Alp Arslan.

Problems with Byzantine intelligence meant that Romanos had no idea where the Sultan's army was and he unwisely divided his force in two. Romanos continued toward Manzikert while the other half of his army marched on Khliat. Even with his army halved, Romanos easily occupied Manzikert, but his hold on it was brief.

After suffering losses in skirmishes with the Turks outside the fortress, Romanos decided to lead his army out to confront the enemy. As the Byzantines advanced the Seljuks fell back, avoiding pitched battle while making harassing raids. At the end of a frustrating day, Romanos ordered a withdrawal. For Alp Arslan's horsemen, this was the signal to attack. Disloyally deserted by part of his forces, Romanos was surrounded by the Turks and captured after a hard fight.

Many of the professional, elite troops of the Byzantine Empire perished at Manzikert and Alp Arslan only released Romanos after the emperor agreed to cede important Byzantine territories. On his return he was overthrown, blinded, and killed by his political enemies. The weakened Byzantine Empire called on fellow Christians in Western Europe to come to their aid, an appeal that led eventually to the mounting of the First Crusade. **TB**

Toledo was the prosperous capital of the Moorish kingdom of al-Andalus, commanding a strategic position in the center of the Iberian Peninsula. Throughout its history, al-Andalus had been in conflict with Christian kingdoms in the north and the tide began to turn in the Christians favor after Alfonso became king of Leon in 1065 and of Castile in 1072.

Alfonso carefully and cleverly exploited divisions within Moorish Spain. In 1075 he defeated the Taifa kingdom of Granada with the help of their rivals in Seville, and later that year, he supported Toledo against its rivals in Córdoba. However, Alfonso lost his influence in Toledo when Al-Qadir succeeded his father as caliph (Muslim head of state) and expelled Alfonso's sympathizers.

Al-Qadir's actions caused further divisions within the Moorish community; a rebellion lost him Córdoba and sent him into exile, and he was forced to ask Alfonso for assistance. The king agreed on the condition that Al-Qadir give up Toledo to Castile in return for the Moors holding onto Valencia. By the time Alfonso's forces arrived at Toledo, the citizens were tired of conflict and invited him to enter. However, a faction linked to the kingdom of Zaragoza resisted and forced Alfonso to besiege the city.

The ultimate fall of Toledo in May 1085—after four years of mostly desultory military activity—was a significant milestone in the Reconquista of Muslim Spain, allowing King Alfonso to claim the leadership of Spain for Leon-Castile. **TB**

Losses: No reliable figures

◁ *Kleidion 1014*   *Dorylaeum 1097* ▷

Losses: No reliable figures

◁ *Covadonga c. 720*   *Valencia 1094* ▷

Valencia 1094

The Spanish nobleman Rodrigo Díaz, commonly known as El Cid, was a mercenary soldier who became a powerful figure during the wars between Muslims and Christians in the late eleventh century. The climax of his career came in 1094, when he captured the city of Valencia from its Muslim ruler.

El Cid commenced his career with campaigns against the Moors in the service of Alfonso VI of Castile's brother, Sancho II, in which he won victories at Zaragoza and also defeated Ramiro I of Aragon.

After the death of his brother, Alfonso forced El Cid into exile, possibly for reasons of jealousy. The Castilian military leader and diplomat survived by becoming a mercenary and selling his skills to the highest bidder, the most notable of his clients being the Muslim king of Zaragoza.

By the time the Almoravids of Morocco invaded Spain in 1086, El Cid was a significant independent player in Iberian power struggles, leading a combined army of Christian and Muslim soldiers and exercising suzerainty over the Muslim-ruled city of Valencia. When the Almoravids replaced El Cid as the city's suzerains, he fought back and started to win victories.

In 1093, attempting to take advantage of an uprising in Valencia, El Cid began his siege. A mixture of a blockade, which reduced the city's population to near starvation, and the bombardment of the walls with siege engines eventually forced Valencia into submission. El Cid took control of the city on 15 June 1094 and held it for the last five years of his life against Almoravid counterattacks. After his death, his victories for Christendom were immortalized in the epic medieval poem *The Lay of the Cid* and he became a hero of the Reconquista. El Cid's widow ruled Valencia for three years until it was eventually retaken by the Almoravids in 1102. **TB**

"My Lord Cid don Rodrigo straight for the gateway made, and they that held it . . . fled in great fear."

from The Lay of the Cid, *1207*

Losses: No reliable figures

 Toledo 1085

Ourique 1139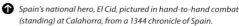

 Spain's national hero, El Cid, pictured in hand-to-hand combat (standing) at Calahorra, from a 1344 chronicle of Spain.

Dorylaeum 1 July 1097

The first clear victory of the First Crusade opened the route to the Holy Land. It showed the superiority of crusader armor over light Turkish Seljuk weaponry, while the unfamiliar crusader tactics confused the Seljuks and were largely responsible for the victory.

After the defeat at Manzikert, the Byzantines appealed to Christian Europe for help. The result was the First Crusade, a Christian army marching from Western Europe, not to help the Byzantines, but to regain the Holy Land from the Muslims. After passing Constantinople, the crusaders marched in two columns into the territory of the Seljuk ruler, Kilij Arslan.

The column of Bohemond of Taranto consisted of 2,000 knights, 8,000 infantry, and a large number of pilgrims. The column of Raymond of Toulouse was of similar size. At dawn on 1 July, Bohemond's camp at Dorylaeum was attacked by many lightly armed cavalry, including horse archers, led by Kilij Arslan. The crusader knights charged, but the swift Seljuk cavalry evaded the charge and attacked the crusader camp. Bohemond pulled his knights back, to dismount and form a defensive line with more heavily armed infantry. The light Seljuk weapons made little impact on the crusaders and attempts to lure them into a hasty charge were unsuccessful. However, Seljuk arrows struck many pilgrims.

After about seven hours of near stalemate, the knights of Raymond's column arrived and charged into the flank of the Seljuk army inflicting heavy casualties. Kilij Arslan rallied his men and was contemplating his next move when the infantry of Raymond's column arrived under the papal legate, Adhemar Le Puy, to storm and capture the Seljuk camp. Kilij Arslan then retreated and allowed the crusaders free passage across his lands. **RM**

Losses: Crusader, 4,000 of 50,000; Seljuk, 7,000–15,000 of up to 60,000

◁ *Dorylaeum 1097*   *Antioch 1097* ▷

Antioch 20 October 1097–28 June 1098

This marked the arrival of the First Crusade in the Holy Land. Events set a pattern of betrayal, massacre, and heroism that was to mark future campaigns. By capturing Antioch, the crusaders secured lines of supply and reinforcement to the west.

Having marched through the Seljuk lands, the crusaders captured Edessa and arrived at the huge city of Antioch on 20 October 1097. Bohemond of Taranto, Raymond of Toulouse, and Godfrey de Bouillon each commanded a section of the blockading lines. The Turkish garrison was commanded by Yaghi Siyan, who summoned a relief army from Damascus and another from Aleppo, only for both to be defeated by the crusaders before they reached Antioch.

Some time during the winter, Bohemond made contact inside the city with a Christian soldier named Firouz, who had command of the Gate of Two Sisters. On 2 June, Firouz opened the gate, allowing the crusaders to enter and join the Christian inhabitants in a massacre of the Turks. Yaghi Siyan was killed but his son Shams held out in the citadel. Two days later a huge Turkish army led by Kerbogha of Mosul arrived and laid siege to the crusaders inside Antioch. On 10 June, a monk named Peter Bartholmew had a vision of where the Holy Lance was hidden; when found, it boosted crusader morale.

On 28 June, the crusaders marched out to do battle with the Holy Lance as their standard. The crusader knights charged, scattering the lightly armed Turkish cavalry. At this point many of Kerbogha's allies deserted him and the Turkish army disintegrated. Bohemond rushed back into Antioch to take the surrender of Shams, occupy the citadel, and announce that he was now Prince Bohemond of Antioch. **RM**

Losses: Crusader, 2,000 of 30,000; Turkish, 10,000 of 75,000

◁ *Dorylaeum 1097*   *Jerusalem 1099* ▷

The capture and sacking of Antioch in 1098 from a fifteenth-century French manuscript.

son entreprise fu se referilloit auec
quelle feust a complie. Et fen re
tourna a vne des grans fenestres
et creneaulx des mirs pres de
sa tour deuant la quelle estoiet
la semis iusques au pied Duy
mond et les aultres Princes et
Baros qui fauoiet lentrepri
se dont chasam auoit vnu de
ses gens auec soy pour la com

purfuier. mais bone triffants
et loyaulx. Em ferrus mist
fu teste bue et ses falaa. Et les
aultres fur. Apres il amasbue
corde et ils fur souoiet vne eschel
le auffi de corde dont ils auoiet
attachie le pied a vnne cue de
fer par bue et Emferrus fat
tachie tresbien au verde de la
fenestre. Et combien quelle

Jerusalem 7 June–16 July 1099

The culminating victory of the First Crusade, the capture of Jerusalem, seemed to justify the faith of the crusaders and the huge effort involved in mounting the campaign. It allowed for the establishment of the Christian Kingdom of Jerusalem, which was to endure for two centuries and provide a focus for future crusades.

After capturing Antioch, the crusaders rested for six months before setting out for Jerusalem. Iftikhar ad-Daula, the Fatimid governor of Jerusalem, gathered food and livestock, poisoned wells around the city, cut down the trees to deny shade to the enemy, expelled all Christians, and sent messengers to his Fatimid masters in Egypt requesting a relief army be sent as soon as possible. His garrison of about 1,000 men was composed mostly of Arabs and Nubians. Iftikhar did not have enough men to

man the entire city walls and placed his hopes on famine and thirst driving the crusaders away.

The crusaders arrived on 7 June and settled down to bombarding the walls with mangonels, trebuchets, and other siege engines. On 17 June, a fleet arrived at Jaffa with the hardware needed to make siege towers. These were unloaded and set off for Jerusalem with an escort that had to fight off a sustained Muslim assault. The construction of the siege towers began on 21 June.

On 6 July, a priest named Peter Desiderius announced that he had been visited in a vision by the spirit of the recently deceased papal legate, Adhemar Le Puy, who told him that the crusaders should imitate Joshua at the Battle of Jericho. They should walk barefoot around the walls of Jerusalem in penitent procession and the city would fall in nine days. The procession duly took place, while Iftikhar and his men jeered from the walls, and

fresh heart was put into the thirsty crusaders. On the night of 13 July, the siege towers were trundled forward and at dawn the grueling task began of filling the city ditch so that they could be pushed up against the walls. Men swarmed up the towers and scaling ladders while the siege engines hurled massive rocks into the city. The defenders tried to burn the towers with flaming oil, bales of hay, and Greek fire, and shot back with their own catapults and archers.

By dawn on 15 July, only two towers remained and several engines had been destroyed by Muslim shot. Then, just before noon, a pile of straw caught fire, blowing choking black smoke onto the walls in front of one of the siege towers. The bridge was hurriedly pushed into place and two Flemish knights, Litold and Gilbert of Tournai, led the charge across to the walls. At noon the crusaders entered the city in force. Iftikhar barricaded himself, his bodyguard, and his treasure chest into the Tower of David. The crusaders butchered indiscriminately anyone they could find. At dusk the nobles attended a service of thanksgiving in the Church of the Holy Sepulchre while the killing continued.

The slaughter ended about dawn, after which the survivors were kept as slaves or permitted to leave if they paid a ransom. Iftikhar was allowed to march out with his bodyguard a few days later once he had handed over the city's treasure chest. Godfrey de Bouillon was then declared King of Jerusalem and the lands captured by the crusaders. **RM**

Losses: Crusader, up to 10,000 dead, wounded, and sick of about 15,000; Fatimid, 950 of garrison of 1,000 along with up to 40,000 civilians

◁ *Antioch 1097*   *Harran 1104* ▷

Harran 7 May 1104

The religious fervor of the First Crusade was over by 1104 as the new crusader lords attempted to secure their hold on the captured lands and to fend off further Muslim assaults. The defeat at Harran was the first suffered by the crusader states and demonstrated the limits to Christian expansion.

An army of Seljuks under Sokman of Mardin and Jikirmish of Mosul lay siege to the city of Edessa. To distract the Seljuks, Prince Bohemond of Antioch and Count Baldwin of Edessa led an army to the city of Harran. The crusaders had not yet properly laid siege to Harran when the army of Sokman appeared. After a brief battle in sight of Harran, Sokman fell back to the south. Bohemond and Baldwin then gave chase. The retreat was probably merely a ruse to draw the crusaders away to allow Jikirmish to enter Harran with supplies and reinforcements.

On the third day of the retreat, Sokman halted just south of the River Balikh where he was joined by Jikirmish whose 7,000 cavalry remained out of sight of the crusaders. Baldwin and the Edessans formed the left of the crusader army and Bohemond with his Antioch troops were on the right. The battle opened with a general attack by Sokman, which was driven off. Sokman then fell back toward the waiting Jikirmish, luring Baldwin to follow him in disorder. Jikirmish's cavalry charged and inflicted heavy casualties, taking Baldwin prisoner.

Bohemond had not taken the bait and retreated in good order, although he lost men as he fought his way back to Edessa. Baldwin was freed in 1108 after paying a ransom and later became King of Jerusalem. However, the crusader state of Edessa never recovered its strength and in 1144 would become the first of the crusader states to fall to the Muslims. **RM**

Losses: Crusader, half of the 3,000 cavalry and 7,000 infantry; Muslim, 2,000 of 20,000

◁ Jerusalem 1099   Edessa 1144 ▷

Kaifeng December 1126–January 1127

In 1127 Jurchen steppe nomads captured the Chinese capital of Kaifeng and with it the Song emperor. This was a major event in Chinese political history, but it was also a turning point in military technology, being one of the earliest occasions on which gunpowder was used in battle.

A confederation of tribal horsemen, the Jurchen had developed imperial pretensions, declaring the foundation of the Jin dynasty in 1115. From 1125 they began a war against the Song dynasty, rulers of most of China. As so often in Chinese history, horsemen proved superior in open battle, but had difficulty taking walled cities.

The Siege of Kaifeng began in December 1126. The Song had been experimenting with gunpowder, placing it on the tips of arrows as an incendiary device and bundling quantities of it in bamboo or paper, tied up with string, to make a primitive bomb. Hurling these "thunderclap bombs" from the walls shocked the Jurchen—a Chinese source states that "many fled, howling with fright"—but the "bombs" were in truth no more than noisy firecrackers.

No relief army arrived to save the city, which fell to the Jurchen in mid-January 1127. There followed an orgy of looting and wanton destruction. The fate of the population was grim: the survivors were subjected to rape and other cruelties, or sold into slavery. The imperial family was not spared. Song Emperor Qinzong was carried off into the Jurchen heartland and lived out his days there with the status and dress of a servant. A new Song emperor was chosen to rule southern China, but the north was lost to the Jin dynasty, which ruled until the arrival of Genghis Khan's Mongols in the thirteenth century. **RG**

Losses: No reliable figures

Tangdao 1161 ▷

A woodblock print showing another use of gunpowder in Chinese warfare—a revolving wheel explosive. ➡

車輪砲

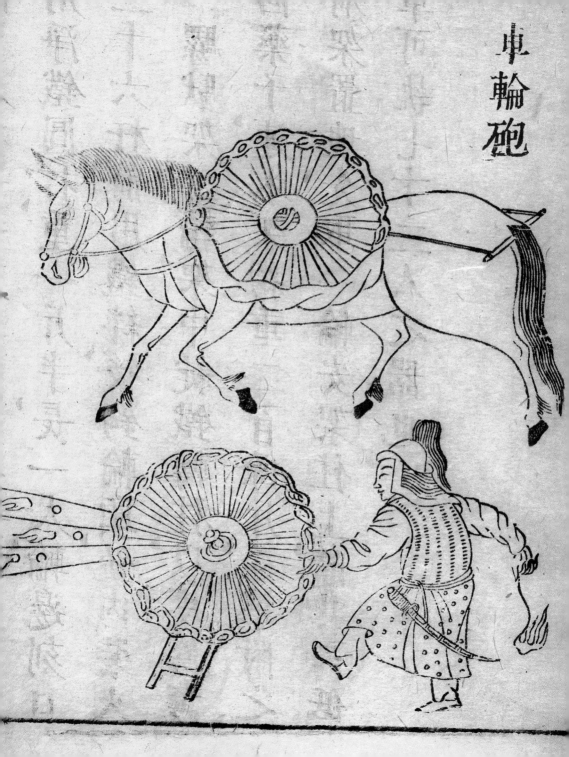

Ourique   25 July 1139

Afonso Henriques, victor of the Battle of Ourique, is seen as the founder of Portugal as an independent kingdom. The victory over the Almoravid Muslim forces in southern Portugal extended the area of Christian rule and allowed Afonso to be proclaimed King of the Portuguese.

Afonso was the son of Henry of Burgundy, Count of Portugal, who owed his title to Alfonso VI of Leon and Castile, whose daughter Teresa he married. Henry died when Afonso was still a child. By the age of eleven the boy was at odds with his mother, who exiled him from Portugal. However, Afonso was ambitious. He raised an army when he became fourteen, the age of adulthood in medieval times, and won a victory over his mother at Sao Mamede in 1128.

Asserting Portugal's independence of Leon and Castile, he declared himself first duke and then prince of Portugal. His realm was what is now northern and central Portugal;

the south was ruled by Almoravid Muslims. By attacking the Muslims, Afonso could both extend his territory and hope to win the support of the pope (Pope Innocent II) for his claim to independence.

Little detailed information about the battle fought at Ourique survives, and the location itself is a matter for speculation. Afonso apparently defeated a larger force than his own, but one that was weakened by the divisions affecting Moorish Iberia at the time. Some medieval chroniclers claimed he benefited from the intervention of Saint James. Whatever the facts, the importance of the battle as a turning point in Portuguese history is undisputed. After the battle, Afonso Henriques was proclaimed king of the Portuguese by his troops as King Afonso I. He would continue to fight the Muslims until his death in 1185. **TB**

Losses: No reliable figures

◀ *Valencia 1094*   *Lisbon 1147* ▶

Detail from a sixteenth-century illumination, depicting the victorious Afonso. ⬆

Edessa 28 November–24 December 1144

The fall of the crusader city of Edessa to the Muslims was the spark that ignited the Second Crusade. The victory entrenched Zengi as leader of the Muslims in the Holy Land, a mantle that would be taken up by his son Nur ad-Din and then by Saladin.

After victory at Harran, the Muslim forces in the Holy Land fractured into warring factions. In 1128 Zengi of Mosul captured Aleppo and cowed neighboring Muslim rulers into submission. In 1144 Zengi learned that Count Joscelin of Edessa had argued with Prince Raymond of Antioch, and then taken almost his entire army to Diyarbakir to interfere in a dispute between Seljuk princes. Zengi marched a large army to Edessa hoping to overwhelm the city before Joscelin could return. He arrived on 28 November and began battering the walls with trebuchets and mining under the foundations. The city walls were, however, exceptionally strong and the defenders put up determined resistance despite their low numbers. Queen Melisende of Jerusalem mustered a relief force that marched for Edessa, but Prince Raymond of Antioch refused to help. On 24 December, a section of the walls collapsed into a mine and Zengi's troops poured into the city, capturing everything except the citadel. Zengi had the local Christians separated from foreign Christians, and then had all the latter executed. The men holding the citadel surrendered on 26 December on condition that their lives be spared. Joscelin and the troops sent by Melisende arrived a few days too late to save Edessa, but did hold on to the lands west of the Euphrates River. When news of the fall of Edessa reached Rome, Pope Eugene III called for the raising of the Second Crusade. This would greatly strengthen the remaining crusader states, although Edessa was never recaptured. **RM**

Losses: Unknown, although all of the crusader garrison was killed

◁ Harran 1104   Damascus 1148 ▷

⬆ *A twelfth-century fresco showing the departure of the crusaders for the Holy Land.*

Lisbon 1 July–25 October 1147

The capture of the city of Lisbon from the Almoravid Muslims was a by-product of the Second Crusade to the Holy Land and one of the few Christian victories of that campaign. It proved to be a pivotal turning point in the history of Portugal as it mutated from being a subordinate vassal of Leon into an independent Christian kingdom.

When he announced the start of the Second Crusade, Pope Eugene III stated that Christians in the Iberian Peninsula could crusade against the Muslims there rather than travel to the Holy Land. On 16 June 1147, 164 ships carrying 6,000 English, 5,000 German, and 2,000 Flemish crusaders put in to Porto to escape a storm. Afonso Henriques, self-proclaimed King of Portugal, asked them to join his own personal crusade to capture Lisbon from the Muslims. He offered them the moveable goods of the Muslims in the city and any ransoms that could be extracted.

The crusaders agreed and, on 1 July, laid siege to Lisbon while Afonso and his army occupied the surrounding countryside. The crusaders built mangonels and other devices and bombarded the city. The Muslims launched a sortie and burned the siege engines. Thereafter the fighting almost stopped as the crusaders settled down to a blockade. On 21 October, the garrison agreed to surrender on condition they were allowed to march out freely. The gates of Lisbon were opened four days later.

Owing to the agreed surrender, the crusaders did not get as much loot. Many English crusaders opted to stay in Portugal—one of them became Bishop of Lisbon—while the Germans and Flemings continued to the Holy Land. Lisbon became capital of Portugal, which won papal recognition as an independent kingdom. **RM**

Losses: Crusader, minimal of 15,000; Muslim, few of 7,000-strong garrison; civilian, unknown but minor

[<] Ourique 1139 Alarcos 1195 [>]

Damascus 23–28 July 1148

The defeat of the Second Crusade at Damascus ensured that the Christian crusader states in the Holy Land would remain on the defensive for the foreseeable future. There was no longer any realistic prospect of expansion so the Christians were confined to small states surrounded by larger and more powerful Muslim enemies.

The Second Crusade started badly as the armies of Louis VII of France and Conrad III of Germany both suffered heavy losses at the hands of the Turks on the arduous journey to Jerusalem. Joining with Baldwin III of Jerusalem, Louis and Conrad marched with some 30,000 men to attack the Syrian city of Damascus. Arriving on 23 July, they moved to occupy the vast orchards and walled fields west of the city, suffering heavily at the hands of Damascene archers who fought a skillful retreat to the city walls. Having failed to assault Damascus from the west, the crusaders moved on 27 July to the open plains to the east of the city.

A dispute broke out between the leaders of the crusade and the local Christian noblemen over how to pursue the siege and who should be ruler of Damascus once it was captured. This disagreement was interrupted by news that a large Muslim army under the skilled general Nur ad-Din had arrived at Homs. From there Nur ad-Din could either march south to relieve Damascus or strike directly at Antioch or Jerusalem. The local Christian lords melted away, taking their men back to defend their own lands.

On 28 July, Louis, Conrad, and Baldwin began their own retreat to Jerusalem, where they too fell out in mutual recriminations over who had been to blame for the failure at Damascus. The crusaders went home with nothing accomplished. **RM**

Losses: Crusader, unknown of more than 30,000; Muslim, unknown of 10,000

[<] Edessa 1144 Hattin 1187 [>]

Crema   2 July 1159–26 January 1160

The Holy Roman Emperor Frederick Barbarossa campaigned in northern Italy to impose his authority over the wealthy city of Milan and its allies. His siege of Milan's ally, Crema, is a classic example of medieval warfare both in its hideous cruelty and its inventive use of pre-gunpowder technology.

The city of Crema was protected by a double circuit of walls and a moat. Inside were 400 Milanese knights and foot soldiers as well as the Crema's own militia. Frederick Barbarossa was able to assemble a large enough army for a full encirclement by combining his imperial army with forces supplied by various German princes and by Italian cities hostile to Crema, notably neighboring Cremona.

Large rock-hurling siege machines were built by both sides for bombardment and counterbombardment. The besiegers used armored mobile roofs to cover men advancing to fill in the moat with barrels of earth and dig tunnels under the walls. A 100-foot (30 m) tall siege tower was rolled up to the walls by 500 men and a bridge lowered for an assault force to cross to the top of the outside wall, while archers shot down on the defenders from higher in the tower.

Yet Crema's inner ring of defenses held firm and the city could not be taken. Both sides used terror to intimidate and demoralize their enemy. Barbarossa tied prisoners, some of them children, to the front of the siege tower as it advanced into battle, so that they were killed by their own friends and relatives. The Cremese answered by hacking prisoners into pieces in full view of the besieging army. Eventually, hunger forced Crema's defenders to surrender. Their lives were spared but the city was emptied of its population and razed to the ground. **RG**

"Barbarossa understood his election as a mission to restore the lost dignity of the Roman Empire.... His sheer ruthlessness in attempting to do so [made] him one of Hitler's heroes."

Dana Facaros, Lombardy and the Italian Lakes

Losses: No reliable figures

A fifteenth-century manuscript depiction of Frederick Barbarossa (below, center) invading Italy.

Legnano 1176 ▷

Tangdao 16 November 1161

In 1132 the Song dynasty rulers of southern China created the country's first permanent navy. This extraordinary force—equipped with gunpowder artillery and including ships propelled by human-powered paddlewheels—enabled the Song to win the crucial Battle of Tangdao in the East China Sea.

Driven out of northern China after the triumph of Jurchen invaders at Kaifeng in 1127, the Song dynasty still controlled the south of the country. In 1161, the Jurchen Jin dynasty planned a seaborne invasion of southern China. Some 70,000 soldiers embarked on a fleet of transports down the coast of China. Their commander, Zheng Jia, was not expecting to engage in a naval battle, a form of warfare of which the Jurchen, as steppe horsemen, had no experience.

The invasion fleet was intercepted by a squadron of Song warships, under the command of Li Bao, among the islands off the Shandong peninsula. The Song force included oared "tower ships" that mounted a trebuchet: a large catapult of the kind used in siege warfare on land. These trebuchets hurled gunpowder projectiles at the Jurchen ships, setting fire to the inflammable vessels. The Song also had smaller, faster ships driven by paddlewheels rotated by crews below deck. As they closed on the enemy, soldiers on board fired crossbows and fire lances—a primitive flamethrower. Much of the Jurchen fleet was soon ablaze. Zheng Jia was among many who drowned leaping into the East China Sea to escape the flames.

This victory, together with a naval success in the same year at Caishi on the Yangtze River, allowed the southern Song to survive for another century, before the dynasty was finally defeated by Kublai Khan's Mongols. **RG**

Losses: No reliable figures; much of the Jurchen fleet of 600 ships destroyed

◁ *Kaifeng 1126* *Xiangyang 1268* ▷

Legnano 29 May 1176

Holy Roman Emperor Frederick Barbarossa's ambition to control Italy came to grief at Legnano. His German knights were humiliated by the citizen soldiers of Milan and other cities of the Lombard League. This victory ushered in the golden age of the Italian city-states, the cradle of the Renaissance.

In spring 1176, Holy Roman Emperor Frederick Barbarossa was campaigning in northern Italy with some 3,000 mounted knights. Henry the Lion, Duke of Saxony and Bavaria, refused to support the campaign, sharply reducing the strength of Barbarossa's army. The citizens of Milan and its Lombard League allies had used their wealth to equip themselves for war. The two armies met at Legnano about 20 miles (32 km) outside Milan.

The key to the battle's outcome was the performance of the disciplined, highly motivated Milanese infantry. Although the German knights easily worsted the Lombard cavalry, they then had to charge the foot soldiers drawn up in tight formation in front of their *caroccio*, an ox-drawn cart carrying the city's standard. Had the infantry formation broken, the armored horsemen would have massacred them, but they stood firm and the knights' charges broke against their bristling pikes.

At the climax of the battle, Barbarossa was unhorsed and disappeared. Believing their emperor dead, the German knights abandoned the field. They were mourning his death in Pavia when he turned up at the gates of the city three days later, battered but alive. In the following years, Barbarossa was obliged to recognize the independence of the Lombard cities. The full weight of his wrath was turned upon Henry the Lion, who was exiled and stripped of his dukedoms. **RG**

Losses: No reliable figures

◁ *Crema 1159*

Uji 23 June 1180

The Battle of Uji was the first encounter of Japan's Genpei War, fought from 1180 to 1185 between samurai of the Taira and Minamoto families. It is renowned for the dramatic suicide of the defeated commander, Minamoto Yorimasa, which set a standard for future generations of samurai.

Rivalry between the Taira and Minamoto families had been growing for some years. The Taira, based mainly in the west of Japan, had married into the imperial family and came to dominate the government. The Minamoto challenged them in 1160 during the so-called Heiji Incident, a minor revolt after which the Minamoto leaders were executed or exiled.

Among the latter was Minamoto Yoritomo, who started a campaign in eastern Japan. While he was still gathering troops in 1180, however, his uncle Minamoto Yorimasa raised his revolt within the monastery of Miidera, where his meager force was supplemented by warrior monks. The Taira advanced against them and—hoping to join up with their fellow monks of Nara—Yorimasa and his troops withdrew to the south, pursued by the Taira, and made a stand at the bridge across the river at Uji.

A long section of planking from the bridge was torn up and the Minamoto awaited a dawn attack. Many deeds of heroism were performed on the broken bridge until the Taira succeeded in crossing by swimming their horses across the river. Yorimasa withdrew to the nearby temple of Byodo-In, where his sons held off the enemy. After writing a farewell poem on his war fan—a fan designed for use in warfare—he then committed hara-kiri, an act that was to be regarded as the exemplar of how a defeated samurai should end his life. **ST**

Losses: Taira, very few, mainly from individual combat; Minamoto, considerable, particularly during the pursuit

Kurikara 1183 [>]

Kurikara 1–2 June 1183

The Battle of Kurikara (or Tonamiyama) was the point at which the tide of Japan's Genpei War turned against the Taira. It is famous for the deception shown by Minamoto Yoshinaka, resulting in a victory that left the road to the imperial capital of Kyoto open to the Minamoto army.

Minamoto Yoshinaka was the cousin of Minamoto Yoritomo, and began his contribution to the defeat of the Taira when he raised a rebellion in the mountainous center of Japan. The Taira sent an expeditionary force—under Taira Koremori, the nobleman son of a great warrior, from Kyoto—against him, and made excellent progress until they reached the mountainous border between Kaga and Echigo provinces.

Yoshinaka allowed them to proceed unmolested into the mountain pass of Kurikara, where he forced them to halt by rigging up an array of dummy flags. He then kept them in position by conducting a formalized battle involving individual arrow duels and challenges to combat. This was enthusiastically joined by the Taira samurai, who enjoyed the fights in classic samurai style, unaware that they were being held in a trap.

Meanwhile a group of Yoshinaka's samurai made their way along winding mountain paths to the Taira rear. When all was ready, Yoshinaka unleashed a herd of oxen along the pass. They had burning brands attached to their horns, and their panic disordered the Taira ranks. Many samurai were knocked down into the valley below, and then Yoshinaka's forces attacked from both sides. The main means of escape was a narrow gully that appeared to promise safety, but which turned out to be a further death trap. The few survivors fled back toward Kyoto with Yoshinaka's victorious troops in pursuit. **ST**

Losses: Minamoto, few, mainly during individual combat; Taira, considerable

[<] *Uji 1180*   *Mizushima 1183* [>]

Mizushima 17 November 1183

The Battle of Mizushima, one of the lesser-known encounters of the twelfth-century Genpei War in Japan, is significant because it was a naval battle fought using land-based tactics—archery and swordsmanship—the forms of combat most prized by the samurai of the Taira and the Minamoto.

Following the death of warrior leader Minamoto Yorimasa —he committed suicide after defeat at the Battle of Uji in 1180—the Genpei War continued in areas distant from the imperial capital. Having lost central Japan to Yoshinaka, the Taira concentrated their resources in three bases, each of which had easy access to the Inland Sea.

One of these bases was Yashima on the island of Shikoku, which allowed them to exploit their superiority at naval warfare. Seeking to destroy this base, Minamoto Yoshinaka sent an army under his general, Yada Yoshiyasu, from the nearby island of Mizushima in the Inland Sea opposite Shikoku. Unlike the Taira, who had risen to power partly because of their expertise in driving pirates from the Inland Sea, the Minamoto were inexperienced at fighting from ships. Taira Tomomori and Taira Noritsune sailed out to meet them, and before encountering the Minamoto fleet they tied their ships together using ropes and stretched planks across them. This enabled the Taira to engage the Minamoto on a flat platform where sword-fighting skills could be best shown.

The battle began with a duel of arrows. Then numerous individual encounters with swords took place on the artificial battlefield, off which the wounded would have drowned. The Minamoto were hopelessly outclassed. They eventually disengaged their ships and withdrew to the mainland. From this time on, raids on the Taira bases were launched from the land, with attempts being made to prevent escape by sea. **ST**

Losses: Unknown; high casualties on both sides

◁ *Kurikara 1183*   *Dan no Ura 1185* ▷

The Minamoto and Taira samurai in battle in Echigo province, Japan, in an 1850 woodcut. ⬆

Dan no Ura 24–25 April 1185

This sea battle, fought in the straits of Shimonoseki, was a decisive encounter resulting in the triumph of the Minamoto in the Genpei War and the foundation of the Minamoto shogunate, or military dictatorship. It also provided a rich vein of samurai tradition, legends, and ghost stories.

Throughout the Genpei War, the Taira family's superiority in naval matters had allowed them to escape from otherwise crushing defeats on land. By 1185, they had been driven out of all their other bases to seek safety on an island at the western end of the Inland Sea, close to the narrow strait of Shimonoseki that divides Japan's main island of Honshu from Kyushu.

In 1185, the Minamoto—who, by now, had acquired naval expertise of their own—sailed against the Taira. On being approached by the Minamoto fleet under Minamoto Yoshitsune, the Taira took to their ships and were so confident of victory that they kept the infant Emperor Antoku on board with them. At first, the battle —fought within sight of land at the beach of Dan no Ura, off the southern tip of Honshu—went their way. But when the tide turned, a traitor general among the Taira declared for the Minamoto cause. Many individual combats took place, including a pursuit of Minamoto Yoshitsune from boat to boat.

When the battle appeared lost, the young emperor's grandmother drowned him by jumping into the sea with the child in her arms. Many more suicides followed, and the result was the complete extinction of the Taira family, whose only surviving supporters became fugitives. The spirits of the dead Taira were believed to reside in the crabs with warriorlike faces that inhabited the shore, and many stories of ghostly sightings developed. **ST**

Losses: Taira, almost total; Minamoto, few by comparison

◁ *Mizushima 1183*　*First Mongol Invasion of Japan 1274* ▷

⬆ *The Battle of Dan no Ura shown in a nineteenth-century Japanese woodcut.*

Hattin   4 July 1187

Muslim warrior Saladin's crushing defeat of the army of the crusader states at Hattin in 1187 sent shock waves through the Christian world. It opened the way for Saladin to retake Jerusalem, lost to the Christians in 1099, and triggered the counteroffensive of the Third Crusade.

By 1187 Egypt, Damascus, Mosul, and Aleppo—the major centers of Muslim power throughout the Holy Land—had been united under the Kurdish leader Saladin. On 2 July, Saladin laid siege to the Christian stronghold of Tiberias. King Guy of Jerusalem thought this gave him a chance to catch Saladin far from his base. Count Raymond of Tiberias assured that his wife, Eschiva, could hold the castle perfectly well and that the crusaders should remain in a strong defensive position at Sephoria.

Guy ignored him and the army left Sephoria at dawn on 3 July, camping for the night on a pair of curved hills known as the Horns of Hattin where there was no source of water. Late in the night, Saladin ordered the grass to

> *"Saladin's victory ... destroyed the Latin field army, and without it, the isolated strongholds proved vulnerable."* Jim Bradbury, The Medieval Siege

be set alight sending clouds of choking smoke into the crusader camp. At dawn a force of mounted archers rode up to pour showers of arrows into the crusader camp. Most of the 14,000 Christian foot soldiers grabbed their weapons and fell back to the hilltop without orders. Guy ordered them to form up to advance, but they refused and squatted on the waterless hilltop. The 2,000 knights and mounted men at arms, however, charged and drove off the mounted archers. They reformed and together with the 2,000 or so light cavalry charged again, and

again. Each time the crusader cavalry hoped to break through the Muslim lines to reach Lake Tiberias and slake their growing thirsts.

By noon the fighting was becoming less coordinated as individual lords and their followers launched charges at the Muslims. The crusader cavalry managed to inflict some casualties, but without their infantry were unable to make any lasting gains. Some charges were made toward springs of fresh water at the nearby village of Hattin, but these were no more successful than attempts to reach the lake. A few groups of crusaders managed to break out of the tightening circle of Muslims, but were then unable or unwilling to break back in again with supplies of water.

Among these was Count Raymond, who rode north to Tripoli on the coast. Fighting died down at night, and several groups of crusaders slipped away under cover of darkness. The battle resumed at dawn, but the crusaders were now exhausted and collapsing through thirst. The Bishop of Acre lifted the True Cross over his head and led a renewed assault. He was killed, the True Cross captured, and most of those involved in the attack were killed.

Toward noon, Guy surrendered. His men simply could not stand up any longer. Saladin ordered the execution of the Knights Templar, together with a few other individuals that he named. The remainder of the crusader army was sold into slavery. Guy and a few nobles were later ransomed. Within two months of his victory at Hattin, Saladin had captured Tiberias, Acre, Nablus, Jaffa, Sidon, Beirut, and Ascalon. Finally, on 2 October, he captured Jerusalem. When news of Hattin and the fall of Jerusalem reached Rome, Pope Urban III died of shock. His successor, Gregory VIII, called for a Third Crusade to recover the Holy Land. **RM**

Losses: Crusader, 17,000 dead or captured of 20,000; Muslim, unknown of 30,000

◁ *Damascus 1148*   *Acre 1189* ▷

In a twentieth-century painting by S. Tahssin, a crusader surrenders to Saladin, who let King Guy sit beside him.

Acre   4 October 1189

Fall of Acre   July 1191

The battle fought at Acre on 4 October 1189, during the siege of that city, was a bloody engagement that displayed the crushing power of a charge by crusader mounted knights on lightly armored Muslims. It was also a lesson in the values of discipline and the costs of prematurely enjoying victory.

Acre had been put under siege by Christian forces in October 1189. The Muslim warrior Saladin arrived with a relief army and besieged the besiegers. The city's defenses were finally reduced after the arrival of fresh crusading armies from Europe—its fall was the occasion for a notorious massacre.

After defeat at Hattin, the Christians held Tripoli, Antioch, and a few other strongholds. King Guy of Jerusalem laid siege to the Muslim-held port-city of Acre so that it could form a base for the expected Third Crusade. Saladin led a relieving force that was driven off on 15 September, but he returned with a larger army on 4 October.

Saladin had his army in three divisions, commanding the center himself with the right wing under Taqi ad-Din. Guy left a strong force to guard his camp against a sally from Acre, and then advanced in three divisions with the Templars on the left. Guy pushed forward his infantry and crossbowmen to engage the Muslims and probe for weaknesses to be exploited by charges of heavily armored mounted knights. The Templars charged first, sweeping Taqi ad-Din from the field. In the center and right Guy's advance was slower, but repeated charges by knights eventually caused the Muslim army to flee.

The crusaders surged forward to pillage the enemy camp, but Saladin was rallying his light cavalry in nearby hills. Some 5,000 men from Acre sallied out but, instead of attacking the crusader camp, they headed north. There they ran into the Templars, returning from their pursuit of Tariq ad-Din. Both sides lost heavily in the confused struggle that ensued. Later in the day, Saladin returned to attack the scattered crusaders and inflict heavy casualties on them before Guy's camp guard moved up to drive the Muslims off. The Siege of Acre continued. **RM**

The fall of Jerusalem to Saladin inspired the three most prominent rulers of Christian Europe—Philip Augustus of France, Richard the Lionheart of England, and German Emperor Frederick Barbarossa—to embark on the Third Crusade. Frederick died en route, but Philip and Richard reached the Holy Land in April and June 1191 respectively.

Joining in the Siege of Acre, they brought great catapults capable of battering breaches in the city walls and built a massive wooden siege tower. Each time a breach was made, however, Saladin launched an attack on the ramparts and ditches with which the crusaders had surrounded their camp, forcing them to divert men from assaulting the breach to defensive duties. Suffering from disease and quarreling among themselves instead of cooperating, the crusaders were in poor shape by the start of July. The Muslim defenders of Acre, however, were in even worse condition.

The Genoese and Pisan ships in which Richard had arrived were able to complete the blockade of the port-city from the sea. Without supplies, surrender was inevitable. On 11 July, the city's garrison held out against a furious Christian assault. The following day they surrendered with the promise that their lives would be spared. Negotiations with Saladin over an exchange of prisoners stalled, however, and a month after the city's fall Richard ordered the 2,700 Muslims under his command to be killed, along with their wives and children. **RG**

Losses: Crusader, 6,000 dead or captured of 12,000; Muslim, 2,500 of 20,000

◁ Hattin 1187

Fall of Acre 1191 ▷

Losses: Crusader, light casualties of 25,000; Muslim, unknown

◁ Acre 1189

Arsuf 1191 ▷

Arsuf 7 September 1191

The Battle of Arsuf was an exhibition of the military and leadership skills of England's crusading King Richard the Lionheart. Richard's Muslim opponent, Saladin, held the strategic initiative, however, and although tactically defeated avoided any major negative consequences.

On 24 August 1191, after the Fall of Acre, Richard led a 20,000-strong force southward down the coast road to lay siege to Jaffa, which he intended to use as a base for attacking Jerusalem. His army moved slowly in the extreme heat, accompanied by supply ships off shore. The crusader column was shadowed by Saladin and his army on higher ground inland.

The Muslims launched a series of attacks on the left flank and rearguard of the crusaders, hoping to break their formation. Richard arranged his marching army in five divisions with the elite Knights of the Templars as the advance guard and the Hospitallers forming the rearguard. The knights were shielded on the landward side by the infantry, including crossbowmen. To keep formation, Richard instructed that no counterattack was to be launched against the Muslim skirmishers without his order.

On 7 September, Saladin launched a major assault on the crusader rearguard. The Hospitallers charged without Richard's order to drive off the attack. Richard then launched all his knights, except the Templars, in a massed charge that caught many of the Muslim cavalry dismounted and skirmishing on foot. Richard himself was in the thick of the fighting, in the words of a chronicler "cutting down the Saracens like a reaper with his sickle." Saladin ordered his army to withdraw, apparently shaken by the ferocity and effectiveness of the crusader knights. Richard continued his march to Jaffa unmolested. **RM**

Losses: Crusader, 700 of 20,000; Muslim, more than 7,000 of 45,000

◁ Fall of Acre 1191   Jaffa 1192 ▷

Jaffa 5 August 1192

The final battle of the Third Crusade led directly to a peace deal between England's King Richard the Lionheart and Muslim leader Saladin that restricted the Christian presence in the Holy Land to a thin coastal strip, but ensured its survival for another century.

After his victory at Arsuf, Richard spent months capturing castles and winning skirmishes, but never reached his goal of retaking Jerusalem. He was in Acre planning his return to England when, in late July, Saladin attacked Jaffa, taking the town but not the citadel. Richard arrived unexpectedly by sea with a force including 80 knights and 400 crossbowmen and waded ashore to drive the Muslims out of the town.

A few days later Saladin attacked Richard's camp outside Jaffa at dawn. Richard put his infantry in the front line and the crossbowmen behind them with orders to aim at the enemy horses. Richard and seventeen mounted knights were positioned at the rear ready to deliver a charge where and when it would do the most good. The sixty-three knights without horses were put among the infantry. Several Muslim cavalry charges were driven off with loss. Richard countercharged several times to cut down dismounted Muslims and hasten the retreat of the rest. In a chivalrous gesture, Saphadin, Saladin's brother, noticing Richard's horse was wounded, sent him a fresh mount.

About mid-afternoon Saladin launched a ferocious assault designed to mask a column of cavalry hurrying around Richard's flank to make a surprise attack on Jaffa. Richard saw the move and led his mounted knights back to block the city gates. Desultory fighting continued until nightfall, when Saladin retreated from Jaffa and then opened peace negotiations. **RM**

Losses: Crusader, 2 dead of 80 knights and a small number of 2,000 infantry; Muslim, 700 dead of 7,000

◁ Arsuf 1191   Constantinople 1204 ▷

Alarcos   18 July 1195

The Battle of Alarcos was fought in the southern Spanish region of Seville between the Almohad Moors of al-Andalus, led by Abu Yusuf al-Mansur, and the forces of Alfonso VIII, king of Castile. Alfonso's heavy defeat at Alarcos was a disaster for Castile and a major setback for the Reconquista.

In the late 1180s, the Almohad caliph, Abu Yusuf al-Mansur, had been hard pressed to deal with problems in North Africa while at the same time defending his Iberian possessions against the Reconquista. A brief truce between al-Mansur and the kingdoms of Castile and Leon provided temporary respite but, in 1190, the expiration of the truce coincided with renewed unrest in Marrakech.

In the absence of the caliph, King Alfonso attacked al-Andalus, sacking several Moorish towns. Caliph al-Mansur responded by crossing the Strait of Gibraltar with his Almohad army in 1195, moving rapidly northward. Alarmed by the speed of the Moors, Alfonso made a tactical error by not waiting for reinforcements from the king of Leon. Instead he assembled his army and marched south from Toledo to engage al-Mansur's larger force. The two armies met at Alarcos near the banks of the River Guadiana, on the present-day Portuguese-Spanish border.

Alfonso gambled on a huge cavalry charge, a tactic that won much success in the Reconquista. At first, the king's gamble seemed to work, smashing the Almohad lines. However, al-Mansur's force was large, and its huge contingent of archers continually rained down missiles on the heavily armored knights, who struggled in the heat. The charge faltered; Alfonso was outflanked and forced to retreat, losing much of the army of Castile. The defeat was a severe turnaround for Castile and halted the progress of the Reconquista for nearly twenty years. **TB**

"An innumerable quantity of arrows flew across the air and . . . hurt the Christians with a deadly blow." Latin Chronicle of the Kings of Castile

The Almohad governor of Seville (seated) holds a council of war in his fortified castle before recalling caliph al-Mansur to Spain.

Losses: No reliable figures

Lisbon 1147   Las Navas de Tolosa 1212

Constantinople   April 1204

The diversion of the Fourth Crusade from the Holy Land to attack, capture, and pillage the Byzantine city of Constantinople divided and dissipated the efforts of the Christians to maintain the war against the Muslims. It is widely regarded as a shocking betrayal of principles out of greed.

The Fourth Crusade was corrupted from its purpose early on. In order to repay Venice for shipping most of the crusaders eastward, they were obliged to seize Zara on the Adriatic from Christian Hungary on Venice's behalf. Meanwhile exiled Byzantine prince Alexius offered a cash reward if he were put on the Byzantine throne.

The crusaders therefore sailed to Constantinople and in July 1203 set up Alexius as emperor. In February 1204 the new emperor was murdered and replaced by courtier Alexius Doucas, who told the crusaders to leave. The crusaders responded by laying siege to Constantinople. A first assault on the city's defenses was repelled with heavy losses, but on 12 April the crusaders were successful. Men swarmed up the masts of ships and scrambled across catwalks to reach the tops of the city walls. Other ships landed men on the shoreline to hack at a bricked-up gateway with picks and shovels. When a hole was broken through, Aleaumes of Clari crawled in to find the street beyond almost deserted. Hundreds of crusaders came through the enlarged hole, fought their way to a main gate, and opened it to their comrades. For three days the army pillaged at will, and then the nobles imposed order and began a more systematic looting of the greatest city in Christendom. The crusader nobleman Baldwin of Flanders was set up as emperor, but most Byzantines refused to recognize him and the empire fragmented into four quarreling states. **RM**

Losses: Crusader, unknown of 20,000; Byzantine, unknown of 30,000, plus unknown civilian losses

◁ Jaffa 1192   Damietta 1219 ▷

Béziers   21 July 1209

This brutal massacre was the first major battle in the Albigensian Crusade called by Pope Innocent III against the Cathars, a religious sect. The French city of Béziers, a Cathar stronghold, was burned down and 20,000 residents killed after a papal legate, the Abbot of Cîteaux, declared, "Slaughter them all!"

The Cathars—also known as "Albigensians" after the French town of Albi, sometimes identified as their headquarters—were "dualists," meaning that they believed in two gods: a greater embodiment of goodness and a less powerful evil deity that created the world. Emerging in 1000–50, they established their own church in c. 1140 and by the late twelfth century had eleven bishops in France and Italy with a large number of followers in the Languedoc region of southern France. Cathars denied the divinity of Christ and the authority of the pope; the Roman Catholic Church declared them heretics in 1176.

Pope Innocent III sent preachers to convert the Cathars, but called a crusade after his legate, Pierre of Castelnau, was killed in January 1208. Many were attracted to the crusade by Innocent's declaration that they would be entitled to keep any land seized from heretics. In 1209 the 10,000-strong crusade army gathered in Lyon and marched south under command of another papal legate, Arnaud Amalric, Abbot of Cîteaux. Arriving at Béziers, the crusaders called for the surrender of the Cathars and local Catholics. The defenders of the city made a sortie to attack the besieging army, but were overwhelmed and the crusaders poured through the open gates of the city. The abbot wrote to the pope, "The city was put to the sword. So did God's vengeance give vent to its wondrous rage." Nevertheless, Cathar resistance remained strong elsewhere and the crusade lasted twenty years. **CP**

Losses: Albigensian, and citizens, 20,000; Crusader, minimal of 10,000

Muret 1213 ▷

Las Navas de Tolosa 16 July 1212

Las Navas de Tolosa was a decisive encounter between the Christian allies of Castile, Navarre, Aragon, and Portugal against the Moorish Almohad forces of the Iberian Peninsula. The battle was an important victory for the Reconquista and hastened the decline of the Almohad Empire.

Following the disastrous defeat at Alarcos in 1195, the kingdom of Castile was weakened and the Almohads forced the surrender of key fortresses in southern Iberia. For a time, it appeared that the Almohad Moors might take Toledo and move northward. However, their aging and ailing leader, al-Mansur, wished to return to North Africa, and Toledo escaped capture. With the Reconquista stalled, Moorish al-Andalus seemed secure enough for al-Mansur's successor, Muhammad an-Nasir, to bring an army to Iberia in 1211 with the objective

of restoring Moorish control in northern Iberia. After a number of Muslim victories, most notably the capture of the stronghold of the Order of the Calatrava of Castile at Salvatierra in the north, the future of the Christian kingdoms in Spain seemed bleak. In response, Pope Innocent III called Europe to arms in a crusade against the Moors to revitalize the Reconquista. This led to an alliance of the rival Christian kingdoms of Castile, Navarre, Aragon, and Portugal, with knights from France also joining the army led by Castile's Alfonso VIII.

The Christians were disunited and quarrelsome. Many were unhappy at fighting under the banner of Castile and some deserted in disgust at Alfonso's lenient treatment of Moorish and Jewish prisoners. However, despite deep divisions, the crusaders approached an-Nasir's camp in the summer of 1212, which he had established on a high plain behind a canyon—an apparently impregnable

defensive position. However, using a path known only to local shepherds, the Christians outflanked the canyon and sprang a surprise attack on an-Nasir's camp. The Muslims fought largely as lightly armed skirmishers, their bowmen trying to wear down the Christian knights by attrition without engaging at close quarters. However, at the climax of the battle Alfonso ordered his reserve of armored knights to charge and the horsemen turned the tide decisively in the crusaders' favor.

Medieval chronicles tell how a force led by King Sancho VII of Navarre broke through the caliph's bodyguard, causing the Almohad leader to flee and slaying the slaves who were chained together to defend him. As in all battles linked to the events concerning the birth of a nation and the clash of religions, statistics written in subsequent years concerning the size of the forces that fought and the relative casualties must be treated with caution. Nevertheless, there is little doubt that the battle was a crushing victory for the Christian alliance. A large proportion of the caliph's army perished in the summer heat and the rest were forced to retreat. After the capture of key fortified towns in the south, the Moorish territory of al-Andalus tottered on the brink of defeat and the Almohad military machine was severely weakened.

The years following the Battle of Las Navas de Tolosa saw the Christians capture Cordova, Seville, and ultimately Cadiz. By the late 1240s, the Almohad Empire was practically extinct and most of the Iberian Peninsula lay in Christian hands. **TB**

Losses: No reliable figures; Crusader, 2,000 claimed of 50,000; Muslim, 100,000 claimed of 200,000

◁ *Alarcos 1195*　　　　　　　　　　*Rio Salado 1340* ▷

Muret   12 September 1213

In a major victory for the Albigensian Crusade against the Cathars, French nobleman Simon IV de Montfort defeated Raymond VI of Toulouse and King Peter II of Aragon. Peter—a celebrated crusader against the Islamic Moors in Spain—was killed, dealing a heavy blow to the Cathar cause.

The crusade began as a religious war but developed political overtones as northern French barons set out to seize land in southern France. The crusaders won a series of victories following the massacre at Béziers in July 1209: French nobleman Simon IV de Montfort took control of the campaign after arguing with Raymond VI of Toulouse.

In 1211 Raymond was excommunicated and embarked on liberating more than thirty towns for the Cathar cause. Then in 1213 Raymond's brother-in-law, King Peter II of Aragon, brought an army of 30,000–40,000 infantry and around 4,000 cavalry to France to support Raymond in besieging Montfort's fortress at Muret. Montfort led an army of 870 cavalry and around 700 infantry out from Muret, dividing his force into three squadrons.

Raymond suggested setting up in a defensive formation, then harrying Montfort's troops with crossbow fire before counterattacking and driving them back into Muret. However, King Peter declared this unchivalrous and opted to attack. He himself fought in the front line, wearing the armor of one of his knights.

In Montfort's first charge, the Aragonese cavalry was overwhelmed, and King Peter was knocked from his horse and then killed, despite identifying himself as the king. The Aragonese army broke and fled, relentlessly pursued by Montfort's cavalry. Peter's death was a shock, and Raymond was forced to flee into exile in England, but Cathar resistance revived swiftly. **CP**

"The signal defeat of the Albigensian heretics at the Battle of Muret in 1213 … legend has attributed to the recitation of the Rosary by St. Dominic."

H. Thurston, The Catholic Encyclopedia *(1912)*

The forces of Simon IV de Montfort pitched against Raymond VI of Toulouse at Muret, from the Grandes Chroniques de France.

Losses: Crusader, few of 1,600; Toulouse and Aragonese, up to 20,000 of up to 45,000

◁ Béziers 1209   Toulouse 1217 ▷

Beijing (Zhongdu) 1214–15

Sweeping southward from the steppes of central Asia, Mongol emperor Genghis Khan and his army besieged Beijing (then Zhongdu), the former capital of China's ruling Jin dynasty. After a siege of several months, the army captured the city, establishing Mongol control of northern China.

The campaign of 1214–15 was the fourth Mongol invasion of the Jin empire of northern China in just three years. Genghis Khan—born Temüjin c. 1162—had established his power over the nomadic tribes of Mongolia and in 1206 established himself as khan or emperor of all the steppe peoples.

During the third invasion, in 1213, the Mongols had besieged Beijing: this fortified city was formidable, with clay walls forty feet (12 m) tall, 900 towers, and three moats—and the Mongols knew little of siege warfare. Genghis Khan lifted the siege after accepting lavish tribute from the Jin emperor, Xuan Zong, but when Xuan Zong moved the capital south to Kaifeng (Nanching), Genghis Khan invaded in autumn 1214 with an army of 50,000 and besieged Beijing once more: this time he had the assistance of rebel Jin forces and siege machines.

The defense of Beijing lay in the hands of prince Shu Zong along with two generals, Fu Xing and Moran Jinzhong. After a Jin relief army of 39,000 men was defeated near Heijang by a Mongol force of just 3,000, Fu Xing committed suicide while his fellow general and the crown prince fled; the terrified people of Beijing stayed put within the city. As the months passed, they grew desperate and reputedly resorted to cannibalism. By the time the city surrendered in May 1215, Genghis Khan had returned to his summer capital of Xanadu. Beijing was sacked and looted by his army, and burned for a month. **CP**

"The Jin khan . . . offered 500 young men and women, 3,000 horses, and massive wealth, and Genghis Khan agreed to go home. When the Jin khan fled to Kaifeng, Genghis Khan felt betrayed."

Sanderson Beck, China, Korea, and Japan to 1800

Losses: Mongol, unknown of 50,000; Jin, many thousands through months of starvation and deprivation

A fifteenth-century Persian miniature of Mongolian horsemen in battle.

◁ Tangdao 1161   Kalka River 1222 ▷

Bouvines   27 July 1214

French king Philip II Augustus defeated a coalition of Holy Roman Emperor Otto IV, King John of England, and Counts Ferdinand of Flanders and Renaud of Boulogne. The victory strengthened the standing of the French crown, confirming its sovereignty over Brittany and Normandy.

The coalition's leaders planned for Otto, Ferdinand, and Renaud to march on Paris from the north, while John would land in western France and march from there. However, after John was defeated by royal troops near Angers on 2 July, Philip Augustus confronted the northern army on the plain near Bouvines in Flanders. Otto deployed his army of around 25,000 facing southwest, with knights in two groups on the flank, infantry in the center, and a reserve of cavalry to the rear; Philip's forces, 15,000 strong, took up an identical formation.

The battle began with cavalry fighting on the French right wing. In the center, the imperial army—containing powerful infantry from the Low Countries—drove forward, but the central French cavalry, commanded by Philip, forced the imperial infantry back. The French triumphed on their left wing, and William Longsword—Earl of Salisbury—was taken prisoner. The French cavalry were also victorious on the right, and Count Ferdinand of Flanders was captured. Finally, in the center, the two blocks of mounted reserves met and France triumphed once more: the two wings closed in to cut off the retreat of the imperial army's central parts. Renaud of Boulogne made a brave last stand but was eventually captured.

In the aftermath, Emperor Otto was deposed by Frederick II Hohenstaufen, and King John was so badly weakened that he was forced to sign the Magna Carta charter of rights. **CP**

Losses: French, 1,000 of 15,000; Coalition, 1,000 dead and 9,000 captured of 25,000

Dover 1217 ▶

The Battle of Bouvines, painted in a Romantic style by nineteenth-century artist Horace Vernet.

Dover 24 August 1217

For an island nation, defeat at sea could mean invasion and conquest. The battle that took place in the Straits of Dover in 1217 saved England from French occupation, but it has also gone down in history as the first battle fought by sailing ships in the open sea.

King John of England had clashed regularly with his leading barons and, in June 1215, was forced to sign the Magna Carta (Great Charter), an agreement guaranteeing baronial, church, and other rights in relation to the crown. The decree by Pope Innocent III two months later, which declared that John need not adhere to the charter, caused the barons to rise in revolt. They sought French help against John, promising the throne to Prince Louis of France. Louis landed in Kent while the rebellious barons seized the Tower of London.

After John's death in 1216, the rebel army was defeated at Lincoln by William Marshal—regent for the new young king, Henry III—and forced onto the defensive. In the south, the French were more successful and managed to besiege Marshal and his supporters in Dover. A French invasion fleet of seventy supply ships and ten escorting warships crossed the English Channel but was met by a forty-strong English fleet, led by Hubert de Burgh, that had sailed out of Dover. The English fleet first sailed past the French before turning to attack them in the rear, grappling the enemy ships before boarding them.

The French commander, Eustace the Monk, was found hiding in the bilges, or bottom of the ship's hull, and was immediately executed as the English towed sixty-five French ships into Dover. With his fleet captured, Louis was forced to abandon his invasion of England and made peace later in the year. **SA**

Losses: English, none of 40 ships; French, 65 of 80 ships captured

◁ *Bouvines 1214*   *Evesham 1265* ▷

⬆ *An English ship maneuvers into close battle off the coast of Dover in this drawing from 1754.*

Toulouse 1217–18

Damietta 1219

Simon IV de Montfort, military leader of the Albigensian Crusade against the Cathars in southern France, mounted a siege of Cathar sympathizer Raymond VI of Toulouse. Montfort's death effectively ended the siege and severely weakened the crusade leadership.

The encounter at Damietta in 1219 was one of the few pitched battles of the poorly organized Fifth Crusade. It exposed the weaknesses of divided command and showed the difficulties crusaders had in achieving any strategic advantage, even when they held a position in the Muslim heartland.

For two years after his victory at the Battle of Muret, Simon IV de Montfort led the troops of the Albigensian Crusade in victories over the Cathars: in 1216 he captured Toulouse and proclaimed himself count while the rightful count, Raymond VI of Toulouse, was in exile in England. Raymond returned that same year and recaptured Beaucaire before he retook Toulouse on 7 November, 1217. Montfort besieged the city, but found its defenses robust and well manned.

In spring 1218 the defenders of Toulouse built a trebuchet (artillery engine) while the besiegers built a cat (wooden tower used to scale city walls). On 25 June 1218, the defenders broke out to destroy the cat and, during the fighting, Simon de Montfort was fatally injured when he was hit on the head by a large stone, probably launched from the trebuchet. The siege was lifted soon afterward; leadership of the crusade passed to one of Simon's sons, Amaury VI de Montfort.

The French king, Louis VIII, led a fresh wave of the crusade in 1226, and Cathar resistance dwindled. Under Louis VIII's successor, Louis IX, a 1229 peace treaty ended the crusade: Raymond VII of Toulouse (son of Raymond VI) was recognized as count of Toulouse but was forced to give his castles into royal control and to undertake to suppress the Cathars. Cathar resistance continued until March 1244 when their castle, Montségur, was captured and 220 Cathars were burned at the stake as heretics. **CP**

King John of Jerusalem brought a small force to join a mixed German-Dutch-Italian army—under the papal legate Pelagius of Albano and Oliver of Cologne—to invade Egypt, ruled by the Ayyubid dynasty, the main opposition to the crusader states in the Holy Land.

The crusaders laid siege to the port of Damietta to gain a supply base before marching inland. When a relief army under Sultan Al Kamil arrived, Pelagius ignored King John's advice and ordered an attack. King John commanded the right with his men, plus a force of Templars; the center was formed by Oliver commanding the Germans and Dutch; Pelagius commanded the left. After a short fight, the Muslim center fell back, luring the crusader center forward where it could be outflanked.

At the same time, a force of Bedouin horsemen raced around the crusader right to attack the Christian camp. King John saw them and sent some of his knights to head them off. Pelagius saw the move, concluded John was retreating, and ordered his own men to fall back, a move that soon became a rout. The Germans in the center realized they were about to be outflanked and ran in turn. King John moved forward with his men to block the Muslim advance and allow the disorganized crusaders to flee to the camp. Al Kamil pulled his army back a few weeks later and Damietta surrendered. Yet the crusaders drew no advantage from this success and were later defeated on an attempted march to Cairo. **RM**

Losses: Unknown

Losses: Crusader, 300 knights and 2,000 infantry of 15,000; Egyptian, unknown of 20,000

◁ *Muret 1213*

◁ *Constantinople 1204*   *Harbiyah 1244* ▷

Crusaders disembark in Egypt—from the fifteenth-century Le Miroir Historial, *by Vincent de Beauvais.*

Kalka River June 1222

During the first Mongol invasion of Russia, an army led by Jebei and Subedei defeated an alliance of Russian princes and the Cuman tribal group. The victory, part of a prolonged raiding campaign, devastated the Russian princes' armies and demonstrated the raw power of the Mongol cavalry.

In 1221 Mongolian generals Jebei and Subedei led an army of 20,000 on a raid through Azerbaijan, into Georgia and along the Caspian Sea into Russia. The raiders defeated an alliance of Turkic tribes from the steppes, including the Alans, Cherkes, and Kipchaks, then wiped out two armies of Cumans (another Turkish tribe); the few Cuman survivors appealed for help to Russian princes.

These princes—including Mstislav III of Kiev, Mstislav of Galich, and Yuri II of Vladimir-Suzdal—raised an army of 30,000 men in alliance with the Cumans and, by advancing on three separate fronts, attempted to encircle the Mongol force on the banks of the River Dnieper. The Mongols made a feigned retreat to the east, leaving a rearguard of 1,000 men to fight under the command of Hamabek; this rearguard was wiped out by an army commanded by Mstislav of Galich, who then pursued the main Mongol force.

After nine days in retreat, the Mongols turned to engage Mstislav on the banks of the Kalka River (probably the modern Kalchik River). They attacked the Russian army head-on and on the flanks, with typical ferocity. The Cumans fled, causing disarray in the Russian ranks, and the Mongols swept through the gap this created. Afterward Jebei and Subedei forced the surrender of the Russian contingent under Mstislav of Kiev and pursued the remnants of Mstislav of Galich's army, before giving up the chase and allowing him to escape. **CP**

Losses: Russian, 20,000 of 30,000; Mongol, very few

◁ Beijing 1214 Kaifeng 1232 ▷

Kaifeng 1232–33

A Mongol army commanded by Subedei captured the northern Chinese Jin dynasty capital, Kaifeng, overcoming defenders equipped with gunpowder bombs. The Jin emperor committed suicide, handing control of Jin territories in northern China to the recently elected Mongol khan, Ogödei.

Although the Mongols captured Beijing (Zhongdu) in 1215, the Jin maintained resistance. After Genghis Khan's death in 1227 and the election of his son, Ogödei, as supreme khan in 1229, they attempted to reassert themselves. Jin leaders recaptured territory in Shensi Province and Honan and built fortresses along the Huang Ho (Yellow River), manned by a defensive army of 300,000. The Mongols launched a three-pronged invasion, with one army under Ogödei's brother Tolui passing with permission through Song territory in the south.

The invaders began a siege of the vast city of Kaifeng in summer 1232. The defenders reportedly used a "thunder bomb," an iron vessel containing gunpowder that was fired by a large catapult and on explosion either blew attackers to pieces or injured them with flying debris. They also used cannon. In the course of the siege, Tolui was taken ill and died, leaving the campaign in the hands of Subedei. He requested reinforcements from the Song, and—after the arrival of a Song army of 20,000—victory was inevitable. The defenders were weakened by famine and illness, and many thousands died within the city.

The Jin emperor Ai-tsung ceded control to his general Tsui Lui, then fled and committed suicide. The city surrendered but, under orders from Ogödei, the Mongols did not massacre the population. Nonetheless, the Jin dynasty was at an end and northern China was in the possession of the Mongols. **CP**

Losses: Mongol, unknown; Jin, thousands of subjects died during the siege, thousands more escaped when the city fell

◁ Kalka River 1222 Xiangyang 1268 ▷

Saule 22 September 1236

Saule was a battle of the Northern Crusades, a series of Christian campaigns against pagan peoples around the Baltic. The crushing defeat of the Order of the Knights of the Sword (or Livonian Knights) at the hands of the pagan Lithuanians and Samogitians destroyed the Order.

The Livonian Knights were already subject to papal criticism for their brutal treatment of converts and their acquisitive, rather than spiritual, agenda when a party of crusaders from Holstein arrived among them and demanded to be led on a campaign against the pagans. They undertook a raid deep into Samogitian territory and were returning heavily laden with loot when they encountered a large party of Lithuanians and Samogitians barring their way at a river crossing.

An immediate attack to break through was the obvious solution, but the ground was swampy, and the knights did not want to risk losing their horses by charging across it. They disdained to fight on foot, so they simply set up camp and surrendered the initiative. The next day Lithuanian light cavalry attacked. Fast moving and hurling javelins, they easily outmaneuvered the heavily armored knights, who were soon taking substantial losses. This course of events appears to have so shaken the auxiliary troops—recruited (perhaps forcibly) by the knights from their conquered peoples—that they broke and fled.

It was the first serious defeat the knights had suffered and it triggered a revolt among the conquered peoples; the Samogitians cut down many knights as they fled. The battle and the revolt it caused gave birth to a mythology of the underlying unity of the Baltic peoples. As for the broken Order, the survivors were forced by Rome to merge with the Teutonic Knights. **JS**

Losses: Livonian Knights, 50 to 60 dead, auxiliary, unknown; Pagan, unknown

Lake Peipus 1242 ▷

The Neva 15 July 1240

Some battles are significant for the imprint they leave upon national mythology. Such was the Battle of the Neva, in which Russians of the Republic of Novgorod, under the leadership of Prince Alexander Yaroslavich—later known as Alexander Nevsky— repelled an army of Swedish invaders.

A Mongol invasion of Russian lands from 1236 gave the Swedes an opportunity to exploit the resulting weakness of Novgorod. A Swedish force, possibly including Norwegians, under the command of Jarl Birger landed at the mouth of the River Izhora.

Russian accounts state that Alexander rushed to meet them with only his household troops and whatever volunteers he could raise in Novgorod. He advanced on Birger's camp under the cover of fog and forest. Birger, supposedly, was expecting no attack; his camp was strung out along the shore and had set no guards. A rapid cavalry charge, quickly supported by infantry, took Birger by surprise and he was unable to get his largely infantry force into an effective defense formation. Indeed, Russian sources assert that many Swedes were unable even to draw their swords before being overwhelmed.

It is claimed that only three ships escaped the terrible slaughter and that Novgorod's losses were insignificant. However, given that Sweden was embroiled in civil strife and threatened with war by Norway, a serious invasion and a great battle seem doubtful. It is likely that this was a relatively minor piratical raid or a trivial border skirmish. But later, Russians needed a heroic figure to counter the humiliation of Mongol conquest: Alexander was nicknamed "Nevsky" (of the Neva), and ultimately canonized, becoming a great symbol of Russian resistance to invaders. His deeds, therefore, required exaggeration. **JS**

Losses: Unknown

Lake Peipus 1242 ▷

Liegnitz (Legnica) 9 April 1241

Mongol raiders in Poland defeated a European army containing much-feted Christian knights from the military orders of the Teutonic Knights, the Hospitallers, and the Templars. The raiders had been sent to Poland as a diversion from the Mongolian invasion of Europe through Hungary and afterward rejoined the Mongol army there.

After the Mongol victory at Kalka River, some 40,000 Cumans fled into Hungary, converted to Christianity, and requested the protection of the Hungarian king, Béla IV. The Mongols claimed the Cumans as their subjects and used these events as a cause to invade Europe. Under a daring invasion plan drawn up by General Subedei, three armies totaling 80,000 men—led by Batu, Shiban, and Subedei himself—would invade Hungary. A fourth force of 20,000, commanded by Princes Kadan and Baidar, was to be sent into Poland with the aim of destroying opposition there before sweeping southward to reunite with the main force.

> *"They collected nine large sacks of ears and sent them back to the Khan as proof of the victory."*
>
> Friar Giovanni Da Pian del Carpini, chronicler

The plan was put into effect in winter/spring 1241: in Poland, Kadan and Baidar won a string of victories and on Palm Sunday, 24 March, burned the Polish capital Cracow. Polish resistance was weakened by rivalry between competing lords, but Duke Henry II the Pious of Silesia succeeded in raising an army of 30,000, which met the Mongols at Liegnitz (now known as Legnica). This army contained poorly equipped infantry raised from the local peasants but also members of the Teutonic Knights and a small group of Knights Templar and Knights Hospitaller

from France, some of the most redoubtable mounted warriors in the Christian world. Meanwhile, a second European army—50,000 strong—was a few days' march away under the command of King Wenceslas of Bohemia. Kadan and Baidar determined to engage Duke Henry's army before it could link up with Wenceslas's troops.

At Liegnitz, on 9 April, a lightly armed Mongol vanguard advanced toward Duke Henry's archers, then turned and feigned retreat, drawing Henry's knights into an attack. The Mongols then created a smokescreen that effectively cut off Henry's cavalry from his infantry. Confused by the smoke, the European knights rode around trying to find the enemy but came under heavy fire as Mongol archers unleashed a hail of arrows. Next, a group of Mongol light cavalry attacked the now-isolated European infantry from the flanks. Finally, the Mongols sent in the heavy cavalry.

Throughout these maneuvers, the Mongol archers kept up a deadly storm of arrows, and—according to some accounts—also used rockets fired with gunpowder. The European army was virtually wiped out. Duke Henry attempted to flee, but was captured, killed, and beheaded; the Mongols paraded his head around the town of Liegnitz on the end of a spear. As was customary among the Mongols, the number of fallen victims was counted by cutting off one ear from each, these being collected together in sacks.

Afterward, hearing of the catastrophic defeat, King Wenceslas retreated to Bohemia. The Mongols sent a small army to pursue him, but this force was driven off by the Bohemian cavalry at Klodzo. Then Kadan and Baidar broke up their army into raiding parties that terrorized the Polish people and ravaged the countryside before heading southward across the Carpathian Mountains to join General Subedei and the main army in Hungary. **CP**

Losses: Mongol, unknown of 20,000 engaged; European, entire army of 30,000

◁ Kaifeng 1232   Mohi 1241 ▷

Matthäus Merian's copper engraving of the Battle of Liegnitz, later colored and published in 1630.

Mohi (Sajo River) 10 April 1241

During the Mongolian invasion of Europe, Batu Khan and General Subedei inflicted a crushing defeat on King Béla IV's Hungarian army, which was renowned for having the best cavalry in Europe. The Mongols burned the city of Pest and seized control of the Hungarian plain.

Mongol general Subedei planned an invasion of Europe in which a three-pronged assault on Hungary was supported by a campaign in Poland. The main invasion force destroyed Hungarian defenses in the Carpathians and swept across Hungary, stopping on the banks of the River Sajo. King Béla IV encamped on the opposite bank, his army of 100,000 outnumbering the Mongols by at least 20,000.

On 10 April, Batu Khan attacked: he and his brother, Prince Shiban, led a frontal assault across the river while Subedei rode northward in search of a ford by which his troops could cross and attack the Hungarians from behind. Batu and Shiban struggled to make headway, but then unleashed catapult-fired explosives that drove the Hungarians back. Once across, they wheeled around and turned the Hungarian position so it would be vulnerable to Subedei when he arrived; then Batu ordered his men to retreat and line up in single file.

Subedei's troops arrived and deployed in the same way behind the Hungarians, who—realizing they were about to be encircled by archers—charged out to regain their camp. Subedei pursued them and bombarded the camp with explosives, finally sending in his heavy cavalry. A column of Hungarians fled back toward Pest but was pursued and shot down by the mounted Mongol archers. Europe was saved from further Mongol depredations by the death of the great khan Ogödei and consequent withdrawal of Mongol forces to select a new leader. **CP**

Losses: Mongol, unknown of 80,000; Hungarian, 60,000 of 100,000

◁ Liegnitz 1241   Fall of Baghdad 1258 ▷

Lake Peipus 15 April 1242

At Lake Peipus, the Novgorodian prince, Alexander Nevsky, built on the reputation he had won at the Battle of the Neva, although again his exploits may have been exaggerated. His defeat of the crusading Catholic Teutonic Knights reputedly saved Orthodox Russia from extinction.

The Teutonic Knights had long been fighting a crusade to convert Orthodox Russians to the Roman Church. A Mongol invasion beginning in 1236 offered them an opportunity to succeed. They invaded Novgorod lands and captured the city of Pskov. Novgorod recalled Nevsky, who had been exiled after the Neva for being overpowerful, to resume command. He retook the city and met the knights and their Estonian auxiliaries on the narrow straits connecting Lakes Peipus and Pskovskoe. There he lured them onto the ice, where their heavy cavalry could only move with difficulty.

Russian sources suggest that the knights managed to charge across the frozen lake, but the momentum of their attack was absorbed by infantry of the Novgorod militia. Several hours of exhausting battle followed before Nevsky ordered his own cavalry, which appears to have included Mongol horse archers, to envelop both flanks and encircle the knights. The appearance of fresh Novgorod cavalry supposedly settled the issue. The knights fled; as they attempted to regroup on the opposite side of the lake, the thinner ice broke and hundreds were drowned.

This encounter ended the last serious attempt at a crusade against Russian lands, and later generations further hailed Nevsky as a national hero. There are questions about the size and importance of the battle, but any exaggeration usefully obscured the fact that Nevsky was soon to offer homage to the Mongols. **JS**

Losses: Unknown

◁ The Neva 1240   Kulikovo 1380 ▷

 Detail from a sixteenth-century illustrated manuscript chronicling Batu Khan's invasion of Western Europe.

Harbiyah 17–18 October 1244

Sometimes called La Forbie, the fight at Harbiyah was the last time that the kingdom of Jerusalem took the offensive against the Muslim states that surrounded it. The loss of men and leaders in the fighting was never made good, leaving the kingdom reliant on erratic aid from Europe.

In 1244 the kingdom of Jerusalem formed an alliance with Al Mansur, emir of Homs, and other minor Muslim rulers against the powerful Egyptian sultan, As-Salih Ayyub. The allied army was marching south through Gaza under the command of Walter of Brienne when it was confronted by Emir Baibars with 5,000 Egyptian cavalry and a similar number of Khwarizm mercenary cavalry. Al Mansur suggested fortifying the camp for a defensive battle, but Lord Philip of Tyre ordered an attack. He placed his 6,000 Christians on the right, beside the sea, with Al Mansur's 2,500 men in the center and 3,000 other Muslim allies on the left. Baibars placed his Egyptians facing the Christians and the Khwarizm facing the Muslims. On 17 October, only desultory skirmishing took place, but the armies formed up again on 18 October.

The battle opened with a charge by the Khwarizm against Al Mansur. The men of Homs were pushed back, suffering heavy losses, whereupon the other Muslim allies fled. The Christians, meanwhile, attacked the Egyptians and broke through on the right. The Khwarizms returned from pursuing the Muslim allies in time to attack the victorious Christians from the rear, penning them up against the sea. Philip of Tyre, with sixty-five Christian knights and about 1,000 others, managed to break out and escape. The rest were captured and sold into slavery. Count Walter died in captivity, and Al Mansur returned to Homs with only 180 men of the 2,000 with which he had left. **RM**

Losses: Crusader and allied, 7,000 of 11,000 engaged; Ayyubid, 2,000 of 10,000 engaged

◁ Damietta 1219   Al Mansurah 1250 ▷

Matthew Paris's thirteenth-century illustration of the Battle of Harbiyah, or La Forbie. ↥

Al Mansurah   8 February–6 April 1250

The defeat of the Seventh Crusade at Al Mansurah expunged the popular fervor for crusading among the Christians in Europe. The final two crusades would be limited military campaigns by kings intent on bolstering their reputations. This victory made the Mamluks the rulers of Egypt.

The Seventh Crusade was led by King Louis IX of France. He landed in Egypt to fight the powerful Ayyubid sultan, As-Salih, and force him to hand over Jerusalem as the price of peace. Louis captured the key port of Damietta in June 1249, and his good fortune continued when As-Salih died on 22 November, leaving Egypt to his inexperienced son, Turanshah.

Louis ordered most of his army to march on Cairo, leaving a garrison at Damietta and men to guard the ships. The advance was held up by a wide canal at Al Mansurah, but on 8 February, the crusaders fought their way across, defeated the Egyptian army, and captured Al Mansurah. A counterattack by Mamluks, elite Muslim slave soldiers, inflicted heavy losses on the crusaders and forced them to fortify their camp on 11 February. Mamluk leader Baibars al-Buduqdari placed a fleet on the canal to cut the crusaders off from supplies and began a siege of their camp.

On 4 April, with disease and hunger weakening his men, Louis ordered a retreat to Damietta. The crusaders fought a running battle against the circling Mamluks, but on 6 April, at Farskur, Louis decided to surrender. Baibars ordered the instant death of the 7,000 Christians deemed too sick to be useful as slaves. Louis later paid a vast ransom for himself and 12,000 other survivors. The Mamluks then killed Turanshah and took supreme power in Egypt for themselves. **RM**

Losses: Crusader, entire army of 25,000 dead or captured; Egyptian, unknown of 35,000

◁ *Harbiyah 1244*   *Acre 1291* ▷

⬆ *Miniature from a twelfth-century chronicle showing Louis IX at the point of surrender.*

Fall of Baghdad February 1258

Kressenbrunn July 1260

A Mongolian army under Hulegu Khan sacked Baghdad, capital of the Islamic Abbasid caliphate. The army destroyed the city's palaces, mosques, and libraries and killed al-Mustasim, last of the Abbasid rulers, sending an immense haul of booty back to the Mongolian capital, Qaraqorum.

The battle fought between Bohemia and Hungary at Kressenbrunn was for control over the duchy of Styria. The victory of the Bohemian king, Premysl Ottokar II, made him briefly the most powerful man in Europe, but he also became the object of fear and jealousy among his neighbors.

Under Mongke Khan, grandson of Genghis Khan, the Mongols embarked on new campaigns of expansion. Mongke sent his brother, Hulegu, into Iran and then Iraq. His vast army of 150,000 encamped outside Baghdad, capital of the Islamic Abbasid caliphate.

In November 1257, Hulegu offered a peaceful takeover but was rebuffed by the Abbasid caliph al-Mustasim, who sent out a pitifully small force of 20,000 to confront the invaders. These men were surprised when the Mongols flooded the battlefield by smashing nearby dams, and then were wiped out by the Mongol heavy cavalry. Hulegu's troops occupied Baghdad's western suburbs and built a rampart right around the city; on 30 January 1258, they began bombardment. The Mongol army was equipped with Chinese explosives and the newest siege equipment, including catapults capable of firing flaming missiles. On 6 February, the besiegers captured the city's east wall: Baghdad surrendered on 10 February. Hulegu took al-Mustasim and his courtiers prisoner and had every remaining member of the garrison executed.

The sacking of Baghdad began on 13 February: this great city—for centuries under Islamic rule a center of the arts and learning—was utterly destroyed. According to one account, the Tigris River turned black from the ink of ancient manuscripts hurled into its waters. Al-Mustasim was forced to watch, then was rolled in a carpet and trampled to death by the hooves of the invaders' horses. **CP**

When Ottokar became king in 1253, he was already the duke of Austria and Styria through a fortunate dynastic marriage. However, new to the throne, he was unable to prevent the Hungarian king, Béla IV, from wresting Styria from him. He always intended to win it back when the time was right.

In the summer of 1260 Ottokar and Béla clashed again. Their armies met on opposite banks of the River Morava. It was to be one of the biggest battles of medieval Europe—although claims that each army numbered 100,000 or more must be treated with skepticism—but it might never have taken place because neither side was prepared to risk attacking across the river.

Ottokar, however, wanted to fight and decide the issue that day. He therefore offered to withdraw some distance to allow the Hungarians to cross safely before the fighting began. As he retreated, a contingent of Hungarian cavalry charged and a fierce melee developed around Kressenbrunn. Any advantage the Hungarians might have gained was wiped out quickly by the return of the main Bohemian army. The Hungarians were soon retreating in disorder, and many drowned in the river. Béla was forced to surrender Styria, and soon Ottokar ruled territories stretching from Silesia to the Adriatic. However, the German princes were alarmed at his power and elected Rudolf of Hapsburg as their emperor. They were clearly intent on bringing Ottokar down. **JS**

Losses: Mongol, minimal; Baghdadi, some sources claim up to 2 million dead

Losses: Unknown

◁ Mohi 1241   Ain Jalut 1260 ▷

Marchfeld 1278 ▷

 In this fourteenth-century illumination, the Mongols launch their attack on Baghdad's city walls.

Ain Jalut September 1260

An army of the Islamic Mamluk sultanate of Egypt inflicted a comprehensive defeat on the Mongols at Ain Jalut in Palestine. The battle did away with the myth that the Mongols were invincible and marked the end of any concerted effort by the Mongols to conquer the Middle East.

After the sack of Baghdad, Mongol leader Hulegu Khan captured Damascus and Aleppo in Syria, then began to move southward to depose the Mamluk sultans of Egypt. However, when news arrived from the east of the death from dysentery of his brother Mongke Khan, Hulegu withdrew the bulk of his army from Syria to Maragheh in Iran, leaving a much-reduced presence under General Ked-Buqa to counter the Mamluks.

The Mamluks saw their opportunity: an army under Sultan Qutuz marched north to defeat a small Mongolian force at Gaza, then came up against a Mongol army of around 20,000 at Ain Jalut (Goliath's Spring), so called because it was held to be the place where King David

> "Our horses are swift . . . our swords like thunderbolts, our hearts as hard as the mountains."

Hulegu Khan

of Israel killed the Philistine warrior Goliath, as described in the book of Samuel. The Mongol army contained a sizable group of Syrian warriors, as well as Christian Georgian and Armenian troops. The two armies were roughly matched in numbers, but the Mamluks had one great advantage: one of their generals, Baibars, was familiar with the terrain because he had been a fugitive in the area earlier in his life. Baibars reputedly drew up the battle strategy, which used one of the Mongols' most successful tactics: that of the feigned retreat.

At Ain Jalut the Mamluks concealed the bulk of their army among trees in the hills and sent forward a small force under Baibars; his group rode back and forward repeatedly in order to provoke and occupy the Mongols for several hours, before beginning a feigned retreat. Ked-Buqa fell for the trick and ordered an advance; his army poured forward in pursuit only to be ambushed by the main Mamluk army in the hills. Then the Mamluks attacked from all sides, unleashing their cavalry and a heavy storm of arrows, but the Mongols fought with typical ferocity and succeeded in turning and breaking the left wing of the Mamluk army.

In this close fighting, the Mamluks used hand cannon—known as "midfa" in Arabic—primarily to frighten the Mongolian warriors' horses and cause confusion. Contemporary accounts report that Mamluk sultan Qutuz threw down his helmet and urged his men forward to fight in the name of Islam, and that after this inspiring speech the Mamluks began to gain the upper hand. Then Mongol general Ked-Buqa was killed in battle—or, according to one account, was taken prisoner by the Mamluks and, after he declared defiantly that the khan would inflict savage revenge for this defeat, was beheaded on the battlefield. Finally, the Mongols turned and began to retreat, heading for Beisan, eight miles (13 km) away. The Mamluks pursued them all the way.

At Beisan, the Mongols turned to fight once more, but were heavily defeated. The Mamluks made the most of the propaganda value of their remarkable victory over the seemingly invincible Mongols, dispatching a messenger to Cairo bearing Ked-Buqa's head on a staff. Subsequently, General Baibars formed a conspiracy against Qutuz, who was murdered as he made his way back to Cairo. Baibars seized power for himself. **CP**

Losses: Mongol, most of 20,000; Mamluk, heavy losses of 20,000

◁ *Fall of Baghdad 1258*

A fourteenth-century Persian miniature depicts Mongol warriors advancing on the Egyptians.

كوروفا براستان دواند وحله را مسرو كرد و بادشاه اسلام ازوادى ان أوازى شنند كه لتخفضوت من القوم الطلبين
وبدان صارب فوى همه نما متى در نفس مبارلش طاهر لشب وحون شر عرس معرفد وصف لسكرى دربد و رخم سنان
كهدان ابنازا مى انداخت وملك برسكرهند واو ودامدند وسراران كه ند و بازسوارشدند و سر مصربان لرك تا ن
كردند وارووت جاشت نا بسرحلل بود عاقبت الامر مصربان بشكسند و منعرف كشته منهم شدند

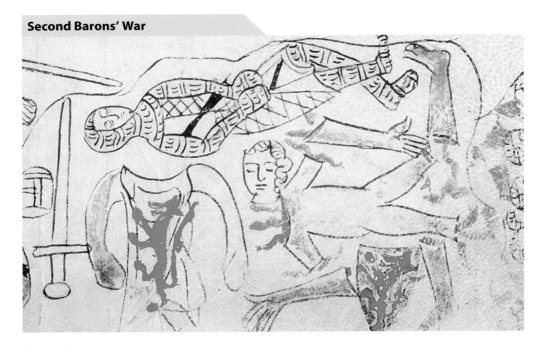

Evesham 14 August 1265

The long-running disagreement between English kings and barons over how England should be ruled came to a climax at Evesham in 1265. The battle ended in a bloody massacre of the outnumbered baronial army, settling the argument comprehensively in favor of the king, Henry III.

The fifty-six-year reign of Henry III was marked by royal misrule and incompetence, Henry relying on the advice given by relatives of his French queen, Eleanor of Provence. A rebellion in 1258, led by Simon de Montfort, Earl of Leicester, forced Henry to sign the Provisions of Oxford, limiting his royal power. Henry, however, repudiated the Provisions in 1261, leading to the outbreak of war against him in 1264.

Simon de Montfort defeated Henry and his son Edward, the future Edward I, at Lewes and took both captive. Edward, however, escaped and raised an army in western England. Montfort, in the meantime, forged an alliance with Prince Llewelyn of Wales and raised a large army in the principality. From there he moved east to join up with an even larger army led by his son, also called Simon. Edward acted quickly, realizing he must stop the two Montfort armies meeting. Marching eastward, he surprised and defeated the younger Simon's army at Kenilworth. The older Montfort was unaware of this defeat and marched into Evesham. Edward advanced through the night and surrounded Montfort's men on a loop of the River Avon. Montfort led the charge against Edward's lines, but his forces were soon overwhelmed and Simon was killed.

So one-sided was the encounter that Robert of Gloucester, a contemporary chronicler, referred to it as "the murder of Evesham, for battle it was none." **SA**

Losses: Prince Edward, few of 10,000; Simon de Montfort, 4,000 of 5,000

◁ *Dover 1217*   *Stirling Bridge 1297* ▷

Simon de Montfort's dismembered body lies at Evesham in a thirteenth-century depiction. ⬆

Benevento 26 February 1266

This battle was the result of the long-running power struggle in Italy, between the Guelfs (supporters of the papacy) and the Ghibellines (supporters of the Holy Roman Empire). The defeat of Manfred of Sicily marked a triumph for the papacy and all but destroyed the Hohenstaufen dynasty.

Having usurped the throne of Sicily (which ruled much of southern Italy) from his infant nephew, Manfred—son of Frederick II of Hohenstaufen—quickly and ruthlessly established his authority over his realm, allying himself with Muslim Saracens at Lucera in southern Italy. However, he faced the undying hostility of a series of short-lived popes, who sought a challenger whom they could recognize and support. Eventually Charles of Anjou, brother of Louis I of France, was invited to Rome, crowned by the pope as the true king of Sicily, and—with the help of Genoese and Florentine bankers—raised an army of Italian Guelfs and French mercenaries.

Manfred took up a strong position on the plain of Grandella, near Benevento. As the French infantry advanced, he unleashed his Saracen archers and light cavalry, and the French were scattered. But the Saracens left themselves exposed to the French heavy cavalry and were, in turn, overwhelmed. To regain the advantage, Manfred ordered his own heavy cavalry, mostly German mercenaries, into the attack. Initially they seemed to be succeeding, but they were seriously outnumbered and began to take heavy losses.

The role played by Manfred's Italian cavalry is disputed: either they attempted a flanking attack and were quickly beaten, or they were so appalled at the butchery of the Germans that they fled the field without a fight. Either way, it was clear to Manfred that all was lost, and he rode into the thick of the fighting to meet his death. **JS**

Losses: Unknown

◁ *Legnano 1176*

Bay of Naples 1284 ▷

Charles of Anjou opposes Manfred in a fifteenth-century manuscript "Roman de la Rose," by Jean de Meun.

Xiangyang 1268–74

Having conquered the Jin, the Mongols besieged the Southern Song for five years in one of the greatest sieges in Chinese history, an operation during which much ingenuity was shown on both sides. Weapons included exploding bombs and huge, stone projectiles hurled from counterweight trebuchets—the first in China.

Xiangyang (present-day Xiangfan in Hubei) consisted of the twin cities of Xiangyang and Fancheng, which lay across the Han River. They formed the northern outpost of the Southern Song and withstood a sustained siege by Kublai Khan from 1268 to 1274.

In 1272, the Song built a pontoon bridge to link the two cities, but the Mongols constructed mechanical saws, operated probably from the treadmills of paddle boats, which cut the bridge into sections, after which it was burned. A successful provisioning operation of Xiangyang was carried out later on in the siege when the Song ships were equipped with fire lances, siege crossbows, and trebuchets shooting fire bombs. Yet even when a blockade was established, the Mongol traction trebuchets proved incapable of causing any real damage to the walls. Something stronger was needed, and this was supplied in the form of counterweight trebuchets. Projectiles could now be launched weighing ten times more than any stone thrown hitherto, and one particular shot—perhaps exceeding 200 pounds (75 kg)—brought down a tower with a noise like thunder. A commentator wrote that the projectiles were several feet in diameter, and when they fell to the earth, they made holes three to four feet (about one meter) deep.

Massive stones therefore triumphed where both traction trebuchets and explosives had failed, and the city finally surrendered in 1274. **ST**

Losses: Unknown, but considerable on both sides

◁ *Kaifeng 1232*　　　　　　　　　*Yamen 1279* ▷

　　The Mongol cavalry, from a thirteenth-century Japanese scroll attributed to Tosa Nagataka.

First Mongol Invasion of Japan 2–20 November 1274

Kublai Khan turned his attentions toward Japan to neutralize any support likely to come from that direction when he advanced farther into southern China. In spite of unfamiliar tactics and exploding bombs, the samurai drove the invaders back, although a brief raid may have been the original intention anyway.

The Mongol invasion of Japan in 1274 was the samurai's first experience of foreign attack. Sailing from Korea on Korean ships and with Korean and Chinese soldiers, the Mongols first ravaged the islands of Tsushima and Iki, where great heroism was displayed by the samurai warriors. Seeking to instill terror into the defenders of mainland Japan, the Mongols tied captive women and children to the bows of their ships as they sailed into Hakata Bay.

The raid lasted little more than twenty-four hours and was more of a reconnaissance in force; the Mongols tested the defenses of the samurai and observed their reaction to Mongol innovations in warfare, such as the use of exploding bombs fired from catapults. These caused terror and alarm among the samurais' horses. The samurai were also disappointed that they were unable to challenge the Mongols to single combat, although one managed to kill a senior Mongol with a long-range arrow.

Instead, the Mongols fought in dense phalanxes and, by using these tactics, drove the defenders back to the ancient earthwork known as the Mizuki. The samurai responded with cavalry charges in small groups of mounted warriors. Yet, very soon, the Mongols withdrew to their ships, where they were subjected to severe storms on the way home. The resistance had impressed them, and they were to return with a much larger force seven years later. **ST**

Losses: Mongol, 3,500, mostly Korean, mainly lost at sea; Japanese, unknown but heavy

◁ *Dan no Ura 1185*   *Second Mongol Invasion of Japan 1281* ▷

⬆ *A samurai delivers the heads of two Mongol invaders during the First Mongol Invasion of Japan.*

Marchfeld (Durnkrut)   26 August 1278

Marchfeld was a battle between the armies of Premysl Ottokar II of Bohemia and Emperor Rudolf of Hapsburg, supported by Ladislaus IV of Hungary. The defeat of Ottokar made the Hapsburg dynasty secure in Vienna for centuries and permanently broke the power of Bohemia.

Since his election as emperor, after the Battle of Kressenbrunn, Rudolf had used his imperial authority to cut down Ottokar's power. Lands (including Austria) were stripped from Ottokar and, at one point, Rudolf forced him to offer homage as his vassal. In 1278 Ottokar chose to fight and sought allies by presenting himself as the defender of all Slav peoples from the rapacity of the German princes. He invaded Austria at the head of a powerful army and marched on Vienna. But Rudolf had a superior set of alliances, and his army included a powerful contingent of Hungarian cavalry who were happy to have the opportunity to avenge their defeat at Kressenbrunn.

When the two armies met, Hungarian light cavalry and horse archers were the first to attack and, after some hours of indecisive combat, the heavily laden Bohemian horses were exhausted. It was at this point that Rudolf threw in the heavy cavalry he had kept concealed in reserve. They attacked the Bohemians from the rear, and Ottokar's forces were overwhelmed and soon in headlong flight. Ottokar himself was killed, and Premysl's power was shattered.

Now secure in Vienna, Rudolf was too cautious to try and annex Bohemia, but he limited its frontiers and appointed his own son-in-law, Otto IV, Margrave of Brandenburg, as regent for Ottokar's six-year-old heir, Wenceslaus II—a brutal regency that was deeply detested. **JS**

Losses: Unknown

◁ Kressenbrunn 1260

Morgarten 1315 ▷

Yamen   19 March 1279

The Song dynasty made its final stand against the Mongols in the naval battle of Yamen on China's southern coast. After a campaign of many years against the Song, this victory delivered southern China into the hands of Mongol leader Kublai Khan, founder of the Chinese Yuan dynasty.

Mongke Khan launched a campaign against the Song dynasty in southern China in 1252 that continued intermittently for decades. In 1276 the main Song rulers surrendered their capital Linan (Hangchow) and were granted refuge by new Mongol leader Kublai Khan, but two princes remained as figureheads of Song resistance.

In the course of their long campaign in China, the Mongols had gathered a navy. Kublai Khan's general, Zhang Hongfan, now led a naval assault against the remaining Song court in the port of Yamen. Song general Zhang Shijie had 1,000 ships chained together in the bay, with the one containing the Song boy emperor, Zhao Bing, in the center. These ships were painted with fire-resistant mud; so the Mongols' "fire ships"—burning vessels filled with explosives—had little effect. Then Zhang Hongfan blockaded the Song vessels, and the sailors and courtiers onboard quickly ran out of supplies and grew weak. The Mongol general sent his ships in three groups to attack from north, south, and east, while reserving one group to make a frontal assault. The attack from the north was beaten back.

The Mongols used a trick, playing music to suggest that the men were resting, before making a sudden frontal assault of great ferocity. The Song attempted to break out with twelve ships, including the one with the boy emperor, but failed. Zhao Bing jumped into the sea and was drowned. The Song dynasty was at an end. **CP**

Losses: Song, 100,000 of 200,000; Mongol, unknown of around 20,000

◁ Xiangyang 1268

Lake Poyang 1363 ▷

Second Mongol Invasion of Japan 22 May–14 August 1281

The lessons learned during the first Mongol invasion of Japan were applied by both sides, and when the Mongols returned in 1281 their larger force faced prepared defenses and stone walls. Samurai bravery kept the Mongols at sea, where they were destroyed by the "kamikaze" typhoon.

The second of the two Mongol invasions of Japan was carried out in two stages. The first phase left Busan and traveled via the islands of Tsushima and Iki to make landfall in Hakata Bay, where the Japanese had built a wall along the shore with a sloping rear side, up which horses could be ridden. A steady arrow barrage was kept up, and—combined with individual attacks by samurai—the Mongols were prevented from establishing a beachhead.

The Mongols were then harassed on their ships by a series of raids launched from small boats. While this phase of the battle was being controlled, a much larger invasion fleet set sail from southern China and began to attack an area of Japan, farther to the west, that had not been defended by a wall. However, once again, the samurai confined the Mongols to their ships.

There was still great danger, and prayers were offered to the gods. These prayers appeared to be answered when a typhoon arose and hit the Mongol fleet as it lay at anchor off the island of Takashima. The ships, tied together to provide protection against the Japanese raids, crashed into each other. Many were sunk with a huge loss of life. The storm was dubbed the "kamikaze," the wind from the gods, and when Japan again faced invasion in World War II, this name was to be used in reference to the suicide pilots who used their planes themselves as weapons against enemy targets. **ST**

"The effect on Japanese pride was colossal, for the kamikaze was literally regarded as a weapon from heaven."

Stephen R. Turnbull, The Samurai

Losses: Mongol, 60–90 percent dead, mainly because of the kamikaze; Japanese, unknown

A nineteenth-century woodcut by Utagawa Kuniyoshi, in which Nichiren summons a storm to drive off the Mongols.

◁ First Mongol Invasion of Japan 1274   Minatogawa 1336 ▷

Bay of Naples 5 June 1284

The battle fought by oared galleys in the Bay of Naples in 1284, an episode in the War of the Sicilian Vespers, was among the most celebrated victories of Roger di Lauria, the greatest of medieval European naval commanders. His Aragonese fleet trounced the hapless Charles of Salerno.

In 1282 Sicily rebelled against the rule of Charles of Anjou, imposed after the Battle of Benevento in 1266. The kingdom of Aragon intervened to aid the Sicilians. Roger di Lauria, the commander of the Aragonese naval forces, had a personal grudge against the Angevins, who had seized his family's lands in southern Italy.

In spring 1284, Lauria blockaded the port of Naples. Inside the city Charles of Anjou's son, Charles of Salerno, longed for a chance to attack the blockade fleet. On 5 June, Lauria offered him the opportunity he wanted by sending away part of his force. Seeing his enemy depleted, Charles hastily sortied with his Neapolitan and Provençal galleys. Lauria turned and fled with the impetuous Angevin in pursuit. It was a trap. At a prearranged point, Lauria was rejoined by the rest of his galleys, which had hidden behind a headland. His whole force turned and bore down upon the enemy.

The Aragonese were experienced and disciplined fighters, their ships packed with Catalan crossbowmen and *almughavars*, lightly equipped Spanish mercenaries sometimes used as combat swimmers to assault enemy galleys. About a dozen of the Provençal galleys, which had been in the van of the original pursuit, were surrounded and forced to surrender. Charles of Salerno was among those taken prisoner. He was later released in return for a promise to hand Sicily to the Aragonese—a promise he subsequently broke. **RG**

Losses: Aragonese, no galleys sunk of 36; Angevin, 12 galleys sunk or captured of 30

◁ Benevento 1266

Meloria 6 August 1284

The city-state of Pisa was a major Mediterranean naval power and a commercial rival to Genoa and Venice—until the Battle of Meloria. This decisive encounter, which took place off Italy's Tuscan coast, ended in a triumph for Genoese admiral Oberto Doria that sent Pisa into terminal decline.

Mercantile and political rivalry between Genoa and Pisa had raged throughout the thirteenth century. Both cities had war fleets of sleek, oared galleys that they used freely in the ongoing struggle for trading rights and colonies. In 1241, the Pisans had attacked a Genoese naval convoy in a first battle near Meloria and destroyed twenty-five ships. The decisive victory led to Pisan ascendancy over Genoa. Pisa was able to dominate Sardinia, in addition to the control it already exercised over neighboring Corsica. However, the career of Oberto Doria, a powerful leader in Genoa from 1273, changed Genoese fortunes.

Under Doria, the city became wealthier and could afford a larger war fleet. In 1284, Genoa deliberately provoked a war. Doria besieged Sassari in Sardinia, forcing the Pisan fleet to engage him, again at Meloria, in retaliation. Doria cleverly arranged his fleet in two lines, with many of his larger ships in the rear to hide them from the Pisan fleet. Pisa attacked the first line in one large formation, ramming into the Genoese ships and boarding them. As the battle raged, Doria's second line of galleys moved forward, outflanking the Pisan fleet. Completely encircled, the core of the Pisan navy perished. Doria followed up his victory by capturing Porto Pisano, Pisa's seaport, and filling it in so it could no longer be used. The victory left Genoa and Venice in a head-to-head fight for the fortune to be gained from Mediterranean trade. **TB**

Losses: Genoese, unknown; Pisan, 10 ships sunk and 25 captured, more than 5,000 dead

Curzola 1298 ▷

Acre   4 April–18 May 1291

The fall of Acre marked the final defeat of the Christian crusader states in the Holy Land. Thereafter, Christianity in the eastern Mediterranean would suffer a string of defeats and conquests that would not end until the Muslim tide was finally halted at the gates of Vienna in 1683.

By 1291 the kingdom of Jerusalem consisted of Cyprus, Acre, and Tyre. Sultan Khalil of Egypt marched on Acre with ninety-two siege engines, including the largest trebuchet yet built. He laid siege to the city while his vast army swept over the surrounding lands. The Templars launched a moonlight attack on the Mamluk camp and, although they inflicted much damage, they lost heavily.

On 4 May, King Henry of Jerusalem, who had been in Europe trying to raise support, sailed into Acre harbor with only 700 men. By 15 May, the lower outer wall had been breached and the Mamluks launched an attack, which was driven off with heavy loss by the Templars and Hospitallers. Henry decided the outer wall was indefensible and that night retreated to the inner wall. On 18 May, a section of the inner wall near the Accursed Tower collapsed, prompting a suicidal assault by Mamluks from the fanatical Chages sect. This achieved a breakthrough, but at horrific cost, allowing the main Mamluk army to enter the city. A day of confused street fighting followed, which ended with King Henry fleeing by ship to Cyprus, the Templars and others holding out in the harborside Templar castle, and hundreds of civilians dead. On 28 May, a breach opened in the Templar castle and the Mamluks stormed in. There were no Christian survivors, and 2,000 Mamluks died in the assault.

King Henry ordered the evacuation of Tyre in early June. The crusader states were extinguished. **RM**

Losses: Crusader, 17,000 of 18,500, unknown number of civilians; Mamluk, unknown of 60,000

◁ Al Mansurah 1250

Stirling Bridge   11 September 1297

The kings of England repeatedly sought to extend their rule north of the border into Scotland. The death of the Scottish queen in 1290 gave Edward I of England the chance to take over the country, but his intentions were dashed with a major defeat at the hands of William Wallace.

The death of the seven-year-old Scottish queen, Margaret, in 1290 left the throne of Scotland vacant. The Scottish lords gave Edward I the task of choosing a new king. He picked the weak John Balliol, a distant descendant of the great Scottish king David I, in the expectation that he would do Edward's bidding. The English king, however, was quickly disabused of this idea when Balliol refused to join him on campaign in France and, in 1295, signed an alliance with France, England's traditional enemy.

Edward was furious and in 1296 marched north to invade Scotland. He massacred the garrison at Berwick and then defeated Balliol at Dunbar, deposing him and ruling Scotland directly. The next year, the Scots, led by William Wallace, predictably rose in revolt against English rule. The two sides met at Stirling Bridge. A large English army commanded by the Earl of Surrey attempted to cross the River Forth via a narrow bridge in front of the Scottish lines. The smaller Scottish army, led by Wallace and Andrew de Moray, took advantage of their position up on a slope and hurled spears and other missiles down onto the advancing English knights.

The knights soon floundered in the marshy ground and many thousands of them were killed. Those English soldiers yet to cross the bridge fled the scene, ceding victory to William Wallace and the Scots. It was an ignominious defeat. **SA**

Losses: Scottish, unknown of 2,300; English, 5,000 of 8,000–12,000

Falkirk 1298 ▷

Falkirk   22 July 1298

The Scottish victory over the English at Stirling Bridge in 1297 was soon avenged at the Battle of Falkirk. English rule was re-established over Scotland, forcing William Wallace to wage a lengthy guerrilla campaign until he was hunted down, betrayed, and eventually executed for treason in 1305.

After the disaster of Stirling Bridge, King Edward I of England determined to crush the Scots once and for all. He headed north to invade the country in 1298, advancing with an army of around 2,500 mounted knights and 12,500 infantry, including large numbers of Welsh and English archers armed with longbows. In response, Wallace tried to avoid a pitched battle, because his own forces were smaller than the English, totaling around 1,000 mounted knights and 5,000 infantry. Wallace preferred to conduct guerrilla warfare against the invading army, but was eventually forced into battle at Falkirk.

On the morning of battle, Wallace formed his pikemen up into four schiltrons, hedgehoglike circular formations of pikemen standing shoulder to shoulder with their pikes facing outward through an outer row of men in armor. The gaps between the schiltrons were filled with archers. The four schiltrons withstood the initial English cavalry and infantry attacks but then became vulnerable to steady fire from Edward's longbowmen, the first time significant use had been made of this deadly weapon in battle. As the arrows poured down, supplemented by crossbow and slingshot, the schiltrons were soon broken up by the charging English cavalry. The Scots then fled into the neighboring woods. Wallace escaped, although he lost many supporters. English losses, too, were high, testimony to the effectiveness of the schiltrons in battle. **SA**

Losses: English, 2,000 of 15,000; Scottish, 2,000 of 6,000

◁ Stirling Bridge 1297   Bannockburn 1314 ▷

Curzola   9 September 1298

Curzola was a hard-fought naval encounter between the war fleets of Genoa and Venice, a part of their ongoing struggle for control over Mediterranean trade. An indirect consequence of the battle was the creation of one of the world's most influential books: Marco Polo's account of his travels to China.

After Genoese leader Oberto Doria's victory over Pisa at Meloria in 1284, Genoa saw Venice as its last serious rival in the Mediterranean. In 1295, the Venetians attacked and defeated a Genoese fleet off the coast of Turkey. The Genoese sought revenge three years later at Curzola.

The Genoese fleet was led by Oberto Doria's brother, Lambda Doria. The Venetian galleys, about a hundred in number, were commanded by Andrea Dandolo, the son of the doge of Venice. It is thought that Marco Polo, a Venetian merchant who had returned from China in 1295, was serving in some capacity with Dandolo's fleet.

The battle took place off the southern Dalmatian coast near modern-day Korcula. Although the Venetians had a slightly superior number of galleys, Doria compensated by tactical acumen. He employed a similar strategy to that used at Meloria, arranging his ships in two groups. The first group was used to draw the Venetian galleys into attack, and the second group was used to outflank and surround the enemy. The Venetians suffered a heavy defeat, losing most of their hundred ships. Dandolo and Marco Polo were among those taken prisoner. Genoese chroniclers later wrote that Dandolo committed suicide by banging his head against the hull of a ship. It was while in captivity that Marco Polo is reputed to have dictated *The Travels of Marco Polo* to a fellow prisoner. The struggle between Venice and Genoa continued unabated. **TB**

Losses: Genoese, unknown; Venetian, 90 ships sunk or captured, 5,000 dead and several thousand captured

◁ Meloria 1284   Chioggia 1379 ▷

Courtrai 11 July 1302

Fought outside the Flemish town of Courtrai (Kortrijk), the battle was a famous victory for low-born Flemish foot soldiers over mounted noblemen and knights of French king Philip IV. It is also known as the Battle of the Golden Spurs, after the 700 spurs stripped from fallen knights that were displayed in Courtrai's Church of Our Lady.

In 1302, artisans' guilds of wealthy Flemish manufacturing cities led protests against French king Philip IV's mistreatment of the Count of Flanders. In Bruges anyone who spoke French was killed. Philip sent his brother, Count Robert of Artois, to Flanders to punish the rebels.

The cities of Bruges, Ghent, and Ypres assembled an army of foot soldiers—merchants, guild workers, and peasants, plus a few Flemish nobles—armed with pikes and the heavy wooden club ironically known as a *goedendag* (good day). Outside Courtrai they faced Count Robert's army of splendidly armored nobles and knights on horseback, supported by crossbowmen and infantry. The Flemish force took up a position on marshy ground behind a stream, digging ditches as further obstacles to a French cavalry charge. Their leader, William of Julich, ordered them: "Do not allow the enemy to break through your ranks. Do not be afraid. Kill both man and horse."

The tightly-packed Flemish suffered losses at the start of the battle when the crossbowmen advanced to shoot. But the French cavalry charge that followed was a fiasco. Horses floundered in the marsh and fell in the ditches. The Flemish foot soldiers halted the disrupted charge with their pikes and then rushed forward to attack, killing the mounts and butchering unhorsed nobles and knights. As many as a thousand may have been killed, including Count Robert. **CP**

Losses: French,1,000 of 8,000; Flemish, several hundred of 9,000

> *"[The Flemings] were . . . immensely enriched by booty and spoil taken from their enemies."*
>
> Annales Gandenses (Annals of Ghent)

↑ *The defeat of the French at Courtrai by Master of Mary of Burgundy from* Chronicles of the Counts of Flanders *(1477).*

Bannockburn 24 June 1314

Bannockburn was one of the most important battles in Scottish history. The heavy defeat of the English by Robert Bruce's army led to the eventual recognition of Scotland's independence by the English. Tactically, the battle was significant for the rout inflicted by a humble infantry force on noble mounted knights.

The defeat of the Scottish patriot William Wallace at Falkirk in 1298 and his eventual capture and execution in 1305 did not end the campaign by the Scots for independence from English domination. In 1306 Robert Bruce took up the mantle of Wallace and was crowned king on the Stone of Destiny at Scone Abbey, the traditional coronation site for Scottish kings. In response, Edward I of England launched a new invasion of Scotland in 1307 but died on his way north. Bruce gathered his forces slowly before capturing several castles. By 1314 he was strong enough to attack Stirling Castle, one of the key fortresses held by the English in Scotland. The new

> *"Both in number and in equipment . . . our troops are far superior to those wretched Scots."*
>
> *Edward II, before the Battle of Bannockburn*

English king, Edward II, immediately headed north with an army to relieve the castle and put down Bruce's rebellion.

Bruce drew up his 9,000-strong army on a site he chose carefully: a slope above a stream called Bannockburn, a few miles south of Stirling Castle. The width of the battlefield was about 1 mile (1.6 km), restricted on either side by marsh to the Scottish left and woodland to the right. Bruce commanded his men to dig many small holes in front of their lines and cover them with branches and grass in order to trip the English horses. After initial

skirmishes between mounted knights on 23 June, the main battle commenced the following day.

The Scots drew their infantry up into schiltrons, their pikes protruding through their shields in all directions. Mounted knights led the English advance, foolishly shielding their own archers behind them and thus preventing them firing off volleys of arrows onto the Scots' formations, as they had done at Falkirk. A series of English cavalry charges failed to break the schiltrons, while those few knights who did break through were immediately hacked to death. The English army soon collapsed into confusion on the narrow battlefield as retreating knights got tangled up with those trying to advance. To make matters worse, the English archers, in attempting to fire over the knights' heads into the schiltrons, managed to shoot many of their own countrymen in the back. At this point, a large number of Scottish camp followers emerged from the woods to the English left as if to attack. The English left began to crumble. Edward II then took the decision to leave the battlefield, causing many of his knights to follow. The Scots seized their chance and pursued the fleeing English, killing thousands of them as they attempted to escape across Bannockburn.

Despite their decisive victory, the Scots did not gain their independence, and warfare with England continued. A declaration signed in Arbroath in 1320 by Scottish lords and bishops appealing to Pope John XXII to recognize Scottish independence failed to achieve much, and it was not until Edward II was deposed in favor of his young son, Edward III, in 1327 and Robert Bruce launched an invasion of England to force the issue did the English give up. By the simultaneous treaties of Edinburgh and Northampton, signed in 1328, England finally recognized Scotland's independence. **SA**

Losses: Scottish, 4,000 of 9,000; English, up to 11,000 of 25,000

◁ *Falkirk 1298*　　　　　　　　　　　*Halidon Hill 1333* ▷

Effigy of King Edward II on his tomb at Gloucester Cathedral, England. ➜

Morgarten 15 November 1315

In medieval Europe, the independent people of the Swiss cantons were renown for their fighting qualities. That reputation was founded at the Battle of Morgarten, a victory of Swiss foot soldiers over Hapsburg mounted knights that marked a major step on the road to Swiss nationhood.

In the early fourteenth century, the Swiss Confederacy consisted only of the rural Alpine communities of Uri, Schwyz, and Unterwalden. The powerful Hapsburg family aspired to control an area strategically placed between Germany and Italy, but the Swiss traditionally enjoyed self-rule within the Holy Roman Empire.

In 1315, on the pretext of a dispute over grazing land in Schwyz, Hapsburg Duke Leopold I of Austria led an army into the Swiss mountains. With a force of more than 2,000 mounted knights, Leopold expected an easy victory over the farmers of Schwyz. Led by Werner Stauffacher, the Swiss prepared to defend themselves by exploiting their knowledge of local terrain, which was ideal for ambushes and unsuitable for cavalry warfare. Unterwalden did not take part, but Schwyz was aided by the men of Uri. They prepared a trap near the Morgarten pass, at a point where Leopold would have to ride through a narrow defile. They blocked the exit from the defile and waited in hiding. Once the Hapsburg force was engaged in the confined space, boulders and logs were hurled down on them, followed by charging Swiss fighters armed mostly with halberds—a combination of pike and axe.

As common people not covered by the conventions of chivalry, the Swiss were merciless, slaughtering the Hapsburg knights and taking no prisoners. The Swiss Confederacy not only preserved its independence, but also began to expand on the back of this success. **CP**

Losses: Hapsburg, most of 8,000; Swiss Confederacy, light casualties of 1,500

◁ Marchfeld 1278   Sempach 1386 ▷

Halidon Hill 19 July 1333

The Scottish success at Bannockburn in 1314 eventually forced England to recognize Scottish independence in 1328. Within five years, however, the English were back, their victory at Halidon Hill a precursor of the successful infantry tactics they would use during the Hundred Years' War.

A year after Scottish independence was agreed, Robert Bruce died. David II, his five-year-old son, succeeded him. In 1332 Edward Balliol, son of the king who Edward I had tried to foist on the Scots in 1292, seized his chance and invaded Scotland with a group of exiled Scottish nobles and English adventurers. He deposed David II and sent him into exile, but was himself quickly ambushed by David's remaining supporters and fled into England. He asked Edward III for support, promising to cede southeast Scotland to him. Edward grabbed the opportunity and invaded Scotland to reestablish English control.

The two armies met outside Berwick-upon-Tweed. Edward took up position on Halidon Hill and formed the English into three divisions, his dismounted knights supported by rows of archers. Opposite them, on the other side of a marshy dip, the Scots formed themselves into schiltrons. To reach the English, they had to march downhill, cross the marshy ground, and then advance up Halidon Hill. As soon as the Scots reached the marsh, they were assailed by torrents of arrows. Those who managed to reach the English lines were attacked with spears and swords. Thrown back in disarray, the retreating Scots were finished off by mounted English knights.

The English victory brought them the strategic town of Berwick. More importantly, it taught them how to best use infantry in battle, a lesson that would soon make them supreme in European warfare. **SA**

Losses: English, 14 of 9,000; Scottish, unknown but most of 13,000

◁ Bannockburn 1314   Otterburn 1388 ▷

Minatogawa 4 July 1336

In 1331 Japanese emperor Go-Daigo attacked the institution of the shogun (hereditary military dictator) by overthrowing the ruling Hojo family. But his ally, Ashikaga Takauji, then formed a new dynasty of shoguns. The Kusunoki family, opposing him for the emperor, was defeated at Minatogawa.

The Battle of Minatogawa is famous for the loyalty to the emperor displayed by his leading general, Kusunoki Masashige. Masashige had been in favor of withdrawing to the mountains to fight a guerrilla war, a tactic that had succeeded several times before, but Emperor Go-Daigo wanted to make a stand against the Ashikaga. Kusunoki Masashige's sense of duty forced him to agree, although he knew the situation was hopeless.

At Minatogawa, Kusunoki Masashige and Nitta Yoshisada defended a position against Ashikaga Takauji. Takauji advanced by sea, while Ashikaga Tadayoshi—whose vanguard was led by Shoni Yorihisa—advanced by land. They were joined by a large seaborne reinforcement from Shikoku that tried to land but was driven off and forced to land farther along the coast. Nitta was attacked by Shoni and forced back, leaving Kusunoki Masashige perilously isolated. From his command position, Masashige launched desperate charges against the Ashikaga troops. Wave after wave of samurai horsemen rode up and discharged their longbows against the enemy, following the archery exchange with sword fighting. Yet the Ashikaga had superiority in numbers.

Masashige was soon totally surrounded, and committed suicide as his army collapsed. His sons would continue the fight against the Ashikaga for many years to come, and Masashige is today honored as the greatest exponent of samurai loyalty to the emperor of Japan. **ST**

Losses: Unknown, but very high on the Kusunoki side

"I could not return, I presume / So I will keep my name / Among those who are dead with bows."

Emperor Go-Daigo

⬆ Mount Yoshino Midnight-Moon *(1886) by Yoshitoshi: the ghost Kiyotaka giving advice to Emperor Go-Daigo that led to defeat.*

◁ *Second Mongol Invasion of Japan* 1281   *Kyoto* 1467 ▷

Sluys 24 June 1340

Rio Salado 30 October 1340

In 1337, Edward III of England laid claim to the French throne, thus starting the lengthy series of conflicts known as the Hundred Years' War. The first major contact between the two sides was a naval battle off the coast of Flanders. England's victory ended the threat of a French naval invasion and brought it dominance of the English Channel.

In 1340, Moroccan ruler Abu al-Hasan—a sultan of the Marinid dynasty—mounted a large-scale seaborne invasion of southern Spain. It was the last serious attempt by Muslim forces to reverse the Christian Reconquista in Spain and Portugal. Defeat at Rio Salado foiled Moroccan ambitions and ensured a Christian future for Iberia.

In June 1340 a large English fleet commanded by Edward III set sail across the Channel to assert his claim to the French throne. Opposing him was a large French fleet, reinforced with galleys from Genoa, that was drawn up in the inlet of Sluys in Flanders. The French placed their fleet in a defensive position, their anchored ships lashed together with cables to create a floating platform on which to fight. The Genoese commander, Egidio Bocanegra, known as Barbavara, kept his galleys free behind the French lines. In response, the English placed one of their ships filled with knights and swordsmen between two ships packed with longbowmen. Ships of both sides were filled with soldiers because, at this time, naval battles were only fought on the restrictive confines of the ships' decks.

Battle started at around noon and continued for most of the day and night. Both sides used grappling hooks to hold an enemy ship fast while it was boarded, but it was the English who eventually got the better of the battle. This was because their ships were free to attack the anchored French ships as and when required, and also because their longbowmen produced a more rapid and accurate rate of fire than the French and Genoese crossbowmen. The result was a disaster for the French, with almost all their 190 ships captured or sunk and both their commanders killed. Only the Genoese managed to gain something, seizing two English ships. **SA**

Abu al-Hasan's immediate aims were to help Granada, the only Muslim kingdom left in Iberia, defend itself against the Christian kingdom of Castile, and to establish Moroccan control over the Straits of Gibraltar. In the longer term, he hoped to regain the extensive Iberian lands ruled by his Muslim predecessors.

The invasion of Spain was impressively organized. Moroccan war galleys established naval superiority by crushing the Castilian fleet, which allowed troops and supplies to be ferried unopposed from Ceuta in north Africa across to Gibraltar. As the large Muslim force established itself ashore, the Christian kings Alfonso XI of Castile and Afonso IV of Portugal—until recently at war with one another—responded to the threat by forming an alliance to fight the Moors. They sent galleys to contest command of the sea and assembled an army to march southward.

Abu al-Hasan was besieging the coastal town of Tarifa with his Granada allies when the Castilian-Portuguese army arrived on the scene. He drew up his forces behind the Salado River. The Castilians mounted a charge across the river and a fierce fight swayed to and fro. The Tarifa garrison sortied and attacked the Moroccans from the rear while the Portuguese worsted the Granada army. Caught between the various Christian forces, the African troops were routed, fleeing under hot pursuit. Abu al-Hasan hastily crossed back to Ceuta, never to return. **RG**

Losses: English, 2 ships captured of 210; French and Genoese, 170 ships captured or sunk of 190

Losses: Unknown

Crécy 1346 ▷   ◁ Las Navas de Tolosa 1212   Granada 1492 ▷

Crécy 26 August 1346

In 1346 Edward III of England landed in northern France to protect his lands there as part of the ongoing Hundred Years' War. The battle at Crécy shocked European leaders because a small but disciplined English force fighting on foot had overwhelmed the finest cavalry in Europe.

Edward landed near Cherbourg and then headed southeast toward Paris, capturing Caen and pillaging other towns as he went. The French, led by Philip VI, destroyed all the bridges on the lower Seine in an effort to cut him off, but Edward found a repairable bridge and escaped over the river to the north.

The French eventually caught up with the English near the coast in Picardy. Edward drew his army up on a slope, dividing it into three divisions, each comprising knights and other armored men who fought dismounted, longbowmen, and Welsh light infantry. The English also deployed some primitive gunpowder artillery—one of the first uses of cannon in European warfare. The French, although far larger in number, were tired, disorganized, and wet from a thunderstorm. They were also disadvantaged by having to fight uphill into the evening sun.

The battle started as Genoese crossbowmen in the pay of the French king advanced up the slope. Their first volley fell short and they were quickly overwhelmed by a furious volley of arrows from the English longbowmen that decimated their ranks. As the crossbowmen retreated, the French knights charged through their ranks and up the slope, straight into the fire of the English archers. Those few who managed to reach the English lines died in fierce fighting. Some fifteen or sixteen further attacks continued throughout the night, each one mown down by the English archers. **SA**

Losses: French, 14,000 of 35,000; English, 200 of 16,000

◁ *Sluys 1340*   *Calais 1346* ▷

Calais 4 September 1346–4 August 1347

After his magnificent victory at Crécy, Edward III of England marched north and besieged Calais. The siege lasted for almost a year and, although it was an English victory, both sides were exhausted. A truce was soon declared in the long-running Hundred Years' War that was to hold for eight years.

After Edward landed in France in summer 1346, he sent his fleet home. He therefore needed a secure port from which he could receive fresh supplies and reinforcements. Calais was ideal. The city was surrounded by walls and a double moat and boasted a moated citadel. Its position on the English Channel meant that, once captured, the city could be supplied and defended by English ships easily. Edward's army numbered around 34,000 men, but such a force was inadequate to penetrate the city's defenses. The English also had twenty cannon, but these crude devices made no impression on the city's walls, despite many attempts to breach them.

At first, stalemate reigned as the French failed to intercept the English lines of supply, and the English failed to stop French sailors bringing in new supplies. By February 1347 Edward managed to prevent supplies getting into Calais by sea and dug in for a long siege, starving the 8,000 citizens into surrender. Supplies of fresh water and food were reduced to almost nothing. In July, 500 children and elders left the city so that the remaining inhabitants might survive. Edward, however, refused to accept these expellees, who then starved to death outside the city walls.

Eventually, Calais surrendered. The city was to remain in English hands until 1588, but Edward's finances were now in ruins and the black death was killing large numbers of soldiers. A truce was quickly signed with the French. **SA**

Losses: Unknown

◁ *Crécy 1346*   *Les Espagnols Sur Mer 1350* ▷

Les Espagnols Sur Mer 1350

Despite a truce signed in 1347 between the English and French, the enmity between the two nations continued. In 1350 Edward III of England took the opportunity to weaken France's Spanish ally, Castile, by attacking its fleet. The English victory was hard fought, but the impact was minimal.

The Castilian fleet was under the command of Don Carlos de la Cerda, a Franco-Castilian nobleman and a solider of fortune. On its way to Flanders, the fleet had captured a number of English merchant ships, throwing their crews overboard. Edward decided to seek revenge, intercepting the Castilians as they sailed down the Channel on their way home to the Basque coast of northern Spain. The English fleet, gathering at Winchelsea, was fifty strong, while the Castilian fleet consisted of forty ships. However, their vessels were generally larger in size and well protected by crossbowmen and other mercenaries hired in Flanders in anticipation of battle.

The battle could have been avoided had the Castilians stayed well out in the Channel, but instead they sailed close to land, searching for the English fleet. The English responded by sailing directly at the Castilian fleet, the English flagship *Cog Thomas*—with Edward on board—ramming an enemy ship with such force that the flagship itself began to sink. The crew quickly grappled another enemy ship alongside and boarded it as their flagship sunk. Although the Castilians used the greater height of their vessels to drop heavy weights onto the English decks and their crossbowmen killed many of the enemy, the English gradually got the better of the encounter.

Their eventual victory gave England control of the English Channel but did little to affect the overall outcome of the war. **SA**

Losses: English, 2 ships of 50; Castilian, 14–26 ships of 40

◁ *Calais 1346*   *Combat of the Thirty 1351* ▷

Combat of the Thirty 1351

Battles are usually fought by many thousands of armed men on either side. One battle, however, was very limited in numbers, with only thirty knights fighting on each side. Although its impact was limited, the Combat of the Thirty has gone down as one of the most chivalrous battles in history.

From 1341 to 1364, the succession to the duchy of Brittany was contested between the rival houses of Blois and Montfort: the French king supporting Blois, the English king favoring Montfort. The contest therefore formed part of the much larger conflict between France and England known as the Hundred Years' War.

A truce arranged by Jean de Beaumanoir, governor of Brittany and a supporter of Blois, was being ignored by Sir Robert Bramborough, the captain of Ploërmel and a supporter of Montfort. Beaumanoir issued a challenge that thirty knights and squires on each side should decide the matter in battle, midway between their two castles of Josselin and Ploërmel. Beaumanoir commanded an all-Breton army, while Bramborough led a mixed force of twenty Englishmen, six German mercenaries, and four Bretons. The battle was fiercely fought, the soldiers either mounted or on foot. Victory finally came when Guillaume de Montauban, a squire fighting for Beaumanoir, mounted his horse and overthrew seven English horsemen. Casualties were heavy on both sides but Bramborough's force suffered a higher loss of life and surrendered. All the prisoners were treated well and were released promptly on the payment of a small ransom.

The impact of the conflict on the succession was limited—the house of Montfort eventually won—but contemporaries considered it to be one of the finest examples of chivalry yet displayed. **SA**

Losses: Franco-Breton, 2 of 30; Anglo-Breton, 9 of 30

◁ *Les Espagnols Sur Mer 1350*   *Poitiers 1356* ▷

Poitiers   19 September 1356

An English raiding party in France led by Edward, Prince of Wales, was caught and engaged by the French king Jean II outside Poitiers. The bitterly contested battle ended in catastrophe for France. Many of the French nobility were wiped out and King Jean was left a prisoner of the English.

An eight-year truce in the Hundred Years' War ended in 1355 as neither England nor France could agree to a permanent peace treaty. Edward III of England crossed the Channel and raided deep into northern France. His second son, John of Gaunt, raided Normandy while Edward, Prince of Wales, the "Black Prince," set out from English-held Aquitaine in southwest France to raid central France. His army, consisting of around 4,000 knights, 4,000 mounted cavalry, 3,000 archers, and 1,000 infantry, avoided fortified locations as they plundered undefended towns. On hearing that the French army, led by King Jean II, had crossed the Loire to challenge him, Edward headed south as quickly as his slow-moving baggage

"The king was taken, and his son; and a great number of other great people were both taken and slain."

Edward, in a letter to the people of London

train would allow. Moving at greater speed, the French intercepted the English 3 miles (5 km) east of Poitiers.

Forced into a battle he did not want, Edward chose his position carefully, a slope protected on the left by a marsh and stream while in front his narrow line was covered by a hedge with only a single gap in it through which four knights might ride abreast. On his exposed right flank he placed his wagons. Although the site was ideal, Edward was obviously concerned about the coming battle and, in the early morning of 19 September, attempted to slip

away. The French spotted his move and began their attack, forcing Edward to return quickly. Edward lined up his archers behind the hedge and dismounted all his knights apart from a small reserve force on his right flank. The larger French force was broken into four divisions, or battles, each around 10,000 men. Apart from the knights of the first battle, these, too, were all dismounted, in the mistaken idea that this was the way to engage the English; instead, it deprived them of mobility and surprise.

The first French battle rode toward the English and attempted to storm through the gap in the hedge. As they reached the gap, the English archers opened fire, knocking the knights off their horses only for them to be finished off in fierce, hand-to-hand fighting. French crossbowmen lined up behind their knights had no opportunity to open fire. The second French battle, led by the Dauphin, then marched up the slope toward the English, encountering heavy fire before engaging the English in heavy fighting. The French almost broke through but were repulsed when Edward brought up his reserves. As the French prepared for a third attack, the English archers retrieved arrows from bodies in order to replenish their supplies. The third French battle, however, led by the young Duc d'Orléans, was intimidated and fled the battlefield. With just one battle left, the French king himself advanced toward the English.

Edward responded by ordering his entire army to attack, his small reserve cavalry force sent around the French flank to attack them in the rear. The fighting was intense, with many English archers fighting with knives as their arrow supply was exhausted. Eventually the king and his bodyguard were overwhelmed. Jean was taken into captivity and held until a vast ransom was paid in 1360, but many of his leading nobles had lost their lives. **SA**

Losses: English, 1,000 dead of 12,000; French, 2,500 dead and 2,600 captured of 40,000

◁ Combat of the Thirty 1351   Cocherel 1364 ▷

A fourteenth-century illumination depicting the Black Prince and King Jean II of France at Poitiers.

y parle de la bataille de poi
entre le prince de galles e

Mello 10 June 1358

After the French defeat at Poitiers and the imprisonment of King Jean in England, France was convulsed by a popular uprising against the nobility. This movement, known as the Jacquerie, was savagely suppressed after an ill-equipped rebel army was destroyed at Mello in the Beauvais.

From spring 1358 French peasant bands attacked the isolated houses of the nobility, destroying property and massacring the inhabitants. They were supported by a commune under Etienne Marcel that had taken control of Paris. French nobles assembled an army to fight back, finding a leader in a pretender to the French throne, Charles II of Navarre, and additional troops in English mercenaries, unemployed in the post-Poitiers truce. This army—makeshift but consisting of, and led by, men highly experienced in warfare—marched from Normandy into Beauvais to confront a rebel force mostly recruited from the region's peasantry, equipped with agricultural implements and led by a local man, Guillaume Cale.

The nobles regarded their opponents as having no right to the protection of the laws and customs of war. When the two armies faced one another outside Mello, Charles invited Cale to negotiate, promising safe passage. When Cale arrived for talks, he was seized, tortured, and executed. The nobles' army then attacked the leaderless peasants and drove them from the field. In a merciless pursuit, fleeing men were hunted down and killed.

Meanwhile in the neighboring town of Meaux, where hundreds of rebels from Paris had arrived and were being entertained by the local population, a handful of knights sortied from the town's keep and slaughtered Parisian rebels and local citizens alike. The Jacquerie was suppressed in an orgy of summary executions. **CP**

Losses: Noble, few casualties of around 2,000; Rebel, most dead of around 5,000

☐ *Poitiers 1356*   *Cocherel 1364* ☐

Lake Poyang 30 Aug–2 Sep 1363

Zhu Yuanzhang, the future Ming emperor of China, was opposed by the Han and the Wu Chinese, and a classic Chinese naval battle occurred when a Ming fleet came to the relief of the besieged city of Nanchang in Jianxi province, which lies on the Gan River south of Lake Poyang.

The relieving Ming fleet was divided into eleven squadrons. The greater maneuverability of the Ming ships allowed their men to set fire to more than twenty Han ships using catapult bombs, but this failed to break the Han line. Indeed the opposite was happening because the flagship of the Ming vanguard had caught fire and the Han ships were naturally concentrating their attacks on it. Zhu Yuanzhang went to the rescue in person and the fires were extinguished as the Han attackers drew off to concentrate on the enemy commander, for whom disaster struck when his ship ran aground.

Other Ming ships came bravely to the rescue of their leader, but when battle resumed on the morrow some cowards among the Ming commanders refused to advance; they were beheaded for their treason. Zhu Yuanzhang then changed his tactics and ordered the construction of fireships. In the carnage that followed Han troops were either burned or drowned, and the Ming forces boarded the stricken vessels, taking many heads.

On 2 September, battle had recommenced when Zhu Yuanzhang was presented with the good news that the hostile army sent to cut off Nanchang had been defeated and his forces had succeeded in relieving the city. His objective in the Poyang campaign had thus been achieved, but a long war of attrition was not to his liking. Zhu consequently ordered his men to make a withdrawal, which took a full month to achieve. **ST**

Losses: Unknown, but likely high on both sides

☐ *Yamen 1279*   *Ningyuan 1626* ☐

 Knights massacre Jacquerie supporters in Meaux, from Froissart's fourteenth-century Chronicles.

Cocherel 16 May 1364

Constant fighting with England during the early stages of the Hundred Years' War had left the French kingdom weak and divided. However, the Battle of Cocherel, fought to resolve a dispute over the succession to the Duchy of Burgundy, showed that France had found a brutally effective military commander in Bertrand du Guesclin.

In 1361 Philip I, Duke of Burgundy, died unexpectedly. Charles II of Navarre, closely related to the French royal family and a major landowner in Normandy and eastern France, claimed the duchy as a step toward a bid for the French throne itself. The French king, Jean II, responded by claiming the duchy himself. In April 1364 King Jean died and the Dauphin took the throne as King Charles V. He entrusted the Breton knight Bertrand du Guesclin with the task of fighting Navarre for control of Burgundy.

The two sides met at Cocherel in Normandy. In command of the Navarran force, which included some 900 knights and 300 English archers, was Jean de Grailly, Captal de Buch. Du Guesclin was a tough, uncompromising fighter known for his ugliness—he was once described as a "hog in armor." In contrast, the Captal de Buch was renowned in his day as the ideal of the chivalrous nobleman.

Emulating a tried and tested English battle tactic, the Navarran army stood on the defensive on a hill, obliging Du Guesclin to attack. The royal force managed to break their opponents' lines by first attacking and then pretending to retreat, tempting the Navarran troops to leave their strong positions and give chase. A flank attack by the French reserve then won the day. The Captal de Buch was captured but later released without ransom. The position of the French king was much strengthened and the threat of Navarre to the French throne ended. **SA**

Losses: No reliable figures

◁ *Poitiers 1356*   *Auray 1364* ▷

Bertrand du Guesclin's force attacks the Navarrans in a fifteenth-century French illustration. ⬆

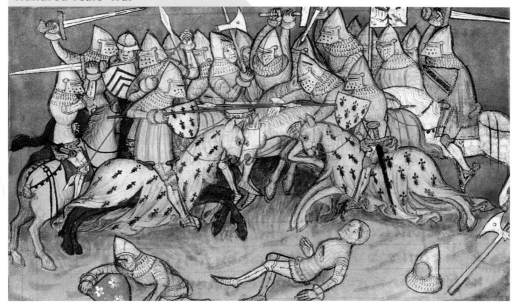

Auray 29 September 1364

Although officially at peace after an agreement at Brétigny in 1360, England and France continued to fight for control over Brittany, supporting opposing claimants to the dukedom. The Battle of Auray was militarily a decisive victory for the English side, but it proved impossible to translate battlefield success into political advantage.

After his success at Cocherel, French military commander Bertrand du Guesclin was sent to Brittany, where the coastal town of Auray was under siege by an Anglo-Breton force. The Bretons were led by the English-backed claimant to the dukedom, Jean de Montfort, and the English troops by Sir John Chandos. This force invaded the town and surrounded its inner citadel. Running short of food, the citadel's defenders agreed to surrender if not relieved by 29 September.

In the two days before that deadline, both Du Guesclin and Montfort's rival for the dukedom, Charles de Blois, arrived with their armies. The Anglo-Breton forces came out to face them and on 29 September battle was joined.

The fighting had no hint of the chivalry associated with the period. The men-at-arms on both sides mostly fought on foot, hacking and stabbing with swords, daggers, and lances in a vast melee. Usually in medieval warfare the lives of men of high rank were spared, but at Auray quarter was not always given. Charles de Blois, floored by a thrust from a lance, was unceremoniously finished off by an English soldier. Du Guesclin had better fortune. As his army broke and fled, his surrender was accepted by Chandos. He was later ransomed by French king Charles V. Installed as undisputed Duke of Brittany, Montfort quickly changed allegiance, swearing fealty to the French king. The English gained nothing. **RG**

Losses: Anglo-Breton, no reliable figures; Franco-Breton, more than 1,000 dead

⟨ *Cocherel 1364*　　　　　　　　　　*Najera 1367* ⟩

Knights on horseback battle at Auray in an illustration by Jean Cuvelier, c. 1400.

Najera 3 April 1367

The kingdom of Castile was plunged into civil war between rival claimants to the throne, Pedro and his brother Enrique. The French under Bertrand du Guesclin and the English under Edward, the Black Prince, intervened in the dispute. Victory at Najera carried the Black Prince to the peak of his renown.

The Anglo-French conflict known as the Hundred Years' War was interrupted by the Peace of Brétigny in 1360. This agreement brought no peace to French towns and villages, which were ravaged by roaming companies of unemployed soldiers. It was largely to free France of this human plague that Du Guesclin assembled an army to campaign in Castile, where they could make a living by plundering someone else.

After Du Guesclin backed Enrique, Pedro appealed to Edward, the Black Prince, for help. Abetted by Sir John Chandos and John of Gaunt, the Black Prince led an army south from Aquitaine. The rival forces met at Najera in the Rioja region of northern Spain. The Franco-Castilian army outnumbered the English and Pedro's Castilians, but experienced French commanders advised Du Guesclin to avoid a pitched battle, and instead maneuver to cut the Black Prince's supply lines. The advice was militarily sound but politically impossible, since Enrique could not be seen to run away from a battle. Du Guesclin had to fight and duly lost. The English longbowmen decimated their enemy's cavalry and the English men-at-arms outfought the French on foot. As at Auray three years before, Du Guesclin was taken prisoner and ransomed.

Pedro took the Castilian throne, but never repaid the Black Prince for the expense of his army. The French were cheered by the heavy casualties as it reduced the number of soldiers who returned to prey on civilians. **RG**

Losses: Anglo-Castilian, 200 of 28,000; Franco-Castilian, 7,000 of 60,000

◁ *Auray 1364* *Pontvallain 1370* ▷

Pontvallain 4 December 1370

The Peace of Brétigny signed in 1360 between England and France—designed to end the Hundred Years' War—broke down in 1368. Now better led than before, the French managed to achieve a significant victory against their foe, ending a period of English invincibility on the battlefield.

In 1368 Gascon nobles revolted against the rule of their English duke, Edward, the Black Prince. They were quickly supported by the French, ably led by Bertrand du Guesclin, soon to be promoted Constable of France; a position that, in effect, placed him as second-in-command to the king. In response, Edward III—father of the Black Prince—overturned the Peace of Brétigny and renewed his claim to the French throne.

Du Guesclin cleverly avoided tackling the English in set-piece battles, where their superiority in archers would win the day, but harried them instead when they were unprepared. A small but significant battle took place in the Loire valley at the end of 1370. The battle, at Pontvallain, actually consisted of two separate skirmishes, with the smaller of the pair taking place in nearby Vaas—the two are sometimes named as separate battles.

Du Guesclin left Normandy in November in pursuit of a large English raiding party and arrived near Le Mans on 3 December. On hearing that some of the English force was spread out near Pontvallain, he ordered a night march and surprised them at dawn. The English tried to escape but were caught at Château de la Faigne and overwhelmed in tough hand-to-hand fighting. A second English contingent was massacred near the fortified abbey of Vaas. As the English survivors fled south, they were pursued by Du Guesclin and most were killed outside the castle of Bressuire. The thirty-year English reputation for invincibility in open battle was at an end. **SA**

Losses: No reliable figures

◁ *Najera 1367*

Aljubarrota 1385 ▷

⬆ *As the Battle of Pontvallain rages, Gregory XI is made pope at Avignon in December 1370.*

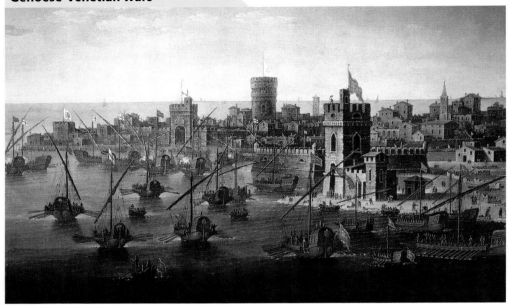

Chioggia 16 August 1379–14 June 1380

The Battle of Chioggia was the decisive and climactic encounter in the long struggle for naval and commercial supremacy between the Italian cities of Genoa and Venice. After looking certain to be defeated in the early stages of the prolonged battle, the Venetians emerged triumphant and went on to dominate the Mediterranean.

In August 1379 Venice lay wide open to Genoese attack. One fleet of Venetian war galleys, commanded by Vettor Pisani, had been destroyed by the Genoese at Pola in May; the rest of the Venetian galleys under Carlo Zeno were far away in the eastern Mediterranean. The Genoese fleet was able to enter the Venice lagoon and, with the aid of the land forces of Hungarian and Paduan allies, occupy the port of Chioggia. This allowed the Genoese to place Venice under blockade by land and sea.

Threatened with destruction, the Venetian government gave way to popular pressure and reinstated Admiral Pisani, who had been disgraced and imprisoned after the defeat at Pola. On 21 December Pisani turned the tables on the Genoese. Mustering all available forces, under cover of darkness he moved into the lagoon and formed a blockade of Chioggia. Ships were scuttled in the shallow channels, trapping the Genoese fleet and cutting off their supply routes and their means of escape. Less than two weeks later, the Venetians were reinforced by the arrival of Carlo Zeno's fleet, on 1 January 1380. The desperate Genoese fleet attempted to break out, but the Venetian commanders had the advantage of superior knowledge of the lagoon and defeated them in a series of skirmishes.

In June the once-proud Genoese fleet surrendered. Victory enabled Venice to exclude the Genoese from the Adriatic and dominate the eastern Mediterranean. It was a disaster from which Genoa never recovered. **TB**

Losses: No available figures

◁ *Curzola 1298* *Zonchio 1499* ▷

In a sixteenth-century painting, the Venetian fleet arrives to relieve the port of Chioggia. ⬆

Kulikovo   8 September 1380

The Battle of Kulikovo, fought near the Don River in 1380, is celebrated as the first victory for Russian forces over the Tatars of the Mongol Golden Horde since Russia was subjugated by Batu Khan in the thirteenth century. Even more significant, the victory was a giant step for the Duchy of Moscow in its rise to leadership of the Russian people.

Previously a backwater, Moscow grew in importance in the fourteenth century because its princes acted as agents of the Golden Horde, whose khans were overlords of the Russian lands. In the late 1370s, however, Dmitri, Prince of Moscow, took advantage of divisions among the Tatars to assert a measure of independence.

One claimant to leadership of the Golden Horde, Mamai, led an army to assert authority over Russia. Dmitri crossed the Don to face the Tatars. Chronicles narrate that the battle opened with a fight between champions from each side, both of whom were killed. Around noon a general engagement began. Dmitri cunningly exchanged his armor with one of his followers, who was duly sought out and killed by the Tatars. Dmitri escaped this fate, although he was wounded. After about three hours of fighting, a flanking charge by Russian cavalry forced the Tatars to withdraw. Although collapsing from loss of blood, Dmitri had his victory. He was accorded the name "Donskoy" to mark his triumph on the Don.

The result of the battle was decisive for Mamai, who lost the struggle for leadership of the Golden Horde. Russia had not gained freedom from Mongol domination, however, for the Horde's new leader, Tokhtamysh, sacked Moscow two years later. But the Battle of Kulikovo did much to erase the memory of the Duchy of Moscow's collaboration with the Mongols and established Dmitri Donskoy as a heroic figure in Russian history. **CP**

Losses: No reliable figures

◁ *Kalka River 1222*   *Orsha 1514* ▷

⬆ *Massed Russian and Tatar troops clash at Kulikovo in a seventeenth-century Russian depiction.*

Aljubarrota 14 August 1385

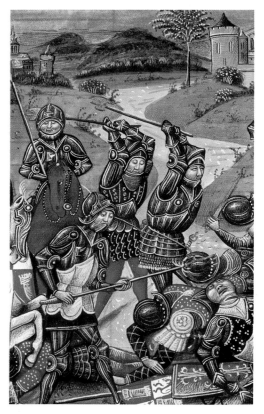

Portugal exists today as a separate country from Spain in large part because of victory at Aljubarrota. Had the Portuguese lost, they would have lost their autonomy to Spanish Castile. The battle was also an episode in the Hundred Years' War, with English contingents supporting the Portuguese and the French siding with Castile.

In 1383 the succession to the Portuguese throne was contested. King Juan of Castile claimed the throne through marriage to a Portuguese princess. But the Grand Master of the Military Order of Aviz emerged as a Portuguese contender, to be declared King João I. As Portugal's ally, England sent men-at-arms and longbowmen to aid João, while the French supplied 2,000 knights to the Castilian army that invaded Portugal.

Castile had by far the larger force, but the Portuguese employed the tactics that had allowed the outnumbered English to triumph over the French at Poitiers. João selected a defensive position between two creeks, digging trenches to block the charge of the Franco-Castilian cavalry. His men were to fight on foot, supported by English bowmen. Juan of Castile tried to avoid a frontal assault on this strong position. He marched his army around the Anglo-Portuguese to attack from the other side. But this flanking march, on a hot day, exhausted his troops and they still had to attack a resolute enemy occupying a restricted battlefield. French cavalry charges suffered grievous losses in the face of English archers.

When the French and Castilian knights dismounted to fight on foot, a furious melee developed with heavy casualties on both sides. Finally the French and Castilians were routed, and through the following days hundreds were killed by Portuguese civilians as they fled. **CP**

"King Juan, despairing of victory, fled the field, taking refuge in Santarem before boarding a ship for Seville."

Thomas M. Izbicki, Medieval Iberia, 1997

⬆ *Portuguese knights battle with Castilians at Aljubarrota, from Jean Batard de Wavrin's fifteenth-century* Chronicle of England.

Losses: Portuguese and English, 1,000 of 7,000; Castilian and French, 5,000 of 30,000

◁ *Pontvallain 1370* *Agincourt 1415* ▷

Sempach 9 July 1386

After its triumph over the Austrian Hapsburgs at Morgarten, the Swiss Confederacy continued to expand. In 1386 Hapsburg duke Leopold III of Austria responded to the adhesion of yet more towns and rural communes to the upstart Confederacy by leading an army to attack the Swiss town of Sempach, near Lucerne.

The Swiss cantons mobilized an army to counter the Hapsburg offensive. Both sides were acutely aware of the divide in social status between them—the Hapsburg forces led by nobles and their knights, the Swiss army made up of common townsmen and peasants.

The vanguard of the Swiss marching column unexpectedly encountered Leopold's army on the road outside Sempach. The Hapsburg knights chose to fight on foot. At first they had the better of the fighting and the Swiss looked beaten. But as more Swiss troops reached the battlefield it was the Hapsburg force that began to wilt under pressure. At some point, according to Swiss accounts of the battle, a certain Arnold von Winkelried threw himself on to the Hapsburg spears, thus opening a gap for the Swiss infantry to push through. Duke Leopold led more dismounted knights into the melee, but could not turn the tide of the battle. The Hapsburg rearguard took to horse and fled the field. So did many of the squires entrusted with the dismounted knights' warhorses, taking away their masters' only means of escape. Butchery ensued, with Duke Leopold himself falling among the slaughtered nobility and knights.

The battle effectively settled the issue of Swiss independence. In the medieval European view, the victory of commoners over the chivalric elite in an equal fight, man to man, was an especially shocking event. **CP**

Losses: Hapsburg, 700 of 4,000; Swiss Confederacy, unknown of 4,000

◀ Morgarten 1315   Murten 1476 ▶

Otterburn 5 August 1388

England's attention was diverted away from its northern neighbor, Scotland, during the Hundred Years' War with France. Warfare and border skirmishes continued between the two countries, however. A Scottish raiding party achieved great success at Otterburn in Northumbria, although at the cost of the life of its leader, James Douglas.

Exact details of this battle are somewhat contentious, as the main source, Jean Froissart's *Chronicles*, gets many distances and other facts wrong. What is known is that James, the Second Earl of Douglas, took the opportunity of leadership divisions on the English side to launch a massive border raid south. Douglas divided his forces, sending his baggage train southwest toward Carlisle while he led a raiding party that ravaged the countryside around Newcastle and Durham to the east.

On 4 August, Douglas destroyed Ponteland castle, moving on the next day to besiege Otterburn castle. The English lord Henry Percy, First Earl of Northumberland, seized his chance and launched a surprise attack on the besieging Scots during the afternoon. However, his attack gave the bulk of the Scottish army time to muster their ranks and attack the English flank later that evening. Although Douglas himself was killed in the fighting, and the Scottish army was outnumbered almost three to one by the English, Scottish discipline and good leadership brought them a major victory. When the Bishop of Durham arrived from Newcastle with 10,000 reinforcements, he was so impressed with the orderly formations of the Scottish troops and their unassailable position that he declined to attack them.

As a result of the battle, Scotland and England remained largely at peace for more than twenty years. **SA**

Losses: Scottish, 500 of 2,900; English, 1,860 dead and 1,040 captured of 8,000

◀ Bannockburn 1314   Flodden 1513 ▶

desconfirent lauant garde de lamo
raquin z quant il se repentit de son ep

Amorath baquin ne mist p
en oubli son emprinse ma

Kosovo 28 June 1389

At the Battle of Kosovo Serbians under the overall command of Czar Lazar were defeated by a much larger force of invading Ottoman Turks, led by Sultan Murad I. Both leaders were killed in the battle, which became central to the formation of Serbian national identity.

Under Sultan Murad's rule the Turks had been expanding their rule from Anatolia into the Balkans, where the Serb Empire was potentially their strongest opponent. At the Battle of Marisa in 1371 the Serbs suffered a severe defeat that fragmented their empire into rival princedoms.

Murad resumed his campaigns against the Serbs in the 1380s. In the summer of 1389 he halted at Kosovo, from where he had options to attack Serbia or Macedonia. While Murad consulted with his commanders, Lazar mustered all his forces in alliance with Vuk Branković, a Serbian noble, and advanced on Kosovo. Lazar's army is thought to have been less than half the size of Murad's force. The battle began with Ottoman archers bombarding the advancing Serbian cavalry, which blunted their impact on the Turkish lines. However, inroads had been made and the Serbian charge was followed up by heavily armored knights. Fearing that the Serbians might break through, the Turks counter-attacked, routing the Serbian infantry.

Some records claim that Lazar was captured and executed; others claim that he was deserted by the jealous Branković and fought valiantly until hacked to death. Murad is thought to have been killed by a Serbian knight, Miloš Obilić, in the immediate aftermath of the battle. Although both sides suffered huge losses, the Ottomans possessed the resources to raise another army and Serbia became part of the Ottoman Empire. **TB**

Losses: Heavy on both sides, including both leaders and much of the Serbian nobility

Nicopolis 1396 ▷

Terek River 14 April 1395

The Central Asian warrior Timur, known as "the Lame" and hence Timurlane, conquered an ephemeral empire that stretched from India to Turkey. His rise to prominence, which occurred relatively late in life, began with the defeat of a rival nomadic warrior, Tokhtamysh.

Of Mongol and Turkish origins, Timur was in his early years a lawless leader of mounted bandits. Despite being half-crippled by an arrow wound—he was unable to walk unaided—by the age of fifty, in the mid-1380s, he had made himself ruler of Samarkand and Heart. Wider ambitions were sparked by rivalry with Tokhtamysh, who was leading the Mongol Golden Horde on raids through the rich lands of Persia. Timur first imitated his rival, plundering Persian cities such as Shiraz and Isfahan, but soon rivalry turned to war, with the two armies of nomadic horsemen pursuing one another across the immense spaces of Central Asia.

An initial victory over Tokhtamysh at the Kundurcha River in 1391 proved inconclusive, but four years later Timur settled the issue for good in a battle on the Terek River north of the Caucasus. According to contemporary chronicles, Tokhtamysh attacked first, penetrating his enemy's lines to threaten Timur in person. But Timur was defended by his bodyguards and all Tokhtamysh's charges were repulsed. The battle raged with fearful intensity, hand-to-hand fighting spreading across the breadth of the field, until Tokhtamysh at last despaired of success and withdrew. Timur, it is said, flung himself down in prayer of thanks to Allah after this narrowest of victories. He exploited it to the full. Tokhtamysh's horde was pursued mercilessly. Controlling Central Asia, Timur had a base for wider conquests. **CP**

Losses: No reliable figures

Delhi 1398 ▷

 Death of Sultan Murad I, *from the fourteenth-century* Chronicles of Jean Froissart.

Nicopolis   25 September 1396

"*King Sigismund . . . fought badly at Nicopolis and lost his army with great slaughter and ruin for his followers.*"

Giunio Resti, chronicler

⬆ *Bayezid I routs the crusaders at the Battle of Nicopolis in a sixteenth-century watercolor from the* Hünername *in Istanbul.*

In 1394 Pope Boniface IX called for a crusade against the rising power of the Muslim Ottoman Turks, who were taking over southeast Europe. The result, two years later, was the Battle of Nicopolis, a catastrophic defeat for Christian knights at the hands of the Ottoman Turks.

After their victory at Kosovo, the Ottomans gained control of much of the Balkans under the leadership of Bayezid I, known as "the Thunderbolt." In response to the pope's call, nobles from across Christian Europe eventually signed up for the venture, including large contingents from France, Hungary, and Germany and from the Knights of the Order of the St. John. Led by Sigismund, King of Hungary, they embarked on the long journey to the Danubian fortress of Nicopolis in modern-day Bulgaria.

From the outset the crusade was riven by disputes of precedence and status. The knights reached Nicopolis in the late summer, ill-equipped to take the fortress by force. After weeks of siege, it was discovered that Bayezid was only hours away at the head of a large army. The crusaders panicked, and despite a council of war, their actions were rash and uncoordinated. The French knights insisted on leading a charge, not fully knowing the size of the Sultan's army. The charge was initially successful, but Bayezid responded with his reserves. In their rush to secure the glory of victory for themselves, the French knights had become separated from their Hungarian support, and as Bayezid counterattacked they were destroyed. The Hungarians tried desperately to support the French but failed to notice an outflanking move by the Ottoman *sipahis* (light cavalry). Enveloped, the crusaders were overcome. Sigismund was among the few to escape. After the battle Bayezid had most of his prisoners executed. **TB**

Losses: Ottoman, considerable of 15,000; Crusader, most dead or captured of 10,000

◁ *Kosovo 1389*   *Ankara 1402* ▷

Delhi 17 December 1398

In 1398 the Mongol-Turkish warrior Timur, ruler of Central Asia from his capital at Samarkand, found a pretext to strike south into India. His victory over the sultan of Delhi confirmed the irresistible fighting qualities of his army and the awesome destructiveness that made him a legend of cruelty.

A devout Muslim, Timur alleged that his co-religionist Sultan Nasiruddin Mahmud of Delhi was being too lenient toward his Hindu subjects. On this pretext he marched into the Indian subcontinent in late summer 1398, his tribal steppe horsemen plundering and massacring as they advanced. By the time Timur approached Delhi, his army was so encumbered with loot and captured slaves that military efficiency was imperiled. Timur's solution was to order his followers to kill all their slaves—possibly around 100,000 people. Thus prepared, the invaders faced Sultan Mahmud's army outside the walls of Delhi. The sultan had a force of war elephants, creatures with which the steppe warriors were unfamiliar. Timur had his men dig elaborate field fortifications—a system of trenches and ramparts—to block the charge of the pachyderms and give his nervous followers a sense of security.

The course of the battle is hard to piece together from the historical record. Incendiary devices played a part, including catapults that hurled pots of inflammable liquid. By one account, Timur had camels loaded with kindling that was set on fire, releasing them to spread panic among the Indian elephants. The charge of Timur's horsemen was certainly decisive, reportedly scattering the Indian soldiers "as hungry lions scatter a flock of sheep." Victorious in the field, Timur unleashed his warriors upon Delhi in an orgy of destruction from which the city took a century to recover. **CP**

"He loved bold and valiant soldiers, by whose aid he . . . tore men to pieces like lions, and overturned mountains."

Ahmad ibn Arabshah, on Timur

Losses: No reliable figures, although some sources give the Indian death toll as 1,000,000

⬆ *A manuscript depicting Timur's late-fourteenth-century invasion of India.*

◁ *Terek River 1395*   *Aleppo 1400* ▷

Aleppo 11 November 1400

Mynydd Hyddgen June 1401

After the success of his devastating invasion of India, Timur turned his army to the west. His attack on the Syrian domains of Sultan Faruj, Mameluke ruler of Egypt, was an astonishingly bold enterprise. In the event, the renowned Mameluke forces proved no match for Timur at Aleppo.

The English had ruled Wales ever since Edward I invaded the principality and incorporated it into England in 1284. Welsh resistance to English rule continued, however, erupting into open revolt, led by Owain Glyndwr, a descendent of the last independent Welsh prince, in 1400.

By 1400 Timur's steppe warriors were showing signs of battle fatigue, but Timur himself, although more than sixty years old, still lusted for conquest. He was handed a pretext to attack the wealthy cities of Syria when an ambassador whom he had sent to Damascus was executed by the city's Mameluke viceroy. Overriding the protests of his weary followers—no doubt intimidated by the Mamelukes' high military reputation—Timur marched into Syria. Sultan Faruj called on all his emirs to concentrate their troops at Aleppo. Timur advanced with caution, constructing a fortified camp each night as he approached the city.

The Mamelukes meanwhile, after a heated council of war, decided to face Timur's army in open battle outside the city walls. It was an unfortunate decision. After two days of skirmishing, largely favorable to the Mamelukes, full battle was joined. Timur threw his horsemen in wide arcs around the flanks of the enemy line, while his center held firm, strengthened by war elephants brought from India. Thrown into disorder by the fierce cavalry attacks, the Mamelukes broke and fled for the safety of the city. Timur had kept a reserve for the pursuit and threw these horsemen forward to slaughter the mass attempting to force themselves through the city gates. While a few succeeded in reaching the citadel, it was soon made to surrender. A massacre ensued, and Timur's trademark pyramid of skulls was erected as a warning to all. **CP**

The first battle in Wales's war of independence occurred when English settlers in Pembrokeshire, in the far southwest of Wales, and settlers of Flemish descent living in the area since the early 1100s, attacked Glyndwr's army camped at the bottom of the Hyddgen valley. Mynydd means "mountain" in Welsh but the exact location of the battle is not known. It is assumed to be on the western slopes of Pumlumon, the highest point of the Cambrian mountains, on the present-day borders of Ceredigion and Powys. The English settlers were aided by a large force of English soldiers and Flemish mercenaries, their total numbering perhaps 1,500 men. Most of these troops were foot soldiers, with some light cavalry. In contrast, Glyndwr's army consisted of no more than 500 men— some records suggest that the total did not exceed 120.

Most of the Welsh army were archers, riding small hill ponies that were well suited to the region's boggy and mountainous conditions. Despite their numerical disadvantage, and having to fight from low ground, the Welsh troops soon overcame the undisciplined English and Flemish force. They quickly set out in pursuit of the routed attacking force, killing 200 and capturing many more. Exact details of the battle are not known, but Glyndwr's success was probably the result of the better maneuverability of his troops against their more heavily laden attackers, who struggled to fight effectively in the marshy terrain of the valley floor. **SA**

Losses: No reliable figures, but at least 20,000 Syrians reportedly massacred

◁ *Delhi 1398* *Ankara 1402* ▷

Losses: Welsh, unknown of 500; English, 200 dead and more captured of 1,500

Usk 1405 ▷

Ankara 20 July 1402

In 1402 two feared warriors met in combat outside the city of Ankara: Ottoman Sultan Bayezid, "the Thunderbolt," victor of Nicopolis, and Timur, the conqueror of Asia from Delhi to Damascus. The battle ended in humiliating defeat for Bayezid and came close to destroying the Ottoman Empire.

Bayezid I was at the height of his power, besieging the Byzantine capital, Constantinople, when he was drawn away from fighting the Christians by the threat of Timur's army advancing from eastern Anatolia. Bayezid marched his army across Anatolia in the summer heat to face Timur, but the wily Asian warrior outmaneuvered him. As Bayezid marched eastward, Timur cut behind him and besieged the vital Ottoman city of Ankara.

Thirsty and exhausted, Bayezid's troops had to turn back to attempt the relief of the city. Timur drew up his forces in battle order and forced Bayezid to attack by sending troops to divert the only source of water for his army—the Ottomans had to fight or die of thirst. Serbian cavalry, fighting as auxiliaries of the Ottomans, opened the battle with an effective charge, but Timur's mounted archers took a heavy toll of Bayezid's army. Thousands of Ottoman infantry were slaughtered. Bayezid fled from the battle with a cavalry force, but Timur pursued and surrounded him.

Bayezid became the only Ottoman sultan ever to be captured by an enemy. He died in captivity in 1403, after allegedly being kept by Timur in a golden cage as a trophy. Timur advanced to the Aegean, forcing Bayezid's son to flee Anatolia. Yet ultimately Timur's army were only raiders; they established no permanent presence. The Timurid Empire declined rapidly after Timur's death in 1405. For the Ottomans, decline was only temporary. **TB**

Losses: Timurid, 15,000 dead or wounded; Ottoman, 30,000 dead or wounded

◁ *Nicopolis 1396*   *Varna 1444* ▷

Usk Spring 1405

The Welsh campaign for independence from England led by Owain Glyndwr had begun in 1400. The guerrilla campaign achieved huge success, but was halted by a major defeat at Usk in South Wales during the spring of 1405. From then on, the tide would turn against Glyndwr and his cause.

In early 1405 a Welsh force was defeated at Grosmont in what is now northern Monmouthshire. In an attempt to regain the initiative in the area, Glyndwr's eldest son, Gruffudd, launched an attack on Usk castle. What Gruffudd probably did not know was that the castle defenses had recently been strengthened, and that large numbers of extra troops had been drafted in to augment the garrison. As a result, his risky attack was easily repelled.

The troops inside the castle then went on the offensive, pursuing the Welsh across the River Usk and into the forest of Monkswood toward Mynydd Pwll Melyn, the "mountain of the yellow pool." In the words of Adam of Usk, a local priest who later recorded the events, the English "there slew with fire and the edge of the sword many of them, and above all the Abbot of Llanthony, and they crushed them without ceasing, driving them through the monk's wood, where the said Griffin [Gruffudd] was taken."

Welsh losses were high, with perhaps 1,500 deaths, including that of Tudor, another of Glyndwr's sons. Gruffudd was captured and imprisoned in the Tower of London, where he died six years later, while around 300 other prisoners were beheaded in front of Usk castle. The battle and its bloody aftermath ended the rebellion in southeast Wales. With the loss of so many men, Glyndwr was unable to contemplate tackling the English in battle again, and by 1415 his rebellion had petered out. **SA**

Losses: English, no reliable figures; Welsh, 15,000

◁ *Mynydd Hyddgen 1401*

Grunwald (First Tannenberg) 15 July 1410

The defeat of the Teutonic Knights by a Polish-Lithuanian army is an event embedded in racial legend—seen as a tragic or triumphant moment in the epic struggle between the Germanic peoples and the Slavs. More prosaically, it marked the emergence of Poland-Lithuania as one of Europe's most powerful states.

The Order of the Teutonic Knights, originally founded during the Crusades in the Holy Land, had become rulers of a state in Prussia. From there they mounted crusading campaigns against their non-Christian neighbors, including the Duchy of Lithuania. In 1386 Lithuania's ruler converted to Christianity and married the queen of Poland, on her death becoming ruler of Poland as King Ladislav II Jagiellon. The Teutonic Knights contested the sincerity of Jagiellon's conversion and, in 1409, their choleric Grand Master, Ulrich von Jungingen, declared war on Poland and Lithuania. He had underrated the joint power and unity of the newly conjoined states.

"The forces of the Polish king were so numerous that there is no number high enough in the human language." *Prussian Chronicles*

In the summer of 1410, an army led by King Jagiellon and Grand Duke Witold of Lithuania advanced upon the Teutonic Knights' capital at Marienberg. The Teutonic Knights confronted the invaders between the villages of Grunwald and Tannenberg, in what is now northern Poland. Although outnumbered, the Knights were confident in the strength of their disciplined armored cavalry. The opposing lines were drawn up early in the morning, but until noon a standoff prevailed. Exposed to the summer sun, the Knights cooked inside their armor. An attempt to fire a pair of bombards—unwieldy siege cannon—against the Polish-Lithuanian troops had no effect. Grand Master von Jungingen, reduced to insults in his desperation to provoke his enemy to action, sent swords to Jagiellon and Witold with the ironic advice that they might find them useful if they ever fought a battle.

Eventually the fighting began, with swift success for the Teutonic Knights. Clashing with Lithuanian cavalry on the enemy right, the charging Knights swept them from the field. Returning from the pursuit, they then joined in the tougher fighting against the Poles on the Polish-Lithuanian left. Again the Knights gained the upper hand. King Jagiellon was narrowly saved from capture or death as von Jungingen led the charge in person. But at this crucial juncture the survivors of the Lithuanian cavalry returned to the battlefield and crashed into the rear of the Teutonic Knights. The Grand Master was killed by a lance-thrust through the throat as the rest of the Knights made a fighting withdrawal to their camp. Their attempt to secure a defensive position behind wagons failed and many of them were cut down. By the end of the day most of the Teutonic Knights' troops were either dead or prisoners.

Despite the scale of their victory, the Polish-Lithuanian army failed to take Marienberg and peace was made the following year on mild terms. The Teutonic Knights never regained their dominance, and Poland-Lithuania became the major power in eastern Europe. The victory is celebrated in the national histories of Lithuania, Poland, and Belrus. In the Soviet period it was also retrospectively claimed as a Russian triumph, because of the presence of some troops from Smolensk. When the Germans triumphed over the Russians in the early stages of World War I, they called the battle Tannenberg so they could claim revenge for the defeat after half a millennium. **CP**

Losses: Polish-Lithuanian, 5,000 dead of 39,000; Teutonic, 8,000 dead and 14,000 captured of 27,000

[<] *Lake Peipus 1242*   *Swiecino 1462* [>]

Teutonic Knights grapple with their neighbors in a painting by Carl Wilhelm Kolbe (1757–1835). ➡

Agincourt 25 October 1415

In 1413 the new king of England, Henry V, took the opportunity of a power struggle inside France to renew English claims to the French throne and invade. His victory against a much larger French army repeated the successes of Crécy and Poitiers, enabling him to dominate northern France.

In 1396 England and France signed the thirty-year Truce of Paris to end the long-running Hundred Years' War. However, the French continued to support England's enemies in Scotland and Wales and in 1403 raided several Channel ports. Inside France, the intermittent insanity of King Charles VI prompted a power struggle between the rival dukes of Orléans and Burgundy, with both sides appealing for English help. In 1413 Henry V came to the English throne. He formed an alliance with Jean, Duke of Burgundy: the duke promised to remain neutral in return for gaining land as Henry's vassal.

With one side of the French conflict neutralized, Henry prepared for war. In August 1415 he sailed for Normandy

"We cried out that God would have compassion upon us and upon the crown of England."

A chaplain traveling with Henry V

with an army of 12,000 men. After a six-week siege he captured Harfleur, with the loss of half his army from casualties and disease. Henry then marched overland toward English-held Calais but found his way blocked by a far larger French army led by Charles d'Albret, Constable of France. Henry drew up his army where the road to Calais passed through thick woods. It had been raining hard for several days and the fields on either side were newly plowed. Placing his archers on either flank, with more archers and dismounted knights in the center,

he hammered rows of pointed stakes into the road. Confronted by this narrow battlefield, the French formed up into three battles or divisions, one behind the other, the first two consisting of dismounted men with some crossbowmen, the third mostly mounted men.

At first the two armies faced each other down the road, probably about 1 mile (1.6 km) apart. The French knew of Henry's youthful enthusiasm and hoped he might attack them first. Henry, however, decided to force a French attack and moved his army forward a short distance. The trick worked, for, unable to control his eager men, the French Constable ordered an attack. As the first French battle advanced, mounted knights from either flank galloped past them toward the English lines. Under intense fire from the English archers and hampered by the weight of their armor, the muddy ground, and the rows of stakes, they were soon in trouble. This initial cavalry attack had been completely repulsed before the first battle arrived on foot. Fighting their way through to the English line, they were then attacked by the English archers wielding axes, swords, and daggers in close combat. Within minutes, the entire first battle had been killed or captured. The second French battle then surged forward but fell back with heavy losses.

At this point Henry received reports that his camp a mile to the rear was under attack. In reality, this was just a group of peasants out for plunder but, knowing that his small army could not fight on two fronts and guard the many prisoners, Henry ordered all French prisoners to be killed. When the third and final French battle assault was thrown back, Henry ordered his few mounted men to charge the French lines. The result was a rout, with more than a hundred French noblemen, all supporters of the Orléans faction, dead and many more captured. Henry had won against overwhelming odds. **SA**

Losses: English, 400 of 6,000; French, 5,000 of 30,000

◁ *Pontvallain 1370*   *Rouen 1418* ▷

The English and French armies at Agincourt in an illustration from a fifteenth-century French manuscript.

Rouen   31 July 1418–19 January 1419

"And flesh save horse they had none / They ate dogs, they ate cats / They ate mice and horse and rats . . ."

John Page, "The Siege of Rouen"

⬆ *A detail of a pen-and-ink illustration of the Siege of Rouen from The Pageants of Richard Beauchamp, c. 1484–90.*

In his campaigns to capture Normandy during the Hundred Years' War, Henry V of England besieged and took the city of Rouen. With more than 70,000 inhabitants, it was one of the most important cities in France, and its capture was consequently a major success for the English army.

After his dramatic victory at Agincourt in 1415, Henry V returned to England. He spent the next year building up a powerful fleet to clear the English Channel of Genoese ships supporting the French, at the same time forming an alliance with the Holy Roman Emperor, who was previously a supporter of the French king.

In 1417 Henry returned to France and in three campaigns captured all of Normandy except Mont St. Michel. The highlight of these campaigns was the seizure of Rouen. Expecting an attack, the French had strengthened the city's defenses. The city walls were studded with towers and lined with crossbowmen. Cannon were trained at the English army.

With only a small force at his disposal, Henry could not attempt to breach the walls and storm the city, so he settled down to a long siege with the object of starving the defenders into submission. The siege began at the end of July 1418. By December the inhabitants were reduced to eating dogs, cats, horses, and mice, if they could catch them. More than 12,000 poor people were expelled from the town to save food. Henry refused to allow them passage, so they were forced to huddle in defensive ditches recently dug around the walls. Two priests gave them food on Christmas Day, but that was the limit of English largesse. The French garrison tried to break the English siege on several occasions, but to no avail. In January 1419, the French surrendered. **SA**

Losses: No reliable figures

◁ *Agincourt 1415*   *Orléans 1428* ▷

Kutná Hora 21 December 1421

Hussites—followers of Jan Hus, a preacher who had called for national and church reform in Bohemia—proved the effectiveness of armed "war wagons" in defeating a crusade army raised to defend the authority of the Roman Catholic Church and led by King Sigismund of Hungary.

Jan Hus, a popular preacher and dean at Prague University, had made powerful enemies and in 1415 had been declared a heretic and burned at the stake. His followers, who included knights and nobles, launched a protest movement. On the death of King Wenceslas IV of Bohemia they rejected the claim of his half-brother, King Sigismund of Hungary, to the Bohemian throne, instead declaring their own government and the "Hussite Revolt." Pope Martin V called a crusade and Sigismund led a large army—swelled by crusaders from all over Europe—into Bohemia. The crusaders took control of Kutná Hora in central Bohemia (now Czech Republic) and on 21 December 1421, encountered there a dramatically smaller army of Taborites, a radical subgroup of the Hussites.

Commanded by the brilliant, one-eyed general Jan Zizka, the Taborites deployed a new military tactic, using horse-drawn "war wagons," ordinary farm wagons made effective by the use of handguns and other artillery. These were usually deployed in a defensive circle or square behind a ditch. The crews of gunners and bowmen fired at the enemy cavalry before, in a second phase, bursting out to attack. At Kutná Hora the Taborites were initially surrounded, but the wagon crews kept Sigismund's heavy cavalry at bay. Then Zizka drew the wagons into a column and drove them outward, guns firing, to burst right through the crusade army. Some historians identify this as the first maneuver using mobile artillery. **CP**

Losses: Crusader, 12,000 of 100,000; Taborite, unknown of 12,000

Lipany 1434 ▷

Chi Lang October 1427

Guerrilla leader Le Loi is a national hero in Vietnam, renowned for his successful struggle against the oppressive domination of Ming China. His defeat of a Chinese army at the Chi Lang defile in northern Vietnam led to the restoration of Vietnamese independence for another four centuries.

China took over northern Vietnam early in the fifteenth century after the Vietnamese kingdom had been torn apart by a dynastic conflict. Chinese rule proved deeply unpopular, with imposition of heavy taxes, forced labor, and alien Chinese dress and customs. Le Loi launched his insurrection in 1418, initially operating in remote mountain areas, but building up support from discontented peasants. By 1426 he was ready to attack the Red River Delta, the heart of northern Vietnam.

The main Ming occupation force was besieged in Dong Quan (modern-day Hanoi). An attempted breakout by the trapped army was defeated at Tot Dong, after which the Ming government sent a large force from China to relieve the city. The relief force marched toward Dong Quan in two columns. Le Loi decided to concentrate his guerrillas against the larger column, some 100,000 men commanded by Liu Sheng, which chose the route through the Lang Son pass. As the Chinese soldiers marched through the narrow Chi Lang defile, the Vietnamese guerrillas sprang an ambush. Liu Sheng was killed along with thousands of his men. Tens of thousands more were taken prisoner. The other relief column, fearing a similar fate, retreated into China.

News of the Chi Lang catastrophe utterly demoralized the Ming troops inside Dong Quan. They accepted an offer from Le Loi of safe passage back to China. Le Loi became Vietnam's emperor, founding a new dynasty. **RG**

Losses: Chinese, heavy, and 30,000 captured; Vietnamese, unknown

◁ *Bach Dang 938*

Orléans   12 October 1428–7 May 1429

Successes at Agincourt and later in Normandy brought England the French throne in 1422. The English ruled the country from Paris, with the French Dauphin in retreat to the south of the Loire. An English attempt to capture the Loire River crossing at Orléans, however, marked a turning point in French resistance to English rule.

The English king Henry V's campaigns in France after 1415 led to the Treaty of Troyes, signed between the two nations in 1420. Under this treaty, Henry became regent of France and heir to the ailing Charles VI, marrying his daughter Catherine. In 1422, however, Henry died, and the English throne passed down to his nine-month-old son, Henry VI. Two months later, Charles VI died too. As the infant Henry was too young to rule, John, Duke of Bedford, became regent of France, ruling from Paris with the help of England's Burgundian allies. The French Dauphin, the future Charles VII, however, continued to resist English rule from south of the Loire River, although he had neither the

> *"I will raise such a war cry against you as shall be remembered forever."*
>
> *Joan of Arc*

forces nor the vision to do so effectively. In 1428 Bedford decided to seize the Loire River crossing at Orléans prior to invading Berry, the Dauphin's stronghold.

Bedford's army of 5,000 men, led by the Earl of Salisbury, started operations by attacking a fortress guarding a bridge south of the city. The mining operations against the fortress were successful, although Salisbury was killed by cannon shot from across the river as he observed the French fortifications. His place was taken by the Earl of Suffolk, who began the Siege

of Orléans itself by constructing a line of fortifications in earth and wood around the city on the north bank of the river. However, the English, numerically weak despite the presence of 1,500 Burgundian reinforcements, could not prevent French supplies from entering the city. Their own supplies came under French attack, although one attack on 12 February 1429 was successfully repelled by the supply convoy's commander, Sir John Fastolf.

Operations at Orléans might have dragged on for some time had it not been for the appearance at the French court of a young girl, Joan of Arc. Opinion is still divided as to whether she was a superb military tactician, despite her youth and inexperience, or whether indeed she was a divinely guided inspirational force. Whatever the truth, her appearance revived French morale, as did the defection of a Burgundian force to the Dauphin's ranks.

In April 1429 Joan was given command of a force to relieve the Siege of Orléans. Her army of 5,000 men evaded the English lines by sailing up the river in boats. Once in the city, she organized a series of sorties against English strongpoints outside the walls. By 7 May, only a few positions remained in English hands. In a final attack against an English bridgehead on the south bank of the Loire, Joan received a serious arrow wound but continued to fight on until, in the evening, her forces took the stronghold. Faced with the failure of their siege, the English tried to force the French to fight an open battle. When the French refused, the English abandoned the siege the next day and dispersed to English-held towns along the Loire.

Orléans had been relieved within nine days of Joan's arrival in the city. The lifting of the siege marked the first major French victory for years against the English. Owing to Joan's leadership, the tide of the Hundred Years' War was now running strongly in favor of the French. **SA**

Losses: No reliable figures
◄ *Rouen 1418*　　　*Patay 1429* ►

Joan of Arc enters Orléans in a painting by Jean Jacques Scherrer (1855–1916). ➜

Patay 18 June 1429

Carried by their successful raising of the Siege of Orléans in May 1429, the French under Joan of Arc gained a series of victories over the English along the Loire valley, culminating in a decisive victory at Patay a month later—the last action of the French Loire Campaign. English superiority on the battlefields of France was now at an end.

The French campaign against English-held towns along the Loire culminated in a major battle at Patay, slightly north of Orléans. The English army, led by John Talbot, First Earl of Shrewsbury, and Sir John Fastolf, relied on the successful use of archers, just as it had at Crécy, Poitiers, and Agincourt. Longbowmen were deadly when firing, but their lack of armor seriously weakened their effectiveness if forced into hand-to-hand combat. The French exploited this weakness to great effect at Patay.

As preparations for the battle began, French scouts sallied forth to search out any weaknesses in the English positions. They noted that the English archers had yet to secure their front with stakes, which they usually drove into the ground to slow down the advance of the cavalry. Worse, the English archers gave their positions away when they raised a hunting cry as a stag wandered into an open field. The French grabbed the opportunity and quickly threw 1,500 mounted knights against the English lines.

The attack soon turned into a rout, with the English knights retreating on their horses and leaving the infantry to be cut down where they stood. Joan of Arc herself played no part in this surprise victory, but, helped by increasing French popular resistance to English rule, she and her army went on capture Troyes, Châlons, and, in July, Rheims, where the Dauphin was crowned Charles VII, King of France. **SA**

Losses: French, 100 of 1,500; English, 2,500 dead, wounded, or captured of 5,000

◁ Orléans 1428   Formigny 1450 ▷

San Romano 1 June 1432

The Battle of San Romano is a famous example of warfare in early Renaissance Italy, in which victory was contested between armies recruited and led by condottieri—literally "contractors"—who were mercenary military entrepreneurs or warlords. In this case the rival armies were contracted by the neighboring Tuscan cities of Florence and Siena.

Wars between the wealthy and powerful city-states of the Italian peninsula were a frequent occurrence. The Florentines had managed to defeat Milan, ruled by the Visconti family, but were then drawn into a conflict with Siena, which was loyal to the Visconti cause. San Romano was the major clash of the war that followed.

The forces of Florence were led by the condottiere Niccolo da Tolentino and those of Siena by another mercenary, Francesco Piccinino. Such professional soldiers usually avoided pitched battles, but at San Romano the fighting raged for several hours. Tactics consisted almost entirely of heavy cavalry charges by armored horsemen. Losses were evenly distributed until, as exhaustion threatened to wear both sides down, the battle was turned to Florentine advantage by a relief force of cavalry led by condottiere Micheletto Attendolo da Cotignola.

The Florentines were able to claim the victory, but the city's coffers were empty and taxes had to be raised. This increased the unpopularity of the government, resulting in the reinstatement of the rule of the Medici family in 1433. In 1456 the Florentine painter Paolo Uccello was commissioned by Cosimo de' Medici to produce three paintings commemorating the battle. In the first two paintings the battle is clearly depicted as a struggle between two cavalry-based armies, while the third painting depicts the final decisive Florentine attack. **TB**

Losses: Florentine, fewer than 200 cavalry; Sienese, 600 dead or captured

Lipany (Český Brod)   30 May 1434

The "Bohemian League"—an alliance of moderate Hussites and Roman Catholics—inflicted a crushing defeat on the radical Hussites or Taborites of Bohemia at Lipany in Bohemia. A feigned retreat by the League drew the Taborites out of their defensive deployment of "war wagons," after which their foe returned and massacred them.

Wars between the Hussites in Bohemia continued for fifteen years after the invasion of a crusading army led by King Sigismund of Hungary was defeated at Kutná Hora. The great Taborite general Jan Zizka died of plague in 1424 and thereafter his bereaved troops called themselves "the Orphans." The wars, predominantly fought and won by the infantry, proved the effectiveness of hand-held guns and field guns against mounted cavalry. The two factions of the Hussites—the radical Taborites and the more moderate Ultraquists—fought several pitched battles.

At the Battle of Lipany, the Orphans and the Bohemian League both used "war wagons." The Taborite army commanded by Prokop the Great had them deployed in a defensive formation on a hill; the Bohemian League concealed a group of heavy cavalry and then advanced their own wagons and infantry toward the Taborite position. After a period of bombardment, ineffective because the armies were still quite far apart, the wagons of the Bohemian League began to retreat and the Taborites broke out of their defensive formation in pursuit. The Bohemian League wagons then stopped and began firing while their heavy cavalry swept in to attack. The Taborite leaders were killed and key elements of their forces broke and fled. The battle became a massacre. As a result, the Hussite Wars finally ended with a peace treaty, the Compact of Basel, signed on 5 July 1436. **CP**

Losses: Taborite, 1,300 of 10,700; Bohemian League, unknown of 13,000

◁ *Kutná Hora 1421*

"You who make a stop here, think on where the disunity of a nation may lead."

Inscription on monument at site, erected 1881

⬆ *Densely packed soldiers file out of a Hussite encampment surrounded by war wagons in a codex illumination c. 1450.*

Varna 10 November 1444

سلطان مراد غازی ابن محمد

"To escape is impossible, to surrender is unthinkable. Let us fight with bravery and honor our arms."

János Hunyadi

⬆ *Murad II, a watercolor from John Young's* Series of Portraits of the Emperors of Turkey *(1808).*

At Varna on the Black Sea coast in eastern Bulgaria, a Christian retaliation against the advance of the Muslim Ottoman Turks came to a disastrous end. The victory of Sultan Murad II over the great Hungarian commander János Hunyadi opened the way to the Ottoman conquest of Constantinople.

Murad II had resumed the Ottoman expansion in Europe, interrupted for a period after the disastrous defeat at Ankara in 1402. Fearing that the Ottomans would advance farther into central and western Europe, Pope Eugene IV called for a crusade. János Hunyadi, serving Władysław III, king of Poland and Hungary, at first inflicted some sharp setbacks on the Ottomans, before a truce was agreed. The Christians made an elaborate plan for a campaign in 1444, in breach of the truce, considered nonbinding by the Christians since it was agreed with an infidel. The Venetian and Papal fleets were to cut the Ottomans off from reinforcement from Anatolia. This would allow a Christian army to destroy their forces in Europe.

But the naval blockade never happened and by the time the crusader army reached Varna, it faced a numerically far superior Ottoman army. At first, the battle seemed to go well for the crusaders, as Hunyadi formed and held a strong defensive line. But as the Ottoman troops fell back in the face of a cavalry charge, King Władysław rejected Hunyadi's cautious advice and led the bulk of his forces against the Ottoman center in a rash attempt to capture the Sultan. The Sultan's elite bodyguard repelled the attack and the king was killed, his head displayed on a pike. The crusaders eventually retreated after taking enormous losses. The defeat of the crusade left the Ottoman Empire with no threat from the west and free to turn its attention to Constantinople. **TP**

Losses: Christian, heavy casualties of 20,000; Ottoman, minimal of 50,000

◁ *Ankara 1402*   *Fall of Constantinople 1453* ▷

Formigny 15 April 1450

The final years of the Hundred Years' War were marked by English ineptitude and French discipline, the French establishing a standing army with great skills in deploying artillery. These skills were put to great use at Formigny, where French cannon were used to devastating effect.

The French resurgence that began with the campaigns of Joan of Arc in 1429 continued despite her death in 1431. The civil war between the rival dukedoms of Orléans and Burgundy ended in 1435, bringing unity to the country, while Paris was recaptured from the English in 1436. A five-year peace with the English was then signed at Tours in 1444. Acting on sound military advice, Charles VII of France set up the basis of a standing army that kept the mercenary soldiers paid while not fighting, rather than roaming around the countryside and causing mayhem. He also hired the brothers Jean and Gaspard Bureau to create an efficient artillery organization, giving the army tactical superiority over the English.

When the truce ended in 1449, the French began a campaign to retake Normandy, capturing Rouen the same year. In 1450 the two armies met at Formigny, outside Bayeux. The English drew up their archers behind a thicket of stakes and earthworks. The French responded by placing a cannon on each flank and bombarding the English lines, causing great loss of life. The English archers charged the guns, which they briefly captured, but were then met by a French counterattack by dismounted knights and infantry that recaptured the cannon and engaged the archers in hand-to-hand combat. French reinforcements then dealt the final blows against the English flanks. The French victory was decisive, bringing them total control of Normandy four months later. **SA**

Losses: French, 500–600 of 4,500; English, 4,000 of 4,500

◁ Patay 1429   Châtillon 1453 ▷

"The French guns at Formigny ... rather well marked the end of the longbow's special advantage on the continent."

Albert D. McJoynt, 1997

⬆ Mounted French knights charge English knights in a depiction of Formigny, from The Vigils of King Charles VII (1477–83).

Fall of Constantinople 29 May 1453

After ten centuries of wars, defeats, and victories, the Byzantine Empire came to an end when Constantinople fell to the Ottoman Turks in May 1453. The city's fall sent shock waves throughout Christendom. It is widely quoted as the event that marked the end of the European Middle Ages.

By the mid-fifteenth century the Byzantine Empire had long been in decline, but it remained an important bastion of Christian Europe facing Muslim Asia. The Ottoman Turks, however, had extended their territories to include the Balkans as well as Anatolia. Only Constantinople held out behind its supposedly impregnable walls, as the Ottoman Empire spread around it. For the Ottomans, the city had enormous prestige, both as a center of the rival Christian faith and a symbol of imperial power. A attempted siege conducted by Sultan Murad II in 1422 failed, but Murad's young successor, Mehmed II, leader of the Ottomans from 1451, was determined to carry out the operation that would cap all previous Turkish triumphs.

> *"After the fall of our city, the Sultan celebrated his victory with a great, joyful triumph."*
>
> George Sphrantzes, Byzantine eyewitness

When Mehmed II set out to take Constantinople in the spring of 1453, the city was a shadow of its former glory, but it remained highly difficult to capture by assault. Its formidable fortifications had held out through numerous sieges in the past. It was poorly garrisoned, its defenders, under Emperor Constantine XI, numbering around 8,000 men despite having been bolstered by the arrival of Christian volunteers from across western Europe. Mehmed besieged the city in early April with a force of between 75,000 and 100,000 and a large fleet. His

preparations were extensive. He had built a castle on the Bosphorus with guns that would prevent any relief ships sailing to the city from the Black Sea. He also employed a Hungarian artillery expert, Urban, to build him the most powerful cannon ever seen to batter the city's walls. Access to the inlet of the Golden Horn, Constantinople's port alongside the walls, was blocked by a chain, so Mehmed had his ships dragged from the Bosphorus across land on logs, then refloated in the Golden Horn to menace the fortifications from the sea.

Initial attacks on the city's ancient but formidable walls failed with heavy casualties, but after attempts to negotiate a surrender came to nothing, the attacks began again, with increasing frequency and ferocity. Finally, on 29 May, Mehmed launched simultaneous assaults from the sea and land sides of the city that overcame the defenders. Pouring into the city through one of the gates that was forced (some claimed that it had been unlocked), the Ottomans killed the emperor as he attempted a counterattack with his remaining defenders. The Turks spread out to sack the city, massacring so many that, in the words of eyewitness Nicolo Barbaro, "blood flowed in the city like rainwater in the gutters after a sudden storm" and bodies "floated out to sea like melons along a canal." Mehmed, still only twenty years old, rode a white horse through the streets to Hagia Sophia, Constantinople's famed cathedral, which was immediately used as a mosque to say prayers of thanks for victory.

The fall of Constantinople was a huge blow for the Christian world but, although Pope Nicholas V called for a crusade to regain the city for Christendom, no concerted military response was made. Now styled "the Conqueror," Mehmed declared the city his new capital and claimed to be the rightful successor to the Roman Empire. **TB**

Losses: Byzantine, 5,000; Ottoman, no reliable figures

◁ *Varna 1444*　　　　　　　　　　　*Belgrade 1456* ▷

　　　Sultan Mehmed II at Constantinople, in a painting by Panagiotos Zografos, 1836.

Δ Κωνσταντινούπολις · ή πόλεως αὐλή

Β ὁ ὀχλικός

Châtillon 17 July 1453

The Hundred Years' War between England and France, begun in 1337, ended 116 years later in Aquitaine, southwest France. Here the final remnants of English rule were swept away, leaving only the port of Calais in English hands. After centuries, France was now a united kingdom.

After their successful recapture of Normandy from the English in 1450, the French armies headed south to take the duchy of Aquitaine, which had been in English hands since 1154. The capture of Bordeaux in June and Bayonne in August 1451 brought the French control of the duchy, but the local nobles still felt loyal to the English king and resistance soon began against French rule. The nobles of Aquitaine appealed for English help in ousting the French. In October 1452 John Talbot, First Earl of Shrewsbury, landed near the mouth of the Garonne River with an army of 3,000 men and retook Bordeaux.

In July of the following year, Shrewsbury attempted to raise the Siege of Châtillon, the walls of which were under attack from artillery commanded by Jean Bureau, the French master of artillery. Bureau prepared for the attack by turning his cannon around to face the advancing English. Deceived by the withdrawal of the French horses into thinking that their troops had also left their camp, the English launched a hasty attack over the earthworks thrown up by Bureau without waiting for reinforcements. They were met with a barrage of cannon fire and crossbow bolts that threw their cavalry into confusion. When the French mounted a counterattack, Shrewsbury and many of his men were killed and the English army fled in great disarray. Three months later, the French retook Bordeaux for the final time. The Hundred Years' War had ended in complete French victory. **SA**

Losses: No reliable figures

◁ *Formigny 1450*

Belgrade 4–22 July 1456

The Siege of Belgrade was a decisive encounter in the war between the Kingdom of Hungary and the Ottoman Empire. At Belgrade, a force of Hungarians, under János Hunyadi, defeated the Ottomans, led by Sultan Mehmed II. The defeat halted the Ottoman advance into central Europe.

With the fall of Constantinople in 1453, the Hungarians knew that they stood in the way of Ottoman expansion into Europe. Under the command of their great general, János Hunyadi, who had fought at Varna, the Hungarians prepared for war. By 1456, Mehmed had mustered an invasion force of around 50,000 and set sail for Belgrade. Mehmed arrived in early July and besieged the fortress, bombarding the walls and positioning his fleet of almost 200 ships close by on the Danube to blockade the city. Inside the fortress were 6,000 Hungarian defenders who desperately repelled the early attacks.

Hunyadi's fleet arrived in mid-July and he immediately attacked the Ottoman fleet, sinking a number of Ottoman vessels and breaking the blockade so that Belgrade could be re-supplied. Defense was then turned to attack when a number of Hungarians launched a surprise raid that gathered momentum, prompting Hunyadi into the action against his wishes. The Hungarians rushed the Ottoman lines, causing chaos in the complacent Ottoman army. Mehmed was hit in the leg by an arrow and was rescued by his bodyguard as the Ottomans retreated in disarray.

Mehmed later withdrew under cover of darkness and returned to Constantinople. Victory for Hungary soon turned to tragedy, however, when Hunyadi died of a plague that swept through his camp one month later. But the Ottoman Empire would have to wait seventy years before attempting further advances into Europe. **TB**

Losses: Ottoman, 10,000, 75 galleys; Hungarian, unknown

◁ *Fall of Constantinople 1453*   *Mohacs 1526* ▷

Sultan Mehmed II's forces lay siege to Belgrade in a Turkish representation.

قلعه صالدی عدویه خرق عاده

Swiecino (Schwetz)   17 September 1462

After their catastrophic defeat at Grunwald, the Teutonic Knights were fatally weakened. In 1454 the cities and nobles of Prussia rebelled against them, allying with Poland. Swiecino, the decisive encounter in the ensuing Thirteen Years' War, was a conflict that humbled the once-proud Knights.

The war with the Teutonic Knights came at a difficult time for Poland's King Casimir IV Jagiellon. He was at odds with the Lithuanian half of his domains, which gave him no military support. The Teutonic Knights, employing mercenaries to do their fighting, had some striking successes against Poland's feudal army. Finally Casimir himself turned to employing paid soldiers, many of them Czechs. Led by Polish military commander Piotr Dunin, this largely mercenary force adopted the tactics practiced in the Hussite War. Wagons were chained together to form a defensive position protected by cannon. The army had a powerful force of crossbowmen, as well as cavalry. The Teutonic Order's army adopted similar tactics.

Dunin opened the battle with a charge by armored cavalry, but the able Teutonic commander Fritz Raveneck drove them back. When the Teutonic Order's mercenaries took the offensive, however, they stalled in front of the Polish wagons and were cut down by concentrated crossbow fire. Raveneck was killed trying to rally his retreating troops and a withdrawal turned into a rout. The Polish cavalry overran the Teutonic wagons and captured their valuable artillery. The defeated Teutonic Knights were forced to accept humiliating peace terms—the Second Peace of Thorn—in 1466. **CP**

Losses: Polish, 250 of 2,000; Teutonic, 1,000 of 2,700

◁ *Grunwald 1410*   *Orsha 1514* ▷

A Great Battle of the Onin War, *a nineteenth-century woodblock print by Utagawa Yoshitora.* ⬇

Kyoto   May 1467–77

By 1467 the Ashikaga dynasty of shoguns in Japan had grown so weak that a succession dispute provided the trigger for a civil war and the collapse of central authority. The Onin War, largely fought within the imperial capital of Kyoto, was the precursor of the so-called Age of Warring States.

The Onin War was fought between the families of two samurais who were close to the Ashikaga Shogun. Each had a mansion that acted as a military base within Kyoto, where the Shogun was also located. The first was Yamana Sozen, nicknamed the Red Monk. His rival was his son-in-law, Hosokawa Katsumoto. The spark for their conflict was a succession dispute within the Shogun's own family.

The fighting began when the Hosokawa family attacked the mansion of Isshiki, one of the Yamana generals, that lay across the street. The battle consisted of arrow exchanges, swordplay, and the use of fire. Soon the rivals were facing each other across a charred wasteland. Sporadic fighting took place for about a year.

The recently renewed contact with China, severed during the Mongol invasions, allowed several Chinese weapons to appear in Japan. The first were exploding arrows launched by catapult, while in 1468 there is a record of fire-spears being used.

The Onin War dragged on with sporadic attacks as the fighting spread to neighboring province. Where the families had fought, looting mobs moved in, leaving the imperial capital almost in ruins. Yamana and Hosokawa both died in 1473, but by then the cause of their dispute was almost forgotten. **ST**

Losses: No reliable figures

◁ *Minatogawa 1336*   *Kawagoe 1545* ▷

Tewkesbury 4 May 1471

"Now is the winter of our discontent / Made glorious summer by this sun of York / And all the clouds that lour'd upon our house / In the deep bosom of the ocean buried."

William Shakespeare, Richard III, *referring to Edward IV*

⬆ *A late-fifteenth-century manuscript illustration of the Battle of Tewkesbury.*

Rival claims to the throne of England from the royal houses of Lancaster and York led in 1455 to an intermittent civil war known as the Wars of the Roses, after their symbolic red and white roses respectively. York won at the Battle of Tewkesbury, confirming Edward IV's hold on the throne.

In 1454 the saintly but weak Lancastrian king Henry VI was seized by mental incapacity. His cousin, Richard, Duke of York, became regent. A year later, Richard was dismissed; as a result, he rose in revolt against Henry, claiming the throne for himself. Lancastrian forces killed Richard in battle in 1460, but his son Edward defeated the Lancastrians the following year and took the throne as Edward IV. Ten years later, Edward was deposed in a Lancastrian coup and fled into exile as Henry VI was restored to the throne.

In 1471 Edward returned to reclaim his throne. His Yorkist army met the Lancastrians at Tewkesbury, his opponents led by Margaret of Anjou, the remarkable and formidable queen of Henry VI. The Lancastrian army formed up in a strong position on a slope, where they were first bombarded by Yorkist artillery. The Earl of Somerset responded by leading a sortie along a hidden lane to attack the Yorkist left wing, but then came under fierce attack from reserves led by the Duke of Gloucester, Edward's brother. As Somerset's troops broke under the pressure, Edward charged the Lancastrian center.

In the ensuing rout, some 2,000 Lancastrians were killed, including the Prince of Wales. Somerset was captured and executed, while Margaret was captured and held prisoner until the French king ransomed her in 1476. Within a month her husband Henry VI was killed in the Tower of London, ending the Lancastrian line of kings. **SA**

Losses: Yorkist, unknown of 3,500; Lancastrian, 2,000 of 5,000

Bosworth Field 1485 ▷

Murten (Morat) 22 June 1476

The battle between Burgundy and the Swiss Confederacy at Murten in Switzerland was a pivotal moment in European warfare, marking the arrival of massed formations of pikemen as a decisive element in battlefield tactics. The collapse of Burgundy's independence was now imminent.

Charles the Bold, Duke of Burgundy, was an ambitious ruler who sought to expand his domains through war. His army, advanced in organization and technology, was a permanent force of professional soldiers with Europe's best field and siege artillery. His expansionist ambitions brought him into conflict with the Swiss Confederacy.

In summer 1476 Duke Charles besieged the town of Murten on Lake Morat, in the Swiss canton of Berne. He had already been defeated by Swiss infantry at Grandson in the previous year, so he took pains to defend his besieging army against an attack by a relief force, constructing a defensive line of ditch-and-palisade field fortifications covered by cannon. On the wet and stormy day of 22 June, however, the Burgundian troops were caught off guard by the rapid approach of a column of Swiss foot soldiers supported by cavalry from the Confederacy's ally Lorraine.

Marching in a dense formation of perhaps 20,000 men, armed with long pikes or halberds, the Swiss did not halt to deploy for battle but headed directly for the Burgundian defenses. Duke Charles's cannon managed a few shots as his soldiers rushed to arm themselves and take up their positions, but the Swiss tide swept over the trenches and advanced on the Burgundian camp. Unable to coordinate a defense, Charles ordered a retreat that swiftly turned into a rout. The Swiss allowed no quarter, killing every Burgundian soldier they caught. **CP**

Losses: Burgundian, 7,000 of 20,000; Lorraine and Swiss Confederacy, light casualties of 20,000

◁ Sempach 1386 Nancy 1477 ▷

Nancy 5 January 1477

Six months after suffering a crushing defeat at Murten, the Burgundian army fought its last battle at Nancy. Another military catastrophe led to the absorption of the Duke of Burgundy's lands by France and the Austrian Hapsburgs. The Swiss were confirmed as the finest infantry in Europe.

Duke Charles the Bold of Burgundy laid siege to Nancy, the capital of Lorraine, and Duke René of Lorraine organized a relief army in alliance with the Swiss Confederacy. For the relief force the Swiss supplied some 10,000 pikemen and halberdiers, while Lorraine furnished an approximately equal number of cavalry and infantry.

There was snow on the ground when the two armies met south of Nancy. Charles, his army weakened by losses at Murten, took up a strong defensive position near the top of a slope behind a stream, his flanks anchored in woodland. He hoped to cut down the enemy with the fire of his field cannon as they advanced up the slope. The Lorrainers and Swiss, however, did not oblige with a frontal attack. Instead, a large part of their forces carried out a flanking march through the woods in a snowstorm, emerging behind and above Charles's army. The Swiss infantry swept down the hill, charging in a tightly massed formation. Charles swiveled his cannon around but they lacked the elevation to fire effectively up a slope. The Burgundian army was overrun and disintegrated, men fleeing for their lives.

Charles's body was identified on the battlefield three days later. His head had been split open by a blow from a halberd. Along with Murten, the victory made the Swiss infantry feared and coveted. Fighting as mercenaries, their massed pikemen featured in almost every major European battle of the fifty years following. **CP**

Losses: Burgundian, 4,000 of 8,000; Lorraine and Swiss Confederacy, unknown of 20,000

◁ Murten 1476

Taximoaroa 1478

In pre-Columbian America, military expansion by the Aztecs or México—creators of the vast Aztec empire in central Mexico—was temporarily halted by a crushing defeat in a two-day battle near Taximoaroa at the hands of their archenemies, the Tarascans of Michoacán.

The Aztecs founded the city-state of Tenochtitlán at Lake Texcoco in 1325, and their empire began to grow after 1428 when Tenochtitlán formed a Triple Alliance with the city-states of Texcoco and Tlacopan: military campaigns after 1458 under leaders Moctezuma I Ilhuicamina and Axayácatl greatly expanded Aztec territory. The Tarascan empire was a rival power founded c. 1300 and centered on its capital at Tzintzuntzan (in present-day Michoacán).

From 1469 onward Axayácatl conquered several Tarascan border towns but his campaign ended at Taximoaroa in 1478. The Aztec army of around 32,000 contained squadrons of Tetzcocans, Tepanecs, Chalcas, and Xochimilcas, as well as Aztecs. The Tarascans sent four envoys to warn the army against invading, and when Axayácatl learned that the Tarascans had gathered a force of about 50,000, his instinct was to retreat, but his generals persuaded him to engage the Tarascans.

The squadrons in the Triple Alliance army were sent one after another into battle but to little effect; many were captured, including one of the members of Axayácatl's four-man inner council. At the close of the first day's fighting, the Aztec troops began to flee but the army commanders inspired them to rally. However, on the second day the Aztecs were catastrophically defeated and Axayácatl was forced to withdraw. Aztec-Tarascan conflict reignited in the 1480s and continued until the conquest of both empires by the Spanish after 1519. **CP**

Losses: Aztec, 28,400 from various forces of 32,000; Tarascan, presumed few of 50,000

Night of Sorrows 1520 ▷

Bosworth Field 22 August 1485

The Wars of the Roses, between the rival houses of York and Lancaster for the English throne, had apparently ended in the Yorkist victory at Tewkesbury in 1471. But another Lancastrian claimant appeared in 1485, successfully seizing the throne as Henry VII, the first Tudor king of England.

Henry Tudor's claim to the throne was remote, but force of arms could often override such dynastic quibbles. In early August 1485, Henry landed in west Wales with around 3,000 French mercenaries. Picking up support as he headed into England, he met the Yorkist king, Richard III, at Bosworth Field in Leicestershire. The exact site of the battle has long been in dispute, but in October 2009 archaeologists discovered a number of primitive pistol bullets and cannonballs in a field, locating once and for all the site of the battle some 2 miles (3.2 km) away from where it was once thought to have been fought.

The battle itself was very strange. Henry fielded around 5,000 men; Richard had around 8,000, but sections of his Yorkist army, led by two powerful nobles, the brothers Lord Thomas Stanley and Sir William Stanley, refused to join in and watched events from a distance before defecting to Henry's side. When Richard then ordered an advance, his entire left wing under the Earl of Northumberland refused to move. Faced with disgrace and defeat, Richard led a small group of loyalists straight into the center of the Lancastrian army, hoping to engage Henry in one-to-one combat. He got close enough to kill Henry's standard-bearer before he was cut down, his crown apparently rolling into a thorn bush before it was retrieved and brought to the new king, Henry VII. The Wars of the Roses were now at an end and a new and famous dynasty took the throne. **SA**

Losses: Tudor, 100 of 5,000; Yorkist, 1,000 of 8,000

◁ *Tewkesbury 1471*　　　　　*Flodden 1513* ▷

Fall of Granada   2 January 1492

The Emirate of Granada in southern Spain was the last surviving Muslim state in the Iberian peninsula. A siege undertaken by the Christian kingdoms of Aragon and Castile led to the capitulation of Granada, marking the end of the long struggle known as the Reconquista.

In 1482 war broke out between Muslim Granada and the Catholic kingdoms of Isabella I of Castile and Ferdinand II of Aragon. Castile was the more prominent member of the alliance, with Isabella supplying and financing the bulk of the army that Ferdinand led. While Granada was riddled with internal conflicts, the Christian kingdoms were more stable and gained the ascendancy as many nobles flocked to the Christian banner, enticed by the prospect of land and plunder.

In the course of the conflict the Christians made increasing use of cannon, which allowed them to take many towns without prolonged sieges. The last ruler of Granada, Emir Muhammad XII, was a devious figure who for a time acted as an ally of the Christian kingdoms while they reduced his Muslim political enemies. Eventually he turned against the Christians, however, and in April 1491 the forces of Aragon and Castile placed the city of Granada under siege. Emir Muhammad sought support from the Muslim powers of North Africa, but neither Egypt nor Morocco was prepared to come to his aid.

In January 1492 the city of Granada surrendered and the Reconquista was complete. The intolerance of the Christian kingdoms was shown in the Alhambra Decree, issued in March 1492, which ordered the expulsion of Jews, soon followed by the forced conversion of Muslims to Christianity. Within two decades, the crowns of Castile and Aragon were united as the kingdom of Spain. **TB**

Losses: No available figures

< Rio Salado 1340

"Woe to Granada! The hour of its desolation is at hand. The ruins of Zahara will fall upon our own heads."

Reaction of a Moorish scholar to the defeat

⬆ Muslim women are forcibly baptized after the surrender of Moorish Granada, in a relief by Felipe Bigarny (c. 1475–1542).

Fornovo   6 July 1495

In 1494 Charles VIII of France marched into Italy with a powerful army, initiating more than half a century of complex conflicts known as the Italian Wars. The Battle of Fornovo, the final encounter of Charles's campaign, revealed the shortcomings of his primitive cannon as field artillery.

The pretext for the invasion of Italy was to uphold the French king's claim to the throne of Naples. The leaders of the various Italian states were shocked by the speed with which the French army crossed the Alps and by its unprecedented artillery train of cannon on wheeled carriages. Moving swiftly southward, Charles took Naples without much difficulty, but his success provoked an alliance against him. The Holy Roman Empire, Spain, Naples, Milan, Venice, and the papacy formed the League of Venice, creating an army led by the condottiere (mercenary commander) Francesco Gonzaga.

This alliance threatened to cut Charles off from France. His baggage train laden with plunder, Charles quit Naples and marched northward. The king and much of his army were incidentally infected with the new syphilis epidemic in southern Italy, which they spread along their route. Gonzaga intercepted the French at Fornovo on the Taro River, 20 miles (32 km) from Parma. There were substantial bodies of mercenaries on both sides—Swiss halberdiers serving Charles and Greek-Albanians paid for by the Venetians. Charles's army was hampered by the rainy weather, which wetted the powder of the cannon, rendering them ineffectual. Although taking fewer losses than the League, Charles retreated to save his army from the League's repeated cavalry attacks. The baggage full of loot was lost to plundering League troops. Charles returned home empty-handed and died two years later with his country heavily in debt. **TB**

Losses: French, 1,000; League of Venice, 2,000

Cerignola 1503 ⊳

Zonchio   12–25 August 1499

For more than a century after its victory over Genoa at Chioggia, Venice dominated the eastern Mediterranean with its naval power. In the 1490s, however, the decision of the Ottoman Empire to build a war fleet challenged Venetian supremacy and, at the Battle of Zonchio, ended it.

The Battle of Zonchio occurred at a time when naval technology and tactics were changing rapidly. The introduction of cannon led to the use of larger vessels as gun platforms. The Ottoman admiral Kemal Reis's flagship, *Goke*, could carry more than 500 troops as well as cannon. The war fleet sent to sea in 1499 by the Venetians included twelve "great" galleys as well as forty-four regular galleys and twenty-eight sailing ships—although at that time tactics for combining oared galleys with sailing vessels in action were ill-developed.

An Ottoman army was besieging the Venetian fortress of Lepanto in the Peloponnese. Venice intended its fleet to prevent the resupply of the Ottoman forces by sea. Following the arrival of an Ottoman fleet, Venetian admiral Antonio Grimani made an attack on 12 August, but without the desired result. Two Venetian vessels were sunk by Turkish gunfire, and another two of their largest ships became entangled with an Ottoman ship that caught fire, all three being destroyed by the flames.

Unnerved by this initial setback, Grimani, an ineffectual commander, failed to press further attacks with any vigor over the following two weeks, and the Ottoman force was able to place itself between the Venetian fleet and the besieged fort. The fort's garrison surrendered and the Venetian fleet eventually withdrew. This defeat, a severe shock to Venice, was confirmed by another Ottoman naval victory at Modon a year later. The Ottomans were now the primary naval power in the region. **TB**

Losses: No available figures

⊲ *Belgrade 1456*   *Chaldiran 1514* ⊳

Ottoman and Venetian ships clash at Zonchio in a detail from a sixteenth-century Italian woodcut.

3 1500–1699

Detail from a painting of the Battle of Orsha (1514) by an artist known as the Master of the Battle of Orsha.

Cerignola 21 April 1503

In 1499 French king Louis XII invaded Lombardy, northern Italy, reigniting the Italian Wars. France and Spain then went to war over control of southern Italy. At Cerignola, Spanish General Fernández de Córdoba's army was heavily outnumbered by the French forces of Louis d'Armagnac, Duke of Nemours, but new defensive tactics won the day.

General Córdoba was the first commander to realize the effectiveness of combining gunpowder weapons with field fortifications. He took up a defensive position on high ground, which he fortified with ditches and ramparts. Behind these earthworks he placed infantry, armed with the arquebus (the forerunner of the musket) and cannon. Pikemen and cavalry were held in reserve. Their opposing French force had plenty of cannon, but they depended on armored cavalry as their shock troops, supported by Swiss mercenary pikemen.

The Duke of Nemours launched frontal assaults on the Spanish position, which appeared flimsy to him, but both cavalry and pikemen were stopped by the ditch and rampart and there slaughtered by close-range arquebus and cannon fire. Nemours himself was killed by a shot from an arquebus, the first commander slain by an infantry firearm. When the French forces had been sufficiently weakened and disordered, Córdoba ordered an advance by pikemen and light cavalry that drove the surviving enemy from the field.

The battle initiated the dominance of disciplined, professional Spanish infantry on European battlefields that would last until their defeat at Rocroi in 1643. In addition to being the first battle won by infantry firearms, it also established the reputation of Córdoba—henceforth hailed with the epithet "El Gran Capitan"—as one of the great commanders of his age. **TB**

Losses: Spanish, 250 of 10,000; French, 5,000 of 30,000

[<] *Fornovo 1495*   *Garigliano 1503* [>]

Garigliano 29 December 1503

If the Battle of Cerignola demonstrated the defensive genius of Spanish commander Gonzalo Fernández de Córdoba, his follow-up success at Garigliano revealed an exceptional flair for attacking maneuvers. For a second time the French were defeated by a numerically inferior force. Spain established its rule over southern Italy.

After the Spanish victory over the French at Cerignola, a period of stalemate followed. The armies of France and Spain camped on an unhealthy marshy plain 40 miles (64 km) north of Naples, observing each other across the only bridge spanning the Garigliano River. Córdoba resolved to break the stalemate by crossing the river at another point and launching a surprise flank attack.

The Spanish installed a makeshift bridge, a pontoon made out of boats and barrels, 4 miles (6.4 km) upstream of the French camp, and crossed unobserved with an initial force of around 1,500 infantry and 300 cavalry, led by Bartolomeo d'Alviano. Córdoba followed with the main Spanish force and attacked the French who were oriented to defend the bridge. The French were pushed back, and their commander, Ludovico of Saluzzo, ordered a retreat toward the port of Gaeta. Córdoba pursued the retreating French army, but successful rearguard actions gave the bulk of Ludovico's army time to regroup and avoid being totally surrounded. However, strengthened by reinforcements arriving from Naples, the Spanish advanced again and besieged the French army inside Gaeta.

After several days, in which illness spread through the French army, the Marquis of Saluzzo surrendered. The French were defeated and gave up their campaign to capture Naples. The Spanish ruled the city and southern Italy for the following two centuries. **TB**

Losses: Spanish, 1,000 of 12,000; French, 8,000 of 25,000

[<] *Cerignola 1503*   *Ravenna 1512* [>]

Diu 3 February 1509

The Battle of Diu was fought between a Portuguese fleet of ocean-going sailing ships—carracks and caravels—and a fleet of Arab and Indian galleys and dhows. Victory at Diu meant that the Portuguese would become the dominant naval power in the Indian Ocean, and therefore able to take control of the lucrative spice trade.

After a Portuguese fleet commanded by Vasco da Gama reached India in 1498, Portugal became a threat to the established spice trade through the Mediterranean and Red Sea. The island of Diu, lying off the south coast of the Gujarat region of northwest India, was an important staging post in this trade.

The sultan of Gujarat, Mahmud Begada, had the support of other established beneficiaries of the spice trade: Egypt, the Ottoman Empire, and Venice. With Ottoman and Venetian backing, the Egyptians assembled a fleet of war galleys to send in support of Gujarat, which had its own force of Indian Ocean dhows. The Portuguese commander in the Indian Ocean was the viceroy Dom Francisco de Almeida. It was his decision in 1509 to seek out the Egyptian-Gujarati fleet, partly because he wanted revenge for the death of his son in an earlier naval clash. Almeida found the enemy ships in harbor at Diu. He bombarded them with his cannon, exploiting the stronger firepower of his naval artillery, before closing to board.

The Portuguese had manned their superior ships, built to withstand the rigors of the Atlantic Ocean, with experienced sailors and soldiers armed with arquebuses. The ships of the alliance were no match for them and Diu was lost. Prisoners taken by the Portuguese in the fight were put to death with barbaric cruelty. Portugal was to control the Indian Ocean spice trade for a century. **TB**

Losses: Unknown

Goa 1510 ▷

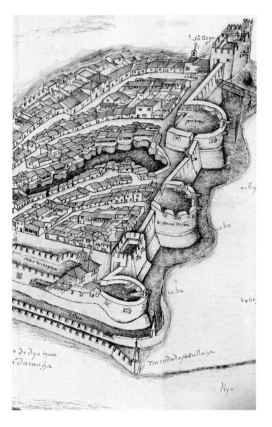

> "As long as you may be powerful at sea, you will hold India as yours."

Dom Francisco de Almeida, after the Battle of Diu

↑ *Part of the Portuguese colony of Diu in western India, in a 1531 depiction from Gaspar Correia's* Legends of India.

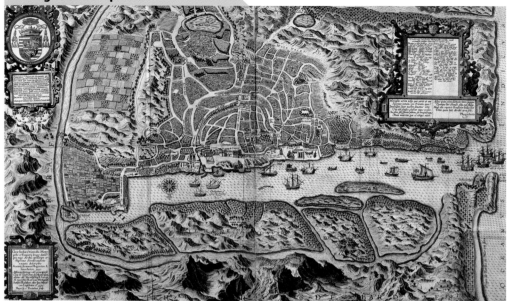

Goa   9–10 December 1510

The first part of India to fall to European colonial rule was Goa on the west coast. Its conquest was the work of energetic Portuguese viceroy Afonso de Albuquerque, who recognized that the port-city would make a perfect permanent base for Portugal's navy and commerce in the Indian Ocean.

After the Portuguese naval victory at Diu in 1509, Francisco de Almeida was replaced as Portugal's overall commander in the Indian Ocean by Albuquerque. He had at his disposal a fleet of twenty-three ships and more than a thousand men.

In January 1510, he was approached by a Hindu bandit chief, Timoji, with a suggestion that he should attack Goa while the city's Muslim ruler, Ismail Adil Shah, was distracted by a rebellion inland. Timoji hoped to emerge as Goa's ruler with Portuguese support. In March, Albuquerque duly occupied the city, but his hold on the conquest was tenuous and he soon withdrew to avoid facing a counterattack that might have been supported by the restive population. Fortuitously, reinforcements arrived in the form of a Portuguese fleet bound for Malacca. Albuquerque hijacked this fleet and diverted it to a second attack on Goa. The seaborne assault was made with overwhelming force. Within a day the Goan defenses were overcome, despite brave resistance by the Muslim garrison. About two-thirds of the Muslim defenders are said to have been killed, either struck down in the fighting or drowned trying to escape the Portuguese fury.

Timoji was assigned only a subordinate role as Albuquerque set about turning Goa into the capital of Portugal's naval and commercial empire in Asia. Goa was destined to remain under colonial rule until 1961; it was the last—as well as the first—European possession in India. **RG**

Losses: Muslim, 6,000 of 9,000; Portuguese, unknown

◀ *Diu 1509*   *Cape Rachado 1606* ▶

An engraving from 1595 of a map of Goa, showing its port, rivers, and mountainous regions. ⬆

Ravenna 11 April 1512

The Battle of Ravenna is chiefly remembered for the tragic death of the brilliant young French commander, Gaston de Foix. This loss overshadowed an extraordinary triumph for the French forces, which inflicted appalling casualties upon a largely Spanish Holy League army.

Amid the shifting alliances that marked the Italian Wars, the French found themselves in conflict with a papal Holy League dependent on Spain for its military strength. In 1512 Gaston de Foix, Duke of Nemours since the death of his father at Cerignola, was appointed commander of the French army in Italy at the age of twenty-one.

His bold leadership immediately invigorated the French campaign. He took Brescia by storm in February and then marched on Ravenna, intending to provoke the Holy League into battle. Ramon de Cardona, Spanish viceroy of Naples and commander of the Holy League forces, duly obliged by leading an army to relieve Ravenna. Battle

was joined on Easter Sunday. Both sides had learned the new rules of warfare in the gunpowder age. Reluctant to assault well-defended earthworks with cavalry or infantry, they indulged in an artillery duel, maneuvering unwieldy cannon to find effective lines of fire. After two hours, unable to stand passively taking losses, cavalry and infantry threw themselves forward in often disorganized assaults. Casualties were heavy as horsemen clashed in swirling melees and infantry swarmed over ramparts and ditches. The issue was decided when the French cavalry, having driven the opposing horsemen from the field, returned to attack the Spanish infantry. Amid the general slaughter of his forces, Cardona was taken prisoner. With the battle effectively over, de Foix was killed in a pointless skirmish with retreating Spanish infantry. **RG**

Losses: French, 4,500 of 23,000; Holy League, 9,000 of 16,000

[<] *Garigliano 1503*　　　　　　　　　　*Novara 1513* [>]

The Death of Gaston de Foix at the Battle of Ravenna, *a nineteenth-century painting by Ary Scheffer.*

Novara 6 June 1513

The crushing defeat of a French army at Novara was the greatest victory of the Swiss pike-wielding mercenaries, who were omnipresent on battlefields of the era. A major reversal of fortunes for France, this military disaster forced French king Louis XII to withdraw entirely from Italy.

Despite their extraordinary victory at the Battle of Ravenna in April 1512, the French were driven out of Milan by their enemies in the Holy League. In 1513 they returned to Italy with an army of 12,000 under the command of the experienced Louis de la Trémoille, retook Milan, and besieged Novara, an important city in the Piedmont region.

The city was defended by Swiss mercenaries, famed for their tight-knit battle formations of pikemen. As the French dug in to besiege the Swiss inside the city, they were unexpectedly attacked from the rear by a relief force. More than 10,000 Swiss pikemen, advancing at a trot in dense, well-organized columns, surged toward and around the French siege lines. The French were unprepared to fight a pitched battle and had little time to turn their cannon from the direction of the city and fire on the pikemen. The guns were quickly overrun.

German Landsknecht mercenary infantry employed by the French were also overwhelmed by the sheer speed of the Swiss onslaught. French armored cavalry, their strongest arm, was unable to organize itself in time to fight and played little part in the battle. De la Trémoille retreated in disarray. The Landsknecht and the Swiss were bitter enemies, and all the captured Landsknecht were executed after the battle. Some of the Swiss pursued the French army over the Alps, and only stopped at Dijon when the French king agreed to pay them a hefty tribute. **TB**

Losses: French, 7,500 of 10,000; Swiss, 2,000 of 13,000

◁ *Ravenna 1512*　　　　*Marignano 1515* ▷

Johann Stumpf's sixteenth-century illustration of the Battle of Novara. ⬆

Flodden   9 September 1513

Ever anxious to protect themselves against their old enemy, the English, the Scots formed an alliance with France in 1295. The Auld Alliance, as it was known, proved to have disastrous consequences when, in 1513, James IV invaded England in support of his French ally.

In 1513, King Henry VIII of England declared war on France and invaded the country. King James IV of Scotland then promptly declared war on his old enemy and headed south in an attempt to divert Henry's attention away from France. Thomas Howard, the Earl of Surrey, hurriedly raised an English army and headed north to meet the Scots.

The two sides met at Flodden in Northumbria in what became the largest battle that the two nations ever fought against each other. The Scottish army drew itself up on a hill and prepared to fight a defensive battle. Surrey responded by boldly moving his entire army around to the back of the Scots, forcing them to reverse their positions. Surrey covered his move with a long-range artillery bombardment and archery volleys from the English longbowmen. Thoroughly unsettled by this bombardment, the impatient Scottish pikemen charged down the hill. A violent melee then took place, the English infantry mainly armed with bills—a curved blade on the end of a long pole—gradually repulsing repeated Scottish assaults. By the time the battle ended that evening, some 10,000 Scots lay dead, including James IV and most of his leading nobles.

Militarily the battle is very important, and has been described as the last great medieval battle that took place in the British Isles. This was the last time the longbow played a decisive role in battle, and the first time artillery proved crucial in Britain. **SA**

Losses: English, 1,500 of 26,000; Scottish, 10,000 of 30,000

◁ *Otterburn 1388*   *Solway Moss 1542* ▷

⬆ *The Earl of Surrey (center) inflicts a crushing defeat on the Scots at Flodden.*

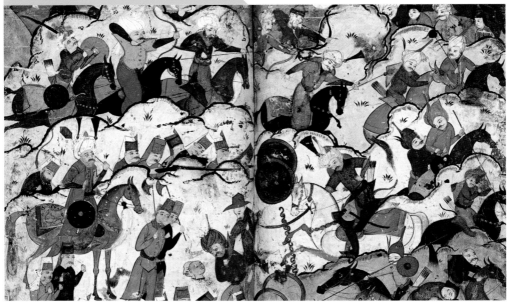

Chaldiran   23 August 1514

The Battle of Chaldiran was fought between the Ottoman Empire, under Selim I, and the invading Safavid Persian Empire, led by Shah Ismail I. Although possession of artillery ensured a decisive victory for the Ottomans, the battle heralded the start of a long war between the rival Muslim powers for control of Anatolia and Iraq.

Sultan Selim I (Selim the Excellent or Brave) had deposed his father, Bayezid II, in 1512 and consolidated his rule by executing many of his cousins, who had rival claims on the throne. Selim set about turning the attention of the Ottoman Empire from the West to the East by embarking on a campaign to overcome the threat posed to Sunni Islam by the Shia Islamic Safavid Persian Empire, which had become a power in the region after the demise of the Timurid Empire.

Selim assembled a huge army—more than 100,000 strong—and marched into Iran, where they engaged the shah's smaller and less well-equipped army at Chaldiran, a county in the northwestern West Azerbaijan province. Drawing on lessons gained in wars against European armies, the Ottoman army was disciplined, equipped with heavy cannon, and deployed musket-armed Janissary infantry. In contrast, the Safavid army relied on the cavalry charge and possessed no artillery.

As they repeatedly attacked the Ottoman positions, the Safavid cavalry took heavy losses from the Ottoman cannon and were repulsed by banks of musket fire. The Safavid army was routed, and the Ottomans advanced to take the Safavid capital at Tabriz, forcing future shahs to move their capital farther to the east. The battle and subsequent Ottoman advance was instrumental in forging a frontier between the two empires that defines the modern-day border between Turkey and Iran. **TB**

Losses: Ottoman, 3,000 of 100,000; Safavid, 6,000 of 20,000

◁ *Zonchio 1499*   *Marj Dabiq 1516* ▷

The Battle of Chaldiran, as depicted in the Sharafnama *(1597), a history of the Kurdish nation.* ⬆

Orsha   8 September 1514

At the Battle of Orsha, a Polish-Lithuanian army triumphed over the Grand Duchy of Muscovy during the Russo-Lithuanian War (1512–22). Muscovy had invaded with the intention of capturing territory in Lithuania. In spite of its victory, Poland-Lithuania was still forced to cede lands to Muscovy when the war ended.

In 1514 the Muscovite army captured Smolensk, a fortress town on the Dnieper that held the approaches to Lithuania. A Polish-Lithuanian army of 35,000 men was sent to meet the Muscovites. Its commander was Konstanty Ostrogski, a Lithuanian nobleman and soldier, who had spent seven years in captivity in Muscovy after being captured in battle in 1499 and was eager for revenge. The Muscovite commander, Boyar Ivan Chelyadnin, led 80,000 soldiers west out of Smolensk to meet the enemy.

The first encounter was on the Berezina River. The Polish-Lithuanians crossed the river and formed up while the Muscovites drew their infantry up in three lines with cavalry on both sides. The Muscovite right flank attacked first, but their charge had no support and was forced back in disorder. Polish cavalry pursued and then shattered the Muscovite center, breaking their first two lines. Meanwhile, the other Muscovite flank had attacked, but artillery fire and Lithuanian armored cavalry forced them back. The Polish-Lithuanian horsemen now aggressively surged forward, trapping the Muscovite cavalry between the Dnieper and swampy land. The Muscovite infantry attempted to stop the slaughter by attacking the rear of the Polish-Lithuanian cavalry, but a detachment was able to swing around and defeat them. When the battle was over, the Muscovites had lost all of their artillery and their commander Chelyadnin, who was taken captive. **JF**

Losses: Polish-Lithuanian, few of 35,000; Muscovite, 30,000 of 80,000

◁ *Swiecino 1462*

⬆ *It is thought that the unknown artist of* Battle of Orsha *(1524–30) may have fought in it himself.*

Marignano   13–14 September 1515

Francis I, newly crowned king of France, won a hard-fought victory over Swiss mercenary pikemen at Marignano, near Milan. The battle showed how heavy artillery in conjunction with cavalry could overcome the tight formation tactics of the Swiss, who lost their aura of invincibility.

The Battle of Marignano was revenge for the French defeat at Novara in 1513. Francis led his army with some seventy bronze cannon over the Alps in a march that was compared with the achievement of Hannibal. Marching into Piedmont, he intimidated his enemies. The Spanish held back their troops farther south and even the Swiss, in control of Milan, considered seeking terms. Hoping to repeat their success at Novara, the Swiss finally decided to sortie from the city and attack the French in their camp at Marignano.

The Swiss achieved an element of surprise with their rapid movement, but this time the French organized themselves more swiftly, forming their divisions and preparing their huge battery of cannon to fire. The Swiss attacked the battery in their usual dense columns of pikemen, but they were counterattacked by French armored cavalry and by the German Landsknecht mercenaries serving the French, known as the Black Band. The Swiss launched repeated attacks on the artillery but their formations were first broken by cannon fire and then harried by cavalry. Later in the day, the French were joined by Venetian troops and this finally turned the battle decisively against the Swiss, who retreated in disarray. Victory saw France gain control of Milan and the Swiss evicted from Italy. **TB**

Losses: French, 4,000 of 40,000; Swiss, 10,000 of 20,000

Marj Dabiq   24 August 1516

The Battle of Marj Dabiq was a decisive encounter between the forces of the Ottoman Empire, under Selim I, and the Mamluk sultanate of Egypt and Syria, led by Al-Ashraf Qansuh al-Ghawri. Ottoman victory led to the conquest of Syria, which remained under Ottoman rule into the twentieth century.

After his victory at Chaldiran in 1514, Selim I continued his conquest of the Muslim Middle East by turning his attention to the Mamluk sultanate. Despite Selim's offer of peace, al-Ghawri did not trust the Ottomans and raised an army, allying himself with the son of one of the cousins executed when Selim came to power. In so doing, al-Ghawri hoped to cause defections in the invading Ottoman army. On his way to meet the invasion, al-Ghawri received mixed messages from Ottoman emissaries, and became unsure of the Ottoman leader. As he approached Halab, news of the size and capabilities of his army was sent to Selim by the city's governor, who bore a grudge against the Mamluk sultan. As a result, Selim was able to prepare his army, especially his cannon, because he now knew that the Mamluks had no guns.

The outcome of the battle was never in doubt because the Ottomans were able to bring the power of their artillery to bear on the advancing Mamluks. Al-Ghawri retreated to Damascus but found the city barred to him and was killed when the Ottoman army slaughtered most of his army. The Ottomans were welcomed into Damascus as liberators, and Syria became part of the rapidly expanding Ottoman Empire. Syria remained under Ottoman control until the empire's dissolution after World War I. **TB**

Losses: Ottoman, 10,000 of 75,000; Mamluk, 65,000 of 85,000

◀ *Novara 1513*   *Bicocca 1522* ▶   ◀ *Chaldiran 1514*   *Ridaniya 1517* ▶

Ridaniya   22 January 1517

Ridaniya was the final battle in the war between the Ottoman Empire, under Selim I, and the Mamluk sultanate of Egypt and Syria. Victory for the Ottomans led to the conquest of Egypt and allowed Selim to claim the title of caliph, leader of the Islamic world.

After the victory at Marj Dabiq, Selim I continued his advance, taking Gaza in December and invading Egypt in January 1517. Tuman Bay II, the new Mamluk sultan, was visited by Ottoman emissaries who offered a peace treaty, provided that Tuman ruled Cairo in the name of Selim I. Tuman wanted to accept, but his advisors had the Ottoman ambassadors executed and instead prepared for war.

As at Marj Dabiq, four months earlier, Tuman's force was no match for the Ottomans and, despite a long battle in which Tuman fought alongside his personal guards, the Egyptians were taken apart and defeated. As Tuman retreated up the Nile with the remnants of his army, Selim moved into Cairo. The citadel's defenders were massacred, and Selim garrisoned the city before stationing his weary army at a nearby fortress. As night fell, Tuman counterattacked and took the lightly defended city, killing the entire Ottoman garrison. Two days later, the Ottoman army returned and swept into Cairo causing Tuman to flee once more. Tuman continued to resist Ottoman rule, launching raids from his base at Giza.

After an unsuccessful attempt to agree to the terms of a treaty, Tuman was finally defeated in a battle near the Pyramids in May 1517. He was captured and executed. Selim took the title of caliph, which the Ottoman emperors were to hold until the 1920s. **TB**

Losses: Unknown

◁ *Marj Dabiq 1516*   *Rhodes 1522* ▷

Night of Sorrows   30 June 1520

Spanish invaders of Mexico commanded by Hernán Cortés were invited into the Aztec capital Tenochtitlán but then attempted to retreat by night and were attacked. Many Spaniards were killed in an encounter that was dubbed "La Noche Triste" (The Night of Sorrows).

When an exploratory expedition from the Spanish colony of Cuba landed on the Mexican coast in April 1519, the Aztec ruler, Moctezuma II Xocoyotzin, welcomed the Spaniards—perhaps because portents suggested that expedition leader Hernán Cortés might be the Aztec god Quetzalcóatl making a prophesied return.

After being invited into the Aztec capital, Tenochtitlán, the Spaniards took Moctezuma prisoner then attacked and killed a group of Aztec nobles; the Aztecs elected Moctezuma's brother Cuitláhuac leader before attacking the palace in which Moctezuma was held captive. The deposed ruler was killed. Spanish troops stormed and set fire to the Aztec temple, the Great Pyramid, and Cortés attempted to lead a retreat by night along a causeway leading across Lake Texcoco to Tlacopan. The Aztecs attacked from canoes, firing arrows and swinging clubs, while attempting to pull down bridges and break up the causeway; the fleeing Spaniards retaliated with crossbows and arquebuses. In pouring rain, hundreds of Spaniards were killed and some drowned as their weapons and looted gold weighed them down when they tried to escape by leaping into the water; others were captured as prisoners of war and afterward sacrificed to the gods, in the Aztec tradition. A core group of Spaniards escaped to Tlacopan to fight the Aztecs at Otumba. **CP**

Losses: In Cortés's account, Spanish, 150, native allies, 2,000; in Cortés's chaplain's account, 450 Spanish and 4,000 natives; other sources suggest as many as 1,150 Spanish; Aztec, unknown

◁ *Taximaroa 1478*   *Otumba 1520* ▷

Otumba   7 July 1520

Hernán Cortés and the Spanish conquistadores defeated a vast Aztec army at Otumba when the Aztecs were surprised by the power of the Spanish mounted knights in battle. This crucial victory prevented the beleaguered Spaniards from being wiped out, paving the way for their victory over the Aztec empire in 1521.

After their retreat from Tenochtitlán on the Night of Sorrows, the bloodied Spaniards regrouped and marched on toward Tlaxcalan. However, at the Otumba Valley, they encountered a large Aztec-Texcocan force sent to pursue and confront them. The two sides met in battle on 7 July. The conquistadores were greatly outnumbered, and many were exhausted and ill equipped to fight after losing artillery, horses, and crossbows during the chaotic retreat.

In the first phase of the battle, Spanish foot soldiers under the command of Diego de Ordaz were surrounded, but held their own. Meanwhile Spanish *caballeros* (mounted knights) made a powerful impact on the Aztecs, riding at full tilt with lances at the ready. Cortés himself rode into battle and killed several captains, whom he could identify by their golden plumes. Then he spotted the Aztec army commander, arrayed in a magnificent feathered costume and standing on the hillside from which he directed his troops. Cortés rode in to attack. He killed the commander with his lance, and this proved the turning point of the battle as the Aztecs began to retreat. According to one account, a vast army of Aztec allies was preparing to march in support but melted away when they saw the battle was lost. In the aftermath of the battle, the Spaniards proceeded to Tlaxcala while the Aztecs withdrew into Tenochtitlán. **CP**

Losses: Aztec, considerable of up to 200,000; Spanish, some contemporary Spanish sources suggest fewer than 73 dead

⟨ *Night of Sorrows 1520*   *Tenochtitlán 1521* ⟩

Seventeenth-century painting of Hernán Cortés at the turning point of the battle. ⬆

Pamplona 20 May 1521

The Battle of Pamplona was part of the war between France and the Hapsburgs from 1521 to 1526. Spain had conquered part of Navarre in 1512, but in 1521 it rebelled with French backing. The Navarrese captured Pamplona by defeating the Spanish garrison, which included Ignatius of Loyola, who subsequently founded the Jesuits.

Navarre had straddled the Pyrenees until Spain conquered the Iberian part of the kingdom in 1512. Henry d'Albret—the son of the last king of Navarre before the Spanish annexation—was eager to reclaim his lands. When war between France and Spain started in 1521, Henry crossed the Pyrenees with a strong French army. This ignited revolt across Spanish Navarre.

The most important position was Pamplona, the capital of Navarre. When the town rose up, with assistance from the French army, the Spanish governor wanted to surrender immediately. Loyola—a Basque soldier who had more than a decade of military experience—opposed this, arguing that the garrison should attempt to hold out. The Spanish retreated to the citadel of the fortress, where a Franco-Navarrese force besieged their position. On 20 May, after a six-hour bombardment, a cannon ball severely wounded Loyola as he patrolled the ramparts. It passed through his legs, wounding one and shattering the other. Shortly afterward, the defenders surrendered and Pamplona was lost.

Loyola was allowed to return home. During his convalescence, he underwent a religious conversion and gave up his military career for a religious life, eventually founding the Jesuit order and becoming Saint Ignatius of Loyola. Spain was able to reverse its setback after Pamplona and recapture the southern part of Navarre that year, with the kingdom north of the Pyrenees only enduring as a French client state. **JF**

Losses: Unknown

Detail from a late sixteenth- or early seventeenth-century painting depicting the besieged fortress.

Tenochtitlán 22 May–13 August 1521

Spanish conquistadores commanded by Hernán Cortés and supported by an alliance of local Indian groups conquered the Aztec empire after a ninety-three-day siege of the capital Tenochtitlán, capturing and much later executing the Aztec ruler Cuauhtémoc. The invaders incorporated the vast Aztec lands into the colony of New Spain.

After surviving an attack by the Aztecs and allies at Otumba in July 1520, the invading Spanish army settled in Tlaxcala, where Cortés built alliances with Indian groups as he prepared to launch an attack on Tenochtitlán. In October 1520 an epidemic of smallpox, a disease brought to Mexico by the Spanish, decimated the population in Tenochtitlán and killed the ruler Cuitláhuac. He was replaced by Cuauhtémoc; many others died of starvation.

Cortés determined to besiege Tenochtitlán, which was built on an artificial island on Lake Texcoco connected to the mainland by three causeways that ended in the cities of Tlacopan, Coyoacan, and Ixtlapalapan. On 22 May

"With such wonderful sites to gaze on, we did not know what to say, or if this was real that we saw …"

Bernal Díaz, witness to siege

1521, he mounted the siege, stationing an army at the end of each causeway—one under Pedro de Alvarado at Tlacopan, one under Cristobal de Olid at Coyoacan, and one under Gonzalo de Sandoval at Ixtlapalapan. Each army had up to thirty cavalry, around twenty to twenty-five artillerymen, 150 to 175 Spanish infantry, and up to 30,000 native allies. Cortés also ordered armed brigantines to patrol the lake to prevent the Aztecs leaving the city by boat; the brigantines each contained one cannon and were manned by twenty-five troops and artillerymen. Aztec water supplies largely came into the city by aqueduct from the springs at Chapultepec, and Cortés next moved to cut off this supply.

The first military encounter followed an advance along the causeway at Tlacopan by the armies of Alvarado and Olid; after a long battle, the Aztec defenders won and drove the attackers back. Fighting on the causeway, the Spanish and their allies came under savage attack from both sides by Aztecs firing arrows from canoes, while the brigantines could only fight on one side of the causeway. Cortés ordered the digging of a break in the causeway to allow his brigantines to pass through and fight on both sides; meanwhile the Aztecs attempted to damage the Spanish vessels by concealing spears in shallow water.

Gradually the attackers tightened their hold on the city; more native groups joined the Spanish side, providing supplies and manpower. Finally the attackers broke into the city and fought the Aztec defenders in the streets. Cortés sent Indian allies ahead to draw the Aztecs out of hiding to a battle. When the allies were attacked they retreated quickly and the Spanish troops swept forward to fight. Each day, the invaders made progress through the city; the Aztecs fought with pride and ferocity to the end, but finally were too weak to resist. They surrendered on 13 August 1521, after Cuauhtémoc and his chief warriors attempted to escape by canoe and were captured.

The invaders gained control of an empire containing 500 small states spread over 80,000 square miles (207,000 sq km) and with a population of 6 million people. Cortés took Cuauhtémoc on an expedition to Honduras, and the last ruler of the Aztec empire was hanged in Chiapas in 1524. On the ruins of Tenochtitlán, Cortés built a capital (now Mexico City) for the colony of New Spain. **CP**

Losses: Aztec, 240,000, plus 100,000 dead of starvation, disease, or in-fighting during the siege; Spanish, 850, plus 20,000 Tlaxcalan allies

◁ Otumba 1520   Cajamarca 1532 ▷

An engraving of Tenochtitlán by Franz Hogenberg from the atlas of cities, Civitates Orbis Terrarum. ➜

MEXICO, REGI
ET CELEBRI
HISPANIÆ N
VAE CIVI A

Cum Priuilegio.

Bicocca   27 April 1522

France's victory over Swiss mercenaries at Marignano in 1515 failed to win it a long-term advantage in the struggle for supremacy in Italy. In 1522 it was the turn of France's enemies to win a battle outside Milan. The Swiss lost again—but this time they were in the pay of the French.

In 1519 Hapsburg king Charles I of Spain became Holy Roman Emperor Charles V. Combining the German imperial forces with the army of Spain created a formidable opponent for France's Valois king Francis I, opening a new phase in the long-running Italian Wars.

In the winter of 1521 a French army under the Vicomte de Lautrec fought a losing struggle against an offensive by Spanish-Imperial forces, commanded by Prospero Colonna. Forced to abandon Milan, Lautrec strove to strengthen his forces, mostly with additional mercenary infantry and contingents sent by France's ally Venice. By spring 1522, however, he had no more money to pay his Swiss mercenaries and faced the choice of seeking battle immediately or seeing his army disintegrate.

Colonna had adopted a formidable defensive position at Bicocca outside Milan, with his cannon and arquebusiers ranged behind ramparts and a sunken road. On 27 April, the Swiss pikemen launched a frontal attack that stalled in the sunken road. Cut apart by a storm of artillery and infantry fire, the Swiss were driven back by German Landsknecht mercenaries. An attempted flanking maneuver by French cavalry had no greater success. Colonna rejected calls to take the offensive, aware that he had already won. Within a few days, the decimated Swiss army marched home and the remnants of the French army withdrew, leaving Milan in imperial control. The word "bicocca" entered the Spanish language, meaning "easy" or "cheap." **RG**

Losses: French, 3,000 of 20,000; Spanish-Imperial, light casualties of 7,000

◁ *Marignano 1515*   *Pavia 1525* ▷

Rhodes   June–December 1522

Led by Sultan Suleiman the Magnificent, the Siege of Rhodes was the second attempt by the Ottoman Empire to defeat the Knights Hospitaller and take control of Rhodes. Control of the Greek island would consolidate Ottoman control of the eastern Mediterranean.

Selim I had vastly expanded Ottoman territory in the Muslim Middle East. His successor, Suleiman, now took the Christians as his target. Suleiman learned from the failed attempt of 1480: this time the Ottomans doubled the size of their fleet to more than 300 ships and, along with a force of 75,000, besieged the island in June 1522, blockading the harbor and bombarding the town.

The walls had been strengthened after the first siege but, after several weeks, the cannons breached a section allowing the Ottomans to launch an attack on the English section. For a day, the Ottomans attacked, but English and German knights repelled them. After attacks on other parts of the ramparts failed, the Ottomans decided to explode mines under the walls but these attacks were repelled, too. In early December, the bombardment ceased while the two sides negotiated. However, peace talks broke down and the bombardment continued with increased ferocity as more artillery had been brought from Anatolia.

The Grand Master could see that the situation was hopeless and surrendered in December to avoid loss of civilian life. Suleiman was generous, in recognition of the bravery of the defenders. In late December, the knights marched out of the town carrying their banners and were transported safely to Crete aboard Ottoman ships. Although costly, the capture of Rhodes was a significant victory for the Ottomans. The Knights Hospitaller relocated to Malta. **TB**

Losses: Ottoman, 25,000 of 75,000; Knight Hospitaller, 3,000 of 7,500

◁ *Ridaniya 1517*   *Mohacs 1526* ▷

Pavia   24 February 1525

Ten years after his triumph at Marignano, French king Francis I invaded Italy a second time, only to suffer a catastrophic defeat at Pavia. This military disaster left Francis a prisoner of his archenemy, Hapsburg Emperor Charles V, and exposed Italy to Hapsburg domination.

In late 1524 Francis marched into Lombardy and occupied Milan. He then laid siege to the imperial-controlled city of Pavia. Emperor Charles sent an army under the Marchese di Pescara to relieve the siege. The imperial forces arrived outside Pavia and took up a position facing the French on the opposite side of a stream.

After three weeks of wary skirmishing, Pescara led a bold attack. He staged a night march several miles to the north and forded the stream. By daybreak a large part of his army was in place, threatening the open French left flank. Confused by fog that obscured the battlefield, the French commanders struggled to reorient their forces to meet this unexpected attack. Showing impeccable personal courage but limited judgment, King Francis led his armored cavalry in a medieval-style charge with couched lances. Unfortunately his horsemen rode in front of his cannon, making it impossible for the artillery to fire on the enemy. Francis's Swiss mercenary pikemen showed no eagerness to fight, and forces under the Duke of Alençon failed to engage in the general confusion.

Spanish arquebusiers took a heavy toll of the French, the veteran Duke of Tremoille falling with a ball through the heart. The imperial Landsknecht mercenaries, under Georg von Frundsberg, surrounded the renegade Black Band Landsknecht fighting for the French and annihilated them. Francis was carried off to captivity in Spain, where he was held for more than a year. **RG**

Losses: French, 8,000 of 20,000; Hapsburg, 1,000 of 23,000

◁ Bicocca 1522   Sack of Rome 1527 ▷

"To inform you of how the rest of my ill-fortune is proceeding, all is lost to me save honor and life."

Francis I, writing to his mother after his capture at Pavia

⬆ Detail from The Battle of Pavia by sixteenth-century artist Ruprecht Heller; the encounter embarrassed the French military.

Panipat 12 April 1526

An overwhelmingly outnumbered Mughal force prevailed at Panipat. This was due to the resourcefulness of its commander, Babur, demonstrated in his use of field fortifications and his instinctive sense of the value of the firepower of gunpowder. The victory enabled him to lay the foundations for the Indian Mughal Empire.

A descendant of Timur, Babur became a refugee at the age of twelve when the Uzbeks seized Samarkand in 1494. At age fifteen he was back with his own warband. He laid siege to his home city, but without success. Undaunted, he headed south into Afghanistan. Capturing Kabul in 1504, he made it his base for raids into Central Asia's Transoxania region. Increasingly, however, he found himself tempted by the unimaginable wealth of India. In the years that followed, he mounted a series of incursions into the Punjab.

These territories had for three centuries belonged to a Muslim empire, the Delhi sultanate. Although its prestige

> *"Everywhere the leaders of the Afghan tribes set themselves up as independent chiefs . . . in convenient strongholds."* Babur

had been badly damaged by Timur's triumph of 1398, it remained a powerful presence in northern India. At this time, the sultanate was under the control of an Afghan elite. A capricious and divisive ruler, Sultan Ibrahim Lodi had alienated many of his nobles. It was indeed a local lord in Hindustan who, in 1523, invited Babur to undertake a full-scale invasion.

Although he clearly was attracted by the idea of invasion, Babur was in no hurry. His army numbered only 10,000 men, so he made sure that they were well-equipped and superbly trained before committing to his assault on Hindustan. He took the time to train them in the use of gunpowder weapons, while making sure their skills in traditional steppe warfare were not neglected. Only at the end of 1525 did he embark on his invasion.

His army swept aside the Afghan force that marched out to meet it, so Sultan Ibrahim himself led a second army into the field, taking up a position at Panipat, to the north of Delhi. On 12 April 1526, Babur found himself confronted with an enormous multitude: 100,000 men and 1,000 elephants. Unfazed, he set about constructing an impromptu fortress on the open plain, tying 700 carts together and fronting them with earthen ramparts as protection for his cannon and for his musketeers with their matchlocks. As the days passed and a hesitant Sultan Ibrahim stayed his attack, Babur was able to consolidate his position still further. He dug trenches and felled trees, constructing barriers to the left and right, while leaving gaps through which his cavalry could charge.

On 21 April, Ibrahim finally made his move. His troops surged forward, only to be brought up short by Babur's fortifications. As they milled about in confusion, the Mughal cavalry came wheeling in from the wings: the sultan's force was effectively surrounded. At this point, Babur's gunners opened up their bombardment from behind their barrier, firing at point-blank range into this close-packed mass. Unable either to advance or retreat, the Afghan army was cut down cruelly.

Not only was Babur now the undisputed ruler of Hindustan, but also the road to Delhi and the domains of the sultanate lay wide open. On the basis of this victory, he was able to establish a glorious new ruling line. In honor of its founder's Timurid origins—and of the Mongol antecedents of Timur himself—this was to be known as the Mughal, or Mogul, dynasty. **MK**

Losses: Mughal, unknown; Afghan, 20,000–50,000

Khanwa 1527 ⊳

Babur leads his army into battle, from a nineteenth-century miniature by Charpentier. ➔

Mohacs   29 August 1526

The Battle of Mohacs was a decisive defeat for Hungary, led by King Louis II, at the hands of the Ottoman Empire, led by Sultan Suleiman the Magnificent. The victory at Mohacs led to the Ottomans controlling a large part of Hungary for almost two centuries.

In order to expand the Ottoman Empire into the heart of Europe, Suleiman would have to conquer the kingdom of Hungary. The first stage to accomplishing this goal was the capture of Belgrade in 1521. Suleiman could then use Serbian territory to launch an invasion.

The Hungarians knew that an attack was coming but could not win any support from other Christian powers. Suleiman's army made an uncontested crossing of the Drava River on a pontoon bride, which took five days, while King Louis waited to face the invaders on a large marshy plain at Mohacs. The Hungarians intended to rely upon the shock effect of their charging armored knights, but Suleiman had better balanced forces, including infantry Janissaries armed with arquebuses, sipahi light cavalry, and formidable banks of cannon.

The charge of the Hungarian cavalry caused serious casualties to the Ottoman vanguard, but Suleiman's elite Janissaries pushed back the Hungarians, who were also torn apart by Turkish cannon fire. As the Hungarians fell back, they were outflanked and encircled by the fast-moving Ottoman light cavalry. King Louis of Hungary was thrown from his horse and killed as he tried to escape the carnage. A large part of his army was cut down. The defeat at Mohacs was a disaster that ended the existence of Hungary as an independent united kingdom and led to its effective partition between the Ottoman and Hapsburg empires. **TB**

Losses: Ottoman, 2,000 of 60,000; Hungarian, 18,000 of 35,000

◁ Rhodes 1522   Vienna 1529 ▷

Khanwa   17 March 1527

A year after Babur's victory at Panipat, Hindu Rajput ruler Rana Sanga threatened to destroy his new Muslim Indian Empire before it had even properly come into being. The Battle of Khanwa was long and bitter, but modern firepower (and a promise to Allah) were to prove decisive.

India's Hindu kings were alarmed to see a new and aggressive Islamic empire establishing itself along their borders, but—after years of warring—they were too disunited to resist. Then Rana Sanga of Mewar rallied the Rajput caste—the Hindu warriors—and by early 1527, he had an enormous force under arms.

At Khanwa, outside Agra, this vast force confronted Babur's. As at Panipat, the previous year, the Mughals were massively outnumbered. Rana Sanga had up to 120,000 men; Babur only about a tenth that number, including steppe-style mounted archers. But his army also included musketeers and heavy artillery—up to twenty cannon. Sanga's elephants would have seemed a formidable asset just a few years before, but Babur had transformed warfare in the subcontinent. Even so, if only for its sheer size, the Rajput army was seriously daunting, and Babur saw the demoralization of his men. In desperation, he is is said to have called on Allah for help—much as he loved it, he would give up wine, he vowed.

The Rajputs attacked on 17 March with overwhelming force. The Mughal soldiers barely managed to stand firm. Hour by hour, however, their ceaseless matchlock fire ravaged the attacking ranks from the front, while the cavalry kept harrying from the flanks. Finally, the crash of cannon terrified Sanga's advancing elephants; their stampede threw his whole army into disarray. Babur's Mughals were masters of northern India. **MK**

Losses: Unknown

◁ Panipat 1526   Second Panipat 1556 ▷

Detail showing triumphant Ottoman troops, from the Hünername *by Lokman published in 1588.*

Sack of Rome 6 May 1527

Vienna Sep–Oct 1529

Victory over the French at Pavia in 1525 left the forces of the Holy Roman Emperor, Charles V, dominant in Italy. In 1527 these forces stormed the city of Rome and embarked on an orgy of destruction and massacre, terrorizing the population and humiliating Pope Clement VII.

In 1529 the Ottoman Empire made a determined effort to capture Vienna, the capital of the Hapsburg Austrian Empire. The failure to take Vienna marked the end of Turkish expansion into Europe and was followed by the diversion of Ottoman effort toward Asia and the Mediterranean.

Pope Clement had unwisely formed an alliance, the League of Cognac, to challenge Charles's supremacy in Italy. Rome was not, however, attacked on the emperor's orders, but on the initiative of imperial troops angry at not being paid. These ragged and hungry soldiers, including German Landsknecht mercenaries and Spanish infantry, mutinied and marched on Rome, under the command of renegade French aristocrat the Duke of Bourbon.

The walls of Rome were poorly defended, the city's garrison numbering only 8,000 men, including the 2,000-strong Swiss Guard. On 6 May the rebellious imperial army launched an assault in the face of cannon and arquebus fire. The Duke of Bourbon was shot dead but the men he had led swept into the city, killing everyone in sight, armed or not. The Swiss Guards fought bravely to defend St. Peter's Basilica and created enough delay to allow Pope Clement to escape down a tunnel into the fortress of Castel Sant'Angelo. There he was besieged while the city was laid waste. The Protestant Landsknecht felt particular hatred for Catholic Rome and its idolatrous Renaissance treasures—they stabled horses in St. Peter's—but the Catholic Spanish equaled them in cruelty and destructiveness. Clement surrendered in June, agreeing to pay a huge ransom and cede substantial territory to Charles V who, although embarrassed by the brutal conduct of his troops, was happy to accept the advantage he had gained. **TB**

After the defeat of the Hungarians at Mohacs, the Ottoman Empire and Austria were brought into direct contact along a border across Hungary. In 1529, Suleiman launched a campaign against Austria's Archduke Ferdinand I with an army of more than 100,000.

Suleiman's advance from the Black Sea, which began in May, was arduous because the weather had been particularly wet, with many lives lost due to the spread of illnesses through the soaked ranks of the sultan's army. Much of the heavy artillery that would have been vital in the siege had to be abandoned when it became stuck in mud. Suleiman reached Vienna in September with his army greatly weakened. Ottoman attempts to mine the walls were hampered by a counterattack, and more heavy rains in October dampened much of the gunpowder.

Attack after attack was repulsed by the Austrian defenders, who picked off the Ottoman troops with arquebuses from the high walls of the city and forced back those who scaled the walls by using long pikes. In late October, Suleiman ordered one last all-out assault, but this was also repulsed. Suleiman then ordered a retreat of his battered army, which turned into a disastrous ordeal as winter snows came early causing many deaths and loss of the remaining artillery. Defeat at Vienna forced Suleiman back into Ottoman Hungary and, after a second failure to take Vienna in 1532, he abandoned thoughts of conquering Europe. **TB**

Losses: Roman, 1,000 Swiss Guards and 25,000 civilian casualties; Holy Roman Empire, unknown

◁ *Pavia 1525*

Losses: Austrian, unknown; Ottoman, 16,000 of 100,000, thousands more dead in the retreat

◁ *Mohacs 1526*   *Baghdad 1534* ▷

Cajamarca 15 November 1532

The noise and smoke of fire-flashing European weapons, as much as their deadly destructiveness, carried the day for the Spanish conquistadores at Cajamarca. Sheer shock made a nonsense of the numbers as Francisco Pizarro's 128 invaders defeated the Inca army to take Peru.

A complacent King Atahuallpa had allowed Pizarro's expedition to pass unhindered into his realms. The Incas were observing a religious fast and decided that so negligible an enemy could wait. On 15 November 1532 the Incas finally confronted the Spaniards in the main square of Cajamarca, but Atahuallpa left the bulk of his 80,000-strong army outside the provincial city.

Pizarro's "plan" appears to have been to improvise: trusting to the advantages of surprise and shock that the sight of horses, firearms, and iron weaponry and armor had given his compatriots wherever they went in the Americas. A nerve of steel also helped, however: Pizarro stayed calm as Atahuallpa and his staff came out to parley and dismissed with contempt his claim to have brought word of the true God. Handed a prayer book, the Inca king threw it down: Pizarro needed no further excuse to attack. His men opened fire and threw themselves upon the astonished Inca bodyguard. Blazing away with their muskets, slashing and thrusting with their swords, they slew 7,000 Incas; not a single Spaniard was badly hurt.

For all the power of their firearms, the conquistadores' real secret weapon was their obliviousness toward the Inca people's taboos: in physically laying hands on Atahuallpa and taking him prisoner, they did the unthinkable. The king was a god to his subjects; his humiliation turned Inca reality upside down. They were now allowed to occupy Atahuallpa's empire unopposed. **MK**

Losses: Inca, 7,000; Spanish, none

◁ *Tenochtitlán 1521*　　　　　　　*Cuzco 1536* ▷

Baghdad 1534

The Ottoman capture of Baghdad occurred during the first campaign of a twenty-year war between the Ottoman Empire and the Persian Safavid Empire of Shah Tahmasp I. The famous city was to remain in Ottoman hands almost continuously until it was captured by the British in 1917.

War between the Ottoman and Safavid empires was brought about chiefly by territorial disputes along their Asian frontier, but also by Persian efforts to forge an alliance with the Hapsburg-controlled states, at the head of which sat the powerful Holy Roman Emperor, Charles V of Spain. Such an alliance would open up a double front against the powerful Ottoman Empire.

These tensions ignited into war when Tahmasp had the governor of Baghdad—a supporter of the Ottoman cause—killed. The murder caused Suleiman to turn his attention away from his campaigns in central Europe to focus on the Safavid threat. The Ottomans invaded Safavid territory in 1531 and captured the Kurdish town of Bitlis in 1532 after a three-month siege. The force then advanced on the Safavid capital of Tabriz in eastern Persia, which was taken with ease. Tahmasp continued to fall back, evading capture and avoiding engaging the Ottomans in battle. Baghdad fell in 1534, and Tahmasp again withdrew.

From this point onward, he began harrying the Ottomans, launching guerrilla attacks and adopting a scorched-earth campaign that hampered Suleiman's ability to supply his army. Frustrated by Tahmasp's tactics, Suleiman garrisoned his gains and withdrew in 1534, ending the first phase of the war with no decisive conclusion. After a further phase of fighting in 1548 to 1549, the war finally ended in 1555, leaving the Ottomans with key gains in Mesopotamia, including Baghdad. **TB**

Losses: Unknown

◁ *Vienna 1529*　　　　　　　*Fall of Tunis 1535* ▷

Fall of Tunis June 1535

In 1535 the Ottoman Empire of Suleiman the Magnificent and the Hapsburg Holy Roman Empire of Charles V were both at the height of their power. The port-city of Tunis in north Africa became the focus for a bold and successful counterattack by Charles upon the expansionist Ottomans.

Tunis fell to the Ottoman Empire in August 1534, following a naval attack by the Ottoman admiral Hayreddin Barbarossa. The city's Berber Hafsid ruler, Muley Hasan, who had been an ally of Charles V, was driven into exile.

By capturing Tunis, the Ottomans gained a strategic base from which to launch seaborne raids into the western Mediterranean, most notably against Hapsburg possessions in Italy. In 1535, Charles V sailed to recapture the city with a large army and a fleet of galleons armed with powerful bronze cannon. The expedition was financed by gold plundered from the Incas in Peru, and thus Charles began a process whereby wealth gained from

Hapsburg Spain's transatlantic empire was used to finance the campaigns deemed necessary to fulfill Hapsburg rulers' responsibilities as champions of Catholicism.

In June 1535, Charles's fleet, supported by a number of Genoese vessels under Andrea Doria, attacked Tunis and destroyed the Ottoman galleys there. The city was retaken after a short siege. The fall of Tunis, which resulted in the restoration of Muley Hasan as vassal to the Hapsburg Empire, was a blow to Ottoman prestige. The scale and efficiency of the operation brought Charles great renown and appalled his enemies, the French, who renewed efforts to ally with the Ottoman Empire. Tunis was recaptured by the Ottomans in 1574, an event which ensured that the future of north Africa would be Muslim rather than Christian. **TB**

Losses: Spanish, unknown; Ottoman, 70 ships destroyed and 20,000 civilians dead

◁ Baghdad 1534   Preveza 1538 ▷

Detail from a sixteenth-century engraving depicting Charles sailing into battle near Tunis. ↑

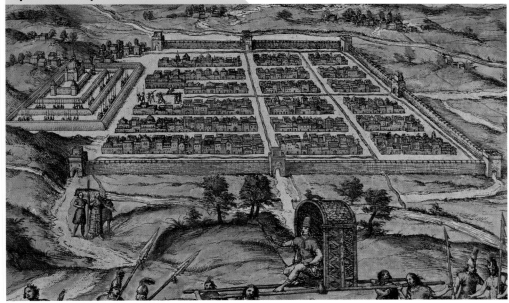

Cuzco   May 1536–March 1537

Manco Inca, son of Atahuallpa, brought a force of 400,000 warriors with him when he launched his assault on Cuzco early in 1536. Holed up in the Inca capital, the Spanish conquistadores resorted to desperate measures, but still succeeded in withstanding a ten-month siege.

The Inca paid an enormous ransom in gold for the release of Atahuallpa—their king and god—but the conquistador leader, Francisco Pizarro, still had his prisoner garrotted in the end. Manco took his place as Inca ruler. At first content to be a puppet ruler, Manco rebelled when he realized how little authority he would have. Taking refuge in the Yucay Valley, he raised an army: warriors flocked there from all corners of Peru, and from Inca realms in Ecuador and Chile. Although Pizarro's troops had been reinforced by fresh arrivals in the years since he had taken the Inca Empire with just 128 men, the Spanish were still overwhelmingly outnumbered.

In May 1536, the Inca attacked. They took the Spanish by surprise and managed to occupy most of the city. Crucially, they took the formidable citadel of Sacsahuaman. The conquistadores were forced to mount their own countersiege. Meanwhile, cut off from all support, they sent out parties to seek help from New Spain (Mexico). These excursions were intercepted, their members killed or captured. Manco set these Spanish prisoners to instruct his Inca warriors in the use of horses, swords, and guns. However, after months of fighting, the Spanish succeeded in cutting off supplies to Sacsahuaman: they then sallied forth to attack Manco's headquarters at Ollantaytambo. This attack was repelled but, as Manco moved in upon Cuzco for the kill, his own force was taken by surprise. The Inca were defeated, and the reign of the Spanish over Peru was confirmed. **MK**

Losses: Unknown

⟨ *Cajamarca 1532*

S. ACQVISTA.   IL DI III DI MAGGIO
M.DCV. LA PREVESA. IN ALBANIA.
CITTA GIA DETTA. NICOPOLI
DA AGVSTO.

Preveza 28 September 1538

The Ottoman fleet under Admiral Hayreddin Barbarossa was raiding the coast of Italy at will and threatening Venetian possessions in Greece. In desperation, an alliance of Christian states—the Holy League—sent a fleet to attack Barbarossa. The result was a triumph for Ottoman naval power.

The Holy League, called into existence by Pope Paul II, included Venice, Spain, Portugal, Genoa, and the Papal States. It assembled its armada at Corfu during the summer 1538 under the command of the experienced Genoese admiral, Andrea Doria. Meanwhile, Barbarossa took up a position at Preveza—a Turkish fort, on the coast of northwest Greece—with landing troops to take Actium, a Christian fortress on the facing shore.

The Holy League fleet, a mix of oared galleys and sailing ships, arrived and made attacks on Preveza and Actium. It was repelled, taking heavy losses. Barbarossa, who had a smaller fleet, could shelter under the guns of the two forts, while the Holy League forces could not come ashore for resupply. Barbarossa could have waited for the Christians to leave, but instead confidently chose to give battle. The League's ships were arranged in four ranks, while the Ottoman galleys formed a crescent, with the wings composed of faster, more agile ships, ready to perform an outflanking maneuver. As the two fleets clashed, Andrea Doria held back his own Spanish and Genoese ships, while the Venetian and Papal ships were attacked, a move later blamed for the League's defeat. The Christians' superior firepower was negated by the maneuverabilty of the skillfully handled Ottoman galleys.

With this victory, the Ottoman Empire consolidated its control of the eastern Mediterranean, and Venice was forced to cede territory to the Ottomans. **TB**

Losses: Holy League, 50 ships sunk or captured of 100, 2,500 men captured; Ottoman, no ships lost

◁ Fall of Tunis 1535   Djerba 1560 ▷

Solway Moss 24 November 1542

At Solway Moss in Cumbria, northern England, an English and a Scottish army clashed in 1542. After a brief engagement, the Scots fled back across the border, a humiliation that may have hastened the death of Scottish king James V, bringing his infant daughter Mary to the throne.

After the death of James IV at Flodden in 1513, his infant son succeeded him as James V. Relations between England and Scotland were mainly peaceful until tension, caused by the renewed Franco-Scottish alliance and the Henrician Reformation, led to war.

On 24 November 1542, a Scottish force of about 18,000 men crossed the border. James V had accompanied them but did not lead the invasion in person and remained in Scotland. He had not designated a commander, but shortly before the battle his favorite military man, Sir Oliver Sinclair, was declared general. Most of the other senior officials in the Scottish army refused to listen to Sinclair. In addition, he had little chance of creating any cohesion because each noble and gentleman had their own retainers who would heed only their orders.

Sir Thomas Wharton led a smaller English force from Carlisle to intercept the Scots. When the English cavalry attacked, it pinned the Scots between the boggy Solway Moss and the River Esk. Chaos ensued, and many of the Scots fled. Rumors that another English army was approaching added to the panic. Several hundred Scots drowned in their retreat, and many others surrendered. The English took Sinclair prisoner, as well as several other influential Scottish aristocrats. Three weeks after hearing of the defeat of his army, James V died, leaving his six-day-old daughter, Mary, as queen. Fighting continued with the English until 1547. **JF**

Losses: English, negligible of 3,000; Scottish, 20 dead and 1,200 captured of 18,000

◁ Flodden 1513

A nineteenth-century painting of the Battle of Preveza by Ohannes Umed Behzad.

Ethiopian-Adal War

Wayna Daga 21 February 1543

In 1543, at Wayna Daga in northern Ethiopia, an Ethiopian-Portuguese force comprehensively bested the army of the Muslim Adal sultanate, which had invaded and occupied large swaths of Ethiopia. The battle ended the Ethiopian-Adal War (1529–43), and the Adal presence in Ethiopia.

In 1541, the Portuguese had sent an expeditionary force to aid the Ethiopian emperor Gelawdewos, but the Adal army and their Ottoman allies had routed it at the Battle of Wofla in 1542. The next year Gelawdewos, along with the remaining Portuguese soldiers, marched toward the Adal army's position near Lake Tana and camped nearby.

After initial skirmishing, the two armies lined up against each other on 21 February. The Portuguese troops, along with around half the Ethiopian soldiers, advanced in the first line, with the rest of the Ethiopian army in a second line. The Adal army was also divided into two roughly equal lines, along with 200 Ottoman musketeers in the van, commanded by Imam Ahmad.

At first the Adal army made steady progress. However, an allied countercharge pushed them back. Imam Ahmad rode to the front to rally his men but the allies spotted him and he was killed by their musket fire. Shortly after, the command of the second Adal line was killed in a fierce hand-to-hand struggle. The Adal lines were in total chaos, and their soldiers began to flee. The allies pursued and looted the Adal camp. With their leader dead, the Adal sultanate was unable to maintain its position in Ethiopia, and Gelawdewos conquered the territory he had lost. **JF**

Losses: Unknown of 8,500 Ethiopians and 120 Portuguese; unknown of 15,000 Adal and 200 Ottomans

The Solent   19–20 July 1545

In 1543 Henry VIII of England declared war on France and seized Boulogne. In response, Francis I prepared a fleet to invade England. The opposing naval forces met off the English coast in a tentative encounter that deterred a French invasion but is chiefly remembered for the sinking of the *Mary Rose*.

As the French assembled their fleet of 150 sailing ships in Le Havre, joined by twenty-five galleys brought from the Mediterranean, the English under Admiral John Dudley launched a largely fruitless preemptive strike. His fleet returned to Portsmouth for essential repairs but was far from ready when the French fleet crossed the Channel to the Sussex coast and then sailed west to the mouth of the Solent, between Portsmouth and the Isle of Wight. On the fine, still morning of 19 July, the French galleys entered the Solent in sight of Henry VIII,

who was reviewing his fleet in Portsmouth. The English fleet set sail, taking advantage of a freshening breeze to approach the galleys. One ship, the large but elderly *Mary Rose*, fired her starboard guns at the galleys and then turned to prepare to fire her port side guns. As she did so, she floundered, either as a result of enemy gunfire or more probably as a result of a sudden gust of wind that caused her to keel over and submerge her open starboard gun ports. As the sea poured in, the ship quickly sank, killing all but thirty of its 415 crew.

The French failed to capitalize on this disaster. Both fleets exchanged long-range cannon fire the next day, and some French soldiers went ashore briefly on the Isle of Wight. While the English tried to salvage their sunken ship, the French headed home across the Channel. **SA**

Losses: English, 1 ship of 80; French, no ships of 175

Kawagoe   31 October 1545

The Odawara Hojo were typical of the successful lords of Japan's Age of Warring States that lasted from 1467 to 1615. The Hojo took over the Kanto Plain, the area where modern Tokyo now lies. When Kawagoe Castle was besieged, the Hojo relieved it in a daring night attack.

In 1545, samurai commander Ogigayatsu Tomosada allied himself with Ashikaga Haruuji and marched against Kawagoe Castle, which was defended by Hojo Ujiyasu's brother, Hojo Tsunanari. Tsunanari's garrison were only 3,000 strong, but they managed to hold out against 85,000 besiegers. Hojo Ujiyasu marched to the castle's relief with 8,000 samurai, and one brave warrior managed to slip past the siege lines to tell his brother that they were on their way.

The relief force was another pitifully small army, but Ujiyasu was confident and so offered a deal to Ashikaga Haruuji, whom he perceived as the weakest of the allies. His offer was rejected, but intelligence suggested that the besiegers were so sure of victory that their vigilance had slackened. Ujiyasu decided to make a night attack, which was to be coordinated with a sortie from the castle by his brother, Tsunanari. Ujiyasu issued orders that his men should not overburden themselves by wearing heavy armor and should wear white paper jackets to be seen in the dark. They also should not waste time taking heads. It says a lot for the loyalty of the Hojo samurai that they willingly suspended this most basic of samurai privileges for the common good.

The plans worked perfectly and, despite the odds of ten to one against them, the Hojo triumphed. The coalition was utterly destroyed, and the Hojo control of the Kanto was dramatically confirmed. **ST**

Losses: Ashikaga allied, up to 16,000; Hojo, few

◁ Kyoto 1467   Okehazama 1560 ▷

Second Panipat   5 November 1556

The Mughal Empire's expansion, stalled after the death of its founder Babur in 1530, began anew under Babur's grandson, Akbar. Fighting on a field that had proved so propitious for his grandfather, the young Akbar won a vital victory over the powerful Hindu ruler, Hemu.

Babur's son Humayun had encountered serious setbacks, even losing his kingdom after it was conquered by the Pashtun warlord Sher Shah Suri in 1540. Rebuilding his forces in exile, he eventually took back his realms fifteen years later, leaving his son and successor, Akbar, with a great empire.

To the east of Akbar's realms, the Suri general Hemu had set himself up as a strongman ruler; calling himself a king, he built a powerbase in Bengal. Aged just thirteen, Akbar seemed singularly ill-equipped to cope with this threat. However, he had rare gifts—and the support of his guardian, the accomplished general Bairam Khan. Hemu had unstoppable momentum, it seemed—having already taken Agra and the strategic fortress of Tughlaqabad, in October 1556 he captured Delhi. Too late to save the city, Akbar's army let it go and stopped on the plains to the north, at Panipat.

On 5 November, battle was joined. Repeated elephant charges failed to break the resolve of the outnumbered Mughal soldiers. An inspiring figure, Hemu led from the front, perched high up on an elephant, an important talisman for his troops. He was also a tempting target for the Mughal archers, and initially they showered him with shafts to no avail, so impregnable was the head-to-foot armor he was wearing. Eventually, though, one arrow found its way in through an eye-slit and killed him. Seeing their leader fall, the Hindus broke and fled. **MK**

Losses: Unknown

◁ Khanwa 1527   Talikota 1565 ▷

Saint-Quentin 20 August 1557

The Hapsburg-Valois War (1551–59) was a French attempt to challenge Hapsburg dominance of Europe. In 1557 the Spanish invaded northern France and won a great victory at Saint-Quentin. The Hapsburg cause emerged victorious when the war ended in 1559.

Henry II of France declared war on Charles V of Hapsburg in 1551. In 1556, Charles abdicated, splitting his lands between his sons Philip and Ferdinand. In addition to Spain, Philip's inheritance included the Netherlands, and it was from here that he launched his campaign in 1557. His target was Saint-Quentin, which commanded the approach to northern France.

The French commander, Duke Anne of Montmorency, was unable to send substantial reinforcements to Saint-Quentin before the Spanish army of about 47,000 arrived to besiege the town on 12 August. The Spanish camped on both sides of the River Somme, which ran through Saint-Quentin. On 20 August, Montmorency attacked with a relief army of 24,000. He was able to surprise the Spanish on the south of the Somme and push them north across the river. The French were slow to follow up their initial success as they had to wait for boats to ferry them across the Somme. The Spanish regrouped and counterattacked, outflanking the French and devastating them with mounted arquebus charges and heavy cannon. Montmorency retreated with only half of his army remaining, leaving northern France defenseless. The Duke of Savoy wanted to advance to Paris but Philip ordered him to take Saint-Quentin, which fell seventeen days later. The French then reorganized their armies, and the Spanish were unable to follow up their triumph at Saint-Quentin. **JF**

Losses: French, 6,000–7,000 dead and 6,000 captured of 24,000; Spanish, few dead of 47,000

Djerba May 1560

The Battle of Djerba was fought off the coast of Tunisia between the fleets of the Ottoman Empire and a Spanish-led alliance, commanded by the Genoese admiral, Giovanni Andrea Doria. Victory for the Ottomans marked the pinnacle of their naval superiority in the Mediterranean.

Victory in 1538 for the Ottoman fleet at Preveza was followed by increasingly threatening Turkish incursion into the western Mediterranean, putting the Spanish coast and the Balearic Islands at risk. To counter this, a new Christian alliance was formed that assembled a fleet of around fifty ships under the command of Giovanni Andrea Doria, a nephew of Andrea Doria.

In February 1560, the Christian fleet embarked to capture Tripoli in north Africa. However, the primary objective of the mission was cancelled because of sickness spreading through the fleet and adverse weather conditions. Instead, in March, the fleet reached the coast of Tunisia and easily took the fortress island of Djerba. The Ottoman network of north African forts quickly relayed news of the fall of Djerba to Admiral Piyale, who immediately gathered a fleet of one hundred ships and sailed for Djerba.

The Ottomans reached the island in May, catching the Christians by surprise and attacking their fleet as it lay anchored in port. The unprepared state of the Christian fleet meant that the battle was a walkover for the Ottomans and, within a few hours, more than half of the Christian fleet had been captured or sunk. The Christians sought refuge in the fort and were besieged for a few months before surrendering later in the year. Victory at Djerba prepared the way for the Ottoman siege of Malta in 1565. **TB**

Losses: Christian allied, 30 ships sunk or captured, 15,000 dead or captured; Ottoman, fewer than 5 ships lost, 750 dead

◁ Preveza 1538   Malta 1565 ▷

Okehazama 12 June 1560

During Japan's Age of Warring States, strong lords appropriated the lands of lesser ones. In the Battle of Okehazama, the future unifier of Japan, Oda Nobunaga, achieved his first great victory when he defeated the ambitious Imagawa Yoshimoto, who had invaded his province on route to Kyoto.

Yoshimoto chose to rest with his troops at a place called Okehazama, a wooded gorge, where they performed a celebratory head-viewing ceremony. It was territory that Nobunaga knew well, and therefore provided the perfect opportunity for a surprise attack. Nobunaga rigged up a dummy army, and led 3,000 men on a circular route through the wooded hills to drop down beside Okehazama from the north. As Nobunaga's men drew near, a terrific thunderstorm began, which cloaked Nobunaga's final approach toward Imagawa's men, who were huddled under trees from the torrential rain. As the clouds blew away, the Oda troops poured into the gorge.

The Imagawa troops were so unprepared for an attack that they fled in all directions, leaving Yoshimoto's curtained field headquarters quite unprotected. Yoshimoto had so little knowledge of what was going on that he drew the conclusion that a drunken fight had broken out among his men and, on seeing an angry-looking samurai running toward him, barked out an order for the man to return to his post. He only realized that it was one of Nobunaga's men when the samurai aimed a spear-thrust at him, but by then it was too late. He drew his sword and cut through the shaft of the spear but, before he could do any more, a second samurai grabbed him and lopped off his head.

All but two senior officers of the defeated Imagawa army—thought to number around 20,000—were killed, and the remaining troops joined the Oda army. **ST**

Losses: Imagawa, very high; Oda, comparatively few

◁ Kawagoe 1545 Kawanakajima 1561 ▷

Woodblock print titled The Great Battle at Okehazama *(1864) by Tsukioka Yoshitoshi.*

Kawanakajima   16–17 October 1561

Takeda Shingen and Uesugi Kenshin, typical lords of the Japanese Age of Warring States, fought five battles between 1553 and 1564 on the flat plain of Kawanakajima in Shinano province. All proved indecisive, but the fourth battle—fought in 1561—was one of the fiercest battles in samurai history.

The fourth Battle of Kawanakajima was the largest of the five encounters. Uesugi Kenshin advanced into the plain to threaten Takeda Shingen's castle of Kaizu (modern Matsushiro). He established a camp high on the mountain of Saijoyama, from where he could observe the Takeda movements. Yamamoto Kansuke, Shingen's chief strategist, suggested a clever move: the Takeda should leave Kaizu under cover of darkness and take up a prearranged position across the river. A detachment would then attack Saijoyama to the rear, driving the Uesugi samurai in panic down the hill, across the river, and into the waiting guns of the Takeda army.

Kenshin anticipated the move, and evacuated Saijoyama before the Takeda realized. In great secrecy he guided his army across a ford and positioned them across the river to meet the Takeda. As dawn broke, he attacked the Takeda from the flank. According to legend, Shingen and Kenshin fought a single combat when Kenshin broke into the Takeda field headquarters. By this time, the detached force sent up from Kaizu castle had discovered that Saijoyama had been abandoned. Highly alarmed, they came hurrying down to the river, where they encountered Kenshin's rearguard. Fierce fighting continued and, taking full responsibility for the presumed disaster, Yamamoto Kansuke committed suicide. However, the Takeda rallied, and the Uesugi were driven away. Both sides claimed victory, which was an expensive one. **ST**

Losses: Uesugi, 72 percent of its army; Takeda, 62 percent of its army, including several leaders

◁ *Okehazama 1560*   *Anegawa 1570* ▷

⬆ The Forces of Takeda Shingen Returning after the Victory at Kawanakajima *(1856) by Utagawa Sadahide.*

Dreux 19 December 1562

Dreux was one of the first major engagements of the Wars of Religion that tore France apart in the second half of the sixteenth century. In a hard-fought battle, the Catholic side narrowly won as the Huguenot army retreated from the field, but both sides had their commanders captured.

Calvinism had spread through France in the first half of the sixteenth century. Its followers were known as Huguenots. They had been persecuted, but in January 1562 a royal edict granted them limited freedom of worship. On 1 March, Catholic troops brutally murdered a Protestant congregation in Vassy, exacerbating the tension between Catholics and Huguenots. Both scaled up their military capabilities and raised large armies.

In December 1562, a Huguenot army led by Louis de Condé, came upon a royal army near Dreux, in northwest France. Battle began early on 19 December. In the first stage of fighting, the Huguenot cavalry devastated the royal left and captured their commander, Anne, Duke of Montmorency. The only sustained royal resistance was from their Swiss mercenaries, but the Huguenots eventually forced them to retreat.

The successful attack left the Huguenots dispersed across the battlefield, and the royal army launched a strong counterattack. They captured Condé and were able to force the surrender of the German mercenaries whom the Huguenots had hired. Just as the royal army was on the verge of total victory, the Huguenots rallied with a cavalry charge, and the rest of their army was able to retreat in good order as night fell. Three months later, a truce was agreed at Amboise, which ended the fighting. However, it did not lead to a definitive peace, and war resumed in 1567. **JF**

Losses: Catholic, 5,800 of 19,000; Huguenot, 3,000 dead and 1,500 mercenaries surrendered of 12,000

Jarnac 1569 ▷

Talikota 26 January 1565

The firepower of gunpowder weapons proved crucial in inflicting a crushing defeat on the Hindu Vijayanagara Empire in this fiercely fought battle beside the Krishna River. Victory allowed the Deccan sultanates to extend Islamic rule across much of central and southern India in the following years.

The Deccan sultanates—a confederation of Muslim kingdoms that had broken free from the medieval Bahmani sultanate in the late fifteenth and early sixteenth centuries—spanned central India by the 1550s. At best an uneasy alliance, the sultanates could really unite only in the face of a common enemy—hence the decision to attack the Vijayanagara Empire, the vast and powerful Hindu state that held sway through the whole of India to the south. It should have been a foolhardy venture: the empire's armies were much bigger, with more than 140,000 infantry, 10,000 cavalry, and at least 100 elephants. The sultanates had only 80,000 foot soldiers and 30,000 cavalry, although they did have more than twenty cannon with skilled gunners.

As the Mughals had done before them, the Deccan forces brought modern weapons and tactics into play to spectacular effect when the armies met on 26 January 1565. Aging Hindu commanders proved too conservative, too inclined to "fight the last war." Startled by the bang and flash of firearms, and bewildered by the acrid smoke, elephants were no longer the key to military victory in India, more a lumbering liability. The Hindu ranks were ravaged by repeated cannonades, their cavalry outmaneuvered by Muslim horsemen who had learned cavalry skills originally developed on the Central Asian steppes. Even so, the empire's forces might have won had it not been for the defection of key Muslim generals in their service. **MK**

Losses: Unknown

◁ Second Panipat 1556 Chittor 1567 ▷

A shila shamana (sculptural inscription) dedicated to Krishna Deva Raya, the Vijayanagara king.

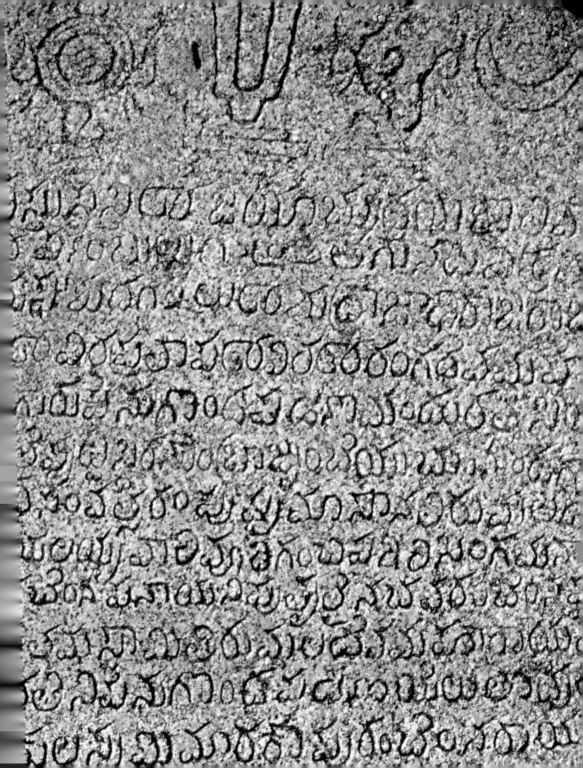

ಸ್ವಸ್ತಿ ಶ್ರೀ ವಿಜಯಾಭ್ಯುದಯ
ಶಾಲಿವಾಹನ ಶಕ ವರುಷ
ಪ್ರಭವ ಸಂವತ್ಸರದ ಶ್ರಾವಣ ಬ
ಹುಳ ಪಾಡ್ಯದೊಳೆ ತರಂಗದ ಮ
ಹಾರಾಜ ಶ್ರೀಂ ಕೃಷ್ಣ ರಾಯ ಮಹಾ ರ
ಜ್ಞ ಅರಸೊಂಗೆ ತಮ್ಮಂ ಶ್ರೀ ಮೂ
ಲ ಸಂಸ್ಥಾನ ಪ್ರತ್ಯ ಮಹಾ ಸಂಪ ನ್ನ ರಾ
ಚಾಯ ನಾಳ ಪ್ರತಿಗಂಡ ಭೈರ ಸಿಂಗಾ
ಮೆಂಕ ಮಹಾ ರಾಯ ನ ವಿಪ್ಪ ಲ ನ ಬ ವಲ ಬ ಹ
ಪ್ರಭುಸ್ವಾಮಿ ತಿರುಮಲ ದೇ ವ ಮಹಾ ರಾಯ
ಟಿ ನ ವ ಸಗೊಂಡ ಪ ಡ ನ ಯ ರ ಲ ನ ವ ಮ
ಚ ಲ ಸ ವ ಮ ಮ ರ ನ ವ ಸ ಗಂ ಬೆ ನ ಸ ರ ಯ

Malta   May–September 1565

The Siege of Malta, one of the most savagely contested encounters of the sixteenth century, followed after the forces of the Ottoman Empire invaded the island. The successful defense of Malta by the Knights Hospitaller shattered the Ottomans' reputation of invincibility and halted their advance into the western Mediterranean.

Controlled by the Knights Hospitaller since their expulsion from Rhodes, Malta was the key to Christian defenses against Ottoman expansion in the Mediterranean. The Maltese knights had expected an attack since the Ottoman naval victory at Djerba in 1560. The Ottomans took five years to launch their attack; the delay gave the Knights Hospitaller the opportunity to strengthen their fortifications and Christian Europe time to rebuild its fleets.

The Ottoman armada arrived off Malta in May 1565 and anchored at Marsaxlokk close to Fort St. Elmo at the entrance to Grand Harbour. The sheer scale of the force—around 180 ships and 40,000 soldiers—may have been

> *"Their orders were to … try and capture a stray Turk so that he could be questioned."*
>
> Balbi di Correggio, eyewitness

one reason why it took so long to invade. The commanders were Ottoman Admiral Piyale, supported by the Barbary corsair Admiral Turgut Reis, and grand vizier Mustafa Pasha leading Sultan Suleiman's land army. Rivalry between Piyale and Mustafa became open disagreement when the invasion started. Mustafa preferred to take the capital Mdina, followed by a land attack on the coastal forts. Admiral Piyale preferred to take the forts first, by means of a heavy bombardment, and managed to convince Mustafa that his plan could be

accomplished swiftly. However, the decision proved to be a blunder because the Grand Master of the Knights, Jean de Valette, had gambled on the Ottomans invading St. Elmo first and had moved his heavy artillery into the fort. To Mustafa's dismay, the capture of the fort took several weeks, and he was forced to keep his army idle while the cannon did their work. Eventually, the fort was reduced to rubble and the Ottomans attacked, killing almost all of the defenders but taking very heavy losses themselves from the fort's artillery. Admiral Turgut was among those killed.

Mustafa seized the initiative and ordered an offensive, transporting his troops wide of the Grand Harbour to avoid Fort St. Angelo's heavy artillery and attacking Fort St. Michael on the Senglea peninsula. A cleverly planned assault from sea and land was rebuffed, the Ottomans taking more heavy losses. The Ottomans suffered one of the heaviest sustained bombardments the world had yet seen. Eventually an all-out attack was ordered in August, and the Ottomans were on the brink of success when, in an audacious move, a small force of knights attacked the Ottoman camp. Thinking that the knights had Spanish reinforcements, Mustafa retreated and the advantage was lost. By the end of August, and after a series of costly attacks, Mustafa attempted to break through with siege towers, but each time the towers were destroyed.

As Mustafa settled in for a long siege, news arrived that a Christian relief force had landed on the north of the island. Mustafa retreated, but the forces clashed and less than half of the Ottoman force managed to board the boats. The invasion had failed, and the Maltese received the admiration of Christian Europe and funds to build stronger defenses. For the Ottomans, this was their worst reversal in more than a century, and it gave Christian Europe hope that Turkish expansion could be halted. **TB**

Losses: Knight Hospitaller, 3,000 of 6,000; Ottoman, 20,000 of 40,000

◁ Djerba 1560   Szigetvár 1566 ▷

Detail of The Siege of Malta *fresco by sixteenth-century cartographer Ignazio Danti.* ➡

Szigetvár August–September 1566

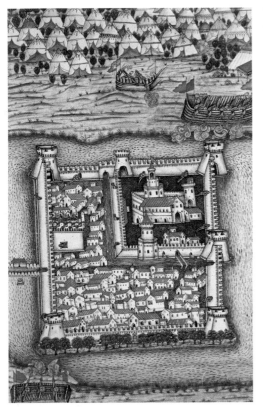

"I will go first, and what I do, you do. And God is my witness— I will never leave you, my brothers and knights!"

Count Nicholas Zrinsky, at Szigetvár

⬆ Sixteenth-century depiction of the siege of Szigetvár: Suleiman the Magnificent took no part but died here of natural causes.

The Battle of Szigetvár was fought between the forces of the Ottoman Empire, under the aging Suleiman the Magnificent, and an army of the Hapsburg monarchy in Hungary. The Ottoman victory was overshadowed by the death of their great sultan, whose campaigns had taken the Turks to their peak of glory.

Sultan Suleiman had been grieved by the Ottoman defeat at the Siege of Malta. In 1566, although succumbing to old age and infirmity, he embarked on one last effort to realize his ambition to conquer central Europe.

In August, the sultan's huge army besieged the Hungarian city of Szigetvár. Suleiman's condition had deteriorated during the long march from Constantinople and he was forced to rest in his tent for the duration of the siege. Croatian count Nicholas Zrinsky commanded the Hungarian and Croatian defenders, who desperately repelled the early attacks and lost more of their number with each new assault. As the numbers of defenders became critically low, Zrinsky ordered a retreat into the old town where they would make a last stand. The final Ottoman attack destroyed the fortress and the Ottoman forces swarmed into the old town. Zrinsky gathered his remaining forces and attacked the Ottomans, dying in the hand-to-hand combat.

While these dramatic events were taking place, however, Sultan Suleiman died in his tent. Although the Zrinsky army was virtually wiped out, the battle was hailed by Christians as a great turning point in European history, partly because Ottoman losses were so heavy, but mostly because of the death of the Turks' all-conquering leader. Preoccupied with the succession issue, the Ottomans abandoned plans for a further advance toward Vienna. **TB**

Losses: Hapsburg, almost all of 3,000; Ottoman, 40,000 of 125,000

◀ Malta 1565   Lepanto 1571 ▶

Chittor 1567–68

An ancient stronghold of India's Rajput warriors, Chittorgarh (the fort of Chittor) already had a heroic history when it was besieged in 1567 by the Mughal emperor Akbar. Its defenders' self-sacrifice on this occasion was very much in the heroic tradition, but could not prevent Mughal military might predominating.

Akbar had to capture the kingdom of Mewar, Rajasthan, in order to complete the conquest of northern India. This meant taking the big and redoubtable fort of Chittor. It was partly a matter of symbolism—Chittorgarh was a long-standing center of Rajput power—but the fortress was strategically vital, too.

Mewar's ruler, Rana Udai Singh II, is said to have quarreled with his son, who ran off to Akbar—accusing his father of disloyalty to the Mughals—before regretting his action and running home to warn him of Akbar's anger. This warning allowed the king to escape to the nearby hills. Chittorgarh itself was left in the hands of two brave young warrior chiefs; Jaimal and Patta were both sixteen.

With only 8,000 Rajput fighters to help Jaimal and Patta hold the fort against Akbar's vast army, the stage was clearly set for a heroic last stand. Hindu pride was at stake and the mood of religious sacrifice underlined by the news that Akbar had vowed a pilgrimage to the shrine of Moinuddin Chisti, a celebrated Muslim mystic, if he succeeded. The defenders fought bravely, exacting heavy casualties, but as time went on and it became clear that defeat was inevitable, they resolved to take their own lives rather than submit to Islamic rule. They were inspired, it is said, by the example of the royal princesses and aristocratic ladies, who hurled themselves onto a burning pyre. **MK**

"We would not have found the way had it not been that Allah had guided us."

Emperor Akbar, justifying the deaths of 32,000 Rajputs

Losses: Unknown

⬆ Emperor Akbar crosses the Ganges River with his forces in 1567, in an illustration from the Book of Akbar, c. 1590–95.

◁ Talikota 1565   Haldighati 1576 ▷

Jemmingen 21 July 1568

Jemmingen was an early battle in the Dutch Revolt, a conflict that turned into an eighty-year war for independence from Spain. At Jemmingen, in East Friesland, Fernando, Duke of Alva, the ruthless Spanish governor-general of the Netherlands, decisively crushed a Dutch rebel army.

The Dutch Revolt against Catholic Spanish rule stemmed from anger at high taxes and religious unrest caused by the spread of Protestantism. When armed conflict began in 1567, Philip II of Spain dispatched the Duke of Alva to restore order. Alva's persecution of Protestants and suspected rebels increased unrest and forced thousands into exile, including William of Orange, who would emerge as the rebel leader.

In 1568, Alva's army of 15,000 to 20,000 was marching toward a Dutch rebel army in Friesland. Its commander, Louis of Nassau, William of Orange's brother, led 10,000 to 12,000. Louis was low on money so mutinies were constantly breaking out. On hearing of Alva's approach, Louis concentrated his army near Jemmingen. His forces were protected by the River Ems, and the only crossings were two heavily guarded wooden bridges. Alva entered the town of Groningen and then, on 21 July, sent a small force of 500 musketeers, later joined by another 1,000, to draw the rebels out of their position. After nearly a day of skirmishing, a large group of Dutch rebels took the bait and charged. They were quickly pushed back. This led to panic in the Dutch camp and soon a chaotic retreat started. The rebel army had set fire to the bridges but the Spanish skirmishing force, joined by 2,000 more, charged over the burning crossings or waded across the river. The Spanish chased the fleeing rebels across the swampy countryside, completely routing them. **JF**

Losses: Spanish, 7 of 3,500; Dutch rebels, 6,000 of 10,000–12,000

Zuiderzee 1573 ⊡

San Juan de Ulua 24 Sept 1568

An English flotilla led by John Hawkins was badly mauled by a Spanish naval force at San Juan de Ulua, Veracruz, Mexico. A major step toward open warfare between England and Spain, the clash inspired Hawkins's young cousin, Francis Drake, with a lifelong hatred of the Spanish.

Hawkins and Drake had been trading slaves to Spain's empire in the Americas—an illegal trade as only Spanish ships were allowed to carry goods to their colonies. The Spanish regarded them as pirates because they carried out attacks on shipping and colonial ports, but they had the backing of Queen Elizabeth as "privateers."

Hawkins's decision to take his six ships into port at Veracruz was a bold gamble. He needed repair and resupply before sailing home with his booty and guessed the Spanish would prefer not to pick a fight with such dangerous visitors. Shortly after the English ships docked at the fortress island of San Juan de Ulua, a Spanish naval force sailed in bringing a new viceroy to Mexico. After a nervous standoff, fighting broke out, according to the English, a sneak Spanish attack in breach of a truce. The engagement in enclosed waters was furious and destructive. The aggressive English sailors, expert gunners and ruthless close-quarters fighters, destroyed one Spanish galleon and damaged another. But Hawkins's ships could not survive under the fire of the Spanish fortress's guns. Only two small English vessels, one captained by Drake and the other by Hawkins himself, escaped to open sea. After many hardships, they reached England in early 1569. Only eighty of the flotilla's original crew of 400 survived. The embittered Drake redoubled his attacks on Spain's empire, although war was not formally declared until 1585. **RG**

Losses: English, 4 ships of 6; Spanish, 1 ship of 13

Cadiz 1587 ⊡

⊙ *An oil painting by Louis Eugene Gabriel Isabey depicting the Duke of Alva arriving in Rotterdam in 1567.*

Jarnac 13 March 1569

VOICI·LES·COVPS·MORTELS·LA·RAGE·ET·LA·FVRIE
DE·DEVX·CAMPS·ANIMES·PAR·VN·CONTRAIRE·EFFORT
OV·CEVX·QVI·SE·DEVROINT·SECOVRIR·EN·LEVR·VIE·
CE·SONT·CEVX·MAINTENANT·QVI·SE·DONNENT·LA·MORT

"[Pope Pius V] commanded that his enemies should be 'massacred' and 'totally exterminated.'"

Samuel Smiles, The Huguenots *(1869)*

Detail from a sixteenth-century tapestry that describes the Battle of Jarnac and the death of Louis de Condé.

The Battle of Jarnac was a battle of the French Wars of Religion between the Catholics, led by Henry of Anjou—the future King Henry III—and the Protestant Huguenots, led by Louis de Condé. The conflict raged for more than thirty years and was fueled by rivalries among the French aristocracy.

The French Wars of Religion had at their roots the domination of a weak monarchy by the deadly rivalry between the Catholic Guise and Protestant Huguenot Bourbon factions. After the Peace of Longjumeau of 1568 had granted freedoms to the Protestant faction, many Catholics continued to persecute Protestants, causing many Huguenots to flee, including Louis de Condé. The Edict of Saint-Maur overturned the terms of Longjumeau, and the French Protestants mustered an army under Condé, with the support of German mercenaries and English finances. After the Protestant force had captured a number of French cities, the Catholics responded, led by the Duke of Anjou and supported by the papacy.

The forces of the rival factions met at Jarnac in western France on the banks of the River Charente. The Catholic force was superior to the Protestant and launched an attack that took Condé by surprise. The battle was characterized by a series of attacks by the superior Catholic cavalry, which wore down the Protestants. Some of Condé's army were pushed into the river and others fell back but were eventually defeated. Condé was captured and killed in the aftermath of the battle, his body paraded through Jarnac in front of jeering Catholic crowds. However, a significant section of the Protestant force escaped under the command of Gaspard de Coligny, who then assumed the overall leadership of the Huguenot cause. **TB**

Losses: Unknown

Dreux 1562   Moncontour 1569

Moncontour   30 October 1569

Anegawa   9 August 1570

The clash at Moncontour was a decisive battle of the French Wars of Religion between the Catholics, led by Henry of Anjou, and the Protestant Huguenots, led by Gaspard de Coligny. The battle resulted in defeat for the Protestants but did not put an end to the war.

In Japan's Age of Warring States, Oda Nobunaga's victory at Okehazama in 1560 gave him the allies to expand his own territories. In 1568 he entered Kyoto, only to be opposed by the allied forces of the Asakura and the Asai. Defeated once, Nobunaga returned to the fray in 1570 to win at Anegawa.

After the Battle of Jarnac, the Protestant army regrouped under Gaspard de Coligny. In June, Coligny was victorious at La Roche-l'Abeille but, after failing to take Poitiers, the Huguenots then set about committing atrocities in which Catholics were massacred. These murders were most likely against the wishes of Coligny, who wished to use the advantage his victory had gained to secure concessions from the crown. However, the atrocities led to a Catholic army confronting Coligny at Moncontour at the end of October.

The battle was preceded by a parley, in which the Catholics warned Coligny that they had increased their numbers. However, Coligny was advised that the Catholics were trying to trick him into an unfavorable peace. Instead, he was persuaded to give battle and win a decisive victory for the Protestant cause.

As it turned out, the Battle of Moncontour was fought with bitter acrimony, with the Catholics incensed by the recent Huguenot atrocities. Coligny was wounded in the action after he had personally killed the Marquis Philibert of Baden. The melee was so chaotic that Coligny's officers had great difficulty in extricating their commander from the battle. The Catholic warning that their force had been strengthened turned out to be true, and the Protestant army was soundly defeated. Coligny continued to champion the Protestant cause up until his death during the St. Bartholomew's Day Massacre of 1572. **TB**

The Battle of the Anegawa (Ane River) was fought between Oda Nobunaga and the allied armies of Asai Nagamasa and Asakura Yoshikage. Nobunaga's troops had advanced against the Asai castle of Odani and faced the allied forces across the Ane River, while other troops laid siege to Yokoyama castle.

The battle was effectively a huge hand-to-hand melee in the middle of the wide river—near Lake Biwa in Ōmi Province—fought during the day in the blazing sun. The samurai strode boldly into the shallows of the river. At first it was almost as though two separate battles were being fought: Nobunaga's allies under Tokugawa fighting against the Asakura, and the Oda upstream fighting against the Asai.

On the allied side fought a brave father and son team from the Makara family, who wielded enormous *nodachi* (field swords) from the saddle until they were cut down. The Tokugawa made better progress, but a samurai of the Asai—Endo Kizaemon—had resolved to take Nobunaga's head personally, and was only cut down by another samurai—Takenaka Kyusaku—when he was quite close to his target. Seeing Nobunaga's army in dire straits, the Tokugawa, who were by now relieved of the pressure from the Asakura, attacked Asai's right flank. Expert swordsman Inaba Ittetsu, who up until then had been held in reserve, fell on to their left. Even the besiegers of Yokoyama castle left their lines to join in. The result was a victory for the Oda forces. **ST**

Losses: Catholic, unknown; Huguenot, 10,000

◁ Jarnac 1569   Coutras 1587 ▷

Losses: Allied, 3,170; Oda, unknown

◁ Kawanakajima 1561   Mikata ga Hara 1573 ▷

Lepanto 7 October 1571

One of the world's most famous naval encounters, Lepanto was the last major battle fought by oared galleys. It pitted the fleet of the Muslim Ottoman Empire against a Christian Holy League, which included Spain, Venice, Genoa, and the Knights of Malta, commanded by Don John of Austria.

Despite failure at Malta, the Ottoman Empire, under Selim II, continued to dominate the Mediterranean. A Holy League formed by Pope Pius V failed to stop the fall of Cyprus, but in October, the League engaged the Ottoman fleet at Lepanto in the Ionian Sea. The League had 200 ships, of which a small number were Venetian galleasses, transport ships twice the size of galleys with cannon mounted along the sides. Spain provided few ships because her fleet was needed in the western Mediterranean. However, Philip II of Spain supplied a large proportion of the 20,000-strong force that manned the fleet plus his own commander, Don John of Austria. The Ottoman fleet, made up of the imperial navy and

"Don John of Austria is going to the war / Stiff flags straining in the night-blasts cold . . ."

G. K. Chesterton, "Lepanto"

Barbary corsairs, consisted of 280 ships and a fighting force of 30,000. The Holy League possessed a two-to-one advantage in cannon, and their soldiers were mostly equipped with firearms; the Turks depended more on bows.

The Christians deployed their fleet in four sections, with the new galleasses pushed forward of the main force. They were faced by the Ottomans, arranged in three sections with a small reserve at the rear. Both fleets were aligned in a long north-south line to prevent outflanking moves. The Ottomans opened by attacking the Venetian

galleasses, thinking the clumsy ships were an easy target, but the Turkish galleys were subjected to broadsides from the side-mounted cannon and many were sunk. This was followed by a series of attempts at outflanking maneuvers by the relatively nimble Ottoman galleys, which put the Christian fleet under severe pressure.

As the battle raged, the two fleets became entangled, with the Knights of Malta taking heavy losses and losing their flagship. The commander of the Venetian squadron, Agostino Barbarigo, was killed by an arrow in the eye. Don John ordered an attack into the Ottoman center, supported by Andrea Doria's Genoese galleys. The Ottoman flagship was rammed and crippled. A number of Ottoman ships quickly rallied to protect their flagship, while the Holy League reserve, commanded by the Marquis de Santa Cruz, piled into the fighting. At this point, the Spanish infantry proved their superiority as they boarded the Ottoman flagship and fought on its deck, killing the Ottoman fleet's commander, Muezzinzade Ali Pasha. Ali Pasha's head was quickly raised on a spike for all to see. This dented the morale of the Ottomans who tried desperately to disengage their battered fleet, with some men fighting until they had nothing left to fight with.

The corsair Uluj Ali took command of the Ottoman forces and managed to escape with less than a third of the proud Ottoman fleet. Lepanto was a crushing defeat for the Ottoman Empire. The battle had destroyed the best ships of its navy and, perhaps more significantly, a large proportion of its experienced naval expertise had perished. However, the Ottomans had the resources to recover—their grand vizier claimed that the Christians had merely shaved the Ottoman beard, which would "grow better for the razor." **TB**

Losses: Holy League, 20 ships of 200, 7,000 dead of 20,000; Ottoman, 80 ships sunk, 130 ships captured of 280, 18,000 dead of 30,000

◁ Szigetvár 1566　　　　　　Keresztes 1596 ▷

This original plan for the Battle of Lepanto indicates how the fleet was positioned in the gulf. ➡

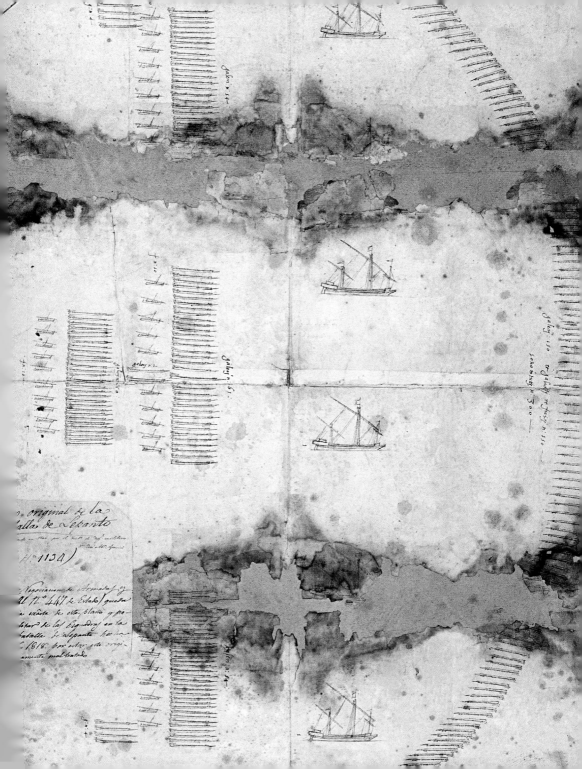

Molodi 30 July–2 August 1572

In 1570, Crimea—a client of the Ottoman Empire— had invaded Russia, which led to the beginning of the Russo-Ottoman War. In 1571, the Crimean army set fire to Moscow itself, but the following year it was defeated soundly by a Russian army at Molodi, definitively ending any Crimean ambitions to expand north.

The Crimean khan, Devlet I Giray, launched an invasion north in summer 1572. Czar Ivan IV had deployed troops and fortifications along the Oka River to block the Tatars. In command was Prince Mikhail Vorotynsky, who was in a *gulyay-gorod*, a huge wheeled fortification made of wooden screens—with holes for firearms—that housed thousands of soldiers. After some skirmishing, the Tatars forced their way across the Oka and were close to Moscow when Russian cavalry attacked their rearguard at Molodi. Devlet decided to fight before advancing.

On 30 July, the Tatars attacked the *gulyay-gorod* but met with heavy casualties from the Russian guns. Rather than launch another attack, the Tatars surrounded the *gulyay-gorod* to starve it out. This would have worked had the Tatars not intercepted a message to Vorotynsky stating that reinforcements were coming. These reinforcements never existed, but Devlet believed they were real and ordered an all-out assault on 2 August.

As the Tatars attacked, they were driven back by axes and gunfire, and by the evening they were exhausted. Vorotynsky secretly led cavalry out of the *gulyay-gorod* and attacked the Tatars from the rear. At the same time, a sortie of infantry and a concentrated volley of gunfire were launched from within the *gulyay-gorod*. The Tatars could not endure the attack and fled, ending their invasion. Russia's fortitude had been decisively proven. **JF**

Losses: Crimean, heavy casualties of 40,000–60,000; Russian, fewer casualties of 30,000–40,000

Mikata ga Hara 25 January 1573

In 1572, Tokugawa Ieyasu—the future shogun— received his most serious military challenge when Takeda Shingen advanced south and threatened Hamamatsu castle. Rather than stay inside Hamamatsu and suffer a siege, Ieyasu advanced to meet Shingen in pitched battle at Mikata ga Hara, during which his force was almost destroyed.

Ieyasu was outnumbered by about three to one in a total army of 11,000, of which 8,000 were his own troops and 3,000 were reinforcements from Nobunaga. In late afternoon, as the snow was beginning to fall, the front ranks of the Tokugawa opened fire, apparently by first throwing stones; when bullets followed, the Takeda knew it was time to respond.

At this point, Shingen withdrew his forward units to rest and sent in fresh troops. It was getting dark and, seeing the Tokugawa troops reeling, Shingen ordered a general assault by the main body. Very soon, the Tokugawa army was in full retreat. Ieyasu wanted to charge back into the Takeda ranks, but Natsume Yoshinobu rode out from the fortress to persuade his lord to withdraw. Three more samurai sacrificed themselves for Ieyasu during the retreat. Ieyasu ordered the gates to be left open for their retreating comrades, and huge braziers were lit to guide them home.

To add to the confident air, Sakai Tadatsugu beat the large war drum in the tower beside the gate. The Takeda vanguard saw the open gates and the light and heard the drum, so there was no immediate attack. Ieyasu ordered a night attack on the Takeda lines at Saigadake, and Shingen withdrew the following morning, leaving Hamamatsu castle safe. Mikata ga Hara may therefore be regarded as Ieyasu's most successful victory. **ST**

Losses: Tokugawa, almost all of 11,000; Takeda, 500–3,000

⟨ *Anegawa 1570*   *Nagashino 1575* ⟩

Woodblock of Takeda Shingen with one of his Twenty-Four Generals, Kansuke Yamamoto, at his feet.

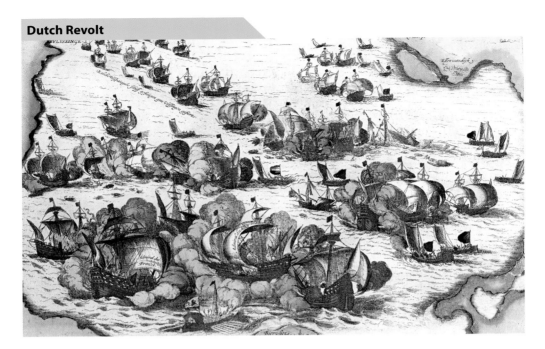

Zuiderzee 11 October 1573

After the Battle of Jemmingen, the Spanish appeared to have suppressed the Dutch Revolt but they were unable to destroy it completely. Rebel fleets, who called themselves the Sea Beggars, enjoyed continued success, and in 1573 they bested the Spanish at Zuiderzee, an inland sea in the northern Netherlands.

In 1569, the Spanish had occupied Amsterdam, but the Sea Beggars continued to disrupt their shipping to the city through the Zuiderzee. Seeking to prevent this, the Spanish sent a fleet of thirty under Count Bossu into the Zuiderzee.

On 11 October Bossu met the Sea Beggars between the towns of Hoorn and Enkhuizen. The Sea Beggar commander, Admiral Kornelius Dirkszoon, had five fewer ships than the Spanish, and they were smaller and more lightly armed than the Spanish vessels. Under a strong easterly breeze, the Sea Beggars bore down on the Spanish and captured five of their ships. Most of the other Spanish ships fled,

leaving only Bossu's flagship, the heavily armored *Inquisition*. Four Sea Beggar ships attacked the *Inquisition* and one was destroyed immediately. The other three grappled to the larger ship, locking the four ships together. A bitter hand-to-hand struggle commenced. Bossu drove back the boarding parties with boiling oil and molten lead.

At sunset, the four ships struck a shoal and the combat continued through the night. At dawn, a Sea Beggar managed to climb on board and tear down the *Inquisition*'s colors, but he was shot down after doing so. By now, the Sea Beggar ships were receiving fresh supplies of men and ammunition, and Bossu realized his position was untenable. He surrendered his men and his ship, and he and his surviving crew were taken prisoner. The Sea Beggars had maintained their control of the Zuiderzee. **JF**

Losses: Spanish, 300 sailors captured and 6 ships captured of 30; Dutch rebels, 1 ship of 25

◁ *Jemmingen 1568* *Gembloux 1578* ▷

Naval Combat between the Beggars of the Sea and the Spanish in 1573, *engraved by Franz Hogenberg.* ⬆

Nagashino   28 June 1575

In Japan's Age of Warring States, Nagashino castle held out against the Takeda in a classic siege. The besiegers tried attacks by river, mining, and through fierce hand-to-hand assaults. Eventually a relieving army arrived and defeated the Takeda using an innovative combination of firearms and simple defenses, revolutionizing Japanese warfare.

The Takeda army that laid siege to Nagashino castle consisted of 15,000 men, of whom 12,000 took part in the subsequent battle. They were therefore considerably outnumbered by the Oda-Tokugawa force of 38,000 who advanced to meet them, and whose positions looked across the plain of Shidarahara toward the castle. Oda Nobunaga also had the advantage of a unit of 3,000 matchlock musketeers, whom he realized would need some form of physical protection, so his army built a palisade between the forested edge of the hills and the river. It was a loose fence of stakes, staggered over three

layers, and with many gaps to allow a counterattack. The total front stretched for about 6,890 feet (2,100 m).

Nobunaga's plan was for the matchlockmen to fire volleys as the Takeda cavalry approached. As they had only a short distance to cover, it was likely that there would be some casualties, but not enough to break the momentum of the charge. The horsemen would then be upon the hopeless ashigaru (foot soldiers) as they tried to reload. Horses and men carefully negotiated the shallow riverbed and mounted the far bank. At this point, with the horsemen close to the fence, the volley firing began. This broke the charge, but the battle lasted until mid-afternoon, when the Takeda began to retreat and were pursued. **ST**

Losses: Takeda, 10,000 dead, including 54 of 97 samurai leaders and 8 of the Twenty-Four Generals; Oda, comparatively few

◁ *Mikata ga Hara 1573*   *Yamazaki 1582* ▷

Katsutaka is depicted trying to return to his compatriots in the besieged castle in a 1868 woodblock by Yoshitoshi.

Haldighati 21 June 1576

The capture of Chittorgarh in 1568 had enabled Emperor Akbar to conquer Mewar for the Mughal Indian Empire, yet the kingdom's warrior clans kept up their fight. Maharana Patrap Singh's defiance brought defeat in an epic encounter at the Battle of Haldighati outside Gogunda. Rajput resistance continued nonetheless.

Rana Udai Singh II had escaped the slaughter at Chittorgarh. On his death in 1572, he was succeeded by his son, Pratap Singh, who refused to recognize the authority of Akbar and his Mughal reign. As a series of envoys from Akbar was sent packing by Pratap, hostility spiraled quickly into open war.

Akbar sent an army to Rajasthan under the command of Raja Man Singh, his most trusted general, despite his Hindu faith. Pratap Singh marched out to meet him; the sources are vague on how many fought on either side, but the Mughals clearly outnumbered the Rajput— perhaps by as much as four to one. The Mughal troops were tough and battle-hardened. Superbly trained and ably led, they also had the advantage of heavy cannon. The battle was a heroic fight but a foregone conclusion—Pratap is said to have engaged with Raja Man Singh in person, his horse rearing up and placing its forehoofs on the trunk of the Mughal general's elephant. Man Singh saw Pratap hurl his spear and ducked, although his mahout was not so lucky and was killed.

After four hours' fighting, the battle was over. Facing certain defeat and determined to live another day, Pratap swapped clothing with a friend and fled, while his double fought on to a valiant death. Akbar had his victory but, since the dream of Rajput resistance remained alive, both sides took something from the fight. **MK**

Losses: Unknown

◁ Chittor 1567   Samugarh 1658 ▷

Gembloux 31 January 1578

Three years after the Dutch rebels' success at Zuiderzee, the unpaid Spanish army in the Netherlands mutinied violently, sacking several cities. As a result, most of the Netherlands joined the revolt. In 1578, Spain was able to begin to reestablish its authority after routing the Dutch rebels at Gembloux.

In 1576, Philip II appointed his half brother, Don John of Austria, governor of the Netherlands. By 1577, Philip II had been able to resolve his financial troubles and sent reinforcements led by the Italian general, Alexander Farnese. The Spanish army of 20,000 mustered at Marche in Luxembourg and prepared to attack. The Dutch commander, Antoine de Goignies, led an army of equal size, but it was less disciplined than the Spanish army.

The Dutch rebels were camped at Namur, Wallonia, but, on 31 January, they fell back to Gembloux when they heard the Spanish were approaching. The rebels lined up with a vanguard of infantry and light horse, the main body on foot in the center and heavy cavalry in the rear. The Spanish pursued, and when the rebel army was spotted, Don John deployed 600 horses and 1,000 foot soldiers to harass their rearguard until the main body of infantry arrived.

Farnese had other ideas. He saw that the rebels were marching along a deep ravine and launched a surprise attack by leading a cavalry charge. The charge shattered the Dutch, who were now under attack from the rear and the flank. The rebel cavalry fled, and the Spanish were able to attack the exposed infantry in the center. Thousands were killed or captured. Don John died eight months later; Gembloux was to be the last major victory of his illustrious military career. **JF**

Losses: Spanish, 10 of 1,600; Dutch rebels, 3,000–10,000 dead or captured of 20,000

◁ Zuiderzee 1573   Antwerp 1584 ▷

Alcazarquivir 4 August 1578

The defeat of Portuguese king Sebastian's invading army at Alcazarquivir (Ksar el-Kebir) in Morocco was one of the worst humiliations ever inflicted by an African army upon European forces. The battle was a catastrophe for Portugal, which lost not only its young king but also its independence as a direct consequence.

Twenty-four-year-old Sebastian was besotted with visions of crusading glory. He found a pretext for military action when a deposed sultan of Morocco, Mohammed II Saadi, asked him for help in regaining his throne from a usurper, Abd al-Malik. Sebastian emptied his treasury to finance an expedition, assembling some 500 ships to carry an army of Portuguese noblemen, Spanish volunteers, and German, Flemish, and Italian mercenaries, the Italians led by English Catholic adventurer Thomas Stukely.

This variegated force landed in northern Morocco and, joined by Sultan Mohammed, trekked inland. Abd al-Malik awaited them with a large army partly supplied by the Ottoman Turks, who were backing his claim to the throne. It combined Moroccan cavalry with Ottoman musket-armed infantry and cannon. Abd al-Malik died of natural causes early in the battle, but this did not trouble his troops' fighting spirit. After four hours, the invading army was vanquished. Stukely died in battle, his legs shot off by a cannonball. Sultan Mohammed drowned attempting to flee the battlefield. Sebastian disappeared in the thick of the fighting and was never seen again. Without a king and bankrupt, Portugal was taken over by Spain's Philip II within two years. Philip had a body purporting to be Sebastian's buried in Lisbon, but he could not suppress Portuguese popular belief that the young king had survived and would one day return to save his people. **RG**

Losses: Moroccan, unknown; Portuguese allies, 8,000 dead and 10,000 captured of 18,000

Tondibi 1591 ▷

Ponta Delgada 26 July 1582

Fought off the Azores in the mid-Atlantic, Ponta Delgada was a Spanish victory that ended Portuguese resistance to the takeover of their country by Spain's king Philip II. It inspired the Spanish with a confidence in their naval power that led directly to the Armada expedition against England six years later.

Philip II claimed the Portuguese crown and annexed the country in 1580. A Portuguese pretender to the throne, Antonio, Prior of Crato, intended to use the Azores as a base for a fightback against the Spanish. With the backing of France, he fitted out a fleet and manned it with Portuguese exiles and an international band of military adventurers.

Sixty ships sailed to the Azores under the command of Filippo Strozzi, a Florentine mercenary with impressive military experience. Spain, however, had an inspired naval commander in Alvaro de Bazan, Marquis de Santa Cruz, one of the heroes of the Battle of Lepanto. Although Santa Cruz's experience was with oared Mediterranean galleys, he assembled a fleet of twenty-eight oceanic sailing ships, consisting mostly of large Portuguese-built galleons and armed merchantmen, that located Strozzi's force off São Miguel island.

The battle began with the Spanish galleon *San Mateo* blundering in among enemy ships that bombarded it from all sides. Santa Cruz formed his ships in line abreast, like a galley fleet, and sailed to the rescue. The heavier cannon fire of the larger Spanish ships proved decisive. At the climax of the battle, Strozzi's flagship was battered and boarded by Santa Cruz's *San Martin*; Strozzi himself was killed. Enthused by his success, Santa Cruz persuaded Philip II to begin construction of a large fleet of galleons to be used against the impudent English. **RG**

Losses: Portuguese, 11 ships destroyed or captured and 1,500 dead; Spanish, no ships lost and 224 dead

◁ Alcazarquivir 1578   Spanish Armada Channel Fights 1588 ▷

Yamazaki   2 July 1582

In Japan's Age of Warring States, Toyotomi Hideyoshi was Oda Nobunaga's general and he was fighting in the west of Japan when he heard that his master had been murdered. Hideyoshi quickly arranged a peace settlement and hurried to Kyoto in a forced march. The usurper Akechi Mitsuhide was surprised and soundly beaten at Yamazaki.

On arriving at Yamazaki, Toyotomi Hideyoshi sent a detachment under Nakagawa Kiyohide to secure the nearby hill of Tennozan. On the night of 1 July, two of Hideyoshi's generals, Nakamura Kazuuji and Horio Yoshiharu, sent ninja into the Akechi camp, where they set fire to abandoned buildings and generally caused confusion. On the morning of 2 July, Hideyoshi's army moved forward to confront the Akechi force across the Enmyōji River while a fierce battle began on the slopes of Tennozan. Mitsuhide's samurai, under Matsuda Masachika and Nabika Kamon, attempted to fight their way up the hill paths, but were driven back by arquebus fire and suffered many casualties. With the dominance of Tennozan thus assured, Hideyoshi sent his right wing across the Enmyōji to perform an encircling movement.

In spite of fierce resistance, they managed to penetrate the forward troops and turned toward the Akechi main body. Hideyoshi committed his left wing from upstream, which was supported by a fierce surge of troops down from Tennozan. The impetus was too much for the Akechi army, who broke and ran. As the Akechi army retreated, Akechi Mitsuhide abandoned his men and fled for his life. He made it only as far as a village called Ogurusu, where he fell victim to a gang of bandits. Its leader thrust a spear at him from within the protection of a bamboo grove, and he fell dead from his horse. **ST**

Losses: Akechi, almost total, although many fled; Toyotomi, few, mainly in the fight for Tennozan

[<] *Nagashino 1575*   *Shizugatake 1583* [>]

A triptych by Utagawa Yoshitora entitled The Great Battle of Yamazaki in the Taiheiki *(1864).*

Shizugatake   20 April 1583

The victory of territorial lord Hideyoshi at Yamazaki in the Japanese Age of Warring States made him Nobunaga's natural successor, but he was opposed by Nobunaga's sons and other generals. Hideyoshi picked them off one by one, culminating in the Battle of Shizugatake, where Shibata Katsuie's general, Sakuma Morimasa, met his end.

After the spring thaw, a number of Hideyoshi's frontier mountaintop fortresses had fallen to Sakuma Morimasa, but Sakuma's master, Shibata Katsuie, sent orders for him to abandon his open siege lines for the security of the newly captured Oiwa castle. Sakuma disobeyed the orders of his commanding officer and stayed fighting in the open. Hideyoshi made ready to advance quickly by a forced march in order to catch Sakuma unprepared. Hideyoshi's army of 1,000 mounted samurai and their exhausted personal attendants hurried along, while the main body of 15,000 men brought up the rear.

The first that Sakuma Morimasa knew of their arrival was the sudden appearance of 1,000 burning pine torches down in the valley. Hideyoshi paused only to collect his brother Hashiba Hidenaga's troops in Tagami and to be apprised of the situation. The first armed contact was made as dawn was breaking. All along the mountain paths and in among the trees took place numerous small-group and individual combats.

As the first of Sakuma's retreating troops came hurtling down into the valley, Shibata Katsuie realized that the day was lost. Hoping to save as many of his army as he could, he ordered a general retreat and made it back safely to Kita-no-sho castle—which he had built in 1575—but with Hideyoshi in hot pursuit. It was a hopeless situation and, when the castle was surrounded, Shibata Katsuie committed hara-kiri among the flames. **ST**

Losses: Shibata, considerable; Toyotomi, very few

◁ *Yamazaki 1582*   *Busan 1592* ▷

⬆ Valiant and Renowned Warriors at the Great Battle of Shizugatake, *a woodblock print by Utagawa Yoshitora.*

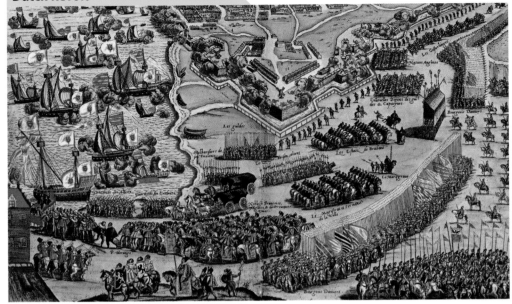

Antwerp   July 1584–17 August 1585

In the years after the Battle of Gembloux, the Spanish governor-general, Alexander Farnese, slowly consolidated his control of Flanders and Brabant. Spanish control of the southern Netherlands was complete when Farnese captured Antwerp in one of the most technically brilliant actions of the Dutch Revolt.

Antwerp was the richest and most populous city in the Netherlands and a rebel stronghold ever since Spanish soldiers sacked it in 1576. In July 1584, Farnese laid siege to Antwerp. He constructed a network of forts that cut off access to Antwerp by land. Next, he decided to block the Scheldt River, which connected Antwerp to the rebel-controlled north. Huge piers were thrown out from heavily armed forts on either side of the Scheldt. Between them, a floating bridge of connected barges armed with cannon was constructed. The massive structure was completed on 25 February 1585.

Meanwhile the Dutch rebels had cut the dykes around Antwerp, hoping to flood the region, allowing their ships to bypass the blockade. Farnese still controlled the last dyke before Antwerp, the Kouwenstein, so his bridge was not outflanked. On the night of 4 April, an attempt was made to destroy the bridge by floating explosive ships down the Scheldt from Antwerp. The plan caused considerable damage, but Farnese's engineers were able to repair the bridge. A similar attempt on 20 May failed. Elsewhere, rebels from the north failed twice to capture the Kouwenstein on 6 and 26 May. On 17 August, Antwerp surrendered. After taking control of Antwerp, Farnese decreed that all its Protestants must convert to Catholicism or be exiled. Consequently, just under half of Antwerp's population of about 80,000 migrated north. **JF**

Losses: Spanish, at least 1,600 of 11,700; Dutch rebels, several thousand of 20,000

◁ *Gembloux 1578*   *Zutphen 1586* ▷

Illustration from a manuscript showing how Farnese cut off all access to Antwerp. ⬆

Zutphen 2 October 1586

The Battle of Zutphen was symbolic of England's brief formal involvement in the Dutch Revolt: mostly disorganized, sometimes heroic, but ultimately doomed. In the action, the English failed to prevent a Spanish relief convoy from entering Zutphen, and the famed poet Sir Philip Sidney died after being wounded during the battle.

Shortly after the fall of Antwerp, the Dutch rebels signed an alliance with England. Elizabeth I sent an expedition force to the Netherlands, led by Robert Dudley, Earl of Leicester. In 1586 Leicester sought to wrest full control of the River IJssel from Spain by capturing Zutphen, sending a force of 6,000 men to besiege it. In response, the Spanish governor-general, Alexander Farnese, sent a large convoy of supplies to provision Zutphen. It was guarded by 4,000 soldiers, including cavalry, pikemen, and musketeers.

As the convoy approached Zutphen on 2 October, the English attempted to ambush it at nearby Warnsveld.

Their numbers were small, around 550, because the English had not thought the convoy would be heavily protected. In the late afternoon, the English cavalry began the first of many charges. They were met with heavy fire, and promised reserves of soldiers never arrived. In the last charge of the day, Sir Philip Sidney was struck in the thigh by a musketball and died of his wound two weeks later.

In spite of the ambush, the convoy reached Zutphen safely from whence a force of 1,000 Spanish soldiers emerged to ensure the supplies' successful arrival. The siege ended in January 1587 when the English troops at Zutphen (and numerous other towns) surrendered to the Spanish. This exacerbated ongoing tensions between Leicester and the rebel leaders, and by the year's end he had returned home, bringing England's Dutch adventure to a close. **JF**

Losses: Spanish, 200 of 5,000; English, 35 of 550

◁ *Antwerp 1584*   *Nieuwpoort 1600* ▷

⬆ *In* The Last Days of Sir Philip Sidney *(1882) by Robert Hillingford, the poet accepts his fate.*

Cadiz 29 April–1 May 1587

Intense rivalry between England and Spain during the reign of Elizabeth I led Philip II of Spain to prepare an armada to invade England. In response, Elizabeth ordered a preemptive strike against the Spanish fleet, a daring raid its leader, Francis Drake, termed the "singeing of the king of Spain's beard."

Tension between Protestant England and Catholic Spain grew during the reign of Elizabeth I. English privateers attacked Spanish ships, while the English aided Dutch rebels in their revolt against Spanish rule. In 1587, Elizabeth executed her Catholic cousin and heir, Mary Queen of Scots, for treason. In response, Philip prepared a large armada to invade England to overthrow Elizabeth and restore Catholicism. Elizabeth ordered Francis Drake to disrupt Philip's plans.

The English fleet arrived at Cadiz on the afternoon of 29 April, and sailed through the defending galleys into the harbor. The English quickly sunk a Genoese merchantman and then began to attack the many ships at anchor, removing their cargoes and setting them alight. The Spanish defenders launched a number of hit-and-run attacks and managed to seize one isolated English ship. The next day, the English continued their attacks, despite the Spanish use of heavy onshore guns and fireships sent in to disrupt the English fleet. Unfavorable winds kept the English fleet in harbor a second night before Drake made his escape the next day. After he read a report on the raid, Philip II stated, "The loss was not very great, but the daring of the attempt was very great indeed." However, the English destruction of thousands of barrel staves, crucial to the manufacture of storage barrels, was to prove significant when the armada of 1588 set out to sea with too few barrels of food and drink. **SA**

Losses: English, 1 ship captured of 21; Spanish, 33 ships destroyed

◁ San Juan de Ulua 1568   Spanish Armada Channel Fights 1588 ▷

Coutras 20 October 1587

Twenty-five years after the Battle of Dreux, the French Wars of Religion were still continuing their destructive, tortuous progress. In 1587, King Henry of Navarre—the military leader of the Huguenots— won a commanding victory over a royal army near Coutras, in southwest France.

France was enjoying one of its sporadic spells of peace from 1580. However, when King Henry III's younger brother died in 1584, the Huguenot Henry of Navarre became heir presumptive to the throne. This was unacceptable to the Catholic League, an organization created to destroy Protestantism in France. Its powerful leader, Henry, Duke of Guise, forced Henry III to rescind Henry of Navarre's right to the throne, and eventually war restarted in 1585.

After a tiring campaign season in 1587, Henry of Navarre's small army was falling back to Huguenot territory in southern France. He was pursued by a considerably larger royal army, led by Anne, Duke of Joyeuse. Eventually the two armies faced each other on a plain east of Coutras. The Huguenot artillery launched a devastatingly accurate bombardment, creating havoc in the royal lines. In response, Joyeuse ordered a cavalry charge, but his forces were cut to pieces by the counterattack of the Huguenot horsemen. The battle lasted for two hours, and Joyeuse himself was killed in the fighting.

Henry of Navarre showed great mercy after his victory. He ordered the dead to be given an honorable burial, the wounded to be cared for, and he allowed many prisoners to be released without ransom. Coutras was an important victory for Henry of Navarre, although he did not follow it up, which allowed his army to disperse. The Catholic League had suffered a terminal setback. **JF**

Losses: Catholic, 2,000 of 19,000–23,000; Huguenot, 30 of 5,200–6,500

◁ Moncontour 1569   Ivry 1590 ▷

Spanish Armada Channel Fights 29 July–6 August 1588

The great armada that sailed from Spain to invade England in 1588 arrived in the English Channel with the intention of escorting a large Spanish army from the Netherlands across the North Sea to Kent. Its progress up the Channel was disrupted by English attacks that kept the fleet at sea.

The armada that left Coruña in northern Spain on 22 July, commanded by the Duke of Medina Sidonia, was an impressive fleet. It comprised 138 ships carrying more than 24,000 men. Fifty of these ships were galleons and other warships, the rest slower transport vessels for men and supplies. The English would eventually have a total of 197 ships at their disposal in various ports, most of them faster and more maneuverable than their bigger, heavier opponents.

The Spanish fleet was spotted off the Lizard in southwest England on 29 July, the news broadcast to the rest of the country via a string of beacons. Confined to harbor by unfavorable winds, fifty-four English ships, commanded by Lord Howard of Effingham and Francis Drake, emerged from Plymouth the next day and sailed around to the rear of the Spanish armada so that they could shadow its progress up the Channel. The armada stuck to a crescent formation, its warships protecting the transport ships in the center.

An English attack on the Spanish rearguard off Plymouth on 31 July was inconclusive, but informed both sides about the strengths of their opponents. Two stray Spanish ships were picked off on 1 August, with a larger skirmish occurring off Portland Bill on 2 August. Further actions—and a lack of ammunition—convinced both sides not to risk a pitched battle and so, on the evening of 6 August, the armada dropped anchor off Calais. **SA**

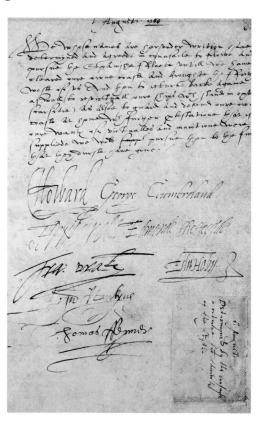

> *"Much ammunition was expended, but the Spanish formation held together well."*
>
> *Dr. Simon Adams*, The Spanish Armada

Losses: Spanish, 2 ships captured of 138; English, no ships of 54

◁ Cadiz 1587   Gravelines 1588 ▷

⬆ *A resolution to oppose the Spanish, signed by commanders including Francis Drake (two lines below Lord Howard).*

Gravelines 8 August 1588

With its passage up the English Channel safely accomplished, the Spanish armada anchored off Calais in the Straits of Dover to await the invasion army it was to escort over to England. The English attack wrecked these plans and forced the armada on a dangerous and ignominious voyage home.

The armada dropped anchor in open waters off Calais on 6 August. The next day, its leader—the Duke of Medina Sidonia—received bad news that the barges due to carry the invasion army across the Channel were not ready and that the army's leader, the Duke of Parma, was still some distance away and would not be ready to sail for at least two weeks.

That night, the English attacked the armada in earnest, sending in eight fireships packed with gunpowder. None did any damage, but they caused such panic that the armada cut its anchor cables and fled the scene. The next morning, the Spanish ships lay in scattered formation off Gravelines. The English fleet pounced, their rate of fire and maneuverability greater than anything the Spanish could match. The Spanish saw the use of cannon as a necessary preliminary to grappling and boarding an enemy ship, whereas the English used cannon to attack and sink the enemy from a distance. In an often closely fought encounter, the English inflicted greater damage, but both sides pulled back in the evening as ammunition stocks ran low. By then, the wind had swung around to the northwest, threatening to drive the Spanish onto the coastal shoals. With no chance of liaising with Parma's army, Medina Sidonia took the only decision open to him: to sail up the North Sea and return home to Spain around the rocky coasts of Scotland, Ireland, and western France. Losses on the voyage home were immense. **SA**

Losses: English, no ships of 140; Spanish, 1 ship sunk, 4 driven inshore and captured of 136

[<] *Spanish Armada Channel Fights 1588*   *Flores 1591* [>]

A sixteenth-century depiction of the defeat of the Spanish armada, probably a design for a tapestry. ⬆

Ivry   14 March 1590

Nearly two years after his victory at Coutras, the Huguenot Henry of Navarre became king of France—as Henry IV—after the assassination of Henry III. At Ivry, the decisive battle of the French Wars of Religion, Henry IV defeated a Catholic League army, cementing his position as king.

Despite holding the throne, Henry IV still faced the powerful Catholic League, which held Paris. Henry IV was besieging the town of Dreux in northwest France when a large League force, commanded by Charles, Duke of Mayenne, approached to raise the siege. Outnumbered, Henry IV retreated north and drew up his army near Ivry. Mayenne pursued him, and the armies faced each other on 14 March.

Battle opened at noon with an exchange of artillery fire before a mass cavalry charge. The struggle was evenly balanced until Henry IV led a devastating cavalry attack. He used a tactic called the *pistolade*, which involved charging close to the enemy and firing pistols before attacking with swords. At such close quarters, the League cavalry, which favored the lance, were not effective. Once Henry IV's cavalry reserves also entered the fray, the League cavalry were utterly routed and fled the field, along with Mayenne. After a brief pursuit, Henry IV wheeled around against the remaining League infantry. They were now completely isolated and were slaughtered by the hundreds, before Henry IV offered them the chance to surrender. The Battle of Ivry destroyed the Catholic League as a military force, but Henry IV was only able to enter Paris and fully consolidate his control of France after converting to Catholicism in 1593. In 1598, Henry IV issued the Edict of Nantes, which gave Huguenots freedom of worship and ensured peace in France for more than twenty years. **JF**

Losses: Catholic League, 6,000 dead and 4,000 captured of 17,000; French, 500 of 11,000

◁ *Coutras 1587*   *La Rochelle 1627* ▷

⬆ *In* Battle of Ivry *(1590), Peter Paul Rubens paints Henry IV centerstage in crimson velvet, sword raised.*

Tondibi 13 March 1591

Ahmad al-Mansur, ruler of Morocco, sent an army south across the Sahara desert to take control of Mali, at the time a source of gold and slaves and fabled for its wealth. This unprecedented military expedition destroyed the West African Songhai Empire and raised Morocco to the peak of its power.

Ahmad al-Mansur had inherited the Moroccan throne on the death of Abd al-Malik during the Battle of Alcazarquivir in 1578. He was an ambitious ruler whose projects of military expansion and prestige-building were costly. The decision to attack the Songhai Empire was a bid for a fresh source of finance. No one had sent a substantial army across the wastes of the desert before.

Ahmad al-Mansur planned his expedition meticulously, with supplies carried on 8,000 camels, animals that outnumbered his military personnel by two to one. His troops were a hand-picked, battle-hardened force, many of them Muslims who had been expelled from Spain by the Christians, bringing with them European military skills. Their equipment included arquebuses and cannon.

The sultan entrusted leadership of the expedition to a palace eunuch, Pasha Judar. The Moroccan army followed trade routes for the 1,500-mile (2,424 km) march across the desert, benefitting from the aid of the Tuareg desert nomads who hated the Songhai. The army's arrival in Mali achieved total surprise. Songhai ruler Ashak II hastily called on his feudal lords to supply cavalry and infantry, which confronted the Moroccans at Tondibi, north of the Malian city of Gao. The Moroccan army was outnumbered, but it had gunpowder weapons and the Songhai did not. The novel experience of being fired upon soon put the Songhai army to flight. The Moroccans were able to occupy the major Malian cities, including legendary Timbuktu. **RG**

Losses: Unknown

◁ Alcazarquivir 1578

Flores (Azores) 30–31 August 1591

The battle between Spain and England off Flores Island in the Azores was a Spanish victory, showing the resurgence of Spain's naval power after the debacle of the 1588 armada. For the English, the heroic fight put up by Richard Grenville's *Revenge* became a national legend.

Led by Thomas Howard, an English squadron sailed to the Azores in the mid-Atlantic, hoping to intercept the annual Spanish treasure fleet laden with silver and gold from the Americas. For months they waited for the treasure ships in vain, their crews progressively depleted by disease. Meanwhile, Spain organized a powerful fleet, under Alonso de Bazan, to attack Howard's squadron.

The English were taking on water at Flores Island when the Spanish arrived on 30 August. Although Bazan tried to trap them with a pincer movement, all of the English ships slipped away except one. Lagging behind, Grenville's *Revenge* was rammed by a Spanish galleon and surrounded by enemy warships. Grenville was a fighting man with a fearsome reputation—arrogant, brutal, and intransigent—and his ship was credited as the finest galleon in the English navy. Without a thought of surrender, he fought off Spanish boarding parties and kept his men firing, taking on five enemy ships simultaneously and succeeding in sinking one of them. The battle lasted fifteen hours. On the morning of 31 August, with further resistance impossible, Grenville gave the order to blow up his shattered ship rather than surrender. His crew refused to obey. Gravely wounded in the head, Grenville had the chagrin of seeing his ship taken over by the Spanish before he died of his injuries. The Spanish never succeeded in taking *Revenge* home as a prize; the ship sank in an Atlantic storm within a fortnight. **RG**

Losses: English, 1 ship captured; Spanish, 1 ship sunk

◁ Gravelines 1588 Cadiz 1596 ▷

Busan 24 May 1592

In Japan's Age of Warring States, Toyotomi Hideyoshi had reunited Japan by 1591, but in 1592 he ordered an invasion of Ming China to be carried out through Korea. The Koreans resisted, and a fierce war began. Busan, Korea's most important port, was the first gain by the Japanese invaders.

The taking of Busan, the most important port on the southern coast of Korea, was the engagement by which the first invasion of Korea began. The first group of invaders to land were the advance party commanded by So Yoshitomo, who was the daimyo of Tsushima—the island of Japan that is closest to Korea—and personally acquainted with the local area. In command of the garrison was the Korean general, Chong Bal. He sank all his ships in the harbor and withdrew all his forces within the gates of Busan. Refusing to surrender, he ordered his men to fight to the death, but was shot dead during the assault. Korean casualties numbered 8,000, with 200 being taken prisoner.

While So Yoshitomo attacked the main fortress of Busan, Konishi Yukinaga launched a simultaneous assault on a naval fort near the harbor, which was defended by some 6,000 Koreans. Yukinaga led the attack with his troops scaling ladders while musket fire prevented the Koreans from counterattacking. The governor of the fort stated that he would take orders to surrender only from the king of Korea. Yukinaga pretended to withdraw while the required orders were obtained, but instead launched a surprise attack at 4:00 AM the following morning. The moat was filled in quickly with rocks and earth, and the Japanese climbed over the walls. The fort surrendered after two hours, and the harbor and city of Busan were secured immediately. **ST**

"The Japanese use of the arquebus was a considerable element in their success."

Stephen Turnbull, Japanese Castles in Korea 1592–98

Losses: Busan, almost the complete garrison; Japanese, very light

↑ *So Yoshitomo's Japanese invasion force storms ashore to attack the fortress of Busan, in a painting by Byeon Bak.*

Hansando 1592 ▶

Hansando   14–16 August 1592

During the Japanese invasion of Korea, its military superiority on land was soon to be reversed at sea. Under the command of Admiral Yi Sunsin, the Korean navy gradually cut off the Japanese supply lines. When the Japanese tried to destroy the Korean fleet, they were led into a very costly trap at the decisive Battle of Hansando.

Looking for Admiral Yi and his fleet, the Japanese ships under Wakizaka Yasuharu sailed southwest into the narrow straits of Kyŏnnaeryang, which divided Kŏje Island from the mainland, and anchored there for the night. Contact was made early the following morning when Yi's fleet headed for the straits and observed eighty-two enemy vessels. Yi's strategy was determined by the fact that the channel was narrow and strewn with sunken rocks; it was not only difficult to fight in the bay for fear the Korean ships might collide with one another but the narrowness of the channel also made it likely that the Japanese would escape to land. Yi therefore decided to

"The fish in the cooking pot jumped out, to our great indignation."

Admiral Yi, on the escape of some sailors back to Japan

try his well-rehearsed maneuver of a false retreat, in order to lure the Japanese out to the southwest where a wide expanse of sea, fringed by several uninhabited islands, would provide an ideal location for a sea battle.

The bait was taken, and from the northeast came Yi's vanguard of six ships, beating down the straits with Wakizaka Yasuharu's entire fleet in hot pursuit. When the Japanese were well clear of the narrow, rocky strait and out into the bay before Hansando (Hansan Island), they found Yi's main body waiting for them. The Korean ships

were spread out into a semicircular formation, which Yi's report calls a "crane's wing." With three turtle ships acting as the vanguard once again, the Korean fleet rowed toward the focal point of their crane's wing formation. The fight became a bloody free-for-all, the Korean ships initially trying to keep the Japanese at a distance so they could bombard their victims without the risk of a boarding party being sent against them.

Much hand-to-hand fighting took place, but Yi only allowed this close combat if the Japanese vessel was already crippled. Accounts of the battle record individual achievements: a turtle boat captain, called Yi Kinam, captured one enemy vessel and cut off seven Japanese heads; and a certain Chŏng Un—a captain from Nokdo—holed and destroyed two large enemy pavilion vessels with cannon fire and burned them completely, cut off three Japanese heads, and rescued two Korean prisoners of war. Wakizaka Yasuharu himself had a very narrow escape. The Japanese fleet was bombarded with wooden arrows tipped with iron that smashed their planking, and also by iron fire bombs shot from mortars similar to those used in Korean sieges. These weapons would probably have been fired from the open ships rather than from the confined space of a turtle ship.

The destruction of Wakizaka's fleet was almost total. Hardly a single ship escaped, and countless numbers of Japanese were hit by arrows and fell dead into the water. However, not all the Japanese troops were killed, because about 400 exhausted soldiers—finding no way to escape—deserted their boats and fled ashore. The victorious Koreans, similarly exhausted, withdrew for the night. The following morning, Admiral Yi Sunsin conducted a mopping-up operation among the islands in the bay. The Japanese naval power was broken. **ST**

Losses: Japanese, 47 ships destroyed and 14 captured, 9,000 dead; Korean, no ships lost, 19 dead

◁ *Busan 1592*   *Byeokjegwan 1593* ▷

An extract from Admiral Yi Sunsin's war diaries.

十二日甲辰時早朝劉雪崖來同賦船
其破鳴濕申八亘向結晴空云員冷水
船華舵出海君驅船百三千餘我
似讀於水自發象寮窩之勢運生四頃之社
右水使雪濤新而蒲船之左二三場的客促
窩為孤放此言各櫓眉昏如風雷了
麻三艦上如雨私射賦虎石破披畫高下返
然間之破重勢將石以一船之又求額生
余案亦論解日城城雀

Byeokjegwan 27 February 1593

Haengju 14 March 1593

Following the Japanese invasion of Korea, a vast Chinese army, entering the war in support of the Joseon dynasty, crossed the Yalu River and drove the Japanese out of Pyongyang. From that time onward, the Japanese were in retreat, and the Battle of Byeokjegwan—the largest conflict of the Korean invasion—was to be their only victory.

Despite its unexpected victory at Byeokjegwan, the morale of the Japanese army remained low after its invasion of Korea. Instead of taking the offensive, it had retreated to Seoul and was now preoccupied with defending the city. Meanwhile, Korean general Kwon Yul inflicted a heavy defeat at Haengju castle to the northwest of Seoul.

The Battle of Byeokjegwan was a rearguard action by Kobayakawa Takakage to allow the Japanese army time to regroup in Seoul, a short distance to the south. In addition to Kobayakawa's unit of 10,000 men, Kato Kiyomasa supplied 3,000 troops. The Japanese stationed themselves in two divisions on the hill of Byeokjegwan, with the main body behind.

The Chinese attacked at dawn and began to force the Japanese to retreat down the road through the mud and slush, then they began a vigorous pursuit down the reverse slope. The Japanese calmly withdrew, allowing the Chinese force to become dispersed. Finally, seeing their opportunity as the Chinese army became detached from their own rearguard and mired in the soggy ground, Kobayakawa Takakage led the Japanese into a counterattack, with support from their wings.

The fighting developed into a huge melee. The Japanese were victorious largely because of the superior quality of their swords. The Chinese commander, Li Rusong, was unhorsed and only saved from death by the intervention of his quick-thinking comrades. In a change of tactics, Kobayakawa pulled back his samurai in order to allow his musketeers to pour fire into the mass of Chinese and Korean troops. Byeokjegwan was a stunning victory for a Japanese force that had looked beaten, but it did not change the overall trend. **ST**

Haengju castle lay on a hill with the Han River as its natural southern defense. On the other three sides, the area of the fort was surrounded by a zone of swampy land. The whole Korean army is said to have totaled 10,000 men, including 1,000 priest soldiers under the command of the priest general, Cho Yon. Kwon Yul moved 2,300 men up to Haengju castle under his own command, repaired the castle walls, prepared palisades, and made ready for a siege. Approximately 30,000 Japanese troops in total surrounded the fort.

At about 6:00 AM, the battle began when Konishi Yukinaga's army advanced, but the resistance was fierce. Rockets were fired from multiple-rocket fire wagons and a hail of stones fell. The Koreans also threw powder at the enemy to blind them. Even women took part in the siege and used their aprons to carry stones for throwing. Volleys of rockets and arrows hit the densely packed advancing troops, and the morale of Konishi's troops was severely shaken. At this point, the Japanese army launched a full attack, and a fierce hand-to-hand fight began. Kwon Yul drew his own sword and engaged in individual combat while still giving orders. Although the fight ebbed and flowed, the Japanese were faced with the problem of a relieving army that arrived for the Korean army, so they retreated. Haengju was an important Korean victory, which was to lead to the evacuation of Seoul. **ST**

Losses: Chinese, 2,000–8,000, with many more unaccounted for; Japanese, possibly as many

Losses: Korean, unknown; Japanese, 24,000 of 30,000

◁ Hansando 1592

Haengju 1593 ▷

◁ Byeokjegwan 1593

Jinju 1593 ▷

Jinju 21–29 June 1593

Jinju was the most important fortress in southern Korea. The Japanese had failed to capture it on previous attempts, and in the summer of 1593 a renewed attempt on the fortress produced the final land battle of the first Japanese invasion. Success at Jinju provided some satisfaction within the general gloom of the Japanese retreat.

On 21 June 1593, a huge Japanese army advanced on Jinju castle, eager to succeed where Hosokawa Tadaoki had failed the previous year. The army was made up of the troops of Konishi Yukinaga, Kato Kiyomasa, and Ukita Hideie, with Kobayakawa Takakage's army held back as a reserve corps on a hill to the north. The Japanese attack began across the Chinyang River, while the defenders were occupied by arquebus fire from a tall siege tower.

The attack was a violent assault designed to take the castle at a single stroke, but it was driven off three times. The Jinju garrison met the Japanese scaling ladders with rocks, tree trunks, and boiling water, as well as some ingenious siege engines using spiked boards. Seeing the garrison so determined not to let them scale the walls, Kato Kiyomasa ordered the construction of some heavy wooden wagons, reinforced by fireproofed hides, and as rocks bounced off the roofs of the wagons, the Japanese prized at the stones of the castle walls with large crowbars.

After several days, a section of the wall collapsed. The Jinju garrison had now withstood the Japanese army for seven days, but on 29 June the attackers managed to enter through this breach in the castle wall. The fall of Jinju at this second attempt was regarded by the Koreans as the biggest loss to the Japanese since the beginning of the war. **ST**

Losses: Japanese, unknown; Korean, 60,000 including civilians

⟨ *Haengju 1593*   *Chilchonryang 1597* ⟩

Cadiz 20 June–5 July 1596

The defeat of the Spanish armada in 1588 was a diplomatic and military disaster for Spain, but it only encouraged a rebuilding and strengthening of the fleet in order to restore Spanish maritime power. A second attempt to invade England in 1596 was met, as before, with a preemptive strike against the fleet in Cadiz.

Maritime rivalry between England and Spain intensified after 1588. An English counterarmada against Spain the following year proved to be a fiasco, while English attacks on Spanish treasure ships returning from the New World caused great controversy, although they often failed in their mission. It was, therefore, no surprise when Philip II of Spain ordered a second armada to invade England.

In response, a large English and Dutch fleet of around 120 ships left Plymouth on 3 June 1596, to scupper the Spanish plans. Once at Cadiz, the English destroyed two Spanish galleons and captured two more. The Earl of Essex, co-commander of the expedition, then led his men to storm the walls and occupy the city. Cadiz was ransacked, but the English failed to seize the rich merchant ships in the inner harbor, allowing the Spanish to scuttle them in time. Essex wanted to occupy and garrison the city permanently, but the other English commander, Lord Howard of Effingham—hero of the previous armada's defeat—refused to agree because many of the English wanted to return home with their loot.

Leaving the city in flames, the English withdrew on 5 July. A success in terms of hurt Spanish pride, the raid failed to prevent the second armada setting sail four months later. However, once again, the weather intervened, and the Spanish fleet was forced home before it had reached its destination. **SA**

Losses: English, no ships of 120; Spanish, 2 ships sunk and 2 ships captured

⟨ *Flores 1591*   *Santa Cruz 1657* ⟩

Keresztes   24–26 October 1596

If Christian Europe harbored any illusion that the power of the Turkish Ottoman Empire had been undermined by its defeat at the Battle of Lepanto, the illusion was dispelled at the hard-fought Battle of Keresztes. Instead of retaking Hungary and Bulgaria from the Turks, the Christians were heavily beaten on the battlefield.

In 1593, war erupted between the Hapsburg monarchy and the Ottoman Empire in southeast Europe. In 1595, after some initial Ottoman gains, a Christian alliance was formed by Pope Clement VIII to stop the Turks from taking Vienna. Led by Archduke Maximilian of Austria and Sigismund, Prince of Transylvania, the alliance took the offensive, attempting to take Ottoman territories across the Danube. The Christian capture of the fortress at Hatvan prompted the Ottoman sultan, Mehmed III, to take action, and he led his army in a successful siege of the strategic fortress of Eger. Persuaded by his advisers to seek battle with the Christian army, Mehmed was confronted by an entrenched army at Keresztes. The Ottomans attacked the trenches but were repeatedly pushed back by artillery and small arms fire, and appeared to have been defeated.

On the second day of the battle, the sultan's camp was penetrated by some Christian soldiers. However, they were distracted by the prospect of loot, and the Turkish cooks and camel minders fought back fiercely with improvised weapons. The Christian soldiers fled. When the main body of the sultan's army saw this, they thought the whole Christian army was in retreat and advanced in one mass. The Austrian and Transylvanian forces were surrounded and slaughtered. Defeat had been turned to triumph for the Ottoman Empire, ensuring that large parts of Bulgaria and Hungary stayed under Ottoman control. **TB**

"The Christian soldiers got on the treasure chests of gold coin . . . and started to dance around them."

İbrahim Peçevi, chronicler, describing looters at Keresztes

⬆ Mehmed's successful siege at Eger, depicted in this sixteenth-century painting, encouraged him to attack at Keresztes.

Losses: Unknown

◁ *Lepanto 1571*   *Khotyn 1621* ▷

Chilchonryang 28 August 1597

Three years after their initial victory, the Japanese launched a second invasion of Korea in 1597. Their success was due in part to the spectacular failure of the Korean navy to stop the invasion. This was because Korean admiral Yi Sunsin had been replaced by an incompetent rival, who was trounced by the Japanese at Chilchonryang.

The night sea Battle of Chilchonryang was Japan's only naval victory of the entire war. The Korean fleet left Hansando to make contact with the enemy on the open sea near Busan. Weon Gyun ordered the Korean navy into the attack. Thirty ships were lost before Weon Gyun called a withdrawal and pulled his men back to the apparent safety of nearby Gadeok Island. Unfortunately, Gadeok was one of the islands that the occupying Japanese had chosen to fortify, and the garrison wasted no time in attacking the Koreans as they came ashore in search of water and provisions. Some 400 men were lost in this brief encounter, after which the Korean fleet hastily set sail again and rounded the north coast of Geoje in order to seek a temporary sanctuary in the narrow straits of Chilchonryang.

The Japanese decided to launch a night attack. It was the sort of naval battle at which Admiral Yi Sunsin had always excelled. The Japanese fleet bore down upon the hapless Koreans, whose state of shock prevented them from using their traditional tactics of destroying the Japanese fleet from a distance with superior artillery fire. When the battle was over, more than 150 Korean ships floated in the straits as pieces of burned wreckage, and any survivors who had struggled ashore were killed by the Geoje Island garrison. Among them was Weon Gyun himself. **ST**

Losses: Korean, 157 ships of 169, loss of life almost total; Japanese, unknown

◁ Jinju 1593　　　　Myongyang 1597 ▷

Myongyang 26 October 1597

Admiral Yi Sunsin was reinstated in charge of the Korean navy's attempts to repel Japan. After the defeat at Chilchonryang, he made his base much farther west than before—at the southwestern tip of Korea—in a narrow strait called Myongyang, which was known for the fierceness of the changes of its tides. There he defeated the Japanese navy.

The Japanese ships continued to press farther along the coast, and Yi Sunsin began planning how he could employ the unusual tidal conditions in Myongyang to defeat the Japanese. The tidal race passing through the strait is one of the fastest in all Korean waters, running between 9.5 and 11.5 knots at its highest rate. It was also known to change direction from north to west and then back again every three hours. This phenomenon was the only advantage Yi had, because the Japanese possessed 133 ships whereas he had only the twelve vessels saved from Chilchonryang.

The battle, which the Koreans call the "Miracle at Myongyang," began when the heavily armed Japanese fleet approached the strait from the direction of Oranpo on a favorable tide. Yi took up his position in the open sea just to the north of the strait. When the Japanese had advanced midway up the Myongyang strait, Yi sailed into the attack. His tiny flotilla was surrounded immediately, but Yi stuck firmly to his time-honored tactics of keeping the Japanese ships beyond boarding distance and bombarding them with cannon and fire arrows. As the fight progressed, the tide turned and began to carry the Japanese ships back along the strait. The Korean ships continued to harass them, destroying vessels out of all proportion to their relative numbers. Korean naval superiority was reconfirmed. **ST**

Losses: Japanese, 31 ships, 8,000–12,000 dead or wounded; Korean, no ships, 2 dead, 3 wounded

◁ Chilchonryang 1597　　　　Sacheon 1598 ▷

Barrills of Powder
Burnt

Bagnoll over the water slow

Battaile

Yellow Ford   14 August 1598

The Nine Years' War that broke out in Ulster in the north of Ireland in protest against English rule culminated in a battle fought at the Yellow Ford by the River Blackwater in County Armagh. The defeat of the English troops at the hands of the Irish was the heaviest England had ever suffered in Ireland.

War broke out in the north of Ireland in 1593 after the English lord-deputy of Ireland, Sir Edward Fitzwilliam, threatened the power of the northern lordships. Hugh O'Neill, second Earl of Tyrone, rose in revolt, creating a well-disciplined army that several times defeated the English troops.

In 1597, the English had built a fort on the River Blackwater, some 5 miles (8 km) northwest of the garrison town of Armagh, to help support military expeditions into neighboring Tyrone. Soon after the fort was built, the Earl of Tyrone responded by besieging it. In August 1598, an English expeditionary force of six regiments set out to relieve the fort but was immediately attacked by musket fire and a volley of spears thrown by rebels hiding in the nearby woods. The six regiments became separated: the regiment at the back was left behind guarding an ox-drawn artillery piece with a damaged wheel stuck in a bog; the regiment in the front crossed a wide trench but was forced to retreat again under heavy fire. To make matters worse, the leader of the expedition, Henry Bagenal, was shot in the head and the English gunpowder store exploded. O'Neill seized his chance and his cavalry attacked the front of the expedition, followed by his infantry. The English were cut down quickly, suffering heavy losses, and the remnants of their force retreated to Armagh under constant attack. **SA**

Losses: Irish, 300 dead of unknown total; English, 900 dead and 900 deserted of 4,000

Kinsale 1602 ▷

Sacheon   30 October 1598

After the death of Toyotomi Hideyoshi, the Japanese evacuated Korea, protected by the garrisons of the *wajo*, Japan's chain of coastal fortresses. In order to hinder the withdrawal, the Chinese and Koreans launched massive attacks against the three largest *wajo*—at Ulsan, Sacheon, and Suncheon—and were defeated at each.

The castle of Sacheon held a garrison of 8,000 troops who were commanded by the father and son team, Shimazu Yoshihiro and Tadatsune. It protected a natural harbor and was a key element in the communications with Japan. By the middle of September 1598, the Chinese general Ton Yuan had assembled an army of 34,000 Chinese troops together with 2,000 Koreans. On 1 October 1598, the allied army arrived at Sacheon, just too late to stop reinforcements from joining Shimazu Yoshihiro inside the castle.

Both sides used great ingenuity in their attack and defense. The Chinese brought up a combined battering ram and cannon against the main gate. The Japanese managed to destroy it and also launched exploding fire bombs by catapult into the midst of the Chinese army. One shot hit the Chinese gunpowder store. Shimazu Yoshihiro took the initiative on the last day of the siege and led his army out to meet the Chinese and Koreans in a field battle. Three divisions attacked simultaneously from out of the three landward gates. The force of the attack broke the besieging army, who were driven back as far as the river with many casualties. There was a brief rally, but the Chinese and Koreans were defeated. More than 37,000 heads are believed to have been taken, from which the noses were removed and sent back to Japan as trophies. **ST**

Losses: Korean and Chinese, very high, 37,000 heads taken although Ming sources say 80,000 dead; Japanese, very few

◁ Myongyang 1597   Noryang 1598 ▷

A depiction of the Battle of the Yellow Ford, c. 1600, now in Trinity College Library, Dublin.

Noryang 17 December 1598

The final evacuation of Korea by Japanese troops was intercepted by Korean admiral Yi Sunsin as the fleet passed through the Strait of Noryang. The action was to provide the last Korean success of the war, but the victory was marred by the fatal shooting of Admiral Yi on board his flagship at the moment of triumph.

Renewed Korean naval activity led to the Japanese decision to head for the shortest route along the coast, which lay between Namhae Island and the Korean mainland through the narrow Strait of Noryang. Anticipating the move, Admiral Yi Sunsin drew up his fleet in the open sea just to the west.

Late at night, Yi was told that the Japanese fleet had sailed into the Noryang strait and was anchored for the night. This state of affairs provided the Koreans with the perfect opportunity to launch a surprise attack, and within hours almost half of the Japanese fleet was either broken or burned. Admiral Yi was in the thick of the fighting and personally wielded a bow when he rowed to the aid of the Chinese Admiral Chen Lin, whose flagship had come under heavy attack from a group of Japanese ships.

By the time the dawn was breaking, the Japanese were retreating, and, sensing that this could be the last opportunity for the Koreans to force a victory, Admiral Yi ordered a vigorous pursuit. It was at that moment, when victory was certain, that a Japanese sharpshooter put a bullet into Yi's left armpit. He was dead within minutes. Only three close associates saw the incident, and the dying Yi asked them to keep his death a secret. His body was covered with a shield, and the battle continued toward its victorious conclusion. Out of 500 Japanese ships, only fifty survived. **ST**

Losses: Japanese, 450 ships of 500; Korean, no ships lost, 500 dead

◁ *Sacheon 1598*   *Sekigahara 1600* ▷

Nieuwpoort 2 July 1600

Nieuwpoort was one of the most famous examples of the brilliance of Maurice of Nassau's military reforms, which revolutionized warfare. In command of the army of the nascent Dutch United Provinces, he drove the Spanish from the field—the first time the Dutch had routed their former rulers in a pitched battle.

In the years after the Battle of Zutphen, the Low Countries had been divided into the Protestant United Provinces in the north and Catholic Flanders, ruled by Spain, in the south. In an attempt to reduce attacks against Dutch shipping, Maurice had been ordered into Flanders to capture the pirate strongholds of Nieuwpoort and Dunkirk. The invasion force (including some English regiments) crossed the Scheldt on 22 June, and advanced along the coast. The Dutch hoped that recent mutinies in the Spanish army would make their task an easy one. This was not to be.

On 30 June, the governor-general of Flanders, Archduke Albert of Austria, arrived with an army of seasoned troops. After a series of skirmishes drove the Dutch back, Maurice's army was pinned down on the dunes near Nieuwpoort. Dutch artillery drove back an initial charge of the Spanish cavalry; the Dutch innovation of placing wooden mats underneath their guns meant they could be moved and fired without sinking into the dunes. However, the renowned Spanish infantry, the finest in Europe at the time, slowly forced the Dutch back. Even in retreat, years of drill training meant the Dutch kept in formation and did not break rank. As the sun set, Maurice unleashed his reserves of cavalry on the tired Spanish army, which broke their resolve and scattered them. Strategically the victory was unimportant, but it showcased Maurice's brilliance. **JF**

Losses: Spanish, 2,000–3,000 of 10,000; Dutch, 2,000–3,000 of 15,000

◁ *Zutphen 1586*   *Ostend 1601* ▷

Two phases of the Nieuwpoort battle, from the atlas collection of Frederik Willem van Loon (1644–1708).

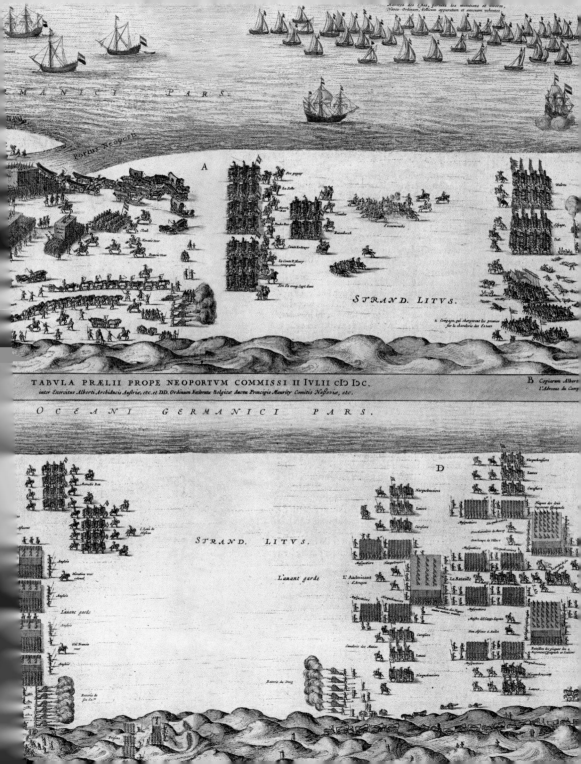

OCEANI GERMANICI PARS.

Portus Neoporti

A

STRAND. LITVS.

TABVLA PRÆLII PROPE NEOPORTVM COMMISSI II IVLII cIↄ Iↄc.
inter Exercitus Alberti Archiducis Austriæ, etc. et DD. Ordinum Fœderatæ Belgicæ ductu Principis Mauritij Comitis Nassoviæ, etc.

B Copiarum Albert
L'Abrense du Camp

OCEANI GERMANICI PARS.

D

STRAND. LITVS.

L'avant garde

Sekigahara   21 October 1600

The death of Toyotomi Hideyoshi left Japan under the rule of his five-year-old son, Hideyori. Regents were appointed but two factions emerged: a coalition of generals and Tokugawa Ieyasu, who controlled much of eastern Japan. Ieyasu defeated the alliance at Sekigahara and founded the Tokugawa shogunate.

The coalition (western army) was under the leadership of Ishida Mitsunari, who arranged his army at the western end of the valley of Sekigahara. His plan was that the main body would hold the Tokugawa (eastern army) in the center, then Kobayakawa Hideaki would fall on them from the left, while other generals would attack them in the rear.

By daybreak the eastern army had advanced to meet the coalition troops on as wide a front as the narrow valley would allow. There was a thick fog that persisted until about 8:00 AM, when the fighting started. The central divisions were the first to engage, the first shots of the battle probably being fired by coalition troops onto

> *"Evil-doers and bandits were vanquished and the entire realm submitted to Lord Ieyasu."*
>
> Hayashi Gahō, Tokugawa historian

those of Ii Naomasa of the eastern army. The coalition was successful in driving the easterners back but they rallied, and the fight swayed to and fro. The front ranks of the eastern army pushed toward Ishida Mitsunari, while the second rank moved up to attack troops led by Ishida's fellow commander Konishi Yukinaga.

All the main divisions were now engaged, and Ishida thought the moment opportune to light the signal fire that would bring Kobayakawa down from his position. But Kobayakawa did not move a man, for one side or the other, and Ieyasu became concerned that the reports he had heard that Kobayakawa would defect to his side were not correct. He sent some men to fire on Kobayakawa's division to see what the reaction would be. Kobayakawa responded positively by sending his army down to assault the flank of Otani Yoshitsugu, whose contingent was the nearest of the coalition troops. Otani had obviously been expecting something like this, for his men turned calmly and repulsed the treacherous attack, but with considerable loss. Ieyasu then ordered a general attack along the line, and further contingents of the coalition army, led by Kuchiki Mototsuna and Wakisaka Yasuharu, showed their true colors. Soon the Otani were being attacked from three sides. Otani, who was a leper and crippled from the disease, leaned out of the palanquin in which he was carried and asked a retainer to put an end to him.

In the meantime, Konishi Yukinaga's division had been driven back gradually. Kobayakawa's men swept through the defeated Otani troops and attacked Konishi from behind. The coalition army began to break up. Only the army of the Shimazu was intact, but soon many of them were killed, too, including the brother of the commander, Shimazu Yoshihiro. Putting himself at the head of eighty survivors, Yoshihiro succeeded in cutting his way through the eastern army and back down the road toward Ogaki castle. Unfortunately, this route took him southwest of Mount Nangu where Ishida's reserve troops were stationed, a sight that convinced his men the battle was lost. Some troops had already decided to join Ieyasu; others were wavering, unsure what to make of the battle noise they could hear and the garbled reports they were receiving. Consequently, the very contingents who might have been able to reverse Ishida's defeat retreated from Sekigahara. **ST**

Losses: Ishida, as many as 32,000; Tokugawa, unknown but much fewer

◁ Noryang 1598   Osaka 1615 ▷

Detail from a seventeenth-century screen depicting Nijo castle, home of the Tokugawa family in Kyoto.

Ostend 15 July 1601–22 September 1604

Kinsale 3 January 1602

The Spanish struggle to wrest the port of Ostend, the last Protestant settlement in Flanders, from the hands of the Dutch lasted more than three years and was the bloodiest battle of the Dutch Revolt. Such was its length and violence that it became known as the "New Troy."

The Nine Years' War that broke out in Ulster in northern Ireland against English rule reached its climax in the Siege of Kinsale. The English victory ended the revolt and led to the economic and religious transformation of Ulster, with implications that have continued to the present day.

After the Battle of Nieuwpoort, the rulers of the Spanish Netherlands turned their attention to capturing the last Dutch enclave in Flanders. On 15 July 1601, a Spanish army of 20,000, commanded by Albert of Austria, laid siege to Ostend. The city's garrison numbered 3,500, commanded by the English general Francis Vere.

By winter 1601, sickness and death had considerably weakened the defenders. To stall an imminent Spanish attack and give time for reinforcements to arrive by sea, Vere called for a parley with Albert. The ruse worked and allowed time for 1,200 men to land. When the Spanish launched an all-out assault on 7 January 1602, they were driven back and suffered 1,000 casualties after miscalculating the tides.

By March 1602, the Anglo-Dutch garrison had risen to 7,000, regular supplies were getting through, and Ostend's resolve seemed unshakable. Hope came for the Spanish in the form of the Italian general Ambrogio Spinola, who arrived in the Low Countries with an army of 9,000. The wealthy son of Genoese bankers, Spinola offered to finance the siege in return for command of the armies, and did so in September 1602.

Spinola's Italian engineers used mines to destroy Ostend's defenses, and the defenders were driven back slowly but surely in bloody skirmishes in trenches around the city. Ostend finally surrendered on 22 September 1604, and Spinola entered the city in triumph. **JF**

The Irish Catholic rebels—led by Hugh O'Neill, the second Earl of Tyrone and uncrowned "king of Ireland"—first rose in revolt in 1593. They had long sought aid from Catholic Spain—the traditional enemy of Protestant England—which was eventually forthcoming in 1601.

A Spanish force of 4,000 landed at Kinsale, south of Cork in southern Ireland, on 2 October 1601, and fortified the town. The English lord-deputy of Ireland, Lord Mountjoy, headed south from Dublin to besiege the attackers, bringing in English reinforcements through Oysterhaven, just east of Kinsale. In the north, two rebel armies, led by O'Neill and his ally, Hugh Roe O'Donnell, set out on a long march south to link up with the Spanish troops.

Leaving a few regiments to guard the camp and watch over the Spanish still besieged in Kinsale, Mountjoy moved out to meet the rebels to the northwest of the town. O'Neill held the high ground, but when his allies failed to move to help him, he abandoned his position and retreated into nearby marshes in the hope of disabling the English cavalry in the boggy ground. His plan failed, however, as the English cavalry charged through his men and broke up his army. Most then fled back to Ulster, with the Spanish agreeing to return home.

Two years later, the Irish rebellion ended. O'Neill and his fellow Catholic earls fled to Europe, allowing the English to destroy Irish rule over Ulster, seize their land, and bring in Protestants from Scotland to settle the province. **SA**

Losses: Spanish, 60,000 dead; Anglo-Dutch, 30,000 dead

Losses: English, 400 dead of 7,200; Irish, 1,200 dead of 6,000

◁ Nieuwpoort 1600   Gibraltar 1607 ▷   ◁ Yellow Ford 1598   Rathmines 1649 ▷

Polish-Swedish War

Kircholm   27 September 1605

Sweden and Poland-Lithuania had been at war since 1600 in a struggle for control of the southeast Baltic. At Kircholm, near Riga, the Polish-Lithuanian cavalry annihilated the Swedish infantry, although they were not able to bring about a decisive end to the war.

The Swedish leader, Charles IX, had been besieging Riga, when a Polish-Lithuanian army—commanded by Grand Lithuanian Hetman Jan Karol Chodkiewicz—approached to raise the siege. Charles pursued them for six miles (9.5 km) with a force of 10,868 (8,368 foot soldiers and 2,500 cavalry), many of whom were foreign mercenaries. Chodkiewicz's army was a third of the size (1,000 infantry and 2,600 cavalry).

Charles occupied the crest of a ridge above a plain and drew his army in four lines: infantry in the first and third, cavalry in the second and forth. The infantry was drawn up in the new western style, in squares of pike bordered with shot. Chodkiewicz aimed to draw the Swedes out of position by launching a series of light cavalry feints and then pretending to withdraw. Charles took the bait and ordered his army to advance onto the plain.

At this moment, the Polish-Lithuanian winged hussars—elite heavy cavalry units armed with five-meter lances (their name stemmed from wings attached to their saddles, which produced a strange whirring sound when they charged)—charged into the Swedish infantry with great success. Charles was able to hold the line temporarily by deploying reserves of cavalry on both flanks, but these were soon driven back, leaving the Swedish infantry completely isolated. The Polish-Lithuanian hussars and infantry massacred the Swedish foot soldiers, and Charles was forced to abandon the siege of Riga. **JF**

Losses: Swedish, 9,000 of 10,868; Polish-Lithuanian, 100 of 3,600

Klushino 1610 ☑

Dutch-Portuguese War

Cape Rachado   18 August 1606

Fought between the Dutch and Portuguese, Cape Rachado was a naval battle between European commercial powers fighting for control of the valuable spice trade. Although the Portuguese claimed a victory, the battle marked an important step in the rise of Dutch power in the East Indies.

In 1511, the Portuguese seized the port-city of Malacca from its Muslim sultan, taking control of trade through the straits between the Malay peninsula and Sumatra. They turned Malacca into a fortress, defending it against counterattacks from descendants of the sultan, at the time rulers of neighboring Johor.

In 1606, the Dutch East India Company—set up to develop Dutch colonial interests in Asia—sent eleven ships to blockade Malacca. The Portuguese responded by dispatching a fleet from their base at Goa in India. Commanded by Portuguese viceroy Dom Martin Afonso de Castro, the fleet arrived on 14 August.

Four days later, shifting winds gave the Portuguese the chance to close with their opponents off Cape Rachado, seeking to grapple and board the smaller Dutch ships. Some Dutch vessels collided while trying to flee; Portuguese ships rammed their entangled enemy. Interlocked vessels were the scene of furious hand-to-hand fighting and point-blank cannonades. Outbreaks of fire on board threatened both sides.

The Dutch finally withdrew, taking refuge in Johor. There they reaped the reward of their courage. Impressed by their fighting spirit, the sultan agreed to an alliance against the Portuguese. In the long term, this deal was decisive. Portugal did not have the resources to defend Malacca against both Dutch ships and Johor land forces. The vital city was lost to the Dutch in 1641. **RG**

Losses: Dutch, 2 ships lost, 150 dead; Portuguese, 2 ships lost, 500 dead

Salvador de Bahia 1625 ☑

Gibraltar 25 April 1607

After the loss of Ostend, the Dutch United Provinces geared up their maritime campaign against Spain. This culminated in the breathtakingly bold raid on the Spanish fleet in harbor at Gibraltar, one of the most celebrated Dutch naval victories in their war of independence.

The United Provinces had been sending warships to the southern Spanish coast since 1599 in an attempt to disrupt enemy shipping. In the wake of recent losses in Flanders, the Dutch launched a daring surprise raid against the Spanish fleet. The Dutch commander, Jacob van Heemskerk, sailed his fleet of twenty-six warships into the Bay of Gibraltar, where a Spanish fleet was anchored. The Spanish admiral, Don Juan Alvarez de Avila, had a force of twenty-one ships, which included ten large galleons, and outgunned the Dutch.

In the first approach, Van Heemskerk—in his flagship, *Aeolus*—targeted his opposite number's flagship, *San Augustin*. As the ships engaged, a cannonball severed Van Heemskerk's leg and he was mortally wounded. The captain of the *Aeolus*, Verhoef, took command of the fleet, but did not reveal the death of its admiral, and in the next broadside, the Spanish admiral was killed.

The smaller Dutch vessels lethally harried the larger Spanish ships, with two attacking each galleon. One of the Spanish galleons exploded when its magazine was ignited, and the flames spread to other ships, leaving the Spanish fleet in total disarray. With all other ships sunk or burned, the devastated *San Augustin* managed to raise the white flag, but the Dutch did not accept the surrender. Instead, they rowed among the ruined Spanish fleet, shooting and stabbing survivors as they floated in the water. **JF**

Losses: Spanish, entire fleet of 21 ships and 2,000–4,000 men; Dutch, no ships and 100 men

◁ Ostend 1601   Breda 1624 ▷

The Spanish admiral ship explodes in The Battle of Gibraltar *(c. 1622) by Cornelis Claesz van Wieringen.*

Klushino   4 July 1610

Muscovy was dragged into the ongoing war between Poland-Lithuania and Sweden when Czar Basil IV allied with Charles IX to fight off a usurper to his throne. As at the Battle of Kircholm, the Polish-Lithuanian cavalry triumphed against a numerically superior enemy.

The Muscovite-Swedish army was heading to relieve the besieged fortress of Smolensk when they were intercepted by a Polish-Lithuanian army of 6,500 cavalry and 200 foot soldiers. Its general, Stanisław Żółkiewski, had led his men in a forced night march through dense forest to meet the enemy just before dawn. He was outnumbered by more than five to one. The Muscovites, commanded by Prince Dmitrii Shuiskii, had troops of 30,000 (although around half were peasant auxiliaries) and the Swedish had a force of 7,000 (mostly French, German, and British mercenaries), led by Christoph Horn and Jacob de la Gardie.

The Swedish had been in Muscovy since 1608 and had trained their allies in the latest western military tactics. Żółkiewski could not launch an immediate attack on the enemy camp because his men had to negotiate a palisade and a small village when they emerged from the forest. Even without the element of surprise, the winged hussars smashed the numerically superior Muscovite cavalry in their first attack. Aided by their small force of infantry, two guns, and a canny deployment of reserve cavalry, they forced the Swedish cavalry, and their generals, from the field. The Muscovites followed. The foreign mercenaries, now totally abandoned, gave up and many switched sides. The charge of the winged hussars had once again won the day. Soon after Klushino, Basil IV was dethroned, and Żółkiewski entered Moscow without opposition. **JF**

Losses: Polish-Lithuanian, 500 of 6,700; Muscovite-Swedish, 5,000 of 37,000

◁ *Kircholm 1605*   *Dirschau 1627* ▷

⬆ *A seventeenth-century painting of the Battle of Klushino, with the Polish hussars center-left in the foreground.*

Osaka (Tennoji)   4–5 June 1615

After Sekigahara, Tokugawa Ieyasu became shogun, but many Japanese still supported Toyotomi Hideyori. In 1614, thousands of Toyotomi supporters packed themselves into Osaka castle. After laying siege, Ieyasu finally defeated them at the Battle of Tennoji. The Tokugawa shogunate went on to rule Japan until 1868.

The Toyotomi plan was to sally out for a pitched battle at Tennoji to the south of Osaka castle. Sanada Yukimura and Ono Harunaga would deliver a frontal assault on the Tokugawa main body, who would be held while Akashi Morishige swept around to deliver a surprise rear attack. Once all the Tokugawa troops were engaged, Toyotomi Hideyori would lead the garrison out of the castle. However, the lack of discipline on the Osaka side resulted in an uncontrolled advance, so Yukimura urged Toyotomi Hideyori to join in the battle at once. Chance was on his side, because the complex maneuvering of the Tokugawa troops had caused many to believe that some had turned traitor. This was not the case, but Tokugawa Ieyasu himself was forced to join his men in the thick of the fighting in order to steady their nerves.

It was Honda Tadatomo who saved the day for the Tokugawa. He led his troops in a fierce charge against Sanada Yukimura, who was killed. Yukimura's death was proclaimed throughout the Tokugawa army, and the tide of the battle began to turn. The Tokugawa flag was planted on the outer castle gate, and as civilians fled the Tokugawa swarmed into the castle. Dragging their guns forward, the Tokugawa artillery opened up on the keep. The following morning flames were seen. Toyotomi Hideyori had burned the castle that had once seemed impregnable, and committed suicide. **ST**

Losses: Tokugawa, 8,000; Toyotomi, 15,000–18,000

◁ *Sekigahara 1600*   *Hakodate Bay 1869* ▷

Japanese warriors clash head-on in this detail from Siege of Osaka Castle *by Kuroda Nagamasa.* ↑

Pilsen   19 September–21 November 1618

The Siege of Pilsen was the first major battle of the Thirty Years' War, one of the most destructive conflicts in European history. It followed the Defenestration of Prague on 23 May 1618, which saw Bohemian Protestants declare independence from the Catholic Hapsburgs by throwing two Catholic regents out of a window.

Prior to 1618, Bohemia's Protestants had been allowed freedom of worship. However, the election of the staunchly Catholic Hapsburg Ferdinand of Styria (elected Holy Roman Emperor in August 1619) as king of Bohemia led to fears that this freedom would be revoked, and eventually to a Protestant rebellion.

The rebels gave command of their armies to the German mercenary general, Ernst von Mansfeld. He had been sent, with 4,000 troops, by the Protestant Elector of the Palatinate, Frederick V, an early supporter of the rebels. Mansfeld's first target was Pilsen, a city loyal to the Hapsburgs, where many Catholic refugees from the new regime had fled. Despite commanding forces of 10,000 troops, Mansfeld was unable to launch an all-out assault on the well-defended city, so he blockaded the gates of the city in an attempt to starve it out.

The rebel artillery arrived on 2 October, but it was not powerful enough to bring down the city walls straight away. Pilsen lacked gunpowder and soldiers to man its defenses, but it held firm. However, its supplies of food and water were running low. After two months of siege, breaches were finally made in the fortifications, and Mansfeld's soldiers stormed the town. The capture of Pilsen meant that almost all of Bohemia was controlled by the Protestant rebels. By 1619, their separation from the Hapsburgs was complete when Frederick V accepted the throne of Bohemia. **JF**

Losses: Unknown

White Mountain   1620 ▸

White Mountain   8 November 1620

After the Siege of Pilsen in 1618, the Bohemian Protestant revolt had spread across the Austrian Hapsburg lands. The Battle of White Mountain, near Prague, was the first major pitched action of the Bohemian revolt, and proved to be a decisive imperial victory over the rebels.

This battle was part of a broader imperial offensive in 1620, where the Hapsburgs, and their allies Spain and the League of German Catholic states, swept through the Palatinate, conquering the lands of the rebel king of Bohemia, Frederick V. In Bohemia, an imperial-Bavarian army of 24,800, which included Spanish and Flemish veterans and Polish Cossacks, had advanced to within 5 miles (8 km) of Prague. There it was intercepted by a rebel army of 23,000; their commander, Christian of Anhalt, had occupied the higher ground, but his position was not ideal; he had been unable to entrench the ridge where his troops were arrayed, he was lacking most of his artillery, and he only had light cavalry.

The imperial-Bavarian army, commanded by Count Bucquoy and Count Tilly, was deployed into ten large infantry blocks accompanied by cavalry. Following an artillery barrage, the army advanced at midday. Christian sent his cavalry down the slope to engage the enemy, and his infantry followed. Within an hour, the rebel cavalry was in retreat, and the infantry soon followed in disarray, many without firing a shot. Their panic stemmed from reports that the Polish Cossacks had outflanked them and were approaching from the rear.

The bulk of the rebel forces were defeated in just over an hour and the victorious army swept into Prague. However, they failed in one important objective, that of capturing Frederick V; he had fled the city. **JF**

Losses: Protestant rebels, 4,000 of 23,000; Imperial-Bavarian army, 800 of 24,800

◁ Pilsen 1618   Fleurus 1622 ▷

Khotyn   September–October 1621

The battle fought at Khotyn in Moldavia was a remarkable defensive victory for the outnumbered forces of the Polish-Lithuanian Commonwealth, led by the veteran Grand Hetman of Lithuania, Jan Karol Chodkiewicz, over the army of the Ottoman Empire, under Sultan Osman II.

In response to raids by Cossacks into Ottoman Moldavia, Osman II advanced toward Poland with an army in excess of 100,000. To confront the Ottomans, Poland-Lithuania raised an army of approximately 50,000 and placed it under Chodkiewicz, a distinguished nobleman and military commander. The Commonwealth men dug themselves into a series of trenches around the fortress of Khotyn, with gaps through which their elite Cossack cavalry could pass. The Commonwealth objective was to stop the advance of the Ottomans, and, as the Turkish army advanced, Cossacks attacked to buy time for the main force to entrench itself. Although the Cossacks were wiped out, they delayed the Ottomans long enough for the Commonwealth to dig in.

Ottoman attacks on the trenches were repelled many times, resulting in heavy casualties. In late September the Commonwealth force pulled back to a second level of trenches and the Ottomans launched a number of attacks, again with no overall success and with heavy losses. As winter approached the Ottomans withdrew, having suffered the loss of almost half of their army.

A tactical victory for the Commonwealth, the battle showed how an entrenched army could hold a larger force. However, the subsequent Treaty of Khotyn allowed both sides to claim victory. Osman II's heavy losses in the battle prompted him to attempt military reforms that led to an uprising in 1622 in which he was assassinated. **TB**

Losses: Ottoman, 45,000 casualties of 100,000; Polish-Lithuanian, 13,000 of 50,000

◁ Keresztes 1596   Fall of Candia 1669 ▷

Fleurus 29 August 1622

Fleurus was a victory for Spain over a German Protestant army during the Thirty Years' War. The Protestant leader, Frederick V, who had lost Bohemia after the Battle of White Mountain, had just disbanded his mercenary army, led by Ernst von Mansfeld and Christian of Brunswick.

Mansfeld and Brunswick's unemployed army was hired by the Dutch to assist them in raising the Spanish siege of Bergen-op-Zoom. They left the Palatinate, but after a forty-seven day march to the Spanish Netherlands, their numbers had been reduced from 25,000 to 14,000. At Fleurus, in Hainaut, they met a Spanish army of 8,000 that had moved to intercept them. The Spanish commander, Gonzalo Fernández de Córdoba, had entrenched his forces, with forest protecting his flanks. There was a short artillery barrage, and then Mansfeld led his infantry against the Spanish, but he could not overwhelm them, as their defensive position was too strong. In five hours of bloody fighting, the Spanish musketeers shot down hundreds of Protestant soldiers.

After five cavalry charges, Brunswick was able to break through the Spanish lines on the right hand side. At this point, all of the Protestants who were able to do so broke through and sped past the Spanish lines. The Spanish were too exhausted to pursue the German Protestant army that day, but the next day the Spanish cavalry cut down most the surviving German infantry. The remnants of the German Protestant army were able to rendezvous with the Dutch at Breda. Mansfeld and Brunswick had lost all of their artillery and baggage, and the majority of their infantry. Brunswick himself had been wounded so severely he had to have his lower left arm amputated. **JF**

Losses: German Protestant, 5,000 of 14,000; Spanish, 300 dead and 900 wounded of 8,000

◁ White Mountain 1620   Stadtlohn 1623 ▷

Stadtlohn 6 August 1623

Catholic League commander Count Tilly bested Christian of Brunswick's Protestant army in this Thirty Years' War encounter. Brunswick had joined the Dutch service, but left after three months. After wintering in the Low Countries, he led his army into the Lower Saxon Circle in March 1623.

Brunswick could not find any allies in Germany. Facing attack from Tilly's approaching Catholic League army, Brunswick retreated toward the Netherlands. The first contact between the two armies occurred on 4 August, but Brunswick's rearguard delayed Tilly for two days.

When the rearguard finally gave way, Brunswick was forced to make a stand at Stadtlohn, Westphalia. He deployed his main infantry on the high ground in an arrowhead formation, with marsh to the left and forest to the right. He then sent a detachment of foot soldiers, artillery, and horse to obstruct Tilly.

At 2:00 PM, the Catholic army approached and engaged the Protestant vanguard, which was only able to delay them for ninety minutes. A sustained artillery barrage had already unsettled the Protestant infantry, and Tilly's infantry closed to within musket range, while his cavalry bore down on the Protestant right flank. Brunswick's position quickly became hopeless, and he fled with his cavalry. Most of his infantry were massacred, and the survivors who fled the field were cut down by Croat and Cossack horsemen. Brunswick reached the Netherlands with 5,500 men, and entered the Dutch service for ten weeks. Tilly captured all of the Protestant artillery and most of their baggage train. Five months later, the Protestant general, Ernst von Mansfeld, disbanded his troops, leaving no armed opposition to the Hapsburg Catholics in Germany. **JF**

Losses: German Protestant, 6,000 dead and 4,000 captured of 15,000; Catholic, 1,000 dead and wounded of 20,700

◁ Fleurus 1622   Dessau 1626 ▷

Breda   28 August 1624–5 June 1625

The capture of the fortress city of Breda, in Brabant (now part of Belgium and the Netherlands), was the last great Spanish victory of the Dutch Revolt. It was the finest moment of the illustrious military career of Ambrogio Spinola, who had previously taken Ostend after another lengthy siege.

The United Provinces and Spain had declared a twelve-year truce in 1609. When conflict resumed in 1621, the main Spanish tactic was an embargo of Dutch sea trade, as many in Spain thought land war too costly. In spite of this, in August 1624 Spinola besieged Breda, a vital stronghold in the ring of fortresses defending the United Provinces. The fortified city had a garrison of 9,000 and was well defended.

Spinola placed his army of 23,000 around the city and set about consolidating his position. He made a double circumvallation of siege works, and then pierced a nearby dyke, which flooded the lower ground and hindered any attack on his position. His intention was to starve Breda into submission. There were repeated efforts to break the siege or draw the Spanish away, but Spinola was able to repel them. First, Maurice of Nassau attempted to relieve Breda. When he died in April 1625, command of the Dutch armies passed to his half-brother, Frederick Henry, who, despite the assistance of an English army led by Sir Horace Vere, was also unable to save Breda.

In June, Breda's governor, Justin of Nassau, surrendered to Spinola (a moment recorded by Spanish court artist Diego Velázquez). The surviving garrison of 3,500 was allowed to march out with the honors of war. The Spanish had gained a vital victory, but it had been an expensive one, leaving them unable to follow it up with a sustained land campaign. **JF**

Losses: Dutch, 13,000 civilians and soldiers; Spanish, 5,000 of 23,000

◁ *Gibraltar 1607*   *Matanzas Bay 1628* ▷

Detail from Diego Velázquez's Las Lanzas, *or* The Surrender of Breda *(1635).* ⬆

Salvador da Bahia   April–May 1625

In the seventeenth century Brazil became a battleground between rival European powers who coveted its slave-worked sugar plantations. The recapture of the port-city of Salvador da Bahia by the Spanish and Portuguese in 1625 helped to prevent Brazil from becoming a Dutch colony.

Colonized by the Portuguese in the sixteenth century, Brazil had become a Spanish possession when Spain absorbed Portugal in 1580. The Dutch were engaged in a long war for independence from Spain, and so had no compunction in attacking its South American colonies. In 1623 a Dutch fleet sailed to the Brazilian capital Bahia and seized control of the poorly defended city. Spanish king Philip IV responded by organizing a large-scale naval expedition, totaling fifty-six Spanish and Portuguese ships with some 12,500 sailors and soldiers on board.

The force assembled at Cape Verde Island, off the African coast, in February 1625 and sailed for Brazil under the command of a Spanish nobleman, Alvarez de Toledo. Reaching Bahia, his ships adopted a sickle formation, blocked the bay, and landed troops. These Spanish *tercios* were joined by waiting Portuguese colonists.

Bahia was placed under siege. Spanish artillery bombarded the Dutch defenses while sappers dug trenches toward the city walls. The defenders, including Dutch, English, French, and German soldiers, mounted sorties against the besiegers and inflicted substantial casualties, but their only real hope lay in breaking the naval blockade. After mounting a fireship attack that failed to shake Alvarez's fleet, the Dutch and their allies surrendered. Bahia became a base from which to oppose the spread of Dutch power elsewhere in Brazil. **CP**

Losses: Dutch, 1,912 men captured, unknown dead of 2,500; Spanish and Portuguese, several hundred dead or wounded of 12,500

◁ *Cape Rachado 1606*   *Guararapes 1649* ▷

⬆ *Bahia is recaptured from the Dutch in a 1634 painting by Jean-Baptiste Maino.*

Ningyuan 1626

In the early seventeenth century, Ming China was the world's largest, wealthiest empire. Yet it struggled to defend itself against the rising power of Nurhaci, a chieftain of the Manchu horsemen of Manchuria. A Ming victory at Ningyuan delayed, but could not prevent, the fall of the dynasty.

Nurhaci's forces, organized into eight "banners," inflicted numerous defeats upon the Chinese north of the Great Wall. Proclaiming himself emperor, the Manchu leader aspired to rule both China and Korea. The Ming, however, found a general who was loyal, gifted, and courageous: Yuan Chonghuan. Refusing to withdraw behind the Great Wall, Yuan turned the northern city of Ningyuan into a fortified position, defended by 10,000 troops and European-supplied cannon. Backed by the Wall, his soldiers had orders to stand firm and fight.

Nurhaci could field ten times the number of soldiers that Yuan possessed and was thus confident he could take the city. When his host attacked, however, both Yuan's soldiers and the city's population mounted a vigorous defense. The cannon took a heavy toll of the attackers. After two days Nurhaci, himself wounded by a cannonball, called off the assault.

Yuan pursued the retreating Manchu back to Mukden, inflicting further casualties. Nurhaci died of his wounds. Yet the Ming were incapable of building upon this victory. Nurhaci was succeeded by his son, Huang Taiji, who continued the Manchu campaigns. Meanwhile Yuan, rather than being rewarded for his achievement, was falsely accused of treason and condemned to death. He was executed and cut into pieces in front of the crowd in Beijing's main marketplace on 22 September 1630. The Ming dynasty survived him by only fourteen years. **RG**

Losses: No reliable figures

Fall of Beijing 1644 ▷

Dessau 25 April 1626

Following the catastrophic defeat it suffered at Stadtlohn, the German Protestant cause in the Thirty Years' War seemed lost. There was new hope when Christian IV of Denmark entered the war in 1625, but the next year a Protestant army was bested at Dessau by imperial forces.

The Protestant general Ernst von Mansfeld led an army into Magdeburg, aiming to break the imperial line west of the Elbe River. In command of the forces there was Albrecht von Wallenstein, a minor, but wealthy, Moravian noble who had risen to command the imperial armies. Mansfeld attacked at Dessau, the most important crossing between Magdeburg and Saxony.

Wallenstein had been able to secure a bridgehead by entrenching four infantry companies on the eastern side. Mansfeld arrived in force on 12 April, but despite having superior numbers he was unable to overcome the imperial fortifications. Deciding to take the position by siege, he dug trenches and brought up his guns. He made no headway and by 24 April substantial imperial reinforcements had arrived. Wallenstein occupied a wood on the Protestant right to outflank them.

Mansfeld was now completely outnumbered, but at 6:00 AM on 25 April he ordered an all-out attack. Fighting went on for five hours until Wallenstein, through weight of numbers, was able to force Mansfeld back. Mansfeld ordered his guns and baggage to pull back and carried on fighting to cover their escape. At noon fresh reserves of imperial cavalry and infantry charged from the woods and a counterattack was launched from the bridgehead. The Protestants were forced to retreat. Dessau was the first of many setbacks for Christian IV's overall strategy, and in 1629 he pulled out of the war. **JF**

Losses: Imperial, 1,000 of 14,000; Protestant, 3,000 captured and 1,000–2,000 dead of 7,000

◁ *Stadtlohn 1623*   *Magdeburg 1630* ▷

Dirschau   17–18 August 1627

This Swedish victory over Poland-Lithuania was the first time the Swedes had bested the famous Polish "winged hussars" that had so decisively routed them at Kircholm and Klushino. The battle almost brought the military career of King Gustavus Adolphus of Sweden to a premature end.

Poland-Lithuania had been brought into conflict with Sweden when the Swedes invaded Prussia, a Polish vassal, in May 1626. In summer 1627, King Gustavus Adolphus of Sweden was laying siege to the vital port of Danzig, and a Polish-Lithuanian army led by Stanisław Koniecpolski was sent to dislodge him. They met at Dirschau, a town on the banks of the Vistula on 17 August.

Both armies dug in. First the Swedes attempted to lure the Polish-Lithuanians into attacking their excellent defensive positions by sending out skirmishers. This tactic failed. In turn, Koniecpolski advanced his hussars to try to draw the Swedes out. After two hours there was no movement so they retreated back to their camp, along a narrow causeway over marshy ground. Seeing an opportunity, Gustavus Adolphus launched a sudden cavalry charge. The surprise attack drove two Polish-Lithuanian columns into the marsh. A complete rout seemed possible, but shot from Polish-Lithuanian infantry and a flanking attack from their reserve cavalry drove back the Swedish.

On the next day, Sweden attacked the Polish-Lithuanian camp. Just as victory seemed imminent, a musket ball from a sniper struck Gustavus Adolphus in the shoulder, close to his neck. This stopped the Swedish advance and put their king in bed for three months. Unable to launch any further offensives that campaign season, they remained unable to capture Danzig. **JF**

Losses: Polish-Lithuanian, 80–100 of 7,500; Swedish, negligible of 10,000

◁ Klushino 1610   Oliwa 1627 ▷

"If you hold with God, come over to me. If you prefer the devil, you will have to fight me first."

King Gustavus Adolphus of Sweden

⬆ *Gustavus Adolphus (right) fights in the Battle of Dirschau, in a detail from a 1634 painting by Jan Maertszen de Jonghe.*

La Rochelle 1627–1628

The Siege of La Rochelle effectively ended the final Huguenot rebellion against the French crown, and was a marker in the rise of the French absolute monarchy. Cardinal Richelieu's royal forces captured the city after a fourteen-month siege in which they also saw off three fleets from England.

Eight years after Ivry, Henry IV of France enacted the Edict of Nantes, which guaranteed Huguenots freedom of worship. After Henry's assassination in 1610, his son Louis XIII ascended, and crown policy became more pro-Catholic. This led to Huguenot risings in the 1620s.

In June 1627, Charles I of England sent the Duke of Buckingham to promote revolt in La Rochelle, the most important Huguenot stronghold. On 20 July, leading a hundred ships and 7,000 men, Buckingham landed at Ré, an island at the mouth of the inlet leading to La Rochelle. He was unable to wrest control of Ré from the royal garrison there and was forced to retreat on 17 November.

Elsewhere, a French royal army had begun to construct fortifications close to La Rochelle. When they were fired on from the city in September, La Rochelle was formally at war with the crown. Richelieu, Louis's chief minister, oversaw the construction of 9 miles (14.5 km) of entrenchments studded with forts and redoubts, which completely cut off La Rochelle from land. To prevent the English relieving the city from sea, Richelieu constructed a huge seawall that blockaded the channel leading to La Rochelle. Two English fleets tried, and failed, to bypass the blockade. La Rochelle held out despite famine and disease but finally surrendered on 28 October. Revolt continued until 1629, but the loss of La Rochelle was the death knell of Huguenot resistance. **JF**

Losses: La Rochelle, 14,000 dead and 5,000 fled of 25,000 citizens and sailors; Buckingham, 4,000 of 7,000; French Royalist, negligible of 30,000

◁ Ivry 1590   Faubourg Saint-Antoine 1652 ▷

Oliwa 28 November 1627

The Battle of Oliwa, near Danzig (now Gdansk), was a rare and famous victory for the Polish-Lithuanian navy. Sweden, a dominant naval power with strategic control of the Baltic Sea, suffered a humiliating defeat at the hands of a country with no substantial naval tradition.

A Swedish fleet of twelve ships had blockaded the Baltic shore since summer 1627, but in the fall half of them sailed home. The Swedish admiral left in command of the blockade, Niels Göranson Stiernsköld, now had six ships, armed with around 140 guns. The recently formed Polish-Lithuanian fleet was anchored at Danzig, commanded by a Dutchman, Arend Dickmann. Of his ten ships, only four were comparable in size to those of the Swedish; they were armed with 170 guns, although most of them were of a smaller caliber than those of the Swedes.

On 26 November the Polish-Lithuanian fleet tried to break the blockade, but was repulsed. Two days later, when the Swedish fleet sailed toward Danzig, the Polish-Lithuanian fleet sailed out to meet them head-on. This reaction surprised Stiernsköld, who did not expect a direct assault. The Polish-Lithuanian flagship, the *Saint George*, attacked its Swedish counterpart, the *Tiger*. After a bitter struggle, the Polish-Lithuanians were able to board and capture the enemy flagship. In the engagement, both admirals were killed—Dickmann had his legs shot off by a cannonball. Elsewhere, the Polish-Lithuanian vice-admiral's ship, the *Aquarius*, attacked a larger Swedish ship, the *Sun*, whose crew blew up their ship rather than let it be captured. The four remaining Swedish ships fled the battle. Poland-Lithuania had shown its navy was able to successfully challenge the Swedes. **JF**

Losses: Swedish, 1 ship captured and 1 destroyed of 6, 350 dead; Polish-Lithuanian, no ships out of 10, and 50 dead

◁ Dirschau 1627

Matanzas Bay   8 September 1628

The great Dutch admiral Piet Hein captured a Spanish treasure fleet near Matanzas Bay, Cuba, in this encounter during the Dutch Revolt. Negating their recent success at Breda, this was a major financial and naval disaster for the Spanish.

By the seventeenth century, the struggle between Spain and the United Provinces was no longer confined to the Low Countries. Control of the shipping routes to Asia and the Americas had become vital to both states, and the Dutch West Indies Company was financing attacks on Spanish and Portuguese shipping in the Caribbean.

In 1628 Hein led a squadron of thirty-one ships armed with 700 cannon and around 4,000 sailors and soldiers. One of his targets was the famed Spanish treasure fleet, which carried riches from the New World back to Europe. After four months of cruising, Hein intercepted the Spanish fleet on the northern coast of Cuba. It was an easy victory. He immediately captured nine ships with musket fire from shallops. The remaining six fled into Matanzas Bay, where the crews abandoned ship under fire from the Dutch. The booty, worth more than 11 million guilders, included over 175,000 pounds (79,380 kg) of silver, as well as gold, pearls, indigo, cochineal, sugar, wood, and furs. Spain lost one-third of its ships engaged in the Atlantic trade, a huge blow to its economy. The Dutch West Indies Company was able to distribute a cash dividend of fifty percent to its shareholders that year. The money also contributed to Dutch military conquests in Brazil, as well as financing their armies in Europe. **JF**

Losses: Spanish, entire treasure fleet of 15 ships with all of their contents; Dutch, none of 31 ships

◁ *Breda 1624*   *The Downs 1639* ▷

ALBIS   FLVVIVS

Imperial artillery commences the destruction of Magdeburg, in a 1637 engraving by Matthäus Merian. ⬇

Magdeburg   November 1630–20 May 1631

After defeat at Dessau and Denmark's withdrawal, the Protestants had received a boost when Sweden invaded Germany in 1630, but they could not prevent the imperial army's sack of Magdeburg, the most infamous episode of the Thirty Years' War.

Magdeburg had been under a loose imperial blockade, commanded by Count Pappenheim, since November 1630. Gustavus Adolphus of Sweden had given Magdeburg assurances of protection, and when Count Tilly led a substantial army to besiege it in earnest on 3 April, Gustavus Adolphus moved to protect the city. He had sent one of his officers, Dietrich von Falkenburg, to command the defense. Tilly had a powerful siege train and carefully picked off the outworks one by one.

By 1 May, Tilly had taken all of Magdeburg's outer defenses. Two days later the suburbs fell and the city was reduced to its inner defenses. Gustavus Adolphus was unable to reach Magdeburg as local rulers were unwilling to allow him to march through their territories. Although desperate, Magdeburg still refused to surrender. On 20 May at 7:00 AM, Tilly launched his final charge. Within two hours his infantry had breached the inner defenses, followed by heavy cavalry. During the attack, fires broke out across the city, and imperial soldiers began to massacre the citizenry and loot the city. Tilly, unable to control his men, lost all of the supplies he had hoped to gain. By day's end, 20,000 of Magdeburg's inhabitants had been killed—the single greatest tragedy of the war. **JF**

Losses: Protestant, 20,000 defenders and civilians of 25,000; Imperial, 300 dead and 1,600 wounded of 25,000

◁ *Dessau 1626*　　　　　　　*First Breitenfeld 1631* ▷

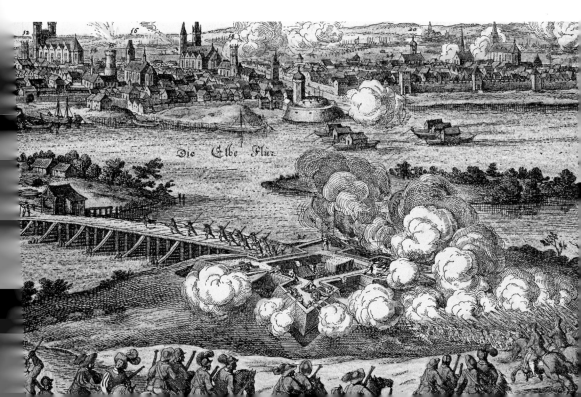

Die Elbe Flur

PRÆLII.
INTER
SERENISS: SUECOR:
REGEM ET SAXONIÆ.
ELECTOREMNECNON
CATHOLICÆ LIGÆ GENE
RALEM CON: A TILI VII.
SEPTEMBER ANNI MDCXXXI
PROPE LIPSIAM COMMISSI,

First Breitenfeld   17 September 1631

The First Battle of Breitenfeld was also the first major Catholic defeat of the Thirty Years' War. The winning general, King Gustavus Adolphus of Sweden, showed exceptional skill as a commander. His victory boosted Protestant hopes, which had been dashed by the sack of Magdeburg.

On 15 September Gustavus Adolphus's army of 23,000 joined 16,000 soldiers from the Electorate of Saxony. Gustavus Adolphus was eager for a victory to convince other Protestant states to join him. Twenty-five miles (40 km) away in Leipzig, the imperial commander, Count Tilly, had an army of 35,000. On 17 September the two armies met on a plain near the village of Breitenfeld.

Tilly's army drew up with his infantry flanked by cavalry. Gustavus Adolphus formed up in a similar fashion, but kept his lines separate from the raw Saxon army, which occupied a position to the left of the Swedes. From noon to 2:00 PM there was an artillery exchange in which the

Swedish guns outnumbered those of the Catholics by fifty-one to twenty-seven. The Swedish cavalry moved to outflank their enemy, who in response launched a charge, which was unable to make any headway after two hours of fighting. Meanwhile, imperial forces attacked the Saxon army, which quickly fled the field. The rapid advance unsettled the imperial lines and the Swedish were able to reorder, creating a new left flank. At 5:00 PM Gustavus Adolphus launched a counterattack through the center. His highly trained troops forced back the imperial army, whose resistance ceased at dusk when thousands, including Tilly, fled the field. Gustavus Adolphus was thence feted as the "Lion of the North," and was able to draw several Protestant states into a major alliance. **JF**

Losses: Catholic, 7,000 dead, 6,000 surrendered on the field (and 3,000 the next day at Leipzig) of 35,000; Swedish, 2,100 of 23,000; Saxon, 3,000 of 16,000

◁ *Magdeburg 1630*   *Rain 1632* ▷

The First Battle of Breitenfeld, in a colored engraving by Matthäus Merian the Elder from 1637. ⬆

Rain (Lech)   15 April 1632

King Gustavus Adolphus of Sweden, the "Lion of the North," followed his triumph at Breitenfeld by again defeating the Catholics on the Lech River near Rain, Bavaria, in this battle of the Thirty Years' War. Rain was also the final battle of Count Tilly, the most famous Catholic general.

In March 1632 Gustavus Adolphus left his base at Mainz and, after capturing Donauwörth on 8 April, marched toward Bavaria. Standing in the way of his army of 37,500 was an imperial army commanded by Count Tilly.

Tilly had firmly entrenched his forces of 22,000 on the eastern bank of the Lech River. On 14 April Gustavus Adolphus drew up opposite Tilly's fortifications and commenced a sustained artillery bombardment. His intention was to provide cover for his planned crossing of the river 3 miles (5 km) to the south, as Tilly's position was too strong for a direct assault. The next day, Gustavus Adolphus sent a small unit of Finns across the river at this location by rowboat under cover of cannon barrage and a smokescreen of burning wet straw mixed with gunpowder. The men secured prefabricated bridge sections that had been floated across the river, allowing the rest of the army to cross and establish a bridgehead.

Tilly sent out forces to meet them and fierce fighting ensued. At 4:00 PM a squadron of elite Swedish cavalry arrived, having crossed the river farther to the south. The imperial army was now exposed to attack on both flanks. An hour later, Tilly was seriously wounded by artillery fire and command passed to the militarily inexperienced Elector of Bavaria, Maximilian I. With his position now terminal, Maximilian ordered a retreat.

Tilly died two weeks after the battle and Gustavus Adolphus was able to lead his army into Bavaria. **JF**

Losses: Catholic, 2,000 dead and 1,000 captured of 22,000; Swedish Protestant, 2,000 of 37,500

◁ First Breitenfeld 1631   Lützen 1632 ▷

The Battle of Rain depicted by Matthäus Merian the Elder in 1633, with the Lech River bisecting the battlefield.

Lützen   16 November 1632

The Battle of Lützen, near Leipzig, saw Sweden triumph over a Catholic army during the Thirty Years' War. However, the victory was Pyrrhic. The Swedes' famed commander, King Gustavus Adolphus, was killed during the battle, and the Protestant cause was robbed of its most dynamic strategist and inspirational figure.

In October 1632 the imperial commander Albrecht von Wallenstein invaded Saxony. On 14 November he decided to disperse his forces for winter. Wallenstein pulled back toward Leipzig with the bulk of his army, about 20,000, while 3,000 withdrew to Halle under the famed cavalry commander Count Pappenheim. When Gustavus Adolphus learned the imperial army had split, he decided to attack Wallenstein on 15 November. However, he lost the element of surprise when he met an advance imperial contingent and was forced to delay battle until the next day. Hearing of the Swedish approach, Wallenstein sent for Pappenheim, requesting his return.

Wallenstein rallied his troops near Lützen, drawing up with infantry flanked by cavalry. His position was parallel to the road to the village, which he fortified by widening the ditches around it and stationing musketeers there. The left wing was weak, but Wallenstein counted on Pappenheim's arrival to strengthen it. Gustavus Adolphus roused his army at 5:00 AM, planning an early attack, but it was delayed by heavy fog. The Swedish drew up with infantry in the center, with wings of cavalry on each side. Gustavus Adolphus personally commanded the horse on the right and Bernhard of Saxe-Weimar, a German general, led the left. At 11:00 AM the fog cleared and the Swedish advanced. Fifteen minutes later the Swedish right met the fortified road, which they took after thirty

minutes of fighting. The hilly terrain held up the Swedish left wing, but by noon their army had reformed and was on the offensive. At that time Pappenheim arrived with 2,300 cavalry (his infantry would follow later). This reinvigorated imperial efforts, and they launched a counterattack at 12:30 PM Pappenheim took command of the imperial left and charged the Swedish right; the attack was a success, although he was killed. The Swedish were now in difficulty across their line.

Gustavus Adolphus personally led a detachment of horse to relieve his infantry, and they were able to fall back and consolidate their position. At 1:00 PM Gustavus Adolphus charged into the gunsmoke and mist and lost most of his men. A group of imperial musketeers attacked him, and he was shot dead. At 1:30 PM the Swedish launched a counterattack, but when Gustavus Adolphus's body was found at 2:00 PM, their momentum stalled. It seemed that the imperial army was going to be victorious. Bernhard, now in command of the Swedish army, rallied his troops by telling them their king was not dead, only wounded. At 3:30 PM Bernhard ordered what would be the final Swedish attack. Wallenstein fought back by deploying his reserves, but his army was forced back and, as night fell at 5:00 PM, the fighting tapered off. At about that time Pappenheim's infantry reserves had arrived, but Wallenstein's only use for them was to guard the retreat of his exhausted army. The Swedish had won the day as Wallenstein later withdrew from Saxony into Bohemia, but in the long term the victory was no compensation for the loss of Gustavus Adolphus. **JF**

Losses: Swedish Protestant, 5,000–6,000 of 19,000; Catholic, 6,000 of 23,000

◁ *Rain 1632*   *Nördlingen 1634* ▷

Nördlingen 6 September 1634

The Spanish-imperial victory at Nördlingen forced the rebelling German Protestants to abandon their Swedish alliance and make peace with Emperor Ferdinand II. France, fearing Hapsburg dominance in Germany, entered the conflict, turning it from a religious war to a war between nation states.

The Protestant war effort had lost momentum after the death of Gustavus Adolphus at Lützen. The emperor's son, Ferdinand of Hungary, had led the imperial army to a series of successes. On 18 August he commenced the Siege of Nördlingen, Bavaria. Marching to join his well-entrenched forces was a Spanish army under Cardinal-Infante Fernando, the brother of Philip IV of Spain, who arrived on 2 September. The Protestant commanders, Field Marshal Gustav Horn of Sweden and Bernhard of Saxe-Weimar, decided to relieve Nördlingen.

On 5 September Horn and Bernhard attacked the hills overlooking the Spanish-imperial lines, capturing all but one. They were unable to take the most important hill, the Albuch, which blocked the route to the Spanish-imperial left flank. The main battle commenced on 6 September with a sustained Swedish bombardment, followed by an infantry charge on the Albuch. Horn's troops made good progress until a powder wagon exploded in their midst and crack Spanish troops launched a successful counterattack that forced them back to their original positions. On the other flank, Bernhard had also failed to break through. The Protestants retired and were pursued by cavalry. Horn himself was captured, along with thousands of other Protestant soldiers and most of their artillery and baggage. The Catholic victory was complete when Nördlingen surrendered soon after the battle. **JF**

Losses: Spanish-imperial, 1,500 dead and 2,000 wounded of 33,000; Swedish-German Protestant, 8,000 dead and 4,000 captured of 27,500

◁ *Lützen 1632* *Second Breitenfeld 1642* ▷

Protestants and Catholics clash outside the walls of Nördlingen, in a painting by Jacques Courtois (1621–76).

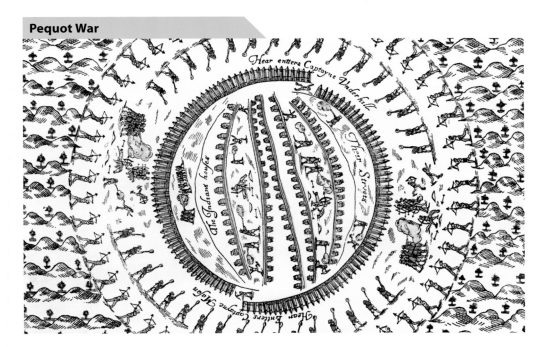

Mystic 26 May 1637

The murder of a slave trader in North America provoked English colonists and their American Indian allies into mounting a punitive attack. Falling upon defenseless villages along the Mystic River, they slaughtered hundreds of women, children, and elderly men in the "Mystic Massacre."

The Pequot people had made their homes in the valley of southern Connecticut's Thames River. Relations with the region's growing number of English colonists had been growing fractious for some time as the incomers expanded their area of settlement ever farther beyond their base on the shore of Massachusetts Bay.

In July 1636 slave trader John Oldham was killed when his ship was robbed by American Indian attackers—the finger of suspicion pointed to the Pequot. In the months that followed, Governor John Endicott raised a settlers' militia under the command of Captains John Mason and John Underhill. The Narragansett and Niantic—both

enemies of the Pequot—offered their support. Winter intervened, but on 26 May the English and their allies attacked the Pequot villages. Since the young men were in the field preparing to fight the settlers, only women, children, and elderly men remained at home, so the "Battle of Mystic" was a one-sided affair. Claims for the number of casualties range from 200 to 800 dead—a figure of 500 does not appear excessive.

Pequot survivors fled inland and hid out in swamps where, in the weeks that followed, they were hunted down while the young warriors waged an increasingly hopeless guerrilla war. The other Indian tribes in the area were intimidated into refusing them support; indeed, in the end it was they who finally defeated the rebels, killing the Pequot leader Sassacus and delivering his head in tribute to the English. **MK**

Losses: Pequot civilian, several hundred

Great Swamp Fight 1675 ▷

⬆ *Militia under Captain John Mason attack a large Pequot village, in a hand-colored woodcut.*

The Downs 31 October 1639

This encounter in the English Channel between Spain and the United Provinces during the Dutch Revolt was a famous victory for Dutch Admiral Maarten Tromp. Like Matanzas Bay, the Downs was symptomatic of Spain's naval decline and the rise of the Dutch as a major maritime power.

In an attempt to resupply its armies in Flanders by sea after the land route had been cut, Spain outfitted a fleet of sixty-seven ships carrying 24,000 soldiers and sailors, commanded by Antonio de Oquendo. The ships left Spain, bound for Dunkirk, at the end of August. Tromp's Dutch fleet engaged it on 25 September, inflicting serious damage. This forced Oquendo to seek shelter at the Downs, an anchorage on the English coast near Dover.

The Dutch government was reluctant to attack there, not wishing to offend England, so Tromp set up a blockade. However, the Spanish began to ferry supplies and soldiers from the Downs to Flanders using English

ships, so the Dutch could not allow the stalemate to continue. By 31 October, Tromp had a fleet of ninety-five warships and eleven fireships, and informed the English he planned to move against the Spanish. The English did not challenge the Dutch when they attacked.

Tromp launched a series of broadsides, forcing twenty Spanish ships to ground themselves to escape destruction. The rest of the Spanish tried to flee but were attacked by Dutch fireships and cannon. By nightfall, the Spanish fleet was in disarray, with many of its ships burned or destroyed, and only thanks to heavy fog cover was Oquendo able to reach Dunkirk with the remnants of his fleet. The Dutch had secured effective control of the Channel, further complicating Spain's land-war effort. **JF**

Losses: Spanish, 54 ships destroyed or captured of 67, more than 7,000 dead and 1,800 captured of 24,000; Dutch, 1 ship of 106 and 100 dead

◁ *Matanzas Bay 1628*　　　　　　　*Dover 1652* ▷

　　　The Battle of the Downs *(c. 1640) by Pieter Cornelisz Soest (c. 1642–67).* ⬆

Montjuïc 26 January 1641

Montjuïc was an early battle of the Catalan Revolt (1640–59) that saw a Spanish army repulsed from Barcelona. The defeat ended any likelihood that Philip IV and his chief minister, the Count-Duke of Olivares, would quickly crush the revolt, which eventually lasted nearly twenty years.

Engagement in the Thirty Years' War put tremendous pressure on all of Spain. The Catalonians felt particularly aggrieved, as they were forced to house soldiers. In 1640, after a period of social unrest, the Spanish viceroy was murdered and a Catalan Republic was declared. Olivares tried to raise an army to restore order but Spanish military resources were severely stretched.

He eventually succeeded in raising an army of 20,000, which invaded Catalonia at the end of 1640, marching toward Barcelona. Command was entrusted to the new viceroy of Catalonia, the Marquis of Los Vélez, a man of little military experience.

On 23 January 1641, Pau Claris, the president of Catalonia, proclaimed his allegiance to the French king, Louis XIII, who sent soldiers to help defend Barcelona.

After meeting little sustained resistance on his march, on 26 January Los Vélez approached the city walls. Francesc de Tamarit, the Catalan commander, had massed many his forces at the fortress on Montjuïc, a hill overlooking Barcelona. These included civic militia, irregular Catalan troops known as "Miquelets," and French soldiers. Surprisingly, Los Vélez ordered a direct assault on Montjuïc. The Spanish charged up the slope, but were continuously repulsed and took heavy, but not disastrous, casualties. Los Vélez, who had advanced without securing his supply chain, was now running low on provisions and faced a difficult struggle. He peremptorily ordered a retreat to Tarragona; the rebels had held Barcelona. **JF**

Losses: Spanish, 1,500 casualties of 20,000; Franco-Catalan, light casualties of 6,000

Battle rages at Montjuïc near the walls of Barcelona, in a painting by Pandolfo Reschi (1643–99).

Edgehill   23 October 1642

Religious and political differences between King Charles I and his opponents in Parliament broke out into open civil war in England in 1642. The first major battle was fought at Edgehill in the Midlands, although the result was inconclusive and neither side gained the upper hand.

On 22 August 1642, Charles I, realizing that war with his Parliamentary opponents was now inevitable, raised the royal standard at Nottingham. He then headed west into more favorable Royalist territory at Shrewsbury, where he raised an army. Parliament too raised an army, under the Earl of Essex. As Charles headed south toward London, he encountered the Parliamentary army in south Warwickshire and issued orders to his troops to prepare for battle on top of the Edgehill escarpment.

The Parliamentary army drew up on lower ground to the north. The Royalist cavalry was superior, but the Parliamentary infantry was better equipped. After an ineffective opening artillery duel, the Royalist cavalry leader, Prince Rupert of the Rhine, attacked. His cavalry charge prompted one Parliamentary troop to change sides and forced another off the field. Rupert gave chase as the Royalist infantry then advanced, to be met by two Parliamentary infantry brigades that stood their ground. Cavalry then emerged through their ranks and charged the Royalist infantry. With Rupert still giving chase away from the battlefield, they swept the Royalist infantry. Having no reserve and with his center collapsing, Charles I withdrew, temporarily losing his standard.

Both sides held their positions overnight, but neither side wanted to resume fire the next day. Charles headed southward to establish his headquarters in Oxford while Essex headed back to London. **SA**

Losses: Royalist, 2,000 casualties of 12,400; Parliamentary, 2,000 casualties of 15,000

Newbury 1643 ▷

Second Breitenfeld   2 Nov 1642

France's formal entry into the Thirty Years' War after Nördlingen did not fatally weaken the cause of the Hapsburg Empire. However, the tide turned at the Second Battle of Breitenfeld, when the Swedish army won a major victory over an imperial army, enabling the Swedes to occupy Saxony.

In command of the Swedish forces was Lennart Torstensson. He had risen from a royal page to the rank of field marshal, and was the finest artillery commander of his day. The imperial commander was Archduke Leopold Wilhelm, Emperor Ferdinand III's brother. Torstensson had marched into Saxony and besieged Leipzig to force the imperial army to meet him in battle. The plan worked, and the two armies met at Breitenfeld, on the same plain where Gustavus Adolphus had triumphed in 1631.

At dawn on 2 November both armies drew up with infantry in the center, flanked by cavalry. At around 10:00 AM both forces of infantry at the center advanced to around 90 yards (82 m) of each other and exchanged small arms fire. The Swedish cavalry made significant headway against the imperial left wing, which quickly collapsed. On the other flank the imperial horses had been more successful and repulsed the Swedish charge. However, at 11:30 AM Torstensson led a cavalry charge from the Swedish right wing that swung around and smashed into the imperial right flank from the rear, devastating their position. Meanwhile, both sides threw reserves into the center, which quickly became a fierce hand-to-hand struggle. By 1:30 PM, after a series of sustained attacks, the Swedish infantry was able to finally triumph over the stubborn imperial army. Torstensson went on to capture Leipzig, but he did not follow up his victory with a major offensive into Bavaria. **JF**

Losses: Swedish, 4,000 casualties of 20,000; Imperial, up to 5,000 casualties and 5,000 captured of 26,000

◁ Nördlingen 1634   Rocroi 1643 ▷

Rocroi 19 May 1643

After France declared war on Spain and the Hapsburg Empire in 1635, a new theater opened in the Thirty Years' War around Flanders. At Rocroi, the young Duke of Enghien, later Prince of Condé, won his first victory, defeating the Spanish *tercios* formations that had long been in the ascendant.

Despite the triumph of its ally Sweden at the Second Battle of Breitenfeld, France found itself in a vulnerable position in 1643. Louis XIII had died on 14 May, leaving his four-year-old son, Louis XIV, as king. On 15 May the Spanish, led by the Portuguese nobleman Francisco de Melo, besieged the town of Rocroi, in the Ardennes. Late on 18 May, Enghien deployed his army on a plain near the town. De Melo set his army out opposite, both of them lining up with foot soldiers in the center flanked by cavalry.

During the night, Spain had slipped 1,000 musketeers into woods on their left flank, hoping to surprise any French cavalry charge. However, a Spanish deserter informed Enghien of this and he destroyed them in the early hours of 19 May. At 5:00 AM the main battle began with a French cavalry charge. The French left wing was routed and the Spanish cavalry wheeled around against the infantry in the center. On the other flank the French were more successful. Enghien was able to divide his right into two parts, one to pursue the Spanish left and the other to attack their right and center. This plan worked with stunning success.

By 8:00 AM all of the Spanish cavalry had been dispersed and their only coherent formation was their central infantry. After two hours of heavy fighting the defiant Spanish foot soldiers finally gave way, and Enghien was able to relieve Rocroi. **JF**

Losses: French, 2,000 dead and 2,500 wounded of 21,000; Spanish, 5,000 dead and 5,000 captured of 23,000

◁ *Second Breitenfeld 1642*   *Freiburg 1644* ▷

Newbury 20–21 September 1643

In the summer of 1643 King Charles I still hoped for a speedy and decisive victory over Parliament in the civil war in England. A pitched battle at Newbury, however, showed how tenacious the Parliamentarian forces could be and how costly victory was going to be, whichever side won.

The Royalists besieged Gloucester, and a Parliamentary army under the Earl of Essex marched to relieve the city. King Charles and his cavalry commander, Prince Rupert, saw an opportunity to block Essex's route back to London. In a race to reach Newbury, the Royalists won by a few hours, on 19 September taking up a position that cut off the London road.

Essex's exhausted and hungry men lay in the open fields all night. The Royalists, however, carelessly allowed them to occupy Round Hill, a dominant feature among the hedges and farmland. The following morning the Royalists attacked. Their cavalry launched charge after charge, but the Parliamentary musket-and-pike infantry resisted unflinchingly, supported by well-handled field artillery. The militia of the London Trained Bands, inspired by their commander Philip Skippon, especially distinguished themselves. The fighting lasted twelve hours and was a murderous business. One sergeant of the Trained Bands recalled that as cannon fired on their ranks, "men's bowels and brains flew in our faces." The king's secretary of state, Viscount Falkland, was killed by a musket ball in the stomach as he charged through a gap in a hedge. He may have sought his own death, horrified by the butchery of the war. By nightfall the Royalists were out of gunpowder. They had no choice but to quit the field, leaving Essex to continue toward London the following day, where he and his men were greeted as heroes. **CP**

Losses: Royalist, 2,000 dead of 14,000; Parliamentary, 1,500 dead of 14,000

◁ *Edgehill 1642*   *Marston Moor 1644* ▷

Fall of Beijing April–June 1644

By the 1640s Ming China was disintegrating, racked by peasant revolts and regional rebellions. In April 1644 rebel warlord Li Zicheng captured Beijing and overthrew the Ming, but before the year's end the city fell again, this time to Manchu invaders who were destined to inherit power in China.

Li Zicheng, a former soldier in the Ming army, had built up a large following over more than a decade's rebel activity in Shaanxi province, northwestern China. In spring 1664 he led a mass advance on Beijing, laying waste cities along his route and attracting thousands more of the disaffected to his banner. Most of the Ming soldiers who should have opposed him defected to his side.

When he reached Beijing, the city's gates were opened by traitors within. The last Ming emperor, Chongzhen, hanged himself from a tree in the imperial garden. Seeking to consolidate his hold on power, Li then marched out of Beijing to meet in battle the Ming loyalist general Wu Sangui. General Wu was guarding the Shanhaiguan pass on the Great Wall, beyond which lay territory dominated by the Manchu horsemen and their armies, organized under banners rather than by clans.

As Li approached, Wu decide to ally himself with the Manchu—partly, it is said, because Li had taken one of Wu's favorite concubines. Wu's army halted the advance of Li's forces, and then Wu and the Manchu leader Dorgon together marched on Beijing. Li's followers lacked discipline and morale, pillaging the city rather than organizing its defenses. On 4 June they marched away westward, loaded with loot, and two days later Wu and the Manchu entered the city. A new dynasty, the Manchu Qing, was founded. Manchu forces hunted Li down, until in summer 1645 he died, probably by suicide. **RG**

Losses: No reliable figures

◁ Ningyuan 1626   Yangzhou 1645 ▷

Marston Moor 2 July 1644

Two years after the outbreak of civil war in England, King Charles I was on the defensive in the north. A Royalist army was besieged in York by a Parliamentary army now supported by Scottish allies. The decisive battle, fought outside York, gave Parliament full control of the north.

In spring 1644 a Royalist army led by the Marquis of Newcastle headed south to York, where it was soon besieged by a joint Parliamentary and Scottish force led by Sir Thomas Fairfax and the Earl of Leven. Charles I ordered his nephew, Prince Rupert of the Rhine, to take forces and relieve the siege. Rupert's advance caused the Parliamentary army to break the siege and head out to meet the advancing Royalist army.

The two sides met at Marston Moor, 7 miles (11 km) from York. Both sides had around 7,000 cavalry, but the 11,000 Royalist infantry were easily outnumbered by the 20,000 combined Parliamentary and Scottish infantry. The two sides drew up with infantry in the middle and cavalry on either wing. A short artillery exchange at around 2:00 PM produced no movement, leading Prince Rupert to believe that battle would not be joined until the next day. At 7:30 PM, however, Parliamentary forces attacked during a thunderstorm. A cavalry troop led by Oliver Cromwell—later nicknamed "Ironside" by Prince Rupert, a name that was then applied to his troops—attacked and defeated the Royalist cavalry on their right wing. On their other wing the Royalist cavalry, led by Lord George Goring, held back a Parliamentary cavalry charge and then smashed the Scottish infantry. Cromwell responded by turning in to attack Goring's cavalry in their rear, after which his cavalry helped the Parliamentary infantry to crush the Royalist center. **SA**

Losses: Parliamentary and Scottish, 2,000 of 27,000; Royalist, 4,150 of 18,000

◁ Newbury 1643   Naseby 1645 ▷

A wounded Cromwell directs his troops at Marston Moor, in an 1817 painting by Abraham Cooper. ➔

Freiburg   3, 5, and 9 August 1644

The struggle for the city of Freiburg in 1644 between French and Bavarian-imperial armies was one of the bloodiest and longest battles of the Thirty Years' War. Although the French suffered heavier casualties, they forced a retreat and went on to gain mastery of the middle Rhine region.

Following the French victory at Rocroi, preliminary peace talks had begun in 1643, but fighting carried on regardless. In the summer of 1644, the Bavarian-imperial armies—under Field Marshal Franz von Mercy—had gone on the offensive in the Rhine and taken the French stronghold of Freiburg (in present-day Germany) on 29 July. The commander of the French armies in Germany was Henri, Viscount of Turenne, an experienced soldier. Joining him to help retake Freiburg was Belgium's Duke of Enghien. Together they commanded 20,000, outnumbering von Mercy by 3,500.

Von Mercy's cavalry was in poor condition so he decided to conduct an infantry-based defense on the earthworks and wooded high ground around Freiburg. At 5:00 PM on 3 August, the French launched a frontal assault against the first line of von Mercy's fortifications. The French ended the day in control of the field, but had taken heavy casualties. Von Mercy pulled his forces back and they were able to entrench their new positions on 4 August because the French were exhausted.

On 5 August the French attacked but they were again forced back at the cost of 4,000 killed or wounded. Von Mercy's army was too tired to counterattack and Enghien called on reinforcements of 5,000. The French moved to attack Freiburg again on 9 August. Von Mercy, sensing the danger, withdrew and was able to retreat without any great losses under pressure from the French. **JF**

"In twenty-two years of my bloody trade I have never seen such a slaughter."

Jan van Werth, commander of the Bavarian cavalry

⬆ *Detail from an oil painting of the Battle of Freiburg by Sauveur Le Conte (1659–94).*

Losses: French, 7,000–8,000 of 25,000; Bavarian-Imperial, 2,500 of 16,500

◁ Rocroi 1643   Jankov 1645 ▷

Jankov 6 March 1645

Following the Battle of Freiburg, the imperial cause in the Thirty Years' War was desperate. France consolidated its position in the Rhine and its ally Sweden advanced into Bohemia in 1645. At Jankov, a decisive Swedish victory over an imperial army opened the way to threatening Hapsburg Vienna.

Swedish field marshal Lennart Torstensson had led his army into Bohemia. The imperial commander, Melchior von Hatzfeld, moved his army to block them at Jankov. Hatzfeld occupied a strong position, although he was vulnerable on his left, which was dominated by high ground. At 6:00 AM on 6 March, the Swedish army feinted toward the imperial right. Hatzfeld left his command position to examine the threat. In his absence the imperial left wing advanced toward the Swedish on the higher ground, where they were torn apart by musket fire. At 11:30 AM the imperial army fell back and assumed a defensive position, hoping to retreat at sunset.

When Torstensson realized that the imperial force had not completely left the field, he ordered an assault. At 1:00 PM he launched an artillery attack and then engaged the imperial center, which held firm. The Swedish devastated the imperial cavalry on the right flank, but on the other wing the imperial horses achieved great success, advancing to the Swedish baggage train. When looting ensued, the Swedish were able to regroup and scatter the horsemen. The imperial infantry were now isolated and their resistance collapsed by 4:00 PM.

The Swedish army took thousands of prisoners, including Hatzfeld, and Torstensson crossed into Austria. However, he was unable to capture Vienna because his exhausted army had run out of supplies, and he withdrew in December. **JF**

Losses: Swedish, 2,000 dead and 2,000 wounded of 16,000; Imperial, 4,000 dead and 4,500 captured of 16,000

◁ Freiburg 1644   Zusmarshausen 1648 ▷

Yangzhou May 1645

The Fall of Beijing in 1644 was followed by years of costly warfare, as the newly victorious Manchu fought to extend their rule over all of China. The siege of the city of Yangzhou was among the bloodiest episodes in the large-scale conflicts that preceded the establishment of the Qing dynasty.

When the Manchu declared the Qing dynasty rulers in Beijing, officials loyal to the Ming set up an alternative administration in China's old capital, Nanjing. A member of the Ming family, the prince of Fu, was named Emperor Hongguang. In response the Manchu sent a vast army under Prince Dodo—a son of the original Manchu leader Nurhaci—south from Beijing, following the Grand Canal toward Nanjing. In their path stood the prosperous commercial city of Yangzhou, and loyalist Ming general Shi Kefa persuaded his soldiers to defend the city.

Prince Dodo had brought with him a train of siege guns, but Shi also lined the city walls with cannon. The Manchu made furious assaults on the walls, suffering heavy casualties. It is said that after a week the bodies were piled so high outside the walls that Manchu soldiers were able to climb on top of the dead and from there onto the battlements. Once the Manchu had entered the city, resistance soon ceased. Prince Dodo unleashed his men upon the city's population for ten days. According to traditional accounts, 800,000 people were killed in the terrible massacre that followed, although this figure must certainly be highly exaggerated. Shi Kefa was executed after refusing to join the Manchu. Intimidated by the example of the massacre at Yangzhou, Nanjing surrendered almost without a fight. Emperor Hongguang fled, but was captured and executed in 1646. **RG**

Losses: Manchu, unknown; Ming, unknown, 800,000 civilians dead

◁ Fall of Beijing 1644   Nanjing 1659 ▷

Naseby   14 June 1645

The English civil war between king and Parliament reached its climax at Naseby in June 1645. Parliament's New Model Army scored a convincing victory, dashing Royalist hopes. Within a year the king, Charles I, was a prisoner of his enemies.

Soldiers on both sides of the conflict were largely inexperienced, with only their officers having had some exposure in Europe to warfare. Despite several Parliamentary victories, its army was unable to deliver the knockout blow required to end the war. In January 1645 Oliver Cromwell proposed to Parliament that a new army be set up, modeled loosely on his Ironsides, who first saw success at Marston Moor. The New Model Army was to be raised through conscription and paid for by taxation. Around 22,000 strong, its infantry would consist of twelve regiments and 14,000 men; the cavalry, eleven regiments and 6,600 men; and 1,000 dragoons or mounted infantry. All these men were to be properly trained and dressed in a red uniform, the first time the famous "redcoat"

> *"I wish this action may beget thankfulness and humility in all that are concerned in it."*
>
> Cromwell reports the victory at Naseby to Parliament

was seen on the battlefield. This new professional force overcame the reluctance of the local militias to fight outside their own counties, and soon became a highly mobile, motivated army.

After a brief truce over the winter, the war resumed in May 1645 when the Royalists captured Leicester. The New Model Army under Sir Thomas Fairfax ended its siege of the Royalist stronghold of Oxford and moved north to challenge the Royalist army, where Cromwell's cavalry joined it. The two sides met near Naseby, south of Leicester. As at Edgehill, the Royalists, led by Prince Rupert of the Rhine, the king's nephew, drew up on a ridge, the Parliamentary forces taking lower ground to their south. Again, as before at Marston Moor, both sides placed their infantry in the center with cavalry on both flanks, the Parliamentary dragoons hiding behind a hedge to the left. The land between the two sides was waterlogged, so Cromwell advised Fairfax to withdraw to higher ground. Mistaking this movement, Prince Rupert decided to attack. His cavalry on the Royalist right flank broke though the cavalry and dragoons on the Parliamentary left flank but instead of turning back to confront the infantry, rode on in pursuit of the enemy cavalry, just as Rupert had so impetuously led them to do at Edgehill. The Royalist infantry then overwhelmed the Parliamentary infantry.

At this point, Oliver Cromwell stepped in with a decisive move to exploit Rupert's reckless blunder. With Rupert's cavalry off the field, Cromwell's cavalry carried out a disciplined charge against the Royalist left flank that broke through their cavalry. He then charged the Royalist infantry in the center, who were also under attack from the remnants of the Parliamentary cavalry and dragoons from the left flank. Many of them surrendered, while Rupert's returning cavalry refused to reengage.

After Charles was dissuaded from risking his reserves, he fled to Leicester. The outcome was decisive. Within months, the remaining Royalist strongholds in the south and west of England fell to Parliamentary forces, while Charles's army met its final defeat not far from Oxford. On 5 May 1646, Charles surrendered, circumspectly handing himself over not to Parliament but to its Scottish allies, in the hope of dividing his opponents and saving his skin. The first civil war between king and Parliament was thus brought to an end. **SA**

Losses: Parliamentary, 400 of 13,500; Royalist, 1,000 dead and 5,000 captured of 8,000

◁ *Marston Moor 1644*   *Preston 1648* ▷

The Roundheads of Cromwell and Fairfax face Charles I's Royalist army at Naseby. ➔

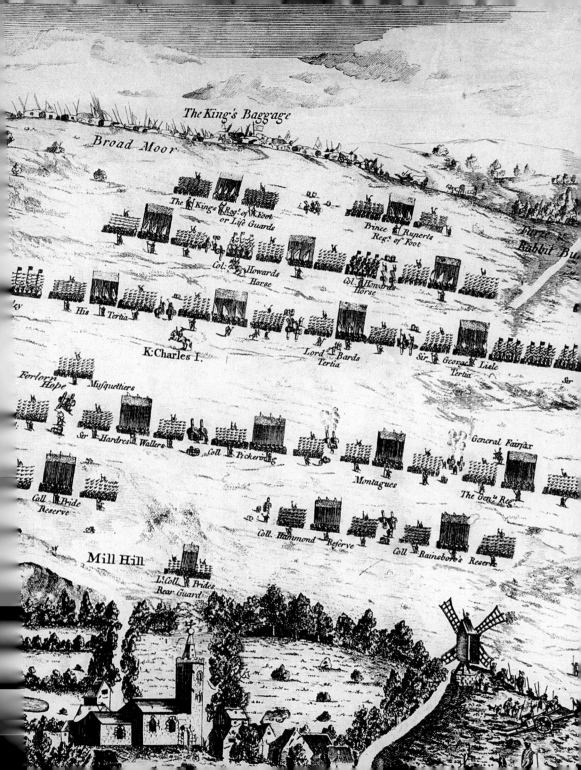

The King's Baggage

Broad Moor

The Kings Reg.t of Foot
or Life Guards

Prince Ruperts
Reg.t of Foot

Burze
Rabbit Bu

Col: Howards Horse

Col: Howards
Horse

His Tertia

K: Charles I.

Lord Bards
Tertia

Sir George Lisle
Tertia

Sir

Forlorn
Hope

Musquettiers

Sir Hardres Wallers

Coll Pickering

General Fairfax

Montagues

The Gen.l Reg

Coll Pride
Reserve

Coll. Hammond Reserve

Coll Rainsbro's Reserve

Mill Hill

L.Coll Prides
Rear Guard

Kilsyth 15 August 1645

After the Battle of Naseby, the Royalist cause in England had effectively collapsed. However, in Scotland the Royalists enjoyed a major victory at Kilsyth over the Presbyterian Covenanters. This military success marked the height of Royalist fortunes in Scotland during the British civil wars.

In April 1644 the Marquis of Montrose led a Royalist uprising in Scotland against the Covenanters, the Presbyterian faction allied with the English Parliament that had ruled there since 1639. Drawing on forces from the Scottish Highlands and Ireland, Montrose won a series of victories. The beleaguered Covenanter armies at Perth had an experienced general in William Baillie, but his orders were subject to advisement from the Committee of Estates, a body of Presbyterian noblemen and clergy. Marching to join them from Glasgow was an army of 1,500 led by the Earl of Lanark.

When Montrose's army marched south from its camp at Dunkeld, Baillie was ordered to intercept. On 14 August Montrose camped near Kilsyth. Baillie arrived the next day and deployed his men on the high ground overlooking the Royalists. He wanted to wait for Lanark's reinforcements but the Committee ordered him to immediately flank around the Royalist army to prevent it from escaping. As they marched, fighting broke out on Montrose's left flank. Troops from both sides weighed in and Montrose launched a devastating cavalry charge. The Covenanter lines broke under the onslaught, taking heavy casualties. Montrose marched to Glasgow and summoned a parliament in the name of the king, and the Covenanter leaders fled to England. However, a month later Montrose was routed at Philiphaugh and the Covenanters were able to regain control of Scotland. **JF**

Losses: Covenanter, 5,000 of 7,500; Royalist, negligible of 5,000

◁ Naseby 1645   Preston 1648 ▷

Zusmarshausen 17 May 1648

Zusmarshausen was one of the last major battles of the Thirty Years' War. The retreating imperial army narrowly avoided annihilation at the hands of a French-Swedish army. This, and later setbacks at Lens and Prague, forced Emperor Ferdinand III to come to terms in October 1648, ending the war.

Since the Battle of Jankov, the imperial cause appeared hopeless. However, in 1648 they still had one significant army in the Rhine, commanded by Peter Melander, a Calvinist peasant who had risen through the ranks to become a field marshal.

Despite being joined by a Bavarian contingent, Melander faced the prospect of fighting a larger French-Swedish force, so he decided to retreat to Augsburg. His large baggage train and the rough forest terrain slowed progress. Pursuing him were the allied forces of France and Sweden, commanded by the Viscount of Turenne and Gustav von Wrangel, respectively.

At 7:00 AM on 17 May the French-Swedish army engaged the imperial rearguard of cavalry near Zusmarshausen, two hours later forcing them to make a final stand. Turenne launched a frontal assault while Wrangel swung round to attack from the rear. In the fighting Melander, who had arrived with reinforcements, was shot dead. Wrangel and Turenne then advanced to capture the imperial baggage train. This, and the rearguard action, gave the imperial survivors enough time to escape across the Schmutter River and destroy the bridge. The Bavarians formed a solid defensive position and were able to force back an attempted river crossing by the French-Swedish force. The pursuit was broken. Melander had saved his army at the cost of his life, but the French and Swedish still went on to overrun Bavaria. **JF**

Losses: French-Swedish, negligible of 25,200; Bavarian-Imperial, 2,200 of 18,000

◁ Jankov 1645

Preston   17–19 August 1648

In war, victors often fall out among themselves. Two years after the end of the English civil war, the victorious Parliamentary army took on its former allies, the Scots, at Preston. The battle was to become yet another famous victory for Parliamentary commander Oliver Cromwell.

After the Battle of Naseby in June 1645 and subsequent Parliamentary victories, Charles I surrendered to the Scots on 5 May 1646. He hoped to negotiate with them alone, splitting them from their Parliamentary allies. His plans did not work out, however, and in January 1647 the Scots handed over the king to Parliament in return for £400,000. Oliver Cromwell and the army offered the king a peace deal but he refused it, escaping to the Isle of Wight in November. There he concluded a deal with the Scots that would put him back on his throne.

The following July a Scottish army invaded England in the king's support. Led by the Duke of Hamilton, it moved south through Lancashire, prompting Cromwell to head north from Wales to meet it. The two sides were ill-matched, the Scots having 18,000 men to Cromwell's 8,600, but neither side could field artillery—Cromwell had marched too fast for his guns to keep up with his army. Crucially, the Scots were poorly equipped, commandeering horses on route to carry their ammunition, and their units straggled over more than 50 miles (80 km). On 17 August Cromwell pounced on the Scottish advance guard on the road into Preston and seized the town. The next day he attacked the rest of the Scottish army in hand-to-hand fighting, both sides relying on the skills of their pikemen. Totally outmaneuvered, the Scots fled, surrendering to Cromwell at Warrington on 19 August. The second civil war was now over. **SA**

"There came no band of your foot to fight that day but did it with incredible valor and resolution."

Cromwell, in his report of Preston to Parliament

⬆ *Detail from* The Battle of Preston and Walton, August 17th, 1648, *a watercolor by Charles Cattermole, 1877.*

Losses: Parliamentary, 100 of 8,600; Scottish, 2,000 dead, 9,000 captured of 18,000

◀ Kilsyth 1645   Rathmines 1649 ▶

Guararapes 18 February 1649

Despite their loss of Bahia in 1625, the Dutch extended their presence in Brazil, with Recife in the Pernambuco region as their principal city. But an insurrection of Portuguese colonists, black former slaves, and American Indians ended the prospect of a future Dutch Protestant Brazil.

The revolt against Dutch rule in Pernambuco broke out in 1645. Portuguese landowners, partly provoked by Dutch-imposed restrictions on their Catholic worship, assembled an army of 1,800 men under João Fernandes Vieira. They were joined by a column of 330 black former slaves fighting under a black captain, Henrique Dias, himself the son of slaves. There were also some 400 American Indian fighters under a tribal leader given the name Felipe Camarão. Portugal, asserting its independence after sixty years of Spanish rule, backed the rebellion, providing covert help that included 150 soldiers.

The rebels were better adapted to fighting in the jungles and swamps of Pernambuco's Guararapes hills than the Dutch, who stuck to strictly European tactics. In 1648 a force of more than 4,000 Dutch soldiers with cannon marched south from Recife in search of the insurgents. Beaten in an initial clash in April, they retired to a defensive position across the coastal road to Recife. Using forest paths, the insurgents outflanked these prepared defenses and, on 18 February 1649, launched a full-scale attack. Appearing from unexpected directions, firing their muskets from the cover of trees, and making rushes forward to stab and slash with their short swords and knives, they routed the nervous and demoralized Dutch troops. The Dutch soldiers scuttled back to Recife, from which they were finally evicted after a Portuguese naval blockade in 1654. **CP**

Losses: Dutch, 1,500 casualties of 4,000; Insurgent, unknown

◁ Salvador da Bahia 1625

Rathmines 2 August 1649

The execution of English king Charles I in January 1649 and the establishment of a republic by the English Parliament led to a pro-Royalist revolt in Ireland. The first battle took place at Rathmines, just outside Dublin. It was the precursor of a bloody campaign to come.

Irish Catholics had been at war with their king, the Protestant Charles I, since 1641 in a conflict that predated the English civil war. With the king's execution, the Catholics and their Protestant Royalist opponents put aside their differences to fight on behalf of the crown against the new English republic.

A Royalist leader, James Butler, First Duke of Ormond, marched toward Dublin in order to seize the city from English control. However, he was not expecting the English commander, Michael Jones, to march out to meet him and had not drawn up his troops for battle. The attack on 2 August came as a complete surprise. Thrown back toward their camp in great confusion, Ormond and his commanders responded by sending individual units into the attack in order to hold up the English advance. Jones's cavalry outflanked each advancing force, driving the Royalists south through Rathmines. The battle soon became a rout as the fleeing Royalists were picked off by the pursuing English. The battle was finally ended by a rearguard action by the Royalist Earl of Inchiquin that allowed the remnants of his army to escape.

After the battle, Ormond withdrew from Dublin, allowing Oliver Cromwell and 15,000 battle-hardened English troops to land there unopposed in order to quell the rebellion. Cromwell described the victory at Rathmines as "an astonishing mercy," but he was to show no mercy to the Irish in the months to come. **SA**

Losses: English, few of 5,000; Irish Royalist, 3,000 dead and 2,500 captured of 11,000

◁ Preston 1648   Drogheda 1649 ▷

Drogheda   11 September 1649

Cromwell *taking* Tredagh *by Storm*

"[A] judgment of God upon these barbarous wretches, who have imbrued their hands in so much innocent blood." Cromwell, after Drogheda

↑ *This elegant depiction of Cromwell taking Drogheda (here Anglicized as "Tredagh") gives no hint of the butchery to come.*

The Royalist rebellion that broke out in Ireland against the new English republic in 1649 was met by a prompt English response. On 15 August Oliver Cromwell and 15,000 troops landed in Dublin. His merciless policy toward the Irish Royalists would become brutally clear within a month.

The defeat of the Irish Royalists at Rathmines in early August was fortuitous for Cromwell, for without it, the English would have held only the small port of Derry (known as Londonderry from 1662) in the north, making his invasion almost impossible to effect. Cromwell quickly found that the Irish Royalists had retreated into fortified towns. He therefore prepared for a series of sieges.

The first occurred at Drogheda, 28 miles (45 km) north of Dublin. The town was surrounded by high, thick walls and its governor, Sir Arthur Ashton, was confident of his defenses and refused an order to surrender. On 10 September Cromwell began an artillery bombardment of the walls. These were breached the next day, but the gap created was too small to allow troops to enter the city. Twice they were repelled until Cromwell himself led an assault and overwhelmed the defenders.

The carnage inside the city was appalling. Cromwell's troops killed priests and monks on sight and set light to a Catholic church sheltering some soldiers. Civilians as well as soldiers were massacred, and Ashton was bludgeoned to death with his own wooden leg. The few Royalist soldiers who survived were transported to Barbados. What happened at Drogheda was replicated at Wexford the following month and Clonmel the next May. By the time Cromwell had put down the rebellion and returned to England in that same month, he had become forever hated by Irish Catholics. **SA**

Losses: English, 150 of 12,000; Irish, 2,800 dead and 200 captured of 3,100

◁ Rathmines 1649   Dunbar 1650 ▷

Dunbar   3 September 1650

The execution of King Charles I and the establishment of a republic in England in 1649 led to a Royalist revolt in Scotland, as it had in Ireland. Two months after returning from crushing the Irish rebellion in May 1650, Oliver Cromwell was pressed into service to suppress its Scottish counterpart.

Incensed by the execution of their king by the English Parliament, the Scots declared for Charles's successor, his eldest son Charles II. On 22 July 1650 Cromwell headed north with 16,000 men to preempt a Scottish invasion. The canny Scottish commander, General David Leslie, although he had a larger force, avoided direct confrontation. Cromwell soon lost 5,000 men to sickness and was forced to withdraw to the east coast port of Dunbar, where the English fleet could reinforce him.

The Scots pursued Cromwell and took up position above the port on Doon Hill, trapping Cromwell's army between themselves and the sea. On 2 September Leslie led his men down the hill to prepare for an attack the next day. Only a narrow ravine separated the two sides. Cromwell took the initiative and, under cover of darkness, ordered his men across the ravine to launch a surprise attack at daylight. Leslie was caught unprepared, having ordered almost all his musketeers to extinguish their matches. The Scots resisted well at first, but then Cromwell noticed that the cavalry on the Scottish right wing was cramped between the ravine and the hill behind it. He launched his reserve cavalry against this force, pressing the horsemen back onto their own infantry. Losing formation, the Scots were soon routed, retreating north to Stirling and leaving Cromwell in control of southern Scotland. Dunbar is often considered to be the greatest of Cromwell's victories. **SA**

Losses: English, 30 of 11,000; Scottish, 3,000 dead and 9,000 captured of 20,000

◁ Drogheda 1649   Worcester 1651 ▷

Berestczko   28 June–10 July 1651

The Ukraine was part of the Polish-Lithuanian Commonwealth. In 1648 the Ukrainian Cossack leader Bohdan Khmelnytsky led a revolt against the Commonwealth, only to suffer heavy losses at Berestczko in one of the largest European battles of the seventeenth century.

In June 1651 King John II Casimir Vasa's Commonwealth army faced Khmelnytsky at Berestczko. Khmelnytsky's army, joined by Tatars led by Khan Islam III Giray of Crimea, vastly outnumbered the Commonwealth forces. However, the Commonwealth army was better trained and equipped than the Cossack army, which included large numbers of peasant volunteers.

Fighting started on 28 June, and carried on to the next day. Numerous closely fought cavalry charges produced no decisive result. On the evening of 29 June the Khan harangued Khmelnytsky for not warning him of the numbers and expertise of the Commonwealth forces. On 30 June the Commonwealth cavalry pierced the Cossack ranks, causing chaos. The Commonwealth infantry, supported by artillery, then advanced with great success. At this point the Khan fled with his army, with Khmelnytsky trying to persuade the Khan to return. After waiting under siege for more than a week for a sight of Khmelnytsky, the Cossacks decided to retreat under cover of darkness. The regular forces departed, and when day broke the peasants realized they had been abandoned and rioted. At this point the Commonwealth army attacked the camp and butchered many of those remaining.

In September Khmelnytsky was forced to sign a peace treaty with the Commonwealth but the next year he rallied his armies again and eventually managed to secure virtual independence for the Ukrainian Cossacks. **JF**

Losses: Polish-Lithuanian, minimal of up to 60,000; Cossack-Tatar, 40,000 of 150,000

Warsaw 1656 ▷

Worcester   3 September 1651

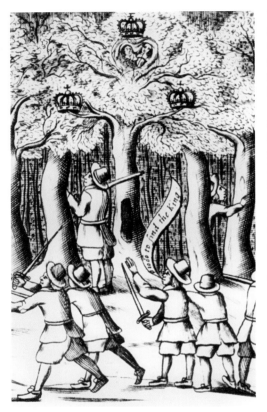

The long-drawn-out conflict between Royalists and their opponents across the British Isles, which had started in Scotland in 1639 and spread to Ireland and then England by 1642, finally came to an end at Worcester in 1651. It was a scrappy battle, but it ensured the survival of the English republic.

Oliver Cromwell's defeat of the Scots at Dunbar in 1650 had not ended the threat from Scotland. In June 1651, after a lengthy illness had halted his campaign, Cromwell headed north to threaten the Scottish stronghold of Stirling. He deliberately left open the road to England. The new king, Charles II, fell into the trap. At the head of the Scottish army, he marched south down the west coast. Cromwell ordered Lieutenant-General John Lambert's cavalry troop to follow him, ordered a second force to move across country from Newcastle to Warrington, and a third, militia from the midlands, to move north.

Once he had taken Perth, Cromwell led his main army south down the east coast, covering around 20 miles (32 km) a day and collecting reinforcements as he went. All four English armies then converged on the Scots at Worcester. The Scots were hopelessly outnumbered, their 16,000 troops facing 30,000 English, of whom 20,000 were well-trained and disciplined members of the New Model Army. The initial English assault from the south and east of the town pushed the Scots back toward Worcester. Stubborn Scottish resistance in the south forced Cromwell to send reinforcements, leaving his east flank exposed. Charles ordered two sorties to exploit this weakness, which was quickly filled by Cromwell's return. English troops were then able to push the Scots back into Worcester, soon capturing the city itself. The Royalist cause lost, Charles fled into exile in France. **SA**

"The dimensions of this mercy are above my thoughts. It is, for aught I know, a crowning mercy."

Cromwell, in his report of the battle to Parliament

⬆ *In a 1660 engraving, Charles II is shown hiding in an oak tree at Boscobel after his defeat at the Battle of Worcester.*

Losses: English, 200 of 30,000; Scottish, 3,000 dead and at least 10,000 captured of 16,000

◁ *Dunbar 1650*

Dover (Goodwin Sands) 29 May 1652

The first of many battles between the English and Dutch fleets was triggered by a question of etiquette: should the Dutch dip their flag to the English? Two fiery admirals—Maarten Tromp and Robert Blake— found this sufficient pretext to launch a twenty-year struggle for naval supremacy.

The background to the Battle of Dover lay in mounting commercial rivalry between the Dutch, established European leaders in merchant shipping, and the English under Oliver Cromwell's Commonwealth, keen to seize their own share of wealth from maritime trade. In 1651 the English government passed the Navigation Acts, insisting that goods imported to England must be carried in English ships. A campaign of harassment was launched against Dutch merchant ships. As part of the assertion of English naval power, Cromwell ordained that all foreign vessels in the North Sea and Channel should dip their flag to English ships, in acknowledgement that these were English waters.

On 29 May 1652 a fleet of warships under General-at-Sea Robert Blake encountered a Dutch merchant fleet escorted by warships under the command of Lieutenant-Admiral Maarten Tromp on board *Brederode*. A hardened sailor from boyhood and victor of the Battle of the Downs, Tromp was not a man prone to servile gestures. Seeing *Brederode*'s flag defiantly undipped, Blake fired three warning shots. By accident or design, one cannonball hit the Dutch flagship. Tromp replied with a full broadside and the battle had begun. For five hours the two fleets blasted at one another. Tromp had the worst of the fight but cleverly shielded his merchant convoy as it slipped away toward home and safety. Six weeks later England formally declared war on the Dutch United Provinces. **RG**

> *"The issue was one of hegemony at sea and its recognition by the competing nations."*
>
> W. Frijhoff and M. Spies, 1650: Hard Won Unity *(2004)*

Losses: English, none of 25 ships; Dutch, 2 captured of 40 ships

◁ The Downs 1639   Kentish Knock 1652 ▷

 Smoke billows from a broadside fired during the Dover confrontation of Tromp's Dutch fleet and Blake's English ships.

Faubourg Saint-Antoine   2 July 1652

At Faubourg Saint-Antoine in Paris, two of the great French generals of the Franco-Spanish War—Louis, Prince of Condé and Henri, Viscount of Turenne—met on opposite sides in battle. It was one of the final engagements of the Fronde civil war, which lasted from 1648 to 1653.

The Fronde was a reaction to the increase of royal power at the expense of the liberties of the French provinces and nobility. Figures like Condé and the king's own uncle, Gaston, Duke of Orléans, sided against Louis XIV's chief minister, Cardinal Jules Mazarin. During the Fronde, neither side was able to win consistent control over Paris.

In summer 1652, the royal and Frondeur armies were maneuvering around Paris without engaging each other. Eventually, the royal general, Turenne, managed to trap Condé's Frondeur army at Faubourg Saint-Antoine, with the city walls behind him. Paris, traditionally hostile to the presence of any army, had closed its gates, cutting off

Condé's escape route. Turenne rushed to confront Condé, leaving his artillery to follow him.

At 7:00 AM Turenne launched the first in a series of cavalry charges through the streets; these were all fought back with heavy casualties on both sides. When Turenne's cannons arrived in the early afternoon, Condé was doomed, as his army was pressed against the wall and vulnerable to artillery fire. Just as a rout seemed imminent, the city gates were opened because Gaston and his daughter had persuaded the Parisian authorities to admit Condé's army. Condé was able to retreat into the city, covered by guns of the civic militia, and Gaston's daughter herself, in the Bastille. But the Frondeurs could not maintain their hold on Paris and the movement petered out by 1653, leaving Mazarin in control to lay the foundations of the absolutist regime of Louis XIV. **JF**

Losses: Fronde, 1,500 of 6,000; Royal, 1,500 of 8,000

Valenciennes 1656 [>]

Overlooked by the Bastille, cavalry of Condé and Turenne clash outside the Paris city walls. ⬆

Kentish Knock   8 October 1652

The First Anglo-Dutch War, initiated at Dover, was a naval conflict for which neither side was well prepared. The encounter at the Kentish Knock was a chaotic tragicomedy that revealed divisions in the Dutch camp and underlined the difficulty of fighting coherent battles in sailing ships.

The Dutch United Provinces were thoroughly disunited, riven by disputes between provinces and factions. Political machinations led to the sacking of admiral Maarten Tromp and his replacement by Witte de With, a notoriously brutal disciplinarian who was widely disliked. De With abandoned Tromp's cautious policy of protecting merchant convoys and sailed out to attack the English fleet in its anchorage at the Downs.

Bad weather soon drove all plans awry. The Dutch fleet was scattered by gales and the English under Robert Blake sailed out to take advantage of their disarray. As battle was joined in the shallows around the Kentish Knock sandbanks, the larger English ships pounded the Dutch with their broadsides. De With struggled in vain to assert authority. When he tried to shift his flag to *Brederode*, Tromp's old flagship, the crew refused to let him on board and threatened to fire on him if he insisted. The English had their own problems, two ships running aground on the sandbanks and others losing formation in shifting winds. By the time nightfall halted the fighting, one Dutch ship had exploded and several others had been boarded or forced to withdraw. In a fury, De With vowed to fight on the following day, but the entire contingent from the province of Zealand sailed home regardless. Depleted in numbers, De With was persuaded by his subordinate, Michiel de Ruyter, to make a prudent withdrawal to the protection of the shoals off the Dutch coast. **RG**

Losses: English, none of 68 ships; Dutch, 1 ship destroyed, 1 captured of 62

◁ *Dover 1652*   *Portland 1653* ▷

⬆ *Witte de With's Dutch fleet is repelled by the English in the Battle of Kentish Knock.*

Portland 28 February–2 March 1653

In the First Anglo-Dutch War, Maarten Tromp was reinstalled as commander of the Dutch fleet after the Battle of Kentish Knock. Tromp's heroic demonstration of fighting skill at the three-day Battle of Portland could not disguise the inferiority of his ships or the rise of English naval power.

Tromp's essential task was to maintain the foreign trade on which the wealth of the Dutch United Provinces depended. He used his fleet to escort merchant convoys between Dutch ports and the Atlantic, through waters dangerously close to England.

At the end of February 1653 he was shepherding 150 merchant vessels eastward along the Channel when he sighted Robert Blake's fleet off Portland. Blake's ships were scattered and downwind of the Dutch. Tromp attacked while he held a brief advantage. Blake found himself with twelve ships surrounded by thirty Dutch vessels. Tromp's flagship *Brederode* closed with Blake's *Triumph* and swept her decks with broadsides at point-blank range. Commodore Michiel de Ruyter, leading one of Tromp's squadrons, captured another English warship by boarding after a fierce fight. But as more English ships sailed in to join the melee, the Dutch were driven onto the defensive. For the next two days a running battle was fought along the Channel as Tromp maneuvered to keep his warships between the English and the merchant convoy. By the end of the third day's fighting the Dutch were almost out of powder and shot, but valiantly held position. On the morning of 3 March the English found themselves in an empty sea; the surviving Dutch vessels had slipped away for home. Tromp received a rousing reception on arrival in port, but the Dutch had suffered heavy losses, including a third of the merchant convoy. **RG**

Losses: Dutch, 8 ships of 70, 50 merchant ships captured; English, 2 warships of 80

◁ Kentish Knock 1652   The Gabbard 1653 ▷

The Gabbard 12–13 June 1653

The battle fought near the Gabbard bank, off eastern England, was a climactic moment in the First Anglo-Dutch War. The English demonstrated the superiority of warships fighting in a disciplined line of battle, a tactical doctrine that would dominate the future of warfare in the age of sail.

Since the outbreak of war with the Dutch the previous summer, the English had striven to bring order to the chaos of naval warfare, adopting the Articles of War, which imposed strict rules upon naval captains. Whereas the Dutch sought to engage the enemy in a free-for-all, close-quarters melee, English captains were expected to maintain a line and execute maneuvers as ordered.

When the two fleets met at the Gabbard, the Dutch enjoyed an initial stroke of luck as one of the two generals-at-sea commanding the English fleet, Richard Deane, was killed by almost the first shot fired. But the other English commander, George Monck, kept his nerve and admiral Maarten Tromp's Dutch ships were soon suffering heavy damage, battered by English broadsides. Because the Dutch ships were smaller and their captains more skilled seamen, they could outdo the English in deft maneuver, but English discipline and heavier weight of guns were decisive. Tromp unwisely chose to renew the battle on the second day, although his powder was almost exhausted and many of his captains—often merchant seamen drummed into temporary war service—had no stomach left for a fight. After heavy losses Tromp was forced into a fighting withdrawal, nursing his holed flagship back to the Netherlands. This victory allowed the English to blockade Dutch ports and prey at will on Dutch merchant shipping. Tromp died leading a bold blockade-busting sortie at Scheveningen the following August. **RG**

Losses: Dutch, 10 ships sunk and 11 captured of 98; English, none of 110 ships

◁ Portland 1653   Lowestoft 1665 ▷

Valenciennes 16 July 1656

After the end of the Thirty Years' War in 1648, war continued between France and Spain. Much of the fighting took place around the Spanish Netherlands, where Spain triumphed at Valenciennes in 1656. As at the Faubourg Saint-Antoine, French generals Turenne and Condé fought against one another.

On 15 June the Viscount of Turenne invested Valenciennes and set about constructing siege-works. A Spanish army arrived to relieve the town. It was led by Don John of Austria, the bastard son of King Philip IV of Spain, and Louis de Condé, who had previously held high command in the French army but joined the Spanish in 1652 after the failure of the Fronde Revolt.

The Spanish flooded the French position by opening the sluices of the Scheldt River, and on 26 June entrenched themselves against the besiegers. In an effort to protect his position against the Spanish, Turenne had spread his forces thinly and warned his officers to be extremely vigilant of any enemy movement. Unfortunately, Marshal Henri La Ferté, in command of the French section most open to attack, was a rival of Turenne and so disregarded his advice. On 16 July Condé and Don John attacked La Ferté's position and quickly advanced through his infantry lines. La Ferté counterattacked by personally leading a cavalry charge, but he could do nothing to rally his men and was captured. Soldiers sent in by Turenne also failed to repulse the Spanish, who broke through and relieved the Siege of Valenciennes.

Turenne managed to reorganize his disheveled forces and lead an orderly retreat to nearby Quesnoy, where he received supplies and reinforcements. The Spanish did not make any full-scale attempt to engage Turenne there and he was able to lead his army to safety. **JF**

Losses: French, 4,400 captured of 25,000; Spanish, light of 20,000

⟨ Faubourg Saint-Antoine 1652

The Dunes 1658 ⟩

Warsaw 28–30 July 1656

Sweden had invaded Poland-Lithuania in 1655, starting the Northern War that would last until 1660. The Swedish advance was swift. In 1656 King Charles X of Sweden and an allied Brandenburg army bested a larger Polish-Lithuanian army near Warsaw before advancing into the city.

In June 1656 Sweden signed an alliance with Frederick William, Elector of Brandenburg and Duke of Prussia. Their joint army of 18,000 marched toward Warsaw from the north. Awaiting them was the Polish-Lithuanian king, John II Casimir Vasa, and an army of around 40,000 largely untrained soldiers. John Casimir ferried part of his army across the Vistula, and marched up the river's right bank toward the Swedish-Brandenburg army. On 28 July Charles launched an unsuccessful frontal assault along the right bank. He was unable to dislodge the Polish-Lithuanian infantry, which had dug in behind earthworks between the river bank and the Białołęka Forest.

The next day, Charles and Frederick William decided to bypass the Polish-Lithuanian lines. Their forces wheeled left through the forest, with infantry shielded by cavalry. Fighting off Polish-Lithuanian attacks, they now occupied an open plain on the Polish-Lithuanian right, thus outflanking them. John Casimir attempted to dislodge their new position with a Hussar charge, but he was unable to press home his advantage. With his position now untenable, John Casimir withdrew across the Vistula that night. On 30 July the Swedish-Brandenburg army marched across the open plain and attacked the retreating Polish-Lithuanian army, which was forced to flee from Warsaw. The Swedish-Brandenburg army marched into Warsaw, but its forces were inadequate to hold the city and it was later forced to withdraw. **JF**

Losses: Polish-Lithuanian, 2,000 of 40,000; Swedish-Brandenburg, 1,000 of 18,000

⟨ Berestczko 1651

Lwów 1675 ⟩

Santa Cruz   20 April 1657

Samugarh   29 May 1658

In 1654, Oliver Cromwell, Lord Protector of the republican Commonwealth, declared war on Spain, unleashing English fleets to attack Spanish shipping and colonies in the Caribbean and Atlantic. In 1657, Admiral Robert Blake destroyed a Spanish treasure fleet in a daring raid at Santa Cruz in the Canary Islands.

The year 1657 saw the start of a bitter struggle for the Mughal succession in India: four brothers fighting frantically for their father's throne. All the pretenders were power-hungry, but only Aurangzeb had the ruthlessness and cunning of a winner. A crucial step toward his seizure of the throne was taken at Samugarh.

In spring 1657, Blake was blockading the Spanish port of Cadiz when he received news that a fleet carrying silver and gold from the Spanish colonies in the Americas was approaching. Consisting of seventeen ships, the fleet docked at Santa Cruz because it was unable to reach Cadiz. Aware of the oncoming threat, the Spanish carried their silver bullion ashore. On 20 April, Blake arrived with a fleet of twenty-three ships. Defending Santa Cruz was a castle and a string of smaller forts, which were all connected with a breastwork manned by musketeers.

Blake sent twelve ships under Vice Admiral Richard Stayner to attack the Spanish fleet. Blake was to attack the fortifications and provide covering fire. Stayner sailed into the harbor and anchored with his broadside facing close to the Spanish. He was able to destroy twelve of the Spanish ships and capture five, which he intended to tow away as prizes. As the English were under heavy fire from the fortifications and having difficulty maneuvering because of the winds, Blake ordered that the five captured ships be destroyed. When the tide turned, the English fleet was able to drift out of Santa Cruz to safety. Even though he had failed to capture the treasure, Blake was hailed as a hero in England, but died four months later on his way home. The Spanish, already low on funds to finance their war effort, were now unable to transport their treasure from the Canary Islands to Spain. **JF**

The Mughal emperor, Shah Jahan, is famous for the Taj Mahal, the splendid tomb he built for his wife, Mumtaz Mahal. Unfortunately, the couple left a more toxic legacy behind in their four sons, who fought frantically for the succession. They did not even wait for their father to die: on hearing he had fallen ill in 1657, Shah Jahan's second son, Shah Shuja, proclaimed himself emperor in Bengal. However, Crown Prince Dara Shikoh defeated Shuja at Bahadapur, and a grateful Shah Jahan handed him his throne.

Shah Jahan's younger sons, Aurangzeb and Murad Baksh, were power-hungry, too. At Aurangzeb's behest, Murad set himself up as emperor in Gujarat, declaring Dara Shikoh a usurper. The brothers marched northeast to Agra, running the gauntlet of the region's Rajput princes but defeating them at Dharmat. They met Dara's army at Samugarh. Inexperienced and indecisive, Dara threw his army forward in a general advance; his cannon, ranged in a line, fired indiscriminately. Even so, he might easily have won, because—equally impetuous—Murad led his left wing to destruction at the hands of one of Dara's Rajput allies. With the battle apparently won, however, Dara dismounted from his elephant. His men believed their commander had been killed; demoralized, they fled. Within months, the victorious Aurangzeb had executed Murad for "treachery" and seized the throne for himself. He ruled India for almost fifty years. **MK**

Losses: English, 40 dead and 110 wounded, no ships of 23; Spanish, all 17 ships

◁ *Cadiz 1596*

Losses: Unknown

◁ *Haldighati 1576*

An eighteenth-century book illumination depicting Aurangzeb later capturing Kandahar.

The Dunes (Dunkirk)   25 June 1658

The Battle of the Dunes was one of the final major battles of the Franco-Spanish War. The French had recovered from their defeat at Valenciennes and were laying siege to Dunkirk in 1658. With help from English Commonwealth soldiers, the French routed a Spanish relief army on the nearby dunes.

The Viscount of Turenne had invested Dunkirk at the behest of Oliver Cromwell, who had joined the war against Spain and sent soldiers, on the condition France capture and deliver the town to England. Spain raised an army to relieve Dunkirk, which included 2,000 English Royalists led by James, Duke of York, son of the late Charles I. The army was commanded by Don John of Austria and Louis, Prince of Condé.

The Spanish drew up along the beach north of Dunkirk and threw up entrenchments on the dunes, but in their haste they had left behind their artillery. Don John commanded the right, next to the sea, and Condé led the left, by a canal. Turenne marched to meet them. He had complete artillery coverage of the Spanish, thanks to French heavy guns and English frigates cruising nearby.

Battle was joined at 8:00 AM on 25 June. The first contact saw Commonwealth soldiers on the left force the Spanish back with a pike charge. A counterattack led by York failed because his cavalry could not maneuver effectively through the sand. In a short time, the Spanish right had collapsed as it was driven back by the French cavalry and artillery. Condé had been able to hold his position on the left under heavy bombardment and even managed to launch a cavalry charge. Eventually, the French infantry overwhelmed Condé and he retreated. The battle ended at noon. Turenne captured Dunkirk, and it was handed over to the English. **JF**

Losses: Anglo-French allied, 400 dead or wounded of 15,000; Spanish, 1,000 dead and 5,000 captured of 16,000

◁ *Valenciennes 1656*

Turenne leads a dramatic charge in Battle of the Dunes *(1837) by Charles-Philippe Lariviere (detail).* ⬆

The Sound 29 October 1658

Sweden, the dominant power in northern Europe, was threatening to exclude the Dutch from Baltic trade. The Dutch government sent a fleet to intervene in a war between Sweden and Denmark, fighting to deny the Swedes control of the Sound (Øresund), the narrow gateway to the Baltic Sea.

Under King Charles X Gustav, the Swedes were besieging the Danish capital, Copenhagen, by land and sea. The Dutch fleet, led by Lieutenant Admiral Jacob van Wassenaer Obdam, sailed into the Øresund to attack the Swedish blockade ships. Obdam had a north wind at his back, giving him a tactical advantage over the more numerous Swedish fleet. However, the wind denied him support from Danish warships, because it pinned them in harbor at Copenhagen. Pulled about by the treacherous currents in the Sound, neither fleet could maintain formation, and individual captains engaged the enemy as best they could.

Obdam's flagship *Eendracht* was surrounded by Swedish vessels and battered; she survived as Dutch captains sailed to their admiral's rescue. Several Swedish ships were boarded by the Dutch and taken after fierce hand-to-hand fighting. *Brederode*—the flagship of the famously bad-tempered Dutch commander Witte De With—ran ashore and was the helpless target of broadsides for two hours before being boarded. Hit by two musketballs, de With died of his wounds. Nonetheless, the Dutch had the better of the fighting before both sides withdrew, the Swedes to their port of Landskrona and the Dutch into Copenhagen.

Swedish King Charles announced a victory and had De With's body exhibited as a trophy. But the Dutch had achieved their objective. Joining with the Danes, they blockaded the Swedish fleet in Landskrona. Charles soon abandoned the siege of Copenhagen. **RG**

Losses: Dutch, 2 ships of 35; Swedish, 5 ships of 45

A pen-and-ink depiction of the Battle of the Sound by Willem van de Velde the Elder.

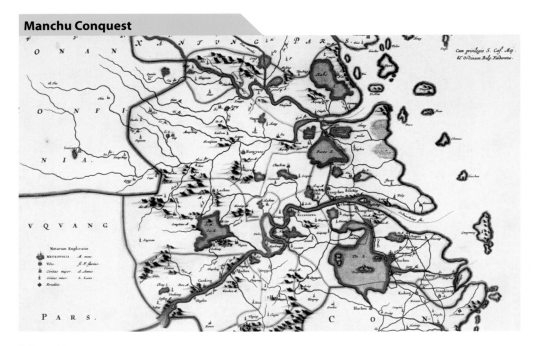

Nanjing   24 August–10 September 1659

Zheng Chenggong, better known as Coxinga, was the most loyal supporter of the final claimant to the throne of the Ming dynasty after it had been replaced by the Manchu Qing dynasty. He led a series of campaigns that culminated in an unsuccessful attempt to capture Nanjing in 1659.

The Manchus had fortified the area of the lower Yangtze River, including a formidable river barrage known as the "Boiling River Dragon." After four days' exchanging artillery fire, Zheng's fleet broke through and secured the riverside forts. Nanjing was their next objective, but conflicting advice reached Zheng. Some of his commanders were in favor of a blockade of Nanjing, but Zheng felt that a quick victory was needed to sustain the momentum.

Unfortunately the wind changed on 10 August, making it impossible to sail upstream, so Zheng and his men had to haul the ships along from the riverbank. This took two weeks, during which time the Manchus sent reinforcements. They then indicated to Zheng that they would be willing to surrender Nanjing after a month. A siege began, and there was so little activity that the besiegers went fishing in the local ponds instead of mounting guard duty. Sorties were made from inside Nanjing, which only served to irritate Zheng.

On 8 September, a major sortie was carried out via a secret passage. This caused many casualties, and Zheng withdrew some of his troops. The following day, another sortie occurred, and Manchu agents within Zheng's army managed to cause a major explosion. Taking advantage of the confusion, the Manchus launched a full attack out of the city, and Zheng was obliged to retreat. After his defeat, Zheng was concerned with his own position rather than restoring the fortunes of the Ming dynasty **ST**

Losses: Zheng, unknown; Manchu, 4,500 bodies in the river alone

◁ *Yangzhou 1645*   *Fort Zeelandia 1661* ▷

Copper engraving from 1655 of a map showing Jiangsu province and its capital Nanjing. ⬆

Fort Zeelandia   21 April 1661–1 February 1662

Fort Zeelandia was a Dutch outpost on the island of Taiwan. Under severe pressure from the Manchus in southern China, Zheng Chenggong decided to capture Taiwan in order to provide a secure base for his own family from which he might one day continue the war against the Qing.

The Dutch had feared an attack by Zheng for some time and had requested supplies and reinforcements for Fort Zeelandia, which had been built in a vulnerable position at a time when an attack from mainland China was not envisaged. Zheng's fleet consisted of 900 warships with a complement of 50,000 men, who were already troubled by a lack of supplies by the time they made the short crossing to Taiwan.

The Chinese fleet was attacked by Dutch ships within sight of Fort Zeelandia, but this failed to prevent them from landing, and a series of land battles began. Hoping to retain the fort, if not Taiwan itself, the Dutch began negotiations, but when these collapsed without success, they prepared for a long siege. Several artillery exchanges took place during which the Chinese suffered heavy losses. Zheng also failed to bring over reinforcements from the mainland, and his men began to suffer food shortages.

On 30 July, a Dutch fleet that had been sent to relieve Fort Zeelandia was spotted, and a battle took place, but the situation did not change for many months. Eventually, the Dutch defenders realized that they could either fight to the death or negotiate a surrender with honor. The latter course was decided upon, and the Dutch sailed away proudly when Fort Zeelandia surrendered on 1 February 1662. Zheng reclaimed Taiwan in the name of the rightful emperor of China and became a national hero. **ST**

Losses: No reliable figures, but considerable on both sides

◁ *Nanjing 1659*   *Penghu 1683* ▷

⬆ *A seventeenth-century Chinese wall hanging depicting the island of Taiwan.*

Lowestoft 13 June 1665

Early in the Second Anglo-Dutch War, the Dutch navy suffered a bloody defeat in a savage battle fought off Lowestoft, eastern England. Yet this catastrophe only stirred the Dutch to greater efforts in the war, and the English failed to draw any lasting advantage from a hard-fought victory.

After the Battle of the Gabbard, the First Anglo-Dutch War had petered out without clear result. However, with the restoration of the English monarchy under Charles II in 1660, England soon resumed its harassment of Dutch merchant shipping and colonies, seizing New Amsterdam —later renamed New York—in 1664.

War was formally resumed in March 1665. Three months later, Admiral Jacob van Wassenaer Obdam was tasked with leading a large Dutch fleet to attack the English in their home waters. The resulting battle was fought in shifting winds that made it difficult for the English commander, James, Duke of York, to keep his ships in formation, and impossible for the Dutch, who were soon engaging as individual ships rather than a coherent fleet. With more than 200 ships and almost 10,000 cannon packed into a small area of sea, broadsides wrought carnage. The Duke of York narrowly escaped death when a cannonball decapitated a row of courtiers standing behind him. Van Wassenaer was less fortunate, killed when his flagship *Eendracht* exploded. After their admiral's death, Dutch captains began to flee for home, some colliding in the general panic. The English launched fireships to finish off crippled Dutch vessels. Only Vice Admiral Cornelis Tromp had the nerve and authority to organize coherent action to cover the withdrawal. In the aftermath of defeat, the Dutch took vigorous steps to improve their naval command and build new warships. **RG**

Losses: Dutch, 8 ships destroyed and 9 captured of 103; English, 1 ship of 109

◁ *The Gabbard* 1653   *Four Days' Battle* 1666 ▷

The Battle of Lowestoft *by Adriaen van Diest (1655–1704).* ⬆

Ambuila   29 October 1665

The Battle of Ambuila, near the border of Angola and Kongo, was one of the largest battles in central African history. In 1665, a Portuguese army from Angola defeated a larger Kongolese army, killing their king, António I, which plunged Kongo into a brutal civil war.

When António I became king of Kongo in 1661, he was determined to use aggression to counter Portuguese expansion in the region. The *casus belli* was a succession dispute in the tiny kingdom of Ambuila, with rival factions appealing to the Kongolese and the Portuguese for help. Consequently, both powers sent armies into Ambuila in 1665. The Kongolese advanced in a half-moon formation with all of their musketeers, joined by infantry and archers, in the first wave. The Portuguese army was deployed in a more defensive fashion, with musketeers and artillery in a central diamond-shaped formation, flanked by two wings of allied African soldiers and a large force in reserve.

When the two armies clashed, the fighting was fierce, but the Portuguese artillery was key in eventually forcing the Kongolese back. António I led a renewed attack against the Portuguese, which succeeded in driving off their flanking troops. However, the Kongolese were unable to dislodge the Portuguese center.

The battle turned when António I was killed in the fighting. The loss of their king totally shattered the Kongolese army, and their casualties quickly mounted. Only a careful withdrawal protected the survivors from total annihilation, although the Kongolese lost all of their baggage in the retreat.

After the battle, Ambuila became a Portuguese vassal, but the real impact was in Kongo. The lack of a recognized heir to António I led to decades of civil war that totally destabilized the once mighty kingdom. **JF**

Losses: Portuguese and allied African, unknown of 7,500; Kongolese, unknown of 70,000

A nineteenth-century plate showing António I's palace on the hilltop.

Four Days' Battle   1–4 June 1666

The bloodiest fight of the seventeenth-century Anglo-Dutch naval wars, the Four Days' Battle revealed the spectacular recovery of Dutch naval power from the debacle at Lowestoft. Defeat in this prolonged engagement left English shipping and the English coast open to Dutch attack.

By 1666, England much regretted provoking the Second Anglo-Dutch War. With royal finances in chaos, the English could not match the rate of Dutch shipbuilding. The Dutch had also formed an alliance with France, which threatened to shift the naval balance of power even further to England's disadvantage. In desperation, the English chose to attack.

On 11 June 1666, George Monck, Duke of Albermarle, led fifty-six ships against the Dutch fleet at anchor off Dunkirk. It was a bold decision, because the Dutch force numbered eighty-four ships and was under the command of Michiel de Ruyter, his country's most inspired naval

commander. It is hard to do justice to the sheer ferocity of the fighting that followed. The cannon fire was so heavy that, as the battle drifted toward the English coast, the guns could be heard by strollers in London's Hyde Park. Dutch admiral Cornelis Evertsen was cut in half by a cannonball. Many others died in close-quarters fighting as vessels were boarded. Ships continued fighting after catching fire, even though the risks were terrifying on a wooden ship packed with gunpowder.

By the third day, Monck had only twenty-nine ships still in action, but he was reinforced by the arrival of a squadron under Prince Rupert of the Rhine, which allowed the English to keep fighting for another day. By the time they finally disengaged, vanishing behind a fog bank, they had lost one in eight of their ships and almost 5,000 men. **RG**

Losses: Dutch, 4 ships of 84; English, 10 ships of 79

◁ *Lowestoft 1665*   *Raid on the Medway 1667* ▷

Michiel de Ruyter's flagship holds position in the center of The Four Days' Battle *by Abraham Storck (1644–1708).* ⬆

Raid on the Medway 12–14 June 1667

The Dutch raid on the dockyards in the Medway in 1667 was one of the deepest humiliations ever visited upon England and the Royal Navy. Although the material losses inflicted were grave, even more painful was the public proof that the English were powerless to defend their own coastline.

Since the Second Anglo-Dutch War began in 1665, England had suffered a string of misfortunes, including the Great Plague and the Great Fire of London. King Charles II was broke and had no money to pay sailors or dockworkers. England was seeking peace desperately, but the Dutch government leader, Johann de Witt, wanted a crushing victory so he could impose punitive terms. His brother, Cornelis de Witt, was given command of a fleet that first sailed to the mouth of the Thames and then shifted southward, taking Sheerness on the Medway and sailing inland toward the dockyard at Chatham.

The English blocked the navigable channel with a chain stretched from shore to shore, but Dutch engineers made short work of this obstacle. Beyond the chain, English ships with skeleton crews lay defenseless. Three "great ships"—the largest naval vessels—were scuttled hastily; a fourth, *Royal Charles*, was seized by the Dutch. The only resistance came from shore batteries. Nonetheless, De Witt and his captains were nervous, hardly believing the ease of their success, and on 14 June they withdrew, taking *Royal Charles* with them as a trophy. The other ships they had captured were burned.

The shock of the action was great. Diarist Samuel Pepys, then secretary to the admiralty, thought the monarchy would fall. In fact, peace was made with limited advantage to the Dutch. England's desire for revenge helped motivate another Anglo-Dutch War the following decade. **RG**

Losses: English, 13 ships; Dutch, no ships

◁ *Four Days' Battle 1666*   *Solebay 1672* ▷

⬆ The Dutch in the Medway 1667, *by Willem Schellinks (1627–78).*

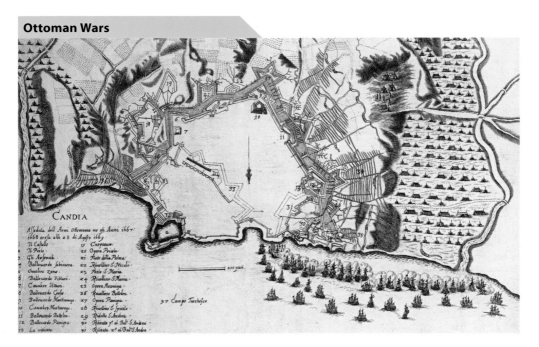

CANDIA

Assedio dell'Armi Ottomane nel gli Anni 1667
1668 presa alli 28 di Agosto 1669.

1 Il Cavallo
2 Il Priso
3 Gli Arsenali
4 Ballouardo Sabionera
5 Cavaliere Zane
6 Ballouardo Vitturi
7 Cavalier Vitturi
8 Ballouardo Giesu
9 Ballouardo Martinengo
10 Cavaliere Martinengo
11 Ballouardo Bettelem
12 Ballouardo Panigra
13 La ritirata

19 Cospetour
20 Opera Priula
21 Forte della Palma
22 Ravellino S. Nicolo
23 Porta S. Maria
24 Ravellino S. Maria
25 Opera Moceniga
26 Ravellino Bettelem
27 Opera Panigra
28 Ravellino S. Spirito
29 Ridotto S. Andrea
30 Riloeata 1° al Bal. S. Andrea
31 Riloeata 2° al Bal. S. Andrea

37 Campo Turchesco

Fall of Candia   5 September 1669

The fall of the Venetian fortress of Candia (modern-day Heraklion) on Crete ended a siege that had lasted twenty-four years—probably the longest siege in history. Its capture completed the conquest of the Mediterranean island by the Ottoman Turks. Crete remained under Ottoman rule until 1913.

The Ottomans launched a surprise attack on Venice's last major overseas territory in 1645, and by 1648, all that remained under Venetian control was the fortress of Candia. The Ottomans besieged the fortress in May 1648. Although the Ottomans could supply their forces with enough to sustain them, Venetian naval attacks in the Aegean and a blockade of the Dardanelles hampered attempts to supply the army with the necessary equipment to launch a decisive assault.

The Ottomans dug extensive earthworks, settled in, and maintained the siege in desultory but effective fashion until 1667, when they sent a large army led by

the grand vizier for a final assault on Candia. The ultimate phase of the siege, from May 1667 to September 1669, was terrible for all involved: Turkish soldiers, Cretan civilians used as slave labor in the siege works, and the Christian defenders. The arrival of French troops and galleys enabled resistance to be maintained for a little longer, but the leader of the French troops, Francois, Duke of Beaufort, was killed in a night sortie against the Ottoman lines in June 1669. The French galleys bombarded the Ottoman positions, but the well-entrenched suffered little, while the French fleet sustained substantial losses.

Discouraged, the French withdrew in August. The siege continued, but the Venetian position became increasingly hopeless. Candia finally surrendered to the Ottomans in September 1669, putting an end to four centuries of Venetian rule. **TB**

Losses: Unknown

[<] *Khotin 1621*   *Lwów 1675* [>]

A seventeenth-century map by G. Bouttats, depicting the Siege of Candia.

Solebay   7 June 1672

In Dutch history, 1672 is known as the "year of disaster." England's King Charles II formed an alliance with French King Louis XIV to attack the Dutch Republic on land and sea. The Battle of Solebay was a crucial moment in the desperate fight to preserve Dutch independence.

In June 1672, the English and French fleets joined up at Southwold, eastern England, under the command of James, Duke of York. Knowing that the allies intended to use their combined naval power to impose a blockade of the Dutch coast, Lieutenant Admiral Michiel de Ruyter decided to launch a preemptive attack.

Appearing off Solebay early on 7 June, De Ruyter achieved total surprise. Sailors ashore rushed to rejoin their ships and captains hastily prepared for battle. The Duke of York struggled to form a coherent line as the Dutch approached, but the commander of the French squadron, the Comte d'Estrées, sailed southward while the English squadrons shifted north. Seeing the allies split, De Ruyter assigned a few ships to keep the French busy while concentrating the weight of his fleet against the English.

The Duke of York was obliged to change ships twice, his flagships battered by Dutch broadsides. The *Royal James*, a one-hundred-gun ship under the Earl of Sandwich, was first shattered by point-blank cannon fire from a Dutch vessel that had grappled it, then set alight by a fireship. In their desperation to escape the burning hulk, many men drowned, including Sandwich, whose body washed up on shore a few weeks later. The Dutch also suffered heavy losses and, at nightfall, broke contact, withdrawing across the North Sea. The Anglo-French alliance, never popular or comfortable, was left in tatters as the allies indulged in bitter recriminations. **RG**

Losses: English and French, 1 ship destroyed of 93; Dutch, 2 ships of 75

◁ *Raid on the Medway 1667*   *Texel 1673* ▷

⬆ The Joining of d'Estrées and the Duke of York, 1672 by Jan Karel Donatus van Beecq (1638–1722).

Maastricht 6 June–1 July 1673

The Siege of Maastricht showed the genius of Sébastien Le Preste de Vauban, the most renowned military engineer of his day. In this siege, during the Franco-Dutch War, Vauban was able to capture the well-fortified city without a prolonged struggle.

The Dutch had helped block French expansion into the Spanish Netherlands in 1669. Louis XIV became progressively more anti-Dutch and invaded the United Provinces in 1672. The French captured many important Dutch cities, but bypassed Maastricht in their rapid advance north. By 1673, Dutch-held Maastricht was a major hindrance to French operations in the area, so Louis moved to capture it.

Maastricht was in a strong position and commanded a crossing of the River Meuse. It also had a garrison of around 6,000, with a skilled commander, Jacques de Fariaux. The siege began on 6 June. On 8 June, 7,000 peasants were conscripted to dig extensive lines to surround Maastricht. When Louis arrived on 10 June, he gave command of the siege to Vauban. Vauban unleashed the might of his battery of twenty-six guns. He ordered trenches to be dug parallel to the walls. Then he used artillery to protect sappers digging diagonal trenches toward a closer position where another trench was started. Using this technique, Vauban moved closer and closer to Maastricht. A direct assault on the walls on 25 June failed, with the loss of 300. Ultimately, it was the effective use of artillery and mines that made the position of the defenders untenable. On 30 June, Fariaux agreed to parlay, and the next day French troops entered Maastricht. **JF**

Losses: French, few of 45,000; Dutch, few of 6,000

Seneffe 1674 >

The Battle of the Texel, *by Willem van de Velde the Younger, depicts the failure of the Dutch to capture the English flagship (center).* ⬇

Texel   21 August 1673

The last engagement of the Anglo-Dutch Wars, Texel demonstrated the indomitable fighting spirit of the Dutch navy led by Michiel de Ruyter, and the fiery temperament of seventeenth-century admirals, two of whom fought a personal duel.

After his attack on the allied English and French at Solebay, De Ruyter fell back on the defensive. The allies blockaded the Dutch coast but De Ruyter was in the safety of shallow home waters and mounted sorties to harass their blockading squadrons. Although outnumbered, the Dutch relied on a lack of cooperation between the French and English.

When De Ruyter sailed out at Texel, French commander the Comte d'Estreés was probably under secret orders from Louis XIV to avoid losing ships and mostly kept out of the battle. The fighting between the Dutch and English was disrupted by a vendetta between English Admiral Sir

Edward Spragge and Dutch Lieutenant Admiral Cornelis Tromp. Spragge had sworn to kill Tromp and pursued him without regard for battle formation. Having shattered one another's flagships—and half their crew—in a savage exchange of fire, the two men shifted ship and repeated the devastation with a second pair of vessels. Finally, as Spragge took to a rowing boat to transfer to a third ship, the boat was cut in half by a cannonball and he drowned.

De Ruyter, meanwhile, pummeled the English before disengaging at will to return to the safety of the shallows. The storm of abuse heaped by the English upon the French in the wake of the battle heralded the end of the Anglo-French alliance and of English participation in the war against the Dutch. **RG**

Losses: No ships lost on either side

◁ *Solebay 1672*

Seneffe 11 August 1674

Despite the success at Maastricht, Louis XIV's progress in the Franco-Dutch War had stalled after the Dutch allied with Spain and the Holy Roman Empire. Their combined forces clashed with the French at Seneffe in a battle that was the bloodiest of the war.

William of Orange led an allied Dutch-Imperial-Spanish force of 65,000 troops. The French commander, Louis, Prince of Condé, led a smaller army of 45,000 so he would not be drawn into battle. Condé saw his chance when the allies split into four groups, eliminating their numerical advantage.

At 10:00 AM, the French attacked the rearmost Dutch group at the village of Seneffe and routed them within an hour. When he heard this news, William ordered the imperial troops in the van, under Field Marshal Jean-Louis Raduit de Souches, to pull back. However, Souches did not hurry back with any great urgency. Meanwhile, the French had been able to advance and to outflank and defeat the second Dutch group. Condé's troops were tiring, but he still advanced to meet the largest of the three Dutch groups, personally commanded by William. The French managed to force the Dutch back, but William was able to rally his troops and retire in good order to a sound defensive position on high ground, where he was at last joined by Souches's reinforcements.

Against all advice, Condé launched his exhausted army into a fourth attack at 3:00 PM. The savage fighting went on past nightfall, with both sides suffering severe casualties. Eventually Condé realized victory was impossible and pulled his army back. William likewise retreated. Condé had not decisively defeated the allies, but his action at Seneffe prevented William advancing into France. **JF**

Losses: Allied, 15,000 dead or wounded and 5,000 captured of 65,000; French, 10,000 dead or wounded of 45,000

◁ *Maastricht 1673*   *Turckheim 1675* ▷

Turckheim 5 January 1675

French progress in the Low Countries slowed after the Battle of Seneffe. In 1675, the French advanced on the German front when the Viscount of Turenne launched an attack into Alsace, gaining control of the region after a stunning victory over Frederick William, Elector of Brandenburg.

At the end of 1674, Turenne had marched his forces in Lorraine south behind the Vosges, and then split his troops into small bodies to approach Alsace through the mountains. This approach allowed a French army of about 30,000 to assemble in Alsace by the end of December.

Turenne's cavalry were tired after a long season but his infantry had been strengthened by reinforcements from the French army in the Low Countries. The allied armies of Brandenburg-Prussia and Austria in the region did not expect an assault, and Frederick William struggled to rally their forces en masse. Eventually he mustered an army 30,000 to 40,000 strong, but it was not well organized. The army deployed between Colmar and Turckheim.

On 5 January, Turenne attacked. He feinted toward Colmar on his right. This caused Frederick William to pull back men from Turckheim. Using the terrain to hide the movement of his soldiers, Turenne redeployed his army and outflanked the enemy by capturing the town with his infantry. The Brandenburg-Austrians attempted to retake it but the French held their position under heavy attacks from artillery and cavalry. The French infantry launched a charge from Turckheim, which pushed the Brandenburg-Austrians back, but nightfall prevented a French pursuit of the enemy. The next day, Turenne found Frederick William's army had retreated across the Rhine to Strasbourg, leaving the French in command of Alsace. **JF**

Losses: Brandenburg-Austrian, 3,000 captured, dead, or wounded of 30,000–40,000; French, few of 30,000

◁ *Seneffe 1674*   *Fehrbellin 1675* ▷

Fehrbellin 28 June 1675

The first major engagement of the Scanian War (1674–79), Fehrbellin was a vital moment in the emergence of Prussia as a major military power. The forces of Brandenburg-Prussia bested an invading Swedish army, which was considered to be the one of the finest in Europe.

At the Battle of Warsaw, Sweden and Brandenburg-Prussia had been allies. When French King Louis XIV offered to increase subsidies to a financially struggling Sweden if it would attack Brandenburg, the Swedish invaded.

Brandenburg's Hohenzollern ruler, Frederick William, heard of the invasion and marched his army home from the Rhine. The bulk of the Swedish army, led by Karl Gustav Wrangel, was at Alt-Brandenburg, west of Berlin, aiming to march west to meet up with an allied Hanoverian army. Wrangel's half brother, Volmar, led another group stationed north at Havelsberg. Frederick William thrust between them by capturing the town of Rathenow, jeopardizing the position of the Swedish armies. Volmar attempted to join up with the other Swedish army by circling to the east and crossing the Rhine at Fehrbellin. However, the bridge there had been destroyed. While they repaired it, Frederick William's army descended and bombarded them with artillery fire from the high ground. The Swedes, bogged down on marshy terrain, were able to construct an improvised bridge under heavy fire. Only a determined rearguard action prevented the armies of Brandenburg from pressing their advantage completely, and Swedish losses were relatively light.

Strategically, the engagement was insignificant as the two Swedish armies were able to join up. The main impact was psychological: Sweden's armies were no longer regarded as invincible. **JF**

Losses: Brandenburg, negligible of 6,000; Swedish, 600 of 13,000

◁ Turckheim 1675   Öland 1676 ▷

Lwów 24 August 1675

In 1672, the Ottoman Empire invaded Ukraine, then part of the Polish-Lithuanian Commonwealth, starting the Ottoman-Commonwealth War. The Turks, joined by Tatars from the Crimean khanate, won a series of victories until King John III Sobieski led a Commonwealth army to victory outside Lwów.

In summer 1675, Sobieski faced an Ottoman-Tatar army of nearly 100,000. It successfully advanced through the Ukraine toward Poland. Its likely route ran through the city of Lwów. It was there that Sobieski decided to make his stand, and he arrived on 18 July with 6,000 men, posting troops on all of its approaches.

He planned to draw the Ottomans into attacking the enclosed spaces around Lwów, where their superior numbers could not be utilized. An advance force of 20,000 Tatars was sent to test Lwów's defenses, and they arrived on 24 August. At noon, Sobieski received news that the Tatars were going to approach over a marsh and via a narrow ravine. In the hills surrounding their approach, he ordered civilians to stand with spears and planted lances in the ground to give the illusion of reinforcements and deter any flanking attack. The Tatars entered the pass at 3:00 PM, and the Commonwealth infantry immediately fired from point-blank range, driving them out of the ravine. The Tatars regrouped and charged again, but were forced back by cavalry and were now pinned between the ravine's entrance and marshy ground.

Sobieski personally led a cavalry charge against the Tatars, inflicting heavy casualties, before forcing them to retreat. He had successfully broken the Ottoman momentum, although when the war ended in 1676 the Commonwealth still had to cede some of their Ukrainian territory to the Turks. **JF**

Losses: Polish-Lithuanian, few of 6,000; Crimean Tatar, heavy of 20,000

◁ Fall of Candia 1669   Vienna 1683 ▷

Great Swamp Fight 20 December 1675

Mutual animosity fueled by ongoing land disputes between English settlers and American Indians in the Massachusetts and Plymouth colonies erupted into open war in 1675. Chief Metacom (a.k.a. King Philip) organized Indian resistance to colonial authority.

The ill-trained militia of the Council of United Colonies made a poor showing as attacks continued through the summer and autumn of 1675. King Philip and his men eluded efforts to trap them in the coastal swamps, and consistently defeated the militia companies. King Philip's success as a rebel leader brought other tribes to join him.

In September, the Council of United Colonies declared war against King Philip. Each council member was levied to provide militia for a 1,000-man army. Efforts to make a truce failed, and Indian attacks grew in severity with more towns destroyed. King Philip's base remained secret until December, when an Indian deserter guided Governor Josiah Winslow of Plymouth and his small army through a snow storm to a large Narragansett stronghold in the Great Swamp near West Kingston, Rhode Island.

On 20 December, Winslow's force arrived at the fortified camp. Two companies attacked the Indians before the rest of the army was in position. They were driven back with heavy losses. Captain Benjamin Church led another coordinated assault that broke through the log palisade. Despite fierce resistance, the town was finally taken and burned. Philip and a few Indians escaped. **RB**

Losses: United Colonies, 80 dead, wounded unknown; Indian, 600 dead (including women and children), wounded and captured unknown

◁ *Mystic 1637*   *Saint Fe 1680* ▷

A depiction of the Battle of Agosta by French draftsman and engraver Gabriel Perelle (1604–77).

Agosta   22 April 1676

France's success at Turckheim was mirrored in the Mediterranean. Consequently, the Dutch sent a fleet to protect the Italian possessions of Spain, their ally in the Franco-Dutch War. In 1676, Dutch admiral Michiel de Ruyter was fatally wounded in a battle with the French fleet near Agosta, Sicily.

In March 1676, De Ruyter and his Spanish allies pulled into Agosta, on the east coast of Sicily. He had seventeen men-of-war and twelve smaller vessels, with Spain providing ten battleships. On 21 April, a French fleet of thirty ships of the line and ten smaller ships, commanded by Abraham Duquesne, approached. The French fleet had double the cannon of the Spanish-Dutch force, and their ships were of superior quality. The Dutch and Spanish ships sailed out of Agosta at dawn on 22 April. Dutch ships formed the van and rear with the Spanish in the center.

Battle was joined at 4:00 PM. De Ruyter's vanguard bore down on the French, inflicting heavy damage. The Spanish, worried about a lack of ammunition, held back, delaying the Dutch rear joining the fray. After half an hour of fighting, a bullet struck De Ruyter, carrying off his left foot, breaking his right leg, and hurling him back. The injury was kept secret. Eventually the French retreated at 7:00 PM. Neither side lost a ship, although the French fleet had received the more serious damage. However, De Ruyter's injury proved fatal and he died within a week.

The Dutch were forced out of the Mediterranean by October, leaving France with mastery of the area. **JF**

Losses: Spanish-Dutch allied, no ships of 27 battleships and 12 smaller ships; French, no ships of 30 battleships and 10 other ships

◁ *Turckheim 1675*   *Saint Denis 1678* ▷

Öland   11 June 1676

After the Swedish defeat at Fehrbellin, King Christian V of Denmark joined the Scanian War. He aimed to capture the former Danish provinces of Scania and Halland from Sweden. In 1676, at the Battle of Öland, a Dutch and Danish fleet bested the Swedes, giving them control of the Baltic.

The allied Danish-Dutch fleet was eager to gain control of the Baltic so they could transport troops to Sweden. In turn, the Swedish wanted naval supremacy to help relieve their beleaguered forces in Germany.

On 11 June, the two fleets met at Öland, an island just off the Swedish coast. At noon, the allied admiral, Cornelis Tromp, brought his flagship, *Christianus V*, level with his Swedish counterpart, *Kronan*, which was the largest warship in the Baltic. A misreading of signals with other ships caused the Swedish admiral, Lorentz Creutz, to sail the *Kronan* toward the allies. As a result of the maneuver, the ship began to take on water. The crisis continued when a fire onboard ignited the magazine, causing a huge explosion and sinking the ship.

Before the battle had really begun, the Swedish had lost their admiral and flagship. The new Swedish commander, Claes Uggla, was unable to bring his fleet into order and the allied fleet fell on the Swedish ships. Eventually, Uggla's ship, *Svärd*, was destroyed by a fireship after a fierce exchange of cannon fire. The Swedish fleet was in complete disarray, and the remaining ships scattered to avoid being captured or destroyed. The Danes had complete dominance of the Baltic, and their armies prepared to cross into Sweden. **JF**

Losses: Danish-Dutch allied, 1 ship of 47; Swedish, 7 ships captured and 8 ships destroyed of 55

◁ *Fehrbellin 1675*   *Lund 1676* ▷

Lund   14 December 1676

After their naval triumph at Öland, a Danish army was able to cross into Scania in southern Sweden. At Lund, the bloodiest battle of the Scanian War, Charles XI of Sweden led his army to a decisive victory over Christian V of Denmark's invading army.

Danish troops had been able to overrun most of Scania during summer 1676. In October, Charles XI led an army of 12,000 into Scania to retake the province; by December, disease and hunger had cut its numbers by nearly half. The Danish army, which included experienced German mercenaries, was well rested and well equipped and had taken up a position near the town of Lund. When a cold snap froze the nearby Lödde River, Charles XI launched a daring, surprise night attack on the Danish army. This attack failed, and the Swedish center and left were locked in a desperate struggle with the Danes across the treacherous frozen ground around Lund.

Meanwhile, Charles XI had launched a successful cavalry charge on the right wing, which broke the Danish left. In its pursuit, it had reached as far as the Danish camp, and it took an hour and a half to rally and return to the main battlefield. There the Swedish center and left had been pinned back by the superior Danish infantry and artillery. Just as it appeared that the Danes were close to victory, Charles XI's cavalry swept through them from the rear, completely devastating the Danish horse, who quickly abandoned the foot soldiers. The Danes who remained on the field were slaughtered until the Swedish offered quarter to any who laid down their arms. **JF**

Losses: Swedish, 2,300–3,000 of 6,500; Danish, 6,000 of 12,300

◁ *Öland 1676*　　　　　　　　　*Kjöge Bay 1677* ▷

Kjöge Bay   1 July 1677

After their defeat at Lund, Denmark regained the upper hand in the Scanian War by defeating a larger Swedish fleet at Kjöge Bay, near Copenhagen. The action definitively ended any hopes Sweden had of controlling the Baltic, and is remembered as one of Denmark's finest naval victories.

In their attempt to regain command of the Baltic, the Swedish had suffered a heavy defeat at Möen in May 1677. The rest of the Swedish fleet was anchored near Stockholm. Its commander, Henrik Horn, was a soldier who had little experience at sea or knowledge of naval tactics. He wanted to engage the Danes before Dutch reinforcements could arrive. In turn, the Danish admiral, Niels Juel, wanted a victory without any Dutch aide.

On 30 June, Horn tried to engage the Danes, but the two fleets mostly kept their distance, trying to gain a superior tactical position. At 5:00 AM the next day, fighting began as the two fleets tacked along the coast. Suddenly, the Swedish ship *Drake* ran aground, and Horn detached six ships from his fleet to help it while the rest sailed on. Juel sent some of his ships to engage the formation around the *Drake*, and they were able to capture four Swedish ships.

Meanwhile, Juel took the bulk of his fleet to pursue the Swedish, and the two forces engaged in a ten-hour struggle. The fighting was so furious that Juel had to switch his flagship three times to remain on board a fully functioning vessel. He managed to capture a handful more Swedish ships before the rest of the fleet sailed out of reach. On the day of the action, the Dutch reinforcements had arrived and captured some Swedish stragglers, but the glory belonged to Denmark and Juel. **JF**

"Thus have we stilled the tumults of the Baltic. In the year 1677."

Inscription on a medal commemorating Kjöge Bay

↑ *Danish forces engage with their Swedish rivals in this seventeenth-century depiction of the Battle of Kjöge Bay.*

Losses: Danish, no ships of 25, 400 dead or wounded of 6,700; Swedish, 8 ships captured and 2 destroyed of 31, 4,000 dead, wounded, or captured of 9,200,

◁ *Lund 1676*

Saint-Denis 14 August 1678

Saint-Denis was the last battle of the Franco-Dutch War, fought days after the Dutch and France had signed a peace treaty. France had not made peace with Spain, so when France besieged Mons, the Dutch-Spanish army engaged in battle. France triumphed, but was forced to abandon the siege.

The war had gone well for the French after the Battle of Agosta in 1676, and peace negotiations had begun that year. On 10 August 1678, the Dutch and the French made peace by signing the treaty of Nijmegen. France had delayed making peace with Spain so it could capture Spanish-held Mons. The Dutch military commander, Prince William of Orange, was eager that France should not gain such a strategically important town. So, despite having knowledge of the recent peace, William marched toward the French army of Marshal François-Henri, Duke of Luxembourg, which was blockading Mons.

Luxembourg moved to challenge Orange and entrenched his army in two positions: in the abbey of Saint-Denis and in Castean, a ruined fortress. When battle started on 14 August, the Dutch-Spanish army made good early progress and captured both French positions. During the fighting, two bullets pierced William's armor, but he was not seriously injured. The French managed to recover their ground and force the allies back to their starting positions after eight hours of battle. Only determined resistance from 8,000 English troops fighting for the allies prevented William's army being encircled completely.

The next morning, Luxembourg decided to raise the siege, and his army withdrew back to France. William had not secured a victory, but his action had saved Mons from capture. France and Spain made peace the next month. **JF**

Losses: Dutch-Spanish allied, 4,000 of 45,000; French, 4,000

◁ *Agosta 1676*

Santa Fe 1680

The year 1680 saw an uprising of New Mexico's Pueblo people against their Spanish overlords; they successfully besieged the colonial capital, Santa Fe. The Spanish were ousted for more than a decade, and although they did return eventually, the Pueblo managed to retain some autonomy.

In what is now the American Southwest, the peaceable Pueblo enjoyed a degree of security they had not known before. Protection against Apache and Navaho raids came at a price, however: Spanish landowners abused their powers to conscript Native labor, and Christianization was enforced. This was not so hard to bear as long as indigenous traditions were tacitly respected; in the 1670s, however, the Church authorities cracked down. The rounding-up of "pagan" priests and the suppression of ancient rituals caused seething resentment among the Pueblo.

This boiled over in 1680, when, roused by the influential priest Popé, villagers across New Mexico attacked and burned their mission churches. Killing Catholic priests and Spanish settlers, they converged on Santa Fe, sealing it off from the outside world. Several thousand Spanish survivors were holed up in large groups in Santa Fe and in other fortified settlements. So completely had communications been severed, however, that each party was unaware of the others' survival and no concerted response was possible.

Colonial governor Antonio de Otermín felt he had no alternative but to order a general retreat. The settlers streamed south to an encampment near what is now Ciudad Juarez. An attempt to retake the colony the following year was beaten back. Over decades, the Spanish reestablished their hold, but made important concessions to Pueblo culture and beliefs. **MK**

Losses: Pueblo, 21; Spanish settler, 400

◁ *Great Swamp Fight 1675*   *Raid on Deerfield 1704* ▷

Vienna 11–12 September 1683

The Siege of Vienna in 1683 was the last occasion on which the Ottoman Empire offered a serious military threat to Christian Europe. Led by grand vizier Kara Mustafa Pasha, the Ottomans narrowly failed to take the city, driven off by a relief army led by Polish ruler Jan III Sobieski.

In March 1683, the Ottomans, ruled by Sultan Mehmed IV, sent an army from Constantinople to conquer the city of Vienna and open the way for territorial expansion into central Europe. As the Ottomans advanced, passing Belgrade and moving toward Vienna, most of the city's population was evacuated and those who decided to stay prepared for a long siege. The massive Ottoman army of around 100,000 besieged the city in July, and the city's 10,000 troops refused an offer of surrender. Mustafa Pasha set up a magnificent camp for his huge army on

a plain next to the city, and began trying to mine the heavily fortified walls of the city. With its food supplies cut, conditions inside the city were soon desperate and many died of starvation. However, the Ottomans were in no hurry, expecting several months of siege. They finally succeeded in breaching the city walls in September, and a series of attacks was launched with the aim of further sapping the strength of the city's starving defenders.

However, the Ottomans were unaware that forces were gathering north of Vienna. Imperial forces under the Duke of Lorraine had joined with the Poles commanded by Sobieski. These troops united with others from the Holy League and, under the leadership of the Polish king, advanced across the Danube with a force of 50,000 infantry and 30,000 cavalry. On 12 September, the two armies faced each other outside Vienna. One army was fighting for its faith and the survival of its homeland;

the other was divided and unsure why it was there. Mustafa attacked first, feeling secure in his two-to-one numerical advantage, with the objective of not allowing the League's various commanders to arrange their battle formations. As the attack was pushed back by forces from Lorraine, the Polish king ordered a counterattack just as Mustafa's forces became separated by an attempt to storm the city. If Mustafa had planned the assault, it was a serious error. The Ottoman army opened two fronts, and, as the city's defenders pushed the assault back into the main Ottoman force, it caused panic among the Ottoman ranks. This chaos resulted in the Polish charge routing Mustafa's right flank and breaking the line of his center formation.

After several hours of savage fighting, the Polish and Austro-German cavalry moved around to the right of the battlefield, gained high ground, and waited while the League's infantry fought the Ottoman Janissary elite troops. Victory for the League was sealed—and Vienna saved—when it became apparent that many of the Ottomans' Crimean Tatar troops had fled. At this point, the Christian cavalry swept downhill in several separate formations, each attacking a specific part of the Ottoman force, killing many and scattering the rest southward in disarray. The Ottomans retreated back to Constantinople, and Mustafa Pasha was executed—ritually strangled with a bowstring—for presiding over such a huge disaster. The Viennese set about repairing the city defenses, expecting another attack. However, no attack came, and the defeat of 1683 was the last time the Ottomans would try to take Vienna. **TB**

Losses: Unknown

◁ *Lwów 1675*   *Zenta 1697* ▷

Penghu (Pescadores) 1683

For two decades after the victory of Zheng Chenggong at Fort Zeelandia, Taiwan remained a center of Han Chinese resistance to the Manchu takeover of China, protected by its naval strength. In 1683, Qing Emperor Kangxi at last found the ships and the admiral to conquer Taiwan.

Kangxi turned to Shi Lang, an experienced naval commander who had once fought under Zheng but had defected to serve the Qing—a desertion that Zheng punished by executing Shi's family. Shi Lang assembled an expeditionary force of more than 300 fighting ships and 60,000 soldiers. He set sail in July 1683 not only to fulfill a mission for the Qing but also to wage a personal war of revenge on Zheng's grandson, who by then had inherited rule of Taiwan.

Shi was confronted by a fleet under Liu Guoxuan at the Penghu (Pescadores) Islands. While most of his warships took on Liu's fleet, Shi diverted troops to an attack on Liu's island base, where they made an opposed landing in the face of fire from cannon and crossbows. The battle at sea was hard-fought but its outcome inevitable, for Shi's fleet was larger and better supplied with cannon and ammunition. Within an hour, Liu's fleet was effectively beaten, yet he and his most stubborn captains fought on, resorting to hand-to-hand fighting when their cannon ammunition was exhausted. Some committed suicide, jumping into the ocean rather than surrender.

On land, the Qing force was also successful, overrunning its enemy's base after stiff fighting. Liu surrendered when further resistance was hopeless. Soon after, Taiwan's ruler, Zheng Keshuang, accepted defeat and surrendered to the Qing. Taiwan was integrated into the Qing Empire, where it remained until it was forcibly ceded to Japan in 1895. **RG**

Losses: Qing, 5,000; Zheng, 12,000

◁ Fort Zeelandia 1661   Jao Modo 1696 ▷

Sedgemoor 6 July 1685

The battle at Sedgemoor in Somerset, England, was the conclusion of the Monmouth Rebellion, a conflict between a legitimate king and an illegitimate claimant to the British throne. The battle marked the last time a major armed confrontation took place on English soil.

The death of Charles II in 1685 brought his Roman Catholic brother, James II, to the throne. English Protestants feared he would restore Catholicism as the national religion. James Scott, Duke of Monmouth, one of Charles II's many illegitimate children, emerged as a staunchly Protestant claimant to the throne.

Monmouth had been commander in chief of the English army and had fought in the Anglo-Dutch Wars. He sailed from the Netherlands and landed on the English south coast with eighty-two men, soon gathering local support. He marched toward Bristol, fighting skirmishes on the way, but was forced back by the Royalist army to Bridgwater in Somerset. At 10:00 PM on 6 July, Monmouth led his army on a nighttime attack. His troops numbered around 3,500, mostly farmworkers armed with pitchforks. The similarly sized but far better equipped Royalist army was led by the Earl of Feversham, with John Churchill—later the Duke of Marlborough—as his second in command.

The rebel army crossed an open moor and startled a Royalist patrol. One shot was fired, alerting the rest of the Royalists that battle had commenced. The rebel cavalry moved forward but were swiftly engaged by the King's Regiment of Horse. The royal infantry followed, and soon the rebel forces were defeated. Monmouth escaped, only to be recaptured, taken to the Tower of London, and beheaded. James II was overthrown three years later after an unopposed invasion by William of Orange. **SA**

Losses: Royalist, 300 of 3,000; Protestant rebel, 1,000 dead and 500 captured of 3,500

Bantry Bay 1689 ▷

Bantry Bay 11 May 1689

The deposition of the Roman Catholic James II of England in favor of his Protestant son-in-law, William of Orange, brought England into conflict with France. The naval battle that took place off the southern coast of Ireland was the first time the English and French had clashed at sea since 1545.

In 1688, William of Orange took over the English throne from James, ruling jointly with James's daughter, Mary. As effective ruler of the Dutch United Provinces, William was already at war with the French king, Louis XIV, who supported James II in exile as a co-religionist. Setting out from France in the company of one hundred French officers and 2,500 troops, James landed on the Irish coast at Kinsale in March 1689. His intention was to establish control over Ireland and use it as a base for invading Britain.

On 6 May, a supply fleet of twenty-four ships under the Marquis of Chateaurenault left Brest in Brittany and headed for Ireland, where it was intercepted by an English fleet of nineteen ships commanded by Admiral Herbert (later Earl of Torrington). Prevented by the English from landing their supplies at Kinsale, the French fleet anchored to the far west in Bantry Bay. As the French started to unload men and supplies, the English fleet sailed into view.

A running battle took place, the two fleets at first parallel in the narrow bay but then spreading out into the open sea. The English fleet suffered heavy damage, but Chateaurenault failed to press his advantage and Herbert was able to limp back to Portsmouth. The French unloaded their supplies and returned to France. Although neither side delivered a knockout blow, the outcome was ominous for the English, who depended on their navy for protection against invasion. **SA**

Losses: French, no ships of 40, 40 dead; English, no ships of 19, 94 dead

[<] Sedgemoor 1685   Beachy Head 1690 [>]

Beachy Head 10 July 1690

After besting the English at Bantry Bay, the French navy defeated an allied Anglo-Dutch fleet off Beachy Head, southern England. The victory briefly gave France control of the Channel and led to the imprisonment of the English admiral, Arthur, Earl of Torrington, in the Tower of London.

On 23 June 1690, the French admiral, Anne, Count of Tourville, sailed the combined Atlantic and Mediterranean fleets out of Brest. His force of seventy-seven ships of the line outnumbered the Anglo-Dutch fleet in the Channel, which had thinned to fifty-seven ships of the line because many had been sent elsewhere to protect commercial shipping.

On 2 July, the fleets met near the Isle of Wight and sailed up the Channel without engaging. Torrington wanted to withdraw to protect his fleet, but on 9 July Queen Mary II ordered him to engage the French. The next day, near Beachy Head, he sailed toward the French with the Dutch in the vanguard. The Dutch failed to reach the front of the French line, so the leading French ships were able to cut across them while the French center completed an encirclement from the rear. The surrounded Dutch ships were battered mercilessly, the English unable to help them. After hours of fighting, Torrington broke off the fight by ordering his fleet to drop anchor, so the tide carried the French out of range. He then sailed for the Thames, abandoning Dutch ships too damaged to follow.

Imprisoned and court-martialed, Torrington was cleared of failing to support the Dutch but lost his post. Despite his supremacy, Tourville did not exploit his victory, sailing to Le Havre to rest and repair his fleet. By autumn, the Anglo-Dutch had ninety ships in the Channel, and the brief French superiority there was over. **JF**

Losses: Anglo-Dutch allied, at least 7 ships of 57; French, no ships of 77

[<] Bantry Bay 1689   Barfleur–La Hogue 1692 [>]

The Boyne   12 July 1690

The Battle of the Boyne is one of the most significant battles in British and Irish history. The victory of William of Orange over James II blunted attempts to restore Catholicism in Britain and confirmed the Protestant supremacy in Ireland. The battle has since become part of Irish folklore.

Deposed from the English throne by his Protestant son-in-law, William of Orange, the Catholic James II fled to France from where—with French help—he landed in Ireland seeking to regain the crown. His army soon controlled the entire island, except two Protestant strongholds in Ulster in the north—Londonderry and Enniskillen—to which it laid siege in April 1689. Both sieges were eventually ended in August: that of Londonderry by an English naval convoy breaking the blockade of the town, that of Enniskillen by the local militia. Having lost control of Ulster, James then headed with his army toward Dublin. The same month, a 20,000-strong army sent by William landed at Bangor and headed south. With its progress to

> ## "The flight became wild … the fugitives broke down the bridges and burned the ferryboats."
>
> *Lord Macaulay,* History of England

Dublin blocked by James, the army withdrew, and both armies camped for the winter. The following June, William landed at Carrickfergus in Ulster and headed south to join his troops and confront James. The two armies finally met up by the River Boyne, 25 miles (40 km) north of Dublin.

The two sides were quite different in makeup. The Jacobite army of James II numbered 23,500, mostly Irish Catholics reinforced by 6,000 French troops. His Irish infantry were mainly untrained peasants who had been pressed into military service. They were poorly equipped, some with obsolete matchlock muskets and others with scythes and other farm implements. Only the Irish cavalry were of a high caliber.

Facing them was an international Williamite army of around 36,000 men. William was the de facto ruler of Holland and was able to draw on infantry regiments from there and Denmark. These were professional soldiers equipped with the latest flintlock muskets. They fought alongside a large number of French Huguenot or Protestant troops sent into exile from France because of their religion, as well as English and Scottish troops and some Ulster Protestants. Crucially, William commanded eight times as much artillery as James.

William almost lost the battle before it started, because the day before he had been wounded in the shoulder by Jacobite artillery while surveying the various fords across the Boyne over which his men might pass. Patched up, he took command the next day. He sent about 9,000 men to cross the river at Roughgrange. Fearing he might be outflanked, James sent about half his army to challenge this force. What neither side recognized was that there was a deep ravine in the area that kept the two sides apart and forced them to sit the battle out without firing a shot. At the main ford at Oldbridge, the elite Dutch Blue Guards forced their way across the river and drove back the Jacobite infantry. A Jacobite cavalry counterattack pinned them down until the Williamite cavalry crossed the river and forced the Jacobites to retreat. A successful rearguard action then saved many of their lives. James quickly fled the field and returned to France, leaving his demoralized troops behind. Two days later, the Williamite army entered Dublin. The Protestant cause had triumphed, and the threat of a Catholic restoration was, for a time, ended. **SA**

Losses: Williamite, 750 casualties of 36,000; Jacobite, 1,500 casualties of 23,500

◁ Sedgemoor 1685   Barfleur–La Hogue 1692 ▷

Anti–home rule propaganda postcard celebrating the victory of William of Orange at the Boyne.

TRUTH. UNITY &CONCORD

NO SURRENDER.

I VI
II VII
III VIII

LET ALL WHO VIEW THESE EMBLEMS DEAR
WITH HEART AND SOUL IN CONCERT JOIN
TO HONOUR MEN WHO KNEW NO FEAR.
AS PROVED AT DERRY AND THE BOYNE.

FOR TRUTH AND LIBERTY THEY FOUGHT,
FOR ENGLAND'S HONOUR NOBLY FELL,
HIS SUBJECTS GOOD, GREAT WILLIAM SOUGHT
AS FUTURE AGES YET SHALL TELL.

CIVIL & RELIGIOUS
LIBERTY

AUGHRIM
DERRY.

WILLIAM III.
PRINCE of ORANGE.
OF GLORIOUS, PIOUS AND IMMORTAL
MEMORY.

JULY 1, 1690.

WALKER

THE BATTLE OF THE BOYNE. JULY 1ST 1690.
BY THIS GREAT VICTORY, WILLIAM AND HIS BRAVE ARMY SECURED
TO US AND OUR POSTERITY, OUR LIBERTY, LAWS AND RELIGION.

Barfleur–La Hogue
29 May–5 June 1692

After defeating the allied British and Dutch fleets at Beachy Head in 1690, France seemed to have a real chance of achieving naval superiority in the Channel. This hope was destroyed when an Anglo-Dutch fleet inflicted heavy losses on the French in the twin battles of Barfleur and La Hogue.

French king Louis XIV planned to restore the Catholic James II to the English throne. In May 1692, plans were made for a French fleet to join with and escort an invasion force to England before the Anglo-Dutch allies could deploy their fleet in the Channel. However, the French encountered difficulties and only a belated and depleted fleet eventually set sail under the Count of Tourville.

They were engaged by Admiral Edward Russell off the French coast at Barfleur. Tourville attacked, despite inferior numbers, on the morning of 29 May. Exchanging broadsides in line of battles, the center squadrons of the two fleets inflicted and suffered heavy casualties. Tourville skillfully prevented his van being overlapped by the Dutch ships in Russell's van, before calm waters and a fog set in, making it impossible for the ships of the line to maneuver except under tow by rowing boats.

After nightfall, the battered, exhausted fleets disengaged. The French slipped away, but Russell pursued them with his damaged ships. Some of the French fleet escaped, but fifteen damaged ships tried to find refuge on the French coast at Cherbourg and La Hogue. The British soon discovered the location of these vessels and attacked them with fireships. All were destroyed. The actions at Barfleur and La Hogue ended Louis XIV's ambitious plans to invade Britain and were key milestones in the rise of British naval preeminence. **TB**

Losses: French, 2,000 casualties, 15 ships of 40; Anglo-Dutch allied, 2,500 casualties, no ships of 82

◁ Beachy Head 1690   Action of 29 June 1694 ▷

Steenkerque
3 August 1692

The Battle of Steenkerque was fought as part of the ongoing War of the League of Augsburg (or Nine Years' War) between France, led by the Duke of Luxembourg, and allied British, Danish, and Dutch troops, under the personal command of King William III of England.

Having made a number of gains in Wallonia (present-day northern Belgium), most notably the capture of the strategic town of Namur after a month-long siege, the French army formed a defensive line not wishing to expose their army to further engagements. William had lost patience with his supreme commander, Prince Georg Friedrich of Waldeck, following defeat at Fleurus in 1690, and took personal command of his army.

On 3 August, William attacked the right wing of the French army, which had become isolated from the main force. However, William's army did not keep close formation as it moved into battle, and the attack was a shambles. Any advantage gained was lost due to the inability of the allies to back up their front line with their main force. As the isolated allied vanguard pressed the French back with great success, Luxembourg arrived with his main force and ordered a counterattack of his Swiss guards. William struggled to control his disorganized forces and offer his front line the support they badly needed, and they were pushed back by the French counter. At the same time, the progress of his infantry was blocked by an uncoordinated cavalry charge led by the Dutch lieutenant general, Count Solms. The ensuing melee was savage, and both sides took heavy losses. In the end, William had been unable to coordinate his commanders and he ordered a retreat, blaming the Dutch for his unexpected defeat. **TB**

Losses: French, 7,000 casualties of 80,000; Allied, 10,000 casualties of 20,000 (60,000 failed to support the front line)

Neerwinden 1693 ▷

◉ *Detail of a nineteenth-century etching by Chavanne, showing French and British ships in battle off Normandy.*   1500–1699 | **385**

Neerwinden   29 July 1693

The Battle of Neerwinden was the greatest triumph of French commander the Duke of Luxembourg, and his second consecutive major defeat of King William III of England. Luxembourg went on to decorate the interior of Notre-Dame Cathedral in Paris with captured British and Dutch flags.

After their defeat at Steenkerque in 1692, William III's allied army in Flanders held a crescent of fortified trenches from Laer to Neerwinden on the right, and from Neerwinden to Neerlanden on the left. The Duke of Luxembourg sent scouts to survey the allied positions and decided that William's right flank was the weakest because the line was long and the River Gete at William's rear would impede his retreat. In particular, the French commander thought that a concerted assault on William's long, spread-out line would enable him to break through before William could muster support from the flanks.

Luxembourg concentrated his force of 75,000 and attacked William's line at Neerwinden, following a lengthy bombardment of the allied positions. However, the first wave soon faltered because the allied troops put up a solid defense, and Luxembourg sent in a second wave, which managed to break through the allied line. In response, William attempted to close down the attack, and, after a long period of brutal hand-to-hand fighting, Luxembourg called in his last massive wave, which overwhelmed the already exhausted allied infantry. As the allies retreated, there were several rearguard actions, which gave William time to regroup and support his forces from other parts of his entrenchments. However, as the allies sought to turn retreat into attack, the French cavalry charged, pushing William's army back to the river where many drowned in the stampede to escape. **TB**

Losses: French, 8,000 casualties of 75,000; Allied, 20,000 casualties of 60,000

◁ Steenkerque 1692   Namur 1695 ▷

Action of 29 June   29 June 1694

After their crushing defeat at Barfleur–La Hogue, the French navy avoided fleet actions, resorting to commerce raiding and hit-and-run attacks. The Action of 29 June was a triumph for France's most famous privateer, Jean Bart, who boldly recaptured a convoy that had been taken by the Dutch.

By the 1690s, France's continual wars had almost bankrupted King Louis XIV and reduced the French people to near starvation. Unable to match their enemies in terms of shipbuilding, the French began a naval guerilla war, in which privateers used their own ships to attack allied merchant vessels from bases in Channel ports such as Dunkirk.

Jean Bart was the most celebrated of these privateers, carrying out successful attacks on merchant vessels from 1691. His most famous action came on 29 June 1694. Bart had been instructed to escort a convoy of more than one hundred grain ships to France, essential to feed the hungry population. However, the convoy set sail before he arrived and was captured by Dutch warships. Bart hunted down the convoy and discovered it near the Dutch offshore island of Texel. He then launched an audacious attack on the Dutch naval vessels, despite their superiority in numbers and greater firepower. In a short battle, he succeeded in boarding and capturing the Dutch flagship, despite sustaining heavy damage to his own flagship, *Maure*. After two other Dutch ships were also taken, the rest took flight, seeking the safety of port.

Bart recaptured the grain convoy, delivering a major boost to French morale. He became a French naval hero and was ennobled by the king. Several French warships have since borne his name, and he is commemorated with a statue in the town of Dunkirk. **TB**

Losses: Allied, 3 naval ships, 100 grain ships; French, no ships lost

◁ Barfleur–La Hogue 1692   Dogger Bank 1696 ▷

War of the League of Augsburg

Namur   2 July–1 September 1695

The fortress of Namur, in modern-day Belgium, was a key stronghold in the war between Louis XIV's France and the anti-French alliance commanded by William III of England. The French took Namur in 1692 but lost it three years later, partly due to the skill of Dutch siege expert Baron Coehoorn.

France improved Namur's defenses after their capture of the city, but by 1695 Louis XIV's coffers were depleted and his armies were on the defensive. William III and Maximilian of Bavaria led an allied army in to besiege the city in July, with Baron Coehoorn organizing their entrenchments and mining operations.

It took Coehoorn three weeks to breach the outer defenses, after which allied troops assaulted the city and inflicted serious casualties on the French defenders. The French commander, Duke of Boufflers, agreed a truce in order to give time for both armies to attend to their wounded. He ceded control of the city, but pulled his forces back to the inner citadel, which he continued to defend.

The French sought to create a diversion to relieve the city by launching an attack on Brussels under the command of the Duke of Villeroi. The bombardment caused extensive damage in Brussels and widespread outrage in Europe, because an attack against a civilian population was widely considered contrary to the rules of war. However, the diversion failed to break the siege, and Villeroi's army was stopped from marching to relieve Namur. Boufflers surrendered the citadel on 1 September after the French garrison had taken two-thirds casualties. With the French government facing bankruptcy, the loss of Namur impelled France to seek peace terms, which were finally agreed in 1697. The ambition of Louis XIV would start a new European war, however, four years later. **TB**

Losses: Allied, 15,000 casualties of 60,000; French, 9,000 casualties of 15,000

◁ *Neerwinden 1693*

Chinese-Zhungar Wars

Jao Modo   12 June 1696

In the late seventeenth century, following the tradition of Genghis Khan's Mongols, the Zhungar tribes under their inspired leader Galdan created the last of the great Asian nomad empires. Qing emperor Kangxi led a military expedition from China against the Zhungars in 1696.

It was highly unusual for a Chinese emperor to campaign in person, but Kangxi attributed great importance to halting Galdan's rising power. Although China had the military might to defeat the steppe horsemen in open battle, the mobile Zhungars were expert at avoiding combat except on their own terms.

In March 1696, three armies set out from China for the Zhungar heartland on the far side of the Gobi desert. They totaled more than 70,000 men and carried with them more than 300 cannon. Surviving conditions ranging from snow and rain to sand dunes and drought, two of the armies, led by the emperor and his general Fianggyu, closed in on Galdan in June. By then, however, their supplies were exhausted and starvation threatened. The emperor turned back for home to avert disaster, but not before he had driven Galdan's army into flight, and into the path of Fianggyu's 14,000-strong force.

The two armies met at Jao Modo. Once the Chinese had gained control of high ground, their cannon began to decimate the Zhungar fighters. An advance by Chinese infantry, followed by a cavalry charge, routed Galdan's force completely. Emperor Kangxi reached Beijing after ninety-eight days and a journey of some 1,500 miles (2,424 km), claiming a great victory. Nonetheless, the Zhungars continued to be a significant force until crushed with near-genocidal thoroughness in the mid-eighteenth century by Kangxi's successor, Emperor Qianlong. **RG**

Losses: Chinese, unknown; Zhungar, 5,000 dead or captured

◁ *Penghu 1683*

Dogger Bank   17 June 1696

The Battle of Dogger Bank was a naval encounter between a French force, under the command of the famous privateer, Jean Bart, and a squadron of Dutch ships acting as escort to a convoy of more than one hundred merchant vessels. The battle was part of the ongoing War of the League of Augsburg.

Almost one year after his victory over a Dutch squadron in the so-called Action of 29 June, the privateer Jean Bart was patrolling the Dogger Bank area of the North Sea, 60 miles (96 km) off the east coast of England, when he sighted a large merchant convey of more than one hundred vessels being escorted by five Dutch ships. Over the previous few days, Bart had skillfully avoided an English naval squadron that had been alerted to Bart's presence in the area and had been looking to capture him. It was during this dangerous game of cat and mouse that Bart decided to launch an attack on the convoy with his twelve ships.

Although Bart's ships were more powerful, his attack needed to be swift, because the English, under the command of Admiral Benbow, were not too far away. Bart attacked the Dutch flagship, *Raadhuis Van Haarlem*, and, after a few hours, the ship was destroyed and her captain killed. The remaining four Dutch ships surrendered after taking heavy damage, three of which later sank. Bart was able to capture and destroy twenty-five merchant vessels before sighting Benbow's squadron and fleeing toward the coast of Denmark. The game of cat and mouse continued for another two months, but Bart eluded detection as he moved down the coast, arriving in Dunkirk in September. Bart's action was one more success in the guerilla naval war and enhanced his hero status in France. **TB**

Losses: Allied, 5 naval vessels and 25 merchant ships; French, minimal casualties

◁ *Action of 29 June 1694*   *Vigo Bay 1702* ▷

Zenta   12 September 1697

In 1697, Prince Eugene of Savoy, commanding a Hapsburg Austrian army, surprised a larger Ottoman Turkish army at the Tisza River in Serbia and defeated it in a bold attack that made him one of Europe's most celebrated generals. The defeat was another step in the decline of Ottoman power.

Defeated at Vienna in 1683, the Ottomans were driven out of Belgrade and large parts of central Europe. However, Austrian involvement in war with France allowed the Ottoman Empire to launch a counterattack that resulted in the recapture of Belgrade in 1690. In 1697, Prince Eugene resolved to stop the Ottoman army advancing to the Hungarian city of Szeged.

When the Ottomans learned of Eugene's army, they abandoned plans for taking Szeged and started a withdrawal into Romania for the winter months. Eugene was determined to force a battle and caught the Ottoman army at the Tisza River near the town of Zenta. The Ottomans were camped behind field fortifications with their backs to the river, which they had begun to cross by a single bridge. Eugene launched a surprise attack, trapping the Turks between his troops and the river. Eugene's artillery devastated the Ottomans as they tried to complete their withdrawal, and his soldiers succeeded in taking the bridge. The trapped Ottoman troops where subjected to an onslaught that ended with thousands drowning in the river and the deaths of many more thousands in the surrounded camp.

Zenta was a disastrous defeat for the Ottoman Empire. It forced the Ottomans to sign the Treaty of Karlowitz in 1699, which ceded Hungary and Transylvania to Austria, most of Dalmatia to Venice, and permanently ended Ottoman plans for the conquest of central Europe. **TB**

Losses: Ottoman, 30,000 casualties of 60,000; Hapsburg, 1,500 casualties of 50,000

◁ *Vienna 1683*   *Corfu 1716* ▷

Eugene leads a surprise attack on the Ottoman army in the eighteenth-century painting The Battle of Zenta.

4

1700–1799

Detail from a painting of the Battle of Ushant (1778) by French painter Theodore Gudin (1802–80).

Narva   30 November 1700

In 1700, Czar Peter I of Russia challenged the long-established Swedish domination of the Baltic in alliance with Denmark and Saxony-Poland-Lithuania. In November that year, the Swedish triumphed over the Russians in their first major engagement of the Great Northern War at Narva.

After the Russians declared war on Sweden, they invaded Estonia and besieged Narva in September 1700. By November 1700, the Swedish king, Charles XII, had already forced Denmark out of the war. He then transported his army to Estonia to face his remaining enemies. The Saxon-Polish-Lithuanian army had just withdrawn for the winter. This left the way clear for the Swedish army to relieve Narva by surprising the Russian army, which was more than four times its size.

Crucially, the Swedish forces were well led and highly disciplined, whereas the Russians were comparatively poorly trained and often ineffectively led by foreign officers. Czar Peter had been leading his armies personally—but, shortly before the Swedish arrival, he had returned to Russia, leaving an experienced general, Charles Eugène de Croy, in command.

The Swedish army approached Narva on 30 November and quickly took advantage of a snowstorm that blew into the face of the Russian army. The Swedes attacked in two columns of foot and horse, too rapidly for the Russians to deploy their artillery. After a fierce struggle, the Russian cavalry on the left flank fled, and then their infantry on the right flank retreated. The remaining Russians surrendered, and Croy was also captured. Narva had rid Sweden of any immediate Russian threat on its Baltic territory, but Charles XII was unable to follow up his victory with a decisive blow into Russia. **JF**

Losses: Swedish, 2,000 of 8,000–11,000; Russian, 8,000–10,000 of 24,000–35,000

Holowczyn 1708 ▸

Engraving depicting King Charles XII (on horseback) in the thick of the Battle of Narva. ⬆

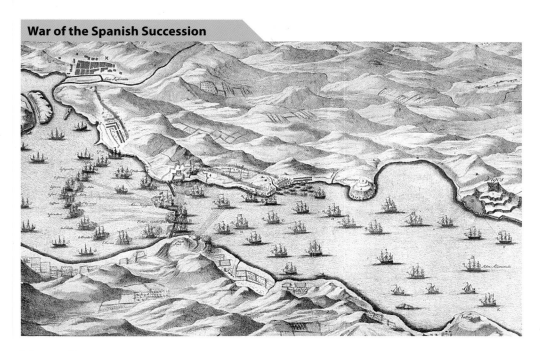

Vigo Bay   22 October 1702

The Battle of Vigo Bay was one of the first naval battles in the War of the Spanish Succession. Fought between the Anglo-Dutch navy and an allied French and Spanish force, the battle was primarily an attempt to capture Spanish silver as it was being transported from America.

The War of the Spanish Succession was fought to prevent Spain and France from uniting under one Bourbon monarch and dominating Europe. Attacks on Spanish treasure fleets were an important aspect of the campaign, and, in October 1702, news came that a major shipment of silver was due to arrive. By mid-October, Admiral Sir George Rooke received intelligence that the treasure had reached Vigo Bay. Rooke sailed north and reached Vigo on 22 October.

A Dutch force was landed, which assaulted and captured Fort Rande, at which point Rooke set about destroying a defensive boom that the French had laid across the port. Rooke sent in his first ship, *Torbay*, an eighty-gun ship of the line, which rammed the boom and broke through. She put up a spirited fight, but a sudden lull in the wind prevented the rest of Rooke's squadron following, which allowed the French to attack the *Torbay* with fireships. The lull was only short, and when Rooke's flagship led the rest of the Anglo-Dutch squadron into the port, the French set fire to their own ships rather than allow their capture. Even so, some treasure was taken.

The long-term impact of the attack was military rather than financial. Vigo was a disaster for the French navy because it lost fifteen ships of the line. However, for Spain the impact was worse because it convinced Portugal that naval supremacy lay with the Anglo-Dutch, and an alliance with these powers was signed in 1703. **TB**

Losses: Anglo-Dutch allied, no ships, 800 casualties; Franco-Spanish allied, 17 ships of the line, 2,500 casualties

◁ *Dogger Bank 1696*   *Schellenberg 1704* ▷

⬆ *This battle plan reveals the intended maneuvers of the Dutch fleet in the waters of Vigo Bay.*

Raid on Deerfield   29 February 1704

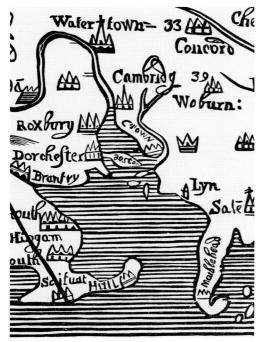

An early map of Massachusetts Bay: Deerfield lies farther inland, west of Cambridge.

> "[My wife] was plunged over head and ears in the water; after which she traveled not far, for the cruel and bloodthirsty savage slew her with his hatchet."

Rev. John Williams's memoir, The Redeemed Captive Returning to Zion (1707)

The attack on the English settlement at Deerfield, in the colony of Massachusetts, was an example of the kind of warfare that occurred in North America during Queen Anne's War (1702–13). The raid resulted in the capture of civilian settlers, who were forced to walk 300 miles (483 km) to Quebec.

Queen Anne's War was fought between France and England for control of North America and was part of the wider conflict known as the War of the Spanish Succession. From 1703, a number of isolated New England settlements had been attacked by French soldiers and French Canadian militia with their American Indian allies. Nonetheless, the raid on Deerfield caught the settlement—with a population of 250 and a garrison of fewer than 20 soldiers—totally by surprise.

The raiders were led by Jean-Baptiste Hertel de Rouville and consisted of forty-seven French and French Canadians and several hundred Algonquin and Mohawk warriors. They attacked before daybreak, advancing silently over snow-covered ground, and swarmed through the settlement's stockade. Despite being caught unprepared, the soldiers and settlers put up a stiff fight, reportedly killing up to forty of the intruders. They were swiftly overwhelmed, however, with about sixty English men, women, and children dying in the onslaught.

In excess of one hundred settlers were taken prisoner and forced to walk through the freezing winter weather to the Mohawk settlement of Caughnawaga in Quebec. Many died on the journey or in subsequent captivity. The New England colonists launched retaliatory raids on French settlements in which they took prisoners who could be exchanged for those taken at Deerfield. **TB**

Losses: English colonists, 60 dead and more than 100 captured (number of survivors unknown); French and American Indian, 50 casualties of 300

◁ Santa Fe 1680

Schellenberg   2 July 1704

In the War of the Spanish Succession, Britain fought in alliance with Austria and the Dutch Republic against France and her allies. In the summer of 1704, the Duke of Marlborough led an army through Germany to save Vienna from an imminent attack by the French and Maximilian II Emanuel of Bavaria.

The Elector of Bavaria learned of Marlborough's plan to cross the Danube at Donauworth and sent an advance Franco-Bavarian force to fortify itself into positions on the Schellenberg heights, which had a commanding position above the town. Upon arrival, Marlborough decided to launch a swift assault on what he deemed to be the weakest part of the fortifications. He knew that casualties would be heavy, but feared that once his enemy had dug in they would be impossible to move. Also, he feared the approach of the main Franco-Bavarian army that was only days away.

Marlborough bombarded the enemy positions, but his first assault failed with heavy losses. A second assault was also forced back by intense musket fire and grape shot. The breakthrough came when the allies launched a two-pronged attack. The Austrians struck at the Bavarian exposed left flank, taking the town; Marlborough's British troops launched an assault straight at the hill. This time Marlborough abandoned tight formations and spread his force in a broad line, which reduced the effectiveness of the Bavarian musket fire. The Bavarians routed and fled for their lives, pursued by Marlborough's cavalry. Marlborough's victory secured the Danube, but it was followed by a period of stalemate in which the allied army devastated Bavaria while Marlborough and his allied commanders debated the best course of action. **TB**

Losses: English-led allied, 5,000 casualties of 20,000; Franco-Bavarian allied, 6,000 casualties and 2,000 captured of 15,000

◁ *Vigo Bay 1702*   *Blenheim 1704* ▷

"He commanded the armies of Europe against France for ten campaigns. He never fought a battle that he did not win, nor besieged a fortress that he did not take. . . . He quitted war invincible."

Winston Churchill, on the Duke of Marlborough

⬆ Prince Eugene of Savoy in the Field, *by Pietro Longhi (1701–85): the prince prepares to partner Marlborough.*

Blenheim   13 August 1704

The Battle of Blenheim was a crushing victory for the Duke of Marlborough and Prince Eugene of Savoy over a Franco-Bavarian army. A decisive turning point in the war of the Grand Alliance against French king Louis XIV, it made Marlborough a British national hero.

After his victory at Schellenberg, the Duke of Marlborough wished to draw the Elector of Bavaria, Maximilian II Emanuel, into battle before he could join with Marshall Tallard's French army and launch an attack on Vienna. However, Maximilian would not be drawn, despite the alliance's attempts to force him into action by adopting a scorched-earth campaign that devastated much of Bavaria. Eventually, Maximilian and Tallard joined forces in early August. Marlborough, meanwhile, was joined by Prince Eugene's Austrian army. Although outnumbered, they decided to take the offensive against the Franco-Bavarian force on the banks of the Danube, near the village of Blindheim (Blenheim).

> *"[I pay tribute to] the glory of Prince Eugene, whose fire and spirit had exhorted the wonderful exertions of his troops."* Winston Churchill

The Franco-Bavarian army had positioned itself along a 4-mile (6.5 km) strip of land. Tallard's French divisions stretched from the Danube and Blenheim on their left through to the village of Oberglau in the center. The Bavarians took the right flank and stretched along the battlefield to high ground and pine woodland near the hamlet of Lutzingen. In front of the Franco-Bavarian army was a long piece of marshy land known as the Nebel.

Prince Eugene was assigned the task of taking Lutzingen, while Lieutenant General John Cutts was ordered to take Blenheim. Cutts began his attack under the cover of an artillery bombardment, but as his infantry ranks marched forward they were repelled by small arms fire from the French barricades, with heavy casualties. However, after repeated attacks, Cutts broke through, pushing the French back. His advance caused the French commander, Clerambault, to break off from the main force, thus weakening Tallard's line and removing the advantage he had over Marlborough in term of numbers. Seeing his opportunity, Marlborough ordered Cutts to contain Clerambault at Blenheim, which kept Tallard's reserve away from where it might have been of more use.

At the opposite end of the battlefield, Prince Eugene was being held at bay by Maximilian's Bavarian army. Eugene launched repeated attacks, but the combination of the difficult terrain and the stout Bavarian defense hampered his attacks. As Eugene continued on the offensive, Marlborough attacked Tallard's center at Oberglau. After several charges and heavy infantry losses, Tallard's cavalry were overcome, and Marlborough's forces broke through, routing the French infantry. With his reserve bogged down by Cutts in Blenheim, Tallard's lines disintegrated and, as his French forces fled, the Bavarians defending Lutzingen also retreated. Clerambault fought on at Blenheim, hoping to hold the village in time for a French counterattack. However, the broken Franco-Bavarian army had retreated southwest, and the French commander surrendered as night approached.

The allied victory at Blenheim was a shattering defeat for Louis XIV. It turned the tide of the war and forced the French alliance onto the defensive. In the short term, Vienna was saved from an attack that might have resulted in the collapse of the Grand Alliance. Marlborough gained an enduring moral ascendancy over his opponents. **TB**

Losses: Grand Alliance, 15,000 of 50,000; Franco-Bavarian allied, 35,000 dead or captured of 60,000

[<] Schellenberg 1704   Ramillies 1706 [>]

Military plan showing troop positions in the Battle of Blenheim. ➜

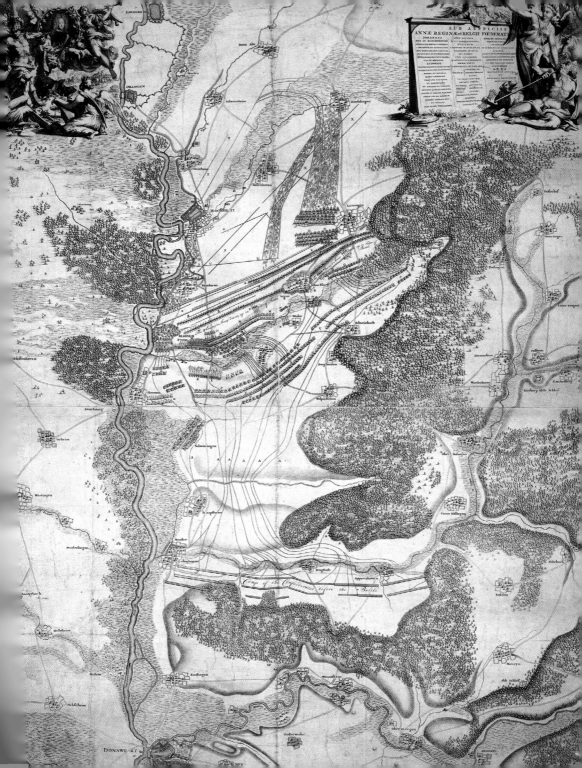

SUB AUSPICIIS
ANNÆ REGINÆ, et FŒDERATI BELGII

Ramillies   23 May 1706

The Battle of Ramillies was an encounter in the War of the Spanish Succession between the Grand Alliance, led by the Duke of Marlborough, and a Franco-Bavarian army, commanded by the Duke of Villeroi. The battle was a failed attempt by King Louis XIV to regain the initiative in the long war.

Although defeat at Blenheim had pushed Louis XIV onto the defensive, the Allies failed to end the war. In 1706, the French won victory in Alsace and—in order to strengthen his hand at the negotiating table—Louis ordered the Duke of Villeroi to attack the Duke of Marlborough. The Franco-Bavarian army met Marlborough's army near the villages of Ramillies and Taviers.

The first attack was launched by Marlborough's Dutch forces on Taviers. After fierce fighting, the French were pushed back, threatening Villeroi's right flank. Villeroi responded with an infantry advance but this was routed by Dutch cavalry. Marlborough ordered the Duke of Orkney to attack the French left. Villeroi responded by moving troops from his center to reinforce his left. Marlborough attacked the weakened French center and withdrew Orkney, shifting his troops to support the attack on Villeroi's vunerable section.

Villeroi had not seen Orkney's move, and the French lines were soon breaking. The French commander hesitated in committing his cavalry reserves, fearing that they might be needed later in the engagement; when he did commit them, it was too late. Allied troops broke through right across the field, putting the Franco-Bavarian army to flight. Victory for the Grand Alliance resulted in the capture of most of the Spanish Netherlands, and Louis XIV was forced to seek a peace settlement to save France from invasion. **TB**

Losses: Grand Alliance, 4,000 casualties of 60,000; Franco-Bavarian allied, 12,000 casualties of 62,000

◁ Blenheim 1704   The Lizard 1707 ▷

The Lizard   21 October 1707

During the War of the Spanish Succession, despite the superiority of its navy, Britain found it hard to secure its maritime lines of communication. The interception of a military convoy off the coast of Cornwall by French privateers and naval ships resulted in a costly defeat for the Royal Navy.

In October 1707, five Royal Navy ships of the line—under Commodore Richard Edwards— were escorting a convoy of eighty troop transports and supply ships, bound for the British army fighting in Spain. The convoy was sighted by a French squadron of six ships under Admiral Claude de Forbin. He tracked the convoy for some time, but the attack was only made when Forbin was joined by a second squadron of ships—led by St. Malo privateer René Dugauy-Trouin—off the Lizard peninsula in Cornwall, southwest England.

Forbin initially hesitated, but the aggressive Dugauy-Trouin led an attack, forcing the convoy to flee while Edwards mounted a defense with his five warships. When Forbin committed his squadron, the French were able to inflict massive damage on the English warships due to their advantage in numbers. In the course of the engagement, three ships of the line—*Cumberland*, *Chester*, and *Ruby*—were captured. After fighting valiantly until dusk, *Devonshire* was destroyed with all hands lost— more than 800 men—when her gunpowder magazine exploded. Only *Royal Oak* survived, reaching safety on the Irish coast at Kinsale.

The brave resistance of the escort ships allowed most of the transport ships to escape, although an uncertain number—much disputed between British and French sources—were captured. Nothing could disguise, however, a British naval defeat of serious proportions. **TB**

Losses: Royal Navy, 4 of 5 ships; French, no ships lost

◁ Ramillies 1706   Oudenarde 1708 ▷

Holowczyn (Golovchin) 14 July 1708

Charles XII of Sweden had been able to force Denmark and Saxony-Poland-Lithuania out of the Great Northern War by 1706. The next year, the Swedish king invaded Russia—his last remaining foe—where he followed up his triumph at Narva with another victory over a larger Russian army.

Charles XII's army set off through Poland-Lithuania to threaten Moscow. A Russian army of 38,000 commanded by Field Marshal Boris Sheremetev congregated at Holowczyn on the River Vabich, intending to halt the Swedish advance. Charles decided to meet the enemy head-on and led 20,000 through the woods. He found the Russians entrenched behind the Vabich. They had split into two groups, with woods and marshy land between them; Sheremetev led one group and General Anikita Repnin the other. Charles spent days surveying the field.

At midnight on 14 July, Charles ordered his army to prepare for battle as quietly as possible, and he brought his artillery up. At dawn, the Swedish put down pontoons and crossed the river. Charles had decided to advance through the space between the Russian camps and attack Repnin. The Swedish infantry engaged the Russian foot and there was a heavy exchange of musket fire. The Swedish horse had to charge the numerically superior Russian cavalry numerous times before their lines broke.

At 7:00 PM Repnin's forces began to flee. The Swedish were unable to pursue the Russians effectively because they had open ground to their rear. Meanwhile, Sheremetev retreated after his attempt to attack the Swedish camp was repulsed. For his part in the defeat, Sheremetev was court-martialed. The Swedish route to Moscow was clear, but the Russians fell back to new defensive positions with their army largely intact. **JF**

Losses: Russian, 1,000 dead and 700 wounded of 38,000; Swedish, 250 of 20,000

◁ Narva 1700　　　　　　　Poltava 1709 ▷

Oudenarde 11 July 1708

The Battle of Oudenarde was a key encounter of the War of the Spanish Succession between the forces of France, under the Duke of Bourgogne and the Duke of Vendome, and the combined forces of the Grand Alliance, commanded by the Duke of Marlborough and Prince Eugene of Savoy.

By May 1708, the French army had launched a new offensive and moved into Flanders, taking Ghent and Bruges and threatening Oudenarde, the one remaining allied fortress. If the fortress fell, the allied army would be trapped in Flanders. Marlborough embarked on one of the most famous forced marches in history, in which several temporary bridges were built to cross the Scheldt, in order to position his army of 100,000 between Oudenarde and the advancing French.

The first crucial phase of the battle was effectively a struggle to control the crossing point at the River Scheldt near the fortress. An advance division of cavalry was sent to capture and hold the crossing while Marlborough marched his army to the scene. The French approached, but were surprised by the strength of Marlborough's vanguard and hesitated long enough for Prince Eugene to cross the river with a large contingent of Prussian cavalry. As the allied forces moved up, the two French commanders disagreed over tactics; Bourgogne favored an attack but Vendome was more cautious. In the end, the French launched two attacks with very little coordination; one unified effort might have defeated the allies.

By all accounts, Marlborough deployed his forces brilliantly, masterminding an audacious outflanking move using the clever deployment of his Dutch army. However, the allies were aided by the French lack of coordination, resulting in another crushing defeat for France. **TB**

Losses: Grand Alliance, 5,000 casualties of 100,000; French, 20,000 casualties and desertions of 100,000

◁ The Lizard 1707　　　　Malplaquet 1709 ▷

Poltava   8 July 1709

The Battle of Poltava was the turning point of the Great Northern War and a key moment in Russia's rise to major power status. In 1709, Czar Peter's army crushed Swedish king Charles XII's invading army in central Ukraine.

In spite of his previous success against the Russians, Charles XII had not been able to challenge Moscow. By winter 1708, facing icy Russian weather and low on supplies, Charles headed south to the Ukraine. He found it difficult to supply his army, and began his spring offensive having lost 5,000 to 8,000 men. However, he still had an army of 25,000, and decided to capture the Russian fortress of Poltava on the Vorskla River. Czar Peter mobilized his forces to defend Poltava.

On 27 June, during the first skirmishes, a stray Russian shot struck Charles in the foot. The wound became serious and for two days Charles's life hung in the balance. Although he recovered, he was unable to lead his army in person. Command was transferred to Field Marshal

> *"I have resolved never to start an unjust war but never to end a legitimate one except by defeating my enemies."* Charles XII

Carl Gustav Rehnskiöld and General Adam Ludwig Lewenhaupt. Knowing the Swedish lacked cohesive leadership, Peter crossed the Vorskla and dug in his army of 40,000 near Poltava. He set up a T-shaped series of redoubts in the woods southwest of his position along the route the Swedish would have to take to attack. The positions would provide flanking fire against the advancing Swedes and help protect the main camp.

On 8 July, the Swedish took the initiative and attacked just before dawn. Lewenhaupt was in command of the infantry, which advanced toward the main Russian camp. His original orders did not take the redoubts into consideration and some officers stopped to capture them, costing the Swedish time and casualties. One infantry battalion of 2,600 had been attacking the redoubts one by one. This left them completely isolated and they were forced to surrender, costing the Swedish one-third of their infantry on the field. The rest of the Swedish infantry had reached the narrow plain in front of the Russian camp by 8:30 AM. They paused for two hours, waiting for the remainder of their infantry. Eventually, Peter decided to march his infantry forces of 20,000 out of the camp and drew up in two lines, supported by sixty-eight guns.

After forty-five minutes' artillery barrage, the two forces advanced toward each other. The superior Russian numbers meant that they outflanked both sides of the Swedish infantry, which also lacked any coherent cavalry support. Lewenhaupt was able to break through the first Russian line, but he could not sustain his momentum and the Russians pushed forward against the exhausted Swedish soldiers, who were soon forced back. When the 10,000-strong Russian cavalry joined the fray, the battle turned into a rout, and the Swedish army retreated in complete disarray.

The Swedish losses at Poltava in terms of casualties and prisoners numbered more than 10,000. Three days later, most of the remainder of the Swedish army surrendered to the Russians at Perevolochna. Essentially, the Swedish army had ceased to exist. Charles managed to flee southward to the Ottoman Empire, where he spent five years in exile. Poltava was a major turning point. Russia could now dominate the Polish and Baltic lands without any Swedish opposition, and Peter became the leading ruler in the region. **JF**

Losses: Swedish, at least 10,000 dead, wounded, or captured of 25,000; Russian, 4,500 dead or wounded of 40,000

◁ *Holowczyn 1708*   *Gangut 1714* ▷

Peter the Great at the Battle of Poltava, *by Gottfried Tannauer (1680–c. 1737), one of the czar's favorite artists.*

Malplaquet   11 September 1709

The last of the Duke of Marlborough's great battles in the War of the Spanish Succession, Malplaquet was won with an excessive loss of lives. Marshal Claude de Villars, the defeated French commander, told King Louis XIV: "If it please God to give your enemies another such victory, they are ruined."

After the Battle of Oudenarde, a concerted campaign in France was delayed by the onset of winter. Marlborough began a new offensive in June 1709, but it was not until September that any significant gains were made. Louis XIV ordered Marshal de Villars to stop the allied advance, and the two armies met in battle at Malplaquet.

Marlborough sent in his Austrian force first and attacked the French left wing, which had positioned itself in front of a wooded area. The attack pushed the French back and, soon after, the Dutch army launched an assault on the French right. Villars repulsed the attack and inflicted surprisingly heavy casualties on the Dutch, who

had fought so decisively at Oudenarde. Prince Eugene of Savoy then threw his forces into the fray to support the depleted Dutch army. This succeeded in weakening the French line, and Boufflers, Villars's second in command, transferred troops from the center to support Villars. The Earl of Orkney saw the French redeployment and charged the center with allied cavalry supported by artillery fire. As the French and allied cavalry fought desperately, the allied infantry moved up and drove back the French, but sustained massive casualties. Villars was wounded by musket fire, and Boufflers took command, ordering a strategic retreat. The French conceded the field so the result must be considered an allied victory. However, this was a Pyrrhic victory, and the scale of the losses damaged Marlborough's reputation. **TB**

Losses: Grand Alliance, 22,000 casualties of 80,000; French, 10,000 casualties of 70,000

◁ Oudenarde 1708   Brihuega 1710 ▷

An eighteenth-century print of Marlborough attacking the French left wing. ⬆

Brihuega   8 December 1710

The issue at stake in the War of the Spanish Succession was whether a Hapsburg or a Bourbon king should occupy the Spanish throne. The defeat of a British army, under Lord Stanhope, by the Duke of Vendome's French and Spanish forces at Brihuega was a serious blow to the Hapsburg cause.

After some key victories in the war in the Spanish peninsula, the Grand Alliance army occupied Madrid, and the Hapsburg Holy Roman Emperor, Charles, was proclaimed King Charles III of Spain. However, the French army regrouped and advanced on Madrid, led by the Duke of Vendome. Faced with the possibility of being trapped in a long and damaging siege, the allied army retreated from Madrid and moved toward Catalonia. However, the problems of moving and supplying troops in winter resulted in the allies becoming divided.

With a Herculean effort that must be rated equal to Marlborough's famous forced march to Oudenarde in 1708, Vendome caught up with Stanhope as he rested at the town of Brihuega in the province of Guadalajara. Stanhope sought to defend the town but was subjected to a savage bombardment. As the French spilled into Brihuega, the British infantry fought desperately with bayonets and began to take heavy losses. In the face of overwhelming odds, Stanhope realized that his position was hopeless and surrendered; the remaining British troops were taken prisoner.

Vendome then moved south and inflicted another defeat on the rest of the retreating allied army at Villaviciosa two days later. By the time Charles reached Barcelona in January 1711, his forces were severely depleted and he formally abandoned his campaign to secure the throne of Spain in April. **TB**

Losses: Grand Alliance, 600 dead, 3,400 captured of 4,000; French and Spanish, 1,200 casualties of 10,000

⟨ *Malplaquet 1709*

⬆ *Philip V and Vendome lead the Bourbon claim to the throne in Battle of Villaviciosa by Jean Alaux (1786–1864).*

Gangut 6 August 1714

Gangut was the first major victory of the Russian navy created by Czar Peter the Great. After his triumph at Poltava, Peter had invaded Finland in 1713. He deployed his navy to secure his seaborne supply lines. His galleys fought a Swedish fleet near the Finnish Gangut peninsula.

Czar Peter had deployed a fleet of galleys around Finland to support his armies there. Its commander, Admiral Fyodor Apraksin, sailed toward Åbo, a Russian military base in Finland. Apraksin found a Swedish fleet blocking his movement west at Gangut. He sought refuge by retreating east toward the coast. He tried to drag his galleys across the peninsula, but quickly gave up on this plan after one was broken up in the attempt.

The Swedish commander, Gustav Wattrang, moved to attack the Russians. He was unable to engage them successfully as the wind had fallen, immobilizing his sail-powered Swedish ships. By 6 August, most of the shallow-hulled galleys had been able to bypass the Swedish fleet by rowing along the coast. At this point, the only thing blocking the Russian movement west was a detachment of nine ships, under Nils Ehrensköld, dispatched to intercept any ships that broke the Swedish blockade.

Ehrensköld positioned his ships in a narrow channel, with his flagship—*Elefant*—in the center. At 2:00 PM, Apraksin sent thirty-five galleys against Ehrensköld, but the attack was repulsed, as was a second wave of eighty galleys. Finally, Apraksin deployed all ninety-five galleys available to him. They attacked the ships flanking the *Elefant*, before surrounding the flagship and boarding it. By 5:00 PM, the battle was over, and Russia was able to supply its forces in Finland without Swedish interference. **JF**

Losses: Swedish, 350 dead and 350 captured of 950, all 9 ships; Russian, 125 dead and 350 wounded, 2 galleys ran aground of 100

[<] *Poltava 1709*　　　　　　　　　　*Dynekilen 1716* [>]

The Swedes trap the Russian fleet at Hango Head (Gangut), from the Illustrated London News. ⬆

Preston   9–14 November 1715

The last important siege of a city in England, Preston pitted the British army of the Hanoverian King George I against a Jacobite army attempting to restore Stuart rule in the person of the Old Pretender: Prince James, son of the deposed King James II.

After a series of campaigns in Scotland in which the Earl of Mar had captured much of the Highlands and the city of Perth, the Jacobite army moved south with little resistance from the British army, expecting to be joined by more than 20,000 supporters in Lancashire. However, the support they found was disappointing, and the Jacobites entered Preston on 9 November 1715, joined by fewer than 2,000 men, under the command of Thomas Forster, a member of the Northumberland gentry.

On 12 November, General Charles Willis besieged Preston. An initial attack was repelled, with the British forces being held back by barricades and taking heavy losses from small arms fire directed at them from houses. During the night of 12 November, many Lancashire Jacobites deserted; the next day, the government forces were swelled by reinforcements, which set about preventing the Jacobites from escaping. Forster opened negotiations for surrender, but Willis refused because he knew that the Highlanders wished to fight on. It was only when Willis received confirmation that the Highlanders had disarmed and assembled in the market square that government forces entered the city on 14 November. Reports on what happened to the Jacobites vary, with some sources claiming that many were transported to the Americas. Other sources cite a number of executions, but also state that numerous Highlanders managed to find their way back to Scotland. **TB**

Losses: British government, 300 casualties of 3,000; Jacobites, 50 casualties of 1,500 (plus a large number of desertions)

Culloden 1746 [>]

⬆ *Government forces battle to prevent the escape of Jacobite horsemen from Preston.*

Dynekilen 8 July 1716

After being defeated by the Russians at Gangut in 1714, the Swedish navy was dealt another blow at Dynekilen in 1716, this time by Denmark-Norway. The victory made the bold naval commander, Peter Tordenskjold, a national hero in both Denmark and Norway.

In 1716, Charles XII of Sweden invaded Norway, which was part of a union with Denmark. Swedish troops were moved to Norway by sea. On 2 July, the Norwegian commander, Peter Tordenskjold, left Copenhagen, charged with stopping Swedish shipping. On 7 July, he learned that a Swedish fleet escorting troop ships to Norway had put in at Dynekilen, a fjord near the Swedish-Norwegian border.

The Swedish had placed a battery of six 12-pound (4.5 kg) guns on an island in the fjord, as well as soldiers on both sides of the harbor to provide crossfire. At 4:00 AM the next day, Tordenskjold sailed into the fjord and ninety minutes later he anchored his ships and opened fire on the Swedes. At 1:00 PM, Tordenskjold's men took the battery. Soon after, the largest Swedish ship, the *Stenbock*, surrendered. By late afternoon, the majority of the Swedish fleet was sinking, burning, or had been run aground. Many of the Swedish sailors had fled. Determined to capture as many Swedish vessels as possible, Tordenskjold ordered the stricken ships to be made seaworthy. Facing volleys of musketballs from the soldiers on the coast, his men put out the fires onboard the Swedish ships and freed the ones that had run aground. At 9:00 PM, Tordenskjold left Dynekilen with his fleet intact and thirty captured ships. The defeat forced Charles XII to put an end to his invasion of Norway in 1716 and he returned to Sweden. **JF**

Losses: Danish-Norwegian, 67 dead or wounded, no ships of 7; Swedish, 11 warships and 19 transports captured and 10 transports destroyed of 15 warships and 29 transports

◁ Gangut 1714   Fredriksten 1718 ▷

Corfu 19 July–20 August 1716

The Siege of Corfu was a key encounter in the Ottoman-Venetian War (1714–18), the last in a series of wars between the two Mediterranean powers that stretched back to the fifteenth century. The failure to take Corfu by the Ottoman forces was hailed as a great victory across Christian Europe.

The Ottoman Empire declared war on Venice in 1714, determined to reverse their losses in the Great Turkish War of 1684 to 1699. After victory at Thebes, the Ottomans conquered Venice's Peloponnesian territories in June 1714, under the command of the grand vizier, Damat Ali Pasha. Venetian forces were no match for the Ottoman Empire, and, after capturing Venetian bases in the Ionian Islands, the Ottomans arrived at Corfu on 8 July 1716. The Ottoman fleet was met by a Venetian fleet, commanded by Andrea Cornaro. The Venetians attempted to destroy the Ottoman fleet with fireships, but failed when the Ottomans withdrew slightly. After several hours, the Venetians withdrew and the Ottomans landed their invasion force. After a swift advance that overran a number of forts, the Ottomans besieged the city of Corfu on 19 July.

Over the next twenty-two days, the Turks launched assaults on the city's defenses; each time the attacks were repelled after savage fighting. The Venetian garrison, led by Count von der Schulenburg, put up a heroic defense and was victorious eventually. However, the victory can also be attributed to the city's formidable fortifications and a huge storm that raged on 9 August. The failure of the siege was a celebrated victory for Venice, but the republic never regained its losses in the Peloponnese despite Austria's entry into the war. The Ottoman Empire was forced into a disadvantageous peace in 1718. **TB**

Losses: Unknown

◁ Zenta 1697   Belgrade 1717 ▷

Belgrade   August 1717

The Siege of Belgrade was an engagement in the Austro-Turkish War of 1716 to 1718, in which Prince Eugene of Savoy led a campaign against the forces of the Ottoman Empire, ruled by Sultan Ahmed III. The fall of Belgrade ended Ottoman control of Serbia and foiled their ambitions to conquer Hungary.

After failing to take Corfu in 1716, the Ottomans turned their attention to the conquest of the rest of Hungary. Prince Eugene engaged the invading Ottoman army, under the grand vizier, Damat Ali Pasha, at Petrovardin, north of the Danube River. Eugene attacked before the Ottomans could seize the fortress and inflicted a decisive defeat on the Turkish army, which resulted in the death of Ali Pasha. The Ottomans abandoned their plans to invade Hungary and retreated in disarray. Eugene advanced quickly on Belgrade, besieging the city in June and subjecting it to a bombardment of several weeks, which destroyed much of the city's walls. However, before Eugene could attack, the rest of the Ottoman army arrived led by a new grand vizier, Halil Pasha. It deployed itself on a plateau overlooking Eugene's army and launched an artillery bombardment of the Austrians.

While Eugene was considering his predicament, an opportunity presented itself. On 16 August, the area around Belgrade was covered by a thick fog, which silenced the Ottoman guns. Seizing the initiative, Eugene sprang a surprise attack on the plateau that caught the vizier's army off guard. The Austrians routed the Ottomans, who then fled leaving Belgrade at the mercy of the Austrians. Belgrade fell one week later, and the war was over. The Ottomans signed the Treaty of Passarowitz in 1718, which finally put an end to Ottoman rule in Hungary. **TB**

Losses: Unknown

"I advanced my camp so near Belgrade that the bullets were constantly flying over my head."

Prince Eugene of Savoy, original manuscript

⬆ *Detail from a painting by Johann Gottfried Auerbach (1697–1753) showing Prince Eugene of Savoy at the Siege of Belgrade.*

◁ Corfu 1716

Fredriksten 1718

After the setback at Dynekilen, the Swedish cause in the Great Northern War was further weakened when Sweden failed to capture the fortress of Fredriksten, as part of their invasion of Norway in 1718. During the siege, Charles XII of Sweden was killed, and his army withdrew from Norway.

In autumn 1718, Charles XII invaded Norway, which was then united with Denmark, with an army of 40,000. One of his first objectives was to take the fortress of Fredriksten near the Swedish-Norwegian border. Fredriksten could be provisioned by sea and if it was left it would be a major threat to the rear of the Swedish army.

Although Fredriksten had a garrison of only 1,400, it was well constructed and had three outworks. By the end of November, the Swedish lines had completely cut off Fredriksten from the surrounding countryside and placed their heavy artillery on a hill overlooking the fortress. On 5 December, the Swedish diggers, covered by guns, began to drive trenches toward the fortress under cover of night. Three days later, they captured one of the outworks. As the Swedish trenches closed toward Fredriksten, the diggers became increasingly vulnerable to musket fire from the defenders, who used flares to illuminate their positions. More than one hundred Swedish diggers were killed, but by 11 December the Swedish trenches and artillery were in a good position to begin the final drive toward the fortress. That evening Charles XII surveyed the siege works from a trench, exposing his head above the breastwork for several minutes. A Norwegian bullet struck him in the head, passing from temple to temple. The Swedish king was dead, and the Swedish invasion of Norway was abandoned quickly. **JF**

Losses: Swedish, 113 of 40,000; Norwegian-Danish, negligible from a garrison of 1,400

◁ Dynekilen 1716   Ezel 1719 ▷

Ezel 4 June 1719

In this naval battle of the Great Northern War, the Russians defeated the Swedes near Ezel Island in the Baltic. It was the first major victory of the Russian deep-sea sailing fleet, and another major setback for the Swedish, who had recently lost their king at Fredriksten.

By 1719, Russia was established as a major naval power in the Baltic, successfully challenging Sweden. On 11 May, news reached the Russian fleet that a convoy of three Swedish ships of the line was sailing from the Baltic port of Baltiysk to Stockholm, aiming to protect Swedish commercial shipping in the area. The Russian Admiral Fyodor Apraksin ordered Captain Naum Senyavin to take a squadron of seven ships from Tallinn and look for the Swedes.

At daybreak on 4 June, Senyavin met the Swedish squadron in open sea between the islands of Ezel and Gotska Sandön. The Swedish fled north, and the Russians pursued and engaged them. The two leading Russian vessels—the flagship *Portsmouth* and *Devonshire*—engaged the Swedish flagship, *Wachtmeister*. In the fighting, *Portsmouth* lost two of her sails, but still managed to damage quite seriously another Swedish ship, *Karlskrona Vapen*. She was forced to surrender, as was the other Swedish ship, *Bernhardus*. *Wachtmeister* attempted to flee and seemed on the verge of escape until two Russian ships—*Rafail* and *Yagudill*—came up on both sides of her. The Swedish fought valiantly to save their ship from capture during two hours of fighting, but they were forced to surrender to the Russians. Senyavin returned safely to Tallinn with his fleet intact and three captured ships. **JF**

Losses: Swedish, 50 dead and 15 wounded, all 3 ships captured; Russian, 18 casualties, no ships of 7

◁ Fredriksten 1718   Grengam 1720 ▷

Grengam   7 August 1720

Grengam was the last major naval engagement between Sweden and Russia during the Great Northern War before they made peace with the Treaty of Nystad in 1721. The Russians had defeated a Swedish squadron in 1719 at Ezel, but at Grengam both sides claimed victory.

In 1720, the Swedish sent out frigates to survey the strength of the Russians in the Åland Islands, situated on an important shipping route between Sweden and Finland. They sighted a Russian fleet of sixty-one galleys and twenty-nine other boats docked at the island of Grengam on 6 August. Against the orders of the Swedish admiral of the fleet, Karl Wachtmeister, a squadron of eight ships commanded by Carl Georg Siöblad attacked the Russians the next day. The Russian commander, General Mikhail Golitsyn, retreated toward the coast in an attempt to lure the Swedish into shallow waters where their larger ships would be less maneuverable.

As the Swedish squadron advanced, the Russian fleet turned and attacked. The Swedes attempted to bring their cannon to bear quickly, but four of their ships ran aground against the shore and were captured. More than one hundred of their men were killed in the fighting. In spite of these difficulties, the Swedes inflicted serious damage on the Russians and destroyed three-quarters of their fleet of galleys. Siöblad was able to make good an escape on his flagship, *Pommern*, and sailed back to safer waters. The Battle of Grengam had no major strategic impact, and Sweden and Russia made peace at Nystad on 10 September 1721. Sweden recognized Russia's conquests in the Baltic lands, and Russia handed most of Finland back to Sweden. **JF**

"[He had] a special reputation for his natural intelligence ... and did not lose his presence of mind in any situation." Biographer of General Golitsyn

⬆ The Battle of Grengam, *an etching from 1721 by Russian artist Alexey Zubov.*

Losses: Swedish, 103 dead, 4 ships captured of 8; Russian, 82 dead and 246 wounded, 45 galleys of 61 galleys and 29 other boats

◁ *Ezel 1719*

Karnal 24 February 1739

The Battle of Karnal in 1739 was the supreme triumph of Nader Shah, the great Persian king and military commander. At Karnal, in northern India, the Persians comprehensively crushed the Mughal emperor Muhammad Shah's larger army, going on to sack their capital, Delhi.

Nader Shah's victory at the Battle of Damghan in 1729 had consolidated his control of Persia, and he became king in 1736. After successfully invading Afghanistan in 1738, he advanced into the Mughal Empire, which had been seriously weakened by wars and internal strife. The Mughal army was encamped near Karnal, north of Delhi.

On 24 February, the Persians advanced toward Karnal, and the Mughals sent a force to meet them, including several war elephants. The Mughal front was more than 2 miles (3.2 km) long, and the same depth. It was to prove no match for Nader Shah's disciplined army. The Persians waited until the Mughal came within close

range and unleashed devastating volleys of gunfire, with the elephants providing especially easy targets. The Mughals lost two of their chief commanders: Khan Dauran was seriously wounded and forced to retire (he died the next day) and Sa'adat Khan was pulled from his elephant and captured. After two hours, the Mughal lines quickly began to fall apart and the soldiers fled back to their camp.

The battle swiftly became a rout. The Persians pursued and were able to capture Muhammad Shah. Nader Shah's army advanced to Delhi and looted the city, capturing a great fortune in jewels and precious metals before returning to Persia. Muhammad Shah remained on the throne, but Karnal and its consequences were hugely damaging to the prestige of the Mughal Empire, whose decline quickly became terminal. **JF**

Losses: Persian, 400 dead and 700 wounded of 100,000 to 125,000; Mughal, 10,000 of 200,000

Eighteenth-century Persian book cover: Nader Shah was a military genius, but he was also known for his cruelty.

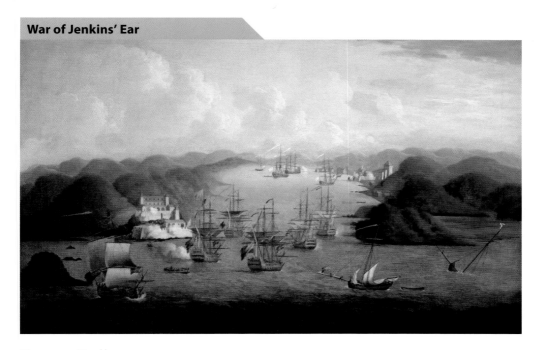

Porto Bello   20–21 November 1739

Disputes over trading rights and the alleged mistreatment of seamen led Britain to declare war on Spain in 1739. The war was mainly fought in the Caribbean and North America and began with this successful British attack on the Spanish base of Porto Bello, on the isthmus of Panama.

The Anglo-Spanish war of 1739 to 1742 was known as the War of Jenkins' Ear. It was named after a British sea captain who was mutilated allegedly by the Spanish authorities in the West Indies, when they did not want to allow British trade with Spain's colonies in the region.

Edward Vernon, an irascible and eccentric British admiral who was also a Member of Parliament, had boasted before the war that he could easily capture the important Spanish trading station of Porto Bello. When the war began, Vernon was commanding the British forces in Jamaica and set out with just six warships to make good his claim.

Vernon planned his attack carefully and made sure his captains had precise orders. In reality, the defenses of Porto Bello were far from formidable; undermanned and with only a few serviceable guns. The British ships arrived off the town on 20 November 1739 and immediately went into action, firing on one battery from close range and sending a landing party against another. The Spanish surrendered the next morning. Vernon's men spent a few weeks demolishing the town's fortifications and then sailed away.

This easy success was acclaimed in Britain as a great victory. Thomas Arne wrote "Rule Britannia" for the celebrations, districts of London and other cities were named for the battle, and George Washington's half brother Lawrence renamed the family estate in Virginia "Mount Vernon" in the British admiral's honor. **DS**

Losses: Fewer than 100 on each side; Spanish, 1 ship sunk

Cartagena de Indias 1741 ▷

⬆ *In* Capture of Porto Bello *by Peter Monamy (1689–1749), Vernon leads his six ships into the harbor to attack.*

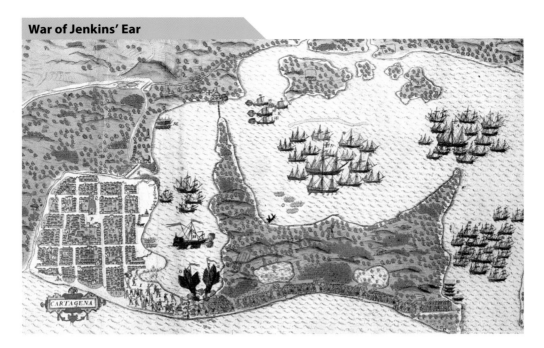

Cartagena de Indias March–May 1741

Following the straightforward, successful attack on Porto Bello, the British decided to continue the War of Jenkins' Ear by capturing Spain's most important port in the Caribbean region, Cartagena de Indias, on the coast of modern Colombia. The attack would fail disastrously.

From the start, the British expedition to Cartagena was plagued by difficulties. The force was so large—more than 30,000 men aboard almost 190 transports and warships—that it was almost unmanageable. To compound the problem, the commanders—Admiral Vernon and General Wentworth—quarreled incessantly. Worse still, European armies and navies of this period lacked the knowledge and techniques to ward off lethal tropical diseases during prolonged operations.

Cartagena had a garrison of around 5,000 men and substantial fortifications, but the British force was strong enough to defeat them if it could make a rapid and organized attack. Instead, when the attackers arrived on 4 March, it took several days to issue the necessary orders to all the ships, giving the Spanish commanders, notably Admiral Blas de Lezo, ample time to prepare.

After a long initial bombardment, land attacks—delayed in part by Wentworth's incompetence—took some of the outlying Spanish forts, but an assault on the main defenses in early April narrowly failed. Thousands of the British troops were dying of yellow fever and the tropical rainy season was beginning. In late April, the British commanders decided to give up and had completed the evacuation of their remaining forces by mid May. After a failed attack on Havana in Cuba later in 1741, the British abandoned offensive operations against Spain's empire for the rest of the war. **DS**

Losses: British, 16,000 dead or wounded, 50 ships abandoned; Spanish, 2,000 dead or wounded, 6 ships lost

◁ *Porto Bello 1739*

Detail from an eighteenth-century map of the naval attack on Cartagena de Indias. ↑

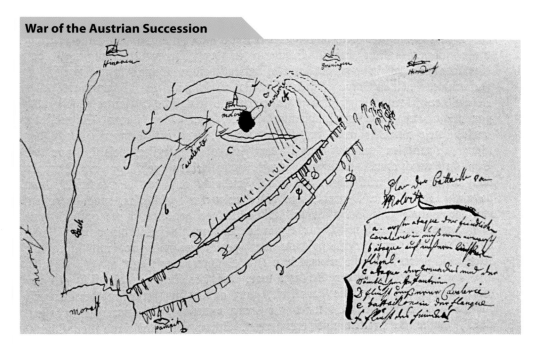

Mollwitz   10 April 1741

In 1740, Frederick II acceded to the Prussian throne and within six months went to war with Austria. He later became known as Frederick the Great, a master of eighteenth-century warfare. However, his first experience of command in battle, at Mollwitz, did nothing to suggest future military genius.

In December 1740, Frederick invaded Silesia, a wealthy province of the Austrian Empire, hoping to benefit from Austrian weakness as a result of the contested accession of a woman, Empress Maria Theresa, to the Austrian throne. The invasion triggered the War of the Austrian Succession, the first general European war since 1714.

Frederick inherited from his father, Frederick William I, a strong army centered around brutally disciplined infantry. However, the young ruler had no experience of command in war. He easily occupied Silesia with his unexpected attack, but was caught off guard by an Austrian counterstroke. Austrian commander Reinhard von Neipperg led an army

into Silesia without waiting for the winter snow to melt. He advanced across Frederick's lines of communication with Prussia, forcing him to give battle.

Frederick located the Austrians at Mollwitz, and the two armies drew up battle lines in the snow. The Austrian cavalry charged and swept aside the horsemen on the Prussian left, leaving the flank of the Prussian infantry in the center open to attack. Skeptical of the military abilities of his young king, the experienced Prussian field marshal, Graf von Schwerin, had Frederick hurried away from the battlefield to safety. Taking over command, Schwerin led a fightback, telling one officer that the only way they would leave the battlefield would be "over the bodies of their enemies." The disciplined musket volleys of the Prussian infantry turned the tide, routing the Austrians who fled the field. **RG**

Losses: Austrian, 4,000 of 20,000; Prussian, 4,000 of 20,000

Prague 1741 >

⬆ *A sketchy military plan for the Battle of Mollwitz, drawn up by Frederick II.*

Prague 25–26 November 1741

The armies of eighteenth-century Europe have often been described as unimaginative, slow-moving, and inflexible. The French seizure of Prague in the War of the Austrian Succession defies these stereotypes; it was an operation using speed and stealth to achieve success with minimal casualties.

While the Prussians invaded Silesia, France sent an army under the command of the Duke of Belle-Isle to attack the Austrian Empire, supporting the claim of Elector Charles Albert of Bavaria to the Austrian throne. Along with Bavarian and Saxon contingents, the French first marched on Vienna, but then veered off into Bohemia, a part of the Austrian Empire.

The Austrians lost track of a French corps, led by Maurice de Saxe, advancing on the Bohemian capital, Prague. An experienced commander renowned for his intellectual grasp of the principles of war, Saxe discreetly went forward to reconnoiter the walled city's defenses in person and recognized the chance for a surprise operation. Calling to his side one of his boldest officers, Colonel François de Chevert, he outlined a plan for a body of grenadiers to assault the walls by night. In order to avoid alerting the Prague garrison, the assault would be made without firing muskets; only bayonets were used to dispatch the soldiers on guard duty.

On the night of 25 to 26 November, Chevert and his men climbed ladders onto the parapet of a poorly defended section of the walls and had taken possession before the garrison realized what was afoot. The city gate was opened, and Saxe's cavalry rode in, leaving Prague's defenders no choice but to surrender. Charles Albert was crowned king of Bohemia the following day and later, briefly, held the title of Holy Roman Emperor. **RG**

Losses: Unknown, but light

◁ Mollwitz 1741   Chotusitz 1742 ▷

Chotusitz 17 May 1742

Humiliated by his first experience of military command at Mollwitz, Frederick II of Prussia vowed never again to quit his army in battle. His tenacious performance in a bloodbath at Chotusitz stilled lingering doubts about his fitness for combat command and secured Prussian control of Silesia.

In spring 1742, an Austrian army led by Charles of Lorraine sought to regain control of the Bohemian capital, Prague. Frederick's Prussian forces maneuvered to block the Austrians' path. The two armies, of roughly equal strength, met at the village of Chotusitz (now Chotusice in the Czech Republic) in the Elbe valley.

The fighting began at around 8:00 AM. Both armies were fully committed to attack. The Austrian infantry broke through to Chotusitz and seized the village, which was soon in flames. On the flanks, Prussian and Austrian cavalry clashed in furious charge and countercharge, the whirling horsemen lost in clouds of dust. The Austrian troops generally had the better of the cavalry duels, but driving back and pursuing the Prussian horse they left their own infantry unprotected. At the height of the battle, Frederick ordered his infantry forward, their advance supported by cannon. The combined musket and cannon fire was too much for the Austrian foot soldiers to withstand.

Around noon, Charles was forced to order a retreat as his infantry center disintegrated. Both sides had suffered heavy casualties, with about one in four of their soldiers killed or wounded. It was a sobering price to pay for a battle, the outcome of which could not be strategically decisive for either side. A month later, Prussia and Austria made peace by the Treaty of Breslau, which gave Prussia control of Silesia. **RG**

Losses: Austrian, 7,000 casualties of 30,000; Prussian, 7,000 casualties of 28,000

◁ Prague 1741   Dettingen 1743 ▷

Dettingen 27 June 1743

An episode in the War of the Austrian Succession, the Battle of Dettingen is famous as the last occasion on which a reigning British monarch commanded troops in combat. Happily for George II, it was also a military success, allowing the British and their German allies to escape a perilous situation.

Britain was drawn into the war on the side of Austrian Empress Maria Theresa in order to counter a possible threat by France to George's German state of origin, Hanover. A combined British-Hanoverian-Austrian force, known as the Pragmatic Army, marched south from the Netherlands through Germany. The experienced French commander, the Duke of Noailles, maneuvered his forces brilliantly to trap the Pragmatic Army, shepherding it into a defile between the River Main and the Spessart hills. The exit from the defile was blocked at the village of Dettingen by French troops under the Duke of Gramont.

Without hope of resupply and vulnerable to French cannon on the heights, it appeared that King George would have to surrender and become a prisoner of France. The chance of a glorious French victory was thrown away by Gramont's indiscipline. He launched piecemeal attacks with his cavalry and infantry that made deep inroads into his enemy's lines, but also left his forces exposed to a counterattack. The resolute Austrians, Germans, and British inflicted heavy losses with musketry and cannon fire.

After stiff fighting, Gramont's infantry broke and fled across the river, some drowning when bridges of boats capsized. The Pragmatic Army was left free to pursue its march to safety at Hanau. King George had fought on foot after his horse bolted early in the battle; he showed great personal courage but no flair for military leadership. **RG**

Losses: Allied (Pragmatic Army), 2,000 casualties of 35,000; French, 4,000 casualties of 23,000

◁ Chotusitz 1742　　　　Fontenoy 1745 ▷

> "Lads, you see they loons [young men] on yon' hill. Better kill them afore they kill you."
>
> *Sir Andrew Agnew of Lochnaw, to his regiment*

⬆ *An engraving of the Battle of Dettingen from 1743 by I. Pano: the British army is commanded by a reigning monarch for the last time.*

Fontenoy 11 May 1745

"War is a science so obscure and imperfect that, in general, no rules of conduct can be given in it."

Maurice de Saxe, Reveries on the Art of War

⬆ *Troops confront each other in tight formation in the nineteenth-century* Battle of Fontenoy *(detail) by Félix Phillipoteaux.*

A hard-fought battle of the War of the Austrian Succession, Fontenoy is remembered by the French as the masterpiece of their celebrated commander Maurice de Saxe, and by the British army as a singular example of the courage and resolution of its infantry under extreme pressure.

In spring 1745, Saxe threatened the Austrian Netherlands (modern-day Belgium), placing Tournai under siege. The Pragmatic Army of allied British, Hanoverian, Dutch, and Austrian troops advanced to relieve the city. Saxe formed a defensive line centered on the village of Fontenoy. His troops were installed at the top of a slope, with the position further strengthened by earthwork ramparts.

The British, under King George II's son—the Duke of Cumberland—attacked the section of the French line between Fontenoy and the Bois de Barry. Two columns of British and Hanoverian foot soldiers advanced up the slope, under the fire of French cannon, grouped in strong points on the flanks of the line. Those who survived to reach the crest were confronted by the bulk of the French army. According to Voltaire's account of the battle, Sir Charles Hay of the British Foot Guards, finding himself face to face with the French Garde Française, doffed his hat and called upon them to fire first—an invitation the French courteously declined.

British musket volleys almost carried the day, driving the French line back in disarray. But Saxe, despite being seriously ill, rode forward to organize repeated counterattacks. Battered by cavalry charges, artillery fire, and a ferocious attack by a brigade of Irish "wild geese" fighting for the French, Cumberland's troops were driven into retreat. The triumphant Saxe went on to occupy most of the major cities of the Austrian Netherlands. **RG**

Losses: Allied, 7,500 dead or wounded of 50,000; French, 7,500 dead or wounded of 50,000

◁ *Dettingen 1743*　　　　　*Hohenfriedberg 1745* ▷

Hohenfriedberg 4 June 1745

In 1744, Frederick II of Prussia reentered the War of the Austrian Succession from which he had withdrawn after Chotusitz. He again attacked Austria, but by spring 1745 found himself on the defensive in Silesia. There, the Prussian king won one of his most admired victories.

The Austrian commander Charles of Lorraine established his troops and their Saxon allies in a solid defensive position behind the Striegau River. Frederick had an army of similar strength, but thought only of attack. Judging the Saxons to be the weaker element, he planned a surprise night attack on their end of the defensive line. Leaving their campfires burning in order to deceive the enemy, the Prussian army marched silently through the darkness to a bridge at Striegau and began to cross it. Surprise was lost when a chance encounter with Saxon outposts led to an outbreak of firing.

As dawn broke, Frederick was, theoretically, in a perilous position, with only half his army across the river. However, Prussian musketry and cannon soon threw the Saxons into disorder, while the rest of the Prussian army found fords to cross. The rigidly disciplined Prussian infantry maneuvered with mechanical perfection amid the storm of fire, but it was the impetuous bravery of the cavalry that carried the day. The Bayreuth Dragoons, under Graf von Gessler, saw an opportunity to charge the Austrian infantry and rolled them up in a series of savage passes, slashing with sabers and taking an astonishing haul of prisoners and standards. By 8:00 AM, the Austrians were in full retreat. A delighted Frederick wrote that there had not been "so decisive a defeat since Blenheim." It required more fighting, however, before Prussian control of Silesia was confirmed. **RG**

Losses: Austrian and Saxon, 8,600 casualties and 5,000 captured of 60,000; Prussian, 5,000 casualties of 60,000

◁ Fontenoy 1745   Kesselsdorf 1745 ▷

Kesselsdorf 15 December 1745

Fought outside the Saxon capital, Dresden, the Battle of Kesselsdorf was a personal triumph for Leopold I, Prince of Anhalt-Dessau. The veteran commander led the Prussian forces to a victory that persuaded Austria to make peace, confirming Prussia in possession of much-coveted Silesia.

After their victory at Hohenfriedberg in June 1745, the Prussians saw some vigorous campaigning. As winter approached, with snow and ice on the ground, the Austrians and Saxons were deflected from an advance on Berlin by a Prussian move against Dresden.

Led by Count Rutowsky, Saxon and Austrian forces took up a defensive position on a ridge by the Elbe River at Kesselsdorf, in the path of a Prussian column led by the seventy-year-old Prince Leopold, who resolved to attack. A devout Lutheran, before the battle he reportedly prayed: "O Lord God, let me not be disgraced in my old age. If you will not help me, do not help these rogues, but leave us to try it ourselves."

Divine help seemed at first denied. Leopold drove his infantry forward in a frontal assault against the town of Kesselsdorf, which the Saxons had fortified and defended with cannon. Twice the Prussian foot soldiers were hurled back with heavy casualties. However, the overconfident Saxons left their defensive positions to pursue the apparently defeated enemy. Counterattacking Prussian cavalry caught them in the open and chased them back through the town. Soon the Saxons were surrendering in droves or fleeing in panic. Joined by the Prussian king Frederick II, Leopold occupied Dresden three days later.

Peace negotiations followed; Austrian empress Maria Theresa accepted the loss of Silesia to Prussia in return for recognition of her right to the Austrian throne. **RG**

Losses: Austrian and Saxon, 4,000 casualties and 6,500 captured of 35,000; Prussian, 5,000 casualties of 30,000

◁ Hohenfriedberg 1745   Lauffeld 1747 ▷

Culloden   16 April 1746

The dream of a Stuart restoration to the British throne ended on a desolate moor in the north of Scotland. The defeat of the Jacobite pretender to the throne, Charles Edward Stuart—known as Bonnie Prince Charlie—was decisive.

Charles Edward Stuart was the grandson of James II, the Stuart king deposed in 1688 by his son-in-law, William of Orange. Charles's father James, the "Old Pretender," had tried but failed to regain the throne from the new Hanoverian dynasty of British kings in 1715. In 1745, Charles, the "Young Pretender," tried again. Britain was at war with France and, after a serious defeat at Fontenoy in Belgium, was vulnerable to a French invasion. Charles grabbed his opportunity and, in July 1745, landed in the Outer Hebrides with French support. Thousands flocked to his cause and he soon marched into Edinburgh.

Defeating a British government army at Prestonpans in September, he crossed the border and headed south to London with around 6,000 men. He reached as far south as Swarkestone Bridge in Derbyshire, but few English Jacobites rallied to his cause and the promised French invasion fleet was still being prepared. With two British armies approaching, his Council of War took the fateful decision that he should return to Scotland. On 6 December, Charles and his men turned north, reprovisioning in Glasgow and defeating a British army at Falkirk before heading up to Inverness. In January 1746, a major British army led by William, Duke of Cumberland, the son of British King George II, arrived in Edinburgh. It marched up the east coast to Aberdeen, where it spent six weeks training, before heading west to engage the Jacobite army.

The two armies were similarly sized but widely different in makeup. The Jacobite army consisted largely of Scottish

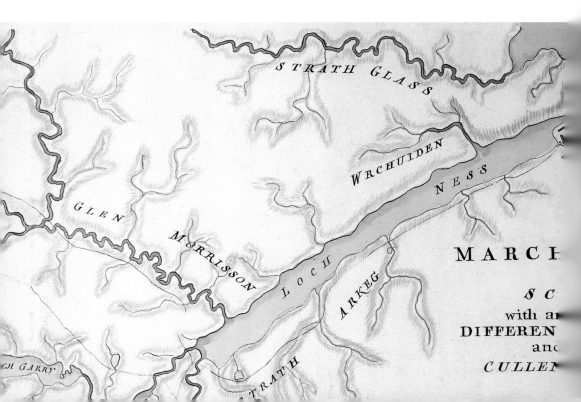

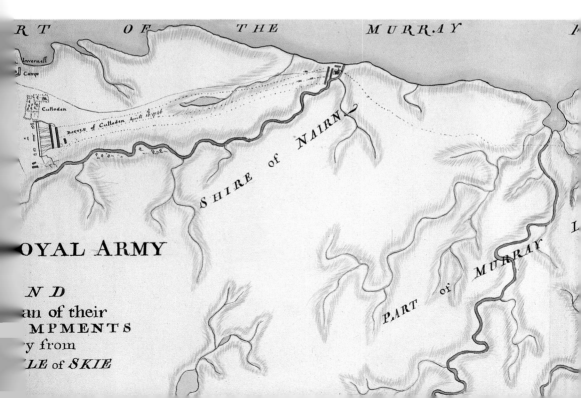

Highlanders, with a few Lowland Scots, some Englishmen from Manchester, 350 French soldiers, and 302 Irish soldiers serving in the French army. The British army was mostly English, with some Highland and Lowland Scots, a battalion of Ulstermen, and a small number of Austrians and Hessians from Germany. Both sides were well equipped with firearms, although the Jacobites were outgunned by the Royal Artillery's heavy guns and were ill trained compared to their British opponents. The Jacobites also suffered from a lack of trained officers, while many of their men had been pressed into service and deserted before the battle.

The battle took place on a bleak, boggy moor just east of Inverness. The British troops advanced forward steadily while the Jacobites marched into driving rain and sleet. A British artillery bombardment softened up the Jacobite ranks before the Jacobite infantry responded by charging the fixed lines of British muskets and bayonets. Their impact was considerable before a British counterattack managed to trap the Jacobite right wing on three sides. On the other Jacobite wing, a charge by the Macdonald regiments was halted, causing them to give way; two other smaller units were decimated. The British swiftly grabbed their chance and attacked, causing the Jacobite left wing to collapse. In the rout that followed, Jacobite regiments retreating on the road to Inverness were cut down by British dragoons. The Jacobite rebellion was over, and, after five months on the run, Bonnie Prince Charlie sailed for France, disguised as a lady's maid. It was the end of a dream. **SA**

Losses: British, 50 dead, 259 wounded of 8,000; Jacobite, 1,500 to 2000 dead or wounded, 376 captured of 7,000

◁ *Preston 1715*

Lauffeld

2 July 1747

In the final years of the War of the Austrian Succession, the French army, commanded by Maurice de Saxe, established superiority on European battlefields, repeatedly defeating the allied armies of Britain, the Dutch Republic, and Austria. Lauffeld was the last major land battle of the war.

Prussia's withdrawal from the War of the Austrian Succession in 1745 should have put an isolated France at a disadvantage. However, Saxe continued to build upon his success at Fontenoy, occupying the Austrian Netherlands and threatening an invasion of the Dutch Republic.

In summer 1747, the allied and French armies were maneuvering for advantage in Limburg, west of the River Meuse. Moving his men in forced marches, Saxe surprised the British commander, the Duke of Cumberland, at Lauffeld, outside Maastricht. The allies hastily arranged a line; the Austrians on the right, Dutch in the center, and Cumberland's British and Hanoverians on the left. Saxe deftly shifted the weight of his forces to his right and attacked the British, who stoutly defended the villages of Lauffeld and Vlytingen, inflicting heavy casualties.

The disintegration of the Dutch in the center, however, left the British flank vulnerable. Driven from the villages, British infantry were exposed to pursuing French cavalry. To cover the retreat, British cavalry commander General John Ligonier led a mass countercharge into the midst of the French foot and horse. With heavy losses—including Ligonier himself, who was taken prisoner—the British cavalry charges allowed their infantry to complete an organized withdrawal. The war concluded the following year with the Peace of Aix-la-Chapelle. France gained no significant advantage from its military victories. **RG**

Losses: Allied, 6,000 casualties of 60,000; French, 9,000 casualties of 80,000

◁ Kesselsdorf 1745   Second Cape Finisterre 1747 ▷

Second Cape Finisterre

25 October 1747

As well as land battles in Europe and the European colonies, the War of the Austrian Succession featured naval clashes in the Atlantic, on the routes between the British and French colonies in the Americas and their home ports. Britain had the best of these clashes, including this notable victory.

In the summer of 1747, the British authorities became aware that a large French merchant ship convoy was being assembled at the port of La Rochelle in order to carry supplies to the French possessions in the West Indies. Admiral Edward Hawke was sent to intercept its progress with fourteen ships of the line. The French force consisted of 252 merchant ships and eight ships of the line, most of which were individually more powerful than the British ships. Hawke's fleet found the French convoy on 25 October.

Although named for Cape Finisterre at Spain's northwestern tip, the battle was fought far out in the Atlantic. Hawke was unsure whether to send his ships into action as soon as each could get into range or to form a line of battle, which was safer but could allow the French to escape. In the end, after delaying to form a line, Hawke signaled "general chase," which allowed his ships to act individually. The French formed line between the British and the merchant ships, which fled as fighting began.

In a hard-fought action, six of the eight French warships were captured. Almost all of the convoy escaped, though about a fifth of its ships was captured later. This success confirmed British naval superiority in the Atlantic, limiting French trade and hurting France economically, important factors in the peace negotiations the following year. **DS**

Losses: British, 600 dead or wounded, no ships lost; French, 6 ships captured, 4,000 dead, wounded, or captured

◁ Lauffeld 1747

↩ The Battle of Lauffeld by Pierre L'Enfant (1704–87), in which Louis XV directs Maurice de Saxe to Lauffeld.

Jumonville Glen 26 May 1754

Imperial ambitions and competition for the rich fur trade with American Indian tribes brought England and France into conflict in the Ohio River Valley. When the French rebuffed a warning and began building outposts, the royal governor in Virginia sent an expedition to secure the Forks of the Ohio.

In January 1754, a company of the volunteer Virginia Regiment was sent to build a fort at the strategic confluence of the Monongohela and Allegany rivers (the "Forks") where the Ohio River began. The Virginians were driven away by French troops, who went on to construct Fort Duquesne on the site. In response, a larger expedition was dispatched in April. Lieutenant Colonel George Washington, the regiment's deputy commander, led the advance element.

On 24 May, his force reached Great Meadow, an open, marshy area about 60 miles (96 km) southeast of the Forks where camp was set up. Three days later, friendly Indians informed Washington that thirty-two French soldiers and Indians were camped in a hidden ravine only 7 miles (11 km) away. Convinced that the French intended to attack, Washington decided to strike first.

During the rainy night of 27 to 28 May, Washington led a raiding party of forty Virginians and Indians to the French location. At dawn, as they moved into position around the glen, a shot was fired. The surprised French, commanded by Lieutenant Joseph de Villiers, returned the musket fire for fifteen minutes before they surrendered. Villiers was among the dead, allegedly wounded and killed by an Indian. One of the French survivors escaped into the woods and returned to Fort Duquesne to report the attack. The rest were made captive and sent to Virginia. **RB**

Losses: French and American Indian, 10 dead, 1 wounded, 21 captured; Virginian, 1 dead, 2 wounded

Fort Necessity 1754 ▷

Fort Necessity 3 July 1754

Lieutenant Colonel George Washington, Virginia Regiment, knew that the escape of a survivor of his raid at Jumonville Glen made a counterattack by the French only a matter of time. Washington fortified his camp at Great Meadows while he awaited the rest of his volunteer regiment.

When the last companies of the Virginia Regiment arrived on 9 June, Washington learned that the colonel had died en route and that he was now the commander of the regiment's 293 officers and men. Washington put his men to work building a small log palisade—with a low trench and earth berm around the perimeter—which he christened Fort Necessity. It was in a poor location on low ground that was subject to flooding, with the edge of the higher woodlands within musket range. Reinforcements arrived when South Carolina's Provincial Independent Company marched in with another one hundred men.

On 3 July, in heavy rain, a force of 800 French and Indians appeared, commanded by the older brother of the officer killed at the glen. Washington formed his men in ranks to fight outside the fort, but this was not what the French or Indians intended. Instead, they surrounded the fort and opened fire from the woods. Four hours later, Washington's trench was flooded and exposed to enfilade fire, much of his low supply of powder was wet, and many of his men were dead or wounded. At dusk, the French commander called a truce and offered terms. Washington, with no hope of reinforcement, signed the surrender not realizing that it was also a confession to "murdering" the French officer in May. At dawn on 4 July, Washington and his surviving men marched out of the fort. **RB**

Losses: French and American Indian, 100 casualties; Virginian and South Carolinian, 100 casualties, 2 captured

◁ Jumonville Glen 1754   Monongahela 1755 ▷

Monongahela   9 July 1755

The defeat at Fort Necessity made it clear to Virginia's royal governor that the colony did not have the resources to drive the French from its western territory. An appeal to London for assistance resulted in the dispatch of two infantry regiments under Major General Edward Braddock.

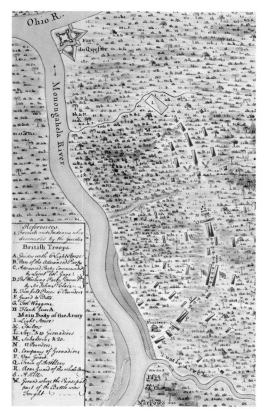

Braddock, commander in chief of British forces in North America, arrived with his men in February 1755. Supplies were gathered and men recruited in order to bring the regular regiments up to strength, as well as the two companies of Virginia volunteers, civilian teamsters, and drovers. By May, Braddock's force numbered more than 2,200 and assembled in western Virginia. Among them was George Washington, serving at colonel's rank on Braddock's personal staff. Although a detachment cut a trail ahead of the main body, it was still very slow going. At Washington's suggestion, a faster detachment of 1,200 with artillery moved ahead of the support train.

On 9 July, Braddock crossed the Monongahela River. Without warning, his advance guard hit a French force of about 900 regulars and Indians coming to intercept it. Volleys were exchanged, and the French reacted quickly. Through heavy brush and ravines, the Indians moved around both flanks of the column. Braddock's advance and flank guards collapsed, entangling men trying to move forward. The Virginia volunteers dispersed to fight from cover, but most regulars tried to fight from ranks on the trail. After three hours, many British officers were killed or wounded, ammunition was exhausted, and troop control lost. Braddock fell mortally wounded, and the army stumbled back. Washington rallied a rear guard while the broken army retreated over the river. **RB**

"[The soldiers] were struck with such a panic that they behaved with more cowardice than it is possible to conceive." George Washington

---

Losses: French and American Indian, fewer than 100 casualties; British and Virginian, 800 to 900 casualties

◁ Fort Necessity 1754   Fort Oswego 1756 ▷

 A detailed plan of the battlefield for the attack at Monongahela River drawn up by a British soldier who fought there.

Minorca   20 May 1756

By 1756, an Anglo-French conflict had already begun in North America, without a declaration of war. This spread to Europe and became part of the Seven Years' War. France's victory at Minorca was only a brief setback to Britain's maritime superiority, but led to the execution of Admiral Byng.

After naval clashes in their undeclared war in 1755, France prepared an expeditionary force at its main Mediterranean base of Toulon. Britain was slow to respond, initially concentrating its mobilization in the Atlantic and off North America. A British fleet, under the command of Admiral John Byng, was sent to block whatever maneuver the French might attempt from Toulon, but the French struck first, landing troops on the island of Minorca—an important British base—and besieging Port Mahon, its main port.

Byng reached Minorca with his fleet of twelve ships of the line on 20 May 1756 and found a French fleet, also of twelve ships (although rather more heavily armed), under the Marquis de la Galissonière, ready to oppose him. Byng attacked straight away, but his approach to the French line went badly wrong and only a few of his ships engaged the enemy. A limited and unimaginative commander, he failed to maneuver his fleet to remedy this initial blunder. After an indecisive battle, he decided to give up any attempt to relieve Minorca and sailed back to Gibraltar. Port Mahon fell a few days later.

Opinion in Britain was one of outrage. Byng was tried for neglect of his duty to do his utmost to engage the enemy. Of this he was undoubtedly guilty, but the charge carried a mandatory death sentence. Appeals for clemency failed, and he was executed by firing squad on the deck of a ship at Portsmouth a year later. **DS**

Losses: Fewer than 200 dead and wounded on each side; no ships lost

Lagos Bay 1759 ⊳

The routed English fleet takes refuge in the Bay of Gibraltar in this eighteenth-century engraving. ⬆

Fort Oswego   12–14 August 1756

After the British defeat at Monongahela in 1755, France sent an experienced professional soldier, Louis-Joseph de Montcalm, to Canada with a body of troops of the French regular army. In summer 1756, he attacked the British outpost of Fort Oswego on the shores of Lake Ontario.

Used to the formality of European warfare, Montcalm had a contempt for the French Canadian militia and disliked the use of American Indian warriors. However, he did not have sufficient regular troops to dispense with local forces. He advanced on Fort Oswego with 1,300 disciplined French infantry and artillerymen, around 1,500 Canadians, and a few hundred Indians.

There were, in fact, two forts where the Oswego River met Lake Ontario—Fort Ontario east of the river and Fort Oswego to the west of it. The garrison of provincial militia, commanded by Lieutenant Colonel James Mercer, was outnumbered and outgunned by the French attackers.

Montcalm set about instituting a European-style siege, digging earthworks outside Fort Ontario in preparation for a bombardment of its wooden palisade. Realizing the fort was indefensible, Mercer abandoned it on 13 August and concentrated his men inside Fort Oswego. This left Montcalm free to mount his cannon on high ground next to the abandoned fort. Fort Oswego was bombarded mercilessly the following morning. Mercer was killed, his head knocked from his shoulders by a cannonball. As French and Indian forces crossed the river and opened fire on the fort from a clearing near the broken walls, the British saw that the situation was hopeless and surrendered. Montcalm triumphantly carried 1,700 prisoners back to Quebec. The victory persuaded many of the Indian tribes to support the French in their war with the British. **TB**

Losses: French, fewer than 50 casualties of 3,000; British, 200 casualties of 1,000, 1,700 captured (including noncombatants)

◁ Monongahela 1755   Fort William Henry 1757 ▷

A south view of Oswego, where the river flows into Lake Ontario, from 1760.

Plassey 23 June 1757

Victory for the British East India Company in the Battle of Plassey was the start of nearly two centuries of British rule in India. For an event with such momentous consequences, it was a surprisingly unimpressive military encounter, the defeat of the Nawab of Bengal owing much to betrayal.

In India, Britain was represented by the British East India Company, a venture that had been given a royal charter in 1600 to pursue trade in the East Indies that included the right to form its own army. The French East India Company had a similar remit. From 1746, the rival companies fought the Carnatic Wars for advantage in India, where they maintained trading posts, and sought influence over local rulers. In 1755, Siraj ud-Daulah became Nawab of Bengal and adopted a pro-French policy. He overran British trading posts, including Calcutta, where British prisoners were allegedly left to die in the infamous "black hole of Calcutta." Lieutenant Colonel Robert Clive was sent from Madras to retake Calcutta and from there began

"All war is so contrary to our interests that we cannot too often inculcate to you our aversion thereunto." British East India Company, 1681

plotting the overthrow of the nawab. One of the nawab's discontented followers, Mir Jafar, was bribed secretly with a promise of the throne if he would back the British. Other Bengali generals were also suborned.

Clive advanced on the Bengali capital, Murshidabad, and was confronted by the nawab's army at Plassey (Palashi) by the Bhaghirathi River. The balance of forces seemed to make a British victory impossible. The nawab's army numbered 50,000, two-thirds infantry armed at best with matchlock muskets. The French had sent

artillerymen to bolster the Bengali cannon to more than fifty guns. Facing this host, Clive arranged his force of 3,000, composed of European and Sepoy troops and a much smaller force of artillery.

The French artillery opened fire first, followed by the Bengali guns. The British guns returned fire. Due to the close proximity of the Bengali cavalry to the French guns, Clive's bombardment missed the artillery but caused damage to the cavalry, forcing the nawab to pull them back for protection. When the nawab's infantry advanced, Clive's field guns opened fire with grapeshot along with volleys of infantry musket fire, and the Bengali troops were held back. Mir Jafar, with around one-third of the Bengali army, failed to join in the fighting, despite pleas from the nawab, and remained isolated on one flank.

The battle appeared to be heading for a stalemate when it started to rain. Clive had brought tarpaulins to keep his powder dry, but the Bengalis had no such protection. Thinking that the British guns were rendered as ineffective as his own by damp powder, the nawab ordered his cavalry to charge. However, the British guns opened fire and slaughtered many of the cavalry, killing their commander Mir Madan Khan. The nawab panicked at the loss of this valued general and ordered his forces to fall back, exposing the French artillery contingent. This was rushed by the British and captured. With the French cannon taken, the British bombarded the nawab's positions without reply and the tide of the battle turned. The nawab fled the battlefield on a camel, and Mir Jafar was duly installed in power as a British puppet. The victory had cost the lives of only twenty-two soldiers on the British side, while achieving a major stride toward British control of Bengal. **TB**

Losses: Bengal and French East India Company, 1,500 casualties of 50,000; British East India Company, fewer than 100 casualties of 3,000

Wandiwash 1760 [>]

Lieutenant Colonel Robert Clive depicted at the head of his army in India. ➜

A copper engraving from 1758 showing the French troops, led by the Duke of Estrées, against the allied troops, led by Cumberland. ⬇

Hastenbeck 26 July 1757

The Battle of Hastenbeck was fought by France against an alliance of Great Britain, Hanover, Hesse-Kassel, and Brunswick. Victory for France led to a short-lived occupation of Hanover, which ended when the allies counterattacked in 1758.

In June 1757, France invaded the Electorate of Hanover, the home of Great Britain's Hanoverian King George II. The Hanoverian army was commanded by the Duke of Cumberland, George's second son. The French had formed an alliance with Austria with the objective of breaking Britain's alliance with the other German states.

As the French advanced, Cumberland took up a defensive stance at the village of Hastenbeck. Cumberland set his right flank by the River Hamel, his center and main battery north of the town, and his left flank of infantry and artillery on heights at Obensburg.

Crucially, Cumberland misread the terrain, thinking that the heights gave more protection than they actually did.

The French attacked on 26 July and made an outflanking move on the exposed Hanoverian left. Cumberland redirected troops from his center, which took the main thrust of the French attack. The Hanoverian battery north of the town inflicted serious casualties on the French and they withdrew. The battle then took a confusing turn when the Hanoverian reserve advanced and regained the left flank while Cumberland's main force retreated. Both commanders were momentarily convinced they had lost the battle, but the Hanoverian reserve was soon expelled by the French who went on to occupy Hanover. **TB**

Losses: French, 2,500 casualties of 50,000; British allied, 1,500 casualties of 30,000

◁ *Minorca 1756*   *Rossbach 1757* ▷

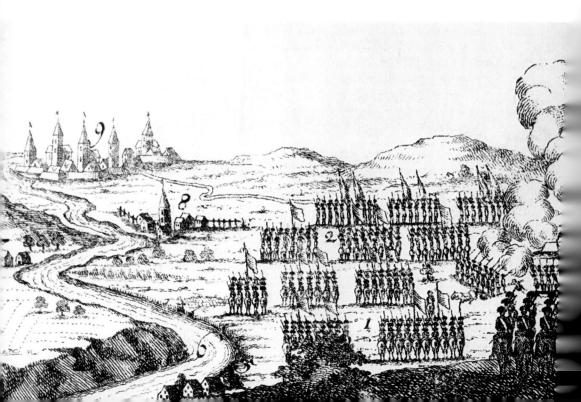

Fort William Henry   3–9 August 1757

For France, success at Fort Oswego in 1756 needed to be followed up. General Louis-Joseph de Montcalm set his sights on Fort William Henry, a stronghold on the frontier between British New York and French-controlled Canada.

The French were able to recruit a large number of American Indians impressed by the victory at Fort Oswego the previous year. Some 2,000 Indian warriors accompanied Montcalm's force of 4,000 French regulars and colonial militia, which brought with it heavy siege guns.

The French launched their attack on Fort William Henry's garrison of 2,500 British regulars and colonial militia on 3 August. The fort's commander, Lieutenant Colonel George Monro, refused to surrender and a bombardment began. The French barrage caused extensive damage, and the French had advanced close to the fort by 8 August. Monro realized it would be best to secure the safety of those inside the fort by seeking terms from Montcalm. On 9 August, it was agreed that the British garrison could withdraw honorably but with no ammunition. Montcalm tried to ensure that the American Indians understood the terms of the surrender but, on the next day, one of the worst atrocities of the war occurred. Monro's defenseless column of regulars, militia, and women and children was attacked by Montcalm's Indian allies. This resulted in the deaths of 185 and the abduction of more than 2,000. The attack outraged the British command in North America and was a key factor in bringing about the mass mobilization of militia in New England. **TB**

Losses: French, fewer than 50 casualties of 6,000; British, 200 casualties and 2,000 captured of 2,500

◁ *Fort Oswego 1756*   *Louisbourg 1758* ▷

Rossbach   5 November 1757

At the Battle of Rossbach during the Seven Years' War, Prussia comprehensively defeated a Franco-Austrian army nearly twice its size without sustaining significant casualties. For Frederick II of Prussia it was a great victory—his speed of thought and decisiveness allowed him to completely surprise and overwhelm his enemy.

The French had temporarily forced Prussia's ally, Hanover, out of the war after the Battle of Hastenbeck in July 1757. Frederick's armies had also been defeated recently in Bohemia and East Prussia while Austria had advanced into Silesia. Frederick aimed to regain the initiative by advancing into Saxony to attack the allied Franco-Austrian army.

After a period of maneuvering without engagement, the two armies faced each other in November. The Prussian army of 22,000 had set up camp north of Rossbach. To their west on higher ground was an allied force of 41,200: two-thirds French, one-third Austrian. Prince Charles of Soubise and Prince Joseph of Saxe-

> *"With plenty of work still to be done, Seydlitz displayed that rare quality in cavalry commanders: control."* Simon Millar, Rossbach and Leuthen 1757

Hildburghausen commanded the French and Austrian forces, respectively. Early in the morning of 5 November, a French detachment, led by the Count of Saint Germain, occupied the heights opposite the Prussians and bombarded them. By noon, the rest of the allies were marching south and then east in an attempt to swing around the Prussians and turn their left flank. At first, Frederick thought they were retreating but he soon realized their true intention, and the Prussian army quickly broke camp and marched east. The allied maneuver would leave their flank exposed, and Frederick sought to exploit this by trapping them as they marched around.

Major General Friedrich Wilhelm von Seydlitz advanced first, in command of the cavalry, to take up a position in advance of the allies, making up the Prussian left wing. Frederick followed with the infantry. Hills masked the Prussian movements, so the allies hastily advanced believing their enemy was retreating. In their rush forward, the allied cavalry and foot soldiers became separated, leaving the 7,000 allied horse without any significant infantry support. Frederick advanced eighteen guns to the high ground, and they opened fire on the allies. Battle was joined in earnest when Seydlitz swung into the right flank of the unprepared allied cavalry with devastating results, routing them within thirty minutes. When the allied infantry joined the fray, a fierce firefight ensued with the Prussian foot soldiers. The allied infantry bravely held their line under a heavy frontal assault from the Prussian infantry and artillery.

Disaster soon struck when Seydlitz rallied his troops and launched a second charge against the retreating allied cavalry, driving them back in disarray into their infantry. The allies were now in complete chaos. The battle was over, and their disordered retreat had scattered the allied army across the countryside. The Prussians were able to capture most of their seventy-two cannons and baggage. The allies had suffered 3,000 casualties and 5,000 captured; the numbers would have been higher but for determined rearguard actions and nightfall putting an end to the Prussian pursuit. Both the French and Austrian armies quickly retreated from Rossbach. Frederick's triumph was complete and he was able to return to Silesia and engage the Austrian army there. **JF**

Losses: Franco-Austrian, 3,000 dead and wounded and 5,000 captured of 41,200; Prussian, 165 dead and 376 wounded of 22,000

◁ *Hastenbeck 1757*   *Leuthen 1757* ▷

Detail from Seydlitz in the Battle of Rossbach (c. 1795) by Johann Christoph Frisch (1738–1815). ➜

Leuthen 5 December 1757

After his victory at Rossbach, Frederick II of Prussia marched his army to Silesia to challenge the Austrians, who were attempting to recapture the region. They met at Leuthen, where the Prussians defeated an Austrian army over twice their size by skillfully outmaneuvering and then routing them.

General Prince Charles Alexander of Lorraine had led the Austrian capture of Breslau in November 1757, and he marched 80,000 men out of the city to meet the Prussian army of 34,000. Early on 5 December Frederick sighted the Austrians, perpendicular to the route of his advance. They were drawn up in a very long line of around 5 miles (8 km), centered at Leuthen. Hills obscured the Prussian movement, so Frederick could march his troops south to attack the Austrian left wing without being observed.

Meanwhile, Charles transferred men to his right wing. The Prussians advanced diagonally against the Austrian left wing at 1:00 PM, quickly defeating it and forcing it to withdraw toward Leuthen. Eventually Charles was able to redeploy his right and center to face the Prussians, and the Austrians held their ground just outside Leuthen. The battle turned when the Austrian right launched a charge against the Prussian left flank that failed and was routed. The Prussians advanced, wheeling around to attack the Austrian rear and flank. The Austrian resolve broke and their army fled, abandoning 116 cannons. Nightfall prevented the Prussians from launching a sustained pursuit, which limited the Austrian losses. However, the damage to the Austrian army was still catastrophic. Charles withdrew to Bohemia and Frederick was able to retake most of Silesia in the aftermath of his decisive victory. **JF**

Losses: Austrian, 10,000 dead and wounded and 12,000 captured of 80,000; Prussian, 6,200 dead and wounded of 34,000

◁ Rossbach 1757   Zorndorf 1758 ▷

Louisbourg 8 June–26 July 1758

The Siege of Louisbourg was an important encounter in the contest between France and Great Britain for domination in North America. The capture of the fort by the British was a key achievement that opened the way for the conquest of Quebec and the defeat of France in Canada.

Fort Louisbourg overlooked the St. Lawrence River and the British knew that they would need to capture the fort before they could attack Quebec. Throughout May 1758, Major-General Jeffrey Amherst assembled the British force at Halifax, where a fleet of ships was brought over to support the army. The French had plans to cut off the Royal Navy, but these were foiled when their squadron was intercepted and captured off the Spanish coast.

For the first few days of June, the British attack on Fort Louisbourg was hampered by bad weather and restricted to a bombardment from a group of frigates. However, the land assault began on 8 June when Brigadier James Wolfe established a beachhead and moved forward, forcing the French back into the fortress.

The siege itself began on 19 June, when the British opened fire with their battery, which had been put into position at a high point at the harbor entrance after a successful operation by Wolfe. On 21 June a French naval vessel, *L'Entreprenant*, was destroyed along with two other vessels; two days later, the British battery destroyed the fort's headquarters. The French held out for another month, ending plans for an attack on Quebec in 1758. However, with the fort in British hands, the Royal Navy would be able to sail up the St. Lawrence River and support an attack on Quebec the following year. **TB**

Losses: French, 400 casualties, 6,000 captured, 4 ships destroyed; British, 500 casualties of 20,000

◁ Fort William Henry 1757   Carillon 1758 ▷

In a plan of the battle, ships of the Royal Navy bring troops for the Siege of Louisbourg. ➡

PLAN DU CAP BRETON DIT LOUISBOVRG AVEC CES ENVIRONS PRIES PAR LAMIRALLE BOCKOUNE LE 26 Juillet 1758

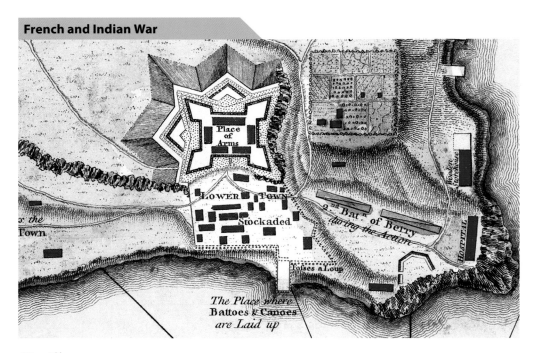

Carillon 8 July 1758

An episode in the French and Indian War, the British attack on Fort Carillon was mounted in retaliation for the massacre of British colonists by France's American Indian allies at Fort William Henry in 1757. It resulted in victory for French commander Louis-Joseph de Montcalm, against heavy odds.

In June 1758 British General James Abercomby gathered a large army of regulars and colonial militia and advanced on Fort Carillon, the base from which the French attack on Fort William Henry had been launched. He landed his army on the shore of Lake George, 4 miles (6.5 km) from the fort, on 6 July. Montcalm hastened to dig earthworks as an outer defense for the fort.

On 7 July, Abercomby sent a column forward to assess the state of the fort's defenses. Despite his column running into a French force, resulting in the death of its commander, Abercomby was heartened to learn that his troops outnumbered the French garrison by four to one.

He ordered an advance on the fort on 8 July, deciding to save time and leave his field artillery behind in the belief that his superiority of numbers would win the day. When Abercomby's force encountered the entrenched French positions, the general ignored the advice of officers who suggested a siege would be the best option, also dismissing suggestions that he attempt a flanking move on the French positions.

Instead, the British general ordered a series of direct frontal assaults without artillery support. The resolute French defenders were able to inflict massive casualties on wave after wave of British attacks. It would take the onset of darkness before Abercomby recognized the scale of the carnage. The British retreated in disarray, withdrawing across Lake George the following day. **TB**

Losses: French, fewer than 500 casualties of 4,000; British, 3,500 casualties of 16,000

◁ Louisbourg 1758   Fort Niagara 1759 ▷

Fort Carillon, later Fort Ticonderoga, commanded the river linking Lakes George and Champlain. ⬆

Zorndorf 25 August 1758

The Prussian cause in the Seven Years' War appeared healthy after their victory at Leuthen. In August 1758 the Russians invaded Brandenburg and Frederick II marched his army back from invading Bohemia to face them. They met at Zorndorf in one of the bloodiest battles of the war.

When Frederick arrived in Brandenburg he drew up with around 35,000 men at Frankfurt an der Oder. Meanwhile, the Russian army of 45,000 under William Fermor was besieging nearby Küstrin and Frederick moved to relieve it. Fermor raised the siege and retired to a defensive position on the high ground at Zorndorf, arraying his forces in three irregular groups.

The Prussians attacked the Russians on the morning of 25 August. The battle was to last ten brutal hours. The Prussians gave no quarter after learning that the Russians had committed atrocities during their invasion of Brandenburg. Frederick's infantry swung around the Russian front to attack their flank, but the Russians fought with dogged determination and did not give way. However, the Prussians made gains when their renowned cavalry commander, Friedrich Wilhelm von Seydlitz, led a charge across marshy ground that smashed the Russians.

Frederick renewed his efforts but the Prussian foot was still unable to make any progress. By late afternoon, both sides were running low on ammunition, and the battle descended into hand-to-hand struggles with swords, bayonets, and musket butts. When the fighting finally ended at nightfall both sides had suffered casualties of nearly 40 percent but neither appeared to have won the day. The Russians eventually retreated to Poland and Frederick was able to march his army to Saxony to relieve his brother Prince Henry from attack by the Austrians. **JF**

Losses: Russian, 20,000 casualties of 45,000; Prussian, 13,000 casualties of 35,000

◁ *Leuthen 1757*   *Hochkirk 1758* ▷

⬆ *Russians (in white coats) battle with Prussians at Zorndorf, in an 1858 painting by Emil Hünten.*

Part of a plan of the Battle of Hochkirk, from an unsigned eighteenth-century copper engraving. ⬇

Hochkirk   14 October 1758

During the Seven Years' War, while Frederick II of Prussia was fighting the Russians at Zorndorf, the Austrians under Leopold Joseph von Daun had invaded Saxony. Hurrying to intercept the Austrians, Frederick met them at Hochkirk but was defeated after a rare tactical misjudgment.

Stationed in Saxony was a Prussian army under Frederick's brother, Prince Henry, which was outnumbered over three times by the Austrian army of 90,000. Before Daun could press his advantage, Frederick's army of 37,000 arrived, having marched 120 miles (193 km) in seven days. Frederick tried unsuccessfully to draw the Austrians into battle, but Daun put his army on the defensive.

Then Daun saw his chance to attack, as Frederick had recklessly camped his army near Hochkirk, in a position commanded by the Austrians. At 5:00 AM on 14 October

the Austrians swept down on the Prussians while they slept. The surprise was complete and the Prussians were caught totally off guard.

Eventually the well-disciplined Prussians were able to take up arms and begin a stubborn resistance around Hochkirk, even managing to launch a counterattack. After a five-hour struggle the Prussians finally retreated from Hochkirk in good order. Although they had lost nearly one-quarter of their army and 101 guns, the surprise never turned into a rout. Thanks to Frederick's effective rallying of his men, Daun could not take full advantage of his victory and pursue the fleeing Prussians. Frederick was able to retire 2 miles (3.2 km) away and call up reserves. **JF**

Losses: Austrian, 8,000 casualties of 90,000; Prussian, 9,000 casualties of 37,000

◁ *Zorndorf 1758*   *Minden 1759* ▷

Fort Niagara   6–26 July 1759

The Siege of Fort Niagara was a key encounter in the final stages of the war between Great Britain and France in North America. The siege, part of the final British campaign to defeat the French in Quebec, had been made possible by the British victory at Fort Louisbourg in 1758.

As a result of his successes at Louisbourg and Lighthouse Point, where he had been able to place an artillery battery, James Wolfe was promoted to major general and given command of the campaign to invade Quebec from the east. Wolfe's attack was to be supported by an advance from the west, and Fort Niagara had to be taken in order to open this second front. The French garrison, commanded by Captain Pouchot, had been reinforced.

Leading the attack on Fort Niagara was Brigadier-General John Prideaux, who left Fort Oswego in July and sailed across Lake Ontario with his force of regulars, New York militia, and a significant number of Iroquois. The British invasion fleet skillfully evaded French ships patrolling the lake on the lookout for the enemy, and Prideaux was able to land undetected near the fort on 6 July. As the siege began, the French put up a stout defense and, in an unfortunate freak accident, Prideaux was killed by shrapnel from one of the British guns.

On 24 July a French relief force was intercepted by the British and the Iroquois 2 miles (3.2 km) south of Fort Niagara. The force suffered heavy casualties and was forced to retreat. On 26 July Pouchot surrendered when it became clear that his relief force had been routed. **JF**

Losses: French, 120 casualties of 500; British, American militia, and Iroquois, 250 casualties of 4,000

◁ Carillon 1758   Quebec 1759 ▷

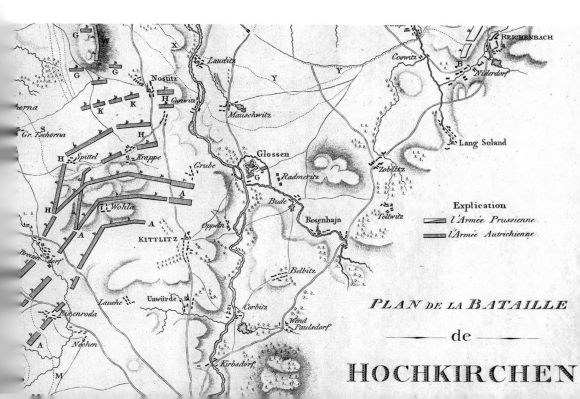

Minden   1 August 1759

The Battle of Minden was a decisive encounter of the Seven Years' War. It was fought between the forces of France, led by the Marquis de Contades, and an alliance of Britain and a number of German states, under the command of the Prussian field marshal, Ferdinand, Duke of Brunswick.

The French occupied Hanover in 1757 following their victory at Hastenbeck, but were forced back across the Rhine in 1758 when Ferdinand of Brunswick counterattacked. However, the French launched another invasion in 1759. After defeating Ferdinand at Bergen, the Marquis de Contades paused at Minden, where he set up a strong defensive position. However, Contades made the grave error of seeking an outright victory in open battle and left his advantageous position to face Ferdinand, who had split his force in an attempt to attack the French supply line. Contades was tempted by the knowledge that a decisive French victory at Minden might end Britain's appetite for the war.

A significant portion of the battle was taken up by both sides trying to bombard the other into submission, and when Lord Sackville, commander of the British contingent, refused to advance his cavalry, a French victory seemed likely. However, the decisive phase of the battle occurred when six divisions of British infantry launched a series of attacks on the French cavalry, which were the only protection that Contades had given his artillery. As the French cavalry were forced back, the French battery was overrun. With the French guns silenced, the allies launched a full advance and drove the French from the field. The French offensive of 1759 had failed and the victory at Minden was a key factor in Britain sending a more substantial army to Germany in 1760. **JF**

"It is the opinion of this court that the said Lord Sackville is . . . unfit to serve His Majesty in any military capacity whatever." Sackville's court-martial

⬆ *Disciplined lines of infantry press forward in a detail from a colored engraving of the Battle of Minden.*

Losses: French, 12,000 casualties of 50,000; British and German allied, 3,000 casualties of 40,000

◁ Hochkirk 1758   Kunersdorf 1759 ▷

Kunersdorf 12 August 1759

Prussia's Anglo-German allies had won a significant victory at Minden but eleven days later the Prussians were trounced at Kunersdorf. A Russian-Austrian army routed Frederick II's army, inflicting his worst defeat not only of the Seven Years' War but also of his entire military career.

In July 1759 a Russian army of 60,000 led by Pyotr Saltykov captured Frankfurt an der Oder. They were joined by 18,000 Austrians under Baron Ernst Gideon von Laudon. The Russians camped on the high ground at Kunersdorf, east of Frankfurt an der Oder. Ready to help to the west were the Austrians.

At noon on 12 August Frederick, leading an army of 50,000, attacked the Russians. The Prussians got the better of this engagement and by 3:00 PM the Russian left was routed. Frederick's generals asked him to stop as the Prussian army was tiring in the hot weather. However, seeking to totally annihilate the Russians, Frederick pressed on. He was so confident of victory that he sent a note to Berlin announcing his success.

This was premature. The Russians, joined by fresh reserves and Austrian soldiers, made a desperate stand against the Prussians. Frederick called up his cavalry but they could not make any headway. By 5:00 PM the Prussians were completely exhausted and they began to be forced back. This swiftly turned into a bloody rout as Austrian cavalry descended on the Prussians, who lost around 20,000 and all their artillery. The rest of their army was so scattered that the disconsolate Frederick could only effectively call on 3,000 troops. Berlin now lay totally open to Prussia's enemies but they did not take the initiative, and within a week Frederick was able to reorganize his surviving soldiers into a coherent army. **JF**

Losses: Austrian-Russian, 15,700 casualties of 78,000; Prussian, 20,000 dead, wounded, or captured of 50,000

◁ Hochkirk 1758   Torgau 1760 ▷

Lagos Bay 18–19 August 1759

As part of the Seven Years' War, in 1759 France planned an invasion of Britain. France's Mediterranean fleet was to join its Atlantic fleet to create a naval force powerful enough to protect the landing of troops on the British coast. A defeat off southern Portugal ended this plan.

In part because of the loss of Minorca in 1756, the British Mediterranean fleet, commanded by Admiral Edward Boscawen, was unable to keep a close watch on the French base of Toulon. On 17 August 1759 Boscawen's fourteen ships of the line were at anchor in Gibraltar for repair and resupply when twelve French ships, commanded by Admiral de la Clue, sailed past, heading out into the Atlantic. Boscawen and his men hurried to get their ships ready to follow them.

That night, five of the French ships became separated, finally making landfall in the Spanish port of Cadiz. On 18 August the British gradually caught up with the rest of the French force, though intermittent winds made this a long process. One French ship was battered into surrender in a running battle that lasted until nightfall. Boscawen's flagship was heavily damaged too. During the night two more French ships escaped and the last four ran into Portuguese waters in Lagos Bay. Ignoring the restrictions on warfare imposed by Portuguese neutrality, Boscawen followed them there on the 19th, destroying two by fire and capturing the other two.

In the aftermath some of Boscawen's ships blockaded the escaped French vessels in Cadiz, while he led the rest north to reinforce the British home fleet. Several of the victors from Lagos Bay would also fight at Quiberon Bay in November, a battle in which the French threat of invasion was finally completely eliminated. **DS**

Losses: French, 3 ships captured and 2 destroyed; British, no ships lost

◁ Kunersdorf 1756   Quiberon Bay 1759 ▷

Quebec (Plains of Abraham) 28 June–13 September 1759

The Battle of the Plains of Abraham was a defining moment in the struggle between Britain and France for control of North America. The British victory was a key factor in the creation of Canada, as well as the moment when General James Wolfe gained immortality as a hero of the British Empire.

In 1759 Great Britain gained victories on all fronts, resulting in the year being hailed as the Annus Mirabilis (year of miracles). The crowning glory of 1759 was the capture of Quebec, and the victory was gained in no small part due to one of the most efficient operations of navy and army that the British military had yet staged. The Royal Navy fleet of fifty ships and almost 150 amphibious craft, under the command of Admiral Charles Saunders, supported Wolfe's force of around 8,000.

Saunders ordered a prolonged period of surveys, led by Captain James Cooke, to find the safest place to land the army. The surveys eventually managed to secure a safe landing for Wolfe's army on the Isle of Orleans on 28 June,

> *"I have led you up these steep and dangerous rocks, only solicitous to show you the foe within your reach."* General Wolfe, address before the battle

while the navy repelled a squadron of French ships that tried to disrupt the landings using fireships. The following day Wolfe landed a force on the southern shore of the St. Lawrence River and commenced a bombardment of Quebec. By the end of July the British guns had caused extensive damage to the town.

Wolfe's first attempt at landing on the northern shore ended in failure, when his force of 4,000 was repelled on 31 July by a combination of French fire and a thunderstorm, which ended the operation. Meanwhile,

the navy continued to probe the French defenses and eventually found a weak point in the French line at the Anse du Foulon. The Royal Navy launched a diversionary attack to draw General Louis-Joseph de Montcalm's French forces and Wolfe landed his army using a flotilla of amphibious landing craft on 12 September. He proceeded to climb a narrow undefended path. By dawn Wolfe surprised the French by assembling a force of 4,500 British regulars and American militia on the Plains of Abraham.

General Montcalm was caught completely off guard. He appealed to the city governor to release cannon from the ramparts but was only permitted to remove three. However, thinking that three would be enough, the French general decided to drive Wolfe from the plains. As the French line advanced toward them, Wolfe ordered his troops to lie down to avoid French fire and then rise up to fire coordinated volleys when the French were within 35 yards (32 m). The tactic was successful, with the first volleys breaking the French line and allowing the British to advance. Repeated instances of volley followed by advance eventually forced the French army from the field. General Montcalm was killed during the battle.

However, at the moment of victory Wolfe was also hit, first in the hand and then in the stomach and chest. As he lay on the ground dying, news was given to him of the French defeat. After ordering General George Townsend to take command and cut off the French retreat, Wolfe died, uttering his famous words, "Now God be praised, I will die in peace." After Townsend had completed the rout, the majority of the French garrison withdrew. Despite a French counterattack and victory at the Battle of Sainte-Foy in 1760, Quebec remained under British control and the future of Canada was decided. **JF**

Losses: French, 1,500 casualties of 4,000 regulars, militia, and American Indians; British, 700 casualties of 4,500 regulars and militia

◁ Fort Niagara 1759   Sainte-Foy 1760 ▷

General Wolfe dies on the Plains of Abraham on 13 September, in a painting by Benjamin West c. 1771 (detail).

A painting of Quiberon Bay by Richard Paton (1717–91) captures the drama of a naval confrontation in stormy conditions.

Quiberon Bay 20–21 November 1759

In the most decisive naval victory of the Seven Years' War, France's last substantial fleet was neutralized by an audacious British attack. French plans to invade Britain were abandoned, France's ailing trade and economy crippled, and its remaining colonies left to fall to British forces.

Despite its naval defeat at Lagos Bay, France still tried to go through with its planned invasion of Britain. The main French warship fleet was at Brest while the invasion transports had assembled in the ports along France's western coast. Brest was guarded by the main British fleet, under Admiral Hawke, but when this was driven out of position during a storm the French (twenty-one ships of the line under Admiral de Conflans) managed to leave the port to try to link with the transport force. Alerted by his scouts, Hawke chased after the French.

The two sides met by the Loire estuary on 20 November 1759, by which time Hawke had twenty-three ships of the line. Conflans's crews were too inexperienced to stand a chance against the British veterans so he sought refuge in Quiberon Bay nearby. The weather was dangerously stormy and the British had no good charts of the bay, but Hawke decided to follow the French nonetheless.

In a wild evening and night of fighting two French ships sank, drowning all their crews. Other ships on both sides were driven ashore and wrecked. Some French ships escaped only after throwing all their guns overboard. By morning eight French ships had managed to escape but the rest were out of action, one way or another. **DS**

Losses: French, 7 ships captured or destroyed; British, 2 ships wrecked

◁ *Lagos Bay 1759*   *Ushant 1778* ▷

Wandiwash (Vandivasi)   22 January 1760

The Battle of Wandiwash was a decisive battle in the Indian campaign of the Seven Years' War between Britain and France. It was a defining moment for the British presence in India and came after the British had successfully repelled a French attempt to capture Madras in February 1759.

Having held out until reinforcements forced the French to abandon their siege of Madras in 1759, the British went onto the offensive in India. Wandiwash, halfway between Madras and the French colony at Pondicherry, fell to the British, under the command of Sir Eyre Coote, on 27 November. The French, commanded by the Count de Lally, counterattacked with the support of 2,000 Maratha troops. The fort was stormed but the small garrison held out long enough for Coote to appear with a relief army and confront Lally's force on 22 January.

Lally ordered his cavalry to attack but they refused to engage because of fear of the British artillery. By the time Lally had replaced their commander any outflanking advantage that could have been gained by an early strike was lost and the British were rapidly advancing on the French line. A lucky shot from the British guns hit an ammunition cart which exploded, causing chaos in the French lines. Lally's position became even more hopeless with the desertion of his Maratha ally.

The French abandoned Wandiwash and retreated to the fort at Pondicherry, which resisted a British siege for four months. The French campaign in India ended when the fort surrendered to Coote in January 1761. **TB**

Losses: British East India Company, 300 casualties of 2,000; French East India Company, 600 of 2,000

◁ *Plassey 1757*   *Third Panipat 1761* ▷

Sainte-Foy 28 April 1760

The Battle of Sainte-Foy was the last victory gained by France in the French and Indian War against Britain in North America. Although the French, under the command of Chevalier de Levis, defeated the British, led by General James Murray, they failed to recapture Quebec after a short siege.

After General Wolfe's decisive victory on the Plains of Abraham in September 1759, the French had retreated to Montreal and regrouped under the command of General Levis. In April 1760 the French counterattacked with a force of almost 8,000. Due to the ruined state of Quebec's fortifications and the poor health of his troops after a harsh winter, General Murray decided on a battlefield engagement. Murray faced Levis's larger force and struck quickly before the French could properly deploy.

The strategy had initial success but was soon halted as Levis moved up troops in support. The battle then developed into a bloody struggle. Levis intended to maneuver his force between the British and the citadel to stop Murray from retreating back into Quebec, but as the British lines collapsed a division of French moved over to the left to press home the advantage, inadvertently allowing Murray to retreat into the citadel.

Although France won at Sainte-Foy, Levis was forced to besiege Quebec and await naval reinforcements. However, Britain enjoyed naval superiority and the ships never came. In May Levis abandoned hopes of retaking Quebec when a squadron of Royal Navy ships came into view. Levis fell back to Montreal but surrendered on 6 September to a large British army under the command of General Amherst. With the fall of Montreal, the French campaign in North America was all but over. **TB**

Losses: French, 500 casualties of 5,000 regulars and militia; British, 1,200 casualties of 3,500 regulars

◁ Quebec 1759

Torgau 3 November 1760

The disastrous defeat of the Prussians at Kunersdorf was followed by a series of setbacks for them and their allies in the Seven Years' War. Frederick II reversed this negative trend in his victory over the Austrians at Torgau, although both armies suffered extremely heavy casualties.

On 9 October, while Frederick was away campaigning, an Austro-Russian army seized and partly burned Berlin. On Frederick's approach to relieve the city, the Russians went home and the Austrians eventually withdrew to Saxony. The Austrian commander, Leopold von Daun, ordered to engage the Prussians, drew up his army in a good defensive position at Torgau, on high ground west of the Elbe River. Frederick moved to engage Daun in a frontal assault from the north. He also sent a detachment under General Hans Joachim von Zieten to swing around the Austrian right and attack their rear from the south.

The plan began to go awry when Zieten's force missed the road nominated for their advance and was forced to engage with a group of Austrians. When Frederick heard the cannonade he immediately attacked the Austrians, ordering his soldiers to charge uphill. He eventually threw his reserves into the battle, but after hours of fighting the Austrians still held the high ground and the Prussians had suffered very heavy losses. Both Frederick and Daun were wounded in the fighting. At sunset the battle swung the Prussian way. Zieten's troops finally arrived on the battlefield and engaged the main body of Austrians. Daun now faced attack from two sides and the Prussians ultimately took the high ground. When dawn broke the Austrian army was in full retreat toward Dresden. Frederick had achieved victory, but at a major cost. **JF**

Losses: Austrian, 4,000–8,000 dead and wounded and 7,000 captured of 55,000–65,000; Prussian, 13,000–16,000 casualties of 45,000–50,000

◁ Minden 1759　　　　　　　　　　Freiberg 1762 ▷

Third Panipat   14 January 1761

A major battle of its century, Panipat was fought between the Maratha Empire, under Sadashivrao Bhau, and the Afghan Durrani Empire, led by Ahmad Shah Durrani. The defeat of the Marathas in the battle weakened an Indian power that might have resisted British imperial expansion.

Following the decline of the Mughal Empire after the death of Emperor Aurangzeb, the Maratha Confederacy had expanded rapidly, threatening the Afghan Durrani Empire, ruled by Ahmad Shah Durrani. Ahmad declared a jihad and launched a campaign that captured large parts of the Punjab. The Marathas responded by raising a large army, under the command of Sadashivrao Bhau, and recaptured Delhi. Ahmad's campaign was aimed at starving the Maratha army of its supplies. At the same time, he led an army of 40,000 into the south to trap the Maratha army in the Punjab.

Cut off and starving, Bhau decided to break Ahmad's blockade and the two armies met at Panipat. Bhau attempted to pulverize Ahmad's army with a massive artillery bombardment and then utilize his superiority in numbers to break the Durrani blockade and move south in a defensive posture. However, he was undermined by rivalries within his ranks and the need to protect many civilians. Durrani launched a surprise attack before the artillery had inflicted serious damage and Bhau's nephew was killed. The Maratha commander entered the battle to recover his nephew's body, but his troops thought him dead and their morale plummeted. The smaller Durrani army took advantage and routed them. Bhau escaped, to die sometime later, but the Maratha army had been destroyed and the unity of the empire was broken. **TB**

Losses: Maratha, 40,000 casualties and 30,000 captured of 80,000; Durrani, 5,000 casualties of 40,000–75,000

◁ *Wandiwash 1760*   *Buxar 1764* ▷

Freiberg   29 October 1762

At the Battle of Freiberg Prince Henry, younger brother of Frederick II of Prussia, defeated an Austrian army. It was the last truly significant battle of the Seven Years' War in Europe, as well as the only major Prussian victory of the conflict not personally commanded by Frederick.

In the aftermath of the Battle of Torgau Prussia's military capacity was severely stretched. It received a major boost when Empress Elizabeth of Russia died in January 1762 and her successor, Czar Peter III, allied with Prussia.

Prince Henry, stung by Frederick's recent criticism of his military prowess, planned to capture Austrian-held Freiberg in Saxony. On 28 October, without waiting for reinforcements to arrive, Henry marched toward his target, a line of fortifications on the hills northwest of Freiberg. Heavy woods screened the position. Henry had divided his forces into four columns, and they advanced toward Freiberg at 5:00 AM on 29 October.

Henry's ambitious strategy relied on the columns acting simultaneously but independently. The strongest column was to attack from the south, aiming to take a hillock called the Three Crosses, which was the key to the position. Another column would attack from the south, creating a pincer movement. A third would make a frontal attack through the woods, which would hide its advance. The fourth column was to protect the Prussian rear. Henry's attacks were well coordinated and the Prussians converged from three sides onto the Austrians, who made no attempt to attack the Prussian rear. After three hours of heavy fighting the Austrians gave way and retreated. This was the last battle of the war in Europe, and by February 1763 Prussia was in control of Silesia. **JF**

Losses: Austrian, 3,000–4,000 dead or wounded and 4,000 captured of 30,000–40,000; Prussian, 1,500–2,500 dead or wounded of 22,000–24,000

◁ *Torgau 1760*

Anglo-Bengal War

Buxar   23 October 1764

The Battle of Buxar was a decisive encounter in eastern India between Britain, represented by the forces of the British East India Company, and an alliance of Indian states including Bengal, Awadh, and the Mughal Empire. The British victory at Buxar resulted in a large area of the Indian subcontinent coming under British control.

After consolidating gains made at Plassey in 1759, the British East India Company assembled an army consisting mainly of Indian sepoys and Indian cavalry and sought to assert its control of Bengal against the Mughal Empire.

In October, the combined Indian force confronted the British near the town of Buxar. The British, under the command of Sir Hector Munro, were divided into three sections. On the left flank, Major Stibbert commanded regular troops; on the right were the Bengalese troops, commanded by Major Champion. Supporting these in the center were the Bengal cavalry backed by four companies of sepoys. Champion advanced first and attacked a small village close to the town. After a series of bloody encounters the Indian forces were pushed back, allowing Champion to occupy the village. Meanwhile, the main Indian force advanced to engage Stibbert's regular troops. However, having secured the village on the Indian left flank, Champion was able move out and outflank the Indian advance. Despite their superiority in numbers, the Indians were encircled and took heavy casualties from British musket volleys. A detachment of Durrani cavalry was unable to turn the battle and the Indians retreated.

The battle resulted in the 1765 Treaty of Allahabad, in which the Mughal Emperor surrendered sovereignty of Bengal to the British. Lord Robert Clive, the victor at Plassey, became the first governor of Bengal. **TB**

Losses: British East India Company, fewer than 1,000 casualties of 8,000; Indian states, 6,000 of 35,000

◁ Third Panipat 1761   Pondicherry 1778 ▷

Corsican Revolution

Ponte Novu   8 May 1769

The Battle of Ponte Novu ended Corsica's brief period of independence. The island had declared independence from Genoa in 1755, and established a progressive republic. In 1769 an invading French army decisively defeated the Corsican republicans under Pascal Paoli at Ponte Novu. In 1770 Corsica was incorporated into the French monarchy.

In 1768 France had purchased the claim to Corsica from Genoa. By May 1769 the French invaders had begun to force back the Corsicans under the leadership of the Count of Vaux. To block the French advance south, Paoli determined to defend the crossing of the Golo River at Ponte Novu, placing detachments in nearby villages.

On 8 May the troops at the bridge heard musket fire from nearby Lento, and swarmed there to join the battle. However, the French had already taken Lento and the shots fired were a token resistance. The Corsicans rushed back to Ponte Novu, but many retreated into the mountains, leaving their position in disarray. One of the Corsican commanders attempted to restore order by ordering a company of Swiss and Prussian mercenaries to hold the southern side of the bridge while the defenses on the north could be reorganized. In the panic some Corsicans attacked the Prussians, who fired on them.

The Corsican lines were now in chaos, with rumors of betrayal flying through the army. When the French advanced to Ponte Novu, they swept away the Corsicans with ease, with some French troops scrambling across the valley to attack the Corsican rear from the south side. The Corsicans were completely broken and by nightfall they gave up and fled into the surrounding woods. In the aftermath of the battle the French secured their control of Corsica, and Paoli fled into exile in England. **JF**

Losses: Corsican, unrecorded but heavy from 12,000–16,000; French, light from their invasion force of 30,000

Chesma (Çeşme)   5–7 July 1770

In 1768 Empress Catherine the Great's Russia went to war against Ottoman Turkey. The Russian Baltic fleet was sent to the Mediterranean, where it imposed a devastating defeat upon the once-proud Ottoman navy at Chesma Bay. The victory provided unmistakable proof that the power of Russia was rising in the face of Ottoman decline.

Russia's Baltic fleet, under the overall command of prominent courtier Count Aleksei Orlov, was sent to the Mediterranean in the hope of stimulating a revolt against Turkish rule in Greece. It found the Ottoman fleet in Chesma Bay, between the island of Chios and Anatolia.

On 5 July 1770 nine Russian ships of the line and eleven other vessels under Admiral Grigori Spiridov found Hassan Pasha's fourteen Turkish ships of the line, numerous smaller warships, and a large fleet of transports anchored in two defensive lines, a position designed to maximize their firepower. Although outnumbered, the Russians attacked, Spiridov's flagship *Yevstafy* taking on Hassan's flagship *Real Mustafa* at close range. A fire broke out and both ships were destroyed, killing most of their crews—some 500 men on the Russian vessel. Shortly after this unnerving event the action was broken off and the Turks withdrew further into the bay.

The next morning more Russian ships arrived, commanded by Admiral John Elphinston, one of a number of British officers then in Russian service. Under his direction the Russian forces sent fireships into the Turkish anchorage, with more fireships that night, covered by a naval bombardment. Shortly after midnight on 7 July a Turkish ship caught fire and exploded. The conflagration spread through the closely packed Turkish fleet with horrible effect. Only one Turkish ship of the line escaped. **DS**

Losses: Turkish, 13 battleships, up to 200 other vessels, and 10,000 dead; Russian, 1 battleship, more than 500 dead

Kinburn 1787 ▷

"Signaling Russia's achievement of a new level of power, Catherine [had] ordered the circumnavigation of Europe." Scott Powell, historian

⬆ The Sinking of the Russian Battleship *St. Yevstafy* in the Naval Battle of Chesma *(1771), by Jacob Philipp Hackert.*

Lanckorona   23 May 1771

The Bar Confederation was created in 1768 to defend the rights of the nobility and oppose increasing Russian encroachment into Polish-Lithuanian affairs. In 1771 Alexander Suvorov beat the Confederates at Lanckorona. This paved the way to the final defeat of the Confederation and the first formal partition of Poland-Lithuania.

The Bar Confederation enjoyed early success, and its armies won several victories over the Russian forces sent to combat their influence. France had dispatched a military advisor, Charles François Dumouriez, to help organize the Confederation armies, and in 1771 they launched a successful offensive and occupied Kraków.

On 23 May, in nearby Lanckorona, a Russian army led by Suvorov encountered Dumouriez. The Frenchman had deployed the Confederates on a ridge with the fortress of Lanckorona and thirty guns on its left flank, with woods protecting the right and center. Thick brushwood covered the slope toward their line. Suvorov's attack on this essentially sound defensive position was audacious. Without waiting for infantry support, he launched a cavalry charge of Cossacks and carabineers against the Confederate center. Dumouriez ordered his men to hold their fire, but at the sight, and sound, of the cavalry the poorly disciplined Confederates began to turn and run.

Dumouriez attempted to rally his men and launch a counterattack against the approaching Russian infantry but the battle was already decided. The Confederate left managed to retire to the fortress, which the advancing Russians were forced to bypass because of a lack of heavy artillery. Shortly afterward, Dumouriez returned to France. The Confederate army was left without a cohesive, experienced leader, and they were defeated by 1772. **JF**

Losses: Confederate, 500 of 2,000; Russian, light of 20,000

Praga 1794 ▷

Concord (Lexington)   18 April 1775

An attempt to seize an arms cache of the rebellious Massachusetts Provincial Congress at Concord sparked the opening engagements of the American Revolutionary War. What was intended as a simple preemptive strike to disarm local militia and demonstrate the power of the British king turned into a bloody retreat.

When 700 British soldiers and Royal Marines under Lieutenant Colonel Francis Smith made a predawn movement by boat from Boston to Charlestown, American agents quickly spread the alarm along the road to Concord where a large store of arms and powder was hidden. No significant resistance was expected, so Smith had no artillery and issued no rations; only thirty-six rounds of ammunition were given to each man.

Fair weather made an easy march to Lexington, where the road passed the village green. Gathered there were 130 local "minutemen," or quick-responding militia. With no orders to fight, the militia commander directed his men to move aside, but without warning a shot was fired and both sides opened fire. The militia soon fled, leaving eight dead. The British re-formed and continued on to Concord, 6 miles (9.6 km) away, where the road crossed a bridge. More militia stood on the far side and others gathered nearby. Smith posted troops for security at the bridge and sent others to search the town.

Around noon, the Americans advanced toward the bridge and the security detachment opened fire. Volleys were exchanged and the British fell back. Lacking ammunition, Smith ordered a withdrawal. As they marched, his men suffered under increasingly heavy fire from over 3,500 militiamen in positions along the road. Only at Lexington did Smith's troops find safety. **RB**

Losses: American, 49 dead, 41 wounded, 5 missing; British, 73 dead, 174 wounded, 26 missing

Bunker Hill 1775 ▷

A column of red-coated British troops files past a burning Lexington, in an undated engraving.

Bunker Hill (Breed's Hill)   17 June 1775

Following the fighting at Lexington and Concord, British forces withdrew into Boston, where they were besieged by a militia army commanded by Massachusetts militia general Artemus Ward. Other colonies sent reinforcements. An attack on American positions on Bunker Hill and Breed's Hill outside Boston resulted in a costly tactical victory for the British that almost ruined their strength.

During the night of 16–17 June, a force of militiamen under Colonel William Prescott was sent to fortify abandoned British earthworks on Bunker Hill, one of several hills dominating the Charlestown peninsula that extended into Boston Bay. However, Prescott decided that Breed's Hill, not quite as high but closer to the bay, was a better position. An earth redoubt overlooking Charlestown, 136 feet (41.5 m) long, was almost completed by dawn, along with some breastworks. In the morning, more militia units arrived for a total of about 1,400 defenders. The American positions extended along a stone and rail fence

"Charleston was in flames, women and children flying from their burning houses sought refuge . . ."

Dorothea Gamsby, eyewitness

to the left of the redoubt down Breed's Hill almost to the Mystic River, where a breastwork covered the beach.

Lieutenant General Thomas Gage, British commander-in-chief, realized the danger that cannon on Breed's Hill presented and he ordered the hill taken immediately. On 17 June, a hot day, a British assault force of 2,500 soldiers and marines commanded by Major General William Howe had barged across the Charles River by noon. Supported by cannon fire from warships that also set Charlestown afire, the British landed unopposed. Howe's plan called for

an envelopment of the American position. A two-prong attack was to be made directly on the redoubt to hold its defenders in place while companies of light infantry moved along the Mystic riverbank to turn the American left flank and attack from the rear.

The light infantry moved rapidly along the level river beach and assaulted the breastwork and fence where several hundred militia, some led by Colonel John Stark, waited. At a distance of 50 yards (45 m) the British line was staggered by a withering volley of musket fire. After two more attempted attacks, the light infantry withdrew with heavy losses, leaving behind their dead and wounded. An assault by grenadier companies against the stone fence also failed with heavy losses.

Meanwhile, with some artillery support, the British regimental line companies began to attack the main American positions. The advancing infantry lines, led by grenadiers, also met a hail of close-range musket fire and were twice driven back with many casualties, especially among the officers. The American militia, however, had depleted their limited ammunition and few had bayonets. Howe re-formed his battered lines and with some fresh reinforcements led a third attack up the hill. The Americans fired one last volley before the British came over the walls and surrounded the redoubt. After a brief hand-to-hand struggle, the panicked militiamen fled to the rear toward Bunker Hill, where reserve positions were supposed to have been prepared. Little was done, so Prescott withdrew the militia to the mainland.

The depleted British were in no shape to pursue. After several days Gage withdrew his men back to Boston. American morale soared despite the defeat and popular support for independence from England increased. In March 1776 the British were to evacuate Boston. **RB**

Losses: American, 140 dead, 301 wounded, 30 captured; British, 1,154 dead and wounded

◁ *Concord 1775*　　　　　　　　　*Long Island 1776* ▷

　　　Detail from a painting of the Battle of Bunker Hill by Winthrop Chandler c. 1776–77.

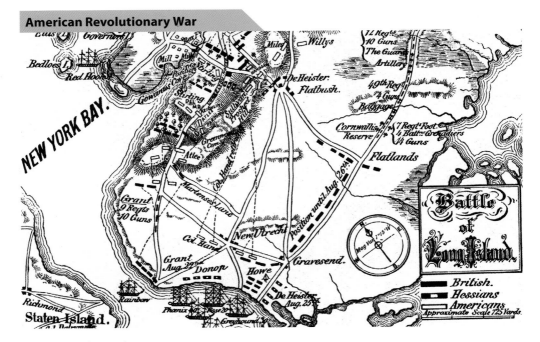

Long Island (Brooklyn) 27–29 August 1776

Major General William Howe wanted to regain the initiative after being forced from Boston by General George Washington's siege. Howe assembled a large fleet and with a reinforced land force he attacked the American army on Long Island as a first step in capturing New York City.

A Continental Army division under Major General Nathanial Greene occupied a line of fortifications on Long Island's Brooklyn Heights, across the East River from New York City. Howe planned to attack by land while warships blocked the river, trapping the Americans. On 22 August, his force of almost 30,000 British regulars and German mercenaries landed on the south beaches of Long Island. The Americans reinforced their strength to 9,000 men, but Greene fell ill and was replaced by Major General Israel Putnam, a less capable soldier. About 6,500 men manned the main American positions while the rest were placed forward to block the three approach roads up to

the Heights. Howe divided his men into three assault columns, one for each road.

After midnight on 27 August, Howe's left and central columns marched forward, causing Putnam to shift units to meet the threat. Meanwhile, the main British attack swung right and, finding the road undefended, attacked the American rear. Surprised and outnumbered, American units fled to the main defense line. Several regiments fought desperate rearguard actions but were overwhelmed. Despite his initial success, Howe paused two days in front of the American fortifications to prepare a final assault. When a storm drove the British warships downriver, Washington used the opportunity to abandon Long Island. During the night of 29 August, the bulk of the American army crossed the river and escaped. **RB**

Losses: American, 300 dead, 650 wounded, 1,100 captured; British and German, 63 dead, 314 wounded

[<] Bunker Hill 1775   Trenton 1776 [>]

A plan of the Battle of Long Island by historian Colonel Henry Beebee Carrington (1824–1912).

Valcour Island   11–13 October 1776

The unsuccessful American campaign in Canada ended in a withdrawal down Lake Champlain in western New York with British forces close behind. The British goal was to take control of the lake before winter. Each side built a flotilla of boats and maneuvered toward their enemy on the lake.

Major General Guy Carleton, British Governor-General of Canada, had five heavily armed boats, including *Inflexible* with eighteen 12-pound cannon, plus twenty gunboats and twenty-eight barges filled with soldiers and Indians. Brigadier General Benedict Arnold led an American flotilla of fifteen assorted schooners, galleys, and gunboats.

As the British moved southward down the lake, Arnold positioned his boats across the narrow passage between Valcour Island and the western shore. On the morning of 11 October the British sailed past, failing to see the Americans until well beyond them. Carleton moved back upwind to block the mouth of the passage. His large boats had limited maneuverability, but he pressed ahead and began a battle that lasted until dark. Early on, the American *Royal Savage* was badly damaged and burned, but the British force also suffered heavily.

As darkness fell, *Inflexible* fired five broadsides that devastated the American boats, rendering many guns unusable. Arnold realized he could not survive another day of battle, so when a fog descended he ordered his crews to muffle oars and led his darkened boats in single file past the British blockade. Arnold's escape was discovered at dawn and a two-day pursuit began. The American boats were finally overtaken and more damage inflicted. In desperation, Arnold ordered his men to reverse course past the surprised British into a nearby bay where the last boats were beached and burned. **RB**

Losses: American, 673 dead or captured; British, 50 dead, wounded, or missing

Fort Ticonderoga 1777 ▸

The British fleet fires a broadside on 11 October, the first day of the battle on Lake Champlain.

Trenton   26 December 1776

The American defeat on Long Island began a series of minor engagements as General George Washington parried attempts by British commander Lieutenant General William Howe to draw the Americans into a decisive battle. Washington successfully evaded Howe until the American army was safely over the Delaware River.

In crossing the river on 8 December, Washington took all the available boats, ending the British pursuit. Howe returned to New York City, leaving Major General Charles Cornwallis in charge for the winter. Cornwallis placed a garrison of 1,200 Hessians under Colonel Johann Rahl in the river town of Trenton to act as an outpost.

With morale low and enlistments expiring, Washington knew he had to have a success to keep his army. When spies reported lax security at Trenton, he saw his opportunity. During the snowy night of 25–26 December, Washington moved his men across the river. He planned to cross units at three sites, but due to the storm only his column of 2,400 men and eighteen cannon made it. Washington organized these into two assault groups, then marched 9 miles (14.5 km) through the blowing snow to Trenton. They arrived well past dawn. One group swung west, the other took the cannon to the north end of town. When the surprised Hessians discovered the attack, they formed ranks in the streets and returned the American musket volleys. Rahl was mortally wounded in subsequent house-to-house fighting. Overwhelming numbers and accurate artillery fire soon drove the Germans out of town into an orchard where they made a short-lived stand before surrendering or fleeing the battlefield. Recrossing the river to safety, Washington had regained some of his reputation with Congress. **RB**

Losses: American, 4 dead, 8 wounded; Hessian, 40 dead, 66 wounded, 918 captured

◁ *Long Island 1776*   *Princeton 1777* ▷

Washington Crossing the Delaware, *the iconic 1851 painting by Emanuel Gottlieb Leutze.* ⬆

Princeton 3 January 1777

Victory at Trenton encouraged General George Washington to seek similar opportunities with British outposts. He recrossed the Delaware River on 30 December, assembled his army at Trenton, and awaited an opening as a British-German force under Major General Charles Cornwallis, the British area commander, made its approach.

Marching to attack Washington, Cornwallis left a detachment of 1,200 men at Princeton, about 12 miles (19 km) north of Trenton. An American delaying force slowed the British advance so that Cornwallis did not arrive at Trenton until 2 January. He found Washington's army deployed on the far side of a creek outside of town, and planned an attack for the next morning.

During the night, Washington left his fires burning and slipped away on a back road with the bulk of his army to attack Princeton. At dawn, as the Americans closed on the town, an American force sent to block the main road ran into two British regiments marching to Trenton, and a hot fight began. Meanwhile, Cornwallis discovered the American trick and hurriedly put his men into pursuit. For almost an hour, the fighting south of Princeton grew in intensity, and the American militia was beginning to give way when more Continental units arrived with Washington, who took command. The reinforced Americans drove the British from the field, then advanced into Princeton where only about 200 British troops remained. These took refuge in a stone house, but a cannon fired into the building brought their surrender. Before Cornwallis could arrive with his force, Washington gathered the prisoners and marched west. The British had lost control of most of New Jersey, attracting serious French interest in supporting the American rebellion. **RB**

Losses: American, 23 dead, 20 wounded; British, 28 dead, 58 wounded, 187 missing or captured

◁ Trenton 1776   Brandywine Creek 1777 ▷

American Brigadier General Hugh Mercer is killed at Princeton, in a painting by John Trumbull (1756–1843).

Fort Ticonderoga   2–7 July 1777

The summer after their success at Valcour Island, the British opened their renewed invasion plan with a three-pronged effort to split the northern American colonies. Accordingly, Major General John Burgoyne sailed with 9,100 British and German troops and Indians down Lake Champlain to seize the American-held Fort Ticonderoga.

Although it was a strong fortification and occupied a strategic position, Fort Ticonderoga was vulnerable to artillery attack from three nearby hills: Mt. Hope, Sugar Loaf Hill, and Mt. Independence. Each was fortified, but thinly manned. Proper defense was beyond the capability of the estimated 4,000 Americans under Major General Arthur St. Clair, whose plan was to hold out as long as possible, then use a pontoon bridge to cross the lake to Mt. Independence and withdraw a safe distance.

Burgoyne with his main body landed on the west lake shore near the fort on 30 June. His Hessians marched on the opposite shore toward Mt. Independence, threatening to cut off the American escape route. On 4 July St. Clair observed British artillery emplaced on Sugar Loaf. After dark on 5 July he evacuated his sick and wounded by boat, and then marched his men over the lake. On the other side, he ordered his last detachment commander, Colonel Seth Warner, to wait for the rearguard, then rejoin the main body.

Warner, however, disregarded the order and halted his men for the night in Hubbarton. At dawn the next day, British pursuers made a surprise attack on Warner and a sharp fight began. Warner's Continentals were close to winning when Hessian reinforcements arrived and tipped the battle in favor of the British. Warner's men were scattered, although St. Clair's main army escaped. **RB**

Losses: American, 40 dead, 40 wounded, 234 captured; British and Hessian, 35 dead, 150 wounded

◁ *Valcour Island 1776*   *Bennington 1777* ▷

Bennington   13–16 August 1777

After capturing Fort Ticonderoga, Major General John Burgoyne pushed into western New York State toward Albany. His long supply line to Canada could not provide adequate supplies, so foragers were sent to seize supplies from the Americans. Raiders sent to Bennington, Vermont, sparked the first battle of the Saratoga Campaign.

Colonel Friedrich Baum, a German officer from Brunswick, was tasked to lead a mixed raiding force of 800 Germans, British, Loyalists, and Indians to seize the American supplies. Departing on 9 August, they plundered the countryside for five days. On 14 August a group of American militia sent by Vermont Brigadier General John Stark lost a skirmish with Baum's raiders near Bennington. The American force grew to 1,100 men the next day when Stark arrived with reinforcements in a heavy rain. Baum realized he was badly outnumbered. He sent a courier to Burgoyne requesting more troops, and had his men build earth breastworks for defense.

On 16 August Stark led his militia in a multipronged assault against Baum's positions. The complex American plan worked perfectly, hitting the positions simultaneously from several directions. The Loyalists and Indians ran at the first volley, but the British and German regulars fiercely defended their redoubt for two hours until their ammunition was gone. In a vain attempt to break out, Baum had his dismounted Hessian cavalrymen draw sabers and made a charge on foot. Baum fell fatally wounded and the survivors surrendered. Reinforcements sent by Burgoyne were delayed by the rain and arrived after the battle. Stark reformed his celebrating men and attacked the arriving Germans. In the fight, the German commander was killed and the rest forced to retreat. **RB**

Losses: American, 14 dead, 42 wounded; British and Loyalist, 207 dead, 700 captured

◁ *Fort Ticonderoga 1777*   *Saratoga 1777* ▷

Brandywine Creek   11 September 1777

British Lieutenant General William Howe's campaign to capture Philadelphia, the American capital, began in mid-1777. The forces had skirmished earlier as General George Washington avoided committing his retrained but untested Continental Army. Confident of success, Howe hoped to draw Washington into a decisive battle.

In July Howe embarked a force of British, Germans, and Loyalists and sailed up Chesapeake Bay, landing about 50 miles (80 km) south of Philadelphia. Washington assembled his Continentals and sent units to harass the British advance. Howe divided his army, leading one column of about 6,000 while Lieutenant General Wilhelm von Knyphausen commanded another of 5,000. Washington selected positions blocking several fords across Brandywine Creek, 25 miles (40 km) from Philadelphia. Two divisions with artillery were posted at Chadd's ford on the main road.

When Knyphausen's advance guard arrived early on 11 September, it was taken under fire. After an American foray was repulsed, fighting slackened. Meanwhile, Howe marched upstream to a unguarded ford and crossed to attack the American right flank and rear. Washington did not respond at first, but at 2:00 PM Howe's advance was confirmed, and Washington sent all but one division to face Howe. The complex maneuver became confused and the American units, though fighting stubbornly for two hours, could not form a cohesive defense.

Washington committed his last division, but it was too late, and it could only act as a rearguard for the other units. At the same time Knyphausen pushed through the weakened defense at Chadd's ford and joined Howe. Only at nightfall did the pursuit of the Americans end. **RB**

Losses: American, 200 dead, 500 wounded, 400 captured; British and German, 89 dead, 488 wounded, 6 missing

◁ Princeton 1777   Germantown 1777 ▷

Regiment von Bose.

Fusilier regiment von Donop.

"Notwithstanding the misfortune of the day, I am happy to find the troops in good spirits; and I hope another time we shall compensate for the losses now sustained."

General Washington, in a letter written to John Hancock after midnight, 12 September 1777

⬆ Illustrations of the Regiment Von Bose (top) and the Regiment Von Donop of Fusiliers, commanded by Knyphausen.

Saratoga 19 September–17 October 1777

The August defeat at Bennington put British Major General John Burgoyne's dwindling army in more serious straits than he realized. British campaign plans called for three expeditions to converge on Albany, New York, but only Burgoyne's army had made any progress—and it was stalled.

In September 1777 General Horatio Gates, the recently appointed senior northern American commander, positioned his army of 7,000 Continentals and militia in a blocking position across Burgoyne's advance down the Hudson River. Gates had his men prepare extensive fortifications along Bemis Heights overlooking the river. Burgoyne had little information as to the size or location of Gate's larger force and tried to break through.

When British troops advanced to Freeman's Farm, about 3 miles (5 km) from Bemis Heights, American Brigadier General Benedict Arnold convinced the hesitant Gates to send him and Colonel Daniel Morgan with riflemen and light infantry to attack the advance guard.

"That officer is General Fraser. . . . Take your stations in that clump of bushes, and do your duty."

Colonel Daniel Morgan orders sharpshooters to kill Fraser

Many British officers were picked off in the open fields by long-range American rifle fire from marksmen concealed in the thick woods. As the disheartened British advance guard began to break, the main British force arrived, followed soon after by German reinforcements that struck the American flank. The American Continentals stood fast, however, and heavy fighting lasted for several hours until at dusk the Americans withdrew. An angry Gates removed Arnold from command. Burgoyne, expecting reinforcements from Lieutenant General Henry Clinton,

decided to wait and built his own defensive works from Freeman's Farm to the river. Gates also strengthened his positions as more American units arrived, raising his strength to 11,000. Burgoyne, on the other hand, was growing weaker as supplies became desperately short.

Finally, Burgoyne could wait no longer for Clinton. Rejecting a proposal from his officers to retreat, he decided to test the American strength. On 7 October he sent a reconnaissance in force, using 1,500 troops in three columns under Brigadier Simon Fraser to probe the American left. Less than a mile from the American earthworks, Fraser halted to reform his units. A division of Continental infantry, including Morgan's riflemen, were positioned nearby in the dense woods and they opened fire on the exposed British before attacking. Fraser was fatally shot trying to rally his men as the American assault drove the British and Germans back to their redoubts on Freeman's Farm. Just as the American attack began to falter, the insubordinate Arnold appeared on horseback, leading a fresh brigade in a wild charge into the British positions until he was wounded. The Germans in their redoubt stubbornly resisted the American assaults, but they were finally overwhelmed.

The fall of the redoubt made Burgoyne's other redoubt and works vulnerable, but nightfall ended the fighting before these could be attacked. During the night Burgoyne ordered a retreat back north to Saratoga. He reached the town, but realized he could go no farther and opened negotiations of surrender with Gates. On 12 October Brigadier General John Stark arrived with his troops from Bennington and cut the road north out of Saratoga, blocking Burgoyne's exit. Gates and Burgoyne reached agreement and on 17 October the survivors of Burgoyne's army laid down their arms. **RB**

Losses: American, 215 dead, 300 wounded, and 36 missing; British and German, 1,200 dead or wounded, 5,800 captured

◁ Bennington 1777   Germantown 1777 ▷

General Burgoyne (right) surrenders his sword after Saratoga, in a painting by John Trumbull (1756–1843). ➡

Germantown 4 October 1777

American defeats at Brandywine and Paoli forced Congress and its rebel supporters to evacuate Philadelphia. On 26 September a British detachment occupied the city while Lieutenant General William Howe's main army of 11,000 remained 5 miles (8 km) away at Germantown. General George Washington moved to strike back.

Washington's strategy was to push the British into Philadelphia and then cut their land-bound supply line. He moved 11,000 Continentals and militia against Germantown after nightfall on 3 October. Washington's tactical plan was to hit Howe simultaneously with three columns converging from different directions. It was a difficult plan for his inexperienced army, which, delayed in the dark, was then confused by thick fog at dawn.

Washington led the central attack that forced the British back through the town. The attack on the right, however, was stalled by Hessian resistance, while the American units on the left remained lost in the fog until the fighting was well underway. A British group used a stone house as a strongpoint that Washington's troops initially bypassed, then tried in vain to reduce with cannon fire. Hearing the fighting at the house, a brigade from the American left column moved in that direction and, confused by powder smoke and fog, fired into the flank of a center unit. Believing themselves attacked by British troops and low on ammunition, that unit fell back. This exposed the flanks of joining units to the continued British resistance, and started a general withdrawal. British reinforcements arrived, and, sensing the American lines wavering, Howe counterattacked, trapping one of the advanced Continental units. Washington made a skillful fighting retreat for 10 miles (16 km), ending the battle. **RB**

Losses: American, 152 dead, 521 wounded, 400 captured; British and Hessian, 71 dead, 450 wounded, 14 captured

◁ *Saratoga 1777*　　　　　　*Monmouth 1778* ▷

Monmouth 28 June 1778

The British surrender at Saratoga brought the French into the war as American allies in February 1778. The new British commander, Lieutenant General Henry Clinton, received orders to follow a defensive strategy and consolidate forces in New York City. He abandoned Philadelphia and marched his army north.

To catch Clinton, General George Washington marched his army on a road that intersected the British route at Monmouth County Court House near Freehold, New Jersey. An American advance guard of 5,000 under Major General Charles Lee caught the 1,500-man British rear detachment at the court house and opened the battle. Lee had no battle plan and when a British force of about 5,000 under Clinton appeared, Lee lost control, his vague instructions causing confusion and a retreat.

Washington arrived about noon, ahead of his main army, in time to see Lee's men fleeing the battlefield. Outraged, Washington rallied and re-formed the men to delay until his following units were in a battle line. There were attacks and counterattacks by both sides throughout the hot afternoon, with numerous casualties as American and British cannon swept the field in the largest artillery duel of the war. The American left held steady while the advanced right wing under Major General Nathanial Greene was pushed back. Greene re-formed his units as part of the main battle line and fought on. Benefiting from their winter training at Valley Forge, the Continentals repulsed the British regulars and made bayonet counterattacks. By late afternoon both sides were exhausted and fighting stopped. Clinton rested his men until midnight, then he slipped them away to the coast and evacuation by the Royal Navy. **RB**

Losses: American, 109 dead, 161 wounded, 130 missing; British, 207 dead, 170 wounded

◁ *Germantown 1777*　　　　　*Savannah 1778* ▷

Ushant 27 July 1778

In the summer of 1778 France went to war with Britain as an ally of the Americans in their struggle for independence. The Battle of Ushant demonstrated that Britain was in serious trouble at sea, the Royal Navy being incapable of preventing the resurgent French navy from influencing the course of the war taking place across the Atlantic.

Since the end of the Seven Years' War in 1763, the French had invested large-scale resources in shipbuilding and reformed its naval organization and training, while Britain's navy had been run down and starved of funds. Britain needed to keep the French Atlantic and Mediterranean fleets cooped up in Brest and Toulon respectively, but lacked the naval strength to do so.

In July 1778 the Atlantic fleet, commanded by the Comte d'Orvilliers, sortied into the Bay of Biscay. It was brought to battle by the British Western Squadron under Admiral Augustus Keppel 100 miles (160 km) off Ushant. In the best traditions of the Royal Navy, Keppel sailed in to attack, but he was outmaneuvered by the French, who succeeded in bringing the guns of their best modern ships of the line to bear upon the British rear, commanded by Admiral Sir Hugh Palliser. Trained to a high standard, the French gunners inflicted heavy structural damage on Palliser's ships and decimated their crews. Keppler ordered a pursuit as the French sailed for home, but Palliser had seen enough combat for the day and failed to execute the necessary maneuver. The battle was followed by a prolonged dispute between Keppler and Palliser over responsibility for the Western Squadron's substandard performance, which did nothing to improve naval morale. Meanwhile, the French Mediterranean fleet had crossed the Atlantic unopposed and arrived off New York. **RG**

"If the enemy really seeks to force [a naval engagement], it will be very hard to shun."

Comte d'Orvilliers

Losses: British, no ships lost of 30, 1,200 casualties; French, no ships lost of 27, 500 casualties

🔼 *A detail of an eighteenth-century French engraving of the confrontation between the British and French navies at Ushant.*

◁ Quiberon Bay 1759   Cape St. Vincent 1780 ▷

Pondicherry   21 Aug–18 Oct 1778

The outbreak of war between Britain and France over French support for the rebel United States of America had repercussions in India. The hostilities provided a convenient opportunity for the British to make inroads into the remaining French possessions in the Indian subcontinent, which had their capital at Pondicherry.

The British were commanded by General Hector Munro and the French garrison at Pondicherry was commanded by Guillaume Leonard de Bellecombe, its governor. Bellecombe set about improving Pondicherry's defenses. Gun batteries were moved close to the shore to counter a move by the Royal Navy, and the French garrison was swelled by French troops who had retreated following the fall of Karikal on 10 August.

General Munro besieged Pondicherry on 21 August, and this was followed by a series of naval encounters that resulted in the French ships withdrawing to the south. The British brought up batteries to begin bombarding the fortress in September and launched a first assault soon after. However, the British took heavy losses and withdrew to settle in for a long siege. Throughout September the French launched a number of sorties to sabotage the British artillery under the cover of nightfall, with mixed success. In one sortie, on 4 October, Bellecombe was injured and had to withdraw, whereupon the British increased the ferocity of their bombardment, leveling parts of the south and northwest bastions. With an all-out assault looking imminent, Bellecombe, who was ill from his injury, surrendered on 18 October. As a tribute to their sixty days of resistance, Munro allowed Bellecombe's force to march out of the fort with full military colors. **TB**

Savannah   29 December 1778

Stalemate in their war with the Americans in the north and concern over French attacks against British-held Caribbean islands caused the British to focus on securing American colonies in the south. A primary objective was the capture of the port of Savannah, in Georgia. A force of British regulars was sent to bolster that operation.

Lieutenant General Henry Clinton envisaged a combined British effort with troops coming from East Florida, but the small Florida force was easily repulsed by the American outposts before British ships arrived with 3,500 men under Lieutenant Colonel Archibald Campbell. These sailed up the Savannah River and landed Campbell with his men 3 miles (5 km) east of Savannah on 29 December. He then worked his way overland toward the town.

The mixed American defense force of Continentals and militia under Major General Robert Howe could muster only 850 effective men. Howe positioned his men around the southern edge of Savannah with the untrained local militia on his far right, farthest from the point of expected British arrival. He then waited, thinking the surrounding swamps would disrupt Campbell's advance.

However, a local slave showed Campbell a hidden path around to the American right flank. Campbell sent an assault force in that direction while another group with artillery made diversionary probes against the center defenses. The American militia on the right broke and ran almost immediately on seeing the British approach. Campbell then led an assault against the center. Howe's defense collapsed and the city was captured after less than an hour of light fighting. Howe and others escaped, but Britain now had a southern operational base. **RB**

Losses: British, 200 casualties of 1,500 regulars, 800 casualties of 7,000 sepoys; France, 300 casualties of 800 regulars, 150 casualties of 500 sepoys

Losses: American, 83 dead or wounded, 453 captured; British, 3 dead, 10 wounded

◀ Buxar 1764   Pollilur 1780 ▶   ◀ Monmouth 1778   Camden 1780 ▶

Flamborough Head 23 Sept 1779

Since its creation in late 1775, the American navy had increased in strength and capability. Under aggressive captains, a few American warships were prowling international waters as early as 1776, looking for British supply ships. Many of the force were converted merchantmen, including *Bonhomme Richard*, which was provided by France.

Major General John Burgoyne's surrender at Saratoga encouraged French support of the Americans. An agreement was reached to modify a merchant ship into a man-of-war of forty-two guns for "loan" to Captain John Paul Jones. Jones named the ship *Bonhomme Richard* and took her to sea. In September 1779, off Flamborough Head, Jones encountered the large Baltic fleet of British merchantmen escorted by HMS *Serapis*, which carried forty-four guns on two decks and seven more cannon.

As Jones approached, a suspicious Captain Richard Pearson prepared *Serapis* for action. At 100 yards (90 m), Jones raised the American ensign and both ships opened fire. In the second broadside, two of Jones's guns exploded, causing serious damage and limiting his firepower. Jones turned his ship across the bow of *Serapis* to rake her decks, but he lost the wind. The bow of *Serapis* rammed *Bonhomme Richard*, entangling the ships. Jones had his crew lash the ships together bow to stern as they blasted away point-blank. After three hours, *Bonhomme Richard* was terminally damaged and sinking, yet Jones refused to surrender. As the fight raged, an American crewman crawled into the rigging and dropped a grenade into the hatch of *Serapis*, setting off a explosion that killed many crew and destroyed her lower gun deck. Unable to continue, Pearson surrendered. **RB**

Losses: American, 150 dead or wounded of 322; British, 130 dead or wounded of 284

Cape St. Vincent 16–17 January 1780

By 1780 Britain was not only fighting the rebel United States in the American Revolutionary War, but the nation was also at war with France, Spain, and the Dutch Republic—all major naval powers. Victory over the Spanish in the "moonlight battle" at Cape St. Vincent thus came as a welcome relief for the hard-pressed Royal Navy.

A British force of twenty ships of the line and six frigates under Admiral Sir George Rodney was sent to relieve Gibraltar, which the Spanish were besieging by land and sea. Off the Algarve coast of southern Portugal, Rodney ran into a Spanish squadron of nine ships of the line and two frigates led by Commodore Don Juan de Lángara. The commodore was a courageous officer, but faced with a far superior force he sensibly chose to bolt for a safe haven in Cadiz. Rodney unleashed his captains in a "general chase," allowing each to pursue the Spanish at his own best speed.

Benefiting from the newly introduced copper sheathing of their hulls, the fastest British ships overhauled the Spanish within two hours and commenced their cannonades at around 4:00 PM. The winter night soon closed in, but the British were not to be denied their prey and were able to continue the fight in fitful moonlight. With a gale driving the ships toward the Algarve coast, the night battle was risky for both sides. The Spanish fought bravely but the balance of forces was hopelessly against them. *Santo Domingo*, a seventy-gun ship of the line, exploded, killing all its crew. De Lángara's flagship, *El Felix*, was the last to be battered into submission, striking its colors at around 2:00 AM. Six of the Spanish ships escaped when the British had to turn their attention to avoiding being driven ashore by the gale. **RG**

Losses: British, no ships lost; Spanish, 1 ship destroyed, 4 ships captured

◁ *Ushant 1778*   *Chesapeake Bay 1781* ▷

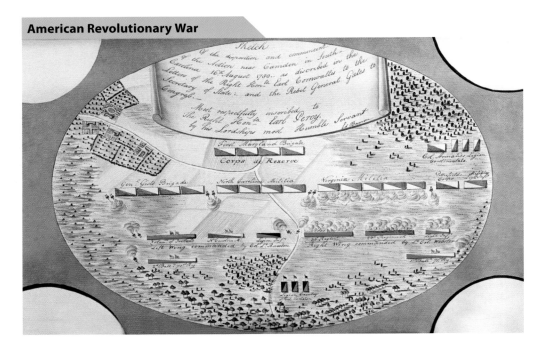

Camden 16 August 1780

British subjugation of rebel American colonies in the south depended on control of outposts and supply depots. The largest was at Camden, South Carolina, about 115 miles (185 km) inland from the coast. In August 1780, an American force under Major General Horatio Gates marched to capture it.

When Lieutenant General Charles Cornwallis learned of Gates's approach, he assembled 2,200 regulars and Loyalists and marched north from Camden to confront the Americans. Gates was a poor field commander whose victory at Saratoga, which earned him the southern command, was due to more talented subordinate leaders. His southern army of about 3,700 was mostly local militia with a small core of 900 veteran Continentals from Maryland and Delaware. Unaware of the other's presence, the armies marched toward one another.

On 15 August Gates fed his men a meal of molasses and cornmeal that gave many of them diarrhea. Despite this, he ordered a night march toward Camden. Before dawn the next morning his advance party encountered British scouts, and both armies halted until daylight.

Both commanders placed their most reliable troops on their right, so the British regulars under Lieutenant Colonel James Webster faced the weaker American militia. As at Saratoga, Gates placed himself to the rear. As Webster's line of regulars advanced, the militia line crumbled with hardly a shot fired. Webster then wheeled left and attacked the flank of the two Continental regiments that had been pressing the Loyalists hard. Outnumbered and trapped, the Continentals were overwhelmed. Few escaped except Gates, who fled on horseback. It was the worst American defeat in the field and left the British in temporary control of the southern colonies. **RB**

Losses: American, 250 dead, 800 wounded and captured; British and Loyalist, 68 dead, 256 wounded

◁ Savannah 1778   Kings Mountain 1780 ▷

A 1780 engraving of the Battle of Camden, with the British regulars positioned at bottom right.

Pollilur 10 September 1780

The Battle of Pollilur was one of the most calamitous defeats ever suffered by British forces in India, and a memorable victory for Tipu, the future Sultan of Mysore. Tipu so relished the victory that he had scenes of the battle painted as murals to decorate his summer palace.

After the capture of Pondicherry in 1778, the British East India Company continued to extend its control at the expense of the French. This brought the British into conflict with France's ally, Haider Ali, ruler of Mysore. Haider formed an alliance not only with the French but also with the Marathas and the Nizam of Hyderabad. He was thus able to field an impressive army that invaded the state of Karnataka and caught the British forces disorganized and dispersed.

The British commander, Sir Hector Munro, decided to concentrate his forces at Conjeeveram (modern-day Kanchipuram), but on 6 September 1780 a detachment led by Colonel William Baille, making its way to join Munro, was cut off by a large force under Haider's son, Tipu. Munro sent a mere 1,000 men to aid Baille, far too few. On 10 September Baille attempted to break through to Conjeeveram but was caught in the open by Tipu's 10,000-strong army. Baille formed a large defensive square, but this buckled under repeated charges by Tipu's cavalry and fire from the formidable Mysorean rocket troops. Baille surrendered to avoid complete annihilation.

Two hundred British soldiers were taken prisoner, enduring a gruesome ordeal in the Mysore dungeons that many, including Baille, did not survive. The British were able to launch a counterattack in 1781, defeating Haider Ali at Porto Novo, but two decades would pass before Pollilur was truly avenged, at Seringapatam in 1799. **TB**

Losses: British, heavy, a minority of survivors of more than 4,000; Mysorean, casualties unknown

◄ *Pondicherry 1778*   *Trincomalee 1782* ►

⬆ *Tipu's army attacks the British at Pollilur, from an eighteenth-century mural at Tipu's summer palace.*

Kings Mountain   7 October 1780

After the British victories at Charleston in May and Camden in August, Major General Charles Cornwallis felt confident to move his army against the Americans in North Carolina. He assigned Major Patrick Ferguson and his force of Loyalists to secure the region to the west of the mountains.

Ferguson was a competent British officer, familiar with the frontier style of warfare, who used a silver whistle to direct his Loyalists in battle. At first Ferguson was successful in dispersing the numerous but uncoordinated rebel militia bands east of the Blue Ridge Mountains. However, when he threatened to cross west of the mountains and lay waste to the countryside of the "over-mountain men" living there who did not swear allegiance to the king, he reignited their resistance.

A large number of American militia groups gathered under Colonel William Campbell and began searching for Ferguson and his 1,000 Loyalists. Concerned, Ferguson requested reinforcements from Cornwallis and set up camp on "Kings Mountain," a long, narrow ridge with wooded, boulder-strewn slopes. He did not prepare defensive positions, but concentrated his men at either end. Campbell divided his 900 men into eight smaller groups to surround and attack the ridge. Campbell's militiamen advanced up the ridge, firing their rifles.

When the Loyalists made bayonet counterattacks, the Americans withdrew in the rugged terrain, then returned to the attack. Gradually the ring closed around Ferguson's Loyalists until they were squeezed into a small area at the northern end of the ridge. Ferguson was shot dead off his horse as he tried to break out and a senior Loyalist officer raised a surrender flag. The American victory devastated Loyalist support in the south and stalled Cornwallis. **RB**

Losses: American, 29 dead, 58 wounded; Loyalists, 250 dead, 163 wounded, 668 captured

[<] Camden 1780   Cowpens 1781 [>]

Cowpens   17 January 1781

Major General Nathanial Greene took command of the shattered American southern army after the disaster at Camden. He asked Brigadier General Daniel Morgan to join him in South Carolina, where they plotted the defeat of the British commander, Lieutenant General Charles Cornwallis.

Greene gave Morgan about 1,000 men to operate against the British. Cornwallis was determined to catch Greene and could not afford to have a threat to his rear area. He detached Lieutenant Colonel Banastre Tarleton to eliminate Morgan. In January Tarleton learned that Morgan was at a large meadow called the "Cowpens," and he hastily marched there. Morgan had selected the location to suit his mix of veteran Continentals and raw militia. Morgan arrayed his militia in two lines backed by a third line of Continentals with riflemen and mounted troops on each flank and in reserve.

Tarleton first sent his cavalry to scatter the skirmishers, but deadly rifle fire forced the cavalry to withdraw. Next, Tarleton ordered his infantry forward. The front line of militia fired twice, then fell back. The British advanced and the second American line fired, inflicting more casualties before also moving to the rear. As the British continued forward and exchanged volleys with the Continentals, Tarleton committed his infantry and mounted reserves.

The American position had almost collapsed when men misunderstood a unit realignment as a general retreat. Morgan and his officers regained control at the critical moment. The Continentals turned and blasted the British at close range, and then charged with bayonets. At the same time, the militia rejoined the battle as Morgan's dragoons hit the British right flank. The British infantry dropped their weapons and Tarleton's Loyalists fled. **RB**

Losses: American, 12 dead, 60 wounded; British, 110 dead, 229 wounded, 600 captured

[<] Kings Mountain 1780   Guilford Court House 1781 [>]

Americans battle the British on horseback at Cowpens, in an 1845 painting by William Ranney.

Guilford Court House   15 March 1781

British Lieutenant General Charles Cornwallis, smarting from the Cowpens defeat and his fruitless pursuit of Major General Nathanial Greene's American army, moved quickly when he learned of Greene's presence at Guilford Court House. He led 1,900 veteran regulars and Loyalists in a forced march to catch Greene and reverse his fortunes.

Reinforcements gave Greene confidence to risk open battle, though he was determined not to lose his army. He picked a battlefield and waited with 4,500 Continentals and militia, though few were veterans. Greene arranged his force in three battle lines with cavalry and riflemen on each flank, but kept no reserve. His least dependable militia and two cannon were in the first line with orders to fire, retreat, and reform. Veterans manned the third line.

Cornwallis's troops deployed immediately, light artillery in the center, grenadiers and Germans on the flanks. They fired at the first American line waiting behind a fence and received a heavy volley in return. As ordered, the militia withdrew, but to Greene's dismay most left the battlefield. The British continued forward into thick woods where they encountered Greene's second line and a longer and much tougher fight, but the British regulars finally forced the Americans back. Separate fights took place on the flanks and units were drawn away from the center. The British left pushed against the main American line and was sharply repulsed. However, in the center, Cornwallis's troops fought the Americans in a fierce hand-to-hand melee. Counterattacks by American cavalry and Continentals were unable to break the determined British, whose artillery fire and a charge by Cornwallis's reserve cavalry finally carried the day. Greene gave orders to disengage and withdrew his army. **RB**

Losses: American, 78 dead, 183 wounded, 1,046 missing; British, 93 dead, 413 wounded, 26 missing

◁ Cowpens 1781   Chesapeake Bay 1781 ▷

A nineteenth-century illustration of Greene's force retaking British artillery at Guilford Court House.

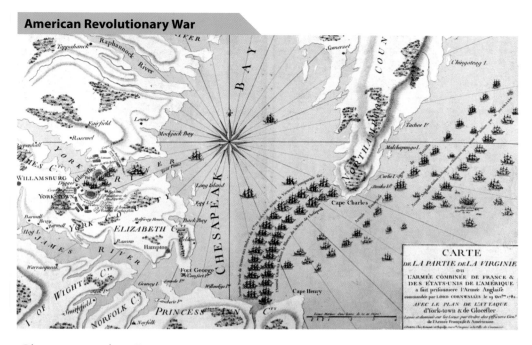

Chesapeake Bay (Battle of the Capes)   5 September 1781

Irreplaceable losses of men and supplies at Guilford Court House forced British Lieutenant General Charles Cornwallis to end his southern campaign in late summer 1781. When Lieutenant General Henry Clinton ordered him to find a defensible deepwater port for use as an operations base, Cornwallis marched his army into Virginia.

For his base, Cornwallis chose Yorktown, Virginia, a port where the York River joins Chesapeake Bay. As Cornwallis fortified the town, Clinton received information that a large French fleet was on route to the Chesapeake from the West Indies. He sent a British fleet—nineteen ships of the line and seven frigates—under Rear Admiral Thomas Graves to intercept the French. However, Graves was slow and when he arrived at the bay on the morning of 5 September, the French armada (twenty-five ships of the line and six frigates) under Rear Admiral François de Grasse was already there.

De Grasse's fleet sailed out on the afternoon tide and formed an in-line battle formation. Graves's fleet approached from the northeast, sailing with the wind. He ordered his ships of the line into a similar battle formation as the two fleets sailed south on slightly converging courses. The two-hour battle began at about 4:00 PM with an exchange of broadsides fired at close range. Some confused signals among the British commanders resulted in a number of their ships not entering the fight. The firepower of the larger French ships took a severe toll on the British, and after two hours of pounding each other, and with darkness coming on, Graves pulled away. Both fleets moved slowly south until de Grasse lost sight of Graves and returned north to block the bay. **RB**

Losses: British, 90 dead of 13,000, 246 wounded, 1 ship scuttled, 6 ships badly damaged; French, 200 dead or wounded of 19,000, no ships lost

◁ Guilford Court House 1781   Yorktown 1781 ▷

⬆ *An eighteenth-century French map shows French ships of the line blocking the British fleet's reinforcement of Yorktown.*

Yorktown   28 September–19 October 1781

On 22 August British Lieutenant General Charles Cornwallis brought his army of 7,200 men to Yorktown, Virginia, and began converting the river port into a fortified base. The move was shadowed by Major General Maria Joseph de Lafayette, who informed General George Washington.

Washington was with the main American army in New York when he learned of the expected arrival in Chesapeake Bay of Rear Admiral François de Grasse with a French fleet and troops. Washington saw an opportunity to trap Cornwallis. Gambling on de Grasse's timely arrival, Washington and Lieutenant General Jean Baptiste Rochambeau, commander of the French force, began to move their armies to Virginia. To deceive the British and keep them pinned in New York, half the American army was left behind while the rest joined Rochambeau's force and moved toward Maryland ports on the bay. The victory of de Grasse in the Battle of the Capes on 5 September permitted the ferrying of Washington's

> *"I have the mortification to inform your Excellency that I have been forced to give up the posts of York and Gloucester."* Cornwallis, to Clinton

heavy artillery, troops, and supplies down the bay. By mid-September, nearly 16,000 American and French soldiers were assembled, and on 28 September they were only a mile from Yorktown.

Cornwallis had built earthworks at Yorktown and across the river at Gloucester Point. He had been informed by Lieutenant General Henry Clinton that a second British fleet with reinforcements was being sent, so he decided to hold Yorktown using the inner defenses. Accordingly, two days later the allies were surprised to find three of the

British outposts abandoned. Allied artillery was rolled into these for the siege bombardment, and troops including French cavalry were sent to block the British positions on Gloucester Point. After a minor cavalry fight on the point on 3 October, the British there remained quiet.

Washington organized his Americans into three divisions and placed them to occupy the right and center of the siege line while Rochambeau's French troops took the left side of the line. On 6 October, as the French pressed against the British right redoubt at Yorktown, Washington's troops began digging the first trench parallel to the British earthworks. Ten allied cannons opened the bombardment of the town on 9 October, and more cannons were brought up until forty-six were in action, forcing Cornwallis and others to seek shelter behind the river bluffs. Several small British vessels in the river were also hit and sank. An approach trench was soon completed, but work on a second, closer parallel trench was endangered by fire from two British redoubts.

During the night of 14–15 October, two assault parties, one French and one American, simultaneously attacked the redoubts and captured them after brief hand-to-hand fights. A British sortie two nights later to spike the cannon being emplaced in the second parallel was only a partial success, and the guns were quickly repaired to fire at close range into the British defenses.

A fierce storm on the night of 16–17 October frustrated a desperate attempt by Cornwallis to evacuate his army to Gloucester Point. With no other choice, he sent a British officer at dawn with a drummer and white flag to ask for a truce. Surrender terms were agreed the next day, and on 19 October Cornwallis's army marched out and laid down its arms. The end of the war was in sight. **RB**

Losses: American, 23 dead, 65 wounded; French, 52 dead, 134 wounded; British, German, and Loyalist, 156 dead, 326 wounded, 7,157 captured

◁ *Chesapeake Bay 1781*   *The Saintes 1782* ▷

A depiction of the American army filing toward British-held Yorktown, with the York River to the rear. ➤

The Saintes   12 April 1782

After the Siege of Yorktown, the independence of the new United States was assured, but Britain and France still fought over colonial territories in the Caribbean. A victory at the Saintes restored British naval mastery in the West Indies, although the British fleet initially failed to follow it up .

The French planned an attack on British-owned Jamaica, and a British fleet, under Admiral Sir George Rodney, was sent to block the move. In early April 1782, Rodney's fleet met the French force, led by Admiral de Grasse, off the north of Dominica—near a group of islands called the Saintes—for which the battle is usually named. After some initial maneuvers and minor clashes, a full-scale battle was joined on 12 April, by which time the British had thirty-six ships of the line in action against thirty French ones.

The engagement began with the two fleets sailing parallel to one another in line of battle, the British having the better of the exchange of broadsides partly because some of their guns were equipped with new flintlock firing mechanisms. The French line was somewhat loosely formed and, at a crucial moment, Rodney exploited a shift in the wind and cut across the line, raking the French ships on either side with his broadsides. Other British ships imitated their commander, and the French lost all formation, their ships suffering heavily as a melee developed. De Grasse surrendered his flagship late in the day with some 400 of his crew killed. Four other French ships were also captured, one of them destroyed at nightfall by an explosion. The victory could have been more complete if Rodney, actually a rather conservative admiral, had organized a more vigorous pursuit of the remainder of the French fleet. **DS**

Losses: British, no ships, 1,000 dead or wounded; French, 4 ships captured, 1 destroyed, 5,000 dead, wounded, or captured

⟨ *Yorktown 1781*   *Trincomalee 1782* ⟩

The Battle of the Saintes by Thomas Luny (1759–1837), in which the British wreak havoc with their broadsides.

Trincomalee 3 September 1782

French efforts to counter British expansion in India were undermined by British naval superiority. In 1781, France found a skillful naval commander in Admiral Pierre André de Suffren. Although unable to achieve any durable progress in India, Suffren did redeem the reputation of the French navy.

The Battle of Trincomalee was the last in a series of fiercely fought engagements between Admiral Suffren and British Admiral Sir Edward Hughes in 1782. The French captured Trincomalee, in present-day Sri Lanka, on 1 September when Suffren seized the anchorage and forced the garrison to surrender. Two days later, Hughes approached the port, and Suffren ordered his ships to raise anchor and engage the British fleet.

The battle was a savage encounter. Suffren, aboard his flagship *Heros*, moved into the center of the British squadron, supported by two ships, and engaged Hughes's flagship, the seventy-four-gun *Superb*. Hughes had the support of three other ships of the line but took heavy damage from the French. Suffren was forced to withdraw when his mainmast broke and his ammunition ran out. However, at either end of the British formation, French ships were causing havoc, disabling the sixty-four-gun *Exeter* and killing her captain. The battle continued for several hours, and the French, assisted by a favorable wind, were able to inflict serious damage on the British ships. In the end, darkness forced the two fleets to withdraw. The British limped back to Madras while the French returned to Trincomalee to effect repairs. Although the Royal Navy lost no ships, the damage was so severe that Madras effectively had no naval cover and troops were brought in just in case the French decided to launch an invasion. **TB**

Losses: British, 320 casualties, severe damage to all 12 ships; French, 350 casualties, severe damage to most of the 14 ships

◁ *The Saintes* 1782   *Cuddalore* 1783 ▷

This painting by Dominic Serres (1719–93) highlights the discipline of the fleets in battle at Trincomalee.

Cuddalore 20 June–25 July 1783

Cuddalore was the end of the war between Britain and France in India that accompanied the American Revolutionary War, and also that of the Second Anglo-Mysore War. The fighting was in full flow when news of a peace agreement arrived from Europe.

Although the British had more success in their war with Mysore after the disaster at Pollilur, there was no end to the conflict in sight when Haider Ali, Mysore's ruler, died suddenly in December 1782. This spurred the British to seek a decisive victory over Mysore and its French allies by attacking the key southeastern port of Cuddalore.

On 20 June, a British land force, commanded by Major General James Stuart, advanced on the fortress. The French garrison and their Mysore allies managed to spring an attack on the British and inflict heavy casualties, taking a key fortified position. The British siege operations were further disrupted when a French fleet, under the command of Admiral Suffren, renewed hostilities with their British adversaries, led by Admiral Hughes. Suffren forced Hughes to withdraw to Madras and abandon his plans to support the British siege. The French fleet anchored in the port and Suffren landed more than 2,000 troops to bolster the French garrison.

Meanwhile, in Europe, France and Britain had agreed a cease-fire that would eventually lead to the signing of the Treaty of Paris on 3 September. However, the news of the cease-fire did not reach India before the garrison launched a second attack on the British siege positions. Although the British redoubts were damaged and casualties sustained, the attack did not break the siege, which continued until a British ship of the line approached the port on 25 July flying a white flag. **TB**

Losses: British, 1,500 casualties of 12,000; French and the kingdom of Mysore, 1,100 casualties of 9,000

◁ *Trincomalee 1782*　　　　　　*Seringapatam 1799* ▷

Kinburn 1 October 1787

The Russo-Turkish War saw the Ottoman Empire challenge Russian control of territories they had lost to Russia after their conflict of 1768 to 1774. In 1787, the Turkish attacked the Russian fortress of Kinburn but were forced back by a determined defense.

When war started between Russia and the Turks, General Alexander Suvorov was put in command of the Crimean theater. His first major act was to organize the defense of the Russian fortress at Kinburn, on the western point of a long and narrow peninsula in the Black Sea, to the south of the Dnieper estuary.

The Turks commenced a three-day bombardment of Kinburn on 29 September. At 9:00 AM on 1 October, some 5,000 Turkish soldiers landed on the peninsula to storm the fortress. Suvorov made no attempt to stop the landing, nor the construction of fifteen lines of fortified entrenchments that reached within 1,000 yards (915 m) of the fortress. At 3:00 PM, Suvorov launched an artillery salvo and gave the order to attack the Turkish lines. The Russians advanced in two lines of infantry followed by cavalry, and a fierce hand-to-hand struggle commenced.

The initial Russian charge drove the Turks back ten trenches, but the Turks fought back, advancing again, and Suvorov was nearly killed by a Turkish soldier. The Russians rallied and forced the Turks back once more, only for the Turks to launch another successful counterattack. Suvorov then mustered all of his available forces and launched a third, and final, attack. The Russians advanced and swept the Turks back into the sea, ending the battle. At the day's end, more than eighty percent of the Turkish army lay dead in the trenches or had drowned in their attempt to escape. **JF**

Losses: Turkish, 4,000 of 5,000; Russian, 250 dead and 750 wounded of 3,000

◁ *Chesma 1770*　　　　　　*Ochakov 1788* ▷

 The Anglo-Mysore wars lasted for three decades; Tipu Sultan was killed in 1799 at Seringapatam.

Ochakov
June–17 December 1788

During the year after their defeat at Kinburn, the Ottomans lost Ochakov on the Black Sea in this engagement. The siege ended when Prince Grigory Potemkin stormed and captured Ochakov and massacred the whole Turkish garrison.

Ochakov was a vital position, overseeing the mouths of the Dnieper and Bug rivers, and essential to controlling Crimea. Modern fortifications and a garrison of around 20,000 made Ochakov a difficult target. Potemkin's army of 40,000, joined by Alexander Suvorov, decided to take the fortress by siege in June 1788 and commenced a sustained artillery bombardment, hoping to force the Turks to surrender. There was, however, no surrender.

Suvorov urged Potemkin to take Ochakov by storm. Potemkin disregarded this plea and the siege continued. In August, the Turks launched a sortie. Suvorov pursued them and, without Potemkin's permission, recklessly threw men into the fray. The Russians lost 200 in the struggle; Suvorov was disgraced temporarily and ordered to leave the army and recuperate in Kinburn. There was another attempted Turkish breakout that month but, after that, the siege became a drawn-out stalemate.

The Russian navy prevented any Turkish reinforcements arriving. By December, winter was setting in and Potemkin decided to launch a direct assault. At 4:00 AM on 17 December, in freezing temperatures, the Russians advanced on Ochakov in six columns. They surged over the walls and entered the city, which they captured within hours. By the end of the fighting, the entire Turkish garrison had been destroyed, and the Russians commenced plundering the undefended city. **JF**

Losses: Russian, 15,000 of 40,000 (1,000 dead and 2,000 wounded in final assault); Turkish, entire garrison of 20,000, (9,500 dead in final assault)

◁ Kinburn 1787   Focsani 1789 ▷

Focsani
1 August 1789

After its victory at Ochakov, the Russian army advanced into Wallachia and inflicted another defeat on the Ottomans in this battle. With his Austrian allies, Alexander Suvorov smashed the Turkish army and forced it to withdraw to the Danube.

In 1789, the Russian and Austrian forces in Romania were scattered. The Turks who were massed near Focsani aimed to take advantage of this by attacking the Austrians, led by Prince Josias of Saxe-Coburg at Adzhud, before moving on to the Russians. Saxe-Coburg appealed for help, and Suvorov left his position at Buirlad at 6:00 PM on 28 July. He arrived at Adzhud at 10:00 PM the next day, having marched 40 miles (64 km) in twenty-eight hours.

The Russo-Austrian armies then advanced to attack the Turks in two columns, with the Russians on the left and the Austrians on the right. On 31 July, they made first contact with the Turks, and pushed them back toward Focsani. Battle began in earnest at 9:00 AM the next day when the Russo-Austrians approached Focsani itself, where the Turkish army lay behind a line of entrenchments. The Turks charged on all fronts, but musket and artillery drove them back. Suvorov then attacked the Turkish right. Initially his cavalry was repulsed, and it was the Russian infantry that was crucial, forcing the Turks back to their trenches and firing on them from close range. The Austrian foot on the other side had proved similarly successful, and the Turks began to flee in all directions. By 4:00 PM, the Russo-Austrian victory was complete. It was not, though, strategically important because the Russians and the Austrians did not have the resources to follow it up with an advance into the Ottoman Empire. **JF**

Losses: Turkish, 1,500 dead and 2,500 wounded of 30,000; Russo-Austrian, 800 of 25,000

◁ Ochakov 1788   Tendra 1790 ▷

Second Svensksund
3 and 9 July 1790

The Second Battle of Svensksund—the final stage of the war between Sweden and Russia—was the last major naval battle in which oar-powered ships played a significant role. The Swedish victory helped secure a favorable peace treaty the following month.

The war began with a Swedish attack on Russia, but this met various setbacks, including a naval defeat off southern Finland in the First Battle of Svensksund in August 1789. Further minor Swedish defeats in 1790 saw the main Swedish naval force bottled up in Vyborg Bay by the Russian forces in early June.

Both sides had substantial forces of sail- and oar-powered ships—the comparatively sheltered waters of the Baltic and the shallow, narrow channels between the numerous small islands meant that galleys and oared gunboats played a significant part in this region long after they had largely been abandoned by other European navies. Both sides had at least forty major sailing warships and numerous supporting sail- and oar-powered vessels.

In the first stage of the battle, on 3 July, the Swedes broke out from Vyborg Bay and headed for a safer anchorage near their fortress at Sveaborg. The Swedish forces lost heavily, however, in the confusion after a fireship went off course and ended up exploding in the middle of the Swedish fleet. This engagement is sometimes known as the Battle of Vyborg. On 9 July, the Swedes got their revenge, smashing a disorganized attack by the overconfident Russians and destroying about one-third of the Russian force. The Swedes lost only six vessels to their opponent's fifty in probably the largest naval battle ever fought in the Baltic. **DS**

Losses: Russian, 55 ships and 9,000 dead; Swedish, 25 ships and 4,500 dead (both engagements)

Tendra
8–9 September 1790

In this naval engagement, the Russians clashed with the Ottomans near Tendra on the Black Sea. One year after the Russian army's victory at Focsani, Admiral Fyodor Ushakov led the navy to victory. It gave them total strategic command of the Black Sea.

At 6:00 AM on 8 September, Ushakov's fleet was cruising in the Black Sea when they spotted Turkish vessels anchored at Tendra. The Turkish admiral, Hussein Pasha, immediately ordered his fleet to weigh anchor and sailed away; Ushakov pursued. After some maneuvering, the two fleets were sailing in two parallel lines. Soon the ships began to exchange fire, with the Russians gaining the upper hand. By around 8:00 PM, the Turkish ships had managed to escape the Russians without any losses, although many of their ships had been badly damaged.

The next morning, the Russians sighted the Turkish fleet and sailed toward them. One of the Turkish ships—*Melike Bahri*—immediately gave up without a fight. Another, *Kapitana*, put up a fierce struggle that started at 10:00 AM, with Russian ships surrounding it by noon. Two hours later, Ushakov's flagship—*Rozhdestvo Christovo*—managed to shoot away the masts of *Kapitana*, and she surrendered within an hour. Unfortunately, the ship caught fire and exploded, with most of its crew aboard, before the Russians could capture it. Meanwhile, other Russian ships had been tracking the rest of the Turkish fleet but had been unable to engage them, and were recalled. The remaining Turkish ships sailed on to Constantinople, but several foundered en route or were captured by other Russian vessels. There was no other major fighting in the Black Sea that year. **JF**

Losses: Turkish, 1 ship captured and 1 sunk of 22, 1,500 captured and 700 dead; Russians, no ships lost of 16, 25 dead and 25 wounded

◁ Focsani 1789   Izmail 1790 ▷

Izmail   March–22 December 1790

Russia had gained control of the Black Sea after the Battle of Tendra. In December 1790, General Alexander Suvorov led the capture of Izmail, which the Russians had besieged since March. During the attack, most of the Turkish garrison were killed in the bloodiest episode of the Russo-Turkish War.

Prince Grigory Potemkin had been laying siege to Izmail, situated on the Danube's outlet to the Black Sea, since March 1790. His efforts had made little progress, so he sent for Suvorov to capture Izmail. Suvorov arrived on 13 December to face a formidable challenge.

Izmail had an impressive garrison of 35,000, was surrounded by 4 miles (6.4 km) of earth walls and ditches, and was protected by 200 guns as well as armed boats patrolling the Danube. Suvorov threw up two batteries to the west and east of Izmail, and his 30,000 men made preparations to attack. At dawn on 21 December, the Russian artillery commenced an intense bombardment of Izmail, which continued until 3:00 AM. The Russians eventually stormed Izmail at 5:30 AM. Six columns attacked from the north, east, and west, and three boat landings were made from the south. The first advances were made on the east and west, where the Russian guns had done the most damage to the walls. To the north, where the walls were mostly intact, progress was slower, but the Russian troops managed to force their way in after a fierce struggle.

By 8:00 AM, Russian soldiers has entered Izmail from all directions and advanced through the streets house by house. The combat was vicious. By 11:00 AM, Izmail had fallen: 26,000 of the garrison had been killed and the rest had been captured. The victorious Russians spent three days sacking and looting Izmail. **JF**

Losses: Russian, 10,000 casualties of 30,000; Turkish, 26,000 dead and 9,000 captured of 35,000

◁ *Tendra 1790*

Izmail is enveloped in flames in Capture of the Turkish Fortress, Izmail *(1953) by Mikhail Grachev.* 🔊

Wabash 4 November 1791

One of the U.S. Army's most disastrous defeats was sustained on U.S. soil, outside what is now Fort Recovery, Ohio. Here, the Western Confederacy of Indian nations overwhelmed an ill-equipped and ill-prepared U.S. force in a major humiliation for the forces of the new republic.

In the Treaty of Paris (1783), the European powers had agreed to U.S. authority over the area south of the Great Lakes and east of the Mississippi. However, the people of this northwest territory had not been consulted, because they were considered by participating governments to be no more than "savages."

Little Turtle, the chief of Ohio's Miami people, saw the situation very differently, as did Blue Jacket of the Shawnee, and the Delaware chief, Buckongahelas. They could call on thousands of highly motivated warriors from a coalition of nations at a time when their U.S. adversaries were struggling to field a credible fighting force.

General Arthur St. Clair had difficulties both in getting hold of seasoned soldiers and in securing supplies and horses for those he had. The collapse of morale that this caused was evidenced in a desertion rate approaching 50 percent. Despite this, President George Washington insisted that St. Clair pursue an aggressive strategy, striking north into Ohio to take on the region's tribes.

On 4 November, Little Turtle and Blue Jacket led a surprise attack at dawn. St. Clair's trained troops were quick to grab their muskets and fire off volleys. However, the inexperienced majority fled in terror; those who escaped slaughter at the hands of the attacking warriors milled about in confusion, hampering their comrades' attempts at self-defense. A brave but unavailing bayonet charge ended in complete carnage; only forty-eight U.S. soldiers made it through unscathed. **MK**

Losses: American Indian, 40; U.S., more than 500

Fallen Timbers 1794 ▷

Nineteenth-century engraving of a view of New Harmony, on the banks of the Wabash River.

Valmy 20 September 1792

Although little more than a skirmish, Valmy was one of history's decisive battles; the Prussian march on Paris to restore the French monarchy was halted and the French Revolution saved. The Prussians and their allies withdrew, allowing the French to renew their invasion of the Austrian Netherlands.

Alarmed by the growing radicalization of the French Revolution, Austria and Prussia signed the Declaration of Pillnitz in August 1791; it threatened military action if the trend toward republicanism in France continued. It served only to encourage the revolutionaries to take more extreme action, which eventually led to the imprisonment of the French monarch, Louis XVI. Prussia and Austria began to mobilize their forces, joined by French émigré Royalists determined to overthrow the revolution. With conflict inevitable, the French government anticipated events by declaring war against Austria on 20 April 1792 and invading the Austrian Netherlands (roughly modern-day Belgium and Luxembourg).

"Kellermann's army ranged on the plateau of Valmy projected like a cape into the midst of the lines of the Prussian bayonets." Edward Shepherd Creasy

The turmoil of the revolution had seriously affected the efficiency of the French army, with many of its aristocratic officers fleeing abroad. The extent of the army's instability was revealed in the failed invasion of the Austrian Netherlands—some French units broke and fled after killing their officers. The monarchist powers were encouraged by this turn of events, and Prussians, Austrians, German mercenaries, and French émigrés began to assemble their forces. A Prussian army, under the command of the Duke of Brunswick, invaded eastern France in August, capturing the fortress cities of Longwy and Verdun as a preliminary act to a march on Paris itself.

Two small French armies opposed the Prussian advance: the Army of the North, led by General Charles Dumouriez, and the Army of the Center, under the command of General François Kellermann. In the manner of eighteenth-century warfare, the two national sides maneuvered against each other until Dumouriez placed his troops against the Prussian line of march. He was joined by Kellermann, who advanced beyond Dumouriez's Army of the North to take up a position on high ground around the village of Valmy, directly in front of the Prussians. Kellermann set up his command post by a windmill at the center of the French line. The French forces were a combination of enthusiastic but ill-trained volunteers and experienced regulars from the old royal army, supported by the technically proficient French artillery.

As the mists cleared on 20 September, Prussian and French artillery opened fire in a long-range duel that caused few casualties on either side. Brunswick then ordered his troops forward in the hope that the French would break and run at the sight of the famed Prussian infantry. However, the French held firm, and Brunswick withdrew his troops to allow his artillery to continue to soften up the French positions. A second assault was ordered, which coincided with a lucky Prussian cannon shot detonating a French ammunition wagon by the windmill. Again the French line did not waver, and, in the face of heavy musketry fire, the Prussians retreated.

This marked the end of the battle, although the armies remained facing each for some days until the Prussians withdrew from French territory. The poet Goethe witnessed the battle and prophetically wrote: "From this day forth begins a new era in the history of the world." **AG**

Losses: French, 300 casualties of 32,000 engaged; Prussian, 180 casualties of 34,000

Jemappes 1792 ▶

Detail from Battle of Valmy, *1835, by Jean Baptiste Mauzaisse in which the French troops stand their ground.*

Jemappes 6 November 1792

The engagement at Jemappes demonstrated the ability of the French revolutionary armies to mount complex offensive operations against regular soldiers. The French victory opened the way for the Army of the North to seize Brussels and the rest of the Austrian Netherlands.

The French victory at Valmy allowed General Dumouriez, the commander of the French Army of the North, to pursue his plan of invading the Austrian Netherlands. Advancing along the main road to Brussels, the French encountered the Austrian force of Duke Albert of Saxe-Teschen, which was defending a low ridge between Mons and Jemappes. The French enjoyed a decisive numerical advantage over the Austrians, and Dumouriez grandly decided to launch a double outflanking maneuver to cut off the Austrians from any chance of retreating to Brussels.

After a preliminary artillery bombardment in the early morning, the French attacked on both flanks; however,

despite their overall superiority, little progress was made against the enemy. Duke Albert had been obliged to send troops to reinforce both his flanks and in the process had weakened his center.

At midday, Dumouriez ordered an attack on the Austrian center, but, as his troops deployed from column into line—in accordance with the tactical theories of the day—they were caught by an Austrian cavalry charge and scattered. The French swiftly re-formed, however, and advanced in a large column, which forced the Austrians back off the ridge. At the same time, the flank attack against Jemappes began to make progress. Fearing that his forces might be overwhelmed, the Austrian commander ordered a general retreat, which was carried out in good order. **AG**

Losses: Austrian, 1,250 casualties of 14,000; French, 2,000 casualties of 40,000

[<] *Valmy 1792*   *Neerwinden 1793* [>]

Engraving of the Battle of Jemappes, showing the French troops in decisive action against the Austrians. ⬆

Neerwinden   18 March 1793

In this battle of the French Revolutionary Wars, French overconfidence was a key factor in their defeat by a resolute Austrian force. This setback cost the French temporary control of the Austrian Netherlands, and led to the downfall of the victor of Jemappes, General Charles Dumouriez.

Emboldened by their success in the Austrian Netherlands, the French revolutionary government declared war against the Netherlands and Britain in February 1793. The French commander, Dumouriez, invaded the Netherlands and had some success until an Austrian counterattack forced him back to the Austrian Netherlands. Strengthened with new troops, Dumouriez resumed the offensive.

The Austrian force, led by Prince Josias of Saxe-Coburg, held a position on the road between Liège and Brussels around the village of Neerwinden. Dumouriez divided his army into eight columns—three on the right wing, two in the center, and three on the left—and gave a

general order for all eight columns to attack. The French right and center made some limited progress but the French left wing was repulsed with heavy losses by the Austrian defenders under the command of the Archduke Charles. Dumouriez had counted on the impetuous dash of the French troops being sufficient to break the enemy line, but the Austrian regular infantry had proved to be doughty opponents. With his center now dangerously isolated, the French commander ordered a general retreat, which the Austrians did not follow up.

A further casualty of the battle was Dumouriez himself. He had made a number of enemies in the revolutionary government, and, fearful that he might be recalled to face the wrath of the National Convention and the guillotine, he defected to the Austrians on 5 April. **AG**

Losses: Austrian, 2,000 casualties of 39,000; French, 4,000 casualties of 45,000

◁ Jemappes 1792   Wattignies 1793 ▷

↑ *The head of William Pitt is offered on a plate to Dumouriez in this caricature from 1793 by James Gillray.*

Wattignies   15–16 October 1793

The superior numbers of the French revolutionary force at Wattignies proved too much for the Austrians, who nonetheless fought with great fortitude and inflicted heavy casualties on their opponents. The French victory achieved its objective of forcing the Austrians to abandon the siege of Maubeuge.

On 30 September 1793, an Austrian army under Prince Josias of Saxe-Coburg invested the French fortress of Maubeuge. This move greatly concerned the French revolutionary government because if Maubeuge fell then a gap would open up in the frontier defenses that might allow an advance on Paris. General Jean-Baptiste Jourdan was given command of the Army of the North, with instructions to raise the siege and defeat the Austrian force. He was accompanied by the influential French minister of war, Lazarre Carnot.

As Jourdan's force was twice as strong as his opponent's, he wasted little time in launching an attack along the Austrian line on 15 October. The French advanced in skirmish order with little thought of tactical maneuver, and they were repelled by steady volley fire from the Austrian infantry and a series of cavalry counterattacks. As dusk fell, the armies disengaged, with Jourdan and Carnot arguing how best to defeat the enemy when battle resumed the following day.

The French commanders decided to concentrate on the Austrian left wing. They made repeated charges, suffering heavy casualties against an Austrian line that refused to buckle. Eventually, French numerical superiority began to tell, and the Austrian left wing slowly fell back, surrendering the village of Wattignies. In order to conform with the left wing, the rest of the Austrian army also began to withdraw, leaving the battlefield to the French. **AG**

Losses: Austrian, 3,000 casualties of 21,000; French, 5,000 casualties of 45,000

◁ *Neerwinden 1793*   *Cholet 1793* ▷

Etching after an 1837 painting by Eugène Lami: both sides suffered sizable losses on the plateau of Wattignies. ⬆

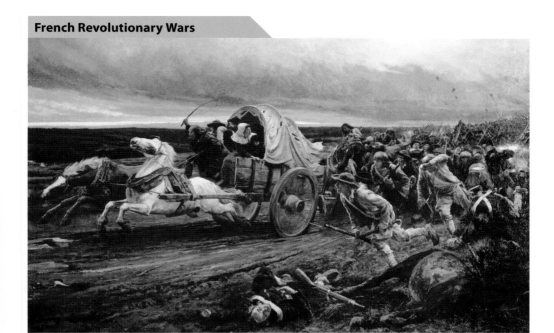

Cholet 17 October 1793

The rebellion in France's Vendée region against the French Republican government in Paris was a serious threat to the revolution. At the Battle of Cholet, the rebel forces were crushed and, although the uprising was to continue, any hope of victory had been dashed.

Many areas in rural France opposed the revolution, and nowhere was this resistance stronger than in the Vendée region of France. When the French government restricted the freedoms of the Catholic clergy and imposed conscription, opposition broke out into open insurrection in February 1793. The Vendéan rebels attacked and killed representatives of the revolutionary government, which provoked a violent counterreaction from the authorities. Initially, the rebels enjoyed considerable success, defeating not only local militias but also regular forces.

During September and October 1793, reinforcements dispatched by the Republican government began to tip the scales against the rebels. On 15 October, they were defeated at the Battle of Tremblaye by a strong Republican force—under the effective command of General Jean-Baptiste Kléber—and were forced back to positions around the town of Cholet. Although short of ammunition and artillery, the rebels decided to attack the Republicans a short distance away. The rebels advanced in good order and in one part of the line set fire to the heathland, causing smoke to obscure their advance from the Republican artillery. At this point, the Republicans fell back in some disarray, but Kléber's timely intervention with his reserves restored order. Following the deaths and wounding of several Vendéan leaders, the rebels began to fall back to the Loire River. There they were covertly ferried over to the north bank to escape further fighting. **AG**

Losses: Republican, 4,000 casualties of 26,000; Vendéan, 8,000 casualties of up to 40,000

◁ *Wattignies 1793*   *Toulon 1793* ▷

⬆ *The rebels make a dramatic escape toward the Loire in this nineteenth-century painting by Jules Girardet.*

Toulon   27 August–19 December 1793

As France's major naval base, Royalist-held Toulon was an important prize, and French Republican forces devoted much effort to its capture. On a more personal level, the engagement saw the emergence of a brilliant military leader who would soon set his stamp on the nations of Europe: Napoleon Bonaparte.

The surge of anti-Republicanism in southern France during 1793 led to the seizure of Toulon in August by Royalist forces, who handed it over to an Anglo-Spanish fleet led by Admiral Sir Samuel Hood. The Royalists occupied the surrounding defenses and in the process seized some seventy ships, almost half the French fleet.

The Republican response was to surround the port, and a siege began on 8 September. Among the Republican troops was a young artillery officer—Napoleon Bonaparte—who drew up a plan to eject the enemy from Toulon. Unfortunately, Napoleon had to deal with two incompetent superiors, until they were replaced by General Jacques Dugommier, who immediately saw merit in Napoleon's plan. With the young officer in command, the Republicans seized the outer forts overlooking the port, before preparing for the main attack on the Little Gibraltar fort, which dominated Toulon's two harbors.

On the night of 16 December, the Republicans launched their offensive. Napoleon was bayoneted in the thigh by a British soldier, but the Royalists were ejected. The guns in the fort were immediately turned inward to fire on the ships in the port. In a desperate scramble, the Anglo-Spanish fleet took advantage of a favorable wind to escape, leaving Toulon to the Republicans. They advanced into the city on 19 December and took vicious revenge on the remaining Royalists. **AG**

"I have no words for Bonaparte's merit: much technical skill, an equal degree of intelligence, and too much gallantry." General Dugommier

⬆ *James Gillray lampoons Admiral Hood's retreat from Toulon in this 1793 cartoon.*

Losses: Allied, 4,000 casualties of 16,000; French Republican, 2,000 casualties of 62,000

◁ Cholet 1793   Tourcoing 1794 ▷

Tourcoing 17–18 May 1794

Austrian and British hopes of inflicting a decisive defeat on the French revolutionaries in the Austrian Netherlands were dealt a blow by their failure to coordinate their forces effectively. The ill-handled battle is said to have provided the origin for the satirical nursery rhyme "The Grand Old Duke of York."

British participation in the war against France provided the Austrian army with much-needed reinforcements in the Austrian Netherlands, although the British contribution came mainly in the form of Hanoverians and German mercenaries. The Austrian commander, General Karl Mack von Leiberich, proposed a plan to destroy the French Army of the North, then under the temporary command of Major General Joseph Souham. The French were relatively dispersed in positions to the north of Lille, and the allied armies were scattered in a wide arc around the French. Mack ordered the Anglo-Austro-German forces to concentrate on the battlefield, a wildly ambitious plan, considering the inherent problems of directing a multinational army.

The allies marched against the French in six columns. Operating on interior lines, a French division held superior Austrian forces advancing from the north, while the bulk of the French army attacked the columns led by Frederick, Duke of York, and Field Marshal Otto. In a series of confused engagements, the allies fared slightly worse, but their position was made untenable by the failure of the columns led by the Archduke Charles and Count Franz Josef von Kinsky to advance into battle. The allied troops then began to retreat ignominiously, leaving the battlefield to the French, who did not follow up their advantage, presumably through exhaustion. **AG**

Losses: Allied, 5,500 of 48,000 engaged (74,000 in total); French, 3,000 of at least 70,000

◁ Toulon 1793   First of June 1794 ▷

First of June 1 June 1794

The British referred to the first major naval battle of the French Revolutionary Wars as "the Glorious First of June" after having the better of the fighting. The British success was based on Admiral Howe's precise plan to break through the enemy line of battle. However, the French succeeded in getting a vital grain convoy through.

In the spring of 1794, France was threatened with a serious famine and a convoy of 300 grain ships was making its way from the United States. Admiral Howe's British Channel Fleet was tasked to intercept the convoy, and Villaret de Joyeuse, commanding France's Brest squadrons, to protect it.

Howe's twenty-five ships found the twenty-six French ships on 28 May, and fought a small action that day. They closed in for battle on 1 June, after being delayed by fog. The battle was fought some 450 miles (724 km) west of France's northwestern tip and is known by its date rather than its location because it took place so far out to sea.

Howe was one of a growing number of senior British officers who believed that his men and ships were superior to their opponents in a close-quarter battle and that by abandoning rigid formation they could force such an encounter and win it decisively. Howe wanted each of his ships to break through the enemy line individually and predicted that one enemy ship would be lost for every British ship that achieved this. He was exactly right. After several hours of fierce combat, the fleets separated; seven British ships had broken the French line and seven French ships were captured or sunk. The survivors on both sides were too battered to continue the fight; crucially, the nearby convoy of grain ships managed to avoid interception by the British. **DS**

Losses: French, 7 ships and 5,000 dead, wounded, or captured; British, no ships, 1,200 casualties

◁ Tourcoing 1794   Cape St. Vincent 1797 ▷

Fleurus   26 June 1794

The French revolutionary victory at Fleurus had far-reaching strategic consequences: it convinced the Austrian court in Vienna that the Austrian Netherlands was not worth fighting for and effectively ceded it to the French, who were then able to invade and conquer the Netherlands.

At the end of May 1794, General Jean-Baptiste Jourdan was assigned command of a newly created force—the Army of the Sambre and Meuse—with orders to capture the fortress of Charleroi as part of a general advance to retake the Austrian Netherlands. The French revolutionary government attached great importance to this operation, dispatching Louis Antoine de Saint-Just—Robespierre's sinister lieutenant from the Jacobin Committee of Public Safety—to help supervise operations.

Charleroi was besieged by the French in June, and a mixed Austrian and Dutch army, under the command of Prince Josias of Saxe-Coburg, was sent to counter this move and raise the siege. Jourdan deployed his forces in

> *"To serve his country with zeal, courage, loyalty, and disinterested affection are the duties imposed on all Republicans." Jean-Baptiste Jourdan*

a ring around Charleroi, to protect the besiegers from the advancing allies. Fortune favored Jourdan; not only did he possess a considerable numerical advantage over Saxe-Coburg, but also the garrison in Charleroi surrendered as the allied forces arrived at the French positions. Thus, the besieging troops of Major General Hatry's division could be redeployed as an additional reserve for the French army.

The allies deployed their forces into five columns and advanced against the entire French line. The attack was delivered with fierce determination. On the far right of the

allied line, the Prince of Orange's Dutch troops pushed the French back in confusion; they were saved only by the timely arrival of Charles Daurier's brigade to stabilize the line. On the allied left flank, General Beaulieu was similarly successful, breaking through the stretched French defenses. In the center, Archduke Charles and General Peter Quasdanovich made good progress, although the French line remained unbroken.

The situation seemed critical for the French, but Jourdan acted coolly and decisively. He was also helped by a new weapon of war, a hydrogen observation balloon. The tethered balloon stayed aloft for the duration of the battle, its two observers surveying the fighting below; messages were slid up and down a cable to provide information on enemy dispositions and movements. On Jourdan's order, the French reserve cavalry charged against Archduke Charles's troops, breaking the first line of Austrian infantry and forcing the second to form square. This brought the Austrian advance to a halt. With his center secure, Jourdan then dispatched Hatry's division, which had been besieging Charleroi, to shore up the wavering French right. General Beaulieu's advance had lost its momentum, and his Austrians were forced back by the fresh French reserves.

Realizing that the tide of battle had turned against him, Saxe-Coburg ordered a general withdrawal. The Austrians retired back across the Rhine to leave the Austrian Netherlands firmly in French hands. Now that the fear of an allied thrust on Paris had disappeared, so the Jacobin's control over the revolution diminished, ultimately leading to their overthrow. In an ironic twist of fate, Saint-Just would find himself under the guillotine's blade on 28 July, just a few weeks after his triumphant return to Paris from Fleurus. **AG**

Losses: Allied, 5,000 casualties of 52,000; French, 5,000 casualties of 70,000

◀ First of June 1794   Lodi 1796 ▶

Jacques-Marie-Gaston Onfray de Bréville's 1908 depiction of the first use of the hydrogen observation balloon.

Fallen Timbers 20 August 1794

Praga 4 November 1794

The U.S. Army suffered its two worst defeats at the hands of the American Indian tribes in the Ohio territory in 1790 and 1791. Determined to avenge the defeats and clear the territory of the recalcitrant Indians, President Washington recalled veteran Major General Anthony Wayne to active duty.

In the years after the Battle of Lanckorona, Russia had twice partitioned Poland-Lithuania, annexing half of its territory. In 1794, Tadeusz Kosciuszko led an uprising against the Russians. It met a brutal end at Praga, where the Russian army massacred 20,000 people in the last battle of the revolt.

Wayne recruited and trained a new army organized under a unique "legion" concept that combined infantry, cavalry, and artillery into a single unit called a "sub-legion." Throughout 1792 and 1793, Wayne trained the raw recruits, drilling them into a disciplined team.

In spring 1793, when legion field strength was about 1,200, plus mounted Kentucky militia and Indian scouts, Wayne launched his march into Indian country, destroying villages and fields. On 20 August, the legion advanced north along the Maumee River with the four sub-legions abreast, their flanks and rear screened by light infantry and mounted troops. This broad front formation countered the favored Indian tactic of flank envelopment.

Some 5 miles (8 km) from Fort Miami, the British supply post, about 1,000 Indians waited, hidden in a massive tangle of brush and fallen trees. As the legion approached, one group of Indians charged, scattering Wayne's advance party. The advancing line, however, put the Indians to flight. The charge was premature and ruined the ambush planned by the larger group of Indians and Canadians. The legion moved forward, fired one volley, and charged into the timber with fixed bayonets. After forty-five minutes of fighting, the enemy scattered with dragoons in pursuit. Wayne's demand that the British evacuate the fort was refused. He lacked the strength to force the matter and, after several days, he withdrew. **RB**

In 1794, Kosciuszko had taken control of the Polish armed forces and led them to a series of victories over Russia. But in October that year, he was captured, and the Russians advanced toward Warsaw. The Praga suburb, divided from Warsaw by the Vistula River, stood in their way.

The people of Warsaw had strengthened Praga's defenses, constructing a formidable line of earthworks, redoubts, and batteries. In addition to soldiers, several hundred untrained civilians manned the fortifications. The Russian army, under Alexander Suvorov, drew up outside Praga on 2 November and the next day launched a sustained artillery barrage. Suvorov ordered an all-out surprise attack on Praga early the next morning. Seven columns were to attack the emplacements directly, and, at 5:00 AM, Russian troops advanced, swarmed over Praga's defenses, and entered the suburb. Many Poles began to retreat across the Vistula, but any chance of escape was eliminated when Russian soldiers burned the bridges between Praga and Warsaw. The flames spread to Praga, and thousands of Polish soldiers and civilians were trapped in the burning streets.

The battle became a massacre as the Russians slaughtered combatants and civilians alike. Warsaw quickly surrendered. The Russians now dominated Poland, which would not reemerge as an independent nation for more than a century. **JF**

Losses: U.S., 33 dead,100 wounded; American Indian,19 dead, 2 wounded

Losses: Russian, 2,000 of 25,000–30,000; Polish, 13,000 dead and 11,000 captured of 30,000, as well as 7,000 civilians dead

◁ Wabash 1791

Tippecanoe 1811 ▷

◁ Lanckorona 1771

Lodi 10 May 1796

Given command of the French Army of Italy at the age of twenty-six, General Napoleon Bonaparte transformed a semimutinous, ill-equipped body of troops into a victorious army. His small-scale victory over the Austrians at Lodi was a first step in the creation of the Napoleonic legend.

After defeating Piedmont, Austria's ally in northern Italy, Napoleon wasted no time in celebration. He advanced eastward along the south bank of the River Po in the hope of outflanking the main Austrian army, retreating in parallel on the north bank. The French managed to cross the Po at Piacenza on 6 May and then pressed northward to the town of Lodi on the River Adda. However, by then, the main Austrian army had escaped successfully, leaving a small force—under the command of General Karl Philipp Sebottendorf—to act as a rearguard.

The French had little difficulty in clearing Lodi itself, the Austrian rearguard having positioned itself on the far side of the Adda, with infantry in place, supported by artillery. A wooden bridge separated the two combatants, which, surprisingly, the Austrians had not destroyed. While Napoleon waited for the arrival of General André Masséna's reinforcements, he sent his cavalry to find and cross a ford to outflank the Austrians. On Masséna's arrival, Napoleon assembled a column of grenadiers to storm the bridge. Halfway across, withering Austrian fire caused the assault to falter, at which point new troops—led by senior officers, including Masséna and two other future marshals of France, Louis Berthier and Jean Lannes—successfully renewed the attack. Desperate fighting continued, but the arrival of the outflanking French cavalry on the far side of the Adda led to an Austrian retreat. **AG**

Losses: Austrian, 2,000 casualties of 10,000; French, 1,000 casualties of 15,000

"Bonaparte is not known for any striking feat, but he is understood to be a profound theorist and a man of talent." Allies' chief of staff, 1796

⬆ Napoleon's direct leadership of troops at Lodi, painted here by P. Bignami, helped convince him of his own military effectiveness.

◁ Fleurus 1794   Arcole 1796 ▷

Arcole   15–17 November 1796

The battle for the village of Arcole set the aggressive flexibility of the French soldiers of Napoleon Bonaparte's Army of Italy against the doggedly resolute troops of the Austrian army. In the end, Napoleon was lucky to prevail, saved by the well-timed intervention of General André Masséna.

During November 1796, the Austrians sent two armies into northern Italy to relieve the besieged garrison in Mantua. Napoleon organized a holding force to bottle up the smaller Austrian army marching down the Adige valley in the Alpine foothills, while he faced the larger Austrian army commanded by General Joseph Alvinczi. Napoleon hoped that the Austrians in Mantua would make no attempt to break through the thin line of French besiegers.

Seizing the initiative, Napoleon ordered his troops to cross the Adige at its confluence with the smaller River Alphone, situated in marshy ground near the village of Arcole. On 15 November, French soldiers marched along a built-up causeway to cross the Alphone at Arcole, but they were left vulnerable to well-directed Austrian fire. Napoleon attempted to rally his wavering troops by grabbing a standard and waving it on the exposed causeway (an incident later embellished to include a daring assault across the pontoon bridge to Arcole itself).

Despite Napoleon's best efforts, the French could make no headway and were forced to retreat. A similar result occurred on the second day's fighting, with the French again unable to gain ground. On 17 November, it seemed that the exhausted French might be defeated, until the timely arrival of Masséna's division threatened to outflank the Austrian position, at which point Alvinczi ordered a general retreat to Vicenza. **AG**

Losses: Austrian, 2,500 casualties and 4,000 captured of 24,000; French, 3,500 casualties and 1,300 captured of 20,000

⟨ *Lodi 1796*   *Rivoli 1797* ⟩

A nineteenth-century painting of Arcole by Louis Bacler d'Albe, strategic adviser to Napoleon. ⬆

Rivoli   14–15 January 1797

Napoleon Bonaparte's victory at Rivoli transformed the Italian campaign, forcing the surrender of the fortress of Mantua and ejecting the Austrians from northern Italy. It raised Napoleon to new heights of popularity in France and forced the Austrians to accept the punitive Peace of Campo Formio.

As part of the continuing Austrian attempt to relieve Mantua and win back northern Italy, General Alvinczi conducted a march through the Alps into the Adige valley. The bulk of Napoleon's army was awaiting an attack in the Po valley, and the only formation defending the Adige valley was the 10,000-strong division of Major General Barthélemy Joubert, positioned on a plateau to the north of Rivoli.

The Austrian plan was imaginative—involving a double envelopment of Joubert's position—but overelaborate. On 14 January, three Austrian columns launched a frontal attack on the Rivoli plateau, while General Quasdanovich's column of 7,000 men tried to outflank the French right (supported by Austrian artillery on the far side of the Adige). A further column, led by General Lusignan, was sent on a wide sweeping march to attack the French from the rear.

Once Napoleon was aware that the main threat was coming from Alvinczi in the north, he immediately dispatched troops to support the outnumbered and increasingly beleaguered Joubert. Masséna's division helped shore up the French center—with a brigade deployed to cover the threat of Lusignan—while Napoleon and Joubert redeployed their forces to repulse Quasdanovich's attack. Lusignan's column was overwhelmed by French reinforcements under the command of Generals Rey and Victor. The following day, as the Austrians began to retire, Joubert initiated a full-scale counterattack, capturing 11,000 Austrian troops. **AG**

Losses: Austrian, 14,000 casualties, 11,000 captured of 28,000; French, 4,000–5,000 casualties of 20,000

◁ *Arcole 1796*   *Cape St. Vincent 1797* ▷

⬆ *Napoleon changes his horse in* The Battle of Rivoli *(1844) by Felix Philippoteaux.*

Cape St. Vincent   14 February 1797

After the "Glorious First of June," the Battle of Cape St. Vincent was the second in a series of major British naval victories in the wars against France and its allies. The qualitative superiority of Britain's navy over its enemies was confirmed, while Nelson established an enviable reputation for boldness and aggression.

Spain had allied with revolutionary France in 1796, a move that forced Britain to withdraw its Mediterranean fleet—greatly outnumbered by its enemies—into the Atlantic. In early 1797, the Spanish sent their fleet into the Atlantic to escort a valuable convoy to Cadiz, at the time watched by Britain's former Mediterranean force.

By 1797, this fleet, under the formidable command of Admiral Jervis, was an elite force, with the highest standards of gunnery and seamanship in the world. When Jervis's fifteen ships met the twenty-seven Spanish vessels (under Admiral de Cordova) off Cape St. Vincent

at Portugal's southern tip, he did not hesitate to attack. The Spanish fleet had split into two sections and Jervis headed for the stronger group of about eighteen.

As the battle began, Horatio Nelson, then a junior admiral whose ship was stationed near the rear of Jervis's line, realized that his commander had misjudged his maneuver and that the Spanish might be able to reunite their force. Although he could have been court-martialed for breaking formation, Nelson did just that and headed for Cordova's flagship. This delayed the Spanish just enough for the rest of Jervis's ships to engage. After a close-range melee, four Spanish ships were captured; the rest escaped but only with considerable damage. Although Spain's losses were comparatively small, its navy was demoralized and would be reluctant to challenge Britain again. **DS**

Losses: Spanish, 4 ships captured, 800 dead or wounded, 3,000 captured; British, 500 dead or wounded

◁ *Rivoli 1797*   *Camperdown 1797* ▷

A depiction of the Battle of Cape St. Vincent made in 1798 by an unknown artist. ⬆

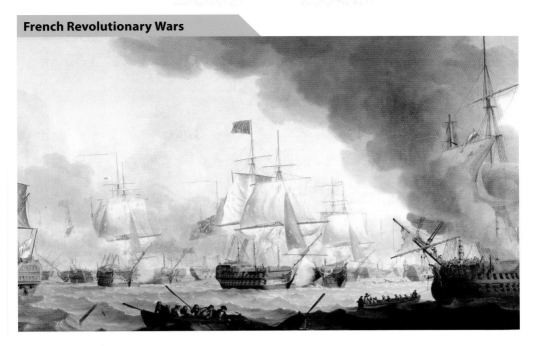

Camperdown   11 October 1797

The Dutch had become somewhat reluctant allies of France against Britain in 1795. In October 1797, Dutch leaders sent their fleet to sea hoping to score a victory over the British North Sea forces, which they knew had been thrown into disarray recently by a sailors' mutiny. In fact, the Dutch had missed their chance.

French leaders wanted to mount an invasion of Ireland, despite fumbling their chances over the winter of 1796 to 1797 and the defeat of their Spanish allies at Cape St. Vincent. The mutinies in the home-based forces of the British navy in May to June 1797 gave the French a new opportunity, in conjunction with the Dutch, but they were too slow to take advantage. By the time the Dutch fleet put to sea on 8 October, Admiral Duncan's British squadron was back in the fight.

Duncan caught up with the Dutch three days later, off Camperdown (or Kamperduin) on the Dutch coast.

Duncan had fourteen ships of the line against Admiral de Winter's eleven. On both sides, a number of slightly smaller warships played a full part in the fighting, although this was unusual in battles of the period.

When the two fleets met, Duncan ordered an immediate attack without waiting to get his ships into formation. Like the British in this and other battles, the Dutch directed their fire into the hulls of enemy ships, rather than follow the French practice of firing at masts and rigging in order to disable them. This meant that casualties on both sides were heavy, but in the end the Dutch were overwhelmed. Almost half their fleet was captured; the rest escaped but was so badly damaged and the sailors so demoralized that the Dutch navy played no further significant part in the war. **DS**

Losses: Dutch, 11 of 26 ships, 1,160 dead or wounded; British, no ships, 825 dead or wounded

◁ *Cape St. Vincent 1797*   *The Pyramids 1798* ▷

⬆ *A Dutch crew abandons a burning ship at Camperdown in a painting by Thomas Whitcombe (1760–1824).*

Vinegar Hill   21 June 1798

In 1798, the United Irishmen rose in revolt against British rule. Influenced by the American and French revolutions, they hoped to establish an independent Irish republic. Their hopes were dashed at Vinegar Hill in Wexford, the republican dream in abeyance for another century and more.

The United Irishmen were formed in Belfast in 1791 and, unlike later Irish republican movements, drew their strength from both Catholics and Protestants. Taking advantage of Britain's preoccupation with its war against France, the Irishmen rose in revolt on 23 May 1798.

The rebels quickly seized most of County Wexford. Around 20,000 British troops surrounded the county and prepared to suppress the uprising. The rebel leadership called its fighters to gather on Vinegar Hill and meet the British in battle. Around 20,000 men responded to the call, although they were badly armed and mostly relied on pikes rather than firearms. The British, under General Lake, encircled the hill and, just before dawn on 21 June, began an artillery bombardment. Advance units seized rebel outposts and, as they gained ground, moved their artillery forward, tightening the noose around the rebel positions. As the British reached the eastern crest of the hill, the rebels began to withdraw through a gap in British lines. Lake sent his cavalry to pursue and cut down the fleeing Irishmen. Many hundreds were massacred, including women and children who had taken refuge on the hill.

While this battle raged, British troops seized the nearby town of Enniscorthy in order to cut the escape route from the hill over the River Slaney. Although successful, they were unable to prevent some of the rebels escaping along the riverbank into the hills to continue their campaign for another month, until they too were crushed. **SA**

Losses: British, 100 of 18,000; United Irishmen (including civilians), 500–1,000 of 20,000

Easter Rising 1916 ⊳

Defeat of the Rebels at Vinegar Hill (1854) by George Cruikshank: the British edge forward to gain ground. ⬆

The Pyramids 21 July 1798

In 1798, Napoleon Bonaparte sought glory by leading a military expedition to Egypt. At the Pyramids, he lured the Egyptians into fighting a pitched battle against his superior forces. The victory left the way open for the occupation of Cairo and French domination over Egypt.

After landing in Ottoman-controlled Egypt and capturing Alexandria on 2 July 1798, Napoleon's French army marched down the Nile toward Cairo. The French were opposed by Murad Bey, who had mobilized a force of 6,000 elite Mamluk cavalry and 15,000 fellahin (peasant militia). On the far side of the Nile was a substantially larger Egyptian army, commanded by Ibrahim Bey.

As the French closed in on the Egyptians guarding the approaches to Cairo, Napoleon adopted the novel tactic of deploying his army into five large divisional "squares" (rectangular in shape), with cavalry and stores in the middle and artillery at the corners. As the squares slowly advanced toward the fortified position of Embabeh, Murad Bey's Mamluks suddenly attacked. The well-disciplined French infantry were not overawed by the mass charge, and their accurate volley fire caused massive casualties to the scimitar-armed cavalry.

On the French left, Embabeh was stormed successfully by the French. The survivors leaped into the Nile to escape, but hundreds were shot in the water by the French or drowned before they gained the opposite bank. Murad Bey's Mamluk cavalry, unable to make any impression on Napoleon's squares, simply melted away and retreated southward along the Nile. The army commanded by Ibrahim Bey had been unable to influence the battle, and, on seeing the disaster suffered by Murad Bey, it evacuated Cairo and retreated back toward Palestine and Syria. **AG**

Losses: Egyptian, 2,000 Mamluks and several thousand fellahin of 21,000; French, 29 dead and 260 wounded of 25,000

◁ Camperdown 1797　　　　　Aboukir Bay 1798 ▷

The Battle of the Pyramids by Louis Lejeune (1775–1848), in which Napoleon's men outclass the Egyptians.

Aboukir Bay (Nile)   1–2 August 1798

Nelson is remembered as the finest fighting admiral. At the Nile, he led an audacious attack on a superior enemy force anchored in a shallow bay and won the most overwhelming of his great victories, ending Napoleon's dream of an eastern empire.

In early 1798, the British discovered that Napoleon was planning a major expedition from Toulon, although they did not know his objective was Egypt. Admiral Jervis maintained his blockade of the Spanish fleet in Cadiz but sent the best of his ships into the Mediterranean, under Admiral Nelson, to intercept the French.

The French left port on 19 May, and Nelson was soon trying to track them down. One of history's great "might have beens" is the fact that the British twice narrowly missed finding their quarry and quite possibly ending Napoleon's military career. Instead, by the time Nelson found the French fleet anchored in Aboukir Bay near Alexandria, Napoleon's army was ashore and had won the Battle of the Pyramids.

> *"The whole bay was covered with bodies, mangled, wounded, and scorched, not a bit of clothes on them but their trousers."* John Nicol, seaman

Nelson was no great seaman but was proving to be an inspirational and far-sighted leader. Jervis's stern discipline and equal care for the welfare of the men had given Nelson superbly trained crews with high morale; Nelson made sure that his captains understood his plans and would carry them out intelligently whatever the circumstances.

The French, by contrast, were ill-prepared. Admiral Brueys must have assumed that the shallow waters of the bay would make the British reluctant to attack, because he did little to prepare for such a possibility. Perhaps a quarter of the French ships' crews were ashore when the British came in sight in the late afternoon of 1 August.

Nelson ordered an immediate attack. He intended some of his ships to sail down each side of the French line to overwhelm its leading vessels one by one, despite the danger of sailing into obviously shallow water in the growing darkness. Indeed, one of Nelson's thirteen ships of the line did run aground on the approach, but the rest followed his plan exactly. The French also had thirteen ships of the line, with substantially more gun power overall. Sailors of the period, however, seldom attempted to use the guns on both sides of their ships simultaneously, a difficult operation even with well-trained crews at full strength. By forcing the French to fight in this way, Nelson gained a vital advantage.

The battle began shortly before sunset. At the start, eight British ships concentrated their fire on the five leading French ships and battered them into submission. Other British vessels moved farther down the line until eventually only the last three French ships were unengaged. The French flagship, the massive 120-gun *L'Orient*, caught fire and blew up in a huge explosion. Admiral Brueys was not among the few survivors. The fighting continued into the morning until only two French ships and two supporting vessels were left for the French to make their escape from a bay strewn with bodies and wreckage.

The victory made Nelson a British national hero. It guaranteed the failure of Napoleon's adventure in Egypt and helped persuade Russia and Austria to join a new anti-French alliance. Britain went on to capture new bases in the Mediterranean and used them to help extend its maritime supremacy. **DS**

Losses: French, 11 ships captured or destroyed, more than 6,000 dead, wounded, or captured; British, no ships lost, 900 dead or wounded

⟨ *The Pyramids 1798*   *Acre 1799* ⟩

The Battle of the Nile, *a lithograph from* British Battles on Land and Sea *(c. 1910), by Bernard Finegan Gribble.* ➡

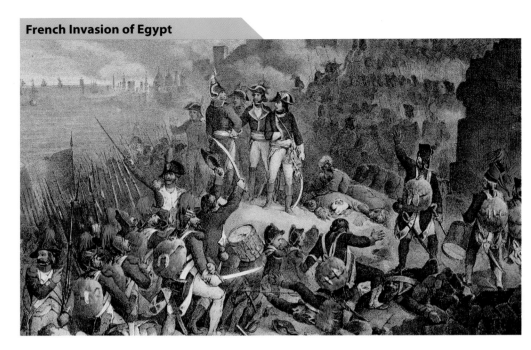

Acre   18 March–20 May 1799

Napoleon's unsuccessful siege of the city of Acre was his first setback in the Egyptian campaign and marked the end of any hopes of carving out an empire in the east. More to the point, British command of the Mediterranean Sea made the whole expedition to Egypt increasingly irrelevant.

Effectively marooned in Egypt through the loss of the French fleet at the Battle of the Nile, Napoleon decided to continue his war with the Ottoman Turks and marched into Palestine. On 18 March, his forces encountered the walled city of Acre, whose 5,000-strong garrison was supported by two Royal Navy ships of the line under Admiral Sir William Sidney Smith. The British had captured a flotilla containing half of Napoleon's siege guns, and the town's fortifications were improved by Smith and Phélippeaux, a French émigré officer.

A series of French infantry assaults was repulsed, forcing Napoleon to instigate formal siege operations.

To add to his difficulties, the Turks sent a large army to raise the siege. General Jean-Baptiste Kléber was ordered to repel this force, and, despite being heavily outnumbered, he inflicted a crushing defeat on the Turks at the Battle of Mount Tabor on 16 April.

By the end of April, the French had secured sufficient artillery to make a breach in Acre's walls. Five desperate assaults were launched by the French from 1 to 10 May, and when the attackers had fought their way onto the walls, they discovered that the defenders had built a series of equally formidable internal fortifications. While Acre continued to be resupplied by sea, the demoralized French were suffering grievous shortages, with disease starting to take hold. Reluctantly, Napoleon accepted defeat and began the long retreat back to Egypt. **AG**

Losses: French, 2,200 dead, 2,000 wounded or ill of 13,000; Ottoman Turkish, unknown

[<] *Aboukir Bay 1798*   *Aboukir 1799* [>]

The French attempt to battle their way through Acre's fortifications in this nineteenth-century illustration.

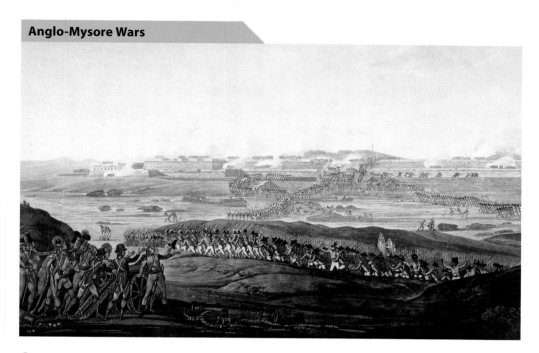

Seringapatam (Srirangapatana)   5 April–4 May 1799

The Battle of Seringapatam was the final encounter in the long series of conflicts between Britain, represented by the British East India Company, and the kingdom of Mysore. Mysore's ruler, Tipu Sultan, was killed when British forces stormed the citadel, bringing the kingdom under British control.

Tipu Sultan, known as the Tiger of Mysore, was a lifelong enemy of the British. He decorated a palace with murals showing the defeat of the British at Pollilur in 1780, and owned an automaton representing a tiger savaging a British soldier. In 1799—with Napoleon Bonaparte's invasion of Egypt potentially posing a threat to British power in India—Britain decided that an independent hostile Mysore, as a potential ally of France, could no longer be tolerated.

A British and East India Company army was sent from Madras to attack Seringapatam, Tipu Sultan's capital, supported by other forces sent by the nizam of Hyderabad. On 5 April, the British besieged Seringapatam and a bombardment began, which eventually breached the oldest part of the city's walls. Leading the storming of the breach was Major General Sir David Baird, who had survived four years as a prisoner of Tipu Sultan after Pollilur. Colonel Arthur Wellesley, the future Duke of Wellington, led a larger force following on behind to secure positions gained.

On 4 May, the vanguard broke through the breach and forced its way onto the ramparts. The main force then stormed through, including many Hyderabad infantry. A savage battle with the Mysore troops followed, in which Tipu Sultan was killed bravely defending his citadel. After the fall of Seringapatam, Mysore became a princely state under British control. **TB**

Losses: British and Indian allied, 1,500 casualties of 50,000; Mysore, 6,000 casualties of 30,000

◁ *Cuddalore 1783*   *Assaye 1803* ▷

⬆ *Baird and his men engage in the assault in* The Capture of Seringapatam in 1799 *(1801) by Antoine Cardon.*

Aboukir 25 July 1799

"So these are the French whose presence you found so intolerable. All I need do is show my face, and they flee before me!" Mustapha to Murad Bey

Detail from The Battle of Aboukir by Louis Lejeune (1775–1848), in which Turkish foot soldiers face a surprise French cavalry charge.

The Battle of Aboukir, the last attempt by the Ottoman Turks to regain Egypt from the French, ended in abject failure. Although this easily won victory came as a relief to Napoleon Bonaparte, the French general had already made up his mind to desert his troops and return to France.

Shortly after the French army's return to Egypt, a Turkish force of 15,000 men, led by Mustapha Pasha, landed at Aboukir Bay, close to Alexandria. Hearing news of the landings in Cairo, Napoleon assembled all available forces and marched toward the enemy. In previous actions, Napoleon had relied on his infantry, but, realizing that the Turks had few horsemen of their own, he decided that his own cavalry—1,000-strong, under the command of General Joachim Murat—could play a lead role in the coming battle.

The Turks had established a series of entrenched positions from which to defend their beachhead. The French infantry started the battle and broke into the Turkish lines. In the fierce fighting that ensued, the French were helped by the Turkish tradition of breaking off combat to plunder the dead and cut off their heads. In the confusion of this situation, Murat seized the moment and led a thunderous cavalry charge. The Turks were surprised at the ferocity of the French attack and fell back in disarray. At the head of his troops, Murat hacked his way into Mustapha's tent and captured the enemy commander, receiving a wound to the face for his trouble. The lack of a commander signaled the end for the Turks, who broke and ran. Many drowned as they attempted to swim out to the British transports in the bay, while others managed to retreat to Aboukir castle, only to be starved into surrender a week later. **AG**

Losses: French, 220 dead, 750 wounded of 10,000: Turkish, at least 8,000 casualties of 15,000

◁ Acre 1799　　　　　　　　　　　　　　　　Novi 1799 ▷

Novi 15 August 1799

With Napoleon in Egypt, the entry of Russia into a renewed round of the French Revolutionary Wars put France on the defensive. At Novi, a powerful Russo-Austrian army, inspired by the brilliance of Russian general Alexander Suvorov, temporarily ended French control of northern Italy.

During 1799, the French in Italy suffered a series of military setbacks at the hands of a combined Russian and Austrian army. General Joubert was dispatched to help restore French fortunes. Drawing together the French formations scattered across the country, he advanced from his base in Liguria into the Po valley in northern Italy, but he almost immediately encountered the combined Russian and Austrian armies, commanded by General Alexander Suvorov and General Michael von Melas, respectively.

Surprised at the size of the coalition force, Joubert adopted a defensive position. Under Suvorov's leadership, the allies ordered a general assault, hoping to push in both French flanks. The Austrians attacking the French left came under heavy fire, their attack halted. Aware of the importance of holding this part of line, Joubert galloped over to supervise operations and led a column of grenadiers that threw back the Austrians. It was at this moment that Joubert was mortally wounded by a musketball, and command of the French army passed to General Jean Victor Moreau.

Under new command, the French maintained their position repulsing several more allied attacks. The situation changed dramatically in the late afternoon, however, following the arrival of Melas, whose fresh troops broke through the enemy defenses. The tired French troops began to retreat, and under strong Austro-Russian pressure had many men captured. **AG**

Losses: Allied, 1,800 dead, 5,200 wounded of 50,000; French, 1,500 dead, 5,000 wounded, 4,600 captured of 35,000

◁ Aboukir 1799   Zürich 1799 ▷

Zürich 25 September 1799

The French success in this engagement outside Zürich expelled the allies from Switzerland and led to the withdrawal of Russia from the allied coalition against France. The battle also confirmed General Masséna's stature as one of the more able French revolutionary commanders.

The allied coalition armies of Austria, Russia, and Britain inflicted a series of reverses on the French during the summer of 1799. Allied forces, under the Austrian Archduke Charles, advanced into French-held Switzerland and defeated an army led by General André Masséna outside Zürich in June, ejecting the French from the city. The allies failed to exploit this victory, however, transferring Charles to the campaign on the Rhine while assigning command of allied troops in Switzerland to General Alexander Suvorov, the victor of the Battle of Novi. While Suvorov advanced toward Switzerland, command of allied forces in Switzerland temporarily passed to the Russian general, Alexander Korsakov.

Masséna had a numerical advantage over his opponent; he took the initiative and fell upon Korsakov's dispersed forces before they could be reinforced by Suvorov. Major General Nicolas Soult attacked and defeated a smaller, nearby Austrian force, whose commander, General Friedrich von Holtze, was killed in the encounter. At the same time, Masséna advanced against Korsakov, whose troops were holding a defensive line in front of Zürich. While the French pinned down the main body of Russians, a French division began to drive back the Russian units deployed north of Zürich, threatening their line of retreat. When Korsakov heard news of Holtze's defeat, he ordered a general withdrawal. The French followed up their victory, capturing eighty artillery pieces. **AG**

Losses: Allied, 8,000 casualties of 27,000; French, 4,000 casualties of 35,000

◁ Novi 1799   Marengo 1800 ▷

American Civil War
Anglo-Afghan Wars
Anglo-Ashanti Wars
Anglo-Egyptian War
Anglo-Maratha Wars
Anglo-Sikh Wars
Anglo-Zanzibar War
Anglo-Zulu War
Argentine Civil War
Argentinian-Brazilian War
Austro-Prussian War
Barbary War
Boer-Zulu War
Boshin War
British Abyssinia Expedition
Carlist Wars
Creek War
Crimean War
First Boer War
First Franco-Moroccan War
First Italian-Ethiopian War
First Sino-Japanese War
First Turko-Egyptian War
Franco-Prussian War
French Civil War
French Conquest of Algeria
French Conquest of Benin
French Intervention in Mexico
French Revolutionary Wars
Greek War of Independence
Hungarian Revolution
Indian Rebellion
Italian Wars of Independence
Lower Canada Rebellion
Mahdist War
Maori Wars
Mexican-American War
Napoleonic Wars
Northwest Rebellion
Opium Wars
Peninsular War
Philippine-American War
Plains Indian Wars
Russo-Turkish Wars
Satsuma Rebellion
Schleswig War
Second Boer War
Second Turko-Egyptian War
Seminole Wars
Sino-French War
South American Independence Wars
Spanish-American War
Taiping Rebellion
Tecumseh's War
Texas Revolution
Texas-Mexican War
War of 1812
War of the Pacific
War of the Triple Alliance

Detail from a painting of Napoleon Bonaparte during his 1814 campaign by Ernest Meissonier (1815–91).

Marengo   14 June 1800

Although Napoleon considered Marengo to be one of his finest victories, his overconfidence prior to the battle almost led to disaster. His ultimate success owed much to the determination of the French infantry and the decisive interventions of his subordinate commanders.

Following his return from Egypt in October 1799, Napoleon exploited the muddled state of French politics and effectively seized power in France, naming himself First Consul in December. Turning his attention to the strategic situation in Europe, he decided to lead an army over the Swiss Alps to attack the Austrians in northern Italy, while French forces under General Jean Victor Moreau marched into southern Germany.

Napoleon's Army of the Reserve secretly crossed the St. Bernard Pass, reaching the Po valley on 24 May with 40,000 men but only six guns. One of the French aims of the campaign had been to relieve the French garrison besieged by the Austrians in Genoa, but the city fell to the

"Through a powerful charge, [General Kellermann] managed to tilt the balance in our favor."

Murat's "Official Report"

Austrians on 4 June. Despite this, Napoleon's daring move through the Alps had placed his army squarely across the Austrian lines of communication. As a result, the Austrian commander, General Michael von Melas, withdrew his forces from the Franco-Italian border to give battle to the French near the fortified town of Alessandria.

Napoleon believed that the Austrians were about to retreat and he detached several formations to prevent them evading his net. Thus, when the Austrians decamped from Alessandria and crossed the River Bormida, the French were caught by surprise. Initially, Napoleon thought the Austrians were conducting a diversionary action, but it soon became clear that this was a full-scale assault; urgent dispatches were sent to the now dispersed French divisions to march to Marengo.

The Austrians advanced in three columns, Melas in the center with Generals Ott and O'Reilly attacking on the flanks. Major General Claude Victor's corps bore the brunt of the Austrian attack, but it fought a determined delaying action. Ultimately, Austrian numerical superiority forced the exhausted French to retreat to a new position at St. Guiliano Vecchio. French counterattacks were repulsed repeatedly and it seemed that the Austrians would be victorious. This was certainly Melas's impression; he retired from the battlefield to have a minor wound dressed, handing over command to his chief of staff, General Anton Zach.

Unknown to the Austrians, French reinforcements were beginning to arrive on the battlefield, and included the formations of Major Generals Louis Desaix and Jean Boudet. Desaix, one of Napoleon's most trusted lieutenants, spearheaded the counterattack. Supported by French artillery and the heavy cavalry of General François Kellermann, the French closed in on the Austrians. Although Desaix was killed, sustained French pressure and the chance explosion of an Austrian ammunition wagon provided Kellermann with an opportunity; his cuirassiers charged into the Austrian flank, causing confusion that turned into dismay when General Joachim Murat's light cavalry joined in the attack. The whole French line went over to the offensive, forcing the Austrians back into Alessandria with heavy losses. Bottled in by the French, Melas was obliged to ask for an armistice, which led to the loss of Lombardy to France. **AG**

Losses: Austrian, at least 9,500 casualties of 31,000; French, 5,000 casualties of 28,000

◀ *Zürich 1799*   *Hohenlinden 1800* ▶

Napoleon looks on in a detail from the nineteenth-century Death of General Desaix *by Jean Broc.* ➡

Hohenlinden 3 December 1800

Comprising a series of confused engagements, the Battle of Hohenlinden revealed the superior initiative of the French divisional commanders, who worked closely together and deftly exploited opportunities as they arose, in contrast to their timid Austrian opponents who operated in isolation.

While Napoleon was fighting to regain northern Italy, General Moreau launched an offensive deep into southern Germany. By December 1800, Moreau's forces were threatening the Bavarian capital of Munich. The Austrian response was to send an army, under the youthful and inexperienced Archduke John, to repel the French. The Austrians—supported by a small Bavarian contingent—moved against Moreau's position in four uncoordinated columns. Their advance was made all the more difficult because of the hilly, wooded terrain and cold weather.

The French were deployed in two corps, each of three infantry divisions, with cavalry in support. On the French left, Major General Paul Grenier's corps was the first to see action, conducting an astute defensive battle against the Austrians emerging from the woods. On the French right, two divisions from Moreau's reserve corps began an outflanking move against the Austrian left, spearheaded by Major General Antoine Richepanse. One of Richepanse's brigades was badly mauled in an attack by Austrian grenadiers. Undeterred, he carried on with his enveloping move, destroying the left-hand Austrian column, which turned the battle in favor of the French. Sensing victory, Moreau ordered an all-out attack, with the Austrians retreating in disorder, losing many prisoners and at least fifty guns in the process. After the battle, Moreau advanced into Austria, and with his troops only 50 miles (80 km) from Vienna, the Austrians sued for peace. **AG**

Losses: Austro-Bavarian, 4,600 dead or wounded, 9,000 captured of 57,000; French, 3,000 dead or wounded of 55,000

◁ *Marengo* 1800   *Copenhagen* 1801 ▷

Battle of Hohenlinden, 1800 *by François Louis Couche (1782–1849).* ⬆

Copenhagen   2 April 1801

While at war with France, Britain's naval operations against French trade also hurt neutral nations' shipping. Such hostility brought Britain into conflict with Denmark in 1801 to 1802, resulting in a successful British attack on Copenhagen and, shortly after, the demise of an anti-British alliance.

In early 1801, Russia, Prussia, Sweden, and Denmark formed a coalition to protect their own shipping and cut Britain's supplies from the Baltic of timber and other products vital to the navy. The British sent a fleet to break the coalition. Admiral Parker, a suitably senior but rather unenterprising officer, was in charge; Nelson was his second in command.

The fleet reached Denmark on 21 March. After fruitless negotiations, Nelson, on board HMS *Elephant*, led twelve ships of the line on an attack on the Danish ships and land batteries near Copenhagen on 2 April. The plan was bold because the British were moving into shallow waters without proper charts; three British ships ran aground in the early stages. Parker thought Nelson's force was taking unacceptable losses and ordered him to retreat. Nelson, who was blind in one eye from an old wound, made a joke about not being able to see the signal flags and fought on. By late afternoon, the Danish were taking a battering, and the British were in a strong position. They reopened negotiations—with eventual success—and were aided by the news that Czar Paul of Russia had been assassinated; his successor Alexander was known to be more pro-British. Copenhagen is often listed as one of Nelson's great victories; it was scarcely that—the Danes were far from beaten—but it did help end an important threat to British power. **DS**

Losses: Danish, 12 ships captured or destroyed, 1,000 dead or wounded; British, several ships grounded but later refloated, 1,000 dead or wounded

◁ *Hohenlinden 1800*   *Algeciras 1801* ▷

⬆ *A toast to battle in* Before Copenhagen: The Ward Room of HMS *Elephant (1898) by Thomas Davidson.*

Algeciras   6 July and 12–13 July 1801

After an initial setback in this two-stage battle, an inferior British fleet eventually defeated Franco-Spanish opponents, ending the last hopes of rescue for France's abandoned army in Egypt. Once again, the discipline and skill of the British crews contrasted strongly with their enemies' timidity and incompetence.

As part of preparations to help the French army in Egypt, France and Spain planned to assemble a naval force at the Spanish port of Cadiz. The first stage of the plan was to send four French ships from Toulon to Cadiz. These vessels were spotted passing the British base at Gibraltar and stopped in Algeciras Bay, a fortified Spanish base short of their destination.

On 6 July 1801, six British ships attacked the French in Algeciras but were badly defeated, partly because of intermittent winds. One British ship went aground and had to be surrendered; all the rest were damaged heavily. British Admiral Samaurez took his ships back the short distance to Gibraltar for repair while French Admiral Linois sent a message to Cadiz asking for reinforcements.

By 12 July, nine French and Spanish ships were at Algeciras, while four of the British ships had been partly repaired and a fifth had reached Gibraltar. Despite their superior strength, the allied force headed for Cadiz, chased by the British. The only British ship fast enough to catch up was the undamaged, newly arrived *Superb*. In a running night battle, *Superb* engaged the two largest Spanish ships then sailed off to attack and capture a French vessel. Unaware that *Superb* had moved on, the Spanish pair kept firing—at each other—then both caught fire and blew up. A further French ship was captured the next day while the rest escaped to Cadiz. **DS**

Losses: Spanish, 2 ships sunk; French, 2 ships captured, more than 2,000 dead; British, 1 ship captured, 150 dead

◁ Copenhagen 1801   Trafalgar 1805 ▷

Assaye   23 September 1803

The Battle of Assaye was fought in western India between the Maratha Confederacy, led by the mercenary Hanoverian, Anthony Pohlmann, and forces under the command of Major General Arthur Wellesley, future Duke of Wellington. Later in life, the duke described the victory at Assaye as his greatest military achievement.

The Treaty of Bassein of 1802 split the Maratha Confederacy and led to war with the Maratha chieftains who opposed the Peshwa. Wellesley split his army into two and sought to trap the Confederacy before it could advance southward and attack Hyderabad. However, this strategy failed when Wellesley stumbled upon the Marathas in a position contrary to the intelligence he had received. Even though Wellesley was surprised by the size and resources of the Maratha army, which had been swelled by several divisions of infantry, he resolved to attack quickly rather than wait for his second force, under the command of Colonel Stevenson.

The ensuing battle was a costly one for the Marathas, who were unable to deploy their cavalry decisively. Wellesley's infantry charged with bayonets fixed directly at the Maratha battery because the cannonade was causing damage to the British lines. The battery was taken, and many of the Maratha fled. Wellesley's right flank was less successful and was saved only by the redeployment of a division of cavalry. The battle was decided by the eventual success of Wellesley's strategy to silence the Maratha artillery; when Wellesley ordered a full-scale bayonet advance on Pohlmann's center, the Maratha army was put to flight. The British did not pursue the Marathas, but Assaye was soon followed by victory at Aragon, which led to British dominance of central India. **TB**

Losses: British, 1,500 casualties of 10,000; Maratha Confederacy, 6,500 casualties of 50,000

◁ Seringapatam 1799

🔄 The Battle of Algeciras, 6 July 1801, *a watercolor after Alfred Paris, from 1895.*

Tripoli 3 August 1804

Pirates based in the ports of the Muslim north African coast were a serious threat to international shipping in the Mediterranean in the early nineteenth century. In 1804, the U.S. Navy launched an attack on Tripoli, Libya, one of the rogue states supporting these maritime terrorists.

Although the naval squadron sent to the Mediterranean was led by Commodore Edward Preble, the hero of the United States' war with Tripoli was Stephen Decatur from Maryland. As a lieutenant, in February 1804, Decatur led a raiding party into Tripoli harbor by night to destroy a captured U.S. frigate, *Philadelphia*, that Tripoli was turning to its own use. This bold action made him the youngest man to earn a promotion to captain in the history of the Navy. The following August, he was an obvious choice to take part in a larger scale assault on the hostile harbor.

Preble gave him command of half of a force of six gunboats and two bomb ketches—small shallow-draft vessels carrying large cannon and mortars—to enter the harbor and attack Tripolitanian gunboats. The Tripoli shore batteries would be kept quiet by bombardment from the guns of the frigate *Constitution* off shore.

The operation did not go smoothly. The U.S. gunboats faced fierce resistance from fighters on the boats in the harbor. Decatur boarded two enemy gunboats, his boarding parties engaging in close-quarters fighting with pistols and sabers. In one incident, Decatur was wrestling with a pirate and shot the man in the back as they clinched; the spent bullet ended up lodged in Decatur's clothing after passing through his enemy's body.

By the end of the action, the Americans had captured three gunboats and their crews. The following year, the landing of U.S. Marines to threaten Tripoli led to a compromise deal that ended the fighting. **RG**

Losses: Tripolitanian, at least 47 dead, 49 captured, 3 gunboats; U.S., 13 casualties

Detail from a painting (1897) by Edward Moran showing the Philadelphia *burning in Tripoli harbor.*

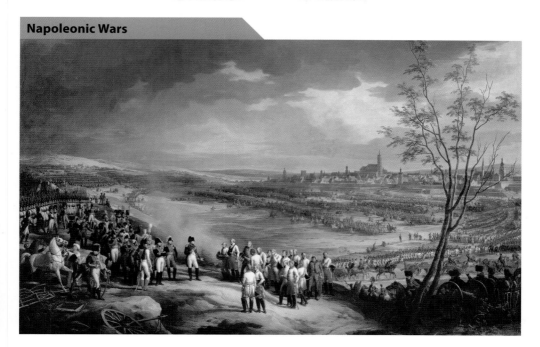

Ulm   26 September–20 October 1805

The destruction of General Mack's Austrian army at Ulm was one of Napoleon's finest victories. Completely outwitting Mack, he coordinated his army over wide distances with clockwork precision. That there was little fighting was testimony to the brilliance of Napoleon's strategic vision.

Faced by a hostile coalition of Britain, Austria, and Russia, the newly crowned Emperor Napoleon Bonaparte opted to launch an offensive against Austria before Russia could come to its aid. The bulk of the powerful French Grande Armée—over 200,000 strong, organized in seven army corps—was spread across northern France, the Netherlands, and Hanover, but in early September it secretly began to march toward southern Germany. The Austrians believed that the main French thrust would be in Italy, although an army commanded by General Karl Mack von Leiberich invaded Bavaria (now a French ally) and marched west to positions around the city of Ulm.

The French crossed the Rhine on 26 September. While Marshal Joachim Murat's cavalry screen advanced through the Black Forest to draw Mack's attention, the bulk of the Grande Armée advanced east of Ulm in a wide arc, cutting off the Austrians from Vienna and further reinforcement. When Mack realized what was happening, it was too late; the French net had closed around the Austrians. Mack made several attempts to break through the French lines but most failed; only at Elchingen was there much serious fighting when Marshal Michel Ney's corps repulsed an attack, inflicting heavy casualties on the Austrians. On 20 October, Mack capitulated to Napoleon, surrendering nearly 30,000 men (including eighteen generals), sixty-five guns, and forty standards. **AG**

Losses: Austrian, 12,000 dead or wounded, 30,000 captured of 50,000; French, 6,000 dead or wounded of 150,000

◁ *Hohenlinden 1800*   *Austerlitz 1805* ▷

⬆ The Surrender of Ulm *(1815) by Charles Thevenin: Napoleon receives the Austrian capitulation.*

Trafalgar   21 October 1805

In probably the most decisive naval battle in history, Nelson's British fleet annihilated any French or Spanish threat to Britain's supremacy at sea. Immune now from invasion, Britain and its trade would prosper, providing the financial resources that would help Napoleon's many enemies to complete his eventual downfall.

When Britain and France resumed their long-standing war in 1803, Napoleon started preparing an invasion of England. This included a complicated scheme for the French and Spanish fleets to converge on the English Channel and control it while the invasion army crossed. In the event, the largest French force remained tightly blockaded in Brest by the British Channel fleet, while the main Spanish fleet and a substantial French squadron ended up in Cadiz.

Nelson arrived off Cadiz in late September 1805 to take command of operations there, a day after the Franco-Spanish commander, French Admiral Villeneuve, had been ordered to head into the Mediterranean. Villeneuve knew that he outnumbered and outgunned his opponents, but he also knew that his crews were unskilled, demoralized, and essentially unfit for battle.

On the British side, confidence was rightly high. The French and Spanish were prepared to fight naval battles when necessary as a means to another objective, but the more aggressive British policy was now to be fully vindicated. The best British commanders sought battle at every opportunity and, in the meantime, kept their ships endlessly at sea, all the time honing their seamanship and gunnery skills. In his prebattle instructions, Nelson wrote that, in the confusion of battle, no British captain "could do very wrong if he places his ship alongside that of an

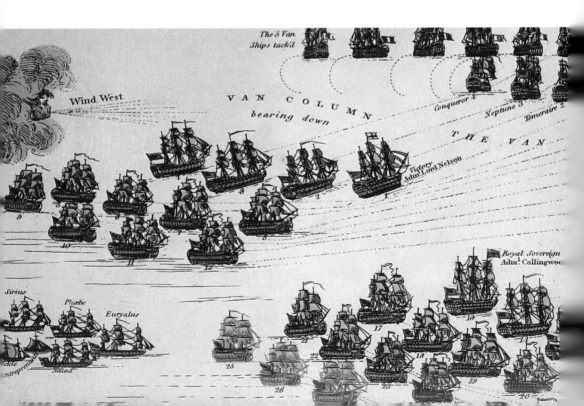

enemy." He wanted the vicious close-quarter battle that these tactics would bring about because he knew he would win. Nelson also decided to attack in two groups, sending one against the center of the allied line and the other against the rear, a scheme explicitly designed to bring about the close-range melee he wanted.

The allied fleet of eighteen French and fifteen Spanish ships of the line began leaving port on 19 October. Nelson, with twenty-seven, closed in on 21 October. The battle was fought essentially as Nelson planned. The allies failed to inflict much damage during their opponents' risky head-on approach and, once the shattering short-range cannonade began, the combat became increasingly one-sided. The first broadside from Nelson's *Victory* killed perhaps 200 men aboard Villeneuve's *Bucentaure*; other allied ships suffered as badly. In the developing clouds of gunsmoke, ships collided and fought at point-blank range. Inevitably there were heavy losses on both sides but the British gunners fired far faster and more accurately.

The *Victory* came alongside the French *Redoutable*, whose crew had been specially trained to use muskets from positions high in the rigging. Soon Nelson fell mortally wounded by a shot from one of these marksmen. When he died some three hours later, the battle was almost over. More than half of the Franco-Spanish ships had surrendered, and the rest were fleeing in total disorder. With this decisive success, Britain was now supreme at sea. For all his land victories between 1805 and his final fall, Napoleon would never again threaten Britain directly. **DS**

Losses: Allied, 18 ships captured or destroyed, more than 7,000 dead, wounded, or captured; British, no ships lost, 1,600 dead or wounded

◁ *Algeciras 1801*   *Santo Domingo 1806* ▷

Austerlitz 2 December 1805

Napoleon's defeat of the Austro-Russian armies at Austerlitz was a tactical masterclass, the French emperor imposing his will on the enemy commanders even before the battle had begun. The allied troops fought with determination, but they were no match for the flexibility and élan of the Grande Armée.

After his victory at Ulm, Napoleon pressed on toward Vienna, which fell on 12 November 1805. His main intention was to engage and defeat General Michael Kutuzov's Russian army, but Kutuzov played for time and fell back northeast hoping to overextend the French while reinforcing his own side with Austrian and other Russian troops. With winter drawing in, the French were placed in a difficult position, and on 23 November, Napoleon called a halt in order to reorganize and resupply his troops.

Napoleon feigned weakness to tempt the Austro-Russian forces into making a full-scale assault near the village of Austerlitz, which had been fully reconnoitered by the French. He abandoned the obvious key topographical position on the Pratzen plateau, withdrawing his troops behind the seemingly weak line of the Goldbach stream. As a further inducement, he deliberately weakened his right wing to tempt the allies into an enveloping move on that flank. Against Kutuzov's advice, the allied emperors—Francis of Austria and Alexander of Russia—decided on a flank attack and so fell for Napoleon's stratagem.

The allies moved onto the Pratzen plateau, while General Frederick Buxhowden's corps marched against the sparsely defended French right. Events looked promising for the allies, until the sudden arrival of Marshal Louis Davout's corps on the French right brought the allied enveloping maneuver to a halt. This encouraged

The Battle of Austerlitz *(1810) by François Gérard, in which General Rapp reports the defeat of the Russian Imperial Guard to Napoleon.*

the allies to divert troops from the Pratzen—in the center of the allied position—to help their comrades on their left flank. This only played into French hands, and Marshal Nicolas Soult's heavily reinforced corps advanced in the early morning mist across the Goldbach stream to storm the Pratzen. Meanwhile, on the French left, the formations under Marshals Lannes and Murat pinned down the allied right wing, preventing it from sending reinforcements to aid their fast-disintegrating center.

Kutuzov, aware of the danger to his troops on the Pratzen plateau, sent in a succession of reserves to steady the line. He played his final card and threw the Russian Imperial Guard into the melee, but was trumped by Napoleon's decision to commit his own Imperial Guard, which cleared the Pratzen of all allied troops. Soult's corps had, meanwhile, turned southward to attack the dangerously extended allied left wing. The allied left wing was completely isolated, and troops tried desperately to escape across the frozen lakes and marshes to the south of the Pratzen. Many were sent to their deaths as their weight—aided by French cannonballs—broke the ice.

Marshal Jean Bernadotte's corps was adroitly transferred from the French left to secure the Pratzen against the last of the Russian counterattacks. As light began to fade, Kutuzov ordered a general retreat, leaving the allied units in the south with little option but to surrender to the French. On the morning of 4 December, the Austrians sued for peace while the remnants of Kutuzov's army retreated back to Russia, the allied coalition against France in tatters. **AG**

Losses: Allied, 16,000 dead or wounded, 11,500 captured of 85,000; French, 8,000 dead or wounded of 73,000

◁ *Ulm 1805*   *Jena-Auerstadt 1806* ▷

Santo Domingo 6 February 1806

Although unwilling after Trafalgar to face Britain in a full-scale fleet battle, the French navy was still able to attempt raids on British commerce and against distant colonies. Often, as here, the raiders achieved early successes, only to be hunted down.

Much of the French fleet had been destroyed at Trafalgar and in its aftermath, but France's Brest squadrons had taken no part in the campaign. At the end of 1805, two squadrons left Brest. One squadron, under Admiral Willaumez, returned home in the late summer of 1806 having taken losses and achieved little. By contrast, within days of setting out, Admiral Leissègues and his five ships of the line—one of them the exceptionally powerful 120-gun *Impérial*—were being pursued to the Caribbean by the British.

The British squadron was led by Admiral Duckworth, who annoyed his superiors by abandoning the blockade of Cadiz to take up the pursuit. The French had headed for the island of Santo Domingo, a Spanish colony then under French occupation. The British closed in on 6 February 1806, with seven ships of the line.

In the battle that followed, the British outfought and captured three of the French ships and then concentrated on *Impérial* and its remaining consort. They were forced ashore and wrecked. Much of the combat took place at close range in a pall of gunsmoke; there were several collisions and examples of ships being hit by "friendly fire." Casualties on both sides were severe. If the British had failed to win this battle, Duckworth would have been in trouble; instead he was praised for saving Britain's immensely valuable West Indies trade from a serious French attack. **DS**

Losses: British, 340 dead or wounded; French, 1,500 dead or wounded, 5 ships captured or destroyed

[<] Trafalgar 1805   Copenhagen 1807 [>]

Jena-Auerstadt 14 October 1806

Napoleon's advance into Prussia revealed his strategic superiority over the Prussians. On the battlefields at Jena and Auerstadt, the Grande Armée demonstrated its tactical skills against an army still living off the legacy of Frederick the Great.

When hostilities broke out between Prussia and France, Napoleon's Grande Armée marched northward from Bavaria in three columns. Marshal Lannes's left-hand column first encountered Prussian forces near Jena on 13 October. Napoleon believed this to be the main Prussian army and ordered all other commanders to march toward Jena in support. Lannes had, in fact, encountered a subsidiary force of 38,000 troops commanded by Prince Hohenlohe; the bulk of the Prussians, led by the Duke of Brunswick, lay to the north, near the village of Auerstadt.

Napoleon's attack on Hohenlohe's troops began on 14 October, and a precipitate advance by Marshal Ney was harshly dealt with by the Prussians, who also repulsed an attack by Lannes. By midday, however, French superiority in numbers began to tell, and, as both Prussian flanks began to waver, Hohenlohe ordered a retreat.

The two French corps under Marshals Davout and Bernadotte lay to the north; as Davout marched on Jena, he encountered Brunswick's army to the east of Auerstadt. (Bernadotte failed to follow Napoleon's order and took no part in the battle.) Heavily outnumbered, Davout's troops conducted a resolute defense before going over to the attack. The death of Brunswick broke the will of the Prussian command, whose troops then retreated in confusion. The French cavalry pursued the Prussians with unrelenting determination, and Berlin was occupied on 25 October. **AG**

Losses: French, 2,500 casualties of 90,000 (Jena), 4,350 casualties of 27,000 (Auerstadt); Prussian, 28,000 casualties of 38,000 (Jena), 18,000 casualties of 60,000 (Auerstadt)

[<] Austerlitz 1805   Eylau 1807 [>]

Eylau 7–8 February 1807

After a succession of victories to 1806, Napoleon was fought to a standstill in a bitter engagement with the Russians at Eylau. The unrelenting winter conditions added to the horror of the fighting, as the wounded froze to death in the battle's aftermath.

After his triumph against Prussia, Napoleon pressed eastward into Poland to attack the Russians. Although it seemed that both armies would settle into winter quarters, a probing action by the Russian commander, General Levin Bennigsen, provoked a response from Napoleon, who advanced toward the Russians holding the town of Eylau. On the afternoon of 7 February, the French attacked and captured Eylau, seeking refuge from the cold.

The following morning, battle resumed amid heavy snow showers. Although outnumbered, Napoleon decided to attack the Russian center, hoping to pin down Bennigsen's troops, while awaiting reinforcements from Marshals Davout and Ney on each flank. Marshal Charles Augereau and his troops advanced toward the Russian line but, in driving snow, lost their way and were all but destroyed by a Russian seventy-gun battery. A Russian counterattack put the French center in danger, too, the position only saved by an epic charge from Marshal Murat's 10,000 cavalry.

The entrance of Davout's corps against the Russian left flank seemed to swing the battle toward the French, but the counterarrival of Prussian reinforcements forced Davout back. The fighting continued after dark, with the arrival of Ney's corps on the French left finally giving the French rough numerical parity with the allies. During the night, Bennigsen withdrew from the battlefield; the French were in no state to pursue their opponents. **AG**

Losses: Allied, 15,000 casualties of 80,000; French, at least 15,000 casualties of 75,000

◁ Jena-Auerstadt 1806   Friedland 1807 ▷

Friedland 14 June 1807

After the Eylau setback, Napoleon's victory over the Russians at Friedland restored his reputation. It forced Russia's emperor Alexander I to accept French terms at the Treaty of Tilsit, which left Napoleon the undisputed master of continental Europe.

Determined to engage the army of General Bennigsen, Napoleon caught the Russians in front of the town of Friedland on 14 June. At first only Lannes's corps held contact with the Russians, but, during the day, the various other corps of the Grande Armée began to arrive on the battlefield. By 4:00 PM, Napoleon was able to utilize some 80,000 men, and, seeing that Bennigsen's forces were badly deployed in front of the River Alster, he launched an immediate attack despite the lateness of the day.

The main thrust of the French attack was made against the congested Russian left, spearheaded by Ney's corps. The assault got underway at 5:30 PM, and Ney met stiff resistance and made little headway until reinforcements arrived from Victor's corps. In the center, Napoleon massed his guns and pushed them forward to case-shot range with the Russians, who suffered devastating casualties. In desperation, the Russians attacked the guns but were repulsed by the infantry of Lannes and Mortier. Ney, meanwhile, began to push in the Russian left flank, fighting his way into Friedland by 8:30 PM.

Realizing that the battle was lost, Bennigsen began to save as much of his army as possible, withdrawing his troops across the Alster. Although many soldiers drowned, the Russian army escaped almost total destruction as a result of General Emmanuel de Grouchy's refusal to commit his cavalry in pursuit of the retreating Russian right wing. **AG**

Losses: French, 8,000 casualties of 80,000; Russian, 20,000 casualties of 60,000

◁ Eylau 1807   Eckmühl 1809 ▷

Copenhagen   2–6 September 1807

Fearful that Napoleon's defeat of Russia and Prussia might lead to him bringing the fleets of the Baltic powers under his control, Britain acted ruthlessly to neutralize the substantial Danish navy. The Danish fleet was surrendered to Britain after Copenhagen was bombarded.

In early 1807, British leaders suspected that Napoleon might get control of the Russian fleet and then perhaps the Danish and Swedish ones, too—together a strong enough force to pose a new threat to Britain's naval mastery. Britain also had valuable trading interests in the Baltic, which was a vital source of naval supplies.

Britain prepared a large expedition—29,000 troops and more than 400 warships and transports—and remarkably managed to keeps its destination secret. The force reached Denmark in early August 1807 and demanded that the Danes allow their fleet to be taken into British control. The Danes refused, and hostilities began.

British troops under Wellesley (later the Duke of Wellington) landed near Copenhagen and surrounded the city. When further negotiations failed, the British fleet, under Admiral James Gambier, began a fierce bombardment on 2 September, making much use of Congreve rockets (one of the first times rockets had been employed in European warfare). Soon much of the city was in flames, and the Danes, suffering heavy civilian casualties, were forced to surrender. The British left with over sixty Danish ships and quantities of naval supplies.

Britain and Denmark remained at war for more than six years. Denmark did manage to capture some British merchant ships and Britain had to convoy and escort its Baltic trade. There were a few minor clashes at sea but no further land battles. **DS**

Losses: Danish, 2,000 dead, 60 ships captured; British, 200 dead or wounded

◁ *Santo Domingo 1806*　　　　　*Basque Roads 1809* ▷

　　　A painting depicting the bombardment of Copenhagen (artist unknown). ⬆

Madrid   2 May 1808

The French commanders in Spain were highly experienced and successful soldiers, but they completely misjudged the inflammatory nature of Spanish political, religious, and social life. What they considered as a simple punishment for dissent was transformed into a rallying cry of insurrection.

In March 1808, the French army marched into Spain to impose Napoleon's Continental System over the Iberian peninsula. Napoleon also began to meddle in Spanish royal politics, which led to the removal of the Spanish monarch, who was replaced by Napoleon's elder brother, Joseph. Not surprisingly, this caused deep consternation among the Spanish people, which came to a head when Marshal Joachim Murat prepared to remove the children of the royal family to France. Although Madrid had been occupied by the French since 23 March, the French were unprepared for the strength of feeling among its citizens, which erupted into violence on 2 May 1808.

A crowd assembled around the royal palace in an attempt to physically stop the removal of the children. On hearing this, Murat dispatched a grenadier battalion of the Imperial Guard and a battery of artillery to clear a way for the royal departure; when the French guns opened up on the Spanish, the protest was transformed into outright rebellion. French cavalry then charged through the streets quelling the protest with their sabers.

The following day, the French instigated measures to repress the revolt; those caught carrying firearms (and many who were not) were shot. Although Murat and his fellow commanders thought that such exemplary punishments would stop the protests, they could not have been more wrong. The events of *Dos de Mayo* acted as the fuse that lit a nationwide uprising against French rule. **AG**

Losses: French, unknown; Spanish, 500 (including more than 100 executed on 3 May)

Bailén 1808 ▷

↑ The Third of May 1808 *(1814) by Francisco de Goya depicts the French suppression of the revolt.*

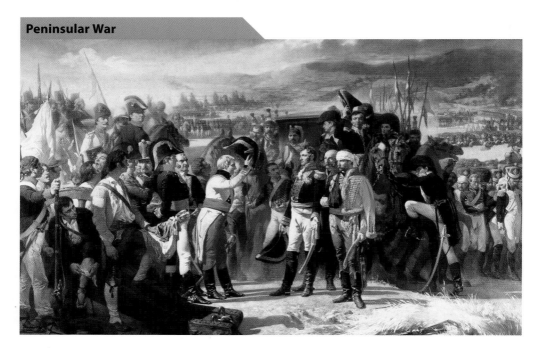

Bailén   15–21 July 1808

The surrender of an entire French army corps at Bailén was a blow to French fortunes, stimulating resistance to Napoleon not only in Spain but also throughout Europe. In Austria, news of the French disaster encouraged the Emperor Francis to prepare for war against the French.

The French reaction to the Spanish uprising of 1808 was to dispatch flying columns against centers of resistance, and General Pierre Dupont was ordered to capture the vital naval port of Cadiz. Reinforced by General Vedel's division of 10,000 men, Dupont's corps began its march across the hostile terrain of southern Spain. Almost immediately, the French found their way disputed by the Army of Andalusia, commanded by General Francisco Castaños and General Theodor von Reding. After reaching the city of Córdoba, Dupont halted his advance; judging that he had no realistic chance of capturing Cadiz, he decided to return across the pass of the Sierra Morena to safety.

The French retreat was painfully slow, encumbered by 1,200 wounded and ill soldiers and 500 wagons of booty. On hearing reports that the Spanish were blocking the road across the Sierra Morena, Dupont fatally weakened his command by sending Vedel's division to clear the Spanish and keep the pass open. While Castaños pinned down Dupont's column, Reding successfully interposed himself between Dupont and Vedel at Bailén on 17 July.

Now surrounded, Dupont made three increasingly desperate attempts to break through the Spanish lines but was repulsed on all occasions. Vedel made several half-hearted attempts to come to Dupont's rescue but achieved little. His troops short of water and food, Dupont (along with Vedel) accepted Spanish surrender terms on 21 July, the entire force marching into captivity. **AG**

Losses: French, 2,500 dead or wounded, 17,600 captured of 24,500; Spanish, 1,000 dead or wounded of 30,000

◁ *Madrid 1808*   *Vimeiro 1808* ▷

The Surrender of Bailén (1864) by José Casado de Alisal, an iconic painting in the style of Velázquez.

Vimeiro 21 August 1808

The arrival of the British army was to transform the war in the Iberian peninsula; in this first engagement General Wellesley revealed his tactical acumen against a series of clumsy and poorly coordinated French attacks—a pattern that was to be repeated in many subsequent engagements.

Britain actively encouraged the Iberian insurrection against the French, and, on 1 August 1808, a British expeditionary force landed in Portugal under the command of Lieutenant General Sir Arthur Wellesley. The French commander in Portugal, General Jean-Andoche Junot, advanced toward the British positions to the north of Lisbon. Although possessing a clear numerical superiority, Wellesley cautiously adopted a defensive line on a ridge stretching either side of the town of Vimeiro and awaited the French assault.

Junot's plan was to pin down the British center while sending a force to envelop the British left flank. Wellesley could see the French plan unfolding and adjusted his line to deal with the French attack on his left wing. Unfortunately for Junot, the rough terrain separated the two elements of his assault, which soon broke down into a series of isolated attacks that was easily repulsed by musket fire from the well-disciplined British infantry on the ridge.

Seeing that he would not be able to dislodge the British, Junot withdrew his army. He realized that his position was critical, being isolated from other French troops in Spain. Consequently, he entered into surrender negotiations with the British. In the meantime, Wellesley had been superseded by two more senior commanders, who, in the Convention of Cintra (30 August), permitted Junot's entire force to be repatriated by the Royal Navy. The lenient terms caused outrage in London. **AG**

Losses: British, 720 dead or wounded of 18,000; French, 2,000 casualties of 13,000

◁ *Bailén 1808*　　　　　　　　*Corunna 1809* ▷

Cavalry suffering heavy losses in The 20th Light Dragoons at the Battle of Vimeiro *by Richard Simkin (1840–1926).*

Corunna 16 January 1809

A British force led by Sir John Moore overreached itself during the advance toward Madrid and was forced to make a desperate withdrawal across much of Spain. However, the resolute British defensive action at Corunna helped to erase the humiliations of the retreat.

To support the Spanish insurrection against France, a British army commanded by Lieutenant General Sir John Moore marched into Spain during November 1808. When Moore reached Salamanca, he received the unwelcome news that Napoleon had just led a large army into Spain and was threatening to trap his own increasingly isolated force. Moore reluctantly began to retreat to the port of Corunna (La Coruña) in northwest Spain, where a Royal Navy fleet would evacuate his troops. Napoleon failed to envelop the retreating British, delegating the subsequent pursuit to Marshal Soult.

The long retreat—much of it through the mountains in grim winter conditions—nearly destroyed Moore's army, but a series of rearguard actions kept the French at bay until the army reached Corunna on 11 January 1809. To Moore's dismay, the transport fleet had not arrived, forcing him to stand against the French. On 15 January, Soult's troops forced in the British outposts and prepared for battle the following day. By now the transports had arrived and the evacuation was progressing, but the French attacked the main British line in the afternoon of 16 January. Most of the fighting centered around the village of Elvina, which changed hands on several occasions. While rallying a unit, Moore was mortally wounded, but the French broke off operations as darkness fell. During the night, the British successfully slipped away from the battlefield to complete the evacuation. **AG**

Losses: British, 900 dead or wounded of 16,000; French, 1,000 dead or wounded of 16,000

◁ Vimeiro 1808

Talavera 1809 ▷

Basque Roads 11–12 April 1809

A French expedition from Brest to reinforce Martinique in the West Indies got no farther than an anchorage off Rochefort on France's west coast. A bold night attack crippled the French force, although its effects were limited by command problems on the British side.

By 1809, Martinique was one of the few French colonies that had not been captured by Britain. To reinforce the colony, a strong French squadron escaped from the blockaded port of Brest, but, instead of joining up with other French squadrons sheltering in Lorient and Rochefort to the south, it ended up taking refuge in the Basque Roads anchorage off Rochefort. The British soon arrived to mount an attack.

The anchorage was covered by shore batteries, and shoal waters made navigation difficult. Admiral Gambier, a rather dull and cautious leader commanding the British Channel fleet, decided not to risk his main battleship force. Instead, he proposed attacking with fireships; his superiors in London agreed, but sent out an enterprising junior officer, Lord Cochrane, to command the actual attack.

Just after dark on 11 April, the British destroyed the protective boom across the entrance to the anchorage using two small ships packed with explosives; a force of twenty fireships followed behind. Most of the fireships came nowhere near the French vessels but the French panicked, cut their anchor cables, and their ships drifted ashore. In the morning, with most of the French ships hard aground and helpless, Cochrane asked Gambier for reinforcements to finish them off. Gambier refused to risk his fleet (and was exonerated by a subsequent inquiry), and the battle petered out with only a few French ships destroyed. **DS**

Losses: British, no ships; French, 4 ships of the line and 1 frigate

◁ Copenhagen 1807

Grand Port 1810 ▷

Eckmühl   21–22 April 1809

As at Austerlitz and Auerstadt, Napoleon relied heavily on the skills of Marshal Davout, who held the line against superior numbers until the emperor arrived on the battlefield to overwhelm the enemy. On this occasion, Austrian Archduke Charles escaped, withdrawing his forces across the Danube.

In April 1809, the Austrian invasion of Bavaria by Archduke Charles renewed war against France, with Napoleon hurriedly departing Paris to organize his forces in southern Germany. As Napoleon advanced along the Danube valley on 21 April, Marshal Louis Davout's isolated and depleted corps found itself under attack from forces totaling around 70,000 men. Unaware of the size of the attack, Napoleon instructed Davout to hold on, although he loaned him a corps of Bavarian troops commanded by Marshal François Lefebvre.

With his usual cool imperturbability, Davout repulsed the Austrian attacks, but, by the morning of 22 April, he once again informed the French commander in chief of his difficult position and a shortage of ammunition. Napoleon realized that Davout was facing the main Austrian army and redirected his forces to come to his aid. Davout and Lefebvre immediately went over to the offensive to pin the Austrians as Napoleon rushed his forces forward to fall upon the Austrian left wing. The Austrians fell back in the face of the French onslaught; sensing danger, Archduke Charles began the process of withdrawing his troops to the fortified city of Ratisbon and then to the safety of the north bank of the Danube. As darkness fell, Napoleon instructed his cavalry to pursue the enemy; despite a number of bloody clashes, they were unable to prevent the Austrians from making a fairly orderly retreat. **AG**

Losses: Austrian, 12,000 of 35,000; French and allied, 6,000 casualties of 36,000 rising to 60,000

◁ *Friedland 1807*　　　　*Aspern-Essling 1809* ▷

Aspern-Essling   21–22 May 1809

The French defeat at Aspern-Essling was the first reverse suffered by Napoleon in Europe, giving hope to his many enemies across the continent. Among the long list of casualties suffered by the French was Marshal Jean Lannes, mortally wounded on the second day of fighting.

After his success at Eckmühl, Napoleon marched into Vienna on 10 May, although the Austrians, led by Archduke Charles, remained a powerful force on the north bank of the Danube. All the bridges in and around Vienna had been destroyed, so Napoleon was forced to deploy pontoon bridges, using the river island of Lobau as a stepping stone to gain the opposite bank.

On the night of 20 to 21 May, Napoleon's engineers laid bridges from Lobau to the north bank, and immediately troops from the corps of Marshals Lannes and Masséna crossed over the river, securing the villages of Aspern and Essling. The Austrians waited until midday—deliberately allowing a sizable French force to cross—before they struck. The French were caught by surprise, and vicious close-quarter fighting ensued, with the villages changing hands several times before nightfall brought the battle to a temporary close.

The French position was made especially perilous when bridges were swept away by rising floodwaters and enemy action, thereby slowing the arrival of reinforcements. During the night, the bridges were repaired, but when the fighting recommenced on 22 May, the French were constrained to the line running between Aspern and Essling. After a final French attack in the center had been repulsed by the personal intervention of Archduke Charles, Napoleon ordered a retreat across the Danube, leaving the field of battle to the Austrians. **AG**

Losses: Austrian, 23,000 casualties of 95,000; French, 23,000 casualties of 70,000

◁ *Eckmühl 1809*　　　　*Wagram 1809* ▷

Wagram   5–6 July 1809

Napoleon inflicted a decisive defeat upon the Austrians, but massed artillery batteries caused heavy casualties to the tightly packed armies on both sides. These were losses that the French army could ill afford, making it increasingly reliant on its allies to shore up Napoleon's empire.

In a controlled display of energy that followed his defeat at Aspern-Essling, Napoleon drew upon reinforcements from Germany and northern Italy and developed the river island of Lobau as a vast, well-defended military park. Learning from the failings of the previous battle, Napoleon built a series of well-made and well-defended bridges to the north bank of the Danube. By contrast, Archduke Charles remained lethargically on the defensive; apart from calling upon the 15,000 troops of Archduke John, he surrendered the military initiative to Napoleon.

Napoleon began by launching a subsidiary attack from Lobau due north—between Aspern and Essling—while the main transfer of troops was directed eastward from the island a little later, on the night of 4 to 5 July. The Austrians were taken by surprise; in the morning more than 130,000 French soldiers were on the Danube's north bank, with more to follow. In contrast to the sound tactics used at Aspern-Essling, the Austrians made an initial and ultimately fatal error in adopting a defensive position a few miles farther back from the river, thereby allowing the French to deploy their forces at leisure. During 5 July, both armies locked horns, inflicting enormous casualties without result; an attempt by the French and their German allies to break the Austrian center was repulsed.

The following day, Archduke Charles attempted to regain the initiative by launching attacks all along the French line, although the main thrust was directed

against the lightly held French left. On the French right, which was held by Marshal Davout's corps, the Austrian attacks came to nothing, and the French advanced steadily forward. On the French left, the Austrians did make progress, but their greatest success took place on the French left-center when Marshal Bernadotte's poorly trained Saxon corps broke and fled. In a daring tactical readjustment, Marshal Masséna's corps was dispatched to cover the exposed French left flank, while the gap in the left-center was filled by the French reserves, which included the Imperial Guard and other elite formations.

Feeling that the battle could be decided in his favor, Napoleon arrayed mass batteries of artillery to break open the Austrian attack against his center, before ordering General Jacques MacDonald's corps to take the offensive. Macdonald formed his 8,000-strong infantry formation into a massive hollow square and advanced on the enemy, taking enormous casualties from their artillery as a consequence. Although supported by French cavalry, MacDonald's unwieldy mass was eventually brought to a halt by the Austrian defenders.

Better progress was made on the French right, as Davout, supported by Oudinot, began to unravel the Austrian left, especially when it became obvious that Archduke John's troops would not arrive in time. With Napoleon in a dominant position, Archduke Charles retreated from the battlefield. After further skirmishes with the French, the Austrians accepted that the war was lost and came to terms with Napoleon, bringing the Fifth Coalition against France to a close. **AG**

Losses: Austrian, more than 40,000 casualties of 160,000; French, 38,000 casualties of 180,000

◁ *Aspern-Essling 1809*   *Smolensk 1812* ▷

Talavera   27–28 July 1809

Although the French army gained some local successes in this battle of the Peninsular War, the fact that the two generals in command operated in isolation was of enormous help to the British, whose well-drilled troops successfully weathered the many assaults made against them.

Having forced Marshal Nicolas Soult's French army out of Portugal in May 1809, Lieutenant General Sir Arthur Wellesley marched into Spain with 20,000 British troops. In July, he combined forces with a 35,000-strong Spanish army, commanded by General Gregorio de la Cuesta, and advanced toward Madrid. The Anglo-Spanish armies pursued Marshal Claude Victor's corps, but, after it was joined by substantial forces under King Joseph Bonaparte, the French went over to the offensive. The allies took up a defensive position, with the Spanish on the right by the city of Talavera and the British on the left, the centerpiece of their position being the Medellin hill.

Stationed on the right of the French line, Victor launched an impetuous attack on the evening of 27 July with only his own troops. Although it caused some confusion among the surprised British, his assault was halted and his troops thrown off the Medellin. The battle proper continued the following day, with the French launching repeated attacks against the British lines, all of them repulsed by heavy musket fire. A French attempt to outflank Wellesley's left was also thwarted, although a sudden British cavalry charge was badly mauled by the French. During the evening of 27 July, the French withdrew toward Madrid, but the allies also retreated when news came that Soult's army was bearing down upon them. Wellesley, granted the title of Viscount Wellington, retired in good order to Portugal. **AG**

"I don't know what effect these men will have upon the enemy, but, by God, they frighten me."

Arthur Wellesley's reported verdict on his new troops

🔼 *Wellesley leads his redcoats as the tide of the battle ebbs and flows in a detail from* Battle of Talavera *(1819).*

Losses: Anglo-Spanish, 5,500 (British) and 1,200 (Spanish) casualties of 55,000; French, 7,300 casualties of 46,000

◁ *Corunna 1809*   *Ocaña 1809* ▷

Ocaña   19 November 1809

One of the worst defeats suffered by the Spanish during the Peninsular War, Ocaña confirmed the Spanish army's inability to wage war against the French on open ground. For the French, Ocaña was revenge for the humiliation of Bailén, opening the way for the conquest of Andalusia.

During the autumn of 1809, the Spanish once more attempted to wrest control of Madrid from the French. Two armies were formed to seize the capital, and the southerly army, commanded by General Juan Carlos Aréizaga, advanced from the Sierra Morena and caught the French by surprise. Unfortunately for the Spanish, Aréizaga failed to press his advantage, providing time for a French force, commanded by King Joseph and Marshal Soult, to march on the Spanish.

Although the Spanish possessed a numerical advantage, their inexperienced and poorly led troops were no match for their opponents. Aréizaga drew up his forces in two lines with his left anchored on the town of Ocaña; his right was left hanging on an open plain, and although protected by cavalry, it remained vulnerable.

On 19 November, after a preliminary artillery barrage, Soult ordered his infantry forward against the Spanish center. The Spanish fought hard and even began to force the French back, until Soult threw in his reserves to prop up the line. On the Spanish right, the cavalry guarding the infantry were completely overwhelmed by a massed French cavalry charge. The Spanish horsemen fled, while the well-disciplined French cavalry wheeled about and attacked the Spanish infantry in the flank, now under renewed attack from Soult's infantry and artillery. At this point, virtually the entire Spanish army broke and ran, the French securing a vast haul of prisoners and guns. **AG**

Losses: French, a few hundred dead or wounded of 34,000; Spanish, 4,000 dead or wounded, 14,000 captured of 51,000

[<] Talavera 1809   Bussaco 1810 [>]

Grand Port   22–27 August 1810

Mauritius was one of the last French overseas possessions to be captured by Britain. The Indian Ocean island was used as a base for raids on British trade into 1810, and Grand Port was the scene of a rare heavy naval defeat for Britain, with four frigates lost.

France's possessions in the Indian Ocean, then known as the Île Bonaparte and Île de France (now Réunion and Mauritius, respectively) had been used throughout the Napoleonic wars as bases from which to launch attacks on Britain's valuable trade with India and the East. After various naval skirmishes and ships captured and recaptured on each side, Île Bonaparte was taken by the British in July 1810, and the remaining fighting then focused around Île de France.

The British began with a series of attacks on Grand Port in the south of the island. Before long, a French squadron of three warships slipped into the anchorage following a brief combat. The British commander, Captain Pym, decided to attack the French, even though he knew that his ships would only be able to move in one at a time through the narrow, twisting channel.

The attack, on 22 August, turned into a complete fiasco. The one British ship that managed to get close to the French could not get most of its guns to bear and consequently was battered into wreckage. The next day, two other British ships were set on fire by their crews after becoming stuck fast, and on 27 August the last ship, which had still been trying to escape out of the bay, surrendered when French reinforcements arrived. The French success was ultimately short-lived. Stronger British forces quickly reached the area and completed the capture of the Île de France in December 1810. **DS**

Losses: British, 4 frigates, 300 dead or wounded; French, no ships lost, 150 dead or wounded

[<] Basque Roads 1809

Bussaco   27 September 1810

Fighting in Portugal in the Peninsular War, the poorly coordinated French attacks on Bussaco were easily repulsed by Wellington's forces. However, Marshal Masséna was not deterred from continuing his advance into a country devastated by Wellington's scorched-earth policy.

In September 1810, in the face of superior French numbers, Wellington and his Anglo-Portuguese army retreated to the prepared defenses in front of Lisbon known as the Lines of Torres Vedras. However, during the retreat, Wellington decided to engage the French, commanded by Marshal André Masséna. Wellington chose a steep-sided granite ridge to make his stand, and, as was his usual practice, deployed the bulk of his forces on the reverse slope in order to hide them from enemy observation and protect them from enemy fire.

The French were confused by the British dispositions, and Masséna ordered a frontal assault of infantry with little thought to effectively reconnoitering the position before going into battle. Major General Jean Reynier led the first corps into action; the troops clambered up the slopes of Bussaco hill and emerged from the early morning mist to be met by controlled fire from the British infantry. The French fought with great bravery, but were attacked on three sides and forced down the hill. Marshal Michel Ney's corps, operating on Reynier's right, fared even worse and were ambushed by the hardened troops of the Light Division and a Portuguese infantry brigade. A British bayonet charge drove them off the ridge with heavy losses. The fighting then subsided before Masséna discovered a route that outflanked the Bussaco position. Wellington retired behind the Torres Vedras Lines, leaving the French army to starve over the winter. **AG**

Losses: Anglo-Portuguese, 1,250 dead or wounded of 52,000; French, 4,500 dead or wounded of 65,000

◁ Ocaña 1809   Fuentes de Oñoro 1811 ▷

Fuentes de Oñoro   3–5 May 1811

A fierce clash in the Peninsular campaign, this battle ended the British siege of Almeida (the French garrison abandoned the fort and slipped back to French lines) and finished Masséna's command in Spain. The old campaigner was recalled in disgrace by Napoleon and replaced by Marshal Marmont.

Having driven Marshal Masséna's starving army out of Portugal, Wellington set about besieging the fortresses that guarded the frontier into Spain. In May 1810, Masséna led a force to raise the siege of Almeida but was blocked by Wellington at the strong defensive location of Fuentes de Oñoro. The first stage of the battle took place on 3 May, with a fierce artillery bombardment against the British left wing and an infantry attack on the village of Fuentes de Oñoro, the key at the center of the British line. The French responded strongly and almost forced their way through the village before a British counterattack expelled them.

The following day, there was little military action. However, on 5 May, Masséna renewed his assault, once more fighting to secure Fuentes de Oñoro but also sending a large force to overwhelm the poorly defended British right wing. The battle for the village was ferocious, with attack and counterattack following each other throughout the day; in one instance, one hundred French grenadiers were trapped by the British and killed at the point of the bayonet. On the British right wing, the French enjoyed initial success, nearly overwhelming the newly constituted 7th Division, before Wellington's reinforcements saved the day. By nightfall, the battle was effectively over. Although the French remained on the battlefield for a few days more, Masséna realized he could not break Wellington's line and so retired to Spain. **AG**

Losses: Anglo-Portuguese, 1,711 dead or wounded of 37,000; French, 2,844 dead or wounded of 48,000

◁ Bussaco 1810   Albuera 1811 ▷

Albuera 16 May 1811

In this shockingly costly engagement of the Peninsular War, a combined allied force managed to repulse Marshal Soult's advance on the city of Badajoz. A significant part of the allied success derived from a steadfast defense conducted by infantry from the often maligned Spanish army.

In May 1811, a combined Anglo-Portuguese force led by Marshal Sir William Beresford was joined by a Spanish army under General Joaquin Blake. Together they advanced to Albuera to oppose Marshal Soult's march on Badajoz. Beresford deployed his forces on a ridge on either side of the village of Albuera: the Portuguese on the left, the British in the center, and the Spanish on the right. He expected the French to strike against Albuera itself, and this seemed to be the case when French infantry advanced on the village. In fact, Soult had decided to launch his main attack on the allied right.

Beresford and Blake were slow to react, but when they saw two French divisions bearing down on four isolated Spanish infantry battalions they immediately dispatched forces to counter the attack. Blake's army contained the best troops in the Spanish army, and, despite being heavily outnumbered, the Spanish infantry held their ground until reinforcements arrived. The first British formation to arrive was Major General William Stewart's 2nd Division, which hastily deployed in line to engage the French just as a thunderstorm broke, rendering infantrymen's muskets useless. It was at this moment that the French cavalry fell upon Stewart's men, a regiment of Polish lancers virtually destroying an entire British brigade. Disaster was only averted when Major General Sir Lowry Cole's 4th Division plugged the gap in the allied line. Unable to advance further, the French retired. **AG**

Losses: Allied, 5,380 dead or wounded of 35,000; French, at least 6,000 dead or wounded of 24,000

◁ *Fuentes de Oñoro 1811*　　　　*Ciudad Rodrigo 1812* ▷

Tippecanoe 6–7 November 1811

Defeat at Fallen Timbers and the subsequent treaties did not end American Indian resistance to U.S. expansion into the Ohio Valley. The U.S. victory broke Tecumseh's power and ended the threat of an Indian confederation. Tecumseh took his followers to join the British in Canada.

Shawnee chief Tecumseh and his brother, "The Prophet," worked to build a confederation of tribes, from Michigan to Georgia, to resist settlers. Indian attacks in the Indiana Territory persisted despite conferences with Tecumseh and warnings by Governor William Henry Harrison.

During the summer of 1811, Harrison assembled a force of 950 territorial militia and regular infantry. In September, he marched north from Vincennes up the Wabash River toward Prophetstown, Tecumseh's main village near the Tippecanoe River. Tecumseh was absent, but on 6 November, a delegation from The Prophet appeared and arranged a conference for the next day. Harrison camped his men on a small rise of ground near the village. Wary of a trick, he placed them into a rectangular defensive formation with orders to remain on full alert. Ammunition was distributed, sentries posted, and bayonets fixed.

At about 4:00 AM on 7 November, hundreds of Indians attacked the north end of the camp, then all sides. The battle lasted more than two hours with hand-to-hand fighting in the dark. Some warriors rushed in seeking to kill Harrison, but missed him. Three times the Indians charged. Harrison, fighting on horseback at the front lines, led his small reserve to repulse each attack. At dawn, as the Indians fell back to regroup, Harrison counterattacked with the regulars and militia. Taken by surprise, the Indians scattered, hotly pursued by the mounted troops. The village and crops were destroyed. **RB**

Losses: U.S., 66 dead, 151 wounded; American Indian, more than 100 dead or wounded

◁ *Fallen Timbers 1794*　　　　*Thames River 1813* ▷

Ciudad Rodrigo   7–20 January 1812

The capture of Ciudad Rodrigo not only gained the French army's siege train for the British but also opened up the northern gateway from Portugal into Spain. This allowed Wellington to move south to besiege Badajoz, which guarded the other major route into Spain.

When Wellington heard news that the French forces facing him directly had withdrawn, he immediately went to besiege Ciudad Rodrigo. In bitterly cold weather, Wellington arrived at the gates of the fortress on 7 January 1812. The following day, his troops seized the Grand Tesson, a redoubt that dominated the position. After this initial engagement, siege work began in earnest.

Ciudad Rodrigo was not a particularly powerful fortress, and the French garrison of around 2,000 men was not sufficient to man the walls. Wellington possessed a small but useful siege train, and his heavy guns opened up two breaches in the city walls, while his sappers dug assault trenches to protect the attacking force. Fearful that he might have to raise the siege if a French relieving army arrived, Wellington ordered the attack for the evening of 19 January.

Major General Thomas Picton's 3rd Division assaulted the "greater" breach and Major General Robert Crauford's Light Division fought its way through the "lesser" breach. Although French guns and booby traps caused heavy casualties—including the loss of Crauford, who was mortally wounded—the British clambered their way up the shattered walls of the two breaches and successfully stormed the city. As was the tradition of the day, the attacking troops comprehensively looted the town, downing copious amounts of alcohol and refusing to obey their officers' orders. **AG**

Losses: British, 1,700 dead or wounded of 10,700; French, 530 dead or wounded, 1,460 captured of 2,000

◁ Albuera 1811   Badajoz 1812 ▷

Badajoz   16 March–6 April 1812

Of the many sieges that characterized the war in the Iberian peninsula, Badajoz stands out for the extraordinary intensity of the fighting on both sides and for the dreadful savagery of the British soldiers after the siege, who indulged in an orgy of destruction within the "liberated" city.

In order to secure their lines of communication into Spain, the British and Portuguese, led by Wellington, advanced on the French-held fortress of Badajoz. The strong French garrison was commanded by the determined and resourceful Major General Armand Philippon, who, after withstanding a British siege in 1811, had greatly reinforced the already strong defenses of the city.

On 16 March, Badajoz was invested by Wellington's troops; trenches were dug as siege artillery was brought up to pound the major outworks protecting the city walls. The French were active in disrupting the Anglo-Portuguese operations, although a major sortie on 19 March was firmly repulsed. On 25 March, the Picurina redoubt was stormed, thereby providing a platform for the British heavy guns to smash gaps in the main walls.

By 6 April, two major breaches had been established, with a smaller, subsidiary breach made in the walls of the citadel. That evening, the Light Division and 4th Division stormed the two main breaches with the greatest determination; despite their best efforts, the attackers were held by the French. Wellington was about to abandon the assault when news reached him that the 3rd Division had scaled the citadel and entered the city. The French garrison retired to the San Vincente bastion and surrendered the following day. British troops went on the rampage for the next three days; when order was restored as many as 4,000 civilians had been killed. **AG**

Losses: Anglo-Portuguese, 4,800 dead or wounded of 27,000; French, 1,500 dead or wounded, 3,500 captured of 5,000

◁ Ciudad Rodrigo 1812   Salamanca 1812 ▷

 Storming of Ciudad Rodrigo, January 19th, 1812, *an illustration of the battle by an unknown artist.*

Salamanca   22 July 1812

A turning point in the Peninsular War, the Battle of Salamanca has been hailed as Wellington's masterpiece. Although the French army was able to escape total destruction, the battle demonstrated that the British commander was more than just a defensive general and could conduct offensive operations with equal ability.

In the spring of 1812, Wellington and his predominantly Anglo-Portuguese army—supported by Spanish units—moved deeper into Spain, to be engaged by a French army under Marshal Auguste Marmont. Both sides tried to outmaneuver the other, each commander hoping to exploit a mistake by his opposite number. Advancing in line almost parallel to Wellington's forces, Marmont pushed forward to the south of the city of Salamanca, hoping to sever Wellington's line of communications to Portugal. Marmont mistakenly believed that Wellington was preparing to retreat and hurried his divisions forward; in so doing he dangerously overextended them. Wellington, with a superb eye for reading a battlefield, saw his opportunity and, on the afternoon of 22 July, he ordered his troops to pounce on the French.

Thomières's force, the lead formation in the French line, was set upon by the British 3rd Division; the French commander was killed and his men routed. General Maucune, the commander of the next French division, saw British cavalry in the area and ordered his troops to form square, the appropriate formation in the circumstances. However, the cavalry were shielding the British 5th Division, whose sustained infantry fire broke the French squares, which were charged by General John le Marchant's Heavy Brigade and dispersed. Marchant then turned on Brenier's troops, but was killed in the

attack. Salamanca was a high point for the British cavalry arm and one of the few engagements where it played a significant part in the outcome of the battle.

To make matters worse for the French, Marmont and his second in command were hit by artillery fire and badly wounded when the British infantry and cavalry smashed into the French line. This left their forces leaderless during a critical phase of the battle. Command passed to General Bertrand Clausel, who displayed the traditional skills of a battle-hardened French divisional commander, steadying the line and beating off an allied attack. Heartened by this turn of events, Clausel initiated a counterattack with his own division and that of Bonet. However, the Anglo-Portuguese forward momentum was too strong and the outnumbered French were driven back.

Clausel realized that the battle was lost and set about organizing a retreat, calling upon the three divisions of

Ferry, Sarrut, and Foy—who had so far played little part in the battle—to cover the French withdrawal. Ferry's division was the first into action and had to withstand the full weight of Wellington's advance. Despite determined resistance, the division eventually broke when its commander was killed. As darkness fell, the British advance began to lose impetus, allowing Foy's division, the last formation in the French line, to protect the retreating French troops from further harassment. With Marmont's army in full retreat, Wellington was able to march into Madrid. Even though he was subsequently forced to withdraw from the city, it was a significant humiliation for the Bonaparte regime in Spain. **AG**

Losses: Allied, 5,000 casualties of 52,000; French, 6,000 dead or wounded, 7,000 captured of 50,000

◁ *Badajoz 1812*   *Vitoria 1813* ▷

Smolensk   16–18 August 1812

When Napoleon invaded Russia in June 1812, he led a multinational army of more than half a million soldiers. He needed a rapid and decisive victory, but although victorious at Smolensk, he was unable to destroy Russian resistance. This meant the campaign would continue deeper into Russian territory.

Napoleon's aim was the strategic envelopment of the Russian army in the first few weeks of the campaign. However, the heavily outnumbered Russians pulled back rather than risk all in a single battle. Napoleon hoped they would be forced to stand and fight at Smolensk, one of Russia's most sacred cities. In this he was correct; Alexander and the Russian people insisted that the city must not be surrendered tamely.

Two French columns crossed the River Dnieper at night, and a forced march took them within 30 miles (48 km) of Smolensk before they met any resistance. However, a stubborn rearguard action allowed the Russians time to man the rather aged and dilapidated city defenses, and in the suburbs a confused battle raged as the French attempted to take the city by storm.

French artillery pounded much of the city to burning ruins, but the Russian infantry defended their positions with a grim tenacity that stunned the French. Having brought the enemy to battle, Napoleon intended to encircle them. However, the Russian commanders feared such a move and ordered a withdrawal during the night. Again the stubbornness of the rearguard proved vital; ten regiments fought determinedly as the first of Napoleon's troops (largely Portuguese and German conscripts) broke into the city. The Russians retreated over the river and burned the bridges behind them. The possession of burned ruins was all that Napoleon had achieved. **JS**

Losses: Russian, 12,000 to 14,000 dead or wounded of 125,000; French, 10,00 dead or wounded of 185,000

[<] *Wagram 1809*   *Borodino 1812* [>]

The Battle of Smolensk,1812, *in which the city suffers damage from both French and Russian forces.* ⬆

USS *Constitution* and HMS *Guerriere* 19 August 1812

The United States declared war on Great Britain on 18 June 1812 in response to accumulated grievances against the British, including a semiblockade of U.S. ports. Among the British warships prowling the U.S. coast was the thirty-eight-gun frigate HMS *Guerriere* under Captain James R. Dacres.

Dacres had no respect for the small U.S. Navy, and he was looking for action. About 3:00 PM on 19 August, some 400 miles (644 km) southeast of Halifax, he spotted a lone U.S. warship approaching with the wind from the north. It was the larger and more heavily armed forty-four-gun frigate *Constitution* under Captain Isaac Hull. As was customary, both ships carried more cannon than their official rating (*Constitution* fifty-four guns, *Guerriere* forty-nine) especially the heavy, short-range carronade.

Dacres fired twice at long range with no effect. Hull waited until he was closer before firing a reply. Marines and marksmen in the rigging of both vessels fired muskets at the crews and officers on deck. As the ships exchanged broadsides, one of Hull's discharges knocked *Guerriere's* mizzenmast overboard, causing the ships to collide briefly. More close-range broadsides were fired as Hull maneuvered *Constitution* to the other side and blasted again.

His guns damaged *Guerriere's* hull and mainmast, which collapsed and brought the ships together again. Before either captain could order boarders away, the ships parted. As *Guerriere's* crew worked to clear the debris, Hull approached ready to rake *Guerriere's* deck with grapeshot. Wounded, unable to control his ship, and with the ship's guns entangled and awash, Dacres consulted his officers. They agreed he should spare further losses, and he struck the colors. **RB**

Losses: U.S., 9 dead, 13 wounded of 476; British, 21 dead, 57 wounded of 263

Fort George 1813 ▶

⬆ Naval Duel between the *Constitution* and *Guerriere, a colored lithograph from 1893.*

Borodino 7 September 1812

After his victory at Smolensk, Napoleon tried once more to destroy the Russian army. At Borodino, he was again victorious, but at the cost of at least 30,000 casualties, and the Russians evaded annihilation for the second time. The road to Moscow was left open, but the war went on.

After Smolensk, Napoleon faced a difficult decision: either to stay in the city—or even retreat to Polish territory for the winter—or advance toward Moscow and immediately gain the complete victory he needed. The latter option risked a winter campaign for which his army was ill-equipped. Instinctively, he always preferred to pursue and destroy a beaten foe; he therefore chose to march. However, while he had been hesitating, the Russians had appointed the aged General Kutuzov to supreme command with orders to defend Moscow.

Kutuzov chose to fight behind the Kalatsha River, across a 5-mile (8 km) front situated in hilly terrain suitable for the defense, and which his troops labored hard to make even more formidable by constructing earthworks and entrenchments. The key to the defense was the Great Redoubt, which was strongly garrisoned and whose artillery was positioned to devastate French attacks. The Russian southern flank was comparatively weak, and an attack here could force the Russians to retreat.

Napoleon did not want a retreat; he wanted a total victory. The French launched a series of frontal attacks, which showed little subtlety—it was a simple matter of brute force. Artillery caused huge losses on both sides, but the tenacity of the Russian infantry was again the Russian army's greatest strength. When forced out of the villages of Utitsa and Borodino, the Russians launched furious counterattacks. If counterattacks proved impossible, they

withdrew in good order to new positions, refusing to be panicked by repeated cavalry charges. The French were disadvantaged by the mistakes of their senior officers; their artillery was sited out of range of the Russians and had to be relocated in the middle of the battle, leaving troops unnecessarily exposed. When the French finally broke into the Great Redoubt, four Russian regiments fought to the last. It seemed that at last the Russians were breaking, and a final effort might turn retreat into a rout. However, a desperate counterattack by the Russian cavalry prevented the French from exploiting their success. After twelve hours of continuous combat, with more and more French reserves being thrown in without much effect—and having fired 90,000 artillery rounds and 2,000,000 musket shots—the French had advanced just 1 mile (1.6 km). The only uncommitted troops were the Imperial Guards, which Napoleon refused to send in.

Mutual exhaustion brought an end to the fighting, and during the night Kutuzov withdrew in good order. Once again, Napoleon had failed to destroy his enemy. The way to Moscow was clear, and seven days later Napoleon's army entered the city. Still the Russians refused to submit; indeed, the character of the war had developed a religious fervor among the Russian people. The Russian armies were growing stronger every day, while the French army was suffering severely from attrition, battle casualties, disease, desertion, and the need to garrison territory. All Napoleon had gained was a salient 350 miles (563 km), deep into enemy territory, which was steadily becoming more vulnerable. **JS**

Losses: Russian, 44,000 dead or wounded of 120,000; French, 30,000–50,000 dead or wounded of 131,000

◁ *Smolensk 1812*　　　*Maloyaroslavets 1812* ▷

Maloyaroslavets 24 October 1812

The French retreat from Moscow in 1812 was a catastrophe for Napoleon. The engagement at Maloyaroslavets with Russian forces shadowing his withdrawal was technically his victory, but it closed his best escape route. The battle played a significant role in the destruction of the French army.

After taking Moscow, large parts of which were burned, Napoleon tarried for several weeks waiting for the Russians to submit. By the time he accepted that this was not going to happen, and he ordered a retreat, little time was left before winter closed in. He chose to march down the Kaluga road and retreat along rich territory, but his troops were wounded and laden down with loot; progress was painfully slow. However, the Russian commander, Kutuzov, was also very slow in his pursuit.

The French arrived at Maloyaroslavets, on the right bank of the Luzha River, and took it easily. However, Russian forces were approaching, and—in a surprise night attack—the French were expelled. Russian artillery was positioned to cover the vital bridges, and the next morning a desperate battle was fought over the town. It took the artillery of an entire French corps to silence the Russian guns pouring fire on the bridges. Italian conscripts who showed determination and courage bore the brunt of the fighting, and they took the town at bayonet point quickly, but lost it again to a counterattack.

The town changed hands several times during the morning, and seven French generals were killed in bitter fighting. The French took the town, but Russian guns still controlled the crossings over the Luzha River. The only line of retreat left to the French was through the territory that had been ravaged during their advance. **JS**

Losses: Russian, 6,000 dead or wounded of 25,000; French, more than 4,000 dead or wounded of 20,000

◁ Borodino 1812

Berezina 1812 ▷

Berezina 27–28 November 1812

The agony of the retreat from Moscow reduced Napoleon's Grande Armée to a shadow of its former greatness. However, Napoleon pulled off an extraordinary feat of arms to escape the pursuing Russians at Berezina. He survived to fight again, but most of his troops did not.

In the freezing retreat from Moscow, the French army began to disintegrate. Napoleon still led some 90,000 men, but nearly half of these were stragglers—men whose regiments had collapsed, or who had abandoned their weapons, or who had no fighting potential and were clinging to the shirttails of the army for fear of marauding Cossacks.

As they approached the River Berezina, they found the Russians holding Berezina town and the vital bridges in force. General Kutuzov's army was approaching from the rear, and disaster seemed at hand. But Kutuzov saw no point in spending lives when the winter was destroying the French anyway, so his pursuit was leisurely. Salvation came when the French cavalry located a ford. Launching diversionary movements to the south, Napoleon was able to get enough troops across the river to cover his engineers while they worked in the freezing water to build two pontoon bridges. A bridgehead was established before the Russians realized French intentions. In bitter fighting, the French held on to their bridgehead, while the rearguard fought to fend off Kutuzov's belated assault. French cavalry launched desperate charges to allow the last of the rearguard to escape, but no thought had been given to evacuating the stragglers, who were abandoned. As the hysterical mob fought to get across the bridges, Napoleon ordered them destroyed. Thousands perished in the crush, drowned, or were left to the Cossacks. **JS**

Losses: French, up to 55,000 dead, wounded, or missing of 89,000; Russian, 15,000–20,000 dead or wounded of 64,000

◁ Maloyaroslavets 1812

Bautzen 1813 ▷

San Lorenzo February 1813

Really no more than a skirmish, the encounter at San Lorenzo was to loom large in the Latin American imagination. It was here that, in the heat of the battle, the great freedom fighter San Martín was saved by the self-sacrificing heroism of one of his men.

The Battle of San Lorenzo was fought by the monastery that stood above the Paraná River, in Santa Fe province. At this time, the Spanish still claimed authority over the whole of Argentina. An independence movement had grown among the colonists, however; it was especially strong among the northern provinces (including those that were subsequently to go their separate way as Uruguay).

In February 1813, a flotilla of eleven ships sailed up the Paraná River, carrying Spanish soldiers and their royal supporters. Their intention was to attack rebel positions in the open country along its banks. The bulk of the trained soldiers were marines. This, the rebel commander José de San Martín realized, set them at a disadvantage against his mounted grenadiers, drawn from the wild *gauchos* (cowboys) of the Pampas.

From the monastery's bell tower, San Martín saw the enemy drop anchor, so he was ready when some 200 troops came ashore and set off uphill. Although outnumbered, his horsemen swept down upon them with the advantage of surprise. The Spanish were caught unprepared. A routine victory was won with an epic flourish after San Martín's horse was shot from under him; as it fell, it trapped his leg and pinned him down. As the Spanish closed in for the kill, Sergeant Juan Bautista Cabral strode into the thick of the throng and freed his commander. San Martín was saved, but Cabral was killed. **MK**

Losses: Spanish, 40; Argentinian, 15

Fort George 25–27 May 1813

U.S. war strategy in 1812 was a four-prong invasion against key Canadian towns and forts. Of special interest were those on the Niagara River, but other battles diverted U.S. forces until the spring of 1813. In April, the Americans crossed the river to raid York, capital of Upper Canada.

The successful but costly amphibious raid on York to burn the shipyard encouraged Major General Henry Dearborn to plan more thrusts into Canada. Men and equipment for his Army of the North were assembled at camps along the Niagara River until more than 4,000 men, many newly recruited regulars, had gathered. Among the arrivals was Winfield Scott, a young, energetic artillery colonel who was appointed as Dearborn's adjutant general (chief of staff). Scott drew up a detailed plan for a 2,500-man joint Army-Navy operation against Fort George.

The fort, located at the mouth of the Niagara on Lake Ontario's south shore, was defended by British Brigadier General John Vincent with 1,100 British troops and Canadian militia. A two-day, cross-river bombardment of the fort was followed on the foggy morning of 27 May by the landing of the first assault wave led by Scott. Resistance was met at the beachhead, but with the help of cannon fire from the Navy ships and the arrival of reinforcements, the British and Canadians were forced back. When a British counterattack failed, Vincent abandoned the fort and withdrew to conserve his outnumbered forces. Fuses were set to blow up the powder magazines in the fort. Scott dashed into the fort just as one of the magazines exploded. He was thrown off his horse, breaking a collarbone, but recovered and extinguished the other fuses. **RB**

Losses: U.S., 39 dead, 111 wounded; British and Canadian, 52 dead, 44 wounded, 262 captured

Chacabuco 1817 >

< *USS* Constitution *and HMS* Guerriere *1812* Chesapeake *1813* >

Bautzen   20–21 May 1813

Despite the catastrophe he had suffered in Russia in 1812, Napoleon was still a formidable force. Faced with a hostile alliance that included Russia, Prussia, Austria, and Sweden, he raised new armies and managed to inflict painful defeats, although he would never regain the strategic initiative.

A Russo-Prussian force had already been mauled by Napoleon at Lutzen when it withdrew and made a stand behind the Elbe River. The force occupied a strong position, with a series of fortified ridges. Napoleon intended a frontal attack with three corps to pin down the enemy and inflict heavy losses, while a fourth corps under Marshal Ney would outflank the enemy right wing and take the village of Hochkirk to their rear. With retreat cut off, the enemy could only draw back to the frontier of neutral Austria, where they must either be destroyed or agree to surrender.

However, Ney, who never seems to have understood his role in the battle, squandered much of the first day getting into position. During that time the French launched furious attacks on Russo-Prussian lines. With great courage, engineers built bridges across the Spree River under intense artillery fire. The infantry attacked and by evening had taken the forward positions. The Russo-Prussian forces felt under such pressure that they ignored the threat from Ney; the battle, they believed, would be decided in the center. The next dawn Ney was in position, but instead of racing toward Hochkirk, he insisted on expending time and lives in attacking the unimportant village of Preititz, and his chance was lost. With it, Napoleon's chance of completely destroying his enemies vanished. His enemies withdrew during the evening, leaving the French too weary to pursue. **JS**

> *"The Allies escaped destruction because Ney . . . delivered the final charge in the wrong direction."*
>
> G. E. Rothenberg, Art of Warfare in the Age of Napoleon

⬆ *French (left) and Prussian infantry clash behind Russian cavalry at Bautzen, in a detail from a nineteenth-century etching.*

Losses: French, 20,000 dead and wounded of 100,000; Prussian and Russian, 20,000 dead and wounded of 96,000

◁ Berezina 1812   Leipzig 1813 ▷

Chesapeake 1 June 1813

From 1812, American strategy dictated that naval operations should focus mainly on attacking British merchant ships. Congress kept a tight string on the U.S. Navy's purse. Many American warships were refurbished older vessels, such as the fifty-cannon small frigate USS *Chesapeake*.

The *Chesapeake* was an unlucky ship, having suffered a shameful search and surrender to HMS *Leopard* in 1807. Thus her new commander, Captain James Lawrence, had trouble recruiting an experienced crew and officers. *Chesapeake*'s luck did not change when he sailed her out of Boston Harbor on 1 June. Eighteen miles (29 km) out at sea waited HMS *Shannon*, a fifty-two-cannon British frigate of equal size. Her experienced captain, Philip V. Broke, was a gunnery expert, and unlike many captains he drilled his guns crews daily for speed and accuracy. He had introduced several gunnery innovations and was eager to prove his crew against an American ship.

At about 5:50 PM, without hesitation, the two ships pulled close alongside each other and opened fire. They pounded each other with broadsides, and heavy damage was inflicted to the hulls of both ships. As shells and splinters flew, Lawrence was mortally wounded and several of his officers were killed or wounded. Some of the inexperienced American gun crews deserted their stations under the accurate British fire.

As they maneuvered, *Shannon*'s anchor snagged *Chesapeake*, drawing the ships closer. Broke's crew tied the ships together and he led a boarding party onto the American deck, where hand-to-hand fighting took place for several minutes. The American Marines were the last to be overcome. Fifteen minutes after the battle started, the American colors were struck. **RB**

Losses: U.S., 61 dead, 85 wounded of 379; British, 33 dead, 50 wounded of 330

◁ Fort George 1813 Lake Erie 1813 ▷

Vitoria 21 June 1813

Although Wellington was deeply frustrated that the bulk of the French army escaped from his trap at Vitoria, the battle signaled the end of Napoleonic Spain. With King Joseph Bonaparte retreating over the Pyrenees, Wellington was able to make preparation for an invasion of France itself.

During their 1813 campaign, Wellington's Allied army advanced across Spain, harrying a French army commanded by King Joseph and his military adviser, Marshal Jean-Baptiste Jourdan. The French decided to regroup their forces and adopt a defensive position along the valley of the Zadorra River (running east–west by the city of Vitoria). Wellington divided his army into four columns; the first under Lieutenant General Sir Rowland Hill was to press along the valley and engage the enemy's front, while the other three were to outflank the French right from the north.

The two central Allied columns, led by Wellington and Lieutenant General Lord Dalhousie, engaged the French right flank with some success; after crossing the Zadorra they began to push the French back toward Vitoria. As Allied pressure mounted, the French retreat degenerated into a rout. The fourth British column, under Lieutenant General Sir Thomas Graham, was to advance directly on Vitoria from the north—from behind the main French army—and cut the French line of retreat, but Graham's lack of drive provided an opportunity for General Honoré Reille to set up a blocking force. The bulk of the French Army thus escaped along the road to Salvatierra.

The French left behind military equipment, including all but one of Joseph's 152 guns, and an extraordinary store of booty that the Allied soldiers began to plunder—at the expense of pursuing the retreating French. **AG**

Losses: Allied, 5,000 casualties of 75,000; French, 8,000 casualties of 57,000

◁ Salamanca 1812 Toulouse 1814 ▷

Lake Erie (Put-in-Bay)   10 September 1813

Control of two of the Great Lakes—Ontario and Erie—was vital to successful operations along the U.S.-Canadian border by either side. In 1813 American and British commanders were in a naval arms race to build and arm squadrons of vessels that could dominate those two bodies of water.

By August an American fleet of ten ships under Commodore Oliver Hazard Perry had formed around the twin twenty-gun brigs USS *Lawrence* and *Niagara*. Perry established a base at Put-in-Bay on Lake Erie while Royal Navy Captain Robert H. Barclay prepared his ships, the largest of which was HMS *Queen Charlotte* (seventeen guns). On 10 September, at 11:45 AM, the two fleets met outside the bay.

Barclay, sailing with six ships, planned to keep his distance and use long-range cannon. Perry, with nine ships, was armed with shorter-range but heavier carronades and so wanted a close-in fight. He sailed within short range of Barclay's ships and both fleets exchanged broadsides. Perry, on board *Lawrence*, planned to engage *Queen Charlotte* while *Niagara* handled HMS *Detroit* (eleven guns), but *Niagara* held back, leaving Perry to fight *Detroit*. He battled both British ships for over two hours while the two fleets fired away at each other.

By 2:30 PM the two British ships were badly damaged, but *Lawrence* was sinking. Perry took a small boat, his battle flag, and his pennant, and rowed to *Niagara* where he took command and sailed back into battle. Barclay was wounded. As *Detroit* and *Queen Charlotte* maneuvered to meet Perry, they became entangled. *Niagara* raked the *Detroit* at close range and broke the line of British ships. Thirty minutes later, *Detroit* and *Queen Charlotte* surrendered and the others followed. **RB**

Losses: U.S., 27 dead, 96 wounded; British and Canadian, 41 dead, 94 wounded

◁ Chesapeake *1813*   Thames River *1813* ▷

Commodore Perry transfers to Niagara, in an 1873 painting by William Henry Powell. ⬆

Thames River   5 October 1813

The American naval victory on Lake Erie, and failure of British and Indian attacks against forts in Ohio, forced Major General Henry Proctor to withdraw his forces to his base at Fort Malden in Canada. The American North Western Army under Major General William Henry Harrison soon followed.

When 4,000 Americans landed near Fort Malden, Proctor retreated up the Thames River. With him was the Indian chief Tecumseh and his followers. On 1 October Harrison with another 3,500 men crossed the Detroit River and invaded Canada. His force consisted of regulars, militia, and a mounted regiment of Kentucky volunteers commanded by Colonel Richard Johnson. Johnson's mounted troops led the way in pursuit of Proctor.

The British march was slowed by supply boats and wagons that were soon abandoned. A brief skirmish with Tecumseh was unsuccessful in delaying Harrison. Proctor finally chose a defensive position along the Thames. He put his infantry regiment (41st Foot) with a cannon on the left, between the road and the river, while Tecumseh and his Indians formed on the right, near a swamp. Johnson, seeing that the 41st was loosely deployed and vulnerable to a mounted assault, convinced a skeptical Harrison to let his regiment charge. Splitting his men into two battalions, Johnson sent one battalion straight up the road into the infantry while he took the other through a wooded area to hit the Indians' flank. The 41st was overrun by the mounted charge and surrendered, but Johnson's battalion met brush too thick for horses. Kentuckians dismounted for fierce hand-to-hand fighting with the Indians, during which Tecumseh was killed. Outflanked, the Indians scattered into the woods. Fighting was over in thirty minutes, but Proctor and his staff escaped. **RB**

Losses: U.S., 15 dead, 30 wounded; British (total campaign), 634 dead or captured; American Indian, 33 dead

◁ *Lake Erie* 1813   *Horseshoe Bend* 1814 ▷

⬆ *A nineteenth-century depiction of Shawnee chief Tecumseh being shot during the Battle of Thames River.*

Leipzig 16–19 October 1813

In the Battle of Leipzig, also known as the Battle of the Nations, Napoleon suffered a crushing defeat from which he never recovered. Pitting France against a grand coalition that included Russia, Prussia, Austria, and Sweden, it was the largest battle in European history before World War I.

Napoleon was determined to exploit his victory at Bautzen and regain the strategic initiative. But the alliance against him was growing, and after the terrible losses in cavalry he had suffered in Russia the previous year he lacked the mobility to locate and defeat his enemies separately. With much of Germany on the brink of revolt, his armies hungry and dispirited, he had no choice but to withdraw across the Elbe River and concentrate his forces at Leipzig. This suited the Allies, who intended to cut his lines of communication from the Rhine.

As huge forces converged, Napoleon took up strong defensive positions in the suburbs and the numerous towns and villages around the city. The rolling terrain was

> *"Had I possessed 30,000 artillery rounds at Leipzig on the evening of 18 October, today I would be master of the world."* Napoleon

suited for defense and there was plentiful open country for cavalry maneuver. Napoleon's plan was to hold off the Swedish and Prussian forces until he destroyed the Russians and Austrians. But Prussia's Marshal von Blücher arrived earlier than anticipated and occupied ground to the north, across Napoleon's planned line of outflanking attack on the Austrians and Russians.

On 16 October four columns of Austrians and Russians advanced on the French from three directions under the cover of mist, but they were poorly coordinated, and the

French held on all fronts, steadily pushing them back. There was an opportunity here for Napoleon to launch a deadly counterstroke and smash them, but he found himself unable to assemble sufficient troops to launch a fatal attack. The arrival of Austrian reserves allowed the columns to withdraw, mauled but unbroken. Throughout the day attack and counterattack meant that positions changed hands repeatedly. Both sides deployed massed artillery, and the infantry suffered terrible casualties as a result. While the day ended in a stalemate, it was one that favored the Allies, whose strength was growing steadily with the arrival of fresh troops.

Napoleon could have ordered a retreat then, but hesitated in the hope of his enemies making some sort of fatal error. But they did not; instead, they managed to improve the coordination of their attacks, landing heavy blows across widely separated parts of the line, spreading out French reserves and weakening them everywhere. By the time orders were given to build a bridge for an orderly withdrawal, the eastern sector was under such pressure that the Imperial Guard had to stabilize the line.

Napoleon then suffered the betrayal of some of his Saxon troops and the situation became critical, with French troops pushed back into Leipzig's suburbs, running short of ammunition and with mounting casualties. A strong rearguard fought a house-by-house battle as the main army began its withdrawal. It seemed that the French would make good their escape, and Napoleon would pull off a feat equal to Berezina, when disaster struck. An officer left in charge of the demolition charges on the bridges abandoned his post, leaving the fuses in the hands of a corporal, who panicked and lit them while the bridge was still crammed with troops. The rearguard and many others were left trapped. **JS**

Losses: French, 73,000 dead, wounded, or captured of 195,000; Allied, 54,000 dead or wounded of 365,000

◁ *Bautzen 1813*   *La Rothière 1814* ▷

A nineteenth-century map of the Battle of Leipzig charts positions of French and Allied forces around the city.

Breitenfeld

Wetteritzsch

Gr. Wetteritzsch

Lindenthal

Mockern

Gohlis

Reudnitz

Mölkau

Mickau

Neutzscha

S. Tecla

Grasdorf

Taucha

Plosti

Panitsch

Eutritzsch

Heiter Blick

Rte de Wurtzen

Paunsdorf

Sellerhausen

Sommerfeld

Luppe R.

Möckern

Gohlis

Hallesdorf

LEIPSIG

Faubourg de Ranstadt

Kohlgaerten

Crottendorf

Thonberg

Reudnitz

Stotteritz

Baalsdorf

Zweinaundorf

Hirschfeld

Lindenau

Schleissig

Kl. Zschocher

Gr. Zschocher

Probstheide

Zuckelhausen

Holzhausen

Tuterie

Meusdorf

Dosen

Mark Kleberg

Wachau

Liebertwolkwitz

Gr. Possna

Seyfartshayn

Knauthayn

Zaulsch

Zobigker

Gaschwitz

Ostewitz

Auenhayn

Grosbern

Cossa

Gohren

Magdeborn

Zwenkau

Pleisse R.

Rte d'Altenburg

Borna

La Rothière 1 February 1814

After their victory at Leipzig the Allies invaded France. Napoleon remained convinced he could recover from his reverses, fighting a brilliant defensive campaign against mounting odds. But his desperately war-weary nation began to crack after yet another defeat at La Rothière.

Napoleon and his weary and bedraggled army faced a huge coalition intending to converge on Paris. He knew he had to prevent his enemies from joining forces and defeat them separately but, despite his victory over the Prussians at Brienne, they had united by the time his pursuit caught up at La Rothière.

Napoleon was now heavily outnumbered, but a blizzard prevented him from realizing his peril. Thinking he was facing merely a screening force, he attacked, and his army was fully committed to battle before the size of the enemy forces became clear. The French enjoyed some successes, and the cavalry attacked the Russian artillery—the guns were elevated too high and many gunners were killed. But Russian cavalry counterattacked and a desperate cavalry melee ensued.

Meanwhile the French infantry stood at La Rothière, blinded by the blizzard and mercilessly pounded by Allied artillery. The Russian infantry advanced on them, seemingly indifferent to the hail of fire they met. Driven from the village, the French counterattacked and retook it, but a furious hand-to-hand battle in the surrounding woods threatened to engulf them. They were saved from disaster when Würtemburg cavalry mistook their Bavarian allies for Frenchmen and attacked. This allowed Napoleon to withdraw in good order, the Imperial Guard providing a stubborn rearguard. However, Napoleon's defeat on home soil was a devastating blow to French morale. **JS**

Losses: French, 6,000 dead and wounded of 40,000; Allied, 6,000 dead and wounded of 110,000

◁ Leipzig 1813

Arcis-sur-Aube 1814 ▷

Arcis-sur-Aube 20–21 March 1814

This was the last major battle before Napoleon was forced to abdicate his imperial throne and exiled to the island of Elba. Though driven from the field, he evaded destruction and was ready to fight on. However, his own officials had had enough and opened surrender negotiations behind his back.

Despite his defeat at La Rothière, Napoleon was still convinced he could prevail. His intention was a sudden dash to the Marne River, where he would collect the large garrisons at Metz and Verdun to replenish his ranks, before threatening the Allied rear. He advanced on Arcis-sur-Aube, believing it lightly held, but the Austrian commander, Marshal Schwarzenberg, had massed his army in the area for an offensive.

The French were stunned at the mass of cavalry they faced, and were soon under intense pressure. Napoleon, possibly seeking an honorable death in preference to defeat, showed great courage in personally leading the Imperial Guard into battle. With great difficulty the French prevailed, and Napoleon, still convinced he had defeated merely the Austrian rearguard, ordered a pursuit the next day. But Schwarzenberg, who spent the night deploying his much superior force into a great arc beyond the sight of the French, only hesitated to attack for fear of a trap.

When the French advanced they were appalled to see the size of the army they faced. Napoleon quickly grasped the danger and ordered a retreat. The determination of his rearguard, coupled with Schwarzenberg's continuing hesitation, allowed the French to withdraw in good order across the Aube River over two bridges, which were then destroyed. But with a Prussian army approaching Paris, it was obvious to all but Napoleon that the end was approaching. He was forced to abdicate on 6 April. **JS**

Losses: French, 3,000 dead and wounded of 28,000; Austrian, 4,000 dead and wounded of 80,000

◁ La Rothière 1814

Ligny and Quatre Bras 1815 ▷

Napoleon arrives at the island of Elba in April 1814 after his forced abdication. ➡

Horseshoe Bend   27 March 1814

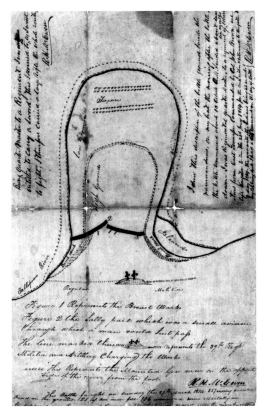

Chief Tecumseh's death did not end conflict between the United States and American Indian tribes. In the southeastern Mississippi Territory, hostile Creeks known as Red Sticks raided settlers, sparking an intratribal war and threatening an alliance with the pro-British Spanish in Florida.

Unable to divert troops from the Canadian campaigns, the United States mobilized territorial militia to attack the Red Sticks. In the fall of 1813, multiple columns of militia were sent into hostile territory with meager results. There were several fights and Indian towns burned, but the Red Sticks defiantly held out. In early 1814 Major General Andrew Jackson's Tennessee militia were reinforced by the regular 39th Infantry Regiment and fresh militia, and these were trained into a disciplined force of 2,700.

On 27 March Jackson's force plus allied Cherokee and "White Stick" Creek warriors surrounded the Red Stick stronghold of Tohopeka. The village was located inside a bend of the Tallapoosa River, with the river on three sides and a strong earth-and-timber breastwork on the fourth. Colonel John Coffee's militia and Indian allies occupied the riverbank opposite the village. Jackson's offer to evacuate the women and children was refused and he began a bombardment by his two small field guns. They did little damage to the earthwork but created a diversion during which Coffee's men took Red Stick canoes and crossed the river to attack the rear of the village.

Jackson then ordered the regulars and militia to charge. They stormed over the breastworks using bayonets and clubbed muskets. The Red Sticks made a desperate stand but were crushed in a five-hour hand-to-hand battle through the burning village. **RB**

> *"If I had known that Jackson would drive us from our homes, I would have killed him."*
>
> Cherokee Chief Junaluska, who aided Jackson in battle

A diagram of Horseshoe Bend drawn by R. H. McEwen, a quartermaster who fought in the battle.

Losses: U.S., 108 dead, 24 wounded; American Indian allies, 23 dead, 46 wounded; Red Stick, 557 dead, 500 captured

◀ *Thames River 1813*　　　　*Chippewa 1814* ▶

Toulouse   10 April 1814

Fought in southern France, this final battle proved that the French were still determined and able to fight. Ironically, it turned out to be a pointless encounter; four days earlier, albeit unknown to the French and British commanders, Napoleon had surrendered to the Allied Sixth Coalition.

During 1814 Field Marshal Wellington and his allies began to advance into southern France. Marshal Nicolas Soult, the French commander, withdrew to Toulouse to replenish his army, closely followed by Wellington and a combination of British, Portuguese, and Spanish troops.

Wellington surrounded the city on three sides. To the west, he dispatched Lieutenant General Sir Rowland Hill with his 2nd Division and the Portuguese Division to capture the suburb of St. Cyprien and draw away Soult's troops. To the north, the 3rd Division, under Lieutenant General Sir Thomas Picton, and the Light Division would provide feint attacks, while, to the east, the main assault would be made against the dominating Heights of Calvinet. This attack would be led by two divisions under Marshal Sir William Beresford, supported by two Spanish divisions commanded by General Manuel Freires.

On the morning of 10 April Hill's force took St. Cyprien with ease, but to the north an overeager Picton pushed on farther than ordered, and his troops were repulsed with heavy losses. Beresford initially had difficulties arriving at his start line, while the Spaniards attacked without British support and were driven off the heights with heavy losses. At last, Beresford managed to capture the position. Realizing the danger, Soult then quietly slipped away from Toulouse to the south, to agree to armistice terms with Wellington after learning of Napoleon's abdication. **AG**

Losses: Allied, 4,600 casualties of 50,000; French, 3,200 casualties of 42,000

◁ *Vitoria 1813*   *Ligny and Quatre Bras 1815* ▷

Chippewa   5 July 1814

Napoleon's defeat in April 1814 raised American concern that fresh British troops would soon be on their way to Canada. To seize the critical Niagara–Lake Huron area before those veteran reinforcements could arrive, Major General Jacob Brown's army crossed the Niagara River in July.

Major General Brown advanced north with Brigadier General Winfield Scott's 1st Brigade in the lead. Scott moved quickly, using his artillery to defeat British efforts to delay them. At dusk on 3 July he reached the Chippewa River. On the far side, defending the bridge over the river, was the main British force of 2,100 under Major General Phineas Riall. Scott withdrew his brigade a mile (1.6 km) over a long cleared area and camped.

Early the next day Brown sent the 3d Brigade (all volunteers) to secure woods on the left and probe toward the river. They encountered Riall's men, who had crossed the river and were advancing in massed columns. Brown saw the volunteers running back and rode to Scott with orders to bring his 1,300 men forward. Scott deployed his artillery, which opened fire on Riall's guns and the advancing British infantry.

Scott's brigade formed ranks and moved forward under fire without faltering, surprising Riall, who thought that the advance would consist of more militia. As the British infantry approached his line, Scott ordered his two flank regiments to incline slightly toward the center and fire. The British were staggered by the deadly crossfire. Scott then ordered his men forward in a bayonet charge that collapsed the British ranks and sent them reeling to the rear. Finally, Riall gathered one regiment as a rearguard and withdrew his men over the river. **RB**

Losses: U.S., 44 dead, 244 wounded (1st Brigade), 54 dead or wounded (3d Brigade); British, 148 dead, 241 wounded, 46 captured or missing

◁ *Horseshoe Bend 1814*   *Lundy's Lane 1814* ▷

Lundy's Lane 25–26 July 1814

Although he had a victory at Chippewa, a lack of supplies and naval support forced Major General Jacob Brown to give up further offensive plans and withdraw the American army down the Niagara River to Fort Erie. British forces under Major General Phineas Riall followed Brown at a distance.

When Brown heard of a possible British raid against his supply base, he ordered Brigadier General Winfield Scott to march his brigade back north as a diversionary threat against Queenston. On the evening of 25 July, Scott arrived north of Chippewa and discovered Riall's force of about 1,000 regulars and militia with cannon occupying a ridgetop road named Lundy's Lane. Scott's brigade was in the open but he refused to retreat. He sent Brown a message for reinforcements and advanced. Thinking he faced the entire American army, Riall began to withdraw just as British Lieutenant General Gordon Drummond arrived with reinforcements and ordered the ridge held.

Scott's brigade took heavy casualties from British artillery, while one regiment worked its way through woods to hit the British flank. Riall was captured, but Drummond reformed and repulsed the attack. When Brown arrived at dusk, he replaced Scott's battered brigade with Brigadier General Eleazar Ripley's brigade. Ripley's men pushed the British off the hill in a confused night battle, holding against three British counterattacks. The artillery changed hands several times in the dark until fighting tapered off after midnight. Americans held the ridge, but as a wounded Brown was evacuated, he ordered Ripley to withdraw and the Americans left. Later, Brown ordered Ripley to return for the guns, but the British were back in strength and Ripley withdrew. **RB**

Losses: U.S., 171 dead, 573 wounded, 117 missing or captured; British, 81 dead, 562 wounded, 233 missing or captured

◁ Chippewa 1814   Bladensburg 1814 ▷

Bladensburg 24 August 1814

In 1814 it was British strategy to relieve American pressure against Canada by creating a diversion on the United States' east coast. The plan called for large, effective raids in the area of Chesapeake Bay, where Rear Admiral George Cockburn's small British fleet had been raiding for over a year.

An expeditionary force under Vice Admiral Alexander Cochrane and Major General Robert Ross entered Maryland's Patuxent River and landed 4,000 British troops about 30 miles (48 km) southeast of Washington. Diversionary ships were also sent north into the Potomac River. As he mobilized a defensive force, Brigadier General William H. Winder, commanding the defense, received conflicting reports of the British movements. Few regulars were available and the majority of his men were inexperienced Maryland militia.

The British opted to take a less direct road that crossed the Anacostia River at Bladensburg. Hearing this, on 24 August Winder deployed 6,000 men and artillery in three successive positions along the west bank of the river opposite Bladensburg. Meanwhile, President James Madison and Secretary of State James Monroe rode out to advise him. Unknown to Winder, Monroe repositioned the units, placing them too far apart for mutual support.

At about noon, British infantry waded the river and attacked. After some fighting, the first militia line scattered. Pressed on the flanks, the militia in the second and third positions also finally collapsed, retreating in what became a disorderly rout. After pausing briefly, the British occupied Washington and burned its public buildings. Lagging American support for the war was galvanized by this event and enlistments jumped. **RB**

Losses: U.S., 26 dead, 51 wounded; British, 64 dead, 185 wounded

◁ Lundy's Lane 1814   Lake Champlain 1814 ▷

Lake Champlain 11 September 1814

With fresh reinforcements from Britain, Lieutenant General George Prevost, governor general of Canada, initiated his plan to seize the American base at Plattsburg, New York, and destroy the American fleet on Lake Champlain. Prevost's objective was uncontested control of the lake.

Prevost planned a joint land and lake attack. He advanced a British force of 10,350 along Lake Champlain's south shore and on 6 September occupied Plattsburg, west of the Saranac River. Across the river were American defensive positions guarding the bridges. Offshore on the lake was anchored the American flotilla, commanded by Captain Thomas Macdonough: USS *Saratoga* (twenty-six guns), *Eagle*, *Ticonderoga*, and *Preble*, plus ten gunboats. Prevost's assault was to be coordinated with an attack on Macdonough by Captain George Downie's naval squadron: HMS *Confidence* (thirty-seven guns), *Linnet*, *Chubb*, and *Finch*, plus twelve gunboats.

Downie arrived on 11 September. He ordered his four ships abreast and sailed directly at the American line, firing his long-range guns. Macdonough's guns were shorter-range but heavier carronades. The wind died, disrupting Downie's formation. When the starboard batteries of *Saratoga* and *Eagle* were damaged, Macdonough used anchors to swing the ships so that their port guns could fire broadsides. Downie was killed and *Confidence*, badly hurt, soon surrendered. *Ticonderoga* and *Preble* forced *Finch* to beach, but *Preble* was heavily damaged. *Chubb* and *Linnet* did little and both struck their colors after being hit by several broadsides. Prevost watched the naval disaster and revoked his already on-going attack. The next day he withdrew his army back to Canada. **RB**

Losses: U.S., 89 dead, 120 wounded; British, 92 dead, 119 wounded, more than 300 captured or deserted

◁ Bladensburg 1814 Baltimore 1814 ▷

Baltimore 12–14 September 1814

Following their raid on Washington and seizure of Alexandria in Virginia, the British commanders— Vice Admiral Alexander Cochrane, Rear Admiral George Cockburn, and Major General Robert Ross— decided to strike next at the Chesapeake Bay port of Baltimore, America's third-largest city.

Baltimore's citizens had worked on its defenses for more than a year. Fort McHenry, south of the harbor entrance, was the main defense, commanded by Major George Armistead with a regular garrison. Militia manned other earthworks. The harbor entrance was blocked by a large chain and scuttled hulks. The British planned a land attack on the city supported by naval gunfire from the harbor.

On 12 September, 4,700 troops under Ross landed north of the harbor. Opposing them was Brigadier General John Stricker's brigade of 3,200 militia. In late afternoon, Ross's infantry encountered Stricker's skirmishers. Ross came forward and was killed. Taking command, Colonel Arthur Brooke attacked, turned the American left, and assaulted the center. After a sharp but short battle, Stricker retreated to a second defensive line, and with nightfall the British stopped and Stricker withdrew into the city.

Meanwhile, sixteen British ships approached Fort McHenry. The following afternoon they began a long bombardment of the fort. Brooke advanced to within sight of the city's strong fortifications and concluded that only a night attack supported by naval cannons could succeed. The ships, however, were unable to engage with the fort because of the chain and Armistead's artillery. That night an attempt to land marines was driven back. On 14 September the British decided that a successful attack was impossible and departed. **RB**

Losses: U.S., 29 killed, 153 wounded, 50 captured; British, 46 killed, 300 wounded

◁ Lake Champlain 1814 New Orleans 1815 ▷

New Orleans 8 January 1815

The Treaty of Ghent was signed on 24 December 1814, too late to stop the British operation to capture New Orleans and block the Mississippi River. On 23 December a fleet under Vice Admiral Alexander Cochrane had secured a beachhead, landed British troops, and camped near the city.

On arrival at New Orleans on 1 December, Major General Andrew Jackson found nothing done to defend the city. He declared martial law and drafted civilians to build breastworks, from the Mississippi on the right to a thick swamp on the left. Logs, earth, and large cotton bales coated with mud were used to protect four batteries of cannon. Behind a dry ditch Jackson placed his army of regulars and militia.

On 24 December Jackson made an unsuccessful spoiling attack on the British camp. British Lieutenant General Edward Pakenham, senior army commander, arrived the next day. A minor British sortie was repulsed

on 28 December. An artillery bombardment also failed, due to accurate American counterfire. Reinforcements trickled in for both sides, ultimately giving the British more than 6,000 and the Americans about 5,300.

On 8 January Pakenham launched a two-part predawn attack. About 1,000 men crossed the river to assault the American batteries on the west bank. A larger British force attacked on the east bank. One reinforced brigade aimed for the left of Jackson's line nearest the swamp, which Pakenham thought the weakest; it was not. Another brigade attacked the right. American cannon, musket, and rifle fire raked the massed British columns. By 8:30 AM Pakenham and many officers were dead and the attacks shattered. The detachment on the west bank captured the battery but too late, and the British withdrew. **RB**

Losses: U.S., 13 dead, 39 wounded, and 19 missing; British, 300 dead, 1,262 wounded, 484 captured

◁ *Baltimore 1814*

Lieutenant General Pakenham lies dying at New Orleans, in an 1817 engraving after Benjamin West.

Ligny and Quatre Bras   16 June 1815

In 1815 Napoleon, returned from exile in Elba, stole a march on the Allies with his daring and swift move into Belgium. But Marshal Ney's vacillation in front of Quatre Bras and the mismanagement of General D'Erlon's corps were to have disastrous consequences for French hopes of ultimate victory.

In June 1815 Napoleon Bonaparte waged a campaign against the armies of Prussia and Britain, then deployed in the Netherlands (modern Belgium). Advancing in secret, Napoleon planned to separate the British from the Prussians and defeat them separately. Aware that the Prussians had decided to stand and fight at Ligny, Napoleon and the bulk of his army marched against them, while Ney, commanding the left wing, was ordered to take the crossroads at Quatre Bras before advancing on Ligny to finish off the Prussians.

At Quatre Bras, Ney hesitated to attack the small Anglo-Dutch force holding the crossroads, thereby allowing time for Wellington to begin reinforcing the position. When the French did attack, it seemed for a while that the Allied line might not hold, but British reinforcements arrived and the position was successfully strengthened.

Ney had hoped to use General D'Erlon's powerful corps of 20,000 men, but Napoleon ordered it to support his attack at Ligny, an order that Ney then countermanded. D'Erlon's troops thus marched back and forth between the two battles without involvement in either. At Ligny Napoleon proved too strong for the Prussians under Marshal Gebhard von Blücher. Beaten but not crushed, the Prussians retreated northward to maintain contact with Wellington's forces. **AG**

Losses: Ligny: French, 8,000 casualties of 70,000; Prussian, 16,000 casualties of 84,000; Quatre Bras: French, 4,000 casualties of 24,000; Allied, 5,000 casualties of 8,000 rising to 36,000

◁ *Toulouse 1814*   *Waterloo 1815* ▷

Anglo-Dutch forces deploy in the foreground of an 1815 aquatint of Quatre Bras by Thomas Sutherland.

Waterloo   18 June 1815

This climactic battle brought an end to the Napoleonic Wars, and to the career of one of history's great commanders, but Napoleon was not at his best at Waterloo, allowing his subordinates to instigate a series of poorly coordinated attacks against the line held by the Duke of Wellington's army.

After the Battle of Ligny Napoleon directed Marshal Emmanuel de Grouchy and the 33,000 troops of the French right wing to pursue the defeated Prussian army of Marshal von Blücher. With the rest of his forces, Napoleon then advanced on Wellington's army, which had withdrawn from Quatre Bras to a better defensive position just to the south of the village of Waterloo, Wellington having been assured of Prussian assistance if attacked by the French.

Wellington's force—composed of British, Dutch, and German troops—was deployed along a low ridge, with the bulk of the army hidden on the reverse slope. His line was buttressed by two strongpoints: the chateau of Hougoumont on the Allied right and the farm complex

"Believe me, nothing except a battle lost can be half so melancholy as a battle won."

The Duke of Wellington, writing on the battlefield

of La Haye Sainte in the center. The French moved into position on 17 June, ready to do battle the following day. Napoleon decided to exploit his superiority in artillery, but because of previous heavy rain he waited for the ground to dry during the morning of the 18th.

This was to prove a fatal mistake, as time was of the essence for Napoleon; Grouchy had failed to engage the Prussians, who were, in fact, marching on Waterloo to support Wellington, leaving only a small corps to face Grouchy. Napoleon's plan was for his left wing to

launch an attack on Hougoumont, in order to draw in Wellington's reserves while a mass infantry attack by D'Erlon's I Corps would drive in the Allied center-left.

The battle began just before noon. The French artillery opened a fearsome cannonade but most of Wellington's troops were either hidden or lying down, minimizing casualties. The battle was going badly for the French. The attack on Hougoumont failed to draw Wellington's reserves and, instead, sucked in large numbers of French troops. D'Erlon's assault by four divisions was halted by fierce and deadly infantry fire before his two lefthand formations were broken by a British cavalry charge.

By 2:00 PM Napoleon was well aware of the Prussian forces advancing against his right flank, and during the afternoon increasing numbers of French reserves were committed to shoring up this exposed flank. The battle was not over, however, as French pressure began to tell on an increasingly battered Allied line. Marshal Ney personally led a series of furious cavalry charges against Wellington's center, while at around 6:00 PM La Haye Sainte was overrun by the French. This was the moment of decision, and Ney desperately asked for reinforcements, but Napoleon initially refused Ney's request, fearful of the growing Prussian threat. At 7:00 PM Napoleon committed the infantry of the Imperial Guard in a last-gasp attack on Wellington's line, but its line of march veered to the left, to be met by some of the best and freshest British troops. Blasted by volley after volley of musketry, the Guard faltered and retreated. Sensing victory, Wellington ordered a general attack by all his troops and, with a simultaneous Prussian advance, the French retreat became a rout. The remnants of Napoleon's army fled the field of battle, pursued by Blücher's cavalry. **AG**

Losses: Allied, 24,000 combined casualties of 68,000 Anglo-allied and 50,000 Prussians; French, 25,000 dead or wounded, 8,000 captured, and 15,000 missing of 72,000

◁ *Ligny and Quatre Bras 1815*

A map originating with the British War Office depicts deployments at the Battle of Waterloo.

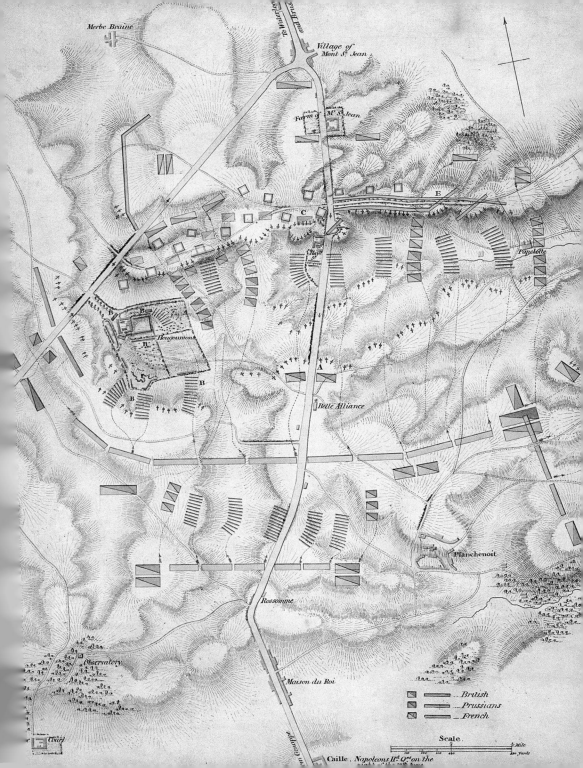

Merbe Braine

To Waterloo and Brussels

Village of
Mont St Jean

Farm of Mt St Jean

C

Olave

E

Papelotte

B
B
Hougoumont
B

B

A

B

Belle Alliance

Planchenoit

Rossomme

Maison du Roi

Observatory

Court

British
Prussians
French

Scale

½ Mile

Caille, Napoleons H^d Q^rs on the

Chacabuco 12 February 1817

During the Napoleonic Wars Spain's hold on its South American colonies had weakened. In 1817 Argentinian General José de San Martín led an army across the Andes, aiming to liberate Chile from Spanish rule. His victory at Chacabuco was a decisive step forward in the struggle for South American independence.

San Martín's crossing of the Andes with more than 5,000 men and all their horses, pack-mules, guns, and munitions was a remarkable military achievement in itself, claiming a heavy toll in lives of men and beasts. The unexpected arrival of his Army of the Andes in Chile sent the colonial authorities into shock. Despite being heavily outnumbered, they decided to stand and fight at Chacabuco, outside Santiago.

The battle opened prematurely when the impetuous Chilean patriot Bernardo O'Higgins threw his men forward into the attack before the rest of San Martín's army had formed up. The Spanish set about slaughtering them, but soon the Irish-descended Chilean general began to receive support he had expected as José de San Martín advanced against the Spanish right with what had been intended to be the reserve. Meanwhile, Argentinian General Miguel Estanislao Soler and his cavalry, having approached undetected over a rugged ridge, rushed upon the left flank of the Spanish force. Beleaguered and confused, the Crown troops thrashed about in panic.

Spanish General Ildefonso Elorreaga was killed, but General Rafael Maroto's elite Talavera Regiment led a courageous Spanish and Royalist counterattack. The outcome was thus again in doubt, but Soler's cavalry succeeded in encircling the Spanish, cutting off their retreat. Trapped, they were cut to pieces by the rebels. **MK**

Losses: Royalist, 600 casualties and 500 captured of 1,500; Republican, 100 casualties of 4,000

<San Lorenzo 1813   Maipú 1818 >

Republican General San Martín (on white horse) at Chacabuco, in a painting by Pedro Subercaseux (1880–1956).

Maipú   5 April 1818

Maipú marked a milestone in Latin America's march to freedom from Spanish rule. Argentinian General José de San Martín's victory broke the Spanish hold on Chile. The boldness of his triumph left the colonial power reeling; San Martín swept on to proclaim the independence of Peru, although the struggle was far from over.

"Chile is ours!" San Martín had exclaimed after the rebel victory at Chacabuco, but he spoke much too soon. Seeing the situation in South America spiraling out of control, the Spanish Crown sent reinforcements. On 16 March 1818 San Martín's Army of the Andes was badly mauled by General Mariano Osorio's force at the Second Battle of Cancha Rayada, where San Martín's botched tactical withdrawal had allowed the Spanish to spring an audacious surprise attack.

San Martín's rebellious resolve was only strengthened by his humiliation, however, and within weeks he had regrouped his rebel force. San Martín was well aware that as time went on the Spanish would only become more firmly entrenched, and that it was now or never for the liberation struggle. Accordingly, he took the fight to Osorio's army as it advanced across a high plateau beside the Maipú River in the Andes south of Santiago.

San Martín's mounted grenadiers attacked the Spanish left, making immediate and significant inroads, but the left proved far more obdurate than expected, the feared and elite Spanish Burgos Regiment exacting heavy casualties. San Martín brought up his reserve, commanded by Colonel de la Quintana, backed by a heavy artillery bombardment. As fighters the reserve were no match for the Burgos Regiment, but the elite force advanced so quickly that its formation fell apart, allowing the rebels to regain the initiative and win the day. **MK**

Losses: Spanish and Royalist, 2,000; Republican, 1,000

◁ Chacabuco 1817   Boyacá 1819 ▷

⬆ *General San Martín (with drawn sword) at Maipú, in a painting by Théodore Géricault (1791–1824).*

Boyacá 4 August 1819

Beside the Boyacá River, Simón Bolívar showed he was more than an idealistic dreamer when he comprehensively outmaneuvered the Spanish commander sent against him. The "Liberator" brought about the independence of Colombia in this engagement to the south of Bogotá.

In 1815 a young Venezuelan, Simón Bolívar, had sworn not to rest until the Americas had cast off the colonial "tyrants' yoke." By the beginning of 1819 he had liberated his homeland in the face of ferocious Spanish resistance. But he wanted to go much further—to build an independent "Gran Colombia" in the viceroyalty of Nueva Granada, which included present-day Panama and Colombia.

Backed by a ragtag army of peasants and *llaneros* (literally "plainsmen," or cowboys), supplemented by the British volunteers of his Albion Legion, he made an epic crossing of the Andes. Exhausted though they were, on 25 July his men defeated José María Barreiro's Royalist army at the Vargas swamp. Barreiro, retreating, raced Bolívar's army toward Bogotá, hoping to occupy the city and bar the Republicans' way.

On 4 August Bolívar feinted toward the town of Chicamocha, withdrawing discreetly after darkness fell. Circling around to avoid an imagined trap, Barreiro fell into a real one when his cavalry crossed a narrow bridge in pursuit of what they thought was a small scouting party of llaneros. Not only did this turn out to be the Republican vanguard, which duly savaged them, but the cavalry's move had left the main column of the Royalists dangerously exposed beyond the river. Stretched out in a straggling line, they were attacked from one side by the Albion Legion and from the other by llaneros. The road to Bogotá—and to Gran Colombia—lay open. **MK**

> *"Those soldier liberators are the men who deserve these laurels."*
>
> Simón Bolívar on the British volunteers

A nineteenth-century engraving depicts the battle between Spanish Royalists and Simón Bolívar's Republican army.

Losses: Spanish, 500; Republican, 13

◁ Maipú 1818   Valdivia 1820 ▷

Valdivia   3–4 February 1820

Despite rebel victories at Chacabuco and Maipú, Spanish Royalists continued to resist independence forces in Chile. In the service of the Chilean rebels, maverick British Admiral Thomas Cochrane carried out an attack—one that he himself described as "madness"—on the Royalist naval base of Valdivia.

Valdivia, in southern Chile, occupied a natural defensive position in a narrow-mouthed inlet whose approaches were guarded by seven separate fortresses, with 120 cannon and a garrison of 1,600 soldiers. Cochrane had a small squadron with only a single effective warship—a frigate—and 300 men.

Lord Cochrane's career with the British Royal Navy had ended shamefully after a stock-market fraud, but the Scottish adventurer certainly lacked neither seafaring skills, experience in command, nor courage. He devised a plan for taking Valdivia, the "Gibraltar of Chile," from the land. Late at night on 3 February 1820, his landing party disembarked on the coast south of the fortifications. They rushed one fort, the "English Fort," taking its garrison completely by surprise, before pushing rapidly on to take two further forts in the confusion that ensued.

Cochrane's daring and the defenders' demoralization conjoined in bringing success to what should have been an impossibly ambitious plan. The rebels' position, despite their early success, was extremely vulnerable once dawn broke on 4 February, but Cochrane called on his tiny squadron to approach the bay. The boats had been left with only skeleton crews, but the boldness of their coming now in broad daylight convinced the Spanish garrisons that a new wave of attackers was arriving. Deserting in droves, they saved Cochrane the trouble of sacking Valdivia by doing it themselves. **MK**

Losses: Spanish, 100; Republican, 7

◁ Boyacá 1819   Carabobo 1821 ▷

Carabobo   24 June 1821

Simón Bolívar's victory over the Spanish and their Royalist South American supporters opened the road not only to Caracas but also to Venezuelan liberty. Bolívar's British mercenaries proved stalwart when his homegrown revolutionaries broke and fled under a storm of musket fire.

Venezuela was Bolívar's native country; he had fought for its liberty before, and apparently won, but the Spanish kept coming back to a colony they saw as key to their American possessions. An uneasy cease-fire had prevailed since the start of 1820 when, in April 1821, Maracaibo city rose up in revolt against the Spanish. Taking advantage of the confusion, Bolívar's chief of staff, Rafael Urdaneta, and his lieutenant, José Bermúdez, attacked Spanish garrisons at Caracas and Puerto Cabello on the Atlantic coast.

"The Liberator" was making for the Spanish stronghold of Puerto Cabello with an army some 7,000 strong when he found himself facing Royalist leader Miguel de la Torre with his force at Carabobo. In hopes of outflanking his enemy, Bolívar sent half his troops sweeping around on either side of the road through rough scrubland and forest, but La Torre, whose men occupied higher ground, dispatched his own forces to cancel out this maneuver.

Bolívar's risky maneuver had failed, it seemed, especially when his main column, mounting a frontal attack on La Torre's force, was greeted by a hail of fire from 3,000 Spanish muskets. Utterly demoralized, they broke and fled. But the "British Huntsmen" mercenaries saved the day—and the future of an independent Venezuela. Holding firm, with desperate courage they met the enemy fire with volleys of their own before fixing bayonets and blindly charging. The astonished Spanish simply broke and ran. **MK**

Losses: Republican, 200; Spanish, 3,000 dead, wounded, or captured

◁ Valdivia 1820   Pichincha 1822 ▷

Infantry courageously follow the Republican flag of Ecuador in a heroic depiction of the Battle of Pichincha. ⬇

Pichincha   24 May 1822

The slopes of an active volcano high above Quito formed a fittingly spectacular backdrop for one of the most dramatic battles of Spanish America's war of liberation. Antonio José de Sucre defeated Melchor Aymerich's Royalist army, giving Ecuador its independence from the Spanish Crown.

Armies from newly liberated Colombia had tried to free Ecuador in 1820, and again in 1821. Only at the third attempt did Simón Bolívar's friend Sucre succeed in toppling Spanish rule. Both earlier attacks had involved a direct advance on the capital, Quito, from coastal Guayaquil. This time, Sucre decided instead to approach the city from the south, up through the Andes, and make his final attack over the heights of the volcano Pichincha.

The idea was that he would take the Spanish by surprise, and it might have worked had his advance not slowed to a crawl as his men picked their way across the volcano's slopes. At 11,000 feet (3,350 m), the toughest troops were afflicted by altitude sickness, while steady rain turned the volcanic ash beneath their feet to mud. In full view of the Spanish by now, Sucre was compelled to call a halt while the men rested and regrouped. His force was especially vulnerable since the Albion Legion was toiling at an unknown distance behind.

Watching this whole scene unfold from the valley below, Aymerich could plan at leisure. His crack Aragón battalion crested the volcano and fell on Sucre's army from the rear. But Republican rout turned to Royalist disaster as—just in time—the Albion Legion arrived and carried the day. Sucre swept triumphantly into Quito. **MK**

Losses: Republican, 200; Spanish, 400

◁ *Carabobo 1821*   *Lake Maracaibo 1823* ▷

Lake Maracaibo 24 July 1823

José Prudencio Padilla led the little fleet of Simón Bolívar's Republic of Gran Colombia to victory over Ángel Laborde y Navarro's superior Spanish squadron. Against unequal odds, his remarkable daring and tactical resource won the day, finally guaranteeing Venezuela's independence.

Lake Maracaibo is something between a bay and a lake, with a narrow strait separating its sluggish waters from the sea. Here, at the start of July 1823, the Republican and Spanish fleets fought a few skirmishes before the former withdrew into the lake-port of Moporo for repairs and resupply. On the afternoon of 23 July Padilla received Laborde's formal challenge: the Spanish fleet was lined up in battle formation close to Maracaibo's western shore.

Spain's hold on Venezuela had been uncertain since its dismal defeat at Carabobo two years before, but its continuing colonial presence had been assured by naval power. So it seemed set to continue, with Padilla, apparently eager to avoid a confrontation, steering for the safety of the mouth of the lake, in the east.

The following dawn he briefed his captains, but even then he did not give the order to weigh anchor until almost noon. As though making up for lost time, his fleet now sailed with startling swiftness into the attack. The well-armed Royalists opened up with their cannon first; the Republicans held their fire until, at point-blank range, they sent off a salvo to truly devastating effect. Closing fast, they quickly captured those vessels that had not been sunk in the opening bombardment. Only three succeeded in limping away after this savaging. **MK**

Losses: Unknown

◁ *Pichincha 1822*　　　　　　　　　*Junín 1824* ▷

Junín 6 August 1824

Not a shot was fired as cavalrymen fought in the medieval style with lance and sword, on open ground beside a mountain lake at Junín. But, for all its romantic circumstances and setting, the battle brought real bloodshed—and real consequences in Simón Bolívar's liberation of Peru.

"Soldiers," cried Simón Bolívar, "you are going to . . . save a whole world from slavery!" Somehow, the battle at Junín managed to live up to that exhilarating speech—even if it never quite delivered on the promise of global liberation. Bolívar's army had already completed a nightmarish journey over burning deserts, rugged passes, and freezing snowfields before it reached the basin of Lake Junín, at an altitude of more than 12,000 feet (3,650 m) in the Andes.

General José de Canterac of Spain, ignoring his superiors' orders, had headquartered himself here in the mountains, safe, as he imagined, from Bolívar the Liberator's forces. Events, however, quickly spiraled out of the control of both commanders. De Canterac, shocked to find himself threatened by his enemy, marched his army down the lakeside slopes to meet them, but abruptly turned back when he realized that Bolívar's men were advancing up the opposite shore and threatening to cut off his force from its base at the head of the valley.

A race resulted in which the cavalry on both sides naturally outstripped their infantry. The horsemen met on marshland, the Spanish taking the Republican llaneros ("plainsmen") by surprise. As the Spanish swept triumphantly across the plain, however, they overshot a detachment of Republican hussars, who now attacked them from the rear while the llaneros regrouped and charged from the other side. In itself a minor victory, the battle at Junín robbed de Canterac of the initiative; Bolívar marched, more or less unhindered, into Peru. **MK**

Losses: Republican, 150; Royalist, 250

◁ Lake Maracaibo 1823   Ayacucho 1824 ▷

Simón Bolívar personally leads his Republican troops at Junín, in a mural (1931–33) by Fernando Leal. ⬆

Ayacucho 9 December 1824

Antonio José de Sucre led from the front in the battle that underlined the independence not only of Peru but of Spanish America as a whole. Surrender here left the position of the Spanish colonial power irretrievable; Simón Bolívar's dream of liberation had been realized.

Bolívar was busy on the coastal plain of Peru, preparing to take Lima, when his friend Antonio José de Sucre engaged the army of the Viceroy, José de la Serna. Caught on low ground, below the Royalist army, the Republicans were badly outnumbered and outgunned. And, to begin with, at least, comprehensively outmaneuvered.

General Jerónimo Váldez, leading the Spanish center, sensed the weakness of the Republican volunteers facing him. Ordering his artillerymen to pound away with their cannon, he not only ravaged their ranks but, by drawing down reinforcements to fill the gaps, eroded the integrity of Sucre's army as a whole.

The tide of a battle that seemed to be flowing steadily the Royalists' way was then changed by a commander's desperate theatrics. Sucre, alighting from his horse, histrionically slew it on the spot before his awestruck soldiers; why would he need it, he asked, when he was resolved to stand and fight, to win or die?

As the Spanish cavalry poured down the hillside to administer the coup de grâce, they were taken aback to find the Republican footsoldiers surging forward, spears presented toward their horses, which pulled up in terror, all impetus gone. Half an hour's hand-to-hand fighting followed, in which Váldez's cavalry were cut down while the Republicans forced their way steadily uphill to take the Spanish artillery. When the Viceroy was captured, it became clear that the game was up. La Serna surrendered and was given safe passage back to Spain. **MK**

Losses: Republican, 310; Royalist, 1,900
⟨ *Junín* 1824

A nineteenth-century impression of the Ayacucho battlefield, on a valley floor dominated by the Andes.

Messolonghi 10 April 1826

The Greeks began a war of independence against Ottoman Turkey in 1821. In 1826, after a siege lasting a year, Turkish and Egyptian forces took one of the chief centers of the rebellion, Messolonghi in western Greece. Yet this military disaster proved to be a publicity triumph for the Greeks.

Messolonghi was a site famous throughout Europe because the aristocratic poet Lord Byron had died there in 1824 after devoting himself to the cause of Greek freedom. In the year after Byron's death the war had turned sharply against the Greeks with the arrival of an army sent by the Turkish sultan's nominal vassal, Muhammad Ali of Egypt, and led by Muhammad's son, Ibrahim Pasha. The Egyptians were well equipped, disciplined, and ruthless. Faced with both Ibrahim Pasha and the Turkish forces of Reshad Pasha, the Greek rebellion wilted.

In April 1825 Messolonghi was placed under siege. The Turks and Egyptians settled down to a blockade, an assault being deemed too costly. The trickle of supplies into Messolonghi was eventually stopped, so that by April 1826 the defenders faced the choice of surrendering or attempting a breakout. On 10 April Georgios Karaiskakis, one of the heroes of the Greek independence struggle, led a diversionary attack while all the able-bodied Greeks inside Messolonghi—about 7,000 people—attempted to escape. The plan was not a success. As the enemy forces opened fire, only about 1,000 Greeks reached safety. The rest fell back into Messolonghi, which was then taken by assault. About 3,000 Greeks were slaughtered, the rest enslaved. European liberal opinion was appalled by the fall of Messolonghi and its aftermath. Pressure on the governments of Britain and France to intervene became irresistible, with decisive results at Navarino in 1827. **RG**

Losses: Greek, at least 3,000 dead; Ottoman, unknown

Navarino 1827 >

Juncal 8–9 February 1827

The decisive naval engagement of the war between the Argentinian republic and imperial Brazil, which lasted from 1825 to 1828, was fought off Juncal Island, Argentina. The Argentinian fleet commander, Irish-born Admiral William Brown, was consequently celebrated as a national hero.

The war between Argentina and Brazil was fought over control of the Banda Oriental—land that was to become Uruguay. The Argentinian navy was comprehensively outnumbered and outgunned by its Brazilian opponent, but the Argentinians had key assets in the maneuverability of their little ships and the skills, experience, and daring of their commanders. The conditions of the Río de la Plata seemed to suit them; its confined spaces and unpredictable shoals gave them a clear advantage over the Brazilians' bigger ships.

By February 1827 the Brazilians had divided their naval forces for different tasks, giving Brown the chance to fight at more equal odds. The Brazilians' Third Division, under Jacinto Roque de Sena Perreira, was tasked with controlling the Uruguay River to cut the Argentinian land forces' lines of communication in the Banda Oriental.

Determined to prevent this, fifteen Argentinian ships under Brown confronted Sena Perreira's squadron of seventeen vessels at Juncal. On the first day of the battle the Brazilians had the advantage of the wind and used it to avoid close fighting. The following day the wind favored Brown and he launched a swift and devastating attack. The Brazilians, responding chaotically to confused orders, failed to maintain formation and all of their ships were captured or destroyed. Sena Perreira's flagship *Oriental* was boarded and the admiral taken prisoner. Brown returned to Buenos Aires to a hero's welcome. **MK**

Losses: Brazilian, 12 ships captured, 3 destroyed; Argentinian, no ships lost

Ituzaingó 1827 >

 The Siege of Messolonghi, one of a series by Panagiotis Zografos depicting the Greek War of Independence.

Ituzaingó   20 February 1827

General Carlos María de Alvear led Argentina's army to a significant—but not quite convincing—victory over the forces of imperial Brazil. The battle took place in a little valley near the border between Brazil and the territory now known as Uruguay.

The Banda Oriental (Eastern Band) between the Río de la Plata and the Uruguay River corresponded roughly with what is now Uruguay. In 1821 the region was annexed by the Portuguese and added to their vast territories in Brazil. Four years later, with the backing of Argentina, people who had settled in the Banda Oriental declared their independence from both Portugal and Brazil. In 1826 King Pedro IV of Portugal, who was brought up in Brazilian exile with his country under occupation by Napoleonic France, proclaimed himself Emperor Pedro I of Brazil. In reaction to the Banda Oriental declaration of independence he declared war on Argentina.

Argentinian General Carlos María de Alvear crossed the Brazilian border from Banda Oriental on 20 January 1827. The Marquis of Berbacena, commanding the Brazilian army, marched out to meet him. Alvear's move had been a calculated ploy, designed to bring Berbacena onto ground he had chosen at Ituzaingó, beside a tributary of the Santa María River. Although the Brazilians forced back the Argentinians at first, and even captured their artillery, the ground favored the Argentinian cavalry, which now swept down to devastating effect. Despite this success, the Argentinians were unable to follow through, and Berbacena's men retreated in good order, ready to fight another day. Ituzaingó was the only serious battle of the war but, together with the naval victory at Juncal, it sufficed to hold Brazil in check. In 1828 a British-brokered peace treaty brought independence to Uruguay. **MK**

Losses: Brazilian, 200; Republican, 150

◁ *Juncal 1827*

Navarino   20 October 1827

The Turks, with assistance from Egypt, had gained the upper hand in the Greek Independence War. Britain, France, and Russia intervened decisively, defeating the Turkish and Egyptian navies in the last fleet action of the sailing-ship era.

The Greek struggle for independence won considerable popular support in Britain and France; Russia was traditionally hostile to Turkey and sympathetic to its Orthodox coreligionists in Greece. Faced with the prospect of a Greek defeat and reports of massacres of the Greek population, the allied powers each sent a naval squadron to back up their calls for an armistice.

A blockade of the Turkish and Egyptian fleet in Navarino Bay, on the west coast of the Peloponnese, had no effect. British Admiral Sir Edward Codrington agreed with his allies to sail into the bay and force the Turko-Egyptians to agree an armistice or else have their ships destroyed. The allied fleet was outnumbered, but most of the opposing vessels were small and poorly armed. Sailing past shore batteries, the allies anchored among the Turkish and Egyptian ships and tried to open negotiations—they had orders not to fire first. The Turks unwisely fired on a boat carrying a British message and the whole allied fleet opened fire.

It was a hopelessly one-sided combat. The British and French gunnery in particular was vastly superior. Within a couple of hours about two-thirds of the Turkish and Egyptian ships had been sunk or set on fire by their own crews to avoid capture. The encounter turned out to be the last full-scale battle between traditional wooden sailing ships. Within a few months Russia declared war on Turkey in support of Greek independence, which was achieved by a treaty of 1832. **DS**

Losses: Allied, 700 dead and wounded; Turko-Egyptian, 4,000 dead and wounded, 60 ships destroyed

◁ *Messolonghi 1826*   *Konya 1832* ▷

The Battle of Navarino, by Greek painter Panagiotis Zografos. ➡

Conquest of Algiers 14 June–4 July 1830

France's first great colonial venture began with a flourish in 1830, when Charles X launched an expedition against the North African port-city of Algiers. The city's Ottoman ruler had no answer for European military technology and firepower, but the Algerian people were not so easily suppressed.

His reign rocked by unrest, Charles X, Bourbon ruler of France, sought some distraction for his subjects. What could be better than a foreign war? And what could be more suitable than war with the weak and impoverished possession of an Ottoman Empire in obvious decline?

The persistent charge that Algiers was providing a haven for the Barbary Corsairs who preyed on Western shipping had already led to its bombardment by Britain's Royal Navy in 1816. France was further affronted by the fact that Hussein Dey, the Ottoman ruler of Algiers, had demanded payment of a debt incurred by Napoleon during his Egyptian campaign over thirty years before.

On 14 June the French arrived in overwhelming force. A fierce naval bombardment was quickly followed by the landing of 37,000 troops, who attacked the fort of Sultan-Khalessi, outside the city. Dey was slow to react, but within a few days had mustered some 10,000 troops of his own—Turks, Berbers, and Arabs. They counterattacked courageously but to no avail. Algiers fell on 4 July, to be followed by extensive looting by the French, and further expeditions took cities in the interior and along the coast.

Charles X would not enjoy his triumph long; he was overthrown weeks later in the July Revolution and Louis Philippe inherited his new North African possession. French proprietorship was incomplete, however; though Ottoman rule had been toppled easily, popular resistance at local level would continue for almost half a century. **MK**

"They have rummaged through the tombs of our fathers / And they have scattered their bones ..."

Poem lamenting the desecration in Algiers after the siege

⬆ French gunners bombard the port of Algiers and outlying positions in a nineteenth-century colored engraving.

Losses: French, 415; Algerian, up to 1,500

Isly 1844 ▶

Konya   21 December 1832

The Battle of Konya was fought between the Muslim armies of Egypt and Turkey. It was an important moment both in the rise of Egypt, which, under Viceroy Muhammad Ali, was modernizing its armed forces and its economy, and in the inexorable decline of the Ottoman Empire.

Muhammad Ali in theory ruled Egypt on behalf of the Ottoman sultan and had sent his son Ibrahim Pasha to fight for the Ottomans in the Greek War of Independence in the 1820s. In 1831, seeing the weakness of the Ottoman regime and seeking compensation for the expense and losses of the campaign in Greece, Ibrahim Pasha led an army from Egypt into Ottoman-ruled Syria. By mid-1832 Ibrahim had won control of Syria and Lebanon, but Ottoman Sultan Mahmud II refused to grant the Egyptians authority over these provinces. So Ibrahim resumed his advance, crossing into Turkey.

Mahmud sent an army under his grand vizier Reshid Pasha to confront the invaders outside Konya. The Ottoman army was far larger, but the Egyptian forces were better led, trained, and disciplined. The battle was fought in winter fog. Egyptian guns won an opening artillery duel, firing accurately toward the sound of the enemy cannon. An outflanking movement by cavalry and infantry, commanded by Ibrahim in person, punched in the Ottoman left flank. Reshid Pasha blundered into the midst of Egyptian soldiers and was captured. An attempt to organize an Ottoman counterattack failed in the face of Egyptian cannon fire and at nightfall the Ottoman forces fled. The road to Constantinople was open, but intervention by the European powers prevented Ibrahim from completing his victory. However, the Ottomans were forced to concede Egyptian control of Syria. **RG**

Losses: Egyptian, 262 dead, 530 wounded of 27,000; Ottoman, 3,000 dead, 5,000 captured of 50,000

◁ *Navarino 1827*   *Nezib 1839* ▷

Alegria de Alava   27–28 Oct 1834

The Spanish Carlist Wars, fought between the 1830s and the 1870s, set Spanish liberals, originally known as Cristinos, against traditionalist Carlist rebels. Although fighting against the odds, the Carlists found an inspired military commander in Basque General Tomas de Zumalacarregui.

Zumalacarregui initially fought as a guerrilla leader because the relative weakness of the Carlist forces obliged them to avoid conventional battles. In October 1834 he discovered a liberal army under General Manuel O'Doyle, a Spanish commander of Irish origin, near Vitoria in the Basque country. O'Doyle had superior forces but his troops were dispersed. Moreover, Zumalacarregui knew exactly where O'Doyle's soldiers were, while the Carlists' maneuvers were undetected. O'Doyle himself was to be found in the village of Alegria de Alava.

Zumalacarregui staged a noisy diversionary attack on liberal troops some 6 miles (10 km) distant. As expected, O'Doyle marched toward the sound of the guns, to be ambushed by Zumalacarregui's forces. The Guias de Navarra, a formation of captured liberal troops who had joined the Carlists in return for their lives being spared, fought with particular ferocity. The battle turned into a massacre, with fleeing Cristianos chased through the forest and bayoneted without mercy. O'Doyle and other captured officers were shot by firing squad.

A few hundred Cristianos remained as an organized fighting force, reaching the town of Arrieta, where they barricaded themselves into the church. The following day a liberal relief column was sent toward Arrieta but this in turn was ambushed by Zumalacarregui's guerrillas at Venta de Echavarri. The troops trapped at Arrieta broke out the next night, bringing the fighting to an end. **RG**

Losses: Liberal, about 1,000; Carlist, unknown

The Alamo   23 February–6 March 1836

The Texas War of Independence opened in October 1835 with a string of Texan victories that drove the Mexican federal forces south of the Rio Grande by December. Success was short lived. A Mexican army under General Antonio López de Santa Anna advanced north to put down the rebels.

In 1835 most of the victorious Anglo and Hispanic Texas volunteer rebel army went home. Small garrisons were left at several towns, including San Antonio de Béxar (San Antonio), where the Texans occupied a former Spanish mission called the "Alamo." It consisted of three one-story adobe buildings, with log palisades enclosing open plaza areas. Nineteen cannon lined the walls.

The co-commanders, William Travis and James Bowie, did not credit warnings that Santa Anna was coming and did little to lay in food, supplies, or ammunition. They were surprised on 23 February when Santa Anna arrived with his advance detachment of about 1,400 men. His demand for unconditional surrender was answered with

> *"Our business is not to make a fruitless effort to save our lives, but to choose the manner of our death."* William Travis, address to garrison

a cannon shot. Angered, he gave orders that no quarter was to be given, and a thirteen-day siege began. The Mexicans set up artillery opposite the south and east walls and began a steady bombardment, with Mexican cannonballs being shot back by the Texans until the order came to conserve powder. Santa Anna's infantry maneuvered closer to the Alamo but were careful to stay outside the range of the Texans' rifled muskets.

Cold winter weather made life difficult for both sides. Small skirmishes took place with few casualties. On two occasions, a small group of Texan reinforcements broke through the Mexican lines, raising the garrison to about 188 men plus families, but 1,000 men joined Santa Anna. Occasionally Texan couriers managed to slip out of the surrounded Alamo with pleas from Travis for reinforcements, but the disorganized provisional Texas government was unable to put together any relief force. On 3 March the last 1,000-man element of Santa Anna's army arrived, and he prepared his attack.

Before dawn on 6 March, four columns of Mexican infantry attacked from different directions. There were no loopholes or firing ports, so the defenders had to expose themselves to fire over the walls. Texan cannon, loaded with nails, horseshoes, and old iron, fired into the Mexicans and, together with the rifle fire, repulsed the first assault. Regrouping, the Mexican infantry tried again but were driven back. Travis died opposing a mass attack against the weak north wall that finally penetrated the compound. When a cannon covering the south was turned around to meet the attack, Mexicans came over that wall and captured the gun.

When Texan defenders retreated to the adobe barracks buildings for cover, Mexican gunners rolled up cannon and blew down the heavy doors. Infantry then rushed in and for more than an hour room-to-room fighting took place. Bowie died there. Two groups of Texans trying to escape were cut down outside the walls by the cavalry posted there. The last bastion to fall was the chapel where a small Texan detachment manned the last cannon. They fired once as Mexican infantry broke through the doors and were then killed in hand-to-hand fighting. The terrified Texan families sheltered there were spared by the Mexicans, but any surviving fighters were executed. **RB**

Losses: Texan, 180 dead; Mexican, 400–600 dead or wounded

San Jacinto 1836 ▶

In his request for aid, William Travis famously spelled out his insistence on "Victory or Death." ➤

& every thing dear to the American Character, to come to our aid, with all dispatch — The enemy is receiving reinforcements daily & will no doubt increase to three or four thousand in four or five days. If this call is neglected, I am determined to sustain myself as long as possible & die like a soldier who never forgets what is due to his own honor & that of his country —

Victory or Death.

William Barret Travis

Lt. Col. comdt.

P.S. The Lord is on our side — When the enemy appeared in sight we had not three bushels of corn — We have since found in deserted houses 80 or 90 bushels & put into the walls 20 or 30 head of Beeves —

Travis

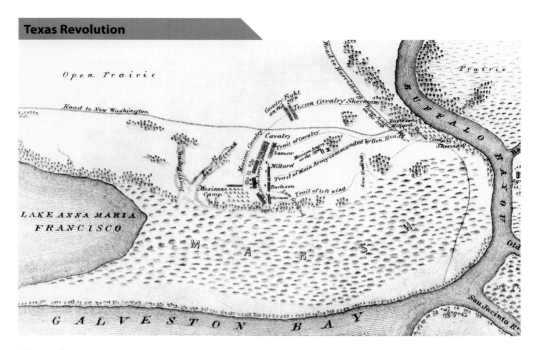

San Jacinto   21 April 1836

Citizens of the new Republic of Texas responded to the destruction of the Alamo and massacre of the unarmed Texans captured at Goliad with outrage. Volunteer companies rushed to join General Samuel Houston's growing Texas army. Meanwhile, Mexican General Santa Anna marched his army to crush the Republican rebels.

Houston avoided contact with the pursuing Mexican army until his Texas army gained strength and training. Santa Anna, on the other hand, split his force, sending some units to secure his long supply line while others sought to capture the provisional Texan government. He personally led the remaining 600 men after Houston.

On 20 April, the two armies met in a low area of marshland and bayous near the San Jacinto River. Santa Anna attempted unsuccessfully to probe the Texan position, and there was an exchange of artillery fire. About 500 Mexican reinforcements arrived. Santa Anna decided

to rest his troops before attacking, but failed to post sentries. A Texan council of war voted to attack, and, at 4:30 PM, Houston launched his 900 Texans in a risky surprise assault. His mounted troops rode around the Mexican flanks while the Texan battle line moved quickly and quietly directly across the open prairie. They were within 200 yards (183 m) of the Mexican camp when discovered. At that moment, Houston's artillery opened fire, and the Texan infantry charged. They fired at close range and rolled over the hasty Mexican breastworks. Santa Anna's defense collapsed as panicked Mexicans tried to flee the cavalry across the marshes. After an eighteen-minute fight, the Mexican last resistance surrendered, but Santa Anna slipped away in a private's uniform. He was finally captured on 22 April and signed a treaty on 14 May. **RB**

Losses: Mexican, 630 dead, 208 wounded, 730 captured; Texan, 9 dead, 30 wounded

◁ *The Alamo 1836*   *Campeche 1843* ▷

A nineteenth-century engraving of the ground plan of the Battle of San Jacinto.

Saint-Eustache 14 December 1837

The Battle of Saint-Eustache was part of the rebellion against British rule in Lower Canada (Quebec), referred to as the Patriot's War. The battle was fought by a French and English Canadian rebel force, under the command of Jean-Olivier Chénier, against a force of British army regulars and colonists loyal to British rule.

The rebellion in Lower Canada broke out in November, and the British declared martial law. The first encounter occurred at the Battle of Saint-Charles, which resulted in Britain regaining control of the Richelieu region of southwestern Quebec. As the British force of 1,200 regulars and 200 militia advanced northward, the patriots built barricades around the church and convent of the village of Saint-Eustache and took over a number of houses in the center of the village.

Field Marshal Colborne commanded the British attack. He surrounded the village and deployed a battery, which commenced firing into the center where the bulk of the patriots waited. After three hours, the British stormed the convent and set it on fire; the church was also attacked and burned. As the patriots stumbled out of the smoking buildings, they were attacked and many were killed. The one-sided affair lasted for several hours, and the British force took only minimal casualties in contrast to the poorly armed patriots who lost almost half their number.

Military defeat for the patriots meant that Canada would remain a British colony but the struggle for self-determination continued. Eventually the British were forced into making concessions, and Upper and Lower Canada were unified into the Province of Canada. The unification was accompanied by the setting-up of a combined legislative assembly in 1841. **TB**

Losses: British, 5 casualties of 1,400 regulars and militia; Patriot, 80 casualties, rest of their force of 200 captured

Batoche 1885 >

⬆ *The British army overpower rebel forces near the church of Saint-Eustache in this 1840 illustration.*

Lake Okeechobee
25–28 December 1837

Conflict in the Florida territory between U.S. settlers and Seminoles (American Indian residents) erupted into major violence in December 1835. Seminole warriors murdered a senior Indian agent and a U.S. army officer, then massacred a column of soldiers, igniting the Second Seminole War.

In September 1837, Major General Thomas Jessup, army commander in Florida, received reinforcements. Among the units was the 1st Infantry regiment under Colonel Zachary Taylor. Taylor was given an area of operations near swampy Lake Okeechobee and 1,032 men: regulars, mounted volunteers, and scouts to hunt the enemy.

On 25 December, a Seminole was captured in an empty camp. He pointed the location of the other warriors: a hammock of dry woodland surrounded by a swamp filled with water and mud and covered with high sawgrass. Led by three war chiefs, 400 Seminole warriors waited behind prepared log breastworks. Shooting lanes had been cut through the grass for musket fire.

Taylor placed dismounted volunteers and scouts in the front line followed by a rank of the 4th Infantry and 6th Infantry. He held the 1st Infantry and artillery men in reserve. Struggling through thigh-deep mud, the volunteers and 6th Infantry sustained heavy casualties. The commander was killed, as were many officers. Most of the sergeants of the 6th were shot down. Seeing his ranks heavily engaged and moving slowly, Taylor sent his reserve, the 1st Infantry, to move against the Seminole's right flank. Movement through the swamp was slow, but eventually the Seminole war chiefs realized they were in danger of being surrounded. After three hours of steady fighting, the warriors' defense collapsed. **RB**

Losses: U.S., 26 dead, 112 wounded, 1 missing; Seminole, 11 dead, 14 wounded, 180 captured

◄ Horseshoe Bend 1814   Wagon Box Fight 1867 ►

Blood River
16 December 1838

Natal's Ncome River in southern Africa gained a new and gory name—Blood River—after the events of December 1838. Dingane's Zulu warriors, hoping to spring a surprise on a small group of migrating Boers, found themselves overwhelmed by European firepower. The river's waters literally ran red.

The 1830s saw successive waves of *Voortrekkers*: Dutch-descended Boers or Afrikaners who left an increasingly British-dominated Cape Colony, South Africa, for fresh lands in the interior. There they came into contact—and conflict—with indigenous peoples who, until then, had been unaffected by the colonization around the coast.

One of these was the Zulu nation. Zulu warriors, armed with stabbing spears and large shields, had become a formidable fighting force, led on campaigns of conquest by King Shaka in the 1820s. Shaka's half brother, successor, and assassin, Dingane, welcomed the Boers at first, mainly because he coveted their livestock. But early in 1838, he massacred some 600 of the immigrants and took their cattle. Andries Pretorius led a punitive expedition against Dingane. Arriving on the banks of the Ncome River, he sensed that a Zulu attack was imminent and had his followers form their wagons into a circle, in a spot that was already partly shielded by a bend in the river, to make a *laager*, or impromptu fortress. Perhaps 20,000 warriors massed for the attack; the Boers numbered 470.

Firepower made the difference. The Afrikaners' two cannon tore holes in the Zulu ranks while they maintained an incessant hail of musket fire; the women and children reloaded for the men. Although the Zulus died in the thousands, the Boers remained untouched; only three of them were wounded. **MK**

Losses: Zulu, more than 3,000; Boer, 3 wounded

Isandlwana 1879 ►

Nezib
24 June 1839

Mahmud II, sultan of the Ottoman Empire, thirsted for revenge after the humiliating defeat of his army by the Egyptian Ibrahim Pasha at Konya in 1832. However, despite the support of Prussian military advisers, the Ottoman forces suffered another major reverse at Nezib.

From his deathbed, Sultan Mahmud sent an army to attack the Egyptians in Syria. He had tried to modernize his armed forces, suppressing the reactionary janissaries and importing military specialists from Europe. However, corruption and incompetence were still the norm.

The army that marched toward Syria had Helmuth von Moltke, future Prussian chief of general staff, in charge of its artillery, but the overall commander was the hapless Hafiz Pasha. As Ibrahim Pasha's Egyptians crossed the border to attack the advancing Turks, advisers argued in vain for the latter to dig into a defensive position. Instead, Hafiz Pasha chose to confront the enemy in open battle.

The Egyptian troops remained resolute under the fire of Moltke's cannon; the Ottoman troops, in contrast, wavered as Egyptian artillery bombarded their ranks. When the infantry clashed, the Ottoman vanguard was driven back and soon thousands of Ottoman troops were in flight. Hafiz Pasha was incapable of pulling together his rapidly disintegrating army. Moltke wrote: "The Turks threw down their arms and abandoned their artillery and ammunition, flying in every direction."

Sultan Mahmud died five days after the battle. His empire survived because European powers intervened to preserve it, but Ibrahim Pasha's father, Muhammad Ali, was recognized as hereditary ruler of Egypt, founding a dynasty that remained in power until 1951. **RG**

Losses: Egyptian, 4,000 casualties of 46,000; Ottoman, no reliable figures, 10,000 captured of 80,000

◁ *Konya 1832*

Retreat from Kabul
6–13 January 1842

In 1839 Britain had invaded Afghanistan from India to block the extension of Russian influence in the country. After initial success, the military intervention ended in ignominy and tragic loss of life. The British were destined never to establish rule over the independent Afghani tribal warriors.

Britain suspected Afghanistan's ruler, Dost Muhammad, of pro-Russian leanings. They intended to install a pro-British candidate, Shoja Shah, on the Afghani throne. Led by Sir Willoughby Cotton, an expedition of British and Indian troops made light of rugged terrain and difficult conditions. They entered Kabul in August 1839. Dost Muhammad fled, and Shoja Shah was installed.

The complacent British replaced Cotton with the elderly William Elphinstone, despite mounting resistance to their presence. In 1841, Dost Muhammad's son, Akbar Khan, called for revolt. After officers who had been sent for talks with Khan were murdered, Elphinstone recognized his predicament. On 6 January 1842, his troops and their dependents left Kabul with a promise of safe passage.

Their goal was to reach British-garrisoned Jalalabad. As they entered the rugged mountain passes, they came under attack from tribesmen. The winter weather was fierce; thousands froze in the snow. Elphinstone, his authority long gone, gave himself up to Akbar Khan as his dwindling band of troops struggled on. In the Gandamak pass on 13 January, the last remnant of the British infantry, surrounded on a hilltop, was either killed or captured. One army surgeon, William Brydon, reached Jalalabad. Asked where the army was, he replied: "I am the army." Sixteen thousand troops and camp followers had died. **MK**

Losses: British, more than 16,500; Afghani, unknown

Maiwand 1880 ▷

Campeche   30 April and 16 May 1843

The naval battle of Campeche, a part of the struggle of the Republic of Texas to assert its independence from Mexico, was arguably the only battle ever won by sailing ships against steamships. It was also the last battle fought between ships crewed by British and U.S. sailors on opposing sides.

After the Battle of San Jacinto, Texas became a self-governing republic, but still feared the Mexican government's intentions. Farther south, Yucatán was also fighting for independence from Mexican rule.

Mexico mounted a blockade of the Yucatán coast, using two British-manufactured, British-crewed steamships: the large, iron-hulled, paddle-wheel frigate *Guadalupe* and the wooden-hulled, ironclad *Moctezuma*. The small Texan navy was in poor shape, its crews mutinous for lack of pay. The head of the navy, Commodore Edwin Ward Moore, accepted payment from the Yucatán rebels to aid them against the Mexicans. Moore commanded two wooden sailing ships: the sloop of war *Austin* and the brig *Wharton*. Aided by small vessels of the Yucatán navy, he broke through to the port of Campeche, surviving a two-hour running fight on 30 April. There he was trapped, with *Guadalupe* and *Moctezuma* waiting for him to emerge. Undaunted, Moore spent a fortnight fitting his ships with longer range guns, which would give him a better chance against the steamships when he attempted a breakout.

The Texans sailed out to take on the steamships on 16 May. In the exchange of fire, *Austin* suffered a good deal of structural damage, but the sailing ships' broadsides took a heavier toll of the Mexican ships' crews. The Texans returned to a heroes' welcome in Galveston, preempting Texan president Sam Houston's intention of arresting them for selling their services to another country. **RG**

Losses: Texan, 30 casualties; Mexican, 90 casualties; no ships on either side

◁ San Jacinto 1836   Palo Alto 1846 ▷

Isly   14 August 1844

Outside the north African city of Oujda, in August 1844, French marshal Bugeaud's army routed a Moroccan force four times its size. Morocco's sultan was allowed to stay in power, but the victory at Isly was vital to the consolidation of France's colonial hold on neighboring Algeria.

It had taken the French no more than a few days to take Algiers and other key centers in 1830; years later, however, resistance continued. Abd al-Qadir had proven a resourceful and remarkably effective guerrilla leader; French forces had struggled to maintain any sort of order. Brutal repression and scorched-earth punitive actions only seemed to stiffen the Algerian rebels' resolve.

France was growing increasingly exasperated at the part played by Morocco, whose sultan was known to be supporting the insurrection. Concerned that his kingdom should be the next colony on France's imperialist agenda, the Alaouite ruler, Mulai Abd ar-Rahman, had been helping Abd al-Qadir behind the scenes. Hence Bugeaud's incursion with an army, 13,000 strong, into a country on which he had no design of conquest. Marching out to meet him came some 60,000 troops under the command of the sultan's son. They were poorly armed, however, and ineptly marshaled. Far from being fazed by the sight of such an enemy, Bugeaud's battle-hardened men advanced. Holding their formation, they pushed forward, routing the Moroccans. Despite their numerical disadvantage, they came through unscathed, while the sultan's army lost 800 men.

Having been shown who was in charge in the region, Mulai Abd ar-Rahman was allowed to remain in power; in Algeria, the counterinsurgency campaign was intensified. Bugeaud was awarded the title Duke of Isly. **MK**

Losses: Moroccan, 800; French, none

◁ Conquest of Algiers 1830   Sidi Brahim 1845 ▷

Marshal Bugeaud's triumph in the desert, from a painting by Horace Vernet (1789–1863).

Sidi Brahim 21–25 September 1845

The campaign of resistance to French colonialism led by Abd al-Qadir in Algeria was a classic exercise in guerrilla warfare. At Sidi Brahim the insurgents surrounded and annihilated a force of French cavalry, although French honor was redeemed by the incredible courage of a handful of heroes.

Algerian resistance to French occupation had been hampered by the loss of Moroccan support after the defeat at Isly, but Abd al-Qadir and his Berber followers were determined that the fight for Algeria's freedom should continue. On 21 September 1845, French Lieutenant Colonel Lucien de Montagnac led a squadron of hussars and a detachment of chasseurs (light infantrymen), numbering about 450 men, into an ambush by a far larger rebel force not far from the border with Morocco. Montagnac ill-advisedly ordered his men to charge the enemy. Overwhelmingly outnumbered, the hussars were cut down quickly as their charge ground

to a halt in the thick of the rebel throng. About eighty surviving chasseurs took sanctuary in the structure of a tomb, from which they fought a desperate defensive action. Holed up there, with their water and their ammunition steadily depleted, they faced certain death but chose to fight on.

The story goes that Abd al-Qadir ordered a captured French officer to demand the men's surrender. Instead, the Frenchman exhorted them to fight on and was beheaded. The rebel leader then told a captive bugler to sound the retreat; defiantly, he gave the signal to charge. Finally, their ammunition long since spent, the few survivors resolved to make a "death or glory" break for freedom, bayonets fixed. Only sixteen survived; Montagnac was not among them. The victory was ultimately to no purpose because Abd al-Qadir surrendered two years later. **MK**

Losses: Algerian, unknown; French, 435

◁ Isly 1844

A nineteenth-century watercolor by Gaspard Gobaut shows the French army forced into a retreat.

Ferozeshah 21–22 December 1845

In the early nineteenth century, Maharaja Ranjit Singh created a powerful Sikh empire in the Punjab, while the British were consolidating their hold on the rest of the Indian subcontinent. In the 1840s the British and Sikhs fought some of the hardest battles in the history of the British Empire.

After Maharaja Ranjit Singh died in 1839, the Sikh Empire became unstable at a time when the British continued to threaten the southern borders of Sikh territory. Eventually, the peace was shattered when the British, under the command of Sir Hugh Gough, advanced toward the state of Ferozepur.

The Sikh Khalsa army, under Lal Singh, responded by moving south, fighting an inconclusive encounter with the British at Mudki on 18 December. The two armies clashed again when the British reached the Sikh defensive positions at Ferozeshah. Gough attacked at once, but took heavy losses from the Sikh artillery, which had been trained by European mercenaries. Gough's second in command, Sir Henry Hardinge, was so appalled at the losses that he sent a rider to Mudki to give the order to prepare for a full British withdrawal.

On the second day, the British army was supported by units of the Bengal army and managed to push the Sikhs back. Almost as soon as the British and Bengalese forces were breaking through, a large contingent of Sikh reinforcements arrived, under the command of Tej Singh. As Gough and Hardinge were contemplating surrender or imminent destruction, the second Sikh force inexplicably withdrew and the battle ended with no clear victor. After the battle, the Sikh Khalsa commanders were accused of treachery in Lahore, and the lull in hostilities gave the British time to reinforce their troops and continue the war. **TB**

Losses: Sikh, unknown; British (East India Company), 2,500 casualties of 16,000

Sobraon 1846 ▶

⬆ *The Sikh army fought well at the Battle of Ferozeshah but was let down by poor commanders.*

Sobraon   10 January 1846

The Battle of Sobraon was fought in the Punjab region of northern India and was the decisive encounter of the First Anglo-Sikh War. It involved the forces of the British East India Company, under Sir Hugh Gough, and a Khalsa army of the Sikh Empire, under Tej Singh and Lal Singh.

Ferozeshah was followed by recriminations on both sides. The Sikhs accused Tej Singh of holding back his Khalsa relief force when victory could have been obtained, and Sir Henry Hardinge accused Gough of recklessness. Seeking to repulse the British and restore their honor, the Khalsa leaders moved south and established a fortified bridgehead across the River Sutlej at Sobraon. Gough was chastened sufficiently by Hardinge's accusations to wait for the arrival of heavy siege guns before marching to meet the Sikhs.

The two armies met at the river on 10 February. Unlike at Ferozeshah, this time Gough was persuaded to pound the Sikh positions with his cannonade before launching an attack, but he was still noted by his fellow officers as being too eager to advance. Gough's attack finally came with a two-pronged assault on the Sikh flanks. However, the action on the right foundered and was chased back by Sikhs who killed the wounded British troops. Spurred on by the outrage of seeing their wounded comrades slaughtered, Gough ordered a full assault that was backed up by cavalry on the right.

The result was a savage fight in which the Sikhs, who refused to surrender, lost thousands of men by the banks of the river. By 13 February, the British had advanced to threaten the Sikh capital, and the Sikhs were forced to cede large parts of the Punjab to the British East India Company in the Treaty of Lahore. **TB**

Losses: Sikh, 12,000 casualties of 25,000; British (East India Company), 2,300 casualties of 20,000

◁ *Ferozeshah 1845*   *Chillianwallah 1849* ▷

Nineteenth-century watercolor by an artist of the Punjab school: British and Sikh troops clash in battle. ↑

Palo Alto 8 May 1846

The Mexican government's refusal of the treaty signed by General Santa Anna after San Jacinto left a disputed area between the Rio Grande, the boundary claimed by Texas, and an ill-defined line farther north claimed by Mexico. Meanwhile, Congress had approved the annexation of Texas.

After the annexation, an army of observation, under Major General Zachary Taylor, was sent to establish a U.S. presence. He landed in July 1845 near Corpus Christi, Texas, and camped on the Gulf of Mexico coast. Talks between the United States and Mexico failed, and in March 1846 Taylor was ordered to the Rio Grande.

He shifted his supply base to Point Isabel on the Gulf and marched his troops to the north riverbank across from Matamoras, Mexico. Patrols from the Mexican army, commanded by Major General Mariano Arista, successfully ambushed several U.S. detachments. When Arista crossed the river in force in order to cut the road to the coast,

Taylor led his troops to Point Isabel for reinforcements and supplies. His small fort on the river was beseiged.

On 7 May, Taylor started back with 2,228 men and cannon, including two batteries of light, six-pounder horse-drawn "flying artillery" pieces. Arista placed his battle line of 3,300 to block the road on the grassy plain of Palo Alto. Taylor advanced with his heavier force on the right. Mexican artillery was ineffective, and Arista's attempts to flank Taylor's right with cavalry were repulsed by U.S. infantry. At the same time, the two U.S. flying batteries moved quickly to a position well forward in order to place deadly flanking fire on the Mexican infantry attacks. Taylor's eighteen-pounders then blasted the attacking cavalry with canister. After three hours, the Mexicans withdrew a short distance. **RB**

Losses: U.S., 5 dead, 48 wounded; Mexican, 102 dead, 129 wounded, 26 missing

◁ *Campeche 1843*　　　　　　　　　　　*Monterrey 1846* ▷

⬆ *Carl Nebel's 1851 depiction of the Battle of Palo Alto.*

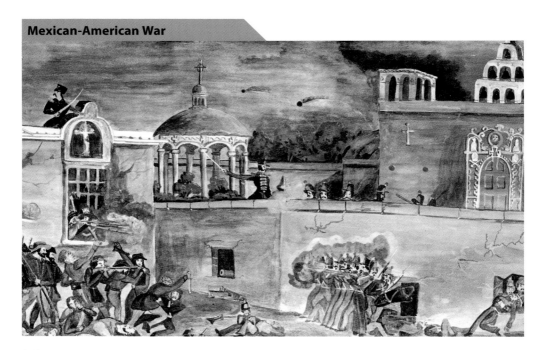

Monterrey 22–23 September 1846

On 13 May the United States declared war on Mexico. Unaware of this, on 18 May Major General Zachary Taylor crossed the Rio Grande into Mexico, after defeating the Mexicans at Palo Alto and the next day at Resca de la Palma. He occupied Matamoros and halted there awaiting orders.

News of Taylor's victories brought untrained volunteer units to join the army. These were shipped to join Taylor, raising his army to more than 6,600 men. When his proposed campaign against Monterrey was approved, Taylor organized the army into three divisions and marched, arriving north of Monterrey on 19 September.

The town was protected by forts, several on prominent nearby hills, and defended by more than 5,000 Mexican regulars led by Major General Pedro de Ampudia. After a reconnaissance, Brigadier General William Worth's division was sent around west to cut the road to Saltillo and to capture Federation Hill and

Independence Hill, while the other divisions attacked on the east. On 21 September, a cavalry attack on Worth was repulsed, and his troops successfully seized the two fortifications on Federation Hill. In the east, Taylor's advance suffered under heavy fire, but succeeded in capturing a fortified bridge and two earthworks, then pushed into town before withdrawing for the night. After dark, a detachment climbed Independence Hill for a surprise attack that captured its two positions.

On 23 September, U.S. forces attacked on the east and west of Monterrey in a bitter house-to-house battle. Cannon were brought into the streets to blast holes through house walls. The next day, at Ampudia's request, Taylor negotiated a surrender of the town, allowing Mexican forces to withdraw and an eight-week armistice. **RB**

Losses: U.S., 120 dead, 368 wounded, 43 missing; Mexican, 430 dead, wounded, or missing

◁ Palo Alto 1846   Buena Vista 1847 ▷

    American Troops Storm the Bishops' Palace in Monterrey (c. 1846–48), by Samuel Chamberlain.

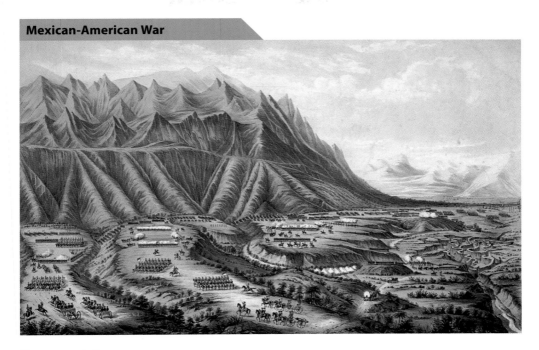

Buena Vista   22–23 February 1847

The Monterrey armistice ended in November 1846. As Major General Zachary Taylor expanded his area of control, he found his army reduced significantly. In January, most of the regular army and some volunteer units were ordered to join Lieutenant General Winfield Scott's new army on the coast.

Taylor's forces were concentrated around Saltillo. In February, Taylor learned that General Antonio López de Santa Anna was approaching with a Mexican army of 15,000. Taylor positioned his 4,700 men near Buena Vista ranch, then took troops to protect his supply base at Saltillo.

On 22 February, Taylor returned in time to refuse Santa Anna's surrender demand. Mexican light troops then used nearby mountain slopes overlooking the U.S. right flank in an attempt to turn it, but Taylor's dismounted cavalry and riflemen held steady. The next morning, Santa Anna began his main attacks. One assault, on Taylor's right, was repulsed with heavy losses. However, on the left, two

Mexican divisions collapsed the U.S. line. Taylor sent two regiments and flying artillery to delay the action until he arrived with more troops. They rallied the retreating men, stopped the advancing Mexicans, and reformed the left flank line.

Meanwhile, Mexican cavalry broke through and attacked the U.S. rear area at the ranch. The defending infantry were hard pressed, but held on with the help of dragoons. A U.S. advance in the center of the battle line ran headlong into another large Mexican assault force, catching many U.S. units out of position. The arrival of flying artillery and two reinforcing infantry regiments saved the dangerous situation and forced the Mexicans to retire. As daylight faded, Santa Anna began a slow withdrawal south with no pursuit by Taylor. **RB**

Losses: U.S., 272 dead, 387 wounded, 6 missing; Mexican, 591 dead, 1,048 wounded, 1,894 missing

◁ Monterrey 1846   Cerro Gordo 1847 ▷

⬆ *At Buena Vista, Taylor restored his reputation as a leader and turned back a major Mexican offensive.*

Cerro Gordo   17–18 April 1847

In February, Major General Winfield Scott arrived at Tampico, Mexico, with an approved strategy to capture Mexico City. He spent a month assembling his army, then landed in early March near Veracruz and captured the port to use as a base. In April, he marched west toward Mexico City.

General Antonio López de Santa Anna hoped to hold Major General Winfield Scott's army of 8,500 on the disease-ridden coast of Mexico. He placed his army of 12,000 to block the road, where it lay in a long narrow valley between high hills and a river. His units held three hills south of the road and two hills north: La Atalaya and El Telégrafo. When heavy fire stopped Scott's advance on 11 April, he sent engineers to scout the Mexican positions in Cerro Gordo. They found a north trail that bypassed the valley. Scott sent Brigadier General David Twiggs's division on this trail around the Mexican left while another division made a secondary attack against the south hills.

On 17 April, Twiggs's infantry were spotted and came under fire from La Atayala. Twiggs diverted a brigade to take La Atalaya while his other two brigades continued on the trail. With artillery support, the infantry cleared La Atalaya, but they were stopped on El Telégrafo. That night Scott directed Twiggs to capture El Telégrafo and also to continue the flanking movement.

The next morning, heavy fighting drove the El Telégrafo defenders off the hill. The Mexican cannon were then used to bombard Santa Anna's camp. At the same time, Twiggs's other brigades emerged in the Mexican rear and charged into the camp, causing a panicked retreat. The secondary attack south of the road failed, allowing many Mexicans to escape. **RB**

Losses: U.S., 63 dead, 368 wounded; Mexican, 1,000 dead or wounded, 1,000 captured

⟨ *Buena Vista 1847*   *Churubusco 1847* ⟩

Churubusco   19–20 August 1847

Following his victory at Cerro Gordo, Major General Winfield Scott moved west on the road to Mexico City. South of the city lay the huge lava field known as "El Pedregal," skirted by roads east and west. To the north these roads converged to cross a fortified river bridge at Churubusco.

On 13 August, Scott's army of 8,500 reached El Pedregal. When his engineers found a trail around the south end of the lava, Scott divided his force. Major General Gideon Pillow took two divisions and followed the trail to reach the western road near Contreras, where he defeated the west wing of General Santa Anna's army on 19–20 August, then marched to Churubusco. Meanwhile, Brigadier General William Worth's division advanced north through obstacles on the east road. He eliminated a Mexican strongpoint at San Antonio and pushed on to the bridge. Two strongpoints guarded the bridge: the stone convent of San Mateo and the bridge's gateway.

On 20 August, Pillow sent four brigades to seize the convent while Worth attacked the gateway. In both places, several infantry assaults were beaten back before hand-to-hand fighting gained footholds for the Americans late in the day. At the convent, an infantry regiment climbed the walls and, in desperate fighting, cornered the Mexicans and the San Patricio battalion of U.S. deserters. A white flag sent out by the defenders was accepted. Determined assaults by Worth's troops at the bridge gateway finally overcame the strong resistance there. Several infantry regiments crossed the river at another location and moved to cut off the Mexican retreat out of Churubusco. Dragoons pursued the fleeing Mexicans almost to the gates of Mexico City. **RB**

Losses: U.S., 137 dead, 865 wounded; Mexican, 10,000 dead, wounded, or captured

⟨ *Cerro Gordo 1847*   *Chapultepec 1847* ⟩

Chapultepec 12–14 September 1847

The fortified castle of Chapultepec sat on a rocky hill overlooking causeways leading to Mexico City's two western gates. It was the last obstacle that Major General Winfield Scott had to secure before attacking the city, defended by the 15,000-man army of General Antonio López de Santa Anna.

To defend the castle, General Antonio López de Santa Anna installed General Nicolas Bravo with 1,000 troops, fifty military cadets, and some artillery in buildings and supporting earthworks. Beginning on 12 September, Major General Winfield Scott's artillery bombarded the castle; on 13 September, he launched his main attack.

Two divisions advanced abreast from the west: Major General Gideon Pillow's division, with Brigadier General William Worth's in support, on his left; Brigadier John Quitman's division approached from the south along a causeway. Pillow's brigades fought through a grove of trees at the base of Chapultepec hill and up the slope, then faltered at the walls when the scaling ladders failed to appear. Quitman's men were also stopped by artillery defending the causeway. He sent a brigade to flank the position and another with ladders to assist Pillow.

When the ladders appeared, the U.S. assault surged over the walls. The troops from the three divisions became intermixed as they scrambled into the castle. By 9:30 AM, the castle was taken. Quitman then led a rush of infantry along the southern causeway to capture one gate, while Worth—with an artillery gun section—pushed forward and seized the other gate. By dusk, Worth's and Quitman's troops were in the city, but had to halt as darkness fell. Early in the morning of 14 September, a Mexican delegation told Scott that Santa Anna and his army had fled the city. **RB**

Losses: U.S., 130 dead, 703 wounded, 29 missing; Mexican, 3,000 dead, wounded, or captured

◁ *Churubusco 1847*

"[Chapultepec] was manned by the most learned and skillful gunners . . . including some French artillerists of distinction."

Edward Deering Mansfield, historian

⬆ *Detail from a fresco (c. 1929–30) in the National Palace, Mexico City, by Diego Rivera depicting the assault on Chapultepec.*

First Custoza   23–26 July 1848

In 1848, Europe was swept by popular rebellions. The Piedmontese monarchy attempted to exploit revolutionary outbursts against Austrian rule in Lombardy and Venetia to drive the Austrians out of Italy. The Piedmontese were defeated at Custoza, but took a step toward assuming leadership of the Italian nationalist movement, the Risorgimento.

King Carlo Alberto of Piedmont hesitated to take advantage of the uprisings, despite the fact that revolution at home meant that Austria could not reinforce its Italian provinces. In fact, he hesitated so long that the revolutionary tide was receding by the time he marched, and Austria was able to send sizable reinforcements.

The Piedmontese took Peschiera, one of the four great Austrian fortresses known as the "Quadrilateral," and took up defensive positions in the hills at Custoza. The veteran Austrian commander, Marshal Joseph Radetzky, closed in on them with a substantially superior army. In two days of bitter hand-to-hand fighting, the Piedmontese troops fought with courage and determination, repelling repeated attacks. However, the troops were let down by their aristocratic officers, many of whom had disdained formal training. Supply provisions were sketchy at best; no thought was given to rotating troops so that those in the front line might rest.

Mutual exhaustion allowed the Piedmontese to retreat under honorable terms, and Austrian rule was restored. However, the Piedmontese had fought under the tricolor Italian flag, and the temporary presence during the war of contingents from other Italian states did suggest a national, rather than simply Piedmontese, dynastic agenda to the campaign, which was, in the long term, perhaps more threatening to Austrian rule. **JS**

Losses: Piedmontese, more than half of 22,000; Austrian, more than half of 33,000

Novara 1849 ▶

Battle of Custoza by Giovanni Fattori (1825–1908), a master of realistic landscapes and military scenes. ↑

Chillianwallah 13 January 1849

In 1848, the Sikhs led a rebellion against British dominance of the Punjab, precipitating the outbreak of the Second Anglo-Sikh War. Although the Sikhs eventually lost the war and their independence, they inflicted a costly defeat upon British forces at Chillianwallah, which was a significant blow to Britain's prestige in India.

The Second Anglo-Sikh War started when rebellion broke out in the city of Multan, resulting in the murder of a number of British officers. Despite misgivings over his competence during the First Anglo-Sikh War, Sir Hugh Gough was given command of the British force sent to suppress the revolt.

Late on 13 January 1849, he encountered a Sikh army under the command of Sher Singh Attariwalla. Despite the lateness of the hour, and ignoring the advice of his officers who urged caution and the commencement of an artillery bombardment, Gough ordered an immediate full-scale attack by infantry and cavalry, just as he had done at Ferozeshah, four years earlier. The result was a disaster. The British struggled to make headway through dense vegetation without any artillery support. Cohesion was lost, and the chain of command broke down. Some units were completely routed, leaving their colors strewn across the bloody field of battle.

As darkness fell, Gough ordered his stumbling army to fall back. Further carnage was averted only by three days of rain, which forced both armies to withdraw. Gough went on to defeat the Sikhs at Gujarat, but was criticized severely for recklessness and was relieved of his command. The battle taught the British to respect the Sikhs as fighting men, and Sikhs later proved an important source of soldiers for the British imperial army. **TB**

Losses: Sikh, 3,700 casualties of 22,000; British (East India Company), 2,500 casualties of 16,000

◁ Sobraon 1846   Cawnpore 1857 ▷

⬆ The Battle of Chillianwallah *(c. 1849) by Charles Becher Young.*

Novara 22–23 March 1849

Despite their defeat the previous year at First Custoza, the Piedmontese reentered the fray against Austria. The result was a second crushing victory for the veteran Austrian Marshal Joseph Radetzky. Yet again, in the long run, the cause of Italian unification was strengthened.

King Carlo Alberto was forced by the weight of public opinion and the rise of republicanism to renounce the armistice he had signed after his defeat at Custoza. He had tried to address the weaknesses of his army, but the other Italian states showed little interest in supporting the campaign, and his own troops lacked enthusiasm.

Lombard volunteers, under the command of General Ramorino, were ordered to occupy territory between the Ticino and Po rivers and delay any Austrian advance while the Piedmontese marched on Milan. However, Ramorino abandoned his position (for which he was later executed), allowing the Austrians free passage to outflank the Piedmontese. The Piedmontese were defeated at Sforesca and Mortara, before the main battle at Novara. Although outnumbered, the Austrians were far more professional, and it was only the dogged determination of the Piedmontese infantry that prevented a rapid collapse.

The control of the town of Bicocca was key to the battle, and here the fighting was bitterest. The town changed hands several times, with Carlo Alberto at the forefront of the fighting, refusing to take cover. With the arrival of Austrian reinforcements, the Piedmontese position became impossible and they were forced to accept harsh peace terms. Carlo Alberto soon abdicated and died in exile; he became a romantic figure—the king who had risked and lost all for the cause of Italy. **JS**

Losses: Unknown

◁ First Custoza 1848   Rome 1849 ▷

Rome 30 April–1 July 1849

The defense of the short-lived Roman Republic made Giuseppe Garibaldi a hero of Italian nationalists. The republic was overthrown by French forces, and the pope restored to power. However, defeat in Rome only strengthened the long-term cause of Italian unification.

In November 1848, revolution in the Papal States swept Pope Pius IX from power, and he called upon Catholic powers to restore his authority. The newly elected French president (soon to be self-appointed emperor), Louis Napoleon Bonaparte, decided to appease French Catholics and forestall an Austrian invasion, by intervening.

By April 1849, the first 10,000 French troops had landed and were marching on Rome, expecting to be hailed as liberators. The Roman garrison, commanded by the guerrilla leader Giuseppe Garibaldi, was a mixture of volunteers from across Italy, as well as papal troops who had joined the revolution; it numbered just 7,000, but the men were determined to fight. The French were shocked to come under cannon fire as they approached the city and retreated. An armistice allowed the French to assemble 30,000 troops equipped with siege artillery. When hostilities were renewed, the Romans neglected to warn outlying positions, and the crucial position at Villa Pamfili was surprised and overwhelmed.

With the city covered by French guns, the issue was effectively decided. Futile but heroic counterattacks were launched, and a determined stand was made on the walls. When they fell, hastily constructed inner defenses were defended with great courage. When the city fell, Garibaldi led volunteers into the countryside to fight on. Italians proved how well they could fight for the ideal of Italy. **JS**

Losses: Unknown

◁ Novara 1849   Magenta 1859 ▷

Temesvar   9 August 1849

Caseros   3 February 1852

In 1848, Hungarian nationalists rebelled against Austrian Hapsburg rule. Austrian and Russian forces crushed this revolution at Temesvar and the autonomy Hungary had enjoyed was overturned. It was a great victory for the forces of reaction, but Hungarian national aspirations remained strong.

The battle fought at Caseros, Buenos Aires, was a significant turning point in the history of Argentina. The confrontation brought an end to two decades of rule by the dictator Juan Manuel de Rosas and set the country on the road to centralized constitutional government.

The bloodless Hungarian Revolution of March 1848 was a great triumph but it left problems in its wake, including the role of the national minorities, who were mostly Slavs. They wanted the same rights that Hungarians claimed, but the Hungarians felt that they could not fragment their fledgling state while the Hapsburg rulers in Vienna were recovering from the revolutionary shockwave that had swept Europe. It did not take long for the Hapsburgs to build an anti-Hungarian coalition among the alienated minorities, proclaim Hungary under martial law, and launch an invasion.

A formal declaration of independence provided the Russians with a pretext to intervene. Soon a ramshackle Hungarian army—which included some Slav volunteers who hated and feared the Russians—was driven toward Temesvar. Heavily outnumbered, and their cause already effectively lost, the outcome was certain before the first shot. The heaviest fighting was around the village of Kisbecskerek. Here Hungarians enjoyed early success through an audacious cavalry charge that sent the Austrians reeling back. An artillery duel developed, which the Hungarians lacked the ammunition to win. As their gunfire died down, the enemy closed in. A retreat began, but any hope of escape vanished when the Hungarian rearguard panicked and fled. The survivors scattered and returned home—the revolution was over. **JS**

As governor of Buenos Aires, Rosas dominated the loose federation of provinces that constituted Argentina in the 1830s and 1840s. In 1851, however, he found ranged against him an alliance between the Brazilian Empire, Uruguay, and two provinces of northeastern Argentina: Entre Rios and Corrientes. The Argentinians made up the bulk of the forces that engaged in the subsequent conflict, which was primarily a civil war. Rosas's opponents were led by General Justo José de Urquiza, the governor of Entre Rios.

On paper, the forces that met at Caseros were well matched, but morale in the Rosas ranks was poor. The anti-Rosas alliance suffered from divided command, because the leaders of the different allied contingents refused to take orders from General Urquiza. The Brazilians provided a relatively small body of 3,000 soldiers, but these were the only professional troops on the field and they played a crucial role, as did Urquiza's cavalry. After three hours' fighting, the Rosas army's resistance collapsed when its artillery ran out of ammunition. Rosas fled the field, resigned his governorship, and sailed into exile onboard a British frigate. Urquiza was brutal in triumph, executing captured soldiers and officers. He became president of Argentina under a new constitution in 1854, but there was further civil strife before genuine national unity was achieved in the 1860s. **RG**

Losses: Hungarian, more than 10,000 dead or wounded, 6,000 captured of 55,000; Austrian and Russian, fewer than 5,000 dead or wounded of 90,000

Losses: Rosas, 1,500 casualties, 7,000 captured of 22,000; Allied, 600 casualties of 24,000

Riachuelo 1865 ▶

Sinope 30 November 1853

The Battle of Sinope, fought between the imperial Russian navy and a fleet of the Turkish Ottoman Empire, was the event that precipitated the Crimean War. It was also a turning point in the history of naval warfare, demonstrating the devastating effect of explosive shells on wooden-hulled ships.

In October 1853, the Ottoman Empire declared war on Russia. Czar Nicholas I retaliated by sending a fleet under the command of Admiral Pavel Nakhimov into the Black Sea. A much weaker Ottoman naval force, commanded by Admiral Osman Pasha, took shelter from bad weather in the harbor at Sinope in northern Turkey.

Nakhimov decided to sail into the harbor and attack the Turkish warships, the largest of which were frigates. Six Russian ships of the line moved into the harbor in two squadrons and anchored in line beside the Ottoman ships. The Russians were equipped with Paixhan guns, innovative weapons that fired an explosive shell in a flat trajectory. The Russian warships fired volley after volley, easily piercing the wooden hulls of the Ottoman ships to devastating effect. Some were completely destroyed, whereas others ran aground in flames.

After an hour of fighting, only *Taif*, a steam frigate, managed to escape. The battle was the first significant operational use of naval guns firing explosive shells and caused naval designers to begin searching for ways of armoring wooden ships, leading to the development of "ironclads." The effect of the battle on public opinion in Britain and France was decisive. Although it was a legitimate act of war, the one-sided combat was denounced in the press as a massacre. The British and French backed the Turks against the Russians, soon intervening directly in the Crimea. **TB**

Losses: Ottoman, 7 frigates and 4 corvettes, 3,200 casualties; Russian, none

Alma 1854 ▶

Russian-Turkish Sea Battle of Sinope (1853) by Ivan Aivazovsky, known for his dramatic seascapes. ↑

Alma 20 September 1854

In September 1854, an Anglo-French expeditionary force landed in the Crimea intending to capture the Russian Black Sea port of Sevastopol. The Anglo-French force was confronted by a Russian army under General Alexander Menshikov. The Battle of Alma was the first of the Crimean War.

The Russian army occupied a defensive position made formidable by cliffs on the south bank of the Alma. In order to advance, the allied army would have to assault Telegraph Hill, and to the east, Kourgane Hill, both of which were topped with Russian redoubts. The valley in between led to Sevastopol, but no advance would be possible if the Russians held the two hills.

The French commander, General Jacques St. Arnaud, planned to cross the river under the cover of a naval bombardment and scale the cliffs with a detachment of French troops. This would divert the Russians and allow the British to attack the redoubts. The French part of the plan began successfully but lost momentum, and the Russians restored their lines. As a result, the British attack faltered and their battalions became entangled in chaos.

Meanwhile, the British commander, Lord Raglan, sought a good vantage point from which to watch the progress of the battle. Advancing fearlessly—even foolhardily—to an exposed forward position, he found a spot that overlooked the Russian rear and ordered guns to be brought up. The guns opened fire with great effect, surprising the Russians and turning the battle in the allies' favor. Both hills were taken after hard fighting by the infantry, with losses heavy in frontal assaults on Russian defenses. The allied army failed to press home its advantage, and the Russians were able to retreat unmolested and regroup. **TB**

Losses: Anglo-French, 3,300 casualties of 60,000; Russian, 5,600 casualties of 37,000

[<] *Sinope 1853*   *Balaclava 1854* [>]

A nineteenth-century illustration of the storming of the heights south of the Alma River Valley.

Balaclava   25 October 1854

The Battle of Balaclava is one of the most famous— or infamous—events in British military history. It is remembered for the performance of the "thin red line" of infantry and for the heroic but misguided "Charge of the Light Brigade"—the latter immortalized in verse by Alfred, Lord Tennyson.

After the defeat at the Battle of Alma, the Russian army regrouped at the heavily fortified port of Sevastopol, which the allies then besieged. The British, under Lord Raglan, took over the southern port of Balaclava, where they could be supplied easily and where they protected the right flank of the allied siege operations. The Russians decided to break the siege before the allied troops could become entrenched and, under the command of General Pavel Liprandi, attacked the allies at Balaclava.

Early in the battle, the Russians occupied the Fedyukhin and Vorontsov heights. From these vantage points, they pounded allied positions with artillery. Russian infantry attacked a series of Turkish-held redoubts and, although

"Not tho' the soldiers knew, someone had blunder'd . . . Charging an army, while all the world wonder'd." Alfred, Lord Tennyson

the Turks fought bravely, the Russians broke through to threaten Balaclava. Between the Russian cavalry and the port stood only the kilted infantry of Sir Colin Campbell's 93rd Highland Regiment and a few marines. Told by Campbell they must win or die where they stood, the infantry beat off two Russian cavalry charges by forming up in line on the plain and firing disciplined volleys. They became known as the "thin red line," an abbreviated version of a description by war correspondent William Russell. The Russian cavalry was then routed by Sir James

Scarlett's Heavy Brigade: Scots Greys, dragoons, and horse artillery. The fact that they attacked uphill at a trot makes the designation of this action as the "charge of the Heavy Brigade" something of a misnomer.

Lord Raglan had, meanwhile, gained a good vantage point over the whole area of the battle. He observed the Russians moving artillery from the captured redoubts on the Vorontsov heights and sent orders for the Light Brigade—lancers, hussars, and light dragoons—under the command of Lord Cardigan, to disrupt the operation. Raglan phrased the order, " . . . advance rapidly to the front, follow the enemy, and try to prevent the enemy from carrying away the guns." However, by the time the order reached Cardigan, it had passed between several commanders and had been shortened to "advance rapidly." Cardigan thought the order was absurd but had to obey what he thought were Raglan's wishes. He led a charge straight down the center of North Valley to attack the Russian artillery battery sited there. The brigade advanced slowly at first and then at full charge, all the time fired on by the Russian guns on the heights as well as the battery in front of them. The allies had suffered heavy losses by the time they reached the Russian battery, where they were also threatened by a counterattack from the Russian cavalry. Out of more than 600 men who embarked on the charge, 110 were killed and about 160 were either wounded or captured.

Lord Raglan had watched the cavalry charge from his position in dismay, powerless to stop it. He abandoned attempts to retake the heights and pulled his infantry divisions back to form up defensive positions against further Russian attacks on Balaclava. The Russians claimed a victory because the positions that they had gained severely hindered the allied siege of Sevastopol. **TB**

Losses: Allied, 615 casualties of 4,500; Russian, 627 casualties of 25,000

◁ *Alma 1854*   *Inkerman 1854* ▷

Detail from The Valley of Death, after the Charge of the Light Brigade *, a photograph by Roger Fenton.* ➡

Inkerman   5 November 1854

The Battle of Inkerman was an attempt by the Russian army, led by General Alexander Menshikov, to defeat the Anglo-French forces, commanded by General Lord Raglan and General François Canrobert, and force the allies to abandon the Siege of Sevastopol during the Crimean War.

After Balaclava, the Russians exposed the allies' weak supply routes and forced them into a long thin line that was vulnerable to attack. Menshikov felt that there was an opportunity to defeat the allies in the field and lift the Siege of Sevastopol. His plan involved seizing a long line of ridges called Mount Inkerman. The ridges were held by Brigadier General Pennefather's 2nd Division.

The British had built a wall, called the "Barrier," and a fortified position, known as the "Sandbag Battery." Menshikov mounted simultaneous attacks on these positions with overwhelming strength; more than 40,000 Russian troops attacked fewer than 3,000 defenders.

However, on the morning of the attack, the ridges were enveloped in thick fog. A large section of the Russian force took the wrong route and was pinned down on the edge of the Careenage ravine. The Russians sustained heavy losses in chaotic hand-to-hand fighting and were pushed back by the 47th Regiment of the Light Division. British and French reinforcements arrived, and the guards pushed the Russians back from the Barrier. Sandbag Battery swapped ownership several times but was held by the allies when a French division counterattacked. Even when the Russians managed to move forward from the Careenage ravine, they met heavy resistance. By 2:30 PM, the Russians called off the attack. Menshikov abandoned hopes of defeating the allies in the field, and the war became focused on the Siege of Sevastopol. **TB**

Losses: Allied, 3,300 casualties of 15,700; Russian, 10,700 casualties of 42,000

◁ *Balaclava 1854*　　　　　　　　*Malakoff 1855* ▷

Captain Arthur Earle, Brigadier General Philip Macpherson, and officers of the 4th Division. Photograph by Roger Fenton.

Malakoff   7 September 1855

The Battle of Malakoff was the climax of the Crimean War. French forces commanded by General MacMahon played the leading role in the defeat of Russian forces commanded by General Pavel Nakhimov. The allied victory led to the capture of Sevastopol by the allies and the end of the war.

The allied Siege of Sevastopol had continued since October 1854. Russian engineer Eduard Totleben organized a masterly defense despite constant shelling from allied siege guns. In August 1855, a Russian sortie tried to force the allies to abandon the siege, but failed with heavy casualties. By 7 September, the French command considered that the fortifications of the Malakoff redoubt on the southern side of the city were sufficiently reduced by bombardment that an assault could succeed.

At midday, when the Russians were occupied with changing their garrison, the French swarmed forward over the rubble and engaged in desperate hand-to-

hand combat. All along the lines, the fighting was bloody and savage, resulting in horrendous casualties on both sides. The French were encouraged when a Zouave detachment took the Malakoff tower and the French flag was raised over the redoubt. The British assault on one of the V-shaped redans was pushed back; the Russians gained heart at this but were targeted by heavy artillery. Eventually, suffering unsustainable casualties, the Russians drew back, and the Malakoff redoubt was taken. With it came the fall of Sevastopol.

On 11 September, the Russians burned what remained of their Black Sea fleet and withdrew completely. The war was over, although an armistice was not agreed until February 1856. In total, the Siege of Sevastopol had cost the allies 128,000 casualties from war and disease, while the Russians had suffered 100,000 casualties. **TB**

Losses: Allied, 10,200 casualties; Russian, 12,900 casualties

⟨ *Inkerman 1854*

⬆ *The ruins of the Malakoff tower and its semaphore. Photograph by George Shaw Lefevre.*

Cawnpore 5–25 June 1857

The Siege of Cawnpore (Kanpur) was a key event during the Indian rebellion of 1857, traditionally known as the "Indian mutiny." The British garrison was unprepared for a long siege and surrendered to the Indian rebels. British women and children were later killed in what came to be known as the "Bibighar massacre."

The Indian rebellion—often called the First War of Indian Independence—started as a small-scale mutiny of sepoys in the town of Meerut. Sepoys were native troops in the employ of the British East India Company. In June, the sepoys in Cawnpore rose up and besieged the town. The British commander at Cawnpore, Major General Sir Hugh Wheeler, had been confident of the support of a local Maratha leader, Nana Sahib, but Nana Sahib assumed the leadership of the rebellion.

The British garrison was not supplied with enough food and water to withstand an extended siege. After three weeks, Wheeler agreed to surrender on the condition that the garrison and its women and children would be given safe passage to Allahabad. As the party traveled to board boats, the rear of the column was attacked by sepoys, and wounded soldiers were killed.

The rebel sepoys then attacked the rest of the column, setting fire to the boats, killing the men, and capturing the women and children. When news came that a British relief force had left Allahabad for Cawnpore, the women and children were hacked to death with meat cleavers in what came to be known as the Bibighar massacre. Their bodies were thrown down a well to hide the evidence; however, when the British retook Cawnpore, the remains were discovered. The British took savage revenge against rebel sepoys and Indian civilians. **TB**

"All the wonted terrors of a multitudinous enemy without, of a feeble garrison and scant shelter within . . ." Sir J. W. Kaye, historian

⬆ *Ruins at Cawnpore, where rebels inflicted the worst massacre of the Indian mutiny. Detail of a photograph by Felice A. Beato.*

Losses: British, all 300 soldiers and 600 civilians dead, except 5 men and 2 women; Indian, unknown

◁ *Chillianwallah 1849*　　　　　*Delhi 1857* ▷

Delhi 8 June–21 September 1857

The hard-fought recapture of Delhi by the British army was a decisive moment in the suppression of the Indian rebellion of 1857. It extinguished Indian dreams of recreating the rule of the Mughal Empire. The rebellion lost its cohesion, allowing the British to defeat any remaining isolated pockets of resistance.

After the capture of Delhi by rebels in May, the British were unable to launch a counterattack because their army was dispersed over vast distances. It took quite some time for the British to assemble an army, but, in June, two columns were combined with a force of Ghurkas.

The makeshift force managed to occupy a ridge overlooking the city but was not large enough to launch an assault. Inside the city were more than 30,000 mutineers loyal to Bahadur Shah, who was holding court as the Mughal emperor. The large numbers of mutineers meant that the British force felt as though they were the ones under siege, and, as the weeks wore on, the British began to suffer from outbreaks of cholera and dysentery. However, reinforcements slowly arrived from the Punjab, including a siege train of thirty-two guns and 2,000 more men under the command of Brigadier General John Nicholson.

By mid-September, the British had assembled a force of 9,000, which consisted of 3,000 regular troops and 6,000 Sikhs, Punjabis, and Ghurkas. The siege guns opened fire and, after a few days, made sufficiently large breaches in the walls to launch an attack. The assault was met with stiff resistance but, after a week of savage street-to-street fighting, Delhi was back under British control. Bahadur Shah was arrested and died in exile in Rangoon in 1862. He was the last of the Mughal emperors. **TB**

Losses: British, 1,200 dead, 4,600 wounded of 9,000; Indian, 5,000 dead or wounded of 40,000

◁ Cawnpore 1857   Lucknow 1857 ▷

Lucknow 16–22 November 1857

The relief of Lucknow occurred during the Indian rebellion and consisted of two attempts by the British to rescue Sir Henry Lawrence and a contingent of British and Indian troops, along with several hundred civilians, from the center of Lucknow where they held out under siege conditions for five months.

On 30 June 1857, Sir Henry Lawrence was forced to retreat into the Residency, the central fortress of Lucknow. The Residency was protected by battery positions but was vulnerable because a number of buildings surrounding it were occupied by rebel snipers and artillery. Despite this precarious position, and the death of Lawrence early in the siege, the troops and civilians managed to hold out thanks to the actions of a number of soldiers who were later awarded the Victoria Cross.

The first relief attempt occurred on 25 September when a force under the command of Major General Sir Henry Havelock fought its way across rebel-held territory to Lucknow. However, by the time he reached the Residency, Havelock had lost so many troops that he considered it too risky to attempt to evacuate the civilians. The relief force joined the garrison, improved the defenses, and waited for a second relief.

On 16 November, a much larger force approached Lucknow, led by Lieutenant General Sir Colin Campbell. The force stormed the Secundra Bagh, a walled enclosure blocking Campbell's route to the Residency. By now, the British soldiers had learned of the massacre at Cawnpore, and no mercy was shown to the rebels. On 22 November, Campbell was able to evacuate the Residency and withdraw. After defeating rebels in December, Campbell returned in March and recaptured Lucknow. **TB**

Losses: British, 2,500 casualties of 8,000; Indian, unknown

◁ Delhi 1857

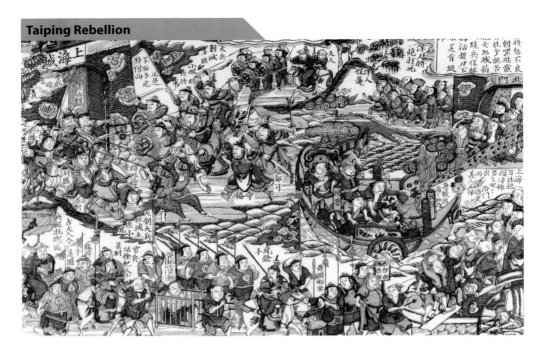

Sanhe 7–18 November 1858

The Taiping Rebellion in China, which lasted from 1851 to 1864, was one of the bloodiest civil conflicts ever, causing an estimated 11 million deaths. The battle at Sanhe in 1858 exemplified the nature of the fighting in the first phase of the war, during which the rebels were mostly triumphant.

The Taiping movement was founded and led by Hong Xiuquan, a visionary who was inspired by a highly individual interpretation of Christianity. China was seething with discontent under the decaying Manchu dynasty, and millions joined the rebel cause.

The Taiping formed mass armies that took the city of Nanjing in 1853 with barely a fight. While the Manchu army seemed incapable of resistance, in Hunan province an official and landowner, Zeng Guofan, recruited and trained local forces—the Xiang army—that achieved a far greater level of effectiveness. In 1858, a Xiang army force under General Li Xubin advanced from Hunan into Anhui province, wresting a series of cities from Taiping control. In November, Li Xubin's force reached Sanhe, a town that the Taiping—using their vast manpower—had surrounded with freshly built walls and forts. Having left garrisons in each captured city, Li Xubin had only 6,000 men, facing a Taiping force of at least ten times that number. The well-trained Xiang troops nonetheless succeeded in taking the outlying forts, pinning the Taiping inside the walled town.

On 16 November, however, the Xiang army force was lured into an open battle in which its elite troops were overwhelmed by the sheer mass of their enemy. Retreating to the forts, the survivors resisted valiantly, but within two days all the forts had fallen and the Xiang force had been annihilated. Li Xubin committed suicide, hanging himself from a tree. **RG**

Losses: Taiping, unknown; Xiang, 6,000 dead of 6,000

Taku Forts 1859 ▶

A nineteenth-century Chinese popular print of fighting during the Taiping Rebellion. ⬆

Magenta 4 June 1859

French ruler Emperor Napoleon III allied himself with the kingdom of Piedmont, intending to drive the Austrians out of northern Italy. Moving 130,000 men to Italy by train—the first mass movement of troops by railroad—Napoleon III then ran into a chaotic encounter with the Austrians at Magenta.

An early offensive by the Austrians against Piedmont, before the kingdom was supported by the French, might have given them some sort of victory. Prevarication prevented this, and the Austrian armies withdrew to the Ticino River and took up defensive positions. As the French approached, the Piedmontese should have supported them, but their commanders were also hesitant and the French fought alone.

They managed to establish bridgeheads across the river, over hastily built pontoon bridges in the north, and at San Martino across a bridge that the Austrians had intended to destroy but only damaged. Around San Martino the fighting was fierce, even desperate. French grenadiers found themselves attacked repeatedly by Austrian columns. French reinforcements had to run in sweltering heat to relieve the grenadiers. It was a battle in which tactics counted for little, but bayonet and sword and fighting spirit predominated.

It seemed that the battle had ended for the day. However, to the north, French troops under General MacMahon, which initially had been repulsed, rallied and assaulted the town of Magenta. Every building had been fortified and manned by sharpshooters, and each house had to be cleared in a series of bloody encounters. Finally the town fell, and the Austrian army retreated. Soon afterward, popular risings were to put Tuscany, Parma, and Modena into Piedmontese hands. **JS**

Losses: French, more than 4,500 dead or wounded of 54,000; Austrian, 5,700 dead or wounded, 4,500 captured of 58,000

◁ Rome 1849   Solferino 1859 ▷

The capture of Magenta was a bloody encounter; the Austrians led by Marshal Gyulai were forced to retreat.

Solferino   24 June 1859

French emperor Napoleon III and Austrian emperor Franz Joseph commanded opposing armies in this bloody battle. France's ally Piedmont achieved a step toward leadership of a united Italy, but the battle is most remembered for its sickening slaughter, which motivated the founding of the Red Cross.

After the victory at Magenta, a Franco-Piedmontese force pursued the retreating Austrians. Piedmont wanted to secure the last two Italian provinces ruled by Austria: Lombardy and Venetia. The Austrians retreated to the River Mincio and chose to fight in front of the river when the French unexpectedly caught up with them. Neither commander—Napoleon III nor Franz Joseph—realized that they were confronting more than screening forces, and the battle was confused and dominated by small unit actions in its first hours.

As the fighting developed, each side worked out a tactical plan. Napoleon intended to break the Austrian center, whereas Franz Joseph decided to stand firm in

> *"I have twice taken the offensive and have engaged my last reserves. I cannot hold out much longer."* General Wimpffen to Franz Joseph

the center and attempt to envelop the French wings. However, the Austrians had one great disadvantage. Senior commanders were drawn from the highest ranks of the aristocracy and obeyed orders when and if they chose. General Wimpffen, on the left, failed to press attacks with vigor. On the right, General Benedek was hard pressed by Piedmontese troops, whose king, Victor Emmanuel, was determined that there would be an unquestioned Piedmontese victory. His troops advanced bravely enough, but his commanders were incapable

of coordinating their attacks, which were repeatedly repelled. In the center, fighting was particularly bloody. Austrian infantry, equipped with the recently introduced rifle muskets, occupied slit trenches and hastily constructed defenses. It took repeated French infantry charges, through withering gunfire, followed by savage bayonet work to push the Austrians back.

The ground was carpeted with the dead and wounded. The losses among officers were very heavy; no fewer than three field marshals and nine generals were killed. French rifled cannon took a particularly heavy toll of the Austrians, who had only smoothbore artillery. With the precipitate retreat of the Austrian left wing, the center began to disintegrate. Orders for a retreat were given, but Benedek ignored them and stayed to inflict a further humiliating reverse on the Piedmontese. They only managed to occupy the Austrian positions after Benedek withdrew in good order, taking his wounded and prisoners with him.

For the rest of the Austrian army, retreat in any sort of order was made possible only by an intense rain storm preventing a French pursuit. The fate of Italy was essentially decided. The Austrians were in a desperately weak position but Napoleon III did not want another battle so bloody because more heavy losses might undermine his popularity in France. Both sides had reasons to agree peace terms at Villafranca, under which Piedmont would receive Lombardy but not Venetia, a compromise greeted with dismay by Italian nationalists. Another impact of the battle was that a Swiss businessman, Jean-Henri Dunant, was so appalled by the suffering of the wounded that he went on to found the International Committee of the Red Cross to ensure the horror was not repeated. **JS**

Losses: French and Piedmontese, more than 17,000 dead, wounded, or captured of 130,000; Austrian, more than 20,000 dead, wounded, or captured of 120,000

◀ *Magenta 1859*   *Calatafimi 1860* ▶

The French celebrate victory at Solferino, from an 1891 article on the anniversary of the battle.

Taku Forts   24–26 June 1859

The Battle of Taku Forts was an Anglo-French attack on the forts that protected the Hai River estuary in the Tianjin area of northeast China. It was part of the Second Opium War, fought to force the Chinese to open their ports to foreign trade.

After the Treaty of Tientsin, the Taku Forts were returned to the Chinese in 1858. However, China continued to resist western trade, and General Sengge Rinchen reinforced the forts with artillery and a larger garrison. In June 1859, a British force of twenty ships, under Admiral Sir James Hope, approached the forts with the intention of landing troops to escort Anglo-French diplomats to Beijing. The Chinese refused entry and broke the terms of the treaty.

On 24 June, the British attacked under cover of darkness. The assault, led by Captain George Willes, saw obstacles in the harbor blown up. The next day, however, only small shallow-draft vessels were able to advance. As the British began shelling, Rinchen's newly installed batteries replied, sinking four gunboats and disabling two others. Hope's flagship, *Plover,* was crippled and most of her crew killed. A U.S. naval steamer, *Toey Wan*, rescued the *Plover* crew and helped the British man their guns.

Although the United States was neutral, the U.S. crew justified its action with the now-famous words: "Blood is thicker than water." This was the first time that the U.S. and British military had fought alongside each other. The attack was abandoned but the war continued, and the forts were taken by a larger British force in 1860. **TB**

Losses: British, 3 gunboats sunk, 3 grounded, 425 casualties of 2,000; French, 35 casualties; U.S., 2 casualties; Chinese, unknown

◁ *Sanhe 1858*   *Palikao 1860* ▷

A relief scene on the ossuary that was built outside Calatafimi in 1892 to commemorate the victims of the invasion of Sicily.

Calatafimi 15 May 1860

Guerrilla leader Giuseppe Garibaldi led a force of 1,000 red-shirted volunteers to invade Sicily, a part of the kingdom of Naples. It was widely deemed a madcap idea, doomed to failure. His first victory meant that eventually all of Italy would be united.

The Piedmontese had never wanted to do any more than unify northern Italy; they had no desire for the Neapolitan kingdom with its dreadful problems of poverty, violence, and corruption. Garibaldi intended to force their hands, but his volunteers had little military training or experience. Naples had a large and professional army, and his mission should have failed. However, he had luck, and his landing in Sicily was unopposed. His first encounter against a Neapolitan force at least twice as large as his own exemplified the advantages of charismatic leadership and revolutionary élan over ill-motivated troops.

Neapolitan troops took up position outside Calatafimi, but they were nervous at the prospect of facing a commander of such prowess. Also, local bandit groups had already harried their advance, destroying supplies and killing stragglers. When the Red Shirts charged, Garibaldi at their head, they showed a reckless ferocity, and the Neapolitans quailed and fled. Soon, rumors spread across Sicily that the Red Shirts were not men but devils, and their shirts were impervious to bullets. Attracted by promises of land reform and justice, and with the knowledge that this force could defeat the regular army, thousands of Sicilians flocked to join Garibaldi. But when he talked of acting in the name of Italy, few of his new followers were sure who or what "La Talia" was. **JS**

Losses: Unknown

◁ *Solferino 1859* *Volturno 1860* ▷

Palikao 21 September 1860

In the Second Opium War, European powers fought to overcome resistance by China's Qing dynasty rulers to their penetration of Chinese markets. Anglo-French forces invaded China, occupied Beijing, and inflicted humiliation upon the imperial regime by burning the Summer Palace.

In August 1860, the Anglo-French naval and land forces captured the Taku Forts that had defied attack the previous year. They then advanced on Beijing. The bridge of Palikao (Baliqiao) marked the outer limits of the Imperial City and stood in the way of an allied capture of the city.

On 21 September, the Chinese fought a last attempt to stop the Anglo-French army. Commanding the Chinese was General Sengge Rinchen, who had defeated the Anglo-French attack on the Taku Forts in 1859. The British were led by General Sir James Hope Grant, and the French by General Charles Montauban. As the allied force reached the bridge, Rinchen ordered waves of Chinese attacks against the volleys fired by the allied infantry. The Chinese took heavy losses, and Rinchen ordered his elite Mongolian cavalry to charge. After several suicidal frontal charges, the cavalry were practically wiped out.

The allies were able to secure the bridge and moved in to capture the capital on 6 October. Emperor Xianfeng fled, and much of the Imperial City was looted shamelessly; the Summer Palace was burned to the ground. The allied victory ended the war, and the Chinese agreed to accept foreign diplomats in the imperial court and to open up markets to European trade. **TB**

Losses: Anglo-French, 900 casualties of 10,000; Chinese, 26,000 casualties of 30,000

◁ *Taku Forts 1859*　　　　　　　　　*Cixi 1862* ▷

Battle of the Volturno *by Giovanni Fattori (1825–1908) depicts artillery in action.* ⬇

Volturno   1–2 October 1860

After his victory at Calatafimi, Garibaldi went on to capture Palermo and Naples. However, Neapolitan forces still barred his advance north. Despite being defeated, their resistance ensured that a united Italy would be led by the Piedmontese monarchy rather than by Garibaldi's republicans.

The Piedmontese viewed Garibaldi's successes with alarm. He was a revolutionary republican bent on uniting all of Italy, including Naples and the Papal States, which might mean war with France. In order to achieve this, he had to defeat the last Neapolitan troops. A brief skirmish on the River Volturno gave the Neapolitans their first victory and made them realize the "red devils" were not invincible. They launched an offensive intending to retake Naples.

Garibaldi's Red Shirts were outnumbered and weary. He would have been in real peril, but fortunately the Neapolitans chose to divide their forces and attack from two sides. Garibaldi took up positions at Santa Maria and Maddaloni, which were connected by a railway line, meaning he could transfer troops rapidly if necessary. The Neapolitans fought bravely, but they divided their forces again at Maddaloni and thus threw away their numerical advantage. Eventually piecemeal Neapolitan attacks were pushed back, but the Neapolitans were not destroyed and still barred the road to Rome. This gave the Piedmontese time to persuade the French that it was preferable that they occupy the Papal States rather than Garibaldi, and for the Piedmontese army to march south and demand Garibaldi surrender Naples to them. **JS**

Losses: Neapolitan, more than 300 dead and 2,000 captured of 30,000; Red Shirt, more than 300 dead of 20,000

◁ Calatafimi 1860   Second Custoza 1866 ▷

Fort Sumter   12–13 April 1861

The Confederate shelling of the Union-held Fort Sumter in North Carolina marked the start of a four-year civil war that would tear the United States apart and cost many thousands of lives. Ironically, in view of what was to come, the shelling of the fort was entirely bloodless.

The election of the Republican candidate, Abraham Lincoln, to the presidency of the United States on 6 November 1860 was perceived in the Southern states as a grave threat to their agricultural economies based on slavery. On 20 December, South Carolina seceded from the Union; it was to be followed by ten more pro-slavery states by June the following year.

The outgoing U.S. president, James Buchanan, did nothing to stop Southern state militias from taking over local military bases and arsenals. On his own initiative, however, U.S. Army Major Robert Anderson occupied Fort Sumter in Charleston Harbor on 26 December and refused to hand it over to South Carolina. A ship sent to supply Anderson in January 1862 was fired on by the Carolinians and turned back. Further fighting was avoided until April, however, when a substantial Union relief fleet was dispatched to supply and reinforce Fort Sumter. The Confederates decided to attack before the ships arrived.

At 4:30 AM on 12 April, around 500 South Carolinian troops, under General Pierre Beauregard, opened fire with forty-three guns and mortars. The Union forces withstood the bombardment for thirty-four hours until, with their supplies exhausted, they surrendered. Along with seven officers and seventy-six men, Anderson marched out of the fort with full military honors, and all were then shipped up north. Two days later, President Lincoln called for 75,000 volunteers to suppress the rebellion. The American Civil War had begun. **SA**

Losses: None on either side

First Bull Run 1861 ▶

Union officers on the parapet of Fort Sumter, 13 April 1861. Photograph by Mathew Brady.

First Bull Run (First Manassas)   21 July 1861

The first major battle of the American Civil War was a chaotic encounter fought by volunteers short of training and organization, and haphazardly equipped. It ended in victory for the Confederates under General Pierre Beauregard. Defeat shocked the Union into mobilizing resources for a long war.

Succumbing to the popular clamor for decisive action, President Lincoln ordered General Irvin McDowell to lead an army from Washington, D.C., toward the Confederate capital, Richmond. Beauregard blocked their path at the Manassas rail junction 25 miles (40 km) from Washington, drawing up his army behind Bull Run River. He was reinforced with troops, under General Joseph E. Johnston, that had been rushed by train from the Shenandoah Valley.

The weather was hot. Unfit Union soldiers arrived at Bull Run exhausted by the march from Washington. Nonetheless, the battle opened to their advantage. McDowell achieved surprise by sending most of his troops around the left of the Confederate line, crossing the river unopposed. The Southerners fought a desperate defensive action; General Thomas Jackson was nicknamed "Stonewall" for holding his Virginian infantry firm in the face of the Union onslaught.

In the afternoon, the arrival of fresh Confederate troops at Manassas demoralized weary Union soldiers. As they wavered, the Southerners raised the blood-chilling rebel yell and drove them back across the river. Once they had begun to run, nothing would stop the panicking Union troops. Journalists and congressmen, who had ridden out to observe the battle, found themselves caught up in a rout. Fortunately for the Union, the Southerners were in no state to mount a pursuit. The day after the battle, Lincoln signed a bill to create an army of half a million men, enlisted for three years. **RG**

Losses: Confederate, 400 dead, 1,600 wounded of 18,000; Union, 460 dead, 1,100 wounded, 1,300 captured of 18,000

◁ Fort Sumter 1861   Fort Donelson 1862 ▷

⬆ *A nineteenth-century Currier and Ives print of Union and Confederate soldiers clashing at First Bull Run.*

Fort Donelson   11–16 February 1862

An early battle in the Western Theater of the American Civil War, the capture of Confederate Fort Donelson propelled Union Brigadier General Ulysses S. Grant from obscurity to national fame. His demand for the "unconditional surrender" of the fort's garrison became an instant legend.

As commander of what became the Army of Tennessee, Grant embarked on a combined land and naval campaign along the Tennessee and Cumberland rivers. On 6 February, Fort Henry on the Tennessee was reduced by the fire of Flag Officer Andrew H. Foote's river gunboats. Grant then switched his forces to attack Fort Donelson on the Cumberland.

The Confederates reinforced the fort and sent Brigadier General John B. Floyd to lead its defense. This time Foote's flotilla had much the worse of a duel with the fort's gun battery, and Grant was obliged to confront some 15,000 entrenched Confederate soldiers with his land forces. The weather was bitterly cold, and many Union troops lacked blankets or overcoats. On the morning of 15 February, while Grant was away conferring with Foote, the Confederates launched an attempted breakout. Caught by surprise, Union troops were driven back in hard fighting. However, Confederate commanders were shocked by heavy casualties and failed to exploit the opportunity; they pulled back to the illusory security of their trenches. Grant returned to reinvigorate his men, announcing that "the enemy will have to be in a hurry if he gets ahead of me." Accepting that he was beaten, Floyd slipped away by river. The following morning, a few Confederates escaped through the Union lines; the rest accepted Grant's demand for "an unconditional and immediate surrender." **RG**

Losses: Confederate, 327 dead, 1,127 wounded, 12,392 captured of 16,000; Union, 507 dead, 1,976 wounded of 24,000

◁ First Bull Run 1861   Shiloh 1862 ▷

Hampton Roads   8–9 March 1862

Hampton Roads, an encounter between the Union and Confederate navies, was the first battle fought between steam-powered ironclad warships. It persuaded naval experts worldwide that unarmored wooden-hulled sailing ships were obsolete. A new era in naval warfare had begun.

Both sides in the American Civil War began work on experimental ironclads during 1861. The Confederacy built CSS *Virginia* at Norfolk Navy Yard, Virginia, encasing a wooden-hulled frigate, called USS *Merrimack*, in iron plates and adding a ram to its prow. In New York, Union engineers developed *Monitor*, an all-metal, semisubmerged raft, with guns in a revolving turret on top.

On 8 March, CSS *Virginia* left the naval yard and steamed toward three wooden Union frigates blockading Hampton Roads. The frigates were powerless, their solid shot bouncing off *Virginia*'s armor. One frigate was sunk by ramming, another shot to pieces after running aground. The following day, *Virginia* reemerged, with Lieutenant Catesby ap Roger Jones in command, intending to finish off the third Union frigate. It was confronted by *Monitor*, which had been hastily towed south from New York. The two ungainly metal machines crawled toward one another, blasting away to little effect. Conditions within the ships were cramped and fume-ridden. *Virginia* ran aground but refloated with a maximum effort of its engine. *Monitor*'s captain, John Worden, suffered flash burns from a shell that exploded in the eyeslit of his armored pilothouse. In the end, a stalemate was admitted, and *Virginia* returned to port. It was scuttled two months later to prevent it falling into Union hands. *Monitor* sank at the end of the year, under tow in an Atlantic gale. **RG**

Losses: Union, 2 frigates, 261 dead; Confederate, no ships, 7 dead

◁ Fort Sumter 1861   Shiloh 1862 ▷

The turret of Monitor, *photographed on 9 July 1862 on the James River, Virginia.*

Shiloh 6–7 April 1862

As Union and Confederate forces battled for control of Virginia in the east, a Union army led by General Ulysses S. Grant was taking Confederate territory in the west. Though it was a close battle, Grant's victory at Shiloh severely weakened the Confederate side.

In February 1862, Union forces under General Grant captured Forts Henry and Donelson in western Tennessee. Nashville fell the same month, allowing Grant to move south down the Tennessee River and disembark at Pittsburg Landing, near a church called Shiloh, not far from the main Confederate base at Corinth in Mississippi. His plan was to await the arrival of the Army of the Ohio, under Major General Don Carlos Buell.

Confederate General Albert Johnson had other plans; before Grant had had time to dig any defensive fortifications, Johnson launched a surprise dawn attack on 6 April. His forces drove the Union army back toward Pittsburg Landing in hard-fought, close-quarters combat, until they were halted by Union artillery reinforced by two Union gunboats on the river. Johnson was killed by a Union bullet while leading a desperate charge; he was replaced by General Pierre Beauregard.

That night, Buell's army arrived on the east bank of the river and some of the troops were ferried across. At dawn, Grant launched a counterattack. With their reserves depleted—which created a numerical disadvantage— the Confederates were pushed back and soon gave up the fight, retreating in the afternoon south to Corinth. The Confederate position was now severely weakened, but many people in the North criticized Grant for his lack of preparation. President Lincoln silenced the critics: "I can't spare this man. He fights." **SA**

Losses: Union, 1,754 dead, 8,408 wounded of 66,812; Confederate, 1,728 dead, 8,012 wounded of 44,699

◁ Fort Donelson 1862   Mississippi Forts 1862 ▷

Mississippi Forts 18–27 April 1862

A major objective of the Union forces was to gain control of the lower Mississippi River valley from the Confederates, thereby splitting the Confederacy in two. The capture of New Orleans was the key to this strategy and seriously weakened the ability of the Confederacy to ship in supplies.

Two forts, Jackson and St. Philip, equipped with 115 heavy guns guarded New Orleans on either side of the Mississippi. In order to take the city, the Union task force, headed by the commander of the West Gulf Blockading Squadron, David Farragut, had first to cross the sandbars at the mouth of the river and then break through the chain barrier that had been installed by the Confederates between the two forts, strung between eight sunken ships. For this task, Farragut had eight steam sloops, nine gunboats, and nineteen barges loaded with mortars able to fire 200-pound (90 kg) shells, as well as transports carrying 15,000 soldiers to attack the forts by land.

The Union mortar bombardment began on 18 April, but despite a daily bombardment of around 1,000 shells, the forts' guns continued to return fire. Farragut, therefore, decided to force a passage. On 20 April, three Union gunboats succeeded in cutting a small passage through the chain barrier. On the early morning of 24 April, the Union fleet sailed through this gap. The forts' guns opened fire, disabling one ship and forcing three to return. Two Confederate cottonclads—gunboats with bails of cotton as armor—managed to ram and sink the steam gunboat USS *Varuna*, but most of the Confederate gunboats were sunk. Once past the forts, the fleet headed up to New Orleans, taking the city the next day after it had been evacuated by the Confederates. The forts surrendered two days later. **SA**

Losses: Union, 1 ship; Confederate, 1 ironclad, 11 gunboats

◁ Shiloh 1862   Murfreesboro 1862 ▷

Puebla   5 May 1862

For Mexicans, the Battle of Puebla is a symbol of resistance to foreign imperialism, celebrated annually in the Cinco de Mayo festivities. Fought against an army sent by Napoleon III's French Second Empire, it demonstrated Mexico's will to resist, but did not end the French intervention.

In December 1861, British, Spanish, and French troops occupied the port of Veracruz after Mexican president Benito Juarez suspended repayment of foreign debts. The British and Spanish did a deal with Juarez and withdrew, but France had wider ambitions.

Taking advantage of the American Civil War, which kept the United States otherwise occupied, Napoleon III hoped to turn Mexico into a French-dominated state. Ignacio Zaragoza Seguin, a general with experience in the civil conflicts that had brought Juarez to power, was tasked with blocking a French advance from Veracruz to Mexico City. He took a stand outside the city of Puebla, where his small army would be supported by the guns of Forts Loreto and Guadalupe. French general Charles Latrille de Lorencez mounted a frontal attack on the Mexican defenses, expecting his experienced Zouaves to carry the day with ease.

Fort Guadalupe became the key focus of the fighting, bombarded by French artillery and assaulted three times by the infantry. In the afternoon, the French ran out of artillery ammunition, and the onset of heavy rain reduced the battlefield to mud. Zaragoza unleashed his cavalry, and the French were forced to pull back. In a message to Juarez, Zaragoza wrote: "The national arms have been covered with glory." But the French returned the following year in greater force to occupy Puebla and Mexico City. **RG**

Losses: French, 462 dead, 300 wounded of 6,000; Mexican, 83 dead, 131 wounded of 4,000

Camarón 1863 >]

Seven Pines   31 May–1 June 1862

In 1862, Union General George B. McClellan's Army of the Potomac tried to take the Confederate capital, Richmond, with an attack up the Virginia peninsula. The counterattack at Seven Pines marked the failure of McClellan's offensive campaign and brought Robert E. Lee to command the Confederate forces.

McClellan was an excellent organizer and was adored by his troops, but he also lacked attacking verve. His plan to avoid the main Confederate defenses between Washington, D.C., and Richmond by transporting troops by sea to the peninsula was an intelligent use of Union naval superiority, but his progress once ashore was slow and overmeticulous.

McClellan's Confederate opponent, General Joseph E. Johnston, was also a cautious commander. Using delaying actions, he withdrew toward Richmond, taking up a strong defensive position behind the Chickahominy River. By late May, McClellan had half of his army across the river, while he remained on the other side with the rest. Prodded into action by Confederate President Jefferson Davis, Johnston devised a plan to attack the divided enemy, hoping to crush the Union force on his side of the Chickahominy.

Launched early on 31 May, the Confederate attack was poorly executed. The left made some progress through the village of Seven Pines; however, on the Confederate right, a Union counterpunch at Fair Oaks halted the attack completely. The battle soon disintegrated into chaotic small-scale actions, fought over waterlogged ground where wounded men were at risk of drowning in mud. Essentially, the battle was a Union defensive success, but the attack unnerved McClellan. Meanwhile, Johnston had been wounded severely and was replaced in field command by Davis's military adviser, General Lee. The Peninsula Campaign had reached its turning point. **RG**

Losses: Confederate, 6,134 casualties, including 980 dead, of 40,000; Union, 5,031 casualties, including 790 dead, of 40,000

[< *First Bull Run 1861*   *Seven Days 1862* >]

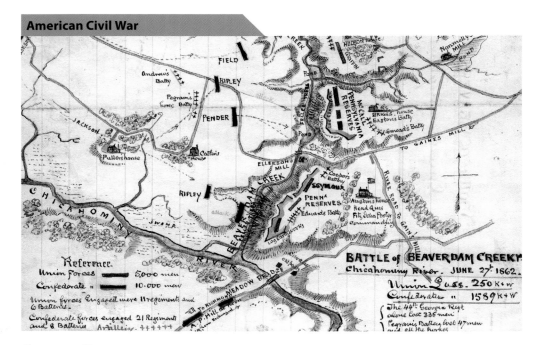

Seven Days 25 June–1 July 1862

Taking command of the Confederate Army of Northern Virginia after Seven Pines, General Robert E. Lee devised an offensive to drive Union forces back and away from Richmond. The battles that followed were marked by errors on both sides, but ended with Lee in the ascendancy.

The Union Army of the Potomac, led by General George McClellan, was close to Richmond. Reconnaissance by Confederate cavalry under J. E. B. Stuart, who rode right around the Union army, revealed an exposed right flank open to attack. Lee ordered General "Stonewall" Jackson's army to return from its successful campaign in the Shenandoah Valley and seized the initiative.

He launched a series of frontal attacks, combined with an envelopment of the Union right, that persuaded the cautious McClellan to withdraw up the Virginia peninsula. Lee maintained pressure, although bold plans to envelop withdrawing Union formations failed repeatedly because

of poor execution—Jackson was especially at fault, reacting tardily to events in an uncharacteristic manner. McClellan was permitted to withdraw his troops to a strong defensive position at Malvern Hill, and took refuge on a ship off shore himself.

On 1 July, the Union army pounded the ill-coordinated Confederate infantry assaults on the hill with its artillery. Despite this success, the carnage unnerved McClellan and he withdrew his forces to a defensive position on the coast, from where they were eventually evacuated in August. Although he had saved Richmond, Lee was appalled by the slaughter and asked General John Magruder why he had persisted in attacking Malvern Hill in the face of such odds. "Because of your orders, twice repeated," he replied. **SA**

Losses: Confederate, 3,494 dead, 15,758 wounded of 92,000; Union, 1,734 dead, 8,066 wounded of 104,100

◁ *Seven Pines 1862*　　　　　　　*Second Bull Run 1862* ▷

　　A map of the Battle of Beaverdam Creek, drawn by hand the following day during the Seven Days Battle. ⬆

Second Bull Run (Second Manassas)   28–30 August 1862

Fought over the same ground as the battle in July 1861, Second Bull Run was the culmination of a fast-moving Confederate offensive against an enemy that was superior in numbers but inferior in morale and leadership. It opened the way for a subsequent Confederate invasion of Maryland.

General Robert E. Lee was convinced that the only hope for the Confederacy lay in taking the offensive. After his success in the Seven Days Battle, Lee and his Army of Northern Virginia headed north to fight Union Major General John Pope's Army of Virginia. Confederate General "Stonewall" Jackson undertook a long flanking maneuver to the north and east in order to capture a Union supply depot at Manassas railroad junction—threatening Pope's communications with Washington, D.C.—before withdrawing to the northwest and taking up position on Stony Ridge. From there, he attacked a Union column on 28 August, although with limited result.

On the same day, General James Longstreet broke through Union lines at Thoroughfare Gap and approached the main battlefield. The next day, convinced he had Jackson trapped, Pope launched attacks against him that were repulsed with heavy casualties on both sides. He did the same on the third day, unaware that Longstreet had taken up position on Jackson's right flank.

As Confederate artillery rained down on the Union lines of General Fitz John Porter's corps, ending his advance, Longstreet's five divisions of 25,000 men launched the biggest simultaneous mass assault of the war, crushing the Union left flank and driving it off the field. An effective Union rearguard action limited the consequences of the defeat, but Pope was relieved of his command in September and sent to fight Indians. **SA**

Losses: Confederate, 1,300 dead, 7,000 wounded of 50,000 engaged; Union, 10,000 dead or wounded of 62,000

[<] *Seven Days 1862*   *Antietam 1862* [>]

Antietam   17 September 1862

The costliest single day's fighting in the American Civil War took place at Antietam creek near Sharpsburg, Maryland. While technically a Union victory, as the Confederacy withdrew from the field, it was for Lee a remarkable escape from a perilous position. Lincoln's Emancipation Proclamation, freeing Confederate slaves, followed the battle.

The Confederate victory on 28–30 August at Second Bull Run confirmed General Lee in his decision to take the war to the Union. On 3 September he marched into the Union state of Maryland with his Army of Northern Virginia. Unfortunately for him, a copy of his detailed battle plans, Special Order 191, was mislaid and then discovered, wrapped around three cigars, by Union soldiers. It was learned that Lee's army was divided, with elements sent to Harpers Ferry in West Virginia and Hagerstown in Maryland. Union General McClellan, who had returned from the Peninsula to take command in front of Washington, had the chance, if he moved quickly,

> ## "I have heard of 'the dead lying in heaps,' but never saw it till this battle. Whole ranks fell together."
>
> *Captain Emory Upton, 2d U.S. Artillery, at Antietam*

to pick off each part of Lee's army in turn. McClellan saw his opportunity but waited eighteen hours before acting.

It was to prove a costly delay, as his approach through the Blue Ridge Mountains was in turn held up by a spirited Confederate defense at South Mountain. Instead of retreating back into Virginia, Lee ordered his forces to concentrate near Sharpsburg, where he intended to fight a defensive battle. General "Stonewall" Jackson, who captured the Union garrison at Harpers Ferry on 15 September, raced to join Lee, but part of Jackson's

corps was still en route when the battle started. At dawn on 17 September McClellan launched his first attack against Lee's army, which was drawn up behind Antietam creek. He had overwhelming force of numbers and equipment, but his legendary caution prevented him from committing all his forces in one strike.

The first charge was led by General Joseph Hooker's corps through a cornfield against Lee's left flank, which barely held in the face of this attack. In the center, Confederate troops fought a lengthy holding action in Sunken (Bloody) Lane against a Union attack that eventually succeeded but was not followed up. During the afternoon, Union General Ambrose Burnside's corps made repeated attempts to cross a small stone bridge over the creek but the men were held up by intense Confederate rifle and artillery fire. Burnside finally got across the bridge and the battle was beginning to turn McClellan's way when Confederate General A. P. Hill arrived from Harpers Ferry, marching toward the sound of the guns; he launched a surprise counterattack that drove back Burnside's men. Crucially, Lee had committed his entire force of 38,000 men while McClellan, grossly overestimating the strength of his opponents, had held back in reserve more than a quarter of his 75,500-strong army. With fighting at a standstill, both men consolidated their lines for the night. The next day there were further skirmishes, but Lee was allowed to withdraw across the Potomac, McClellan declining to resume the fighting.

Antietam was a lost opportunity for the Union. Lee had survived to fight on for another two and a half years. Two months after the battle, President Lincoln relieved McClellan of his command. Most significantly, the battle gave Lincoln the confidence to issue his Emancipation Proclamation, effective 1 January 1863. **SA**

Losses: Union, 2,108 dead, 9,540 wounded of 75,500; Confederate, 1,546 dead, 7,752 wounded of 38,000

◁ *Second Bull Run 1862*   *Fredericksburg 1862* ▷

The dead lie in Sunken Lane after the Union 1st Brigade's costly assault on the Confederate center. ➡

Cixi 20 September 1862

In China in the early 1860s the Taiping Rebellion became a threat to Shanghai, a port city with a substantial Western population. American adventurer Frederick Townsend Ward was an important leader in the fighting around Shanghai, until he met his death at the Battle of Cixi.

In 1860 Ward, a sailor from Salem, Massachusetts, with experience of mercenary warfare, recruited a band of miscellaneous Westerners who had washed up in Shanghai, turning them into a Foreign Arms Corps to fight the Taiping. Although his corps had mixed success, and he was himself seriously wounded, Ward attracted the attention of the Chinese imperial authorities. In 1861 they entrusted him with training a mix of Chinese peasants and Filipinos in the tactics of modern warfare. The force thus created would later become known as the Ever Victorious Army. Through 1862 Ward's army of a few thousand men drove the Taiping back from the environs of Shanghai, repeatedly defeating numerically far superior forces with their modern arms and more flexible tactics.

The attack on the walled town of Cixi, near the port of Ningbo, was like many actions the Ever Victorious Army had undertaken. Clad in Western-style uniforms plus Indian turbans, and trained in the disciplined use of rifle-muskets and artillery, they were quite different from the archaic Chinese imperial forces. Ward always led from the front—he was wounded four times in fighting in 1862. The Taiping were as usual well beaten, partly because of inferior leadership and command structures, but in taking the town Ward was hit by a musket ball in the stomach. He died in agony, at only thirty years of age . His successor in command of the Ever Victorious Army was British army engineer Charles Gordon. **RG**

Losses: No reliable figures

◁ Palikao 1860   Nanjing 1864 ▷

Fredericksburg 13 December 1862

The inconclusive but bloody battle at Antietam was followed within months by one of the most one-sided battles in the entire American Civil War. Despite a new commander, Union forces failed yet again to take the Confederate capital of Richmond, allowing the war to carry on into its third year.

Within days of replacing General McClellan as commander of the Union Army of the Potomac, General Ambrose Burnside drew up plans to capture Richmond. His idea was to deceive Confederate General Robert E. Lee about his intentions in order to achieve an unopposed crossing of the Rappahannock River at Fredericksburg and then move south along the railroad to Richmond.

Burnside's plan fell at the first hurdle, as the pontoons necessary to cross the river were not, as he ordered them, at the head of his advancing army, but at the rear. This muddle allowed Confederate General James Longstreet's corps to arrive in the town. Burnside might still have been able to fight this army before General "Stonewall" Jackson's corps arrived, but he again squandered the opportunity. By the time the pontoons had been brought forward and put in place, Confederate sharpshooters were in position and Lee's men were ready with their artillery in the hills behind the town.

On 11–12 December Burnside's men crossed the river and took up positions. The battle began on 13 December with the first of many Union infantry assaults, all of which were met with heavy cannon and small-arms fire. One Union attack on the Confederate right flank met with some success until it was driven back. The two armies held positions the next day until Burnside asked for a truce to tend to his wounded. The following day, the Union army retreated ignominiously across the river. **SA**

Losses: Confederate, 608 dead, 4,116 wounded of 72,500; Union, 1,284 dead, 9,600 wounded of 114,000

◁ Antietam 1862   Chancellorsville 1863 ▷

The sunken road and stone wall where Longstreet's corps successfully defended Marye's Heights.

Capt. Russell Phot.

Murfreesboro 31 Dec 1862–2 Jan 1863

While major battles were being fought in the east between the Confederate and Union capitals, an equally intense struggle was taking place for control of Kentucky and Tennessee. The Battle of Murfreesboro brought the heaviest casualties, proportional to forces engaged, of the Civil War.

In October 1862 the Confederate Army of the Mississippi, commanded by General Braxton Bragg, called off an invasion of Kentucky and withdrew into Tennessee after fighting the Union army of General Don Carlos Buell at Perryville. Buell's failure to follow up led President Lincoln to replace him with General William Rosecrans, who set off after Bragg in late December.

The two armies met at Murfreesboro in the valley of the Stones River, forming up in parallel lines about 4 miles (6.5 km) long. Both commanders planned to envelop the enemy's right flank, and victory should have gone to the side that attacked first. In the early hours of 31 December the Confederates took the initiative, their dawn attack achieving surprise and driving back the Union flank 5 miles (8 km) until Rosecrans sent in reinforcements to steady the line. A second Confederate attack in the center was held at great cost in Union lives and captured guns until the Confederates withdrew for lack of ammunition. At the end of the first day Bragg believed he had won.

But Rosecrans, his troops pinned into a tight but easily defended horseshoe formation, held firm. Further Confederate attacks on the following two days failed to break through the Union lines, running into heavy Union artillery and small-arms fire. Unable to prevent the Union army receiving reinforcements, and citing the risk of rising river levels splitting his army in two, Bragg conceded defeat by withdrawing. **SA**

Losses: Union, 1,730 dead, 7,802 wounded of 43,300; Confederate, 1,294 dead, 7,945 wounded of 37,712

◁ Shiloh 1862   Vicksburg 1863 ▷

Camarón 30 April 1863

A defensive action fought with suicidal courage during France's ill-fated intervention in Mexico, the Battle of Camarón founded the legend of the French Foreign Legion. Captain Jean Danjou, who led the legionnaires, enjoys the strange distinction of having his wooden hand revered as a relic of war.

Almost a year after their setback at Puebla in 1862, the French expeditionary force in Mexico resumed its push toward Mexico City. Puebla was placed under siege. Danjou was ordered to protect a valuable supply convoy heading for Puebla from Veracruz. With sixty-two men and two lieutenants under his command, he encountered some 2,000 Mexican cavalry and infantry.

Danjou was a battle-hardened veteran who had lost a hand fighting rebels in Algeria. He held off the Mexican cavalry by forming his men into an infantry square, before falling back to a strong defensive position in "Hacienda Camarón," a high-walled inn. The situation was hopeless, but Danjou refused to surrender. His legionnaires swore to fight to the death. Barricaded in the hacienda, they cut down wave after wave of Mexican infantry with disciplined fire. At around midday Danjou was shot in the chest and killed. Resistance continued for another four hours and the number of dead and wounded mounted until only six men were left fighting—Lieutenant Maudet and five legionnaires. Still refusing to surrender, this remnant fixed bayonets and charged the Mexican line. Two survived to be taken prisoner, and their request for an honorable surrender was granted by the Mexicans.

Every subsequent year, the Legion would bring out Danjou's wooden hand for veneration on the anniversary of the Battle of Camarón. France abandoned its fruitless Mexican adventure in 1866. **RG**

Losses: French, 43 dead, 20 wounded of 65; Mexican, 90 dead and several hundred wounded of 2,000

◁ Puebla 1862

Chancellorsville   30 April–6 May 1863

After the Union failure at Fredericksburg, General Joseph Hooker took over as commander of the Army of the Potomac. At Chancellorsville, Hooker was outmaneuvered by a Confederate army half the size of his. However, Robert E. Lee's brilliant victory was marred by the death of "Stonewall" Jackson.

"Fighting Joe" Hooker devised a new plan to capture Richmond. While some of his troops would tie down General Lee at Fredericksburg, his main force would advance through the forests of the Wilderness on the Confederate left. But as before, a Union general had massively underestimated Lee's skill and boldness. Aware of the plan, Lee left a small holding force in Fredericksburg and marched into the Wilderness on 30 April to block the Union advance at the Chancellorsville crossroads.

Lee's most trusted subordinate, General "Stonewall" Jackson, took a large part of the army on a wide flanking move that brought him up against Hooker's right wing. His attack on the late afternoon of 2 May caught XI Corps of the Union army unawares—many were sitting down to dinner with their rifles stacked and unloaded—and more than 4,000 were taken prisoner. Jackson, however, was wounded by "friendly fire" from Confederate pickets as he rode back from reconnoitering Union positions.

Cavalry General J. E. B. Stuart, who had never before commanded infantry, took over Jackson's command and continued the attack on the Union flank the following day, enabling the Confederates to capture Chancellorsville. Union forces stood on the defensive until, on the night of 5–6 May, Hooker withdrew across the Rappahannock River. Confederate joy at the success was dimmed when Jackson died of postsurgery complications on 10 May. He was a grievous loss to the Confederacy. **SA**

Losses: Confederate, 1,665 dead, 9,081 wounded of 60,892; Union, 1,606 dead, 9,672 wounded of 133,868

◁ Fredericksburg 1862   Gettysburg 1863 ▷

"Tell him to make haste and get well. . . . He has lost his left arm, but I have lost my right."

Message from Robert E. Lee to "Stonewall" Jackson

⬆ Wounded soldiers recuperate under trees after Confederate General Lee's victory over the Union at Chancellorsville.

Vicksburg 19 May–4 July 1863

While the epic Battle of Gettysburg was being fought out to the east of the Confederacy, an equally epic siege was drawing to an end in the west, at the Confederate stronghold of Vicksburg on the Mississippi. The Union victory here, as at Gettsyburg, was to be a decisive turning point in the course of the American Civil War.

Vicksburg, Mississippi, stood on the east bank of the Mississippi River, commanding shipping to and from the American interior. The city was strategically vital to the Confederates, their president, Jefferson Davis, stating that "Vicksburg is the nail head that holds the South's two halves together." The city sat on a high, easily defended bluff by the river and was surrounded by swamps that made it difficult to approach.

In December 1862 General Ulysses Grant, commander of the Union Army of the Tennessee, began operations to seize the city. His initial plan was to divide his army in two, with one half reaching the city from the north while

> *"Vicksburg is the key. The war can never be brought to a close until the key is in our pocket."*
>
> *President Abraham Lincoln*

the other half moved east to entice the Confederates out into battle. This plan failed, as did attempts to dig canals around the west of Vicksburg, out of range of its artillery, which would enable him to ferry his troops safely from the north around the city to the south. Grant therefore came up with a new plan, to march his army down the west side of the Mississippi.

On the moonless night of 16 April, a small fleet of seven gunboats and three troop-carriers loaded with stores sailed south down the Mississippi past Vicksburg. Despite keeping silent, they were soon spotted and subjected to fire from Confederate artillery. The Union commander then realized that the shells were only hitting the upper parts of his boats, suggesting that the Confederates were unable to depress the firing angle of their guns. He therefore sailed close in to the east bank, so close as to hear the Confederate commanders giving orders. From that moment the Confederate shells went straight over the top of the fleet, and it survived with little damage. A second flotilla made the same run six days later, with equal success. Grant now had the transports in place to carry his men over the river.

On 29–30 April Grant crossed the river and headed northeast to the state capital of Jackson, which he captured from Confederate General Pemberton on 14 May. From there he had a direct march west to Vicksburg, overcoming Confederate attempts to stop him at Champion Hill and Big Black River Bridge. On 19 May he ordered the first of several frontal assaults against the city, but was unable to break through Confederate lines.

Reluctantly, on 25 May, he began siege operations. Soldiers dug lines of ditches around the north and east to seal up all roads in and out of the city. Unguarded gaps in the fortifications to the south were filled by reinforcements rushed in from across the river, bringing the total number of Union troops to 77,000, more than double the Confederate numbers. Artillery regularly pounded the defenders, soldiers and civilians alike, who also came under fire from Union gunboats on the river to the west. With no Confederate reinforcements in view, the people of Vicksburg began to run out of supplies. The siege lasted through June until, on 4 July, the city surrendered. The Mississippi was now in Union hands. **SA**

Losses: Union, 4,835 dead or wounded of 77,000; Confederate, 3,202 dead or wounded of 33,000

◁ *Murfreesboro 1862*   *Chickamauga 1863* ▷

One of the Confederate riverside batteries that failed to destroy the Union boats at Vicksburg. ➡

Gettysburg   1–3 July 1863

The unplanned three-day Battle of Gettysburg, fought in and around a small town in Pennsylvania, was a disaster for the Confederacy. By the time it was over, almost 8,000 men lay dead and the tide of war had turned decisively in favor of the Union.

After his victory at Chancellorsville, and with the safety of Richmond, the Confederate capital, now assured, General Lee decided to take the war to the Union and invade the North. In June the 75,000-strong Army of Northern Virginia advanced up the Shenandoah Valley into Pennsylvania. Shocked at this unexpected turn of events, President Lincoln sacked General Joseph Hooker from his command of the Army of the Potomac and installed General John Meade in his place.

Meade's instructions were to seek out and destroy Lee's army. As the Union army approached, Lee ordered his scattered men to assemble at Gettysburg, a small road and rail junction town. The first to arrive, in the early morning of 1 July, was one of General A. P. Hill's divisions, which entered the town having heard that there they might find some much-needed boots, of which they were in short supply. Hill's men quickly came under fire from some dismounted Union cavalry, who fought a delaying action until reinforcements could arrive. A major Confederate attack pushed the Union cavalry, by now supported by two infantry corps and artillery, back through the town to Cemetery Hill. By the end of the day, 27,000 Confederate and 22,000 Union troops were engaged in the battle.

The following morning, on 2 July, the rest of the Union infantry arrived and took up position in an inverted U-shaped formation along the ridges and hills to the south of Gettysburg. Facing them to their west, north,

Union and Confederate soldiers lie where they fell on the Gettysburg battlefield. Photograph by Timothy O'Sullivan. ⬇

and east were the Confederate forces, forming a larger U-shape about 5 miles (8 km) long. Lee considered but rejected the idea of outflanking the Union lines in favor of a late-afternoon, direct assault on Cemetery Ridge on the western side of the hills. His men drove the Union troops back through a peach orchard and wheat field but were stopped in Plum Run Valley and were unable to dislodge them from the ridge. Crucially, they failed to take the commanding peak of Little Round Top, from where their artillery could have dominated Union lines.

The next day, 3 July, battle began early in the morning as Union troops on the ridge nearest the town bombarded Confederate lines to drive them away from Culp's Hill. The Confederates responded with an infantry attack and fighting continued all morning. Farther south, at around 1:00 PM, a Confederate artillery bombardment began to soften up the Union lines and was met by a

Union response from around eighty cannon. As the bombardment subsided, at 3:00 PM, around 14,000 Confederate infantry, commanded by General George Pickett, advanced across open fields. They were met with a Union artillery barrage of shot and shell that was joined, when the Confederate infantry came to within 200 yards (180 m), by Union infantry rifle fire from behind stone walls and earthworks. Only around 200 Confederates managed to reach the Union lines before they were finally repulsed. The next day, 4 July, both sides exchanged limited fire, but Lee's men were exhausted, and on 5 July he gave the order to retreat south to Virginia. The invasion threat to the North had been lifted. **SA**

Losses: Union, 3,155 dead, 14,531 wounded of 93,921; Confederate, 4,708 dead, 12,693 wounded of 71,699

☐ *Chancellorsville 1863*   *Wilderness 1864* ☐

Fort Wagner 18 July 1863

In the American Civil War engagement fought at Fort Wagner, South Carolina, the courageous performance of a regiment of black troops, the 54th Massachusetts Infantry, transformed the image of the African American soldier and swung Northern opinion in favor of freeing slaves.

Despite President Lincoln's Emancipation Proclamation of 1862, there was no great enthusiasm among Northern whites for the abolition of slavery and widespread skepticism about the ability of blacks to fulfill combat roles. The 54th Massachusetts Volunteer Infantry Regiment was one of the first Union military units made up of black soldiers under white officers. Its recruitment had been a high-profile event and its commander, Colonel Robert Gould Shaw, hailed from a prominent Boston abolitionist family. The regiment's assignment to lead the assault on Fort Wagner on Morris Island, South Carolina, was thus seen as a crucial chance to prove that African Americans could fight for their own freedom.

The approach to Fort Wagner was a narrow strip of beach 180 feet (55 m) wide with the Atlantic to the east and a marsh to the west. Once on this beach, the Union troops had to cross a shallow moat surrounding the 750-foot- (685 m) wide fort, which was heavily fortified with mortars and other guns. The assault began at 7:45 PM, with a total of ten regiments engaged. The soldiers of the 54th fought their way on to the fort's parapet and held out there for over an hour under heavy fire before the attack was called off at around 10:00 PM. The black regiment had taken more than 50 percent casualties, with Colonel Shaw among those killed. The soldiers were hailed for their valor, and the recruitment of African Americans into the Union army sharply increased as a result of the public recognition. **SA**

Losses: Confederate, 174 dead or wounded of 1,800; Union, 1,515 dead, wounded, or captured of 5,000

◁ *Vicksburg 1863*　　　　　*Chickamauga 1863* ▷

Chickamauga 19–20 September 1863

The Battle of Chickamauga was the most impressive Confederate victory in the Western Theater of the American Civil War, a bloody fight resulting in a toll of casualties second only to that of Gettysburg. It threw the Union forces onto the defensive, but failed to deliver a knockout blow.

In early September 1863 the Union Army of the Cumberland, commanded by General William Rosecrans, drove the Confederates under Braxton Bragg out of Chattanooga and south into Georgia. Confederate President Jefferson Davis was determined that Bragg should counterattack, and reinforced him with troops from Mississippi and two divisions from Virginia under Lieutenant General James Longstreet. On 17 September Bragg turned around and headed back toward Rosecrans's advancing army. After some skirmishes, battle was fully joined on the morning of 19 September.

Bragg's men charged but failed to break the Union line on the western side of Chickamauga Creek. The next day, as they continued to assault Union lines, they were given a lucky break by their opponents. Rosecrans was informed, incorrectly, that there was a gap in his lines. In moving units to close the gap, he created a real gap directly in the path of an eight-brigade Confederate assault led by Longstreet. This attack drove around one-third of the Union army from the field, including Rosecrans. But the remaining Union units regrouped in a defensive line on Horseshoe Ridge under Major General George Thomas, repelling a series of Confederate attacks until evening. As the Union forces fell back on Chattanooga, Bragg refused to pursue, shocked at losing a third of his army, including ten generals killed or wounded. Instead the Confederates instituted a siege of the city. **SA**

Losses: Confederate, 2,312 dead, 14,674 wounded of 65,000; Union, 1,657 dead, 9,756 wounded of 60,000

◁ *Vicksburg 1863*　　　　　*Chattanooga 1863* ▷

 Black soldiers of the 54th Massachusetts storm Fort Wagner, from an 1890 print produced by Kurz & Allison.

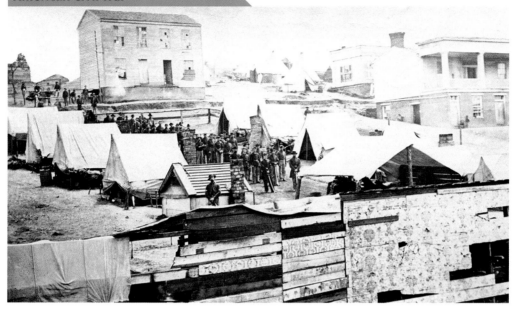

Chattanooga 23–25 November 1863

The battles that took place in and around Chattanooga in November 1863 gave the Union army complete control of Tennessee. Victory here opened the gateway to the Deep South, enabling Union General William Sherman to occupy Atlanta and undertake his March to the Sea the next year.

The Confederate victory at Chickamauga in September 1863 forced the Union Army of the Cumberland back into Chattanooga, where it was blockaded from the surrounding hills by the Confederate Army of Tennessee under General Braxton Bragg. Union General Ulysses S. Grant arrived in Chattanooga to take charge, while substantial reinforcements were brought by railroad, transferred from the the Union Army of the Tennessee and Army of the Potomac.

Grant opened a supply line—the Cracker Line—to feed his men and animals and, when he was ready, seized the initiative. On 23 November the Army of the Cumberland under General George Thomas broke out of Chattanooga and seized the high ground at Orchard Knob. The following day, troops of the Army of the Potomac defeated Confederate forces on Lookout Mountain.

The crucial confrontation took place on 25 November. General Sherman, leading elements of the Army of the Tennessee, was making slow progress in an attack against Bragg's right flank on Missionary Ridge. To distract Bragg, Grant authorized General Thomas to advance to the bottom of Missionary Ridge and seize the line of Confederate rifle pits. This they did, but came under punishing fire from the ridge above. Seeking refuge, Thomas's soldiers fought their way up the ridge and scattered the Confederates, who fled the ridge and retreated into Georgia. Union victory was complete. **SA**

Losses: Union, 753 dead, 4,722 wounded of 56,000; Confederate, 361 dead, 2,160 wounded of 44,000

◁ *Chickamauga 1863* *Atlanta 1864* ▷

Under Confederate siege, Union forces in Chattanooga broke up houses for defense materials. ⬆

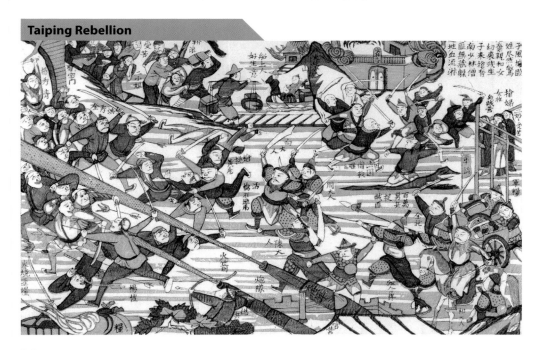

Nanjing   1 March–July 1864

At the time of the Battle of Sanhe in 1858 the Taiping Rebellion in China had seemed capable of overthrowing the rule of the Qing emperors. But by 1864 the bulk of the followers of Hong Xiuquan were besieged in the Taiping capital of Nanjing. Their resistance ended in a bloodbath.

Imperial China had been fortunate to find a loyal and efficient general in Zeng Guofang. Through 1863 and early 1864, aided by the Western-led Ever Victorious Army, Zeng's Xiang Army drew a noose ever tighter around Nanjing, capturing cities and cutting off food supplies.

The defense of the Taiping capital was entrusted to General Li Xiucheng. By March 1864 Zeng had sealed off the city with a line of forts and breastworks. Zeng's soldiers dug dozens of tunnels toward the city, intending to pack them with gunpowder and blow up the walls. The Taiping dug countertunnels, which led to desperate hand-to-hand fighting underground.

As Nanjing's population began to starve and its defenses came under bombardment from Zeng's European-supplied artillery, the Taiping "Heavenly King" Hong Xiuquan fell ill. He died on 1 June and was succeeded by his son, Tiangui Fu. The young monarch's reign lasted six weeks. On 19 July explosives in tunnels were fired, destroying a 60-yard (55 m) section of the city walls. Zeng's soldiers poured into the city, embarking upon a three-day orgy of slaughter and destruction. Li Xiucheng was captured and executed. Zeng wrote to the Chinese emperor: "Not one of the 100,000 rebels in Nanjing surrendered themselves when the city was taken but in many cases gathered together and burned themselves." Fighting continued into 1866, but from the city's fall onward the Taiping cause was doomed. **RG**

Losses: Imperial, 10,000 dead of 200,000; Taiping, 100,000 dead of 400,000 soldiers and civilians

◁ *Cixi 1862*   *Foochow 1884* ▷

⬆ *A nineteenth-century illustration of the capture of Nanjing.*

Dybbol   18 April 1864

In the Second Schleswig War, the Danes fought a German coalition led by Austria and Prussia. When Prussian troops finally stormed the fortress of Dybbol, fighting lasted only four hours, and the war was decided. But the Danes still commemorate the self-sacrifice of their soldiers in the battle.

Forced back from the "Danevirke," their traditional frontier earthworks, the Danes were besieged in the Dybbol fortress, a strong position situated on a peninsula and supported by naval gunfire. The siege began in February 1864, but an infantry attack seemed a futile prospect. Indeed, Prussian General von Moltke suggested simply bypassing the fort. But the fear in Berlin and Vienna was that the longer it held out, the more likely the possibility of British intervention. The coalition commenced what was then the heaviest bombardment in history, using 120 guns (including 24-pound siege guns) and mortars.

The Danish wooden blockhouses and shallow trenches were no match for modern artillery, and casualties mounted. The shorter-range Danish guns could not reply. In the hours before the final assault, 8,000 shells rained down on the Danes, before the Prussian infantry climbed from their trenches and charged. Within the redoubts under attack, fighting was mainly hand-to-hand. The defenders showed great courage; in one redoubt nineteen Danes fought more than 1,000 attackers, inflicting nearly 150 casualties before being overrun.

As the Danish position began to collapse, the 8th Brigade launched a heroic counterattack that temporarily pushed back the Prussians. Though suffering heavy losses, the brigade covered the withdrawal of much of the garrison across a pontoon bridge to the island of Als. Though defeated, the Danes had cause for pride. **JS**

Losses: Austrian and Prussian, 1,201 dead and wounded of 37,000; Danish, 5,000 dead, wounded, or captured of 11,000

Heligoland 1864 ⟩

Gate Pa   29 April 1864

During Britain's phase of imperial expansion, the Maori of New Zealand were among the most formidable adversaries met by the British army. The Maoris defended their fortified strongholds with skill and courage, never more so than at Gate Pa, where heavy losses were inflicted on the British.

The Maori adapted their traditional hilltop strongholds, known as "pa," to meet the demands of fighting British troops equipped with firearms and artillery. They constructed complex systems of palisades, redoubts, trenches, and bunkers to withstand bombardment and resist infantry assault.

Gate Pa, at Tauranga in North Island, was attacked by the British as part of the suppression of the Maori King Movement, formed in opposition to land grabs by white settlers. Crimean War veteran General Duncan Cameron assembled a force of 1,700 troops to take the stronghold, which was defended by fewer than 250 Maori warriors.

On 29 April, Cameron subjected the stronghold to a lengthy artillery bombardment. By mid-afternoon the pa appeared to be in ruins and a column of soldiers was sent forward to take it by assault. As the soldiers entered the pa the Maori, who had been sheltering underground, emerged to fire with their rifle-muskets. Confusion redoubled as a second wave of troops surged into the pa, increasing the density of combatants in a confined space. Many British officers were killed and, in failing light, most of the troops fled from the stronghold in disorder.

By nightfall, the British had dug in outside the pa. The Maori warriors seized the opportunity to slip away under cover of darkness. They had achieved a remarkable feat in inflicting 111 casualties on an altogether better armed enemy that outnumbered them by seven to one. **RG**

Losses: British, 38 dead and 73 wounded of 1,700; Maori, 25 dead

Wilderness 5–7 May 1864

In spring 1864, Union General Ulysses S. Grant initiated the Overland Campaign, a relentless drive toward the Confederate capital, Richmond, Virginia. The first battle of the campaign—a bloody but inconclusive encounter resulting in a high body count—set the tone for what followed.

The battle took place in an area of almost impenetrable scrub and rough terrain known as the Wilderness of Spotsylvania, a few miles to the west of where the Battle of Chancellorsville had been fought a year earlier. The Union Army of the Potomac, under the command of General George Meade but taking orders from Grant, crossed the Rapidan River and converged at the Wilderness Tavern on the main turnpike.

Meade had no wish to fight in the wooded Wilderness, unlike his Confederate opponent, General Lee, who, massively outnumbered and outgunned, preferred to fight in among trees as these would prevent Grant from using his artillery effectively and provide cover for his smaller force. The unfavorable terrain reduced the two-day battle to a series of bloody small-scale skirmishes, each scene obscured by smoke from gunpowder and the fires lit by exploding shells in the dry woods. Both sides endured heavy casualties, and Confederate General James Longstreet was hit by friendly fire only four miles (6.5 km) from where General "Stonewall" Jackson had been similarly hit the previous year. Horrifically, a brush fire broke out between the two armies on the night of 6 May and killed many of the soldiers still lying wounded on the battlefield. On 7 May, further skirmishes took place before the battle ended. Although inconclusive, the battle benefited the Union side because Lee's casualties were high in proportion to the size of his army. **SA**

Losses: Union, 2,246 dead, 12,037 wounded of 101,895; Confederate, 1,495 dead, 7,928 wounded of 61,025

◁ Gettysburg 1863   Spotsylvania 1864 ▷

Heligoland 9 May 1864

A naval battle of the Second Schleswig War, this was a relatively small action, but provided the Danes with their greatest success in the war. It could not change the outcome of the conflict, which ended three days later, but it did much to highlight Prussian naval weakness.

The Danish naval blockade of the German North Sea coast was their most effective effort in the war. German shipping was so much under threat that many German ships were reflagged as Russian to evade interception. The exasperated Prussians persuaded the Austrians to help break the blockade.

The two squadrons met off the British North Sea island of Heligoland. Three Danish, two Austrian, and three Prussian ships were engaged, none bigger than a frigate, all wooden-built and powered by a combination of sail and steam. From the start it was a Danish-Austrian fight— the Prussian ships could not keep up and, although they opened fire, they were too distant to play an effective role in the battle. Taking into account the superior Austrian guns, the forces were fairly evenly matched, and both sides battered each other in a furious cannonade.

However, the Danes were able to concentrate their fire on the Austrian flagship *Schwartzenberg*, dismounting several guns before a lucky shot set fire to her foretopsail. With the ship's pump destroyed, the fire spread and the Austrians were forced to seek sanctuary in neutral British waters. Any chance of the Danes catching them beforehand was frustrated when the Danish flagship *Jylland* suffered damage to its steering gear. The Austro-Prussian slipped away in the night. No ships were lost, but the blockade remained in place, giving the Danes an unquestioned victory. **JS**

Losses: Danish, 14 dead, 55 wounded; Austrian, 32 dead, 59 wounded; Prussian, none

◁ Dybbol 1864   Sadowa 1866 ▷

Spotsylvania 9–18 May 1864

A lull might have been expected after the Battle of the Wilderness of Spotsylvania, with both Union and Confederate armies exhausted and disorganized. But General Grant pressed on relentlessly with his offensive. Two days later, he met General Lee's army again, 10 miles (16 km) to the southeast at Spotsylvania Court House.

On the night of 7 May, hours after fighting ended at the Wilderness, Grant began moving his army forward to resume its advance. He aimed to take the crossroads at Spotsylvania, cutting between Lee's army and Richmond. Lee anticipated this move and reacted swiftly. On 9 May his troops dug a line of field fortifications some 4 miles (6.5 km) long north of Spotsylvania. Its only weakness was an exposed salient known as the Mule Shoe.

After initial probing skirmishes, Union forces attacked the Mule Shoe the next day. An assault by resolute troops charging at a run penetrated the Confederate lines, but the Union soldiers were driven back by counterattacks at the end of the day. As Grant shifted his forces in preparation for another assault, Lee misunderstood the Union activity and pulled back his artillery to meet a potential flanking maneuver. As a result, Grant's attack on 12 May was initially a complete success, breaking through the Confederate lines before Lee rushed in troops to plug the gap. The battle raged into the night, the intense firepower of both sides flattening the landscape as soldiers engaged in hand-to-hand fighting at a position that became infamous as "Bloody Angle."

In the early hours of 13 May, Lee's men completed a fallback trench and retreated to it, ceding the salient to Grant's troops. A Union attack on this new line on 18 May made no impact, forcing Grant to discontinue. **SA**

Losses: Union, 2,725 dead, 13,416 wounded of 100,000; Confederate, 1,467 dead, 6,235 wounded of 52,000

◁ *Wilderness 1864*　　　　　　　　*Cold Harbor 1864* ▷

Cold Harbor 3–12 June 1864

Continuing his relentless drive toward the Confederate capital of Richmond, Virginia, General Grant ordered a frontal infantry assault on General Lee's Confederate troops, who were now entrenched at Cold Harbor. The result, a disaster for the Union that incurred heavy losses, left the end of the American Civil War no clearer in sight.

The twin battles of Wilderness and Spotsylvania Court House, fought in Virginia in May 1864, produced victory for neither side, but attrition reduced the much smaller Confederate army's numbers and sapped its willingness to fight. Union General Grant became convinced that Confederate General Lee's army was "really whipped," but his own casualties had also been high, and those troops who in 1861 had joined up for three years were now leaving the army in large numbers.

Grant therefore gambled on a final push to take Richmond. On 3 June he launched a frontal assault on Confederate defenses at Cold Harbor, six miles (9.6 km) north of Richmond. He believed that Lee's men were overextended, but Lee had taken advantage of a one-day delay in Grant's assault to bring in reinforcements and improve his fortifications. The result of his preparations was carnage; the advancing Union troops were soon felled, with those making it through the first line of defenses soon being slaughtered at the second. More than 7,000 Union troops were killed or injured in one hour before Grant halted the attack.

For the next nine days, the two armies faced each other in opposite trenches, often only yards apart, until Grant marched off his army to threaten the rail junction of Petersburg. His own comment on the battle: "I regret this assault more than any one I have ever ordered." **SA**

Losses: Confederate, 83 dead, 3,380 wounded of 62,000; Union, 1,844 dead, 9,077 wounded of 108,000

◁ *Spotsylvania 1864*　　　　　　　　*The Crater 1864* ▷

 A Confederate casualty of an attack on a Union defensive position at Spotsylvania.

Cherbourg 19 June 1864

During the American Civil War, the Union navy had command of the sea, blockading the Confederate coast, but Confederate raiders were still preying upon Union merchant shipping. The most successful of these, CSS *Alabama*, met its end in a famous ship-to-ship duel off the French coast.

A wooden-hulled steam sloop, *Alabama* was built by a British shipyard in 1862. She cruised the oceans under the command of Confederate Captain Raphael Semmes, destroying more than sixty Union merchant ships, as well as sinking the Union warship USS *Hatteras* off the American coast in 1863. These exploits won *Alabama* renown and the Union was determined to hunt her down.

In June 1864 *Alabama* put into the French port of Cherbourg for repairs and resupply. She was discovered there by the Union sloop USS *Kearsarge*, commanded by Captain John Winslow, on 14 June. As *Kearsarge* waited outside the port, Semmes decided to give battle before

more Union warships arrived; he thus issued a courteous challenge to Winslow, begging him not to leave before *Alabama* was ready for action. On 19 June *Alabama*, shadowed by a French vessel detailed to protect the harbor, sailed out of port toward *Kearsarge*, guns blazing.

The Union ship was fitted with improvised armor in the form of iron chains wrapped around the wooden hull. *Alabama* was unarmored. *Kearsarge* also demonstrated superior gunnery, using its Dahlgren guns relatively sparingly but to better effect. After an hour's fighting, *Alabama*'s steering gear was wrecked and water was pouring through a gash in her hull. Semmes struck his colors shortly before sinking. Most of the crew were rescued by *Kearsarge* and taken prisoner, but Semmes and some forty others were picked up by a British yacht. **RG**

Losses: Confederate, 1 ship sunk, 9 dead, 21 wounded, and 70 captured; Union, 3 wounded

◁ *Hampton Roads 1862*　　　　　　　　*Mobile Bay 1864* ▷

Captain Winslow and his crew pose aboard Kearsarge *in June 1864, prior to engaging* Alabama.

Atlanta   22 July 1864

As General Grant led the Union attack on Richmond, the Confederate capital in the northeast, General Sherman headed southeast from Tennessee toward Atlanta, Georgia. The battle on 22 July that bears the city's name was decisive, but it was to be another six weeks before Atlanta surrendered.

In May 1864, General Sherman and his three Union armies left Chattanooga, Tennessee, and crossed the border into Georgia. His Confederate opponent, General Joseph E. Johnston, retreated in the face of superior numbers, taking up one defensive position after another and then retreating as Sherman outflanked him. Johnston was soon relieved of his command, but his successor, Texan General John Bell Hood, fared no better, suffering a defeat at Peachtree Creek on 20 July.

By now Sherman's army was outside Atlanta. On 22 July, Hood decided to fight. He sent an infantry corps to march around the Union left flank while another corps attacked the Union front line and his cavalry threatened the Union supply line. But Hood had miscalculated the time the flanking march would take, allowing Union General James McPherson to bring up his reserves and repel the Confederate attack. At around 4:00 PM the Confederate assault on the front line broke through but was driven back by heavy artillery fire. Confederate casualties were high—losses that they could ill afford—but they retained control of Atlanta itself. Sherman therefore began to bombard the city into submission, sending raiding parties west and south to cut off its supply lines. On 1 September Hood pulled out of the city, destroying supply depots as he left. The next day, the mayor and other leading citizens surrendered the city to Sherman. "Atlanta is ours, and fairly won," Sherman telegrammed Washington. **SA**

Losses: Union, 3,641 of 112,000; Confederate, 8,499 of 60,000

◁ *Chattanooga 1863*   *Nashville 1864* ▷

⬆ *Union soldiers under General Sherman tear up railroad track after taking Atlanta.*

The Crater   30 July 1864

In the final year of the American Civil War, Union forces besieged the town of Petersburg, to the south of the Confederate capital of Richmond. But a well-conceived attempt to end the stalemate of trench warfare and break through Confederate defenses with gunpowder resulted in a tragic fiasco.

After his failure at Cold Harbor, Union General Grant sent his Army of the Potomac over the James River to attack Richmond from the south. He failed, however, to capture the important railhead at Petersburg. Confederate General Lee rushed to strengthen its fortifications, forcing Grant to dig in for a siege. Having learned his lesson at Cold Harbor, Grant was in no mood to attempt a frontal assault on Confederate earthworks. He made it known that he was seeking alternatives.

Lieutenant Colonel Henry Pleasants, a mining engineer, came up with the idea of digging a mineshaft under Confederate lines and filling it with explosives. Not only would the explosion kill the defenders but it would also breach their front line. Pleasants and his miners dug a sloping tunnel 500 feet (150 m) long that ended in a large chamber. This was filled with 320 kegs of gunpowder that were then detonated in the early hours of 30 July.

The explosion killed around 300 Confederate men and opened up a vast crater, 170 feet (52 m) long and 30 feet (9 m) deep. The way was now clear for Union troops to pour into Petersburg, but the first soldiers to enter the crater decided it was a good place to dig a rifle pit, and stayed put. Within an hour Confederate troops had rallied their strength and begun to fire rifles and artillery down into the crater, killing hundreds. Union reinforcements also came under intense fire until all withdrew. The successful detonation had created a death trap. **SA**

Losses: Confederate, 361 dead, 727 wounded; Union, 504 dead, 1,881 wounded

◁ *Cold Harbor 1864*   *Cedar Creek 1864* ▷

A young soldier lies dead, a victim of the Union catastrophe of the Petersburg Crater. ⬆

Mobile Bay   5 August 1864

During the American Civil War, Union ships imposed a blockade on Confederate ports. One of the few ports to defy the blockade was Mobile in Alabama. In 1864 Union Admiral David Farragut was tasked with closing this gap, which was making the Union stranglehold on the South less effective.

The anchorage in Mobile Bay was well protected by two forts and rows of stakes blocking the shallows, as well as many floating mines, then known as "torpedoes." Farragut planned his attack well. In the early hours of 5 August his fleet of four monitors and fourteen wooden steamships crossed the bar at the entrance to the harbor on the incoming tide. The four monitors steamed on the starboard side of his wooden warships to protect them from Fort Morgan's guns.

Ahead of them, a Confederate squadron consisting of three gunboats and the large ironclad CSS *Tennessee* lay in wait. As the Union fleet approached, the guns of Fort Morgan opened fire. The Union fleet responded, the exchange creating such smoke that Farragut had to climb the mainmast of his flagship USS *Hartford* to see what was happening. Ahead, the Confederate fleet joined in the battle. Maneuvering to engage *Tennessee*, the monitor USS *Tecumseh* struck a "torpedo" and sank with few survivors. As the Union squadron came to an uncertain halt, Farragut urged them on: "Damn the torpedoes! Full speed ahead." The Union ships headed unscathed into the bay and engaged the Confederate squadron. After a long and hard fight, they finally succeeded in blowing a hole in *Tennessee*'s iron armor. The wounded Confederate admiral, Franklin Buchanan, then ran up the white flag. Over the next few weeks, Union forces captured the harbor's two forts, sealing the bay. **SA**

Losses: Union, 1 monitor of 18 ships; Confederate, 1 ironclad and 2 gunboats of 4 ships

[<] *Cherbourg 1864*

The lighthouse at Mobile Point was made a target for Union artillery during the siege of Fort Morgan.

Early on 19 October, Confederates drive back Union troops at Cedar Creek; the tables turned in the late afternoon. ⬇

Cedar Creek 19 October 1864

In 1864 Union General Philip Sheridan was sent into Virginia's Shenandoah Valley to contest a drive by a Confederate army toward Washington. Sheridan's scorched-earth policy was called "the Burning" by terrified local residents. The decisive battle of the campaign was fought at Cedar Creek.

The Washington-bound Confederate army, led by General Jubal A. Early, won a series of victories until General Sheridan led his army into the valley, beating Early's forces in several encounters and systematically burning crops, barns, and factories to deny the Confederate army its food and supplies. Just as Sheridan considered Early as beaten, the Confederate general pursued the Union army and boldly launched a surprise attack at Cedar Creek.

Overnight, Early's men marched around Massanutten Mountain and—just before sunrise and in dense fog—attacked the left of the Union camp. The Union army was caught by surprise, with many still in their bedclothes. Sheridan was 10 miles (16 km) away at Winchester. George Crook's VIII Corps soon collapsed, as did XIX Corps. The final corps, Horatio Wright's VI Corps, fought hard before withdrawing slowly under great pressure.

Mistakenly believing that he had won, Early did not give chase, allowing Sheridan time to reach the battlefield and rally his troops. At 4:00 PM the Union troops counterattacked and broke the Confederate lines, cutting off their escape route to the rear. Many surrendered quickly, giving Sheridan a major victory. The Confederacy would never threaten Washington again. **SA**

Losses: Union, 5,665 of 31,945; Confederate, 2,910 of 21,000

◁ *The Crater 1864*   *Five Forks 1865* ▷

Nashville   15–16 December 1864

After the fall of Atlanta, Union General Sherman's army prepared to march through Georgia to Savannah. Meanwhile Confederate General John Bell Hood's defeated Army of Tennessee aimed to push through Tennessee into Kentucky. Hood's bold venture came to grief in front of Nashville.

Hood was a young, aggressive commander who believed he could beat the Union troops despite his army's inferior numbers, lack of essential equipment, and shaky morale. Meanwhile, Union forces, led by Major General George H. Thomas, were concentrating in fortified positions in front of Nashville, Tennessee, in late November.

Hood began a siege, despite having inferior forces to the enemy inside the defenses. Overall Union commander General Grant fumed at Thomas for failing to attack and was about to travel to Nashville when, on 15 December, Thomas launched his counterattack. Outnumbering the Confederates by almost two to one, the Union forces battered Hood's line, pinning his right flank with an attack in divisional strength while throwing an overwhelming weight of infantry and cavalry against his left.

After a first day of fighting, Hood pulled back to shorten his line, but the pressure on the second day was relentless. Union cavalry with repeater rifles found a way behind the Confederate left flank and toward nightfall, in heavy rain, the defensive line collapsed. Many Confederate soldiers surrendered; others threw away their weapons and ran. Only half of Hood's original force reached Mississippi. It was the last major battle in the Western Theater. **RG**

Losses: Confederate, 6,000 casualties and captured of 30,000; Union, 387 dead, 2,558 wounded of 55,000

◁ *Atlanta 1864*

Five Forks
1 April 1865

The lengthy Union siege of Confederate-held Petersburg in Virginia was brought to a close in what has been called the "Waterloo of the Confederacy." Union troops overwhelmed their opponents, forcing the Army of Northern Virginia to abandon Petersburg and head toward final defeat a week later.

After his successful campaign in the Shenandoah Valley, Union General Philip H. Sheridan pursued the Confederate army of George E. Pickett to Five Forks, southwest of Petersburg. Pickett and his men built a defensive line of logs and earth almost 1 ¾ miles (2.8 km) long, its flanks guarded by cavalry. In response, Sheridan planned to push evenly along the whole line with his cavalry while V Corps under General Gouverneur K. Warren attacked the Confederate left flank.

The approach to the Confederate line was slowed by muddy roads and tangled undergrowth, and Warren was unable to attack until 4:00 PM. Faulty intelligence, however, had led Sheridan to imagine the left flank much further to the east than it actually was. As a result, one of Warren's three divisions missed the line altogether while another was fired at from the side as it brushed past the flank. The two Union divisions floundered for a time while they sorted out their positions until Sheridan led a charge by one of the divisions and broke through the Confederate flank. As the Confederates tried to organize a new defensive line, Warren's third, reserve, division attacked while Sheridan's cavalry swept around the other Confederate flank to attack from the rear. The Union victory was decisive. Faced with this major defeat, Confederate General Lee was forced to evacuate Petersburg, handing it over to the Union the next day. **SA**

Losses: Union, 830 of 17,000; Confederate, 2,950 of 9,200

◁ *Cedar Creek 1864*   *Appomattox Court House 1865* ▷

Appomattox Court House
9 April 1865

Tired, despondent, outnumbered, and outgunned, the Confederate Army of Northern Virginia met its end in Virginia on 9 April 1865. That afternoon, General Robert E. Lee surrendered to Union General Ulysses S. Grant, bringing the four-year American Civil War to a close.

Defeated at Five Forks on 1 April and forced to evacuate Petersburg the next day, General Lee then abandoned the Confederate capital of Richmond, Virginia, and retreated west, hoping to join up with some remaining Confederate forces in North Carolina. Union forces pursued the weary army, forcing the capture and surrender of 10,000 Confederates at Sayler's Creek on 6–7 April. The remaining men marched west toward Lynchburg.

Union General Philip H. Sheridan realized what Lee was doing and managed to intercept Lee's army at Appomattox Court House on 8 April, capturing his supplies and obstructing his route west. At dawn the next morning, the Confederate II Corps attacked Sheridan's cavalry and broke through to the ridge behind them. There they saw the vast numbers of Union infantry from the Army of the James, arriving after an all-night march and lining up for battle. In the face of such overwhelming numbers, Lee accepted the inevitable and asked Grant for a cease-fire. Grant offered to meet Lee wherever he chose.

Lee's aide surveyed the small village of Appomattox Court House and found a brick house belonging to Wilmer McLean. There, around 4:00 PM, Lee surrendered. His men were allowed to return home with their horses and mules after handing in their arms. Attempts to continue Confederate resistance on other fronts soon failed. It was the end of the American Civil War. **SA**

Losses: Union, 164 dead and wounded of 120,000; Confederate, 500 dead and wounded of 28,356

◁ *Five Forks 1865*

Riachuelo
11 June 1865

Second Custoza
24 June 1866

Between 1864 and 1870 Paraguay fought the War of the Triple Alliance, a catastrophic conflict that eventually cost the lives of the majority of the Paraguayan population. The naval battle of Riachuelo, fought on the Paraná River in southern Paraguay, marked an early turning point.

When, on 14 June 1866, Austria went to war with Prussia, the newly founded kingdom of Italy chose to fight Austria for control of Venetia—even though the Austrians would have offered Venetia as a gift in exchange for Italian neutrality. The Italian thirst for glory ended in humiliation.

In the 1860s, Paraguay's president Francisco Solano López built an army and threatened neighboring Brazil and Argentina. Both countries supported rebels in Uruguay. After Brazil invaded Uruguay, López declared war on Brazil in December 1864 and invaded. When his demand to cross Argentina to get to Uruguay was refused, López invaded Argentina as well, prompting a Triple Alliance to be formed by Argentina, Brazil, and Uruguay in May 1865.

López, wishing to attack Brazilian ships at Riachuelo, ordered the Paraguayan fleet—eight steamships plus seven barges laden with cannon—to approach the docked Brazilian ships during darkness and seize them quietly. Instead, the Paraguayan commander, Captain Meza, sailed down the Paraná River, firing at the Brazilian fleet as he passed by. The Brazilians boarded their ships and returned fire, hitting one Paraguayan steamer.

As the Paraguayans formed up in a line below Riachuelo, the Brazilian fleet gave chase. The Paraguayans opened fire, causing one Brazilian ship, *Jequitinhonha*, to turn around mistakenly and head back upstream, taking all but one ship with her. The Brazilians then returned downriver toward the Paraguayan fleet. With the battle evenly balanced, Brazilian Admiral Barroso ordered his steamer, *Amazonas,* to ram two Paraguayan steamers and sink a barge. Two more Paraguayan steamers were heavily damaged, and all the barges sunk. **SA**

While the Austrians were engaged against Prussia, the Italians intended to strike in two thrusts in a coordinated invasion of Venetia, with twelve divisions advancing from the Mincio River and another six from the Po River. In support, the veteran revolutionary Giuseppe Garibaldi and a force of volunteers would invade the Tyrol.

The plan ignored severe weaknesses in the Italian army: its artillery was outdated, leadership at the highest ranks and among junior officers was woefully inadequate, and the troops—mainly unwilling conscripts—had no wish to fight. The Austrians had problems of their own, not least the reliability of some Hungarian and Slav units, but while the Italians advanced at a leisurely pace, detaching units to besiege fortifications, the Austrians struck hard, intending to cut off and annihilate the main Italian force.

At the last possible moment, the Austrian presence was detected and Italian troops raced to dominate the high ground while their commanders scrambled to reassemble their scattered forces. What followed was a confused melee, with Italian infantry launching repeated attacks on Austrian positions, only to be beaten back by superior artillery and determined cavalry charges. A final wild cavalry charge by the Austrians broke the nerve of the Italian infantry, sending them in full flight back to Lombardy. Only Prussian victories gave Italy the prize they were unable to gain by their own prowess. **JS**

Losses: Brazilian, 1 ship sunk of 9; Paraguayan, 4 ships of 8 and all 7 barges sunk

◁ *Caseros 1852*　　　　　　*Campo Grande 1869* ▷

Losses: Austrian, 6,000 dead, wounded, or captured of 75,000; Italian, 8,000 casualties of 120,000

◁ *Volturno 1860*　　　　　　*Sadowa 1866* ▷

Sadowa (Königgrätz) 3 July 1866

The Prussian victory at Sadowa, masterminded by Chief of Staff Helmut von Moltke, ensured that henceforth Austria would play no role in German affairs. The way was opened to the unification of Germany under Prussian leadership, a process completed over the next five years.

Moltke's plan of campaign against Austria was based on the rapid mobilization of some 300,000 men and their movement by train to the war zone with their equipment—a feat of organization that gave the Prussians the initiative from the outset. Two armies were launched on a two-pronged invasion of Bohemia, while a third army entered Saxony. The Prussian advance, to be coordinated by Moltke using the telegraph, was to be united only in the face of the enemy. The Prussians risked their forces being defeated separately, but the risk was worth the speed the maneuver would allow.

In the event, the Austrian commander, Ludwig von Benedek, proved hesitant. By the time he took up a

> ## "The victory of the Prussians . . . was a victory of the Prussian over the Austrian schoolmaster."
>
> *Privy Councillor Peschel, in Ausland, No. 19 (17 July 1866)*

position between Sadowa and Königgrätz, the fighting spirit of his army—and that of his Saxon ally—had been severely undermined by earlier defeats. Benedek urged his government to make peace but his emperor, Franz Josef, required him to fight. Benedek opted for a defensive battle, realizing that frontal assaults with fixed bayonets in the face of Prussian firepower would be disastrous. His infantrymen, armed with muzzle-loading weapons that had to be reloaded from a standing position, were at a severe disadvantage to the Prussians, whose breech-

loading Dreyse needle-guns could be reloaded from the prone position. All did not go smoothly for the Prussians, however. Their supply system almost broke down, as did coordination between the different armies. Approaching Sadowa, the Prussian forces were divided by the Elbe River, and the Second Army opened the attack before the First Army was in position.

This could have proved a decisive moment. The Prussian infantry ran into a storm of artillery fire and for five hours were unable to advance. Hastily constructed Austrian defenses within the forest proved extremely difficult for the Prussian infantry to overwhelm. An Austrian attack in strength at that moment might have provided victory, but, as Benedek hesitated, the headstrong commander of his northern flank, without orders, launched his infantry in a traditional bayonet charge. His flank exposed, Benedek did not dare launch the assault by his center that might have swept the Prussian Second Army from the field.

The Prussian First Army then arrived and launched a flanking maneuver that threatened to encircle the Austrians, whose northern flank was soon thrown back in disorder. Austrian reserves were expended in futile counterattacks. At this point the day was lost, and Benedek could only try to extricate his army, now threatened on three sides, along a single road that was already jammed with men and horses. The withdrawal of the demoralized Austrian infantry soon collapsed into a disordered rout. Only the bravery of the Austrian cavalry (which lost nearly 2,000 men covering the retreat) and artillery saved the Austrians from annihilation. The war was effectively over—there was no possibility of the Austrian army ever fighting another battle. **JS**

Losses: Austrian and Saxon, 44,000 dead, wounded, or captured of 206,000; Prussian, 2,000 dead and 7,000 wounded of 221,000 engaged

◁ *Second Custoza 1866*   *Lissa 1866* ▷

Disciplined Prussian infantry fire on the Austrians and Saxons in this nineteenth-century depiction of the battle.

Lissa   20 July 1866

Fought between Italy and Austria, Lissa was a naval battle at an odd moment in the development of naval technology. Ramming, widely employed by the ancient Greeks, had briefly reappeared as the prime form of attack—with the rams attached to the prows of steam-powered ironclads.

In 1866 Italy was fighting as an ally of Prussia in its war with Austria. The Italian and Austrian fleets both comprised obsolete wind-powered wooden ships and modern, steam-powered ironclads, but the Italian fleet was larger and had better guns. The Austrians had already been defeated on land at Sadowa, and Italy had every reason to expect to dominate the Adriatic.

Peace negotiations had already opened when the Italian fleet attacked the Dalmatian island of Lissa, hoping to improve Italy's position at the talks. After bombarding the island, Admiral Carlo di Persano was preparing to land troops when the Austrian fleet approached. Austrian Admiral Wilhelm von Tegetthoff, attacking in three V-shaped formations with the most powerful ships leading, closed rapidly with the Italians to negate their gunnery advantage and ram their ships.

In this they succeeded, largely due to confusion in the Italian command. Persano ordered his ships to form line of battle, then decided to transfer his flag to another ship. Half of his battle line slowed down, but, failing to read signals, his leading ships carried on, opening a gap in his battle line. The Austrians descended as the Italians were still struggling to gain formation. The melee was chaotic, with both sides combining gunfire with attempts to ram. After losing two ironclads (*Palestro* and *Re' d'Italia*), Persano broke off, conceding defeat. Lissa was the last naval battle fought by ships designed for ramming. **JS**

Losses: Austrian, 38 dead; Italian, 620 dead, 2 ironclads sunk

◁ *Sadowa 1866*

Wagon Box Fight   2 August 1867

With the conclusion of the American Civil War in 1865, land grants to veterans and the discovery of gold resulted in a population surge into the western territories of the United States, reigniting the bitter conflict between nomadic American Indian tribes and the new settlers.

The Bozeman Trail was a main route through Wyoming and Montana, crossing land ceded by treaty to the Sioux and Northern Cheyenne tribes. In 1866 Indians led by Sioux sub-chief Red Cloud repudiated the treaty and took up arms to resist. Confronting Red Cloud, soldiers arrived in July 1866 to construct Fort Phil Kearny.

On 2 August 1867 Red Cloud attacked a detachment of the 27th Infantry, commanded by Captain James Powell, that was protecting woodcutters 7 miles (11 km) from the fort. Powell's base was an oval enclosure of fourteen wooden wagons (with wheels removed) placed end to end on a grassy plateau. Loopholes were cut through the sides of the wagons. The soldiers had newly issued breech-loading Springfield rifles rather than muzzle-loading muskets, plus Colt revolvers and plenty of ammunition. The Indians first attacked the cutters, killing several; Powell intercepted them, then withdrew into the wagon barricade. He had thirty-two officers and men against Red Cloud's several thousand warriors.

The Indians, expecting lulls in the defenders' fire for musket reloading, made repeated mass charges that were broken by rapid, steady fire from the Springfields. Attempts to penetrate the wagon enclosure by dismounted attacks also failed with bloody results for the Indians. When an Army relief force approached, Red Cloud withdrew his shattered force. Fort Phil Kearny was only abandoned after a treaty was signed in 1869. **RB**

Losses: U.S., 1 dead, 2 wounded; Sioux-Cheyenne, 1,000 dead or wounded

Little Bighorn 1876 ▷

Magdala 9–13 April 1868

This battle was fought between an army of the British Empire, under the command of Field Marshal Robert Napier, and the Abyssinian army of the Emperor Theodore II (Tewodros II). It resulted in the fall and subsequent sacking of the Abyssinian fortress capital of Magdala, and the death of the emperor.

In January 1868, the British invaded Abyssinia (present-day Ethiopia) to secure the release of civilian hostages. The terrain was extremely rough and it was not until April that Field Marshal Napier approached Magdala. Between the British and Magdala lay the plateau of Arogi and an Abyssinian army. The British moved onto the plateau and deployed ready for an assault, not expecting an attack from the strong defensive positions held by the emperor's army. But the unexpected attack came, as thousands of Abyssinians rushed the British, who frantically tried to move from an attacking posture to a defensive one.

Napier formed up infantry divisions armed with new Snider-Enfield rifles, capable of firing ten rounds per minute as opposed to the usual three. The British opened fire at close quarters and the effect was devastating; the attackers were routed. This was the first time the British had used the new rifle, and the spears and muskets of the Abyssinians were no match for such firepower.

The battle was a perfect example of the gap in technology that existed between African and European forces. The decision to attack was disastrous for Emperor Theodore, as it destroyed the resolve of his army to protect his capital from the superior British force. Theodore slowly released the hostages for whom the British had come over the ensuing days, but the fortress was stormed on 13 April, and the emperor committed suicide during the attack. **TB**

Losses: British, 20 casualties of 16,000; Abyssinian, 2,200 casualties of 9,000

Adowa 1896 ▶

Hakodate Bay 4–10 May 1869

The Meiji restoration of imperial power in Japan that started with the overthrow of the shogunate or feudal dictatorship in early 1868 ended in imperial victory at a naval battle in Hakodate Bay, off Hokkaido, the northernmost island of Japan. Japanese naval power was now in the ascendant.

The Tokugawa shogunate that had ruled Japan since 1603 began to collapse as Japan opened up her ports to western states after 1854, ending her effective isolation from the rest of the world. In January 1868 a group of imperial courtiers declared the shogunate at an end and supported the Meiji ("enlightened rule") of the emperor. The brief civil war that followed ended when part of the shogun's navy, led by Admiral Enomoto Takeaki, and several thousand soldiers fled to Ezo, now known as Hokkaido, where they established a rebel republic.

The Republican fleet was small, just the paddleship *Kaiten* and four other steamships. The Meiji emperor had little time to construct his own fleet, purchasing the ironclad warship *Kotetsu* from the United States along with seven other ships acquired from friendly Japanese lords. The imperial fleet landed troops on Hokkaido, destroying fortifications and attacking rebel ships. *Chiyodagata,* grounded and abandoned, was captured on 4 May, and *Kaiten* was hit and disabled on 7 May. Although the rebel *Banryu* managed to sink the imperial *Choyo,* she herself sank after sustaining heavy damage.

Defeated at sea, the Republic of Ezo surrendered and ceased to exist on 27 June. The next month, imperial and rebel ships were formed into the Imperial Japanese Navy. The emperor's men at Hakodate Bay included Togo Heihachiro, who later became famous as commander-in-chief during the 1904–05 war with Russia. **SA**

Losses: Imperial, 1 warship sunk of 8; Republican, 2 warships sunk and 3 captured of 5

Shiroyama 1877 ▶

Campo Grande 16 August 1869

The South American War of the Triple Alliance, begun in 1864, reached its tragic climax at Eusebio Ayala in Paraguay in 1869. The defeat of the Paraguayan army—more than half of it children—led in 1870 to the death of its president, Francisco Solano López, and to the end of the war.

Paraguay's attempts to become the major power in its region led to war in 1864 with Brazil, which formed a Triple Alliance with Argentina and Uruguay in 1865. Superior numbers soon gave the Alliance a series of victories. By mid-1869 the Paraguayan army was on the run and the national capital, Asunción, was occupied by the Allies.

López refused to surrender. Most Paraguayan men had been either killed or captured, so López conscripted children into the army, some of them painting on false moustaches to hide their youth. Early on 16 August Allied troops met the remnants of the Paraguayan army, including 3,500 child soldiers, at Campo Grande, also known as Acosta Nu, a vast flat plain.

After an initial exchange of fire, the Paraguayans retreated across the Juquerí River, setting the grass on fire to hide their movements. Allied infantry charged across the river but were repelled. Allied artillery then opened fire, causing huge losses. By now the Brazilian cavalry had reached the battlefield from the rear of their lines and crossed the river, again inflicting huge losses on the Paraguayan infantry, who had formed up into infantry squares to defend themselves. A further Allied infantry charge seized the eight Paraguayan cannon and broke their lines. The eight-hour battle was over. Within a year, Paraguay was defeated, its president and more than half its population dead, and its territory shrunk by half. **SA**

Losses: Allied, 46 dead, 259 wounded of 20,000; Paraguayan, 2,000 dead, 1,200 captured of 6,000

◁ Riachuelo 1865　　　　Fortín Nanawa 1933 ▷

Fröschwiller 6 August 1870

German statesman Otto von Bismarck maneuvered the French into a needless war to complete the process of German unification. The French expected an easy victory, but Fröschwiller, the first major battle of the Franco-Prussian War, was to be the first indication of impending disaster for them.

At the outbreak of war French mobilization was utterly chaotic, with generals separated from their regiments, the supply system tangled, and too many units seriously under strength. The French were heavily outnumbered in their first encounter, in Alsace, with a more efficient and experienced German military machine.

After an initial skirmish near Weissenburg, the French commander, Marshal Patrice de MacMahon, pulled back to a strong defensive position on a heavily wooded plateau at Fröschwiller. Bavarian troops, eager to prove their worth to their Prussian allies, who had recently been their enemies, attacked first, but met ferocious resistance from the French, who included experienced North African troops armed with the latest Chassepot breech-loading rifles. German artillery soon silenced the French guns, and the Germans deployed superior numbers in a move to envelop the French. French counterattacks followed, including suicidally courageous cavalry charges. One unit of 700 cuirassiers was massacred within minutes by German artillery, but further attacks continued.

All this was to no avail; with both his flanks now overlapped, MacMahon's forces had to withdraw. Most reached Châlons-sur-Marne; the Germans, lacking cavalry, were unable to pursue closely. But the road to Paris was left open, and those French troops who escaped only went on to face greater disaster at Sedan. **JS**

Losses: French, 11,000 dead or wounded and 6,200 captured of 46,500; German, 9,200 dead or wounded and 1,400 missing of 125,000

◁ Sadowa 1866　　　　Mars-la-Tour 1870 ▷

Dead infantry pile up before French riflemen at Fröschwiller in a detail from a nineteenth-century engraving.

Mars-la-Tour 16 August 1870

As the Franco-Prussian War, a disaster for France, unfolded, Marshal François Bazaine decided to withdraw his army to the fortress at Verdun. There he himself met disaster, at the hands of a smaller German force. The last successful major cavalry charge in Europe contributed to his failure.

After a series of stinging, if minor, defeats, Bazaine chose to abandon the fortress at Metz and link up with French forces at Verdun. When Hanoverian dragoons located his army at Mars-la-Tour, a force of 30,000 Germans was hastily moved to close his route. A truly desperate fight ensued. This was a "soldier's battle," in which the initiative of unit commanders, and the fighting spirit of individual soldiers, would be the key to victory.

At one point a cavalry melee broke out that lasted nearly an hour as both sides hammered at each other, but without decisive effect. The Germans were outnumbered four to one but Bazaine never recognized this fact.

Proceeding cautiously, he failed to throw his full force into the battle. The Germans, on the other hand, quickly committed every man and gun, and at the same time enjoyed the invaluable advantage of immense self-confidence. Fighting all day, the Germans held off the entire French army until their smaller force was reinforced.

The turning point of the battle came when a German cavalry brigade, in a famous "Death Ride," found concealment in the terrain and smoke from French artillery fire and closed in for a sudden charge that carried them right through the line of French guns. Nearly half of the cavalry fell, but the attack had convinced Bazaine that he could not break through. The fighting died down through mutual exhaustion, and the next day Bazaine withdrew, unmolested, back in the direction of Metz. **JS**

Losses: French, 17,000 dead or wounded of 127,000; German, 16,000 dead or wounded of 80,000

◁ Fröschwiller 1870   Gravelotte–St. Privat 1870 ▷

The German "Death Ride" cavalry charge that won them Mars-la-Tour, in an 1872 painting by Emil Hünten. ⬆

Gravelotte–St. Privat   18 August 1870

Following his defeat at Mars-la-Tour, Marshal François Bazaine was reluctant to return to Metz, which lacked the supplies to withstand a siege. Instead, he chose to offer battle at Gravelotte–St. Privat. Bazaine's failure in an engagement he might have won doomed France to defeat.

The site of Gravelotte–St. Privat was arguably one of the strongest natural defensive positions in Europe. By occupying the ridge, the French would force the Germans to come to them, where they could use their artillery and superior breech-loading rifles to best advantage. The left flank was protected by the Mance ravine. The right flank, resting on the village of St. Privat, was weaker, and the French lacked the trenching tools to prepare it adequately.

Repeated German attacks were beaten back with heavy losses. Only heavy artillery, which caused most of the French casualties, prevented the German attacks from collapsing. Despite being outgunned and outnumbered, the French fought with considerable tenacity. Bazaine himself showed courage in riding from battalion to battalion encouraging his men. The Mance ravine was eventually carpeted with German dead.

After repeated German attacks, during which virtually every officer was killed, the Prussian Guards took St. Privat after desperate house-to-house fighting. But the position of the exhausted German troops was precarious. A major French counterattack that night might have shattered them, but Bazaine was too cautious. Instead, he chose to fall back to Metz, where he passively awaited relief that never came. In effect, his entire army was neutralized as a military force for the rest of the war, a real catastrophe for France. Bazaine tamely surrendered in October. **JS**

Losses: French, 8,000 dead or wounded, 4,400 missing or captured of 113,000; German, 20,000 dead or wounded, nearly 500 missing or captured of 188,000

◁ *Mars-la-Tour 1870*   *Sedan 1870* ▷

⬆ *Bodies litter the cemetery at St. Privat, in a dramatic depiction of the battle by Alphonse de Neuville from 1870.*

Sedan 1 September 1870

Having been defeated at Gravelotte–St. Privat during the Franco-Prussian War, the French only had Marshal Patrice de MacMahon's army in the field. Rather than withdrawing to defend Paris, MacMahon attempted to relieve Marshal Bazaine and his army at Metz, where they were besieged by the Germans. MacMahon's failure at Sedan brought down the Bonaparte dynasty.

Emperor Napoleon III was ill and suffering severe pain, but he could not retreat toward Paris because such an admission of failure would doom the Bonapartes. Despite being repeatedly outmaneuvered by the Germans, MacMahon—accompanied by Napoleon—decided to advance north toward the Belgian border, before swinging to relieve Metz. The Germans were fully aware of these intentions and moved to intercept them.

Harassed by German cavalry and jeered at by French peasants (who refused to feed the hungry troops), the army was dispirited even before two German armies

> *"General Wimpffen made a vain effort to rally his fleeing troops. He shouted, 'Vive la France! En avant!' but there was no reply."* French officer

caught up with them, 60 miles (96 km) from Metz. After sharp clashes at Nouart (29 August), Beaumont-sur-Meuse (30 August), and Bazeilles (31 August), MacMahon was forced to retire to the small fortress town of Sedan. Here the position was truly hopeless. The town could not feed the army for more than a few days; in fact, with its streets clogged with transport carts, artillery, and refugees, Sedan could not contain the army. Many men were trampled in the panic to get within the walls. The only option for the French was to break out of Sedan, but they were encircled and heavily outnumbered, and MacMahon had been wounded. Still, the escape attempt was made.

The only possible route was through the town of La Moncelle, which the French occupied. Unfortunately, the Germans anticipated this maneuver and moved their artillery up to seal off the route. As both sides poured reinforcements into an increasingly ferocious battle, it seemed that a French counteroffensive might prevail. However, the German artillery became increasingly effective, and the French position ever more untenable. In desperation, the French cavalry attacked three times, showing a courage that the German gunners admired even as they obliterated their attackers. Courage was not enough, and, despite their efforts, the way out was closed.

Within Sedan, there was mounting chaos as the French were hammered by more than 400 German guns mounted in a semicircle on the high ground around the town. Napoleon joined the battle line, seeking death in battle to avoid the approaching humiliation, but he was too ill to remain there. By late afternoon, all was lost. Napoleon was urged to place himself at the head of his troops for one final break-out attempt, but he recognized that further resistance would bring only pointless slaughter.

Early the next morning, he ordered a white flag raised, and—with cheeks rouged to disguise his illness—took a carriage to the Prussian king, William I, and surrendered. Disgusted by their disgrace, many French troops turned their backs to him. This was an ominous portent for the dynasty; when the news reached Paris, a popular uprising overthrew the Second Empire, and the Third Republic was born. However, this was not good news for the Germans because the new government was not willing to accept German terms and the war continued. **JS**

Losses: French, 3,000 dead, 14,000 wounded, 103,000 captured of 120,000; German, 2,320 dead, 5,980 wounded, 700 missing of 200,000

◁ Gravelotte–St. Privat 1870   Paris 1870 ▷

Napoleon's letter of surrender after the Battle of Sedan, written to William I, king of Prussia. ➜

Monsieur mon frère

N'ayant pas pu mourir
au milieu de mes troupes
il ne me reste qu'à remettre
mon épée entre les mains de
Votre Majesté

Je suis de Votre Majesté
le bon frère
Napoléon

Sedan le 1er Sept. 1870

Paris   19 September 1870–28 January 1871

"*The gates of the city are guarded. …
We expect another desperate sally
but this will probably be the last.*"

Letter from Helmuth von Moltke to his brother Fritz

↑ Detail from a photograph of soldiers in front of a barricade
at Place Vendome, March 1871, after the Siege of Paris.

**After the defeat at Sedan, the new Third Republic was
not ready to accept German peace terms. In order to
end the Franco-Prussian War, the Germans besieged
Paris. The length of the siege helped to salve French
pride, but also left bitter political divisions.**

The hastily assembled Parisian garrison was of
questionable quality but the city's walls and outlying
fortresses were formidable. Field Marshal Helmuth von
Moltke, commanding the German forces, had no intention
of wasting lives by storming the city. Instead, the Germans
settled down to starve Paris into submission.

The garrison made three sorties to try and break
the siege, but they achieved little. Within the city, as
food supplies dwindled, "siege cuisine" entered French
mythology. Nearly every animal in the zoo was consumed
in the course of the siege, and feline and canine butchers
appeared. However, the poorest citizens suffered most;
few deaths from starvation occurred but infant mortality
soared and working-class resentment simmered.

Losing patience, the Germans finally shelled the city,
firing 12,000 shells in three weeks, but they had yet to
bring up heavy siege guns and killed fewer than one
hundred Parisians, which had little impact on Parisian
morale. However, morale plummeted when the city stood
on the verge of starvation. No relief came, and many
Parisians—especially the working classes—were unaware
of the guerrilla warfare harrying German communications
or the suffering of newly raised French armies and felt
deserted by France. In the end, the city capitulated, regular
troops were taken prisoner, and the city suffered the
humiliation of a triumphal German march through its
streets. Such indignities would not be forgotten quickly. **JS**

Losses: French, 24,000 dead or wounded, 146,000
captured of 400,000, not including 47,000 civilians dead or
wounded; German, 12,000 dead or wounded of 240,000

◁ Sedan 1870   Paris Commune 1871 ▷

Paris Commune   18 March–28 May 1871

After the Franco-Prussian War, a mainly monarchist National Assembly was elected by France. The Siege of Paris left behind a radicalized working class, which seized power and attempted a social revolution, but the army extinguished this revolutionary spirit.

The Paris Commune, as the revolutionary government was known, comprised a mix of anarchists and socialists. Despite having the largest artillery park in France and the largest military force in the National Guard, the Commune was too divided to organize effective military efforts, and the Guard too poorly trained to carry them out. Instead, the Commune was passive and ignored the rest of France.

The rest of France, however, was not willing to ignore Paris—the city's revolutionary tradition had long been a source of antagonism to monarchical, rural France. The government proved willing to pay a higher price than the Germans during the earlier Siege of Paris, and was determined to take the city by storm. Grimly and methodically, they reduced the outlying fortresses, which the Communards were too inept to support effectively, before battering at the defenses of the city.

The end, when it came, was quick. A gate near Point du Jour was badly damaged and its defenders had pulled back to escape the bombardment. Government forces poured into the city, and the *semaine sanglante* (bloody week) began. There was no coherent defense; each district resisting the government built its own barricades and defended with varying degrees of skill. Many public buildings were burned, adding to the rage of government forces. Indeed, the vast majority of Communard deaths occurred in the mass execution of prisoners. Revolution was crushed indeed. **JS**

Losses: Communard, 20,000–30,000 dead, 40,000 captured, 7,000 exiled; Government, 750 dead

◁ *Paris 1870*

Amoaful   31 January 1874

The Ashanti Empire was a state in West Africa that had grown rich through conquest and trade with Europeans. Its warlike independence brought it into conflict with the British, and in 1874 the Ashanti suffered a major defeat at Amoaful.

In 1873, the British took over control of the Dutch Gold Coast, including an area of Ashanti territory. The Ashanti invaded and, in response, General Garnet Wolseley landed a force of 2,500 regulars and several thousand Indian and African troops.

On 31 January, the British attacked the village of Agamassie, but encountered fierce resistance from an Ashanti force that occupied high ground on the other side of a stream, armed with a consignment of rifles supplied by British manufacturers. As the 42nd Regiment advanced through bush, it came under fire and was pinned down on the ground for more than two hours. The British moved artillery closer and opened fire with field guns and rockets, forcing the Ashanti back. The 42nd then rose up, moved through the swamp, and crossed the stream under heavy fire, dispersing the Ashanti and moving into the village. Even though the village was taken and the Ashanti camp overrun, they still fought on for several hours taking massive casualties against the superior rifles of the British, resulting in the death of one of their leaders, Ammon Quatia. In comparison, the losses to the British force were relatively light.

After a further victory at Ordahsu, the British entered and sacked the Ashanti capital, Kumasi. The war was covered by the correspondent Sir Henry Stanley, and thanks to his reports, Wolseley achieved fame in Britain. The Ashanti kingdom survived for another twenty years. **TB**

Losses: British, 200 dead or wounded of 5,000; Ashanti, unknown of 15,000

Little Bighorn 25–26 June 1876

The treaty of 1868 established a Sioux Indian reservation in Dakota Territory and also designated part of Montana as an unceded preserve restricted for the Indians to roam and hunt. In 1874, a report of gold brought waves of illegal fortune hunters and immigrants into the Sioux preserve.

Unable to control illegal encroachment, the U.S. government ordered the removal of all Indians from the preserve to the reservations. Encouraged by the Sioux medicine man Sitting Bull, many Sioux and Cheyenne refused to leave. In spring 1876, a U.S. army campaign was launched. Columns of troops pushed from the west and east looking for the elusive Indian camps. In mid-June, scouts indicated that Sioux were in the vicinity of the Bighorn River.

On 21 June, Brigadier General Alfred H. Terry divided his force into two groups with different but converging paths. The groups were directed to meet on 26 June near the Little Bighorn River. Lieutenant Colonel George A. Custer led his group, composed of the 7th Cavalry Regiment,

> *"The more I study the moves here [on the Little Bighorn], the more I have admiration for Custer."*
>
> *Lieutenant General Nelson A. Miles*

south up the Rosebud River to cut off Indian movement in that direction before he headed to the Little Bighorn. On 24 June, Custer found a large Indian trail, and—in a controversial move—followed it west toward the Little Bighorn. Indications suggested an uncommonly large camp; it held some 1,800 warriors. He marched all night and planned to rest in concealment before attacking at dawn on 26 June. However, by midday on 25 June, Custer was convinced his regiment had been detected and he decided to attack.

He divided the regiment into three battalions. Custer commanded five companies (221 men); Major Marcus A. Reno took three companies (175 men); and Captain Frederick W. Benteen also had three (120 men). One company was assigned as pack train escort (136 men). Benteen was sent to scout farther to the south before rejoining Custer. Reno's battalion moved west across the Little Bighorn River into the valley, then turned north toward the mostly unseen Indian camp. Custer followed, but short of the river he turned north along its east bluffs. The pack train trailed at a much slower pace. As Reno's battalion formed a dismounted skirmish line, it was met head-on by hundreds of mounted warriors coming from the camp. They quickly overlapped the left of Reno's line, and he ordered a withdrawal into woods along the river. The outnumbered cavalrymen fought until Reno panicked and led a confused mounted retreat over the river and up the bluffs to a defensive position.

Custer continued along the bluffs, seeking a place to descend and attack the camp. With Reno pinned down, hundreds of Indians rode back and crossed the river to fight Custer. Surrounded by Indians, Custer's companies fought delaying actions over several ridges. Each company was overrun, until the last members of Custer's command gathered for a final stand before being killed. Benteen's battalion and the pack train soon reached Reno's position. Despite pleas from his officers, Reno resisted moving toward the sound of fighting where Custer was assumed to be. Finally, a late, futile effort was made, which had to turn back. Skirmishes and sniping then continued throughout 26 June. On 27 June, the Indians were gone. However, the U.S. Army began a relentless and eventually successful campaign to eradicate the remaining tribes. **RB**

Losses: U.S., 265 dead, 52 wounded; Sioux-Cheyenne, 30–100 dead

◁ Wagon Box Fight 1867   Wounded Knee 1890 ▷

Battle of Little Bighorn (c. 1900) by Amos Bad Heart Buffalo, an Indian scout for the U.S. Army. ➤

Plevna   19 July–10 December 1877

The heroic defense of Plevna as part of the Russo-Turkish War of 1877–78 earned the Turkish cause considerable international sympathy. Moved by this and by their own perceived interests, the great powers forced the Russians to moderate their peace terms.

Feeling that the Ottoman Empire's day in Europe was done, the Russians hoped to take Constantinople at last. However, as the Russian army marched south, Osman Paşa, a Turkish commander, recognized the strategic importance of the town of Plevna and led his troops on a forced march from his base at Vidin. They prepared the defenses as the Russians approached.

On three occasions, the Russians attempted to storm the town. However, their tightly packed ranks launched in poorly coordinated frontal assaults were mercilessly cut down by the defenders and beaten off with heavy casualties. The Russians therefore decided to encircle the town, cut off its supplies, and starve it into submission.

Realizing that the town must fall eventually, Osman wanted to withdraw, but in Constantinople Plevna's defense was seen as a matter of prestige, and he was ordered to remain and promised relief. It never arrived. By early December, it was clear that the garrison would starve within a few weeks. Osman attempted to break out in a surprise night attack. However, the plan failed and he was wounded. The next day, the garrison surrendered. Osman's heroic stand meant that Russia was forced to accept far more limited rewards than they had hoped for at the Congress of Berlin. **JS**

Losses: Russian, 40,000 dead or wounded of 150,000; Turkish, of the 40,000 garrison, all dead or captured

Catalca 1912 ▷

Surrender of the Satsuma Rebels *(1877) by Yoshitoshi depicts the rebels in surrender to the sharply dressed imperial army.*

Shiroyama 24 September 1877

The last and most serious revolt against the Meiji government of Japan ended in military defeat for the samurai rebels at Kagoshima. The crushing of the Satsuma Rebellion, as it was known, ended the dominance of the samurai class in Japanese society.

The Meiji Restoration of 1868 to 1869 restored power to the Japanese emperor after centuries of shogunate or feudal warlord power. Modernization of the country was opposed by several groups, notably the samurai warrior class, whose privileged status had been abolished.

Opposition was focused in the Satsuma domain. Led by Saigo Takamori, the rebels unsuccessfully besieged Kumamoto castle and then fought a desperate battle at Tabaruzaka before they were caught and almost wiped out at Mount Enodake. Only around 400 samurai escaped to Satsuma, where they seized Shiroyama Hill overlooking the capital, Kagoshima. Here they were surrounded by a large imperial army led by General Yamagata Aritomo. He ordered the construction of elaborate walls and ditches to prevent a samurai breakout and called in five warships to bombard samurai positions from the harbor. On 24 September, a massive bombardment softened up the samurai before the imperial forces stormed up the hill. Samurai swordsmanship prevailed initially until sheer weight of numbers pushed them back. By 6:00 AM, only forty samurai remained alive. After Saigo was shot, the remaining samurai drew their swords and charged the imperial lines, where they were mowed down by Gatling guns. The last stand of the samurai was over. **SA**

Losses: Imperial, unknown of 30,000; Samurai, 350 of 400

◁ *Hakodate Bay 1869*   *Yalu River 1894* ▷

Isandlwana   22 January 1879

The Battle of Isandlwana was one of the worst defeats ever suffered by the British army. When Lord Chelmsford—the general commanding British forces in South Africa—invaded the Zulu kingdom, a large body of Zulu warriors, under King Cetshwayo, all but wiped out a well-armed British column.

Lord Chelmsford completely underestimated the threat posed by the Zulu kingdom and divided his invasion force into three columns. The center column was tracked by Zulus as it moved through their territory and made its camp close to Isandlwana Hill. On 22 January, the camp's commanding officer, Colonel Pulleine, sent messengers to Chelmsford when he learned that the Zulus were close by. However, it was all too late.

A scouting party had stumbled upon the Zulus and were retreating in disarray back to the camp when they suddenly came under attack from several thousand Zulu warriors. The Zulus swept down the slopes and overran British rocket and field gun positions before they could even be fired. The British fought desperately to defend the camp, but the sheer numbers of Zulus meant that, even with superior firepower, the British were soon outflanked and surrounded. With their camp encircled, the British force fired at wave after wave of Zulu attacks until their ammunition ran out and they were overwhelmed. As many soldiers fled, they were hunted down and killed, and only those with mounts managed to escape.

As a sudden total eclipse of the sun plunged the whole area into eerie darkness, the remaining survivors of the British camp stumbled for cover in the bush and were slaughtered. Complacency had led to the unthinkable; when the telegraph broke the news at home, Victorian Britain was shocked. **TB**

Losses: British, 1,300 dead of 1,500; Zulu, 2,000 casualties of 15,000

☑ *Blood River 1838*   *Rorke's Drift 1879* ☑

The isolated hill of Isandlwana, from a series of photographs by George Froom of the 94th Regiment. ⬆

Rorke's Drift 23 January 1879

At the Battle of Rorke's Drift, a small garrison of British troops successfully defended a mission station against the attack of 4,000 Zulu warriors. The battle resulted in the award of eleven Victoria Cross medals for valor, the largest number to be awarded in a single encounter.

After wiping out a British column at Isandlwana, 4,000 Zulu warriors attacked the missionary station at Rorke's Drift. In their way stood a mere 139 soldiers of the 1st Battalion, 24th Warwickshire Foot Regiment—commanded by Colonel John Chard and Major Gonville Bromhead—and of these, only one hundred were fit for duty. As wave after wave of Assegai spear-brandishing Zulus stormed the station, the British repelled the attacks, and Zulu bodies piled up at the mission's walls, which were too high to climb. At one point, the Zulus crawled along the bottom of the walls and climbed over their own dead, grabbing the British bayonets and trying to pull

rifles out of the hands of the defenders. At 6:00 PM, Chard ordered a withdrawal and evacuated the hospital as the Zulus swarmed over it, poking their weapons through the walls and roof.

All through the night, the attacks persisted. Almost all of those who were not killed suffered wounds of some kind as the defenders fell back to make a last stand at the hastily prepared bastion surrounding the storehouse. However, at dawn, the exhausted and starving Zulus left, thinking that a British relief force was on its way. The stand at Rorke's Drift restored British imperial self-confidence after the crushing blow at Isandlwana, and its reputation as a fine example of the "heroic last stand" was popularized in 1964 in the film *Zulu*, narrated by Richard Burton. **TB**

Losses: British, 17 dead, 14 wounded of 139; Zulu, 350 dead, more than 500 wounded of 4,000

[<] *Isandlwana 1879*   *Ulundi 1879* [>]

⬆ *Survivors from the company of the 24th Regiment at Rorke's Drift.*

Ulundi   4 July 1879

The Battle of Ulundi was the final decisive battle of the Anglo-Zulu War. The British force was commanded by Lord Chelmsford, and the Zulu forces were under the command of King Cetshwayo. The battle ended in defeat for the Zulus and the destruction of their royal kraal at Ulundi.

The disastrous battle at Isandlwana forced Lord Chelmsford to adopt a more cautious approach in his second invasion. As he advanced, Chelmsford kept his much larger force together and protected his flanks and rear with cavalry. Chelmsford planned to defeat the Zulus in their heartland by deploying the formation known as the "hollow square." This was a rectangle with the sides formed from lines of light infantry and with cavalry sheltered inside; the firepower of the infantry was bolstered by Gatling guns and seven- and nine-pound field guns.

The British approached the royal kraal at Ulundi and formed the hollow square as the Zulus moved to attack. The Zulu army encircled the British formation and then charged all sides. Each side of the rectangle fired volley after volley, backed up by the merciless firepower of the field and Gatling guns. The Zulus launched waves of attacks; however, after hours of battle, not a single attack had managed to breach the British lines. As the exhausted Zulus fell back, each of the sides of the rectangle formed gaps and the cavalry stormed out, scattering the Zulus to complete the rout.

Chelmsford ordered the royal kraal to be destroyed, but Cetshwayo escaped and was exiled in London. He was restored as Zulu king in 1884 after a campaign by the British press, but the Zulu kingdom was now subordinate to British rule. **TB**

Losses: British, fewer than 100 casualties of 5,300; Zulu, 1,500 casualties of 12,000

◁ Rorke's Drift 1879   Majuba Hill 1881 ▷

Angamos   8 October 1879

In 1879, the War of the Pacific broke out between Chile, Bolivia, and its ally Peru over control of the Atacama desert, which contained valuable nitrate deposits. As there were few roads and rail lines in the desert, most of the initial fighting was at sea between the Chilean and Peruvian navies.

The Chilean plan was to achieve naval supremacy before landing troops in the disputed territory. However, the Peruvian ironclad *Huascar* was at sea, attacking Chilean ports and presenting a considerable threat to the Chilean navy. Accordingly, a Chilean fleet set sail on 20 September with the intention of sinking or capturing the ironclad.

Huascar was located off Punta de Angamos in what was then Bolivia. On 8 October, at 9:25 AM, *Huascar* opened fire on the Chilean ironclad *Almirante Cochrane*, which continued to steam toward *Huascar* until its guns were within range. One shot pierced *Huascar*'s artillery turret while another hit the hull and cut the rudder chain, leaving the ship unable to steer. A few minutes later, a further shot killed Admiral Grau and shattered the rudder wheel. At 10:10 AM, *Huascar* lowered its flag, but rather than surrender, the crew used the opportunity to repair the rudder. That done, the flag was hoisted again, and combat resumed. Two Chilean ships closed in, their shots killing almost the whole of *Huascar*'s crew in the artillery tower.

With many of the crew now dead, the new commander, Lieutenant Pedro Garezon, decided to sink the ship. As the water flooded in, Chilean sailors managed to get on board and close the sea valves. The capture of *Huascar* gave Chile control of the seas, enabling the war to start on land. **SA**

Losses: Chilean, no ships of 2 ironclads, 3 corvettes, and 1 transport; Peruvian, 1 ironclad captured

Tacna 1880 ▷

 The charge of 17th Lancers at Ulundi, 4 July 1879; detail from an 1880 painting by F. Fayel.

Tacna 26 May 1880

The War of the Pacific between Chile and a Peruvian-Bolivian alliance over the nitrate-rich Atacama desert reached its climax in 1880. The five-hour battle resulted in a decisive victory for Chile, knocking Bolivia out of the war and leaving Peru to fight on alone.

After its naval victory over Peru at Angamos in 1879, Chile had control of the seas and could launch an invasion of the disputed territory. By mid-1880, the Chileans had conquered the Bolivian-held parts of the territory and were now attacking the Peruvian-held districts of Arica and Tacna in the far north.

The two sides met on the sandy Intiorko plateau a few miles north of the town of Tacna, the allies drawn up in a long defensive line facing five Chilean divisions. An initial exchange of artillery fire petered out as the shells buried themselves in the sand without detonating. The Chileans then advanced toward the allied line but failed to break through. Artillery fire against the left of the allied line proved effective until two allied elite units—the Colorado and Aroma battalions—forced the Chileans back. With the battle evenly balanced, the Chileans managed to catch the two units in deadly crossfire. Seizing the initiative, the Chilean infantry rushed the allied line with bayonets drawn and managed to break through, splitting the line in two. The allied right wing was outflanked and soon the entire line collapsed, the allies fleeing the battlefield.

The battle was decisive. The Bolivian army withdrew and took no further part in hostilities. Chile scored another victory over the Peruvian army the following month at Arica and occupied the Peruvian capital, Lima, but Peru refused to accept defeat. **SA**

Losses: Chilean, 2,200 casualties of 14,000; Peruvian-Bolivian, 3,500–5,000 of up to 12,000

◁ Angamos 1879　　　　　　　　　　Huamachuco 1883 ▷

Maiwand 27 July 1880

In 1878, British forces from India invaded Afghanistan to counter the expansion of Russian influence. As in their previous campaign in the 1840s, the British found fighting Afghan warriors on their own terrain a formidable task. The costly defeat at Maiwand was a shock to Victorian Britain.

By 1880, Britain was in control of large parts of Afghanistan, with an army under Major General Sir Frederick Roberts installed in Kabul. However, Ayub Khan—a disappointed claimant to the Afghan throne—raised the flag of revolt in Herat. In early July, Brigadier General George Burrows marched his brigade—chiefly Indian troops with some British contingents—out of Kandahar to intercept Ayub Khan's army that was marching toward the city of Ghazni. Burrows was deserted by local allies from Kandahar, many of whom rode off to join Ayub Khan, but nonetheless his troops advanced confidently to attack what turned out to be a much superior force.

Ayub Khan had not only greater strength in numbers, but also better artillery. Burrows faced him on a hot, dusty plain, a poorly chosen position that suited the Afghan cavalry. As the British and Indian troops came under attack from three sides, discipline broke down. Amid the chaos, the regiments that stood their ground—notably the 66th Regiment of Foot and the Bombay Grenadiers—suffered more than 60 percent casualties. The Afghans took no prisoners, finishing off the wounded where they lay. The battered remnants of Burrows's brigade retreated to Kandahar, many stragglers cut down by Afghan cavalry along the road. The military disaster provoked an outpouring of sentimental patriotism in Britain. Bobbie, a regimental dog that survived the battle, was awarded a campaign medal by Queen Victoria. **TB**

Losses: British, 969 dead, 177 wounded of 2,500; Afghan, 3,000 casualties of 12,000

◁ Retreat from Kabul 1842　　　　　　　Kandahar 1880 ▷

Kandahar 1 September 1880

After their defeat by Afghan forces at Maiwand, British troops were besieged in Kandahar. Major General Sir Frederick Roberts, commanding British forces in Kabul, had the task of relieving the siege and restoring the prestige of the British Empire. His success made him a national hero.

While the British garrison at Kandahar bolstered the city's defenses and held out against the army of Ayub Khan, Roberts left Kabul to begin his famous march to Kandahar on 8 August. His army marched in the full summer heat over difficult terrain with full battle kit. At one time, more than 500 troops were falling ill each day, and even Roberts was not immune, needing to be dragged on a litter for the final few days of the march.

By the time Roberts reached Kandahar on 31 August, he had force marched his army of 11,000 some 300 miles (483 km) in three weeks, in some of the most harsh conditions imaginable. There was no respite for the troops because the battle began the next morning, with an artillery bombardment of Khan's positions. This was followed by the 92nd Highlanders and 2nd Gurkhas fighting their way northward village by village and a second similar operation to the south by the 72nd Highlanders and the 2nd Sikh. By midday, both forces converged on the Afghan camp, with the 3rd Brigade moving forward to support the attack.

The exhausted British expected an intense fight, but as they moved into the camp, they found that the Afghans had disappeared into the hills of Herat leaving behind their artillery and most of their supplies. Afghanistan came firmly under British influence. Roberts returned home to receive the thanks of Parliament and numerous honors and decorations. **TB**

Losses: British, 250 casualties of 11,000; Afghan, 1,500 casualties of 13,000

◁ *Maiwand 1880*

Majuba Hill 27 February 1881

Imperial expansion in southern Africa brought the British into conflict with the Boers of the Transvaal. The Battle of Majuba Hill was a crushing Boer victory over a force led by Major General George Colley. Although a small-scale encounter, it persuaded the British to make peace and accept Boer self-rule.

The Boers had no regular army but drew their force from the ranks of farmers, who formed "commandos" when required to fight. They were highly skilled in hunting and firing accurately on horseback or dismounted. They had no uniform, wearing khaki or neutral-colored clothing that camouflaged them on the Transvaal plains. By contrast, the British infantry wore bright uniforms and white pith helmets, which stood out for the Boer marksmen. The British soldiers were not trained as sharpshooters and relied on the firepower of coordinated volleys to take down their enemy. These factors were crucial at Majuba Hill.

Overnight, Colley had led a force to the top of the hill so that he could overlook Boer positions. He had no artillery and did not order his men to dig field fortifications because he was confident that the Boer irregulars would not attempt an assault against his disciplined professional soldiers. However, at dawn, the Boers attacked, making maximum use of any cover that was available as small groups dashed forward while their colleagues delivered accurate covering fire. Around midday, they captured a knoll that overlooked the British positions and from there began to pick off their enemy with accurate shots. Colley was among those killed as the British broke and fled down the reverse slope. Victory gave the Boers great confidence in their military skills, which was reflected in their aggressive stance at the start of the Second Boer War eighteen years later. **TB**

Losses: British, 92 dead, 134 wounded of 400; Boer, 1 dead, 5 wounded of 450

◁ *Ulundi 1879*   *Colenso 1899* ▷

Tel el-Kebir 13 September 1882

The Battle of Tel el-Kebir was a decisive encounter between an army of the British Empire, commanded by Lieutenant General Garnet Wolseley, and the Egyptian nationalist army, led by Colonel Ahmed Urabi. The British victory and the surrender of Urabi led to Egypt becoming a British protectorate.

The war in Egypt began when nationalists loyal to Ahmed Urabi rebelled against the khedive Muhammad Tawfiq Pasha. The British and French governments could not allow Egypt to become unstable because of their interests in the Suez Canal. A British fleet of fifteen ironclads bombarded Alexandria on 11 July 1882, when riots threatened Europeans living in the city. After an advance on Cairo from Alexandria failed, Wolseley shifted his troops by sea to the Suez Canal. Urabi hastily dug in to defend Tel el-Kebir, between Cairo and the British army.

Wolseley advanced under cover of darkness with two divisions of infantry, the Highlanders and Guards, supported by a brigade of cavalry and a contingent of Indian troops. At dawn, the Egyptians found Wolseley's troops within a few hundred yards of their lines. Defying the volleys fired by the Egyptian infantry, the British force fixed bayonets and charged at the poorly prepared entrenchments. They overwhelmed the Egyptian lines in less than an hour; the British cavalry then pursued the enemy as they retreated in chaos.

Urabi and his senior officers surrendered to the chasing cavalry, and Wolseley advanced into an undefended Cairo on 14 September to restore Tawfiq to power. In return, Tawfiq was forced to make concessions that placed Egypt under British military occupation and gave Britain effective control of the Egyptian administration. Urabi was later exiled to Sri Lanka. **TB**

Losses: British, 57 dead, 402 wounded of 18,500; Egyptian, 1,396 dead, 681 wounded of 15,000

El Obeid 1883 [>]

Huamachuco 10 July 1883

The engagement between Chilean and Peruvian forces at Huamachuco in the high Andes was the last battle of the War of the Pacific. A victory for Chile forced Peru and its former ally Bolivia to accept peace terms that involved the loss of valuable territory and left a legacy of bitterness.

After the Chilean victory at Tacna drove Bolivia out of the War of the Pacific, Peru was occupied by Chilean forces. Remnants of the Peruvian army led by General Andres Avelino Caceres sustained a guerrilla campaign in the Andes. By 1883, peace negotiations were under way, but the success of Caceres's guerrillas was weakening Chile's position.

Admiral Patricio Lynch, Chile's commander in Peru, decided to mount a major military effort to crush Caceres. Chilean columns marched into the Andes in search of the elusive guerrillas. In early July, Caceres discovered an isolated column in the town of Huamachuco. As the guerrillas took up positions around the town, the column's commander, Colonel Alejandro Gorostiaga, marched his men out to a defensible hilltop, where Inca ruins provided ready-made fortifications. After initial artillery exchanges, on 10 July the Peruvian guerrillas assaulted the hill. Ferocious fighting ensued. After four hours, the Peruvians had battled their way to the crest, but their troops were desperately short of ammunition. Artillery support for the attack was lost when a Chilean cavalry charge overran the Peruvian guns. The Chilean infantry then launched a counterattack, sweeping down the slopes. Out of bullets, the Peruvians swung their guns as clubs to beat off the Chilean soldiers, but the contest was soon ended. Caceres escaped capture but the guerrilla resistance collapsed. Peru lost two provinces to Chile, and Bolivia lost its access to the sea. **RG**

Losses: Chilean, 68 dead, 96 wounded of 1,500; Peruvian, 800 casualties and captured of 1,700

[<] Tacna 1880

A lithograph depicting the British at the Battle of Tel el-Kebir.

El Obeid   3–5 November 1883

In 1883, Sudan was being governed by the Egyptians from Khartoum. The self-proclaimed Mahdi, Muhammad Ahmad, built up an army to fight for Sudanese independence. The destruction of a British-led Egyptian force at El Obeid demonstrated the growing strength of the Mahdist movement.

Increasingly in control of Egypt's affairs after the 1882 Battle of Tel el-Kebir, Britain wanted nothing to do with a war in Sudan. However, the British allowed the Egyptian governor in Khartoum to raise a force to march against the Mahdists. A large proportion of the soldiers that the governor recruited were from the army who had been defeated by the British at Tel el-Kebir; they were released from imprisonment to serve in Sudan.

European officers were brought in to lead the force, with a retired British colonel, William Hicks, in overall command. Winston Churchill later described Hicks's force as "possibly the worst army that has ever marched

to war." Its morale was certainly low compared with the religious fervor that drove the followers of the Islamic fundamentalist Mahdi. Ordered by his Egyptian bosses to take the offensive, Hicks reluctantly led his army out of Khartoum to search for the Mahdi, reportedly engaged in a siege of El Obeid.

Either through treachery or by accident, the army's scouts led the force into a trap. Hicks was surrounded and outnumbered by at least four to one. Many of the Egyptian troops deserted, making the situation even worse for those left to fight. The force formed squares and repelled the attacks of the Mahdi's fighters for two days, before being overwhelmed. The officers were executed, Hicks among them. Fewer than 500 soldiers escaped the massacre, which brought recruits flocking to the Mahdi's army. **TB**

Losses: Egyptian, 7,000 dead, 2,000 wounded of 11,000; Mahdist, unknown of 45,000

◁ *Tel el-Kebir 1882*   *Khartoum 1884* ▷

Foochow (Fuzhou)   23 August 1884

The French destruction of the Chinese fleet at Foochow was an example of European imperialism at its most cynical. The naval attack precipitated a nine-month Sino-French War that ended with France adding Tonkin, the northernmost part of Vietnam, to its Indochina empire.

China and France had been at odds over Tonkin since 1883, the Chinese aiding local Vietnamese resistance to a French takeover. The two countries remained officially at peace, however, and a French squadron commanded by Vice Admiral Amédée Courbet was able to anchor unopposed in the Min River, on which Foochow stands.

French warships were intermingled with the Chinese Fujien fleet. China had been making efforts to modernize its navy, but its technology deficit was still acute. The Fujien fleet consisted of a few unarmored wooden-hulled steamships, antiquated sailing junks, and two "flatiron" gunboats—metal rafts each mounting a large gun.

Courbet's force included four cruisers with a total of forty guns and two steam launches equipped with spar torpedoes—mines hung on poles in front of the launch.

The French discreetly positioned their ships to fight a battle for which the Chinese were woefully unprepared. Courbet opened fire just before 2:00 PM on 23 August. Every Chinese ship was swiftly sunk or disabled, including the flatiron gunboats. The Chinese flagship, *Yang Wu,* was sunk by a spar torpedo exploded against its hull.

The French gunners turned their attention to shore targets, devastating the docks and the arsenal. The action was over within an hour. Thirsty for imperial glory, the French public went wild with delight, although the subsequent land fighting for Tonkin proved tougher than expected and somewhat dampened this enthusiasm. **RG**

Losses: Chinese, 9 of 11 ships sunk, 1,000 casualties; French, no ships of 13, 60 casualties

Yalu River 1894 ▷

French warships launch a ruthless attack on the Chinese fleet in the harbor of Foochow.

Khartoum   13 March 1884–26 January 1885

The death of General Charles George Gordon at Khartoum in Sudan is one of the most famous dramas of the British imperial era. Gordon resisted a lengthy siege of the city by the Muslim forces of the Mahdi, led by Muhammad Ahmad, but a relief column was too slow to arrive.

In the wake of the Egyptian defeat at El Obeid in 1883, it seemed only a matter of time before Sudan was overrun by Mahdist forces. The British government, in effective control of Egypt and unwilling to fight the Mahdists, told the Egyptians they must withdraw from Sudan. General Gordon, a British officer of high Christian principles renowned for his exploits fighting in China in the 1860s, had previously acted as governor-general of Sudan from 1877 to 1879. He seemed the ideal choice to supervise the evacuation of Egyptians from Khartoum. Reappointed governor-general, he arrived in Khartoum in March 1884 and was greeted with enthusiasm by the population. However, Gordon believed that the Mahdi should

"I fear the future of all engagements. It is not the fear of death . . . but I fear defeat and its consequences."

From the journal of Charles George Gordon

be resisted and was in no hurry to evacuate the city. Soon all routes leading from Khartoum to Egypt came under Mahdist control. The city was cut off, and Gordon prepared the garrison and people for a long siege.

Despite his predicament, Gordon felt confident that Khartoum could hold out long enough for a British relief force to arrive. The city was protected on two sides by the Nile and to the south by fortifications overlooking desert. Gordon had enough food to last six months, a massive store of ammunition, and a garrison of 7,000. However,

William Gladstone's British government had sent Gordon to evacuate Khartoum not to fight the Mahdi, and was reluctant therefore to send a relief force. Only after a long period of press and public outrage was a relief mission authorized. Commanded by General Wolseley, it did not set out from Cairo for Khartoum until November, eight months into the siege, by which time food supplies in the city were running low.

In January 1885, the relief expedition entered Sudan. There, Wolseley divided his forces into two columns; one descended the Nile by steamer, while the other attempted a faster route across the desert on horses and camels. The desert column survived an attack by Mahdist forces at Abu Klea on 15 January, but already it was too late. Alerted to the approach of the relief force, the Mahdi decided to storm Khartoum. This decision coincided with the winter season, when the level of the Nile dropped, exposing the east and west sides of the city that the river had protected previously. The Mahdists waded across the muddy river and rushed into the city, slaughtering the exhausted and starving garrison.

The manner of Gordon's death is disputed. One account has him dying on the steps of his headquarters with a gun in his hand, and in full ceremonial uniform. However, another account tells of him being recognized in the street and hacked down as he tried to escape to the Austrian consulate with his staff. Either way, his head was put on a pike and paraded through the streets.

Two days later, the relief force arrived within sight of the city, too late to stop the slaughter of thousands of Egyptians. Khartoum and most of Sudan were left in Mahdist hands. When news broke in Britain of Gordon's death, there was a public outcry against the government. It was to take thirteen years for the British to gain revenge. **TB**

Losses: Egyptian, all 7,000 soldiers dead, plus 4,000 civilians; Mahdist, unknown of 50,000

◁ El Obeid 1883   Omdurman 1898 ▷

General Charles Gordon, depicted amid some of his officers, is commemorated after his death at Khartoum. ➔

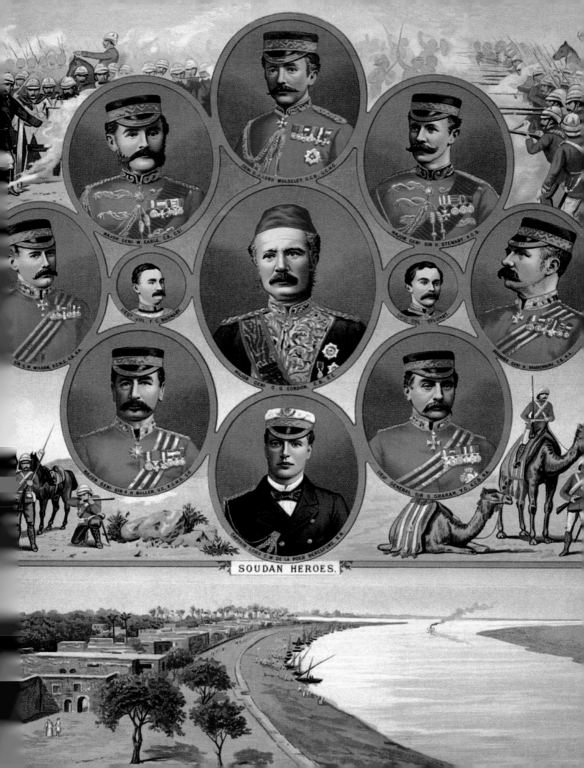

SOUDAN HEROES.

Batoche 9–12 May 1885

The westward expansion of Canada in the nineteenth century was resisted by the Métis, people originally of mixed American Indian and European descent who had formed a distinctive culture in the region. Their resistance, led by the visionary Louis Riel, was crushed at the Battle of Batoche.

The confederation of the British colonies in North America to form the Dominion of Canada in 1867 and the subsequent extension of the Canadian government's rule over the immense expanses of the Northwest Territories led to conflict with the Métis. The brief Red River Rebellion of 1869, which resulted in the founding of the province of Manitoba, brought Louis Riel to prominence.

Forced into exile in the United States for his actions during the rebellion, Riel was called back to lead the movement of discontented Métis in Saskatchewan in 1885. He declared a provisional government in Batoche and awaited the Canadian government response. It was far swifter and more decisive than he had expected. Using the completed sections of the Canadian Pacific Railway, Major General Frederick Middleton quickly moved a force of regulars and militia to the remote region within weeks. Despite suffering losses in an ambush at Fish Creek, Middleton advanced on Batoche accompanied by a transport steamer on the South Saskatchewan River.

Fighting began on 9 May. The transport ship was crippled by a ferry cable lowered across its path, but Middleton's artillery brought the Métis under bombardment. Acting with due caution, the Canadian commander waited until the defenders were low on ammunition, and had been weakened by bombardment and skirmishes, before launching a decisive assault on 12 May that overran the town. Riel was captured and hanged. **RG**

Losses: Canadian, 8 dead, 22 wounded of 916; Métis, 51 casualties of 250

◁ *Saint-Eustache 1837*

Following the Battle of Batoche, the Dominion force burned the homes of the defeated Métis. ⬆

Wounded Knee 29 December 1890

By 1890, the Plains Indians had lost the struggle to defend their territory and way of life against the expansionist United States. Half-starving and desperate, they embraced the Ghost Dance, a religious revival offering a vision of their old world restored, before the arrival of the white man.

Nervous U.S. authorities, seeing in the Ghost Dance a possible cover for an Indian uprising, decided to crack down on the movement. On 15 December 1890, an attempt was made to arrest the famous Lakota Sioux chief Sitting Bull, which resulted in the chief being killed. Seeking safety, a band of Lakota Sioux led by Chief Spotted Elk—known to U.S. soldiers as Big Foot—headed for Pine Ridge reservation.

On 28 December, they encountered a detachment of U.S. 7th Cavalry under Major Samuel Whitside. The cavalry escorted the Lakota to Wounded Knee Creek, where they camped. The rest of the cavalry regiment then arrived under Colonel James Forsyth. They encircled the Indian camp, placing four rapid-fire Hotchkiss guns at points around the perimeter.

The following morning, Forsyth ordered the Lakota to be disarmed. There was a scuffle, and a shot was fired, after which pandemonium broke loose. U.S. soldiers started shooting, and some of the Lakota seized their rifles to hit back in a close-range firefight. Panicking soldiers fired the Hotchkiss guns into the encampment, killing friend and foe alike. The fighting ended after less than an hour with almost half the Lakota dead, including more than sixty women and children. The day after Wounded Knee, there was another firefight between Lakota Ghost Dancers and the 7th Cavalry at Drexel Mission, but the Ghost Dance movement was effectively ended. **RG**

Losses: Lakota, 151 dead, 50 wounded of 350; U.S., 31 dead, 33 wounded of 500

◁ Little Bighorn 1876

⬆ Lieutenant Casey's scouts return from Wounded Knee, where Casey was killed by Plenty Horses.

Cana 2–6 November 1892

Extending its colonial rule in West Africa, France entered into conflict with the kingdom of Dahomey, a well-organized state, used to war and capable of procuring modern weapons. Its army included tough all-female regiments, properly called "Mino," but referred to by the French as "Amazons."

Established on the West African coast at Porto Novo, the French fought a brief war with Dahomey's King Behanzin in 1890. After this indecisive conflict, Dahomey hastened to import Mauser rifles and Krupp guns from Germany, correctly anticipating renewed conflict.

In 1892, the French landed an army at Porto Novo, comprising mostly Senegalese troops and Foreign Legionnaires. It marched toward the Dahomey capital, Abomey, under the command of General Alfred Amédée Dodds. King Behanzin's army made repeated attempts to stop the French, but by November had been driven back to Cana, a sacred city where the "royal road" to Abomey began. Desperate to defend Cana, the Dahomey warriors, both male and female, made fierce assaults on the French camp but were repulsed with heavy losses.

On 6 November, the French launched their own assault on Cana, their artillery blowing breaches in the town's thick walls. The Legionnaires and Senegalese charged with bayonets fixed, forcing a passage into the town. Vicious close-quarters combat continued, and the Dahomey warriors countered bayonets with machetes and short swords. The fighting did not end until after nightfall, the French taking possession of the town at the cost of 200 casualties. Dodds expected another fierce fight for Abomey, but King Behanzin abandoned and torched his capital before the French columns arrived. The war was in effect at an end, and Dahomey became a French colony. **RG**

Losses: French, 200 casualties of 2,000; Dahomey, unknown of 1,500

Yalu River 17 September 1894

In the second half of the nineteenth century, Japan and China put major resources into creating modern navies of armored steamships with guns firing explosive shells. Their battle at the Yalu River in 1894 revealed that the imperial Japanese navy had become a formidable fighting force.

China and Japan went to war over Korea. The Korean Joseon dynasty traditionally accepted the overlordship of Qing dynasty China. By the 1890s, however, Japan was seeking to bring Korea under its own domination.

In 1894, both China and Japan sent troops into Korea. The Koreans had the better of the land fighting, which moved up to the China–Korea border at the Yalu River. On 17 September, a Japanese naval force—under Admiral Sukeyuki Ito—attempted to intercept Chinese troopships heading into the river mouth. The Chinese northern fleet, commanded by Admiral Ting Juchang, was defending the troop landings. The rival warships, of roughly equal strength on paper, steamed into battle. It was one of the first naval engagements between such modern ships.

Combatants were stunned by the sheer violence of the gunfire as explosive shells rained down. The Japanese gunners had superior training, their munitions were of better quality, and their ships were handled with confidence and aggression. The Chinese had failed to grasp the need for antifire precautions, and the flammable paint on their ships ignited too easily. The Japanese flagship, *Matsushima*, was badly damaged when an onboard ammunition store exploded, but by nightfall the Chinese had lost five ships. Short of ammunition and shocked by the experience of modern naval warfare, the Japanese allowed Admiral Ting to escape with his surviving vessels to the fortified harbor of Weihaiwei. **RG**

Losses: Chinese, 5 ships of 14, 1,350 casualties; Japanese, no ships of 12, 300 casualties

◁ *Foochow 1884*   *Weihaiwei 1895* ▷

Detail from a woodblock print by Kobayashi Kiyochika, from October 1894, depicting the fighting at Yalu River.

Weihaiwei   30 January–12 February 1895

The fall of the fortified Chinese port of Weihaiwei to Japan was the climax of the Sino-Japanese War of 1894 to 1895. The defeat of China established imperial Japan as the dominant East Asian power and at the same time advanced Japanese ambitions to win control of Korea.

After its defeat at the Yalu River, the Chinese northern fleet took refuge at Weihaiwei on the Shandong peninsula. There it was protected from Japanese naval attack by mines and steel hawsers blocking the harbor entrance, as well as by the guns of a series of forts around the city. The Chinese warships made no attempt to stop the Japanese landing troops that marched to attack the forts.

The weather was bitterly cold. Military operations were disrupted by blizzards, and soldiers and sailors suffered severe hardship in the freezing conditions. Nonetheless, by 1 February, the Japanese army had taken possession of some of the forts, leaving the Chinese navy trapped between the shore batteries and the blockading Japanese warships, commanded by Admiral Sukeyuki Ito. Clearing paths through the Chinese mines and cutting the steel hawsers, the Japanese navy succeeded in getting small, fast torpedo boats into the harbor under cover of darkness. These night raids sank three of the largest Chinese warships. In despair, Chinese Admiral Ting Juchang sent his thirteen torpedo boats on a mass daylight sortie that resulted in all being sunk or captured.

On 13 February, his position hopeless, Admiral Ting formally surrendered Weihaiwei and the remnants of his fleet, before taking his own life. A peace treaty ended the war two months later. China renounced all interest in Korea, ceded territory to Japan—including the island of Taiwan—and paid a large cash indemnity. **RG**

Losses: Chinese, 1 battleship, 2 cruisers, 13 torpedo boats, 4,000 dead; Japanese, no ships, 235 casualties

⟨ *Yalu River 1894*   *Beijing 1900* ⟩

Detail from a nineteenth-century color woodblock print titled Great Sea Battle at Weihaiwei.

Adowa   1 March 1896

Ethiopia was the only African country to maintain full independence against the wave of European imperial expansion in the late nineteenth and early twentieth centuries. It owed this proud achievement to the victory of an army led by Emperor Menelik II over the Italians at the Battle of Adowa.

Ironically, Menelik partly owed his rise to the Ethiopian throne in 1889 to the support of Italy, which he rewarded by accepting Italian control of Eritrea. He did not, however, accept that Ethiopia should become an Italian protectorate. In 1895, responding to cross-border raids by Italian colonial troops from Eritrea, Menelik led a vast army north to the Tigray region. The Italian commander, General Oreste Baratieri, found himself heavily outnumbered. After an Italian detachment was annihilated at Amba Alagi in December, Baratieri withdrew to a formidable defensive position at Adowa. Menelik faced a dilemma. He did not believe he could

succeed in an offensive against troops with modern weapons in prepared defenses. Yet his army, a medley of forces provided by regional rulers, would soon begin to disintegrate if kept inactive with dwindling supplies.

By the end of February 1896, Menelik was close to abandoning the campaign when the Italians took the offensive. Baratieri's battle plan involved his forces advancing at night to positions from which they would launch an assault at dawn. However, while crossing the unmapped terrain in darkness, the Italians became totally disorganized. The following morning, their forces were split into isolated brigades, surrounded by swarms of Ethiopian warriors with swords, rifles, and spears, and utterly routed. This humiliating defeat ended Italian ambitions to rule Ethiopia until Benito Mussolini's empire-building invasion in the 1930s. **RG**

Losses: Italian, 6,000 dead, 1,500 wounded, 3,000 captured of 17,700; Ethiopian, 12,000 of 100,000

⬆ *A soldier on horseback during the First Italian-Ethiopian War, painted by an anonymous Ethiopian artist.*

Zanzibar 27 August 1896

The war between the British Empire and the East African island state of Zanzibar in 1896 was undoubtedly the shortest in history, lasting only forty minutes. The supporters of Zanzibar's newly installed, anti-British Sultan Khalid bin Barghash were defeated and forced to pay the cost of the war.

When the pro-British Sultan Hamad bin Thuwaini died on 25 August, the British wanted to see Hamud bin Muhammed succeed him. However, Khalid bin Barghash, who was not considered friendly toward Britain, seized power, positioning troops and artillery around the palace and harem. The British were reluctant to attack, and sent a stream of messages and ultimatums to Khalid to stand down and negotiate. Khalid was determined and replied by saying that he did not believe that the British would attack his palace.

Britain rushed a fleet of warships to the scene. When Rear Admiral Harry Rawson arrived on board the cruiser *St. George,* the Royal Navy had five ships off Zanzibar, and Royal Marines and sailors were put ashore to join the pro-British Zanzibari troops. After Khalid refused to stand down on the morning of 27 August, Rawson raised a signal on his flagship, warning Khalid to expect imminent action. Five minutes later, the bombardment of the mostly wooden palace began. Khalid's position was hopeless, although he did deploy *Glasgow*, an armed yacht presented to the previous sultan as a gift from Queen Victoria. *Glasgow* bravely engaged the vastly superior *St. George,* but was soon sunk and her crew rescued. After forty minutes, the shortest and most one-sided war in history was over, and by the afternoon Britain's preferred choice, Hamud bin Muhammed, was proclaimed sultan. **TB**

Losses: British, 1 casualty of 1,000; Zanzibari, 500 casualties of 3,000

Manila Bay 1 May 1898

After an explosion sank USS *Maine* in Havana harbor in February 1898, the United States declared war with Spain on 25 April in support of a Cuban rebellion against Spanish colonial rule. A U.S. "New Navy" attack on the Spanish fleet in the Philippines proved gratifyingly one-sided.

In April 1898, the U.S. Asiatic Squadron, under the command of Commodore George Dewey, was anchored in Mirs Bay on the east coast of China. He was ordered to sail to the Philippines—then a Spanish colony—despite a worrying shortage of ammunition.

The aging Spanish fleet, led by Admiral Patricio Montojo, was outgunned and outarmored by the more up-to-date U.S. fleet. Montojo decided to shelter inshore and rely on land batteries for defense. He chose a site in Manila Bay, away from the capital city, in shallow water off the Cavite Naval Yard. Dewey, on board his flagship *Olympia*, took his squadron into Manila Bay under cover of darkness on the night of 30 April and, soon after dawn, approached the Spanish in single file. The Spanish batteries opened up while well out of range, but Dewey waited for thirty minutes before giving the order to return fire. Passing back and forth in front of Spanish fleet, the Americans pounded the enemy until, fearful that their ammunition was running low, they took a break at 7:35 AM.

Despite inaccurate gunnery, the U.S. ships had sunk most of the Spanish vessels. At around 11:15 AM, they resumed fire, sinking the rest of the fleet and quieting the shore batteries. In the afternoon, Dewey anchored off Manila. Spain's control of the Philippines was over, and— by the Treaty of Paris signed in December 1898—control of the islands was handed over to the United States. **SA**

Losses: U.S., 9 wounded, no ships of 6 warships, 3 support vessels; Spanish, 381 dead or wounded, all 7 warships lost

Las Guasimas 1898 ▶

Las Guasimas   24 June 1898

The United States declared war on Spain two months after the sinking of USS *Maine* in Havana harbor. With confusion, false starts, and disorganization, regular and federal volunteer troops were assembled. In June, an expedition crowded onto transports and steamed for Cuba.

The objective of the U.S. mission was the port of Santiago, on the southeastern tip of Cuba, where the U.S. Navy had the Spanish fleet blockaded in the heavily defended harbor. The plan was to capture the city by a land campaign. U.S. V Corps, commanded by Major General William Shafter, landed at Daiquiri, 15 miles (24 km) from the entrance to Santiago harbor, and also at Siboney. Some 3 miles (5 km) inland, a Spanish force of 1,500 infantry with artillery occupied delaying positions on the Las Guasimas ridge.

Guided by Cuban insurgents, Brigadier General Samuel Young's 2d Brigade, Cavalry Division, advanced at 7:00 AM on 24 June, in two parallel columns, each with between 500 and 550 dismounted troopers. Along a dirt road on the right marched two squadrons under Young, one from the 1st Volunteer Cavalry and the other of the 10th Cavalry, with four small field guns. In thick jungle on the left, Colonel Leonard Wood led two more squadrons of the 1st, with two machine guns.

Firing started as the advance guards made contact with Spanish outposts. Wood's men moved out of the jungle into a field of high grass, and he deployed seven troops on line. As they advanced up the ridge, they were joined by the Regulars from the 10th, led by Captain John J. Pershing, and the other 1st squadron. After a short, but intense firefight, the Spanish commander ordered a withdrawal. The ridge was held by Americans by 10:00 AM. **RB**

"No man was allowed to drop out to help the wounded . . . war is a grim game and there was no choice." Theodore Roosevelt, 1st Volunteer Cavalry

---

Losses: U.S., 16 dead, 52 wounded; Spanish, 9 dead, 27 wounded

◁ *Manila Bay 1898*   *San Juan Hill 1898* ▷

⬆ Black troops, named "Buffalo Soldiers" by American Indians, of the U.S. 10th Cavalry Regiment move forward at Las Guasimas.

San Juan Hill 1 July 1898

After the Battle of Las Guasimas in Cuba, Major General William Shafter planned to take Santiago. Reports of Spanish reinforcements on route to the city caused him to accelerate his plans. He ordered head-on assaults against three hilltop fortified positions that made up the city's outer defenses.

In Shafter's plan, the 2d Division was to take El Caney, then swing south to join in a coordinated attack at 10:00 AM with the 1st Division, led by Brigadier General Jacob Kent, and the dismounted Cavalry Division, led by Brigadier General Samuel Sumner, against the two hills that sat on the San Juan ridgeline: San Juan Hill and Kettle Hill. Entrenchments, block houses, barbed wire, and several cannon protected the Spanish defenders.

Shafter's plan quickly fell apart. The march to attack positions was delayed, and unit deployment was confused by the narrow, crowded trail and enemy fire. At 8:00 AM, 1 July, artillery began firing on the Spanish positions, then ceased to avoid counterbattery fire. Although it was well after noon before all the units were on line, the 2d Division was still heavily engaged at El Caney. Finally, at 1:00 PM, and under galling Spanish fire, an aide of Shafter's gave approval to attack. The Cavalry Division's two brigades, led by the 1st Volunteer Cavalry under Colonel Theodore Roosevelt, charged and captured Kettle Hill.

Meanwhile, the Spanish on San Juan Hill tenaciously held back 1st Division's infantrymen. Two Gatling guns appeared, and their rapid volume of fire let the infantry renew their charge and break into the Spanish trenches. At the same time, cavalrymen attacked from Kettle Hill 500 yards (457 m) away, taking another section of San Juan Hill. By 2:00 PM, the last elements of Spanish resistance had been eliminated. **RB**

Losses: U.S.,124 dead, 817 wounded; Spanish, 58 dead, 170 wounded, 39 captured

◁ Las Guasimas 1898   Santiago de Cuba 1898 ▷

Santiago de Cuba 3 July 1898

Following the United States' declaration of war with Spain in April 1898, Spanish Admiral Pascual Cervera was ordered to take a fleet across the Atlantic to support land forces in the defense of Cuba. With the U.S. Navy equipped with powerful new ships, that proved an impossible task.

Arriving at Santiago de Cuba, the Spanish fleet was immediately blockaded in harbor by superior U.S. warships. As long as the Spanish stayed within the protection of mines and shore batteries they could not be attacked, but nor could they challenge the U.S. blockade squadron. By July, however, the progress of U.S. land forces in Cuba put Cervera's ships at risk from the shore. The Spanish admiral decided to attempt a breakout.

On 3 July, four cruisers and two destroyers steamed out of Santiago de Cuba. By chance, the flagship of Admiral William Sampson, commanding the blockade squadron, was off station. As the Spanish warships steamed along the coast, Commodore Winfield Schley led the pursuit on board USS *Brooklyn*. Cervera's flagship, *Infanta Maria Theresa*, gallantly engaged *Brooklyn* in a delaying action in order to give the other ships a chance to escape, but in vain.

Battered by *Brooklyn*'s guns, the Spanish flagship ran aground, as did the cruiser *Vizcaya*, set ablaze after losing an unequal hour-long duel with the battleship USS *Texas*. The crew of the cruiser *Oquendo* scuttled their ship, and the two Spanish destroyers were sunk. The only Spanish ship to break the blockade was the cruiser *Cristobal Colón*. Fleeing westward, this final survivor was chased for 50 miles (80 km) by the swift battleship USS *Oregon* before it was overhauled. *Colón*'s captain scuttled his ship in shallow water to avoid futile loss of life. **RG**

Losses: Spanish, 474 dead or wounded, 1,800 captured, all 6 ships; U.S., 1 dead, 1 wounded, no ships of 8

◁ San Juan Hill 1898

Theodore Roosevelt and his "Rough Riders" (1st Volunteer Cavalry) at San Juan Hill.

Omdurman 2 September 1898

The Battle of Omdurman was between an Anglo-Egyptian army, under General Sir Herbert Kitchener, and the army of the Muslim Mahdists, who had dominated Sudan since their capture of Khartoum in 1885. For the British, victory avenged the death of their hero, General Gordon, at Khartoum.

Kitchener was serving as commander in chief of the British-officered Egyptian army. The British government authorized him to invade Sudan and suppress the Mahdists. A meticulous, methodical general, Kitchener prepared and executed the expedition with scrupulous attention to logistics. The force he assembled consisted of around 25,000 men, of whom 8,000 were regular British troops and the rest Egyptians and Sudanese. He had a railway built parallel to the Nile to supply his force as he advanced southward from Egypt, and riverboats provided transport for both troops and equipment. The British advance in spring 1898 was observed with concern by Khalifa Abdullah, leader of the Mahdists. He ordered an

> *"The khalifa committed a fatal error in . . . discounting the better disciplined valor of our [army]."*
>
> The Times *(London), 7 September 1898*

army to attack Kitchener's force at Atbara in early April, but they were routed by a preemptive counterattack mounted by the British. The Mahdists then fell back to wait for the invaders at their capital, Omdurman, near Khartoum.

On 1 September, Kitchener set up camp at El Ageiga, on the banks of the Nile, almost within sight of Omdurman. He sent gunboats to shell the town while his cavalry scouts tried to locate the Mahdist army. The khalifa meanwhile had made the fateful decision to engage Kitchener's army in a pitched battle. His force of around 50,000 warriors streamed out of Omdurman to take up positions around the British camp. After a nervous night for the British, fearing an attack under cover of darkness, the fighting began at dawn. The Mahdist forces were arranged into five sections, with some concealed behind hills and the rest directly confronting the British forces on the plain. Kitchener's infantry formed a defensive perimeter with cavalry placed at both flanks. Clad in white under gaudy banners, an 8,000-strong section of the Mahdists charged straight at Kitchener's forces, meeting the fire of artillery and infantry weapons. Especially deadly were the Maxim guns—the first self-powered machine guns—that could fire 600 rounds per minute. The waves of Mahdists were cut down in front of the British lines by the rain of bullets from rapid-fire rifles and Maxims.

With the initial attack defeated, the British moved out of their defenses to advance on Omdurman, unaware of the number of Mahdists present in concealed positions. Sent ahead for reconnaissance, the 21st Lancers, with young war correspondent Winston Churchill temporarily one of their number, rode into a hidden mass of Mahdists, who inflicted sixty-one casualties on the startled horsemen. Elsewhere on the battlefield, the khalifa ordered his concealed forces to attack. A brigade of Sudanese troops, under General Hector Macdonald, found itself isolated in the face of some 15,000 Mahdists; they resisted courageously until support arrived and disciplined firepower drove off the enemy. The failure of this second phase of Mahdist attacks left Omdurman open to be occupied by British forces. Kitchener ordered the tomb of the Mahdi destroyed, while the khalifa retreated into southern Sudan, where he was trapped and killed. Fending off counterclaims by France, Britain made Sudan an Anglo-Egyptian colony. **TB**

Losses: British, 48 dead, 380 wounded of 25,000; Mahdist, 10,000 dead, 14,000 wounded of 50,000

◁ *Khartoum 1884*

A 40-lb. battery at Wad Hamed, Omdurman, 1898. Photograph by Major H. M. Dunn, Royal Army Medical Corps.

Manila   4–5 February 1899

Filipino hopes that the U.S. defeat of their Spanish colonial masters in 1898 would bring independence to the Philippines were dashed when the United States annexed the islands for itself. The war began with a brief but bloody clash between Filipino independence fighters and U.S. troops in Manila.

After their naval victory over the Spanish in Manila Bay in May 1898, U.S. troops occupied the Philippine capital, Manila. Relations between U.S. troops and native Filipinos deteriorated as it became clear that the Americans were there to stay. On 21 December 1898, the U.S. president, William McKinley, issued a Proclamation of Benevolent Assimilation taking over the islands. On 1 January 1899, Filipino leader Emilio Aguinaldo was declared president of an independent republic. A substantial Filipino rebel army dug into positions around Manila, which was occupied by U.S. troops. The Filipinos were short on equipment and lacked leadership, with no clear strategy or tactics.

As tensions rose, two U.S. sentries, who were on guard at Manila's San Juan del Monte bridge on the evening of 4 February, fired shots at a Filipino crowd crossing the bridge. Within minutes, both sides were exchanging fire, and a group of Filipino rebels captured two U.S. artillery pieces. The next morning, at daybreak, U.S. general Arthur MacArthur gave the order to attack the Filipino trenches. U.S. troops captured a ridge to the north, overlooking the city, while troops to the south captured a village containing Filipino supplies. The population of the city failed to rise in support of the rebels. Filipino units continued to skirmish with U.S. soldiers on the city's outskirts for several days until they were finally driven out. The battle for Manila was the prelude to a conflict that would last for three years. **SA**

Losses: U.S., 50–60 dead, 225 wounded of 12,000; Filipino, 2,000 dead or wounded of 15,000

◁ *Manila Bay 1898*   *Balangiga 1901* ▷

Volunteers from Nebraska arrive in Manila in June 1899 as the Philippine-American War continues. ⬆

Colenso   15 December 1899

The Battle of Colenso was the third disaster for British forces in what was dubbed the "Black Week" of the Second Boer War. Sent to reverse early Boer gains, an army corps led by General Sir Redvers Buller suffered heavy casualties against tactically sophisticated, well-armed opponents.

In October 1899, the Boer republics of Transvaal and the Orange Free State went to war with the British in South Africa. The Boers' militia units, known as commandos, had shown their worth in the First Boer War. Now they were armed with German-made weaponry: the smokeless Mauser rifle and Krupp field guns.

Taking the offensive, the Boers besieged the unprepared British forces in Mafeking, Ladysmith, and Kimberley. Arriving from Britain, Buller divided his corps into three columns and set off to relieve the sieges. In Black Week, the British were defeated at Magersfontein and Stromberg, before a column commanded by Buller himself met Boers led by General Louis Botha at Colenso. Botha deployed most of his commando units in camouflaged positions behind the Tugela River and on a flanking hill. After an ineffectual artillery bombardment, Buller launched an assault on the Boer position on 15 December. Sent to cross the river by a ford, one brigade lost its way and was pinned down by Boer rifle fire in an exposed loop of the river. British field guns advanced too far, also coming within range of the Boer Mausers, and the gunners suffered heavy casualties before retreating to cover. Buller's cavalry was equally unable to drive the Boers out of their hilltop position. With no progress being made, the British withdrew, abandoning ten artillery pieces that could not be recovered under Boer fire. The misery of Britain's Black Week was complete. **TB**

Losses: British, 143 dead, 1,100 wounded or missing, 10 field guns; Boer, 23 dead, 27 wounded

◁ *Majuba Hill 1881*   *Spion Kop 1900* ▷

⬆ *British staff and troops view the Boer position at Colenso.*

6

1900–1938

British troops in silhouette march towards trenches near Ypres at the Western Front during World War I.

Spion Kop   23–24 January 1900

After the humiliation at Colenso, the battle at Spion Kop was another costly reverse for British forces, under General Sir Redvers Buller, attempting to relieve Ladysmith from siege by Boer commandos. Reports of the heavy casualties and the failure to hold the hilltop position caused outrage in Britain.

General Buller planned to relieve Ladysmith by launching a dual attack. General Sir Charles Warren would cross the Tugela River at Trikhardt's Drift, and Buller would cross at Potgieter's Drift. Warren's force was spotted by the Boers, who moved to cut off his advance. Pressed by Buller to take decisive action, Warren chose to occupy a hill called the Spion Kop, which dominated the surrounding plain.

Under cover of darkness and mist on the night of 23 January, a detachment of the Mounted Infantry, Royal Lancasters, and Royal Engineers moved up the hill and drove off some Boer pickets. However, the Engineers failed to dig adequate trenches on the rocky ground—a

critical error because the following morning it became clear that the position was particularly vulnerable to artillery bombardment.

The Boers were urged forward by their commanders to retake the hill, launching a frontal assault that was repulsed in hand-to-hand fighting. A British diversionary attack seized a dominant feature, known as the Twin Peaks, but the troops on the Kop continued to take casualties from artillery bombardment, as well as suffering from heat and thirst. All the senior commanders on the hill were killed or wounded, leaving Lieutenant Colonel Alexander Thorneycroft in command. With no clear orders from his superiors, Thorneycroft evacuated the Kop at the end of the day, even though it was by then firmly in British hands. The Boers reoccupied the hill unopposed. **TB**

Losses: British, 383 dead, 1,054 wounded of 13,000; Boer, 350 casualties of 8,000

◁ Colenso 1899   Paardeberg 1900 ▷

A detachment of armed Boer commandos waits in camp on Spion Kop. ⬆

Paardeberg   17–27 February 1900

In response to early disasters in its war with the Boers, Britain sent reinforcements to South Africa under fresh commanders, Lord Roberts and Lord Kitchener. The battle at Paardeberg demonstrated a new British determination to bring superior numbers and firepower to bear against the Boer commandos.

In retrospect, the Boers' decision to besiege British garrisons at Mafeking, Kimberley, and Ladysmith was an error of judgment because holding such fixed positions exposed them to decisive counterattack when more British forces arrived. On 15 February, General John French, commanding a large cavalry division, broke through to Kimberley and pursued the retreating Boer commandos, led by General Piet Cronje. Catching up with the Boers as they were crossing the Modder River at Paardeberg Drift, French opened fire with his horse artillery. Cronje decided to dig in, which gave the British forces time to join the battle with overwhelming strength.

Rejecting the option of reducing the Boers to surrender by artillery bombardment alone, Lord Kitchener launched frontal infantry assaults. These were repulsed by Boer firepower, with the Highland and Canadian troops suffering especially severely. Much criticized, the assaults on 18 February came to be known as Bloody Sunday. However, the Boers remained in a desperate situation, with no defense against the British gunfire that destroyed their supplies and killed most of their horses. Commandos rode in, hoping to relieve the siege, but judged the position hopeless and rode away again.

Cronje surrendered on 27 February after a company of Canadian infantry moved up to his lines under cover of darkness. The defeat and capture of Cronje's army was a turning point in the war. **TB**

Losses: British, 348 dead, 1,213 wounded of 30,000; Boer, 350 casualties, 4,500 captured of 7,000

◁ *Spion Kop 1900*   *Relief of Mafeking 1900* ▷

⬆ *The 82nd Royal Field Artillery cross the Modder River at Paardeberg Drift in pursuit of Cronje and his army.*

Relief of Mafeking   17 May 1900

After a Boer siege lasting 217 days, the British garrison at Mafeking was relieved by a "flying column," led by Colonel Bryan Thomas Mahon. News of the relief was met with unbridled jingoistic celebrations in Britain, although the war was destined not to end for another two years.

Almost as soon as war was declared in 1899, General Piet Cronje advanced an army to Mafeking and ordered the surrender of the British commander, Lieutenant General Robert Baden-Powell. When Baden-Powell refused, the Boers commenced the shelling of the town of Mafeking on 13 October.

The town resisted the Boer siege via a combination of bluff, bravery, and the honorable conduct of the Boers, who allowed cease-fires on Sundays so that civilians could attend church and run a series of cricket matches. The Boers realized that an assault on the well-defended town was too difficult, and their force was halved in November when 4,000 troops were redeployed. The siege continued until 12 May, when news of the approaching British relief force prompted the Boers to attempt a last major assault.

The attackers broke through the perimeter defenses and set fire to parts of the town, before the assault was beaten back. The siege was finally ended on 17 May when a column of 2,000 South African volunteers attacked the Boer force and forced it to abandon the siege. The war had gone badly for the British up to this point, and when news reached Britain that the siege had been lifted, there were celebrations across the country, with Baden-Powell hailed as a hero. There would be no more battles in the war, but there were two more years of brutal struggle as the Boers switched to guerilla tactics and the British carried out a ruthless counterinsurgency campaign. **TB**

Losses: British, 800 casualties of 2,000; Boer, 2,000 casualties of 8,000 (ultimately reduced to 4,000)

⟨ *Paardeberg 1900*

Detail from a photograph taken on 30 November 1899 showing Boer soldiers in the trenches outside Mafeking. ⬆

Beijing   20 June–14 August 1900

Placed under siege by Chinese soldiers, the foreign legations in Beijing held out for fifty-five days until relieved by an international expeditionary force. These events fatally undermined the authority of the Chinese Qing dynasty, which was eventually overthrown and replaced by a republic.

In 1899, Chinese frustration at the arrogant intervention of foreigners in their country found expression in the Boxer Rebellion. Attacks on foreigners and Chinese Christians were orchestrated by the Society of Righteous and Harmonious Fists. By June 1900, the movement had spread to Beijing. After much hesitation, China's ruler, Empress Dowager Cixi, decided to back the rebels.

Foreigners and Chinese Christians in Beijing took refuge in the legation quarter, within an improvised defensive perimeter held by 409 soldiers of different nationalities. Fortunately for the foreigners, the Chinese troops and Boxers attacked only fitfully and with little determination.

On 17 July, a cease-fire was agreed, although the siege was maintained. Foreign powers hastened to organize a relief expedition, landing a large force of British, American, Japanese, French, and Russian troops at Tianjin. On 4 August, they began their advance to Beijing. The Chinese troops made little serious attempt to block the relief column. As it approached the capital, however, assaults on the legation defenses resumed. The expeditionary force reached Beijing on 14 August. While U.S. Marines climbed the city walls, British troops found a way through an unguarded gate and reached the legations first. Empress Cixi fled the city. She was only allowed to return in 1902 after agreeing to humiliating peace terms. The Qing dynasty, its prestige shattered, limped on until it was overthrown in 1912. **RG**

Losses: Legation, 55 dead, 165 wounded of 409, 13 civilians dead, 24 civilians wounded; Chinese, unknown

◁ *Weihaiwei 1895*   *Longtan 1927* ▷

Chinese troops march to Beijing during the Boxer Rebellion in 1900.

Balangiga 28 September 1901

The U.S. annexation of the Spanish-owned Philippine Islands in 1898 prompted the Filipinos to fight for independence against their new imperial masters. The subsequent guerrilla war was brutal, the massacre of U.S. troops at Balangiga the U.S. Army's worst defeat since Little Big Horn in 1876.

Company C of the 9th U.S. Infantry Regiment arrived in Balangiga on the southern coast of Samar Island on 11 August 1901. Relations with the townspeople were initially good, but deteriorated after Captain Thomas W. Connell, the commanding officer, ordered the town to be cleared up ready for a visit from the U.S. Army's inspector general. As part of this effort, he detained the town's male residents and confiscated their *bolos*, the machete-style knives used in the jungle. Valeriano Abanador, the town's local police chief, planned revenge.

Using a local festival as cover, Abanador brought in guerrilla reinforcements, led the women and children away to safety, and covered their disappearance by dressing thirty-four men as women. The U.S. soldiers were then softened up with lots of palm wine. In the early hours of 28 September, the Filipinos attacked the U.S. troops, many of whom were having breakfast. Caught unaware, and unable to grab their rifles, the Americans fought back with kitchen utensils, chairs, and whatever else came to hand. The sentry, Private Gamlin, was knocked unconscious, but when he recovered managed to grab a rifle and caused many casualties. As the initial surprise waned, Abanador called off the attack, leaving the townspeople to bury their dead. Of the seventy-four men of Company C, only four escaped unscathed. The U.S. response was immediate, burning down the town and killing 2,000 to 3,000 local people in reprisals. **SA**

Losses: Filipino, 28 dead, 22 wounded of 500; U.S. 36 dead, 30 wounded, 4 missing of 74

◁ *Manila 1899*   *Bud Dajo 1906* ▷

Port Arthur 9 February 1904

Rival ambitions in Korea and China led to war between Russia and Japan in 1904. The Russian Pacific Fleet was a threat to the movement of Japanese troops to mainland Asia; in response, the Japanese staged a surprise attack on warships in Port Arthur before a declaration of war.

The attack was planned by Japanese Admiral Togo Heihachiro. Ten torpedo-armed destroyers reached Port Arthur just after midnight on 9 February. The unsuspecting Russians had their warships lit up, presenting a tempting target. Slipping undetected into the harbor, the Japanese destroyers torpedoed *Retvizan* and *Tsesarevich*, two of the most powerful battleships in the Russian fleet, and the cruiser *Pallada*. None of the ships was destroyed, however, and the effectiveness of the attack was limited by torpedo nets that protected much of the fleet. After the initial chaos, the Russians turned on searchlights and brought their guns to bear, forcing the Japanese to break off the attack at around 2:00 AM.

Unaware that the torpedo attack had partially failed, Togo steamed toward Port Arthur the following morning with the rest of his warships, confident of finishing off the Russian naval squadron. To his surprise, he was vigorously engaged by the Russian warships as well as by shore batteries. Although no ships were lost on either side, several were damaged, including Togo's flagship *Mikasa*. As the Japanese fleet withdrew to a safe distance, the Russians claimed a victory, but their warships remained blockaded in Port Arthur. Over the following months, several Russian sorties were fought off by Togo's warships. In May, the Japanese landed troops and placed the port under siege. After massive losses on both sides, the Russians surrendered Port Arthur on 2 January 1905. **TB**

Losses: Russian, fewer than 100 casualties, no ships; Japanese, 150 casualties, no ships

◁ *Weihaiwei 1895*   *Yellow Sea 1904* ▷

Russian cruiser Pallada *(left) after being damaged by Japanese torpedoes in the attack on Port Arthur.*

Yellow Sea   10 August 1904

In August 1904, Russian warships trapped in Port Arthur by the Japanese fleet attempted to break out and join the rest of the Russian Pacific Fleet at Vladivostok. The action that resulted was one of the first naval battles fought entirely by steel ships firing explosive shells.

Pessimistic about his chances, Russian Rear Admiral Wilgelm Vitgeft reluctantly attempted the mission in a direct order from Czar Nicholas II. On 10 August, six battleships, four cruisers, and fourteen destroyers made a break for the open sea. Admiral Togo Heihachiro commanded the Japanese blockading fleet, which consisted of four battleships, ten cruisers, and eighteen destroyers. He failed to stop the Russians slipping past his blockade, taking too long to organize his ships into a fighting line, but he pursued and overhauled them in the Yellow Sea.

The two fleets sailed in line, pounding each other for several hours with their heavy guns. Togo's flagship, *Mikasa*, took considerable punishment and was forced to transfer command to the battleship *Asahi*. Soon after, *Asahi* scored a hit on the Russian flagship, *Tsesarevich*, smashing the bridge, killing Vitgeft, and disabling the ship's steering. As *Tsesarevich* veered out of control, the commander of the Russian battleship *Retvizan* carried out an audacious move by swinging his ship around and charging at *Asahi* with all guns firing. The Japanese ships concentrated their fire on the advancing *Retvizan* until it turned away, making smoke to cover its retreat.

Most of the battered Russian squadron turned back to Port Arthur. A few ships, including *Tsesarevich*, sought refuge in neutral ports where they were interned. The ships in Port Arthur were lost when the besieged port surrendered in January 1905. **TB**

Losses: Russian, 444 casualties; Japanese, 226 casualties

◁ Port Arthur 1904   Liaoyang 1904 ▷

Liaoyang   25 August–4 September 1904

The Battle of Liaoyang was a major land battle in the Russo-Japanese War. An extremely costly encounter for both sides, it was fought to gain control of a strategic railway junction on the main railway line connecting Mukden with Port Arthur in the Chinese province of Manchuria.

The Russo-Japanese War provided a large-scale trial of the latest military technology and tactics, including artillery firing high-explosive shells beyond line of sight, directed by observers with field telephones, and infantry equipped with rapid-fire rifles and machine guns. The battle at Liaoyang witnessed the devastation an army could expect when attacking troops equipped with such weaponry.

The Russians, under the command of war minister General Alexei Kuropatkin, attempted an advance to relieve besieged Port Arthur. Their forces encountered the Japanese First and Second Armies, commanded by Field Marshal Oyama Iwao, on 25 August. After several attempts to outflank the Japanese failed, Kuropatkin withdrew and formed a defensive line to the south of Liaoyang on 29 August, intent on stopping the Japanese from taking the city.

Over the next two days, the Russians stood their ground as the Japanese launched waves of futile and costly frontal assaults. At the same time, Oyama sent a large force upriver, which managed to cross to the northeast. Kuropatkin launched a series of attacks against the advancing army, which met the same fate as the Japanese offensive action. Unable to push the Japanese back, Kuropatkin chose to withdraw to Mukden, abandoning plans for the relief of Port Arthur. With no relief forthcoming, it was only a matter of time before Port Arthur fell. The war was now turning toward a Japanese victory. **TB**

Losses: Russian, 6,000 dead, 17,000 wounded of 125,000; Japanese, 3,600 dead, 16,400 wounded of 240,000

◁ Yellow Sea 1904   Mukden 1905 ▷

Mukden   20 February–10 March 1905

The Battle of Mukden (Shenyang) was the climactic land battle of the Russo-Japanese War. Taking place in what is now the Liaoning province of northeast China, the battle was one of the largest fought before World War I, with more than half a million men engaged.

After the Russian defeat at Liaoyang, General Alexei Kuropatkin regrouped at Mukden, assembling an army of around 260,000. With the capture of Port Arthur at the start of the new year, the Japanese were able to redeploy their Third Army to join Field Marshal Oyama Iwao's advance, swelling his force to a similar size. With the entire land forces of Japan committed, Oyama set out to destroy the Russian army at Mukden.

The Russian defensive line was 90 miles (145 km) long, with troops dug into trenches behind barbed wire. The Japanese attempted to envelop the Russians, attacking both flanks, but took massive casualties to machine gun and artillery fire. The Japanese eventually made inroads on the Russian right, to which Kuropatkin responded by ordering troops across from the left on 7 March. However, the transfer of so many troops across such a large front caused chaos. Oyama was aware that Russian forces were preoccupied with this logistical challenge and ordered his forces to redouble their offensive. To escape envelopment, Kuropatkin was forced into a disorderly retreat, leaving behind his wounded and supplies.

With both sides exhausted, Mukden was the last land battle of the war. Popular discontent in Russia—to which news of the defeat at Mukden contributed—had brought the country to the brink of revolution. After a further defeat in the naval battle of Tsushima, the Russians made peace on Japan's terms. **TB**

"The Japanese were morally stronger, and the teaching of all history shows it is the moral factor which really counts."

General Alexei Kuropatkin

 Field Marshal Oyama's infantrymen in a trench on the plains of the Sha River.

Losses: Russian, 15,900 dead, 60,000 wounded of 260,000; Japanese, 8,800 dead, 80,000 wounded or missing of 270,000

◁ Liaoyang 1904   Tsushima 1905 ▷

Tsushima   27–28 May 1905

The naval battle fought in the Strait of Tsushima between Japan and Korea was the final decisive encounter of the Russo-Japanese War. Admiral Togo Heihachiro achieved a victory worthy of his hero, Nelson, and established Japan's place among the world's major naval powers.

In autumn 1904, the Russians hatched an ambitious plan to counter Japanese naval supremacy in the Pacific. The Russian Baltic Fleet would sail 18,000 miles (28,968 km) to the Far East and link up with the Pacific Fleet to launch a combined strike at the Japanese navy, knocking it out of the war. On 15 October, twenty-seven warships set sail from the Baltic, including eleven battleships and nine destroyers, under the command of Admiral Zinovi Rozhdestvenski. Steaming across the North Sea, they fired on British trawlers, mistaken for Japanese torpedo boats, causing a diplomatic furor. It was an unfortunate start to a grueling voyage that placed great strain upon crews and ships alike. Denied the use of the Suez Canal by the British, the fleet steamed around Africa and across the Indian Ocean, finding supplies of coal as best it could.

By May 1905, Rozhdestvenski was in the South China Sea. By that time, Port Arthur—the fleet's original goal—had long since fallen to the Japanese, so Rozhdestvenski headed for Vladivostok where he could join what was left of the Russian Pacific Fleet. However, in order to do this, he would have to either pass between Japan and Korea or sail around the north of Japan. Running low on coal supplies, Rozhdestvenski chose to lead his fleet through the Strait of Tsushima, the shortest, but also the most dangerous, route. Unfortunately for Rozhdestvenski, Admiral Togo guessed that the Russians would choose this option and made ready his fleet to intercept. Togo

had at his disposal a combined fleet of sixty-four vessels, including four battleships, twenty-one destroyers, and twenty-seven cruisers—all more modern than their Russian rivals. Rozhdestvenski's plan was to slip through the strait at night, with his ships observing a total blackout to guard against being seen. However, a light on a hospital ship was spotted, and news of the location of the Russian fleet transmitted to Togo using the new technology, radio. Togo in turn radioed a message to the Japanese government: "The Russian fleet has been sighted. I will attack it and annihilate it."

Exploiting the superior speed of the Japanese warships and the discipline of their crews, on the afternoon of 27 May, Togo located the Russian fleet and steamed at will around it. With his flagship, *Mikasa,* in the van of the line, he executed maneuvers that have delighted aficionados of naval warfare ever since: "turns in sequence" and "crossing the T." For the Russians, it was pure hell, because the exchange of fire at ranges of around 6,000 yards (5,485 m) demonstrated the absolute superiority of Japanese gunnery and range-finding technology. By the time night fell, four Russian battleships had been sunk, taking most of their crew down with them. Rozhdestvenski was put out of action with a shell fragment buried in his skull. After dark, the Japanese destroyers and torpedo boats moved in, launching repeated attacks on the disorganized Russian remnants. The following day, some ships surrendered; a few escaped. Only three ships made it to Vladivostok, and Russia had lost the war. **TB**

Losses: Russian, 4,500 dead, 6,000 captured, 17 ships sunk, 5 ships captured of 27; Japanese, 117 dead, 580 wounded, 3 torpedo boats sunk of 64

〈 *Mukden 1905*

Bud Dajo   5–7 March 1906

Ciudad Juárez   7 April–10 May 1911

Annexing the Spanish-owned Philippine Islands in 1898, the Americans faced not only a war with Filipino republicans but also a rebellion by Moro or Muslim Filipinos living in the south. The conflict, which lasted until 1913, saw at least 20,000 Moros die, including around 1,000 massacred at Bud Dajo.

Seeking to end the dictatorship of Porfirio Díaz, rebel forces, led by Pancho Villa and Pascual Orozco, attacked Federal forces at Ciudad Juárez in the first major battle of the Mexican Revolution. The untrained rebel force emerged victorious, ending Díaz's rule and bringing Francisco Madero to power.

The Moros of the southern Philippines had never accepted Spanish control and continued to resist the incoming Americans. As Muslims, they objected to foreign and Christian occupation and particularly resented U.S. reforms, such as the abolition of slavery and the imposition of *cedula,* or poll tax. Events deteriorated when Pala, a Moro, ran amok in British-held Borneo and then fled to his home island of Jolo. He evaded capture for some months before taking refuge in the extinct volcanic crater of Bud Dajo. Here he was joined by hundreds of Moro rebels and outlaws.

On 2 March 1906, General Leonard Wood, governor of Moro province, ordered Colonel J. W. Duncan of the 6th Infantry Regiment to lead an expedition against the rebel positions. The battle began three days later when mountain guns fired forty rounds of shrapnel into the crater. Three columns of troops climbed the volcano on 6 March, encountering barricades defended by sword-bearing Moros. These overcome, the U.S. troops fought their way up to the crater's edge and, during the night, dragged mountain guns up the volcano's side. In the morning, the guns opened fire, supported by naval guns from the gunboat *Pampanga* stationed in the sea below. The Moros continued to resist, rushing the U.S. lines until they were cut down. The Americans charged the surviving Moros with fixed bayonets, killing all but six of them. The bloodiest fight of the Moro rebellion was over. **SA**

By the end of 1910, opposition to the dictatorship of Porfirio Díaz had resulted in a guerrilla campaign against Díaz's Federal soldiers. The attacks, led by Francisco "Pancho" Villa, Pascual Orozco, and Emiliano Zapata, convinced exiled opposition leader Francisco Madero to return to Mexico. On 7 April, Madero, Villa, and Orozco launched an attack, with a force of 2,500 untrained men, at the strategically important Ciudad Juárez, which lay on Mexico's border with the United States. The city was defended by 700 Federal soldiers commanded by General Juan Navarro.

With the Federal army heavily outnumbered, Díaz attempted to negotiate a truce. Despite Madero ordering a cease-fire, Villa and Orozco continued the offensive. Across the border, in the U.S. town of El Paso, thousands of Americans gathered to watch the battle. Using barricades and machine guns, Navarro had prepared a strong, well-organized defense of the city. To counter this, the rebels avoided an open attack through the streets, instead using dynamite to blow their way through the rows of houses and remain concealed. By 8 May, the besieged Federal troops occupied a few buildings in the city center and had run out of water. With fighting restricted to close combat, the Federal army's superior artillery was of little use. Two days later, Navarro surrendered. Together with the Battle of Cuautla, Ciudad Juárez led to Diaz's resignation, which brought Francisco Madero to power. **ND**

Losses: U.S., 15–21 dead, 75 wounded of 790; Moros, 6 survivors of 800–1,000

Losses: Unknown

◁ *Balangiga 1901*

Cuautla 1911 ▷

Rebel soldiers take up sniper positions outside Ciudad Juárez, 10 May 1911.

Cuautla 13–19 May 1911

A large rebel force led by Emiliano Zapata launched an attack against the Federal army loyal to Porfirio Díaz at Cuautla. In one of the bloodiest battles of the Mexican Revolution, Zapata and his rebel troops defeated the elite federal force, bringing an end to Díaz's dictatorship.

Opposition to Porfirio Díaz's dictatorship in Mexico had grown in late 1910 and early 1911, with unrest spreading throughout the country. In the southern state of Morelos, Emiliano Zapata led an armed agrarian uprising. After the defeat of Díaz's Federal army against rebel forces in Ciudad Juárez, Zapata decided to lead his force of 4,000 fighters in an offensive against the Federal army at the fortified city of Cuautla on 13 May.

The city was defended by around 400 Federal soldiers belonging to the renowned 5th Cavalry Regiment. Although the rebels had a huge advantage in numbers, the Zapatistas were inexperienced fighters and were equipped only with muskets and machetes. The Federal soldiers possessed artillery and machine guns, and occupied better positions. By the second day of fighting, the rebels had surrounded Cuautla and cut off all links into and out of the city. The Federal force refused to surrender, and from behind barricades continued to attack the rebels with artillery fire. The brutal fighting lasted six days, with Federal soldiers and rebels engaged in savage hand-to-hand combat in the city's streets. With ammunition running low, and the majority of the regiment killed, the remaining Federal soldiers pulled out of the city on 19 May. The Federal army's defeat by the Zapatistas in Cuautla led to Díaz's resignation, thereby bringing an end to the first stage of the Mexican Revolution. **ND**

Losses: Rebel, 1,500 casualties of 4,000; Federal, most of 400

◁ Ciudad Juárez 1911 Tierra Blanca 1913 ▷

Catalca 17–18 November 1912

In autumn 1912, an alliance of Balkan states—Bulgaria, Greece, Serbia, and Montenegro—went to war with Turkey. The Bulgarians hoped to seize Constantinople, but at nearby Catalca the Turks held a defensive line in fighting that foreshadowed the trench warfare of World War I.

The Turkish defensive position at Catalca stretched 30 miles (48 km) from the Sea of Marmara to the Black Sea. Although antiquated—originally designed in 1877—it was a formidable network of trenches, machine gun posts, and light artillery posts, supported by heavy artillery to the rear. The Turks also benefited from very short supply lines and were motivated by the fact that defeat here would doom their empire. The Turkish army was weakened by cholera and dysentery, as was almost one-sixth of the Bulgarian army. The exhausted and undersupplied Bulgarian troops faced a monumental task, but their generals were boosted by recent victories and determined to take Constantinople.

There was no attempt at subtlety; the plan was simply for the artillery to blast away at the entire length of the line and for the infantry to charge in. As it happened, heavy fog made any coordination of the battlefield impossible. The artillery barrage was not heavy enough to destroy fixed positions, and the infantry met little success with heavy losses. At one point, part of the line was occupied by a single Bulgarian battalion, but in the confusion, before they could be reinforced, the Turks counterattacked and drove them out. The next day, the attack had to be called off because the Bulgarian troops could endure no more. Turkish morale was boosted by their success, but they were too exhausted to exploit it. **JS**

Losses: Bulgarian, 1,500 dead, more than 9,000 wounded, 1,400 missing of 176,000; Turkish, 10,000 dead, wounded, or missing of 100,000

Adrianople 1913 ▷

◀ Pancho Villa (seated left) and Emiliano Zapata (seated right) with fellow Mexican rebels in 1911.

Adrianople 24 March 1913

"Siege guns split the silence in unison tam-tuuumb … seize it quick smash it scatter it to the infinite winds to the devil." Zang Tumb Tuuum, *Filippo Marinetti*

⬆ *Bulgarian soldiers hold an artillery position as they try to break through the "undefeatable" defenses of Adrianople in 1913.*

Adrianople was one of the largest cities in the Ottoman Empire. When the Bulgarians stormed the city in the First Balkan War, it seemed they would become the predominant power in the Balkans and that the Turks might be evicted from European soil.

Adrianople was strongly defended by a ring of batteries and fortifications incorporating several belts of barbed wire. Lacking precise information about these defenses, the Bulgarians hesitated to launch an attack; they did not relish another failure such as that at the Battle of Catalca. The Bulgarians' Serbian allies agreed to send troops to assist, but an assault on Adrianople's defenses still seemed too hazardous. There was desultory shelling and some attempts at bombing the city from the air, but the Bulgarians did little harm and settled in for a siege. This was risky, however, because a prolonged investment might give the Turks time to bring fresh troops from Asia and attempt to relieve the city.

The intense cold, hunger, and idleness undermined Bulgarian morale, but the Turkish garrison was also suffering severe food shortages and was reaching the limits of endurance. On 24 March 1913, a sudden Bulgarian artillery barrage, followed by an infantry attack, took the Turks completely by surprise. Fearing the main attack would come from the south, reserves were rushed there. However, this was a diversion, and the infantry attacked toward the eastern wall, penetrating the barbed wire.

Initially Turkish resistance was stubborn, but when the Bulgarians broke through the final defenses, Turkish morale collapsed and the city fell within a few hours. This left the Bulgarians with the greatest territorial gains in the war, but their allies were already plotting against them. The Second Balkan War soon followed. **JS**

Losses: Bulgarian, 1,600 dead, 8,000 wounded; Turkish, 15,000 dead or wounded, 60,000 captured

◁ *Catalca 1912*　　　　　　　　　　*Kilkis 1913* ▷

Kilkis   30 June–4 July 1913

In the Second Balkan War of June to August 1913, Bulgaria tried in vain to hold on to gains it had won in the First Balkan War. Defeat at Kilkis ensured that the Bulgarians would fail to become the preeminent power in the Balkans.

When their former Serbian and Greek allies turned against them (and invited the Turks to join in), the Bulgarians found themselves in a desperate position. The Bulgarian troops had suffered heavy losses while fighting the Turks. They were poorly supplied, hungry, unpaid, and mutinous. They launched a preemptive attack on the Greeks, hoping to take Salonika quickly, but simply lacked the strength to achieve their goal.

Facing a much larger Greek force intent on encircling them, and with their coastal positions pounded by the Greek navy, the Bulgarian soldiers pulled back to Kilkis, where they had constructed strong defensive positions, with trenches supported by concealed batteries of captured Turkish guns. The Bulgarians were determined to make a stand here, but the troops were aware of the overwhelming power of the coalition arrayed against them, which caused serious morale problems.

A series of artillery barrages, followed up by concerted infantry attacks, pushed the Bulgarians out of their prepared positions over three days. Greek losses were heavy, but the fighting spirit of the Bulgarian army was falling apart. By the time reinforcements arrived, they could only join in a general retreat that threatened to become a complete collapse. Under attack by the Serbs and the Turks (who retook Adrianople) and the Romanians (only too happy to exploit their neighbors' misfortune), the Bulgarian position became utterly hopeless, and Bulgaria sought whatever peace terms it could secure. **JS**

Losses: Bulgarian, 4,227 dead, 1,977 wounded, 767 missing, and 6,000 captured; Greek, 8,700 dead or wounded

[<] Adrianople 1913

Tierra Blanca   23–25 November 1913

Fighting between Pancho Villa's rebel forces and General Victoriano Huerta's Federal army came to a head at the Battle of Tierra Blanca. The resilience of the rebel army provided Villa with one of his most hard-fought victories of the Mexican Revolution.

After an unsuccessful battle at Chihuahua against General Victoriano Huerta's Federal army in November 1913, Pancho Villa took his rebel Army of the North to the nearby town of Tierra Blanca. Government soldiers soon arrived in the town by train, and fighting began on the night of 23 November.

Although the two armies were of a similar size—around 5,000 men—the Federal army was better equipped with weapons and ammunition supplies. For two days, the battle followed a pattern of attacks and counterattacks. However, the machine guns and heavy artillery of the Federal army enabled it to inflict huge casualties on Villa's men. Facing this continual onslaught and running low on ammunition, Villa decided to gamble and launched an all-or-nothing attack. The rebel troops charged toward the Federal army in a frontal assault, while Villa ordered his cavalry to attack the flanks, sending panic through the enemy ranks. Villa then sent a locomotive loaded with dynamite toward the government soldiers, where it crashed into a train and caused a massive explosion, leaving the Federal troops in further disarray. As they swiftly retreated, the soldiers left behind weapons and ammunition, which Villa's men were able to capture.

Having secured what became his most famous victory, Villa led his men and advanced toward the state capital, Ciudad Chihuahua. With demoralized Federal forces abandoning the city, Villa was declared governor of Chihuahua in early December 1913. **ND**

Losses: Rebel, 300 casualties of 5,500; Federal, 1,000 casualties of 5,500

[<] Cuautla 1911   Veracruz 1914 [>]

Veracruz 21–24 April 1914

The U.S. administration's growing opposition to the military regime of Victoriano Huerta in Mexico led to a naval force being sent to take control of the Mexican port city of Veracruz. Victory for the United States in a one-sided battle resulted in U.S. troops occupying the city for six months.

By early 1914, U.S. support for the military regime of General Victoriano Huerta during the Mexican Revolution had been withdrawn. Woodrow Wilson's election as president led to U.S. opposition to a regime Wilson considered illegitimate, and an embargo was placed on arms transfers to Huerta. Tensions rose in April, following a confrontation between U.S. and Mexican soldiers at Tampico. Shortly after, the United States discovered a German arms delivery due to arrive in Veracruz, and Wilson sent a U.S. naval squadron to take control of the city's port.

On 21 April, warships of the U.S. Atlantic Fleet, commanded by Admiral Frank Fletcher, arrived at Veracruz, and around 500 U.S. Marines and 300 U.S. Navy personnel went ashore. They encountered almost no resistance in taking the port, as Mexican army soldiers loyal to Huerta retreated. However, fierce fighting soon began when the Veracruz Naval Academy cadets, supported by fifty remaining Mexican army soldiers and the untrained citizens of Veracruz, formed a resistance against the U.S. invasion. The Americans suffered a number of casualties in trying to take the Naval Academy, before U.S. warships shelled the building with their long guns, killing all fifteen cadets barricaded inside. With further reinforcements arriving, the U.S. forces were able to take complete control of the city with little difficulty. The U.S. occupation of Veracruz lasted six months and succeeded in forcing Huerta out of office. **ND**

Losses: U.S., 17 dead, 63 wounded of 2,300; Mexican, 126 dead, 195 wounded

[◁] *Tierra Blanca* 1913   *Celaya* 1915 [▷]

Federal troops take up an offensive position in a street in Veracruz in 1914. ⬆

The Frontiers 4–25 August 1914

The commanders of the German and French armies believed that the opening encounters of World War I would decide its fate. Both sides attacked with ruthless intensity, but French tactical ineptitude—massed infantry attacks against artillery and machine guns—nearly brought disaster for France.

German strategy in 1914 dictated that its forces must inflict a swift knockout blow against France before turning east to take on Russia. Seven German armies were deployed, and, according to the Schlieffen Plan, the three larger armies would conduct a sweeping maneuver through Belgium and northern France to trap and then attack the French in the rear. The four smaller armies would act to hold the French attack along the Franco-German borders. The French strategy consisted of a direct advance into German-held Lorraine, with a subsidiary attack in Alsace.

On 4 August, advance elements of the German army crossed into Belgium, with little resistance expected from the Belgium army. However, the unprovoked invasion of a neutral country brought Britain into the war against Germany. Although the Belgians could not stop the German advance, they continued to fight. The arrival of the British Expeditionary Force in Belgium caused the Germans some consternation, although the delaying actions at Mons and Le Cateau did little to slow the German advance.

The French offensive in Lorraine and Alsace swiftly turned into disaster, as attack after attack was repulsed with terrible casualties. Within five days, the French had been thrown back to their start line, except for a small strip of German territory gained near Mülhausen. As the Germans pressed forward, the Allied armies were forced to retreat all along the frontier. **AG**

Losses: Allied, more than 200,000 casualties of 1,500,000; German, unknown of 1,450,000

Liège 1914 ▸

↑ *German soldiers fire from the relative safety of field fortifications.*

Liège 5–16 August 1914

At the start of World War I, the Germans planned to cross Belgium to attack France. Their path was barred by the great fortress complex surrounding Liège. The Germans had allotted just two days to capture the fortress, but the siege lasted eleven days, which bought the Allies valuable time.

Although the German strategists hoped that the Belgians would not contest the German advance through their country, a special task force of 60,000 men—led by General Otto von Emmich—was assembled to capture Liège. The force was equipped with standard 210mm heavy howitzers, but, unknown to the Belgians, the Germans had also assembled the latest superheavy artillery—305mm Skoda howitzers—loaned from the Austro-Hungarian army and two 420mm Krupp howitzers.

The defenses of Liège consisted of a ring of twelve subterranean forts surrounding the city. They were constructed from concrete and well-equipped with artillery mounted in steel cupolas to provided interlocking zones of fire. Many on the Belgian side believed Liège to be impregnable, but the forts had been completed in 1891 to resist only 210mm guns, and there was a shortage of infantry to man the "intervals" between the forts.

On 5 August, the Germans demanded Liège's surrender, which was summarily refused. For the next two days, the Germans suffered heavy casualties, but, under the inspired leadership of General Erich Ludendorff, a brigade of German infantry broke through the outer defenses and captured the city of Liège on 7 August. With their superheavy artillery in place, the Germans began to destroy the forts systematically. The Belgians fought with great determination but, on 16 August, the last two forts fell to the Germans. **AG**

Losses: Belgian, 2,000 dead or wounded, 4,000 captured of 36,000; German, 2,000 casualties of 60,000

◁ *The Frontiers 1914*   *Mons 1914* ▷

The Belgian cavalry reflect on their losses after the German attack on Liège, 6 August 1914. ⬆

Mons 23 August 1914

Although famous as the British army's first battle of World War I, their stand at Mons in Belgium was in effect a minor delaying action. Once the British commanders became aware of the greater strength of the German army, they withdrew from the position and retreated back to France.

After its arrival in France, the British Expeditionary Force—comprising just two corps, each of two infantry divisions and one cavalry division—advanced into Belgium to take up its position on the left of the French Fifth Army. On being told that the Fifth Army was under heavy attack on 21 August, the British commander, Field Marshal Sir John French, agreed to advance to the Mons-Condé canal to protect the exposed French left flank. The British I Corps was effectively held in reserve, the brunt of the coming German attack being directed at II Corps.

On the morning of 23 August, the British came under German artillery fire, prior to an infantry attack by elements of General Alexander von Kluck's First Army. Although the Germans were repulsed by accurate British rifle and machine gun fire, it became clear that a loop in the canal left the British defenses vulnerable to attack from the flank. The Germans exploited this weakness with renewed artillery and machine gun fire.

By the afternoon, as more German units entered the fray, it became clear to the British that they would ultimately be outflanked, and a tactical retreat was ordered. Most units withdrew in good order, and by nightfall had effectively disengaged from the battle. Meanwhile, Field Marshal French had discovered that the French Fifth Army had withdrawn without informing him. Fearful that he might be overwhelmed by the Germans with heavy casualties, a general retreat was sounded. **AG**

Losses: British 2,500 casualties of 80,000; German, 2,400 casualties of 160,000

◁ Liège 1914   Le Cateau 1914 ▷

⬆ *The Royal Fusiliers pictured at Grand Place, the central square in Mons, on 22 August 1914, before the battle.*

Tannenberg   26–30 August 1914

In the opening battle on the Eastern Front in World War I, the Russian army suffered its most disastrous defeat, more from poor leadership than from any inherent weakness. Tannenberg made the reputations of German Generals Hindenburg and Ludendorff; it also started the process of undermining the Russian state.

The Russians would later claim that they attacked too soon, in a spirit of noble self-sacrifice to support their French ally. However, their mobilization went smoothly enough, and they went into battle as ready as they could be. Fearing the much more professional German army, Russia's military plans were hesitant; instead of throwing their whole might against East Prussia, only two armies out of six were committed to this offensive. The rest were to face the much less formidable Austro-Hungarian military.

General Rennenkampf's First Army would advance from the east, and General Samsonov's Second Army from the south. This meant they were too far apart to support each

> *"If the battle had gone badly, the name 'Hindenburg' would have been reviled from one end of Germany to the other."* Paul von Hindenburg

other—not that much cooperation was likely because the two generals hated each other. After winning a victory at Gumbinnen, Rennenkampf halted his advance, effectively abandoning Samsonov completely. Meanwhile the Germans placed veteran Paul von Hindenburg in command, with Erich Ludendorff as his chief of staff. They were to prove both aggressive and decisive. By leaving screening troops facing Rennenkampf and concentrating their forces, the Germans assembled a force larger than Samsonov's. This would have been a very risky maneuver

if Rennenkampf had launched a sudden advance, but the Germans were aided by astonishing Russian security lapses—unciphered radio messages from Rennenkampf saying that he was staying in position and from Samsonov saying that he was advancing anyway told the Germans all they needed to know.

Samsonov's army had been experiencing difficulties en route. In the heavily forested terrain, his infantry could only march 10 miles (16 km) a day, and were unable to maintain this rate for long. In his demand for speed, Samsonov overrode the needs of his men for food and sleep. Consequently, his troops became strung out over a 60-mile (96 km) front, in territory used by the Germans for training. His army blundered into an ambush, with two German corps ahead of him and a third moving behind to cut off a retreat. Too late, Samsonov realized his peril. His bewildered troops were isolated into pockets, which were pounded mercilessly by German artillery. Without effective command, confusion reigned, and many troops threw aside their weapons and fled—directly into German forces to the rear. The rest surrendered in droves.

Rennenkampf finally made efforts to support Samsonov, but did too little, far too late. At Tannenberg, the fighting became a battle of annihilation. Within four days, the Second Army had ceased to exist. Fewer than 10,000 Russians escaped the German trap, but it is likely that far more could have survived if their commander had shown more effective leadership. Whether this battle diverted German forces from the Western Front, where their presence at the Battle of the Marne might have been decisive, is a matter of debate. However, the Russian defeat was the result of failures at the highest level and a severe blow to the prestige of the Russian autocracy. **JS**

Losses: German, 20,000 dead or wounded of 166,000; Russian, 140,000 dead, wounded, or captured of 150,000

First Masurian Lakes 1914 ▶

Smoking ruins testify to the scale of the conflict at Tannenberg. ➔

Le Cateau   26 August 1914

The fight at Le Cateau was a desperate attempt to slow the German advance and give the retreating British time to rally their forces. Although the Germans did not press their advantage after the battle, British casualties were higher than those suffered by Wellington's British troops at Waterloo.

As the British Expeditionary Force (BEF) retreated from Mons, it was pursued by the German First Army. The BEF's I and II Corps were separated by the Forest of Mormal, with the II Corps led by General Sir Horace Smith-Dorrien particularly hard-pressed by the Germans. On the evening of 25 August, Smith-Dorrien decided that his troops were too exhausted to continue the retreat and—in defiance of the wishes of the BEF's commander in chief, Field Marshal French—he halted his corps to fight a rearguard action the following day.

Once battle began on 26 August, German artillery proved particularly effective against the British infantry, who had failed or been unable to dig in and adopt proper defensive positions. Although the British fought tenaciously, their defense was overly static and did not react effectively to the moves made by the Germans. As British casualties mounted during the morning, so the German attackers were reinforced steadily.

Smith-Dorrien realized that he must withdraw or face encirclement. Deploying his remaining reserves, including the British Cavalry Division and some squadrons of French cavalry from General Sordet's Corps as a covering force, the BEF disengaged from the battlefield, although thirty-eight guns were lost to the Germans and as many as 2,600 men taken prisoner. Fortunately for the British, the Germans did not exploit their success, and the BEF was able to continue its retreat relatively unimpeded. **AG**

Losses: British, 8,000 casualties of 40,000; German, 3,000 casualties of a maximum 120,000

◁ *Mons 1914*　　　　　　　　*First Marne 1914* ▷

Heligoland Bight   28 August 1914

In the first major naval encounter of World War I, British and German cruiser and destroyer forces clashed fiercely in the North Sea, with damage on both sides, until the British battle cruiser force intervened and settled the outcome. Poor British planning was set right by bold tactics.

As an opening move in the naval war, Britain planned an attack on German cruiser and destroyer patrols near the island of Heligoland by cruisers, destroyers, and submarines based in southern England. The Admiralty in London also decided to send the battle cruiser force from Britain's main Grand Fleet, based in northern Scotland, in support—but omitted to inform the other attacking commanders.

Fighting began around 7:00 AM on 29 August in difficult hazy conditions and amid confusion on both sides. Several phases of combat continued into the early afternoon as first one side then the other gained reinforcements. The British light cruiser *Arethusa* was hit heavily in two of these phases, but ultimately the Germans had no answer to the firepower of Admiral Beatty's five battle cruisers when they came on the scene—the German capital ships were still raising steam in their anchorage in the Jade River. Beatty took a risk bringing his valuable ships into waters that were known to be heavily mined and with numerous enemy torpedo boats present, but this decision paid off; three German light cruisers were sunk before the British force withdrew.

This undoubted success had important side effects. For the British navy, it helped mask the defective planning and execution of the operation, deficiencies that would come home to roost later in the war. The Germans, for their part, became excessively cautious and unwilling to take risks to disrupt Britain's naval dominance. **DS**

Losses: British, 100 dead or wounded, no ships; German, 1,200 dead, wounded, or captured, 6 ships sunk

Coronel 1914 ▷

　　British sailors look on as flames take hold of the German cruiser Mainz *at Heligoland.*

First Marne   25 August–12 September 1914

The engagements fought to the east of Paris in September 1914 have rightly been considered decisive battles of World War I. By failing to achieve their key aim—of swiftly defeating the French—the Germans were forced onto the defensive to fight an ultimately disastrous two-front war.

The Battle of the Frontiers had been a catastrophe for France, and by 25 August the situation for the Allies was critical. Everywhere, their armies were in retreat, and the steadily advancing German columns had produced panic within government circles in Paris. However, the unflappable General Joseph Joffre, the French commander in chief, was to save the day. The original French plan of attack—Plan XVII—lay in ruins, so he started afresh and set about organizing his troops to counter the German advance. As an initial step, he switched forces from eastern France—using the country's excellent rail system—to form the new Sixth Army (led by General Michael Joseph Maunoury) for deployment on the extreme Allied left.

> *"The hour has come to advance at all costs and to die where you stand rather than give way."*
>
> General Joseph Joffre, to his commanders at Marne

Joffre then ordered General Charles Lanrezac, who was suffering a crisis of confidence because his Fifth Army was increasingly isolated and outnumbered, to launch an attack between Guise and St. Quentin on 29 August. Despite holding reservations about a successful outcome, Lanrezac conducted his forces with considerable skill. The battle opened with a French attack on the German First Army, led by General Alexander von Kluck, but when the German Second Army, under General Karl von Bülow, pinned down the French Fifth Army's right wing, Lanrezac

coolly transferred his troops across the battlefield and inflicted a severe check on the Second Army. Bülow immediately requested assistance from Kluck's First Army, so that instead of swinging around Paris to the west, as originally planned, the First Army altered its direction south and due east of the French capital. This maneuver meant that the Schlieffen Plan of 1905 was compromised, a blunder that was compounded when General Helmuth von Moltke (Chief of the German General Staff) allowed a subordinate general to draw forces away from the critical German right flank to mount his own local offensive.

The farther south the German First Army advanced, the more exposed its right flank became to attack. By early September, Maunoury's Sixth Army was in place to the north of Paris. The military governor of the capital, General Joseph Simon Galliéni, called for an offensive by Maunoury's and his own forces on Kluck's flank. By 5 September, the Allies had retired south of the Marne River, and at that point Joffre authorized Galliéni's proposal to attack, as well as ordering an all-out counterattack along the entire French front.

The French offensive opened with Maunoury's assault on the German First Army along the Ourq River. Kluck held the French attack, but the movement of his forces over to his right flank opened up a gap between his men and Bülow's Second Army. The strength of the French counterattack came as a shock, and when the British Expeditionary Force and the French Fifth Army advanced into the gap, German resolution wavered. On 8 September, the Germans began to retire. Six days later, Moltke was relieved of his command, reflecting the seriousness of the German setback. The Allied follow-up lacked vigor, however, and the Germans were able to fall back in good order and take up new positions on the Aisne River. **AG**

Losses: Allied, 263,000 casualties of 1,050,000; German, more than 220,000 casualties of 1,250,000

◁ *Le Cateau 1914*   *First Aisne 1914* ▷

The French cavalry pursue the Germans across a hastily constructed pontoon bridge at the Marne River. ➔

First Masurian Lakes
9–14 September 1914

Having annihilated the Russian Second Army at Tannenberg, Hindenburg and Ludendorff turned their attention to the First Army. In this Eastern Front battle of World War I, they won another great victory, but it was not quite so decisive—the Russians were not helpless victims this time.

After the disaster at Tannenberg, the Russian commander, Rennenkampf, was determined to risk no more offensive action. His troops took up a defensive line between the Baltic Sea and the Masurian Lakes. They were well supported by artillery, but were spread too thinly. Rennenkampf placed his reserves in the north, where he expected the main attack. In fact, Hindenburg and Ludendorff intended to attack there only to pin down the Russians, and their main assault would come in the south, where they intended to break through and envelop the entire Russian army against the shores of the Baltic.

The Russians in the north fought a stubborn action, and withdrew in good order when pushed back. In the south, the fighting went poorly for the Germans, who were soon in danger of being outflanked themselves, and reinforcements had to be rushed in to save the situation. This turned the tide of the battle; the Germans broke through and threatened the Russians with encirclement. Unlike Samsonov at Tannenberg, Rennenkampf did not wait too long to order a retreat. Indeed, he led by example and his own withdrawal was so precipitate that he effectively abandoned his army, moving his headquarters three times in one day and at one point issuing orders from his staff car. However, most Russian formations withdrew skillfully enough and, although expelled from German soil, they remained a significant force. **JS**

Losses: German, 40,000 dead or wounded; Russian, 145,000 dead, wounded, or captured

[<] *Tannenberg 1914*   *Second Masurian Lakes 1915* [>]

First Aisne
13–28 September 1914

In World War I, the German decision to adopt a defensive position on the heights above the Aisne River was a tacit acceptance that Germany had failed to defeat the French and British in open warfare. The Allied failure to overcome the German defenses initiated trench warfare on the Western Front.

As the Germans fell back from their defeat at the Battle of the Marne, General Helmuth von Moltke made the decision that his armies in the west would go onto the defensive, and that the ridge on the north bank of the Aisne River would be "fortified and defended." The ridge on the Aisne was only a few hundred feet above the river but it provided a first-rate defensive position. Although the German entrenchments were largely invisible to the Allies, the Germans had an excellent view of the advancing Anglo-French forces and were able to direct their heavy howitzers onto their formations with good effect.

The Allied attack on the Aisne comprised a series of frontal assaults by the French Sixth and Fifth Armies and the British Expeditionary Force. The Germans had destroyed most of the bridges over the Aisne, and the Allies were forced to cross the river using pontoon bridges while under heavy fire. Once across, the Allied troops advanced up the ridge, only to come under devastating German fire. Repeated Allied assaults were held by the Germans, and where the Allies made progress, aggressive counterattacks threw them back to their start lines.

By 18 September, Allied progress had slowed, especially as German attacks on Reims (to the east) drew away French reinforcements. On the Aisne, German and French troops began to improve their defenses, digging extended trench lines, reinforced with barbed wire. **AG**

Losses: Unknown

[<] *First Marne 1914*   *Antwerp 1914* [>]

Antwerp
28 September–9 October 1914

The German capture of the Belgian city of Antwerp in World War I showed the weakness of fortifications in the face of the latest German heavy artillery. But the siege also revealed the Belgians' refusal to bow to German demands and their determination to carry on fighting on the Allied side.

After the German invasion of Belgium, most of the Belgian army fell back to the fortress city of Antwerp. Although the German First Army had bypassed it in favor of the advance across Belgium and into France, the Belgian troops in the city were a thorn in the German side. When it became clear that a great victory over France had eluded Germany at the Battle of the Marne, General Helmuth von Moltke redeployed his forces to eliminate this nuisance. General Hans von Beseler's III Reserve Corps—chosen to attack Antwerp—contained only five understrength divisions, but had been reinforced with 173 heavy artillery pieces. These included the superheavy howitzers that had proved so effective against Liège and Namur.

On 28 September, German artillery began to systematically engage and destroy the outer forts that protected Antwerp. The British, fearful that the loss of Antwerp might be the first step in the conquest of the Channel ports, agreed to the Belgian request for reinforcements and began to land naval infantry, with the promise that the newly formed 7th Division would follow.

As the Germans closed in, the Belgian commanders decided to abandon the city. On 7 October, before the British 7th Division had even set off, the Belgians transferred their forces from Antwerp to Ostend to continue the fight in open terrain. Two days later, German troops entered the city; the siege was over. **AG**

Losses: Allied, 30,000 casualties (mainly captured) of 150,000; German, unknown of 66,000

◁ *First Aisne 1914*   *First Ypres 1914* ▷

"I think everything will be all right now, Mr. Burgomaster. You needn't worry. We are going to save the city." Winston Churchill, arriving in Antwerp

⬆ *Soldiers of the Belgian infantry make a hasty retreat from their trenches at Antwerp (detail).*

First Ypres 19 October–22 November 1914

The German failure to break the Allied lines in desperate fighting at Ypres was the final episode in the 1914 campaign in the west. It marked the end of the war of movement, with both sides constructing an elaborate trench network that stretched from Switzerland to the North Sea.

The tactical stalemate at the Battle of the Aisne made German and Allied commanders look elsewhere for the decisive battle. Both sides began a series of outflanking maneuvers, progressing northward to the Belgian coast. Later dubbed the "race to the sea," the rapid deployment of reserves by both the Germans and the French prevented the possibility of a breakthrough by either side.

While the fighting spread northward through France, the Belgian army took up defensive positions along the River Yser, which then formed the northernmost section of the Allied line. As the area around the Yser had been flooded by the Belgians on 24 October, the advancing Germans looked to the open countryside farther south—

> ## "One was not a soldier unless he had served on the Ypres front."
>
> *British soldier Private Donald Fraser*

around the old cloth town of Ypres, in order to make a significant strategic thrust toward the Channel ports.

Reinforced by troops from England, the British Expeditionary Force (BEF) had been ferried by rail north to Flanders, and on 12 October began to take up positions around Béthune, Armentières, and Ypres. Alongside the BEF was the French Tenth Army, and, under the energetic leadership of General Ferdinand Foch, the Allied forces advanced eastward, unaware that the German Fourth and Sixth Armies were marching on Ypres from the other

direction. In the fighting that followed, the Allies were desperately short of artillery and were forced onto the defensive. The Germans had the advantage of superior numbers, although many of their divisions were reserve formations whose recruits were either older men or student volunteers lacking in military training.

A series of attacks made by the Germans from 20 October onward rocked the Allied line, but the close-quarters fighting favored the defenders, the troops of the BEF taking their toll of the attackers with rapid and accurate rifle fire. German attacks were followed by Allied counterattacks to regain ground lost to the enemy, and casualties were correspondingly heavy. The Germans called the losses inflicted on the student volunteers the *Kindermord*, or "the slaughter of the innocents."

The Germans attacked again on 29 October and almost forced the Allies back to Ypres itself. Although the Allied line was stabilized through the judicious use of reserves, most of the high ground around Ypres now lay in German hands, making the city all the more vulnerable to enemy observation and artillery fire. Aware of the vulnerability of Ypres, now surrounded on three sides by the Germans, Foch began to prepare an Allied attack. Timed for 6 November, the Allied plan was forestalled by a resumption of German offensive action on 5 November. The Germans attacked with desperate fury, and twelve crack German divisions were thrown into the battle on 11 November. Although the Allied line was broken in the Menin Road area, the Germans were unable to exploit this success. The fighting died down as winter began to set in; both sides were completely exhausted. For the small BEF, composed of prewar regular soldiers, casualties had been disproportionately heavy, and the battle became known as "the graveyard of the old British Army." **AG**

Losses: Allied, 126,000 casualties; German, 134,000 casualties

◀ *Antwerp 1914*   *Neuve Chapelle 1915* ▶

Troops of the 1st Cameronians at the Houplines Sector in Belgium near Ypres on 18 November 1914. ➡

Coronel 1 November 1914

Although the main British and German naval forces were concentrated in their home waters in 1914, ships based in Tsingtao—Germany's colony in China—set out across the Pacific to attack British trade. They met and defeated an inferior British force off the coast of Chile.

Admiral Maximilian von Spee, commanding Germany's Far Eastern Squadron, had to abandon his base at Tsingtao (modern Qindao) soon after war began, because it was sure to be attacked by Japan's full strength (Japan was allied with Britain). One ship, *Emden*, operated independently, but Spee retained two armored cruisers and three light cruisers. Spee tried to make his way secretly across the Pacific, but an intercepted radio message revealed he was headed for the South American coast. The nearest British force was sent to stop him.

Admiral Christopher Cradock had available an obsolete battleship, two equally old armored cruisers, a light cruiser, and an ill-armed auxiliary. The battleship, outdated as it was, would have outgunned the German ships easily, but Cradock hurried on without it, because it was so slow.

The two squadrons met in the late afternoon of 1 November 1914, some 50 miles (80 km) from the Chilean port of Coronel. The German ships had far more long-range gunpower, and the British were to the west of their opponents, silhouetted against the setting sun. This made them easy targets for the Germans, while the British had to try and aim into the gloom. The two British armored cruisers became battered sinking wrecks within an hour, although the supporting ships were ordered to escape and managed to do so. Shocked at this humiliating defeat, the British authorities deployed new and much more powerful units to hunt down Spee. **DS**

Losses: British, 1,600 dead, 2 armored cruisers sunk; German, 5 wounded

◁ *Heligoland Bight 1914*　　　　*Cocos Islands 1914* ▷

The British armored cruiser HMS Monmouth *was sunk at the Battle of Coronel.* ⬆

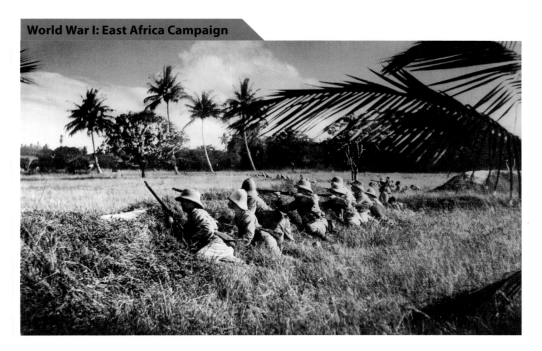

Tanga   2–5 November 1914

In the opening battle in German East Africa (Tanzania) during World War I, an amphibious landing at Tanga ended in total fiasco for the British. Failure to secure the harbor as a base for future operations ended hopes that the German colony would be occupied quickly.

With few troops available in East Africa, Major General Arthur Aitken sailed from Bombay with Indian Expeditionary Force "B." Unfortunately, this command included many poorly trained men. Little intelligence existed regarding German forces, and Aitken chose to ignore advice from men with local knowledge. In addition, the element of surprise was sacrificed when a local truce led to the farce of a British naval officer informing the Germans of the coming attack. This allowed the German commander, Lieutenant Colonel Paul von Lettow-Vorbeck, to reinforce his small, predominantly African Schutztruppe force at Tanga.

Aitken's landing on 2 October was checked by German machine gun fire just east of the town. On 4 October, he attempted a large-scale assault. Indian troops ran into massed rifle and machine gun fire, and casualties were heavy. Lettow-Vorbeck then launched a counterattack. African porters accompanying Indian units fled. Mistaking these men for Schutztruppe, panic spread through a number of regiments, and the Indian attack collapsed. At no time was artillery or naval gunfire called upon to support the assault. With his force totally disorganized, Aitken embarked his men the next day. Even then, chaos ensued when troops abandoned equipment as they ran for the boats. After the battle, Aitken was relieved of his command, and Lettow-Vorbeck went on to wage one of the most successful guerrilla campaigns in history. **AW**

Losses: British-Indian, more than 800 of 8,000; German, 60 of 1,100

Mahiwa 1917 ▸

Soldiers of the Schutztruppe force in a skirmish line during the encounter at Tanga.

Cocos Islands 9 November 1914

While the rest of Germany's Far Eastern Squadron was heading for Coronel, the light cruiser *Emden* was sent to attack British trade in the Indian Ocean. Some two months later, after spectacular successes, *Emden* met the Australian cruiser *Sydney* near the Cocos Islands and was sunk.

While Admiral von Spee took his squadron across the Pacific in August 1914, Captain von Müller and the light cruiser *Emden* headed for the Indian Ocean. In less than two months, *Emden* sank seventeen merchant ships and captured others, using them as colliers and to transport the crews of the other ships to safety. Müller was always scrupulous about treating his prisoners well and was later much praised for this by former captives. British trade in the Indian Ocean was brought to a standstill for several weeks.

In addition to these achievements, *Emden* bombarded the port of Madras (now Chennai) in India, a humiliation for British power even if little material damage was caused. Naturally, various British, French, Russian, and even Japanese warships were hunting for *Emden*, but without success. Instead, on 28 October, *Emden* attacked Penang in Malaya, sinking an ancient Russian cruiser and a French destroyer.

In November, Müller headed for the Cocos Islands in the eastern Indian Ocean in order to attack the British radio station there. Unfortunately for the Germans, an Australian troop convoy was nearby and one of its escorts was sent to investigate an alarm message. HMAS *Sydney* was much more powerful than *Emden*, and their battle could have only one result. In little more than an hour of firing, *Emden* was a battered wreck and had been run aground to stop it sinking. **DS**

Losses: Australian, 10 dead or wounded; German, 200 dead or wounded, 1 light cruiser and 1 supply ship sunk

⟨ *Coronel 1914*   *Falklands 1914* ⟩

The severely damaged light cruiser Emden: *Müller and his crew were made prisoners of war.* ⬆

Falklands   8 December 1914

After the German victory at Coronel the previous month, Admiral von Spee planned to destroy the British coaling station at Port Stanley on East Falkland in the South Atlantic. Spee found a much superior British force in port as he approached. Within hours he was dead.

Coronel had been Britain's worst naval defeat for more than a century. Among the forces deployed to seek revenge was a squadron led by two battle cruisers—*Invincible* and *Inflexible*—vastly more powerful and considerably faster than Spee's principal ships, *Scharnhorst* and *Gneisenau*.

As the Germans came in sight of Port Stanley on the morning of 8 December 1914, they quickly realized that they had sailed into trouble and turned away at full speed to try to escape. All too soon for the Germans, the British were leaving harbor and gathering speed to chase. Conditions were clear, and the British had most of the day to catch up. By early afternoon, Spee accepted escape was impossible and turned back with his two slower big ships, while ordering his three faster light cruisers to flee. British Admiral Sturdee sent his five cruisers after the smaller German ships (two were sunk later and one escaped) and faced Spee with his two battle cruisers.

The British gunnery was poor, and the Germans maneuvered skillfully so that it took much of the afternoon before the British made telling hits. Eventually, however, the big British shells struck home. Both German armored cruisers were sunk before about 6:00 PM, with few survivors. The defeat at Coronel had been avenged—even the German escapee from the battle, *Dresden*, was caught and destroyed while hiding in Chilean waters three months later. **DS**

Losses: British, 10 dead, no ships sunk; German, 100 dead or captured, 2 armored cruisers and 2 light cruisers sunk

⟨ *Cocos Islands 1914*   *Dogger Bank 1915* ⟩

⬆ *A view from the bow of* Scharnhorst *in rough seas during the Battle of the Falklands.*

Dogger Bank 24 January 1915

Dogger Bank was a naval battle of World War I in which British and German battle cruisers clashed in the central North Sea. The weaker German force fled for home, but poor British leadership meant that the battle ended prematurely when a more decisive victory might have been possible.

The first months of World War I had been marked by minor clashes in the North Sea, but in January 1915, Germany planned a new raid. The British were forewarned by naval intelligence picking up German radio signals.

Admiral Beatty's British force had five battle cruisers; Admiral Hipper had three, plus an older ship, *Blücher.* Battle cruisers carried the heaviest guns but traded higher speed for reduced armor protection. Both sides had numerous supporting cruisers and destroyers. The two fleets met to the east of the Dogger Bank on 24 January.

Realizing he was outnumbered, Hipper turned back toward his base and a high-speed chase ensued.

After two hours of firing, *Blücher* was badly damaged and dropping behind the other German ships; at the same time Beatty's own ship, *Lion*, was hit and had to slow down. Beatty signaled his other ships to keep chasing Hipper's main force but was misunderstood. His second-in-command followed what he thought were orders to finish off *Blücher*, and the rest of the Germans escaped.

Poor British command prevented a decisive encounter but—given the inadequate British gunnery and damage control confirmed at Jutland—it is far from certain that Britain would have won the battle if it had continued. **DS**

Losses: British, 50 dead or wounded, no ships; German, 1,100 dead or captured, 1 armored cruiser sunk

◁ *Falklands 1914*   *Jutland 1916* ▷

Second Masurian Lakes 7–22 February 1915

In a winter offensive on the Eastern Front in World War I, German Generals Hindenburg and Ludendorff intended to crush the Russians and force them out of the war. They once again won a great victory, but still failed to achieve the decisive destruction for which they had hoped.

The German plan was to act with an Austrian offensive in the south to destroy the Russian armies in a great envelopment. The initial German objective was to advance from the north and south of the Angerapp Line, running through the Masurian Lakes, and encircle General Siever's Tenth Army. When the Russians were attacked from the south, they were taken completely by surprise. Two days later, with the Russians being pressed back but still capable of fighting a stubborn rearguard action at the town of Lyck, the German army to the north struck.

The Russians were in real danger, but were saved in part by a single—mainly Siberian—corps in the Augustow Forest, which fought a heroic rearguard action for nearly two weeks before it surrendered. This enabled the rest of the Tenth Army to make an orderly withdrawal, again defeated, but not destroyed. Reinforced by the Twelfth Army, they managed to launch a counterattack that effectively halted the German advance. Austrian forces in the south were repelled with heavy losses, and the great envelopment had failed. By the end of the year, the Russians were forced out of Poland, but without suffering the trouncing that Hindenburg and Ludendorff had desperately tried to inflict. **JS**

Losses: German, more than 16,000 dead or wounded; Russian, 56,000 dead or wounded, 100,000 prisoners

◁ *First Masurian Lakes 1914*   *Gorlice-Tarnow Offensive 1915* ▷

Neuve Chapelle 10–13 March 1915

In World War I, the British had high hopes when they mounted the first major offensive against the German trenches, believing that a breakthrough was a real possibility. However, initial success was followed by a series of reverses, setting a gloomy template for so many other battles on the Western Front.

After the heavy losses suffered at First Ypres, the British army remained on the defensive until March 1915 when a limited offensive action was proposed in support of the hard-pressed French forces. The British First Army, under the command of General Sir Douglas Haig, was chosen to make the attack at Neuve Chapelle. The battle plan—which made innovative use of aerial photography—was rehearsed in detail, and secrecy was preserved carefully.

On the morning of 10 March, the battle opened with a short, thirty-five-minute bombardment of the German front line. As the barrage moved forward, the fourteen battalions of the assault force advanced across no-man's-land and quickly overran the battered German front-line trenches. A breakthrough seemed possible, but, after the initial success, the advance began to slow down. German resistance, from isolated strong points, was greater than expected; local British commanders' uncertainty caused delays, and inexperienced British reinforcements were slow in crossing the battlefield. Above all, the breakdown of communications caused by severed telephone lines prevented the proper direction of the battle.

As the British advance slowed, so the Germans recovered. Their reinforcements were not sufficiently cut up by the British guns, and their artillery had little difficulty pinning down the British troops in their narrow bridgehead. The battle continued for three days, and although the British held the village they were unable to push on further. **AG**

Losses: British, 11,200 casualties of 40,000; German, 10,600 casualties

◁ First Ypres 1914   Second Ypres 1915 ▷

Troops in rudimentary trenches at Neuve Chapelle. ⬆

Dardanelles 18 March 1915

In an attempt to knock Germany's ally, Turkey, out of World War I and to open a supply route across the Black Sea to Russia's large but poorly equipped armies, Britain and France planned a naval attack on the Dardanelles Straits en route to the Turkish capital of Constantinople.

The Allied plan was to use warships to force a way through the straits linking the Aegean to the Sea of Marmara. It was assumed that the appearance of a fleet of Allied warships at Constantinople (modern Istanbul) would force a Turkish capitulation, with great benefit to the overall Allied war effort.

The operation was plagued by inept planning and command. The Turks had a series of minefields in the Dardanelles Straits between the Gallipoli peninsula and Asia Minor, with gun batteries covering them, and they were given plenty of warning to strengthen these defenses. When the attack got under way in February 1915, it was carried out with little urgency. The British Admiral Carden (later replaced by John de Robeck) had ample firepower, with sixteen British and French battleships; but, crucially, his minesweepers had unreliable civilian crews, who were reluctant to take the risks their job required.

The Turkish outer defenses were neutralized gradually, and on 18 March, de Robeck advanced with almost his entire force to clear the minefields and batteries at the Narrows, the final barrier to an Allied breakthrough. Turkish gunfire was fierce but was being subdued (unknown to the Allies the Turks were running out of ammunition) when the French battleship *Bouvet* struck a mine, sinking in minutes, with the death of most of the 674 men on board. Panic developed as more Allied ships blundered into the minefield. Six battleships were sunk or badly damaged, and the naval attack was abandoned. **DS**

Losses: Allied, 3 battleships sunk; Turkish, unknown

Gallipoli Landings 1915 >|

⬆ *The Anglo-French fleet maneuver into line at the entrance to the Dardanelles Straits.*

Celaya 13–15 April 1915

The crushing defeat of Pancho Villa's Army of the North at Celaya, against Venustiano Carranza's Constitutionalists, was largely due to the tactical brilliance of General Alvaro Obregón. The battle, which saw some of the fiercest fighting of the Mexican Revolution, signified the end of Villa as a major political force.

By late 1914, Pancho Villa and Venustiano Carranza had become rivals in the struggle for power in Mexico. This rivalry peaked in April 1915, at Celaya, where Villa led his Army of the North against Carranza's Constitutionalists, commanded by General Alvaro Obregón. Despite suffering defeat to Obregón at Celaya one week earlier, Villa launched a new offensive on 13 April.

Villa's force of 20,000 men heavily outnumbered Obregón's 11,000 troops. Confident of a swift victory, Villa ordered his cavalry to launch a frontal charge—a tactic that had brought him success previously.

Obregón, however, was prepared for such an attack. He ordered his forces to dig trenches and put up barbed wire fences. As Villa's men tried to advance, through the barbed wire, Obregón's forces mowed them down with machine guns, inflicting heavy casualties. Obregón then launched a counterattack, using a pincer movement to envelop Villa's forces and secure a decisive victory.

The defeat was devastating for Villa. His forces suffered huge losses, and they also lost large numbers of horses, cannons, and rifles to the Constitutionalists. Celaya was a turning point in the Mexican Revolution because the defeat ended Villa's political influence and Obregón's military brilliance led the United States to recognize Carranza as president of Mexico. **ND**

Losses: Army of the North, 3,000 dead, 5,000 wounded, 6,000 captured of 20,000; Constitutionalist, 200 casualties of 11,000

◁ *Veracruz 1914*　　　　　　　*Columbus 1916* ▷

　　　　　Carranza's forces display guns captured from Pancho Villa's adherents. ⬆

Second Ypres   22 April–25 May 1915

In World War I, the Second Battle of Ypres was notable for the introduction of a new and deadly weapon by the German army on the Western Front: poison gas. Initially, it seemed that the Allies had no choice but to give way; thanks to the extraordinary bravery of the Anglo-Canadian forces, the Allied line remained unbroken.

To divert Allied intentions from their spring offensive on the Eastern Front, the Germans launched a limited attack against the Ypres salient, held by the British Second Army and two second-line French divisions. The German offensive came as an unwelcome surprise to the Allies, but the nature of the assault was an even greater shock.

On 22 April, after some heavy shelling, a bluish-white mist was seen drifting toward the Allied line on the north side of the salient. This was a cloud of chlorine gas, discharged from cylinders against a section of the front held by an Algerian and a French territorial division. Those who inhaled the gas in large quantities died painful deaths; the remainder fled in panic, many choking and gasping horrendously.

By the end of the evening, a dangerous gap of more than 4 miles (6.4 km) had opened up in the Allied line; fortunately for the Allies, the advancing German troops were reluctant to move into the gas cloud (despite wearing gas masks). At a higher level, the German commanders, not anticipating such an early success, failed to develop their initial advantage. The gap was plugged by Canadian and British troops, who suffered heavy casualties in the process. Over the next few weeks, the Germans delivered a succession of attacks, using gas and artillery, and although the Allies were forced to give ground, the Ypres salient held firm. **AG**

Losses: Allied, 70,000 casualties; German, 35,000–40,000 casualties

◁ *Neuve Chapelle 1915*   *Artois-Loos 1915* ▷

Troops of the Liverpool Scottish, 3rd Division, attack Bellewaerde Farm, north of Hooge in the Ypres salient.

Gallipoli Landings   25 April 1915

After the failed attack on the Dardanelles, the British planned landings on the Gallipoli peninsula to revive their efforts to knock Turkey out of World War I. Proponents of the operation hoped to win a cheap but decisive victory; instead they got a bloody stalemate.

While the naval engagements of February and March 1915 were being fought, Britain and France were assembling troops in the eastern Mediterranean to support an attack on Turkey. When the naval commanders reported, after the 18 March operations, that they could not force their way through to Constantinople on their own, Allied leaders decided to make landings on the Gallipoli peninsula. These would clear away the Turkish gun batteries so that the fleet could advance as originally planned. Preparations were slow, and security was nonexistent. The Turks knew that landings were coming—even if they did not know the exact site of the attack—and were given ample time to improve their defenses.

> *"I do not expect you to attack, I order you to die. . . . [Others can] take our places."*
>
> *Mustafa Kemal*

The Allied force included British, Australian, New Zealand, and French troops, under the overall command of the British General Sir Ian Hamilton. Hamilton was an intelligent and cultured man, but lacked drive. His opposite number, General Liman von Sanders, was an able German officer seconded to the Turkish forces, and among his subordinates was the inspirational Mustafa Kemal, in later years Turkey's national leader. Hamilton planned landings in two sectors: a mainly British force on several beaches around Cape Helles at the southern tip of Gallipoli, and an ANZAC (Australian and New Zealand Army Corps) force near Gaba Tepe on the western side of the peninsula. The attack began on 25 April and almost from the outset degenerated into a mixture of bloodbath and near farce.

The ANZAC landings were swept off course on the approach and came ashore north of their intended spot. They then had to advance inland into a maze of barren ravines and jagged ridges. They nearly reached dominating positions on the highest ground but were met and held by virtually suicidal attacks by Kemal's troops. At Cape Helles, the two main landing beaches were well-defended, and the attacking forces suffered dreadful casualties. They were, nonetheless, strongly reinforced by their inept commander, General Hunter-Weston, and eventually gained a foothold ashore. By contrast, troops landing at a subsidiary location met negligible resistance. If they had advanced aggressively, they could have cut off many of the Turkish defenders and perhaps won the battle; instead they stopped to brew a morning cup of tea, and the opportunity slipped away.

By the end of the day, the Allied forces had established their two beachheads, but in subsequent months of ferocious fighting they never came close to advancing far from these to achieve the campaign's objectives. Instead, a nastier version of the Western Front's trench warfare developed, with even less scope for maneuver, and all under a baking Mediterranean sun.

Hamilton tried to get the advance going again, including making new landings at Suvla Bay in August. When these failed to end the stalemate, he was finally relieved, and Allied leaders decided to abandon the campaign. The troops were evacuated in December 1915 and January 1916 in a remarkably successful operation, with negligible casualties. **DS**

Losses: Allied, 6,500 in the first phase of fighting; Turkish, probably similar but unknown

◁ Dardanelles 1915   Lone Pine 1915 ▷

An Australian soldier carries a wounded comrade at Gallipoli. ➔

Gorlice-Tarnow Offensive 2 May–18 September 1915

A combined German and Austrian offensive on the Eastern Front in World War I resulted in a great victory and drove the Russians out of Poland. The Germans and Austrians failed to destroy the Russians, but the political consequences of the campaign would prove fatal to the Romanov dynasty.

The German plan was not as overambitious as Second Masurian Lakes. Instead of a single great encirclement of all the Russian armies, the Germans would break through on several points, and encircle and annihilate Russian forces piecemeal. The Russians were weary, dispirited, and suffering severe supply problems—in some units one-third of the men had no rifle. German General Mackensen's newly created Eleventh Army prepared its attack between Gorlice and Tarnow in great secrecy and achieved complete surprise. As the infantry went in, following an intense barrage, some dazed Russians cut their own wire to facilitate their surrender, and the Russian position rapidly collapsed.

The Germans and Austrians advanced 10 miles (16 km) a day, and it seemed that the Russians were doomed. However, confusion did not reign everywhere. Some units escaped encirclement, often at a terrible cost. The Russian commander, Grand Duke Nicholas, managed to extricate the bulk of his forces skillfully enough, and the Germans and Austrians could not maintain the momentum of the offensive indefinitely. Their exhaustion and extended supply lines meant that the Russians were able to stabilize the lines by autumn. However, the emperor, Nicholas II, took the fateful step of assuming supreme command: henceforth, he would be personally and directly responsible for all the losses and failures of his armies. **JS**

"The Eleventh Army's attack must be carried forward with all speed, if it is to fulfill its assignment."

General Mackensen's "Guiding Orders"

⬆ *Wounded Russian soldiers are transported by truck from the battlefield at Gorlice (detail).*

Losses: German and Austro-Hungarian, 90,000 dead or wounded; Russian, estimates vary, possibly 240,000 dead or wounded, 750,000 captured

◁ *Second Masurian Lakes 1915*   *Brusilov Offensive 1916* ▷

Suvla Bay 6–21 August 1915

Allied troops attacked repeatedly to extend the beachheads at Anzac Cove and Cape Helles that they had taken in the early stages of the World War I Gallipoli landings—but without success. The final serious attempt to break the deadlock was from new landings at Suvla Bay in August 1915.

By June 1915, it was apparent that the Allied forces at Gallipoli were unable to make any significant advance against the Turkish defense. The British government decided to send reinforcements to try to get a worthwhile offensive going, building on an existing ANZAC plan for an attack toward the commanding Sari Bahr ridge. Operations from Anzac Cove had always been hamstrung by the beachhead's limited size so the new divisions were to land at Suvla Bay to the north and advance from there.

Unfortunately, few lessons had been learned from the catalog of errors that had accompanied the April landings. General Sir Ian Hamilton was still in overall command and again failed to ensure that his subordinates had clear orders or were properly briefed about all parts of the operation. Again an utterly incompetent general was in direct control of the Allied landing force.

On 6 to 7 August, 20,000 British troops landed at Suvla, facing scarcely 1,000 Turks. They made little attempt to advance from the beach until late on 8 August, by which time Turkish reinforcements had arrived. The advance was a bloody failure. Fruitless attacks over the next few days culminated in the Battle of Scimitar Hill on 21 August. Inadequate artillery preparations meant that what were essentially uphill frontal attacks had little chance of success. Any prospect of the Gallipoli landings attaining their objectives disappeared with this failure. **DS**

Losses: At least 20,000 on each side

◁ Gallipoli Landings 1915

Lone Pine 1915 ▷

Lone Pine 6–10 August 1915

The Battle of Lone Pine exemplified the courage and skills of Australian troops engaged at Gallipoli. Conceived as a diversionary attack on a quiet sector of the Turkish trenches, Lone Pine developed into a ferocious close-quarters engagement in which seven Australians earned the Victoria Cross.

Brigadier General Harold Walker, commander of 1st Australian Brigade, had no desire to assault well-constructed Turkish trenches as a sideshow to the concurrent landings at Suvla Bay, but his soldiers were keen for action. Much was done to help the Australians cross the 100 yards (91 m) to the Turkish front line successfully. Preliminary bombardment destroyed the Turkish barbed wire; tunnels were dug into no-man's-land to provide a forward jumping-off point, and mines were exploded between the lines to break up the ground and create at least some form of cover.

At 5:00 PM on 6 August, whistles signaled the beginning of the assault. The Australians reached the front-line Turkish trench with light losses, but were startled to find it roofed over with wooden beams and earth. While some soldiers tried to break through, others jumped into uncovered communication trenches. By nightfall, the Australians held part of the Turkish trench system, but they had to defend these gains against determined counterattacks. A vicious battle developed in the warren of trenches, with grenades a principal weapon, sometimes thrown back and forth three times before exploding. Evacuation of the wounded was near impossible; many died where they lay.

By 10 August, the Australians were in control of the trenches, but their success had no strategic significance, and the overall stalemate remained unbroken. **RG**

Losses: Australian, 2,273 dead or wounded; Turkish, 6,390 dead or wounded

◁ Suvla Bay 1915

Artois-Loos 25 September–4 November 1915

The Anglo-French attack was designed to tie down German forces and, if possible, achieve a breakthrough in World War I. It proved a miserable failure for the Allies, however, causing the British commander in chief, Field Marshal Sir John French, to be replaced by General Sir Douglas Haig.

This attack in the Artois sector of the Western Front (known as the Third Battle of Artois to the French) was designed to support the main French offensive, which was taking place farther south (Second Champagne). The French Tenth Army, under the command of General August Dubail, launched an attack on the Vimy Ridge but was repulsed with heavy losses. A number of small territorial gains were made, including the capture of Souchez, but, overall, the French were able to make little impression on the German line. Once the strength of the German defenses became clear to the French, the offensive was abandoned.

The British part of the attack was directed around the village of Loos, to the left of the French assault. The British were short of heavy artillery, and although they used gas dischargers for the first time, these proved ineffective because the gas blew back on the British trenches. Whereas the French were at fault for having their reserves too close to the front, meaning that they were caught by German artillery, the British held their reserves too far back. The result was that early British gains were lost, and the battle degenerated into basic trench fighting in which the Germans held the advantage. Reserves were drawn from the new Kitchener army divisions—inexperienced and somewhat disorganized—and, for them, Loos was a painful baptism of fire. The offensive was renewed on 13 October, but the well-prepared Germans had little difficulty in repelling the British attacks. **AG**

Losses: British, 48,000; French, 40,000; German, 51,000

[<] *Second Ypres 1915*   *Verdun 1916* [>]

The effects of a British gas attack, as photographed by a soldier of the London Rifle Brigade.

Kut   7 December 1915–29 April 1916

In October 1914, the British sent an expeditionary force from India to occupy Basra in Mesopotamia, part of the Ottoman Turkish Empire. A division commanded by Major General Charles Townshend was trapped at Kut al-Amara and forced to surrender after a siege lasting 147 days.

Townshend's Anglo-Indian forces took Kut al-Amara in September 1915. They advanced by river north toward Baghdad but, after a drawn battle at Ctesiphon, fell back to Kut and dug in. The pursuing Ottoman army encircled the British position with earthworks. Their commander, German veteran Field Marshal Wilhelm von der Goltz, correctly expected British forces from Basra to try to relieve the siege and set up defense along the Tigris River.

Between January and April 1916, the British made several attempts to break through to Townshend in Kut. General Fenton Aylmer led the first effort in January, fighting three battles—at Sheikh Sa'ad, the Wadi, and the

Hanna defile—in which his forces suffered thousands of casualties for no effective gain. Aylmer waited for reinforcements to arrive before relaunching his relief attempt in March with an assault on the Dujaila redoubt. Once again repulsed, with the loss of more than 3,000 men, Aylmer was replaced by General George Gorringe. The new commander, further reinforced to a strength of around 30,000, led a determined assault on 5 April, but a series of attacks and counterattacks ended with the last British effort blocked at Sannaiyat on 22 April.

With all hope of relief fading and food supplies running low, Townshend surrendered Kut on 29 April. The Turks captured 12,000 British and Indian soldiers, of whom half would die in captivity. It took another eleven months before British forces captured Baghdad. **TB**

Losses: British and Indian, 17,000 casualties, 12,000 captured; Ottoman, 10,000 casualties of 40,000

Gaza 1917 ☐

⬆ *The British load a barge on the Tigris as the Siege of Kut draws to an end.*

Verdun   21 February–18 December 1916

France's epic defense of the old fortress city of Verdun was perhaps the bloodiest and certainly the longest battle of World War I. Some 40 million artillery shells were fired during the battle, which was a deliberately attritional operation, planned by German General Erich von Falkenhayn to "bleed France to death."

After their limited attack at Ypres in April 1915, the Germans adopted a defensive position on the Western Front. However, in February 1916, the German High Command went over to the offensive. Falkenhayn, the German chief of staff, decided to strike a mortal blow against the French army, which had already been weakened by almost two million casualties since the outbreak of war. Instead of attempting a breakthrough, Falkenhayn planned to inflict maximum losses by attacking a section of the line the French felt compelled to defend, regardless of casualties.

The salient around the fortress of Verdun was chosen as the killing ground; not only was it of strong emotional

> *"The enemy nowhere secured any permanent advantages; nowhere could he free himself from the German pressure."* Erich von Falkenhayn

value to the French, but also it allowed the Germans to bring the maximum amount of artillery to bear on the defenders. Artillery would act as the cornerstone of the German plan; limited attacks by infantry would seize key points in order to suck in French reserves for the "grinding mill" of the German guns.

On 21 February 1916, the 1,200 guns (more than half of heavy caliber) of the German Fifth Army opened their bombardment, the most devastating yet in warfare. Later in the day, assault groups of German infantry advanced into the shattered French trenches. Over the next few days, the Germans advanced steadily and captured the stronghold of Fort Douamont on 25 February.

The French High Command had been caught by surprise, but on the same day that Fort Douamont fell, General Philippe Pétain was appointed to command the French Second Army defending Verdun. Pétain was an excellent tactician. He also had a reputation for caring about his men and immediately set about organizing the supply, reinforcement, and relief of the hard-pressed troops. The only route into Verdun was under constant artillery fire—along "La Voie Sacrée" (the sacred way)—but 3,000 trucks a day persevered and brought men and munitions to defend Verdun.

Throughout March, April, and May, the battle raged with undiminished intensity. Falkenhayn extended the width of the battle zone, and during April and May the Germans waged bitter battles for possession of the hills and ridges on the east bank of the Meuse. Much of the fighting was concentrated around the aptly named spur "Mort Homme" (dead man). For the troops on both sides, the "hell of Verdun" almost developed into a way of life.

To the consternation of the Germans, they too found that their troops were going through the grinding mill. On 1 July 1916, the Allied offensive on the Somme forced the Germans to close down their operations at Verdun. At the end of the month, the French went over to the offensive and, in a series of ferocious counterattacks, won back most of the territory lost to the Germans earlier in the year. While a battered French army hung on to Verdun, the instigator of the German plan, Falkenhayn, was sacked and replaced by the successful team of General Paul von Hindenburg and General Erich Ludendorff, fresh from their victories on the Eastern Front. **AG**

Losses: French, possibly 500,000 casualties; German, possibly 425,000 casualties

◁ *Artois-Loos 1915*   *Fort Vaux 1916* ▷

French troops come under intense artillery fire on the battlefield at Verdun. ➜

Columbus   8–9 March 1916

In need of supplies during the Mexican Revolution, Pancho Villa led his men in a raid across the border into the United States, at Columbus. The raid quickly escalated into a full-scale battle when they encountered the U.S. cavalry. After sustaining huge losses, Villa was forced to retreat to Mexico.

By late 1915, Pancho Villa had lost much of the widespread support he had enjoyed at the start of the Mexican Revolution. Having lost a series of battles, Villa and the remaining 500 soldiers of his Army of the North were desperate for food, horses, and weapons.

In March 1916, Villa planned a raid on the military garrison in the U.S. town of Columbus, New Mexico. The small town lay only a couple of miles across the border. Villa sent spies to gather information, and they returned to report that the garrison consisted of only fifty men. On the night of 8 to 9 March, Villa led the Army of the North into Columbus and attacked the garrison. Villa's men also

began looting and setting fire to houses in the town. However, rather than the fifty U.S. soldiers that Villa had expected, there were actually 350 soldiers, including the 13th U.S. Cavalry, stationed at the garrison.

The raid quickly became a fierce battle when U.S. troops, led by Lieutenant Ralph Lucas, fought back from the garrison with machine guns. A second detachment of U.S. soldiers, commanded by Lieutenant James Castleman, launched a counterattack, which forced Villa and his men to retreat. They were pursued by U.S. cavalrymen back across the border into Mexico. The raid was a disaster, with Villa's forces suffering huge casualties. In response to the attack, U.S. forces later invaded Mexico at Carrizal, in an attempt to capture Villa. **ND**

Losses: Army of the North, 190 casualties of 500; U.S., 7 dead, 5 wounded of 350, plus 8 civilians dead, 2 civilians wounded

◁ *Celaya 1915*

A U.S. soldier remains on duty after the Mexican raid on Columbus leaves the town in disarray.

Easter Rising   24–29 April 1916

Although about 100,000 Irish Catholics served as volunteers in the British army in World War I, Irish Republicans saw the war as an opportunity to throw off British rule. Their uprising at Easter 1916 was a military failure but triggered the collapse of Britain's political grasp on southern Ireland.

The uprising was planned by the Irish Republican Brotherhood (IRB), led by Padraic Pearse, and James Connolly's Citizen's Army. Germany sent a shipload of rifles to arm the insurgents, but through a misunderstanding no one met the ship when it arrived and on Good Friday it was scuttled. The rebel leadership split, but on Easter Monday, 24 April, about 1,300 IRB and 300 Citizen's Army members, with rifles and shotguns, occupied buildings in Dublin, and Pearse read out a florid proclamation on behalf of a provisional government of the Irish Republic.

The British had few soldiers in Dublin and rushed to move in troops in force. The British commander,

Major General William Lowe, used artillery to bombard Republican-held buildings, especially the General Post Office, despite the loss of civilian life this entailed. On 26 April, British reinforcements suffered heavy losses fighting their way across Mount Street Bridge.

Meanwhile, confused by orders and counterorders, Republicans outside Dublin remained largely passive. The city's population, unprepared for the uprising, was mostly indifferent or supportive of the authorities. On 29 April, Pearse announced a surrender. In the aftermath of the uprising, fifteen leaders of the rebellion, including Pearse and Connolly, were executed after secret trial by British military courts. This blood sacrifice transformed them into heroes of the Irish people. **RG**

Losses: British, 132 dead, 400 wounded of 17,000; Irish, 64 dead, 120 wounded of 1,600, plus 300 civilians dead, 2,000 civilians wounded

◁ *Vinegar Hill 1798*   *Four Courts 1922* ▷

⬆ *The devastation was widespread in Dublin's main thoroughfare, Sackville Street, after the Easter Rising.*

Jutland   31 May 1916

Jutland was the only full-scale battle between the British and German fleets in World War I. British naval tradition demanded a victory as crushing as Trafalgar. Instead, after an indecisive clash, the outnumbered Germans fled, never to contest Britain's battle fleet superiority again.

In the prewar arms race, Britain and Germany had built massive fleets in anticipation of great naval battles. Britain won the shipbuilding race and remained paramount in the world's oceans, although its trade would come under increasing attack from Germany's submarine force. If Germany's main High Seas Fleet was to influence events, it had to find a way of whittling down the superior strength of the British Grand Fleet in battles in the North Sea. The British commander, Admiral Jellicoe, was well aware that his superiority could be lost if he blundered into a mine or torpedo attack. He wanted to bring the Germans to battle and destroy them, but he also knew, as Winston Churchill commented, that he could "lose the war in an afternoon."

"The German gunnery was always good at the start . . . it would have been very bad tactics to give them an initial advantage." Admiral Jellicoe

In late May 1916, Germany's Admiral Scheer planned a sortie toward Norway, hoping to lure part of the British fleet into a trap. In fact, the Germans had little chance of achieving the surprise they needed because the British could decipher many of the German radio messages, although poor organization in London meant that this information was not analyzed and distributed properly. Both fleets were at sea in full strength when their scouting forces made contact in the afternoon of 31 May near the Jutland Bank in the eastern North Sea. Jellicoe had some 150 ships, including twenty-eight battleships and nine battle cruisers; Scheer had just fewer than one hundred ships, with sixteen modern battleships, six old battleships, and five battle cruisers. With this disparity in numbers, a prolonged gunnery duel could have only one outcome.

The battle cruiser fleets were the first major units to come into contact. Germany's Admiral Hipper turned away from Britain's Admiral Beatty and lured the British toward Scheer's main force. When this fleet came in sight, Beatty in turn retreated toward Jellicoe's massed battleships. The Germans, unaware that the Grand Fleet was on the scene, blundered into a trap. Although Beatty and his subordinates had failed dismally to send Jellicoe proper information about the enemy deployment, Jellicoe still managed to maneuver into a prime position, ready to pound the German battle line into defeat.

After two brief exchanges of fire, the opportunity to win victory slipped away. Worried about mines and torpedoes, Jellicoe did not try to close in, and, in poor visibility and growing darkness, the two fleets drew apart. Even so, the British were now positioned between the Germans and their home base. Jellicoe hoped to finish the job in the morning, but the Germans managed to break through his patrol lines during the night and reach safety. Once again, Jellicoe's subordinates failed to report German movements; London knew where the Germans were going but did not tell him.

Germany had come off better in the various clashes; three British battle cruisers blew up because of dangerous ammunition-handling procedures, and poor British gunnery meant that fleeting opportunities were missed. In the end, though, a U.S. journalist's verdict summed up the battle: the German fleet had assaulted its jailer, but was still firmly in jail. **DS**

Losses: British, 6,784 casualties, 3 battle cruisers, 11 other ships; German, 3,039 casualties, 1 battle cruiser, 10 other ships
◁ *Dogger Bank 1915*

British battleships off the Jutland Bank, May 1916. ➜

Fort Vaux   31 May–7 June 1916

The French defense of Fort Vaux was a heroic episode in the battle for Verdun. The gallantry of French commander Major Raynal was recognized by the German crown prince, who chivalrously returned the Frenchman's sword after his capture.

The city of Verdun was protected by a circle of forts, one of which was Fort Vaux. Considered too old to withstand the latest heavy artillery, the fort had been dismantled and its guns withdrawn. However, as the German advance closed in on Verdun during May 1916, it once again became an important part of the French defensive line. At the end of May, the French High Command asked for otherwise incapacitated volunteer officers to take control of highly dangerous forward positions such as Fort Vaux. Major Sylvain-Eugène Raynal—recovering from his third serious wound—took command of Fort Vaux with a reinforced infantry company, well supplied with machine guns.

After a short but heavy bombardment, the Germans attacked and cut off the fort from the French lines. The fort was well stocked with food and ammunition, but the water supply was lower than had been thought. German infantry secured the roof of the fort and attempted to oust the defenders with grenades, flamethrowers, and poison gas. Lighting in the almost subterranean fort had failed, and the men battled in darkness with savage intensity. For the defenders, it was terrifying: pools of invisible gas collected in the lower parts of the fort, while above they were pounded with high explosives. Worse was to follow when the water ran out.

With his men literally starting to die of thirst, Raynal surrendered the fort on 7 June. But his heroic resistance was recognized by the Germans, who returned his sword and allowed captured soldiers to leave. **AG**

Losses: Unknown

◁ *Verdun 1916*   *Somme 1916* ▷

A French soldier outside Fort Vaux in 1916. ⬆

Brusilov Offensive   4 June–10 August 1916

At last the Russians had a capable commander, General Aleksei Brusilov. He inflicted a defeat on Austro-Hungarian forces from which their empire never recovered. Unfortunately, the Russians lacked the resources to exploit or repeat his success.

Brusilov was no military genius but possessed common sense and a willingness to learn from past failures. He also had an army that had recovered astonishingly quickly from the Gorlice-Tarnow defeat. Its troops were rested and supply problems eased. Where many Russian generals felt an offensive would be futile, Brusilov insisted that—with surprise and adequate preparation—it could succeed. His troops were trained in full-size replicas of the positions they were to attack, artillery was sighted using air reconnaissance, and secrecy was strictly maintained.

The blow, when it fell, appalled the Austrians who were unable to believe the Russians capable of such a massive assault. Russian shock troops led attacks that broke the Austrian lines on the first day. Soon the Austrians collapsed, and many Slav units, who had no love for their Hapsburg rulers, deserted en masse. So many Austrian guns were captured that Russian factories were converted to manufacture shells for them.

As Russian forces pushed into the Carpathian mountains, it appeared Austria-Hungary would collapse, and the emperor was forced to beg for German help. Russian commanders in the north did not maintain the pressure on the Germans that Brusilov expected, so the Germans were able to send assistance that stabilized the front. However, the blow to Hapsburg prestige was irreversible, especially among the Slav minorities. **JS**

Losses: Russian, 500,000–1,000,000 dead, wounded, or captured; Austrian, 1,000,000–1,500,000 dead, wounded, or captured

◁ *Gorlice-Tarnow Offensive 1915*   *Kostiuchnowka 1916* ▷

⬆ *Russian soldiers attack during the Brusilov Offensive.*

Somme 1 July–18 November 1916

The terrible casualties suffered by the British on the first day of the Somme battle—nearly 20,000 killed in one day—still have the power to shock, but in the months that followed the British army proved itself a capable fighting force that was able to learn from its mistakes.

Although the German attack on Verdun drew away French support from the proposed Allied offensive on the Somme, the assault still went ahead. With Douglas Haig as commander in chief, the British took the lead role. The main attack was made by the eleven divisions of the British Fourth Army, commanded by General Sir Henry Rawlinson, supported by five French divisions south of the Somme River. The British relied heavily on their enormously expanded artillery arm, which included more than 2,000 artillery pieces and substantial supplies of ammunition. In an eight-day preliminary bombardment, 1,732,873 shells were fired, sufficient to destroy the German defenses, in theory. However, the British did not have enough heavy-caliber guns; nearly a third of the shells fired were defective; and the German dugouts proved more shellproof than anticipated.

Confident that the guns had done their work, the British infantry went "over the top" in perfect order on the morning of 1 July 1916, with orders to "push forward at a steady pace in successive lines." The heavily laden men were cut down by well-directed German artillery and machine gun fire. Out of an attacking force of nearly 100,000 men, more than 57,000 became casualties in the first day's fighting, with nearly 20,000 men killed outright. The British attack was virtually stopped in its tracks; over on the right flank, the tactically more sophisticated French army managed to make some gains.

British troops of the 34th Division on the opening day of the Battle of the Somme during the assault on La Boisselle.

Although a terrible setback for the British, 1 July was only the first day of the offensive, which was to continue until November. Lessons were learned, and more flexible approaches adopted. A successful dawn attack on 14 July demonstrated what the volunteer "New Armies" were capable of doing, and represented a marked improvement in British staff work. Increasing numbers of divisions were fed into the battle, including troops from the Commonwealth. The ruins of Pozières fell to a daring Australian assault on 23 July; the South African Brigade battled for Delville Wood, while Canadians and New Zealanders were heavily committed in later attacks.

Every attack soon became bogged down in desperate trench warfare, especially as the Germans operated a policy of vigorous counterattacks. The commander of the German Second Army, General Fritz von Below, instructed his men "to hold our present positions at any cost. The enemy should have to carve his way over heaps of corpses." These orders helped account for the 330 German attacks and counterattacks that punctuated the course of the battle.

On 15 September, tanks arrived at the Battle of Flers-Courcelette. However, after some small, local gains, the hopes invested in them were also dashed. The last phase of the battle ended with the British attack on Beaumont Hamel (launched on 13 November), when cold and rain had turned the battlefield into a sea of freezing mud, which made effective operations impossible. As was the case at Verdun, the fighting on the Somme personified the horror of trench warfare on the Western Front. **AG**

Losses: British and Commonwealth, 420,000 casualties; French, 204,000 casualties; German, at least 465,000 casualties

☑ *Fort Vaux 1916*

Beaumont Hamel 1 July 1916

"The men of the first wave climbed up the parapets, in tumult, darkness, and the presence of death..."

John Masefield, The Old Front Line

⬆ *The corpse of a German soldier at Beaumont Hamel.*

The capture of Beaumont Hamel was one of the objectives of the Somme offensive, but the failure of the attack around this German strongpoint exemplified the overall British failure on the first day of the Somme. The position was eventually captured at the Somme's close in November 1916.

The Germans had full knowledge of the proposed Allied offensive on the Somme in World War I, and developed extensive subterranean fortifications to resist any attack. Beaumont Hamel was one of nine village fortresses that acted to buttress the German front line. The ruined buildings proved excellent concealment, with the many village cellars and newly constructed dugouts connected by tunnels that were virtually shellproof. Machine gun posts were spread around the village, with clearly defined fields of fire overlooking the British lines.

The British 29th Division was given the task of capturing Beaumont Hamel. To help the attackers, a series of mines had been tunneled under the German front-line trenches; these were to be blown two minutes before H-hour at 7:30 AM on 1 July. They included a huge mine under the German redoubt on Hawthorn Ridge, just in front of Beaumont Hamel. However, the mine was blown early, at 7:20 AM, which allowed time for the well-trained German defenders to occupy one side of the vast mine crater and pour down fire on the two infantry brigades slowly advancing toward them.

A mass concentration of German artillery and accurate machine gun fire ripped the British advance to shreds before it reached the German wire. The battalion from the Newfoundland Regiment, held in reserve, was destroyed in just forty minutes. By midmorning, it was clear that the attack had been a complete failure. **AG**

Losses: Newfoundlander, 684 casualties of 778; other British divisions unknown; German, unknown

◁ *Fort Vaux 1916*   *Pozières 1916* ▷

Kostiuchnowka 4–6 July 1916

Kostiuchnowka was fought during the Brusilov offensive and was part of the struggle to create an independent Poland. The Polish Legion fought alongside Austro-Hungarian forces against the Russians; they showed great bravery but gained little benefit from their efforts.

War on the Eastern Front was fought largely on Polish territory, and both sides sought to court Polish goodwill. Many Poles merely questioned which side would win, and to what extent their national aspirations would be fulfilled in exchange for their services.

Józef Piłsudski raised his Polish Legion intending to make it indispensable to the cause of the Central Powers. As the Austrian position began to collapse under Brusilov's assaults, Piłsudski was given his chance, being ordered to hold a position on the Styr River near Lutsk. His forces were heavily outnumbered, and support from Hungarian troops on his flank was uncertain. However, when the first Russian attacks were launched, the Poles held their line and cut down their assailants with machine guns. They were forced to pull back when the Hungarians retreated, but over the next two days the Poles launched furious counterattacks, which either were beaten off with heavy losses or failed due to lack of support.

The Poles fought stubbornly until forced to retreat by overwhelming numbers; their courage ensured the safe withdrawal of other Austro-Hungarian units and earned them the admiration of observers. However, Piłsudski came to the conclusion that the Central Powers would be defeated, and he refused to take an oath of fidelity to their cause. He was arrested, and his Legion unceremoniously disbanded, but he had made himself a national hero and a future national leader. **JS**

Losses: Polish, 2,000 dead or wounded of 5,500–7,300; Russian, 13,000 dead or wounded of 26,000

◁ *Brusilov Offensive 1916*   *Kerensky Offensive 1917* ▷

Pozières 23 July–7 August 1916

The capture of the German stronghold of Pozières was an example of one of the better planned British attacks on the Somme in World War I. It owed much to the determined dash of the Australians in attack and their resilience in defense, although victory came at a high price in casualties.

As part of a general advance on the Somme, the German fortress village of Pozières was selected for attack by the British 48th Division and the three Australian divisions of the I ANZAC Corps. Refusing to be rushed into making a hasty attack, the commander of the 1st Australian Division, Major General Harold Walker, made sure that Pozières was subjected to a heavy bombardment of high explosives and gas. On 23 July, his men crawled into no-man's-land while the bombardment was still in progress; this meant that when the barrage lifted the Australians had to make only a short dash to the German wire. Once through the German front-line trenches, the Australians captured almost the entire village, but the small area still held by the Germans made the Australian position vulnerable to counterattack.

Over the next several days, the Australians endured a series of intense bombardments as the German artillery focused their efforts on Pozières. On 27 July, the battered 1st Australian Division was replaced by the 2nd Division, whose orders were to capture the remaining part of the village. An initial assault failed, but, on 4 August, the objective was gained. The 4th Division took over the line and immediately had to face some of the fiercest German counterattacks of the whole Somme campaign, managing to check desperate German assaults on 6 and 7 August. From then on, the Germans reluctantly accepted that Pozières had been lost to the enemy. **AG**

Losses: British and Australian, 23,000 casualties; German, unknown

◁ *Somme 1916*   *Flers-Courcelette 1916* ▷

Air Battle over London
2–3 September 1916

The first sustained strategic bombing campaign was carried out by German Zeppelin and Schütte-Lanz airships in World War I. London was the favorite target. Night attacks defied British defenses, until Lieutenant William Leefe Robinson shot down airship SL 11 in a turning point of the air war.

On the evening of 2 September, a total of sixteen airships—massive machines around 600 feet (183 m) long carrying several tons of bombs—headed for London. The blacked-out city was ringed with gun batteries and searchlights, but experience showed that the defenders had little hope of success.

Leefe Robinson was part of a home defense wing of the Royal Flying Corps, which had been practicing night flying. He took off in a BE2c biplane—widely regarded as a poor aircraft—around 11:30 PM and spent hours chasing half-glimpsed shadows and finding nothing. He was ready to end his patrol when the sky was lit up by incendiary bombs dropped by Schütte-Lanz SL 11. He closed on the slow-moving airship and raked it from stem to stern. He used newly issued explosive and incendiary ammunition, but nothing happened. Leefe Robinson continued to attack, dodging gunfire from the airship and "friendly" fire from ground batteries, until emptying his third drum of ammunition into the target's tail set SL 11 ablaze. The flames could be seen for miles around as the airship fell in a ball of fire, cheered by crowds in the London streets.

The confidence of the German airship crews was shaken severely. As losses accumulated over the following months, the airship offensive became increasingly ineffectual. Leefe Robinson became an instant celebrity and was awarded the Victoria Cross. He was shot down in his first dogfight over the Western Front the following year. **RG**

Losses: British, none; German, 1 airship with its crew

Gotha Raid on London 1917 ▷

Flers-Courcelette
15–22 September 1916

As one of the final British attacks on the Somme, the assault was notable for the first use of armored vehicles in war. Although they failed to live up to expectations, the British Mark I tanks offered hope— however illusory—that a means might have been found to break the trench deadlock of World War I.

With the thought of a decisive victory in mind, General Haig looked favorably upon the untried tank as a means of smashing a hole through the heavily defended German trench system—one that would open a sufficiently wide gap for his cavalry to exploit. Despite reservations from tank experts, some forty-nine tanks were assembled for the offensive, although just thirty-two were able to begin their slow, uncertain march across no-man's-land when the attack began on 15 September.

The assault was spearheaded by British troops, alongside the New Zealand Division and Canadian Corps. The tanks that reached the German front line caused consternation among the defenders, and the initial objectives fell to the Allies—with the Canadians taking Courcelette—while a tank, with British troops behind, advanced up the main street of Flers. The New Zealanders captured the infamous "switch line," which had caused the British heavy casualties in previous attacks.

Bad weather and determined German counterattacks brought the British advance to an effective close on 17 September. Despite an impressive attack by the British Guards Division, the offensive was called off on 22 September. Unfortunately for the Allies, the tanks had proved too slow and unreliable to be a decisive weapon of war, plagued by mechanical breakdowns and vulnerable to artillery fire. Nonetheless, Haig was impressed and called for 1,000 tanks to be built immediately. **AG**

Losses: Unknown

◁ Pozières 1916   Arras 1917 ▷

◀ German airship SL 11 burns up in midair during the Air Battle over London.

Gaza   26 March and 17 April 1917

During World War I, the British fought the Ottoman Turks for control of the Middle East. In spring 1917, the Egyptian Expeditionary Force, under General Sir Archibald Murray, attempted to break Turkish defenses at Gaza in Palestine and open the way for an advance on Jerusalem.

On 26 March 1917, while cavalry from General Sir Philip Chetwode's Desert Column enveloped Gaza from the east and north, infantry from the British 53rd and 54th Divisions made a morning assault on the main Turkish defenses south of the town. Although the ANZAC Mounted Division achieved complete surprise, taking numerous outposts and even capturing a Turkish general, the infantry assault was delayed due to thick fog. When it finally came, the infantry pushed into the key Ali Muntar strongpoint. There was prolonged hand-to-hand fighting, and gradually the Turks were pushed back into Gaza. With the ANZAC Mounted Division entering the town from the north, victory appeared certain. However, the onset of dusk and appearance of Turkish reinforcements led the British to take a poorly judged decision to withdraw.

On 17 April, a second assault was launched on the much-strengthened Turkish line. Despite support from six tanks—their first use outside the Western Front—and a barrage of gas shells, the assault failed all along the line. Numerous Turkish machine guns and artillery pieces survived the bombardment to contest the dogged British attack and neutralize the small number of tanks. Determined Turkish counterattacks ensured the British had nothing to show for a hard day's fighting and proved the quality of Turkish infantry in a defensive battle. Defeat at Gaza for a second time cost Murray his command. **AW**

Losses: First Gaza: British, 3,867 of 22,000; Turkish, 2,447 of 4,000 engaged (15,000 total); Second Gaza: British, 6,444 of 30,000; Turkish, 2,013 of 20,000

◁ *Kut 1915*   *Aqaba 1917* ▷

Arras   9 April–23 May 1917

The Battle of Arras was intended as a diversionary attack in support of the main Nivelle Offensive in Champagne. It was noteworthy for the swift gains made by the British in the opening phase: above all, the capture of Vimy Ridge—considered virtually impregnable—by the Canadian Corps.

The British attack in Arras opened the Allied offensive in 1917. The Canadian Corps was charged with taking Vimy Ridge in order to safeguard the left flank of the main advance either side of the Arras, which was entrusted to General Sir Edmund Allenby's Third Army. The German position was well defended, but the British had planned the offensive with care, profiting from the lessons of the Somme. Artillery support was increased to nearly 3,000 guns, a substantial proportion of which were "heavies," essential for destroying well-constructed strongpoints.

The British had trained their troops thoroughly in appropriate opening attack maneuvers. On 9 April, the British troops went "over the top" and made good progress. The four divisions of the Canadian Corps struggled up Vimy Ridge, a honeycomb of defenses that had frustrated previous French attacks with great bloodshed. After a bitter fight that cost them nearly 10,000 men, they won control of the position. Farther south, the British were similarly successful, and a few units advanced to a depth of 3 miles (4.8 km) on the first day.

The German command avoided an Allied breakthrough with its usual adroit handling of reserves, and the British advance lost momentum. The original British plan had been to limit the battle once serious resistance was met, but Haig prolonged the offensive to provide aid to the French, incurring heavy casualties for little gain. **AG**

Losses: British, 158,000 casualties; German, 130,000 casualties

◁ *Flers-Courcelette 1916*   *Nivelle Offensive 1917* ▷

Nivelle Offensive 16 April–9 May 1917

The failure of the Nivelle Offensive to secure victory came as a profound shock to the French army, and for a while it teetered on the point of collapse. A strategic consequence of the resulting French mutinies was the emergence of Britain as the senior Allied partner on the Western Front during 1917.

When General Robert Nivelle took over as commander in chief in December 1916, he promised a war-winning offensive that would break through the German lines within forty-eight hours. The Champagne region was chosen as the battlefield, and vast forces were assembled that included 7,000 guns and a number of French Schneider tanks. However, lax security meant the Germans had full knowledge of the coming offensive.

The French attacked on 16 April on a broad 50-mile (80 km) front. Although they smashed their way into the German front-line trenches, the advance soon slowed and progress was minimal. The French casualty lists were not unusually high by Western Front standards, but Nivelle's promises had raised the army's expectations to a dangerously high level and these were dashed when his attack failed to penetrate the German line. There was widespread demoralization, and mutiny was in the air. On 3 May, some units refused to return to the trenches, and by the end of June more than fifty divisions were refusing to obey orders to some extent; many would go into the trenches but refused to attack.

The replacement of Nivelle by the popular General Pétain helped restore order, and with many of the men's grievances met by the authorities, the crisis began to pass. By late August, the French army felt sufficiently confident to mount a limited offensive around Verdun. **AG**

"[Pétain] regarded his handling of the mutiny as his finest accomplishment."

Stuart Robson, The First World War *(1998)*

Losses: French, 187,000 casualties of 1,200,000; German, 163,000 casualties of 480,000

↑ *French infantrymen advance up the Mont des Singes; the area was left in complete devastation after the Nivelle Offensive.*

◁ Arras 1917   Messines 1917 ▷

Otranto   15 May 1917

Allied navies maintained patrols in the Straits of Otranto to try to prevent Austro-Hungarian surface ships and submarines reaching the Mediterranean proper. The Austro-Hungarians had the better of this cruiser and destroyer battle in May 1917, the largest of World War I in the Adriatic.

In 1914, the Austro-Hungarian Empire included extensive territory on the northern and eastern side of the Adriatic. Consequently, as well as many battles on land, Austria fought various battles at sea against Italy (supported by the other Allies). The Allies aimed to keep the Austrian navy bottled up in the Adriatic, away from the important Mediterranean trade routes. This was largely successful as far as surface ships were concerned, but less so in limiting Austrian and German submarine operations.

To keep the enemy submarines penned in, the Allies set up the so-called Otranto barrage, a system of "indicator nets" in the straits—maintained by fishing drifters—intended to detect and entangle submarines. In practice, this largely failed to halt the submarines, but it worried the Austro-Hungarians sufficiently for them to plan a night attack on the drifters and their supporting vessels.

The action began in the early hours of 15 May when three Austrian cruisers, under Captain Miklos Horthy, attacked the hapless drifters—sinking fourteen—while a destroyer force struck a passing convoy. By daybreak, Italian and British light cruisers and destroyers were hurrying to the scene, and several short-lived combats followed as the Austrians made for home. Horthy's cruiser, *Novara,* was badly damaged, and he was wounded. The approach of heavier Austrian ships eventually made the Italians and British break off the pursuit. Horthy survived to become dictator of Hungary after the war. **DS**

Losses: Austro-Hungarian, 2 light cruisers damaged; Allied, 2 destroyers and 16 other ships sunk, 1 light cruiser damaged

◁ *Jutland 1916*   *Zeebrugge Raid 1918* ▷

Messines   7–14 June 1917

The capture of Messines Ridge was a preliminary operation that took place just prior to the Third Battle of Ypres. High-explosive mines placed under the German lines were used to devastating effect, and the blast from the explosions could be heard in London some 130 miles (209 km) distant.

The first stage in the British Flanders offensive was the securing of Ypres through the capture of the Messines Ridge just to the south of the city. Preparation had begun a year earlier with the digging of mines under the ridge. The tunneling companies of General Sir Herbert Plumer's Second Army completed nineteen mines containing around one million pounds of high explosive. Plumer was well aware of the siege-warfare nature of fighting on the Western Front; he planned his offensives with meticulous detail, and his cautious approach saved lives and earned him the affectionate respect of his soldiers.

The British attack at Messines on 7 June opened with the explosion of the mines, causing a virtual earthquake that immediately killed as many as 10,000 German soldiers. A hurricane bombardment by 2,000 guns preceded the advance of nine British and Australian infantry divisions, which proved a complete success. The artillery provided a highly effective "creeping barrage" that protected the infantry as they climbed up the ridge. The infantry met little opposition, with many Germans staggering over the battlefield in a confused state; some 7,000 prisoners were taken that morning. Once the ridge was in British hands, field artillery pieces were brought forward to help deal with the inevitable German counterattacks, which, in the event, were repulsed fairly easily. With the Messines Ridge in British hands, the focus of attention now moved to the breakout from the Ypres salient. **AG**

Losses: British, 17,000 casualties of 216,000; German, 25,000 of 126,000

◁ *Nivelle Offensive 1917*   *Third Ypres 1917* ▷

Gotha Raid on London 13 June 1917

The raid carried out by German Gotha bombers on London in June 1917 had momentous consequences. It led to the creation of the Royal Air Force (RAF) as the world's first independent air arm and to widespread acceptance of the bombing of cities as an inevitable part of modern warfare.

The German army's Gotha G IV twin-engined bomber was the first heavier-than-air aircraft powerful enough to carry a significant bomb load and with sufficient range to reach London from bases in occupied Belgium. Germany's airship offensive against Britain had failed by 1917, but the German government believed the daylight bombing of London by Gothas would undermine British morale and lead to popular pressure for withdrawal from the war.

A Gotha raid on Folkestone on 25 May 1917, which killed ninety-five people, should have acted as a warning. However, the British were hopelessly unprepared when Hauptman Ernst Brandenburg set off for London with the twenty Gothas of Kaghol-3 on the morning of 13 June. Fourteen of the aircraft made it to the target, arriving over the city at noon. Taken by surprise as bombs fell on Liverpool Street station, people ran out into the streets to see the aircraft instead of taking cover. In Poplar, a bomb struck a school, killing eighteen children in one class. The total death toll was 162.

Despite attempts by British aircraft to intercept them, the Gothas returned home unscathed. The withdrawal of aircraft from the Western Front to defend London soon stopped daylight raids, but night raids by Gothas and the even larger R-planes continued into 1918. The British government responded by adopting strategic bombing itself and created the RAF as an instrument for an air offensive against Germany. **RG**

"The whole street seemed to explode, smoke and flames everywhere. Worst of all were the screams of the wounded and dying." Eyewitness

A German soldier loads 50- and 100-kg bombs onto a Gotha bomber in preparation for the raids on Britain.

Losses: British, 162 civilians dead, 432 wounded; German, none

◁ *Air Battle over London 1916*

Kerensky Offensive 1–23 July 1917

The last offensive launched by the Russians during World War I was a complete failure. It undermined the Provisional Government installed after the overthrow of Czar Nicholas, and began the collapse that led to the Bolshevik revolution and the victory of the Central Powers on the Eastern Front.

In February 1917, a revolution in Petrograd overthrew the Romanov dynasty and swept the Provisional Government to power. It was greeted with joy by war-weary Russian soldiers who wanted immediate peace. However, the Provisional Government needed economic support and recognition from the Allies and chose to fight on.

Alexander Kerensky, the Provisional Government's minister of war, ordered an offensive in Galicia, toward Lvov. This ignored the feeble state of the army; every unit had formed its own elected Soviet (council) to run its affairs, officers had lost their authority, there was large-scale fraternization between opposing troops, and mass desertions were commonplace. Indeed the commander, General Brusilov, had to spend hours in discussions with Soviets in order to persuade them to attack and to accept his operational plans. This boded ill for the offensive.

When the attack was launched, the Austrian troops were nearly as war-weary as the Russians and quickly gave way. Kerensky issued heady communiqués about the triumphs of a revolutionary army organized on democratic lines, but it did not last. German troops fought obstinately, and poorly organized Russian assaults were cut down by murderous crossfire. The old tenacity of the Russian armies had vanished; units abandoned their positions, orders were ignored, and soon the Russians were being driven back beyond their starting point. The Russian military collapse had begun and would only accelerate. **AG**

Losses: Russian, at least 40,000 dead, 20,000 wounded; German and Austrian, unknown

◁ *Kostiuchnowka 1916*   *Riga 1917* ▷

Russian troops parade in front of Alexander Kerensky and other officials, July 1917. ⬆

Aqaba   6 July 1917

Fighting the Ottoman Turks in the Middle East, the British supported the Arab Revolt against Turkish rule, led by Emir Feisel. The successful capture of Aqaba gave Arab forces a secure maritime supply line to the British in Egypt. It also established the reputation of Captain T. E. Lawrence.

Lawrence moved north in early May from Emir Feisel's base at Wejh with thirty-six Bedouin tribesmen. Having received little support from the British High Command in Egypt, he was accompanied by Sherif Nasir of Medina and Auda abu Tayi, veteran chief of the Howeitat tribe. He gathered a force of around 2,000 Arabs and raided the Hejaz railway and Turkish military posts, before arriving near Aqaba on 6 July. Lawrence was proved correct in his belief that the Turkish garrison would not expect an attack from the desert. Most of the defenses stood ready to prevent a seaborne landing, with very little between the Arab force and the town.

During the advance, Auda led an attack on a blockhouse between Aqaba and Ma'an. After a fierce skirmish, the defending Turkish battalion was routed. As Lawrence and his men approached Aqaba, the port came under fire from British warships. This bombardment and the surprise appearance of the Arab force led to the town garrison surrendering without a fight. Lawrence then set off with eighteen companions 150 miles (240 km) across the Sinai desert to bring word of the victory to the British High Command. In August, Feisel moved his base to Aqaba, from where he began operating in direct support of the British in Palestine. Lawrence gained a promotion to Major and became the main liaison officer between Feisel's Northern Arab Army and General Allenby's Egyptian Expeditionary Force. **AW**

Losses: Arab, 2 dead, fewer than 10 wounded; Turkish, 300 dead, 700 captured of 1,000

◁ *Gaza 1917*   *Beersheba 1917* ▷

↑ *Lawrence (left) is accompanied by journalist Lowell Thomas, who reported Lawrence's exploits worldwide.*

Third Ypres   31 July–10 November 1917

Fought over difficult, waterlogged terrain, the British offensive at Ypres advanced 5 miles (8 km) in more than three months before coming to a halt at the village of Passchendaele, the appropriately named ruin that was to give the battle its popular name. For the Germans, the battle became "the greatest martyrdom of the war."

After the British success at Messines, Field Marshal Douglas Haig now transferred the main attack northward to General Sir Hubert Gough's Fifth Army, but British preparations were slow and provided the Germans with an opportunity to improve their defenses around Ypres. The concept of flexible or elastic defense was now standard practice in the German army, with the forward line relatively lightly held and the main bulk of troops held back in relative safety but ready to counterattack at a moment's notice. The German army also made good use of reinforced concrete pillboxes to create a series of interlocking strongpoints situated in the forward line.

> *"At times it becomes so terrific … it is simply one great throbbing, pulsating jolting roaring inferno."*
>
> *Lieutenant Cyril Lawrence, Australian Engineers*

The Germans anticipated that most would survive the preliminary bombardment (unless hit by a large-caliber shell) and would then have to be neutralized by the British infantry, slowly and with much loss of life.

On 18 July British artillery began a long, sustained bombardment of the German line, lasting nearly two weeks. On 31 July the Fifth Army opened the assault, with nine divisions attacking to the northeast of Ypres. The German line was pushed back 2 miles (3 km), but exceptionally heavy rain turned the battlefield into a swamp—made worse by the artillery's destruction of the drainage system—and brought the attack to a halt. On 16 August the offensive was resumed against the German positions at Langemarck, but progress here was slow and casualties heavy.

Haig now turned to General Herbert Plumer's Second Army, whose zone of operations was extended northward to include the Menin Road. Once again, preparations were delayed for the offensive, which would comprise three set-piece assaults with limited objectives, directed against German positions on high ground directly to the east of Ypres. Favored by some dry weather the British, Australian, and New Zealand divisions achieved considerable success.

The first advance on the Menin Road Ridge (20–25 September) was followed immediately by the attack on Polygon Wood (26 September), concluding with the advance on Broodseinde (4 October), which was especially punishing for the Germans. At this point the Germans' morale was low and their reserves were limited. To the British commanders, a breakthrough seemed possible. The arrival of fresh German reserves put an end to such hopes, however, and on 7 October the weather turned cold and extremely wet; the battle slowly foundered in a sea of mud in which guns, transport wagons, mules, and men sank without trace.

Although advised to end offensive operations, Haig was determined to secure the Passchendaele Ridge before the onset of winter. In terrible conditions the Australians resumed hostilities on 12 October, but with little success. On 26 October the Canadians were thrown into the attack, finally capturing the ruins of Passchendaele on 6 November. A few days later the battle was closed down with the ridge finally in British hands. **AG**

Losses: British and Commonwealth, 245,000 casualties; German, unknown but probably similar

◁ *Messines 1917*   *Passchendaele 1917* ▷

Australian soldiers walk through the devastation along a duckboard track during Third Ypres. ➔

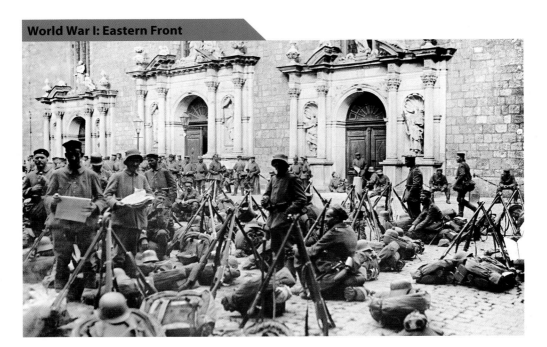

Riga   3 September 1917

By the fall of 1917, the Russian army fighting on the Eastern Front was a shadow of its former might. The rapid German victory at Riga in Latvia, attributed by the Germans to the skilful "infiltration tactics" of General Oskar von Hutier, paved the way for the Bolshevik seizure of power in Russia.

After the Kerensky Offensive of July 1917 there was little fight left in the Russian armies. Their new commander, General Lavr Kornilov, publicly warned that if discipline was not restored he could neither hold Riga nor defend the Russian capital, Petrograd. The Russians reputedly knew precisely when and where the German attack would come. An effective defense should have been possible, but fast-moving German stormtroopers penetrated deep into Russian positions, advancing behind a brief, intense barrage that included a massive use of poison gas.

As the Germans crossed the Dvina River near Uxkull and approached Riga, some Russian units fought with exemplary courage, but so many fled that the Germans were often unaware of any opposition. Riga fell after a few hours of bombardment. The victory was joyously proclaimed in Germany as absolute proof that it could, and indeed would, win the war.

Allied propaganda accused the Germans of using poison gas on Riga's civilians. In Russia, Bolshevik propaganda insisted that the Provisional Government had conspired in the fall of Riga, and would welcome the Germans into Petrograd to destroy the revolution. Kornilov, deciding that the Provisional Government could not reimpose discipline, marched his army toward Petrograd to restore order. The Provisional Government stopped him by arming the Bolshevik militia, thus putting their fate in the hands of their most implacable political enemies, who seized power the following November. **JS**

Losses: Unknown

⟨ *Kerensky Offensive 1917*   *Petrograd 1919* ⟩

German troops assembled in Riga after entering the city with little resistance. ⬆

Passschendaele   12 October–10 November 1917

The British assault on Passchendaele represented the final phase of the Third Battle of Ypres, a calvary of mud and blood for the armies of both sides. The hard-fought capture of the Passchendaele Ridge ejected the Germans from the high ground that dominated the city of Ypres, but at enormous cost.

The attack opened on 12 October with a drive against the German positions at Poelcappelle, just northwest of Passchendaele. Utilizing five British divisions and three divisions from the ANZAC Corps, the advance was an almost complete failure. The mud prevented field artillery from going forward to support the advance, and spirited German counterattacks forced the British and Commonwealth formations back to their start lines with 13,000 casualties. Morale dropped as the rain fell.

The battle resumed with the arrival of the reinforced Canadian Corps with its four infantry divisions. The Canadians would drive directly toward Passchendaele, supported on their flanks by British and ANZAC forces and a French Division. The Canadian battle plan called for three sequential and limited attacks. On 26 October the 3rd and 4th Canadian Divisions spearheaded the advance and in difficult conditions secured most of their objectives. The attack resumed on 30 October and successfully advanced to within striking distance of what remained of Passchendaele village.

There was a brief pause as the Canadians rotated their forces, with the fresh 1st and 2nd Divisions deployed to lead the attack. Hostilities resumed on 6 November as the two Canadian divisions struggled across the mud and within a matter of hours had secured Passchendaele. A few days later the remaining German troops were swept off the Passchendaele Ridge, thus bringing the Third Battle of Ypres to close. **AG**

Losses: Unknown

⟨ *Third Ypres 1917* *Cambrai 1917* ⟩

⬆ *British infantry, wreathed by smoke and poison gas, cross the denuded Ypres battlefield.*

Mahiwa 17–18 October 1917

Using guerrilla tactics in East Africa, German General Paul von Lettow-Vorbeck mostly avoided pitched battles. At Mahiwa, however, the German colonial troops were brought to battle at a serious numerical disadvantage, only to inflict a reverse upon a South African–led British Empire force.

In September 1917 General Jacob van Deventer with three columns of African, British, and South African troops were conducting an offensive southward through German East Africa. The plan was to prevent Lettow-Vorbeck from concentrating his forces and retreating into Portuguese East Africa (Mozambique). On 15 October an attempt was made to surround and destroy a column of German stormtroopers under Major General Kurt Wahle at Nyangao, but Lettow-Vorbeck quickly reinforced Wahle and inflicted heavy casualties on the Anglo-Nigerian Brigade under Brigadier General Gordon Beves.

The following day German forces pulled back 2 miles (3 km) and dug in on a ridge at Mahiwa. The next morning Beves threw his men into a series of frontal assaults against the strong German position. Fighting lasted throughout the day and was often at close quarters. The battle climaxed during the early hours of 18 October when Lettow-Vorbeck launched a strong counterattack. Although forced back, the British and Nigerian troops held their ground. Stalemate was reached with neither side having sufficient forces to settle the battle through offensive action. However, the heavy casualties suffered by Beves led to the cancellation of further assaults and a retreat. Soon after, Lettow-Vorbeck moved his troops south, realizing that with little ammunition his men could not fight another day. On 25 November the Germans crossed into Portuguese East Africa. **AW**

Losses: British-Nigerian, 2,348 casualties of 4,900; German, 519 casualties of 2,800

◁ *Tanga 1914*

Caporetto 24 October–2 December 1917

Italy joined World War I as an ally of Britain and France in 1915. After a long stalemate on Italy's northern border, an Austro-German offensive at Caporetto came close to shattering the Italian army. The British and French had to send troops to strengthen their faltering ally.

In the early hours of 24 October, massed Austrian and German artillery bombarded Italian lines along the Isonzo River with gas, smoke, and high-explosive shells. Despite difficult terrain and poor weather conditions, Austro-German forces quickly tore a large gap through the Italian Second Army. Using infiltration tactics, they bypassed points of resistance, planning to mop them up later. Chaos quickly spread through Italian ranks and by 27 October the Second Army was largely ineffective.

Italian Commander-in-Chief Marshal Luigi Cadorna then ordered a general withdrawal to prepared defenses along the Tagliamento River. This affected the Italian Third Army, still holding the right of the Isonzo line. Mixing with thousands of refugees and stragglers from many units, the Third Army was swept away in the general chaos.

At this crucial time, supply problems and exhaustion began to affect pursuing Austro-German forces. The slight respite allowed the Italians to cross the Tagliamento on 31 October and prepare for defense. The line held for two days until German troops forced a crossing of the river. Cadorna now ordered a withdrawal to the Piave River, where the army would stand. By 10 November this movement was completed although Cadorna was no longer in command, having been replaced by General Armando Diaz. Austro-German attempts to cross the Piave on 16–25 November brought little gain and the offensive was officially shut down on 2 December. **AW**

Losses: Austro-German, 20,000 casualties; Italian, 40,000 casualties and 280,000 captured

Vittorio Veneto 1918 ▷

Italian troops retreat to the Tagliamento River after their defeat at Caporetto. ➡

Beersheeba   31 October 1917

Reorganized after its defeat at Gaza in the spring of 1917, the British Egyptian Expeditionary Force renewed its Palestine campaign. Its new commander, General Edmund Allenby, decided to crush Turkish resistance along the 30-mile (48 km) Gaza defense line by attacking its weakest point, the garrison holding the town of Beersheeba.

To maintain the element of surprise, Allenby shifted four infantry divisions of XX Corps and cavalry of General Henry Chauvel's Desert Mounted Corps east toward Beersheeba in a series of night marches. In particular, Chauvel's approach march over ten nights was a masterpiece of organization and staff work.

On the morning of 31 October, British artillery began shelling Turkish trenches around Beersheeba. Unlike earlier operations at Gaza, plenty of preliminary reconnaissance was undertaken and artillery support was more than adequate for the task. Masked by smoke and dust from the bombardment, infantry from the 60th and 74th Divisions moved forward and took just an hour to secure all their objectives to the west and in front of Beersheeba. This left the Desert Mounted Corps to take the town. Attacking from the east, where Turkish defenses were less extensive, the Australian and New Zealand cavalry took many key positions but were delayed by Turkish machine guns. The 4th Light Horse Brigade, ordered to take the town by nightfall, then charged through the Turkish defenses and secured Beersheeba.

Over the following week, Allenby combined advances from Beersheeba to the west and north with assaults on the main Gaza position. Growing casualties and the threat to their line of retreat forced the Turks to abandon Gaza, opening a line of advance toward Jerusalem. **AW**

Losses: British, 1,348 of 40,000; Turkish, 500 casualties plus 1,528 captured of a garrison of 4,000

◁ Aqaba 1917   Jerusalem 1917 ▷

Cambrai   20 November–8 December 1917

The Battle of Cambrai demonstrated the evolution of technology and tactics on the Western Front that would eventually end the stalemate of trench warfare. Best known as the first effective deployment of tanks, it was also notable for predicted shooting by British artillery and the use of infiltration tactics by German stormtroopers.

The final British offensive of 1917, a surprise attack by General Sir Julian Byng's Third Army, was launched against the German line in front of Cambrai. Uncratered ground allowed tanks to be used on a large scale and surprise was ensured by predicted shooting, in which bombardment would begin without any preparatory shootings by the artillery to "register" their intended targets.

On the morning of 20 November, 1,000 guns simultaneously opened fire on the unsuspecting Germans and 378 tanks rolled through the mist. By midday the British had advanced 4 miles (6.5 km) through the formidable defenses of the Hindenburg Line. The British cavalry were unable to exploit this initial success, however, and the Germans continued to hold strong positions on the flanks of the British advance. More significantly, half the tanks were out of action at the end of the first day's fighting, mainly due to mechanical failure. The battle degenerated into a brutal trench struggle.

On 30 November it was the turn of the Germans to spring a surprise in the form of a counterattack spearheaded by stormtroopers. These specially trained groups used the tactics of infiltration to find and exploit weak points in the British line. The British were caught off balance by the brilliantly executed German attack and fell back in disarray. By 8 December, when the battle ended, the British had lost most of their territorial gains. **AG**

Losses: British, 44,200 casualties; German, 45,000 casualties

◁ Passchendaele 1917   Kaiserschlacht Offensive 1918 ▷

Jerusalem   8–9 December 1917

British General Edmund Allenby's capture and holding of Jerusalem ensured the defeat of the Turks in Palestine in World War I. The victory also brought a welcome morale boost to the Allies in 1917, following a series of reverses including the defeat of the Italian army at Caporetto and the Bolshevik assumption of power in Russia.

Allenby moved his forces through the Judean hills toward Jerusalem. On 27 November his opponent, General Erich von Falkenhayn, launched a counteroffensive against the British. By 3 December the Turks had been fought to a standstill and XX Corps under General Philip Chetwode prepared to capture Jerusalem. Special instructions demanded troops respect the sanctity of religious sites in the Holy City and nearby Bethlehem.

As troops gathered for the advance, their movement was screened by rain and mist. On 8 December infantry of the 60th and 74th Divisions moved forward on a 4 ½-mile (7 km) front west of Jerusalem. All went well until 11:00 AM, when they were checked by heavy Turkish fire. Operations halted for the day and consolidation of captured ground began. This proved difficult owing to the rocky terrain and the fatigue of troops who had endured tough fighting in cold and wet conditions. Transport had difficulty moving in mud, leaving the infantry with little food or water.

The British prepared for a second day of fighting only to discover that their assault had panicked the Turks into abandoning their positions. On 11 December Allenby made a formal entry into Jerusalem on foot, out of respect for its holy status. Two weeks later, Falkenhayn launched a desperate attempt to retake the city. This ended in failure and the British again took up the offensive. Four hundred years of Turkish rule over Jerusalem were ended. **AW**

Losses: British, 18,928 (3 November–15 December); Turkish, 28,443 (31 October–31 December)

◁ Beersheba 1917   Megiddo 1918 ▷

"The procession was all afoot, and at Jaffa gate I was received by the [Allied] guards. . . . The population received me well." General Allenby

⬆ *General Allenby, accompanied by a number of political and military dignitaries, enters Jerusalem on foot via the Jaffa gate.*

Kaiserschlacht Offensive 21 March–18 July 1918

The Germans wagered everything on a last great offensive in the spring of 1918 that would either bring complete victory or defeat. Although the Germans achieved some remarkable tactical successes, in the end the Allies held firm and the exhausted German armies were forced onto the defensive with little hope of success.

The German High Command had decided to launch a massive assault against the armies of Britain and France on the Western Front before the full arrival of the U.S. Army in France tipped the scales irrevocably against Germany. Able to redeploy large numbers of troops from the Eastern Front, the Germans had a numerical advantage in the West. Elite stormtrooper divisions, trained in infiltration tactics, would lead the offensive, which would be supported by artillery using the latest

predicted shooting techniques. Excellent German staff work ensured that guns, ammunition, supplies, and men were brought forward with the utmost secrecy.

Code-named Operation Michael, the German offensive would be conducted by three armies, totaling fifty-nine divisions, and supported by the largest concentration of artillery yet assembled: 6,473 guns and howitzers and 3,532 trench mortars. Along a 50-mile (80 km) front the Germans were faced by the British Fifth and Third Armies, totaling twenty-six divisions. The defenses of the recently arrived Fifth Army were far from complete.

The German guns opened the great offensive with a shattering five-hour bombardment on the morning of 21 March. A thick mist proved invaluable to the attacking storm troops, and the battered British frontline positions were overrun with comparative ease. By the end of the day, both British armies were in full retreat. As the German

advance continued, the Allied forces faced a grave risk of separation. In response, on 26 March, at General Haig's suggestion, General Ferdinand Foch was appointed overall commander-in-chief to coordinate the British and French forces. The French divisions moved north to aid the British.

By 28 March, having penetrated the British line to a depth of 40 miles (65 km), the German effort began to weaken. The British Third Army repulsed an assault against Arras, and the key center of Amiens remained out of German reach. Having failed to break the British with the Michael Offensive, a second blow (Operation George) was delivered farther north in Flanders, along the Lys River. This continued until 30 April but, despite the British forces having, in Haig's words, their "backs to the wall," the Germans once more failed to achieve their objective.

In a last, desperate throw of the dice, the German High Command tried to draw away reserves from Flanders by launching a diversionary offensive against the French sector in Champagne. The attack (Third Battle of the Aisne) began in the early hours of 27 May, taking the French entirely by surprise. Its success surprised the Germans themselves; the first day witnessed the deepest single-day penetration on the Western Front of the whole war. By 3 June the Germans had once more reached the Marne River, but the huge bulge in the German line invited counterattack. German attempts to broaden it met with little success, and the French, reinforced with British and American divisions, prepared to go over to the strategic offensive. Ultimately, the German gamble had failed. **AG**

Losses: British, 418,000 casualties; French, 433,000 casualties; German, 688,000 casualties

◁ *Cambrai 1917*   *Belleau Wood 1918* ▷

Zeebrugge Raid   22–23 April 1918

Desperate to counter the German U-boat offensive in World War I, British Commodore Sir Roger Keyes devised a bold plan to block the Bruges Canal in occupied Belgium, which linked German submarine pens to the open sea. Although resolutely carried out, the raid was an almost complete failure.

Germany's submarine force came close to winning the war with unrestricted attacks on British trade from 1917. One of the most important German U-boat bases was entered via a canal reaching the sea at Zeebrugge. The British planned to block the canal in a night raid by sinking three old cruisers filled with concrete in its entrance. To cover their approach, another old cruiser, HMS *Vindictive*, and supporting vessels were to land seamen and Marines to attack gun batteries on the harbor mole.

On the night of 22–23 April little went according to plan. Battered by gunfire on the approach, *Vindictive* reached the mole in the wrong position. As a result, the landing parties suffered heavy casualties as they attacked along the mole, failing to neutralize the gun batteries. The unsubdued German guns also made conditions extremely difficult for the blockships. With heroic effort two were scuttled in the mouth of the canal, while one was sunk before reaching its target.

Much depleted, the British force withdrew, but in the aftermath it took the Germans only a few days to reopen the port completely. A simultaneous raid on Ostend was equally unsuccessful. Yet the boldness of the operation, contrasting with the caution of most naval activity in World War I, was greeted with fervor by the British authorities and public. Keyes received a knighthood and the heroism of the participants was rewarded with eleven Victoria Crosses. **DS**

Losses: British, 600 dead or wounded; German, 30 dead or wounded

◁ *Otranto 1917*

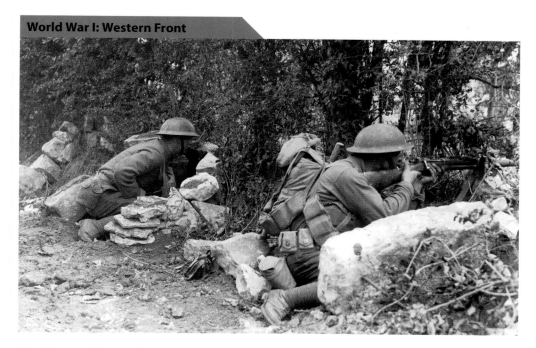

Belleau Wood 1–26 June 1918

The struggle for Belleau Wood announced to the Germans that the U.S. armed forces had arrived on the Western Front in strength and were eager to fight. It was a tough baptism of fire for the Americans but persistence and resolution secured them their first important victory in France.

As the Germans tried to extend and develop their offensive against the French on the Marne River, they came up against the U.S. 2d and 3d Divisions at Château-Thierry and Belleau Wood. Having been checked at Château-Thierry, the Germans advanced through the nearby Belleau Wood and then encountered more of the 2d Division and a brigade of U.S. Marines. Neighboring French troops began to fall back and urged the Americans to do likewise, eliciting the famous response from U.S. Marine Captain Lloyd W. Williams: "Retreat? Hell, we just got here!" The Americans dug in and with a fine display of marksmanship held the German attack on 4 June.

The Americans went over to the offensive and attacked the German positions in front of Belleau Wood on 6 June, suffering heavy losses in the process (the highest in U.S. Marine Corps history until the Battle of Tarawa in 1943). A subsequent attack gained the Americans a foothold on the edge of the wood, but progress was painfully slow, the enthusiasm of the Americans being met by equal determination from the defending Germans. The fighting was relentless, much of it at close quarters and involving bayonets, knives, and even fists. The Americans launched six attacks before the Germans were finally expelled from Belleau Wood on 26 June.

Subsequently, the adjacent villages of Vaux and Bouresche were also secured by the American forces as the Germans fell back to new positions. **AG**

Losses: American, 9,777 casualties; German, 9,500 casualties, including 1,600 captured

◁ *Kaiserschlacht Offensive 1918*   *Le Hamel 1918* ▷

⬆ *A U.S. Marine takes aim with his rifle during the Battle of Belleau Wood.*

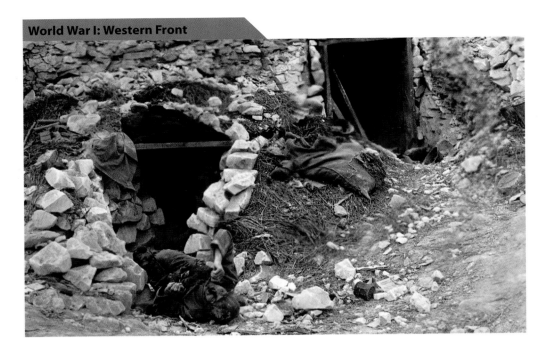

Le Hamel   4 July 1918

The advance against German positions at Le Hamel showed the outstanding fighting qualities of Australian troops, a recognized elite among Allied forces on the Western Front. The assault also exemplified the progress made by the Allies in combining infantry, artillery, tanks, and airpower to bring a set-piece victory for minimal casualties.

Intended to pinch out a German salient facing the British Fourth Army, the attack on Le Hamel was spearheaded by the Australian 4th Division led by Lieutenant General John Monash. Incorporated within the Australian battalions were companies of American infantry, who were there to gain experience of trench warfare. Much thought was put into the planning of the battle. A short, predicted artillery bombardment would precede the attack, which would then be protected by a sophisticated rolling barrage. The latest Mark V tanks would be fighting in support, as well as transporting supplies forward to help the infantry. Aircraft from the newly formed Royal Air Force (RAF) would not only attack the enemy trenches but also parachute packets of ammunition to the troops advancing below.

At 3:10 AM on 4 July, 600 British and French guns opened the bombardment, with the infantry and tanks advancing across no-man's-land. Some of the American troops were so eager to get to grips with the Germans that they ran into their rolling barrage and had to be instructed to hold back. The Germans, caught by surprise, were unable to offer serious resistance. Within ninety-three minutes the Australians had seized their objectives, straightening out the German line. Once in position, the Allied troops were well supplied to repel any German counterattacks, with RAF aircraft parachuting 100,000 rounds of ammunition to the Australian machine gunners below. **AG**

Losses: Allied, 1,300 casualties; German, 3,500 casualties, including 1,500 captured

◁ *Belleau Wood 1918*   *Second Marne 1918* ▷

A German soldier in a dugout at Le Hamel after the battle, 4 July 1918. ⬆

Second Marne 15 July–6 August 1918

The Allied drive against the German salient on the Marne River, achieved during the German Kaiserschlact Offensive, signified the final turn of the tide on the Western Front. With the last German attacks petering out, this Allied offensive was the beginning of a series of operations that would end with final victory in November 1918.

While the Allies were preparing their counterattack against the German salient along the Marne River, the Germans forestalled them by launching an offensive of their own on 15 July. The attack comprised a pincer movement on either side of the French-held city of Reims. The German assault enjoyed some success, with the troops forcing their way across the Marne in a number of places, but it soon faltered when the Allies opened their own offensive on 18 July.

The total forces available to overall commander General Ferdinand Foch comprised forty-four French divisions, eight (large) American, four British, and two Italian divisions. The main thrust was made by the French Tenth and Sixth Armies in the west, with subsidiary attacks made by the French Ninth Army to the south and the French Fifth Army in the east. The now-outnumbered Germans could do little to check the advance.

Fearing encirclement, the German High Command ordered a general retreat on 20 July, and its troops fell back to a securely fortified line along the Aisne and Vesle rivers. General Foch, in keeping with new Allied strategic thinking, did not pursue the offensive, bringing it to a halt on 6 August. From this point onward, the German army would spend its time trying to anticipate where the Allies would strike next. **AG**

Losses: British, 16,500 casualties; French, 95,000 casualties; Italian, 9,300 casualties; U.S., 12,000 casualties; German, 170,000 casualties, including 30,000 captured

◁ *Le Hamel 1918*　　　　　　　　　　*Château-Thierry 1918* ▷

⬆ *German prisoners are led away under the guard of American soldiers after the Allied offensive.*

Château-Thierry 18 July 1918

The battle for Château-Thierry demonstrated the growing confidence of the American forces within the Allied command. Flanking the Moroccan Division—the most decorated formation in the French Army—two U.S. divisions dislodged the Germans from their strongly entrenched positions.

The town of Château-Thierry lay at the apex of the 1918 German advance to the Marne River, and accordingly was a vital sector when the Allies moved over to the offensive during the Second Battle of the Marne. Three divisions were chosen to lead the attack around Château-Thierry: 2d U.S. Infantry Division, the crack Moroccan Division of the French Army, and 1st U.S. Infantry Division. Their goal was to seize the high ground to the south of the town of Soissons and provide a springboard for the general offensive against the German salient.

The attack got underway at 4:35 AM on 18 July, with a short but intense barrage from the Allied guns. The overstretched German line buckled under the pressure. The U.S. 2d Division made excellent progress, advancing 5 miles (8 km) during the first day of fighting and taking 3,000 prisoners, albeit suffering 4,000 casualties of its own in the process. The U.S. 1st Division suffered more heavily, sustaining 7,000 casualties in four days of fighting; during this time it advanced nearly 7 miles (11 km), capturing 3,500 of the enemy and sixty-eight guns. While these two American divisions acted as the spearhead for the U.S. Army, six more American divisions were also fed into the battle over the next few days.

The Americans' readiness and enthusiasm for combat won them the respect of their opponents and the admiration of their French allies, but for this fearlessness there was a high cost in dead and wounded. **AG**

Losses: U.S., 11,000 casualties; German, unknown

◁ Second Marne 1918   Amiens 1918 ▷

Amiens 8–12 August 1918

The British Commonwealth offensive against the Germans near Amiens was arguably the most complete and successful of the whole war on the Western Front. Its effect on German morale was profound: General Erich Ludendorff lamented that 8 August was "the black day of the German Army."

On 8 August the British initiated a series of offensive operations that would push the Germans back across the old Somme battlefield. The Australian, Canadian, and British III Corps from the Fourth Army—with the French Third Army alongside—opened the offensive in front of Amiens. As at Cambrai, the initial success was gained by predicted shooting, followed by an assault by tanks masked by fog, although on this occasion the battle was far better handled by the British commanders. The Canadians and Australians smashed through the German lines and only the British experienced any real difficulties.

By the end of the first day's fighting, the Fourth Army had penetrated the German defenses by a distance of 8 miles (13 km) and had taken 15,000 prisoners and 400 guns. The French—to the south of the British—attacked on 10 August and pushed the Germans, who were already beginning to retreat, back to the vital rail junction at Montdidier. On 12 August the battle was closed down in readiness for an assault elsewhere.

The real importance of the Amiens offensive lay in its effect on German morale. For the first time in the war, whole German divisions had withdrawn without putting up their usual determined resistance, while reinforcements were met with abuse by retreating German troops. For General Ludendorff and the Kaiser, the defeat was a psychological turning point, the latter admitting that "the war must be ended." **AG**

Losses: British and Commonwealth, 22,200 casualties; German, 74,000 casualties, including 50,000 captured

◁ Château-Thierry 1918   St. Mihiel 1918 ▷

St. Mihiel 12–16 September 1918

The Allied attack against the St. Mihiel salient provided the Americans with an opportunity to use their forces on the Western Front en masse. Although lacking some of the tactical skills of the French and British, the U.S. First Army carried the day through sheer determination.

The American commander-in-chief in France, General John Pershing, had, in the main, fought off attempts to use his divisions piecemeal in support of French and British operations, preferring to hold them back to form a separate U.S. army. The attack on the St. Mihiel salient on 12 September gave him the opportunity to use the U.S. First Army in combat for the first time. The American part of the assault was to be conducted by two "super" corps, each with three divisions in attack and one in reserve. Two smaller French corps would provide support on the western part of the salient.

General Erich von Ludendorff—now short of men and aware of the coming Allied offensive—had decided to withdraw from the salient to a shorter and more easily defended line to the rear. As the Germans were withdrawing, the Allies attacked. With much of their artillery not in place, the Germans were poorly prepared to maintain the front line, an advantage that the attacking Americans were quick to exploit. The relative ease of the initial American attack came as a surprise to Pershing, and he sent orders to his commanders to speed up their advance. By 13 September lead units of the U.S. First Army had met up with Allied troops advancing from the west. Three days later, the offensive was halted, with the salient in Allied hands. Pershing now dispatched his forces westward to take part in the forthcoming Meuse-Argonne offensive. **AG**

Losses: U.S., 7,000 casualties; German, at least 17,500, including 10,000 captured

◁ *Amiens 1918*   *Meuse-Argonne 1918* ▷

Megiddo 19 September–1 October 1918

In the culmination of his offensive to crush the Turkish army in Palestine, General Edmund Allenby concentrated his forces, while maintaining the element of surprise. An excellent example of the "all arms battle," the offensive combined artillery, infantry, cavalry, and airpower to achieve victory.

By mid-1918 the Turkish army was poorly fed, clothed, and supplied; disease and desertion were rife. For his initial assault, Allenby concentrated 35,000 infantry, 9,000 cavalry, and 383 guns against 8,000 Turkish infantry with 130 guns. To preserve secrecy, all troop movement was undertaken at night, dummy camps were set up in the Jordan Valley, and the Royal Air Force (RAF) attacked all opposing reconnaissance aircraft. A night of raids on Turkish communications by the RAF and Arab forces under Emir Feisal and T. E. Lawrence opened the battle.

On 19 September, infantry of XXI Corps and cavalry from the Desert Mounted Corps smashed through Turkish lines. By midday the Turks were in general retreat. This became a rout as the RAF bombed and machine-gunned the mass of troops. Success was so complete that, after 21 September, Allenby's men faced no serious infantry fighting. A race then ensued for Damascus between Allenby's cavalry and Arabs under Feisal and Lawrence. Both entered the city on 1 October, Lawrence being just beaten to the prize by Australians of the 3rd Light Horse Brigade. In thirty-eight days, Allenby's troops advanced 350 miles (565 km) and transformed Turkish forces in Palestine from an army into a disorganized rabble. Much of the success was due to the cavalry's rapid advance and the striking power of aircraft. This makes Megiddo a turning point in history as the last great cavalry victory and an early example of the decisive use of airpower. **AW**

Losses: British and Commonwealth, 5,666; Turkish, 8,000 casualties plus 75,000 captured

◁ *Jerusalem 1917*

Meuse-Argonne 26 September–11 November 1918

Meuse-Argonne was the largest and toughest battle fought by the Americans in World War I, where inexperience was ruthlessly exposed by the combat-hardened Germans. But the battle was also a "coming of age" for the U.S. Army, ultimately proving it the equal of allies and opponents.

After its success at St. Mihiel, the U.S. First Army was redeployed to join the French Fourth Army in an advance through the Argonne forest to seize the vital rail junction at Sedan. This attack was part of a series of Allied offensives on the Western Front, whose prime objective was to breach the Hindenburg Line farther north.

General John Pershing's Americans had very little time to prepare for the coming battle, which began with a 17-mile-wide (27 km) attack to the east of the Argonne forest on 26 September. Initially, the Americans met little

resistance from the sparsely manned frontline trenches, but the Germans were employing their elastic defense, in which troops were held back from the front to protect them from the initial enemy barrage and prepare them for counterattacks. The First Army also had problems caused by the rapid move from St. Mihiel; understandably, few staff had previously redeployed large forces so swiftly.

The fast American advance came to a juddering stop as it encountered the well-prepared German second line. The frontline American troops also found that guns and supplies could not get through over the broken ground of the battlefield to support them. The U.S. higher command lost control of several units, while German counterattacks forced Americans to retreat in many places. The line eventually stabilized and the offensive was resumed on 4 October. Progress was slow, but the Germans did retire to new defensive lines by the 10th.

The battle then paused again, providing Pershing with an opportunity to reorganize his forces on 12 October. Command of the First Army passed to Lieutenant General Hunter Liggett, who would lead the offensive, while a new Second Army was created under the command of Lieutenant General Robert L. Bullard. Pershing now became the U.S. Army Group commander. Two days later the offensive was resumed, with slow progress set against heavy American casualties. Liggett decided to break off the offensive to allow his exhausted troops to recuperate.

On 1 November Liggett, his troops rested and resupplied, resumed the attack. Modifying Pershing's plan of a head-on assault against the well-defended Bois de Bourgogne, Liggett directed his troops to outflank the position in conjunction with the French Fourth Army. The tactic worked—the Americans broke through the German line and began to push the enemy back toward Sedan with some rapidity. For the first time in the battle, the Americans were advancing ahead of the French on their left. Greatly improved staff work allowed the advance to continue without delay, denying the Germans any chance to draw breath and regroup. Although Pershing had ordered his troops to take Sedan, Liggett chivalrously drew back to allow the French to occupy the town, partially redressing the humiliation of 1870.

British military theorist and historian Basil Liddell-Hart evaluated the U.S. Army's contribution to the battle as "proof that when purged and refined by experience the American Army could produce leadership and staff work worthy of the gallant sacrifice of the fighting troops." **AG**

Losses: U.S., 117,000 casualties; French, 70,000 casualties; German, 120,000 casualties

◁ *St. Mihiel 1918*   *Canal du Nord 1918* ▷

Canal du Nord
27 September 1918

The Canal du Nord was one of the strongest positions within the German Hindenburg Line defenses on the Western Front, but excellent planning and the determination of British and Commonwealth soldiers produced a victory that opened the way to ultimate success in the war.

After a series of defeats at the hands of the Allies in August and September 1918, General Erich Ludendorff ordered his troops back to the old Hindenburg Line, the strongest—but also the last—line of prepared defenses available to the German army. During 1918 the already impressive Hindenburg Line had been improved further, with key areas comprising fortifications that stretched back from the front to a depth of 10 miles (16 km). One of these areas was the Canal du Nord, close to the old Cambrai battlefield. Although the canal itself was largely dry, it remained a formidable obstacle.

Divisions from the Allied Third Army and First Army were assembled for the attack, the assault troops drawn from British, Canadian, and New Zealand formations. The nature of the terrain was unsuitable for tanks. The main advance was preceded by a bombardment that was spread across a 30-mile (48 km) line in a bid to confuse the Germans as to the point of attack. The Canadians led the way, and on a narrow front they managed the cross the canal and smash their way into the Hindenburg Line.

Once a gap had been made, other divisions could follow. Fighting their way across the old Cambrai battlefield of 1917, the British army now had the satisfaction of achieving a proper exploitation: 6 miles (9.6 km) were gained and 10,000 prisoners and 200 guns taken. With the Canal du Nord in Allied hands, the way was clear for the breaking of the St. Quentin position. **AG**

Losses: Unknown

◁ *Meuse-Argonne 1918*　　*St. Quentin Canal 1918* ▷

St. Quentin Canal
29 September–10 October 1918

The climax of the Allied offensive on the Western Front came in late September with the British-led attack on the Siegfried Stellung (position), the best defended section of the Hindenburg Line. When it was broken, the German High Command had little option but to sue for peace.

The key element of the Siegfried Stellung was the bridge over the St. Quentin Canal at the village of Bellenglise. Taking the bridge was the objective of the British Fourth Army, its attack force drawn from British and Australian formations, plus two divisions from the U.S. Army. The British High Command gave the Americans the task of preparing the way for the main attack, to be conducted by the highly experienced Australians. There was some confusion as the Australians moved through the American units, with the usual whirlwind artillery barrage having to be replaced by a tank attack.

The advance over the canal at Bellenglise by the 46th (North Midland) Division was spectacular; the steep-sided canal traversed in the face of massed machine-gun and artillery fire. As 2 October ended, the division had lost 800 men but captured 4,200 of the enemy. Such success by an "ordinary" fighting division reflected the transformation of warfare on the Western Front in the autumn of 1918—the British army's finest hour.

Beyond the canal lay the Beaurevoir Line—the third and last line of the Hindenburg defenses—which caused the Anglo-Australian force some difficulty until it too fell on 10 October. This was the beginning of the end for the German army, whose commanders concluded that they must make an immediate approach to American President Woodrow Wilson requesting his good offices to set in place an armistice. **AG**

Losses: Unknown

◁ *Canal du Nord 1918*

British soldiers crowd on a bank of the dry St. Quentin Canal following its recapture. ➔

Vittorio Veneto 24 Oct–4 Nov 1918

The final offensive launched on the Italian Front during World War I, this Italian assault coincided with the internal political breakup of the multinational Hapsburg Empire. The defeat of the Austro-Hungarian army consigned the centuries-old empire to the pages of history and dramatically changed the political map of central Europe.

Under political pressure to act before the Austro-Hungarians secured armistice arrangements with U.S. President Woodrow Wilson, Italian commander-in-chief General Armando Diaz launched a major offensive across the Piave River and north against the strongpoint of Mt. Grappa. With the Piave in flood, Diaz first attacked Mt. Grappa on 24 October. Three days of heavy fighting brought little gain against a stubborn defense.

Able to bridge the Piave late on 26 October, Diaz opened the second phase of the operation. On 29 October the Austro-Hungarian line along the river began to crack. The breakdown of the defense coincided with declarations of independence from the provisional Czechoslovak government in Prague and the Hungarian dissolution of their union with Austria.

Short of equipment, rations, and manpower, the Austro-Hungarian army was no longer a coherent fighting force. Some units simply abandoned their positions and began marching home to their new nation states. From 30 October the Italian advance was slowed only by its rapidly growing number of prisoners. On 3 November an armistice was signed, to come into effect on the 4th. The Austro-Hungarian command ordered its men to cease hostilities after the signing, but the Italians continued their advance, taking many more prisoners and reaching the Isonzo River without opposition. **AW**

Losses: Italian, 40,000 casualties; Austro-Hungarian, 35,000 casualties and 430,000 captured

◁ Caporetto 1917

Petrograd 3–24 October 1919

The Bolshevik government installed by Vladimir Ilyich Lenin in Russia in November 1917 was assailed from all sides by internal opponents and foreign troops. But it held the main centers of government, industry, and population. Its success at holding Petrograd, inspired by Red Army founder Lev Trotsky, ensured that it would survive.

The Bolsheviks labeled their Russian enemies in the civil war "Whites," implying, incorrectly, that all wanted to restore autocratic rule. The White commander in the northwest, General Nikolai Yudenich, intended to march on Petrograd, while other forces threatened Moscow from the south and east. Yudenich's forces were small, and his only practical option was to gain support from newly independent Finland and Estonia. However, he was unwilling to recognize their independence and was left to pursue his campaign alone.

Yudenich faced a much larger Red Army, but it was sadly lacking in organization and training. In the face of his more experienced force the Seventh Red Army simply collapsed and abandoned its equipment. It seemed the city must fall. Lev Trotsky arrived in Petrograd to take command, later stating that he found the populace waiting to surrender and his troops falling back in confusion. While Trotsky claimed that he halted the army's retreat and inspired the citizens to construct three lines of defense within and outside the city, it is likely that officers who had begun their careers in the imperial army played a greater one in organizing an effective defense.

At the well-constructed Pulkovo line, Yudenich's force was halted in its tracks. The next day a counterattack was launched, which saved Petrograd and drove Yudenich completely from Russia. **JS**

Losses: Unknown

Warsaw 1920 ▷

A poster by Nikolai Kochergin urges: "The enemy is at the gates! All rise to defend Petrograd!"

ВРАГ У ВОРОТ!!!

ВСЕ НА ЗАЩИТУ
ПЕТРОГРАДА

Warsaw 12–25 August 1920

In a war that pitted Bolshevik revolutionary fervor against Polish nationalism, the Russian Bolsheviks suffered a humiliating defeat. The great Polish victory over the Red Army outside Warsaw ensured the survival of an independent Poland and may have prevented a Bolshevik invasion of Germany.

By 1920 the Bolsheviks had triumphed in the Russian Civil War, but the borders of the Bolshevik-ruled state were still uncertain. The Poles, asserting their newly found independence, pressed eastward into Belarus and Ukraine, leading to clashes as the Red Army extended Bolshevik rule westward. Excited by some quick victories over Polish forces, Lenin conceived of a singularly dubious scheme: he would export revolution on the bayonet points of the Red Army. They would invade Poland, and as they approached Warsaw the Polish Communists would lead the working class into revolution and welcome the Red Army as liberators, a pattern to be followed in Germany and beyond. In vain Poles warned Lenin that an

"The Poles believed earnestly that they were fighting for . . . freedom, language, traditions, and religion."

U.S. Major Michael Fibich, who served in the Polish army

invasion by Russians would unite all Polish classes against Russia, their historic oppressor.

The Polish-born and much feared head of the *Cheka* (Bolshevik secret police), Feliks Dzierzinsky, was made head of a Polish Revolutionary Committee, which would follow the Red Army and form the new government. Lenin was absolutely confident of success. Initially all went well, and within six weeks the Red Army was at the gates of Warsaw. But as the Polish Communists had warned, all classes did indeed unite, and there was no rising in

the city. Also the Polish commander, Józef Piłsudski, drew up a bold, if not foolhardy, plan of counterattack. The Polish army would stand on the defensive in front of the city, and when the Red Army was fully committed to the battle, Poland's best units would launch a flanking attack from the south, cut the Bolshevik lines of communication, and encircle much of the Red Army. Some Polish generals were aghast at the risks involved, but in their desperation there seemed no alternative.

When the Red Army launched what was expected to be the final assault on Warsaw, Piłsudski had to begin his counterattack twenty-four hours early, with some units not yet in position, for fear that Warsaw might fall if he waited. The Red Army fought its way to the village of Izabelin, only 8 miles (13 km) from the city, but the Polish attack succeeded beyond wildest expectations. Driving through a gap in Bolshevik lines, the Poles advanced rapidly against little opposition. In the Red Army, all was chaos; commanders lost control of their units, with some divisions continuing their advance on Warsaw, others fleeing. Three armies disintegrated, and thousands fled into East Prussia, where they were interned. In an encounter that saw Polish lancers charging and overwhelming Bolshevik cavalrymen, the First Cavalry Army, trapped in the "Zemość Ring," was all but annihilated.

The Fourth Army meekly surrendered after being encircled. Marshal Mikhail Tukhachevsky desperately tried to pull his troops back to a defendable line, but the situation was beyond redemption. A few more engagements followed, but the war was effectively won. Lenin was forced to agree to peace terms that surrendered a large tract of territory whose population was in no way Polish—the Red Army returned to reclaim it in 1939. **JS**

Losses: Soviet, uncertain but possibly up to 50,000 dead or wounded, 66,000 captured, and up to 40,000 interned in Germany; Polish, up to 5,000 dead and 22,000 wounded

◁ *Petrograd 1919*

The Legion of Polish Women served in the determined and successful defense of Warsaw. ➔

Members of a Berber war party in the mountains during the Rif War.

Annual   22 July–9 August 1921

The triumph of Berber leader Abd el-Krim over Spanish forces at Annual in the Rif region of northern Morocco was one of Spain's worst military disasters. The shock it gave to the Spanish political system led to the establishment of the military dictatorship of General Primo de Rivera in 1923.

In the early twentieth century, France and Spain divided Morocco between them. The mountainous Rif region fell within the Spanish "sphere of influence," but in practice Spain controlled only the coastal enclaves of Ceuta and Melilla. When it tried to extend its rule into the Rif, Abd el-Krim organized the resistance of the Berber tribes, who were skilled marksmen with a natural ability to fight and survive in their harsh physical environment. In 1921 General Manuel Silvestre led an army of ill-trained Spanish conscripts into the Moroccan interior, garrisoning a series of isolated outposts that were dependent upon lines of communication to the coast. The Berbers began picking off these outposts and massacring their garrisons.

General Silvestre was commanding 5,000 men at Annual when it was besieged in mid-July. Soon out of water and food, the Spanish attempted a withdrawal that turned into a rout. Silvestre was killed along with most of his troops. Spanish soldiers from other outposts fled for the coast, mercilessly harassed by Abd el-Krim's irregulars. General Felipe Navarro was sent from Melilla to organize a stand at the fort of Monte Arruit, but he was surrounded and forced to surrender on 9 August. In September Abd el-Krim declared the Rif an independent republic. **RG**

Losses: Berber, no reliable figures; Spanish, 13,000 dead, wounded, or captured of 20,000

Alhucemas Bay   1925 ▷

Sakariya (Sangarios) 23 August–13 September 1921

The Battle of Sakariya was a crucial moment in the history of modern Turkey. Mustafa Kemal, the hero of Gallipoli, halted a Greek attempt to conquer Anatolia, preserving his project to found a Turkish Republic and frustrating the ambitions of Greek nationalists to create a "Greater Greece."

The collapse of the Ottoman Empire in 1918 was followed by a Turkish national revolution, led by Mustafa Kemal. Britain and France meanwhile encouraged Greek ambitions to take over much of Anatolia. Faced with a Greek invasion, Kemal chose to make a stand on the Sakariya River in front of Ankara, where the undersupplied Greeks would suffer burning days and very cold nights.

Both armies were weary, but the Turks were fighting for their homeland and their morale was higher. Kemal fought a defensive battle, ordering that any unit driven from a position should create a new position as close to the enemy as possible—neighboring units should follow suit only when necessary. This proved extremely frustrating for the Greeks, who were unable to exploit local successes. A grueling battle of attrition developed with heavy losses on both sides. Eventually, Kemal launched 5,000 carefully concealed reserves into a reckless counterattack, stunning their enemy.

Exhausted, the Greeks withdrew toward the coast, and the Turks were too weary to pursue. The French signed a secret peace agreement with Kemal, while Rome and Moscow agreed to supply arms. The Turks would be in a much stronger position when the fighting resumed. **JS**

Losses: Greek, nearly 23,000 dead or wounded; Turkish, 12,000–38,000 dead, wounded, or missing

Dumlupinar 1922 ⊳

Four Courts 28–30 June 1922

In December 1921 Irish nationalists agreed to a treaty with the British government that ended a two-year independence war. But part of the Irish Republican Army (IRA) rejected the treaty, precipitating a civil war that began with the siege of the Four Courts, Dublin's main courthouse building, in June 1922.

Michael Collins, a prominent IRA commander during the independence war, negotiated the Anglo-Irish Treaty and became president of the provisional government of the Irish Free State in 1922. In April the anti-treaty IRA occupied the Four Courts building in Dublin in defiance of the provisional government, turning it into a fortress surrounded with barbed wire, mines, and barricades.

Collins came under mounting pressure from the British, who still had troops in the Free State, to suppress the anti-treaty forces. Eventually he accepted a loan of British artillery and placed field guns opposite the Four Courts. When the IRA refused to leave the building, a bombardment began on 28 June. The anti-treaty irregulars were armed with rifles and light machine guns, plus a single armored car. Free State troops stormed through breaches in the building on 30 June, suffering significant casualties but succeeding in disabling the armored car. Fighting was continuing inside the Four Courts when a massive explosion of munitions stored in the records office shattered the west wing of the building, injuring many Free State troops. A few hours later the anti-treaty garrison surrendered. Street fighting continued across Dublin through the following week until the city was securely in Free State hands.

This small-scale battle had major consequences. The resulting year-long civil war—to be won by the Free State forces—cost thousands of lives, including that of Michael Collins, and left an enduring legacy of bitterness. **RG**

Losses: Anti-treaty irregulars, 172 captured of 200; Free State, 3 dead and 50 wounded of 4,000

< *Easter Rising 1916*

Dumlupinar 26–30 August 1922

In the final battle of the Greco-Turkish War, the Turkish victory was overwhelming. The subsequent burning of Smyrna (now Izmir) marked the end of a Greek presence in Anatolia dating back millennia. Turkish commander Mustafa Kemal was hailed as his country's greatest national hero.

Following the Battle of Sakariya, Kemal spent a year reequipping, reorganizing, and expanding his army. The Greeks withdrew troops from Anatolia to Thrace for an attack on Istanbul (Constantinople) that never materialized. Occupying an apparently secure defensive line 250 miles (400 km) in front of Izmir, along hilly ground well-suited for defense, the Greeks awaited events.

The Turkish attack, when it came, stunned the Greeks. After an extremely accurate and effective barrage that silenced the Greek artillery, an infantry assault was pressed regardless of losses. Within twenty-four hours the Turks had taken the mountain position at Erkmentepe. The Greek lines had been broken and Turkish cavalry swept through. Soon the Greek forces were split in two, and their communications were cut. The Greek I Corps fell back on the town of Dumlupinar, only to find itself encircled by a Turkish pincer movement; one-quarter of the Greek force soon surrendered. The Greek II Corps fell back in a disorder that rapidly became a rout as entire divisions disintegrated. Panic-stricken Greek troops fled, leaving abandoned equipment and burning villages behind them. Pursued all the way to Smyrna, soldiers and civilians thought only of getting aboard a ship.

While Smyrna burned, western warships in the harbor made no attempt to aid refugees or extinguish the fires. Most Greeks escaped, but a population exchange in the peace terms meant that they would never return. **JS**

Losses: Turkish, fewer than 12,000 dead or wounded; Greek, more than 29,000 dead or wounded, 50,000 captured

< *Sakariya 1921*

Alhucemas Bay 8–30 September 1925

The Spanish attack on Abd el-Krim's Moroccan Rif Republic at Alhucemas (Al Hoceima) was a successful experiment in amphibious warfare. With Colonel Francisco Franco playing a prominent role, it was a turning point in the Rif War, restoring Spanish pride after the disaster at Annual.

By 1925 Abd el-Krim was at war not only with Spain but with France, which feared for the security of its neighboring zone of Morocco. The Spanish and French planned coordinated offensives. World War I hero Marshal Philippe Pétain would lead an invasion from French Morocco while the Spanish Army of Africa landed troops on the coast near the Rif capital Ajdir. The forces assembling for the landings included the hardened volunteers of the Spanish Foreign Legion, led by Franco, and tough Moroccan recruits.

On 8 September Spanish and French warships bombarded the landing beaches, which were also strafed and bombed from the air. The Spanish troops headed for the shore in barges pulled by tugs, coming under fire from Rif artillery. An unexpected barrier of shoals forced the troops to disembark and wade ashore, leaving their heavy equipment behind. However, after stiff fighting they established a beachhead, incurring the loss of 124 men. The Rif army delivered ferocious counterattacks, but these were beaten off with the aid of accurate naval gunnery.

By 20 September the Spanish had 15,000 men ashore. The heaviest fighting began two days later with an assault against Rif troops entrenched on Mount Malmusi. Around 700 Spanish soldiers were killed before the feature was taken. Few of the defenders survived. Ajdir fell in early October. Abd el-Krim fought on until May 1926, when he surrendered to the French and went into exile for life. **RG**

Losses: Rif republicans, no reliable figures; Spanish,1,000 dead of 15,000

◁ Annual 1921   Toledo 1936 ▷

Longtan 25–30 April 1927

Chiang Kai-shek, leader of the Chinese Nationalists (Kuomintang), was struggling to unite China under his government but was opposed by powerful regional warlords. His defeat of the northern warlord Sun Chuangfang at Longtan brought all of China at least nominally under Kuomintang rule.

Chiang Kai-shek's push to extend his control over north China was dubbed the Northern Expedition. Early in the campaign, sensing that his Communist allies were becoming too powerful, Chiang attacked them, his troops carrying out a massacre of Communists in Shanghai on 12 April. This threw the expedition into some disarray, allowing Sun Chuangfang's Northern Army to strike, capturing Longtan and threatening Nanjing.

Kuomintang troops put up a strong resistance, holding the vital position of Mount Wulongshan long enough for reinforcements to arrive. They were soon in a position to attack the equally important position of Mount Qixiashan, reputedly aided by gunfire from British warships intended to support Sun's forces. Sun counterattacked and retook Qixiashan twice more but was unable to hold it. Within the city of Longtan, Sun, who established his headquarters at the China Cement Factory, directed the prolonged and bitter battle. Almost continual street fighting lasted six days and nights. The city changed hands twice before six more Kuomintang divisions were thrown into the fray and Sun's forces finally expelled.

Sun fled across the Yangtze River in a small boat. The bulk of his troops were less fortunate and most surrendered. In 1928 Chiang was widely recognized as China's sole legitimate ruler, but his dispute with the Chinese Communist Party led to outright civil war. **JS**

Losses: Northern, 8,000 dead or wounded, 40,000 captured of 60,000–70,000; Kuomintang, unknown

◁ Beijing 1900   Mukden Incident 1931 ▷

Mukden Incident 18 September 1931

An act of aggression by Japanese forces against China, this contrived incident was carried out without the authorization of the Japanese government. It contributed to the international isolation of Japan and is seen as a crucial event on the path to the outbreak of World War II.

Japan had long had strong interests in Manchuria, a theoretically autonomous part of China with valuable mineral and agricultural resources. Japan coveted these after its economy suffered badly in the Great Depression, but the growing power of Chinese nationalism was deemed a threat to these interests. To provide a pretext to drive out Chinese influence, Lieutenant Suemori Komoto of Japan's Kwantung army planted forty-two packs of gun cotton along the Japanese-controlled South Manchurian Railway. The explosion did little damage; indeed, the next train simply passed over the site without stopping. But the Kwantung army claimed it was the work of Chinese

bandits, and that they had to act to restore order. They attacked the city of Mukden, scattered its larger but poorly armed and virtually untrained garrison, and looted the homes of government officials.

Within five months the Japanese had occupied the whole of Manchuria. They met only sporadic resistance—poorly armed and untrained troops were no match for the Japanese. China's leader, Chiang Kai-shek, preferred to leave it to the international community to restrain Japan and offered no resistance, but the Chinese were outraged and a very damaging popular boycott on Japanese goods followed. Demands that Japan be resisted grew ever louder. While the League of Nations did not act, it condemned Japan's occupation, and few would recognize the new puppet state of Manchukuo. Japan, it seemed, had gained little from this adventure. **JS**

Losses: Unknown

◁ *Longtan 1927*　　　*Shanghai 1932* ▷

Japanese troops march into Manchuria on the pretext of restoring order. ⬆

Shanghai   28 January–3 March 1932

After the Mukden Incident, a Japanese attack on the port-city of Shanghai increased pressure upon the Chinese Nationalist government. Japan once again prevailed in a conflict that it had engineered, but stiff Chinese resistance came as an unpleasant surprise to the Japanese aggressors.

Alarmed by the outburst of anti-Japanese sentiment in China and anxious to distract attention from Manchuria, the Japanese military again provoked confrontation, this time instigating riots in Shanghai. Despite the city authorities agreeing to apologize and pay compensation for claimed insults to Japan, Japanese aircraft carriers launched air strikes on the city's civilian population.

As Japanese troops entered Shanghai, Chinese Nationalist leader Chiang Kai-shek decided to defend the vital port. Both sides rushed in reinforcements and fighting escalated. Working-class districts, deemed hotbeds of nationalism, were subject to particularly heavy Japanese air and naval bombardment. Within the city there was brutal house-to-house fighting, and Japanese vehicles came under punishing sniper fire in the narrow streets. Outside the city Chiang brought up some of his best troops, where they fought well—one brigade reputedly launched five bayonet charges in a single hour. When the Japanese breached Chinese lines, heroic but bloody counterattacks drove them back, but eventually Japan's superior airpower and firepower prevailed.

A cease-fire was agreed that was humiliating enough to China—their military was to withdraw from Shanghai and a few other coastal cities, which would be policed by the Japanese. But the Japanese hesitated for five more years before risking renewed conflict in China. **JS**

Losses: Japanese, 385–800 dead, 2,000–4,000 wounded of 47,000–100,000; Chinese, 4,000–6,000 dead, 10,000–11,000 wounded of 50,000–63,000, up to 20,000 civilians dead

◁ *Mukden Incident 1931*   *Marco Polo Bridge 1937* ▷

⬆ *Japanese soldiers search for Chinese snipers from the cover of a rooftop in Shanghai.*

Fortín Nanawa 20–30 January 1933

Between 1932 and 1935 the landlocked South American states of Paraguay and Bolivia fought for control of the arid Gran Chaco region in a war that cost 90,000 lives. The successful Paraguayan defense of Fortín Nanawa was an important step toward Paraguay's eventual victory in the war.

Skirmishes between Bolivian and Paraguayan troops in the sparsely populated region began in the 1920s. By the time full-scale war broke out in the summer of 1932, both sides had imported substantial quantities of modern equipment from Europe, along with military advisers—French on the Paraguayan side, German on the Bolivian. The fighting concentrated on control of isolated "fortín" outposts. Fortín Nanawa, strategically vital to Paraguay, was modeled on field fortifications in Europe—trenches, barbed wire, machine-gun posts, and artillery.

In January 1933, Fortín Nanawa came under attack from Bolivian forces commanded by General Hans Kundt. The Bolivians included 6,000 cavalry reduced to fighting on foot because their horses had died of thirst. The Paraguayan garrison was commanded by the resolute Colonel Luis Irrazábal Barboza. His well-motivated troops succeeded in beating off Bolivian attacks, which suffered the usual fate of frontal assaults on prepared defenses manned by soldiers with modern firearms. Although the Paraguayans soon began to lack ammunition, an airstrip was improvised and the whole of Paraguay's small air force was employed to fly in munitions, landing and taking off under enemy fire. After ten days, the Bolivian attack was called off and the Paraguayans celebrated a major victory. Despite its far smaller population, Paraguay went on to defeat Bolivia in the war. **RG**

Losses: Bolivian, 2,000 casualties; Paraguayan, 248 casualties

◁ Campo Grande 1869

Toledo 20 July–27 September 1936

Early in the Spanish Civil War, the siege of Toledo's Alcázar was a hugely symbolic victory for the Nationalists. The fortress, controlled by Nationalist soldiers, was besieged by Republican militiamen for two months, before General Franco's Army of Africa arrived to relieve the defenders.

Following the Nationalist military rebellion, the Spanish Republican government sent a militia force of around 8,000 men to take the city of Toledo in July 1936. The Nationalist force in Toledo took a number of hostages (family members of known leftists) and retreated into the city's Alcázar, a half-palace half-fortress that had served as a military academy since the nineteenth century.

Around 1,000 Nationalist soldiers commanded by Colonel José Moscardó, the military governor of Toledo, defended the Alcázar against a Republican attack that lasted for around seventy days. The Nationalist resistance held out against heavy bombing and artillery fire until the Army of Africa, commanded by General Franco, arrived to provide relief and defeat the Republicans. While strategically the Alcázar was of little value to either side, symbolically it was very important. The victory was the subject of a huge Nationalist propaganda campaign; the liberation was restaged for news cameras on the next day.

The Nationalists in Toledo then massacred many of the Republican soldiers and supporters, infamously killing 200 wounded soldiers in the Toledo hospital with grenades. Franco's decision to relieve the troops at Toledo, rather than advance to Madrid as many had expected, was taken largely because he recognized the propaganda value of the Alcázar. Franco emerged as the principal leader of the Nationalists and was proclaimed *Generalissimo*. **ND**

Losses: Republican, heavy casualties (figures unknown); Nationalist, 65 dead and 440 wounded

◁ Alhucemas Bay 1925   Badajoz 1936 ▷

Badajoz   14 August 1936

The attack on the Spanish city of Badajoz was one of the first major victories for the Nationalist rebellion against the Republic in the Spanish Civil War. The battle was followed by a bloody massacre in which the Nationalists killed thousands of Republican soldiers and civilians.

By July 1936 the Nationalist military rebellion against the Spanish Republic had gathered momentum. Soldiers of the Army of Africa, commanded by General Francisco Franco, had been airlifted by German and Italian planes to join the Nationalist offensive in southern Spain. The offensive soon connected the Nationalist territories in the north and south of Spain. Badajoz was the final remaining Republican outpost on the Portuguese border, isolated from the rest of the Republican territory.

Under General Franco's instructions, Lieutenant Colonel Juan Yagüe led a Nationalist force, consisting largely of Foreign Legionaries and Moroccan mercenary fighters, in an offensive against the city. Badajoz was defended by Republican militiamen, who had taken control of the city's medieval fortress. On 14 August the attack began with heavy artillery and bombing, which enabled the Nationalist forces to breach the defense. The professional Nationalist soldiers faced fierce resistance from the militia force, but at last took control of Badajoz.

The Nationalists then proceeded to kill thousands of Republican soldiers and civilians in the city. Many of those killed were infamously taken to the city's bullring and executed with machine guns. The massacre of Badajoz was intended to spread fear among citizens loyal to the Republic, particularly in Madrid, the principle target of the Nationalist offensive following the victory. **ND**

Losses: Republican, 750 dead of 8,000 in the initial battle, and 4,000 soldiers and civilians dead in the following massacre; Nationalist, 285 dead of 3,000

◁ Toledo 1936   Cape Espartel 1936 ▷

Cape Espartel   29 September 1936

In the Spanish Civil War many Spanish warships were taken over by their crews, who remained loyal to the Republican government. Nationalist-controlled warships were mostly based at El Ferrol, General Franco's birthplace, which had been seized in July 1936 after two days of bloody fighting.

On 29 September 1936 the Nationalist cruisers *Canarias* and *Almirante Cervera*, commanded by Franco's senior naval officer, Captain (later Admiral) Francisco de Moreno, left El Ferrol to try to break the Republican blockade of the Straits of Gibraltar. Much of the Republican fleet was in the Bay of Biscay, with just a small squadron of destroyers on blockade duty in the Straits.

Cervera skirmished with the destroyer *Gravina*, damaging her and chasing her into Casablanca, before falling upon her consort, *Almirante Ferrandiz*. Purges of Republican ratings had left *Canarias* with a partially trained crew, she was short of one 8-inch gun turret, and her antiaircraft guns had been improvised from whatever was available. Yet her heavier guns gave her the advantage over *Ferrandiz*, commanded by an ensign after her Nationalist captain had also been purged.

Canarias opened fire at 6:40 AM and kept the ensuing one-sided action at ranges of 8–11 miles (13–18 km), far outside the maximum range of *Ferrandiz*. Reduced to a blazing wreck, *Ferrandiz* blew up and sank at 7:20 AM, taking 100 of her crew of 160 with her. *Canarias* suffered no damage or casualties. Although small, the victory was strategically vital, as it opened the Straits of Gibraltar to Nationalist shipping; thousands of reinforcements from the Army of Africa now could be transported from Morocco to the mainland by sea. **NH**

Losses: Republican, 1 destroyer sunk; Nationalist, no ships

◁ Badajoz 1936   Madrid 1936 ▷

Madrid   8–23 November 1936

Following early Nationalist success in the Spanish Civil War, the Republicans looked set to lose Madrid to a powerful Nationalist offensive. However, a desperate defense of the capital followed, crucially supported by the arrival of the International Brigades. The Nationalists were defeated, ensuring Madrid remained in Republican hands.

At the start of November 1936 around 20,000 Nationalist soldiers under the command of General José Varela were poised to launch an attack on Madrid. To avoid open street fighting the Nationalists planned to concentrate the offensive at the Casa de Campo park, with a further attack in the suburb of Carabanchel. The Nationalist uprising against the Spanish Republic had been backed by Fascist Italy and Nazi Germany, so the Nationalist force at Madrid (consisting mainly of Moroccan mercenaries) had support from Italian light armor and German tanks, as well as air support from the German Condor Legion. Believing that this strong Nationalist force would win in

"'They cannot pass,' we tell each other. 'The offensive must be stopped.' It is worker against fascist on Spanish soil." Lise Lindbæk, journalist

Madrid, the Republican government moved to Valencia on 6 November; the defense of the capital was left to General José Miaja.

The attack began on 8 November. The Republicans, having learned of the strategy of the offensive, sent 30,000 ill-equipped and inexperienced troops to Casa de Campo and 12,000 more to Carabanchel. Despite the daunting prospect of trying to defend the city against a powerful Nationalist offensive with an untrained militia force, efforts were made to rally the population of Madrid,

with the famous call *"No Pasarán!"* ("They shall not pass!") booming from the city's radio stations.

General Miaja was assisted by Franco's decision to delay the offensive on Madrid in order to liberate the Alcázar of Toledo. This provided time for the delivery of Soviet aid to the Republic, and crucially allowed the formation of the International Brigades, comprising antifascist volunteers from Europe, North America, and elsewhere who had arrived in Spain to defend the Republic against the Nationalist rebellion. On the evening of 8 November the first International Brigade, consisting of 1,900 men, arrived in Madrid, boosting the city's morale.

The next day, the XI International Brigade launched an attack at Casa de Campo. Forced back, the Nationalists switched the focus of their offensive to Carabanchel. The Moroccan mercenary force had little experience of urban street fighting and incurred huge casualties at the hands of local militia fighters. Over the next few days, the Republicans launched a series of counterattacks, aided by the arrival of reinforcements in the form of 4,000 militiamen from the CNT workers' union, led by the legendary Spanish anarchist Buenaventura Durruti.

On 19 November the Nationalists launched a final offensive on Madrid's University City area. Heavy artillery fire enabled the Nationalist troops to cross the Manzanares River. Fierce street fighting followed, including hand-to-hand combat in university buildings, but the Republican resistance held firm and the Nationalists were forced back. Having incurred extensive losses, Franco decided to abandon attempts to take Madrid in a single offensive, but not before ordering the German aircraft to bomb the city for a number of days. Despite a continued siege of the capital, the Republicans had managed to defeat the Nationalists and keep hold of Madrid. **ND**

Losses: Republican, 5,000 military and civilian casualties of 42,000; Nationalist, 5,000 casualties of 20,000

◁ *Cape Espartel 1936*   *Jarama 1937* ▷

A propaganda poster from the Siege of Madrid. It says: "Defending Madrid is defending Catalonia." ➡

DEFENSAR MADRID ES DEFENSAR CATALUNYA

Jarama 6–27 February 1937

The powerful offensive launched by Franco's Nationalists against the Republicans in the Jarama Valley was halted largely by the efforts of the International Brigades. The Battle of Jarama, destined to end in a stalemate, was one of the bloodiest of the Spanish Civil War.

Following their failed attempt to take Madrid in November 1936, the Nationalist forces launched a major offensive in the valley of the Jarama River. Their aim was to cut off Madrid from Valencia, which had become the Republican capital during the war.

The Nationalists, led by General Luis Orgaz, attacked with five columns consisting of a large number of Moroccan mercenaries and Foreign Legionaries. The initial assaults took the Republicans by surprise. The intense artillery fire, together with the Moroccans' stealth tactics, enabled the Nationalists to advance across the Jarama (despite Republican attempts to blow up the bridge). The Nationalist forces took control of the Pingarrón hills and intense fighting ensued with the International Brigades who were located in Pajares Heights. The International Brigades managed to hold off the Nationalist attack with the support of Soviet aircraft (countering Nationalist planes) and tanks, but experienced horrific casualties.

The Republican forces launched a counterattack on 14 February that, while failing to recapture any of the lost ground, did ensure that the Nationalist advance was stopped. At the end of the battle, the Nationalist front had advanced a few miles, but the failure to take the Madrid-Valencia highway meant that there was no strategic gain. The battle saw some of the fiercest fighting of the war, with both sides incurring heavy casualties. **ND**

Losses: Republican, 25,000 casualties; Nationalist, 20,000 casualties

[<] *Madrid 1936*   *Guadalajara 1937* [>]

Guadalajara 8–23 March 1937

Supported by the Nationalists, Italian forces launched an offensive against the Republicans at Guadalajara. Assisted by adverse weather, the Republicans emerged victorious. While Guadalajara was strategically a minor defensive victory, Republican morale was greatly boosted.

Having failed to take Madrid prior to March 1937, the Nationalists continued their efforts to take the city. Their Italian allies had recently triumphed in Málaga and prepared to launch another offensive. Aiming to encircle Madrid, the Italians launched an attack at Guadalajara, a city 40 miles (64 km) northeast of Madrid, on 8 March.

The Italian offensive began with air raids and intense artillery fire, and then advanced with tanks. The attack led to the capture of numerous towns around Guadalajara, while the retreating Republicans rushed to organize a defense. The Italians continued to press forward, but were held up by thick fog and then a heavy snow storm, which they were ill-equipped to deal with. This delay allowed Republican reinforcements to arrive in support. Following a further advance by Italian and Nationalist forces, a Republican division under the command of General Enrique Líster launched a counterattack on 12 March.

The Italians were further hindered when aircraft of the Italian Legionary Air Force were grounded owing to waterlogged airfields. The Italian positions became easy targets for Republican fighter planes, which took off from airports with concrete airstrips. Despite being heavily outnumbered, the Republican troops pushed the Italians back and recaptured numerous towns. However, the successful Republican defense of Guadalajara was the last major Republican victory in the Spanish Civil War. **ND**

Losses: Republican, 6,000 casualties of 100,000; Nationalist and Italian, 2,200 dead, 4,000 wounded, and 300 captured of 52,000

[<] *Jarama 1937*   *Guernica 1937* [>]

Republican militia give a cheer for the camera at the time of the defense of Guadalajara.

Guernica   26 April 1937

The bombing of the ancient Basque city of Guernica by German and Italian planes is the first-ever example of civilians deliberately being made the target of aerial bombing. The attack—the subject of one of Picasso's most renowned paintings—is the most infamous event of the Spanish Civil War.

By late April 1937, Guernica had become strategically very important to the Nationalist forces in northern Spain, led by General Emilio Mola. The city lay between them and Bilbao, which was seen as the key to winning the war in the north of the country. The Nationalists had the air support of the German Condor Legion, commanded by Lieutenant Wolfram von Richthofen, sent to Spain by Hitler to test the fighting capabilities of the Luftwaffe.

Shortly prior to the bombing, Mola warned the Basques of the coming attack and demanded their surrender. The three-stage attack, named Operation Rügen, took place in the afternoon of 26 April. In the first stage, explosive bombs and hand grenades were dropped. This was followed by the machine-gunning of people running in the streets by fighter planes. In the third stage, the city was subjected to large numbers of incendiary bombs. The repeated strikes left three-quarters of the buildings in the city completely destroyed and the majority of the rest damaged. The use of incendiary bombs—coupled with the fact that the bridge (a key military target) had not been hit—left little doubt that bombing was deliberately directed at civilian targets. As a result of the bombing, the Nationalists faced little resistance in taking the city.

The attack on Guernica is seen as the first example of "terror bombing." Accounts of the event appeared in the French and British press in the days following the attack, prompting an international outcry. **ND**

"The air was alive with the cries of the wounded. I saw a man … dragging his broken legs …"

Juan Silliaco, survivor

⬆ *The bombing of Guernica was targeted on residential areas; anything of potential value to the Nationalists was spared.*

Losses: Republican, 300 civilians dead

◀ Guadalajara 1937   Brunete 1937 ▶

Brunete   6–26 July 1937

Aiming to relieve mounting pressure on Madrid and in the north, the Republicans launched a surprise attack against the Nationalists at Brunete. They had initial success but the Nationalists fought back strongly, inflicting extensive damage on the Republican forces and forcing them to retreat.

In mid-1937 Republican Madrid was experiencing increasing pressure from Nationalist forces. In response the Republicans decided to launch an attack at Brunete, a town 15 miles (24 km) west of Madrid. Brunete lay on the Extremadura road, heavily used by the Nationalists in supplying troops besieging Madrid.

The attack, led by Generals Juan Modesto and Enrique Jurado, began on the morning of 6 July with heavy Republican artillery fire against the Nationalist positions. The Nationalists were taken by surprise, and the Republicans soon captured Brunete and the Extremadura road. A number of days of intense fighting followed, with the Republicans attempting to advance south, but being held by the Nationalists. Finally, by 17 July the Republican offensive ground to a halt.

The following day saw the Nationalists launch a powerful counterattack under the command of General José Varela. The Nationalists—aided by German tanks and a new German fighter aircraft, the Messerschmidt Bf 109—managed to force the Republicans back, after ferocious fighting. When the Nationalist counteroffensive ended on 26 July, the Republican forces had been pushed back to their starting position and had lost control of the Extremadura. The failed offensive proved to be extremely costly for the Republicans. In addition to losing more than 20,000 of their best troops, they also lost a great deal of valuable equipment. **ND**

Losses: Republican, 20,000 casualties of 80,000; Nationalist, 10,000 casualties of 65,000

[<] *Guernica 1937*　　　　　　　　　　*Belchite 1937* [>]

Marco Polo Bridge   7–9 July 1937

It may be claimed that a skirmish between Chinese and Japanese troops at the Marco Polo Bridge outside Beijing was one of the most significant battles of the twentieth century. It precipitated full-scale war between China and Japan, and was in effect the first battle of World War II in Asia.

By summer 1937 the Japanese had control of China north of Beijing. The Chinese Nationalist government of Chiang Kai-shek was eager to resist Japanese encroachment and made an agreement with the Chinese Communists under Mao Ze Dong to suspend their civil war and form a united front against Japan.

In this tense situation, on 7 July Japanese troops carried out night exercises by the Marco Polo Bridge, a historic structure outside the town of Wanping, a key junction on railroads connecting Beijing to the rest of Nationalist China. Local Chinese troops, not informed that maneuvers were planned, randomly opened fire without hitting anyone. The following morning, however, a Japanese soldier was discovered to be missing.

The local Japanese commander ordered an attack on the nearby town of Wanping. The scale of the fighting grew, with several thousand troops engaged and the Marco Polo Bridge changing hands several times in attacks and counterattacks. On 9 July a cease-fire was agreed, but both sides reinforced their troops in the area of the bridge and cease-fire violations multiplied until full-scale fighting broke out in the last week of that month. Chiang Kai-shek announced aggressively: "If we allow one more inch of our territory to be lost, we shall be guilty of an unpardonable crime against our race." Outright war between China and Japan broke out on 13 August with a Chinese attack on Japanese marines in Shanghai. **JS**

Losses: Chinese, 96 dead of 1,000; Japanese, 660 casualties of 5,600

[<] *Shanghai 1932*　　　　　　　　　*Shanghai 1937* [>]

Shanghai   13 August–26 November 1937

The outbreak of fighting between Japan and China in Shanghai in 1937 is sometimes seen as the first battle of World War II. The Japanese eventually prevailed and the Chinese army never again fought so effectively. But Japan found itself trapped in a costly and unwinnable war.

In July 1937 renewed hostilities were imminent between China and Japan. Chinese leader Chiang Kai-shek, aware of his limited industrial base, wanted to shift the focus of the conflict away from the broad plains of northern China, where the Japanese could make the best use of their armor and airpower, to Shanghai, where narrow streets and urban warfare would limit those advantages. Also, the fighting would be seen firsthand by foreigners, attracting sympathy and perhaps even intervention.

Chiang therefore ordered troops into Shanghai, demilitarized after the battle in 1932, to threaten the Japanese Settlement. Japan immediately rushed in reinforcements. It is unclear who opened the fighting,

"More than two-thirds of my 15,000 soldiers died within the initial stages of the battle for Shanghai." *Chinese General Sun Yuanliang*

but initially the Chinese, who heavily outnumbered their enemies, seemed likely to push the Japanese into the Huangpu River. However, the Chinese lacked the firepower to destroy the Japanese concrete bunkers and tanks in the city, and Japanese troops reinforced along the Yangtze River, widening the battle lines to a 40-mile (65 km) front and negating the Chinese advantage. The bulk of Chiang's best troops were poured into the battle, and many fought well; others, from distant provinces, had less taste for the battle. Still, the Japanese troops did not

find the combat easy. Outside the city they faced a tough Chinese defense consisting of cold, muddy swamps with irrigation ditches and deep trenches supported by pillboxes, and the fighting was extremely challenging.

Within Shanghai, house-to-house fighting inflicted carnage on both sides, and thousands of civilians were slaughtered. Japanese warships pounded Chinese positions, and aerial bombing was particularly heavy, with more than 2,500 tons of bombs dropped on the city in just two days. The fighting became a battle of attrition between static lines, with heavy losses on both sides.

Chiang's generals warned him that the battle could not be won, but he refused to permit a retreat. The decisive moment came when 30,000 Japanese troops landed at Hangzhou Bay, 50 miles (80 km) to the southwest. They had to slog through heavy mud, and for two weeks the Chinese fought in every village in a desperate attempt to hold them back. The devastation in these villages was enormous, with bodies reputedly too numerous to count. In the final defensive position, a Chinese battalion ordered to fight to the death literally did so.

Eventually the Japanese were in a position to threaten the Chinese rear. A retreat was finally ordered, and fires were started in the city to cover it. But the retreat was chaotic, suggesting that the Chinese army had been seriously degraded in the battle. Western observers reported serious Japanese atrocities in the city, and certainly the United States was angered by Japanese actions—in October President Roosevelt gave a speech denouncing military aggression that was interpreted by the Japanese as a direct threat. Over time Japan's war with China would lead ineluctably to confrontation and eventually war with America. **JS**

Losses: Chinese, 100,000–270,000 dead or wounded of 600,000; Japanese, 40,000–70,000 dead or wounded of 300,000; civilian, unknown

◁ *Marco Polo Bridge 1937*   *Nanjing 1937* ▷

Soldiers carrying disassembled artillery pieces near the front line in Shanghai. ➡

Belchite   24 August–7 September 1937

In a continued effort to halt the Nationalist advance in the north of Spain, the Republicans launched an offensive at Belchite, in Aragon. The Republicans captured the town after an extremely hard-fought battle but their offensive quickly ground to a halt, and they failed to advance farther.

Having failed in their efforts to capture Brunete in July, the Republicans decided to launch an offensive into the Aragon region. The offensive was an attempt to bring the powerful Nationalist advance in the north to a halt. The Republicans' ultimate aim was to capture the region's capital—Zaragoza—and, along the way, they planned to take the fortified town of Belchite.

The Republicans advanced with a large force of 80,000 men, three air squadrons, and more than a hundred tanks, following a plan by General Vicente Rojo to take Zaragoza using a pincer movement. As in Brunete one month before, they were initially very successful, but soon ground to a halt as a result of poor communication and fierce Nationalist resistance.

At Belchite, the Republicans were held for a number of days by around 7,000 Nationalist fighters—but eventually, having incurred heavy casualties, the Republicans were able to encircle and then take the town. However, the delay meant that the Nationalists were able to send reinforcements to the region and prevent the Republicans from advancing to their target, Zaragoza. Therefore, despite capturing Belchite, the overall offensive into Aragon was a failure. Furthermore, it had done little to hold up the Nationalist advance.

Belchite, recaptured six months later, was completely destroyed in the attack. Franco ordered that the ruins of the town remained untouched as a monument to the Nationalist soldiers who died during the war. **ND**

Losses: Unknown but heavy casualties on both sides

[<] *Brunete 1937*   *Teruel 1937* [>]

Men of the International Brigade, taken prisoner by the Nationalists at Belchite.

Nanjing   13 December 1937

When Japanese troops advanced after the Battle of Shanghai at the start of the Sino-Japanese War, the Chinese government abandoned its capital, Nanjing, and the city fell quickly. The massacre that followed was at that time the worst atrocity that had been committed in the twentieth century.

As the Chinese retreat from Shanghai disintegrated into a rout, the chances of holding Nanjing seemed bleak. So precipitate had been the flight that no thought was given to manning the fairly strong concrete fortifications prepared on the approaches to the city. Nanjing's 90,000-strong garrison was badly shaken. The Chinese commander, Tang Shengzhi, swore he would fight to the death, but quickly tried to negotiate a withdrawal with the Japanese, who were uninterested.

After a two-day barrage that breached the walls, a belated order to retreat was given and the Chinese troops rapidly became a panic-stricken mob. Thousands drowned trying to cross the river and thousands of wounded were simply abandoned. Scarcely any resistance was offered when the Japanese entered Nanjing. The Japanese troops were allowed a free hand in committing atrocities. Tens of thousands of women and girls were dragged away, gang raped, and usually murdered. Prisoners were used for bayonet practice, and many others were burned or buried alive. Two junior officers competed to see which one could behead the most Chinese, both claiming more than 100 victims. The "Rape of Nanjing" lasted seven weeks and shocked the world—even observers from Nazi Germany were horrified by what they saw and tried to protect the Chinese where they could. But the Chinese were not cowed into submission; indeed the atrocity killed any chances of a negotiated peace. **JS**

Losses: Japanese, unknown; Chinese, 40,000–300,000 dead (totals are much disputed)

◁ Shanghai 1937   Wuhan 1938 ▷

Japanese troops follow a Type-89B tank over a partly rebuilt bridge into Nanjing.

Teruel 15 December 1937–20 February 1938

The Republican offensive at Teruel initially brought them success. However, they were again held by Nationalist resistance, with both sides affected by terrible weather in one of Spain's worst winters. Following some of the war's fiercest fighting, the Republicans were forced to retreat.

Having discovered that Franco was planning another major offensive on Madrid, the Republicans decided to launch a preemptive attack on the Aragon front in Teruel. The offensive—mounted in extreme weather conditions—took the Nationalist forces, commanded by Colonel Rey d'Harcourt, by surprise. German and Italian aircraft were grounded by ice, and Nationalist reinforcements were prevented from quickly reaching Teruel. Consequently, as at Brunete and Belchite, the Republicans were initially successful and took the town.

The Nationalists attempted to launch a counterattack but were severely impacted by the weather. As conditions deteriorated further, there was little option available to either side except try to grind the other down. Many soldiers on both sides succumbed to the freezing temperatures. The Nationalists held the advantage as they had more soldiers and weapons, and as Republican morale fell, internal strife surfaced.

In the brutal fighting that followed, both sides incurred enormous losses. The city changed hands a number of times as the battle raged on, with fierce hand-to-hand fighting taking place in the town's buildings. Finally, on 20 February, Republican General Hernández Sarabia ordered troops to withdraw and the Nationalists captured Teruel. The victory sent a clear signal of the military supremacy of the Nationalists, and it seemed only a matter of time before they would win the war. **ND**

Losses: Republican, 30,000 casualties; Nationalist, 57,000 casualties

◁ Belchite 1937   Cape Palos 1938 ▷

Cape Palos 5–6 March 1938

While the Republican navy became listless, the Nationalist navy was extremely active. Concentrated at Palma, on Majorca, Nationalist ships, strongly supported by Italian aircraft, blockaded the Republican coast and escorted convoys of Italian war matériel to the mainland.

On 5 March 1938 a strong force of three Nationalist cruisers supported by destroyers and minelayers put to sea to escort an inbound convoy. At 1:00 AM on 6 March the Nationalist ships steamed headlong into Vice-Admiral Luis González Ubieta's Republican force of cruisers, destroyers, and Soviet-supplied torpedo boats, originally despatched to attack the Nationalist base at Palma. Dodging a Republican torpedo attack, the Nationalist squadron tried to disengage, preferring to delay the action until daybreak, but Ubieta pursued and, at 2:15 AM, his ships opened fire off Cape Palos, near Cartagena.

As the cruisers fought an inconclusive and inaccurate long-range gunnery duel, three Republican destroyers crept unobserved into torpedo range of them. Each ship fired a spread of four torpedoes, at least two of which hit the Nationalist cruiser *Baleares*, flagship of Vice-Admiral Manuel de Vierna, between her two forward turrets. The explosion detonated her forward magazines and wrecked the forepart of the ship, including her bridge, which disintegrated with the loss of all inside, including Vierna. As the smouldering remains of *Baleares* wallowed in the water, slowly sinking, the remaining Nationalist ships fled. Out of a crew of 1,206, 441 survivors were eventually rescued by British destroyers.

Cape Palos was the largest naval battle of the Spanish Civil War, and a significant victory for the Republicans, but the Nationalist blockade remained intact. **NH**

Losses: Republican, no ships; Nationalist, 1 heavy cruiser sunk

◁ Teruel 1937   Ebro 1938 ▷

 A Republican soldier hangs dead in the tree where he was shot while fixing telephone lines at Teruel.

Wuhan   9 June–25 October 1938

Before Nanjing fell to the Japanese, the Chinese Nationalist government withdrew to Wuhan, farther up the Yangtze River. This became the next objective of the advancing Japanese army. Though the invaders eventually prevailed, they failed to gain the decisive victory they desperately needed.

The Japanese offensive, launched up both the Yangtze and Yellow rivers, proved long, costly, and frustrating, despite their superiority in artillery and airpower. In a singularly ruthless act, the Chinese blew up dykes channeling the Yellow River. This certainly delayed the Japanese, but millions of civilians were left homeless and destitute by the resulting floods. The Chinese also opened fire on civilians forced to repair the damage.

In a series of engagements the Chinese often fought well and inflicted some painful reverses on the Japanese. At Taierzhuang Japanese troops were lured into a trap by Chinese General Li Zongren. His troops, supported by a handful of Soviet-supplied tanks, virtually annihilated the Japanese. The Chinese claimed to have inflicted 30,000 casualties. Sometimes the Chinese did not fight so well—they lost the vital river port of Jiujiang despite greatly outnumbering their enemies. Still the Japanese found their progress was slow, the fighting was hard, casualties were mounting, and Chinese morale remained strong.

Eventually airpower enabled the Japanese to advance to within 20 miles (32 km) of Wuhan, at which point the Chinese government withdrew deep inland to Chunking in Sichuan. The Japanese wanted a great climactic battle, but this was denied them. The Chinese melted away into the mountainous interior, where it was unlikely that Japan would be able to force a decisive victory. Frustrated, the Japanese now faced the prospect of a prolonged war. **JS**

Losses: Japanese, 150,000 dead or wounded; Chinese, 400,000 dead or wounded

◁ *Nanjing 1937*   *Changsha 1944* ▷

Artillery pounds a strongpoint outside Wuhan while Japanese infantry await the order to attack. ⬆

Ebro   24 July–16 November 1938

After an initial success in their last-throw offensive at Ebro, the Republicans were once again driven back by Nationalist forces, suffering huge losses. Aided by German and Italian planes, the Nationalists claimed a decisive victory, which sealed the fate of the Spanish Republic.

Having managed to defend Valencia against Nationalist attacks, the Republicans attempted to restore contact with Catalonia with an offensive over the Ebro River. The attack, led by communist General Juan Modesto, once again took the Nationalists by surprise, bringing the Republicans early success. Eighty thousand Republican soldiers crossed the river in boats and attacked General Juan Yagüe's Nationalist troops, inflicting substantial damage. Upon reaching the town of Gandesa, however, the Republicans met fierce resistance. The rocky terrain offered little cover for the fighters, and German and Italian planes were easily able to target Republican positions.

Determined to annihilate the Republicans, General Franco ordered large reinforcements to join the battle, which was to last for over three months. Even when it became clear that they could not win, the leader of the Spanish Republic, Juan Negrín, was unable to withdraw troops as few options remained for the increasingly desperate Republic. In one of the war's hardest fought battles, both sides incurred huge losses, but for the Republicans these losses were unsustainable.

Ebro was the last major battle of the Spanish Civil War. Following the defeat, the Republicans continued to concede territory to the Nationalists until 1 April 1939, when General Franco declared the war over, signifying the end of the Spanish Republic. **ND**

Losses: Republican, 30,000 dead, 20,000 wounded, and 20,000 captured of 100,000; Nationalist, 33,000 casualties of 60,000

◁ *Cape Palos 1938*

↑ *Republican soldiers at the Ebro River, 1938.*

7 1939–Present

An American soldier in a northern Kuwaiti desert, near the Iraqi border, during Operation Desert Storm, 1991.

Khalkin Gol   11 May–16 September 1939

This clash in an undeclared war between Japanese and Soviet forces on the Manchukuo-Mongolia border was largely ignored by the outside world. Yet the battle was to have a major impact on the course of World War II, both in Europe and the Pacific.

The conflict began when cavalrymen from Mongolia (a Soviet client state) came under fire in a disputed border region. Both sides brought in reinforcements, and the confrontation escalated. In June, the Japanese launched an air strike on the Soviet air base at Tamsak-Bulak. It inflicted considerable damage but had not been authorized by the Japanese high command. They forbade further air attacks, effectively denying their army air support when it was about to launch a ground offensive.

The attack on land enjoyed some initial success, but a counterattack by Soviet armor threw back the Japanese. A second attempt saw some localized gains, before the Japanese were forced to retreat when they ran short of

shells. They planned to launch a third attack, but the Red Army, commanded by General Georgi Zhukov, struck first.

Zhukov employed the same innovative mobile warfare tactics that he was to use later with devastating effect against German forces. He launched his infantry against the Japanese center to pin down the enemy—his artillery and aircraft hammering Japanese positions—while his tanks encircled the Japanese on both flanks. After ten days of bitter fighting, the jaws of Zhukov's armored pincer closed, and the battle was won. Japan never again considered fighting the Soviet Union, instead setting upon a course that would lead to Pearl Harbor. Seriously alarmed at the prospect of a two-front war, Stalin made a deal with Germany—the Molotov-Ribbentrop pact—opening the way for Hitler to invade Poland. **JS**

Losses: Red Army, 8,000 dead, more than 15,000 wounded; Japanese, estimates vary, 17,000–61,000 dead or wounded

Invasion of Poland 1939 [>]

Two Russian soldiers congratulating themselves on the victory in Khalkin Gol. ⬆

Invasion of Poland 1 September–5 October 1939

Despite guarantees by Britain and France to aid Poland, Adolf Hitler was determined on war and sure that his secret nonaggression pact with the Soviet Union would give him a free hand in Poland. The German invasion marked the start of World War II.

As dawn broke on 1 September 1939, Germany launched its surprise attack on Poland. Army Group North attacked from Pomerania and East Prussia, while Army Group South drove deep into southern Poland from Silesia and Slovakia. Strategically outflanked and materially outnumbered, the Poles stood little chance, especially because their own forces were deployed too close to the German frontier, unintentionally facilitating Germany's strategy of envelopment.

The powerful Luftwaffe destroyed the Polish air force in days, leaving the Polish army at the mercy of the German panzer divisions. The speed with which the German tank units cut through the Polish lines was to give a new name

to the lexicon of warfare: "blitzkrieg" (lightning war). The declaration of war on Germany by Britain and France on 3 September did nothing to help isolated Poland.

The Poles enjoyed a limited tactical success from 9 to 15 September at the Bzura River, yet it came to nothing as the German armies closed in on Warsaw. Poland's fate had already been sealed, when—in accordance with the secret terms of the Nazi-Soviet pact—the Red Army crossed the Polish border from the east on 17 September. While Warsaw and a few garrisons continued to hold out, the remnants of the Polish armed forces retreated to neighboring countries, at least 90,000 men escaping to fight another day. Poland was divided up between Nazi Germany and the Soviet Union. **AG**

Losses: German, 14,000 dead or missing, 30,000 wounded, of 1,250,000; Polish, 66,000 dead, 130,000 wounded, 400,000 captured of 800,000

◁ *Khalkin Gol 1939*   *Warsaw 1939* ▷

↑ *German forces invade Poland in 1939.*

Warsaw 8–27 September 1939

The German attack on Warsaw included the deliberate bombing of civilian targets in order to strike terror among the city's people. The strategy of mass aerial bombardment would become one of the distinguishing features of World War II, where civilians suffered alongside soldiers.

The Luftwaffe opened its campaign against Warsaw at the outbreak of war on 1 September 1939, subjecting the Polish capital to fearsome and repeated bombing attacks. On 8 September, advance panzer units reached the western suburbs of Warsaw, but it was not until 15 September that the city was encircled and preparations made for a ground assault. The following day, the Germans instigated a series of probing attacks, hoping to exploit weaknesses in the Polish line, but they were repulsed comprehensively by a spirited Polish defense. German artillery and the Luftwaffe continued to pound the city. The German soldiers also prevented any civilians

from leaving Warsaw, thereby increasing the demand for food, which was already known to be in short supply.

The Germans built up their forces in preparation for a main assault by nine infantry divisions with heavy artillery support on 26 September. The Luftwaffe had focused its attacks on power plants, water filtration and pumping stations, and the city's flour mills. As a result, the inhabitants of Warsaw were on the verge of starvation and forced to drink directly from the Vistula River, with a typhoid epidemic a real possibility. Although the Poles continued to defend their positions, the situation was hopeless. In order to avoid further civilian suffering, the Polish commander reluctantly agreed to an unconditional surrender on 27 September. **AG**

Losses: German, 1,500 dead, 5,000 wounded of 175,000; Polish, 6,000 dead, 16,000 wounded, 100,000 captured of 124,000, plus 28,500 civilians dead, 50,000 wounded

◁ Invasion of Poland 1939   Norway 1940 ▷

Adolf Hitler (center right) observes the victory parade through Warsaw, 5 October 1939. ⬆

River Plate   13–17 December 1939

Nazi Germany's hopes of improving on the dismal performance of their country's surface ships in World War I took a blow when one of their most powerful ships was tamely scuttled after an inconclusive battle with a far-from-overwhelming British force at the start of World War II.

The German navy built a class of "pocket battleships," designed specifically for extended raids against British trade. When war broke out in September 1939, one of these ships, *Graf Spee*, was already en route to the South Atlantic. It began operations against British shipping in late September, sinking or capturing nine ships by early December. By then, the British had deployed several groups of warships to search for the raider.

On 13 December, *Graf Spee* met one of these hunting groups off the mouth of the River Plate. It consisted of three cruisers—two British, *Exeter* and *Ajax*, and one New Zealand, *Achilles*—under the overall command of Admiral Henry Harwood. The Germans concentrated their fire on *Exeter*, the most powerful ship, inflicting heavy damage and putting most of its guns out of action. *Exeter* was saved from destruction by the bold intervention of the smaller cruisers, but *Ajax* was also hit heavily. In return, *Graf Spee* received serious but far from fatal damage. The German commander, Captain Hans Langsdorff, decided to retreat to Montevideo in neutral Uruguay in order to make repairs.

While *Graf Spee* was in port, the British tried to rush reinforcements to the area and managed to convince Langsdorff that these had already arrived when, in fact, only one ship had completed the journey. On 17 December, Langsdorff decided to scuttle *Graf Spee* in the River Plate estuary. Two days later, he committed suicide. **DS**

Losses: German, 100 dead or wounded, 1 ship; British and Commonwealth, 100 dead or wounded, 3 cruisers damaged

Sinking the Bismarck *1941* ▷

⬆ *The damaged* Graf Spee *sinks off Montevideo, scuttled by her own crew.*

Mannerheim Line   17 December 1939–15 February 1940

In the Winter War, the Soviet Union attacked Finland, which had rejected demands to concede territory and naval bases. The Red Army was expected to win an easy victory. Its initial failure in attacking the Finnish Mannerheim Line on the Karelian Isthmus had a disastrous impact on Soviet military prestige.

The Red Army, many of whose officers had been removed in Stalin's purges of the late 1930s, proved to have severe shortcomings. Command was split between political and military officers, leading to organizational chaos. Supplies were inadequate, troops dispirited; units became confused by conflicting orders. The Soviets launched a massive barrage, followed by waves of infantry, supported by tanks committed in small packages rather than concentrated into a single thrust. They ran into minefields, murderous machine gun fire, and Finnish infantry growing ever more proficient at destroying tanks. Where localized breakthroughs occurred, there was no hope of exploiting

them. In fact, the Mannerheim Line was by no means impregnable. The defenses were fairly flimsy, comprising lines of trenches supported by firing positions constructed of timber and earth; few contained artillery. Finnish fighting spirit was the impressive factor.

In December, the Finns launched a counterattack, intending to encircle and destroy a large part of the Soviet forces. It failed because of stubborn Soviet resistance in the face of appalling losses. The Soviet leadership responded to the blow to its pride with a new command structure, massive reinforcements, and a concentration of forces. The Soviet offensive resumed in February 1940, and within fifteen days the Red Army took the Mannerheim Line. Finland sued for peace in March, making the concessions the Soviet Union had demanded initially. **JS**

Losses: Unknown, but most of the 25,000 Finnish and 125,000 Soviet killed in the war died in this sector

Suomussalmi 1939 ▶

A Finnish wire-cutter prepares the way for his troops on the Finno-Soviet battle front. ⬆

Suomussalmi   24 December 1939–8 January 1940

When the Soviet Union invaded Finland in the Winter War, its major effort was directed against the Mannerheim Line, but it also attacked to the north between Lake Ladoga and the White Sea. On this flank, the Finns inflicted an astonishing humiliation on the Red Army at Suomussalmi.

When the Red Army launched an attack with the 163rd Division north of Lake Lagoda, the village of Suomussalmi controlled the only road it could use. The Soviets took the village easily, but the Finns were determined to expel them, and had reason to be optimistic at their chances.

There was clear evidence, not least through uncoded radio traffic, that the entire organization of the Soviet campaign was chaotic, with untrained troops unprepared for the winter weather, supplies hopelessly muddled, and an ineffective command system. The Red Army at Suomussalmi was taken completely by surprise by a much smaller counterattacking force. Driven out of the village,

they made a stand, showing considerable resolve and courage for three days against repeated Finnish attacks, before morale collapsed and masses of men fled.

Finnish artillery and bombers were deployed to shatter the ice on frozen lakes as fleeing soldiers crossed, and great numbers perished. The Finns then turned their attention to the Soviet 44th Division, which they ambushed on the road. In the bitter cold, even the Red Army's rifles froze solid, and ill-equipped troops suffered terribly. Again, Soviet soldiers fought bravely but ineptly, and a similar collapse ensued. It was an amazing victory for the Finns, but in the longer term it achieved little. Finland still lost the war. Overall, the Winter War offered a misleading picture of Soviet military capacity, increasing the temptation for Nazi Germany to attack the Soviet Union. **JS**

Losses: Soviet, more than 30,000 dead, 2,000 captured of 35,000; Finnish, 2,000 dead, wounded, or missing

◁ *Mannerheim Line 1939*   *Operation Barbarossa 1941* ▷

⬆ *The bodies of soldiers from the Soviet 44th Division are frozen solid by the roadside at Suomussalmi.*

Norway   9 April–8 June 1940

To prevent Allied interference with the supply of Swedish iron ore to Germany—as it passed through Norwegian waters—Hitler decided to take control of Norway. This World War II campaign was a triumph of planning and execution, in contrast to the blundering half measures of the Allies.

The German invasion of Norway began on 9 April 1940 and adopted a daring plan using air, naval, and ground units to secure Oslo, Kristiansand, Stavanger, Bergen Trondheim, and Narvik simultaneously. Denmark was also seized by the Germans, but the Norwegians were determined to resist. Although caught by surprise, Britain and France dispatched troops to defend Norway.

The Germans relied on gaining maritime superiority in the waters around Norway and, in the process, had several ships sunk by the British and Norwegian navies. Meanwhile, German airborne units seized airfields in Norway, building vital bridgeheads for the invasion and allowing them to redeploy the Luftwaffe as an attack force against the Royal Navy. Overwhelmed by the speed and the scale of the German attack, the Norwegians were unable to mount serious resistance.

Franco-British forces—supported by Polish troops—landed at Narvik (14 April) and Trondheim (18 April), but they lacked adequate equipment, and a confused chain of command militated against decisive action. The Allies' attempt to secure Trondheim failed, their soldiers forced either to surrender or be evacuated. In the northern port of Narvik, the Allies fared better and eventually wrested the town from the Germans on 28 May. However, the isolated Allied garrison in Narvik was abandoned on 8 June, leaving all of Norway under German control. **AG**

Losses: Allied, 6,800 dead, wounded, or missing (including 1,800 Norwegians) of 24,000; German, 5,500 dead, wounded, or missing of 10,000

⟨ *Warsaw 1939*   *Narvik 1940* ⟩

Narvik   9–13 April 1940

The naval battle for Narvik was part of the World War II Norwegian campaign. Although the German navy succeeded in seizing Norway's ports, it took heavy losses. The long-term strategic consequence was that Germany had insufficient naval resources for a potential invasion of Britain later in the year.

Narvik was the most northerly of the ports attacked by the German navy, and the invasion force (Group 1) consisted of ten destroyers—packed with German infantry—and several merchant vessels, protected by the battle cruisers *Gneisenau* and *Scharnhorst*. Group 1 reached Narvik unopposed, and on 9 April, while the two battle cruisers steamed away to open sea, the destroyers made their way along the fjord leading to Narvik. The two aging Norwegian vessels defending the port were hit by torpedoes and sunk, enabling the Germans to begin disembarking their seasick soldiers. After a short engagement, Narvik surrendered to the Germans.

Royal Navy Captain Bernard Warburton-Lee just missed intercepting Group 1. So, on 10 April, he led his five ships—from the British 2nd Destroyer Flotilla—to Narvik. He caught one group of five German destroyers by surprise, sinking two and damaging another, as well as sinking six German merchantmen and a supply ship. The other German destroyers pounced on the British force; one British destroyer was sunk (Warburton-Lee was killed) and one badly damaged, although the force was able to disengage and await reinforcements. On 13 April, nine British destroyers and the battleship *Warspite* sank the remaining German vessels. Unfortunately for the Allies, the British were slow in following up this success, allowing the shaken German garrison in Narvik time to recover. **AG**

Losses: British, 1 destroyer sunk, 6 damaged; Norwegian, 2 defense vessels sunk; German, 10 destroyers, 7 ancillary vessels, 1 U-boat sunk

⟨ *Norway 1940*   *Fall of France 1940* ⟩

↩ *German soldiers arrive at Oslo harbor on 27 April 1940 as part of the Norwegian campaign.*

Fall of France   10 May–25 June 1940

The German offensive in May to June 1940 was a triumph for the Wehrmacht in World War II. In six weeks, Hitler comprehensively defeated France, Belgium, and the Netherlands, and forced the British army to scuttle back across the English Channel, leaving behind its heavy weapons and equipment.

After the defeat of Poland in September 1939, Hitler turned his attention toward the Western Allies. After months of fierce debate, the German Army General Staff adopted a highly imaginative plan of attack. Army Group B would launch a limited offensive through the Low Countries that would knock out Belgium and the Netherlands, and draw French and British troops into the region at the same time. Meanwhile, the main blow would be struck farther south, by Army Group A, in the hilly Ardennes region, the spearhead of the attack provided by ten panzer divisions. While both sides were broadly matched in numbers and firepower, the Germans had a decisive advantage in organization, training, and leadership.

> *"We must be very careful not to assign to this deliverance the attributes of a victory. Wars are not won by evacuations."* Winston Churchill

On 10 May, Army Group B swept into the Netherlands and Belgium, making excellent use of airborne troops to seize key sites and strike fear into the civilian population. The Dutch were overwhelmed swiftly and accepted surrender terms after just five days of fighting. The Belgians fell back to defensive positions and awaited the arrival of French and British reinforcements. As some of the best Allied formations marched into Belgium, the three panzer corps—led by Generals Guderian, Reinhardt, and Hoth—threaded their way through the wooded defiles of the Ardennes, emerging on 13 May to smash their way through the flimsy French defenses on the Meuse River.

Meeting little opposition, the German panzers raced toward the English Channel. The stunned Allied high command made attempts to stem the flow of German armor, but was too late. Just ten days after the opening of the offensive, tanks of Guderian's XIX Panzer Corps reached the English Channel at Abbeville, establishing the "panzer corridor" that cut the Allied armies in two.

As the panzers now advanced northward, the British Expeditionary Force—outflanked and facing disaster—fell back toward Dunkirk to prepare for evacuation. Although this move left the French in a desperate position, the British situation was also proving untenable, especially when the Belgians surrendered on 28 May. The evacuation of around a third of a million men from Dunkirk was a triumph of sorts, but it was a retreat nonetheless.

After a brief period of reorganization, the Germans turned south to deal with the remainder of the French army, which was attempting to build a new defensive line to protect Paris and the French interior. On 5 June, with the panzer divisions to the fore, the German army sliced through the French defenses. The French government fled Paris—which was declared an open city—and on 14 June, German troops victoriously marched along the Champs-Élysées. Advance units of the German army continued to push south, and Marshal Philippe Pétain, the newly installed French president, signed an armistice with the Germans that brought hostilities to a close on 25 June. Hitler's triumph was only slightly marred when Britain completely rebuffed Germany's offer of peace terms. **AG**

Losses: British, 68,000 casualties of 200,000; French, 90,000 dead, 200,000 wounded, 1,450,000 captured of 2,000,000; German, 27,000 dead, 18,500 missing, 111,000 wounded of 2,500,000

◁ *Narvik 1940*   *Bombing of Rotterdam 1940* ▷

Vehicles in a German motorized division advance in northern France in late spring, 1940.

Bombing of Rotterdam   14 May 1940

"The inner city was completely without any military strength … houses and entire streets were ablaze within minutes." Eyewitness

⬆ *German soldiers look on as the buildings of central Rotterdam burn to the ground, having been bombed by the Luftwaffe.*

At the start of their spring offensive in World War II, the Germans needed to break through the Dutch defensive line known as Fortress Holland. They led a devastating bombing raid against Rotterdam, one of the bastions in the line. The raid helped bring about the capitulation of the Netherlands.

On 13 May 1940, German forces captured the bridges to Rotterdam in preparation for an assault on the city the following day. The German commander, General Schmidt, asked the Luftwaffe for a unit of Ju-87 Stuka dive-bombers to support the attack. Instead, the Luftwaffe dispatched a large group of around one hundred Heinkel He-111 medium bombers to attack a range of targets.

Early on 14 May, Schmidt attempted to persuade the Dutch to surrender before the attack began. Negotiations were coming to a conclusion when, in the afternoon, the drone of bomber aircraft was heard overhead. German officers tried to have the bombers recalled, but fifty-four of the He-111s did not receive the message and dropped 90 tons of bombs on the city. Just under 1,000 people were killed in the raid, and such was the destruction that the city center was leveled and 85,000 people made homeless. Although the raid was probably a "mistake," it had a successful strategic outcome for the Germans: the Dutch government surrendered the following day with much of its army still intact.

Allied propaganda portrayed the raid as an example of unbridled German barbarism—as had been the case in the destruction of Warsaw—and inflated the casualty figures to 30,000 in the process. One further consequence of the raid was the decision by the British government to allow the RAF to begin to bomb civilian industrial targets in Germany. **AG**

Losses: Dutch, nearly 1,000 civilians; German, none

◁ *Fall of France 1940*   *Dunkirk 1940* ▷

Dunkirk 26 May–3 June 1940

The evacuation of British troops from Dunkirk in World War II saved the British Expeditionary Force from destruction. More than 200,000 soldiers got back to Britain in a "miracle of deliverance," but the evacuation soured Anglo-French relations and confirmed Germany's battlefield dominance.

Pressed by the Germans from the south and the east, Allied troops in northern France fell back to the port of Dunkirk. While the French prepared to fight a rearguard action, the British had made secret plans to take their troops back to Britain. The evacuation began on 26 May. In the confusion of the operation, French troops were at first forbidden to embark, adding to the bad feeling that already existed between the two nations.

As the evacuation was taking place, the Germans applied increasing pressure to the shrinking perimeter defenses, but the British and French rearguards fought doggedly to hold the line. In the skies, the Luftwaffe and RAF were engaged in a desperate battle, and both sides suffered heavy casualties, while at sea the evacuation vessels faced the gauntlet of German bombers and E-boats as they tried to approach Dunkirk.

On 29 May, the British issued the "Little Ships" appeal, in which a profusion of around 700 civilian vessels were used to ferry men from the beaches to the waiting ships farther out to sea. It was this aspect of the operation that caught the public's imagination and encouraged the "Dunkirk spirit" that raised British morale. By 2 June, the majority of the British troops had been ferried over to Britain, and attention turned to evacuating French soldiers. On 4 June, the Germans fought their way into Dunkirk, by which time 338,226 troops (more than a third French) had crossed the English Channel. **AG**

Losses: Allied, 200 vessels sunk, including 9 destroyers, 177 RAF aircraft; German, 240 aircraft

◁ Bombing of Rotterdam 1940　　　　　Britain 1940 ▷

Mers-el-Kebir 3 July 1940

After France surrendered in June 1940, British Prime Minister Winston Churchill feared the French navy would come under German control and decided he had to prevent this. When negotiations failed, a British squadron attacked France's most powerful ships in the Algerian port of Mers-el-Kebir.

In 1940, France's navy was the fourth largest in the world, far bigger than Germany's. With Italy and its large navy also fighting on Germany's side in World War II from June, British prospects would have been grim if France's ships went over to the enemy. The Franco-German armistice had stipulated that the French fleet would remain neutral, but the British believed that the agreement was as reliable as the rest of Hitler's promises.

Some French ships happened to be in British ports, and these were taken over or disarmed with little bloodshed. It was a different matter at Mers-el-Kebir, where France's most formidable vessels were based. The British sent Admiral James Somerville from Gibraltar with two battleships, a battle cruiser, and an aircraft carrier to present various alternatives to the French for the demobilization of their ships and their removal to distant ports, if they did not want to continue the fight against Germany. Negotiations made no progress, and Somerville—warned that French reinforcements were on their way—opened fire at long range on the evening of 3 July.

One French battleship, *Bretagne*, blew up when a shell penetrated its magazine, killing almost 1,000 crew. The battleship, *Dunkerque,* was also damaged, but its sister, *Strasbourg*, and several destroyers managed to escape to Toulon. For France, it was a treacherous attack by a former ally; for Britain, it was regrettable but necessary in the interests of national survival. **DS**

Losses: French, 1,297 dead, 1 battleship sunk; British, 6 dead

Taranto 1940 ▷

Britain   10 July–12 October 1940

As a preliminary move to their proposed conquest of Britain in World War II, the Germans needed to gain air supremacy over southern England. However, this was denied them as a consequence of the poor command decisions made by the Luftwaffe and the determination and skill of the Royal Air Force.

During July 1940, the Luftwaffe began to target British maritime convoys in the English Channel and attacked a number of ports on the south coast. The tempo of operations increased significantly on 12 August, when the Luftwaffe was ordered to take the battle directly to the RAF. The German Air Force had a considerable numerical superiority over its British adversary. Total German strength at the start of the battle comprised 1,260 long-range bombers, 320 dive-bombers, 280 twin-engine fighters, and 800 single-engine fighters, while the RAF could muster approximately 900 fighters.

The British benefited from other vital advantages. A newly installed radar-based detection system provided

> *"We have now had personal experience of German barbarity, which strengthens the resolution to fight . . . to final victory."* George VI

the RAF with a (usually) good picture of where the Germans would attack, allowing the British Hurricane and Spitfire fighters to vector in on the enemy bomber formations. The RAF also had the advantage of fighting on home ground: downed British pilots parachuting to safety could be back in a plane the same day, while German pilots ended up in a prisoner-of-war camp. Most crucial of all were the differences in leadership. The two main British commanders, Air Chief Marshal Hugh Dowding and Air Vice Marshal Keith Park, fought the battle with cool heads, allocating scarce resources where needed and responding intelligently to changes in German tactics. The German commanders, by contrast, fatally underestimated the RAF and, through poor intelligence, had little idea of how the battle was progressing.

The major German offensive—Eagle Attack—was launched on 13 August. It focused on attacks against RAF airfields and radar stations, but little was achieved because of bad weather. Another mass attack made two days later was savaged badly; the Luftwaffe lost seventy-five aircraft to the RAF's thirty-four. However, the Luftwaffe carried on with its attacks and by early September it was beginning to achieve some success, with a number of key RAF airfields out of action and the RAF pilots under serious strain from near-constant action.

It was at this point that the Luftwaffe changed its strategy from attacking the RAF to bombing London. Initially, Hitler had forbidden direct attacks on London, but when some bombs were dropped accidentally in the south London suburb of Croydon, the RAF mounted a night bombing raid against Berlin. An incensed Hitler demanded retaliation; on 7 September, a daylight raid was launched against the British capital. The RAF was caught by surprise, and the Germans successfully bombed large areas of east London. Another major daylight raid was mounted on 15 September, but this time the defenders were ready and sixty German planes were shot down.

The German aircrews were beginning to feel the strain, and attacks against England were viewed with decreasing enthusiasm as casualty lists grew longer. The plan for an invasion of Britain was postponed indefinitely by Hitler on 17 September, and as September gave way to October the Luftwaffe moved over to night raids to minimize its losses, with London becoming the main target. The Battle of Britain had now merged into the Blitz. **AG**

Losses: British, 788 aircraft; German, 1,294 aircraft

◁ *Dunkirk 1940*   *The Blitz 1940* ▷

A German Heinkel He-111 flies over the Isle of Dogs, London, during the Battle of Britain. ➜

The Blitz   September 1940–May 1941

Having failed to defeat the RAF in the Battle of Britain, the Luftwaffe concentrated on night raids against London and other British cities. Although the German bombers caused enormous destruction and heavy civilian casualties, the raids had little effect on Britain's ability to continue World War II.

The daylight attack against London on 7 September 1940 marked the opening phase of the German bomber offensive against Britain, which came to be called the Blitz (after the German word "blitzkrieg," meaning "lightning war"). The initial daylight attacks soon gave way to night raids, which the British found difficult to counter. The British lacked effective antiaircraft artillery and searchlights, as well as night fighters that could find and shoot down an aircraft in darkness. London was subjected to Luftwaffe attacks for seventy-six consecutive nights.

During November, the offensive spread to the larger provincial cities in Britain. The attack on Coventry was particularly destructive; the German force of 509 bombers

"London stabbed with great fires, shaken by explosions … sparkling with the pinpoints of white-hot bombs." *Ernie Pyle, journalist*

was guided by the X-Gerät intersecting beam system, and much of the old city center was destroyed, with 380 people killed and 865 injured. Although the casualty figures were very small when compared with later Allied raids on Germany, the bombing of Coventry came to be seen as a symbol of the barbarity of modern warfare.

In early 1941, the German navy persuaded Hitler to focus attacks on Britain's maritime resources. In a series of forty-six raids between February and May, ports including Plymouth, Portsmouth, Bristol, Swansea, Merseyside,

Belfast, Clydeside, Newcastle, and Hull were pounded heavily, although they still managed to function.

Civil defense measures to protect the British people were far from adequate in the early stages of the battle. The government had not adopted the idea of building large shelters to protect the public from bombardment—as was the case in Germany—preferring to rely on semiprivate initiatives, such as the inadequate Anderson family shelters. It was only with reluctance that the underground system was made available to the people of London, a decision that ultimately saved many thousands of lives. The stoical manner in which the people of Britain—especially in London—endured the Blitz made a deep impression on neutral commentators, and the radio broadcasts of U.S. journalist Ed Murrow helped persuade the U.S. public that Britain was not a beaten nation and would continue the fight against Nazi Germany.

During the spring of 1941, active British defenses began to improve. The numbers of AA guns and searchlights were increased, and in key areas they were radar-controlled to improve accuracy. The problem of guiding interceptors to their targets was partially solved by the introduction of heavily armed Bristol Beaufighters fitted with their own radar. These improvements were reflected in monthly German casualty figures, which rose from 28 in January to 124 in May.

The Blitz came to an effective close in May 1941 when Hitler decided to invade the Soviet Union. The Luftwaffe did not have sufficient resources to conduct a two-front war, and German aircraft were redeployed to the east. This did not prevent a final, vindictive flurry from the Luftwaffe; on 10 May, a raid against central London led to the highest nightly casualty figure of the battle: 1,364 killed and 1,616 seriously wounded. **AG**

Losses: British, 43,000 civilians dead, 139,000 wounded; German, 600 bombers

◁ *Britain 1940*   *Dambusters Raid 1943* ▷

During the Blitz, some Londoners took cover in tube stations temporarily acting as air raid shelters.

Taranto
11–12 November 1940

Before 1940, proponents of naval air power said that aircraft carriers made battleships obsolete. The British attack on the Italian port of Taranto suggested that they were right—and was studied by Japan, planning a surprise attack of its own.

Britain's Mediterranean Fleet quickly gained the upper hand in early clashes with Italy in the weeks after the Italian declaration of war in June 1940. In November, Admiral Cunningham planned a bold night attack on the enemy base at Taranto, in southern Italy, using aircraft from the carrier *Illustrious*, which had joined his fleet recently. The British strike force was tiny: only twenty-one obsolescent Swordfish biplane torpedo bombers. No similar attack had ever been carried out before, but it proved to be an astonishing success.

The attackers achieved total surprise. Two waves went in, each including a pair of aircraft that dropped flares to illuminate the targets and several bomb-carrying aircraft, as well as the torpedo bombers themselves. Three Italian battleships were crippled by five torpedo hits—the harbor was so shallow that they did not sink completely and would be raised and repaired in due course—and two other ships were damaged; the port's oil tanks and seaplane base were also heavily hit. Only two British aircraft were lost. The raid confirmed the moral superiority of the British over the Italians, and it would be some months before the Italian navy attempted major operations again. The Axis forces had their revenge on *Illustrious*, however, which was badly damaged by Luftwaffe aircraft in January 1941. Meanwhile, the Taranto attack was analyzed carefully by Japanese naval aviators considering a strike against the U.S. base at Pearl Harbor. **DS**

Losses: Italian, more than 600 dead or wounded, 3 battleships damaged; British, 2 dead, 2 aircraft

◁ Mers-el-Kebir 1940   Matapan 1941 ▷

Operation Compass
8 December 1940–9 February 1941

The Italian Tenth Army, which had invaded Egypt in September 1940, was attacked by a small British force that forced it back to Libya. The British followed up their initial success with a classic maneuver that captured almost the entire Italian army.

The British Western Desert Force was placed under the command of Major General Richard O'Connor, with orders to launch a limited offensive against the Italians. The British attacked on the night of 8 to 9 December, taking the Italians by surprise and throwing them back in total disarray. O'Connor then decided to follow up his initial success with an invasion of Libya. At that point, the experienced 4th Indian Division was withdrawn and replaced by the newly arrived 6th Australian Division, untrained in desert warfare. Fortunately for the British, the Australian infantry proved both enthusiastic and efficient, and, after a short delay, they spearheaded the attack on the fortified position of Bardia on 3 January 1941, a successful operation that netted 26,000 prisoners.

O'Conner realized that if he kept pressing the Italians they would have no chance of recovery, and this he duly did, racing forward to capture the key port of Tobruk on 22 January. However, in order to make the victory complete, British armor was dispatched on an imaginative outflanking move. Advance units reached Beda Fomm on the Mediterranean coast just ahead of the retreating enemy. The Italians failed to break through the British blocking force and, effectively surrounded, were compelled to surrender. O'Conner had wanted to push on toward Tripoli but was forced to go over to the defensive because his best troops were withdrawn for the ill-fated campaign in Greece and Crete. **AG**

Losses: Italian, 3,000 dead, 130,000 captured of 150,000; British and Commonwealth, 500 dead, 1,373 wounded of 36,000

Keren 1941 ▷

Keren

3 February–8 April 1941

The capture of the Italian-held stronghold of Keren was vital to the British plan to gain control of the Italian colony Eritrea. The Italians' determined resistance earned them the respect of their foes, but when Keren fell, so too did the rest of Eritrea.

After Italy's declaration of war on 10 June 1940, Italian troops in East Africa captured British Somaliland and raided the British colonies of Kenya and Sudan. However, these would be short-lived successes because, in early 1941, British-led Allied columns set about eliminating the Italian presence in the region with a series of coordinated thrusts made from Sudan, Kenya, and Aden. Lieutenant General William Platt led a combined British-Indian army column (with two battalions of Free French) that advanced from Sudan in January 1941 to capture Eritrea.

The Italian commander in Eritrea, General Luigi Frusci, was instructed to make his stand in the mountainous country to the west of Keren, through which lay the only feasible route to the other key towns of Asmara and Massawa. In order to get to Keren, the British and Commonwealth troops would have to advance through the Dongolaas Gorge. The steep granite mountains that rose up on either side of the gorge provided the Italians with a fine, natural defensive position.

The British attempt to take the Italian positions involved three major assaults between 5 February and 27 March. The first two assaults were repulsed by the Italians, and it was only the third attack, on 15 March, that pushed the Italians back to Keren. From there, the Italians were forced to retreat to the coast, finally surrendering Massawa on 8 April. On 16 May, all Italian forces in East Africa surrendered to the British. **AG**

Losses: British, 536 dead, 3,229 wounded of 13,000; Italian, 3,000 dead, 3,500 wounded, 17,000 captured of 23,000

◁ *Operation Compass 1940*   *Tobruk 1941* ▷

Matapan

28 March 1941

The Italian fleet tried to attack British troop convoys heading for Greece but ended up fleeing for home after ships were hit in an air strike. The British caught part of the retreating force south of Greece's Cape Matapan and achieved an annihilating victory.

In early 1941, Britain was sending troops and supplies to its new World War II ally, Greece. With the promise of German air support, the Italians sent a powerful surface ship squadron to attack this traffic. Unfortunately for the Italians, the British had been warned of the operation by codebreakers and, in the event, the promised German air support did not arrive. The Italians had no aircraft carriers, so the British carrier, *Formidable,* was unchallenged.

Admiral Andrew Cunningham's British fleet included three battleships and supporting light cruisers and destroyers, as well as *Formidable*. Admiral Angelo Iachino had one battleship, *Vittorio Veneto*, six powerful heavy cruisers, and supporting ships. British air reconnaissance found the Italians on 27 March, and fighting began the next day. After morning skirmishes, Iachino decided to turn for home, but by late afternoon the main British force was approaching and an air strike from *Formidable* damaged the Italian battleship and brought the heavy cruiser *Pola* to a standstill. The British hurried on into the night hoping to catch the fleeing battleship but instead found the damaged *Pola*, plus two other cruisers and three destroyers that had been sent back to help. With the advantage of radar and effective night-fighting training—the Italians had neither—the British battleships closed to point-blank range without being detected. The cruisers and two destroyers were shot to pieces within minutes. **DS**

Losses: Italian, 2,300 dead, 800 captured, 5 ships; British, 2 dead, no ships

◁ *Taranto 1940*   *Crete 1941* ▷

Tobruk 11 April–10 December 1941

In 1941, Lieutenant General Erwin Rommel was sent to command the German Afrika Korps in World War II. The British army in Libya was reduced by the transfer of troops to Greece; aware of this sudden reduction, Rommel attacked. Only the defenses of the port of Tobruk held against his onslaught.

The Afrika Korps struck on 24 March, and the disorganized British units retreated in chaos. Tobruk was reached by the German panzers on 10 April and surrounded the following day. As one of the few deep-water ports on the Libyan-Egyptian coast, possession of Tobruk was vital in supporting any potential German advance into Egypt. Rommel ordered an all-out assault in the hope of gaining the port before the British had a chance to organize a proper defense. The attack failed, and the Germans and Italians had to set about mounting a conventional siege.

The defenders comprised the 9th Australian Division, under Lieutenant General Leslie Morshead, and various British engineer, artillery, and tank units, who had energetically improved the various defensive positions first developed by the Italians. During the first month, the defenders faced repeated and intense attacks by the Italian and German besiegers, and were subjected to remorseless artillery and aerial bombardment. These attacks were repulsed with heavy Axis casualties, and Rommel settled down to starve the defenders into surrender. Despite a ferocious series of bombing attacks, the port stayed open, and the Royal Navy was able to get sufficient supplies to the garrison. The siege was lifted finally by the success of the British Crusader offensive at the end of November, the Germans withdrawing to Tripoli. Tobruk had held firm through a 242-day investment. **AG**

Losses: British and Commonwealth, 3,000 casualties of 27,000; German and Italian, 8,000 casualties of 35,000

◁ Keren 1941 Operation Crusader 1941 ▷

Crete 20 May–1 June 1941

The airborne assault on Crete in World War II was a triumph of German determination and a setback for the Allies in the Mediterranean. While the Allies looked to Crete as an inspiration for their own airborne forces, heavy German losses led Hitler to curtail further large-scale airborne operations.

After the abject failure of a British expedition to defend Greece against German attack, remnants of the British and Commonwealth force were evacuated to Crete, an island of strategic importance to both sides. The Germans enjoyed aerial superiority and decided to exploit their advantage by seizing the island in a mass assault by elite parachute and glider troops. They would capture the airfields to allow transport aircraft to ferry in more soldiers before the arrival of seaborne reinforcements. While the British, Commonwealth, and Greek defenders outnumbered the Germans, they were not a coherent force, lacking adequate communications and heavy weapons.

Although plans for the invasion of Crete were known to the British—through the breaking of Enigma codes—German aerial superiority made the long island almost impossible to defend effectively. The airborne assault came on 20 May, with some 9,350 troops landing on the first day. Although German casualties were exceptionally severe, there were sufficient men to hang on until reinforcements arrived. On 26 May, Lieutenant General Bernard Freyberg, the Commonwealth commander on Crete, ordered a general retreat to the south of the island to prepare for evacuation. The Royal Navy, which had already suffered heavy losses, lost more ships as it tried to get the troops away; the operation was abandoned on 30 May, leaving 5,000 men awaiting evacuation from Crete. **AG**

Losses: British and Commonwealth, 4,000 dead, 2,000 wounded, 11,300 captured of 47,500, 9 ships sunk, 18 damaged; German, 7,000 casualties of 22,000

◁ Matapan 1941 Raid on Alexandria 1941 ▷

Sinking the *Bismarck* 23–27 May 1941

The massively powerful German battleship *Bismarck* confirmed the threat it posed to Britain's Atlantic lifeline by sinking the Royal Navy's "mighty *Hood*" in World War II. However, *Bismarck* was hunted down and destroyed three days later after nearly eluding its pursuers in a dramatic chase.

Ready for operations in early 1941, *Bismarck* was the world's most formidable battleship. Accompanied by the heavy cruiser *Prinz Eugen*, it embarked on its first and last mission on 18 May, setting off from the Bay of Danzig and heading for the Atlantic trade routes.

Much of the Royal Navy was deployed to hunt for *Bismarck*, which was spotted in the Denmark Strait between Greenland and Iceland on 23 May. Two British warships arrived to bring *Bismarck* to action the next morning, but within minutes the old and outdated battle cruiser HMS *Hood* was hit; it blew up, killing almost all the crew. The battleship *Prince of Wales* was so new that it was not yet properly ready for action and was soon forced out of the fight. However, *Bismarck* had taken hits, and Admiral Gunther Lutjens decided it should separate from *Prinz Eugen* and head for a French port for repairs.

British ships were still giving chase, and the following night an attack by Swordfish biplane torpedo aircraft from the carrier *Victorious* further damaged the battleship. For a time contact was lost, but on 26 May, *Bismarck* was located again and a Swordfish strike from the carrier *Ark Royal* scored a torpedo hit that wrecked *Bismarck*'s rudders. The next morning, two more British battleships, *King George V* and *Rodney*, finally caught up and pounded the now slow and unmaneuverable *Bismarck* into a sinking wreck. **DS**

"Ship unmaneuverable. We fight to our last shell. Long live the Führer."

Last message sent from Bismarck

Losses: German, 2,000 dead, 1 battleship sunk; British, 1,415 dead, 1 battle cruiser sunk

 *The British cruiser HMS* Dorsetshire *rescues survivors from the sinking of* Bismarck *on 27 May 1941.*

◁ *Matapan 1941*   *Convoy PQ.17 1942* ▷

Operation Barbarossa   22 June–6 October 1941

The opening of the Eastern Front during World War II occurred in June 1941, when the Germans invaded the Soviet Union; many observers assumed the Red Army would collapse within twelve weeks. The ability of the Soviet Union to recover from its appalling early defeats would doom Nazi Germany.

Stalin believed he had bought off Hitler through the Molotov-Ribbentrop pact and refused to accept warnings—reputedly eighty-four in all—of an impending attack. The invasion, therefore, came as a terrible shock. Although the Red Army was being modernized, new equipment—such as the T-34 and KV-1 tanks—was only just coming into production. Too much equipment was obsolete, and too many senior officers had been swept up by the purges. The Germans, perhaps, had reason to be optimistic for a quick victory. Their plans were simple:

Army Group North would advance through the Baltic States and on to Leningrad, Army Group Center would advance on Moscow via Smolensk, and Army Group South would go to Kiev. It was assumed that the resources of these areas were so valuable that the Red Army would commit everything to their defense and be destroyed, ending the war by mid-October.

The initial onslaught was devastating. Hundreds of Soviet aircraft were destroyed on the ground, troops stationed near the frontiers were abandoned without orders, and confused soldiers found German propaganda leaflets informing them that Moscow had already surrendered. Soviet civilians, long assured that their homeland was safe, were bewildered by the unfolding catastrophe. However, after twelve days, Stalin made a radio broadcast to rally his shaken people, whom he addressed for the first time as "brothers and sisters," in

which he appealed to Russian patriotism—rather than Bolshevik ideology—calling for scorched-earth tactics and a partisan war. Large Soviet forces on the approaches to Kiev and Smolensk put up a determined fight—the first real resistance the Germans had met beyond the often suicidal heroism of small units—and although both cities fell, their defense slowed the German advance and allowed new forces to be recruited, as well as for hundreds of factories to be dismantled and evacuated east, with their workers. In the short term, the Red Army would suffer desperate shortages of arms, but the Soviet Union would be amply provisioned to fight a prolonged war.

Hitler did not help his own cause by diverting forces from Smolensk to Kiev, delaying the advance on Moscow. He also insisted that encircled pockets of Soviet troops be destroyed, rather than waiting for them to surrender, consuming resources that might better have been used elsewhere. German troops acted with a brutality that created increasingly troublesome partisan units very quickly. German losses were also severe; after six weeks, they had taken considerably heavier casualties than when they conquered France, and were still meeting tough resistance. Rough terrain and poor roads made resupply, especially of fuel, difficult. Indeed, more German tanks were lost to the terrain than to Soviet action, and some units only had one-quarter battle worthy. By late October, when the advance on Moscow was resumed, many German officers doubted that the city could be reached before winter. The offensive was losing momentum and would be stopped at the Battle of Moscow. **JS**

Losses: German, 250,000 dead, 500,000 wounded; Red Army, 1,000,000 dead, 3,000,000 wounded, 3,300,000 captured

◁ *Suomussalmi 1939*　　　　　*Leningrad 1941* ▷

Leningrad
4 September 1941–27 January 1944

"Some people went quite insane with hunger. The practice of hiding the dead ... and using their ration cards was very common." Eyewitness

⬆ *During the winter of 1941 to 1942, Russian citizens had no choice but to gather their belongings and abandon their ruined homes.*

After Germany invaded the Soviet Union in Operation Barbarossa, Leningrad was placed under siege. The loss of the city would have been a severe blow to Soviet morale, and the 872-day siege came to symbolize the determination of the Soviet people.

Despite the importance of the city, little was done to prepare Leningrad for a siege until the last minute because no one believed that the Germans would progress so far. When action was taken, the first thought was for the city's defenses. Hundreds of thousands of citizens, even schoolchildren, were mobilized to dig 340 miles (547 km) of antitank ditches and 1,600 miles (2,575 km) of trenches. Although the Germans managed to cut all land communications with Leningrad, they were prevented from pushing their tanks into the city itself. Instead, they settled in to starve Leningrad into surrender. This was the Soviets' great weakness. No thought had been given to stockpiling food—there were only thirty-five days of grain reserves in the city—nor had anything been done to evacuate children and the elderly.

As winter set in, the population began to die of starvation. When Lake Ladoga froze over, it was possible to build what became known as "the road of life": an ice road across the lake along which some supplies got through. The city survived, much to the amazement of the besiegers. Terrible battles were fought in 1942 as the Red Army took huge casualties trying to break the siege, but the blockade was only broken the following January. The siege itself continued for another year, with constant shelling from German guns throughout. Leningrad never again suffered the terrible famine of the first winter; it had endured the bloodiest siege in history. **JS**

Losses: German, unknown; Red Army, 1,000,000 dead, wounded, or captured, plus 1,000,000 civilians dead

◁ *Operation Barbarossa 1941*   *Moscow 1942* ▷

Moscow
30 September 1941–7 January 1942

An Eastern Front battle, the fight for Moscow was the climax of Operation Barbarossa. The Germans intended to take the Soviet capital, assuming that this would break the Soviet Union's will to fight on. Their failure ultimately doomed the Third Reich.

The German advance on Moscow was soon in trouble because of atrocious weather conditions. The Germans were also shocked by the Soviet Union's ability to keep bringing forward more reserves. Although some German officers thought Moscow was unattainable, they had no choice but to press forward—they had to end the war before the fierce winter set in.

The Germans managed to encircle large Soviet forces at Viazma in October, but these troops still fought on, delaying the advance. German soldiers pierced the improvised defense lines on the approaches to Moscow and reached within 15 miles (24 km) of the city—they could see the cupolas of St. Basil's Cathedral in Red Square in the distance. However, resistance kept stiffening. Stalin chose to stay in Moscow and appeared at the annual celebrations in Red Square, offering a much-needed morale boost to his people.

By early November, the German army suffered its first cases of frostbite, and soon the soldiers had difficulty firing frozen guns. Then, on 5 December, Siberian troops—transferred from the Chinese frontier—attacked, many wearing the snow camouflage that Germans would learn to fear. The Red Army had high hopes of this offensive, intending to encircle and destroy their attackers. In the event, they did not manage this, but they did drive back the Germans up to 155 miles (250 km) at some points. The Germans had lost their chance for a quick victory. **JS**

Losses: German, 250,000–400,000 dead or wounded; Red Army, 600,000–1,300,000 dead, wounded, or captured

◁ Leningrad 1941 Stalingrad 1942 ▷

Operation Crusader
18 November–10 December 1941

The British advance against Rommel's forces was a rare instance where the panzer commander was defeated in a battle of maneuver. Although his gamble to win failed, he was able to keep his divisions intact by surrendering territory to the British.

On 18 November 1941, the British Eighth Army initiated an offensive to defeat the German-Italian forces on the Libyan-Egyptian border and relieve the besieged port of Tobruk. The British plan was for the armored XXX Corps to swing south and outflank the main Axis position, while the predominantly infantry XIII Corps was to smash its way through the Axis line and advance along the coast road to Tobruk.

Taken by surprise, the Axis troops reacted slowly and with initial confusion. The XXX Corps' advance went well until engaged by the mechanized Ariete Division and the 15th and 21st Panzer Divisions around Sidi Rezegh. In a series of swirling tank engagements, the balance of fortune swung from side to side, but the momentum of the British advance had been lost. Meanwhile, XIII Corps was making steady if slow progress along the coast road, but remained vulnerable to attack by Axis armor.

Rommel suddenly ordered his panzers to disengage from their battle with XXX Corps and race toward the British rear areas—the "dash for the wire." Rommel had gambled on unnerving his opponents, but the British held firm. In a rapid reversal of fortune, the German panzers found themselves in a dangerously exposed position and, running short of fuel and ammunition, they were forced to retreat. The British maintained their pressure and pushed the Germans back across Cyrenaica. Tobruk was relieved on 10 December. **AG**

Losses: Axis, 38,000 (mostly captured) of 115,000; British, 18,000 of 110,000

◁ Tobruk 1941 Gazala 1942 ▷

Pearl Harbor   7 December 1941

The Imperial Japanese Navy's devastating attack on the principal base of the U.S. Pacific Fleet at Pearl Harbor, Hawaii, plunged the United States into World War II. Although the attack brought Japan short-term gains, in the long term it caused her downfall by uniting Americans behind the war effort.

The attack followed years of tension between the two countries, notably over Japan's brutal, undeclared war in China. The Japanese depended on U.S. raw materials, and when the Roosevelt administration imposed sanctions in the summer of 1941, they had to go to war or abandon their expansionist ambitions altogether. The Japanese aimed to lock the United States out of most of the Pacific and simultaneously secure their raw materials by conquering European colonial territories in Asia.

The plan for a surprise raid on Pearl Harbor by naval aircraft was devised by Japanese naval commander in chief Admiral Yamamoto Isoroku. Vice Admiral Nagumo Chuichi's Japanese aircraft carrier task force left Kure under strict

> *"The United States was in the war, up to the neck and in to the death. … As for the Japanese, they would be ground to powder."* Winston Churchill

radio silence in November, vanishing into the Pacific. A fleet of thirty-one ships, including six carriers, sailed 1,000 miles (1,609 km) undetected, refueling from tankers at sea, to arrive within flying range of Hawaii. The first wave of 181 aircraft, led by Commander Mitsuo Fuchida, took off at dawn on 7 December. Although Pearl Harbor's defenders knew a war with Japan was on the cards, an attack on the base seemed unlikely, so when a coastal radar station detected the incoming raiders, the operators were told that they were friendly aircraft. Just before 7:00 AM, a patrolling

destroyer attacked a Japanese midget submarine inside the harbor, but by then it was too late. Nagumo's strike force arrived over the base at 7:53 AM, Commander Fuchida sending the code words "Tora Tora Tora" before his attack. He achieved almost complete surprise, finding defenses unmanned and the island's fighters parked wingtip to wingtip as a precaution against sabotage.

Dive-bombers and fighters swept over the U.S. air bases, strafing the aircraft on the ground. Torpedo aircraft and more dive-bombers made for the battleships anchored neatly in pairs off Ford Island. Within minutes, bombs penetrated the deck armor of USS *Arizona*, detonating her forward magazines, blowing the ship in half, and killing more than 1,000 of her crew. USS *Oklahoma* was torpedoed and capsized with heavy loss of life, and *California* and *West Virginia* were both badly hit below the waterline. After a brief lull, at around 9:00 AM a second wave of attack arrived, concentrating on the ships in dock. The battleship *Pennsylvania* was damaged, and three dry-docked destroyers were destroyed. The raiders finally departed at 10:00 AM, returning to Nagumo's task force, which made off unmolested to the north.

Carried off with light losses, the Japanese raid was an overwhelming success. However, three U.S. aircraft carriers were at sea and escaped attack, and Nagumo's raiders left the base infrastructure largely intact. Japan had, in the apocryphal words ascribed to Admiral Yamamoto, "awakened a sleeping tiger," and a newly unified America prepared for a long war. The escaped carriers later inflicted a devastating defeat on Nagumo at Midway in June 1942, beginning Japan's long retreat that ended with her surrender in Tokyo Bay in September 1945. **NH**

Losses: U.S., 2,400 dead, 1,250 wounded, plus 90 civilian casualties, 4 battleships sunk, 4 damaged, 3 other warships sunk, 7 damaged, 300 aircraft destroyed or damaged; Japanese, 64 dead, 29 aircraft, 4 midget submarines sunk

Prince of Wales *and* Repulse *1941*

U.S. sailors at Pearl Harbor watch USS Shaw *explode after the surprise Japanese attack.* ➜

Prince of Wales and *Repulse*
10 December 1941

Raid on Alexandria
18–19 December 1941

After Pearl Harbor, the only operational Allied battleships facing Japan's advance in World War II were *Prince of Wales* and *Repulse,* from Britain's Force Z based at Singapore. They sought to attack Japan's Malaya invasion force but lacked air support and were sunk by bombers and torpedo aircraft.

An attack by Italian "human torpedoes" sank two British battleships in their Mediterranean Fleet base at Alexandria in Egypt. After other important losses in the previous weeks of World War II, British naval strength in the Mediterranean was left at a low ebb, but the Italians failed to take advantage.

As relations with Japan worsened in late 1941, the British government decided to bolster its naval forces in the Far East. In the event, the new battleship *Prince of Wales* and the old battle cruiser *Repulse* were the only major vessels sent. Designated as Force Z, they reached the region less than a week before Pearl Harbor.

Japan's war plan included an invasion of northeast Malaya—controlled by Britain—from bases in the occupied French colony of Indo-China. This attack began simultaneously with the Pearl Harbor strike, early on 8 December Malaysian time. Later that day, Force Z set out to attack the invaders, but was soon spotted by the Japanese.

On the morning of 10 December, the Royal Navy ships were attacked by land-based bombers and torpedo aircraft operating from Indo-China. The British commander, Admiral Sir Tom Philips, was keeping radio silence, unwisely assuming that his colleagues in Malaya would work out where he was heading and supply air cover. Instead, the Japanese aircraft attacked unhindered, especially after a lucky hit right at the start of the action cut *Prince of Wales*'s speed and disabled most of its antiaircraft capability. Within a couple of hours, both British capital ships had been sunk. Accompanying British destroyers picked up survivors, but Admiral Philips was not among them. **DS**

Although the Italian navy included numerous powerful modern vessels, its main surface forces had been defeated in almost all their battles in 1940 and 1941. However, the Italians had other weapons in their armory. They had pioneered what would become known as "human torpedoes"—a type of midget submarine. Their operators called them "maiali" (pigs) because they were so difficult to maneuver. The two-man crew, wearing diving equipment, sat on top of what was in effect a steerable, low-speed torpedo with a detachable warhead. Their task was to attach the warhead under an anchored enemy ship and then escape before the timed charge went off.

Human torpedoes scored their first success in September 1941—they sank three Allied ships in Gibraltar—but their greatest triumph was at Alexandria three months later. Three maiali were launched from the parent submarine and managed to penetrate inside when the defensive boom was opened for some British ships to return to harbor. Their targets were the battleships *Valiant* and *Queen Elizabeth*—the most powerful vessels of the British Mediterranean Fleet—and a tanker, *Sagona*. All three crews placed their charges correctly and all three targets were badly damaged. For the cost of six men captured, the Italians had put Britain's last Mediterranean battleships out of action. **DS**

Losses: British, 840 dead, 2 ships; Japanese, 3 bombers

Losses: British, 2 battleships and 1 tanker sunk; Italian, 6 ships captured

◁ *Pearl Harbor 1941*

Bataan 1941 ▷

◁ *Crete 1941*

Invasion of Sicily 1943 ▷

Bataan
31 December 1941–9 April 1942

The surprise air attack against U.S. and Filipino installations was followed with amphibious landings by the Japanese 14th Army on the island of Luzon. The Japanese then advanced in pinchers from north and south, barely slowed by the delaying actions of the Philippine army divisions.

The defense of Luzon called for the withdrawal of forces into the mountainous Bataan peninsula and to hold for reinforcement. Instead, General Douglas MacArthur, commander of the U.S. Army in the Far East, tried to defeat the Japanese at the landing sites, and failed. In reality, he lacked the resources for either plan. The U.S. garrison was roughly 30,000, plus about 75,000 poorly trained Filipinos.

As the Japanese approached on 24 December, MacArthur declared Manila an open city and ordered all units to fight a delaying action. On 1 January, the last bridge into Bataan was destroyed and a series of defensive lines established. In January and February, Japanese attempts to land troops behind these lines were repulsed. Desperate fighting continued through March as Japanese infiltrators sought to outflank the defensive lines. A U.S. counteroffensive temporarily regained some ground, but on 3 April, a major Japanese attack decisively breeched the final defensive lines. On 9 April, with food and ammunition gone, a senior commander on Bataan surrendered the 78,000 survivors.

The fall of Bataan provided the Japanese with an artillery base for attacking Corregidor, the last step in the conquest of the Philippines. It was also the death sentence for more than 600 U.S. and 10,000 Filipino prisoners who suffered the Death March, later designated a war crime. **RB**

"Heavy trucks crushed the corpse until it was flattened like a starched suit. . . . Japanese soldiers hollered with delight." Gene Boyt, Death March survivor

⬆ *Japanese soldiers celebrate their success on 1 January 1942, when they seized a vital U.S. gun installation in Bataan.*

Losses: U.S. and Filipino, 21,000 dead or missing, 78,000 captured, 3,000 escaped (to Corregidor); Japanese, 1,500 dead or wounded

◁ Prince of Wales *and* Repulse *1941*   *Guadalcanal 1942* ▷

Fall of Singapore 8–15 February 1942

Singapore was regarded as the base and cornerstone of Britain's empire in Asia, but its defenses proved to be weak and its garrison inadequately trained and incompetently led. Its fall was a humiliating surrender for the British and the Japanese army's greatest victory of the war.

Japanese General Yamashita's Twenty-Fifth Army overran mainland Malaya in less than two months from its landings in the north on 8 December 1941, despite being outnumbered. Surviving British forces withdrew to the island of Singapore, where their leaders hoped to be able to hold out. Singapore had supposedly been made an impregnable fortress by fortifications built before the war, but these had not been designed to meet an attack overland from the north. The garrison of some 70,000 Indian, British, and Australian fighting troops were short of weapons and training, and those units that had fought in the earlier stages of the campaign were demoralized.

The Japanese were far fewer in number—about 35,000—but had tank support and complete command of the air. They began their attack on the night of 8–9 February with landings in the northwest of the island by their veteran 8th and 18th Divisions, joined the next night by the Imperial Guards Division. General Percival, commanding the garrison, had unwisely spread his forces to defend all possible landing points and failed to coordinate effective resistance to the Japanese advance. By 12 February the Allied troops had been forced back to a perimeter around Singapore city itself. Bowing to the seemingly inevitable, Percival abandoned plans for new counterattacks and surrendered on the 15th. Many of his Indian troops later fought for the Japanese; thousands of other prisoners would die during their captivity. **DS**

Losses: British and Commonwealth, 14,000 dead or wounded, 70,000 captured; Japanese, 5,000 dead or wounded

◁ *Bataan 1941*   *Darwin 1942* ▷

    A Japanese soldier escorts the British surrender party (General Percival at extreme right). ⬆

Darwin 19 February 1942

To support their ongoing invasion of the Dutch East Indies, the Japanese high command decided to send their main aircraft carrier force to attack Darwin in northern Australia. Several Allied ships were sunk and heavy damage done to shore installations at negligible cost to the Japanese.

By February 1942, the port of Darwin was being used as a supply base for Allied forces in the East Indies. However, it had been so distant from any Japanese-held territory until a few weeks previously that virtually no thought had been given to defending it. On 15 February, four of the aircraft carriers that had led the attack on Pearl Harbor set out from the major Japanese base at Palau, in the Caroline Islands, to attack it. As at Pearl Harbor, Admiral Nagumo Chuichi was in command.

Having reached a takeoff position in the Banda Sea, the Japanese ships launched 188 aircraft—a mix of torpedo aircraft, fighters, dive-bombers, and conventional bombers—under Commander Mitsuo Fuchida to make the attack on 19 February. In addition to the attack's overwhelming strength it achieved complete surprise, sinking a U.S. destroyer and various merchant ships in the port and wrecking the port facilities. A follow-up raid by land-based aircraft heavily damaged the town's airfield.

The air raids caused a panic in northern Australia and throughout the country about a possible Japanese invasion, but in reality this was never a practical possibility. It is doubtful that attacking such an insignificant target was a good use of Japan's principal naval strike force. After supporting the invasion of the East Indies, its ships would make attacks in the Indian Ocean as far west as Ceylon (Sri Lanka), thousands of miles from their principal enemy, the U.S. Pacific Fleet. **DS**

Losses: Allied, 7 merchant ships and 1 destroyer, 570 dead or wounded; Japanese, 1 aircraft

◁ *Fall of Singapore 1942*   *Java Sea 1942* ▷

⬆ *A U.S. Hudson bomber lies in the ruins of a Darwin hangar following the Japanese raid.*

Java Sea 27 February–1 March 1942

Virtually the last Allied naval forces facing Japan's imperious advance in the East Indies were destroyed in a series of naval engagements off the island of Java. Japan would soon complete its occupation of the archipelago, adding to its conquests in Malaya, Burma, and the Philippines.

By late February 1942 Japanese forces had captured much of the Dutch East Indies. (Although the Netherlands had been occupied by Germany in 1941, its colonial forces continued to fight on the Allied side.) Java was the next Japanese target. Its defenses included a Dutch, British, U.S., and Australian naval force of five cruisers and nine destroyers, commanded by Dutch Admiral Karel Doorman, but these had not trained together and could scarcely communicate with each other. The ships were also outgunned by Admiral Takagi's four cruisers and fourteen destroyers, which had been sent to cover the planned Japanese landings.

The battle began in the afternoon of 27 February off the north coast of Java. In a series of clashes continuing into that night, two Dutch cruisers were sunk by powerful Japanese "Long Lance" torpedoes, and one British cruiser was damaged by gunfire. Before he died aboard his flagship, HNLMS *De Ruyter*, Doorman ordered the two surviving cruisers to escape. The next night, however, these ships, USS *Houston* and HMAS *Perth*, were cornered and sunk while attacking a Japanese landing force. Finally, on 1 March, the damaged British cruiser HMS *Exeter* was caught and sent to the bottom by a superior Japanese force. Five Allied destroyers were also lost in the various battles. The only Japanese ships lost were two transports sunk by *Houston* and *Perth*. For the moment, Japan still retained the initiative seized at Pearl Harbor. **DS**

Losses: Allied, 5 cruisers and 5 destroyers; Japanese, no warships lost

◁ *Darwin 1942*　　　　　　　*Doolittle Raid 1942* ▷

St. Nazaire Raid 28 March 1942

The defeat of France gave Germany control of ports on the Atlantic coast, threatening vital sea-lanes to Britain. The British raid on the Brittany port of St. Nazaire was designed to make it unusable as a base for the powerful German battleship *Tirpitz*. In this it was wholly successful.

The dry dock at St. Nazaire was the only facility on the French coast large enough to service *Tirpitz*. The British planned to ram the dock gates with an old destroyer, HMS *Campbeltown*, packed with explosives. The raid was entrusted to the Royal Navy and the Commandos (special forces trained for attacks on occupied Europe).

Shortly after midnight on 28 March, *Campbeltown* approached St. Nazaire, flanked by a flotilla of motor launches and other small boats. An RAF bombing raid on the port, intended as a diversion, only served to alert the German defenses, and land batteries opened fire almost immediately. Most of the motor launches were destroyed or disabled. Lit up by German searchlights and burning boats, *Campbeltown* pressed on through heavy fire and rammed the dock gates just after 1:30 AM. The explosives in its hull were on a delayed timer fuse.

Commandos disembarked from the destroyer and from the surviving small boats and fought with German soldiers while placing demolition charges. One body of Commandos, deciding withdrawal by sea was impossible, tried to fight through the town to the country, but almost all were killed or captured. In fact, six of the small boats did make it back to open sea. At midday *Campbeltown* was being inspected by German officials when the delayed fuse triggered the explosives, killing some 360 people and destroying the dock. It remained out of action for the rest of the war. **RG**

Losses: British, 169 dead and 215 captured of 612; German, unknown

◁ *Dunkirk 1940*　　　　　　　*Dieppe Raid 1942* ▷

Doolittle Raid   18 April 1942

Bombers launched from a U.S. aircraft carrier made a surprise attack on Tokyo. Little damage resulted, but the raid was a boost to American morale at a low point in the war. The affront of the raid to Japanese national pride motivated Japan's leaders to pursue offensive plans with fresh urgency.

After Pearl Harbor President Roosevelt demanded that the U.S. military find a way of striking back directly at Japan. The only possible method was with carrier-borne aircraft, but standard naval planes had too short a range—carriers launching them would have to sail dangerously close to Japan's well-defended coast.

Instead a special unit of USAAF B-25 Mitchell bombers, far larger than naval aircraft, was trained under Colonel James Doolittle to take off from the carrier USS *Hornet*. They were to drop their bombs on Japan and then fly on to land in an area of China controlled by the pro-Allied Nationalists. Doolittle and his sixteen bombers took off successfully on 18 April—no mean feat for aircraft laden with bombs and fuel. Because the naval force had been spotted by the Japanese, the launch was made 650 miles (1,000 km) from Japan, instead of 400 miles (650 km) as originally intended. The bombers arrived over Japan in daylight but suffered little damage from enemy action. Almost all succeeded in bombing Japanese targets, most in Tokyo but also in Kobe, Yokosuka, and Osaka.

After the attack, all the aircraft ran short on fuel. One diverted to land in Soviet Russia. The other fifteen headed for Nationalist China but had to abandon plans to land at airfields, instead crash-landing or bailing out. All the aircraft were lost but only three crew members were killed, while eight fell into the hands of the Japanese, who subjected them to torture and starvation. **DS**

Losses: Japanese, 50 civilians dead; U.S., 3 dead, 8 captured (4 died in captivity)

◁ *Java Sea 1942*　　　　　　　*Coral Sea 1942* ▷

Coral Sea   6–8 May 1942

In the first major sea battle fought entirely by carrier fleets never within range of one another's guns, the United States came off worse tactically but gained a strategic victory. Japan abandoned its intention to invade New Guinea, its first significant military setback since December 1941.

From their recently captured base at Rabaul on New Britain the Japanese planned to seize new positions in the Solomon Islands and to invade Port Moresby in New Guinea. They deployed several naval task forces for the operation including one led by the fleet carriers *Shokaku* and *Zuikaku*. Unfortunately for the Japanese, American code breakers were now reading their signals efficiently and Rear Admiral Frank Fletcher was ordered to block the attack. He assembled a naval force including the fleet carriers USS *Lexington* and *Yorktown*.

The battle began on 6 May. At first both sides found and attacked minor targets. U.S. naval aircraft sank *Shoho*, a light carrier acting as a convoy escort; the Japanese sank an oil tanker and a destroyer. The main engagement followed on the 8th. The U.S. carriers launched their dive-bombers and torpedo aircraft and hit *Shokaku*, setting it ablaze, but *Zuikaku* escaped under cover of a rainstorm. The Japanese naval fliers also made repeated attacks through the day. *Yorktown* was badly damaged and a bomb exploding below decks caused heavy loss of life. *Lexington*, hit by both bombs and torpedoes, could not be saved and was finally scuttled.

Japan lost fewer ships, but more aircraft and aircrews, than their enemy. But, crucially, whereas *Yorktown* was rapidly repaired, neither *Shokaku* nor *Zuikaku* was ready to fight the following month at Midway. And Japan also abandoned its invasion of Port Moresby. **DS**

Losses: Japanese, 1 light aircraft carrier, 77 aircraft, 1,074 dead; U.S., 1 aircraft carrier, 1 destroyer, 66 aircraft, 543 dead

◁ *Doolittle Raid 1942*　　　　　*Sydney Harbor 1942* ▷

Gazala   26 May–21 June 1942

The German attack on Libya's Gazala Line showed the daring of its commander, Erwin Rommel, and the Afrika Korps's skill in fighting a complex tank battle. The British Eighth Army, comprehensively outgeneralled and out-fought, was left, as one commentator would put it, "brave but baffled."

Rommel's spring offensive of 1942 had come to a halt at the British Eighth Army's Gazala Line, a series of defensive positions, or boxes, running from the coast at Gazala southward to Bir Hakeim, deep in the desert. Both sides reinforced their armies in preparation for a coming offensive, and it was Rommel's Afrika Korps that struck first, on 26 May 1942. Rommel's Italian infantry were committed to a frontal assault against the Gazala Line, while his mainly German mechanized units swung southward around Bir Hakeim to attack from the rear.

The British were prepared for such a move and their armored units, held in reserve, took on the German panzers, forcing them back against the British minefields in the Gazala Line. The British failed to follow up this initial success, however, giving Rommel time to retreat to a position known as the "Cauldron" where he reorganized and resupplied his panzers. Once Bir Hakeim had fallen to the Germans on 11 June, Rommel had a free hand to renew his offensive from a favorable position.

British armor attempted to overrun the "Cauldron" but its uncoordinated attacks were easily fended off by the German antitank screen. With the collapse of the "Knightsbridge" box, the Gazala Line became untenable, and a general retreat was ordered. Rommel seized the opportunity with characteristic energy, capturing Tobruk on 21 June and advancing deep into Egypt to El Alamein, only 60 miles (95 km) from Alexandria. **AG**

"[Retreating from the Gazala Line] was one of the heaviest blows I can recall during the war."

Winston Churchill

⬆ *German general Erwin Rommel in Bir Hakeim during the Libya campaign.*

Losses: Axis, 32,000 casualties of 110,000, plus 560 tanks; Allied, 50,000 casualties of 125,000, plus 850 tanks

◁ *Operation Crusader 1941*   *Bir Hakeim 1942* ▷

Bir Hakeim 26 May–11 June 1942

The stubborn defense of the fortified outpost at Bir Hakeim by Free French forces in the course of the Battle of Gazala in Libya helped delay the advance of Rommel's panzers. It also showed the world that, despite the disasters of 1940, the French had lost neither the will nor the ability to fight.

As the southern bastion of the Gazala Line, Bir Hakeim was a vital part of the British defensive system. The responsibility of holding this position was assigned to the 1st Free French Brigade Group under the command of General Marie Pierre Koenig. Befitting its exposed position, Bir Hakeim was equipped with field and antitank artillery and protected by wide belts of minefields.

The blow fell on 26 May with the advance of German armor around Bir Hakeim. The French could do nothing to stop the maneuver, but their very presence was a thorn in the German side, and an Italian mechanized division was ordered to capture the position. This attack foundered on the minefields and the few tanks that did threaten the French were picked off with antitank guns. The German air force subjected Bir Hakeim to repeated, intense bombardment. But attacks by Italian and German ground forces were repulsed, leading an exasperated Rommel to send Koenig a note on 3 June to discuss surrender terms. This was ignored as the French fought on.

By 10 June the defenders' position had become desperate and a signal was sent from Eighth Army headquarters for the French to break out and retreat eastward to British lines. That night, amid great secrecy, the breakout took place, taking the surrounding Axis units by surprise. From an original force of 3,700 troops, some 2,600 made their way to safety. Conceded Hitler: "The French are still, after us, the best soldiers in Europe." **AG**

Losses: Axis, 3,500 casualties of 45,000; Allied, 1,100 casualties of 3,700

◁ Gazala 1942   Alam Halfa 1942 ▷

Sydney Harbor 31 May–1 June 1942

A direct Japanese attack on Sydney, Australia's largest city, came as a shock to Australians, even if, largely by good fortune, the material damage caused was slight. For Japan it provided a chance to deploy its midget submarines and demonstrate the suicidal courage of their two-man crews.

Strategically the raid on Sydney Harbor was one of a number of diversionary operations intended to distract Allied attention from Japanese preparations for an attack on Midway Island. The midget submarines were carried to the waters off Sydney aboard full-size submarines. Late on the afternoon of 31 May, three were launched about 7 miles (11 km) from their target. Sydney Harbor was not undefended against submarine attack. There were indicator loops to warn of a submarine's approach, an antisubmarine boom net across the harbor entrance, and patrol ships designated for harbor defense. But signals from the indicator loops had come to be routinely ignored, and the boom net was only half finished.

The first midget submarine to arrive nonetheless became entangled in the net, where it was spotted at around 9:30 PM. With an Australian patrol boat preparing to attack, the submariners blew up their craft and themselves with it. The other two submarines penetrated into the harbor. Although they were spotted and attacked with gunfire and depth charges, senior Allied commanders were slow to react, and a blackout was not ordered until after 11:00 PM. One of the submarines fired two torpedoes at the heavy cruiser USS *Chicago*, but missed, instead sinking the depot ship *Kuttabul*, killing twenty-one sailors. The submarine escaped to sea but never reached its mother ship. The third submarine was harried around the area until sunk in the early hours of the morning. **RG**

Losses: Allied, 1 ship sunk, 21 dead, 10 wounded; Japanese, 3 midget submarines sunk, 6 dead

◁ Coral Sea 1942   Midway 1942 ▷

Midway   3–7 June 1942

The Japanese defeat at Midway marked a turning point in the Pacific War. Japan's main aircraft-carrier force was smashed and the initiative passed to the Allied side. Japan was far from beaten but, as the U.S. war effort got into its stride, Japan could only expect further defeats to follow.

Admiral Yamamoto Isoruku, the mastermind of the Pearl Harbor operation, was well aware that strong U.S. Navy forces, centered on aircraft carriers, had eluded his attack. He needed to defeat these in a major battle, and so he planned an attack on Midway Island in the Central Pacific, which the United States would be sure to defend as an outpost of its main base in Hawaii. Yamamoto made a dangerously overcomplicated plan, dividing his Midway forces into several dispersed groups and sending a significant part of his strength on a wasteful diversion against the Aleutian Islands in the North Pacific. In the first phase of operations he expected to surprise the Americans and capture Midway; then he would be well

"They had no right to win. Yet they did, and in doing so they changed the course of a war."

National World War II Memorial, Washington, D.C.

placed to defeat their inevitable attempt to fight back. The most powerful element of his fleet included four carriers commanded by Vice Admiral Nagumo Chuichi.

Admiral Chester Nimitz, commanding the U.S. Pacific Fleet, had other ideas. American code breakers were able to read many Japanese naval messages but Nimitz was instrumental in correctly interpreting these as presaging an attack on Midway and ensuring that the three available aircraft carriers—USS *Yorktown, Enterprise,* and *Hornet*— were deployed far sooner than the Japanese expected.

As well as the carrier aircraft, the land-based planes were available from Midway itself.

Aircraft from Midway located the approaching Japanese fleet on 3 June and made unsuccessful attacks. The main battle began the next morning, with Nagumo still unaware of the American carriers' presence. Japanese naval bombers raided Midway's air base and were being recovered by their carriers when Nagumo first received confused reports of a U.S. carrier force nearby. By this time the U.S. carrier aircraft were already aloft seeking their targets. Torpedo bombers from *Hornet* and *Enterprise* were first to find the Japanese carriers. This was unfortunate, for these slow-moving aircraft attacking at low altitude were easy meat for Japanese Zero fighters. All fifteen torpedo bombers from *Hornet* were shot down without scoring a single hit. But dealing with the torpedo attack pulled the defending Japanese Zeros out of position. At this point groups of dive-bombers from *Enterprise* and *Yorktown* arrived over the Japanese carriers and went into the attack. In rapid succession three of the carriers—*Akagi, Kaga,* and *Soryu*—were crippled; all would later sink.

The Japanese fought back. In the early afternoon aircraft from the undamaged carrier *Hiryu* crippled *Yorktown,* but then a series of hits on *Hiryu* sank her the next morning. Yamamoto briefly hoped to retrieve the situation by catching the U.S. force with his still-powerful battleship fleet, but the Americans wisely stayed out of his reach. Early on 5 June he called off the whole operation. It was little consolation that *Yorktown* was sunk by a Japanese submarine two days later, along with an accompanying destroyer. Midway was a catastrophe for the Japanese navy, causing irreparable damage to its proud carrier fleet and costing the lives of irreplaceable experienced naval pilots. **DS**

Losses: Japanese, 4 aircraft carriers, 225 aircraft, 3,000 dead; U.S., 1 aircraft carrier, 1 destroyer, 151 aircraft, 307 dead

◄ *Sydney Harbor 1942*   *Kokoda Trail 1942* ►

Planes prepare for takeoff on USS Enterprise *for the Battle of Midway.* ➜

Convoy PQ.17 1–10 July 1942

To help Soviet Russia in its fight to the death with the Germans, the western Allies provided supplies and arms in naval convoys from Iceland to northern Russia. These convoys were often heavily attacked from German bases in Norway, with the heaviest losses being incurred by Convoy PQ.17.

Leaving Iceland on 27 June 1942, Convoy PQ.17 consisted of forty merchant ships (though three would turn back early) and an escort force of six destroyers and a dozen smaller vessels. In support was a covering force of cruisers and, at longer range, the main strength of Britain's Home Fleet. But the ships faced a dangerous journey; within easy range of German air bases in Norway and possible attack by the battleship *Tirpitz* and its powerful supporting squadron, they would be permanently exposed by the twenty-four-hour daylight of the Arctic summer. Further, the threat from the air meant that the Home Fleet was not permitted to enter the area of worst danger. The sailing

was a gamble made necessary by the Allies' undertaking to help Russia, but if German reconnaissance detected the convoy and *Tirpitz* attacked, the merchant ships and their escorts would stand little chance.

The Germans duly located the convoy on 1 July near Jan Mayen Island and air and U-boat attacks began. These achieved limited successes at first but on the evening of 4 July the British naval command in London ordered the escorts to withdraw and the merchant ships to scatter. London believed that an attack by *Tirpitz* was imminent and that this move gave the convoy its best chance. Instead a massacre followed. In air and submarine attacks up to 10 July, two-thirds of the convoy's ships were sunk. *Tirpitz* did sail on 5 July, but returned soon after; by then the Germans knew she was not needed. **DS**

Losses: Allied, 23 merchant ships and their cargoes, 153 dead; German, 5 aircraft

[<] *Sinking the* Bismarck 1941   *Convoy ONS.5 1943* [>]

Merchant and escort ships of Convoy PQ.17 assemble at Hval Fjord naval base, Iceland.

Kokoda Trail July 1942–January 1943

Fought in terrible conditions on a track crossing New Guinea's Owen Stanley mountains, the battles along the Kokoda Trail were among the nastiest of the war. After various reverses the Australian forces were able to go over to the offensive and push the Japanese back to their original beachheads.

Despite their losses in the Battle of the Coral Sea, the Japanese command still wished to capture Port Moresby in New Guinea. Maps showed a route crossing from Buna on the north coast, so it was decided to land there and attack overland. In reality the 100-mile (160 km) Kokoda Trail was no more than a muddy track, often only 2 feet (0.6 m) wide, through swampy, disease-ridden jungle and over precipitous ridges. The terrain and the climate were among the worst of any World War II battlefield.

Japanese General Horii's South Seas Detachment initially outnumbered the opposing Australian force. By mid-September the Australians had been pushed back across the mountains to a final defense line only 25 miles (40 km) from Port Moresby. The men of both sides suffered horrible privations throughout; neither side had sufficient supplies or proper facilities for the sick or wounded. The top Allied commanders, Australia's General Sir Thomas Blamey and U.S. General Douglas MacArthur, accused the troops of fighting ineffectively, though neither troubled to visit the front and assess the conditions first hand.

By this time, however, the Japanese supply system had collapsed and the troops retreated back along the trail. They had so little food that some even resorted to cannibalism. By November they were back where they had started. Fresh Australian and U.S. troops were now arriving and these wiped out the fortified Japanese beachheads by mid-January 1943. **DS**

Losses: Australian, 2,163 dead; U.S., 913 dead; Japanese, at least 12,000 dead

◁ *Coral Sea 1942*   *Guadalcanal 1942* ▷

⬆ *Australian troops use horses to haul a 25-pounder gun along the Kokoda Trail.*

Guadalcanal 7 August 1942–9 February 1943

The first major U.S. offensive of the Pacific War developed into a bitter attritional struggle on an inhospitable, jungle-clad island of the southwest Pacific. Although Guadalcanal was thousands of miles from either the United States or Japan, it monopolized the efforts of both combatants for months before the eventual U.S. victory.

The objectives of the U.S. attack were to turn back Japan's drive to cut the routes linking the United States and Australia and to establish an air base to support a northward Allied advance through the Solomon Islands. In the summer of 1942 the Japanese had placed a small force on the island and were building an airfield in preparation for a larger-scale occupation.

Under Vice Admiral Frank Fletcher, some 16,000 troops were assembled, most of them U.S. Marines. On 7 August they began landings on Guadalcanal and two neighboring islands, Florida and Tulagi. Initial Japanese resistance on the ground was soon overcome, but the

> *"Starvation is taking many lives and it is weakening our already extended lines. We are doomed."*
>
> *Major General Kensaku Oda, 12 January 1943*

Japanese immediately attacked the U.S. invasion fleet with aircraft and warships. The U.S. Navy withdrew its carriers to a safe distance and then, after suffering severe losses in the Battle of Savo Island, pulled out all its warships. The Marines on Guadalcanal were left in possession of only part of their supplies and equipment.

Commanded by General Alexander Vandegrift, the Marines formed a defensive perimeter around the airfield, which they labored to render operational and renamed Henderson Field. On 20 August twenty aircraft were

flown in, founding what would be called the Cactus Air Force. Meanwhile a Japanese army counter-offensive got under way. The troops were carried to Guadalcanal on fast destroyers down the "Slot" (New Georgia Sound), and landed by night to avoid air attack. This tactic became known as the "Tokyo Express."

On 12 September the first major fighting took place at Edson's Ridge, named for the Marine officer who led the defense of the feature. Fierce Japanese attacks were driven back, the setback obliging Japanese senior commanders to divert still more forces to the island. The Americans also moved in reinforcements, matching the Japanese numbers. The position of the U.S. soldiers and airmen was unenviable. The island's jungle terrain and climate were viciously hostile and living conditions primitive. Tropical diseases took their toll even when combat subsided. Henderson Field was subjected to aerial bombardment, despite the able air defense mounted by the Cactus Air Force. At night Japanese warships staged raids down the Slot, bombarding U.S. positions with their guns. Troops on both sides were often short of food and medical supplies, but the Japanese eventually suffered far worse because Henderson Field was never put out of action.

The failure of a major Japanese army offensive in October was compounded by a Japanese naval defeat the following month. It became impossible for Japan to continue supplying and reinforcing its troops on the island. In late December Japanese commanders recognized the inevitable and decided to withdraw. The evacuation was skillfully handled. U.S. commanders were given the impression that the Japanese were planning a fresh offensive and remained passive and watchful while 10,000 Japanese troops were extracted on board destroyers in the first week of February 1943. **DS**

Losses: U.S. land forces, 1,700 dead; Japanese land forces, 25,000 dead

◁ *Kokoda Trail 1942*　　　　　　　　　　*Savo Island 1942* ▷

　　U.S. Marines come ashore at Guadalcanal in August 1942; six months of hardship would lie ahead.

Savo Island   8–9 August 1942

U.S. landings on Guadalcanal on 7 August 1942 provoked an immediate and ferocious response from the Imperial Japanese Navy. In the first of a series of hard-fought naval battles nearby, an Allied cruiser and destroyer squadron was heavily beaten by superior Japanese night-fighting skills.

Learning of the U.S. landing on Guadalcanal, Vice Admiral Gunichi Mikawa led seven cruisers and a destroyer to attack their transport ships. Having no air cover, Mikawa decided on a night assault to avoid any interference from U.S. aircraft carriers (they had, in fact, already withdrawn). This left five Allied cruisers and six destroyers on station.

The Japanese achieved complete surprise. Suddenly lit up by flares dropped by Japanese floatplanes, the Australian cruiser *Canberra* was shattered by gunfire and torpedoes from the Japanese warships. The U.S. cruiser *Chicago* escaped with less damage but its withdrawal exposed the rest of the squadron to attack. Unable to distinguish friend from foe in the darkness, Allied ships hesitated to shoot as they were pinned by searchlights. Japanese shells and torpedoes soon destroyed another three U.S. cruisers; two destroyers were also badly damaged. Mikawa's flagship, the heavy cruiser *Chokai*, was the only seriously damaged Japanese vessel.

However, Mikawa failed to follow through with his success. Fearing an attack in daylight by U.S. aircraft, he headed back to base. The only material consolation for the Allied side was that a submarine sank one of the Japanese cruisers, *Kako*, on its return journey. **DS**

Losses: Allied, 4 cruisers sunk, 1,270 dead; Japanese, no ships sunk, 58 dead

◁ *Guadalcanal 1942*   *Milne Bay 1942* ▷

Wounded Allied troops lie on the beach after the Dieppe Raid.

Dieppe Raid   19 August 1942

A mainly Canadian force of nearly 6,000 troops carried out Operation Jubilee, a raid on the heavily defended port of Dieppe in German-occupied France. Ordered by the new Chief of Combined Operations, Vice Admiral Lord Louis Mountbatten, Jubilee was a controversial and costly fiasco.

The cross-Channel attack took place along a 10-mile (16 km) front, with the first troops landing at dawn to neutralize coastal batteries. The German garrison, alerted during the night after a coastal convoy encountered the invasion fleet at sea, fought back hard and many of the troops were unable to move off the beaches. Others arrived late, or landed in the wrong place.

The main frontal assault began at 5:20 AM. Naval gunfire support was insufficient to make an impact, and nearly half of the few supporting tanks were stopped on the beach, their tracks jammed by shingle, or simply unable to cross the town's sea wall. The infantry were pinned down under heavy fire. At 11:00 AM the remnants of the raiding force began to withdraw. More than half of the Canadian troops had been killed, wounded, or taken prisoner, along with 275 Britons. Losses at sea and in the air were equally heavy, the Royal Navy losing a destroyer and thirty-three landing craft, and the RAF 106 aircraft.

If the aim of the operation was to establish whether a cross-Channel invasion was possible and to test the tactics and technology of amphibious warfare under operational conditions, it is debatable whether the lessons learned were worth the price. **NH**

Losses: Canadian, 3,367 dead, wounded, or captured; British, 275 dead, wounded, or captured; German, 591 dead

◁ *St. Nazaire Raid 1942*   *Normandy Landings 1944* ▷

Stalingrad   23 August 1942–2 February 1943

The decisive moment in World War II on the Eastern Front, the Battle of Stalingrad was a catastrophe from which the German army never recovered. In 1942 the Germans might still have beaten the Soviet Union, despite their failure to take Moscow, but after Stalingrad they could only delay defeat.

The German attack on Stalingrad, on the Volga River, was initially a sideshow, a thrust by Hitler's Army Group South through the Caucasus to capture the Baku oilfields. From mid-July the German Sixth Army under General Friedrich Paulus and Fourth Panzer Army drove toward the Volga, sweeping aside outnumbered Soviet forces. In late August waves of Luftwaffe bombers reduced Stalingrad to rubble as the Germans closed in.

The person entrusted with holding Stalingrad was General Vasiliy Chuikov, a blunt, ruthless commander prepared to fight the Germans building by building and street by street. Most of Stalingrad lay west of the Volga. Chuikov established his headquarters on the east bank, from which supplies and reinforcements were ferried to the city's defenders. As German troops pushed into Stalingrad, Chuikov ordered his soldiers to "hug" them, keeping so close that the Germans would not be able to use air support or artillery without hitting their own side. Factories were turned into fortresses, defended for weeks against German assault. The battle was fought within buildings, German and Soviet troops occupying different floors. Snipers operated among the ruins—the Soviets' star sharpshooter, Vasiliy Zaitsev, was credited with 149 kills. The Soviets used terror to keep men fighting, executing thousands of soldiers as cowards or traitors.

While Chuikov held on to shrinking enclaves on the west bank of the Volga, General Georgiy Zhukov, recently

appointed Soviet Deputy Supreme Commander, planned a counter-offensive. The German advance to Stalingrad had created a salient pushed deep into Soviet-held territory. With the best German soldiers fighting inside the city, the flanks of the salient were held by poorly motivated Romanian, Italian, and Hungarian troops. Zhukov massed a million men to the north and south of the salient and, on 19 November, unleashed them in Operation Uranus. In four days they smashed through the enemy defenses and closed around Stalingrad in a pincer movement; 250,000 German troops were trapped.

Hitler refused to countenance a breakout from besieged Stalingrad. Paulus was ordered to hold on, receiving supplies by air, while German forces prepared a counterattack to relieve him. On 12 December the German Don Army Group attacked the Soviet ring around Stalingrad; by Christmas the counter-offensive had failed.

Hundreds of German aircraft were lost trying to supply the army in the Stalingrad pocket through worsening winter weather and in the face of a strengthening Soviet air force. The Luftwaffe never came close to meeting the soldiers' needs. By January 1943 the Germans inside the city were starving, freezing, and short of ammunition and fuel.

Hitler refused to authorize a surrender, promoting Paulus to field marshal to stiffen his resolve. But soldiers began to surrender and on 31 January Paulus joined them. Hitler was furious that his field marshal did not commit suicide. Paulus survived the war; among the 91,000 prisoners in Soviet hands when fighting ended on 2 February, few others lived to see the spring. **RG**

Losses: German, 150,000 dead, 91,000 captured; Soviet, 480,000 dead

◁ *Moscow 1941*   *Kursk 1943* ▷

Milne Bay   25 August–6 September 1942

This outstanding victory for Australian troops in the New Guinea campaign was Japan's first significant defeat on land in World War II. Commentators described it as having a vital morale-boosting effect on all the other fronts where Allied troops were fighting the Japanese.

By mid-1942 Milne Bay, at the eastern end of New Guinea, was a base for Australian troops working with U.S. Army engineers to build airfields. The Japanese decided to capture the area for use in support of their ongoing assault on Port Moresby along the Kokoda Trail. But Allied commanders worked out the Japanese intention from code-breaking information and were able to reinforce the defenders before the enemy attack began.

Some 2,000 elite Japanese marines landed near the Allied positions on the night of August 25–26 and began their assaults. They were joined on the 29th by 600 more troops. The Japanese force was reinforced by a handful of tanks (their opponents had none and no antitank weapons), but it faced more than 4,000 Australian and a few U.S. combat troops as well as several thousand engineers and other support personnel, under the command of Australian Major General Cyril Clowes. In addition the Allied force had significant air support, both from fighters based at Milne Bay itself and other squadrons operating from Australia.

Despite the disparity in numbers there was a series of bitter clashes. The turning point came on 31 August when Australian infantry and U.S. engineers wiped out a series of Japanese charges against one of the Allied airstrips. The Japanese were then pushed back to their landing areas and began withdrawing by sea on 4 September. Almost all the surviving Japanese marines had left by the 6th. **DS**

"Some of us may forget that, of all the allies, it was the Australians who first broke the invincibility of the Japanese army." Field Marshal Slim

⬆ *Australian soldiers advance through jungle in the hot, humid, and wet conditions at Milne Bay in early September 1942.*

Losses: Australian, 161 dead, 373 wounded; U.S., 20 casualties; Japanese, 612 dead

◁ Savo Island 1942   Henderson Field 1942 ▷

Alam Halfa   30 August–7 September 1942

The German advance into Egypt came to a halt around the railway junction at El Alamein. An engagement in July 1942 was inconclusive, and a failed attempt to break through the British lines at Alam Halfa ended Rommel's planned drive to Alexandria and Cairo.

Lieutenant General Bernard Montgomery, who assumed command of the British Eighth Army in August 1942, was determined to build up his forces before opening a new offensive against the now overstretched Axis forces facing him at El Alamein. But at the end of August, the recently promoted Field Marshal Erwin Rommel made a last-gasp effort to break through to the Nile delta. As a result of good intelligence, gained from Ultra decryption of German radio signals, the British had prior knowledge of the German plan and prepared accordingly.

The Axis forces were allowed to begin their flanking attack on the night of August 30–31 without opposition, but they were funneled toward well-defended British positions on the Alam Halfa ridge. As the Axis units advanced they were harassed by RAF bomber attacks, while shortages of fuel also slowed their progress. On reaching the Alam Halfa ridge the Axis met determined British resistance that brought their attack to a halt. Rommel's priceless armor was now in a vulnerable position, and prudently (if reluctantly) he ordered a general retreat. By 6 September the Axis divisions were back on their start line.

The tide of war was now turning against the Axis. While the Eighth Army was gaining in strength and morale, the German and Italian forces had to contend with dwindling stocks of munitions and fuel, which would affect their ability to counter any forthcoming Allied offensive. **AG**

Losses: Axis, 3,000 casualties of 45,000; British, 1,750 casualties of 60,000

[<] *Bir Hakeim 1942*   *El Alamein 1942* [>]

Henderson Field   23–26 October 1942

Exploiting its successes in the naval battles around Guadalcanal, Japan built up ground forces on the island. Its aim was to capture Henderson Field airbase, the main U.S. asset in the campaign, which meant defeating the determined U.S. Marine and Army units manning its defensive perimeter.

By mid-October 1942 the Japanese navy held the upper hand around Guadalcanal. The Japanese were able to land reinforcements on the island and to carry out an effective naval bombardment of Henderson Field. Although many aircraft were lost, Henderson Field (named for a hero of the Midway fighting) remained operational. Japanese General Harukichi Hyakutake thought that his 22,000 men on Guadalcanal now substantially outnumbered their U.S. opponents; in fact numbers were about equal after the recent arrival of U.S. Army units to reinforce the Marines. Confident of his superiority, Hyakutake planned a two-pronged attack on the U.S. beachhead. A diversionary force, including a number of tanks, would assault along the coast from the west, while the main attack went in from the south, heading directly for the U.S. airstrips.

The Japanese plan misfired. The main force had to make a circuitous approach to its starting positions that took several days through near-impossible jungle terrain. It managed to complete this march in secrecy but did not arrive in time. The secondary force did not get orders to delay its attack and was massacred by the defenders. When the main attack commenced, on the night of October 24–25, it was first held and then thrown back during two nights of ferocious combat. The few Japanese who penetrated the defensive perimeter were immediately hunted down. This would prove to be the last major Japanese attack on the island. **DS**

Losses: U.S., 200 dead; Japanese, 2,000 dead

[<] *Guadalcanal 1942*   *Santa Cruz 1942* [>]

El Alamein 23 October–4 November 1942

The Battle of El Alamein marked the beginning of the end for the Axis in North Africa. The charismatic Field Marshal Rommel was comprehensively defeated by the British Eighth Army, and Allied material superiority meant that he had little chance of rallying his broken forces.

Following on from the defensive success at Alam Halfa, Montgomery built up his forces to fight the key battle for North Africa. The British had built a defensive line at El Alamein because the Qattara Depression to the south was impassable to mechanized forces. A narrow choke point prevented the German panzers from operating on their preferred southern flank with open terrain. Now that the British had moved over to the offensive, the proposed battlefield also suited the Eighth Army, whose main strength lay in its artillery and infantry formations.

By mid-October 1942 Montgomery could deploy approximately double the number of men and tanks available to Rommel's German-Italian army. The British also enjoyed the invaluable advantage of air superiority over the battlefield. Aware that an attack was imminent, Rommel had prepared his defenses as best he could, sowing hundreds of thousands of antitank and antipersonnel mines along his front to slow any British advance. Rommel returned to Germany to recuperate from illness shortly before the British offensive was launched, command passing to a subordinate.

Montgomery's plan comprised a diversionary attack to the south, spearheaded by Free French troops, while the main attack would come in the northern sector, close to the coast. The British would break into the Axis line and force them to counterattack. In the process, the British would wear down the enemy's offensive capability.

On the night of 23–24 October a barrage from more than 800 guns heralded the offensive; British sappers, followed by infantry and tanks, advanced to clear paths through the minefields. Although the Axis commanders were taken aback at the violence of the assault, the Eighth Army's progress was painfully slow, the British armor failing to get to grips with the enemy. Rommel, meanwhile, had flown back to North Africa to resume command, and he immediately mounted spirited counterattacks.

For a while it seemed that the Axis might bring the British offensive to a halt. The German minefields and accurate antitank fire produced a mounting toll of knocked-out British tanks. But progress by the infantry, especially the Australian and New Zealand Divisions, opened up corridors through the Axis defenses that the British could exploit. On 2 November Rommel signaled to Hitler that the battle was lost. Although initially refused permission to retreat, Rommel began the withdrawal of his German units, leaving his Italian allies—who lacked motor transport—to be mopped up by the British.

By 4 November the motorized elements of the Axis were in full retreat, and because of the sluggish British follow-up they were allowed to escape virtually unscathed. But this was of limited strategic importance because the British victory at El Alamein was confirmed by Operation Torch, the Anglo-American landings in North Africa on 8 November. The Axis forces were now being squeezed in the Allied vice, and their expulsion from North Africa was only a question of time. **AG**

Losses: Axis, 20,000 dead or wounded and 30,000 captured of 104,000, plus 490 tanks; Allied, 13,500 casualties of 195,000, plus 1,025 tanks

⟨ *Alam Halfa 1942*   *Operation Torch 1942* ⟩

Santa Cruz 26 October 1942

The battles of the Guadalcanal campaign included operations of the two sides' main aircraft-carrier forces. U.S. losses from earlier encounters, and also submarine attacks, meant that the Japanese began the Battle of Santa Cruz with a numerical advantage—but Japan failed to capitalize on it.

Named for the Santa Cruz Islands, the battle was fought well to the east of Guadalcanal and the southern Solomon Islands. The Japanese aircraft-carrier forces, commanded by Admiral Nobutake Kondo, were in the area to support a major land offensive against Henderson Field. The Japanese had two large fleet carriers and two small light carriers equipped with a total of 212 aircraft. The Americans, under Rear Admiral Thomas Kinkade, had two fleet carriers, USS *Hornet* and *Enterprise*, with 171 aircraft. The U.S. force was concentrated for mutual support, but the Japanese were dispersed into several groups.

Both sides found their enemy early on 26 October; the carriers launched attack forces virtually simultaneously—they saw each other in passing while on route to their respective targets. The U.S. attack badly damaged the fleet carrier *Shokaku* and the light carrier *Zuiho*, but in return Japanese strikes crippled *Hornet*, which was hit by bombs, torpedoes, and by aircraft that crashed into the ship. The carrier had to be abandoned and was finished off by the Japanese the following day. *Enterprise* remained operational despite severe damage but was now the only U.S. carrier left in action in the Pacific. As in earlier battles, however, Japanese losses of aircraft and, more importantly, experienced aircrew were severe—many of their planes fell to antiaircraft fire from the battleship USS *South Dakota*, which was in support of the carrier group. Like the battered Americans, the Japanese withdrew. **DS**

Losses: U.S., 1 aircraft carrier and 1 destroyer sunk, 60 aircraft, 260 dead; Japanese, 100 aircraft, 400 dead

◁ *Henderson Field 1942*   *Naval Battle of Guadalcanal 1942* ▷

Operation Torch 8–10 November 1942

About 65,000 Allied troops landed at Casablanca, Algiers, and Oran on the French North African coast in Operation Torch, the first major Allied amphibious assault of the war. It brought U.S. troops into action against Germany, trapping Rommel's army in a pincer as it fled from El Alamein.

Although U.S. planners had favored a direct assault on Europe, the British argued that this was too risky given the limited forces available. Operation Torch offered the opportunity to end the desert war and open the Mediterranean, while trying to meet Stalin's demands for a second front. The operation was preceded by secret negotiations with Vichy representatives in a bid to minimize French and Allied bloodshed. Given French hostility to Britain, due to the Royal Navy's attack on the French fleet in 1940, the first wave was mainly American. U.S. Lieutenant General Dwight Eisenhower was in command. The 33,000 U.S. troops that landed on the Moroccan coast came directly from the United States. The rest of the British and U.S. force were brought from Britain.

Although some Vichy French forces surrendered, others resisted fiercely. At Casablanca, several French warships were sunk and the town only surrendered an hour before the final assault began. In Algiers and Oran, operations to seize the harbor facilities were repulsed with heavy loss of life, but in Algiers resistance evaporated soon afterward and the town surrendered. Capturing the port of Oran took two days and a heavy naval bombardment. On 10 November Marshal Pétain's deputy, Admiral François Darlan, coincidentally in Algiers, concluded an armistice with the Allies, ending French resistance in North Africa but provoking the Germans into occupying the rest of metropolitan France. **NH**

Losses: Allied, 500 dead, 700 wounded; Vichy French, 1,500 dead, 2,000 wounded

◁ *El Alamein 1942*   *Kasserine Pass 1943* ▷

⊙ *A Japanese dive-bomber plane attacks USS* Hornet *at the Battle of Santa Cruz—it crashed on the carrier's bridge.*

Naval Battle of Guadalcanal 12–15 November 1942

While infantry fought on Guadalcanal, the covering U.S. and Japanese naval forces clashed fiercely in two nights of frantic close-range battle. Fighting in what was called "Ironbottom Sound"—for the number of ships sunk there—the Japanese finally came off worse, though both sides lost heavily.

Despite being defeated at Henderson Field in October, Japan was determined to strengthen its land force on Guadalcanal, sending a convoy carrying 13,000 men. Vice Admiral Hiroaki Abe led two battleships, one cruiser, and eleven destroyers to cover the transports and bombard Henderson Field. On the night of 12–13 November, Rear Admiral Daniel Callaghan took five cruisers and eight destroyers to meet Abe's advance.

Unlike the Japanese, the Americans had radar, but they failed to use it properly, and the two sides blundered into close contact. In a ferocious half-hour battle, likened by one U.S. officer to "a barroom brawl with the lights out,"

only one ship on either side escaped damage. Two U.S. cruisers and one Japanese battleship either sank or were finished off later, and Admiral Callaghan was killed.

On 13 and 14 November the U.S. force sank a cruiser and seven transports in daytime air attacks, but the remaining transports continued toward Guadalcanal. Their approach was to be covered by a naval bombardment by Admiral Nobutake Kondo on the night of 14–15 November with a battleship and four cruisers. But Admiral Willis Lee arrived with two U.S. battleships and four destroyers. This time, radar gave the Americans a decisive advantage. All the U.S. destroyers were sunk or damaged gallantly screening the capital ships, but the battleship USS *Washington* sank the battleship *Kirishima* before both sides withdrew. Few Japanese reinforcements reached Guadalcanal. **DS**

Losses: U.S., 2 cruisers and 7 destroyers, 1,700 dead; Japanese, 2 battleships, 1 cruiser, 3 destroyers, 2,500 dead

[<] *Santa Cruz* 1942   *Bismarck Sea* 1943 [>]

An SBD Dauntless dive-bomber flies by two beached and burning Japanese transport ships.

Kasserine Pass   14–15 February 1943

The Axis offensive along the Kasserine Pass in Tunisia was the first large-scale encounter in World War II between the Axis and the U.S. Army. Although the Americans suffered a humiliating setback, they recovered quickly and prevented the Axis from exploiting their initial advantage.

On 14 February 1943 armored units from Rommel's Panzer Army Africa launched an offensive against the Allies to forestall their advance into Tunisia. The spearhead of the Axis advance was directed against the Kasserine Pass, lightly held by inexperienced American troops with some British and French support.

On 19 February a veteran German-Italian assault group smashed into the U.S. troops holding the pass. The German Panzer IV and Tiger tanks were vastly superior to the U.S. M3 light tanks and light antitank guns, and soon the Americans were retreating along the pass in disarray. Confused responses from Lieutenant General Lloyd Frendendall's

U.S. II Corps only made matters worse. For a while a sense of panic pervaded the Corps's command.

Once through the pass, the Axis forces continued their advance, but severe winter weather, increasingly mountainous terrain, and stiffening Allied resistance slowed progress. Simmering disagreements between Rommel and his superiors as to how the advance should proceed now came to a head, and on 22 February Rommel called off the offensive. Two days later, Allied troops reoccupied the pass.

The battle, while a shock to the Americans, had little effect on the continuing advance on Tunis. But one final casualty of the clash was General Frendendall, replaced on 6 March by the considerably more aggressive Major General George S. Patton. **AG**

Losses: Allied, 10,000 casualties of 30,000, plus 183 tanks; Axis, 2,000 of 22,000, plus 34 tanks

◁ El Alamein 1942   Invasion of Sicily 1943 ▷

A U.S. unit prepares for a counterattack on German positions on Kasserine Pass.

Bismarck Sea 2–5 March 1943

Japanese commanders attempted to send troops from their main regional base at Rabaul in New Britain to bolster their garrison at Lae in New Guinea. Their convoy was attacked and wiped out by U.S. and Australian aircraft and torpedo boats. Few of the troops reached their destination.

By early 1943 Allied air forces under Major General George Kenney dominated the skies of the Southwest Pacific Theater, while on land the Japanese outposts on New Guinea were under threat. The Japanese decided to send some 7,000 men of their 51st Division from New Britain to Lae, but their plan was discovered by Allied code breakers.

The Japanese convoy was located on 2 March off New Britain's Cape Gloucester in the Bismarck Sea. Air attacks began immediately, B-17 bombers sinking one of the eight transport ships that day. A Zero fighter shot down a B-17 and reportedly strafed the crew in their parachutes and in the sea. The Japanese commanders unwisely decided not to turn back. On 4 March waves of Allied planes, including U.S. B-25 Mitchell bombers and the Royal Australian Air Force's Bristol Beaufighters, sank all the Japanese transports and four of their eight escorting destroyers. The Allied air attacks were joined late on the 4th by a small flotilla of U.S. torpedo boats.

That night and the next day the torpedo boats and Allied aircraft killed Japanese survivors who had been left in the water and also attacked Japanese rescue vessels, actions they justified as a response to the earlier Japanese machine-gunning of the B-17 bomber crew. Fewer than a thousand Japanese troops reached Lae. The Allies had used superior intelligence information and dominant air power to fight a battle in overwhelming strength against an isolated enemy contingent. **DS**

Losses: Allied, 5 aircraft; Japanese, 4 destroyers, 8 transport ships, 20 aircraft, 3,664 dead

◁ Naval Battle of Guadalcanal 1942   Tarawa 1943 ▷

Convoy ONS.5 28 April–6 May 1943

A struggle was fought to defend merchant convoys, crossing the Atlantic to and from Britain, against attack by German U-boats. The climactic moment of this campaign came in spring 1943, when Allied escort forces first gained the upper hand over the German "wolf packs."

German submarines were attacking in unprecedented numbers in 1943, using coordinated tactics that brought a pack of submarines to bear against a single convoy. They struck on the surface by night, negating the effect of Allied sonar equipment that could detect submerged U-boats. On 28 April the Germans located the westward-bound convoy ONS.5, initially forty-two merchant ships and seven escorts. ONS.5 was to face the largest German "wolf pack" of the war, with around fifty U-boats engaged. But the convoy escorts were better trained and their improved radar sets gave them a good chance of detecting U-boats on the surface.

A single merchant ship was sunk on 29 April and at least two U-boats were damaged in response. Gales then limited German attacks. By 4 May, U-boat commander Admiral Karl Dönitz had two patrol lines of U-boats in position between Greenland and Newfoundland; these now reestablished contact with the slow-moving convoy. On the night of the 4th, picking off stragglers as well as penetrating the center of the convoy, the U-boats sank seven merchant ships for the loss of only one U-boat.

But, on the 5th, the escorts struck back; they found and sank four U-boats that night and the next morning. By the time the Germans withdrew, six U-boats were sunk and four severely damaged, a rate of loss they could not sustain. The Germans were soon forced to abandon submarine attacks on the Atlantic convoys. **DS**

Losses: Allied, 12 merchant ships sunk; German, 6 U-boats sunk

◁ Convoy PQ.17 1942

◉ *A Japanese supply ship burns after an Allied air attack in the Bismarck Sea.*

Dambusters Raid   16–17 May 1943

RAF Bomber Command's "Dambusters" raid—officially designated Operation Chastise—remains one of the most famous air attacks in history. Using specially designed "bouncing bombs," the raid breached crucial dams in Germany's Ruhr valley. While the dams were soon repaired, the raid proved a significant propaganda victory for Britain.

In March 1943 the RAF formed No. 617 Squadron, under the command of Wing Commander Guy Gibson. Flying specially modified Lancaster bombers, they were to strike three dams in the Ruhr valley using a 9,250-lb. cylindrical mine code-named "Upkeep," which had been designed by inventor Barnes Wallis. Dropped at a precise height and speed, the bomb would skip across the water, strike the dam, sink, and explode underwater, fracturing the dam's wall. The weight of water would then destroy the dam.

To ensure the bombs were dropped at the right altitude, two searchlights were fitted on the aircraft; when their beams on the water intersected, the height was correct. The raid, mounted by nineteen aircraft crewed by 133 airmen, was a feat of nighttime flying and navigation. The squadron succeeded in breaching dams at Möhne—destroyed after repeated bombing runs in the face of heavy fire—and at Eder, which, while undefended, was difficult to attack owing to the terrain. A third dam, at Sorpe, survived. Downstream from the breached dams, floodwater swept away homes, bridges, railroad tracks, and industrial facilities. Almost 1,300 Germans were killed.

Although the disruption to German industry was rectified relatively quickly, the raid had enormous political and propaganda value; aerial photographs of the destruction were front-page news around the world. Gibson was awarded the Victoria Cross. **IK**

Losses: RAF, 8 aircraft, 53 dead, 3 captured; German, 1,294 dead

⟨ *The Blitz 1940*   *Bombing of Hamburg 1943* ⟩

The Möhne dam, seen here before the raid, was protected by a heavy anti-torpedo net.

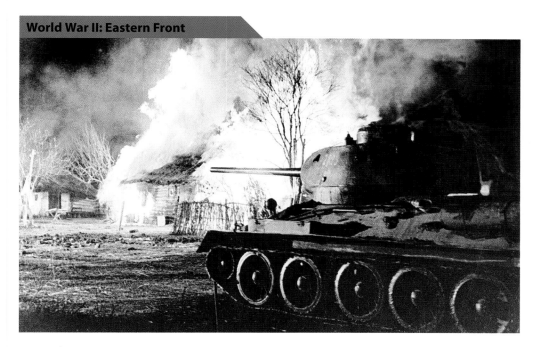

Kursk 5 July–23 August 1943

A key moment in the epic struggle between the Soviet Union and Germany, Kursk was the largest tank battle in history. The Germans were attempting to regain the strategic initiative after their catastrophic defeat at Stalingrad. Their failure to do so meant that henceforth they would be driven inexorably back to Germany.

The salient, or bulge, in the lines around Kursk had been packed with a huge concentration of the Red Army, as it seemed an ideal position from which to launch offensives toward Kiev and Orel. The Germans planned a pincer attack that would seal off the salient, trapping the Soviet forces inside. Germany's entire strategic reserve was committed to the task. But the move was too obvious, and Marshal Georgiy Zhukov had prepared well to face it. Initially he would fight a defensive battle, letting the Germans exhaust themselves, then launch his own encirclements to cut off the enemy. Very deep antitank defenses were built. The Germans were attacking where the Red Army was strongest—the Kursk salient had become one of the strongest defense systems ever seen.

The Germans threw in huge forces, but even by the end of the first day it was clear that they were suffering great losses and making little progress. One German tank commander later noted that, as he repeatedly smashed through Soviet tank formations, only invariably to meet further formations behind them, he realized that the war was lost. After four days of furious attacks, and extremely heavy losses on both sides, the German assault ground to a halt. Then the Red Army counterattacked; the Germans were driven back but escaped encirclement. But if losses on both sides had been immense, Soviet losses were replaceable, German losses were not. **JS**

Losses: German, 250,000 dead or wounded; Soviet, possibly more than 1,000,000 dead or wounded

◁ *Stalingrad 1942*   *Bagration 1944* ▷

Invasion of Sicily
9 July–17 August 1943

The Anglo-American invasion and capture of Sicily was a vital stepping-stone for the campaign in Italy, although the Allies were at fault in failing to prevent the Axis from successfully evacuating their best divisions from the island to continue the defensive battle on the mainland.

While the British wanted to pursue an offensive against Italy after the Allied capture of Tunisia, their U.S. partners were less enthusiastic, but the British prevailed. The Invasion of Sicily, the first part of the plan, was a massive undertaking—in Europe, second only to D-Day—involving 2,600 Allied ships and sustained air support. The invading force was made up of two armies—the U.S. Seventh Army and the British Eighth Army—and once ashore the Allies pressed forward in an attempt to destroy and capture the Axis units on the island. The few German troops on Sicily were quickly reinforced to a total of four elite divisions, along with a substantial Italian force.

Commanded by Field Marshal Albert Kesselring, the Germans skillfully used the island's mountainous terrain to carry out an effective delaying operation. The Allies, especially the British, advanced cautiously against the Germans. Although Hitler insisted that Sicily must be held at all costs, Kesselring soon realized that he must abandon the island if his German formations and their valuable weapons and equipment were not to be lost to the Allies. On the night of 11–12 August the Germans began a well-executed withdrawal that saw 40,000 German and 60,000 Italian troops cross over to the mainland with minimal hindrance from the Allies. **AG**

Losses: Allied, 22,000 casualties of 180,000; German, 10,000 casualties of 50,000; Italian, 132,000 casualties (mostly captured) of 200,000

◁ *Kasserine Pass 1943*　　　　　*Salerno 1943* ▷

Bombing of Hamburg
24 July–3 August 1943

In summer 1943 Allied bombers attacked the north German port city of Hamburg. Favorable weather conditions, with tactical and technical innovations employed by the bomber force, made Hamburg one of the most destructive air attacks ever, killing around 45,000 of the city's population.

By July 1943 the Allied bomber campaign against Germany was maturing. The RAF flew at night and, as precise night bombing was impossible, adopted the tactic of "area bombing" of urban areas. The USAAF bombed in daylight to achieve greater accuracy.

Six major raids were launched on Hamburg, aided by a secret radar countermeasure called "Window": aircraft dropped simple strips of paper, backed with aluminum foil, to blind German radar. This prevented searchlights, antiaircraft guns, or fighters from finding the attacking bombers. An RAF raid on the night of 28 July was accurate and concentrated. Incendiary bombs started many individual fires, while hot, dry weather encouraged fires to join together. These larger fires drew air, becoming ever more intense until entire districts were ablaze. Eventually four square miles (ten sq km) of Hamburg was one enormous firestorm, with temperatures up to 1,500°F (815°C) and winds of hurricane force.

The raid was shockingly destructive, and Nazi leaders feared that more such attacks might end Germany's war effort. But the destruction of Hamburg was a product of specific circumstances, and could not be readily repeated. When the RAF sought to destroy Berlin later in 1943 and 1944, heavy casualties were suffered for far less result. **IK**

Losses: RAF, 87 aircraft, 552 dead; USAAF, 17 aircraft , 46 dead, 106 captured; German, 12–15 aircraft, 8 dead; civilian, 45,000 dead and at least 37,000 wounded

◁ *Dambusters Raid 1943*　　　　*Bombing of Ploesti 1943* ▷

Bombing of Ploesti

1 August 1943

On 1 August 1943 U.S. B-24 bombers based in Libya set out on a 2,400-mile (3,800 km) mission to bomb vital oil refineries around the Romanian city of Ploesti (Ploieşti). Although the attack failed, it is remembered as one of the U.S. Army Air Forces' most daring sorties of the war.

In November 1940, beleaguered by both the Soviet Union and Nazi Germany, Romania joined the Axis powers. Romanian oilfields became vital to the German war effort. During early 1942 the USAAF began to build their strength in North Africa, and in June 1942 mounted a small experimental raid against Ploesti—the first U.S. bomber raid in Europe. The raid proved that such missions were possible, but also prompted the German air commander to implement powerful air defenses.

In summer 1943 the strike against Ploesti was repeated. Hoping to achieve surprise, 178 B-24s attacked at low altitude and in daylight. Due to navigational errors, the bombers could not coordinate their attacks, and two bomb groups ran into alerted defenses around the Romanian capital of Bucharest, 35 miles (55 km) from Ploesti. As the low-level force reached its targets, it was met by a ferocious hail of antiaircraft fire. Flying through gunfire, smoke, and the explosions of time-delayed bombs, the attacking formations suffered severe losses.

Five Medals of Honor were awarded, the most for any single air operation in U.S. history. The refineries were damaged, but excess capacity meant that the raid failed to reduce the output of oil. Ploesti was bombed until August 1944, when the Soviets occupied Romania. **IK**

Losses: USAAF, 54 aircraft, 310 dead, 440 wounded, 108 captured, 78 interned in neutral Turkey; Romanian, 5 fighter aircraft; German, 2 fighter aircraft

◁ Bombing of Hamburg 1943   Schweinfurt-Regensburg 1943 ▷

Schweinfurt-Regensburg

17 August 1943

On 17 August 1943, 376 B-17 Flying Fortresses of the USAAF, based in England, attacked aircraft factories at Schweinfurt and Regensburg in Bavaria. The raid was intended as a crippling blow to the German air industry, but without adequate escort the U.S. bombers suffered terrible losses.

The Regensburg force was to drop its bombs and then fly on to Allied bases in North Africa, while the Schweinfurt bombers were to return to England. Far beyond the range of escorting fighters, the two strikes and several diversionary missions were intended to overtax the German defenses. The B-17 bombers, flying at high altitude and bristling with guns, were expected to be able to fight their way through attacks by enemy fighters.

To prevent the Germans attacking each group in turn, the two forces were to take off within the same ninety-minute period. First to fly, the Regensburg force was intercepted immediately after crossing the European coast and attacked constantly on its inbound flight. The Schweinfurt bombers, whose takeoff was delayed for three hours by bad weather, were likewise attacked constantly on both their inbound and outbound legs, their delayed launch allowing German fighters time to refuel and rearm. Both formations' escorts arrived late, only to return home almost immediately for lack of fuel.

Although both targets were bombed, sixty bombers were shot down and eighty-seven damaged beyond repair. A further raid confirmed that daylight bombers could not operate without fighter escort, and that industries could not be knocked out by single raids. **IK**

Losses: USAAF, 60 bombers, 87 bombers damaged, 3 fighters, 7 dead, 21 wounded, 557 missing or captured; RAF, 2 fighters; German, 40 fighters, 203 civilians dead

◁ Bombing of Ploesti 1943   Berlin 1943 ▷

Salerno 9–16 September 1943

The signing of the armistice between Italy and the Allies on 3 September 1943 might have seemed to support Churchill's claim that Italy was the "soft underbelly of Europe," but the fierce and intelligent resistance displayed by the Germans at Salerno was a portent of things to come.

While Field Marshal Montgomery's British Eighth Army had an easy, unopposed landing at Reggio di Calabria, the Allied amphibious assault against mainland Italy in the Gulf of Salerno did not go as planned. Under the command of Lieutenant General Mark Clark's U.S. Fifth Army, the landing force was drawn from the British X Corps, which would hit the beaches at Salerno, and the U.S. VI Corps, acting as a flank guard and landing farther to the south.

The X Corps troops faced little resistance as they reached the beaches on 9 September 1943, but once ashore they came under sustained attack from the German XIV Panzer Corps. The U.S. VI Corps faced similar problems, unable to push forward from its beachhead. When, on 12 September, the Germans mounted a concerted counterattack, it seemed possible that the Allies might lose their tenuous hold on the Italian mainland. But the arrival of reinforcements—including a parachute drop by two battalions of the U.S. 82d Airborne Division—and the mass redeployment of Allied airpower to the Salerno front turned the tide.

On 16 September the Germans disengaged from the battle and began to withdraw to a specially prepared defensive line farther north; meanwhile, U.S. troops on the right of the beachhead made contact with units from the Eighth Army advancing from the south. As the Germans fell back, the Allies occupied the key port of Naples. **AG**

Losses: U.S., 225 dead, 835 wounded, 589 missing or captured; British, 531 dead, 1,915 wounded, 1,561 missing or captured, of an Allied 80,000; German, 3,000 casualties

◁ *Invasion of Sicily* 1943   *Monte Cassino* 1944 ▷

Allied troops pass by Greco-Roman temples at Paestum, 18 miles (30 km) to the south of Salerno. ⬆

Berlin 18 November 1943–25 March 1944

Between November 1943 and March 1944, RAF Bomber Command mounted a series of heavy night bombing raids against the German capital, Berlin. Although the raids caused massive destruction, the costly offensive failed in its aim of causing a decisive collapse of German morale.

After the firebombing of Hamburg, Air Chief Marshal Sir Arthur Harris, chief of Bomber Command, turned his attention to Berlin. Harris argued that he could "wreck Berlin from end to end," fatally undermining German morale and shortening the war.

The first raid was mounted on 18 November 1943, when 444 RAF bombers attacked the city. By March 1944 9,111 sorties had been flown against Berlin in the course of sixteen major raids. Nineteen raids were also mounted against other cities. Berlin proved a difficult target; it was beyond the range of the RAF's radio navigation aids, and the extra fuel required meant fewer bombs could

be carried. Winter weather also hampered navigation and accuracy. Berlin was formidably defended with concentrated antiaircraft guns, while prowling German night-fighters bristled with radar and innovative weapons such as the upward-firing "Schräge Musik" cannon, which allowed fighters to attack from below in relative safety.

Berlin constituted a defeat for the RAF; the target was too difficult and too well defended. The losses continued; in a disastrous raid on Nuremberg, on 30 March 1944, 795 bombers set out, of which ninety-six were shot down, ten more written off, and seventy-one damaged. That night, 600 airmen were lost. It was a terrible conclusion to a grueling ordeal for Bomber Command. **IK**

Losses: RAF, 1,047 aircraft, 1,682 aircraft damaged, 7,000 dead, wounded, or missing (all targets), 2,690 dead (Berlin); German, probably 4,000 civilians dead, 10,000 wounded, and 450,000 homeless (Berlin)

[<] *Schweinfurt-Regensburg 1943*   *Big Week 1944* [>]

⬆ *Bomb damage in Berlin: a firebomb destroyed the main dome of the cathedral on 24 May 1944.*

Tarawa   20–23 November 1943

"[We] should have let Tarawa 'wither on the vine.' We could have kept it neutralized from our bases to the east . . ." *Marine General Holland M. Smith*

⬆ *A U.S. Marine fires on well-prepared Japanese troops entrenched in their log stockades on Tarawa's main island.*

Tiny Tarawa atoll in the Gilbert Islands became the first target of the U.S. Central Pacific "island-hopping" offensive toward Japan in World War II. In a terrible portent of Pacific War battles to come, the Japanese garrison fought to the last man, inflicting heavy casualties on their U.S. Marine opponents.

The "island-hopping" strategy meant picking off selected Japanese garrisons as stepping stones across the Pacific. Captured islands served as bases for new advances, while other Japanese possessions were isolated and neutralized by air and sea power. By this stage in the war, the United States had formidable forces to bring to bear. For the simultaneous attacks on Tarawa and Makin atolls, Vice Admiral Raymond Spruance had seventeen aircraft carriers under his command, and 18,000 men of 2d Marine Division were transported to Tarawa alone.

After preliminary air and sea bombardments, U.S. troops began landing on Tarawa's principal island on 20 November. Less than a square mile in area, the island was defended by some 4,800 soldiers implanted in bunkers and gun emplacements. The attackers immediately encountered problems. Many landing craft were stranded at the island's coral reef, leaving the Marines to wade from the reef to the shore under fire. By nightfall that day, there were 1,500 U.S. casualties out of a first wave of 5,000 disembarked. That night and the next morning, however, more U.S. troops and tanks managed to get ashore. Gradually they overcame the Japanese positions one by one. Most of the remaining defenders were killed launching suicidal "banzai" charges on the U.S. positions the next night. The only Japanese survivors when fighting ended were seventeen wounded men. **DS**

Losses: U.S., 985 dead, 2,193 wounded; Japanese, 4,800 dead

◁ *Bismarck Sea 1943*   *Imphal and Kohima 1944* ▷

Monte Cassino 17 January–18 May 1944

Anzio 22 January–25 May 1944

The struggle for Monte Cassino in World War II sucked Allied troops on the Italian front into a brutal battle that lasted four bloody months. While Allied material strength was to decide the day ultimately, the Germans again demonstrated their determination and skill in defensive operations.

Intended as a daring outflanking move that would open up the way to the capture of Rome, the Anzio landings degenerated into World War II deadlock: the Allies unable to drive forward from their bridgehead and the Germans without the means to push the invaders back into the sea.

Allied progress up the "boot" of Italy had ground to a halt during the winter of 1943 to 1944, thwarted by the German Gustav Line. The towering hill of Monte Cassino—topped by a historic monastery—was the linchpin in the line, which the Allies were determined to capture.

The battle for Cassino comprised four engagements. The first battle (11 January to 12 February) was conducted by French and U.S. troops, and the Allies were repulsed by the Germans, led by elite Luftwaffe paratroopers. The second battle (15 to 18 February) was controlled by the New Zealand and 4th Indian Divisions and involved an attack on the famous Benedictine monastery. The British divisional commanders demanded that the monastery be destroyed, although the Germans had formally declared that their troops would not use the building. Despite reservations, the monastery was flattened by U.S. bombers. It was a retrograde decision in all aspects, especially because the German paratroopers moved into the ruins, which made an excellent defensive position. The subsequent Allied assault was thrown back with heavy casualties. The third battle (15 to 18 March) was also an Allied failure. The fourth battle, spearheaded by the Polish Corps, finally took the hill. The Germans had already decided to retire to a new defensive line farther north, and when the lead Polish troops gained the summit of the hill on 18 May, they found it unoccupied. **AG**

Having failed to break through the German Gustav Line, the Allies proposed to land an amphibious force on the (western) Italian coast behind German lines. A combined U.S.-British operation, under the command of Major General John Lucas's U.S. VI Corps, it lacked the resources to be effective. The landings on 22 January did, however, achieve complete surprise and were virtually uncontested. Lucas then made the much-criticized decision not to exploit this opportunity; instead of pushing forward, he decided to consolidate his beachhead. Responding with their customary alacrity, the Germans soon had the Allied troops corralled within a tight perimeter. The geography favored the Germans, too; they held a ring of high ground above the Allied position and poured down a massive volume of artillery fire on the soldiers holding the marshy ground below. Both sides reinforced their positions, which further encouraged a tactical stalemate, conditions reminiscent of World War I.

Lucas was made a scapegoat and replaced by Major General Lucien Truscott, but he too could do little to break the deadlock. It was only the slow, relentless pressure applied on land and in the air throughout Italy that forced the Germans to give way. On 25 May, with the Germans in retreat, the men from the Anzio bridgehead met up with Allied troops fighting their way up from the south. On 5 June, the Allies marched into Rome unopposed. **AG**

Losses: Allied, 105,000 casualties of 670,000; German, 80,000 casualties of 360,000

Losses: Allied, 7,000 dead, 36,000 wounded, missing, or captured of 150,000; German, 5,000 dead, 4,500 captured, 30,000 wounded or missing of I35,000

◁ *Salerno 1943*   *Anzio 1944* ▷   ◁ *Monte Cassino 1944*

Big Week
20–25 February 1944

Imphal and Kohima
8 March–3 July 1944

In February 1944, U.S. bombers repeatedly attacked the German aircraft industry in the hope of achieving air superiority in World War II. While the industrial damage inflicted in "Big Week" was limited, the offensive marked an important stage in the progressive erosion of Germany's air power.

Japan planned a major offensive of World War II in Burma in early 1944. The first targets were British bases around Imphal. Indian and British troops were surrounded but fought back. Instead of preparing the way for a Japanese invasion of India, the battle saw the Japanese decisively defeated.

After the failure of the Schweinfurt-Regensburg mission, the United States reconsidered its bombing strategy. It was clear that unescorted bombers were too vulnerable to German fighters and that protection was vital throughout a mission. Fortunately, this realization coincided with increasing numbers of the P-51 Mustang fighter becoming available. Combining high performance and ample fuel capacity, it enabled flights deep into German territory.

With long-range fighters now in action, the Americans could wear down the enemy air force both on the factory floor by bombing and in the air by combat. The Germans, having successfully intercepted previous raids, believed twin-engine heavy fighters and heavily armed single-engine aircraft were the best defense. An offensive of more than 3,000 bomber sorties, "Big Week" began on 20 February with strongly escorted strikes on German cities.

The damage done to German industry was limited, but the defending German fighters suffered heavy losses, especially among the twin-engine crews. The Germans also lost many experienced pilots who, given Germany's limited manpower, were difficult to replace. Allied air forces were now able to inflict losses consistently, and the bombing increasingly disrupted German industry. Big Week itself was not decisive, but it marked an important shift in the air war over Europe. **IK**

General Renya Mutaguchi's Japanese Fifteenth Army advanced across the Chindwin River in early March 1944. General Bill Slim, commanding the British-Indian Fourteenth Army, had expected a Japanese attack and indeed wanted one so that he could weaken the Japanese before beginning his own offensive. However, the speed and size of the Japanese advance took Slim by surprise.

The British IV Corps made a hurried withdrawal, and by early April its three divisions were cut off. Most of the corps manned a defensive perimeter at Imphal while a smaller, massively outnumbered garrison held out at Kohima to the north. Slim's men mounted determined resistance, with the help of air supply, while a relief force fought through to them from Dimapur. Both sieges were ferocious, often fought at point-blank range. The Japanese, however, lacked heavy weapons and were even worse off for supplies than their enemies—to achieve speed and surprise they had neglected logistics and gambled on overrunning British supply dumps, which did not happen. British relief forces made contact with the beleaguered Kohima garrison in mid-April, and the Japanese finally pulled back at the end of May. The ground advance linked up with the Imphal garrison on 22 June. The Japanese eventually retreated in July, by which time they had been outfought completely and their troops were starving and disease ridden. **DS**

Losses: U.S., 190 dead, 111 wounded, 1,156 missing, 261 bombers, 33 fighters; British, 131 bombers; German, 100 dead, 355 fighters

◁ *Berlin 1943* · *Dresden 1945* ▷

Losses: British and Indian, 17,000 dead or wounded; Japanese, 65,000 dead, approximately half were nonbattle casualties

◁ *Tarawa 1943* · *Myitkyina 1944* ▷

Myitkyina
28 April–3 August 1944

Changsha
May–June 1944

U.S., Chinese, and British troops cooperated in this fierce World War II battle for Myitkyina, a small town in northern Burma. The town was brilliantly defended for more than two months by its Japanese garrison in a campaign marked, on both sides, by great bravery and horrific privations.

Japan mounted a major offensive, its largest land battle of World War II, in China in 1944. Code-named Ichigo, its initial targets were in Hunan province. The Chinese Nationalist forces were brushed aside, and the Japanese overran airfields that were being used by the Americans to bomb Japan.

One of the long-term Allied objectives in Burma was to clear the so-called Ledo Road through the northern part of the country into China. The campaign was fought largely by Nationalist Chinese troops, supported by U.S. troops, under the overall command of U.S. General Joseph Stilwell. Despite the rugged terrain and problems with tropical diseases, Stilwell began his offensive in April 1944. The U.S. combat troops at his disposal were Merrill's Marauders: long-distance penetration special forces named for their commander, General Frank Merrill.

The Marauders led the capture of Myitkyina airfield on 18 May; a key success because the airfield was used to fly supplies between China and Burma in the months that followed. However, the town itself was still in Japanese hands, and its commander, General Genzo Mizukami, was determined to hold it with some 4,500 men. Hundreds of U.S. and Chinese troops were already sick and, on the Japanese side, food shortages grew increasingly severe. Even so, both sides fought determinedly for two months.

Eventually, Chinese reinforcements brought in by air, and assistance from British Chindit special forces, helped to decide the battle. On 3 August, a final Allied attack found the town undefended; the last few hundred Japanese had crossed the Irrawaddy River and slipped away. Mizukami committed suicide. **DS**

Japan's attacks in China in 1944 had two objectives. Because their sea communications had become so vulnerable to Allied attacks, they wanted to establish land links between the territory they controlled in North China and their garrison in occupied French Indochina in the south. They also wished to eliminate the bases used by General Chennault's Fourteenth U.S. Air Force to fly B-29 bombing missions into Japanese home territory.

The Japanese Eleventh Army struck southwest from Hankow under the command of General Yosugi Okamura. In a subsidiary attack, Japan's Twenty-Third Army attacked north and west from Canton. The U.S. air units did what they could to halt the attacks, but most of the Chinese Nationalist troops put up little resistance. Chinese troops fought effectively around the city of Changsha, but their local commander lost his nerve and ordered a withdrawal. The Japanese then moved on south to Hengyang and the U.S. bases nearby.

The battle had two important effects. It confirmed the corruption and military ineffectiveness of Jiang Jieshi's (Chiang Kai-shek's) Chinese Nationalist regime and foreshadowed its coming defeat by the Communists. It also forced the Americans to relocate their B-29 bombers to new bases in the Marianas, which would prove much better suited for attacks on the Japanese homeland. **DS**

Losses: Chinese, 4,000 dead or wounded; U.S., 1,200 dead or wounded, plus 1,000 seriously ill; Japanese, 3,000 dead

Losses: Chinese, 50,000 casualties; Japanese, 5,000 casualties

◁ Imphal and Kohima 1944   Saipan 1944 ▷   ◁ Wuhan 1938   Xuzhou 1948 ▷

Normandy Landings   5–6 June 1944

On 4 June, U.S. Army General Dwight D. Eisenhower, Supreme Allied Commander, made the decision to launch Operation Overlord, the Allied invasion of Europe in World War II. Bad weather forced a one-day postponement, but a short period of acceptable weather meant 6 June was marked as D-Day.

Allied soldiers and sailors were already loaded in more than 3,400 ships and began moving across the English Channel. More than 130,000 men were to land on five beaches spread along 50 miles (80 km) of Normandy coast. Before dawn on 6 June, 1,000 air transports and gliders dropped one British (6th) and two U.S. (82d and 101st) airborne divisions—some 18,000 paratroopers—behind the beaches, with the mission to seize key roads and bridges and seal the invasion area from German reinforcements. Although darkness, poor weather, and

pilot confusion caused many paratroopers to land in the wrong locations, the men assembled in small groups and fought their way to their objectives. British gliders brought their troops in on target to seize the important bridges at Caen and Orne. Before sunrise on 6 June, British Royal Air Force planes also began prelanding bombing. Allied deception operations had worked well.

As dawn broke, the surprised German defenders were bombarded by warships accompanying the transports and U.S. bombers. On the right of the invasion area were the two U.S. landing sites designated Omaha Beach (V Corps) and Utah Beach (VII Corps). At 6:30 AM, the first U.S. assault waves from three divisions came ashore under heavy German fire. As with the paratroopers, units were landed in the wrong place and had to adapt. German resistance was heaviest on Omaha Beach, where the assault waves of the 1st and 29th Infantry Divisions

were pinned down. At Point-de-Hoc, between the two beaches, the 2d Ranger Battalion scaled cliffs to seize German coastal guns. On Utah Beach, the 4th Infantry Division used its engineers to blast holes in the cement seawall to let the infantry advance. The two British beaches, Gold (XXX Corps) and Sword (I Corps), were on the left. At 7:25 AM, the British 50th Infantry Division came ashore on Gold while the 3rd Infantry Division waded in on Sword. Between the British beaches was Juno Beach, where the Canadian 3rd Infantry Division landed at 7:45 AM.

Barely acceptable for aircraft, the weather was overcast and windy, with rough seas. The small, flat-bottomed Higgins boats used as landing craft were tossed around as they came in, making many men seasick. Wounded or weighed down by equipment, some soldiers drowned when they stepped off the landing craft into deep water. Most of the specially equipped, amphibious Sherman tanks sent in to knock out German bunkers foundered in the rough surf and sank. However, by noon, German resistance on Utah, Gold, Juno, and Sword was broken, and infantry units were pushing inland to their objectives. U.S. destroyers steamed in close to lend point-blank gunfire support to the troops pinned on Omaha Beach, helping to end the deadlock. Reinforced by more troops, the 1st Division finally broke through. At the day's end, the Allies held small but growing beachheads, while Allied airpower prevented German reserves from arriving. The successful Allied landing opened the door into Europe, which led to the eventual defeat of Nazi Germany. **RB**

Losses: U.S., 1,465 dead, 3,184 wounded, 1,954 captured or missing; British, 2,500–3,000; Canadian, 335 dead, 611 wounded, captured, or missing; German, 4,000–9,000

◁ *Dieppe Raid 1942*   *Normandy 1944* ▷

Normandy   7 June–25 July 1944

Each day after the 6 June invasion in World War II, the Allies poured troops and thousands of tons of supplies over the beaches, which caused a bottleneck. It was imperative that the Allies capture a port and expand the limited beachhead before the German reserves established a strong defensive line.

Initially, Allied ground commanders focused on relieving isolated airborne units, sorting out the confusion on the beaches, and consolidating their battle line. Meanwhile, Allied air forces controlled the roads and kept the German reserves from massing for effective counterattacks. On 8 June, the First Army began an offensive with V Corps to capture the port of Cherbourg and take control of the Carentan area. Progress was slow, the fighting difficult and costly in casualties. German troops fought from prepared interlocking defensive positions using the extensive hedgerows that characterized the Normandy countryside. On 18 June, V Corps crossed the neck of the Cotentin peninsula, trapping German defenders

"Every officer and man must be enthusiastic for the fight and have the light of battle in his eyes."

General Sir Bernard Montgomery

in Cherbourg, but another week of bitter fighting was needed to control the city. Cherbourg's port facilities were destroyed and required months of extensive repair; the Allies faced a critical supply problem.

V Corps continued the bloody war in the hedgerows. On the left, British commander General Sir Bernard Montgomery found progress difficult. British and Canadian troops battled German armored forces in relatively open, flat terrain where the Germans made each village a defensive strongpoint. Montgomery's forces

soon stalled outside Caen. In early July, U.S. First Army launched a general offensive to clear the hedgerows of the Cotentin peninsula and take St. Lo. Stubborn German defenders made the battle costly. At the same time, Montgomery's men waged a difficult street-by-street fight to take Caen. It fell on 9 July and St. Lo on 18 July, but Allied forces remained crowded in the small beachhead. Fortunately, the Germans held back reserves for an expected second Allied landing near Calais.

On 24 July, First Army launched Operation Cobra, a six-division attack—following concentrated bombing by hundreds of bombers—to create a gap in the German line. Poor air to ground communication and thick clouds caused some of the bombs to fall on U.S. troops. Despite this setback, VII Corps's mechanized units rushed through the opening to exploit the disrupted German defenses and kept up the pressure against the German reserves rushing to close the breach. The town of Vire fell after ten days of hard fighting, and the Americans continued to advance south, pushing aside the German blocking efforts. Coutances was liberated on 28 July and Avranches on 30 July, which opened the way to the Breton ports.

In August, Lieutenant General George Patton arrived to command the U.S. Third Army. He moved rapidly into Brittany to seize the ports. A joint American-Canadian effort to pinch off the German salient at Falaise-Argentan was slow, but cost the Germans heavy losses. This forced them to make a general withdrawal toward the Seine River with Allied units in pursuit. By 25 August, the Allies were at the Seine, and the stage was set for the invasion of the German homeland. **RB**

Losses: U.S., 20,838 dead, 94,881 wounded, 10,128 missing; British, Canadian, and Polish, 15,995 dead, 57,996 wounded, 9,054 missing; German, 200,000 dead, wounded, or missing, 200,000 captured

◁ *Normandy Landings 1944*   *Falaise Pocket 1944* ▷

Soldiers gaze across the ruins of the city of Caen during the Normandy campaign.

V-Weapons Offensive   13 June 1944–29 March 1945

On 13 June, Germany launched *Vergeltungswaffen* (vengeance weapons). Aimed at London and Antwerp, V-1 flying bombs and V-2 rockets killed thousands of civilians and caused widespread damage. Despite their powerful psychological effect, they failed to change the course of World War II.

By June 1944, Germany was in dire straits: facing a Soviet offensive in Eastern Europe, constant Allied bombing, and the invasion of Normandy. It retaliated with secret weapons. The V-1 fired at London on 13 June 1944 was the first of 2,419 flying bombs to reach the city. Cheap to produce and launched from simple ramps, the V-1s had a crude jet engine that made an ominous drone that ceased abruptly before the bomb fell to earth. This gave the "doodlebugs" an unnerving psychological impact.

About one hundred flying bombs a day were fired at London in early summer 1944. However, the British soon organized increasingly effective countermeasures, with fighter aircraft, antiaircraft guns, and barrage balloons intercepting the flying bombs over England. By October, Allied armies had overrun the V-1 launch sites within range of London, but a few continued to be launched against Britain from bomber aircraft. Others were targeted at cities on mainland Europe, such as Antwerp.

The first V-2 rocket was fired on 8 September. The V-2 was a complex ballistic missile that flew in a supersonic arc and struck without warning—the sound of its approach arrived after the missile's warhead had exploded—and it was impossible to intercept. In total, 2,790 V-2s were launched at Antwerp, London, and other cities. However, their guidance systems were inadequate and they entered service too late to be decisive. **IK**

Losses: British, 2,917 dead, 1,939 wounded, plus 8,938 civilians dead, 24,504 wounded; Allied, 700 dead, 154 aircraft; Belgian, 30,000 casualties
◁ *The Blitz 1940*

The V-1 flying bomb was used by Germany for the bombing of London.

Saipan   15 June–9 July 1944

While Japan's main fleet was being defeated in the World War II battle of the Philippine Sea, U.S. Marine and Army units were overrunning the island of Saipan in the Marianas. Once the island was captured, the Americans built bomber bases in order to attack Japan directly.

In mid-1944, the next stage in the U.S. plan for the Pacific was to breach Japan's defensive perimeter in the Mariana Islands and build bases there for the new long-range B-29 Superfortress bomber to strike the Japanese homeland.

Two U.S. Marine divisions began landings in the southwest of the island on 15 June; they were joined two days later by an Army division. The joint Japanese army and navy garrison had some 27,000 men. They had prepared effective beach defenses, which caused the attacking Marines significant casualties, but the U.S. troops still managed to fight their way ashore. General Yoshitsugo Saito had hoped to win the battle on the beaches but was forced to switch tactics and withdraw with his troops into the rugged interior of Saipan Island.

The Japanese fought ferociously, holding out in caves and other fortified positions. Slow progress led to a quarrel between the U.S. Marine commander, General "Howlin' Mad" Holland Smith, and the army divisional commander, but gradually the Japanese were confined in a small area in the north of the island. From there, several thousand troops carried out a suicidal night charge on 6 to 7 July, killing many Americans but also being wiped out themselves. Organized Japanese resistance ended on 9 July. Saipan had a significant Japanese civilian population. Many were killed in the fighting but thousands more committed suicide, along with many soldiers, rather than come under the control of the Americans. **DS**

Losses: U.S., 3,400 dead; Japanese, 27,000 troops and 15,000 civilians dead

◁ *Myitkyina 1944*   *Philippine Sea 1944* ▷

⬆ *U.S. troops on the beachhead at Saipan, July 1944, supported by armored Buffalo vehicles.*

Philippine Sea 19–20 June 1944

In mid-1944, Japan's commanders eagerly awaited a U.S. assault on the Mariana Islands, believing it would give them an opportunity to bring the main U.S. forces to battle and turn the tide of the War in the Pacific. Instead, Japan was catastrophically defeated in history's largest aircraft carrier battle.

Japanese dreams of winning a decisive battle were fantasy. By 1944, their carrier fleets deployed only half the number of aircraft of their opponents, and the Americans were better trained—technically superior in every way. They also had detailed intelligence of the Japanese intentions, and in this campaign were led by their shrewdest combat commander, Admiral Spruance.

The battle began after the U.S. landings on Saipan. Admiral Ozawa assembled his nine carriers and headed for the Marianas. He believed that the U.S. forces were already being worn down by attacks launched by land-based aircraft from the islands; in reality, these assaults had already been almost completely wiped out.

Ozawa's sole advantage was that his carrier aircraft had a longer range and so he was able to attack first. On 19 June, Ozawa launched 373 aircraft against the U.S. carriers. Some 240 were shot down by defending fighters and antiaircraft fire, and only one U.S. ship was hit. More Japanese planes were then destroyed over Guam. Only twenty-nine U.S. aircraft were lost. Finally, two Japanese carriers were sunk by U.S. submarines.

The U.S. carriers eventually located their opponents the next afternoon and sent 216 aircraft to attack. These overwhelmed the thirty-five defending fighters and sank another carrier. As the battle ended, the Japanese navy still had various carriers afloat, but hardly any trained aircrew to operate from them. **DS**

Losses: U.S., 120 aircraft (but many crewmen saved); Japanese, 600 aircraft and their crews, 3 aircraft carriers

◁ Saipan 1944 Guam 1944 ▷

Bagration 23 June–19 August 1944

Launched in support of the World War II D-Day landings, Operation Bagration was a large-scale Soviet offensive against the Germans on the Eastern Front. The Red Army showed the world what a formidable fighting force it had become. Its success would carry Soviet power into Eastern Europe.

By mid-1944, German military power was in irreversible decline, and its allies were increasingly unreliable. The Red Army intended to take advantage of this situation by inflicting a catastrophe on the Germans on the scale suffered by the Soviet forces in Operation Barbarossa.

Security was tight, and the Red Army assembled 166 divisions on the Belorussian front, completely surprising the Germans who expected an assault farther south. Attacking on a 450-mile (724 km) front, within five days the Red Army had killed and captured tens of thousands. They went on to Minsk, where, despite desperate German efforts, including laying 4,000 booby traps, another 100,000 were killed or captured, several thousand being paraded in humiliation through Moscow. This left the road open to Poland and Lithuania. Soviet troops were advancing up to 15 miles (24 km) a day, and had entered and liberated all of Belorussia before the end of July.

As the Red Army advanced, it encountered grim evidence of the horrors of German occupation. Mass graves of some of the one million murdered civilians were uncovered; crops and livestock had been destroyed, towns and villages razed, all of which served to infuriate the Soviet soldiers. By the end of the campaign, only the most fanatical Nazi or self-deluded German could fail to recognize that the war was lost. However, as the campaign ran out of momentum, a final tragedy occurred: the Warsaw uprising. **NH**

Losses: German, 350,000–670,000 dead, wounded, or captured; Red Army, more than 750,000 dead or wounded

◁ Kursk 1943 Warsaw Uprising 1944 ▷

Guam   21 July–10 August 1944

In attacking Guam in World War II, U.S. forces were not only acquiring a fine harbor and a number of airfields to use in future operations, but were also liberating U.S. territory—Guam had been captured by the Japanese in 1941. As elsewhere, Guam's Japanese garrison fought practically to the last man.

The attack on Guam was intended originally to start only days after the landings on Saipan, but it was postponed to the next month. The Americans used the delay well, however, to make the preliminary bombardment and air attacks extremely thorough and to ensure that offshore obstacles to landing craft were cleared efficiently. The landing force included both Marine and Army units from General Geiger's III Amphibious Corps, in all 55,000 strong. General Takashina commanded 19,000 defenders, who had built a typically elaborate network of bunkers, artillery emplacements, and other fortifications.

The landings began on 21 July on the west coast of the island. They were soon established solidly ashore despite a series of fierce night attacks by the Japanese over the first few days of the battle. It took a week for the Americans to link their two beachheads, but by then much of the Japanese strength had been dissipated and Takashina himself had been killed. The surviving Japanese units fought on for another two weeks, gradually retiring toward the north end of the island, before organized resistance largely ended.

Even then Guam's particularly mountainous terrain helped a few diehards to hold out. Some small units fought on until after the end of the war, causing occasional U.S. casualties, and one solitary veteran only emerged from the jungle to surrender and return to Japan in 1972. **DS**

Losses: U.S., 1,440 dead, 5,650 wounded; Japanese, at least 18,000 dead

◁ *Philippine Sea 1944*　　　　*Leyte Gulf 1944* ▷

"The theory is simple, gentlemen. It's the old school solution—seize the high ground and hold it."

U.S. Marine commander

 Two U.S. soldiers plant the U.S. flag only eight minutes after arriving on Guam beach (detail).

Warsaw Uprising 1 August–2 October 1944

The Warsaw Uprising was one of the most controversial episodes in World War II. As the Red Army approached Warsaw at the culmination of Operation Bagration, the Polish resistance fighters—the AK—attempted to liberate the city. This ended in disaster, which soured inter-Allied relations.

The Red Army had made good progress and had already reached the Vistula River when Radio Moscow announced the city of Warsaw's imminent liberation and called for its citizens to rise. (Moscow later insisted that the announcement had been routine propaganda, not intended to be taken seriously.) The AK resistance fighters, therefore, decided it was time to act, because if they liberated themselves they could claim a political role in Poland's future. However, the Germans took advantage of Operation Bagration running out of momentum and reinforced the garrison with SS troops, who were to commit the most barbaric atrocities.

The AK was soon in desperate trouble, but the Red Army failed to advance the last few miles to support it. The suspicion arose that Stalin had cynically instigated the rising and then stood back to allow the Germans to destroy the AK for his own political convenience. However, the problems of aiding Warsaw were very real, and an attempt made by Polish troops under Red Army command to cross the Vistula was beaten back with heavy losses. Battered incessantly by air attacks and heavy artillery, the AK was pushed back street by street into an enclave in the city center. After sixty-three days, the AK surrendered on promises that its fighters would be treated as prisoners of war (some in fact were), but the Germans still took revenge on Warsaw, expelling the population and razing many of the city's surviving buildings. **JS**

Losses: German, 16,000 dead; Polish, 165,000–300,000 dead, including civilians

◁ Bagration 1944   Berlin 1945 ▷

SS grenadiers advance through the streets of Warsaw. ⬆

Falaise Pocket | 7–21 August 1944

After the Allied breakthrough in Normandy in World War II, Hitler ordered Field Marshal Gunther von Kluge to counterattack between Mortain and Avranches. The goal was to cut off the Cotentin peninsula and trap U.S. forces in Brittany. The 47th Panzer Corps attacked at night on 6 to 7 August.

German attackers hit stubborn U.S. resistance near Mortain. The 35th Division helped hold the Germans while Allied aircraft pounded the exposed armored columns. Allied units successfully limited the penetration's flanks, and the Germans stalled near Flers. Lieutenant General Omar N. Bradley and General Sir Bernard Montgomery agreed the German salient was an opportunity to trap the attackers. U.S. First and Third Armies made wide swings south, then turned north striking the German left flank near Argentan. At the same time, a Canadian offensive pushed in, but had difficulty taking Falaise, leaving a gap. Time was critical, yet Montgomery provided no reinforcements.

On 12 August, U.S. forces prepared to close the last few miles, but Bradley stopped them to avoid clashing with Canadian units. Contrary to Hitler's orders, the Germans began withdrawing through the gap under intense air and artillery fire. Falaise fell to the Canadians on 16 August, and on 19 August, U.S. and Polish divisions linked up at Chambois. The 1st Polish Armored Division held blocking positions against repeated German efforts to eliminate the Poles. Relatively few Germans escaped. The Canadians joined the Poles on 21 August, firmly sealing the fate of the German Seventh Army. The battle destroyed German resistance in Normandy and forced the defeated Germans to withdraw over the Seine. It also opened the way for an Allied pursuit to the German border. **RB**

Losses: U.S., 3,000; Canadian, 5,500; Polish, 588 dead, 1,002 wounded, 114 missing; German,10,000 dead, 20,000 wounded, 50,000 captured

◁ Normandy 1944   Liberation of Paris 1944 ▷

⬆ *Having driven the Germans from Falaise, U.S. infantrymen hold up a swastika flag, 20 August 1944.*

Liberation of Paris   19–25 August 1944

After Normandy, General Eisenhower intended to bypass Paris. For the Free French forces under General Charles de Gaulle and for French Resistance fighters, however, the liberation of Paris from German occupation was a crucial symbolic goal, which could have weighty political consequences.

On 19 August, elements of the French Resistance took control of much of Paris, including the Hôtel de Ville. The German commander in the city, General Dietrich von Choltitz, wished to avoid a bloodbath and the destruction of the beautiful city. He agreed to a cease-fire that was partially observed over the following days, although local skirmishes caused considerable loss of life.

Meanwhile, General Charles de Gaulle and Major General Philippe Leclerc appealed to the Americans for permission to head for Paris. Faced with French threats to act independently, Eisenhower agreed, but insisted that Leclerc have a U.S. infantry division with him.

Advancing in two columns from the north and south of Paris, Leclerc engaged the German defenses outside the city at dawn on 24 August. The Germans put up a stiff fight, while the French were distracted by the enthusiastic reception they received in the outer suburbs.

By evening, Leclerc had still not broken through, and Eisenhower was threatening to order U.S. forces to do the job. Leclerc instructed Captain Raymond Dronne to lead a small armored column into the city and make contact with the French Resistance. Using back roads, Dronne drove unopposed to the Hôtel de Ville, arriving around midnight. This provoked a wave of popular celebrations that convinced the Germans they had lost. By the following morning, German forces had given up and Leclerc occupied the city. **RG**

Losses: French Resistance, 1,000 dead; Free French, 130 dead, 320 wounded; German, 3,000 dead, 12,800 captured

◁ *Falaise Pocket 1944*   *Hürtgen Forest 1944* ▷

The 2nd French armored division arriving in Paris during the Liberation. ⬆

Hürtgen Forest   14 September–13 December 1944

With the arrival of their armies at the German Westwall–Siegfried Line, Allied leaders looked for a way to break through the extensive belts of bunkers and obstacles. On 14 September, U.S. V Corps began a reconnaissance in force into the Hürtgen Forest, south of Aachen, looking for a pathway.

Unknown to the Allies, the Hürtgen Forest was a sensitive assembly area for German units earmarked to participate in Hitler's Ardennes offensive (the Battle of the Bulge). It also provided a path to the Roer River dams. Two German divisions initially defended the Hürtgen; elements of twelve more reinforced them.

When the U.S. 9th Infantry Division entered the hilly forest, it immediately ran into stubborn resistance and made no headway. Consistent bad weather hampered air and ground operations. After heavy losses, the 9th Division took the town of Schmidt on the main German supply route, then was pushed back to defensive positions near the Kall Trail. A week later, the 28th Infantry Division replaced the battered 9th. The assault on Schmidt was renewed on 2 November, the town repeatedly changing hands in back and forth fighting.

Both sides threw more formations into the battle through November. Heavy fighting occurred as the towns of Hürtgen and Kleinhau were taken, forcing the Germans to withdraw slowly. Capture of Gey and Stras at the forest edge on 13 December ended most of the fighting. The Americans held the forest, but at a very high cost that rendered the U.S. 28th Division ineffective and exhausted the 9th and 4th Divisions. German units suffered, too, but had delayed the U.S. advance and weakened units that might otherwise have withstood the Ardennes offensive two days later. **RB**

Losses: U.S., 23,000 dead, wounded, or captured, 9,000 nonbattle casualties; German, 28,000

◁ *Liberation of Paris 1944*   *Operation Market Garden 1944* ▷

↑ *U.S. infantrymen advance through the dense Hürtgen Forest, 2 November 1944.*

Operation Market Garden   17–27 September 1944

As their armies pursued the retreating Germans across France in World War II, Allied commanders debated alternative strategies how to advance into Germany. Field Marshal Sir Bernard Montgomery, 21st Army Group, proposed using his forces for a single thrust across the Netherlands. Lieutenant General Omar N. Bradley opposed the idea.

Montgomery persuaded the Supreme Allied Commander, General Dwight D. Eisenhower, to approve a two-part airborne-armor assault and to divert supplies to support it. Operation Market landed three airborne divisions at separate locations to seize road bridges along a route through the Dutch towns of Eindhoven, Nijmegan, and Arnhem behind German lines These bridges were to be held open for the British Second Army advance led by XXX Corps (Operation Garden).

Time and distance limited the Allies to only one lift per day. Two days of good weather were forecast when the operation began on the night of 16 September. Air

> *"If the operation had been properly backed . . . it would have succeeded in spite of my mistakes."*
>
> *Field Marshal Sir Bernard Montgomery*

attacks hit German airfields and positions along the path of the 1,567 air transports that followed, carrying the initial 20,000 parachute and glider troops (60 percent of the total infantry) with limited equipment and supplies. The 1st Airborne Division landed 6 miles (9.5 km) west of Arnhem and was soon fighting German units near Oosterbeek. Its 1st Parachute Brigade moved toward Arnhem, but radio problems hindered communications. The 82d Division came down near Nijmegan and soon secured several bridges and Groesbeek Heights. The

101st Division landed north of Eindhoven and within hours held four of five bridges.

At 2:00 PM, XXX Corps started toward Eindhoven behind an artillery barrage, but was soon delayed by German defenders. The surprised Germans in Field Marshal Walther Model's Army Group B reacted quickly. He requested reinforcements and was given priority Luftwaffe support. German resistance stiffened by evening, and several bridges were blown up. Only 2nd Battalion, 1st Parachute Brigade reached Arnhem bridge. The battalion secured the north end and defeated German attempts to cross. The other two 1st Parachute battalions fought into Arnhem with heavy losses, but never reached the bridge. At Nijmegan, the 82d failed to take a key bridge but managed to turn back German counterattacks while the 101st and XXX Corps made contact. The next morning, XXX Corps elements linked with the 82d and joined another unsuccessful effort to take Nijmegan bridge. Eventually, 3rd Battalion, 504th Parachute Infantry secured the bridge, but XXX Corps tanks did not move forward for eighteen hours.

Ahead, British airborne units were in considerable trouble. The 2nd Battalion at Arnhem had been overrun, and the encircled survivors of 1st Airborne Division at Oosterbeek grimly battled against increased German pressure. They withstood a series of heavy attacks from 22 to 24 September. The delayed Polish airborne brigade finally landed, but could not offer assistance. German counterattacks cut the road corridor, and highway sections changed hands several times. Allied leaders decided to abandon the advance and concentrate on defense. The rescue of the 1st Airborne Division survivors ended the operation. **RB**

Losses: U.S., 3,996 dead, wounded, or missing; British and Polish,11,000–13,000 dead or wounded, 6,450 captured; German, 7,500–10,000

[<] *Hürtgen Forest 1944*   *Aachen 1944* [>]

Allied troops parachute near Arnhem at the start of the offensive on 17 September 1944. ➡

Aachen 12–20 October 1944

Collapse of German defenses in France in World War II brought the Allied armies racing to the German border. The first major German town to face the Allied advance was Aachen, situated on the route to the Roer River industrial areas. Hitler ordered Aachen to be held at all costs.

Stiff German resistance along the Westwall–Siegfried Line defense belt caused U.S. First Army to reconsider its plans to bypass Aachen. Instead, during the first weeks of October, the 1st and 30th Infantry Divisions battled to surround the city and block German reinforcements.

Although Aachen was not fortified like the Westwall, urban defensive measures had been built. Defending Aachen was Colonel Gerhard Wilck's understrength 246th Volksgrenadier Division (5,000 men). When Wilck ignored a demand to surrender, a two-day bombardment began, followed on 13 October by simultaneous attacks from two U.S. battalions. On the left, Lieutenant Colonel Derrill Daniel's 2d Battalion operated methodically, clearing a dense urban area of stone buildings. Point-blank fire from tanks and artillery forced defenders into cellars where the infantry eliminated them. On the right, 3d Battalion, led by Lieutenant Colonel John Corley, fought in suburban areas with wooded hills where Wilck had placed his best troops. The hills were key to the control of Aachen.

On 15 October, the two battalions linked up, but 3d Battalion was pushed back by a German counterattack. Corley resumed offensive operations on 19 October, reinforced by an armor task force, and captured the hills. Two days later, Wilck surrendered the Aachen garrison. His delay of the Allied advance gave Hitler time to assemble forces for the Ardennes attack in December. **RB**

Losses: U.S., 75 dead, 414 wounded, 9 missing; German, 5,000 dead or wounded, 5,600 captured

◁ Operation Market Garden 1944   The Bulge 1944 ▷

Leyte Gulf 23–25 October 1944

In the largest naval battle in World War II and history, the Japanese fleet nearly achieved its long-desired victory because of poor U.S. command decisions. Instead, on the brink of success, the Japanese admiral turned away, and the United States won another major victory.

When U.S. troops landed on Leyte in the Philippines on 20 October, Japanese commanders put Operation Victory into action. Japan's aircraft carriers had few planes left, and these would be used as a decoy force to draw the U.S. carriers north. In the meantime, Japan's large remaining force of big-gun vessels would pass through the Philippine archipelago in two groups from the west and close in on the U.S. landing forces off Leyte's east coast.

Things did not begin well for the Japanese. Their main force was sighted far out to the west of the Philippines, and several ships were sunk by submarine and air attacks on 23 and 24 October. However, the Americans made the mistake of thinking that this squadron had retreated when it had only briefly turned away.

A second Japanese battleship force was wiped out in the Surigao strait by a U.S. battleship group on the night of 24 to 25 October. Admiral Halsey, commanding the ten U.S. carriers, had already taken the bait, however, and was heading north against the decoy force. Four of its carriers and several other vessels were sunk eventually. In the meantime, Admiral Kurita's main force had reached the support groups for the U.S. landing force, which should have stood little chance. A combination of heroic defending and Kurita's inept decision-making prevented the Japanese from making progress, and Kurita soon gave up and withdrew. **DS**

Losses: U.S., 1 aircraft carrier, 2 escort carriers, 3 destroyers; Japanese, 4 aircraft carriers, 3 battleships, 20 cruisers and destroyers

◁ Guam 1944   Manila 1945 ▷

U.S. carrier-based bombers attack a Japanese heavy cruiser off Manila Bay; it sank soon after. ➜

The Bulge   16 December 1944–25 January 1945

Despite the advice of senior military commanders, Adolf Hitler ordered a major counteroffensive of World War II through the rugged, densely wooded Ardennes region of Belgium and Luxembourg to pierce the overextended Allied lines and capture Antwerp, the Allies' main port. If successful, it would force the supply-starved Allies to withdraw.

Secretly, Hitler assembled two new armies—the 6th SS Panzer Army (General Joseph Dietrich) and the 5th Panzer Army (General Hasso-Eccard von Manteuffel). Together with the Seventh Army, they struck the V and VIII Corps of U.S. First Army in the Ardennes region.

The Ardennes was regarded as a quiet area. Its 88-mile (141 km) front was held by only four infantry divisions: the 99th (V Corps), 106th, 28th, and 4th (VIII Corps). Other small units held scattered sections. In reserve was the untested 9th Armored Division. On 16 December, German artillery hit the U.S. line and disrupted communications. The 6th Panzer Army in the north made the main attack.

> *"Hell, let's have the guts to let the bastards go all the way to Paris. Then, we'll really cut 'em off and chew 'em up."* General George Patton

On the left was the 5th Panzer Army, and left of that was Seventh Army. The 99th Division repulsed several attacks, but uncoordinated defense between the 106th Division and 14th Cavalry Group opened a gap through which a German parachute division moved. The 106th Division on Schnee Eifel held out by committing its reserve, and the 28th Division stood firm against Seventh Army's attacks. Although German infantry was able to infiltrate U.S. positions, roadblocks prevented tanks from moving toward the key crossroads towns of Bastogne and St. Vith.

When night fell, the U.S. 7th and 10th Armored Divisions were ordered forward. Confused instructions by the 106th Division left two regiments on the heavily forested Schnee Eifel. With orders to defend in place, VIII Corps focused on denying the Germans use of the road net—the only way for vehicles to transit the dense terrain. In the north, V Corps reinforced the shoulder of the penetration with the 2d and 1st Infantry Divisions, then withdrew the 99th Division.

On 17 December, German tanks, under the command of Colonel Joachim Peiper, broke through and raced to the U.S. rear. In VIII Corps, 7th Armored Division's move forward was delayed, leaving the 106th's two regiments to be killed or captured. The third regiment, with 7th Armored Division and elements of 9th Armored and 28th Infantry Divisions, dug in at St. Vith. At Bastogne, the 101st Airborne Division arrived, while engineers blocked the roads and armor teams defended crossroads.

In order to save time, German General von Manteuffel ordered his armored units to bypass the two towns. In the south, 4th Division anchored the defense, squeezing the Germans onto the clogged Loshiem Gap roads. By 19 December, German tanks were sitting 25 miles (40 km) deep. General Dwight D. Eisenhower ordered First Army to defend while Third Army attacked from the south. For better control, British Field Marshal Sir Bernard Montgomery was given temporary command over U.S. First and Ninth Armies.

On 22 December, Third Army turned north and assaulted toward Bastogne, reaching it on 26 December. Fighting continued as German units tried to advance with fuel and ammunition almost gone. Both the First and Third Armies attacked on 3 January, pinching in the sides of the German salient and forcing it to withdraw. On 25 January, the bulge was gone and the front restored. **RB**

Losses: U.S., 76,840; British, 1,408; German, 67,200

◁ *Aachen 1944*   *Bastogne 1944* ▷

American troops capture Germans at Malmedy, Belgium.

Bastogne
17–26 December 1944

On 16 December, the German army launched its last major offensive of World War II. On Hitler's orders, more than twenty divisions burst through the U.S. front line in the Ardennes region. Speed was critical to success, and the Germans sought control of crossroads villages such as Bastogne.

At Bastogne, two roads from Germany led into the U.S. rear area. The U.S. First Army requested the 101st Airborne Division as reinforcement while engineers built roadblocks and barriers to slow the Germans. Combat Command B, 10th Armored Division, arrived on 18 December and engaged the Germans at roadblocks. That night, the 101st Airborne moved to defensive positions north of town.

By 20 December, in addition to four airborne regiments, Bastogne held seven battalions of artillery, a tank destroyer battalion, and assorted surviving tanks, infantry, and engineers from the 9th and 10th Armored Divisions. Rather than be delayed, the commander of 5th Panzer Army ordered his two armored divisions to bypass Bastogne, leaving its capture to the infantry. On 22 December, German artillery surrounded the town. When the order to surrender was refused—General Anthony McAuliffe giving the famous one-word reply "Nuts!"—the Germans opened fire.

For four days, there was heavy fighting around the defensive perimeter. The defenders fought stubbornly while reaction teams of tanks moved to counterattack. On 25 December, Allied aircraft provided aerial resupply and fire support. The next day, 4th Armored Division broke through the encirclement after fighting its way north. The successful defense of Bastogne was a major factor in slowing and ultimately defeating the German efforts to reach the Meuse River and beyond. **RB**

Losses: U.S., 543 dead, 1,775 wounded, 641 missing; German, 7,000 dead, 981 captured

◁ The Bulge 1944

St. Vith 1944 ▷

St. Vith
17–23 December 1944

Early on 17 December, Major General Troy Middleton (VIII Corps) discerned the direction of the massive German attack that had struck his corps the previous day. He focused on blocking the Ardennes road net and defending four critical road junction towns, including Bastogne and St. Vith.

The town of St. Vith lay 12 miles (19 km) behind the front line where the U.S. 106th Infantry Division was losing its battle against overwhelming odds. Two U.S. armored divisions, 7th and 10th, were sent to V Corps as reinforcements. As the 106th fought on, Middleton shifted units to meet the advancing German I SS Panzer and LVIII Panzer Corps.

The U.S. defense was based on the ridge lines and hills to the northeast, east, and southeast. The 7th Armored Division arrived late on 17 December, but still managed to block a German attack north of St. Vith. South of the town, a 106th regiment joined 9th Armored, but on 19 December, the 106th regiments on the Schnee Eifel were destroyed. Two German infantry divisions then moved against St. Vith in heavy fog.

Clogged roads slowed the Germans, and piecemeal attacks were broken up by U.S. fire. Preceded by heavy artillery, German attacks were renewed on 21 December, most severely along the eastern road held by an armored team with engineers and tank destroyers. There the Germans broke through. Defenders fled into the town, followed by the German tanks. Brigadier General Bruce C. Clarke reorganized a new defense line west of the town as chaos at the crossroads halted the German pursuit. On 22 December, U.S. forces withdrew further, helped by a hard freeze of muddy trails and a snowstorm. The last troops crossed U.S. lines at the Salm River on 23 December. **RB**

Losses: U.S., 3,397; German, unknown

◁ Bastogne 1944

Colmar Pocket 1945 ▷

Colmar Pocket

20 January–9 February 1945

Some of the hardest fighting of World War II took place on the Alsace plain in eastern France around the historic town of Colmar. In bitter winter weather, French and U.S. troops drove the German Nineteenth Army out of fiercely defended positions and back across the Rhine.

The "Colmar pocket" was formed in November 1944 when the French First Army and 2nd Armored Division fought through to the Rhine north and south of Colmar. This left the Germans pinned in a semicircle of land with their backs to the river. In January 1945, the Allies undertook an offensive to collapse this pocket.

The opening attack was spearheaded by battle-hardened French Moroccan troops and a French armored division. Their advance ground slowly forward in the face of a stubborn German defense and armored counterattacks. In the northern sector, U.S. 3d Infantry Division suffered heavy losses establishing a bridgehead across the Ill River. Conditions were harsh, with freezing temperatures and deep snow. The frozen ground made it impossible to dig foxholes in terrain that offered little natural cover. Yet, gradually, the Germans were forced to give way.

On 29 January, 3d Infantry crossed the Colmar canal after a massive artillery bombardment. On 4 February, U.S. 12th Armored Division met Moroccan troops at Rouffach, slicing the pocket in two. The German army was supplied and reinforced across a Rhine bridge at Breisach. When the nearby fortified town of Neuf-Brisach fell to 3d Infantry on 6 February, German forces pulled back across the bridge, blowing it up behind them. Fighting continued in the pocket for a further three days, until the last Germans withdrew across the Rhine. **RG**

Losses: U.S., 8,000 casualties; French, 13,000 casualties; German, 25,000 casualties

[<] *St. Vith 1944*　　　　　*Remagen Bridge 1945* [>]

Manila

3 February–3 March 1945

In 1941, when Japan invaded the Philippines, the Allies had chosen not to defend the capital, Manila. It was a different story in 1945, and the city was devastated by a month of the bitterest fighting of the War in the Pacific, before the Japanese garrison was wiped out.

U.S. ground forces landed on the island of Luzon in the Philippines on 9 January 1945. The main Japanese plan, ordered by the overall commander, General Yamashita, was to retreat into the mountainous interior of the island and fight a delaying action. However, Yamashita was an army general, and the capital city, Manila, was defended mainly by navy personnel; their commander, Admiral Iwabuchi, decided to make a stand. Altogether, Iwabuchi had about 20,000 men, including some army troops.

The first U.S. troops reached the city on 3 February, and the carnage began. Three U.S. divisions attacked from different directions—the 1st Cavalry, 11th Airborne, and 37th Infantry. They were assisted by several thousand Filipino guerrillas. An early success came when almost 6,000 Allied military and civilian prisoners were freed.

By 22 February, the Japanese had retreated into the Intramuros district—the old walled city—fighting all the way, demolishing buildings and setting huge fires as they pulled back. In an attempt to protect civilians, General MacArthur ordered that the city was not to be bombed, but the U.S. artillery and tank firepower was so massive that this limitation, in effect, made little difference—and, in any case, the Japanese killed Filipinos with no hesitation. The last Japanese positions were eliminated on 3 March, but by then the city was in ruins and about one-eighth of its population had been killed. **DS**

Losses: U.S., 1,000; Filipino, 100,000 civilians; Japanese, at least 17,000

[<] *Leyte Gulf 1944*　　　　　*Corregidor 1945* [>]

Dresden 13–15 February 1945

In February 1945, British and U.S. bombers attacked Dresden in Saxony, southeastern Germany. Mounted late in World War II, when the Germans were facing defeat, the raid killed 25,000 people and destroyed a city of great cultural importance. It was immediately seen as a bitterly controversial endeavor.

During February 1945, the Soviet Red Army was advancing into eastern Germany. By bombing Dresden, the western Allies sought to disrupt German rail transport and so aid the Russian advance. Dresden also housed important war industries, including artillery and optical instrument factories.

On the night of 13 to 14 February, two Royal Air Force raids dropped 2,650 tons of high explosive and incendiary bombs. Their target was a stadium in the historic old town. With German air defenses now weak, the bombing was accurate and concentrated; it triggered a firestorm that killed up to 25,000 people. Contributing to the death toll was the city authorities' failure to provide adequate air raid shelters. U.S. Army Air Forces followed up with two daylight raids that were largely ineffective.

The destruction of Dresden was controversial instantly. Nazi propaganda claimed a death toll of up to 250,000, and British Prime Minister Winston Churchill tried to distance himself from a bombing policy that he had supported keenly. The raid destroyed much of the city's historic center, including the exquisite eighteenth-century Frauenkirche church. It was condemned as being ineffective, immoral, excessive, and unnecessary, destroying an irreparable cultural heritage. The counterclaim was that Dresden was a strike on a legitimate military target, and part of a legitimate Allied strategic bombing offensive against a determined and resisting enemy. **IK**

Losses: British, 9 aircraft; U.S., 4 dead, 15 wounded, 57 missing, 8 aircraft, 4 damaged beyond repair, 54 damaged; German, 25,000 civilians dead, 1 aircraft

◁ Big Week 1944

Corregidor 14 February–2 March 1945

The U.S. liberation of the Philippine island of Luzon began on 9 January 1945. By 7 February, U.S. forces were closing in on Manila. A major goal was reopening Manila Bay, and the final step in doing this was to retake Corregidor, the rugged island fortress guarding the mouth of the bay.

Intelligence estimated that only 600 Japanese troops were on Corregidor's 1,735 acres (7 sq km); in fact, there were 6,000. During their occupation, the Japanese had expanded the network of underground tunnels and bunkers. On 14 February, a U.S. amphibious and airborne assault to retake Corregidor began with an air and naval bombardment. Hidden Japanese artillery damaged several ships. Two days later, the first of 2,050 U.S. paratroopers landed on two tiny drop zones on the island's higher west end (Topside). Initial Japanese resistance was light, but increased steadily.

The low drop altitude caused a high number of injuries. Navy PT boats circled in the bay looking for men blown to sea by the high wind. The 3d Battalion, 34th Infantry landed by boat at the lower east end of the island. The infantrymen moved quickly to capture Malinta Hill and clear the lower end. By nightfall, Topside and Malinta Hill forces had linked up. A third battalion arrived by boat on 17 February. As clearing progressed, Japanese soldiers raced out of tunnels for hand-to-hand fighting. Others died detonating ammunition stored in tunnels under U.S. positions. Hundreds were killed in night "banzai" attacks. Americans fired 75mm howitzers point blank in order to eliminate entire bunkers. By 2 March, organized Japanese resistance was over, but individual stragglers continued to appear for weeks. **RB**

Losses: U.S., 210 dead, 790 wounded, 5 missing; Japanese, 5,950 dead, 20 captured, 30 escaped

◁ Manila 1945

Iwo Jima 1945 ▷

↩ *The ruins of Dresden after the bombings.*

Iwo Jima   19 February–26 March 1945

Iwo Jima has been described as the most heavily fortified area in the history of warfare. Since the Japanese defenders were, as always, prepared to fight to the last man, the battle for Iwo Jima was ferocious. The U.S. attackers paid a high price for this World War II victory.

Even by Pacific standards, Iwo Jima is a particularly small dot on the map, less than 10 square miles (26 sq km) in size and some 650 miles (1,046 km) southeast of Tokyo. Its importance in 1945 was that it was within fighter range of the Japanese capital and could support the U.S. B-29 Superfortress raids on mainland Japan from the Marianas, both with fighters and by providing emergency landing facilities for bombers in difficulty.

Iwo Jima's barren, rocky volcanic terrain lent itself to defense. In addition, after the fall of the Marianas, it had been fortified by a garrison of 18,000 men commanded by General Tadamichi Kuribayashi. Almost all the garrison and its defenses survived the massive preliminary air and

> *"We shall defend this island with all our strength to the end. . . . We shall not die until we have killed ten of the enemy."* General Kuribayashi

naval bombardment because Kuribayashi had ordered his men not to open fire and reveal their positions until the attackers had actually landed. Two U.S. Marine divisions came ashore on 19 February and soon began taking heavy losses, pinned down on the crowded beaches under artillery and machine gun fire.

Progress inland was generally measured in yards as the Japanese resisted from the many trenches, tunnels, and other strongpoints that honeycombed the island. The first of the island's three airstrips, a few hundred yards

from the landing areas, was captured on 20 February. A small group of Marines managed to gain the summit of Mount Suribachi, the peak dominating the southern tip of the island, on 23 February and raised the Stars and Stripes there. The island's second airstrip was also captured on this day as the main Marine forces pushed north.

The heaviest fighting of the battle came just beyond this position, around a height marked on Marine maps as Hill 382, but generally known as the "meatgrinder." With 60,000 U.S. Marines committed to the battle by General Harry Schmidt's V Amphibious Corps, the outcome was never in serious doubt. However, the Japanese troops fought with astonishing bravery and determination, hiding in caves and other impregnable positions under bombardment, then emerging to take a heavy toll of their attackers, often from positions on a flank or in the rear that the Americans had not located or had overlooked. Kuribayashi had forbidden the traditional "banzai" suicide charges, ensuring his troops sold their lives dearly.

By 1 March, both Hill 382 and the important Hill 362 near the island's west coast had been cleared of almost all their defenders. The level of courage and commitment required of the attackers can be judged from the fact that twenty-seven Medals of Honor were awarded. General Schmidt announced that the island was secure on 16 March, but still the last few hundred Japanese defenders held out in a rocky cleft, known as Bloody Gorge, near the northern tip of the island. They were only wiped out after ten more days of struggle.

Iwo Jima was the only major engagement of the Pacific War in which U.S. casualties, killed and wounded, outstripped the total of Japanese dead. Even before the battle ended, B-29s were making emergency landings on Iwo Jima, possibly saving the lives of their aircrew. **DS**

Losses: U.S., 6,800 dead, 19,200 wounded; Japanese, 18,000 dead, 216 captured

◁ *Corregidor 1945*   *Tokyo 1945* ▷

U.S. Marines raise the American flag on Mount Suribachi, 23 February 1945. ➡

Remagen Bridge   7–17 March 1945

In the War in Europe, units of the U.S. 21st Army Group reached the Rhine River. The German army had withdrawn across it, presumably destroying all the bridges as it went. Allied leaders pondered the problem; a patrol of the 27th Armored Infantry, 9th Armored Division found a bridge intact.

Ludendorff railway bridge spanned the Rhine between Remagen (west bank) and Erpel. The bridge was fitted with demolitions, but why it was still standing is unclear. In any case, with orders from higher command, a German engineer planned to detonate the explosive charges at 4:00 PM on 7 March.

On the same day, a task force led by Lieutenant Colonel Leonard Engeman entered Remagen and discovered the bridge intact. Engeman notified his commander, Brigadier General William Hoge, and was told to secure the bridge. Lieutenant Karl Timmerman from Company A, 27th Armored Infantry got the mission. As Timmerman's men approached, the demolitions were triggered. Only a small number exploded, leaving the bridge weakened but not destroyed. Timmerman and his men were spotted and before long received machine gun fire from the far end. Undaunted, they went ahead; one group of men removed the remaining demolitions while others dodged across and secured the German positions. Resistance was slight. A small number of German soldiers and civilians were captured in the nearby rail tunnel. Hoge rushed troops and tanks across. By nightfall, five battalions were on the east bank; more followed, expanding the bridgehead.

In the following days, the Germans tried without success to destroy the bridge with artillery, bombers, and V-2 rockets. On 17 March, after five divisions had crossed, the bridge collapsed. Pontoon bridges were already in place on either side. The bridgehead was secure. **RB**

Losses: U.S., none; German, 1 civilian dead, 40 captured

⟨ *Colmar Pocket 1945*

An American soldier looks down on Remagen Bridge. ●

Tokyo   9–10 March 1945

The U.S. air raid on Tokyo in the War in the Pacific was one of the most destructive acts of war in human history. Although the precise death toll is unknown, conservative estimates suggest that the firestorm caused by incendiary bombs killed 80,000 people in a single night.

The United States' bombing campaign against mainland Japan was slow to start. The arrival of B-29 Superfortress bombers in 1944 gave the Americans the range to reach Japanese cities, first from bases in China and then from Pacific islands. Bombing raids were conducted on the same lines as U.S. operations in Europe: high-altitude attacks in daylight seeking to strike industrial and military targets. However, a combination of mechanical failures, formidable Japanese air defenses, and strong jet-stream winds made bombing inaccurate and losses substantial.

In January 1945, Major General Curtis LeMay was tasked with revitalizing the campaign. His boss, General "Hap"

Arnold, urged him to adopt incendiary bombing against Japan's cities and abandon the United States' policy of precision bombing. LeMay decided to attack Tokyo by night at low altitude, stripping his bombers of guns and armor to accommodate a larger bomb load.

Using a strategy pioneered by RAF Bomber Command, LeMay sent pathfinder aircraft ahead to mark the target area with napalm bombs. About 275 aircraft followed the pathfinders, dropping 1,665 tons of incendiaries, including napalm and white phosphorus. Dry, windy conditions aided the spread of the conflagration, which turned into a firestorm, destroying almost sixteen square miles (forty-one sq km) of the densely populated city. LeMay later said, "Killing Japanese didn't bother me very much at that time. It was getting the war over that bothered me." **RG**

Losses: U.S., 14 B-29 bombers of 335; Japanese, 80,000–120,000 dead, mostly civilians

◁ *Iwo Jima 1945*   *Okinawa 1945* ▷

⬆ *The U.S. incendiary bombing raids flattened entire blocks in downtown Tokyo.*

Okinawa   1 April–21 June 1945

The capture of Okinawa was the last preliminary of World War II before the planned Allied invasion of the Japanese home islands. The Japanese garrison was annihilated by the attackers' overwhelming firepower, but heavy U.S. casualties on land and hundreds of kamikaze attacks at sea meant that success came at a heavy cost.

The invasion of Okinawa was the largest and most elaborate U.S. operation of the Pacific War. More than half a million U.S. troops and 1,200 U.S. and British ships were involved. The ground forces were formed into General Buckner's Tenth Army, and the naval contingent was led by Admiral Spruance's Fifth Fleet. After preliminary bombardments, obstacle clearing, and the capture of some small outlying islands, the main landings began on Okinawa's southwest coast on 1 April.

The invading forces faced General Ushijima's army of some 130,000 men. Okinawa was within range of Japanese air bases on Formosa and Kyushu so heavy

> *"We have failed to crush the enemy, despite our death-defying resistance, and now we are doomed."* General Ushijima

air attacks by many of Japan's surviving air forces were expected. Ushijima decided not to contest potential landing areas but to concentrate his forces in a fairly small and heavily fortified area in the south of the island, where the rugged terrain would assist the defense.

At sea, the Japanese planned to use kamikaze (divine wind) suicide tactics. First tried systematically during the fighting for Leyte the previous October, this involved pilots deliberately crashing their aircraft into Allied ships. The tactics allowed inexperienced fliers in inferior aircraft to inflict heavy damage on the Allied fleet, while Japan's experienced pilots acted as escorts. During the fighting for Okinawa, kamikaze operations were at their height; more than 400 Allied vessels were either damaged or sunk, with roughly 10,000 casualties. The largest kamikaze operation, however, was a dismal failure. On 6 April, the giant battleship *Yamato* sailed to attack the U.S. fleets off Okinawa. *Yamato* had only enough fuel onboard for a one-way mission, but was sunk on 7 April by strikes from almost 300 carrier aircraft long before it could reach the invasion area; only six U.S. aircraft were lost.

On land, the U.S. forces cleared the northern two-thirds of the island before the end of April. The only notable resistance was in the Motobu peninsula area. The advance south by XXIV Corps was a different matter. After the unexpectedly peaceful initial landings, Japanese resistance soon stepped up. The Americans managed to break through the Japanese forward positions of the Machinato Line by 24 April, but then met the main defenses, the Shuri Line, running across the island just north of the island's capital, Naha. In early May, the Japanese unwisely made a series of counterattacks that not only cost them significant casualties but also revealed many previously hidden positions to the Americans.

By the third week in May, despite appalling weather and ferocious Japanese resistance, the U.S. attacks had ground their way through the Shuri Line. However, it took until 22 June for the advance to clear the last Japanese positions at the southern tip of the island. A final horror of the campaign was the death by suicide of thousands of Okinawan civilians, many of whom killed their children rather than face the cruelties they had been told the Americans would commit. **DS**

Losses: Allied, 12,500 dead, 36,000 wounded; Japanese, 120,000 dead, 7,000 captured, plus as many as 100,000 civilians dead

◁ *Tokyo 1945*   *Hiroshima and Nagasaki 1945* ▷

A Japanese Toni makes a suicide dive on USS Sangamon off Okinawa; it missed by 25 feet (7.6 m). ➜

Berlin 20 April–2 May 1945

In the final battle of World War II in Europe, the Red Army took a terrible revenge for the suffering of the Soviet people since 1941. It was, in fact, a pointless battle, because the Germans were utterly beaten already. At its end, Soviet power would stand astride Central Europe.

Outside Berlin, the Soviet Union assembled one of the largest concentrations of military power ever seen. Within the city, already repeatedly pounded by Allied bombing, terrified refugees and war-weary citizens were protected by a scratch force of stragglers and the remnants of shattered formations, supported by militia and units of the Hitler Youth—one battalion of which was sent into battle with an average age of fourteen.

In a race to win the glory of capturing the city of Berlin, Soviet marshals Ivan Konev and Georgiy Zhukov were willing to accept enormous casualties and inflict colossal damage. Within five days, the two forces had linked up and encircled Berlin. Soviet artillery fired

"The last days of savage house-to-house fighting and street battles had been a human slaughter..."

Eyewitness

nearly two million shells during the final assault. All the frightened Berliners could do was cower in their cellars and desperately hope that rumors of relief, or even that the Americans had joined forces with Germany to expel the Red Army, might be true.

Within the city, there were few fixed defenses. The urban terrain offered some advantage to its defenders, especially because, in their hurry to advance, Red Army tanks went in without adequate infantry support. The Hitler Youth could, and often did, destroy Soviet tanks

by ambushing them with Panzerfaust antitank rockets. Indeed, many defenders fought with suicidal courage; three of them, armed only with a machine gun, held off Soviet attacks on the Helensee bridge for two days. However, the Soviet firepower was overwhelming—a single shot from a sniper could be answered by artillery fire, or by Katyusha rockets, leveling the entire building from whence it came. The suspicion that a cellar might contain defenders would result in Soviet grenades being tossed in, with no regard for civilian lives. For German women, the greatest fear was rape, and Soviet soldiers committed this on a vast scale.

In his bunker, in the center of the city, Hitler remained convinced that Berlin could be saved. He gave utterly hopeless orders for armies that scarcely existed any longer to break the siege. Stalin, too, was not without his own delusions; he was obsessed with taking the Reichstag building, although it had not been used since 1933 and had no strategic value. This obsession cost heavily in the number of Soviet soldiers lost.

Many Berliners, desperate for the nightmare to end, began hanging white or red flags from their windows, offering surrender or even welcome to the Red Army. However, this practice entailed risking execution by SS firing squads, and there is little evidence that Soviet troops paid any attention. As the Red Army closed in around the final enclaves of resistance, Hitler's suicide on 30 April gave the garrison commander, General Helmuth Weidling, the chance to surrender. SS troops were doomed if captured, but some still tried to fight on; others committed suicide. Most were thankful that the ordeal was over. They emerged to take stock of the massive devastation the city of Berlin had endured, and to come to terms with its new masters. The general surrender of German forces was completed five days later. **JS**

Losses: Red Army, 100,000 dead; German, unknown

⟨ *Warsaw Uprising 1944*

A Russian sergeant and a comrade raise the Russian flag onto the Reichstag while Berlin burns. ➲

Hiroshima and Nagasaki 6 August and 9 August 1945

The dropping of atomic bombs on the Japanese cities of Hiroshima and Nagasaki by U.S. B-29 bombers in August 1945 was followed quickly by Japan's surrender, ending World War II. The demonstration of the destructive power of nuclear weapons opened a new era in warfare and international relations.

In July 1945, the first atomic bombs—developed during the war through the Manhattan Project—were delivered to Tinian Island in the Marianas, the base for 509th Composite Group, a bomber formation set up specifically to deliver the U.S. secret weapon. On 26 July, the Allied Potsdam Declaration called on Japan to surrender or face "prompt and utter destruction." When this call was rejected, the atomic bomb attacks were authorized.

Hiroshima had been chosen as a target because it was large, flat, and undamaged, and would thus allow the bomb to show its full effect. The B-29 bomber carrying the uranium bomb Little Boy took off at 2:45 AM on 6 August. It was piloted by group commander Colonel Paul Tibbets, who had had his mother's maiden name, Enola Gay, painted on the aircraft. Accompanied by two other B-29s, "Enola Gay" appeared above Hiroshima in a clear sky and dropped the bomb at 8:15 AM local time.

Thousands were killed within a second of the explosion. Tens of thousands more died through blast injuries or flash burns and as a consequence of firestorms. Deaths from radiation soon began and would long continue. About seventy percent of the city was devastated. The second attack—using the plutonium Fat Boy bomb, carried by B-29 Bockscar—was diverted from its primary target, Kokura, because of cloud cover and instead dropped on Nagasaki. Japan announced its surrender on 15 August. **RG**

Losses: U.S., none; Japanese, 70,000–160,000 dead in Hiroshima, 50,000–80,000 dead in Nagasaki

⟨ *Tokyo 1945*

The remains of the Hiroshima Prefectural Industry Promotion Building, now the Atomic-Bomb Dome.

Xuzhou 6 November 1948–10 January 1949

Sometimes known as the Huaihai Campaign, the large-scale fighting around Xuzhou from 1948 to 1949 effectively determined the outcome of the Chinese Civil War, ensuring that Mao Ze Dong's Communists would come to power in Beijing. The Chinese Nationalists lost more than half a million men, mostly taken prisoner.

Engaged in civil war with Chiang Kai-shek's Nationalists since 1946, Mao announced the transition from guerrilla tactics to conventional warfare in 1948. Largely equipped with arms and vehicles captured from the Nationalists, the Communist Red Army would seek open battle, their forces taking on the enemy in mass encounters.

Communist general Lin Biao defeated the Nationalists in Manchuria in October. When Chiang attempted to regroup and block further Communist advances in northern and central China, Red Army commander in chief Zhu De concentrated his forces against Xuzhou, a vital railroad junction. The Nationalist armies were superior numerically and had a monopoly of air power, but they were demoralized and badly led. In a series of large-scale maneuvers, the Communists encircled sections of the Nationalist forces. Cut off from resupply except by air and subjected to heavy artillery bombardment, Nationalist soldiers began to desert en masse.

The Communists were able to mobilize several million peasants to provide an efficient logistical and intelligence network. The Nationalists were short of ammunition and living off the flesh of their transport horses. Chiang ordered a breakout that the troops were in no position to execute. After sixty-five days' fighting, a Communist offensive overran the Nationalist positions. The Nationalists had no further hope of saving their regime in China. **RG**

Losses: Nationalist, 230,000 casualties, 330,000 captured of 900,000; Communist, 140,000 casualties of 600,000

◁ *Changsha 1944*   *Chosin 1950* ▷

⬆ *Communist troops are supported by an M5 Stuart light tank during the fighting around Xuzhou.*

North Korean Invasion of South Korea   25 June 1950

Korea was divided by the Cold War, with a Soviet-backed communist government installed in the North and a pro-U.S. government in the South. The North Korean invasion of South Korea in June 1950 started a war that was to last three years and cost more than four million lives.

The North Korean attack came as an immense shock to South Korean leader Syngman Rhee and his army. He had a fairly weak army, singularly lacking in armor. North Korea was well equipped with Soviet-supplied T34 tanks and a large, well-motivated, and experienced army; many of its soldiers had fought in the Chinese Civil War.

South Korea was soon in a desperate position. At Chunchon, a single South Korean regiment made a heroic stand until the North brought up tanks. North of the capital, Seoul, the South's 1st Division fought doggedly, with volunteers attempting to destroy T34s with satchel charges; they met little success with high casualties.

After three days, the collapse of the front elsewhere forced the division to retreat. Increasing panic was evident. Rhee ordered the immediate execution of all political prisoners. Army headquarters evacuated from Seoul without informing U.S. liaison officers. The roads were crammed with refugees, and four bridges over the Han River were blown up while refugees were crossing, killing hundreds. Total collapse seemed imminent, but South Korea had been a U.S. creation, and Cold War prestige was at stake. The Soviet Union was boycotting the United Nations, so the United States was able to gain a Security Council resolution authorizing members of the United Nations to intervene militarily. U.S. forces were rushed to Korea, but would they arrive in time? **JS**

Losses: South Korean, 44,000 dead, wounded, or missing of 98,000; North Korean, 58,000 dead or wounded of 260,000; civilian losses unknown

Pusan Perimeter 1950 ▷

A banner in South Korea welcomes Western troops to join the fight against North Korea.

Pusan Perimeter August–September 1950

The United States sent troops to Korea to halt the North Korean invasion of South Korea. Along with surviving South Korean forces, the U.S. Eighth Army was driven back to an enclave around the port of Pusan, which they held at times precariously, as further reinforcements arrived.

The defensive perimeter around Pusan contained an area measuring about 100 miles (160 km) by 50 miles (80 km). U.S. forces felt their position was dire and that they were facing a much larger enemy, capable of taking limitless casualties. In fact, the attacking North Koreans were outnumbered; their armor and artillery had been seriously depleted in the advance south. Their supply problems were colossal, they had great difficulty evacuating their wounded, and their troops were hungry and exhausted. The Americans also enjoyed complete air superiority.

North Korean troops maintained a high fighting spirit, their victories gave them immense self-confidence, and they were aggressive in attack. Several times they managed to achieve relatively deep penetration into the defenses of the perimeter. At one point, the entire North Korean 4th Division managed to cross the Naktong River using submerged bridges, but were driven back after intense fighting. The defenders launched their own counteroffensives; one in the north that was aimed toward the Chinju pass collided with a North Korean offensive, and a desperately confused melee ensued, with U.S. artillery and air power being used to full capacity.

While the northern line was pushed back up to 20 miles (32 km), the Pusan Perimeter was never in serious danger, and, by the end of September, it was clear that North Korea would not win the rapid victory expected. **JS**

Losses: North Korean, heavy casualties of 70,000; U.S., 4,600 dead, 12,000 wounded, 2,500 captured or missing of 140,000; South Korean, unknown

◁ *Invasion of South Korea* 1950   *Inchon Landings* 1950 ▷

⬆ *Elite troops from the United States arrive at the port of Pusan to support South Korea.*

Inchon Landings
15–17 September 1950

With the situation at the Pusan Perimeter stabilized, and United Nations reinforcements arriving in strength, it was time for a United Nations offensive in the Korean War. In an imaginative seaborne landing, the U.S.-led United Nations force would break the North Korean invasion at a stroke.

In order to avoid a costly and brutal land campaign to defeat the North Koreans, U.S. General Douglas MacArthur, commanding United Nations forces, chose amphibious landings at the port of Inchon, far to the rear of the Pusan battle lines, within striking distance of Seoul. This would allow the United Nations to envelop the North Korean invaders and, hopefully, end the war immediately.

There were risks involved: the sea walls at Inchon were very high, the waters could be mined, and offshore currents were fast. However, the North Koreans had few reserves left, their air power was largely destroyed, and the garrison at Inchon was small. As it was, United Nations troops were able to land in broad daylight over two days. Resistance was minimal; a few firefights were concluded rapidly. Belated North Korean attempts to reinforce their garrison were suppressed quickly by air power.

The North Korean leadership, intent on containing United Nations forces at Pusan as long as possible to give themselves time to strengthen their position at Seoul, failed to keep the troops informed. It was a week before news trickled through, and a collapse ensued. Seoul was taken rapidly, and the bulk of the North Korean army was trapped. However, perhaps MacArthur's triumph was too overwhelming; he was now tempted to go beyond expelling the Northern forces from South Korea, and to keep going and destroy the communist state entirely. **JS**

Losses: United Nations, 222 dead, 800 wounded of 40,000; North Korean, 1,350 dead of 6,500

◁ *Pusan Perimeter 1950*   *Invasion of North Korea 1950* ▷

Invasion of North Korea
1 October–24 December 1950

After the success of the Inchon Landings, General Douglas MacArthur, commander of U.S.-led United Nations forces in Korea, was given permission by the U.S. government to invade North Korea. This led to Communist China entering the Korean War and to near disaster for the United Nations forces.

MacArthur planned a two-pronged invasion: one thrust overland to Pyongyang, the other a seaborne landing on the east coast at Wonsan. The original intention was to hold a line across Korea at the 40th parallel. Progress northward proved so easy, however, that MacArthur was tempted to press farther toward the Yalu River, the border with China. This was counter to his orders from his political masters, who were anxious to avoid conflict with China. It was also militarily unwise.

As United Nations forces advanced northward, the Chinese infiltrated lightly armed troops into North Korea, joining remnants of the North Korean army. Ignoring initial clashes with the Chinese, on 24 November MacArthur ordered a last push toward the Yalu. Within two days, advanced United Nations units came under unsustainable pressure from Chinese troops concealed in surrounding mountains. On 28 November, a withdrawal was ordered. United Nations troops had to fight their way southward along roads subject to Chinese ambush and blockade. The retreat turned into a near rout. No defensive line could be stabilized until the troops reached the South Korean border at the 38th parallel. Panic in Washington led to plans to use atom bombs to halt the Chinese. In the event, these were not needed. The Chinese resumed their offensive and retook Seoul in January 1951, but were then driven back to the 38th parallel. MacArthur was sacked in April. **RG**

Losses: United Nations, heavy; Chinese, heavy

◁ *Inchon Landings 1950*   *Chosin 1950* ▷

Chosin
27 November–13 December 1950

After the People's Republic of China's intervention in the Korean War, United Nations forces were soon in headlong retreat. However, the exploits of one group of largely U.S. troops to extricate themselves from the Chosin reservoir proved one of the epic feats of the war.

The sudden Chinese attack trapped more than 30,000 men, mostly U.S. Marines and soldiers of the U.S. Seventh Army, who had been advancing along both sides of the Chosin reservoir. Their only chance of survival was to hold the village of Hagaru-ri, where supplies were stockpiled and an airstrip—the only viable escape route—was under construction. This was carried out by a scratch force with great determination. It was a crucial stand because once all the encircled troops had consolidated there—after bitter fighting and heavy losses—the airstrip was completed, the wounded airlifted out, and supplies delivered.

The weather was atrocious; it was so cold that machine guns had to be fired every thirty minutes to prevent them from freezing solid. On the retreat to the coast, the Americans had to fight to take every hilltop overlooking the road, aware of the constant dangers of infiltration attack. Engineers had to rebuild destroyed bridges under fire, and the wounded needing tending. Linking up with a mixed garrison at Koto, where more wounded were evacuated by air, the column slowly crept toward the coast. Air support was crucial to the escape; at one point prefabricated sections of a bridge were airdropped to the troops. Although harried every step of the way, in the end, courage and endurance got the men to the sea and to safety, and went some way to salving United Nations' pride after the disaster of the Chinese attack. **JS**

Losses: U.S., 1,000 dead, 4,600 wounded, 5,000 missing of 30,000; Chinese, 30,000 dead or wounded of 60,000

◁ *Invasion of North Korea 1950*　　　*Imjin River 1951* ▷

Vinh Yen
13–17 January 1951

After World War II, the Viet Minh—Communist-led Vietnamese nationalists—launched a guerrilla war to oust the French from their Indochina colony. In 1951, Viet Minh commander Vo Nguyen Giap decided to engage French forces in a conventional battle. This was to prove a costly mistake.

Giap chose Vinh Yen as his target because it was only 30 miles (48 km) from Hanoi, and success would allow him to take the city and hopefully end the war. He intended to attack outlying positions, ambush forces sent to support them, and then take the main stronghold.

In the first part of his operation, Giap was almost successful. A French mobile group was ambushed and only extricated itself with difficulty, with heavy losses to two battalions. However, the French had the advantage of air power. Reinforcements were flown in, and when Giap made the mistake of sending in a "human wave" attack in broad daylight, artillery, dive-bombers, and large quantities of napalm wreaked havoc among Viet Minh ranks.

The French also showed considerable courage during the battle. Fewer than one hundred colonial troops withstood an attack from an entire Viet Minh division for a whole day. However, the Viet Minh attacks persisted, and some French positions were lost after running short of ammunition. The French were forced to deploy every aircraft they had capable of dropping bombs, and in the end, it was air power that prevailed. Viet Minh forces had to retreat hurriedly when their casualties became unsustainable. In the long term, this victory did little good to the French, because they never had the resources to defeat the renewed guerrilla warfare that followed the battle. However, the morale boost was welcome. **JS**

Losses: French, 60 dead, 600 wounded of 9,000; Viet Minh, 1,600 dead, 6,000 wounded, 480 captured of 20,000

Hoah Binh 1951 ▷

Imjin River   22–25 April 1951

In 1951, a series of costly encounters saw the fighting in the Korean War sway back and forth, as Chinese manpower was pitted against the firepower of the United States and its allies. A Chinese offensive in April was the occasion for a heroic stand by British troops at the Imjin River.

The position at Imjin was held by the British 29th Brigade (with an attached Belgian battalion). On 22 April, the Chinese threw 350,000 troops against the entire United Nations lines. Under attack from three Chinese divisions, Imjin was in a desperate position.

With orders to hold their ground at all costs, the British were forced by mounting casualties to concentrate their forces and try to survive the night. However, the 1st Battalion, Gloucester Regiment (the Glosters) could not disengage and was surrounded on Hill 235, thereafter called Gloster Hill. Hopelessly outnumbered, the troops showed confidence and courage even as their numbers dwindled. The rest of the brigade was in no position to rescue them, and a misunderstanding in communications meant U.S. help did not arrive in time. (A British officer told a U.S. officer that their position was "a bit sticky"—a classic understatement meaning "desperate," but which the American interpreted as "reasonably stable.")

After three days, during which the British were surrounded by the Chinese and reduced to throwing canned food at them in an attempt to fool them into thinking they still had grenades, the 29th Brigade had to fight its way out. The Glosters could only try to sneak through Chinese lines in small groups. Astonishingly, forty men succeeded; the rest were killed or captured. The savagery of the fighting greatly enhanced the British army's pride and prestige. **JS**

Losses: British, 1,000 dead, wounded, or captured; Chinese 10,000 dead or wounded

◁ Chosin 1950   Kapyong 1951 ▷

Kapyong   22–25 April 1951

The Chinese offensive in spring 1951 that occasioned the famous stand by the British Glosters at Imjin River also gave Commonwealth troops an opportunity to show their best fighting qualities. One Australian and one Canadian battalion held up an entire Chinese division in the Kapyong Valley.

The valley, north of Seoul, was held by South Korean and U.S. forces with 27th British Commonwealth Brigade in reserve. On 22 April, Chinese 60th Infantry Division launched an attack through the valley, driving the South Koreans into retreat. The Commonwealth Brigade was called upon to prevent a breakthrough.

The 3rd Battalion, Royal Australian Regiment and the Canadian 2nd Battalion, Princess Patricia's Light Infantry were designated to hold two dominant positions in the valley: Hills 504 and 677. The Chinese adopted their usual infiltration tactics, flooding soldiers around strongpoints and seeking to overwhelm the defenders in rapid mass infantry assaults. The hills were soon several miles behind the foremost Chinese troops, who were resisted by U.S. tanks and New Zealand and U.S. artillery.

On the night of 23 to 24 April, the Australians on Hill 504 came under intense pressure in fighting dominated by light machine guns, mortars, and grenades. The Chinese coordinated their infantry attacks in the darkness with bugle calls and whistles. Despite suffering a "friendly fire" napalm strike by U.S. Marine aircraft, the Australians held firm and carried out a smooth fighting retreat on 24 April. The Chinese attacks then concentrated against the Patricias on Hill 677. The Canadians held a defensive perimeter, and on 25 April, the Chinese withdrew. Both the Australian and Canadian battalions were awarded the U.S. Presidential Unit Citation for their valor. **RG**

Losses: Australian, 32 dead, 59 wounded, 3 captured; Canadian, 10 dead, 23 wounded; Chinese, unknown

◁ Imjin River 1951   Pork Chop Hill 1953 ▷

 General Matthew B. Ridgway at Imjin; he was recognized for his outstanding leadership in the Korean War.

Hoah Binh   10 November 1951–25 February 1952

With increasing U.S. aid, the French colonialists decided to take the offensive in the First Indochina War against the Communist Viet Minh guerrillas. The campaign was costly to both sides, but in the end it was the French who proved unable to sustain offensive operations.

Situated close to Hanoi, Hoah Binh province was attractive as a battleground to the French. Control of it would cut off supplies from the Viet Minh, who would have to fight on French terms, and the French would have the support of the local Muong people, who opposed the Viet Minh.

They airlifted three battalions of paratroopers to the area, where they were joined by a further fifteen infantry battalions, who advanced against only intermittent resistance. Twenty landing craft were used to clear river communications. Initially, there was no Viet Minh response, but infiltration units began to harry supply lines. The first heavy attack was against the French outpost at

Tu Vu, where a "human wave" assault across a minefield was repelled by murderous machine gun and tank fire. Patrols and supplies were ambushed regularly by Viet Minh guerrillas. Particularly heavy attacks were launched to close the airstrip and road connections. It took twelve French battalions, supported by three artillery groups, eleven days to reopen the roads.

French morale began to sag as losses on both sides escalated. Ultimately, the French could not sustain their losses—they needed their troops elsewhere, and they had to evacuate, if they could. This was a difficult proposition because the Viet Minh were on all sides. However, the French managed to achieve surprise, and a savage running battle was fought, with the French deploying an extra 20,000 troops to rescue the garrison. **JS**

Losses: French, 894 dead or missing, more than 2,000 wounded; Viet Minh, 9,000 dead or wounded

◁ *Vinh Yen 1951*   *Dien Bien Phu 1954* ▷

French prisoners are marched along Route Coloniale 4, October 1951. ⬆

Pork Chop Hill   16 April–10 July 1953

The Korean War became a stalemate in summer 1951, with troops dug into defensive positions and offensives launched only to influence armistice negotiations. U.S. troops fought with great courage at Pork Chop Hill, but the fighting came to symbolize the futility of such engagements.

In March 1953, Chinese forces captured the hill known as Old Baldy. The United Nations was reluctant to expend lives on a position of no strategic significance, despite the political advantage China might gain from such a success. Neighboring Pork Chop Hill, similarly of no particular strategic value, but garrisoned by ninety-six U.S. soldiers, was left exposed.

The Chinese launched a night attack on the U.S. troops. With radio and telephone communications destroyed, the U.S. commander had to appeal for artillery support by signal flares. Most of the hill was occupied within a few hours, with the Americans reduced to a few pockets near the top of the hill. The first U.S. attempts to retake the hill started within hours—it was now deemed imperative that the U.S. Army reestablish the United Nations' credibility in negotiations. Two U.S. infantry companies reoccupied some of the defenses before dawn, but only after suffering heavy losses and urgently needing reinforcements themselves in order to survive. For two days, both sides threw in reinforcements and fired thousands of artillery rounds at the hill. In the end, the Chinese withdrew. Although the hill had no inherent value, for both sides the battle had challenged their prestige, and fighting over the hill was to drag on almost until the last day of the war. At this point, the Americans decided that the cost of holding the hill outweighed the political price of abandoning it. **JS**

Losses: U.S., 347 dead, 1,300 wounded of 20,000; Chinese, 5,500 dead or wounded of 20,000

⊲ *Kapyong 1951*

⬆ *A wounded U.S. soldier is taken back to a position of safety on Pork Chop Hill, July 1953.*

Dien Bien Phu   13 March–7 May 1954

From 1946 the Communist-led Viet Minh fought a successful guerrilla war against French colonial rule in Vietnam. But in 1954 they defeated the French in a conventional battle at Dien Bien Phu. This led to independence for Vietnam—but with the Viet Minh ruling only the north of the country.

By 1953 the long and costly colonial war in Indochina was losing the support of the French electorate. The French army was determined to fight a decisive battle before a new home government committed to withdrawal. But the Viet Minh had a growing supply of heavy weapons and were building a conventional army; their commander, Vo Nguyen Giap, also sought a decisive victory.

In November French paratroopers landed in the remote valley of Dien Bien Phu, near the border with Laos. When the Viet Minh moved in to surround them, the French commander in Indochina, General Henri Navarre, saw a golden opportunity to use artillery and airpower to destroy a concentrated enemy, and reinforced the

> *"The situation is very grave. . . . I feel the end is approaching, but we will fight to the finish."*
>
> *Brigadier General Christian de Castries*

position. The French paratroopers, Foreign Legionaries, and colonial troops depended on air supply through two airfields defended by a series of strongpoints, reputedly named after their commander's mistresses.

Giap had heavy artillery transported over almost impassable terrain to positions on hills surrounding the French base. When the battle began with a massive Viet Minh artillery barrage, the French garrison was shocked by its scale and by the ferocity of the infantry attacks it covered. However, Viet Minh commanders lacked

experience in coordinating large units in combat, and many assaults in the early days were ill-planned and thrown back with great loss. But they learned quickly, and were also more adept in concealing their guns. A Viet Minh commando raid destroyed several French aircraft on the ground, making the garrison ever more dependent upon reinforcements parachuted in.

The fight became a battle of attrition, with the Viet Minh reducing the French strongpoints (which proved inadequate for the artillery used against them) and digging trenches ever closer to the core of the French position. The French will to resist was worn down. Viet Minh losses remained high, but their morale held up and they solved supply problems by the simple expedient of enlisting porters to haul their minimal needs forward. It was becoming increasingly clear to the French that it was only a matter of time before Dien Bien Phu fell.

The U.S. government was so alarmed at the prospect of a Communist Viet Minh triumph, with its likely impact on an international conference on Indochina, soon to be held in Geneva, that it reputedly considered supporting the garrison with battlefield nuclear weapons. But as the Viet Minh overran positions at the center of Dien Bien Phu's defenses, the French defenders finally saw that further resistance would only cause futile casualties, and they surrendered. As far as the French government was concerned, the war was lost. This situation was unacceptable to the United States, which was determined to limit what the Viet Minh should gain from their victory. Thus a "temporary" division of Vietnam was instituted along the 17th parallel. A separate South Vietnamese state was set up, the survival of which was bound up with U.S. Cold War prestige. **JS**

Losses: French, 2,300 dead, 11,700 captured (most died in captivity); Viet Minh, 4,000–8,000 dead, 9,000–15,000 wounded (figures are disputed)

◁ Hoah Binh 1951   Gulf of Tonkin 1964 ▷

A Viet Minh soldier waves a flag atop a French strongpoint at the close of the fifty-six-day battle. ➤

Suez Invasion 29 October–7 November 1956

An invasion of Egyptian territory by a French, British, and Israeli alliance, the Suez operation was a military success but politically inept. Forced to withdraw by pressure from the United States, Britain and France were humiliated and confronted with the demise of their status as imperial powers.

When, in July 1956, Egyptian President Nasser nationalized the Suez Canal Company, a conspiracy was developed, behind the backs of the Americans, by which Israel would invade the Sinai peninsula and approach the canal. Britain and France would then intervene on the pretext of protecting the waterway. The ultimate aim was to overthrow the aggressively nationalistic Nasser.

Israeli operations began with paratrooper landings at the Mitla Pass on 29 October. Israeli forces performed outstandingly, showing the effectiveness of a citizen army that believed it was fighting for national survival. In fact their advance across the Sinai was so rapid that

their campaign threatened to end before the Anglo-French intervention arrived. Then, after initial bombing of Egyptian forces, on 5 November British and French paratroopers landed at the Gamil airport and at strategic bridges over the canal. They faced determined resistance, with sniper fire and accidental attacks from their own support aircraft adding to their difficulties. The next morning the main force came ashore from landing craft.

The operation had its bizarre moments; one tank driver asked his commander on what side of the road he should drive and whether to stop at traffic lights. But civilian casualties were heavy and many troops took little trouble to discriminate targets. The invasion force attained its military objectives, but a U.S.-inspired financial crisis stopped the invasion in its tracks within two days. **JS**

Losses: Israeli, 172 dead; British, 16 dead; French, 10 dead; Egyptian, more than 1,600 military and 1,000 civilians dead

Operation Focus 1967 ⟩

After the battle, British frogmen recover weapons hidden by the Egyptians in the Suez Canal.

Algiers 7 January–8 October 1957

The Battle of Algiers was a major episode in the struggle between the French army and the National Liberation Front (FLN), seeking Algerian independence from French rule. The FLN suffered a crushing defeat in Algiers in 1957, but the methods of the French provoked international outrage.

The FLN was firmly implanted in the Casbah in the center of Algiers, from which they conducted terrorist operations, assassinating government officials and planting bombs in public places frequented by Europeans. In January 1957 the French army under General Jacques Massu was given exceptional powers to suppress the Algerian nationalists. The army imposed a curfew, cordoned off the Casbah, and established checkpoints to control the population.

They also sought intelligence; they needed to identify the leaders of the FLN, who were concealed by a clandestine cell-structured organization. If the leadership could be neutralized, the French reasoned—correctly—

the FLN campaign would collapse. The tactic used was to arrest possible activists just after the curfew, and act on information gained before it was lifted and identified FLN leaders could make their escape.

This restriction did not give the French much time, so they resorted to the most brutal tortures to extract information. A spiral of atrocities and counter-atrocities developed, but by March the FLN was in crisis, and a lull in bombings followed. A renewed effort in June was really the last gasp of a largely defeated movement being hunted to extinction.

The killing of the last FLN leader, Ali Ammar, known as Ali-la-Pointe, by French paratroopers on 8 October signaled the defeat of the FLN in Algiers. But in France and across the world, horror at the conduct of the army fatally undermined France's position in Algeria, which became independent under the FLN in 1962. **JS**

Losses: Unknown

⬆ *A citizen is searched for weapons at one of the French checkpoints around Algiers.*

La Plata   11–21 July 1958

The Battle of La Plata was an encounter during the Cuban Revolution and was part of the summer offensive of 1958, launched by President Fulgencio Batista to defeat Fidel Castro's 26th of July Movement in the Sierra Maestra hills. The battle ended in defeat for Batista's army, undermining its resolve to fight against the revolution.

Batista's summer offensive of 1958, referred to as Operation Verano, was intended to destroy Castro's revolutionary army, which was launching guerrilla-type attacks from the Sierra Maestra hills and gathering support among the Cubans to call for a general strike.

The campaign was planned by General Eulogio Cantillo. On 11 July Cantillo landed a force of two battalions at the mouth of the La Plata River with the objective of surrounding Castro's positions at Turquino Peak. The first operation, involving Battalion Eighteen, was led by Major José Quevedo and was intended to be a swift amphibious

assault that would land and quickly move up to Castro's base and destroy it. The second operation, using Battalion Seventeen, would flank the revolutionary army and attack it from the rear. However, Battalion Eighteen was ambushed by Che Guevara's guerrillas as it moved into the hills. Quevedo formed a defensive position as he came under attack from both sides of the mountain and waited for reinforcements. But Battalion Seventeen had suffered a similar fate and was pinned down. Despite propaganda being transmitted over loudspeakers, Quevedo held out for several days but eventually surrendered on 21 July, later joining the revolution.

Victory at La Plata, and elsewhere, gave Castro valuable propaganda material and weakened the ability of the Batista government to launch further offensives. **TB**

Losses: Cuban regular army, 70 dead and 400 captured; 26th of July Movement, no reliable figures

Santa Clara 1958 ▷

In a mountain camp, Fidel Castro (standing, center) poses with fellow "guerilleros." ⬆

Santa Clara   28–31 December 1958

The Battle of Santa Clara is the name given to the events immediately preceding the capture of the city of Santa Clara during the Cuban Revolution. Over the course of three days, a small force of Cuban revolutionaries led by Che Guevara captured the city and triggered the fall of the president, General Fulgencio Batista.

With Batista on the defensive, Che Guevara advanced toward Santa Clara on 28 December, cheered on by excited crowds. However, government troops were preparing to defend the city. A command post had been set up around an armored train, packed with supplies and ammunition. Guevara sent a small force to capture the train but as they approached the government forces climbed aboard and set off toward the city center.

Guevara needed to stop the train from linking up with government forces in the city. He seized a number of tractors from the university and ordered the tracks to be disrupted to stop the train. The action was successful and the train was derailed, with the troops surrendering. In addition to a minor victory of which much use would be made in psychological terms, Guevara now had additional weapons and ammunition for his campaign.

In fact, the capture of the train turned out to be a huge propaganda coup for Fidel Castro. As news of it spread around the country, more and more troops loyal to General Batista deserted or joined the revolutionaries. Consequently, Castro claimed that little resistance remained to stop him taking Cuba's capital, Havana.

Che Guevara accepted the surrender of the last troops loyal to Batista in Santa Clara on 31 December. In the early hours of 1 January, Batista boarded an aircraft and flew to exile in Honduras. Seven days later, Castro moved triumphantly into Havana. **TB**

Losses: No reliable figures

◁ *La Plata 1958* 　 *Bay of Pigs Invasion 1961* ▷

⬆ *Che Guevara receives the tribute of Cuban revolutionaries after Santa Clara is taken.*

Bay of Pigs Invasion   17–19 April 1961

The Bay of Pigs is an inlet on the southern coast of Cuba. The location became infamous in 1961 as the site of an invasion by a U.S.-backed force of Cuban exiles bent upon the overthrow of the country's revolutionary president Fidel Castro and instatement of a U.S.-approved government. In the event, the invasion was an ignominious failure.

In March 1960 President Dwight D. Eisenhower ordered the Central Intelligence Agency (CIA) to train and equip anti-Castro Cuban exiles. A plan was devised for a seaborne landing to coincide with an uprising against Castro's government. The Cuban air force was to be destroyed by air strikes, carried out by U.S. B-26 bombers piloted by Cuban exiles.

In spring 1961 new U.S. President John F. Kennedy allowed the invasion to go ahead but insisted that U.S. involvement be minimized. On 17 April some 1,500 Cuban exiles sailed from Nicaragua, escorted by U.S. Navy destroyers and an aircraft carrier, and landed at the Bay of Pigs. The anticipated anti-Castro uprising failed to materialize. The exiles' B-26 bombers had been reduced to six, too few to destroy Castro's air force. In control of the air, Castro's aircraft attacked the invasion force on the ground and its supply vessels offshore.

Kennedy refused to allow U.S. air or naval forces to intervene in support of the invasion. Although the exiles fought courageously, within forty-eight hours they were overrun by Cuban soldiers and militia loyal to Castro. Those who were not killed were captured and ransomed back to the United States in 1962. The Bay of Pigs fiasco was a major embarrassment for the U.S. government, which was caught lying about its involvement, and Cuba was driven closer to the Soviet Union. **TB**

"Before the invasion, the revolution was weak. Now it's stronger than ever."

Che Guevara

⬆ *Fidel Castro talks to revolutionary soldiers at his base of operations at Jagüey Grande, near the Bay of Pigs landing zone.*

Losses: Cuban exiles, 120 dead and 1,180 captured of 1,500; Cuban republicans, 3,000–4,000 casualties

< *Santa Clara 1958*

Gulf of Tonkin   2–4 August 1964

In 1964 U.S. personnel were officially involved only as military advisers in the war between the South Vietnamese government and North Vietnamese–backed guerrilla forces. A relatively trivial naval clash in the Gulf of Tonkin, however, gave President Lyndon Johnson authority from Congress to escalate U.S. involvement at will.

In summer 1964 the United States was engaged in covert operations along the North Vietnamese coast, including commando raids and electronic intelligence gathering. The destroyer USS *Maddox*, packed with electronic equipment, was sent in support. At the start of August *Maddox* took up position off Hon Me, a port where a number of North Vietnamese torpedo boats were based.

On 2 August three torpedo boats attacked the destroyer in international waters. After firing torpedoes without scoring a hit, they were driven off by *Maddox*'s guns. Carrier-born Crusader jets then left one torpedo boat dead in the water, and the other two fled.

Initially President Johnson was willing to overlook the incident. *Maddox* was joined by another destroyer, USS *Turner Joy*, and resumed patrol. Washington warned them that intercepted radio traffic indicated another attack was likely. On 4 August radar reported high-speed craft approaching; the ships opened fire. But the radar reports were conflicting. Sonar indicated twenty torpedoes in the water, but none struck. Air support was hurriedly called in, but no enemy craft could be found. Combat hysteria seems to be the only rational explanation for the renewed activity, but Johnson ordered retaliatory air strikes against North Vietnam. Congress authorized the president to use whatever force he deemed necessary to protect allies of the United States in southeast Asia. **JS**

Losses: U.S., none; North Vietnamese, 4 dead, 6 wounded

◁ *Dien Bien Phu 1954*   *Rolling Thunder 1965* ▷

Stanleyville   24 November 1964

The former Belgian Congo in central Africa was thrown into chaos after independence in 1960 by internal revolts and foreign intervention. In 1964 Congolese government forces and U.S.-supported Belgian paratroopers defeated rebels in eastern Congo at Stanleyville (now Kisangani) in an operation justified by the need to save hostages.

The rebels, known as Simbas (Lions), were mainly illiterate tribesmen who believed they possessed magic powers that rendered them invulnerable. They captured Stanleyville in August 1964. The rebels imposed a reign of terror in the region, with thousands massacred.

The Americans and Belgians supported a government counterattack, which advanced on the city. Defeat seemed imminent, but the Simbas took nearly 2,000 U.S. and European hostages, hoping to use them as bargaining chips in negotiations. Several hundred were held at Stanleyville's Victoria Hotel. This led to a daring, but risky, rescue mission. A night landing by a battalion of Belgian paratroopers in USAF Hercules aircraft quickly captured the airport. Mainly armed with spears, the Simbas found their magic little protection against automatic weapons, and any who fought were quickly shot. The paratroopers freed most of the hostages, around sixty of whom had been killed. The survivors were evacuated over the next few days. Government forces, led by white mercenaries and supported by aircraft donated and piloted by the CIA, also entered the city, which they quickly secured.

The Simbas never recovered from this defeat, though it took a year to suppress the revolt completely. But the prestige of Moise Tshombe's Congolese government was tarnished by cooperating with white imperialists, and the following year it was overthrown. **JS**

Losses: Unknown

Rolling Thunder 2 March 1965–31 October 1968

Operation Rolling Thunder was the code name for the air offensive mounted by the United States against North Vietnam between 1965 and 1968. One of the largest air campaigns of all time, with a total of 864,000 tons of bombs dropped, it proved costly, ineffectual, and politically disastrous.

The Rolling Thunder air campaign drew on the resources not only of the USAF but also of the U.S. Navy and Marines. Most of the USAF strike aircraft operated from bases in Thailand, while the large B-52 bombers of Strategic Air Command were based far off in the Pacific at Guam and Okinawa. The Navy and Marine aircraft flew their missions from carriers in the South China Sea. The key aircraft, apart from the B-52s, were F-4 Phantoms for air-to-air combat and F-105 Thunderbirds as fighter-bombers.

The North Vietnamese quickly developed impressive air defenses using Soviet equipment. Their MiG-15 and MiG-17 fighters were primitive in their electronics and armament compared with the U.S. aircraft, but proved

"Letters from residents ... continue to reflect resigned acceptance of the hardships inflicted by the bombings." Extract from CIA and DIA document

nimble and effective in dogfights, often achieving parity with the Americans in aerial combat. Trained to intercept nuclear bombers with long-range missiles, U.S. pilots had to adapt to close-range fights in which Sidewinder heat-seeking missiles or old-fashioned cannon were most effective. On the ground, the North Vietnamese used a combination of radar-controlled antiaircraft guns and surface-to-air missiles that was hard to overcome, the missiles forcing the U.S. strike aircraft to fly at low altitude, where the guns scored most of the kills.

U.S. pilots were frustrated by rules of engagement imposed by politicians determined to keep the bombing campaign under control. The Johnson administration had no intention of conducting a World War II–style no-holds-barred strategic bombing offensive, aimed at crushing the enemy's will and ability to fight. Throughout Rolling Thunder certain areas and targets were ruled out for fear of escalating the conflict. The fearsome B-52s were only used well away from the major cities. The U.S. government used a "stick and carrot" approach to induce the North Vietnamese leadership to withdraw support from the ground campaign in South Vietnam, by upgrading attacks—extending bombing closer to major cities, for example—and occasionally halting the bombing. More effective was the interdiction bombing of targets involved in North Vietnam's war in the South: transport links, industrial production, and fuel supplies. U.S. strike aircraft were armed with Bullpup air-to-ground missiles guided from the cockpit with a joystick, and there were "Wild Weasel" missiles that homed in on radar emissions, for use against antiaircraft defenses. But the technology fell far short of future "smart" weapons, and precision targets such as bridges were almost as difficult for U.S. pilots to hit as they had been in World War II.

The bombing campaign was awesome in its scale. More than 300,000 sorties were flown. U.S. losses of aircraft and pilots were heavy. The bombing probably strengthened popular support for the war in North Vietnam, but in the United States it also provided a key focus for increasingly vocal opposition to the war. From April 1968, succumbing to domestic political pressure, Johnson limited the bombing to south of the 20th parallel. At the end of October, a week before presidential elections, he halted the bombing altogether. **JS**

Losses: U.S., 922 aircraft, 830 aircrew dead or captured; North Vietnamese, tens of thousands dead

◁ *Gulf of Tonkin 1964*　　　　　*Ia Drang 1965* ▷

U.S. B-52 high-altitude bombers pulverize Communist artillery positions. ➔

Chawinda   6–22 September 1965

In 1965, India and Pakistan went to war over Kashmir, an enduring source of hostility between the two countries. At Chawinda, in the largest tank battle that had been fought for twenty years, the Pakistanis halted and ultimately repelled an Indian offensive that might have won the war.

The Indian plan was to launch a surprise attack toward the Sialkot district—six miles (10 km) inside the Pakistani frontier—and seize the Grand Trunk Road, cutting Pakistan in two. Arguably, the Indians simply wanted to attack where the Pakistanis were weak, keep them off balance and prevent them from reinforcing the Lahore sector, where fighting was already fierce.

They had every reason for confidence—their Chieftain tanks were more formidable than the obsolete Sherman and more modern Patton tanks upon which the Pakistanis depended, and they heavily outnumbered their enemy. Surprise was complete and the Indians were soon across the frontier. However, a heroic stand by two squadrons of Pakistani tanks at Phillora seems to have unnerved Indian commanders at brigade level and above.

The Indian staff work was already substandard, with poor planning creating huge traffic jams for their forces. Thereafter they appear to have lost confidence and massively overestimated the enemy forces. The advance was stalled for two days, allowing the Pakistanis time to reinforce and take up strong defensive positions around Chawinda, a town in Sialkot. Here, with little space to maneuver, the Indians launched a series of ill-planned and predictable frontal assaults, which the Pakistanis beat off with great stubbornness and skillful use of Cobra antitank weapons. Let down by their commanders, the Indian soldiers eventually withdrew toward their original positions. **JS**

Losses: Indian, 120 tanks of 700, and 575 dead; Pakistani, 44 tanks of 600, casualties unknown

Indian infantrymen prepare to give covering fire during the Indian advance into Pakistan.

Ia Drang   14–18 November 1965

In March 1965 the United States sent ground forces into South Vietnam. The first major clash between U.S. soldiers and North Vietnamese troops occurred at Ia Drang, near the Cambodian border. Helicopters moved troops into the battle zone in the first large-scale test of air mobility.

The U.S. 1st Cavalry Division (Airmobile) was tasked with carrying troops to seek out Communist forces in South Vietnam's remote Central Highlands. First Battalion, 7th Cavalry, was lifted by Huey helicopters into Landing Zone (LZ) X-Ray on 14 November. The area was a base for two North Vietnamese infantry regiments. The North Vietnamese rapidly moved three battalions to surround the LZ, intending to annihilate the Americans. By mid-afternoon fighting was intense and often hand-to-hand.

The heavily outnumbered Americans called in artillery and air support to pound the North Vietnamese. Some 33,000 rounds of artillery fire were poured in and B-52

bombers, flying from Guam, devastated areas of the surrounding countryside. The North Vietnamese, for their part, sought to fight at close quarters, "hugging" the Americans so that the artillery and air support could not come into play. At night repeated probing attacks harried the surrounded Americans, and in daylight intense assaults continued. One platoon was isolated, and it took three costly attempts before they could be extricated.

By 16 November two more "Air Cav" battalions had been flown in and the North Vietnamese began to withdraw. There was further hard fighting when troops marching to another LZ were ambushed in open country on 17 November, but combat at last subsided the following day. It was clear that the U.S. soldiers were fighting an enemy that would be very hard to defeat. **JS**

Losses: U.S., 234 dead, 242 wounded; North Vietnamese, 1,500 dead

◁ *Rolling Thunder 1965*   *Long Tan 1966* ▷

Engineers of the 173d Airborne Brigade move into position in the Ia Drang valley.

Long Tan 18 August 1966

More than 60,000 Australians served in the Vietnam War as combatant allies of the United States and South Vietnam. In one of their first major encounters with Communist Viet Cong guerrillas at Long Tan, Australian troops showed much valor and won a significant victory despite being heavily outnumbered.

In 1966 the Australian Task Force was based at Nui Dat in Phuoc Tuy province, east of Saigon. On 18 August, D Company of the Royal Australian Regiment, commanded by Major Harry Smith and accompanied by three New Zealand artillery spotters, was on patrol. They met a full regiment of Viet Cong guerrillas, supported by local volunteers, in a rubber plantation south of Long Tan. The Viet Cong later claimed to have ambushed the Australians, who insisted it was a chance encounter.

A fierce firefight broke out under torrential monsoon rains that greatly hampered visibility. The Australians, numbering 108 men, were surrounded by about 2,000 guerrillas. The 3,500 shells fired by supporting New Zealand artillery did much to save the Australians from being overrun. Reputedly, at one point artillery fire was being called in against targets within 150 feet (46 m) of the Australian positions. Poor visibility meant that air support had to be restricted to attacks on Viet Cong rear positions. The Australian infantry repelled repeated Viet Cong assaults. With their ammunition nearly exhausted, fresh supplies had to be airlifted in by helicopter in nearly impossible flying conditions. The Australians held their line with great courage until, toward nightfall, armored forces broke through to assist them. Dawn the following day revealed that the guerrillas had withdrawn. **JS**

Losses: Australian, 18 dead and 24 wounded of 108; Viet Cong, 250 dead of 2,000

◁ Ia Drang 1965   Cedar Falls 1967 ▷

Cedar Falls 8–26 January 1967

The U.S. commander in Vietnam, General William Westmoreland, was determined to carry the war to the Communist enemy and use superior firepower to win decisive victories in the field. But as Operation Cedar Falls showed, they faced an elusive opponent unwilling to cooperate in his own destruction by standing to fight.

Operation Cedar Falls was directed at the "Iron Triangle," a long-established guerrilla base area 25 miles (40 km) from Saigon. It was planned as a "hammer and anvil" operation; troops would attack from the north (the "hammer"), drive the guerrillas into forces waiting to the south (the "anvil"), and crush them. A major target was the village of Ben Suc, considered the center of guerrilla activity in the area.

The "anvil" forces, U.S. and South Vietnamese infantry, were airlifted into position on 8 January. The following day the "hammer" was brought down, spearheaded by an assault by infantry carried in helicopters. The Americans had special troops to explore the network of tunnels the guerrillas had built, and new "Rome plows" that enabled engineers to build thirty-four landing grounds.

But the enemy could not be found. Rather than facing guerrilla concentrations that could be exterminated by artillery and air power, the Americans found themselves engaged in scattered small-unit combats, with the danger coming from ambush, sniper fire, and booby traps.

Considerable amounts of supplies were captured, and civilians were forcibly deported from Ben Suc and their village burned, a much criticized action recorded by television cameras. Within days of the operation ending, hailed as a success by General Westmoreland, the Viet Cong had returned to the area in strength. **JS**

Losses: U.S. and South Vietnamese, 83 dead and 345 wounded of 30,000; North Vietnamese, 750 dead, 280 captured, and 540 defected (U.S. figures)

◁ Long Tan 1966   Tet Offensive 1968 ▷

Operation Focus 5 June 1967

In June 1967, tensions between Israel and neighboring Arab states reached breaking point. Convinced that Egyptian President Abdul Gamel Nasser intended to make war, the Israeli leadership decided to launch a preemptive air strike. Code-named Operation Focus, it proved startlingly successful, gaining Israel command of the air.

The Israeli Air Force (IAF) was inferior to the Egyptian air force in numbers and roughly similar in the quality of its aircraft. Its French-supplied warplanes consisted mostly of Dassault Mirages and Mystères. Egypt had combat aircraft supplied by the Soviet Union, including MiG-21s, MiG-17s, and Sukhoi Su-7s. However, the IAF was superior in leadership and training. Its commander, Major General Mordechai Hod, planned synchronized dawn raids that would destroy the Egyptian air force on the ground.

Taking off from their Israeli bases, the aircraft headed out over the Mediterranean and then swept around to cross the Egyptian coast from an unexpected direction. They flew in flights of four, keeping to low altitude to elude Egyptian radar. Surprise was total. Cannon and rocket fire destroyed lines of MiGs that were not dispersed and had no shelters. Some of the Israeli aircraft dropped French-manufactured runway-cratering bombs to make it impossible for Egyptian planes to take off.

The Israeli air formations were able to return to their bases, swiftly rearm and refuel, and fly back for another wave of attacks on a still immobilized enemy. In two hours most of the Egyptian air force was destroyed. The IAF was then able to turn its attention to the similar destruction of the air forces of Syria and Jordan as they hurriedly entered the war in support of Egypt. **RG**

"For a small country ... this is the only solution. We have to attack them before they attack [us]."

Israeli pilot Elizier Cohen

Losses: Egyptian, 290 fighter and bomber aircraft; Israeli, 10 aircraft

⬆ *Fighter aircraft of the Egyptian air force lie reduced to burned-out wrecks following the preemptive Israeli attack.*

◁ Suez Invasion 1956   Abu Ageila 1967 ▷

Abu Ageila 5–6 June 1967

In the Six-Day War it became evident that a rapid victory over the Egyptians in the Sinai Desert was crucial if the Israelis were to triumph. The scale of their success at Abu Ageila was hailed as a classic example of what can be achieved through superior technology and preparation.

Abu Ageila controlled key routes through the Sinai peninsula and had been particularly well fortified by the Egyptians, with three lines of trenches supported by concrete bunkers. The position had caused severe problems for the Israelis in the Suez invasion. Brigadier General Ariel Sharon drew up a complex plan involving tank, artillery, infantry, and paratroopers; diversionary movements were to draw Egyptian reserves to the south.

Aided by the near-annihilation of the Egyptian air force and the cover of a fortuitous sandstorm, the Israelis reached their positions unobserved. As Israeli tanks moved to encircle Abu Ageila, paratroopers were landed by helicopter to silence Egyptian artillery. Stunned and confused, Egyptian commanders responded slowly, and the heaviest artillery barrage ever unleashed by Israeli artillery added to the chaos. As Israeli infantry entered the trench system and fought hand-to-hand with the garrison, engineers raced to clear a path through the minefields for their armor. Once the tanks were through and engaged with the Egyptians it was clear that their superior technology gave them a huge advantage. The Israelis so outgunned their enemy that they could stand off and pulverize Egyptian armor from a safe range. Surrounded, outnumbered, and poorly led, the Egyptians suffered enormous casualties before resistance collapsed. By 8 June Israeli forces had reached the Suez Canal. **JS**

Losses: Egyptian, 4,000 of 8,000; Israeli, 33 of 14,000

◁ *Operation Focus 1967*   *Jerusalem 1967* ▷

Jerusalem 6–7 June 1967

Jordan's unwise decision to join Egypt and Syria in the Six-Day War against Israel led to the Israelis storming the Old City of Jerusalem, which had been in Jordanian hands since the cease-fire of 1948. The Israelis won a stunning military victory that caused immense political complications.

The Israelis had planned to avoid fighting on their Jordanian front while carrying out their preemptive attack on Syria and Egypt, but King Hussein of Jordan ordered his Arab Legion to take the offensive. For the Israelis, the most pressing concern in Jerusalem was the protection of Mount Scopus, a vulnerable Israeli enclave within Jordanian territory. A reservist brigade of paratroopers was assigned the task of linking up with the enclave, a mission they fulfilled after a sharp fight.

By 7 June powerful Israeli forces, including Mordechai Gur's 55th Parachute Brigade, were tightening a noose around the Jordanians in Jerusalem. Despite fears of damaging Jewish holy places, Defense Minister Moshe Dayan decided to attack the Old City in strength, aiming to seize control before a cease-fire could come into force. Gur's paratroopers stormed through the Lion Gate and fought a fierce street battle with Jordanian troops. Despite coming under fire from all sides, they burst through and raced on to Temple Mount, sacred to both Jews and Muslims. Jordanian troops were still firing when Israeli soldiers stopped to pray at the Wailing Wall.

Shaken by the loss of Jerusalem, King Hussein ordered his forces to withdraw to the east bank of the Jordan River, allowing the Israelis to occupy the west bank. Israeli control of the west bank and east Jerusalem was to prove an immovable block to peace in the Middle East. **JS**

Losses: Israeli, fewer than 200 dead; Jordanian and Palestinian, unknown

◁ *Abu Ageila 1967*   *Karameh 1968* ▷

Khe Sanh   20 January–8 April 1968

Launched in parallel with the Tet Offensive, the North Vietnamese siege of Khe Sanh was intended to inflict a shattering defeat on the United States. Had the military base fallen, it would have been as much a catastrophe for the Americans as Dien Bien Phu had been for France in 1954.

Khe Sanh was an outpost close to the Laotian border and the Demilitarized Zone between North and South Vietnam. When four divisions of the North Vietnamese Army (NVA) closed in on the base in January 1968, General Westmoreland welcomed an opportunity to inflict losses on the enemy. The base's garrison of U.S. Marines and South Vietnamese troops was ordered to hold. Political leaders in the United States were less sanguine, dreading a "second Dien Bien Phu."

The NVA opened their attack with an artillery barrage, destroying every structure above ground and detonating stockpiled munitions. They dug trenches around the base and attempted to reduce its hilltop outposts. The position seemed desperate, but the Americans had the advantage of overwhelming airpower. Khe Sanh was successfully supplied from the air, and aircraft dropped nearly 100,000 tons of bombs and rockets on the NVA in the course of the battle. For the base's garrison, under siege for seventy-seven days, it was a brutal and exhausting battle, with the constant threat of enemy bombardment and infiltration. But for the North Vietnamese conscripts, under artillery and air attack that included use of napalm, it was even more brutal. When the Americans launched Operation Pegasus, the relief of Khe Sanh by land, on 1 April, the North Vietnamese could not prevent relief forces breaking through and had to abandon the siege. **JS**

> "At Khe Sanh, you're not really anywhere. You could lose it and you really haven't lost a damn thing."

Brigadier General Lowell English

Losses: U.S. and South Vietnamese, 233 dead and 1,014 wounded; North Vietnamese, 1,600 dead and more than 14,000 wounded

⬆ *A Chinook CH-47 transport helicopter flies over U.S. troops sheltering at Khe Sanh, where fighting lasted for eleven weeks.*

◁ Cedar Falls 1967   Tet Offensive 1968 ▷

Tet Offensive 31 January–24 February 1968

In the Tet Offensive, cities and towns throughout South Vietnam were attacked by Communist forces. The intention was to trigger a national uprising against South Vietnam and its U.S. supporters. In this the Communists failed, but politically the result was disastrous for the Americans.

In 1968 North Vietnamese leaders adopted a strategy of "General Offensive–General Uprising." They intended a complete victory to end the war. The plan had three phases: first, attacks at the periphery of South Vietnam would disperse U.S. forces; second, assaults on the cities would be carried out by South Vietnamese guerrillas, aided by North Vietnamese soldiers; and third, U.S. forces would be defeated in a conventional battle.

The Americans, aware that forces were assembling near the cities, expected some fighting and crucially reinforced Saigon. But the attacks, timed to coincide with the annual Tet holiday, stunned the Americans by their scale and ferocity. North Vietnamese troops and Viet Cong guerrillas

"We are beginning to win this struggle. We are on the offensive. Territory is being gained."

U.S. Vice President Hubert H. Humphrey

took control of most of the city of Hue, where some grisly atrocities were committed. In Saigon, nineteen Viet Cong guerrillas broke into the grounds of the U.S. embassy and were only defeated after a firefight lasting several hours. The national radio station was seized, causing power lines to be cut to prevent the Viet Cong from broadcasting a proclamation of the liberation of Saigon. Across the city guerrilla teams assassinated government officials and army and police officers. This provoked the notorious incident in which a police officer shot dead a Viet Cong

prisoner in front of the world's press. Every major town and city in South Vietnam experienced guerrilla attacks.

All seemed chaos, but in fact the Americans responded quickly and competently, using helicopter mobility to reinforce where needed. South Vietnamese troops fought well and not a single unit defected or collapsed during the fighting. In Saigon, as in most cities, the fighting was over in a few days. Even more disastrously for the Viet Cong, there was no national uprising—the popular support they expected to receive in the cities never materialized, a massive blow to a revolutionary army. The majority of the South Vietnamese guerrilla forces committed were destroyed. The guerrillas never recovered as a military force, the war on the Communist side henceforth being fought almost exclusively by North Vietnamese troops.

The Tet Offensive led to a U.S. military victory of the type they had been seeking since their arrival. Indeed they were able to follow up their success by making big inroads into Communist-controlled territory. But the perception of events by the U.S. media and public was very different. Images of U.S. troops fighting house-to-house in cities they had controlled for years, of the Viet Cong seemingly attacking anywhere at will, of the confusion, the violence, and the destruction all seemed to suggest that the United States really controlled nothing and had no supporters. U.S. opinion was shocked out of the assumption that the war was nearly won, and questions were raised about whether the war was a stalemate and should not be prosecuted further. The Viet Cong had aimed for a military victory, not to undermine the U.S. willingness to fight, but the latter, despite their terrible losses, is what they achieved. Within months the Americans were seeking a negotiated withdrawal. **JS**

Losses: U.S. and South Vietnamese, 10,000 dead; North Vietnamese, at least 37,000 dead and 6,000 captured; civilian, up to 13,000 dead

◁ *Khe Sanh 1968*   *Hue 1968* ▷

U.S. Marines during the battle in Hue, South Vietnam. ➔

Hue   31 January–24 February 1968

The capture of Hue, the old imperial capital of Vietnam, was a prime objective of the Communist Tet Offensive. The city was retaken from North Vietnamese forces after twenty-five days of bloody combat, during which appalling atrocities were committed against civilians.

Attacking under cover of heavy fog in the early hours of 31 January, North Vietnamese troops and South Vietnamese guerrillas seized control of much of the city, which was poorly defended. Their gains included most of the imperial citadel, but no popular uprising materialized.

South Vietnamese and U.S. forces were quickly ordered to drive the enemy out. This proved slow and bloody work. The battlefield was ideally suited for snipers and ambushes, and losses mounted. As two U.S. Marine battalions fought from house to house, retaking the city one block at a time, their casualties reportedly averaged one man killed or wounded for every yard of ground

gained. After twelve days of this, air strikes and artillery were deployed, despite the immense damage this would inevitably cause. Napalm was dropped on the citadel. Meanwhile the Communists took a grim revenge on those they regarded as enemies, including foreigners, academics, religious leaders, and government officials. Thousands were murdered and buried in mass graves.

Eventually, on 24 February, the imperial palace in the heart of the citadel was retaken. Surviving North Vietnamese troops and guerrillas slipped away. The city was left in ruins, with 116,000 of a population of 140,000 homeless. The battle was a success for the South Vietnamese and U.S. forces, but, as with the Tet Offensive in general, it brought them no political benefit. **JS**

Losses: U.S. and South Vietnamese, more than 600 dead; North Vietnamese, more than 5,000 dead; civilian, more than 5,000 dead

⟨ *Tet Offensive 1968*   *Hamburger Hill 1969* ⟩

A bomb bursts not far from U.S. troops resting in the Hue battle zone. ⬆

Karameh 21 March 1968

The clash at Karameh between Palestinian guerrillas of Yasser Arafat's Fatah movement and the Israeli army was a key moment in Arafat's rise to leadership of the Palestine liberation struggle. The Israelis prevailed in the fighting but the guerrillas fought well, greatly enhancing Fatah's reputation.

Israel's triumphs in the Six-Day War forced Palestinians to accept that nationhood could only come through their own efforts, not through the victories of the Arab nations. Hit-and-run raids from Jordan became an increasing nuisance to Israel. After a school bus hit a landmine, the Israelis opted for punitive action against Karameh, a Jordanian town known to be a center of guerrilla activity.

An armored column struck at the town at dawn. But the Fatah guerrillas had been forewarned and chose to stand and fight. They were supported by Jordanian troops, but the Palestinians insisted that they should be at the forefront of the fighting—although in reality Jordanian armor and artillery played a decisive role. Israeli troops, accustomed to operating largely with impunity, were stunned to come under fire outside the town from fighters concealed in caves. Within the town a street battle broke out, with Israelis being forced to clear neighborhoods house by house. Although they took the town, they were still under fire and taking casualties. Air strikes failed to silence the Jordanian guns and the Israelis withdrew with some difficulty after a day-long battle.

Both sides claimed victory, but Fatah was to gain considerable credit from the encounter. Palestinian self-respect surged and volunteers poured in from across the Arab world. Fatah became a force to be reckoned with and could plausibly present itself as the leader of the Palestinian national movement. **JS**

Losses: Palestinian, 120 dead, 200 wounded or captured; Jordanian, 200 casualties; Israeli, 28 dead, 69 wounded

◁ *Jerusalem 1967* 　　　　　　　　　 *Operation Badr 1973* ▷

⬆ *Israeli troops approach the Damia Bridge on their way to Karameh in Jordan.*

Hamburger Hill 10–20 May 1969

In spring 1969 a U.S. operation was launched against North Vietnamese forces in the A Shau Valley. After many attempts U.S. troops stormed a well-defended position on Ap Bai Hill, but heavy losses caused an outcry in the United States and led Ap Bai to be dubbed "Hamburger Hill."

Troops of the 101st Airborne Division were airlifted to the valley, near the Laotian border, to destroy army bases of the North Vietnamese. A battalion came across North Vietnamese forces strongly entrenched on Ap Bai Hill and attacked. The engagement proved to be much tougher and bloodier than the Americans had expected. The North Vietnamese had constructed strong and well-concealed bunkers. Heavy jungle growth made artillery spotting ineffective—indeed, the difficulty in identifying targets meant that the Americans were repeatedly attacked by their own helicopters. It was very much an infantry battle, fought by small units, to neutralize

individual bunkers, each of which proved costly. Repeated assaults on the hill were repelled and casualties mounted.

The hill itself was of little strategic value, and the attack might have been called off, but the press were reporting failure, and three more battalions were sent in to ensure victory. After a heavy artillery barrage and the liberal use of napalm on the crest of the hill, all four U.S. battalions launched a simultaneous attack that reached the crest after bitter fighting. U.S. commanders claimed victory as North Vietnamese losses were heavy. But in the United States a public outcry followed, with demands for an explanation for the sacrifice of so many young American lives for an allegedly worthless objective. Stung, President Richard Nixon quietly instructed that U.S. military casualties must henceforth be minimized, effectively ending U.S. Army "search and destroy" missions. **JS**

Losses: U.S., 56–72 dead; North Vietnamese, 610 dead

◁ Hue 1968   Quang Tri 1972 ▷

101st Airborne Division troopers on Hamburger Hill.

Quang Tri 1 March–1 May 1972

In an attempt to achieve a rapid victory, the North Vietnamese army launched a massive conventional offensive at Easter 1972. The province of Quang Tri lay in the path of a thrust toward Hue and was overrun, but the offensive ultimately failed in the face of overwhelming U.S. airpower.

The North Vietnamese leadership believed that, with only 65,000 U.S. troops left in Vietnam, a sudden violent blow against the South Vietnamese army might cause a collapse. The intention was to strike at Hue, then attack in central South Vietnam and cut the country in half.

At the end of March the North Vietnamese invaded Quang Tri province across the Demilitarized Zone separating North from South Vietnam, stunning the South Vietnamese by the effectiveness of their heavy artillery. South Vietnamese morale sagged under the barrage and after several days of fighting an entire regiment surrendered. A battalion of South Vietnamese

Rangers broke and fled after being mauled by two North Vietnamese regiments. South Vietnamese marines could not hold the vital bridge at Dong Ha, and had to fight their way out of encirclement. By 1 May the North Vietnamese had achieved a significant victory. But as troops and civilian refugees fled southward, the South Vietnamese army rallied in front of Hue, supported by U.S. air strikes and naval gunfire, and the offensive ground to a halt.

President Richard Nixon, although unwilling to commit U.S. ground forces to the fighting, unleashed Operation Linebacker, an air assault on North Vietnam that destroyed communications and cut supplies to the North Vietnamese army by two-thirds. Quang Tri was eventually retaken by the South Vietnamese in a hard-fought campaign from June to September. **JS**

Losses: South Vietnamese, more than 5,000 dead; North Vietnamese, unknown

◁ *Hamburger Hill 1969*　　　　*Hanoi and Haiphong 1972* ▷

⬆ *A South Vietnamese soldier carries a young victim of a truck mine explosion.*

Hanoi and Haiphong 18–29 December 1972

The bombing of North Vietnamese cities by B-52s over Christmas was the last massive use of U.S. airpower in the Vietnam War. It succeeded in forcing the North Vietnamese to return to negotiations and sign a peace agreement, but the terms hardly suggested a U.S. victory.

Peace terms had been agreed between North Vietnam and the United States in October 1972, but had been rejected by the South Vietnamese. When the North refused further talks, President Richard Nixon authorized Operation Linebacker II, a brief but devastating bombing campaign intended to render North Vietnam defenseless.

The key element in the raids was the deployment of B-52 bombers with a massive conventional payload. The air defenses of Hanoi and the main port at Haiphong were formidable by this time and at first losses of B-52s were, from a U.S. viewpoint, worryingly high—largely because they had approached their targets from predictable

heights and directions. Tactics were quickly changed, but the campaign cost the Americans fifteen B-52s, as well as nine other aircraft. Nearly every surface-to-air missile possessed by North Vietnam was fired, but the size and power of the air raids overwhelmed the defenders.

The B-52s flew over 700 sorties and more than a hundred electronic-warfare aircraft helped suppress the air defenses. After more than 20,000 tons of bombs had been dropped, nearly every military target around the cities was destroyed. In fact, after eleven days there were few military targets left to bomb in the country. Stray bombs did kill people in a Hanoi hospital, to the outrage of antiwar protesters, but overall civilian casualties were fairly modest given the intensity of the attacks. A peace agreement was signed on 27 January 1973. **JS**

Losses: U.S., 24 aircraft, 43 dead, 49 captured; North Vietnamese, more than 1,600 dead

◁ *Quang Tri 1972*   *Fall of Saigon 1975* ▷

In response to constant U.S. air raids, bomb shelters were improvised everywhere in Hanoi.

Operation Badr 6–8 October 1973

In the opening engagement of the Yom Kippur War, Egyptian forces launched a surprise attack on Israelis stationed on the east bank of the Suez Canal. For the first time ever, Arab troops achieved complete victory over the Israelis. Arab pride surged and Israeli confidence was badly shaken.

Since the Six-Day War of 1967, the Israelis, confident of their military superiority, had disdained to negotiate seriously the return of the Sinai peninsula to Egypt. In 1973 Egypt's President Anwar Sadat decided to fight a limited offensive to force the Israelis out of their defensive positions on the Suez Canal (the Bar Lev Line) and compel them to negotiate seriously.

The Egyptian attack, code-named Operation Badr, was launched on the day of the Israeli Yom Kippur religious festival. While the Bar Lev Line was subjected to air strikes and a massive artillery barrage, 4,000 Egyptian troops crossed the canal in dinghies under a smokescreen. As Egyptian reinforcements followed behind, the 550 Israelis occupying the Bar Lev Line were overwhelmed. The well-planned operation proceeded with great efficiency, with pontoon bridges laid across the canal and gaps blasted in sand ramparts that blocked passage from the canal bank into the Sinai desert. Within ten hours Egyptian tanks and artillery were across the canal.

Egypt's Soviet-supplied surface-to-air missiles denied the Israelis their usual aerial dominance, and air strikes against the bridges were a failure. The Egyptians dug in to defend the bridgehead. When the Israelis sent in ill-coordinated counterattacks with armor, the Egyptians' antitank missiles wrought fearful carnage—170 tanks were lost by 8 October. Egypt had recorded an impressive success that electrified the Arab world. **JS**

Losses: Israeli, 3,700 dead, wounded, or captured; Egyptian, fewer than 300 dead

◁ *Karameh 1968*   *Golan Heights 1973* ▷

⬆ *Egyptian troops salute a portrait of their political leader, President Anwar El Sadat.*

Golan Heights   6–22 October 1973

At the same time that the Egyptians launched their attack on Israeli defenses across the Suez Canal in Operation Badr, Egypt's ally Syria took the offensive in the Golan Heights, an area occupied by the Israelis in the 1967 Six-Day War. After initial setbacks, Israel achieved a convincing victory.

Supported by artillery and air strikes, the Syrians pushed 700 tanks forward into the maze of minefields and antitank ditches that constituted the Israeli defensive line. There was a real possibility that the Syrians might break through. Outnumbered Israeli armored formations fought desperate delaying actions, taking heavy losses, as did Israeli aircraft flying ground-attack missions.

The Syrians scored a notable success on the first day when their commandos captured an Israeli position on Mount Hermon in a helicopter assault. By 7 October Syrian tanks had penetrated the Israeli defenses in the southern sector of the Golan, pressing toward the Jordan River. But the arrival of Israeli reserves in growing numbers began to turn the tide. Although Israel's 7th Armored Brigade's strength was reduced to seven functioning tanks after four days' attritional fighting, by 10 October the Syrians had mostly been pushed back to their start lines.

As the United States airlifted in equipment to replace Israel's losses, the Israeli government decided to move over to the offensive, invading Syrian territory and threatening Damascus. Syria found itself fighting for survival and by 12 October it appeared nothing could stop Israel occupying the Syrian capital. However, the unexpected arrival of armored forces from Iraq and Jordan on their southern flank took the momentum out of the Israeli charge. International diplomatic pressure brought a cease-fire on 22 October. **RG**

Losses: Syrian, 3,500 dead, 7,000 wounded; Israeli, 772 dead, 2,453 wounded

◁ Operation Badr 1973

Chinese Farm 1973 ▷

Chinese Farm   15–18 October 1973

The success of Egypt's Operation Badr saw Egyptian forces establish bridgeheads east of the Suez Canal. After heavy fighting for the position known as the Chinese Farm, however, an Israeli counter-offensive crossed the canal in the opposite direction, giving final victory in the war to Israel.

Intoxicated by the success of Operation Badr, the Egyptians were tempted to push on into the Sinai. Four armored brigades launched a new offensive, but were cut to pieces by the Israelis. The engagement allowed the Israelis to exploit a serious Egyptian error, revealed to them by U.S. spy flights: there was a gap between the Egyptian 2nd and 3rd armies east of the Suez Canal, at a place called the Chinese Farm. Major General Ariel Sharon was tasked with punching a corridor through to the canal, where a successful crossing would wreak havoc in the Egyptian rear, cut off the Egyptian forces east of the canal, and even threaten Cairo.

When the attack began on the night of 15–16 October, Egyptian troops defended the Chinese Farm in close-quarters fighting, exploiting its extensive network of irrigation ditches and using antitank missiles to great effect. Sharon was able to open his corridor to the canal, however, and defend it against desperate armored counterattacks. After Israeli paratroopers established a bridgehead west of the canal, a huge, specially designed pontoon bridge capable of carrying Israeli tanks was dragged into position under heavy fire. The Chinese Farm fell to the Israelis on 18 October and Israeli forces spread out west of the canal. The Egyptian 3rd Army, trapped in its position east of the canal, was in a desperate plight, but the United States forced the Israelis to accept a cease-fire, reluctantly observed on 25 October. **JS**

Losses: Unknown

◁ Golan Heights 1973

Raid on Entebbe 1976 ▷

Israeli tanks cross a bridge built by their troops over the Suez Canal. ➡

Fall of Saigon   4 March–30 April 1975

The Fall of Saigon was the last event of the Vietnam War. The Paris Peace Accords of January 1973 had allowed the Americans a face-saving way to extricate their troops from the war. Few expected the peace to hold, but the speed with which South Vietnam collapsed stunned the world.

The peace agreement left North Vietnamese army units where they were in the South, and low-intensity fighting continued. The South Vietnamese were profligate in the expenditure of munitions and, with rapidly rising fuel prices, faced a financial crisis. Rampant inflation, glaring corruption, and the loss of U.S. support undermined army morale, with 24,000 troops deserting every month.

The North Vietnamese, resupplied and scenting a final victory, were eager to fight. In December 1974 they tested whether the United States would resume bombing if they blatantly violated the peace by invading Phuoc Long province, only 40 miles (65 km) from Saigon. Congress rejected President Ford's appeals for increased aid for

"We shouldn't be arrogant about our power and the use of our power."

Walter Cronkite

South Vietnam and there was no U.S. response. The speed and ease of the operation showed that the South's willingness to resist was disintegrating.

In March 1975 the North Vietnamese launched offensives in the Central Highlands and in Quang Tri province in northern South Vietnam. South Vietnamese counterattacks failed as large numbers of troops deserted to protect their families. On 13 March South Vietnam's President Thieu ordered his army to withdraw southward, where supply lines would be shorter, but

retreat rapidly became a rout as deserters, refugees, and troops clogged roads and spread panic. Emboldened, the North Vietnamese ordered their entire strength on the offensive—Saigon was to fall that spring. With only three divisions left to defend the capital, there was no question about the outcome. A desperate scramble to escape the approaching North Vietnamese army ensued. Some South Vietnamese units fought on with great courage—the 29th Division made a heroic last stand at Xuan Loc on the approaches to Saigon. But one air force pilot bombed the presidential palace before flying off to defect.

On 21 April Thieu announced his resignation on television, denouncing the United States for betraying South Vietnam in its hour of need. By 27 April, Saigon was encircled by 100,000 North Vietnamese troops, but there was hardly a need for such a force. U.S. citizens were already being evacuated, and Vietnamese thronged around the U.S. embassy, frantic for a seat on the helicopters. Operation Frequent Wind did evacuate 7,000 people, but they were only a fraction of those with reason to fear the North Vietnamese. Desperate people tried to get aboard already overcrowded boats on the Saigon River. The North Vietnamese did not hinder the flight.

When an artillery barrage announced that the final assault was about to be launched, there was little resistance left. North Vietnamese troops began to occupy strategic points in the city, and within hours the South Vietnamese government offered to surrender, but they were ignored. The North Vietnamese army saw no need to deny themselves a military victory to crown decades of struggle. At noon on 30 April, a T-54 tank burst through the gates of the presidential palace, an act seen on television across the world. A few South Vietnamese units fought on in the Central Highlands and Mekong delta for a while longer, but the war was effectively over. **JS**

Losses: Unknown

⟨ *Hanoi and Haiphong 1972*

U.S. helicopters evacuate residents of Saigon on 29 April 1975. ➔

Quifangondo 10 November 1975

The Angolan Civil War began as a struggle to determine which liberation movement would run the country on independence from Portugal in November 1975. The battle at Quifangondo, which also involved foreign intervention forces, established a left-wing government in Angola.

Holden Roberto, the leader of the FNLA (Angolan National Liberation Front), was supported by South African and Zairian troops, as well as by Portuguese mercenaries. He planned to enter the capital, Luanda, before independence from Portugal was declared on 11 November, and prevent the Marxist MPLA (Popular Movement for the Liberation of Angola) forming the government. He was warned that advancing down the only road to Luanda without any flanking movements to warn of ambush was foolhardy. But in his haste he ignored such concerns, and anyway FNLA troops had no desire to leave the road to enter a crocodile-infested swamp.

Unfortunately for Roberto, Cuban leader Fidel Castro had rushed troops across the Atlantic to support his fellow Marxists, the MPLA. The role played by Cuban troops in the battle at Quifangondo is disputed; there were either fewer than 200 supporting a mainly MPLA action, or 800 fighting the battle with limited MPLA support. But they certainly played a crucial part. Dug in along hilltops overlooking the road, they ambushed the FNLA with a murderous barrage from Soviet-made multiple rocket launchers—the fact that the fuses had arrived late meant that this was their first use in Angola, making them even more devastating to Roberto's poorly trained troops. South African artillery was outranged, the Zairian soldiers simply fled, and within three hours the FNLA had virtually ceased to exist. The MPLA still ruled Angola in 2010. **JS**

Losses: FNLA, hundreds dead or wounded of 2,300–3,300; Cuban, fewer than 6 dead or wounded; MPLA, unknown

Raid on Entebbe 3–4 July 1976

In the 1970s Palestinian terrorists found that hijacking airliners was the easiest way to attack Israel and its allies. In 1976 the Israeli response to a hijacking at Entebbe turned the tide against the terrorists, proving that hostage-takers could be defeated by a well-planned rescue mission.

On 27 June two members of the Popular Front for the Liberation of Palestine and two German terrorists hijacked an airliner bound from Tel Aviv for Paris. They flew to Uganda's Entebbe International Airport in Uganda, knowing that Ugandan ruler Idi Amin Dada was a declared enemy of Israel. At Entebbe they were joined by other Palestinian militants. After freeing all non-Jewish passengers, they demanded the release of imprisoned terrorists, or the Jewish hostages would be killed.

Since Entebbe was 3,000 miles (4,800 km) from Israel and inside hostile territory, a rescue attempt appeared unlikely. However, a plan was approved for a mission to be led by Major General Dan Shomron. Four C-130 Hercules transport aircraft took off from Sharm el-Sheikh and flew to Entebbe undetected. Arriving after dark, they came in to land behind a scheduled cargo aircraft and taxied to an unlit area of the airport to disgorge their troops. The assault on the transit hall where the hostages were being held was entrusted to Lieutenant Colonel Jonathan Netanyahu. His commandos burst into the building and killed the terrorists; three hostages also died.

As the freed hostages were taken to the aircraft, fighting broke out between Ugandan troops and the Israelis. The Israelis destroyed Ugandan MiG fighters on the ground to prevent them following and the Hercules aircraft took off, fifty-seven minutes after landing. Their arrival in Israel occasioned delirious rejoicing. **RG**

Losses: Ugandan, 35 dead; terrorist, 7 dead; Israeli, 1 dead and 5 wounded; hostages, 3 dead

◀ Karameh 1968   Lebanon 1982 ▶

San Carlos 21–25 May 1982

Britain sent a Task Force to retake the Falkland Islands from Argentinian forces, which had occupied them in April 1982. The Royal Navy was tasked with protecting landings of men and equipment from attack by enemy aircraft based in Argentina. It succeeded, but at a cost.

The threat posed by Argentinian aircraft had already been shown during the British approach to the Falklands, when the destroyer HMS *Sheffield* was crippled by an Exocet missile. The Task Force's only air cover was provided by short-takeoff vertical-landing Sea Harriers operating from small carriers. The carriers had to be kept at a distance, for their loss to air attack would have been disastrous. Destroyers and frigates, positioned in San Carlos Sound to screen the landings with their antiaircraft missiles, bore the brunt of the Argentinian attacks.

The first landings on 21 May were quickly detected and Argentinian aircraft began their onslaught within hours. Both sides threw themselves into the fight with courage and determination. To the British, San Carlos Sound became known as "bomb alley." The Argentinian pilots, chiefly flying A-4 Skyhawks and IAI Daggers, attacked at low altitude, mostly dropping unguided 1,000-lb. bombs.

The Royal Navy's Rapier surface-to-air missiles proved less effective than had been hoped and the Sea Harriers struggled to gain command of the air. Among the picket ships, the frigates HMS *Antelope* and *Ardent* and the destroyer *Coventry* were sunk. Losses might have been worse; dropped at too low an altitude for their fuses, the bombs often failed to explode. The container ship MV *Atlantic Conveyor* was sunk by Exocet missiles, its irreplaceable supplies including eleven helicopters, but by 25 May the British forces were safely ashore. **JS**

Losses: British, 2 frigates, 1 destroyer, and 1 container ship sunk, 49 dead; Argentinian, 22 aircraft, 11 dead

Stanley 1982 ⊳

Khorramshahr 24 May 1982

Iran and Iraq went to war in September 1980. The loss of Khorramshahr, a major Iranian port and oil-refining facility, early in the war was a grievous blow to Iran. Its reconquest in 1982 marked a turning point in the war, signaling that the Islamic Revolution would survive.

In the early days of the war the Iranian army had been ravaged by the excesses of the Islamic Revolution, with officers purged and supply and maintenance systems in chaos; it was in no state to fight the highly professional Iraqis. But, despite the turmoil of revolution and colossal economic problems, Iran managed to rebuild an effective military machine remarkably rapidly. The *Pasdaran*, or Revolutionary Guards, were formed as shock troops fueled with religious fervor. But more importantly, officers who had served the former regime were rehabilitated and proved competent in combining the *Pasdaran* and their human-wave tactics with artillery and airpower.

The Iranians mounted Operation Jerusalem to retake Khorramshahr, largely reduced to rubble after two years of bombardment. Attacks in the north and south cut off Iraqi communications to the city. In the center, massed infantry attacks at night—mainly by the *Pasdaran* supported by fighter aircraft and helicopters—and major armored thrusts broke through the two main defensive lines. Within the city, Iraqi troops took up strong defensive positions and fought well, few relishing the thought of capture, but they were simply overwhelmed by the weight of the assaults they faced. After two days of savage street fighting the city was retaken. Of more than 4,000 square miles (10,360 sq km) of Iranian territory conquered by Iraq, a mere 200 square miles (520 sq km) remained. Iran seemed poised to go on to defeat Iraq completely. **JS**

Losses: Iraqi, 25,000–35,000 dead, wounded, or captured; Iranian, at least 10,000 dead or wounded

Basra 1982 ⊳

Lebanon 6 June–4 September 1982

The Israeli invasion of Lebanon in 1982 was intended to end cross-border attacks by the Palestine Liberation Organization (PLO). Although the PLO was dislodged from Lebanon, the invasion was traumatic for Israel, which stood accused of complicity in the massacre of Palestinian civilians.

The arrival of the PLO in Lebanon, after being expelled from Jordan, upset a delicate political balance and plunged the country into civil war in 1975. Syria soon intervened and established a presence in the Bekaa Valley. From bases in southern Lebanon the PLO shelled Israeli settlements. Israel helped arm Lebanese Maronite Christian militiamen, but in 1982 decided to deal with the PLO itself. The Cabinet assumed that the invasion would be a limited operation, venturing only a few miles into Lebanon. But Defense Minister Ariel Sharon intended to take Beirut. He believed that if he smashed the PLO there, its influence would be destroyed.

Four armored columns, aided by marine landings and supported by the entire Israeli Air Force (IAF), dashed north. The IAF engaged the Syrians and inflicted a spectacular defeat on them, shooting down ninety-six jets without loss. The Syrians hurriedly agreed to a cease-fire. But Beirut was tougher; it took two weeks and the aid of Maronite militiamen to encircle the city. Massive air strikes and artillery bombardment of Palestinian-held West Beirut followed, with the city's electricity and water supplies targeted in order to persuade the Lebanese to expel the PLO themselves. It took another seventy days of hard fighting before the PLO fighters negotiated their withdrawal. Israelis entered Beirut to restore order, but were censured for complicity when militiamen massacred undefended Palestinians in camps at Sabra and Chatila. **JS**

Losses: Israeli, fewer than 700 dead; Palestinian and Syrian, nearly 10,000 dead; civilian, nearly 18,000 dead

◁ *Raid on Entebbe 1976*   *Lebanon 2006* ▷

A rocket is fired from a Palestinian area of Beirut. ⬆

Stanley 11–14 June 1982

The Argentinian forces on the Falkland Islands were chiefly concentrated around the town of Stanley. At the culmination of a tough campaign, they were forced to surrender after multiple attacks by British troops. The Argentinian surrender brought down the dictatorship of General Leopoldo Galtieri.

Lacking helicopters after the sinking of MV *Atlantic Conveyor*, British commandos and paratroopers had to foot-slog to Stanley over rough terrain, heavily laden with supplies in atrocious weather conditions. On the way the paras won a fierce battle at Goose Green on 28–29 May. Meanwhile another brigade was arriving from Britain, and heavy casualties were experienced when ships carrying combat troops were hit by an air strike in Bluff Cove.

As they approached Stanley, the British needed to break through a defendable ring of hills around the port. They threw in their elite units in a series of night attacks. The first night, 11–12 June, saw assaults on Mount Harriet,

Two Sisters, and Mount Longdon. The paratroopers assigned to Longdon had the hardest task, against Argentinian bunkers, which stalled their advance several times. It was a battle of grenade, bullet, and bayonet in the bloodiest single ground engagement of the war.

Two nights later, Wireless Ridge, Tumbledown, and Mount William were attacked, and again there was hand-to-hand fighting, with the Scots Guards at Tumbledown facing the only well-executed Argentinian counterattack of the war in a ten-hour battle. The British prevailed in every engagement. The key to their success lay not in their equipment or in numbers, but in professionalism and self-belief. The Argentinians often fought well, but conscripts were no real match for elite troops. Their commander, Brigadier General Menendez, surrendered on 14 June. **JS**

Losses: British, 46 dead; Argentinian, 124 dead, 9,800 captured

◁ *San Carlos 1982*

⬆ *Argentinian soldiers catch up on news in Port Stanley.*

Basra   11–28 July 1982

After its victory at Khorramshahr in May 1982, Iran glimpsed an opportunity of overthrowing Iraqi dictator, Saddam Hussein, and spreading the Islamic Revolution. The failure of an Iranian offensive at Basra would mean that the war would drag on in a costly stalemate for six more years.

Although Iraq had suffered severe reverses, Saddam had one huge advantage—the West was appalled at the prospect of an Iranian victory, and rushed to aid the man they deemed a bastion against fundamentalism. Modern weapons arrived in considerable quantities from Europe, Soviet advisers helped design the defenses of Basra, and U.S. satellite and signals intelligence proved vital. Also, the Iraqis were fighting to protect their homeland, which helped to offset the religious fervor of their enemies.

The Iranians launched a two-day artillery barrage and sent in human waves of *Pasdaran* (Revolutionary Guards). By this time many of the *Pasdaran* were child soldiers, as young as thirteen, sent into battle—often ordered to charge across minefields to clear a passage—with plastic keys to paradise and jackets stencilled with Ayatollah Homaini's permission to enter. Three major assaults were launched, each one failing with enormous casualties. The defenses, based on a network of canals and moats, held. Newly supplied helicopters and missiles inflicted severe damage to Iranian armor. Human waves were cut down by machine gun and artillery fire. Where breakthroughs threatened, Iraqi armor counterattacked and stemmed them, though with heavy losses. The death toll was appalling, and all Iran gained from it was a strategically worthless strip of swamp 10 miles (16 km) deep into Iraqi territory. With assured outside aid, Iraq could endure the resulting war of attrition as long as necessary. **JS**

Losses: Unknown, but probably in tens of thousands on both sides

◁ *Khorramshahr 1982*   *Desert Storm 1991* ▷

Iraqi soldiers behind sandbags, near Basra. ⬆

Grenada   25–28 October 1983

The invasion of the Caribbean island of Grenada was the first major outing for U.S. forces since the Vietnam War. It was hailed by President Reagan as a return to form after the demoralization of the 1970s, but the operation was militarily far from flawless and politically highly controversial.

Grenadan leader Maurice Bishop had pursued left-wing policies with Soviet and Cuban aid since 1979. In Washington he was seen as a communist stooge and a new airport under construction was deemed a transfer point for weapons destined for Latin American revolutionaries. Bishop's assassination, by a more hard-line Military Revolutionary Council on 19 October 1983, was taken as the signal to act. Publicly justified by the need to protect U.S. students in Grenada, Operation Urgent Fury was hastily thrown together. The only resistance was likely to come from a contingent of Cubans, claimed to be construction workers by Havana.

Marines and paratroopers, supported by air strikes, led the invasion on 25 October. Fighting was fierce, especially around the airport defended by the Cubans—and, unexpectedly, the Grenadan militia put up a stout fight. Inadequate communications and intelligence led to "friendly fire" casualties and accidental attacks on civilians. Helicopter gunships, naval gunfire, and reinforcements were deployed until, after three days, resistance ended.

The U.S. public largely supported the invasion but internationally many were outraged at the violation of Grenada's sovereignty on such a flimsy pretext. Even Britain, whose queen was also Grenada's nominal head of state, condemned it. The United States had overthrown a communist dictatorship and restored democracy, but many Grenadans were alienated from the new regime. **JS**

Losses: U.S., 19 dead and 150 wounded of 7,000; Cuban, 25 dead and 59 wounded of 600–800; Grenadan, 45 dead, 337 wounded of up to 1,500

⬆ *Helicopters bring U.S. soldiers into Grenada.*

Desert Storm   16 January–26 February 1991

In Operation Desert Storm, a U.S.-led, U.N.-authorized coalition of thirty-four nations set out to expel Saddam Hussein's Iraqi forces from Kuwait, which they had invaded in August 1990. The operation was a rapid and complete success, providing an astonishing display of the capabilities of the latest military technology.

A huge coalition force was assembled in Saudi Arabia under the command of U.S. General Norman Schwarzkopf. Once diplomatic moves to dislodge Saddam Hussein's troops had failed, on 16 January an air campaign began. Over the next thirty-eight days coalition aircraft flew over 100,000 sorties and Baghdad became the most heavily bombed city since World War II. Especially effective were the F-117A stealth ground-attack aircraft, seeing their first major use in warfare. Hundreds of cruise missiles were fired from warships in the Gulf. "Smart" precision munitions kept civilian casualties relatively low. With some targets struck up to thirty times, Iraqi communications,

> *"The great duel, the mother of all battles, has begun. . . . The dawn of victory nears."*
>
> *Saddam Hussein*

electricity, and water supplies collapsed. Iraqi military positions in Kuwait were also systematically pounded.

Saddam ordered Scud missile attacks on Israel, attempting to widen the war and detach Muslim nations from the coalition, but U.S. pressure prevented Israeli retaliation. British SAS troops were deployed within Iraq to locate the mobile Scud launchers so they could be destroyed. Despairing at seeing his forces steadily degraded, one Iraqi general launched a brief and unsuccessful counterattack on the Saudi town of Khafji,

but most Iraqi soldiers crouched in their dugouts along the Kuwaiti border and tried to survive the bombing. Amphibious exercises by U.S. Marines fooled the Iraqis into expecting a seaborne invasion, while the coalition main force assembled far inland.

On 23 February the coalition ground offensive was launched. A stunning opening barrage by M270 multiple missile launchers was followed by bulldozers tearing gaps through the sandbanks denoting the border with Kuwait, followed by a tank assault. Unfortunate Iraqis positioned there were crushed under the tracks or buried alive. It rapidly became clear that Iraqi troops were totally demoralized, and thousands surrendered immediately. Sporadic artillery fire was the only resistance offered. Superior U.S. tanks, when they encountered Iraqi armor, destroyed their enemy without loss. Within forty hours such resistance as there was had effectively ceased. Even Iraq's elite Republican Guard collapsed after a brief fight.

By the second day of the ground battle coalition forces were penetrating deep inside Iraq. Anti-Saddam Shia Arabs and Kurds were encouraged to revolt, expecting imminent liberation. Saddam needed to save the remnants of his army simply for his regime to survive. He began a withdrawal from Kuwait, after ordering around 700 oil wells to be set alight. A panic-stricken retreat ensued. The last column of fleeing Iraqi troops was caught by coalition aircraft on the Kuwait-Iraq road and incinerated. The road to Baghdad was open, but coalition leaders had already decided that the destruction of Saddam's regime would destabilize the region and break up the coalition. Instead a cease-fire was agreed that left Saddam in power. The Shia Arabs and Kurds who had risen in open rebellion were abandoned to their fate. **JS**

Losses: Coalition, fewer than 400 dead of nearly 1,000,000; Iraqi, 25,000–35,000 dead of 260,000-545,000 (estimates vary); civilian, up to 5,000 dead

◁ *Basra 1982*   *Invasion of Iraq 2003* ▷

Destruction lines a road in northern Kuwait after coalition forces attacked fleeing military personnel.

Sarajevo   5 April 1992–29 February 1996

The collapse of Yugoslavia in 1991–92 led to conflict between ethnic groups. Bosnian Muslims in Sarajevo resisted the Serbs through the longest siege in modern European history. The plight of the city's population outraged world opinion and eventually led to Western military intervention.

Before fighting broke out in Bosnia in April 1992, the Serbs constructed reinforced artillery positions in the hills overlooking Sarajevo, reasoning that if they could crush Bosnian resistance there, they might crush it everywhere in Bosnia. Once the conflict began they occupied the positions and some of the city suburbs, and imposed a total blockade, denying Sarajevo food, power, and water. Although far better armed than the Bosnian militia defending the city, the Serbs lacked the numbers to storm it, and settled in to pound it into submission. The Bosnian militia, despite superior numbers, lacked the weapons to break the siege. It became a contest of endurance.

Serb artillery inflicted great damage—on average more than 300 shells struck Sarajevo every day, and targets such as schools, hospitals, and homes were not spared. Nearly every building in the city was damaged. Snipers added to the dangers and nowhere in the city was safe. Sarajevo came near to starvation before the United Nations, in control of the international airport, organized humanitarian relief. A tunnel, completed in mid-1993, connected city and airport, allowing supplies through. But malnutrition became a serious problem, and in winter the elderly perished in unheated homes. The shelling, especially two ugly incidents at the Markale market, infuriated world opinion. In May 1996 NATO launched air strikes against the Serbs, eventually forcing them to accept the Dayton Accords, which lifted the siege. **JS**

Losses: Serbian, more than 2,000 dead of 30,000; Bosnian, more than 6,000 dead of 40,000; civilian, about 10,000 dead

Kosovo 1999 [>]

A resident looks out from the window of a bullet-riddled building. ⬆

Mogadishu 3–4 October 1993

U.S. forces, intervening in war-torn Somalia for humanitarian reasons, ran into trouble on a mission to seize a Somali militia leader in the capital Mogadishu. Most of the troops were extricated, but the affair was widely deemed a fiasco and, for a time, discouraged U.S. military adventures.

U.S. forces entered Somalia to protect the distribution of food aid, which was being hampered by local warlords. The Americans decided they had to neutralize the worst offender, Mohamed Farrah Aidid. Major General William Garrison was tasked with leading a raid by special forces on the Olympic Hotel in Mogadishu, where Aidid was thought to be hiding.

Landed from helicopters, an assault group secured the hotel and took twenty-four prisoners—although not Aidid, who was absent. Special forces in a column of vehicles following to extract them from the hotel were delayed by Somali road blocks and subjected to continual fire. Two Black Hawk helicopters were shot down by rocket-propelled grenades—an incident dramatized in the 2001 film *Black Hawk Down*—leaving surviving aircrew at risk at the helicopter crash sites. Most of the special forces troops fought through to the first crash site, but were then pinned down under heavy fire. The troops could only shelter in nearby houses and wait for morning. Two special force troopers reached the second crash site and fought off the Somalis for a short time before they were killed and the helicopter pilot captured.

The next morning a U.S. and U.N. relief force of around 100 vehicles fought its way to the first crash site and extracted survivors, fighting a running battle every step of the way. The bodies of dead Americans were dragged through the streets by the Somalis. The failure effectively spelled the end of the U.S. mission in Somalia. **JS**

Losses: U.S., 19 dead and 84 wounded of 180; U.N., 13 casualties; Somali, 700–1,500 of 2,000–4,000

A girl watches as U.S. Marines head for the American embassy in Mogadishu.

Grozny 31 December 1993–6 March 1994

The Muslim Chechens fought for independence from Russia after the breakup of the Soviet Union in 1991. Though eventually victorious in taking the Chechen capital, Grozny, Russian forces suffered humiliating reverses against a separatist revolt that became increasingly intransigent.

Blithely ignoring the Chechen tradition of centuries of resistance to Russian rule, the Russians assumed that the Chechen claim to independence did not need to be taken seriously. The Russian defense minister, General Pavel Grachev, asserted that a single regiment of paratroopers would rapidly bring them to their senses.

Russian military plans proved to be pitifully inadequate. It was assumed that the Chechen "bandits" would flee if faced with tanks in Grozny, even without infantry support. But the tank crews lacked maps, information, or experience in urban warfare, and were without clear orders; they were simply told to occupy the city. Entering Grozny on New Year's Eve, they met no resistance until they entered the city center and were ambushed by Chechens who tossed grenades into the tanks from upper windows. Russians trying to escape burning vehicles were cut down by automatic weapons, or, if they reached a building, greeted by a Chechen *kinzhal* (dagger).

Horrified Russians watched the disaster unfold on live television. Thereafter bruised Russian national pride would settle for nothing less than complete victory. Artillery and high-altitude bombing were used to reduce Grozny to rubble. It still took three weeks of heavy fighting and high casualties for the Russians to secure the city center, and fighting in the southern sector continued several weeks before the Chechens withdrew to fight on from the hills in an increasingly ferocious war. **JS**

Losses: Russian, 2,000 dead admitted, probably many more; Chechen, tens of thousands dead

Kosovo 24 March–10 June 1999

In 1999 NATO carried out a bombing campaign against Serbia to end the "ethnic cleansing" of Albanians in the former Yugoslav province of Kosovo. British Prime Minister Tony Blair, the most committed advocate of the bombing, saw it as opening a new era of international intervention.

From 1996 there was fighting between the Kosovo Liberation Army (KLA) and the Serbian forces of President Slobodan Milošević. After the breakdown of peace negotiations in March 1999, NATO announced it would take military action to stop Serbian massacres of ethnic Albanians. NATO political leaders were unwilling to commit ground troops, fearing that the level of casualties involved would be unacceptable to their electorates. Bombing seemed the better option, holding out hope of a quick victory with minimal NATO casualties.

Operating from bases in Italy or from carriers stationed in the Adriatic, NATO aircraft pounded military targets, but also bridges, factories, government buildings, and water and electricity supplies. Tomahawk cruise missiles were also fired from ships and aircraft. There was little the Serbs could do to defend themselves—they shot down only two NATO aircraft, though one, embarrassingly, was an F-117 Nighthawk stealth bomber. There were some serious mistakes in targeting—an Albanian refugee convoy, a passenger train, and even the Chinese Embassy were struck. Frequent bad weather made operations more difficult than they had been in Iraq in 1991.

Ethnic cleansing in Kosovo actually accelerated. NATO was reluctantly contemplating a ground invasion of Kosovo when Milošević finally submitted in June. NATO troops entered Kosovo unopposed and the alliance had won a victory without a single casualty. **JS**

Losses: NATO, none; Serbian, nearly 600 military dead and 500–3,000 civilians dead

◁ *Sarajevo 1992*

Tora Bora   12–17 December 2001

In October 2001 a U.S.-led coalition launched a military intervention in Afghanistan, backing the Afghan Northern Alliance against the Taliban government and its al-Qaida allies. In a coalition attack on a cave complex at Tora Bora in December, al-Qaida leader Osama bin Laden evaded capture.

The invasion of Afghanistan was an operation in the "war on terror," following the September 11 attacks on the United States, for which the Americans believed al-Qaida was responsible. Al-Qaida was known to operate from bases in Afghanistan and had close links with the Islamic fundamentalist Taliban, who refused to surrender bin Laden. After the U.S.-led intervention, Taliban resistance quickly crumbled.

Bin Laden led several hundred of his followers to a network of fortified caves in the mountains of the Tora Bora region outside Jalalabad, where he was determined to make a stand. The Americans were equally determined to hunt him down and launched massive B-52 air strikes on the area as Northern Alliance militiamen and special forces from the United States, Britain, and Germany were assembled for an assault. Al-Qaida fighters, armed with rocket launchers and mortars, were in easily defendable terrain, and were expected to fight to the finish.

The area was secured within days after some extremely fierce engagements. But bin Laden, although reportedly reluctant to flee, was apparently persuaded to do so by his followers and found sanctuary in Pakistan's tribal territories. The U.S.-led coalition failed to deploy sufficient special force troops in time to close all escape routes. Taking the cave complex without capturing bin Laden meant that he could continue to be a talisman for angry and alienated young Muslims throughout the world. **JS**

"Tora Bora was teeming with operatives . . . but Mr. bin Laden was never within our grasp."

General Tommy Franks

Losses: Coalition and Northern Alliance, unknown; Al Qaida, probably 200 dead

Marjah 2010 ▷

⬆ *In the distance, the payload of a B-52 bomber explodes on the Tora Bora mountain range.*

Invasion of Iraq 19 March–1 May 2003

A U.S.-led coalition invaded Iraq in 2003 to overthrow the dictatorship of Saddam Hussein. The invasion, enormously controversial even at the time, was a notable military success, achieving its main objectives in twenty-one days. However, the unexpected insurgency that followed required a long and costly military occupation.

Publicly justified by the claim that Saddam possessed weapons of mass destruction, the invasion was pressed through by the administration of U.S. President George W. Bush with the support of British Prime Minister Tony Blair, despite a failure to secure backing from the United Nations. It was assumed that coalition forces would be greeted by many Iraqis as liberators, and that the Iraqi people would contribute to their own liberation by rebelling; in fact, this only happened in Kurdish areas.

Coalition commander General Tommy Franks took a very different military approach from Operation Desert Storm in the 1990–91 Gulf War. There was no preparatory strategic air campaign or buildup of overwhelming troop strength. Franks had less than one-third of the forces that were used in Desert Storm. His aim was to pursue the offensive with a combination of relentless speed and precision firepower that would stun the enemy and make them incapable of reacting effectively. This policy, known as "shock and awe," was epitomized by initial air and missile strikes on 19 March that disrupted Iraqi command and communications, most notably by destroying Saddam's palaces and ministries in Baghdad. Precision weapons caused few civilian casualties, which did not prevent the occasional mistake, such as the bombing of a civilian market, being interpreted as deliberate murder.

The ground invasion began on 20 March. An amphibious operation captured oil fields around Basra and in the Al-Faw peninsula to prevent them being destroyed by the Iraqis. A main thrust was made from the Kuwaiti border across the desert toward Baghdad.

Coalition command of the air was key. Using bombs guided by GPS technology, aircraft hit concentrations of troops and vehicles with considerable accuracy. The vulnerability of concentrations of Iraqi vehicles to air attack, plus the disruption of command and control, made it hard for the Iraqis to mount a coherent defense. Nonetheless, there was some hard fighting. At Nasiriyah, on the Euphrates River, U.S. Marines encountered strong resistance from Iraqi guerrillas in battles to secure two main bridges. Polish, British, and U.S. forces took six days to clear the port of Umm Qasr, while Basra was taken by the British after two weeks' fighting against regulars and guerrillas.

A severe sandstorm held up the advance on Baghdad; it took sixteen days for U.S. troops to reach the city. Saddam insisted the battle for Baghdad would destroy the invaders, but the elite Republican Guard melted away, as did government officials, and the city fell on 12 April. Once it became clear that Saddam was doomed, cheering crowds appeared. A tearing down of Saddam's statue in Baghdad by Iraqi civilians and U.S. troops seemed to symbolize the spirit coalition leaders had hoped for. On 1 May, President Bush declared major military operations over, but coalition forces proved unable to provide basic security and an insurgency developed very rapidly. **JS**

Losses: Coalition, 172 of nearly 300,000; Iraqi, 8,000–45,000 of 375,000; civilian, 3,200–7,300

◁ *Desert Storm 1991*   *Fallujah 2004* ▷

Fallujah   7 November–23 December 2004

The U.S.-led coalition that occupied Iraq in 2003 faced a fast-growing resistance movement. An operation to crush a center of resistance at Fallujah, in the Sunni Muslim province of Al Anbar, was a costly military success that failed to prevent the spread of armed opposition to the occupation.

Fallujah was a stronghold of the deposed Saddam Hussein's Baath Party. An ugly incident in the first days of the occupation, in which demonstrators were shot dead by U.S. forces, meant the insurgency began early there. After four U.S. military contractors were killed in the city at the end of March 2004, the Americans attempted to retake control of Fallujah but, after heavy fighting, largely failed. With insurgents in complete control, the city became a magnet for Iraqi resistance fighters and foreign Muslim volunteers.

In November, the occupation forces decided to turn Fallujah into a trap where they would encircle the insurgents and destroy them. The city was surrounded with checkpoints to prevent insurgents from arriving or leaving. Realizing what was to come, 300,000 civilians fled Fallujah. Intense shelling and air strikes pounded the city before the coalition troops moved in on 8 November. The fighting was hard, with concealed sniper positions and booby traps a severe danger. A great deal of destruction was caused by troops blowing holes in the walls of houses rather than risk a possibly booby-trapped door.

After several days of street fighting, the city center was secured, but pockets of resistance endured for several weeks, each having to be reduced at a high cost in lives. The insurgents in Fallujah were largely destroyed, and the resistance never again challenged the coalition in open combat, but small-scale attacks across Iraq multiplied. **JS**

"Years from now ... Americans will speak of the battles like Fallujah with ... awe and reverence."

President George W. Bush

⬆ *The 1st Battalion 3d Marines clear houses in Fallujah.*

Losses: Coalition, 110 dead; Insurgent, nearly 3,000 dead or captured

◁ *Invasion of Iraq 2003*

Lebanon 12 July–14 August 2006

Confronting Palestinian and Islamic militants, Israel invaded Lebanon to suppress guerrillas attacking their settlements. Expecting their superior firepower and control of the air to provide a conclusive victory, the Israelis were faced by an Arab militia that fought them to a standstill.

After the 1982 invasion of Lebanon, a new radical Shia Muslim militia emerged, the Hezbollah (Party of God). Its suicide bombers essentially drove the Israelis from their buffer zone in southern Lebanon. Rocket attacks on Israeli settlements—generally wildly inaccurate but highly alarming—raised demands for reprisals. But the final straw came when Hezbollah attacked an Israeli patrol on 12 July 2006, killing three soldiers and apparently kidnapping two (who in fact probably died in the ambush). Five more soldiers died in a botched rescue attempt.

Israel imposed a major naval blockade on Lebanon, targeted air strikes on institutions and private homes associated with Hezbollah, and advanced ground troops to destroy their positions in southern Lebanon. But despite the destruction of many missile launchers, the scale of rocket attacks increased. Hezbollah fighters were determined to prove that Israeli technology was no match for devout warriors unafraid of death.

Fighting around Bint Jbeil was particularly fierce, and often hand-to-hand, and the Israelis never fully dislodged Hezbollah from the town. The Israeli Air Force pounded much of the infrastructure of Lebanon, their cluster munitions rendering parts of southern Lebanon uninhabitable—an indication of Israeli frustration. Eventually an Israeli withdrawal was negotiated, with international peacekeepers stationed to prevent further missile attacks, but they had failed to crush the militia. **JS**

Losses: Lebanese, more than 1,000 dead; Israeli, around 120 dead

◁ *Lebanon 1982*

Marjah 13–18 February 2010

The largest offensive mounted by the U.S.-led International Security Assistance Force (ISAF) against Taliban insurgents in Afghanistan centered on Marjah in Helmand province. The bold strike was hailed, perhaps prematurely, as a turning point in the long counterinsurgency war.

The offensive, code-named Operation Moshtarak, took place in a region where the ISAF had previously struggled to maintain isolated outposts. It was on an impressive scale, involving some 15,000 ISAF and Afghan army troops. Weeks earlier, special forces had prepared the way with small-scale attacks on Taliban positions.

Early on 13 February, under cover of darkness, waves of U.S. Marines and British, French, and Afghan troops were carried into the Marjah area by helicopter. As always in Afghanistan, they had to cope with large numbers of improvised explosive devices, as well as sniping and hit-and-run attacks from an elusive enemy. Pushing forward into Marjah, U.S. Marines encountered machine gun and rocket fire from houses and compounds. Strict rules of engagement placed limits on the use of air and missile strikes, in order to minimize civilian casualties.

Many Taliban had withdrawn before the operation was launched or slipped away after putting up token resistance. ISAF soldiers discovered caches of weapons, bomb-making equipment, and facilities connected with the opium trade, the main source of Taliban finance. By 18 February Afghan government soldiers were able to raise their flag over Marjah's marketplace, and ISAF and Afghan soldiers settled in to secure and extend the area of government control. They could not, however, prevent Taliban attacks recurring or convincingly win the "hearts and minds" of local people. **RG**

Losses: Taliban, 120 dead of 2,000; ISAF and Afghan government, 6 dead of 15,000

◁ *Tora Bora 2001*

General Index

952 | General Index

954 | General Index

Contributors

Adrian Gilbert (AG) has written extensively on matters of military history, and has a special interest in weapons and the battlefields of Europe. Among his many publications are *Germany's Lightning War: From the Invasion of Poland to El Alamein*; *The Imperial War Museum Book of the Desert War*; *Sniper: One-on-One*; *An Illustrated History of World War I*, and *POW: Allied Prisoners in Europe 1939–1945*.

Alan Wakefield (AW) is a curator at the Imperial War Museum, London. He holds an MA in War Studies from King's College London. Alan has written a number of books and articles on various aspects of World War I. He is a member of the British Commission for Military History and currently holds the position of Chairman of the Salonika Campaign Society.

Charles Phillips (CP) is the author of more than twenty books, including *The Illustrated History of the First Crusades*, *The World of the Medieval Knight*, and *The Lost History of Aztec and Maya*. He is a graduate of Oxford University and holds an MA from the University of Westminster.

Donald Sommerville (DS) is a writer and editor specializing in military history. He holds degrees in History and War Studies from Oxford and London Universities and his previous books include *Monty: A Biography of Field Marshal Montgomery*; *1916: The Year of Attrition*; *Revolutionary Warfare*; and *The Complete Illustrated History of World War II*.

Ian Kikuchi (IK) is a historian and museum curator. He studied War Studies and History at King's College London and is presently studying for a PhD at Queen Mary, University of London.

Jacob F. Field (JF) is an early modern historian based at the University of Cambridge. He was an undergraduate at Oxford, received his PhD from Newcastle for his thesis on the Great Fire of London, and also has written for several popular books on war and history.

John Swift (JS) is a Senior Lecturer in History at the University of Cumbria. His publications include *The Palgrave Concise Historical Atlas of the Cold War* (2003) and *Labour in Crisis: Clement Attlee and the Labour Party in Opposition 1931–40* (2001).

Michael Kerrigan (MK) has written many books, including volumes on Greece and the Mediterranean and Rome for the BBC Ancient Civilizations series and *Ancients in their Own Words* (2009). Coauthor of *The Reader's Digest Illustrated History of the World*, he was also a contributor to *War* (2009).

Nick Hewitt (NH) is a naval historian with numerous publishing and broadcasting credits. He studied history at Lancaster University and War Studies at King's College London before joining the Imperial War Museum as a Research Assistant in 1995. He is currently Head of Attractions and Collections for Portsmouth Naval Base Property Trust.

Niheer Dasandi (ND) is a doctoral student in political science at University College London focusing on international development issues. He also conducts research on civil conflicts in a global context.

R. G. Grant (RG) is a historian who has written extensively on many aspects and periods of history. Among his more than fifty published books are: *Battle*, *Soldier*, and *Battle at Sea* (2005, 2007, 2008). He was also a major contributor to the *ITV Visual History of the Twentieth Century* (1999) and consultant for *Chronology of World History* (1995).

Raymond K. Bluhm Jr. (RB) is a retired U.S. Army Colonel and military historian, author, and former professor of American History. After thirty years of service in the U.S. Army, he now works as a historical consultant to museums and leads battlefield tours. He has published several articles and coauthored and edited six books on Army history.

Rupert Matthews (RM) has been fascinated by battlefields since his father took him to Waterloo when he was nine years old. As an adult, Rupert has written about numerous battles from the ancient world to the present day, making a point of visiting as many battlefields as possible to gain an insight into how the conflict unfolded on the ground. The results of his studies and travels are included in this volume.

Simon Adams (SA) is a historian and writer living and working in London. He studied history and politics at universities in London and Bristol and has written numerous books for adults and children about modern history and warfare.

Stephen Turnbull (ST) is Visiting Professor of Japanese Studies at Akita International University in Japan and Lecturer in Japanese Religiuous Studies at the Universaity of Leeds. He also specializes in premodern Japanese military history and has written over seventy books. He holds a first degree from Cambridge University together with two MAs (in Theology and Military History) and a PhD from Leeds University.

Tony Bunting (TB) is a historian who has recently completed a research project at the University of Central Lancashire on the evolution of nineteenth-century British imperialism. He was a contributor to *1001 Days That Shaped the World*.

The Bridgeman Art Library **442-443** The Art Archive/Harper Collins Publishers **447** © Fine Art Images/Heritage Images/Imagestate **449** akg-images **451** Museum of Fine Arts, Boston, Massachusetts, USA/ Gift of Mr. and Mrs. Gardner Richardson/The Bridgeman Art Library © 2010 Museum of Fine Arts, Boston. All rights reserved. **452** The Art Archive **453** © Collection of the New-York Historical Society, USA/The Bridgeman Art Library **454** The Art Archive/Metropolitan Museum of Art New York/Superstock **455** Digital Image 2008 © Yale University Art of Gallery/Art Resource New York/Scala, Florence **457** Digital Image 2010 Photo Scala, Firenze **457** Digital Image 2010 Photo Scala, Firenze **459** The Art Archive/United States Capitol Building/Superstock **461** akg-images **464** Alnwick Castle, Northumberland, UK/The Bridgeman Art Library **465** Frédéric Soltan/Sygma/Corbis **467** The Art Archive/Superstock **468** akg/North Wind Picture Archives **469** © Costa/Leemage/Lebrecht Music & Arts **471** Digital Image 2010 De Agostini Picture Library, Scala, Firenze **472** Berrington Hall, Herefordshire, UK/National Trust Photographic Library/John Hammond/The Bridgeman Art Library **473** The Gallery Collection/Corbis **474** The Art Archive **478** Central Naval Museum, St. Petersburg, Russia/The Bridgeman Art Library **479** The Art Archive/Culver Pictures **481** The Gallery Collection/Corbis **482** The Art Archive/Musée Carnavalet Paris/Marc Charmet **483** Digital Image 2010 Hip/Scala, Florence **484** akg-images **485** Digital Image 2009 White Images/Photo Scala, Florence **486** © Courtesy of the Warden and Scholars of New College, Oxford/The Bridgeman Art Library **489** Æ White Images/Scala, Florence **491** Digital Image 2010 De Agostini Picture Library, Scala, Firenze **492** Digital Image 2009 White Images/Photo Scala, Florence **493** Digital Image 2009 White Images/Photo Scala, Florence **494** Digital Image 2010 White Images/Photo Scala, Florence **495** Digital Image 2010 White Images/Photo Scala, Florence **496** akg-images/ British Library **497** Digital Image 2009 Hip/Scala, Florence **499** Private Collection/The Bridgeman Art Library **500** © Leemage/Lebrecht Music & Arts **501** © National Museums of Scotland/The Bridgeman Art Library **502** akg-images/VISIOARS **504-505** The Art Archive/Musée d'Orsay Paris/Alfredo Dagli Orti **507** Digital Image 2009 White Images/Photo Scala, Florence **508** Historical Picture Archive/Corbis **509** Private Collection/Bourne Gallery, Reigate, Surrey/The Bridgeman Art Library **510** Photos **12**/Alamy **510** Æ White Images/Scala, Florence **512** The Art Archive/Superstock **513** The Gallery Collection/Corbis **514-515** The Art Archive/Eileen Tweedy **516-517** Private Collection/ Photo © Christie's Images/The Bridgeman Art Library **520** Digital Image 2010 White Images/Photo Scala, Florence **521** The Art Archive/Museo del Prado Madrid/Gianni Dagli Orti **522** Prado, Madrid, Spain/The Bridgeman Art Library **523** John Spink Fine Watercolours, London, UK/The Bridgeman Art Library **526-527** Musee de l'Armee, Brussels, Belgium/Patrick Lorette/The Bridgeman Art Library **528** akg-images/British Library **532** Stapleton Collection/Corbis **534-535** National Army Museum, London/The Bridgeman Art Library **536** akg-images/Erich Lessing **537** The Art Archive/Kharbine-Tapabor/Coll. Jonas **538-539** The Art Archive/British Library **542** Digital Image 2010 BPK, Berlin/Photo Sca la, Florence **544** The Art Archive/United States Capitol Building **545** Corbis **547** Photos **12**/Alamy **549** The Art Archive/Fondation Thiers Paris/Alfredo Dagli Orti **550** Getty Images **554** National Army Museum, London/The Bridgeman Art Library **555** National Army Museum, London/The Bridgeman Art Library **556** Digital Image 2010 Hip/Scala, Florence **558** Private Collection/Index/The Bridgeman Art Library **559** Digital Image 2009 White Images/Photo Scala, Florence **560** The Art Archive/ Museo Nacional Bogota/Gianni Dagli Orti **562-563** Digital Image 2010 De Agostini Picture Library, Scala, Firenze **564** The Art Archive/Simon Bolivar Amphitheatre Mexico/ Gianni Dagli Orti **565** akg-images/De Agostini Picture **566** Stapleton Collection/Corbis **569** Stapleton Collection/Corbis **570** Musee de la Ville de Paris, Musee Carnavalet, Paris, France/Archives Charmet/The Bridgeman Art Library **573** Private Collection/Peter Newark American Pictures/The Bridgeman Art Library **574** Private Collection/The Bridgeman Art Library **575** Leonard de Selva/Corbis **579** © Leemage/Lebrecht Music & Arts **580** Musee Conde, Chantilly, France/Giraudon/The Bridgeman Art Library **581** Digital Image 2010 De Agostini Picture Library, Scala, Firenze **582** The Art Archive/National Army Museum London/National Army Museum **583** Getty Images **584** Stapleton Collection/Corbis **585** Æ WGBH Stock Sales/Scala, Florence **587** The Art Archive/National Palace Mexico City/Gianni Dagli Orti **588** The Art Archive/Galleria d'Arte Moderna Rome/Alfredo Dagli Orti **589** Digital Image 2010 Hip/Scala, Florence **592** Central Naval Museum, St. Petersburg, Russia/The Bridgeman Art Library **593** © Leemage/Lebrecht Music & Arts **595** Private Collection/Ken Welsh/The Bridgeman Art Library **596** National Army Museum, London/The Bridgeman Art Library **597** The Art Archive/National Army Museum London/National Army Museum **598** Getty Images **600** The Art Archive/School of Oriental & African Studies/Eileen Tweedy **601** The Art Archive/Museo del Risorgimento Turin **603** Mary Evans Picture Library/Alamy **604-605** akg-images/Schütze/Rodemann **606-607** Digital Image 2008 Photo Scala, Firenze **608** The Art Archive/National Archives Washington, D.C. **609** Museum of the City of New York/Corbis **610** Bettmann/Corbis **611** Corbis **614** Getty Images **615** Bettmann/Corbis **617** © Collection of the New-York Historical Society, USA/The Bridgeman Art Library **619** The Art Archive/National Archives Washington, D.C. **621** akg-images **623** Getty Images **624-625** The Art Archive/National Archives Washington, D.C. **626** The Art Archive/Culver Pictures **628** Medford Historical Society Collection/Corbis **629** The Art Archive/School of Oriental & African Studies/Eileen Tweedy **632** Getty Images **634** Time & Life Pictures/Getty Images **635** Corbis **636** The Art Archive/Culver Pictures **637** Getty Images **638-639** Corbis **643** Mary Evans Picture Library/Alamy **647** The Art Archive/Musée Carnavalet Paris/Gianni Dagli Orti **648** Digital Image 2010 BPK, Berlin/Photo Scala, Florence **649** Digital Image 2009 White Images/Photo Scala, Florence **651** Interfoto/Alamy **652** Hulton-Deutsch Collection/Corbis **655** Æ Photo Scala Florence/Heritage Images **656-657** Asian Art & Archaeology, Inc./Corbis **658** National Army Museum, London/The Bridgeman Art Library **659** Popperfoto/Getty Images **660** The Art Archive/17/21st Lancers Museum/Eileen Tweedy **664** bpk/Dietmar Katz **666** The Art Archive/National Army Museum London/ National Army Museum **667** akg-images **668** Phil Yeomans/Rex Features **669** Pictorial Press Ltd/Alamy **670** Private collection **671** Corbis **673** © Museum of Fine Arts,Boston /Lebrecht **674** Arthur M. Sackler Gallery, Smithsonian Institution, USA/Gift of Gregory and Patricia Kruglak/The Bridgeman Art Library **675** Photo Scala, Florence 2006 **677** Private collection **678** Bettmann/Corbis **681** The Art Archive/National Army Museum London/National Army Museum **682** Corbis **683** The Art Archive/Alamy **684-685** Hulton-Deutsch Collection/Corbis **686** Getty Images **687** The Art Archive/War Museum of the Boer Republics, Bloemfontein **688** dpa/dpa/Corbis **689** Popperfoto/ Getty Images **691** akg-images **693** Hulton-Deutsch Collection/Corbis **694-695** © Interfoto/Lebrecht Music & Arts **697** Private Collection/The Stapleton Collection/The Bridgeman Art Library **698** The Art Archive/National History Museum Mexico City/Gianni Dagli Orti **700** akg-images/ullstein bild **702** Roger Viollet/Getty Images **703** Corbis **704** The Art Archive/Culver Pictures **705** The Art Archive/Imperial War Museum **707** © Sueddeutsche Zeitung Photo/Lebrecht **709** Bettmann/Corbis **711** Bettmann/Corbis **713** Bettmann/Corbis **715** The Art Archive/Imperial War Museum **716** Photos **12**/Alamy **717** Digital Image 2010 BPK, Berlin/Photo Scala, Florence **718** akg-images **719** Getty Images **720-721** Popperfoto/Getty Images **722** © Sueddeutsche Zeitung Photo/Lebrecht **723** Hulton-Deutsch Collection/Corbis **724** Bettmann/Corbis **725** The Art Archive/Imperial War Museum **726** © Mirrorpix/Lebrecht Authors **727** The Art Archive **728** Digital Image 2010 BPK, Berlin/Photo Scala, Florence **730** The Art Archive/Imperial War Museum **731** © Leemage/Lebrecht Music & Arts **733** Getty Images **734** Corbis **735** Bettmann/Corbis **737** akg-images/ullstein bild **738** The Art Archive **739** © Interfoto/Lebrecht Music & Arts **740-741** © Mirrorpix/Lebrecht Authors **742** © RA/Lebrecht Music & Arts **744** Time & Life Pictures/Getty Images **747** Æ White Images/ Scala, Florence **749** Digital Image 2010 BPK, Berlin/Photo Scala, Florence **750** The Print Collector/Alamy **751** Bettmann/Corbis **753** The Art Archive/Australian War Memorial **754** © Sueddeutsche Zeitung Photo/Lebrecht **755** Mary Evans Picture Library **757** Digital Image 2009 De Agostini Picture Library, Scala, Firenze **759** © Leemage/Lebrecht Music & Arts **760-761** Bettmann/Corbis **762** © Sueddeutsche Zeitung Photo/Lebrecht **763** Getty Images **764** The Art Archive/Imperial War Museum **765** © RA/Lebrecht Music & Arts **768-769** Time & Life Pictures/Getty Images **771** Hulton-Deutsch Collection/Corbis **773** © RIA Novosti/Lebrecht Music & Arts **775** Bettmann/Corbis **776-777** LAZARO (ARCHIVO VIDAL)/EFE/Corbis **780** Getty Images **781** Hulton-Deutsch Collection/Corbis **785** © RA/Lebrecht Music & Arts **787** EFE/Corbis **788** akg-images/ Imagno **791** © Sueddeutsche Zeitung Photo/Lebrecht **792** © Sueddeutsche Zeitung Photo/Lebrecht **793** akg-images/ullstein bild **794** Robert Capa/International Center of Photography/Magnum Photos **796** akg-images/ullstein bild **797** Mary Evans/AISA Media **798-799** Peter Turnley/Corbis **800** Getty Images **801** © Sueddeutsche Zeitung Photo/Lebrecht **802** akg-images/ullstein bild **803** Hulton-Deutsch Collection/Corbis **804** Hulton-Deutsch Collection/Corbis **805** Hulton-Deutsch Collection/Corbis **806** Getty Images **808** Popperfoto/Getty Images **809** © RA/Lebrecht Music & Arts **810** Corbis **813** The Art Archive/Alamy **815** Bettmann/Corbis **819** © SZ Photo/The Bridgeman Art Library **820-821** Hulton-Deutsch Collection/Corbis **822** akg-images **825** Photos **12**/Alamy **827** Getty Images **827** Popperfoto/Getty Images **828** Getty Images **829** Getty Images **832** © RA/Lebrecht Music & Arts **834** © SZ Photo/The Bridgeman Art Library **835** Cody Images **836** Imperial War Museum **837** Interfoto/Alamy **839** Bettmann/Corbis **840-841** The Art Archive **842-843** © RIA Novosti/Lebrecht Music & Arts **844** Interfoto/Alamy **846-847** Getty Images **848** Corbis **848** Corbis **850** Corbis **851** Bettmann/Corbis **852** Imperial War Museum **854** Popperfoto/Getty Images **855** © Sueddeutsche Zeitung Photo/Lebrecht **858** Bettmann/Corbis **859** akg-images **860** Getty Images **864-865** © www.lebrecht.co.uk **867** Time & Life Pictures/Getty Images **868** © RA/Lebrecht Music & Arts **869** The Art Archive/Culver Pictures **871** Corbis **872** akg-images/ullstein bild **873** Time & Life Pictures/Getty Images **874** © Tallandier RA/Lebrecht **875** Time & Life Pictures/Getty Images **877** Private Collection/ The Bridgeman Art Library **879** Corbis **881** The Art Archive/Culver Pictures **884** © RA/Lebrecht Music & Arts **887** Corbis **888** © RA/Lebrecht Music & Arts **889** Corbis **891** Corbis **893** Gamma-Keystone via Getty Images **894** AFP/Getty Images **895** Private collection **896** Gamma-Keystone via Getty Images **897** akg-images/ullstein bild **900** Bettmann/Corbis **902** Gamma-Keystone via Getty Images **903** Bettmann/Corbis **905** AFP/Getty Images **906** Hulton-Deutsch Collection/Corbis **907** The Art Archive/ Kharbine-Tapabor **908** akg-images/ullstein bild **909** Alain Nogues/Sygma/Corbis **910** AP/Press Association Images **913** Popperfoto/Getty Images **914** Hulton-Deutsch Collection/Corbis **915** Tim Page/Corbis **917** Getty Images **919** Christian Simonpietri/Sygma/Corbis **921** Bettmann/Corbis **922** Bettmann/Corbis **923** Micha Bar Am/ Magnum Photos **924** Bettmann/Corbis **925** Bettmann/Corbis **926** Hulton-Deutsch Collection/Corbis **927** Christian Simonpietri/Sygma/Corbis **929** Getty Images **931** Bettmann/Corbis **934** © Sueddeutsche Zeitung Photo/Lebrecht **935** STRINGER/ARGENTINA/X01488/Reuters/Corbis **936** Peter Jordan/Alamy **937** Sipa Press/Rex Features **939** Peter Turnley/Corbis **940** Tom Stoddart/Getty Images **941** Les Stone/Sygma/Corbis **943** © The Times, London/Lebrecht **944-945** Corbis **946** Getty Images

Quintessence would like to thank the following individuals for their assistance in the creation of this book:

Helena Baser, Jodie Gaudet, Ann Marangos, Fiona Plowman, Sunita Sharma-Gibson, Olivia Young

960 | Picture Credits • Acknowledgments